PUBLIC PAPERS OF THE PRESIDENTS
OF THE
UNITED STATES

PUBLIC PAPERS OF THE PRESIDENTS
OF THE
UNITED STATES

George Bush

1990

(IN TWO BOOKS)

BOOK II—JULY 1 TO DECEMBER 31, 1990

UNITED STATES GOVERNMENT PRINTING OFFICE
WASHINGTON : 1991

Published by the
Office of the Federal Register
National Archives and Records Administration

For sale by the
Superintendent of Documents
U.S. Government Printing Office
Washington, DC 20402

Foreword

Iraq's brutal aggression against Kuwait, begun on August 2, dominated events during these six months. In response, the United States and 28 other nations joined together to send to the Persian Gulf region an international coalition of forces designed to deter further Iraqi aggression. At the same time, the United Nations imposed a series of even more severe economic and military sanctions on Iraq, while the United States organized a multi-billion dollar effort to provide economic assistance to countries in the area adversely affected by the crisis. In late November, in a move almost unprecedented in its history, the UN Security Council authorized the use of "all necessary means" to compel Iraq to end its brutal and illegal occupation of Kuwait.

In this crisis, we took heart in the world's united response—political, economic, and military—to Iraq's unlawful aggression and the concomitant functioning of the United Nations as its founders envisioned. This gave rise to hopes that out of this conflict we might enter a historic period of cooperation—a New World Order. I laid out my vision of this New World Order in remarks before a Joint Session of Congress on September 11 and again in remarks to the United Nations General Assembly on October 1. The basis of this idea is a world in which international relations are conducted according to the rule of law and nations can live together in harmony and prosperity, in which there is real consensus that force may not be used to settle disputes and where that consensus is broken responsibility for restoring order will be borne by many nations.

Although attention naturally focussed on the Gulf crisis, there were other pressing matters to which the Administration devoted attention. In July, I attended two very important summits—the NATO Summit in London and the Summit of Industrialized Nations in Houston. In London, the leaders of the Member States of the North Atlantic Treaty Organization took great strides in delineating the future of Europe and the United States' continuing role in it. In Houston, the leaders of the world's seven largest industrial democracies examined the conditions of our economies and also agreed to study the Soviet economy with a view to assisting its transition to a market system.

During the summer, Mexico indicated its willingness to enter negotiations to liberalize trade between our two nations. In September, I notified the Congress of the Administration's intent to negotiate a free trade agreement with Mexico.

In that month, I also met with President Gorbachev of the Soviet Union in Helsinki. Our meetings were intense and productive. At the end, we issued a joint statement that proved to be an important milestone in our cooperative efforts to resolve the Persian Gulf crisis.

In November, the leaders of the member states of the Conference on Security and Cooperation in Europe gathered in Paris to advance an agenda of deepening cooperation and witness the signing of a CFE Treaty between the members of the Atlantic Alliance and the Warsaw Pact designed to reduce conventional armed forces in

Europe. From France, I traveled to Czechoslovakia for meetings with President Havel, marking that nation's transition to democracy, and then to the Middle East for important consultations with our partners in the international coalition against Iraq. Most important, Barbara and I spent Thanksgiving Day with the brave men and women in our Armed Forces who had been deployed to defend Saudi Arabia.

I addressed the American people twice during this period on the conflict in the Gulf—first on August 8 as the first troops were deployed for the defense of Saudi Arabia, and again in September in a Joint Session of Congress. If ever there were a time to put country before self, and patriotism before party, this was that time. The response of the American people and the world was overwhelming. They rallied behind the forces deployed in support of Operation Desert Shield.

These months were also an active time here at home. Guided by the principles of freedom, growth, opportunity, and responsibility, my Administration continued to move forward on an ambitious domestic agenda.

Working with the Congress, we developed landmark budget deficit reduction legislation, reducing Federal borrowing requirements by almost $500 billion over the next five years and introducing important new budget process reform. I signed the Americans with Disabilities Act, landmark legislation to preserve the civil rights of Americans with disabilities. I had the duty and honor of appointing a member of the United States Supreme Court. History will show Justice Souter to be an impartial and superior Justice.

We provided record funding for drug treatment, prevention, and State and local law enforcement through block grants and began to see a decline in drug use. We continue to support a comprehensive crime package, including an increase of over $1 billion for Federal prison expansion and additional law enforcement agents and prosecutors.

The environment has remained at the forefront of our agenda. In November, I signed the Clean Air Act Amendments of 1990. This comprehensive and innovative clean air legislation broke a decade-long stalemate on clean air legislation and reaffirmed America's place as the global leader in environmental protection. The Administration proposed programs to plant a billion trees per year, restrictions on offshore drilling in environmentally sensitive areas, and proposed and negotiated an agreement for the phase-out of all chlorofluorocarbons and other ozone-depleting chemicals. I also signed legislation to expand and protect the Everglades National Park as well as the North American Wetlands Conservation Act.

We also continued our crusade for educational excellence. Building on our partnership with the Nation's Governors, we established the National Education Goals Panel to monitor progress towards the National Education Goals.

On the frontier of space, Vice President Quayle and the National Space Council took a fresh look at America's space program and developed a new commercial space launch strategy.

Our Nation and world are changing, and those changes are producing exciting new challenges. Working together, our great Nation is meeting these problems head-on as we move to the 21st century. America is a mighty nation, but we are only as great as those who are willing to help their fellow Americans. There is no greater example of this than the brave men and women willing to sacrifice the comfort of home and closeness of family to protect the values of this country and her citizens in Operation Desert Shield.

George Bush

Preface

This book contains the papers and speeches of the 41st President of the United States that were issued by the Office of the Press Secretary during the period July 1–December 31, 1990. The material has been compiled and published by the Office of the Federal Register, National Archives and Records Administration.

The material is presented in chronological order, and the dates shown in the headings are the dates of the documents or events. In instances when the release date differs from the date of the document itself, that fact is shown in the textnote. Every effort has been made to ensure accuracy: Remarks are checked against a tape recording, and signed documents are checked against the original. Textnotes and cross references have been provided by the editors for purposes of identification or clarity. Speeches were delivered in Washington, DC, unless indicated. The times noted are local times. All materials that are printed full-text in the book have been indexed in the subject and name indexes, and listed in the document categories list.

The Public Papers of the Presidents series was begun in 1957 in response to a recommendation of the National Historical Publications Commission. An extensive compilation of messages and papers of the Presidents covering the period 1789 to 1897 was assembled by James D. Richardson and published under congressional authority between 1896 and 1899. Since then, various private compilations have been issued, but there was no uniform publication comparable to the Congressional Record or the United States Supreme Court Reports. Many Presidential papers could be found only in the form of mimeographed White House releases or as reported in the press. The Commission therefore recommended the establishment of an official series in which Presidential writings, addresses, and remarks of a public nature could be made available.

The Commission's recommendation was incorporated in regulations of the Administrative Committee of the Federal Register, issued under section 6 of the Federal Register Act (44 U.S.C. 1506), which may be found in title 1, part 10, of the Code of Federal Regulations.

A companion publication to the Public Papers series, the Weekly Compilation of Presidential Documents, was begun in 1965 to provide a broader range of Presidential materials on a more timely basis to meet the needs of the contemporary reader. Beginning with the administration of Jimmy Carter, the Public Papers series expanded its coverage to include all material as printed in the Weekly Compilation. That coverage provides a listing of the President's daily schedule and meetings, when announced, and other items of general interest issued by the Office of the Press Secretary. Also included are lists of the President's nominations submitted to the Senate, materials released by the Office of the Press Secretary that are not printed full-text in the book, acts approved by the President, and proclamations and Executive orders. This information appears in the appendixes at the end of the book.

Volumes covering the administrations of Presidents Hoover, Truman, Eisenhower, Kennedy, Johnson, Nixon, Ford, Carter, and Reagan are also available.

The Public Papers of the Presidents publication program is under the direction of Gwen H. Estep. The Chief Editor of this book was Karen Howard Ashlin, assisted by Sheli Fleming.

White House liaison was provided by Marlin Fitzwater, Assistant to the President and Press Secretary. The frontispiece and photographs used in the portfolio were supplied by the White House Photo Office. The typography and design of the book were developed by the Government Printing Office under the direction of Robert W. Houk, Public Printer.

Martha L. Girard
Director of the Federal Register

Don W. Wilson
Archivist of the United States

Contents

Cabinet

Secretary of State... James Addison Baker III

Secretary of the Treasury............................... Nicholas F. Brady

Secretary of Defense...................................... Richard B. Cheney

Attorney General.. Richard L. Thornburgh

Secretary of the Interior............................... Manuel Lujan, Jr.

Secretary of Agriculture .... Clayton Yeutter

Secretary of Commerce................................... Robert Adam Mosbacher

Secretary of Labor.. Elizabeth Hanford Dole

Secretary of Health and Human Services ... Louis W. Sullivan

Secretary of Housing and Urban
Development... Jack Kemp

Secretary of Transportation .... Samuel Knox Skinner

Secretary of Energy.. James D. Watkins

Secretary of Education .... Lauro F. Cavazos

Secretary of Veterans Affairs........................ Edward J. Derwinski

Director of the Office of Management and
Budget.. Richard G. Darman

United States Trade Representative............. Carla Anderson Hills

Administration of George Bush

1990

Exchange With Reporters in Kennebunkport, Maine
July 2, 1990

Q. Mr. President, are you changing your policy on nuclear use?

The President. We're discussing the NATO agenda here today, and we'll discuss it with our colleagues when we get over there.

Q. Well, it sounds like your proposal changes from flexible response and no first use.

The President. I'm anxious to hear from Secretary Cheney and General Powell and others on this matter that you've raised. And then we've got a wide array of other issues we're talking about there—economic and political dimension of NATO. So, we're trying to get our act totally together. We're in good shape for the meeting. I think our side is generally agreed on the big questions. And then, before we comment on these items, we're going to talk to our allies. That's the way I've tried to do it from the very beginning with NATO, and I'm going to continue that. We don't dictate; we just say, here's our views, and then represent them as best we can.

Q. But your views seem to represent a change.

The President. Well, we'll wait until we see what comes out of the NATO meeting; we're not going to prejudge it. But I'm encouraged because I think we've got a good position here. You know, the other day Marlin bawled me out. I said there's nothing earthshaking about all of this. [*Laughter*] But he and Scowcroft went into a frenzy, saying, well, maybe others will interpret it as this. So, I don't want to understate where we're going or overstate it, but some will look at it as this major change in direction and others won't. But I want to take this opportunity to get myself off the hook.

Q. Have you had any responses from the allies here?

The President. Oh, sure. That's one of the things I want to hear about from Secretary Baker today. They've been in close contact. And he'll go off and—what, tonight do you head off?

Secretary Baker. Tomorrow morning.

The President. Tomorrow morning, and iron out some of the differences before we get there.

Q. Do you expect policy changes to be made at the summit?

The President. Well, what I expect is a document that is unanimously agreed to that will set the course for the future. And as conditions have changed, NATO will change. And I've addressed myself to that. But some will call it dramatic policy changes, and others won't. And so, I don't want to understate it. I don't want to be in trouble saying, Well, you said there would be no changes. But there will be some changes, but I don't happen to believe that it's of a bombshell dimension. Remember the last time we went over there we had a troop policy change. And so, I don't want to mislead you, but there will be some very interesting developments out of it.

Q. Are the allies in agreement with you in the responses that you've gotten to your proposals?

The President. Well, as I say, Jim's going over. We've gotten broad general agreement on a lot of issues, but there's still some work to be done. That's one of the things we're talking about in here today.

President Gorbachev of the Soviet Union

Q. Have you had any contact with Mr. Gorbachev going into his party congress?

The President. No, I haven't talked to him since he was over here—or been in telegraphic. Now, maybe Jim has with Mr. Shevardnadze.

Secretary Baker. Not since——

Q. What are the keys to watch for in

terms of that congress? What are your expectations?

The President. Stay tuned to CNN [Cable News Network]. [*Laughter*] We've got to go to work.

Note: The exchange began at 8:45 a.m. at the President's home at Walker's Point. In

his remarks, the President referred to Colin L. Powell, Chairman of the Joint Chiefs of Staff; Marlin Fitzwater, Press Secretary to the President; Brent Scowcroft, Assistant to the President for National Security Affairs; and Soviet Foreign Minister Eduard A. Shevardnadze.

Statement by Press Secretary Fitzwater on the Deaths of Moslem Pilgrims in Mecca, Saudi Arabia
July 3, 1990

The Government and people of the United States are deeply saddened by the deaths of the many Hajj pilgrims near Mecca on the eve of Eid al-Adha, the Feast of the Sacrifice, this very significant holy day in Islam. On behalf of the people of the United States, the President extends his sincere condolences to the families of those individuals killed in the accident and to King Fahd, the Custodian of the Two Holy Mosques.

Note: On July 2, over 1,000 Moslem pilgrims suffocated or were trampled to death in a stampede in a pedestrian tunnel near holy shrines in Mecca.

Exchange With Reporters in Kennebunkport, Maine
July 3, 1990

The President. Smile. [*Laughter*]

Houston Economic Summit

Q. ——a few surprises at Houston, Mr. President?

The President. No surprises. I think we're in good shape for that meeting, though—those meetings. We'll have a chance to get a preview talking to some of the leaders at the NATO summit about Houston, too—but it will go well. There are some big issues to discuss—trade, particularly.

Q. What would you like to see come out of the Houston summit?

The President. Well, I'd like to see us move forward on the Uruguay round, which means we've got to get moving on the question of agriculture. I've been saying that for some time, and that's very important. We spent a lot of time on that this morning, and it's important work.

NATO

Q. Have you got any feedback from the allies yet on the language concerning last resort——

The President. I'm ready to discuss that with them. I talked to the Prime Minister of Belgium and the Prime Minister of Denmark just now, and we didn't go into that specific, but I think the general approach that we're proposing seems to be getting wide acceptance. I don't want to comment, Jim [Jim Miklaszewski, NBC News], on that one because we didn't discuss that particular issue.

Q. Well, why is it now that we have to assure the Soviets that NATO is a threat? What's different? Or not a threat—I'm sorry—[*laughter*].

The President. Well, I think as things change we want to be sure that everybody understands that NATO is the stabilizing factor that we think it should be and will be. And it's not a question—we don't have to assure them of anything, but I want them to understand the facts. I spent a lot of time working with Mr. Gorbachev when he was here to see that he did understand that a unified Germany in NATO is not a threat to the Soviet Union. And if there are certain things we can do to expand NATO's role that drive that point home, so much the better.

Q. Is there anything really different about this last resort?

The President. Well, you have to wait and see what comes out of it. You'll notice I'm not even commenting on your question because I told you, I think, yesterday that I wanted to discuss the specifics with our NATO partners.

Economic Assistance for the Soviet Union

Q. Mr. President, are you going to still reject the Soviet economic aid package in Houston?

The President. Well, I've explained to our economic summit partners and to the Soviets and to others that we have specific problems with, you know, giving money to the Soviet Union at this point. So, we'll be discussing that at Houston, and we had a good briefing on that here today.

Q. Are you afraid that the money might be wasted?

The President. Well, I still feel the same way I did: that economic reform is essential. And to Gorbachev's credit, he's trying to reform the economic system there.

Q. What are you proposing on the environmental front?

The President. We've tried it the other way, you see, with Poland several years ago and before economic reform, and I think everybody recognizes that that money did not help do what it was intended to.

Houston Economic Summit

Q. Any proposals on the environmental front in Houston?

The President. There will be a good discussion of the environment, yes.

Mr. Fitzwater. Thank you, Mr. President. [*Laughter*]

The President. What do you think, Marlin?

President Gorbachev of the Soviet Union

Q. How do you think Gorbachev handled himself yesterday? He was pretty tough, wasn't he?

The President. I haven't gotten a full report on that, so I can't comment on it.

Interest Rates

Q. How about bringing down interest rates in Houston, worldwide? Is that one of your goals?

The President. It's always a goal. I don't think that's a specific agenda item—worldwide interest rates.

Golf With the President

Q. Mr. Vice President, did you throw the golf game yesterday? There was a story that you went into the tank to purposely lose— [*laughter*]——

Q. Widely speculated.

The Vice President. I went into the tank, and I stayed there. The President won, as he should.

The President. I think he played well.

Q. Well, he was in the sand all the time. Every time I saw a picture, he was hitting out of the sand.

The President. He got five birdies—no, six birdies. That's pretty good golf.

Q. You got six birdies?

The President. Yes. That's not bad.

Q. You started the story then, that you lost.

The Vice President. That's because when the camera was there, I double-bogied the 9th hole and I hit it in the sand on the 18th hole—just record it. I wanted the bad part of the golf game recorded——

The President. Secretary Brady's team won the match. Did you get credit for that, Nick?

Q. No, he wouldn't tell us.

The President. He didn't? They were the victors.

Q. I thought you won. The Vice President said you won.

The President. No, no. Oh, he was just being pleasant, I'll bet.

The Vice President. He won on the first tee.

The President. Won one hole. That's what he meant.

Well, let's go suit up.

Note: The exchange began at 11:20 a.m. at the President's home at Walker's Point in Kennebunkport, ME. During the exchange, *the President referred to Wilfried Martens, Prime Minister of Belgium, and Poul Schlüter, Prime Minister of Denmark. Marlin Fitzwater was Press Secretary to the President.*

London Declaration on a Transformed North Atlantic Alliance
July 6, 1990

ISSUED BY THE HEADS OF STATE AND GOVERNMENT PARTICIPATING IN THE MEETING OF THE NORTH ATLANTIC COUNCIL IN LONDON ON 5TH–6TH JULY 1990

1. Europe has entered a new, promising era. Central and Eastern Europe is liberating itself. The Soviet Union has embarked on the long journey toward a free society. The walls that once confined people and ideas are collapsing. Europeans are determining their own destiny. They are choosing freedom. They are choosing economic liberty. They are choosing peace. They are choosing a Europe whole and free. As a consequence, this Alliance must and will adapt.

2. The North Atlantic Alliance has been the most successful defensive alliance in history. As our Alliance enters its fifth decade and looks ahead to a new century, it must continue to provide for the common defence. This Alliance has done much to bring about the new Europe. No-one, however, can be certain of the future. We need to keep standing together, to extend the long peace we have enjoyed these past four decades. Yet our Alliance must be even more an agent of change. It can help build the structures of a more united continent, supporting security and stability with the strength of our shared faith in democracy, the rights of the individual, and the peaceful resolution of disputes. We reaffirm that security and stability do not lie solely in the military dimension, and we intend to enhance the political component of our Alliance as provided for by Article 2 of our Treaty.

3. The unification of Germany means that the division of Europe is also being overcome. A united Germany in the Atlantic Alliance of free democracies and part of the growing political and economic integration of the European Community will be an indispensable factor of stability, which is needed in the heart of Europe. The move within the European Community towards political union, including the development of a European identity in the domain of security, will also contribute to Atlantic solidarity and to the establishment of a just and lasting order of peace throughout the whole of Europe.

4. We recognise that, in the new Europe, the security of every state is inseparably linked to the security of its neighbours. NATO must become an institution where Europeans, Canadians and Americans work together not only for the common defence, but to build new partnerships with all the nations of Europe. The Atlantic Community must reach out to the countries of the East which were our adversaries in the Cold War, and extend to them the hand of friendship.

5. We will remain a defensive alliance and will continue to defend all the territory of all of our members. We have no aggressive intentions and we commit ourselves to the peaceful resolution of all disputes. We will never in any circumstance be the first to use force.

6. The member states of the North Atlantic Alliance propose to the member states of the Warsaw Treaty Organization a joint declaration in which we solemnly state that we are no longer adversaries and reaffirm our intention to refrain from the threat or use of force against the territorial integrity or political independence of any state, or from acting in any other manner inconsistent with the purposes and principles of the

United Nations Charter and with the CSCE Final Act. We invite all other CSCE member states to join us in this commitment to non-aggression.

7. In that spirit, and to reflect the changing political role of the Alliance, we today invite President Gorbachev on behalf of the Soviet Union, and representatives of the other Central and Eastern European countries to come to Brussels and address the North Atlantic Council. We today also invite the governments of the Union of Soviet Socialist Republics, the Czech and Slovak Federal Republic, the Hungarian Republic, the Republic of Poland, the People's Republic of Bulgaria and Romania to come to NATO, not just to visit, but to establish regular diplomatic liaison with NATO. This will make it possible for us to share with them our thinking and deliberations in this historic period of change.

8. Our Alliance will do its share to overcome the legacy of decades of suspicion. We are ready to intensify military contacts, including those of NATO Military Commanders, with Moscow and other Central and Eastern European capitals.

9. We welcome the invitation to NATO Secretary General Manfred Wörner to visit Moscow and meet with Soviet leaders.

10. Military leaders from throughout Europe gathered earlier this year in Vienna to talk about their forces and doctrine. NATO proposes another such meeting this Autumn to promote common understanding. We intend to establish an entirely different quality of openness in Europe, including an agreement on "Open Skies".

11. The significant presence of North American conventional and US nuclear forces in Europe demonstrates the underlying political compact that binds North America's fate to Europe's democracies. But, as Europe changes, we must profoundly alter the way we think about defence.

12. To reduce our military requirements, sound arms control agreements are essential. That is why we put the highest priority on completing this year the first treaty to reduce and limit conventional armed forces in Europe (CFE) along with the completion of a meaningful CSBM package. These talks should remain in continuous session until the work is done. Yet we hope to go fur-

ther. We propose that, once a CFE Treaty is signed, follow-on talks should begin with the same membership and mandate, with the goal of building on the current agreement with additional measures, including measures to limit manpower in Europe. With this goal in mind, a commitment will be given at the time of signature of the CFE Treaty concerning the manpower levels of a unified Germany.

13. Our objective will be to conclude the negotiations on the follow-on to CFE and CSBMs as soon as possible and looking to the follow-up meeting of the CSCE to be held in Helsinki in 1992. We will seek through new conventional arms control negotiations, within the CSCE framework, further far-reaching measures in the 1990s to limit the offensive capability of conventional armed forces in Europe, so as to prevent any nation from maintaining disproportionate military power on the continent. NATO's High Level Task Force will formulate a detailed position for these follow-on conventional arms control talks. We will make provisions as needed for different regions to redress disparities and to ensure that no one's security is harmed at any stage. Furthermore, we will continue to explore broader arms control and confidence-building opportunities. This is an ambitious agenda, but it matches our goal: enduring peace in Europe.

14. As Soviet troops leave Eastern Europe and a treaty limiting conventional armed forces is implemented, the Alliance's integrated force structure and its strategy will change fundamentally to include the following elements:

—NATO will field smaller and restructured active forces. These forces will be highly mobile and versatile so that Allied leaders will have maximum flexibility in deciding how to respond to a crisis. It will rely increasingly on multinational corps made up of national units.

—NATO will scale back the readiness of its active units, reducing training requirements and the number of exercises.

—NATO will rely more heavily on the ability to build up larger forces if and when they might be needed.

15. To keep the peace, the Alliance must maintain for the foreseeable future an appropriate mix of nuclear and conventional forces, based in Europe, and kept up to date where necessary. But, as a defensive Alliance, NATO has always stressed that none of its weapons will ever be used except in self-defence and that we seek the lowest and most stable level of nuclear forces needed to secure the prevention of war.

16. The political and military changes in Europe, and the prospects of further changes, now allow the Allies concerned to go further. They will thus modify the size and adapt the tasks of their nuclear deterrent forces. They have concluded that, as a result of the new political and military conditions in Europe, there will be a significantly reduced role for sub-strategic nuclear systems of the shortest range. They have decided specifically that, once negotiations begin on short-range nuclear forces, the Alliance will propose, in return for reciprocal action by the Soviet Union, the elimination of all its nuclear artillery shells from Europe.

17. New negotiations between the United States and the Soviet Union on the reduction of short-range nuclear forces should begin shortly after a CFE agreement is signed. The Allies concerned will develop an arms control framework for these negotiations which takes into account our requirements for far fewer nuclear weapons, and the diminished need for sub-strategic nuclear systems of the shortest range.

18. Finally, with the total withdrawal of Soviet stationed forces and the implementation of a CFE agreement, the Allies concerned can reduce their reliance on nuclear weapons. These will continue to fulfil an essential role in the overall strategy of the Alliance to prevent war by ensuring that there are no circumstances in which nuclear retaliation in response to military action might be discounted. However, in the transformed Europe, they will be able to adopt a new NATO strategy making nuclear forces truly weapons of last resort.

19. We approve the mandate given in Turnberry to the North Atlantic Council in Permanent Session to oversee the ongoing work on the adaptation of the Alliance to the new circumstances. It should report its conclusions as soon as possible.

20. In the context of these revised plans for defence and arms control, and with the advice of NATO Military Authorities and all member states concerned, NATO will prepare a new Allied military strategy moving away from "forward defence", where appropriate, towards a reduced forward presence and modifying "flexible response" to reflect a reduced reliance on nuclear weapons. In that connection, NATO will elaborate new force plans consistent with the revolutionary changes in Europe. NATO will also provide a forum for Allied consultation on the upcoming negotiations on short-range nuclear forces.

21. The Conference on Security and Co-operation in Europe (CSCE) should become more prominent in Europe's future, bringing together the countries of Europe and North America. We support a CSCE Summit later this year in Paris which would include the signature of a CFE agreement and would set new standards for the establishment, and preservation, of free societies. It should endorse, inter alia:

—CSCE principles on the right to free and fair elections;

—CSCE commitments to respect and uphold the rule of law;

—CSCE guidelines for enhancing economic cooperation, based on the development of free and competitive market economies; and

—CSCE cooperation on environmental protection.

22. We further propose that the CSCE Summit in Paris decide how the CSCE can be institutionalised to provide a forum for wider political dialogue in a more united Europe. We recommend that CSCE governments establish:

—a programme for regular consultations among member governments at the Heads of State and Government or Ministerial level, at least once each year, with other periodic meetings of officials to prepare for and follow up on these consultations;

—a schedule of CSCE review conferences once every two years to assess progress

toward a Europe whole and free;
—a small CSCE secretariat to coordinate these meetings and conferences;
—a CSCE mechanism to monitor elections in all the CSCE countries, on the basis of the Copenhagen Document;
—a CSCE Centre for the Prevention of Conflict that might serve as a forum for exchanges of military information, discussion of unusual military activities, and the conciliation of disputes involving CSCE member states; and
—a CSCE parliamentary body, the Assembly of Europe, to be based on the existing parliamentary assembly of the Council of Europe, in Strasbourg, and include representatives of all CSCE member states.

The sites of these new institutions should reflect the fact that the newly democratic countries of Central and Eastern Europe form part of the political structures of the new Europe.

23. Today, our Alliance begins a major transformation. Working with all the countries of Europe, we are determined to create enduring peace on this continent.

Note: Paragraphs 12 and 13 of the declaration refer to confidence- and security-building measures (CSBM). The declaration was made available by the Office of the Press Secretary but was not issued as a White House press release.

The President's News Conference Following the North Atlantic Treaty Organization Summit in London, United Kingdom
July 6, 1990

The President. I'd like to begin by thanking Prime Minister Margaret Thatcher for hosting this splendid meeting, and I want to express my appreciation also to Manfred Woerner not only for his kind remarks just now but for his outstanding leadership in NATO and in this alliance which is at a turning point in its history.

I'm pleased to announce that my colleagues and I have begun a major transformation of the North Atlantic alliance, and we view it as a historic turning point. NATO has set a new path for peace. It's kept the peace for 40 years and today charted a new course for stability and cooperation in Europe.

We, as you know, are issuing a document, the London Declaration; and it makes specific proposals and establishes directions for the future in four key areas.

First, the London Declaration transforms our relationship with old adversaries. To those Governments who confronted us in the cold war, our alliance extends the hand of friendship. We reaffirm that we shall never be the first to use force against other states in Europe. And we propose a joint declaration between members of the alliance and member states of the Warsaw Pact which other CSCE states could join in, making a solemn commitment to non-aggression. We say to President Gorbachev: Come to NATO. We say to all the member states of the Warsaw Pact: Come to NATO and establish regular diplomatic liaison with the alliance.

And second, the London Declaration transforms the character of NATO's conventional defenses. We can start, and must start, by finishing the current CFE [conventional forces in Europe] talks this year. Once CFE is signed, we would begin follow-on negotiations to adopt additional measures, including measures to limit manpower in Europe. With this goal in mind, a commitment will be given when the CFE treaty is signed concerning the manpower levels of the armed forces of a united Germany. We will also seek in the nineties to achieve further far-reaching measures to limit the offensive capability of conventional armed forces. We'll change our strategy for a conventional defense. We agreed to move away from NATO's current strategy of forward defense to a reduced forward presence. We agreed, in addition, to make the principle of collective defense even more evident by organizing NATO troops into multinational corps.

And third, the London Declaration transforms NATO's nuclear strategy. For 23 years we've had a nuclear strategy called flexible response, developed to meet a danger of sudden overwhelming conventional attack. As that danger recedes, we've agreed to modify flexible response.

Nuclear deterrence has given us an unprecedented period of peace, and it will remain fundamental to our strategy. But by reducing its reliance on nuclear weapons, NATO in the new Europe will adopt a new strategy making its nuclear forces truly weapons of last resort.

This new strategy will require different forces. We've decided that once negotiations begin on short-range nuclear forces we are prepared to eliminate all NATO nuclear artillery shells from Europe in return for reciprocal action by the Soviet Union. We agreed that this review should report its conclusions as soon as possible.

And fourth, the London Declaration transforms the alliance's vision for the CSCE and the structure for building a Europe whole and free. We know the CSCE process—bringing together North America and all of Europe—can provide a structure for Europe's continued political development; and that means new standards for free elections, the rule of law, economic liberty, and environmental cooperation. And we agreed today on six initiatives to give life to CSCE's principles and realize its potential.

As you can see, the London Declaration will bring fundamental change to every aspect of the alliance's work. This is indeed a day of renewal for the Atlantic community. For more than 40 years, we've looked for this day—a day when we have already moved beyond containment, with unity on this continent overcoming division. And now that day is here, and all peoples from the Atlantic to the Urals, from the Baltic to the Adriatic, can share in its promise.

I'd be glad to take some questions. Helen [Helen Thomas, United Press International]?

Economic Assistance for Eastern Europe and the Soviet Union

Q. Mr. President, with the end of the cold war, the drawdown in forces, and eventual denuclearization of Europe, are you now ready to give some economic help—as other allies want—to include the Soviet Union and Eastern Europe so that they can get back on their feet, as we did after World War II with Germany and Japan?

The President. Well, we have given substantial help to certain countries in Eastern Europe. I have had a discussion—not here at NATO but with Mr. Gorbachev and others at different times—about support for the Soviet Union. We are most interested in helping them go forward with their reforms.

But there was no decision taken, certainly, to send money to the Soviet Union. I have some big problems with that one. I think the American people do. But there are ways that we can assist in this transformation, in this reform that is taking place in the Soviet Union.

Q. Well, you're not opposed to other countries giving it?

The President. If the Germans decide they want to do that, that's their business. But I have made very clear to those who have spoken to me about this that at this juncture we have some serious problems, and I've not been under any false colors about that at all.

Q. President Gorbachev has imposed a 2-year deadline on himself and the Communist leaders for reversing their country's economic tailspin. Does your reluctance to give the Soviets any financial aid complicate his chances for success in meeting that deadline?

The President. I hope not, because as you know, not only have I spoken very fondly of and enthusiastically about what he's trying to do in terms of reform but I've spoken about him personally and about our interest in seeing him succeed. And he's got some extraordinarily difficult problems, but I don't think that our position on financial aid at this time should—hopefully, it will not complicate his standing. He deserves support for this reform.

Q. Do you view Western aid for the Soviet Union now as a subsidy for its military machine?

The President. Well, I'll tell you, we've got some problems that I've been very frank with concerning the Soviets. And one of them is a great percentage of their GNP going into the military. Another is some regional problems that perhaps are unique to the United States, but things that concern me—spending $5 billion a year in Cuba, for example, to sustain a totalitarian regime that is highly critical of the Soviet Union from time to time. So, we have some regional problems. We have some reform problems that should take place before financial support can be given. But perhaps there are ways that we can assist them as we go forward with credit or other matters before we go to direct government loans.

U.S. Armed Forces in Europe

Q. Mr. President, with the threat receding, in the way your communique describes, do you think it's inevitable that at some point in the next few years the Europeans will decide it's better that American troops just go home? And what do you say to American taxpayers to convince them that it's worth continuing to pay the bill to have them in Europe?

The President. Well, I don't think the American troops will stay against the will of the host country. I don't want to see American forces deployed where American forces are not wanted. I don't want to see Soviet forces deployed where Soviet forces are not wanted. And I expect the same would be true of other nationalities' forces as well. But I don't foresee that day because I think the alliance has spoken rather eloquently about the need for a common defense. And all the members of the alliance are united in their view that a U.S. force presence in Europe is stabilizing and very, very important. So, I don't see that day looming up on the horizon.

Q. But do you fear that American taxpayers' support for that continuation might be eroding?

The President. Well, I see some attacks on this, and I think this NATO declaration should help in that regard. But I view it as my responsibility to make clear to the American taxpayer why it is in our interest to help keep the peace. And that's exactly what these forces are engaged in.

Economic Assistance for the Soviet Union

Q. Mr. President, in light of the stress that's been placed here on the continued cohesion within this alliance sir, would it not be a major breach of that cohesion if a country like West Germany were to provide direct aid to the Soviet Union in light of the deep concerns which you have expressed about such aid from the West?

The President. No, I don't feel that that's a breach of alliance cohesion. The Germans have their own bilateral relationship with the Soviet Union, and it doesn't concern me one bit. I've not made one single effort to try to have the Germans look differently at that question.

Q. Mr. President, would it not then be possible that aid from our ally West Germany would, at least arguably or indirectly, flow to a country like Cuba?

The President. Well, if you want to say that anything that goes to the Soviet Union facilitates aid to Cuba, I suppose we could say the same about our trade. But I don't think that would be a fair charge to make against the Germans.

Chinese Dissident Fang Lizhi

Q. Tonight, in an interview to be broadcast in the United States, Fang Lizhi, the recently released Chinese dissident, says you owe him a dinner. He couldn't make it to the one you threw in Beijing, and he would like to be invited to the White House for dinner. Would you do that? I have a followup.

The President. Well, he's here in this country. I thought he wanted to stay out of the public eye. I thought he himself said so. So, you've got a little different information than that. We'll just defer the rest of your question. What's your followup?

Human Rights

Q. If I can follow up: If you do meet him, he is going to complain that you have a double standard for human rights—that you have one standard for the Soviet Union where you complain about human rights violations—or have in the past, at least pre-

Gorbachev—and that you don't complain so much about human rights violations—you're not as tough with the Chinese. He complains about sending Brent Scowcroft [Assistant to the President for National Security Affairs] and Larry Eagleburger [Deputy Secretary of State], et cetera. What would you say to him?

The President. I'd say that he's wrong. He's got a little time warp here because we spoke out at the NATO meeting. Indeed, I think we took the lead at a meeting in Europe—I guess it was the G–7 meeting, not NATO—where we took the lead in expressing our joint indignation in terms of the abuses of human rights at Tiananmen Square. We've kept certain sanctions on China. I am heartened that Fang Lizhi is free and free now to say what's on his mind like this. So, I would say that if he feels that way he's simply not expressing the facts as they are. I don't agree with that. I notice some of my critics in the United States Congress say that, and I think they're just as wrong as they can be.

Eastern European Membership in NATO

Q. Mr. President, back to the declaration. You're inviting the Warsaw Pact countries to come to NATO as observers. What if they want to become members of NATO—Hungary, for instance, or even Poland? Are you saying by inviting them to just be observers that you do not look favorably on them becoming full members?

The President. I'm saying NATO views this as a open invitation, and who knows what will happen in terms of membership down the line? That's not in the cards right this minute. We're just coming out of an adversarial environment of varying—I think there's varying degrees of enthusiasm for what you're talking about amongst the members of the Warsaw Pact at this juncture, so I'd say it's premature.

Q. Would you oppose any country—for instance, Hungary—becoming a member of NATO?

The President. Not forever. But at this juncture, I support the NATO doctrine.

Strategic Nuclear Weapons

Q. Mr. President, in your communique you talk about nuclear weapons becoming truly weapons of last resort. You say the fundamental strategy of the alliance is being transformed here. As part of this review, are you considering going back home and taking another look at some of the strategic nuclear modernization programs that you have supported—looking at some of the very expensive weapons programs that some say should be a bonus, a part of the "peace dividend"?

The President. Not as a result of anything that's transpired here in NATO, no. We are interested in strategic arms agreements with the Soviets. The Soviets, as we all know, have indeed modernized their forces. We're on the horns of a dilemma in that question, you might say, because we have not to the degree they have. But that was not a consideration here at NATO, nor has anything transpired here that will make me go home with a different approach to strategic arms.

Q. If I may follow up, sir: You'll proceed across the board with strategic modernization? Your commitment to that——

The President. Yes. I will proceed in negotiating with the Soviets to achieve a strategic arms agreement.

NATO Policy

Q. Mr. President, how much did threats to *perestroika* and reforms in the Soviet Union play in changes you've announced today at NATO?

The President. You mean, what's going on at the Congress [28th Communist Party Congress of the Soviet Union]? None, in my view. I mean, I think what's contributed to the changes in our approach—NATO—are the changes that have taken place, particularly since our last meeting, in terms of Eastern Europe and in terms of the Soviets' willingness to withdraw forces, hopefully, through a CFE agreement. So, I don't think anything was short—that there was short-term thinking as a result of the debates that are going on in Moscow this very day.

Q. Well, if I can follow up then: What kind of messages do the changes announced today send to Gorbachev?

The President. They send to him that here's an alliance that you should view, Mr. Gorbachev, as defensive and not threatening. And, please, convince your military and others in the Soviet Union of this fact.

You see, from my discussions with Mr. Gorbachev and others, I've had the feeling that they have viewed NATO as much more threatening to them than the way in which I've looked at NATO. But now, as a result of the actions that we've taken here, I think it should be clear to the Soviet military, to Mr. Gorbachev, to his adversaries, and to his friends inside the Soviet Union that NATO is changing. And to the degree they had seen it as a threat to their shores or to their borders, they should look at it not as a threat to their borders or to their people.

Anytime you sit down with people from the Soviet Union, they tell you of the fact that they lost from 20 to 27 million lives. It's ingrained in them. They do it not as a defensive mechanism but they do it because they feel very strongly about that. I hope that they will look at the changes that NATO has taken and say: Well, if NATO had been a threat to us, it no longer is a threat to us. And then I hope we can go forward to further document that spirit by mutual agreements on arms control.

Q. How are you going to communicate what's in this document to Mr. Gorbachev and the people there? Are you going to talk with him personally? Did the NATO leaders decide on some other method of communication with him to let him know what it means, what the communique means?

The President. The NATO leaders have decided that the Secretary General will be going there, and that will be a very good face-to-face chance to discuss these matters. I believe our Secretary of State is meeting soon with Mr. Shevardnadze [Soviet Foreign Minister], you can be sure the matters will be discussed then. And then, in all likelihood, I will discuss it personally by telephone with Mr. Gorbachev.

I think it's very important that the leader of the United States and the leader of the Soviet Union stay in touch. In fact, when he was here in Washington, we talked about more such contacts. So, perhaps within the next couple of weeks, I will be talking to him about what transpired, because I want to make some of these points here again, particularly that they ought not to view

NATO as a threat and certainly ought not to view it as a roadblock to progress in arms control or withdrawal of conventional forces or whatever it might be.

Soviet Response to NATO Policies

Q. Mr. President, what kind of tangible response would you like to see from President Gorbachev now to this? And I'm thinking particularly of the issue of Germany and NATO.

The President. In terms of the question of Germany and NATO, I would like to see the tangible response be an acceptance of the concept that a unified Germany in NATO is not only good but that it certainly is no threat to them. And we've had long talks with Mr. Gorbachev about that. And perhaps this declaration will be a document that he can use to convince others that a unified Germany in NATO is in the interest of stability and world peace. So, I think that is probably the most important message. And then I'd like to think that out of this he would feel more confident in going forward with arms control, bringing the two-plus-four talks to a conclusion, and a wide array of other things as well.

Middle East Peace Process and Talks With the Palestine Liberation Organization

Q. Did the topic of the Middle East come up during your discussions in the margins of the NATO summit? And can you comment on press reports which indicate you might be considering resuming your dialog with the PLO? And what conditions would you attach to such a resumption?

The President. The discussion of the Middle East in the NATO meetings did not come up. It may have been discussed in the corridors, but it was not a discussion in the meetings at all, and I didn't have discussions in a NATO context about the Middle East.

My position on the dialog with the PLO is that one of the preconditions for discussion was a renunciation of terror. And I viewed the aborted attack on the shores of Israel by some Palestinian commandos as a terrorist act. So, we didn't cancel; we suspended the talks with the PLO. And I would like to think that Mr. Arafat [PLO leader] could some way bring his council not only to denounce that particular terrorist act but also to take some action against the person that perpetrated it. And then I think we would certainly give rapid consideration to renewal of the dialog. I happen to think the dialog has been useful. I don't think Mr. Arafat particularly agrees with that, and I'm quite confident that Mr. Shamir [Prime Minister of Israel] doesn't agree with that, but nevertheless, that's the view of the United States.

Soviet President Gorbachev's NATO Address

Q. Mr. President, Mikhail Gorbachev is already under fire from conservatives for essentially giving away Eastern Europe. Are you at all concerned, sir, that by inviting him to speak to NATO you're further undermining him? And I have a followup.

The President. No, not only do I think we're not undermining him but I would think that would send a signal that NATO has no hostile intentions to the Soviet Union. So, I would hope nobody at home would consider this an effort to undermine Mr. Gorbachev, nor would it have the effect of undermining a man who has clearly tried to move forward, who has presided over the Soviet Union at a time when this fantastic change towards democracy and freedom has taken place in Eastern Europe. And you're seeing that same kind of quest for change—democratic change and economic change—inside the Soviet Union. So, I don't think it would have the effect that the question suggests.

Q. If he accepts your invitation, sir, will you attend that meeting, or would it be an occasion for some sort of a superpower summit?

The President. The level of the Gorbachev meeting at NATO has not been determined. And I would be guided by what the other NATO members think is appropriate. The level at which Mr. Gorbachev would speak to NATO has not been set. If it was a head of state level, why, of course, I would attend. Others have addressed NATO at varying levels.

East-West Relations and Political and Economic Change

Q. Having attended quite a number of these things, these NATO conferences, I'd like to ask a question, Mr. President, that I asked—[*inaudible*]—is this to some extent a celebration of the victory of NATO in the cold war—the cold war is over and NATO has won? Or don't you believe it's the idea that NATO has won the cold war?

The President. Excuse me, back up, now. I've tried to avoid code words, and the cold war being over is something that I'd rather not comment on. I don't think we're dealing in terms of victory and defeat. We're dealing in terms of how do we stabilize and guarantee the peace and security of Europe. So, to the degree a chief of state or head of government dwells on the kinds of rhetoric that you understandably ask about, I think it is counterproductive. Does that answer it?

Q. Would you say that NATO has to a great extent caused Gorbachev to be—that the whole changes in Eastern Europe have to some extent been caused by what's been going on in Western Europe for the last 40 years?

The President. I would say to some degree that the changes in Eastern Europe and in the Soviet Union have been because they have seen the success of market economies. They've seen a craving for freedom and democracy on the parts of people. And to the degree NATO countries contributed to that proper perception, so be it. I'd like to think that—I'm convinced that NATO's solidarity during the last 40 years has guaranteed the peace for Europe. And when you look back at history, it is a long peace, given some of the conflagrations on this continent. So, I think NATO deserves a lot of credit.

But I think the yearning for freedom and democracy is pretty fundamental. NATO has nothing to do with the changes in our own Western Hemisphere, and yet you're seeing now the emergence of democracies, and you've seen the emergence of free people there. So, it's fundamental: People want democracy and freedom. But I think NATO's major contribution has been to keeping the peace, and yet it has set an example that I think many in Eastern Europe now want to follow.

Changes in the Soviet Union

Q. Mr. President, how do you square your concern over stability in Europe, which is the new purpose of NATO, with increasing signs of instability in the Soviet Union, particularly on the political and economic front? And what can you do to put those two pieces of the puzzle together?

The President. A very good and very difficult question because, frankly, one thing we do is stay out of the internal affairs of the Soviet Union. I realize that some think that I'm not staying out of the internal affairs of the Soviet Union when I speak pleasantly about Mr. Gorbachev.

But I think they have to sort it out now. They have to decide what they want, how much of their gross national product ought to go into arms, whether the threat is much less than they have historically perceived. And once they take that decision, then we in the West will stand ready to work very cooperatively with them. But I think the next move, what I'm saying, is up to them. I think they have to make these determinations. And in the meantime, NATO, having seen the changes that have taken place in Eastern Europe and the predicted changes in terms of force levels, can go forward with what I think people will view as a historic document.

Excuse me, I did tell you I'd get over here.

Nuclear Artillery

Q. Thank you very much. How conditional is the proposal to remove nuclear artillery from Europe? Are you actually saying that you will not do this unless the Soviet Union does likewise? Are you saying it should be part of negotiations, or are you actually merely inviting the Soviet Union to withdraw their nuclear artillery?

The President. Well, I'd certainly invite them to do it, and the document is fairly clear on that point. I think that the withdrawal of nuclear artillery on the part of the West is conditioned on the withdrawal of Soviet nuclear artillery.

German Membership in NATO

Q. On paragraph 12—"manpower levels of united Germany"—what happened to nonsingularization of Germany?

The President. Well, I don't see that as singularization. That was a question that had to be addressed anyway. And I think that you're going to see the United States addressing its force levels through CFE talks. So, I would think that this is not what I have always thought of as singularization, trying to single Germany out, for example— a united Germany—from being a part of NATO. I think what it simply says is this question, at an appropriate time, will be addressed. And we are going forward, addressing ourselves now to U.S. force levels under our conventional force talks. So, I don't see any contradiction in that.

There was a guy on the aisle that I identified back there—no, I'm afraid it wasn't you, but right there—that had his hand up. Well, he's vanished. The guy in the open shirt here. Then I have to go. Go ahead, we'll get these two, and then I really have to take off.

East-West Relations

Q. Would you say that you are hoping that Gorbachev can convince other people that through this document that they do not have to fear NATO? Are you saying that some of the people in the Soviet Union are imposing this fear to NATO—to Mr. Gorbachev, and who are these people? I have a followup question, please.

The President. If I got the first part of it correctly, I think there's been a historic fear on the part of some about the West because of the Soviets' own history. I happen to believe that that fear has been misplaced all along. But to the degree people still have that fear, and they look at this document, it would seem to be de minimus. I can't single out which people they are, but I think there has been a historic concern on the part of the Soviets because of their own history in—certainly as recently as World War II, with an enormous loss of life. I think over the years, as we have improved our relations with the Soviet Union and, indeed, as they have changed, those fears have diminished. I think—given the new openness, the *glasnost*—I think they're going to diminish even more.

What was the followup?

Q. How do you expect that Mr. Gorbachev can be helped in his present problems in the Soviet Union with this London Declaration?

The President. I think he will say: Look, NATO has indeed changed in response to the changes that have taken place in Eastern Europe. If I were him, I'd say: I've been right. They're changing. And now I want to go forward with the United States and negotiate some more deals. I want to see us reform. I want to see us stop some of what we've been doing in various regions around the world that others view as detrimental to the interests of freedom and democracy. And so, if I were him, I would take a hard look at this document. I'd listen carefully to what he hears from Manfred Woerner when he goes there. And I would think he could say: We've been right to reach out as we have tried to do to the United States and, indeed, to improve relations with countries in Western Europe. They're changing. They have now changed their doctrine because of steps that I, Mr. Gorbachev, have taken. And I get on the offense. Then let the rest of us help him with some of his hardliners. And there's plenty of work to do.

But I would think that he would view this as a very positive step forward and one that vindicates some of the moves that he's made over the past year or two.

Q. Will he join NATO?

Middle East Peace Process

Q. Mr. President, now that you've had time to digest Prime Minister Shamir's letter to you of last week, how does that letter leave you feeling? Does it leave you feeling, as Secretary Baker said, that maybe we should just leave him with the White House phone number and to call when he's serious; or does it leave you feeling you're ready now to get involved in a prolonged negotiation with him, once again spending another few months or years to try to modify his position?

The President. It leaves me feeling we need further clarification in terms of the questions that I've put to him, clarification on some of the answers. But, look, we want to see the peace process go forward. We had good talks with—I did, and so did Jim Baker—with the Egyptian Foreign Minister [Ahmed Esmat Abdel Meguid] the other day. I've been on the phone to Mr. Mubarak [President of Egypt], to King Hussein [of Jordan], to others. And we want to see the process go forward. We have the United States policy, and we're going to stay with the policy in terms of settlements and other things of this question.

But we will do everything we can to encourage a discussion that will end up in peace. There has got to be talks; Palestinians have to attend these talks. And so, the ground rules are out there, and we've got to go forward. But we need more clarification, and very candidly, I'd like to think that Israel would now move forward again. And that's about where we stand.

Thank you very much.

The President's Hand

Q. What's wrong with your hand?

The President. It's skewered. I was cleaning the mackerel, and I plunged the knife into it. Minor wound.

Note: The President's 53d news conference began at 12:18 p.m. in Churchill Auditorium at the Queen Elizabeth II Conference Center. In his opening remarks, he referred to Prime Minister Margaret Thatcher of the United Kingdom and NATO Secretary General Manfred Woerner. Following the news conference, the President traveled to Houston, TX, for the economic summit of industrialized nations, which took place July 9–11. A complete tape was not available for verification of the content of these remarks.

Statement by Press Secretary Fitzwater on the President's Meeting With Prime Minister Toshiki Kaifu of Japan Prior to the Houston Economic Summit
July 7, 1990

President Bush and Prime Minister Kaifu have just finished 2 hours of wide-ranging discussions on our bilateral relationship and the global partnership of international cooperation between our two countries. The two leaders have a very warm, personal relationship, calling each other by first names.

They agreed that the state of U.S.-Japan relations today is excellent and that both countries need to continue to work together in a spirit of cooperation to strengthen their bilateral relationship and support democracy, freedom, and economic liberty around the world.

The President took this opportunity to thank the Prime Minister for his outstanding leadership, which contributed so much to achieving an excellent joint report in our Structural Impediments Initiative (SII). The commitments for reform in this report, when implemented, will strengthen the economies of both our countries and lead to a better life for the Japanese and American peoples and a healthier economic relationship. The progress we have made these past 4 months in the SII process and our other trade discussions has laid a firmer foundation for our overall relationship. But we cannot become complacent in the days to come; we must ensure that our relationship continues to rest on a solid economic base.

The President and the Prime Minister emphasized that the time has come for the United States and Japan, as two of the world's greatest trading nations, to devote their full energy to securing the benefits of an open world trading system through successful completion of the Uruguay round this year.

The President took this opportunity to brief the Prime Minister on the results of the NATO summit just concluded in London. The Prime Minister and the President reaffirmed in this, the 30th anniversary year of the security treaty, the continuing importance of the alliance to peace and stability in Asia.

Japan and the United States agreed to continue to promote important global cooperation in this era of great change, in cooperation with our other summit partners. The President welcomed and encouraged Japan's growing international role, as evidenced by the contributions it is making in support of political and economic freedom in Eastern Europe, Central and South America, and elsewhere. Cooperation among Japan, the United States, and their summit partners in support of common goals will form a central part of the talks to be held during the next few days and is a manifestation of the trialog to which both leaders committed themselves at their meeting in Palm Springs.

The President and the Prime Minister discussed the issue of lending to China. They had useful talks on this matter and agreed to continue these discussions with the other summit leaders.

Finally, the President and the Prime Minister, looking back at the progress our two governments have made toward the goals at the Palm Springs summit last March, agreed to continue to work to build the kind of economic, security, and political relationship between our two countries that will be appropriate to our two great nations in this dramatically changing world.

Note: The President met with the Prime Minister at approximately 11:30 a.m. at the Houstonian Hotel's Manor House in Houston, TX. Later, the two leaders were joined by U.S. and Japanese officials and participated in a working luncheon.

Remarks Announcing Canada-United States Air Quality Negotiations and an Exchange With Reporters in Houston, Texas
July 8, 1990

The President. Well, we're here to comment on the acid rain agreement. The joint statement that we're issuing today on beginning negotiations is long overdue. I know that this is very important for the Canadian side; and I want to say to you, sir, I appreciate your patience and understanding.

Both Houses now in the United States Congress have passed clean air bills, similar to mine, by huge margins; and the House-Senate conference will begin this week. And I think it will be of enormous benefit to both our countries. Bill Reilly, the head of the EPA, plans to be in Ottawa on July 16th and will be prepared to open preliminary discussions. We should be able to begin formal negotiations shortly after that.

And we've made great progress. And I think we ought to both be very pleased about that. Great progress has been made, but we still have a long way to go. We recognize that. And I pledge to my Canadian friends that we want to do our part, and I think this clean air legislation—that I hope I'll be able to sign soon—is but one manifestation of that.

Welcome to Houston, sir. And the floor is yours.

Prime Minister Mulroney. Thank you, Mr. President.

I'm pleased to confirm that the President and I have agreed to begin negotiations for an air quality accord. Our two countries share a long history of cooperation on transboundary environmental problems. An acid rain agreement will safeguard the natural health of our respective ecosystems, and we both fought—President Bush and I—have fought long and hard to get to where we are today.

Bill Reilly and Bob De Cotret [Canadian Minister of the Environment] will discuss this issue when they meet in Ottawa in about a week's time, and as the President has indicated, negotiations will begin shortly thereafter.

And so, we have worked hard for a bilateral accord, and I think that this day will long be remembered in the history of our relationship for the significant departure that it constitutes from past positions in regard to the environment and the protection of the environment in North America.

Thank you, Mr. President.

Q. Are you going to take some from the Canadian press?

The Prime Minister. I think I'll—the Canadians have been in the heat too long.

Q. Mr. President, can I just clear——

Q. ——an accord will give Canada any more protection than it already gets from legislation?

The President. I simply refer you to the statement.

Q. Mr. Mulroney, we'd like to talk to you.

Economic Assistance for the Soviet Union

Q. ——Canadian credit to the Soviet Union, sir? Does that not undercut your policy?

The President. Nothing undercuts our policy like that——

Q. Mr. Mulroney, what would the accord give you that the clean air legislation does not?

Q. He subsidizes aid to Cuba if he gives him credit?

Q. Mr. President, we're still confused about whether Mr. Gorbachev, who specifically asked this summit last year for a role—whether he has made any direct appeal to you as host of the summit to——

The President. We'll have more to say about that later. What I want to do is talk to our summit partners on that very question. We had a good discussion with the Prime Minister on new ideas from the Canadian side. But I don't want to get out ahead of the process here, and I have some responsibility to be sure that our summit partners are briefed on that Gorbachev letter before we go public.

Note: The President spoke at 11:42 a.m. in the front foyer of the Houstonian Hotel's Manor House, following a meeting with Prime Minister Brian Mulroney of Canada.

Joint Statement Announcing Canada-United States Air Quality Negotiations
July 8, 1990

Our two countries share a great legacy of bountiful natural resources and scenic grandeur, as well as a long history of cooperation on transboundary environmental problems. It is critical to the future well-being of Canada and the United States that we assure the continued productivity and environmental health of these natural systems: the Great Lakes and other shared water bodies, the forests, the wildlife, and the soils and farmlands.

Thus, we announce with great satisfaction that our countries have agreed to begin negotiations for a practical and effective air quality accord. U.S. Environmental Protection Agency Administrator William K. Reilly and Canadian Environment Minister Robert de Cotret will discuss this issue when they meet in mid-July in Ottawa. We expect to begin negotiations shortly thereafter.

The initial focus of these negotiations will be on reduction of sulfur dioxide and other precursors of acid rain. With clean air legislation now before a Conference Committee of the House and Senate of the U.S. Congress, the United States anticipates substantial progress in the years ahead in curbing acid rain and improving air quality. Since 1985 Canada has had in place its own control program which will reduce both acid rain damage in Canada and the export of pollution to the United States. We look forward to a close working relationship between Canada and the United States to assure that our agreement on air quality and our other bilateral programs yield tangible environmental improvements and benefits.

Statement by Press Secretary Fitzwater on President Bush's Meeting With President François Mitterrand of France Prior to the Houston Economic Summit
July 9, 1990

President Bush and President Mitterrand met for about an hour this morning to discuss the summit agenda. They had lengthy talks on the Uruguay round and the prospect for a summit statement that moves the Uruguay round forward.

They talked about a number of environmental issues, including the general progress that summit countries have made in cleaning up various pollutants, in preserving their forests, and in balancing economic and environmental objectives.

The two Presidents were encouraged by the Soviet response to their recent NATO communique. Both the United States and France want to support *perestroika* and *glasnost* and encourage the success of President Gorbachev. They discussed the role of economic support and considered the economic possibilities raised in the letter to the [economic] summit from President Gorbachev. President Bush reiterated the U.S. position that we believe technical economic assistance is appropriate; and he has proposed several steps, both at Malta and in Washington, which should be helpful. However, the United States continues to believe that further economic reforms and spending priorities in the Soviet Union are necessary before direct aid is justified.

Note: The two Presidents met at approximately 9 a.m. at the Houstonian Hotel's Manor House in Houston, TX.

Statement by Press Secretary Fitzwater on the President's Meeting With Chancellor Helmut Kohl of the Federal Republic of Germany Prior to the Houston Economic Summit
July 9, 1990

President Bush met with Chancellor Kohl for approximately an hour this morning and discussed the summit agenda. Chancellor Kohl congratulated President Bush on the success of the NATO summit. Both Presidents expressed appreciation for the Soviet response.

The two leaders discussed President Gorbachev's letter to the [economic] summit and their positions on aid to the Soviet Union. President Bush said he understood the German desire for unilateral support to the Soviet Union. President Bush emphasized that the United States supports *perestroika* and *glasnost* and had suggested a variety of technical economic assistance measures in support of President Gorbachev's efforts. President Bush indicated that we

continue to believe that further economic reforms and changes in Soviet military spending are necessary before we can consider direct aid.

The two leaders discussed the progress of change in Eastern Europe and reviewed the democracies emerging in Poland, Hungary, and Czechoslovakia.

Both the President and the Chancellor expressed great concern about the world environment and pledged to continue efforts at reducing pollution and preserving forests on a global basis.

Note: The President met with the Chancellor at approximately 10:30 a.m. at the Houstonian Hotel's Manor House in Houston, TX.

Remarks at the Welcoming Ceremony for the Houston Economic Summit
July 9, 1990

Welcome to Houston. And we think this city is a very appropriate place to host this economic summit not of the postwar era but of the post-postwar era.

Over the past decade and a half, the leaders of the largest industrialized democracies have held these summits to address common problems and challenges. These economic summits have become framework for frank and constructive dialog, a dialog for progress that I believe will be advanced greatly in these next 3 days. And together, we're called upon as allies and as friends to work toward decisions here in Houston that

will bring a new stability and prosperity to the world by tapping the power and energy of free wills and free markets.

A new world of freedom lays before us, hopeful, confident—a world where peace endures, where commerce has conscience, and where all that seems possible is possible. So, let us begin in good faith to set the stage for the new millennium. Thank you for coming to Houston, and thank all who have made us feel so at home here. Thank you very much.

Note: The President spoke at 2:13 p.m. in

the Academic Quadrangle at Rice University in Houston, TX. The 1990 economic
summit of industrialized nations was
hosted by the United States. The following
foreign leaders, accompanied by their foreign and finance ministers, attended the
summit: Prime Minister Brian Mulroney of
Canada, President Jacques Delors of the European Community, Chancellor Helmut
Kohl of the Federal Republic of Germany,
President François Mitterrand of France,
Prime Minister Giulio Andreotti of Italy,
Prime Minister Toshiki Kaifu of Japan, and
Prime Minister Margaret Thatcher of the
United Kingdom. A tape was not available
for verification of the content of these re-
marks.

Houston Economic Summit Political Declaration: Securing Democracy
July 10, 1990

1. We, the Leaders of our seven countries and the Representatives of the European Community, salute the men and women around the world whose courage and wisdom have inspired and brought about the historic advances of democracy we have witnessed over the past year. As we enter the final decade of this century, which we intend should be a Decade of Democracy, we reiterate our commitment to support the strengthening of democracy, human rights, and economic reconstruction and de-velopment through market-oriented econo-mies. We emphasize the important opportu-nity provided in this forum for representa-tives from Europe, Japan, and North Amer-ica to discuss critical challenges of the coming years.

2. Europe is at the dawn of a new era. We welcome enthusiastically the profound and historic changes sweeping the conti-nent. The London Declaration on a Trans-formed North Atlantic Alliance provides a new basis for cooperation among former ad-versaries in building a stable, secure, and peaceful Europe. We are determined to seize all opportunities to achieve a Europe whole and free and recognize the European Community's contribution to that effort. We applaud the unification of Germany, which is a tangible expression of mankind's inalienable right to self-determination and a major contribution to stability in Europe. We welcome the replacement of repres-sive regimes in Central and Eastern Europe by governments freely chosen by their peo-ples. We applaud the introduction of the rule of law and the freedoms that are the bedrock of a democratic state. We urge Ro-mania, following recent events, to adhere to the positive trend taking place in other countries of Central and Eastern Europe.

3. We welcome the intention of the Soviet Union to move toward a democratic political system, as well as Soviet attempts to reform their economy along market prin-ciples. We commit ourselves to working with the Soviet Union to assist its efforts to create an open society, a pluralistic democ-racy, and a market-oriented economy. Such changes will enable the Soviet Union to ful-fill its responsibilities in the community of nations founded on these principles. We are heartened by indications that a constructive dialogue is underway between the Soviet government and the Baltic states, and we urge all sides to continue this dialogue in a democratic spirit.

4. The advance of democracy accompa-nied by market-oriented economic reforms is not just a European phenomenon. Since we last met, we have witnessed the spread of democratic values in many parts of the world.

In Asia, there are encouraging signs of new political openness in Mongolia and Nepal. In the Philippines, the government continues to engage in courageous efforts to consolidate democracy.

We acknowledge some of the recent de-velopments in China, but believe that the prospects for closer cooperation will be enhanced by renewed political and economic reform, particularly in the field of human rights. We agree to maintain the measures put into place at last year's Summit, as modified over the course of this year. We will keep them under review for future adjustments to respond to further positive developments in China. For example, in addition to existing lending to meet basic human needs, we will explore whether there are other World Bank loans that would contribute to reform of the Chinese economy, especially loans that would address environmental concerns.

5. In Africa, we hope that Namibia's attainment of independence and democracy will be a positive example for freedom, pluralism, and market-oriented economic reform throughout the continent. We also welcome the positive developments that have taken place in South Africa, especially the launching of talks between the government and representatives of the black majority. We hope this will lead to a peaceful transition to a non-racial democracy and the complete dismantlement of the apartheid system. We will continue to support this process and we call on all parties to refrain from violence or its advocacy.

6. In Latin America, we welcome the reestablishment of freedom and democracy in Chile. We applaud the recent fair and free elections in Nicaragua, as well as progress on the path to peace through dialogue in El Salvador and Guatemala. We encourage the efforts of the Panamanian government to re-establish democracy and the rule of law. We note with satisfaction the positive evolution in Haiti. We hope that Cuba will take steps to join the democratic trend in the rest of Latin America.

7. While we applaud the reduction of ideological conflicts that have divided much of the world since the end of the Second World War, we note with deep concern the reemergence of intolerance affecting ethnic and religious groups. We agree that such intolerance can lead to conflicts, which can threaten fundamental human rights, as well as political and economic development.

8. We reaffirm our commitment to the fundamental principles we seek to realize in our own societies, and we underscore that political and economic freedoms are closely linked and mutually reinforcing. Each of us stands ready to help in practical ways those countries that choose freedom, through the provision of constitutional, legal, and economic know-how and through economic assistance, as appropriate.

In drawing from our different constitutional and historical experiences, we stand ready, individually and jointly in relevant fora, to:

—assist in the drafting of laws, including bills of rights and civil, criminal, and economic framework laws;

—advise in the fostering of independent media;

—establish training programs in government, management, and technical fields;

—develop and expand people-to-people contacts and exchange programs to help diffuse understanding and knowledge.

In the same spirit, the recent G–24 Ministerial agreed to extend its assistance in Central and Eastern Europe in parallel with progress in political and economic reform.

We agree the challenge facing the industrialized democracies is to continue the effort already underway in Europe while expanding efforts to support political reform and economic development in other parts of the world. We call on our people and the people of other democracies to join in this great endeavor.

Note: The declaration was made available by the Office of the Press Secretary but was not issued as a White House press release.

Houston Economic Summit Statement on Transnational Issues
July 10, 1990

Terrorism

We, the Heads of State or Government, reaffirm our condemnation of terrorism in all its forms, our commitment to make no concessions to terrorists or their sponsors, and our resolve to continue to cooperate in efforts to combat terrorism. We demand that those governments which provide support to terrorists end such support immediately. We are determined not to allow terrorists to remain unpunished, but to see them brought to justice in accordance with international law and national legislation.

We welcome the recent release of several hostages, but remain deeply concerned that hostages are still being held, some for more than five years. Their ordeal and that of their families must end. We call for the immediate, unconditional and safe release of all hostages and for an accounting of all persons taken hostage who may have died while being held. We call on those with influence over hostage-takers to use their influence to this end.

We note with deep concern the continuing threat presented to civil aviation by terrorist groups, as demonstrated by such outrages as the sabotage of civil aircraft over Lockerbie, Scotland on December 21, 1988, above Niger on September 19, 1989, and over Colombia on November 27, 1989. We reiterate our determination to fight terrorist assaults against civil aviation.

Accordingly, we will continue our cooperation to negotiate a convention requiring the introduction of additives into plastic explosives to aid in their detection. We pledge to work to strengthen international civil aviation security standards. Consistent with this objective, we note the importance of making available training and technical assistance to other nations. We support initiatives undertaken through the International Civil Aviation Organization (ICAO) regarding this issue. We will work together with ICAO to expand such assistance.

Non-Proliferation

We discussed the threat to international security posed by the proliferation of nuclear, chemical and biological weapons, and of ballistic missile weapons delivery systems.

With regard to nuclear proliferation, we take special note of the recent declaration issued by the European Council in Dublin on that subject. That document underscored the great importance attached to the maintenance of an effective international nuclear non-proliferation regime and the need to make every effort to contribute to strengthening non-proliferation and encouraging the participation of further countries in the regime. The Treaty on Non-Proliferation of Nuclear Weapons (NPT) is an important element of that regime. We further endorse the EC's call for all states to apply IAEA safeguards on as universal a basis as possible.

We also urge all nuclear suppliers to adopt nuclear export control measures equivalent to the Nuclear Suppliers Group Guidelines.

Whether NPT parties or not, we commit ourselves to working actively to secure a satisfactory outcome to nuclear non-proliferation discussions in the forthcoming months, including those at the Fourth Review Conference of the NPT.

We hope that these discussions will contribute to the achievement of as broad a consensus as possible in favor of an equitable and stable non-proliferation regime. Such a regime should be based on an indispensable balance between the non-proliferation of arms and the development of peaceful and safe uses of nuclear energy.

The global community has focussed for decades on nuclear proliferation, especially when combined with advanced missile delivery systems. Today we also face new and growing problems from the proliferation of chemical and biological weapons.

With regard to chemical and biological proliferation, we commit ourselves to pursue efforts to prevent the diversion of chemical precursors at a national level, as well as in the relevant Western fora. We similarly commit ourselves to be vigilant about the danger of potential diversions in the field of biological technologies.

We endorse a complete ban on chemical weapons, through an effective and verifiable treaty, as the only long-term guarantee against the proliferation of chemical weapons. We believe an important step toward achieving such a treaty was made in the recent U.S.-Soviet agreement on destruction and non-production of chemical weapons and the recent declaration of intent by NATO states to become original signatories to the Chemical Weapons Convention. We reiterate our determination, first expressed at the 1989 Paris Conference on Chemical Weapons, to redouble the effort at the Conference on Disarmament in Geneva to resolve the remaining issues and to conclude the Convention at the earliest date. We also urge all states to become parties as soon as it is concluded. Similarly, as the 1991 Review Conference on the Biological Weap-

ons Convention approaches, we call on all nations that have not become party to the Convention to do so and to participate in confidence-building measures designed to strengthen its effectiveness.

We wish to highlight the importance of dealing with the related threat of ballistic missiles capable of delivering nuclear, chemical and biological weapons. We note especially the contribution of the Missile Technology Control Regime (MTCR) to our joint efforts to control missile proliferation. We applaud the recent decisions of additional nations to adhere to the MTCR, and we call upon all nations to observe the MTCR Guidelines.

Note: The portion of the statement concerning nonproliferation referred to the International Atomic Energy Agency (IAEA). The statement was made available by the Office of the Press Secretary but was not issued as a White House press release.

Houston Economic Summit Economic Declaration
July 11, 1990

1. We, the Heads of State and Government of the seven major industrial democracies and the President of the Commission of the European Communities, meeting in Houston for our annual Economic Summit, celebrate the renaissance of democracy throughout much of the world. We welcome unreservedly the spread of multiparty democracy, the practice of free elections, the freedom of expression and assembly, the increased respect for human rights, the rule of law, and the increasing recognition of the principles of the open and competitive economy. These events proclaim loudly man's inalienable rights: When people are free to choose, they choose freedom.

2. The profound changes taking place in Europe, and progress toward democracy elsewhere, give us great hope for a world in which individuals have increasing opportunities to achieve their economic and political aspirations, free of tyranny and oppression.

3. We are mindful that freedom and economic prosperity are closely linked and mutually reinforcing. Sustainable economic prosperity depends upon the stimulus of competition and the encouragement of enterprise—on incentives for individual initiative and innovation, on a skilled and motivated labor force whose fundamental rights are protected, on sound monetary systems, on an open system of international trade and payments, and on an environment safeguarded for future generations.

4. Around the world, we are determined to assist other peoples to achieve and sustain economic prosperity and political freedom. We will support their efforts with our experience, resources, and goodwill.

THE INTERNATIONAL ECONOMIC SITUATION

5. In recent years, substantial progress has been achieved in promoting a stronger world economy through sound macroeconomic policies and greater economic effi-

ciency. The economic expansion in our countries, now in its eighth year, has supported notable income growth and job creation in the context of rapid growth of international trade. However, unemployment remains high in a number of countries. Inflation, although considerably lower than in the early 1980s, is a matter of serious concern in some countries and requires continued vigilance. External imbalances have been reduced in the United States and Japan, whereas in other cases they have increased. Continuing adjustment remains a priority in order to counter protectionist pressures, alleviate uncertainties in financial and exchange markets, and contribute to avoiding pressures on interest rates. Sound domestic macroeconomic policies, which may differ according to conditions in each country, will make a major contribution to further external adjustment.

6. In the developing world, the experience of the late 1980s varied widely. Some economies, particularly in East Asia, continued to experience impressive domestic growth rates. The economies of a number of other developing countries have been stagnant or declined. Nonetheless, serious efforts—in some cases by new leadership—to implement economic adjustment and market-oriented policies have begun to yield positive results and should be continued.

INTERNATIONAL MONETARY DEVELOPMENTS AND POLICY COORDINATION

7. At a time of growing economic interdependence, the Summit countries have developed a cooperative process based on a common appreciation of the need for market-oriented policies and the importance of sound domestic budgetary and monetary policies. This process has contributed importantly to the strengthened performance of the world economy and to improved stability of exchange rates by concentrating attention on multilateral surveillance and close coordination of economic policies, including cooperation on exchange markets. It is important to continue and, where appropriate, to strengthen this cooperative and flexible approach to improve the functioning of the international monetary system and contribute to its stability.

8. To sustain the present economic expansion to the benefit of all countries, each nation must pursue sound policies. Balanced expansion of demand with increasing productive capacity is key, while external imbalances and structural rigidities require correction. Price pressures warrant continued vigilance.

9. Countries with sizable current account deficits should contribute to the adjustment process by the reduction of fiscal deficits, and undertake structural reforms to encourage private saving and increase competitiveness.

10. Countries with large external surpluses should contribute to the adjustment process by sustained non-inflationary growth of domestic demand with structural reform in order to improve the underlying conditions for growth and adjustment and to promote increased investment relative to saving.

11. The investment needs of the world as a whole are expected to grow in the coming years, particularly in Central and Eastern Europe and in developing countries undertaking market reforms, as well as in some industrial countries. To meet these needs, industrial and developing countries alike should foster saving and discourage dissaving.

12. The market-oriented restructuring of Central and Eastern European economies should stimulate their growth and increase their integration into the global economy. We support these changes and seek to assure that this difficult transformation will contribute to global growth and stability.

13. Within the European Community, the European Monetary System is leading to a high degree of economic convergence and stability. We note the European Community's decision to launch the Intergovernmental Conference on Economic and Monetary Union and the beginning of the first stage of that union. During this first stage, closer surveillance and coordination of economic and monetary policies will contribute toward non-inflationary growth and a more robust international economic system.

14. We welcome the prospect of a unified, democratic Germany which enjoys full

sovereignty without discriminatory constraints. German economic, monetary, and social union will contribute to improved non-inflationary global growth and to a reduction of external imbalances. This process will promote positive economic developments in Central and Eastern Europe.

15. We call on the member countries of the International Monetary Fund (IMF) to implement the agreement by the IMF to increase quotas by 50 percent under the Ninth General Review of Quotas and to strengthen the IMF arrears strategy.

Measures Aimed at Economic Efficiency

16. Considerable progress has been made over the past few years in supplementing macroeconomic policies with reforms to increase economic efficiency. We welcome the progress in the realization of the internal market in the European Community and the continuing efforts to reduce structural rigidities in North America and Japan. Nonetheless, we emphasize the widespread need for further steps to promote regulatory reform and liberalize areas such as retail trade, telecommunications, transport, labor markets, and financial markets, as well as to reduce industrial and agricultural subsidies, improve tax systems, and improve labor-force skills through education and training.

17. We welcome the major contributions of the Organization for Economic Cooperation and Development (OECD) in identifying structural policy challenges and options. We encourage the OECD to strengthen its surveillance and review procedures, and to find ways of making its work operationally more effective.

THE INTERNATIONAL TRADING SYSTEM

18. The open world trading system is vital to economic prosperity. A strengthened General Agreement on Tariffs and Trade (GATT) is essential to provide a stable framework for the expansion of trade and the fuller integration of Central and Eastern Europe and developing countries into the global economy. We reject protectionism in all its forms.

19. The successful outcome of the Uruguay Round has the highest priority on the international economic agenda. Conse-

quently, we stress our determination to take the difficult political decisions necessary to achieve far-reaching, substantial results in all areas of the Uruguay Round by the end of this year. We instruct our negotiators to make progress and in particular to agree on the complete profile of the final package by the July meeting of the Trade Negotiations Committee.

20. We confirm our strong support for the essential broad objectives of the negotiations: reform of agricultural policies; a substantial and balanced package of measures to improve market access; strengthened multilateral rules and disciplines; the incorporation of new issues of services, trade-related investment measures, and intellectual property protection within the GATT framework; and integration of developing countries into the international trading system.

21. As regards agriculture, achieving the long-term objective of the reform of agricultural policies is critical to permit the greater liberalization of trade in agricultural products. Experience has shown the high cost of agricultural policies which tend to create surpluses. The outcome of the GATT negotiations on agriculture should lead to a better balance between supply and demand and ensure that agricultural policies do not impede the effective functioning of international markets. We therefore reaffirm our commitment to the long-term objective of the reform, i.e., to allow market signals to influence agriculture production and to establish a fair and market-oriented agricultural trading system.

22. The achievement of this objective requires each of us to make substantial, progressive reductions in support and protection of agriculture—covering internal regimes, market access, and export subsidies—and develop rules governing sanitary and phytosanitary measures. Variations among countries in the mechanisms of agricultural support reflect differences in the social and economic conditions of farming. The negotiations on agriculture should therefore be conducted in a framework that includes a common instrument of measurement, provides for commitments to be made in an equitable way among all coun-

tries, and takes into account concerns about food security. The framework should contain specific assurances that, by appropriate use of the common measure as well as other ways, participants would reduce not only internal support but also export subsidies and import protection in a related way.

23. Agreement on such a framework by the time of the July meeting of the Trade Negotiations Committee is critical to the successful completion of the Uruguay Round as a whole. Accordingly, we commend to our negotiators the text submitted by the Chairman of the Agricultural Negotiating Group as a means to intensify the negotiations. We intend to maintain a high level of personal involvement and to exercise the political leadership necessary to ensure the successful outcome of these negotiations.

24. Negotiations on market access should achieve agreement on a substantial and balanced package of measures. As regards textiles, the objective is to liberalize the textile and clothing sector through progressive dismantling of trade barriers and its integration, under a precise timetable, into GATT on the basis of strengthened GATT rules and disciplines.

25. Negotiations on multilateral rules and disciplines should strengthen GATT rules in areas such as safeguards, balance of payments, rules of origin, and updated disciplines for dumping and antidumping measures. Concerning subsidies, rules are needed which will effectively discipline domestic subsidies so as to avoid trade distortions, competitive subsidization, and trade conflicts. Improved disciplines must also cover countervailing measures so that they do not become barriers to trade.

26. As regards the new areas, the aim is to develop new rules and procedures within the GATT framework, including: a framework of contractually enforceable rules to liberalize services trade, with no sector excluded *a priori*; an agreement to reduce trade distorting effects of trade-related investment measures; and an agreement to provide for standards and effective enforcement of all intellectual property rights.

27. A successful Uruguay Round is essential for industrialized and developing countries alike. We seek the widest possible participation of developing countries in the Round and their further integration into the multilateral trading system. To achieve this objective, developed countries are prepared to accept greater multilateral disciplines in all areas and to offer improved market access in areas of interest to developing countries such as textiles and clothing, tropical products, and agriculture.

28. For their part, developing countries should substantially reduce their tariffs and increase the percentage of tariffs that are bound; subscribe to balanced and effective restraints on all forms of exceptions, including measures imposed for balance-of-payments difficulties; and participate meaningfully in agreements covering the new areas. The end result should be a single set of multilateral rules applicable to all GATT contracting parties, although some developing countries, especially the least developed, may need longer transition periods or other transitional arrangements on a case by case basis.

29. The wide range of substantive results which we seek in all these areas will call for a commitment to strengthen further the institutional framework of the multilateral trading system. In that context, the concept of an international trade organization should be addressed at the conclusion of the Uruguay Round. We also need to improve the dispute settlement process in order to implement the results of the negotiations effectively. This should lead to a commitment to operate only under the multilateral rules.

DIRECT INVESTMENT

30. Free flows of investment increase global prosperity by complementing the open international trade system. In particular, foreign direct investment can help restructure the economies of developing and Central and Eastern European countries, create new jobs, and raise living standards.

31. All countries should therefore seek to reduce their barriers to investment and resist protectionist pressures to discourage or discriminate against such investment. The OECD and the GATT should continue to promote investment liberalization. The multilateral development banks and the

IMF should require investment liberalization in their programs in Central and Eastern Europe and developing countries.

EXPORT CREDITS

32. We welcome the important negotiations that are underway in the OECD on a balanced package of measures to strengthen multilateral disciplines on trade- and aid-distorting export credit subsidies. This package, to be completed by spring of 1991, should reduce substantially, through improved discipline and transparency, distortions resulting from the use of officially supported commercial and aid credits. It is also important to avoid introducing trade distortions in financial flows to the nations of Central and Eastern Europe.

REFORM IN CENTRAL AND EASTERN EUROPE

33. We welcome the political and economic reforms taking place in Central and Eastern Europe. At the recent Conference on Security and Cooperation in Europe (CSCE) in Bonn and by the agreement to establish the European Bank for Reconstruction and Development (EBRD), the participating countries of the region accepted the key principles underpinning market economies. However, the degree of implementation of economic and political reform varies widely by country. Several countries have taken courageous and difficult measures to stabilize their economies and shorten the transition to a market economy.

34. We and other countries should assist Central and Eastern European nations that are firmly committed to economic and political reform. Those providing help should favor countries that implement such reforms.

35. Foreign private investment will be vital in the development of Central and Eastern Europe. Capital will flow to countries with open markets and hospitable investment climates. Improved access for their exports will also be important for those Central and Eastern European countries that are opening up their economies. Western Governments can support this process by various means, including trade and investment agreements. The recent decision by the Coordinating Committee for Multilateral Export Controls (COCOM) to liberalize export controls is a positive step.

36. We commend the work done by the Commission of the European Communities on the coordination by the Group of 24 (G–24) of assistance to Poland and Hungary inaugurated at the Summit of the Arch, which has made a significant contribution to helping these countries lay the foundation for self-sustaining growth based on market principles. We welcome the decision of the G–24 to enlarge the coordination of assistance to other emerging democracies in Central and Eastern Europe, including Yugoslavia.

37. We recognize that these countries face major problems in cleaning their environment. It will be important to assist the countries of Central and Eastern Europe to develop the necessary policies and infrastructure to confront those environmental problems.

38. We also welcome the recent initiatives in regional cooperation, e.g., in transport and the environment, that will make a positive contribution to economic progress and stability in the region.

39. We expect the new EBRD to play a key role in fostering investment in those countries and to contribute to orderly transitions toward market economies and a sound basis for democracy. We urge the rapid entry into force of the Bank.

40. The Center for Cooperation with European Economies in Transition at the OECD will encourage reforms and strengthen relations between these countries and the OECD, as will the OECD's follow up work from the CSCE Economic Conference in Bonn.

41. We invite the OECD to consider a closer relationship with those Central and East European countries that are committed to political and economic reform.

THE SOVIET UNION

42. We discussed the situation in the Soviet Union, and exchanged views regarding the message that Soviet President Gorbachev sent us several days ago on his economic plans. We welcome the efforts underway in the Soviet Union to liberalize and to create a more open, democratic, and

pluralistic Soviet society, and to move toward a market-oriented economy. These measures deserve our support. The success of perestroika depends upon the determined pursuit and development of these reform efforts. In particular, we welcome President Gorbachev's suggestion for a sustained economic dialogue.

43. We have all begun, individually and collectively, to assist these reform efforts. We all believe that technical assistance should be provided now to help the Soviet Union move to a market-oriented economy and to mobilize its own resources. Some countries are already in a position to extend large scale financial credits.

44. We also agreed that further Soviet decisions to introduce more radical steps toward a market-oriented economy, to shift resources substantially away from the military sector and to cut support to nations promoting regional conflict will all improve the prospect for meaningful and sustained economic assistance.

45. We have taken note of the decision of the European Council in Dublin on June 26. We have agreed to ask the IMF, the World Bank, the OECD and the designated president of the EBRD to undertake, in close consultation with the Commission of the European Communities, a detailed study of the Soviet economy, to make recommendations for its reform and to establish the criteria under which Western economic assistance could effectively support these reforms. This work should be completed by year's end and be convened by the IMF.

46. We took note of the importance to the Government of Japan of the peaceful resolution of its dispute with the Soviet Union over the Northern Territories.

47. The host Government will convey to the Soviet Union the results of the Houston Summit.

THE DEVELOPING NATIONS

48. We reiterate that our commitment to the developing world will not be weakened by the support for reforming countries in Central and Eastern Europe. The poorest of the developing nations must remain the focus of special attention. The International Development Association replenishment of SDR 11.6 billion, agreed to last December, will provide needed resources for these countries, and marks the incorporation of environmental concerns into development lending. It is our intention to take a constructive part in the Paris Conference on the least developed countries in September.

49. The advanced industrial economies can make a number of major contributions to the long-run development of the developing countries. By sustaining economic growth and price stability, we can offer stable, growing markets and sources of capital for the developing world. By providing financial and technical support to developing countries undertaking genuine political and economic reform, we can reinforce their ongoing liberalization. The industrialized nations should continue to make efforts to enhance their development aid and other forms of assistance to the developing countries, including reinforcing the effectiveness of the aid.

50. In the developing world, there is a growing acceptance of the view that growth can be encouraged by a stable macroeconomic framework, sectoral reform to provide more competition, and an opening of markets. Open, democratic, and accountable political systems are important ingredients in the effective and equitable operation of market-oriented economies.

51. Important contributions to a hospitable investment climate can be made by the protection of intellectual property, and by liberalization of investment regimes, including transparent and equitable investment rules, and equality of treatment for foreign and domestic investors.

52. The recent Enterprise for the Americas initiative announced by the U.S. President will support and encourage more market-oriented policies in Latin America and the Caribbean. We believe that such U.S. efforts hold great promise for the region and will help improve prospects for sustained growth in the Americas through the encouragement of trade, open investment regimes, the reduction of U.S. bilateral concessional debt and the use of debt for equity and nature swaps.

53. In a number of countries, sustainable development requires that population

growth remains in some reasonable balance with expanding resources. Supporting the efforts of developing countries to maintain this balance is a priority. Improved educational opportunities for women and their greater integration into the economy can make important contributions to population stabilization programs.

54. In the Mediterranean basin, the initiatives of economic integration, which are underway, deserve encouragement and support.

THIRD WORLD DEBT

55. Significant progress has been made during the past year under the strengthened debt strategy, which has renewed the resolve in a number of debtor countries to continue economic reforms essential to future growth. In particular, the recent commercial bank agreements with Chile, Costa Rica, Mexico, Morocco, the Philippines, and Venezuela involve significant debt and debt-service reduction. Important financial support for debt and debt-service reduction is being provided by the IMF and the World Bank, as well as by Japan. The Paris Club has agreed, in order to support medium term IMF-supported reform and financing programs, to provide adequate restructuring agreements, notably through multiyear reschedulings and through lengthening of the repayment period. The combination of debtor reform efforts and commercial bank debt reduction has had a notable impact on confidence in debtor economies, as clearly demonstrated through flows of both new investment and the return of flight capital to Mexico, in particular.

56. These measures represent major innovations in the case by case debt strategy and are potentially available to all debtor nations with serious debt-servicing problems which are implementing economic adjustment policies.

57. The adoption by debtor nations of strong economic reform programs with the IMF and World Bank remains at the heart of the debt strategy, and a prerequisite for debt and debt service reduction within commercial bank financing packages. It is vital that debtor countries adopt measures to mobilize savings and to encourage new investment flows and the repatriation of flight capital to help sustain their recovery. In this connection, the recent U.S. Enterprise for the Americas initiative to support investment reform and the environment in Latin America needs to be given careful consideration by Finance Ministers.

58. For countries implementing courageous reforms, commercial banks should take realistic and constructive approaches in their negotiations to conclude promptly agreements on financial packages including debt reduction, debt-service reduction and new money.

59. Creditor nations will continue to play an important role in this process through ongoing contributions to the international financial institutions, rescheduling of official debt in the Paris Club, and new finance. We encourage the Paris Club to continue reviewing additional options to address debt burdens. In the case of the lower middle-income countries implementing strong reform programs, we encourage the Paris Club to lengthen the repayment period, taking account of the special situations of these countries. We welcome the decisions taken by France with respect to Sub-Saharan Africa and by Canada with respect to the Caribbean to alleviate the debt burden of the lower middle-income countries.

60. Creditor governments have also provided special support for the poorest countries through the implementation of Toronto terms in Paris Club reschedulings. All of us have cancelled official development assistance (ODA) debt for the poorest countries. We encourage the Paris Club to review the implementation of the existing options that apply to the poorest countries.

61. We note and will study with interest the Craxi Report on debt commissioned by the UN Secretary General.

THE ENVIRONMENT

62. One of our most important responsibilities is to pass on to future generations an environment whose health, beauty, and economic potential are not threatened. Environmental challenges such as climate change, ozone depletion, deforestation, marine pollution, and loss of biological diversity require closer and more effective

international cooperation and concrete action. We as industrialized countries have an obligation to be leaders in meeting these challenges. We agree that, in the face of threats of irreversible environmental damage, lack of full scientific certainty is no excuse to postpone actions which are justified in their own right. We recognize that strong, growing, market-oriented economies provide the best means for successful environmental protection.

63. Climate change is of key importance. We are committed to undertake common efforts to limit emissions of greenhouse gases, such as carbon dioxide. We strongly support the work of the Intergovernmental Panel on Climate Change (IPCC) and look forward to the release of its full report in August. The Second World Climate Conference provides the opportunity for all countries to consider the adoption of strategies and measures for limiting or stabilizing greenhouse gas emissions, and to discuss an effective international response. We reiterate our support for the negotiation of a framework convention on climate change, under the auspices of the United Nations Environment Program (UNEP) and the World Meteorological Organization (WMO). The convention should be completed by 1992. Work on appropriate implementing protocols should be undertaken as expeditiously as possible and should consider all sources and sinks.

64. We welcome the amendment of the Montreal Protocol to phase out the use of chlorofluorocarbons (CFCs) by the year 2000 and to extend coverage of the Protocol to other ozone depleting substances. The establishment of a financial mechanism to assist developing countries to tackle ozone depletion marks a new and positive step in cooperation between the developed and developing worlds. We applaud the announcement in London by some major developing countries, including India and China, that they intend to review their position on adherence to the Montreal Protocol and its amendments. We would welcome their adherence as a crucial reinforcement of the effectiveness of the Protocol, which would ultimately lead to a worldwide phase out of ozone depleting substances. We urge all parties to ratify the amended

Protocol as quickly as possible.

65. We acknowledge that enhanced levels of cooperation will be necessary with regard to the science and impacts of climate change and economic implications of possible response strategies. We recognize the importance of working together to develop new technologies and methods over the coming decades to complement energy conservation and other measures to reduce carbon dioxide and other greenhouse emissions. We support accelerated scientific and economic research and analysis on the dynamics and potential impact of climate change, and on potential responses of developed and developing countries.

66. We are determined to take action to increase forests, while protecting existing ones and recognizing the sovereign rights of all countries to make use of their natural resources. The destruction of tropical forests has reached alarming proportions. We welcome the commitment of the new Government of Brazil to help arrest this destruction and to provide sustainable forest management. We actively support this process, and we are ready for a new dialogue with developing countries on ways and means to support their efforts. We are ready to cooperate with the Government of Brazil on a comprehensive pilot program to counteract the threat to tropical rain forests in that country. We ask the World Bank to prepare such a proposal, in close cooperation with the Commission of the European Communities, which should be presented at the latest at the next Economic Summit. We appeal to the other concerned countries to join us in this effort. Experience gained in this pilot program should immediately be shared with other countries faced with tropical forest destruction. The Tropical Forestry Action Plan must be reformed and strengthened, placing more emphasis on forest conservation and protection of biological diversity. The International Tropical Timber Organization action plan must be enhanced to emphasize sustainable forest management and improve market operations.

67. We are ready to begin negotiations, in the appropriate fora, as expeditiously as possible on a global forest convention or agree-

989

ment, which is needed to curb deforestation, protect biodiversity, stimulate positive forestry actions, and address threats to the world's forests. The convention or agreement should be completed as soon as possible, but no later than 1992. The work of the IPCC and others should be taken into account.

68. The destruction of ecologically sensitive areas around the world continues at an alarming pace. Loss of temperate and tropical forests, developmental pressures on estuaries, wetlands and coral reefs, and destruction of biological diversity are symptomatic. To reverse this trend, we will expand cooperation to combat desertification; expand projects to conserve biological diversity; protect the Antarctic; and assist developing countries in their environmental efforts. We will work within UNEP and other fora to achieve these objectives, and will participate actively in UNEP's work to protect biodiversity.

69. Efforts to protect the environment do not stop at the water's edge. Serious problems are caused by marine pollution, both in the oceans and in coastal areas. A comprehensive strategy should be developed to address land-based sources of pollution; we are committed to helping in this regard. We will continue our efforts to avoid oil spills, urge the early entry into force of the existing International Maritime Organization (IMO) Convention, and welcome the work of that organization in developing an international oil spills convention. We are concerned about the impact of environmental degradation and unregulated fishing practices on living marine resources. We support cooperation in the conservation of living marine resources and recognize the importance of regional fisheries organizations in this respect. We call on all concerned countries to respect the conservation regimes.

70. To cope with energy-related environmental damage, priority must be given to improvements in energy efficiency and to the development of alternative energy sources. For the countries that make such a choice, nuclear energy will continue to be an important contributor to our energy supply and can play a significant role in reducing the growth of greenhouse gas

emissions. Countries should continue efforts to ensure highest worldwide performance standards for nuclear and other energy in order to protect health and the environment, and ensure the highest safety.

71. Cooperation between developed and developing countries is essential to the resolution of global environmental problems. In this regard, the 1992 UN Conference on Environment and Development will be an important opportunity to develop widespread agreement on common action and coordinated plans. We note with interest the conclusions of the Siena Forum on International Law of the Environment and suggest that these should be considered by the 1992 UN Conference on Environment and Development.

72. We recognize that developing countries will benefit from increased financial and technological assistance to help them resolve environmental problems, which are aggravated by poverty and underdevelopment. Multilateral development bank programs should be strengthened to provide greater protection for the environment, including environmental impact assessments and action plans, and to promote energy efficiency. We recognize that debt-for-nature swaps can play a useful role in protecting the environment. We will examine how the World Bank can provide a coordinating role for measures to promote environmental protection.

73. In order to integrate successfully environmental and economic goals, decision-makers in government and industry require the necessary tools. Expanded cooperative scientific and economic research and analysis on the environment is needed. We recognize the importance of coordinating and the sharing the collection of satellite data on earth and its atmosphere. We welcome and encourage the ongoing discussions for the establishment of an International Network. It is also important to involve the private sector, which has a key role in developing solutions to environmental problems. We encourage the OECD to accelerate its very useful work on environment and the economy. Of particular importance are the early development of environmental indicators and the design of market/ori-

ented approaches that can be used to achieve environmental objectives. We also welcome Canada's offer to host in 1991 an international conference on environmental information in the 21st Century. We support voluntary environmental labelling as a useful market mechanism which satisfies consumer demand and producer requirements and promotes market innovation.

74. We note with satisfaction the successful launching of the Human Frontier Science Program and express our hope that it will make positive contributions to the advancement of basic research in life science for the benefit of all mankind.

NARCOTICS

75. We urge all nations to accede to and complete ratification of the UN Convention Against Illicit Traffic in Narcotic Drugs and Psychotropic Substances (the Vienna Convention), and to apply provisionally terms of the Convention.

76. We welcome the conclusion of the UN Special Session on Drugs and urge the implementation of the measures contained in the Program of Action it has adopted.

77. We support the declaration adopted at the ministerial meeting on drugs convened by the United Kingdom that drug demand reduction should be accorded the same importance in policy and action as the reduction of illicit supply. Developed countries should adopt stronger prevention efforts and assist demand reduction initiatives in other countries.

78. We endorse the report of the Financial Action Task Force (FATF) and commit our countries to a full implementation of all its recommendations without delay. As agreed at the May meeting of Task Force Finance Ministers, the FATF should be reconvened for a second year, chaired by France, to assess and facilitate the implementation of these recommendations, and to complement them where appropriate. All OECD and financial center countries that subscribe to the recommendations of the Task Force should be invited to participate in this exercise. The report of the new FATF would be completed before we next

meet. We also invite all other countries to participate in the fight against money laundering and to implement the recommendations of the FATF.

79. Effective procedures should be adopted to ensure that precursor and essential chemicals are not diverted to manufacture illicit drugs. A task force similar to the FATF should be created for this purpose, composed of Summit participants and other countries that trade in these chemicals, with the involvement of representatives of the chemical industry. The task force should address the problems which concern cocaine, heroin and synthetic drugs and report within a year.

80. We support a strategy for attacking the cocaine trade as outlined in particular in the Cartagena Declaration. We recognize the importance of supporting all countries strongly engaged in the fight against drug trafficking, especially Colombia, Peru, and Bolivia, with economic, law enforcement, and other assistance and advice, recognizing the need to make contributions within the framework of actions against drug trafficking carried out by the producer countries.

81. The heroin problem is still the most serious threat in many countries, both developed and developing. All countries should take vigorous measures to combat the scourge of heroin.

82. We should support an informal narcotics consultative arrangement with developed countries active in international narcotics control. Such a group could strengthen efforts to reduce supply and demand, and improve international cooperation.

83. We welcome the current review of UN drug abuse control agencies and urge that it result in a more efficient structure.

NEXT ECONOMIC SUMMIT

84. We have accepted the invitation of Prime Minister Thatcher to meet next July in London.

Note: The declaration was made available by the Office of the Press Secretary but was not issued as a White House press release.

Remarks on Presenting the Final Communique of the Houston Economic Summit
July 11, 1990

I would say to my distinguished colleagues that we've had a chance to review the declaration that was agreed this morning by the eight of us. And I first want to thank all of you for the spirit of full cooperation that I think we all agree existed here in this summit. The eight of us—representing the people of France, the United Kingdom, the Federal Republic of Germany, Canada, Italy, Japan, the United States, and the European Communities—all met; and our declaration reflects decisions taken during the past 3 days here in Houston to extend our long economic expansion, strengthen the world trading system, reiterate our support for the strengthened debt strategy, ensure open investment, assist reform in central and eastern Europe and the Soviet Union, safeguard the environment, help developing nations, and reduce the scourge of drugs.

On behalf of my colleagues, I'd like to note several points of particular importance to us, summarizing—not reading in its entirety but summarizing—some key points out of this declaration.

We are enormously heartened by the resurgence of democracy throughout much of the world. We welcome the spread of multiparty democracy, the practice of free elections, the freedom of expression and assembly, the growing respect for human rights and the rule of law, and the increasing recognition of the strength of open and competitive economies. These events proclaim loudly man's inalienable rights: When people are free to choose, they choose freedom.

We, the G–7, are now in the 8th year of an economic expansion which has created millions of jobs, accelerated the growth of world trade, and provided tangible support for developing countries. The process of economic policy coordination, which we have developed over the years, has contributed importantly to this economic performance. However, we cannot rest on current accomplishments. Each of us will continue efforts, individually and together, to maintain and improve conditions for growth.

Economic prosperity depends critically on an open world trading system, and we will devote close personal attention in the months ahead to achieving a successful outcome of the Uruguay round of multilateral trade negotiations. We have given our trade negotiators clear instructions on our commitment to conclude a comprehensive agreement which expands trade worldwide while bringing the greatest number of participants into a strengthened General Agreement on Tariffs and Trade—the GATT. Each of us recognizes that reaching this goal will require difficult steps by all participants. We will not hesitate to take them. This is especially true for agriculture, where we are committed by this declaration to provide the strong political leadership necessary to ensure a successful and enduring result.

We agreed on the significance of the steps underway in the Soviet Union to liberalize and democratize its society and to move toward a market economy. We welcome President Gorbachev's message to us, in particular, his desire for a sustained economic dialog with the West. We want to support the reforms underway in the Soviet Union, and all agree that technical assistance can help the Soviets move toward a market-oriented economy. Some of us are already prepared to extend large-scale credits to the Soviet Union. We all agree, however—all of us—that the Soviet Union could greatly improve the prospects for sustained Western assistance if it introduced further market reforms, cut its military spending, and ceased supporting governments which promote regional conflicts. We also took note of the importance to the Government of Japan of peaceful resolution of its dispute with the Soviet Union over the Northern Territories.

We see the need for a considered, comprehensive Western response in support of Soviet reform efforts. We've asked the major international economic institutions to provide us by year's end their recommendations for reform of the Soviet economy and possible criteria for Western assistance.

We are keenly aware of our responsibilities to pass on to the future generations a world environment whose health, beauty, and economic potential are safeguarded. Environmental challenges such as climate change, ozone depletion, deforestation, marine pollution, and the loss of biological diversity require closer and more effective international cooperation and action. We are united on the goals and measures to be taken now, particularly in relation to climate change and the protection of forests. And in this regard, we have agreed to complete by 1992 the work of the IPCC [Intergovernmental Panel on Climate Change] on a framework convention on climate change; to begin work immediately on developing a pilot project to address tropical deforestation in Brazil; commence negotiations—this is the third point—to commence negotiations on a global forest convention or agreement to curb deforestation, promote biodiversity, and encourage sound forestry practices and reforestation.

We recognize the difficult economic challenges facing many developing countries, including reduced growth and severe debt burdens. We have been in the forefront of addressing these problems, and we are encouraged by the progress that has been made under the international debt strategy over the past year. We have agreed to review options for helping those countries that are heavily indebted to our governments. Economic and political reform are essential for economic prosperity and political stability. For those countries undertaking these difficult steps, we offer our experience, resources, and good will.

We leave Houston renewed by the strength of our common commitments to healthy economic growth and prosperity and freedom for peoples everywhere. And in conclusion, we have accepted Prime Minister Thatcher's kind invitation to meet again next July in London.

Again, my thanks to my colleagues. I think the plan is we now go and have our own opportunity to respond to questions from the press. But I want to thank my colleagues for what I, at least, feel has been a good summit. And we're very pleased you were here. And might I just take one more opportunity to thank the people of Houston for their hospitality. Thank you all very much.

Note: The President spoke at 12:11 p.m. in Assembly Hall at George R. Brown Convention Center in Houston, TX.

The President's News Conference Following the Houston Economic Summit
July 11, 1990

The President. Thank you all very much. And I have a brief opening statement, and then I'll be glad to respond to your questions.

My colleagues from France and the United Kingdom, Germany, Canada, Italy, Japan, and the European Communities and I have just completed this 16th meeting of the leaders of the largest industrialized democracies. This, the first economic summit of the postwar period, celebrates the resurgence of democracy and free markets around the world. Over the past 3 days, we've had full discussions on the key issues of our times: advancing political and economic freedom; promoting sustained economic growth, both in developed and in developing countries; assisting the transition to market economies in central and eastern Europe and, indeed, in the Soviet Union; and protecting the environment. We are united in a common goal to extend to those who seek political and economic freedom a helping hand with our resources, talents, and experience. As our declaration states, when people are free to choose, they choose freedom.

We identified the successful completion of the Uruguay round of global trade talks as one of the highest economic priorities. We recognize that agreement on fundamental reform of agriculture is critical to achieving this goal. We commended the report by the chairman of the GATT agricultural group, the De Zeuuw report, to our negotiators as a vehicle to move these talks forward; and we also committed to maintain our personal involvement and to exercise political leadership at every step along the way as we move toward the final ministerial meeting in December.

On the Soviet Union, we discussed our common efforts to assist the Soviet reform effort, the success of which is in our common interest. In addition to offering the Soviets technical assistance, we've asked the IMF to coordinate a major study of the Soviet economy and make recommendations for its reform. In keeping with the agreements reached here, I will be conveying to President Gorbachev the results of our deliberations.

We achieved major progress on the environment, particularly on climate change and forests. We committed to finish the negotiations on a framework climate change convention by 1992. In a first, we agreed that implementing protocols should consider all sources and sinks of greenhouse gases, consistent with the comprehensive approach that we recommend. We agreed to launch a special effort to address the deforestation in the rain forests, a concern that was very forcefully raised by Chancellor Kohl [of the Federal Republic of Germany]. I found a very receptive audience for my proposal that a freestanding global forest convention be negotiated without delay, and we agreed to move ahead on this rapidly.

In short, this was a summit that addressed itself to a rapidly changing world. We agreed to welcome, respond to, and manage the changes on behalf of free markets, free political systems, and a better life for people everywhere. It is no small achievement that we came to a positive and unanimous conclusion on so many important and difficult issues, and I would stress those two words: positive and unanimous.

And I want to congratulate my colleagues on the results of the collective effort. I think they left feeling good. We had a very generous letter to our Secretary of State just now from Prime Minister Mulroney [of Canada], and he's a veteran of these summits. And I must say to the Canadians here: I once again benefited from not only his commitment—learned from his commitment on certain issues like the environment but benefited from his advice.

I also want to thank the two Secretaries that were at my side, Secretary Baker and Secretary Brady; Ambassador Carla Hills, Secretary Yeutter, Secretary Mosbacher, who worked with their colleagues and others at this summit. I want to thank the sherpas—I understand they all stayed up until 4 o'clock this morning in ironing out this Final Communique.

So, it was a team effort, and I think most of our—well, I think all of our summit participants left feeling good about this particular summit.

And now I think Terry Hunt [Associated Press] has the first question.

Economic Assistance for the Soviet Union

Q. Mr. President, I'd like to ask you about Soviet aid. Is this 6-month study of Soviet needs a way of delaying the political decision on aid, or at the end of that, will the United States make a commitment to send some cash to Moscow?

The President. It's not an effort to delay anything. It is, as we said in the report, a step towards assisting the reforms. And I'll make clear to President Gorbachev that he ought to view this outcome of this summit very positively. You may remember that in London only a few days ago I gave my views on the U.S. lending money at this time. So, it's not an effort to forestall anything; it's an effort to move forward, encourage forward motion, and be helpful to the Soviet Union in terms of reform. They need much, much more reform, and they're the ones that say this. And in Gorbachev's letter, he asked for assistance in many areas—personnel management and how they change their systems. And we've already started bilaterally, as have other countries, in trying to assist. So, it's really a coordinated effort to help the Soviet Union.

Q. Well, in 6 months, then, can Mr. Gorbachev expect that the United States would be sending some financial assistance to meet these needs?

The President. Not particularly. Not necessarily. But what he can expect is that we will have been helpful to him in the reforms that he knows that he has to undertake, and maybe this could lead to support. But there are things that have to happen, and I've been very up front with him personally and then in public statements as to what has to happen for the United States to send money. And incidentally, I don't—I'm trying to think on the Gorbachev letter—I don't think there was a request for sending money. And then I also told our Soviet partners that we had some problems—legal problems—the settlement of this Kerensky debt, for example—before we would be free to give more like financial support.

So, I wouldn't set a timeframe on when and if the United States decides to go forward. But I must say that I hope the Soviets will view this as positive. And, indeed, I've contacted Mr. Gorbachev already by cable telling him I want to talk to him about the summit and telling him why I felt that it is positive—and also congratulating him on his landslide win. Certain readings I was doing before then—I wasn't sure that it was going to work out quite that way. But he's in the political arena, and he did pretty darn well, and I congratulated him.

Q. Mr. President, for 40 years we've spent untold billions to fight the Soviet Union. Is it conceivable, as you and Secretary Baker have portrayed, that the American taxpayer would not be willing to spend a dime to help them now?

The President. We are trying to help them now; and I think we're going to send the kind of help that, in the long run, will be most beneficial to them. And they need reform, and they know it. And we're going to try in every way to facilitate that reform because we are in a very different age. But we have some problems. I'm not particularly enthusiastic about the intercontinental ballistic missiles aimed at U.S. cities. I find it a little contradictory to think that they will continue to spend $5 billion a year for Cuba, a totalitarian system whose leader is

swimming against this tide of democracy and freedom that is lifting up most hopes in the Soviet Union. So, certain things have to happen before I, as President, will make recommendations for direct financial aid. So, what we're trying to do is carry our part of the load in helping the reforms.

Q. In your discussions, why did Germany and other countries think it's necessary now?

The President. Well, Germany has some very special interest that we understand. As I said over in London, Helen [Helen Thomas, United Press International], we're not urging everybody to march in lockstep. Just as in our programs for Central America—I want to see more help from the G–7 and the G–24 and anybody else who will listen to help the democracies in Central and South America. And they've got certain priorities, and I hope they will be able to help in this way. But if we go forward as we have in assisting Nicaragua and Panama, I don't feel that everybody has to move in lockstep on that support for democracy.

Agricultural Subsidies

Q. Mr. President, the Final Communique here, reflecting your views in no small part on agriculture subsidies, calls upon each nation to "make substantial progressive reductions in support and protection of agriculture." Does this mean, sir, that you're prepared to ask Congress to abolish some of the more notorious forms of support and subsidy that are part of our farm program?

The President. Absolutely! And we have to do it, and it's a two-way street. And I expect there would be some political opposition because, like many of these countries, we protect. But I am convinced—and I believe Congress would support the concept—that if we all do this and we all reduce barriers and we all make a freer trading system, that the United States can compete. But I'm sure I would have some obstacles from the supporters of certain programs that have been in existence for a long time.

But that's a little down the road now, and I think as far as the EC goes, it's a little down the road. So, what we're trying to do is move the whole thing forward without saying that we have to have tomorrow totally unprotected trade. I'd like to shoot for that some day. I've said that before.

Q. Well, how soon, sir, will you be going to Congress with a legislative package to begin to undo——

The President. As soon as we see what progress is made in the GATT. That's where the next action is, is in these talks that are coming up—I think it's just on the 23d of this month or sometime. That's why I think this language that we worked out and that all of you have, I think, now is encouraging, because we all know that agriculture has been a major stumbling block.

And my special Trade Representative, Carla Hills, impressed on me the need to move that particular category forward, and we did get agreement. But the next step before we talk about needing a legislative package is to get agreement out of the GATT.

Economic Assistance for the Soviet Union

Q. Mr. President, if the study delays a decision on aid to the Soviet Union beyond German reunification, would it not be expected that there would be a lessening of interest in the summit countries in helping the Soviets if the German unification question is resolved by that time?

The President. No. I think events are changing so fast that different countries are going to look at this with slightly different senses of priority. But in the meantime, this study will go forward. We have sent, in a bilateral sense, many missions to the Soviet Union. Alan Greenspan [Chairman of the Federal Reserve Board] was over there on his own. We've had Dick Thornburgh over there talking about helping reorder the justice system. We have people from the stock markets over there. We've had a wide array of individuals and groups of business people go. And so, that process of trying to assist in change and in reform is underway bilaterally.

But this look that the IMF will coordinate and be done by these other agencies will kind of give an official—at least for the G–7, we will look at it in rather an official way and then see if we can decide on more collective action at the next summit or whether we proceed individually on a case-by-case basis.

Environmental Policy

Q. Mr. President, on the question of the environment, you, in the past, and your Chief of Staff [John H. Sununu], to say at least two, have always said that there has not been enough information—you needed to study more. Now you're prepared to move, particularly on the global warming question. Who twisted your arm? What changed your mind, sir?

The President. I think we're moving forward because we recognize there is a problem. I thought we called for more data in here. Clearly, we need more. When you take the NASA study—and then some people point to that as challenging the concepts of global climate change—why, I think everybody—well, put it this way, everybody at this summit agreed that we needed more scientific information.

But the steps that we've recommended here in this communique we can enthusiastically endorse. So, I think we came out with a reasoned position, not a radical position that's going to throw a lot of American men and women out of jobs. And yet we've done an awful lot—and I think others at the summit recognized it—in terms of cleaning up the air. We've got a proposal—and I told them proudly of it—to redo our Clean Air Act, and they were very much impressed with that. You might have heard Prime Minister Mulroney's supportive comments about that. So, there's a lot of things working bilaterally in terms of emissions, and I think we have a very reasonable position at this point.

Q. If I could follow, there seems to be a little wiggle room on CO_2. Are you making a clear commitment to do something about it?

The President. I wouldn't read anything into these texts beyond what is actually printed there.

Economic Assistance for the Soviet Union

Q. I understand that it would take some time for the Soviet economy to reform. But are you suggesting, when you link Soviet aid to arms control, that you could never imagine any direct aid so long as there are any Soviet weapons aimed at the West?

The President. No, I didn't say that. But I

would really prefer to stand on what I've simply said. The world is changing very fast. But they know that we've got some big difficulties on the regional questions and on the fact that a lot of missiles are aimed at the United States. A good way to start in doing something about that is to have a successful conclusion on the START treaty. So, I don't want to go beyond where we are right now. If you'd have asked me last year at this time if I could have predicted the rapidity of change, the changes that have taken place, I couldn't have predicted them. So, I don't know exactly where we will be, but I do know that this proposal we've made is sound.

Q. Do you think if the IMF does say that some direct aid is necessary that perhaps that would spur greater arms control movement?

The President. Excuse me, the IMF says what?

Q. If the IMF study suggests that direct aid is appropriate, do you think that in turn could stimulate or speed up the arms control on behalf of the Soviets?

The President. I would hope so. I think Gorbachev is committed to a fast track on strategic arms.

Q. On aid to the Soviets, you keep saying that the American people simply aren't ready to give cash to Gorbachev. Now, if the IMF comes back with a report, Gorbachev accepts some of those recommendations, they cut way back on aid to Cuba—largely which consists of oil shipments, after all, not money—he does these things you want, are you ready before the 1992 Presidential campaign to go out there and tell the American people you would send American cash or supply credits to Gorbachev?

The President. Your question is too hypothetical. I can't go into a hypothesis like that. And we will wait and see. We've taken a path. It's based on the facts right now. And I would just say that I think Mr. Gorbachev understands that at this juncture sending money from the United States is not in the cards. And he knows what needs to be done to change the formula, and I'd like to think he's going to try. And maybe he'll come out of this Congress where many predicted his demise and feel encouraged to go

forward. But I'm not going to answer a hypothetical question of that nature.

Economic Summit

Q. Let me ask you this. You got some sort of a delay on aid to the Soviets because of this study, which will not be completed until December. A lot of people are painting this summit as they did the NATO summit: as a victory for George Bush across the board, whether it's cutting agricultural subsidies for Europeans or whether it's the environment. What didn't you get at this summit that you wanted? What did you lose here?

The President. In the first place, I don't— I'm glad to hear that—but really, honestly, we don't look at it as a victory for one side and a defeat for another. That's the good thing about this G–7 group. And so, there weren't any winners or losers in it, but there was compromise along the way. But again, I'm not going to reopen the hard work that went into this agreement by saying what we would like to have had that was different. But it did work out in a way that I can strongly support. But again, excuse me for not projecting winners or losers or helping you with what we got and what we didn't get.

West German Chancellor Kohl

Q. Mr. President, at the NATO summit and then again here, it seems as though you have developed a special working relationship with Chancellor Kohl. I wondered—one of the German delegation also said that after you had supported him on Soviet aid he couldn't come back and not support you on the environment. Can you describe that relationship, and would you say that's a fair assessment?

The President. It's not a fair assessment because he's a bulldog when it comes to the environment. He's a fighter for what he believes in. And I think he felt satisfied with what he got. And maybe he would like to have had more. But when we focused in on this forestry agreement and on the question of the rain forests, I think Chancellor Kohl felt that he had achieved something that he came here to achieve.

But the relationship is—it's hard to explain. I do think that the Germans appreciate the fact that we have stood at their side on this question of German reunification. I think that's an element. But there isn't any quid pro quo. There was no "I owe you one" or "I want to pay you" for taking what we feel is a principled position in terms of German reunification. And he fought hard. And there were some compromises in terms of wording. But I think the declaration in terms of reforestation and the forestry agreement and the Amazon all speak to his keen interests. And so, I hope that he will be able to tell his constituencies and all the German people that there is a new awareness and a heightened awareness because of the eloquence that he brought to bear on the question.

Q. Would you say, however, that you find more common ground or common interest with Chancellor Kohl now than you would perhaps with Margaret Thatcher [Prime Minister of the United Kingdom]?

The President. No, I wouldn't say that at all. But I find plenty of common ground with both. Nice try. [*Laughter*] You're going to get me in trouble; they haven't even left town here.

Economic Assistance for the Soviet Union

Q. I have two questions about the summits' kind of do-your-own-thing on Soviet aid. One, is it really good for the alliance? And number two, doesn't it bode poorly for America's leadership in the alliance?

The President. No, I think, without reopening the hypothesis of the earlier question about how the Americans fared, I think we're doing all right in the alliance. And it doesn't work, Cragg [Cragg Hines, Houston Chronicle], that you have to march in lockstep on all these questions. I don't feel that I have to defer on a lot of questions that we initiate on loans to the G–7. And I don't think they should have—these individual countries who have very special agendas and special relationships—I don't think that they should defer to us on these questions.

Now, when you get into some arms control initiatives or matters of that nature, why, obviously, you want to stay together as much as you can. And as the world—I don't worry about that; I don't worry about it all.

Q. Isn't it drawing it a little fine, though,

to say arms control, yes, but aid to the Soviets—which, really, there were no conditions placed on, that could be used for anything, German aid that could be used for anything. Isn't that——

The President. Well you may be a little ahead of me on what the Soviets plan to use the German aid for, aid that has not yet been forthcoming. I understand that Chancellor Kohl is going to Moscow, I think—is that correct?—within the next couple of weeks. But we don't know that as to what conditions will be on the funding and how it will be used in the Soviet Union. But I gave him our position. He gave me his. But that's not enough to break up a strong alliance and a very comfortable and strong bilateral relationship between the Federal Republic and the United States.

Environmental Policy

Q. Mr. President, on the forestry issue, there are a number of sentences in the declaration talking about the importance of preserving forests globally. What impact would that have on the American domestic field? Would it, for example, change the balance that your administration has been trying to strike on the issue of the Pacific Northwest forests and the spotted owl there?

The President. No, we are committed to prudent forest management, but we're also committed to planting a billion trees a year and putting real emphasis on reforestation. So, I don't think there's any contradiction. Some would argue—some of the purists in the environmental movement—that you've got to stop where we are, not harvest any lumber at all. And some of it would be done in the protection of the owl, and some because they're opposed to harvesting the old growth forests. I don't share that view. And I do think we can find a balance where the net is an increase in the numbers of trees.

Q. If I could follow up: What response do you have to the people in Third World countries who argue that you're asking them to make sacrifices on their economic development, that you're not willing to ask American workers to make parallel sacrifices?

The President. I think we have to find

ways to assist those who would take that view. And I think many of our countries will move forward—and did not have great respect for the environment and now are doing a good job on it—and I would put the United States in that category, with pride, I might say—should find ways to assist these countries.

Agricultural Subsidies and Assistance for Latin America

Q. Back on agriculture, Mr. President. You said that you were encouraged about the language on agricultural subsidies. Could you say why, specifically, when the U.S. gave in on the key question of allowing one common measure to be used for all subsidies? And also, on a separate matter, could you tell us whether you got any commitment for help from your allies on the Latin American aid initiative?

The President. Not being a technical expert on these highly technical GATT negotiations, I relied heavily on advice from experts like Carla Hills, who is one—such an expert. And Clayton Yeutter, Bob Mosbacher, involved also. And these people who have been wrestling with the technicalities of the trade question were very pleased at the formulation we came up with. They felt without such formulation the whole successful conclusion of the GATT round was at stake. But they think that the wording we have that refers peripherally to this De Zeuuw report is enough now to move the agricultural discussion forward when they meet soon again.

What was the second part? I don't know on the others. I know that some of them have expressed an interest in helping, but I didn't ask for a collective decision out of the G–7 on that question.

Economic Assistance for the Soviet Union and China

Q. Mr. President, the Soviets have already reacted negatively to advance word of the part of the communique that says that reform would help them get further aid. What would you tell Mr. Gorbachev when you speak to him—why he should not view this as the allied countries saying: The cold war is over; you lost. Here's what you

have to do; here are our conditions for integrating you back into Western society?

The President. I think you phrase it well, because we've got to be careful that we don't send the signal that we don't want to send. But I don't worry about this one because I sat up there at Camp David with Mr. Gorbachev in a very frank discussion and told him the problems that I have with going forward with financial aid. I've been quite open about it in the press conference following a highly successful NATO summit.

And incidentally, I think the reaction from the Soviet Union on the NATO summit has been extraordinarily positive, extraordinarily so; and some of that, I think, has been masked by the understandable attention given to the G–7 meeting here. But it's been extraordinarily positive.

And so far, I think—put it this way: It just totally diminishes the risk of the kind of misunderstanding that your question implies. Now, you saw the lively debate in the peoples Congress [Soviet Union's Communist Party Congress]. It looks like our own Congress up there—yelling at each other and debating and calling people names and doing all these frantic things. So, I'm not saying that somebody's not going to jump up, having finished trying to filet Gorbachev, and jump on me for the way we've reacted in this summit. I am saying that I am not going to have misunderstanding creep in because of failure to communicate. And, indeed, I've already sent off a communication to Mr. Gorbachev, and I will be in touch with him personally very soon to discuss this. But I don't think there's too much of a danger of that.

Q. If I could follow up: In his letter to you in your role as host of this summit, did he ask for direct cash aid?

The President. I need help on that, but I think not. My reaction is that he did not ask for that. I know he didn't have a price tag on it, but he listed several categories of places where we could give support, including credits.

Bob [Robert D. Blackwill, Special Assistant to the President and Senior Director for European and Soviet Affairs at the National Security Council], was that a proper answer? I don't want to—okay. So, I was right.

Q. Some of your colleagues accused you of a double standard, Mr. President, in supporting language yesterday that opened the door to lending to China, particularly if it moves toward economic reforms, and yet taking the much less flexible position regarding the Soviet Union. How do you respond to that?

The President. I respond by saying we already have sanctions on China because China has not moved forward far enough on human rights. Those sanctions remain. We have offered the hope that if they take further steps in the human rights field more can be done. We've said that all of us together would consider World Bank loans—which right now are discouraged by the G–7—consider World Bank loans that would contribute to the reform of the Chinese economy. And then I think we added a little thing about especially those that would help on this world environmental problem.

So, my answer to those is that they're wrong and that the pressure is still on. And let's hope it will not be counterproductive. Again, my position is—and I think every summit leader there agrees with me, everyone, I believe—that we should not further isolate China. There have been some things that we can take some encouragement from. But the sanctions are on China. We took the lead on this question a year ago at the G–7 summit, and some who criticize me fail to realize that. But I want to see them move forward, and I want to see restored good relations with China. But we're not there yet.

Q. Do you believe that financial aid could play a role in stimulating reforms in the Soviet Union?

The President. Well, some think that. I don't particularly agree with that. I think when you see the Japanese move forward, as they plan to do, to keep a commitment—they feel a solemn commitment—to China for this third yen loan, that they feel that way—I have great respect for Prime Minister Kaifu, and I had a long talk with him about that. As you know, they plan to move forward. Just as I can't get all exercised over what Chancellor Kohl does, I feel the same way about what Prime Minister Kaifu

is doing. But he feels that the step he is about to take would encourage reformers. I'm not sure that he's right in this regard, and I think that the people in power there can build on the steps that they've taken in a way to satisfy the rest of the people in the G–7 that we should go back to more normal relations.

Changes in the Western Alliance

Q. Mr. President, a followup on Craig's question. In the past, the United States did call the tune on allied relations with the Soviet Union. Now that we're seeing key allies going their own way on aid to the Soviet Union, aren't we seeing at least a subtle change in the way the United States has to lead the alliance? Aren't you having to give a little more leeway to the allies now that the cold war is over?

The President. We're dealing in entirely different times. Earlier on, in terms of the alliance, we had a much more formidable military opposition. Now we see the Warsaw Pact in almost a state of disarray: we see troops coming out; we see democracies replacing totalitarian systems. So, you have an entirely different era. For the United States side, I think we have very good understanding inside the G–7 about the Soviet Union. But if your question is, is it bad or does it alter the U.S. role if Chancellor Kohl, for very special reasons, goes forward, I would argue that it does not.

Soviet President Gorbachev

Q. Mr. President, there's a lot of concern over President Gorbachev's ability to hold on to power. Does his victory yesterday suggest he will be around for a good while despite his serious economic problems?

The President. I don't know yet, but certainly he's surprised a lot of us in this room, hasn't he—including me. Who would have thought he'd have a 3 to 1 victory or whatever it was? I had the figures at the tip of my tongue a while back, because it was an impressive landslide inside a body where, if I had gone by just some impressions, I wouldn't have thought he had gotten quite that big a landslide. So, I don't know. And I think there's some discontent inside the Soviet Union. I think he's got enormous problems. I hope that what we're doing to help here will help with those problems. But certainly, I'd have to leave it there because I couldn't go beyond that. And I think if you go to experts you'll find divisions on that question.

Q. You don't think the election proves that he has a grip on power now?

The President. Well, I think it does at this juncture, certainly in terms of the party. And certainly, I think, the way he's handling his foreign affairs is probably getting great credit at home. I do understand there's consumer concern and that everybody, including Mr. Gorbachev and Mr. Shevardnadze, recognize that they have enormous economic problems inside the Soviet Union.

Neil Bush

Q. Mr. President, on an issue outside the purview of this summit, your son Neil has suggested that the savings and loan regulators are conducting something of a vendetta against him, largely because his last name is the same as yours. Do you agree with that charge?

The President. I agree that the President ought to stay out of it and that the system ought to work. And I have great confidence in the integrity and honor of my son, and beyond that, I say no more. And if he's done something wrong, the system will digest that.

This is not easy for me as a father. It's easy for me as a President because the system's going to work. I will not intervene. I have not discussed this with any officials and suggested any outcome. But what father wouldn't express a certain confidence in the honor of his son? And that's exactly the way I feel about it, and I feel very strongly about it. And for those who want to challenge it, whether they are in the Congress or elsewhere: Let the system work; and then we can all make a conclusion as to his honor and his integrity.

And it's tough on people in public life to some degree. I've got three other sons, and they all want to go to the barricades. Every one of them, when they see some cartoon they don't like, particularly those that are factually incorrect and demeaning of the honor of their brother, they want to do

what any other kids would do. And I say: You calm down now. We're in a different role now. You can't react like you would if your brother was picked on in a street fight. That's not the way the system works.

But we have great emotions that I share with Barbara, I share with my sons and my daughter, that I won't share with you except to say: One, as President, I'm determined to stay out of this and let it work and let it work fairly. And secondly, I have confidence in the honor and integrity of my son. And if the system finds he's done something wrong, he will be the first to step up and do what's right.

Chairman of the Federal Deposit Insurance Corporation

Q. Does the same confidence, sir, extend to William Seidman, who has Democrats as well as Republicans——

The President. He wouldn't be there if I— well, I don't know about—I was about to say he wouldn't be there if I didn't have confidence in him. I have confidence in his integrity and his honor.

Last question.

Environmental Protection Agency Administrator Reilly and Environmental Policy

Q. Mr. President, the environmental groups that were very much in evidence here don't seem too happy with the results of the summit.

The President. They haven't seemed happy with me for a long time, and I'm not too happy with them. I think their grading system is absolutely, essentially absurd. But what's the question? [*Laughter*]

Q. Sir, the question is: They're calling your forestation initiative a figleaf to cover up your inaction on the environment. A second portion of this question is why did you leave Bill Reilly home, when last year you brought him to Paris when you weren't even planning to put him in the Cabinet?

The President. Last year many of the environmental ministers were there, and including some of the people—you remember that was the Paris centennial. And many from other countries were there as well. So, he was not here for that reason, nor were other Secretaries whose counterparts were not here. So, that was the reason. This is predominantly an economic summit. But lest anybody have any doubt about it, Bill Reilly retains my full confidence and my full support. I have great respect for him.

What was the rest of your question?

Q. They call the forestation initiative a figleaf to cover up your inaction on global warming.

The President. Look, come on, I'm not going to respond to those groups that have been attacking us every time we turn around. And you cannot appeal—I have to be careful because there were some reasonable people involved—but on the environmental extreme, they don't want this country to grow. They don't want to look down the road at the human consequence of men and women thrown out of work and families put into a whole new state of anxiety. And I, as President, have to be concerned about that as well as being a good custodian, a good steward, for the environment. And so—but we cannot govern by listening to the loudest voice on the extreme of an environmental movement.

And I did not rely heavily on them for support in getting elected President of the United States, and I'm not going to be persuaded that I can get some brownie point by appealing to one of these groups or other. And the attacks that they made on some of my summit partners—I resent them, too, because it's not just the United States, in attacking the President or the policies of the Government, it's the attack on some of these other leaders. So, they're entitled to their opinion. Their signs can be held just as high as others. And their rating systems can attract as much or as little attention as you care to give them. But I am not going to shape the policies—when I know we have sound environmental poli-cies—by the loudest voice or the biggest sign.

So, they're welcome to Houston. I hope they've enjoyed it. I hope they feel they've had an opportunity to get their message out. But I had a little cloakroom conversation with some of the participants, and I think most of them are disinclined to change policies in their countries that they think are sound because of some of the statements that I saw and perhaps some that you were referring to here. So, I'd say, welcome, and we'll listen and keep trying to do better. But I'm determined that we can find a sound environmental path—and I think we've found it—continue to be good stewards for the environment and still have some concern for the workingman and the workingwoman in this country. And that really is what it boils down to when you talk about no growth. And I'm not going to talk about no growth for the United States because I feel a deep concern about the human equation as well as the environment.

I was very pleased with the mood amongst the summit leaders as a result of the common ground that we hammered out on the environment here.

Thank you all very much.

Note: The President's 54th news conference began at 12:59 p.m. in Assembly Hall at George R. Brown Convention Center in Houston, TX. In his remarks, he referred to the Kerensky debt, which was incurred by Russia's Kerensky government after the fall of the czar. The President also referred to the Group of 7 (G–7), the industrialized nations that participated in the economic summits, and the Group of 24 (G–24), the industrialized democracies that pledged support for economic and political reform in Poland and Hungary.

White House Fact Sheet on the President's Proposal for a Global Forest Convention
July 11, 1990

President Bush today proposed to the leaders of the summit of industrialized na-tions that negotiations begin on an international convention on forests.

Background

The U.S. Forest Service estimates that the world is losing about 27 million acres of tropical forest each year. A recent study estimated even higher losses—in the range of 40–50 million acres per year. Severe and widespread forest declines have occurred in eastern and western Europe, and a body of evidence is accumulating that forests in North America and elsewhere are being damaged by stresses caused by air pollution.

The world's forests are the lungs of the Earth, absorbing carbon dioxide from mankind's activities and releasing oxygen critical to human existence. Forests serve as air-conditioners and filters to protect us against heat, dust, and pollutants. They are essential in the protection of water supplies on which agriculture, industry, and cities depend. Not only are they a vital source of wood for fuel and shelter but we are increasingly learning of other resources which can be extracted in a way that provides economic benefits. And forests provide vital habitat for all manner of animal species. The Amazon Basin alone contains over 50,000 species of higher plants and a fifth of all the species of birds on Earth.

The U.S. Proposal

President Bush today proposed at the summit of industrialized nations to begin negotiations as expeditiously as possible on a global convention on forests. This would be a freestanding convention, similar to the highly successful Vienna convention on chlorofluorocarbons. The President proposed that negotiations be completed and the convention be ready for signing by 1992. The President expressed the hope that the convention would, to the maximum extent possible, emphasize market-based mechanisms and flexibility for achieving its goals.

The President outlined several areas in which international cooperation could help to address threats to the world's forests and could lead to positive action:

Research and Monitoring. The convention could accelerate cooperative research in programs to protect natural forests and to improve forest management practices,

the development of more cost effective reforestation techniques, and the development of sustainable yield strategies consistent with each country's economic, environmental, and forest management objectives. The President suggested, as a first step, that the Tropical Forestry Institute in Puerto Rico be expanded into a full-fledged International Tropical Forests Institute.

The President proposed the launching of a worldwide network to monitor the world's forests to improve understanding of their health and vigor, the effects of pollution, and the rate at which they are being converted to other uses. The President called for cooperation in developing an inventory of the resources of the world's forests, as a tool for analyzing their potential for new products and uses.

Education, Training, and Technical Assistance. The convention could help establish vehicles for formal and technical training in forest conservation and forest practices, reforestation, and related subjects; for the provision of technical assistance, extension services, and project expertise.

Reforestation and Rehabilitation. The convention could be used to develop national and international strategies for reforestation, timber stand improvement, and restoration of the health of the world's forests. The President highlighted the commitment of the United States to reforestation through his proposal to plant a billion trees a year in America. That proposal is now awaiting funding by the U.S. Congress.

Noting the importance of economics and trade, the President reaffirmed U.S. support for the International Tropical Timber Organization.

Tropical Forestry Action Plan Reform. The President also reiterated U.S. support for the goals of the Tropical Forestry Action Plan and called for strengthening and reform of the programs contained therein, with an emphasis on wise stewardship and sustainable management.

Reduction of Air Pollution. International action is needed to curb acid rain and tropospheric ozone, which are believed to cause damage to forests. This is essential to relieving stress on forests in Europe and to ensure that the restoration and replanting of forests in eastern Europe will be successful. The President has proposed in his Clean Air Act legislation dramatic reductions in emissions which contribute to acid rain (sulfur dioxide and nitrogen oxides) and ozone formation (volatile organic compounds). The Clean Air Act proposal has passed both Houses of Congress and is awaiting final action by a House-Senate conference committee. The convention could lay the groundwork for bilateral and multilateral agreements with respect to air pollution.

Bilateral and Multilateral Assistance Program. The convention might also address the need for a review of bilateral and multilateral assistance programs to put greater emphasis on conservation of forest areas and sustainable use of forest resources. In addition, it could explore possible ways to promote sound forestry practices and reforestation and to ensure that such programs

are not designed in ways which adversely affect forests.

Debt-for-Nature Swaps. The convention could promote sound use and protection for forests through debt-for-nature swaps, particularly with the support of the multilateral developments banks. In addition, it could encourage local currency environmental trust fund programs and similar devices to help finance environmental programs. The United States recently proposed to pursue such arrangements in Latin America as part of its Enterprise for the Americas Initiative.

Removal of Harmful Subsidies. The convention could address itself to identifying and, where appropriate, changing subsidies and other market distortions which inadvertently encourage deforestation or discourage afforestation of lands which could be best used as forest. One possibility is the reduction of subsidies that encourage the conversion of marginal lands that are economically more productive as forest lands into crop or grazing lands.

Remarks at the Thank You Houston Celebration in Houston, Texas
July 11, 1990

Listen, Barbara and I really wanted to come over and say thank you to all of you. To Judge Lindsey and to Mayor Whitmire, to Ken Lay and George Strake, Fred Malek, and so many others, I am very, very grateful—and so is Bar—and to our entertainers for tonight, Randy Travis and Jaclyn Smith, Marilyn McCoo. You know, when Marilyn was last here with the Fifth Dimension, she sang a hit called "Last Night I Didn't Get to Sleep at All." Well, we understand that, and I expect that Secretary Baker and Secretary Brady—from the hard work they put in in the summit—understand it. But let me tell you that, in the views of the United States delegation to this important summit, it has been a howling success. And much of the credit goes to Houston, Texas, and the thousands of volunteers that made all of us feel so at home.

And so, it's this celebration that tops off 3 days—I would say 3 historic days—for the

people of Houston and, indeed, for the people of the world. For decades, we've kept the faith of freedom burning, we've borne the banner of liberty, and now the people of Berlin and Budapest and so many other parts of the world have lifted that liberty banner for themselves. And in Houston, the Presidents and the Prime Ministers who lead the largest industrialized democracies met to build a world beyond the cold war; to uphold the Revolution of 1989; to help liberated nations enter the 21st century as enduring democracies; and to support free world, free wills, and free markets for all mankind. So, you see, this hasn't just been a successful summit; in a broad foreign policy sense, it's been a celebration—a celebration on behalf of all nations and of all peoples, a celebration of their victory over barbed wire and concrete walls and discredited despotism.

The tone of this summit was set by the

people of Berlin last fall. And the success of this summit is a tribute to my six colleagues from abroad. But it is also a tribute to you, those who made this summit work, the people of the city of Houston, Texas. You know, I know that you've put up with a lot having us here—closed streets, tail-bumper driving, nerve-racking regularity of helicopters, and constant security—and I know how tough this can be on a town. But even more to the point, I want to thank you, thank you all, for all you have done to make this summit such a success.

You know, Houston, in my view, has always been a clean city; but thanks to the people of Clean Houston, this volunteer effort, this city sparkles. And I wish I could go out there and just shake hands and thank each and every one of the thousands—literally thousands—of volunteers who pitched in during their spare time to make Houston a showcase for the world. And just look at what you've done: thousands of volunteers—we call them Points of Light, Texas Points of Light—who scoured the streets and the alleys for litter, planting flowers in the parks, painting over graffiti. And by June 23d, Ken Lay and George Strake told me, 5,261 Houstonians put in 26,200 hours to remove 2.7 million pounds of trash and debris. And what a record—what an example for the rest of our country.

You know, I really do believe that you've shown the world what Houston pride is all about. So, in closing, let me say that I know that Houston, our great city, has had a rough go in the last few years; but as I travel around town, I see more and more signs of a city not just on the mend, which we all know is true, but a city totally rebounding, a city on the go—and not just a city with a future but a city of the future.

One other comment on today. I know that Barbara and I will never forget when the seven leaders and I moved through that downtown area how the whole city turned out—the newscast this evening said more than 100,000 people along the streets with the balloons and the bands and the welcoming signs and the friendly smiles. And you turned this ordinary procession of motorcades into a parade, a moment of unforgettable international hospitality that the visiting Presidents and Prime Ministers and Chancellor will take home with them. Every single one of them commented to me on that warm outpouring of hospitality and friendship.

So, in short, you've shown the world what Houston hospitality is all about. You set it— you set the background for a highly successful and very important meeting between these countries. And you made this Houstonian very, very proud of his hometown tonight. Thank you. Thank you all very, very much.

Note: The President spoke at 7:13 p.m. in Butler Plaza at the University of Houston. In his remarks, he referred to Harris County Judge John Lindsey; Kathryn J. Whitmire, mayor of Houston; Ken Lay and George Strake, cochairmen of the Host Committee of the Houston Economic Summit; Ambassador Fred Malek, Director of the Houston Economic Summit; and Gov. Bill Clements. Following his remarks, the President returned to Washington, DC.

Remarks Following a Meeting With Greek Patriarch Dimitrios I
July 12, 1990

May I just say that it's a great honor for me as President of the United States to receive His All Holiness in the Oval Office. And as I survey the changes that are taking place in Eastern Europe and around the world, my thoughts go to the faith of individuals in so many countries, a faith that is sustained and strengthened by the church and by the leadership of His All Holiness. And so, it is appropriate to be received respectfully in the Oval Office, and that I have an opportunity to tell him that I see faith of people as a driving force for change in the world today and have an opportunity to salute him for his principles and leader-ship.

So, it's been a joy to have you here, a joy to have you here. And to have the various metropolitans [ecclesiastical officials] here, too, is special. Thank you all.

Note: The President spoke at 11:50 a.m. in the Rose Garden at the White House.

Remarks to the 30th Biennial Greek Orthodox Church Clergy-Laity Congress
July 12, 1990

Thank you very, very much. Thank you. Who would have thought that I would be introduced by Peter Jennings before a beautiful evening like this? [*Laughter*] It's just wonderful. Ted, thank you very, very much. Barbara and I are delighted to be here this evening. When Ted said that "a person we hold in such reverence," I was ready. You see, I'm used to it now. I thought he was talking about Barbara, not the All Holiness. [*Laughter*]

I am so pleased to be with you. Your All Holiness, once again, welcome to the Cap-ital of our great nation. It was an honor and, I think, an appropriate honor for us to greet you in the Oval Office today. And I was proud to be at your side in the Rose Garden. And it's an extraordinary privilege tonight to be with you and your distin-guished delegation, and also to be with our respected and revered friend Archbishop Iakovos, who's distinguished himself in the 30 years that he's been the spiritual leader of your church in the Americas. I apologize for the order of the program and speaking before dinner, but Archbishop Iakovos said you were having broccoli, and I figure I have to get out of here. [*Laughter*]

But to more serious things, Your All Holi-ness, meeting with you earlier today was a rare and an inspiring opportunity. Once again, I want to express my profound re-spect. You are a holy man of great spiritual-ity and vision and humility, a gentle and revered pilgrim on this mission of peace. We are especially blessed to be part of this historic journey—the first time in the 1,400-year history of the Patriarchate that the successor to St. Andrew has visited the Western Hemisphere.

Greetings to all of you, the members of the 30th Clergy-Laity Conference from 555 parishes across the sweep of the Americas. I still remember the outpouring of warmth that you gave me when I had the privilege of addressing you 2 years ago and 2 years before that. It is a delight to see you again because I feel that we do have a special bond. In particular, I cherish the Greek-American legacy of putting family values first. This is the finest example of what our country needs in order to be strong and wise and flourishing. We admire your un-flinching devotion to the passing on of clear moral values and your emphasis on the im-portance of a good education.

I noted that in the census returns for the last three decades, you have ranked the highest of any community in education. And I'm not just saying that because John Brademas is here, either. [*Laughter*] Also, you stress hard work and the individual ini-tiative that creates opportunity and, thus, have become the backbone of small busi-nesses throughout this country. And statis-tics show that through your shining exam-ple of love and faith and, of course, family tradition, you've almost no crime and drug problems. And how wonderful that 3,000 of your young people this week took part in a forum about the bitter plague of drugs.

I also admire your strength as a commu-nity in which your Greek Orthodoxy means your deeply rooted spiritual beliefs, as well as the richness of your cultural life. In any age when so many challenges threaten the fabric of our society, your intense devotion to your faith and traditions have made you messengers of hope. You share the richness of your ancient, undivided faith. You've impressed us with the vibrant ethnic vitality of your immigrant parents and grandparents—and I love what Ted Koppel said about that earlier—and with your commitment to Christian service both here and in the lands of your ancestors' birth. They were drawn here by the beacon of Liberty's torch. And now, you are shining your own beacon of promise back to your homelands, always remembering the words of the Greek national anthem: "Now as ever valor prizing/Hail, all hail sweet Liberty!"

And what a splendid place Washington is for you to meet. Here in his hometown, you can proudly tell the story of your Greek-American predecessor, Constantino Brumidi—Brumidi, the Michelangelo of the U.S. Capitol. More than 100 years ago, Brumidi produced those eloquent friezes showing scenes from American history and said with reverence: "My one ambition is that I may live long enough to make beautiful the Capitol of the one country on Earth in which there is liberty."

In Washington, you can rejoice in the magnificence of your Cathedral of St. Sophia. When I was Vice President, I used to live just down the road from Hagia Sophia, the Cathedral of Holy Wisdom. How impressive is its rich Byzantine style; how moving the sight of its candlelit icons and those astonishing mosaics. And it must have been a place of rare beauty much like this that, back in the 10th century, inspired the envoys of Prince Vladimir to bring your Orthodox faith to Kiev. For they said that upon their first glimpse inside an Orthodox church in Constantinople, "We knew not whether we were in heaven or on Earth."

Your All Holiness, you are today trying to bring the peace of heaven to this earthly life. Your global vision is one of hope, hope for what we can do with and for your 250 million spiritual children, so many of whom have lived in the chilled darkness of religious persecution. The world rejoices that the new freedoms of the past year mean that your Orthodox followers in so many lands are now once again able to follow freely and openly the road of holy light.

We celebrate the dawn of hope for these people, particularly those for whom you speak in Eastern Europe. We also celebrate the tremendous strength of spirit which has sustained them through these generations of repression, spirit like that of the 50 million Russian Orthodox believers who still dream of the day when they can worship openly in their faith which is, after all, 930 years older than communism itself. And we know—we know with certainty that day will come because, as a persecutor of Orthodoxy admitted: "Religion is like a nail. The harder you hit it, the deeper it goes into the wood." But while the events of this past year have been a glorious beginning, there is still much to do—because peace is more than just the absence of war.

As we continue the struggle for liberty for all, our way will be lit with the inner radiance of pastoral pilgrims of peace like Your All Holiness. I have often spoken of hope as a Thousand Points of Light ablaze in the black sky, and so, I was struck by this conference's theme: "Walk as children of light." I noticed how this first began—in Ephesians: "For you were once darkness but now you are light."

Eastern Europe was once in dark bondage and now begins to see by the pale glow of a new dawn. It's like your own Easter midnight service. As the priest calls, "Come and receive the light," he brings a candle, I'm told, from the altar into the unbroken blackness of the church. And then he passes the flame to each worshiper's own individual candle until the church is ablaze with flickering lights proudly shining together to defeat the dark.

Your All Holiness, you are that candle. Your faithful here and around the world are that congregation which takes the light of your vision and spreads it through all lands. I was touched to hear that during this trip you will be walking across the Peace Bridge that links our great country, the United States, and Canada. And really, if you think about it, what a wonderful symbol of what all individuals and nations must do: build peace bridges that link—not separate—nations, and then walk upon those bridges to meet others halfway in order to celebrate our similarities, not to battle our differences.

Together, we ask your prayers, Your All Holiness, that God will guide us in our efforts for peace and that the wide arms of faith and forgiveness will one day soon embrace a world with justice and compassion for all.

God bless you, Your All Holiness, and God bless every one of you gathered here tonight. Barbara and I were honored to be your guests. Thank you very, very much.

Note: The President spoke at 7:40 p.m. in the Sheraton Ballroom at the Sheraton Washington Hotel. In his remarks, the President jokingly referred to Ted Koppel, of ABC News, as Peter Jennings, also of ABC News. The President also referred to His All Holiness Ecumenical Patriarch Dimitrios I, His Eminence Archbishop Iakovos of the Greek Orthodox Archdiocese of North and South America, and John Brademas, president of New York University.

Message to the Congress Transmitting a Report on Hungarian Emigration Policy
July 13, 1990

To the Congress of the United States:

In October 1989 I determined and reported to the Congress that Hungary meets the emigration criteria of the Jackson-Vanik amendment to the Trade Act of 1974. This determination allowed for the continuation of Hungary's most favored nation (MFN) status without the requirement of an annual waiver.

As required by law, I am submitting a formal report to the Congress concerning emigration laws and policies of the Republic of Hungary. You will find that the report certifies continued Hungarian compliance with U.S. and international standards in the areas of emigration and human rights policy.

GEORGE BUSH

The White House,
July 13, 1990.

Message to the Congress Reporting on the Economic Sanctions Against Libya
July 13, 1990

To the Congress of the United States:

1. I hereby report to the Congress on developments since my last report of January 25, 1990, concerning the national emergency with respect to Libya that was declared in Executive Order No. 12543 of January 7, 1986. This report is submitted pursuant to section 401(c) of the National Emergencies Act, 50 U.S.C. 1641(c); section 204(c) of the International Emergency Economic Powers Act, 50 U.S.C. 1703(c) ("IEEPA"); and section 505(c) of the International Security and Development Cooperation Act of 1985, 22 U.S.C. 2349aa–9(c).

2. Since my last report on January 25, 1990, there have been no amendments to the Libyan Sanctions Regulations, 31 C.F.R. Part 550 (the "Regulations"), administered by the Office of Foreign Assets Control ("FAC") of the Department of the Treasury. Additionally, since January 25, 1990, there have been no amendments or changes to orders of the Department of Commerce or the Department of Transportation implementing aspects of Executive Order No. 12543 relating to exports from the United States and air transportation, respectively.

3. During the current 6-month period, FAC has issued a limited number of specific licenses to individuals and corporations to permit them to engage in activities that would otherwise be prohibited by the Regu-

lations. Under FAC licensing procedures, 15 individuals registered to travel to or remain in Libya with Libyan immediate family members. Fifteen licensing decisions were made authorizing or prohibiting transactions in connection with Libya. The most significant licensing activity since the last report was the authorization of U.S. involvement in a U.N. Food and Agriculture Organization program to eradicate the screw worm, an infestation that threatened both humans and animals in North Africa.

4. Various enforcement actions mentioned in previous reports continue to be pursued. In February 1990, in the U.S. District Court for the District of Minnesota, Sealed Air Corporation and two of its former corporate officers each received criminal sentences for engaging in shipments of rust inhibitor chemicals to Libya in violation of the Regulations. The corporation was fined $500,000, the maximum penalty permitted for a violation of IEEPA. A senior vice president of the firm was fined $100,000 and was ordered to perform 400 hours of community service. A general manager was fined $40,000 and was ordered to perform 200 hours of community service.

In April 1990, FAC closed the offices of a Libyan student group for failure to abide by the terms of its FAC license. All tangible property of the organization and all bank accounts of the organization were blocked. The student group has since elected a new board of directors and has agreed to renew its licensed contractual arrangements for

outside monitoring of financial transactions and to obtain funds from Libya in order to resume its operation in accordance with FAC licensing requirements.

5. The expenses incurred by the Federal Government in the period from January 25, 1990, through June 1, 1990, that are directly attributable to the exercise of powers and authorities conferred by the declaration of the Libyan national emergency are estimated at $442,541. Personnel costs were largely centered in the Department of the Treasury (particularly in the Office of Foreign Assets Control, the Customs Service, the Office of the Assistant Secretary for Enforcement, the Office of the Assistant Secretary for International Affairs, and the Office of the General Counsel), the Department of State, the Department of Commerce, the Department of Justice, the Federal Reserve Board, and the National Security Council.

6. The policies and actions of the Government of Libya continue to pose an unusual and extraordinary threat to the national security and foreign policy of the United States. I shall continue to exercise the powers at my disposal to apply economic sanctions against Libya as long as these measures are appropriate and will continue to report periodically to the Congress on significant developments as required by law.

GEORGE BUSH

The White House,
July 13, 1990.

Message to the Congress Transmitting the Annual Report on Nuclear Nonproliferation
July 13, 1990

To the Congress of the United States:

I have reviewed the activities of the United States Government departments and agencies during calendar year 1989 related to preventing nuclear proliferation, and I am pleased to submit my annual report pursuant to section 601(a) of the Nuclear Non-Proliferation Act of 1978 (Public

Law 95–242, 22 U.S.C. 3281(a)).

As the report demonstrates, the United States continued its efforts during 1989 to prevent the spread of nuclear explosives to additional countries. This is an important element of our overall national security policy, which seeks to reduce the risk of war and increase international stability. I want to build on the positive achievements cited in this report and to work with the Congress toward our common goal: a safer and more secure future for all mankind.

GEORGE BUSH

The White House,
July 13, 1990.

Statement on Congressional Action on the Americans With Disabilities Act
July 13, 1990

I am delighted that Congress has now approved the conference report on the Americans with Disabilities Act. I am looking forward with great pleasure to signing this important civil rights legislation. This is a great day in the history of our country because for the first time Americans with disabilities will enjoy full civil rights protection with respect to employment, transportation, places of public accommodation, public services, and communications. Further, it is proof that individual rights can be given full and necessary protection without undue regulatory burdens. In this month of the 214th anniversary of the independence of our nation, this legislation will serve as a declaration of independence for millions of persons with disabilities in this country.

Remarks on the Proposed Balanced Budget Amendment and an Exchange With Reporters
July 13, 1990

The President. Let me just say before I leave here that on Tuesday the House is going to vote on a balanced budget amendment. And if enacted, that would halt the steady buildup of the national debt. I think it will bring much-needed discipline to the process, discipline on the executive branch, discipline on the legislative branch, on the Congress of the United States.

We've had one surplus in 30 years. And 30 State legislatures—more than that—have already called for this action. I think this would be a very important tool. This passage is important too, I think, to the current budget negotiators. It would send them a good signal. We are very, very serious not only in the budget negotiations now in process but the commitment to the balanced-budget process. I think this vote on Tuesday is important, so I wanted to urge strong support for it.

Q. What about the civil rights compromise?

Q. How practical is it, Mr. President?

The President. Phase it in and it will be very practical, and it will work. And it ought to be tried. We've tried a lot of other things, and it hasn't worked. And we hear a lot about controlling spending, and then we see bills up there—we're going $4 billion over the President's request in 1 day. Turn around and that's what happens. So, I'd like to give this a shot, and I think the country would like to give it a shot.

Q. When you can't meet Gramm-Rudman in 1 year, sir, how can you reach zero?

The President. We're not going to reach it in 1 year.

Q. Has the budget bogged down?

Civil Rights Legislation

Q. Are you feeling optimistic about the civil rights compromise now, after Sununu's letter?

The President. Well, we're trying very hard on that.

Do I get credit for a full press conference here? Otherwise, I'm leaving.

Q. Half credit on it.

Q. We'll give you credit.

Federal Budget Negotiations

Q. How about tax increase revenues? Have you decided——

The President. The budget process? I think they're working in seriousness as of today, and I've vowed to stay out of it. I notice others are positioning themselves on what they will or won't accept. I made a deal with the leadership that I wouldn't do that, and I'm going to keep my pledge as long as I can—I may be the only one in town doing that, but——

Q. Have you gotten closer to a package on taxes?

The President. I think—well, I don't know, Helen [Helen Thomas, United Press International]. That's a good—and I can't tell you. Sometimes I think our negotiators—Brady, Darman, and Sununu—are optimistic, and sometimes they come back with a little less optimism. But I hope that this statement today will be supportive of the process, and I hope that what I've suggested will happen because I think in the long run that's what's required to keep our fiscal house in order.

Civil Rights Legislation

Q. Where do things stand on civil rights?

The President. Negotiations going on. John Sununu was back today and had a fairly, I would say, reasonably optimistic proposal. My position on that one remains clear: I want to sign a civil rights bill; I will not sign a quota bill. And that's about where we are, but I think it's looking encouraging. I saw [Senator] Ted Kennedy down here yesterday and had a chance to share my views with him once again. And he's been working, I would say, quite cooperatively with us—Republican side, under Senator Hatch—most cooperative. So, as I leave here for the weekend, I hope I'm right in saying that it looks like we can work something out on that. I want to do it.

Federal Budget Negotiations

Q. Can you say, sir, if in fact the administration has signed on for the need for about $25 billion in tax revenues as part of this overall package?

The President. No. I've said I wasn't going to discuss the specifics of the negotiations. And I really think I—I know it's not too specific, but I really feel I ought to keep my share of the bargain on that. I see a lot of speculation and a lot of people saying what we will or won't do or what they will or won't do—Republicans and Democrats—and, look, I understand that. But I gave my commitment to the leadership—Republican and Democrat—in the House, and I'm going to stay with that. And at some point, I may have to go out and say, look, this is all we can do, or here's where we go. But I'm not going to do that now.

Q. Is your commitment——

The President. I'm going to try.

Q. Is your commitment to a capital gains tax cut waning or weakening in any way?

The President. I'm not going to—you know, if I start going into even one facet of the negotiations, I will, in my view, be violating a commitment I made to the Congress. So, I really want to ask to be forgiven for not answering that nice-try question.

Q. When do you think you'll have some answers?

The President. Well, we're moving along, Helen. We all know what the dates are out there. You'll see some figures next week on the magnitude of this problem. The figures are out there pretty much in the public domain, and certainly, the Congress has them. But the American people want something done. And so, I'm going to keep pushing, and our negotiators are working in total good faith. And I think the problem is so important nationally that something positive will happen. It has to.

Russian Republic President Yeltsin

Q. What do you think about Boris Yeltsin bolting the Communist Party?

The President. Boris bolting his party—very interesting development, very interesting.

Hey, I'm tired, come on, and so are the rest of you guys. I can tell from the quality of the questions.

Note: The exchange began at 1:33 p.m. on the South Lawn at the White House, prior to the President's departure for Camp David, MD. In his remarks, the President referred to John H. Sununu, Chief of Staff to the President; Secretary of the Treasury Nicholas F. Brady; and Richard G. Darman, Director of the Office of Management and Budget.

Statement by Press Secretary Fitzwater on President Bush's Meeting With President-Elect César Gaviria of Colombia
July 13, 1990

Colombian President-elect César Gaviria, who is in the United States on a private visit, met today with President Bush for 30 minutes.

President Bush again congratulated him on his May 27 victory in the Colombian election, a completely open and democratic process. He told President-elect Gaviria that the United States looks forward to working closely with his administration. President Bush asked Gaviria to convey his warmest best wishes to President Barco upon his return to Colombia.

The two leaders also touched on bilateral issues, concentrating principally on the fight against drugs and cooperation in economic relations. With regard to drugs, President Bush briefed President-elect Gaviria on our budget requests for the drug fight for the coming fiscal year. There is currently a request for $80.5 million in drug-related assistance pending before the Congress, along with an additional request for a regional Economic Support Fund which would include Colombia. In the area of economics, both sides pledged to continue working toward mutually satisfactory agreements on various trade issues.

President Bush also informed President-elect Gaviria that there was no foundation to recent press reports about massive U.S. military involvement in Colombia or other Andean countries. He reaffirmed that our drug interdiction activities in the Andean countries are and will continue to be fully coordinated with the countries.

On economic issues, the two leaders reviewed President Bush's Enterprise for the Americas Initiative as it might apply to Colombia. Colombia was the first country to take up President Bush's offer to negotiate bilateral trade and investment framework agreements, and we have been holding discussions on this.

Statement on the Federal Budget Deficit
July 16, 1990

The midsession budget review shows the Nation is facing a budget deficit which, if Congress fails to act responsibly, will dictate a $100 billion across-the-board cut in Federal spending. Absent congressional action, this cut will go into effect automatically on October 1. Such a cut would be required by law.

If a fully responsible deficit reduction program is not enacted by the Congress, this automatic $100 billion cut will affect almost all that the Federal Government touches, from military readiness to air safety to vaccinations for children to programs for the elderly to drug abuse prevention to prison violence. It is, therefore, all the more important that the budget summit reach agreement promptly and that the Congress act responsibly to bring the deficit down.

Statement on German Membership in the North Atlantic Treaty Organization
July 16, 1990

I welcome President Gorbachev's statement, at his press conference with Chancellor Kohl, accepting a united Germany's right to choose to remain a member of NATO. This comment demonstrates statesmanship and strengthens efforts to build enduring relationships based on cooperation. It can be seen as a response, perhaps in part, to the outcome of the NATO summit in London, where the alliance displayed its readiness to adapt to the new realities in Europe and reach out to former adversaries in the East.

Five months ago, in February, Chancellor Kohl and I agreed that a united Germany should remain a full member of the North Atlantic alliance, including its military structures. East German Prime Minister de Maiziere joins us in supporting continued German membership in NATO. The Helsinki Final Act guarantees Germany's right to make this choice. And we think this solution is in the best interests of all the countries of Europe, including the Soviet Union.

Note: The statement referred to Mikhail Gorbachev, President of the Soviet Union, and Helmut Kohl, Chancellor of the Federal Republic of Germany.

Nomination of Wayne Lee Berman To Be an Assistant Secretary of Commerce
July 16, 1990

The President today announced his intention to nominate Wayne Lee Berman to be an Assistant Secretary of Commerce (Counselor). In this capacity, he will serve as the senior adviser on policy matters to the Secretary and will coordinate the external affairs of the Department of Commerce.

Since 1989 Mr. Berman has served as Counselor to the Secretary of Commerce in Washington, DC. Prior to this, he served as Director of the Commerce Department transition team; director of congressional relations for the Bush-Quayle 1988 campaign and for the George Bush for President campaign; and partner with the consulting firm of Berman, Bergner and Boyette, Inc., in Washington, DC. In addition, Mr. Berman has served as director of corporate and political affairs at the Center for Strategic and International Studies and as deputy to the director of the resources group for the 1980 Reagan-Bush transition.

Mr. Berman graduated from the University of Buffalo (B.A., 1978). He was born November 8, 1956, in Rochester, NY. Mr. Berman is married, has one child, and resides in Washington, DC.

Letter to Congressional Leaders on the Balanced Budget Amendment
July 16, 1990

Dear Mr. Speaker: (Dear Mr. Leader:)
I am writing to urge prompt adoption of H.J. Res. 268, which proposes an amendment to the Constitution to provide for a

balanced budget for the United States Government and for greater accountability in the enactment of tax legislation. In order to help restore fiscal integrity to the Government, we need such a balanced budget amendment, along with a line-item veto constitutional amendment, and enhanced rescission authority for the President. Together with political courage and discipline, these tools are vital to solving the problem of budget deficits.

A constitutional amendment to require a balanced budget is the most fundamental change needed in the Federal budget process. A balanced budget amendment is both necessary and appropriate to protect the interests of citizens not now able to represent themselves: the citizens of future generations. The seriousness of this issue is reflected in the fact that more than 30 State legislatures have already called for a constitutional convention for this purpose. As for alternatives that would require statutorily a balanced budget, such alternatives are an inadequate substitute for a constitutional amendment.

Sections 2 and 4 of H.J. Res. 268 raise technical concerns related to the public debt and taxes, respectively. These concerns are addressed separately in a Statement of Administration Policy on H.J. Res. 268.

I am prepared to continue working with the Congress to enact meaningful, credible, and effective budget reforms. Adoption of H.J. Res. 268 will be an important first step toward this goal, which is crucial to our Nation's long term economic health and prosperity.

Sincerely,

GEORGE BUSH

Note: Identical letters were sent to Thomas S. Foley, Speaker of the House of Representatives; Richard A. Gephardt, House majority leader; and Robert H. Michel, House Republican leader.

Remarks and a Question-and-Answer Session With the Magazine Publishers of America
July 17, 1990

The President. Apologies for keeping you waiting. Let me just open with a brief—I don't want to filibuster—but open with a brief statement on a word about Germany. And then I'll be glad to respond to your questions.

I talked this morning with both Chancellor Kohl and Mikhail Gorbachev and had a fairly long conversations—about 30 or 40 minutes—with each one. I feel that the agreement that was announced yesterday between Gorbachev and Kohl is very, very significant and very important, and I'd like to reflect on how we got—I say "we" because the U.S. has been in the forefront of suggesting the best way for stabilization and peace would be a united Germany, a unified Germany as a full-fledged member of NATO. So, let me reflect on how we got here.

First, everybody had to recognize that this unification was going to take place, was going to happen, and that it was right. And you don't have to go very far back in your minds to remember there was some debate about the speed of unification and whether a unified Germany indeed would be a factor for peace. I remember telling the press last October, before the Berlin Wall came down, that when we said we supported German unity we really meant that, and we meant it without qualifications. After the East German elections in March, people began to realize that unification could actually occur this year, and my view was the sooner the better. And I know the German people have appreciated that stand by the United States.

And the second step was to put together a solid Western position on the external aspects of German unification. In February Chancellor Kohl and I had a very long talk out there at Camp David about the alignment of a united Germany, and we came out after those meetings and agreed unequivocally that a united Germany needed to remain in NATO, including its full membership in the integrated military structures. Prime Minister Thatcher and President Mitterrand, as well as other leaders in the alliance, developed a solid meeting of the minds on German unification.

And the third step, though, was to persuade the Soviet Union. And President Gorbachev and I discussed this in Washington. We discussed it in considerable depth on that Saturday up at Camp David. And then in our joint press conference, I said that I thought we both agreed that Germany should be free to choose the alliance that it would belong to.

President Gorbachev, if you remember, didn't challenge that; and we all thought that that was a good sign then—the Soviet having been positioned, as you remember, against Germany in NATO. But he didn't challenge that idea that everybody ought to choose what alliance they want to be in.

We also had to show him that the NATO alliance was not his enemy but was a force for stability that could, indeed, adapt—could, indeed, change—adapt to the new realities in Europe. And that's why the recently completed NATO summit was so important, where all of our colleagues agreed to our proposals for the transformed alliance. And I'm very proud of my collaborators here—the top foreign affairs and national security people, Jim Baker, Brent Scowcroft—in formulating this position, this leadership position, on behalf of the United States.

I sent a paper around prior to the NATO meeting, and it was that paper from which everybody worked, and it became the basis for this agreement. Then yesterday, President Gorbachev commented that—and here's what he said—that without the "very important impulse" from the London Declaration it would have been difficult to make headway. So, the Soviets viewed the NATO agreement as something that was very important to them and demonstrated less of a threatening mode on the part of NATO.

Both Kohl and Gorbachev have displayed, I think, exceptional qualities of leadership during this challenging period. I commended—as a politician—commended President Gorbachev on the outcome of the Party Congress over there. You talk about a guy getting hit from all sides—I mean, I felt just—[*laughter*]—totally relaxed about what's happening in this country.

So, anyway, I don't know—but I must say, I take pride in the way Europe is moving into this new era of freedom. It's a goal that we Americans have long worked to achieve. We've still got some very important problems that lie out there ahead of us. But it's a challenging and very exciting time to be President of the United States, and I expect my other co-leaders in the alliance would feel that way. I'm not sure Mr. Gorbachev feels that way yet, but isn't it exciting when you think back a year and a half ago to where we stand today?

Now, with no further ado and without this opening designed to deflect you away from matters domestic, I'll be glad to respond to questions on any subject.

Yes, sir?

Media Literacy Campaign

Q. Mr. President, my name is Peter Diamandis, and I'm the chairman of the magazine publishers association. First of all, I'd like to thank you for spending some time with the representatives of the industry. We're planning a party next year—this is sort of a statement, not a question. [*Laughter*]

The President. All right, I'll take it. [*Laughter*]

Q. Okay. We're going to plan a party next year. We're having a 250th anniversary of the first magazine in America. It started in 1741, appropriately titled the American Magazine. This industry has now grown to 10,000 titles on every conceivable subject. And in honor of that celebration, we're going to devote a big part of our budget and our time to fighting illiteracy—I know that's a big subject for you and your wife. I would just like for you to know that and hopefully support that in 1991.

And on that note, I'd like to introduce a fellow Texan, Mr. Reg Brack, who's the president of Time, Inc., magazine.

The President. Well, first, I'm delighted to hear that. And it is very important. This whole media support for the antinarcotics and for education, with literacy being in the forefront, has been dramatic. I will say this—not to avoid my responsibilities as President, but it couldn't be done—the Federal Government—there are not enough chips around to do what your industry and others are doing on a pro bono, Thousand Points of Light basis.

Excuse me Reg, go ahead, sir.

Postal Service

Q. Well, Mr. President, first of all, I'd like to congratulate you on your most recent accomplishment regarding the German issue and the handling of NATO and the development of Europe in general.

I would like to take this opportunity, on the heels of yesterday's troublesome news about the deficit, to address some issues domestically. And in that respect, I hope you know that I'm sure all magazine publishers are supportive of the administration's apparent willingness to begin to seriously address the deficit crisis.

But in that respect, I'd like to just make a quick comment and then ask a question. The comment has to do with the fact that magazines are particularly dependent on two things if we're going to continue our contribution to America's knowledge and vitality and diversity. Those obviously are advertising—and you just mentioned how advertising functions on some important national matters—the other is the United States Postal Service. And since advertising is, by a large measure, the machine or the engine that drives the consumer demand in this country, we would all hope that you would agree that anything that constrains or restricts advertising of any kind is actually a restriction, really, on the free enterprise system.

As you can imagine, as an industry we're more dependent than any part of the knowledge business on the United States Postal Service. Now, we know we have to pay more; and in fact, the Nation, next year I believe, will be confronted with a cost for its mail $7 billion greater than it pays this year.

My question really has to do with your view of the Postal Service in general and, specifically, your position on the Postmaster General's strategic initiative to address costs in general and reduce labor costs in particular, because it's vital to the way the Nation gets its information.

The President. In the first place, I would obviously support bringing the Postal Service even more significantly into the end of this century. I mean, I think most people that look back historically have found that there are certain inefficiencies there. The whole concept of getting it more out of the political patronage business was to be able to overcome some of those inefficiencies. You people would probably be in a better position than I to judge how successful those efforts have been.

But certainly, I would be for encouraging the ultimate in that. I happen to not be fearful of the competition that has been brought to bear on the Postal Service. I know that some are critical of it, but on the other hand, I think it's a good thing. And I think if that's the way to stimulate efficiency, more efficiency on the part of the public side, the Postal Service itself, so much the better. So, it's a very general answer to a rather specific question, but clearly, I'd like to think the answer is in reducing costs through efficient management as opposed to raising more revenues to support what historically most people think has been politically abused and, to some degree, inefficient system.

Who's next? Yes, sir?

International Competitiveness

Q. Ed Torrero, executive editor, IEEE Spectrum magazine. I'd like to change the topic to international competitiveness, if I might. There are three technologies which are generally agreed upon to be essential to the national security. They are electronics, computers, and telecommunications. Their vitality depends on a vibrant commercial industry. Sir, are there any conditions or scenario under which you would support a somewhat more focused support of critical technologies by a stronger buttressing of commercial activities?

The President. I'm not sure I understand what you mean by "buttressing commercial activities." I mean, clearly, you put your finger on the future. And what we are trying to do, recognizing America's historic ability to lead in these areas, is to open up markets. But I'm not sure I understand what you mean in buttressing——

Q. If I might clarify. In the commercial area, there have been three specific examples in recent years where we may have been able to do something in terms of public policy, but thought better of doing it. One is in the supercomputer area, where we've lost some companies; another is in HDTV, where the former speaker gave some information; and a third is—if I may continue the specifics—in the area of semiconductor equipment manufacturers, which was almost lost to this country. A government agency recently predicted, therefore, that by 1994 the Japanese will, among other Asian technologies, dominate this particular area. So, the previous speaker outlined a very exciting program to help R&D and so on. The question is: Is that enough in time?

The President. I think it's enough in time for the Government. In other words, we are trying to take a look at antitrust to see that we're not giving our producers and our industries a disadvantage. We are trying to open up markets so that we can compete, and we are putting a lot of emphasis on research. I forget the total budget figure for research this year, but it's enormous, not just as it relates to electronics, computers, and telecommunications. But I think that I would draw the line in terms of R&D and then trade policies that give us a chance to compete.

I've just come from an appeal by a United States Senator for support on—this is a little off your question—for the textile industry, to protect the textile business further. And I can't do that. I can't say that I think the answer to the problem of textiles is further protection. Nor can I say that I think the answer to these three very important elements of our technology is further protection. So, that leads you then to R&D and to opening the markets abroad.

Fundamental Values

Q. Mr. President, I'm Jim Guthrie of the MPA. I'd like to address you as our spiritual leader who would like to keep us looking

ahead. We're coming out of a decade that could probably be politely defined and characterized as one of self-indulgence and immediate gratification. There were inquisitive yuppies. There were junk bond LBO's that led to certain decrements in our own economic fabric. There were Wall Street convictions. And now we're at the S&L crisis. Secretary Mosbacher talked about the Baldrige Award. You've talked about a Thousand Points of Light. What else is going on that will keep us looking ahead to the quality and the value that we're talking about restoring to all areas of our life?

The President. You know, I've never been too pessimistic about America in this regard. I'll make you a slight confession: I still am trying to find the appropriate way to discuss, using the bully pulpit of the White House, these matters you talk about—talking about religious values, family values, or whatever. I think there is a danger that one can overdo it, and yet I think it's appropriate that the President try to not only adhere to those values but to discuss them.

Having said that, I'm not pessimistic about America. We go through cycles. We went through a cycle in the Vietnam war where our own sons and, to some degree, daughters were told that our cause was immoral—people feeling as strongly as they did. I was old enough or blind enough, or whatever, not to accept that view. I still don't accept that view, because when I look at Southeast Asia and I see a Vietnam where the charge was against us—if we'd only get out; this is an indigenous civil war; you'd have a little more democracy there—that hasn't worked out that way. And in your line of work, where there were many publications, there are now but a few. And you see, still, people going out in these boats.

But the point is, as it relates to your question, we had a generation of Americans that were taught about a deep conviction by professors and politicians and others that our purpose, our cause, was wrong. And then we condoned as a society certain excesses that we should have condemned. And I'm talking about an elevation of understanding about narcotics, for example, which gets right to the core of values.

Well, you've got to understand. I even think that we condoned graffiti as an expression of people's—wasn't this marvelous—creativity, when all it was, was littering and cluttering up not exactly beautiful subway cars but—[*laughter*]—nevertheless, we condoned things we should have condemned. I have confidence that the country goes somewhat cyclically, but always moves forward to our fundamental values.

I'm not discouraged about it. I wrestle with things that I think are important—and I don't want to get into a debate with you all about the flag amendment. I happen to feel strongly about it, and I'd like to see the debate done so you could do it without having to call the other guy a demagog. I may be wrong, but I feel strongly about it. And I've fought for it because I do think there was a unique symbol there. And there's pretty good understanding on the part of the American people. The debate can go on without denigrating the other person's convictions that disagrees or feels that amending the Bill of Rights or the Constitution would be an egregious error.

But I keep coming back, as I listen to the debates on all these questions—the National Endowment of the Arts—all of them—that we have a way of finding our way through, in the United States, these—what appear to be—dilemmas or these challenges. And the reason is, I think, there is a fundamental understanding that we are one nation under God, that we have great respect for religion diversity, and that as we see the social problems of the day we return more and more to the importance of the family.

So, I don't know what we can do about it. I want to be very careful about censorship and about demagoging these issues, whatever they are. But I don't feel that I ought to address myself, in a legislative sense, to helping with this question because I think we can sort it out as people. And I'm confident not only of our decency and honor as a country but of our tremendous generosity as a country. We've got some big problems here at home, and I've got to address myself perhaps more effectively to some of those. But I don't put down one of them the weakening of the moral underpinning of this country. I hope I'm right.

Here we've got a couple of more. I was late getting over. Yes? [*Laughter*] Thank you, Kristin [Kristin Clark Taylor, Director of White House Media Relations]. I don't want to overrule my leader here. [*Laughter*] She'll kill me when we get out of here.

Federal Budget Negotiations

Q. Mr. President, I'm Tom Ryder, from American Express. After yesterday's disappointing budget news, does the administration's game plan on deficit reduction change?

The President. No——

Q. Where do we go from here?

The President. The news in the Congress has been somewhat discounted because the numbers have been shared with them. And that news is one of the reasons I tried to make very clear that we would go with no preconditions to these talks.

We're getting to a crunch. The debt ceiling vote is going to drive some of the action. I'm still optimistic—or put it this way, fairly optimistic—that we're going to get a budget bill. But it can't be on one side of the equation or not. By that I mean it can't be done by all spending increases, it darn sure can't be done by revenue increases, and it cannot and will not be a budget agreement unless we get budget reform. The American people ought not to be asked to put a Band-Aid on a problem because of the budget process on Capitol Hill.

So, we've got three ingredients to the question, and I think we're going to have to move forward on all three of them. I believe that we can get something done, and I think it is essential, given yesterday's public news—which I think has been discounted by the budgeteers—but I think it is absolutely essential something be done. I will do my part. And I have felt constrained on talking about what kinds of revenues or what kinds of spending cuts or what kinds of reforms because I made a deal with the congressional leaders that I wouldn't do that.

As I said as I departed for Camp David the other day, I'm perhaps the only guy in town abiding by those constraints—[*laughter*]—which isn't all that bad. Because people on both sides of the aisle feel strongly. We've got to make progress. And given yesterday's news, Tom, it is essential. The time for game playing is over. And we have to get something done that is not only a sound budget agreement but is seen by the American people to be a sound budget agreement. And I worry that if we don't get one—about the confidence in the marketplace that, obviously, you know a good deal more about than I do.

So, we will be pushing in the next couple of weeks. And the meter is running. We're getting close to adjournment of the Congress. And we're getting close to a deficit ceiling that has to be raised. But I'm very serious about it, and I will stay with them just as long as is required to get a sound deal.

But the news is disturbing. It's big. It's strong—most of it or a lot of it coming because the economy has been more sluggish. But I still feel—and I'm going to filibuster here—but I still feel that there isn't quite the acute awareness on the part of the average American as deserves to be there. And maybe that means I'll have to do a little bit more once I feel unfettered from my agreement with the leaders.

Let me take three more, and then I will go peacefully.

Space Program

Q. Mr. President, Terry McGraw, McGraw-Hill. Since the completion of the Apollo space program, the U.S. space program has seemingly struggled for a definitive notion of its mission. Could you comment on your priority the space program has in your agenda and, more specifically, what your expectations are in this new investigation of NASA?

The President. One, I have great confidence in Dick Truly, the Administrator of NASA. And so, to lay that part of the question to rest, what we are doing is asking him to form an outside committee of the best minds he can find to look to the future, not go try to assign blame because a mission is delayed getting off the ground. I mean, these shots are highly complex. We have been the leaders in space, and I want to see us continue to be the leaders in space.

So, the group that was advertised a

couple of days ago or heralded as an investigation of NASA is nothing of the kind. I saw the stories and, once again, went semiballistic, thinking, my heavens, how could somebody write this when that is not what the President intends? But I think the Vice President, who is doing a good job as head of the Space Council, clarified that.

In terms of goals, we've got some broad objectives that go far beyond lunar landings now. But the first one obviously would be this space station, but with continued shots back and forth to do what's almost becoming journeymen's work in space. I'm confident we can do it. Obviously, we're in tight budget times, so we've set the goals for Mars and beyond out there many, many years. But I have confidence in NASA. And it's a perilous business, I guess, anytime you put people up there into space; but the record has been very good.

And yet, I think the management is such a complex—it's such a complex organization that it is appropriate that the Administrator now call on the best minds he can find to see how we're going to meet these next goals and meet them, hopefully, within budget. And I'm talking about the space station; I'm talking about what Sally Ride [shuttle astronaut] talked about, Mission to Planet Earth, where we actually utilize to the fullest extent possible space shots in improving matters on Earth—obviously, the environment comes to mind, and agriculture comes to mind. And then taking that third step, how do we organize NASA to meet this big, tremendous management challenge that will come about for this next quantum leap forward—and discuss the cooperation with other nations in all of this.

I mean, as the whole world is changing—and it has dramatically changed—there may be some real opportunities now to do more with the Soviet Union, for example, or with other countries. So, all of this requires a new look, and that's what this story was about.

Two more. Who's got them? Right here. Yes, sir?

South Africa

Q. Mr. President, Ed Lewis, publisher of Essence magazine. Mr. Nelson Mandela, who has visited us, had great impact on many Americans. What are you doing to— or are you—doing to negotiate an agreement between Mr. Mandela and Mr. de Klerk [President of South Africa] to facilitate a hopeful, peaceful resolution for all South Africans?

The President. What we're doing now is encouraging Mr. de Klerk to come here. And I think it is important, having had good visits with Mr. Mandela—and they were good, and I'll tell you about that in a minute—that de Klerk come here. It will be somewhat controversial. There will be a lot of picketers out here. I think they're wrong. I think in de Klerk you have a new kind of leader in South Africa.

I detected quite a respect on Mandela's part for de Klerk. And thus, I have concluded that it is important for the President to sit down with Mr. de Klerk. In the meantime, why, we're having a lot of diplomacy going on as to how we can encourage further change on the part of South Africa towards the elimination of apartheid.

We are not going to change our sanctions position until there is more progress. And you can argue that. I've sometimes felt that sanctions might be counterproductive, but I'm not going to change them now. And I think we're right—nor am I going to strengthen—nor am I going to acquiesce in their being increased right now. And I think that position is understood by Mandela as head of the ANC [African National Congress], and I think it's understood by de Klerk. They may not agree with it.

So, that's about where we are. I will say that the visit with Mr. Mandela was very interesting. I had a long talk with him over here, and then took him and his wife over for lunch. What impressed me—this is kind of a personal observation and off the substance—is how a man who had been incarcerated for so long could retain this quiet sense of dignity and, I thought, reasoned understanding. I disagree with him on, at this juncture in history, the use of violence. He made his position clear. And I happen to think that my position is correct for the United States to keep emphasizing peaceful resolution to this question as opposed to a violent one.

But I talked to him very frankly about the differences we have on Castro [President of Cuba] or Qadhafi [leader of Libya], and yet he didn't take offense by that. But I felt if these talks are going to be meaningful at all, you might as well tell him what he's running into in the United States in terms of Castro, Qadhafi, Yasser Arafat [leader of the Palestine Liberation Organization].

So, we had a good, frank discussion; and I hope that he went away—I think he did— he called me up just before he left—with a feeling that the United States Government had been responsive and certainly interested. And we'll see where we go. But I think more than any of the European countries we can be catalytic. We were not a colonial power, and we are united in our opposition to apartheid. And then we have an Afro-American population here that feels fervently—this is a gut issue. And I think that's a good thing. That might not be quite as prominent in other countries as well.

So, I think those ingredients make our country uniquely able to serve as a catalyst between the various factors in South Africa, and that's what I want to try to do.

Last one. Who's got it? Yes, ma'am?

President's Reading Habits

Q. Marie Petersen, Crafts 'n Things magazine. Our business is communicating via the written word. But many of us in this room are so busy doing our business we don't have time to read. When you have time to read, Mr. President, what is it that you choose to read for pleasure?

The President. What do I read as President?

Q. And for pleasure.

The President. For pleasure? Thank God you added that, because—[*laughter*]—because really, this job is—and I don't want to single out—well, he's not even here to defend himself—but his able deputy and my trusted friend, Bob Gates [Assistant to the President and Deputy for National Security Affairs], is here from the National Security Council—and Brent Scowcroft, who's not here. Part of the job—I'll address myself just to the concept of reading—is endless numbers of papers. I do better getting briefed in person where I can ask questions of our Cabinet or of our national security team, but I have to have reading ahead of that. So, most of my reading is formal and heavy going. But in terms of process, I have enough confidence in our people that when they take those yellow, underlining-highlighting pens, they can take a 40-page document and convert it into 10 pages of reading. I cite this as process.

And it's not just foreign affairs. It's Bob Mosbacher's business or Dick Darman's business, the budget stuff. And so, there's plenty of that to do. The CIA, in which I have great confidence, has some marvelous studies of things all round the world. They've got a good economic part of the house out there. So, I have to do a lot of that reading.

What I do in terms of pleasure is to read mostly novels, some of them not so—I wouldn't say that they would be particularly weighty. "Bonfire of the Vanities" is one which was pretty darn good and was up near the top of the list. I'm reading "Network News" right now. I'm halfway through that. I read a couple of books on Teddy Roosevelt. I'm reading Caro's

"Lyndon Johnson." I say reading—I've got about two or three books going right now. There's a plain mystery by a guy named Beschloss called "Mayday" that I started and put aside because Barbara gave me the other one. [*Laughter*] But it's relaxed reading. It is relaxed kind of reading, and it's novels. I find I can do that just before—instead of taking one of these Halcion sleeping tablets, a good novel will help. [*Laughter*]

But I wish I could tell you that I was doing more serious historical reading; I am not at this moment.

Listen, thank you all very, very much for coming, and I'm glad to have had this opportunity.

Note: The President spoke at 11:35 a.m. in Room 450 of the Old Executive Office Building. In his opening, remarks, he referred to Chancellor Helmut Kohl of the Federal Republic of Germany, Prime Minister Thatcher of the United Kingdom, and President François Mitterrand of France. A tape was not available for verification of the content of these remarks.

Statement by Press Secretary Fitzwater on the President's Meeting With British Labour Party Leader Neil Kinnock
July 17, 1990

The President met for about 35 minutes this afternoon with the leader of the British Labour Party, Mr. Neil Kinnock, in a wide-ranging discussion of East-West relations, including the just-concluded summit meetings in London and Houston. The two men had a good exchange of views. It was the first opportunity in this administration for the President to meet with the leader of Britain's opposition.

The President expressed his pleasure with the July 16 announcement after the Kohl-Gorbachev meetings that the Soviet Union was prepared to accept a united Germany as a full member of NATO if that was the German choice. The President emphasized his support for the continuing process of reform in the Soviet Union. While the London summit had shown the alliance's readiness to adapt to the new European realities, the President stressed that the United States remains fully committed to the North Atlantic alliance.

Following his meeting with the President, Mr. Kinnock was scheduled to meet separately with Vice President Quayle and the national security adviser, Gen. Brent Scowcroft.

Remarks to the National Council of La Raza
July 18, 1990

Thank you all very much. Well, thank you so much for that welcome. I'm delighted to be here, and I had a little visit in the hall with the *jefes* [chiefs], Raul and Tony—[*laughter*]—and Rita, Patricia—gave me the warm welcome. And I rode over here with Dr. Cavazos, our Secretary of Education, who is with us and of whom I'm very, very proud. And, of course, I'm delighted to see Lou Sullivan, who's doing a superb job over at HHS, a major position in our administration.

I shouldn't quote Larry Cavazos, but he says, "You know, it's a strange world." He says, "Here I am Secretary of Education for the United States, and I just met with the Minister of Education from Mexico. The Minister from Mexico's name is Bartlett; the Secretary from the United States' name is Cavazos." So, I tell you—[*laughter*]—things are really moving.

But again, I'm very proud of him. And I am grateful for this opportunity to appear before this distinguished group, to greet the National Council of La Raza, and pleased to see so many distinguished leaders from America's Hispanic service, education, and business communities, all gathered here in our Nation's Capital. And I want to thank the person whose brilliance, foresight, and tenacity made this July gathering in Washington possible. I'm talking about the man who invented air conditioning. [*Laughter*] It is hotter than blazes out there! [*Laughter*] And I'm delighted to be here.

Something about me, I'll tell you. It was hotter than blazes in Houston last week. We should have known it was coming because the weatherman that we consulted was the same guy who set up our summit with Gorbachev at Malta. [*Laughter*] Some of you may remember that one.

But today, I did want to drop in—I'm on my way out to California in just a little bit—but to welcome you to Washington and really to tell you how important I believe and our administration believes your efforts are.

I mentioned Dr. Cavazos and, of course,

Lou Sullivan. But I also wanted to salute an old comrade of mine in Congress, now a Secretary: Manuel Lujan, from New Mexico, the Secretary of the Interior. But he and Larry, outstanding Cabinet Secretaries, they do represent not only the new energy and, I would say, leadership Hispanic-Americans are bringing to our country but also two of the most important priorities: the protection and use of our natural resources and the excellence in education—the quest for all-across-the-board excellence in education. And, indeed, our administration has made educational assistance for Hispanic-Americans one of the top priorities of our campaign to revive national educational excellence. And you heard from Larry yesterday in some detail, I understand. But, look, we will seek and we will demand educational excellence for all America, and that means reforms, like giving parents a choice in their children's education and educational excellence for all Americans.

Let me just touch—without being redundant here and repeating what Dr. Cavazos has said—on just a few of our most important efforts. Last December, we launched a new effort specially designed to assist Hispanic-Americans and developed in part with the assistance and advice that we received from many right here at this table and in this room today. They helped us develop—you all helped us develop this program. And I directed our Secretary of Education to form what we call the Hispanic education task force. And it is aimed not only at identifying educational obstacles but also—and I'd say this is more a part of it—educational opportunities. Larry has told me that the work of the task force is well underway, seeking new ways to improve Federal education programs that basically serve Hispanic-Americans and seeking ways to make them better. We need to focus on finding solutions.

And you who are a proud part of the La Raza tradition have also been one of those solutions, efforts like Project Second Chance, the Family Reading Program—and

I wish Barbara Bush were here to tell you how moved she is by that effort on a nationwide basis—and Project EXCEL, all designed to help Hispanic community organizations become effective partners with the schools. And they're already making a difference for thousands of young Americans. And, look, I view it as a national goal that this unacceptable dropout rate for Hispanic kids come down, way down below the national average.

I don't want to overstay my welcome. I was told to have very brief remarks, and our time today is short. And if I'm not out of the hotel by 2 o'clock, they'll probably charge me for an extra room. [*Laughter*] So, another day, you know. [*Laughter*]

Let me just address briefly one of the most important priorities of our administration, and this is a current subject: helping to build a better America where the doors of opportunity are open to every citizen and every child. And I hope you know where I have stood and always stand on the civil rights matters. And the Civil Rights Commission has been reauthorized. I think that's proper. The Hate Crimes Statistics Act is now the law of the land. And I will sign another, I would say, historic piece of legislation next week, and I'm talking about the Americans with Disabilities Act.

And for the past several months, we have been working diligently to make another civil rights law a reality. And I met with many of you at the White House back in May—several of you—Mario Moreno of MALDEF, Mexican American Legal Defense and Education Fund, you know him. Jesse Quintero of LULAC was there. Raul was there. But I told Raul that I wanted to sign the civil rights bill of 1990 and not a quota bill of 1990.

Morris Abram, a very respected American now serving as an ambassador over in Geneva, but really I think it's fair to say known as a champion of civil rights, recently wrote me about the bill that's before the Congress right now, urging me to oppose the bill as currently written. And he told me, look—here's this quote: "All my life, even in the darkest days of segregation in Georgia, I fought against the principle of color preference, then known as white supremacy." This bill, he pointed out, would

"achieve precisely what the '64 Civil Rights Act stood four-square against."

And he recalled Frederick Douglass' famous statement of 1871. And here was that quote: "Equality of numbers has nothing to do with equality of attainment." And we all know quotas aren't right. They are not fair. They divide society instead of bringing people together. And as leaders and representatives of the Hispanic-American community, I owe it to you to see that this legislation does not say to the young kids, you only fit in if you fit into a certain numbered quota. That is not the American dream.

And I gave Raul a commitment back in May that I want desperately, I want very much, to sign a civil rights bill. And I did then, and I still do. And yesterday's announcement marked only the end of a chapter, not the end of a campaign, because today I just met with some on the Republican side of the aisle. Talks are still going on. And we renew the fight for a civil rights bill that I can sign. But I want to ask for your help to make the changes. And we're talking now about legal changes—they're relatively small—to make the changes needed to ensure that a bill does not result in quotas that could somehow inadvertently work to the detriment of the very kids you all are trying to help, changes needed to ensure a bill that will protect the rights of all Americans and injure the rights of none.

From the time it was first launched in '68, your National Council, Council of La Raza, has played a unique role in helping to improve opportunities for Americans of Hispanic descent. I know sometimes you see only the problems out there, and it's proper you keep them in focus, but I think the success of your efforts is evident in the many success stories that are represented throughout this room. And so, I came over here today to salute you for the important work that you do. By working today for Hispanic-Americans, you're building a better tomorrow for all Americans.

As President of the United States, I want to do my part. I want to lead for equity. I want to lead in the field of education. And I again am grateful for the support I receive there. I want to take the crusades that Dr.

Sullivan is involved in to get better health care out there for our people and be as of the much leadership and support for those initiatives as I possibly can. And some of you know that with me this is more than a passing interest. And I would just say to you, keep up the good work for La Raza. It inspires the American people. And I want to do my part.

Thank you all, and God bless you. Thank you very, very much.

Note: The President spoke at 1:17 p.m. in the Regency Ballroom at the Omni Shoreham Hotel. In his remarks, he referred to Tony Salazar, Raul Yzaquirre, Rita DiMartino, and Patricia Asip, chairman, president and chief executive officer, and executive committee members of the national council of La Raza.

Exchange With Reporters Aboard Air Force One
July 18, 1990

The President. ——say welcome. No questions, of course, because we've just finished this press conference, and you know——

Q. Press conference?

The President. Well, 2 days ago, that one that we had, the one with the magazine editors. Had the one with——

Federal Budget Negotiations

Q. How did the budget meeting go?

The President. Well, we've agreed to meet again Monday, and we'll see how it goes. A lot of work still to be done.

Q. Did you make any progress?

The President. Well, I think every time we sit down we get rid of some of the differences. But in the meantime, Dick Darman is going to have more meetings with Dick Gephardt [House majority leader], who, incidentally, I will say is, I think, doing a first-class job—both Dick Darman and Nick Brady on our side, and certainly, Dick Gephardt trying to hold this big group together and lead it. And I think we all owe him a vote of thanks for the way he's proceeding as chairman of the process.

But, no, we've still got some problems out there. But they're going to be meeting while we're on this trip, and then we'll get back together early in the week.

Q. Do you have basic agreement yet just on the outlines, on the size of the package?

The President. Well, that's what Darman and Dick Gephardt are going to be talking about further. We've had some discussions, and the way it was outlined to me, there's some agreement, but I don't think you can call it total agreement at this time.

Q. Are you more optimistic now than previously?

The President. Well, it's hard to say; it's hard to quantify that. But it's not a question of optimism or pessimism; it's a question of having to get this done. The deficit problem is so serious that there must be a bipartisan, responsible answer. And I will keep saying that and keep encouraging the White House negotiators and the Republicans to go forward, but it's hard. It's a good question, and I don't know how to answer it.

Q. Did you do taxes today?

The President. We just had the kinds of discussions I talked to you about, about getting the problems in shape. And there's five major ingredients, and all of them are being discussed.

Thank you all. I hope you have a wonderful trip out here.

Richard M. Nixon Presidential Library

Q. Are you glad to be honoring Richard Nixon?

The President. What?

Q. Are you glad to be out here for Richard Nixon?

The President. I'm very pleased to be going to this dedication of this library, and I'm very pleased that President Nixon's daughter is with us. And I only regret that a previous commitment on the part of Mrs. Nixon and President Nixon prevented them from being with us today. Yes, I'm glad to be going out.

Note: The exchange occurred in the after-noon while the President was en route from

Washington, DC, to Anaheim, CA. A tape was not available for verification of the content of these remarks.

Nomination of Steven B. Kelmar To Be an Assistant Secretary of Health and Human Services
July 19, 1990

The President today announced his intention to nominate Steven B. Kelmar to be an Assistant Secretary of Health and Human Services for Legislative Affairs. He would succeed Gerald L. Olson.

Currently Mr. Kelmar serves as Principal Deputy Assistant Secretary for Legislative Affairs at the Department of Health and Human Services in Washington, DC. Prior to this, he served as an administrative assistant for Representative Sherwood Boehlert,

1982–1989; deputy assistant for Representative George C. Wortley, 1981–1982; special assistant to Senator S.I. Hayakawa, 1979–1981; a lead advance representative in the Office of the Vice President, 1983–1989; and campaign manager for Boehlert for Congress, 1982–1986.

Mr. Kelmar graduated from Pennsylvania State University (B.A., 1979). He was born May 6, 1953, in Philadelphia, PA. Mr. Kelmar resides in Alexandria, VA.

Remarks at the Dedication of the Richard M. Nixon Presidential Library in Yorba Linda, California
July 19, 1990

The President. Thank you all very, very much. What a wonderful reunion. And I am very proud to have been introduced to this gathering by Ronald Reagan. I know how I got here. [*Laughter*] President Reagan is my mentor and my esteemed friend, and I will always be grateful to him.

But to President and Mrs. Nixon, Barbara and I are delighted to be with you on this memorable day. My special greetings to all my predecessors—to President and Mrs. Reagan, to President and Mrs. Ford—to members of the Nixon family, who are right out here; to Secretary Simon, who has done such a superb job on all of this; to my current Secretary of Commerce, Bob Mosbacher; and of course, to our old friend, your own Governor, George Deukmejian; to all these Cabinet officials out here—former Secretary Haig and Secretary Schultz, and I'm told that Chief Justice Warren Burger was there—all the senior

members of the Nixon administration; of course, all of our friends—Reverend Billy Graham and Reverend Peale and Ambassador Moore, all the way from Ireland, and Ambassador Annenberg and Ambassador Zhu-qizhen of China—welcome, sir—to Hugh Hewitt and Vicky Carr, and ladies and gentlemen. Thank you, Mr. President, once again, for that introduction.

I'm not sure, President Reagan, whether it's you or me that attracted this noise over here; but I remember as Vice President, you had your share of this kind of attention. [*Laughter*] But let me just say to all of you: Our thanks for the privilege of helping to dedicate this beautiful library of the 37th President of the United States of America.

To Lincoln, the Presidency helped play, as he put it, "America's mystic chords of memory." Shall we wait just one minute? And to Teddy Roosevelt, the Presidency meant the "bully pulpit"—calling on America's boundless energy. And it was Dwight Eisenhower, beloved Ike, who described its power "to proclaim anew our faith" and summon "lightness against the dark." To occupy this office is to feel a kinship with these and other Presidents, each of whom in his own way sought to do right and, thus, to achieve good. Each summoned the best from the idea we call America; and each wondered, I suspect, how he could be worthy of God and man.

This year an estimated 1½ million people will visit Presidential museums and libraries, exploring the lives of these Presidents, passed down, like oral history, from one generation to another. And they will see how each President is like a finely cut prism with many facets—their achievements and their philosophy, their family and their humanity.

For instance, not far from here, as we've heard, visitors will soon see the library of my distinguished predecessor, the 40th President of the United States, and Mrs. Reagan. President Reagan, we will not soon forget how you truly blessed America.

Look next to Michigan, where a museum and library honor the 38th President of the United States, Gerald Ford, and Mrs. Ford. An entire nation is grateful for your decency, your leadership, and your love of country.

And tomorrow morning the first visitors will enter our newest Presidential library; and they will note that only F.D.R. ran as many times as Richard Nixon—five—for national office, each winning four elections, and that more people voted for Richard Nixon as President than any other man in history. They will hear of Horatio Alger and Alger Hiss; of the book "Six Crises"; and the seventh crisis, Watergate. And they will think of Checkers, Millie's role model. [*Laughter*] And, yes, Mr. President, they will hear again your answer to my "vision thing"—"Let me make this perfectly clear." [*Laughter*]

And many of these visitors will know of your times as President, perhaps as tumultuous as any since Lincoln's, and of your goal as President: a world where peace would link the community of nations. And yet others, young visitors, will not remember the years 1969 to '74. They'd not even been born when Richard Nixon became President. So, to help them understand our 37th President, here is what I would tell those who journey to Yorba Linda.

I would say first: Look at perhaps the truest index of any man—his family. Think of his mother, a gentle Quaker, and his father, who built their small frame house that we see less than 100 yards from here, and his daughters, Patricia and Julie. Any parent would be proud of children with the loyalty and love of these two women. And think finally of a very gracious First Lady, who ranks among the most admired women of postwar America, the woman who we know and love as Pat.

As First Lady, we remember Pat Nixon championed the Right To Read program, helped bring the Parks To People program to the disadvantaged. She refurbished the White House and opened it to more people than ever before. And she was our most widely traveled First Lady, visiting five continents and 22 nations, overcoming the poverty and tragedy of her childhood to become a mirror of America's heart and love. And when, in 1958, foreign mobs stoned the Nixons' car, she was, an observer said, "stronger than any man." And yet it was also Pat who moved pianist Duke Ellington at a White House dinner to improvise the melody—"I shall pick a name," he said, "gentle, graceful, like Patricia." Mrs. Nixon, the Secret Service called you Starlight, and your husband has said it best: "You fit that name to a T." So, once again, I won't ask you to stand up again—you've already done it. But let us show our appreciation for the grace and the beauty that Pat Nixon brought to the White House. [*Applause*]

And then next I would say to visitors here: Look at Richard Nixon the man. He had an intellectual's complexity. Knowing how you feel about some intellectuals, Mr. President, I don't mean to offend you. [*Laughter*] But he was an author—eight books, each composed on those famous yellow pads—who, like his favorite author, Tolstoy, admired the dignity of manual labor. And he worked in the most pragmatic of arenas, and yet insisted that politics is poetry, not prose. And he believed in love of country and in God, in loyalty to friends and protecting loved ones. And he was also a soft touch when it came to the kids— believe me, I can empathize with that.

Let me repeat a story which President Nixon himself enjoys—I hope he enjoys it. One day, greeting an airport crowd, he heard a young girl shouting, "How is Smokey the Bear?"—and at that time living in the Washington zoo. And the girl kept repeating the question. And not understanding her words, the President turned to an aide for translation. "Smokey the Bear," the aide mumbled, pointing to the girl, "Washington National Zoo." Triumphant, President Nixon walked over, extended his hand and said, "How do you do, Miss Bear." [*Laughter*] I'd be the last to criticize verbal confusion. After all, I confess, some say English is my only foreign language. [*Laughter*] President Nixon—the point is—he was merely being kind, just as he mailed those handwritten letters to defeated rivals, like his friend Hubert Humphrey, or saw that when the POW's returned home in early '73 to a White House dinner each wife received a corsage.

Just as Richard Nixon was extraordinarily controversial, he could also be uncommonly sensitive to the feelings of other people. This brings me to what I would next tell those who travel to Yorba Linda. What President Nixon said of Dwight Eisenhower in a '69 eulogy was true, also, of himself: "He came from the heart of America, not geographically, perhaps, but culturally." And Richard Nixon was the quintessence of middle America and touched deep chords of response in millions of our citizens. As President, upholding what he termed the "silent majority" from Dallas to Davenport and Syracuse to Siler City, he loved America's good, quiet, decent people. And he spoke for them. He felt deeply on their behalf. Theodore White would say: "Middle America has been without a great leader for generations, and in Richard Nixon it elevated a man of talent and ability." For millions of Americans, this President became something they had rarely known: a voice speaking loudly and eloquently for their values and their dreams.

And finally, and most importantly, I

would say to visitors: Richard Nixon helped change the course not only of America but of the entire world. He believed in returning power to the people—so he created revenue sharing—and that young people should be free to choose their future—so Richard Nixon ended the draft. And he helped the United States reach new horizons in space and technology. He began a pioneering cancer initiative that gave hope and life to millions. And he knew that the great outdoors is precious but fragile, and so he created the Environmental Protection Agency, a historic step to help preserve and widely use our natural resources.

And all of this Richard Nixon did, and yet future generations will remember him most, in my view, for dedicating his life to the greatest cause offered any President: the cause of peace among nations. Who can forget how he endured much in his quest for peace with honor in Vietnam. He knew that true peace means the triumph of freedom, not merely the absence of war. And as President, he served this country's special mission to help those around the world for whom America has always been a morning star of liberty, engaging in diplomatic summitry and helping change the postwar bipolar globe.

Who can forget how in Moscow Richard Nixon signed the first agreement to limit strategic nuclear arms, giving new hope to the world for lasting peace, or how he planted the first fragile seeds of peace in the Middle East. And Golda Meir [former Prime Minister of Israel], whose statue is inside, credited him with saving Israel during the Yom Kippur War. And even now memories resound of President Nixon's trip to China—the week that revolutionized the world. No American President had ever stood on the soil of the People's Republic of China, and as President Nixon stepped from Air Force One and extended his hand to Zhou En Lai, his vision ended more than two decades of isolation.

"Being President," he often said, "is nothing compared with what you can do as President." Mr. President, you worked with every fiber of your being to help achieve a generation of peace. And today, as the movement toward democracy sweeps our globe, you can take great personal pride that history will say of you: Here was a true architect of peace.

Yes, there have been literally millions of words written about this President, but let me close with a passage from the President himself that comes from his first Inaugural Address, January 20, 1969, where the new President spoke of how the greatest honor history can bestow is the title of peacemaker. And he began by noting that within the lifetime of most present mankind would celebrate a new year which occurs only once in a thousand years, the start of a new millennium, and that America had the chance to lead the world onto that high ground of peace that man has dreamed of since the dawn of civilization. And finally, Richard Nixon concluded, "if we succeed, generations to come will say of us that we helped make the world safe for mankind. I believe the American people are ready to answer this call," he said.

Mr. President, you helped America answer its summons to greatness. Thank you for serving the cause of peace. God bless you and your wonderful family. And

now it is my honor, as President of the United States, to introduce the 37th President of the United States, Richard M. Nixon.

Note: President Bush spoke at approximately 10:55 a.m. outside of the library. In his opening remarks, he referred to William E. Simon, Secretary of the Treasury during the Nixon administration and head of the foundation responsible for the Richard M. Nixon Presidential Library; Alexander M. Haig, Jr., national security adviser to President Nixon and Secretary of State during the Reagan administration; and George P. Shultz, also Secretary of the Treasury during the Nixon administration. President Bush also referred to the shouting of hecklers present at the ceremony. Presidents Gerald R. Ford, Ronald Reagan, and Richard M. Nixon also spoke at the dedication ceremony. Following the library's dedication, President Bush had lunch with President Nixon. Earlier in the morning, President Bush attended a fundraising breakfast in Anaheim for the California Republican Party.

Remarks at a Fundraising Dinner for Senatorial Candidate Larry Craig in Boise, Idaho
July 19, 1990

What a great crowd. My heavens, this is wonderful! Thank you all. Please, be seated. Thank you all very much. Larry, thank you. I hope you enjoy your dinner tonight. Rest assured, the Idaho potato is one vegetable I approve of. [*Laughter*] But I'm not going to put myself at risk that the other vegetable might be served, so I have to leave before dinner. [*Laughter*] I hope you'll forgive me. But thank you all, really. You have a wonderful way of making me feel at home.

I want to salute Steve Symms, a great Senator, fierce advocate for Idaho and, indeed, for the fundamental principles of the United States. I want to salute the Lieutenant Governor, an old friend of mine, Butch Otter. I see my fellow aviator down there, Pete Cenarusa. He presented me

with a model of the plane I flew a thousand years ago. The only good news is he got his wings 3 months before I did, so he's older and perhaps more experienced. I want to salute the attorney general, Jim Jones; State Treasurer Edwards; and also Roger Fairchild, our distinguished nominee for Governor of this State—and I want him to win. I want him to win the governorship. Our outstanding successor—and this has to be also—successor to Larry Craig, Skip Smyser—we want to see him hold this seat that's so important to us. And we have another superb candidate running in the other seat, Sean McDevitt. And it's important you give him your support—a distinguished veteran of the United States military. And a special salute to a 15-year-old from Boise whom I just met, Olen Hsu, who won this year's Idaho State essay contest. There he is, way down, tethered down on the end down there.

And we just had a receiving line in there, and so I say this from the bottom of my heart: I wish that the pride of Wellesley was with me here tonight—Barbara Bush. She was with me at the library with the four Presidents there, but now she's campaigning next door in Washington State. But, you know, I say this not just with husbandly pride, but, I think, with some objectivity: I thought Barbara did a great job up at Wellesley talking about values and family. And so, that leads me to pay tribute to Suzanne Craig, who is such an important part of all of this—important part in lifting a great career to new heights, doing so much for family. Let us all give a round of applause to Suzanne, and to the kids as well—Mike, Shae, and Jay.

And it is a delight to be back among friends in Idaho. I know you feel I'm like the bad penny turning up every couple of years for the last 8 or 10, but you have this wonderful way of making somebody feel at home. It's especially delightful to be with you during this centennial year. Of course, we know that the history of this great State reaches beyond a century. If we had to choose the one day that Idaho history began, it would undoubtedly have to be March 4, 1863, when the first Republican President, Abraham Lincoln, created a new territory of the United States with a stroke of his pen. And as I look around this room, at Senator Symms and Congressman—Senator-to-be—Larry Craig and at our outstanding candidate for Governor, Roger Fairchild, I can't help but reflect how fitting that this great State of Idaho and our Republican Party were born together. Now a new century is beginning for Idaho. So, let us make it a century of promise and prosperity. Let us do that by sending Larry Craig to the United States Senate.

You know, Larry is a white-water rafter. And he's just the kind of guy who would enjoy a hair-raising adventure, with chills and spills, ups and downs, where you're knocked around and never sure if you're going to make it through in one piece; and that's just what it's like to run for the United States Senate. But nevertheless, he's going to make it, and come November, I'm sure he will have forded the river with this marvelous skill that he has demonstrated in the Congress. I believe that this is his destiny: to join the ranks of great Idaho statesmen, to follow in the footsteps of Borah and Symms and my dear friend and former classmate in the Congress, Jim McClure.

Of course, I don't want to break any myths here, but Larry hasn't been a statesman all his life. In fact—we did a little homework for this meeting—Larry, I understand that when you were a boy, a farm boy in Midvale, you house-trained a pig. [*Laughter*] Imagine that, your Senator-to-be house-training a pig. [*Laughter*] That ought to help him in Congress. [*Laughter*] And at a community car wash, you washed the hood of a farmer's brand new car—unfortunately, using SOS pads. [*Laughter*]

Well, given his decade of achievement in Congress and service to the people of the First District, I reckon that even that farmer has forgotten about his car and cast his vote for Larry Craig—a strong, consistent, steady voice for Idaho and for the bedrock principles and beliefs that Idahoans hold dear: the freedom to own land, to reap the rewards of hard work, to provide for one's family; and then an undying faith in God and country. Larry embodies these values. That's why I have looked to him for advice as Congressman Craig. And I want to rely on Larry Craig's advice and consent in the years ahead, when he is Senator Craig.

As you know, I presided over the Senate as Vice President when that body was controlled by Democrats, and earlier, by Republicans. And I can tell you this: When it comes to an administration and a Congress working together, compromise is often necessary if you're going to make this great country go forward, but there is no substitute for having a United States Senate that shares our outlook, that will work with us to build a better America. And that means, in my view, with considerable experience in Washington, a Republican Senate. And I need Larry Craig to hold that McClure seat to give us a chance to have a Republican Senate.

Electing Larry to the Senate would be a major step toward a Republican future, giving me a partner in leadership. After all, he and I share the same outlook. When it comes to our national defense, he says that it is strength, not weakness, that brought about the Revolution of '89. Larry and I believe that the marvelous changes—and are they ever exciting—taking place in Eastern Europe are a result of 40 years of American and allied vigilance. This is no time for America to turn its back on world leadership nor to fundamentally weaken the defense of this country.

As you know, in the last few weeks, I've attended three summits: one with Mr. Gorbachev, one NATO summit over in London, and then the G–7 economic summit recently concluded in Houston. And the outcome of each summit has convinced me that we are on the right path—keeping America strong, but keeping America strong for peace.

The first summit, with Mikhail Gorbachev, made new progress toward an important goal: engaging the Soviet Union as a constructive partner in the international community. The second summit, with my NATO colleagues in London, confirmed the vitality of the alliance of the Western democracies and reached out to the East to establish a lasting peace in Europe. And our third summit, in Houston, recently concluded with the great industrial democracies, led to a consensus that we need to open up world trade to give farmers, like those right here in Idaho, like those right here in this room, a better chance to compete. We also discussed how we can help the nations of the East move toward freer economies and freer societies. But our message in Houston was clear: We must take the trade barriers down—not just us, but all countries. Let's have a free and fair playing field for American products, and let's not us start throwing up new trade barriers of our own. The best answer for America is a level playing field because I am convinced not only our farmers but our businessmen can compete with anybody, anywhere in the world, if the rules are fair.

And no one can convince me or Larry Craig that this extraordinary new world would have come about if America had fol-

lowed the liberal path of military weakness and unilateral concessions. Of course, there are still some liberal Democrats who would take America back to the days of big-spending, malaise, self-doubt, and drift. Well, there's a river here in Idaho that sums up the course these liberals would have America take—the River of No Return. [*Laughter*]

Well, America isn't taking that course. And Idaho voters want elected officials who will protect us from all threats—threats from afar and from just down the street. And it's for this last reason that Idaho is going to support the candidate who sides with our policemen against the crooks, families against fear, and kids against drugs—and Larry Craig stands for all three of those.

And I would like to take this opportunity to thank the mayor and those leaders in the antidrug coalition, volunteers who met with me before this meeting to explain to me what Boise is doing—trying to fight drugs, trying to help in education, trying to do what they're doing in law enforcement. It is an impressive program that I think has significance for the entire country.

Larry has been a strong champion, leading the fight for laws every bit as tough as the criminals we convict; but our war against drugs and crime will not, cannot, be won from Washington alone. In this war, we will also need to count on local heroes. And right here in the Treasure Valley, a Boise policeman is doing his part by creating and leading, along with Senator Symms and Louise McClure, a volunteer organization that teaches substance-abuse education: Parents and Youth Against Drug Abuse. Prevention is our most critical tool against drug abuse. And that's one reason why I've come to Boise to thank all of the many people who have been on the front lines fighting against drugs. Once again, I was mightily impressed by what I heard this afternoon, and I want to thank you for not only what you are doing for your community but for what you're doing for the entire United States.

There are so many issues: Larry Craig and I will also work together for and not against the right for a kid to pray voluntarily in the school. We will work to pass our Educational Excellence Act and encourage reform of America's entire educational system. And we will work against needless Federal regulation of your schools. But Larry and I will work against unnecessary Federal regulations that stifle opportunity and kill the aspirations of working men and women.

We agree that the congressional budget process is, at best, clumsy and illogical and, at worst, cynical and chaotic—in short, a metaphor for what's wrong with Washington today. As you know, that's why I am currently negotiating with the congressional leadership to bring this budget back towards balance. The deficit is estimated to be over $160 billion. Congress, as the American people know, appropriates every dollar and tells the President how to spend every single penny.

And I have said I will negotiate without preconditions, and I will. And you've seen the firestorm about revenues on the table. Well, I've done my part, and now it's their turn. A truly comprehensive package, not a temporary Band-Aid—there must be reform of the budget process and there must be real spending control. And the American people are entitled to it. And that's why this man's leadership is so valuable. He and I know that this problem stems from too much spending, not too few taxes.

And Larry Craig believes Congress must be forced to act responsibly. That's why he's been fighting, as the founder and chairman of Congressional Leaders United for a Balanced Budget, for the balanced budget amendment to the Constitution. It would discipline my branch of the Government, the executive branch, and it would discipline the congressional branch. Larry was the leader in signing up hundreds of Republicans and conservative Democrats in support of the amendment and in forcing congressional liberals to show their true colors in a direct, up-and-down floor vote just this past Tuesday. And we lost by just a handful of votes—a tremendous majority voted for the amendment, but we missed getting the required two-thirds by just seven votes—seven votes.

And finally, let me say just a few words about the philosophy that Larry and I share

concerning something that's near and dear to the heart of everybody in Idaho. I know it is. I've been here. Every time I come here, I sense it. And of course, I'm talking about the great outdoors; I'm talking about the environment.

We know that from Bear Lake to Pend Oreille, from the shadow of the Sawtooth clear up to Sandpoint, the Idaho way of life is special. I saw it—I've just had a little fringe tastes of it—but I saw it for myself when Jim McClure and I floated and fished the middle fork of the Snake River. And Idaho truly is the Gem State, as bright and clear as one of your deep mountain lakes. And your land is unique, and yes, it does deserve to be protected.

But Larry and I also believe in protecting yet another kind of delicate ecology. And I'm talking about jobs. I'm talking about homes. I'm talking about families. And we believe multiple-use land policies should govern most of our public lands. And we can have a sound economy and a healthy environment. They are not mutually exclusive. And I'm going to continue to fight to protect and enhance both.

I think everybody here would agree that the environmental policy of this country cannot be set by those who have no regard for our precious inheritance. That is a given. And I think of myself as an environmentalist. I care about the great outdoors. I love the recreational places in this country. And I guess one of the best things that happens to me is when I can see the wonders of nature through the eyes of my grandchildren. But the environmental policy of this country cannot and will not be set by the extremes on the fringe of the environmental movement. They're not going to do that to the working men and women in this country. No, Idaho needs a strong, reasoned voice on natural resource policy. That's why, once again, Idaho needs Larry Craig in the United States Senate.

So here we are, and this is the Republican approach: a philosophy of environmental commitment, keeping America strong, laws tougher than the criminals who threaten us, and less government interference in the way you run your schools and in your State. And all this adds up to a very special kind of freedom, the Idaho way of life.

I want to thank each and every one of you for all you have done and all you are pledged to do to advance Republican leadership. And with Larry Craig on his way to the United States Senate, I know that Idaho is on its way to a great second century.

Thank you from the bottom of a grateful heart for this warm Idaho welcome. God bless you all. Thank you.

Note: The President spoke at 6:42 p.m. in the Eyries Ballroom at the Boise Convention Center. In his remarks, he referred to Pete Cenarusa, candidate for secretary of state; Skip Smyser and Sean McDevitt, candidates for the U.S. House of Representatives; and Dirk A. Kempthorne, mayor of Boise. Mrs. Bush spoke at the Wellesley College commencement ceremony. Prior to his remarks, the President attended an antidrug briefing by community leaders at city hall.

Remarks at a Fundraising Breakfast for Senatorial Candidate Allen Kolstad in Billings, Montana
July 20, 1990

Thank you all, and, Allen, thank you for that wonderful introduction. First, it's a delight to see our Governor, your friend and mine, Governor Stephens here. What a job he's doing. And I felt this warmth when I was with him not so long ago at the centennial. Of course, in a very short period of time, Conrad Burns, our unique Senator— [*laughter*]—you can interpret that any way you want to. He hasn't been there that long, but he hasn't forgot how he got there. [*Laughter*] And people understand that, and they respect it in Washington. And clearly, you love him here, as I do. And, Conrad, I appreciate the effort you made to get out here, rushing off to all kinds of connecting airplanes, because he had to work up until the gong sounded yesterday in the Senate. And as for our State chairman, Barbara Campbell, I salute her. She's doing a great job for the party, and she gave me a wonderfully upbeat assessment just now about Allen's chances to win this important Senate seat. Barbara, thank you for what you're doing. And then to our [Republican National] committee members: Jack Galt, Ione Brownson; and my old friend of long-standing, Chuck Heringer. And then, of course, to your outstanding congressional candidate, Brad Johnson—we've got to see him win. I also want to salute one who's not here but who is doing a superb job. I'm talking about Ron Marlenee, who was with me early on—very, very early supporter.

And that brings us at last to the next Senator from the State of Montana, Allen Kolstad.

Let me just say it is great to be back in Montana, near some of the best fishing streams and forests in the country. I remember coming to Glacier National Park last year with a grandson and being told that Montana has 896 catchable fish per square mile. [*Laughter*] My question is, why don't they count the uncatchable fish? [*Laughter*] I've found from my vast experience there are quite a few of those. But there is nothing better for the soul than seeing the grandeur of the snowcapped mountains in the distance or a Montana sunset, as we saw it last night, streaked across the fading skies. Montana is, proudly, the Big Sky State, a State of big skies.

And America still is a country of big dreams. But to help make those dreams come true—and I know Conrad would agree with this—we have got to have more grassroots, sound representation in the United States Senate, and to help make those dreams come true for America and Montana, I need Allen Kolstad working with me in the United States Senate.

Allen Kolstad and Iva, sitting over here next to me, know Montana as few others do. Five generations of Kolstads have called Montana home. Allen is a farmer, rancher, who has given over 20 years of his life to public service, to the people of this great

State. He was elected to the Montana Legislature back in 1968, the first Republican to serve Liberty County in almost 50 years. Then, in 1988, Stan Stephens and Allen Kolstad stunned the Democrats by giving them their first loss in a Governor's race in 20 years. And just like our friend Conrad Burns did in the last Senate election, Allen Kolstad's about to hand the opposition another stunner. We need him in the Senate, and we need him there now.

You see, I am convinced that with more people like Allen there and more Republicans we can build a better America. Despite its minority status on Capitol Hill, the Republican Party has fought hard for what's right. They're fighting to preserve and protect the longest peacetime economic expansion in history, the lowest unemployment rate in the Nation in 16 years, and the 22 million jobs created in the last 7½ years.

Having said that, I am very concerned about problems that remain out there ahead of us. And, Iva, thank you for those lovely words of prayer from your heart. The outrageous deficit, for example, is over—fasten your seatbelts—over $160 billion a year. That is not acceptable, and I am determined to do something about it.

We Republicans have a good record at home and abroad, one we can stand on with pride. And it was our policy of peace through strength that helped bring freedom to the lives of millions from Panama to Poland. And with a Republican majority in Congress working with me, we could do much, much more to ensure that America remains economically strong and becomes fiscally sound.

Instead, with the Democrats now in the control of the United States Congress—both Houses—we're facing government by gridlock in Washington, with spending skyrocketing out of control, good legislation thrown aside for pork-barrel programs, and a budget deficit looming over our children's children. And while the Republican Party is using everything we've got to build a strong, competitive America, the Democratic stranglehold on the United States Congress has finally taken its toll.

Unfortunately, it is the American people who are paying the price. Let me just give you a few specific examples. In April of 1989, our administration sent to the Congress the Educational Excellence Act. Our proposals would advance education reform, reward achievement, and encourage educational choice. And yet, as the bill moved through the Congress—and Conrad knows this so well—some of its most sensible and cost-effective programs were scrapped, ripped out of the bill, substituting tired, old, expensive Democratic substitutes. Almost $1 billion worth of unnecessary, unrelated, and costly changes were heaped on top of our original $400 million education bill. So, it came out not $400 million but it totaled $1.4 billion, more than triple our original request. In fact, they even changed the name of the bill.

I know Allen Kolstad would have said no to these unnecessary changes. Listen, Montana's graduation rate is 87 percent. And that's terrific; you ought to take great pride in that. But Allen and I want to make it even higher. Montana ranks third among the 28 States which administer the ACT test. You've done it by rewarding excellence, putting choice in the hands of parents and students, and building in something that is essential—and that is accountability. And that's exactly the thrust of our Federal program: Choice, accountability, flexibility, excellence is the key—national goals to challenge our students, our teachers, and our schools to succeed. This is the program.

And that's just part of the Republican agenda. Twenty-nine out of the last 35 years of Democrat control is long enough. We must have more Republicans in Congress.

But there's more. We proposed new child-care legislation. Based on our belief that there is nothing more precious than America's children, we asked for $9 billion in funding spread over a 5-year period. We proposed a bill that put choice in the hands of all families, whether low- or middle-income, by helping them get the kind of child care that they wanted—at home or, yes, in a church or a church-related facility or from a local child-care provider. And the Senate passed a child-care bill at double the money—remember I proposed $9 billion; they come up with $18 billion in the

Senate. And then the House, under solid Democratic control, outdid the Senate by tripling my request to $29 billion. In short, we started at $9 billion, and the last word from Congress was $29 billion. And if Congress has its way, the Federal Government will intrude upon one more area of your lives, using that money to pile more redtape on child-care providers, including friends and neighbors providing the child care. Democrats still believe that the Federal Government knows better how to do all this than parents or local communities. And I know what that tells me: It tells me that we must have more Republicans in the United States Congress.

Just this year, in February, March, I requested $800 million in dire emergency—this is a term that's used when you have to do something special—dire emergency funds for immediate assistance to the Governments of Panama and Nicaragua to help those fledgling democracies build their shattered economies, to help them strengthen their democracies. And I challenged the Congress to act in 30 days. I said this is a dire emergency, and we need to have action now. One hundred eight days later, the Congress acted. Who am I to complain? It's been over 20 years since Congress produced a balanced budget.

But here's what caused the delay: some so-called dire emergency additions to the bill by Congress—almost $3½ billion more in spending than I requested. Everyone on Capitol Hill knew how important this bill was, and for 108 days, Congress decided to hold it hostage. For 108 days, Congress calculated how much spending they could pile on top of this emergency request that they knew I needed to support the democracies that were just beginning in Panama and in Nicaragua. And for 108 days, inaction by the Congress jeopardized not only the economic recovery of these two critically strategic nations, it jeopardized the hard-won freedom of the brave people of Nicaragua and Panama. That's more than a difference between parties. In my view, that was a disgrace. And I say we must have more Republicans in the United States Congress.

You know Republicans like what works. We think that finding a cure to the budget deficit means funding those programs that we know work, not throwing billions of hard-earned tax dollars at untested ideas with no track record or built-in accountability. Americans are fed up. Year after year after year, they hear about budget wrangling in Washington, DC. They hear about the President trying to hold the line on spending and the Congress spending money it doesn't have. And I think now, given the magnitude of this problem, enough is enough. We must end this deficits-don't-matter mentality. And I do not want to preside over these god-awful deficits that are saddling these young people here with billions of dollars of debt.

The deficit is estimated to be over $160 billion for 1 year. And Congress, as the American people know so well, appropriates every single dollar we spend. And at this very moment, our White House negotiators are trying to do something meaningful about this deficit. And, frankly, I think in fairness to say, we are getting some good cooperation with the leadership on the Democratic side of the aisle—I'd say on both sides of the aisle. And we must control spending; we must reform the budget process itself. And I've taken a few shots—you've heard it rebounding around out here. I've said before that I'll negotiate without preconditions, and I will, in spite of the outcry about revenues, but there must be budget reform and true spending control. We owe it to the young people in this country.

Some people think that there's no difference between the two parties. I've come here to tell you probably something you already know: to tell you there is. And it's as big as the Great Divide. On one side—the Republicans out there, our side—that side lies opportunity, growth, choice in child care, choice in education, the creativity of the marketplace, and a government that understands it works for you and not the other way around. And I'll tell you something: That's why I think Conrad Burns has what I know Allen Kolstad will have when he comes to Washington—the full confidence of the people of Montana. You have the feeling, and properly so, that he works for the people of this State that sent him to the United States Senate.

And on the other side, the far side, lies the Democratic Party, the party of redtape and bureaucracy. Still pushing for higher and higher spending; still telling the States how to conduct their affairs; still pushing for mandated benefits. Dictation from Washington to every drug program in the country or every education program or every program of whatever nature—mandated benefits—that's the hallmark of the Democratic Party. And now we're getting to the election cycle, and the choice is up to America.

And right here in Montana you know that there's a better way of doing things, a Republican way. I remember the last time I was in this State. It was for Montana's 100th birthday, when Allen was chairman of the centennial commission. For my part, I planted a tree. Now, you may know that my record's not too good in that respect. [*Laughter*] I planted a tree in North Dakota, and regrettably, it got attacked by gypsy moth. [*Laughter*] And I planted a tree in Spokane, Washington, and I hadn't left town before some vandals ripped off the whole tree. [*Laughter*] And so, you can understand why they've asked me not to dedicate any buildings here. [*Laughter*] But the tree—when I climbed off the plane I got a firsthand report from the Governor, who confessed to a certain nervousness about the tree. But the tree I planted in Helena—believe it or not, it's alive, and it's well—[*laughter*]—and it's flourishing. Well, in that spirit, what a great job Allen did for the centennial commission. First of all, he didn't use one penny of taxpayer money, not one. And secondly, the centennial is expected to give thousands of dollars back to the State treasury. And that is the kind of fiscal responsibility that America needs on Capitol Hill.

Allen Kolstad agrees—and most Americans, I believe, when we take the case to them, will, too—we must have budget process reforms. We must have budget process reforms. And your Senator sitting there in Washington now understands exactly what I'm talking about. We must have spending cuts, and frankly, I'd like to have that line-item veto. And if the Congress can't do it,

let the President have a shot at it. And I'd like to see the balanced budget amendment. In the House it missed by seven votes. It would have disciplined the executive branch that I head, and it surely would have disciplined the legislative branch. And I think that kind of disciplinary measure would be good for the United States. We like what works, and our budget process is simply not working.

It was one of the most famous Democratic Presidents, Franklin Roosevelt, who said, about some 50 years ago: "The future lies with those wise political leaders who realize that the great public is interested more in government than in politics." The Republican Party is ready to govern in the United States Congress, and Allen Kolstad is ready to be your next United States Senator.

As for my part, I like my line of work. I like the challenges that face me. I like the fact that Barbara Bush is spelling out a lot of fundamental values that we all believe in for the country. I've dwelt here on what we must do and the things we're trying to do on the domestic side, but when you look around the world, you can't help but wonder and be excited about the changes that are taking place all through Eastern Europe and in our own hemisphere—changes toward democracy and freedom. It's a very exciting time to be the President of the United States. But we cannot succeed without your help, the help of the American people.

And once again—we had a little reception earlier on that Barbara put on and then one that Allen arranged, and I couldn't help but feel the warmth and the genuineness of the people of this country and, in this instance, the people of Montana, as I shook hands with several who were nice enough to greet me once again to this State.

I like my line of work, but I need help. Send Allen Kolstad to the United States Senate.

Thank you, and God bless you, and God bless the United States of America. Thank you.

Note: The President spoke at 8:11 a.m. at the Billings Plaza Trade Center.

Remarks at an Antidrug Rally in Billings, Montana
July 20, 1990

Thank you for that warm welcome on this cool day, and thank you, Governor. I am so very happy that so many of you could join us this morning in this Daylis Stadium, home of the Big Sky State Games. Cycling, golf, handball, shooting, swimming, tennis, track and field—sounds like a weekend at Camp David. [*Laughter*] How come no horseshoes around here? [*Laughter*] I am very pleased to see sports play a prominent role in education, drug awareness programs, and scholarship activities. And first, best of luck to all tomorrow's participants. Good luck to each and every one of you.

I want to thank everybody and single out a few for this special hospitality: Doris Poppler, the Acting United States Attorney, has done a superb job on pulling all this together; the attorney general, Marc Racicot; Senators Baucus and Burns; and Governor Stephens and Mayor Larsen. We're honored to have with us also Robert Helmick, the president of the U.S. Olympic Committee. And then, of course, a very special hello to a special guest, Edwin Moses, whom I just was chatting with earlier—an Olympic hurdler and, would you believe, a bobsledder, too? [*Laughter*] But you got a great turnout and great participants.

And I'm especially honored to be able to congratulate the 5th and 6th grade graduates of the D.A.R.E. program who are out there in the crowd. You see, these kids are setting a wonderful example not only for their friends and classmates but for all the adults as well. And they're proof that each of us, no matter how young or how old, has a part to play in this war on drugs.

The drug problem facing America is the reason that I'm out here today with you. For over 100 years now, the people of Montana have been known as proud, hardworking, community-minded people. And that is where the answer to this nation's drug problem lies—right here in the community. And there is no problem so great that all of us working together cannot solve.

We're beginning to see signs that our national efforts against drugs are working.

And last summer, a major nationwide survey found that the number of current drug users in this country had dropped by almost 40 percent in just 3 years. That's good news for America. It's good news for the next generation. And then in February, mid-February, another survey showed that the number of high school seniors using drugs declined in 1989, a long-term trend that has brought seniors' drug use to its lowest level in 15 years. So, that's all good news. But the good news isn't limited to just these national statistics. Last year the State of Montana reported a decrease in the number of drug abuse violations. It is news like this that deepens my faith, my conviction, that together we can win this national war against drugs.

But like all wars, we must be united in our efforts as a country and as a community. Parents, teachers, children, law enforcement officials must join as one. Business, labor, the professions—all must be a part of this crusade for a drug-free America. Each of you here today, by your presence, is sending the dealers of death a strong Montana message: We will not surrender our children. We will not surrender our community. Billings, Montana, is in this fight to win—and win it you will, win it we will.

You know, I know you're going to win because this State, like so many others across this great land, is taking the initiative. You're fighting back. You've had enough. Last year the Montana Board of Crime Control began the innovative Drug Abuse Resistance Education program throughout the State. For those of you not familiar with that, with D.A.R.E., it is a unique program that targets primarily 5th and 6th graders by using well-trained uniformed officers to teach the kids about the dangers of drug use. The program helps students recognize and resist the subtle pressures that influence kids to experiment with drugs and alcohol. Over 7,500 children statewide received instruction in the program's first year, and this number does not include the kids in kindergarten through

4th grade who were taught about drugs through another program designed especially for them. So, let's give a pat on the back to all the kids who have said no to drugs, and our thanks to the law enforcement officers who help them say no. We're very proud of all of them. Keep up the good work. In your own way, you are making America proud.

Another example of community involvement with young people are the antidrug programs supported by the Freemasons of America, like the Center for Adolescent Development's Montana Teen Institute. This innovative center takes at-risk teens who are willing to commit to swear off drugs and gives them the tools they need to avoid drug use, teens like Manuel Zuniga. An alum of the teen institute, Manuel's new goal in life is to be a U.S. marshal so he can help others. Manuel says, "all kids need the help of parents and all adults to fight the bad guys. I would rather be a role model to my community and have made a stand to live a drug-free life."

Often kids themselves are some of our best troops on the front line against drugs. They understand the enormous power of friendship in helping one another avoid drugs. One such program gaining recognition not just around the country but around the world is Youth to Youth, a community drug prevention program for middle school and high school age young people. Recognizing the influential force of peer pressure, the Youth to Youth program uses that pressure to encourage young people to live alcohol and drug-free lives. Proof that kids talking to kids can make a difference is reflected in the words of a young man in Landisville, PA, who said, "All my friends are drug-free, so I've learned that drug-free is the way to be." Wise, wise words.

Parents will agree that there is nothing more heart-wrenching than to witness something as sinister as drugs and alcohol dim the sparkle of your children's eyes, steal their exuberance, destroy their dreams. But parents don't have to stand by and hope their kids are spared from this devastation. Instead, each and every one of us—that means grandparents, aunts and uncles, cousins, neighbors, friends, anyone— can make a huge difference by setting a

good example and by watching for the overt signs of abuse, the overt signs of trouble. But the most effective way to reach our kids is by talking to them about drugs, and even more important—listening to them. Then, through caring and, yes, discipline, help them turn their backs on drugs. When a kid has someone who cares enough to listen, he will not care about drugs.

But kids, communities, families, and friends have some special allies in this battle. In towns as small as Laurel and as big as Los Angeles, brave men and women who believe that this country is worth fighting for face danger and face death every single day. They form the "thin blue line" between good and evil, protecting our children from drugs, protecting all of us from the terrible threat of crime.

Right here in Montana, you know all too well that sometimes these modern day champions are called upon to pay the ultimate price. You've lost one of the town of Hardin's finest in Janet Rogers, and our hearts go out to George Rogers and his three boys—Jace, Logan, and Chad—whom I'm told are here today. Your wife, your mother, was a true American hero.

But let's face it, heroes alone can't win wars. So, in Washington the administration, under the able leadership of our tough drug czar, Bill Bennett, is taking action to help support our law enforcement officers across the country. As we meet today in Montana, this beautiful State, we're still waiting for the House to act on our anticrime package. Earlier this year, we were pleased that Congress passed our request for more agents, more prosecutors, and more prisons to get criminals off the streets and behind bars, where they belong. But we must do more.

I urge the House of Representatives to pass a major portion of the Violent Crime Act, legislation that will back up our new lawmen with new laws—laws that are fair, fast, and final. Fair—an exclusionary rule designed to punish the guilty and not punish the good cops who have acted in good faith. And when I say fast—we need habeas corpus reforms to stop the frivolous appeals that are choking our courts. And final—I'm talking about fair and constitutionally sound death penalty provisions for these major traffickers. To win the war on drugs, we must have a united effort. This isn't Republican or Democrat or liberal or conservative: it's got to be bipartisan. But now, it's time for Congress to act. Our children, our communities, and our cops have waited long enough.

As I look out over this magnificent audience—an ocean of red, white, and blue, I see America at her best. This country's strength has always been her people, people who for generations have always helped not only for the neighbor next door but for the stranger in trouble down the street. This was true over a hundred years ago, when this great land, Montana, became a State. Back then, the sight of smoke on the horizon, a sure sign of trouble, farmers would drop their plows and mountain men

would leave their traps and shopkeepers would abandon their stores to help a neighbor in distress—some of our first what I call Points of Light. In 1990, this sense of community, this sense of caring, still remains, as Americans support one another in this battle against drugs. Today there is again smoke on the horizon, and every single one of you in this stadium are here to help. You're a community bound together not by geography but by caring, and you should be very, very proud.

So, thank you for having me here, and God bless the great State of Montana. Thank you all very, very much. Thank you.

Note: The President spoke at 9:10 a.m. at Daylis Stadium, a day prior to the start of the Big Sky Games.

Remarks at the Frontier Days and State Centennial Parade in Cheyenne, Wyoming
July 20, 1990

Thank you, Mike. Thank you very much, Governor Sullivan, thank you for that warm introduction, and I am very pleased to be here. And Barbara sends her love to Jane, and we hope someday you'll come back and have supper at the White House—the Sullivans.

It's great to be back in Cheyenne and great to be back under—I would call it—a big open sky—I had other words planned. [*Laughter*] But in the place that as you say, the pavement ends and the West begins. Let me salute, in addition to Mike Sullivan, two former Governors who I just spot out here in the crowd, both friends, both admired Americans—Governor Cliff Hanson and Martha, and Governor Stan Hathaway—Stan and Bobbie—right down in front. It's a great pleasure to see you here. There are also some other special friends here: Senator Malcolm Wallop, an ardent worker for so many things that Wyoming people hold dear. And of course, Senator Al Simpson—as a key member of the leadership in the Senate, he takes on the tough fights and sticks with them and always has

this—don't quite know how to describe it— sense of humor. [*Laughter*] Something he's going to need later when he takes me fishing. I'm not sure if I'm up to your State's cutthroat trout. I have trouble with the kinder, gentler rainbow kind of trout. [*Laughter*]

And to Dick Hartman, the chairman here; and Jerry Jessen, the chairman of the Frontier Days; and Dick, the chairman of the centennial, thank you for this warm welcome. Thank you for letting me and those with me be a part of this great day. And, of course, I want to salute Congressman Craig Thomas, with whom I work closely in the United States House of Representatives—glad to have Craig with us. And special thanks to the mayor. I'm sure he'll be glad to see us leave town, but nevertheless, you couldn't tell that from the warmth of his welcome. Mayor Gary Schaeffer, congratulations on this wonderful day and thank you very, very much, Craig.

So, it's great to be here for this 94th Frontier Days, for the "granddaddy of them all." It reminds me of rodeo atmosphere in

Texas. But I want to say a special thanks first to the Casper Troopers. I've heard of them, but never heard them in action before. I haven't known him too long, but you ought to ride in a parade with Timber Jack and have Toughy at your feet when you're in that wagon out there.

Timber Jack. Yahoo!

The President. Thank you, Timber Jack. I listened to that for three blocks. [*Laughter*] You know, I really do feel at home here. It's wonderful, watching them get hurled about by bucking broncos, wrestling steers, struggling to ride wild horses, not to mention bull riding. Enough about trying to deal with Congress. [*Laughter*] I'm really disappointed, though. I was looking forward to taking place in the chuckwagon races until I discovered the menu: barbecue, beans, and—you guessed it—broccoli. No thanks, I'm going on. [*Laughter*]

But on a more serious vein, I'm pleased to be here because there really is so much to celebrate about Wyoming: the exhilaration of the land, of course—we talked about that—crystal streams, some of the cleanest air in our entire country. And yours is the land where the passage of time and man have had little impact. And our Native Americans understand the meaning of land. A wonderful Native American poet, Peter Blue Cloud, writes of what land can tell to those who listen. And he says: "Each day a different story is told me by the rain and wind and snow, the sun and moon shadows, this wonderful Earth, this Creation."

But what we're celebrating most of all today is that you're keeping alive the most unique period of our communal history. For the West does begin here—the special, sacred place that still fires our imaginations and swells our hope. There's a magic in it, a magic that's felt most of all here in Wyoming, the closest State we have to the Old West—a State whose values, whose fundamental values, continue to inspire America, for its spirit is the most uniquely American that there is. And the values I speak of reject temporary fashion. Instead, they are values which are always in fashion. For a century they've shaped Wyoming, uplifted it, just as they mold it today. And they are as pertinent to 1990 as that year 1890 when Wyoming became a star in the American constellation.

To begin, Wyomingites believe in self-reliance and this drive, this insatiable rugged pioneer drive. And that's why, when it comes to our young people, you believe that the Federal Government doesn't have all the answers and doesn't know best, that families right here in Wyoming know what's best. You walk down any street here and ask about the kids, and you want to make the choice—you want to make it—about their care. You want to ensure that parents, not bureaucrats, decide how to care for America's children. And Wyomingites don't want to expand the budget of the bureaucracy, you want to expand the horizons of our kids. And so, you know that education is best which is closest to the people.

Education—it's not a Republican issue or it's not a Democratic issue. It's not liberal or it's not conservative. It is an American issue. And we must do better in the United States of America. But here in Wyoming, your graduation rate is second in the entire Nation. And you rank seventh in the entire Nation of States who administer these ACT tests. You can ask Mike Sullivan here. He's of a different party from me, and I don't think he wants more red tape. And I know he doesn't want more mandated benefits out of Washington, DC, and as long as I'm President we are going to resist saddling Wyoming people with mandated decrees from Washington.

Because these Members of the Congress with me and the Governor agree that what we ought to do is reward excellence and seeing that the Federal dollars help those most in need. We've got to demand accountability. We've got to give parents and students greater flexibility. We've got to give them choice and ideas, in short, based on the values of local trust and local autonomy—values as revered in Wyoming as love of freedom and love of God. You talk to Wyomingites and they'll tell you that political values without moral values simply cannot sustain a nation. So, you want voluntary prayer restored to America's classrooms. And so do I. Together, somehow, we've got to put the faith of our fathers back in our schools. And I think one of the reasons that Barbara's speech at Wellesley touched a chord is she was talking about these Wyoming values of family and faith. And the American people are crying out for just that. So, you go to any Wyoming county and see these values in action.

And here, too, we agree with a noted preacher who said, "A thoughtful mind, when it sees a nation's flag, sees not the flag only, but the nation itself." And I have a funny feeling, in spite of some of the criticism that I took for my recent attempt—ably assisted by those right here—to protect our flag, I have a funny feeling that Wyoming's sons and daughters might understand more than most why I feel so strongly about the flag of the United States. I have great respect for the Constitution and great respect for the Bill of Rights. But I'm determined to push through an amendment that protects that unique symbol of America—I emphasize the word unique—the American flag.

Finally, let me close with perhaps the greatest Wyoming value of all—neighborhoods and hearts as big as the open sky. No one has had to tell you to lend a hand. You've done it. You are doing it. Building homes from sod, and schools to be constructed so kids could learn. You've all heard me talk about a Thousand Points of Light of community service, of one American helping another. In the last few months, I've named two Wyoming groups as America's daily Points of Light—the Cheyenne Botanic Gardens and the Yellowstone Recovery Corps. The volunteers—the descendants of heroes who forded rivers and tilled your farms, fought off everything from claim-jumpers to grizzly bears. In Wyoming, "do unto others" is, indeed, a century-old creed.

My friends, this stunning sculpture of "The Spirit of Wyoming" says so much about you and your State and about the values I've talked about: generosity, self-reliance, love of country, love of God. Not only does it preserve a wonderful moment of Old West history for generations to appreciate but also, by being located between the capitol and your new Herschler Building, it leads us all from the past to the future. That is what the centennial is all about. By recapturing our history and by renewing the bonds between past and present and between each other, we can discover the way to move ahead together to face the challenges of future frontiers.

Ladies and gentlemen, we are living in exciting times. We're seeing these dramatic changes in the world where totalitarian states are giving way to democracy and freedom. It is an exciting time to be a member of the United States of America family. And I came out here to salute you for keeping the underpinnings of America's greatness alive. Thank you, and God bless each and every one of you. Thank you very, very much.

Note: The President spoke at 1:15 p.m. on the steps of the capitol building.

Remarks at the Francis Earl Warren Air Force Base in Cheyenne, Wyoming
July 20, 1990

Let me just say that I did want to stop by here at Warren, and it's wonderful to be with you all. I understand that you've had your share of visitors lately, so I promise not to overstay. [*Laughter*] Not only the Soviets, but the Inspector General just were here.

But you and other missileers throughout the SAC [Strategic Air Command] are working hard every single day to maintain a strong deterrent. Your ears should be burning when you hear the colonel telling us about the quality of the men and women serving here, a view also expressed by those Senators and our Congressmen from Wyoming who take pride not only in having you as professionals but in the work that this command does to help others in the community. So, I salute you not only for your professionalism but for the way you're doing something here to help others. You work hard every day, maintaining this strong deterrent. Along with the strategic bomber crews and the submarine crews, your commitment to vigilance has helped create the conditions for the changes we are witnessing today. There can be no doubt about that whatsoever.

As we strive for strength and stability, we must maintain an effective deterrent especially in the face of continuing across-the-board modernization of the Soviet strategic forces. Now, this won't be easy in the fiscal environment that we face now. We all recognize that we must get the deficit under control, and the defense will contribute its share. But I don't want defense to contribute more than its share, and I'm asking Congress to hold the line at the already painful reduction in the defense budget set down by the Senate Armed Services Committee earlier this week. There were some positive things for the committee, especially their support of strategic modernization—as well as some actions, on the other hand, that cause me problems.

One point I want to emphasize today is that the deeper and more painful the cuts in the defense budget, the greater is my need for flexibility from the Congress in order to manage these funds. We must have an orderly build-down, not some kind of a fire sale. I especially need that flexibility so that the bedrock of the military, its highly trained, highly motivated, and exceptionally dedicated men and women—people such as you—will be protected. I cannot support reductions in the defense budget that would unfairly penalize those of you who have given so much to our country.

When senior Soviet officers visited the United States military bases several years ago, the thing that impressed them the most was the talent, confidence, commitment, and responsibility of junior officers and enlisted men and women. The Soviets know what deters, and so does this President. And I just wanted to come by, thank you, encourage you to keep up the great work.

Actually, I'm personally well-acquainted with the quality people that serve here at F.E. Warren. John Gordon—you may remember Colonel John Gordon, your commander through May of last year—he's now back in Washington, advising us on a host of questions on our strategic forces, on our arms control. So, you've got a voice in the White House. And, John, thank you. Pleased to see you, and great to visit with all your fellow wingmates and fellow missileers.

Thank you very much for what you're doing. I hate to hit and run like this, but I did want to come by and pay my respects, learn something, and thank you for your dedication and commitment to the greatest country on the face of the Earth. Thank you very much.

Note: The President spoke at 1:25 p.m. in the Peacekeeper missile training silo area. In his opening remarks, he referred to Col. Richard Farkas, wing commander. Following his remarks, the President went fishing at Middle Crow Creek and then returned to Washington, DC.

Remarks at the Christening of the U.S.S. *George Washington* in Newport News, Virginia
July 21, 1990

Thank you very much. What a great day in Newport News. And to all of you out there, thank you for the warm welcome. And Dick Cheney, our able Secretary of Defense, thank you, sir, for those kind words.

You know, we're living in changing times, very exciting times for world peace. We're living in tough times in a lot of ways. But it is so important that we have an able Secretary of Defense leading for our country's best interests, our security interests. And I just want to say to this marvelous gathering today, I can think of no one better to be Secretary of Defense at this critical time than Dick Cheney. I am blessed to have him at my side.

And I'm very proud to have other strong supporters of defense with us today: Our distinguished Senator from Virginia, Chuck Robb, a longtime friend and a strong supporter of all that the Navy undertakes. And it's a pleasure to see the Tidewater contingent from Congress—Herb Bateman and Owen Pickett, Norm Sisisky—all who understand the Navy's mission, all who understand national defense. And of course, I'll single out one other Member of Congress I recognize—though he's known as "B-1" Bob Dornan from California, he, too, a strong supporter—Congressman Dornan. I don't want to reminisce too long, but I see Senator Harry Byrd out here. Harry, stand up—[*applause*]—a great Virginian and another one who has stood for defense. Ed Campbell, my thanks to you, sir, president of Newport News Shipbuilding. And then my dear friend from Houston, Jim Kettleson, who is the CEO of Tenneco. Secretary Larry Garrett—doing a superb job for the Navy; and of course, our new CNO [Chief of Naval Operations], my friend Admiral Kelso; all our other distinguished guests.

I am very pleased to be here this morning with my daughter, Dorothy. She's today's matron of honor. And I know that Barbara—the Silver Fox, we call her—[*laughter*]—is deeply honored that you've chosen her to christen this magnificent ship, the *George Washington.*

Coming to the shipyards today put me in mind of my first government job that Dick referred to. I was commissioned at the age 18, an ensign in the Navy and a carrier pilot, and things were quite different then. The planes were slower. The ships were smaller. And as I look around at these admirals and some of the enlisted men and women that I've been privileged to meet with, they all seem a lot younger today. Captain Nutwell looks too young to drive a great big ship like this. [*Laughter*]

But what I think it sums up to is that I've been told by our Chief of Naval Operations, by General Powell, by the other Chiefs, that we have never had finer officers or enlisted men and women in the armed services than we have today. And they look young to me, but they're the best, and we are very, very proud of them. I don't want to get too nostalgic here—notice my Navy tie, however. [*Laughter*] But on my ship, the *San Jacinto*—it was one of those "fast carriers," built atop a cruiser hull in the early months of our entry into the war—the deck wasn't much wider than the wing span of the plane I flew, a TBF Grumman *Avenger.* Now, looking up at the *Washington,* I'm not sure that the *San Jacinto* itself wouldn't fit on a hangar deck of this behemoth here.

For all of you—and I now speak to those who are doing the work of building this magnificent vessel, who have put months and years of your best work into this aircraft carrier—this has got to be a very proud day for you, as it is for me. The *George Washington* joins a noble line that begins with the first aircraft carrier built here—that was the *Ranger,* back in 1934.

Many of you out here are sons and daughters of shipbuilders. In some families, I'm told, four generations have worked here, turning steel into ships—men like Edgar Davis, 80 years old now, who followed his father and four brothers into these yards, and whose son and two grandsons work here today. When Edgar started work in 1926, there were no portable electric lights, so the steel workers went down into the hull holding candles. And yet before he retired 48 years later, Edgar Davis and his fellow workers here at Newport News had helped launch the nuclear Navy.

Edgar said he'd be here today if the weather was good. We tried to oblige him. He said, "I've seen so many launchings, but I'll tell you, I'm just as enthused about this one as I was about my very first."

This magnificent ship is a tribute to your talents. Few realize the magnitude of your task: what it means to build a state-of-the-art supercarrier—a warship, a floating city, an airport all rolled into one. But here she is, about to be launched, one step closer to service, one step closer to the sea.

The carrier came of age, I think, in the Second World War. And the ships built in this yard helped us turn the tide in the

Pacific: the Battle of Midway, the greatest naval contest in history; at Leyte Gulf, where our Navy captured control of the Western Pacific. When Jimmy Doolittle led his legendary raid on Tokyo, he took off from the deck of the *Hornet,* built right here at Newport News. Today the carrier remains an indispensable element in the American arsenal, projecting power, preserving the peace.

Today, fortunately, is not a time of war. A new chapter is opening, a day of great promise, a time of triumph for the ideals all Americans hold dear. But while freedom has made great gains, we have not entered an era of perpetual peace. What George Washington said in the 18th century is truer today than it ever was: "To be prepared for war is one of the most effective means of preserving the peace." American power is still the world's paramount force for freedom. And as in the time of war, when

America waged the fight for freedom far from our shores, so today we must maintain a policy of peacetime engagement and armed forces sufficient to sustain our vital national interest. We are inescapably the leader of free world defense, the connecting link in a global alliance of democracies, the pivotal factor of stability. We will not shrink from this responsibility. Let the *George Washington* proclaim America's commitment to remain forever free.

Once again, Barbara, Dorothy, and I thank you for this warm welcome. We are pleased and honored to be a part of these proceedings. May God bless the *George Washington* and all who sail in her and all who fly from her deck. Thank you very, very much.

Note: The President spoke at 11:21 a.m. in the Newport News Shipbuilding Yard. In his remarks, he referred to Colin L. Powell, Chairman of the Joint Chiefs of Staff.

Statement by Press Secretary Fitzwater on the Importation of Semiautomatic Weapons
July 23, 1990

The importation of weapons that meet the legal criteria for sporting purposes will continue to be allowed. The current ban on semiautomatic assault weapons was implemented last July, after comprehensive review, because these weapons have features which render them unsuitable for sporting purposes under the 1968 Gun Control Act. As manufacturers redesign these weapons to eliminate the undesirable features, the manufacturers may reapply for approval to import the redesigned weapons. If the redesigned weapons meet the criteria of the 1968 Gun Control Act, the application will be approved by ATF [Bureau of Alcohol, Tobacco and Firearms]. Thus, the requests for imported weapons reported in

today's Washington Post were granted because the weapons had been redesigned. This is entirely within the law.

The crime bill which the administration proposed limits the number of rounds in detachable magazines. However, it will not influence the redesign of weapons within the configuration of traditional sporting rifles. I was wrong to suggest that the new crime bill will influence redesigned weapons. The goal of keeping firearms out of the hands of felons is deeply held by this administration. The crime bill will go a long way toward ensuring the right of every American to be free from fear of violent crime.

Remarks Following Discussions With President Rodrigo Borja Cevallos of Ecuador
July 23, 1990

President Bush. It has been a great pleasure to talk once again to my colleague, President Borja, with whom I had this marvelous tennis game yesterday. You know, when we met in Costa Rica, we enjoyed some good conversation, and we also found time to work in a little tennis. And so, today we had stimulating, substantive talks, and yesterday we worked in a little tennis. And I can say unequivocally that we thoroughly enjoyed the rematches on both fronts.

For many years, the whole world has been watching the progress of this courageous Pacific nation. A little over a decade ago, Ecuador became one of the first to set sail in the rising tide of democracy in Latin America, and like so many of its neighbors, it's raised our hopes for a fully democratic hemisphere. And today the people of Ecuador can be proud of their free press and their exemplary record on human rights, hallmarks of both true democracy and true leadership, I might say.

When he first came to office, President Borja faced difficult economic challenges. Inflation was up at about 100 percent; a debt, a staggering 110 percent of GNP, all payments suspended. But undaunted by the great political pressures he faced, President Borja began taking the kind of courageous steps that characterized the new generation of democratic leaders in this hemisphere. He made important economic reforms, such as improving the tax and tariff systems, and there's also been movement toward reforming market mechanisms and government programs, including steps taken toward the elimination of price controls that have created serious distortions in the past.

As a followup to the Cartagena [antidrug] summit and because of my special concern for the needs of the Andean countries, I am today announcing a package of new measures for the Andean region. These measures will build on my Enterprise for Americas Initiative and will be steps en route to achieving our ultimate objectives of trade and investment liberalization and economic reform in the region.

First, I will ask Congress for legislative authority to enter into a one-way tariff preference arrangement for duty-free entry for selected imports from Ecuador, Bolivia, Peru, and Colombia, to give these countries a special boost in fighting drugs and promoting their transition into a comprehensive free trade zone for the Americas.

And second, I am proposing that we expand U.S. cooperation in technical assistance with the countries of the entire Latin American and Caribbean region, and particularly with Andean countries to enhance the immense potential for agricultural trade.

Third, in fulfillment of my commitment last year to consider additional GSP access for Andean products, this morning I signed a proclamation granting GSP treatment to 67 new products.

And fourth, concurrent with the transitional preferential tariff regime, we propose to negotiate with the Andean countries comprehensive, long-term undertakings on trade and investment liberalization. Bilateral framework agreements are appropriate vehicles for achieving these goals. Today our governments will be signing such an agreement establishing a joint council to help our efforts to expand trade and investment between our countries.

Ecuador has also led the way in environmental reforms, becoming one of the first countries to engage in a debt-for-nature swap program. When we visited Ecuador in 1984, I saw a beautiful country—an extraordinary mix of animal and plant life, the towering Andes, the sweeping vista of the Pacific, and the Galapagos beyond. And we are committed to assist Ecuadorean efforts to preserve their unique environmental heritage.

Ecuador has collaborated closely with the United States in our global effort to deal with the scourge of cocaine. And Ecuador is a leader in rolling back coca cultivation. In fact, several years ago, Ecuador eradicated all coca plantings. And the antidrug legislation you have sponsored not only has kept the destructive cocaine culture from taking root in Ecuador, it also aids us in stanching the drug flow here.

President Borja, I look forward to continued close cooperation with you across the full range of our common concerns, from strengthening democracy throughout our hemisphere to working for expanded trade and investment opportunities to the fight against cocaine trafficking. Our talks have served to reconfirm the great value of our partnership.

Thank you, and Godspeed in your journey ahead. Thank you for coming here.

President Borja. Mr. President Bush and ladies and gentlemen, it has been truly a pleasure to have been invited to this country and to have been received by Mr. Bush and by his family, to have enjoyed the warmth of a close personal association with the family, and especially to have had the opportunity of continuing our tennis match, which started in Costa Rica. And yesterday, fortunately, not due to any diplomatic reasons or—of that nature—the results were tied.

I would like to take advantage of this opportunity to offer you some reflections and some comments as to the nature of the world in which we are living and the nature of the relationships in which we live in this environment between Ecuador and the United States.

Every day, we are witnessing surprising and astounding events. I am certain that the years of 1989 and 1990 will go down in history as 2 years of extraordinary interest and extraordinary events. All of these events that we have witnessed have come with surprising speed and agility. We have been present at the fall of the Wall of Berlin. We are also witnessing the destruction and the disappearance of the Marxist monocracies that are giving way to a new concept of socialism and liberty. We are also witnessing that there is a decrease in the armament race. There are changes in what is NATO and the Warsaw Pact. There are also indications of the unification of Germany, and Korea is also attempting to do the same.

I think that all of these things bring to mind that there are two basic elements that are worthy of mentioning. One is the end of the cold war, which began in World War II. And the second element of importance is the fact that we are witnessing the appearance of a new opening as far as international relations—an era where there will be more just and equitable relations between the various countries.

We are present here at these various elements of this new international order; and we hope that this new international order will be based upon a system of equity, of justice, and of equal participation. We applaud and commend the initiative of President Bush, his Enterprise for the Americas, which is based on three basic columns: one is the participation and growth of trade, the second one is a promotion of investments in all of these other countries, and the third is a reduction of the international debt that weighs so heavily upon us.

We admire the words that have been mentioned by President Bush and his concept that prosperity for Latin American nations depends basically on trade and not so much on foreign assistance that our countries may receive. We are sure that this prosperity will be the result of the work and of the creativity that we ourselves can develop.

Therefore, we are a country that, at present, together with other countries in Latin America, have very low saving rates in our population. The capital transfers are beyond any reason in this sense, and they can provide better opportunities for the future to have better investments that will allow us to find the solutions to the social and economic problems of the countries.

Ecuador is truly a nation of peace. It is an oasis where you find a great deal of tranquillity and peacefulness. We have a group of citizens that are hard-working people, and we have a government that is responsible not only for its mandate but also is projecting the future of Ecuador. And we are also having the basic foundations laid out for a democracy that will continue to survive. Our country, therefore, offers an excellent environment for foreign investments, and we will welcome all foreign investments that come into our country, and that they will also comply with the needs of our country and meet the social and legal elements.

President Bush, Mr. Baker, and Mr. Brady have been extremely courageous in attempting to find solutions to the problems of the foreign debt. This foreign debt, as they have indicated, is not only a financial problem but it also constitutes a political problem with different expressions. The foreign debt for Latin American countries is basically a matter of survival. And we are seeing that this debt, the burdens that it weighs upon our countries, provides the risks of placing our governments into a position of incompetence, of inability of being able to find and solve social and economic problems.

I have mentioned to Mr. Bush and his associates that our government in Ecuador has dedicated the decade of the nineties as the decade for ecological development. We, as all the nations of the world, wish to breathe pure, crystalline air, we wish to have healthy, good, fertile lands, and we also want to have clear waters running through our countries. As Ecuador is a member of the Amazon Basin pact, we are aware that the Amazon region is the largest humid tropical forest that exists in the world. This provides 40 percent of the oxygen that the world breathes. One fifth of the fresh water supplies are residing in this section. We have over 4,000 vegetable species in these lands. Just to give you an idea: 1 square mile of Amazon jungle has more species than all of the United States and Canada together. Therefore, we must take care of this environmental concern, to

handle it properly, and to give it the necessary balance and equilibrium for future generations.

First, I want to thank President Bush for this opportunity of visiting the United States and also for being the first Latin American President that has been invited to hold talks at the issuance of the Enterprise for the Americas. Also, a special word of thanks for the family, for the warmth, for the cordiality that we received during yesterday. And further thanks for the important statements that Mr. Bush has just issued.

We wish to hold the President and the Government of these people responsible in the future to assist us in their commitment to achieve the progress and the well-being of Latin America and the Caribbean nations. And furthermore, a special expression of appreciation for the very kind and warm hospitality that President Bush has given us during these few hours in this wonderful country.

Thank you.

Note: President Bush spoke at 1:12 p.m. at the South Portico of the White House. President Borja spoke in Spanish, and his remarks were translated by an interpreter. In his remarks, President Borja referred to Secretary of State James A. Baker III and Secretary of the Treasury Nicholas F. Brady. Prior to their remarks, the two Presidents met privately in the Oval Office and with U.S. and Ecuadorean officials in the Cabinet Room, and then attended a luncheon in the Old Family Dining Room. The proclamation is listed in Appendix E at the end of this volume.

Remarks Announcing the Nomination of David H. Souter To Be an Associate Justice of the Supreme Court of the United States and a Question-and-Answer Session With Reporters
July 23, 1990

The President. My oath to the Constitution charges me to faithfully execute the Office of President and, to the best of my ability, preserve, protect, and defend the

Constitution of the United States. Few duties are more important in discharging that obligation than my responsibility, under article II, section 2 of our Constitution, to select from among all possible choices one nominee to fill a vacancy on the Supreme Court of the United States.

The task of narrowing the selection to one highly qualified jurist, committed to the rule of law and faithful to the Constitution, could never be easy; but I have found it enormously satisfying. My choice will serve the Court and the Constitution well.

I am most pleased to announce that I will nominate as Associate Justice of the United States Supreme Court a remarkable judge of keen intellect and the highest ability, one whose scholarly commitment to the law and whose wealth of experience mark him of first rank: Judge David Souter of the United States Court of Appeals for the First Circuit.

Judge Souter, I believe with all my heart, will prove a most worthy member of the Court. His tenure as an Associate Justice of the Supreme Court of the State of New Hampshire, as Attorney General of that State, and more recently as a Federal appeals judge unquestionably demonstrates his ability, his integrity, and his dedication to public service. And he has a keen appreciation of the proper judicial role rooted in fundamental belief in separation of powers and the democratic principles underlying our great system of government.

Let me pay tribute, too, to the Justice whose retirement from the Court created the vacancy: Justice William Brennan. His powerful intellect, his winning personality and, importantly, his commitment to civil discourse on emotional issues that, at times, tempt uncivil voices have made him one of the greatest figures of our age. No one can question his dedication to the Nation and the energy that he has brought to his high office. His retirement is marked by the dignity and honor that characterized his 34 years of service on the bench. And I told him the other day when I talked to him of the respect that Mrs. Bush and I have for him, for his wonderful service. In choosing to nominate Judge Souter—who, like Justice Brennan, is largely a product of the State court system—I have looked for the same dedication to public service and strength of intellect exemplified by Justice Brennan.

My selection process was not geared simply to any legal issue. It is not appropri-

ate in choosing a Supreme Court Justice to use any litmus test. And I want a Justice who will ably and fairly interpret the law across the range of issues the Court faces. Our country serves as a model for the world at a time of special significance, and I stress within the White House and to the Attorney General that our process could not be dominated by politics or special interests. And I believe that we've set a good example of selecting a fair arbiter of the law.

Judge Souter will bring to the Court a wealth of judicial experience on the Supreme Court of his State, and before that as a State trial court judge. Prior to his appointment to the State bench, he was Attorney General of the State of New Hampshire. Judge Souter is a graduate of the Harvard Law School, Phi Beta Kappa graduate of Harvard College. He was also a Rhodes scholar.

My respect for his outstanding record led me earlier this year to nominate him to his present position on the court of appeals. The Senate unanimously confirmed him to that position because of his exceptional qualities and his experience. His opinions reflect a keen intellect as well as wise balance between the theoretical and practical aspects of the law. Judge Souter, committed to interpreting, not making the law—he recognizes the proper role of judges in upholding the democratic choices of the people through their elected representatives with constitutional constraints.

Judge Brennan's retirement took effect last Friday. The Court is now reduced to eight members. It is important to restore the bench to full strength by the first Monday in October, when the Court begins its 1990 term. I look forward to presenting Judge Souter's nomination to the Senate as quickly as possible, and I look forward, as well, to a fair and expeditious confirmation process.

Helen [Helen Thomas, United Press International]?

Q. Did you ask Judge Souter his views on abortion? Do you know what his views are? And affirmative action—all of these things that have become so controversial, the major issues of the day.

The President. No. And I had one meeting with Judge Souter. I was very impressed. But in my view, it would have been inappropriate to ask him his views on specific issues. This process has been going on—this selection process—not with any specific seat in mind but just being prepared for a long, long time. Judge Souter was considered for the High Court back when Mr. Justice Kennedy was selected, and so there's a lot. And then, of course, his name was very much in the forefront when he was nominated and subsequently confirmed for the appeals court. So, I am familiar with him, with his general views; but I did not and would not, as I think I've said before when I talked about—not just here but at other times—the litmus test approach—I wouldn't go into that with him.

Q. Sir, does that mean you do not care what he thinks on these issues?

The President. It means that I have selected a person who will interpret the Constitution and, in my view, not legislate from the Federal bench.

Q. Mr. President, barely 3 days have passed since you learned of Justice Brennan's resignation. Why did you move so quickly on this appointment? And you also called the leaders of Congress and others over the weekend for their advice. When did you come to the choice of Justice Souter?

The President. I came to the choice this afternoon. And I think I told the leaders that I talked to over the weekend that I wanted to move very fast. As I've said, this isn't precipitous in the sense that we just started looking for names last Saturday. I remember meeting with the Attorney General and Boyden Gray [Counsel to the President] perhaps within the first month I was President—at least the first 2 months. And I've had a couple of meetings with them, and they've been in discussion with each other for a long time on this. Just the prudence would dictate that one be prepared lest there be a vacancy. So, we've been talking about who I might want to appoint for a long time.

Q. Sir, if I could follow up: You're not certain in your own mind how Justice Souter will vote if *Roe* v. *Wade* comes before the Court next term?

The President. What I'm certain of is that

he will interpret the Constitution and not legislate from the Federal bench.

Q. Mr. President, I believe Judge Souter is about 50 years old, as many of the candidates you've considered were younger than the current Justices. What kind of lasting legacy do you want to leave on the Supreme Court? Do you expect this to be a long-term shifting of the center of balance for the Court?

The President. I'm not looking—he's in good health. I was looking over there to see how he's looking at 50—[*laughter*]—but he seems to be in very vigorous health, and I would expect he'd serve a long term on the bench. But, Ann [Ann Compton, ABC News], I'm not viewing this as some personal Bush imprint on the Court. I've pledged to seek out excellence, and I've pledged to look for somebody who would interpret the Constitution, and I am satisfied I have found the very best in that regard.

Q. Do you expect the Court would shift to the right, philosophically?

The President. I haven't put it in terms of shifting left or right. I read a great deal of speculation about all that, but all I'm saying is that we've got a nominee here who is extraordinarily intelligent, has a record, has been confirmed by the Senate, and who has satisfied inquiry at the State and Federal level as to his objectivity and as to his judicial philosophy. And I'm satisfied as to all those counts.

Lesley [Lesley Stahl, CBS News]?

Q. Mr. President, as you know, the whole issue of abortion has, over this choice—is major in all of this. Do you know if the judge has written on this issue? Does he have a record on this issue that either side can point to, to make it an even bigger issue; or is it unknown and, therefore, more difficult to get at?

The President. In the first place, I think it would be inappropriate, although I'll let him make up his own mind, for Justice Souter—[*laughter*]—to make any comments on any specific issue. Out of respect for the Senate, I would urge that he not do that. Any specific questions on specific issues should be addressed in an orderly confirmation process by the Senate. But beyond that, Lesley, you know, I think what I said earlier responds to your question.

Q. You said you hadn't asked him, but I wonder if he has a record, if it's in print or if he's made——

The President. Well, I don't know about that. I didn't consider that, as I thought I had made clear.

Q. Mr. President, if you've concluded that it's inappropriate to ask about a specific case like *Roe* versus *Wade*, do you also therefore consider it to be inappropriate for the Senate committee that'll do the confirmation to ask about a specific case like that?

The President. I would let the Senate do whatever they want. They're a separate and an independent body of our government, and there are certain precedents for how they approach these issues. But listen, I've got enough problems down here without trying to tell the Senate how to conduct its confirmation hearings.

I've been handed a protocol note. Marlin Fitzwater [Press Secretary to the President], who is not known for his protocol—[*laughter*]—he says it would be most appropriate to let Judge Souter respond at this juncture. So, with your permission, we'll proceed.

David?

Judge Souter. Thank you, Mr. President. I'm really not sure how to do that. If it were possible for me to express to you the realization that I have of the honor which the President has just done me, I would try, and I would keep you here as long tonight as I had to do to get it out. But I could not express that realization, and I'm not going to try to do the impossible. Beyond that, I hope you will understand that I think I must defer any further comments of mine until I am before the Senate in the confirmation process.

Q. Mr. President, conservatives recently have expressed some disappointment with what they call the flip-flop on no-new-tax pledge, your position on China, Lithuania, and the like. [*Laughter*] And since Governor Sununu [Chief of Staff to the President] is recognized as the champion of conservatives in the White House, is the Judge's connection to Governor Sununu—is this meant as an appeasement to the conservative right? Do you think it will appease them?

The President. Sununu's got problems with his own credentials. I mean, he's not going to help on that. [*Laughter*] And that's not what this is all about. This matter, as I've indicated, was—there was almost a certain recusal on the part of Governor Sununu on this. Clearly, he knows Judge Souter. He has great respect for Judge Souter. But this process, as I'm sure Boyden Gray and Dick Thornburgh will tell you, came up through a system. Excellence came to the top. And so, there is no politics of this nature in this kind of an appointment.

If I was looking to shore up one factor or another, there would be plenty of more visible ways to do it. Here, we are talking about excellence, judicial excellence, and the highest degree of qualification based on excellence to be on the Court.

Q. Mr. President, earlier today Marlin Fitzwater said that whomever you chose as your candidate, your nominee, would reflect your general philosophy of government. Is it still your philosophy that *Roe* versus *Wade*, the abortion law, should be overturned?

The President. Look, you all can keep trying all day long to get me to comment on abortion in relation to this nomination. And please stop trying, because I'm not going to respond in that vein. It would be unfair to Judge Souter. It would be untrue because I haven't looked at the nomination in that manner. And so, I simply cannot, and—you get another question, though, instead.

Q. Well, my other question would simply be: Let's not respond in the connection of Judge Souter. How about just your own personal philosophy?

The President. I haven't changed my views, if that helps you any.

Q. Mr. President, I'm still not totally certain by why you feel it was inappropriate to ask the judge's views on issues.

The President. Because I understand that's the customary way of doing it, and that more important are the broad concepts of excellence: Is the man qualified? Does he share a broad view that what he ought to do on the bench is interpret the Constitution and not legislate? And so, that's all I need. And when you see the background of this man, I'm confident that the Senate will share my views. You're looking for fairness. You're looking for equity. I wrote down a bunch of words to help me make the determination, and I wish I had them because they're all along those lines—experience. And I did say that I'd like somebody that will interpret the Constitution, not legislate.

Q. But to even be sure of that, sir, does that mean that you've at least studied some of his rulings?

The President. There's been a great deal of work done in the Justice Department at several levels, in our General Counsel's shop on all that kind of thing. But again, it would be inappropriate to go into those cases that he may have ruled on when he was on the State court or on the Federal bench. And I would simply leave that to the Senate. But, yes, there has been a thorough study of Judge Souter's tremendously impressive record.

Maureen [Maureen Dowd, New York Times]?

Q. Mr. President, given the reality of getting a person confirmed to the Supreme Court these days, are you braced for a big battle?

The President. I'm not going into this nomination or thrusting Judge Souter into the nomination expecting a highly contentious battle. The man was confirmed by the Senate unanimously—and after testimony. So, I'm not suggesting there has to be or should be. I remember calmer days when there weren't. So, I would not anticipate a contentious battle. I would anticipate thorough questioning. I would anticipate each Senator having enough information to make up his or her mind based on the record or responses to questions. But, no, we're not bracing for some horrendous fight with the United States Senate. And given his record, I would expect that the chances of that are minimal.

Q. Do you think a President these days has to do more of a selling job than in the past?

The President. I don't know, Maureen. I don't think so—if the record speaks for itself. If I had selected somebody out of the political arena that had never been on the bench and never had any experience but

was in my view well qualified, there might well have been more intervention on my part. I'm prepared to do whatever is appropriate in not only defending but advocating this confirmation. But I don't believe there's going to be a lot of personal involvement necessary because I think his record and his standing will speak for itself.

Q. Mr. President, I'm going to make one more try. You say it's inappropriate to ask. But you also admit there is a lot of background paperwork on someone. Judge Souter was appointed to the New Hampshire court by Governor Sununu, whose feelings on abortion are well-known. Your feelings on abortion are well-known. Why should we not believe that that is a factor in your selection—even in making a list?

The President. Because I've told you it's not, and because you ought to listen to the testimony on the Hill, and then you can make up your mind better when you've seen the evidence. And I expect people will be raising this question. I've seen a lot of speculation on it over the last 48 hours, or whatever it was, since Justice Brennan retired. But I'm telling you—you asked me what my view was, and I've told you how I approached this matter. And that's all I can do.

Q. Mr. President, you said a moment ago that there are Senate precedents on how questioning happens in the Judiciary Committee. In fact, there are two very contrasting precedents. There was the Bork precedent where the nominee answered all sorts of questions, and there was the Justice O'Connor-Justice Kennedy precedent, in which the nominee declined to answer a lot of specific questions about how the nominee felt. Do you have any preference about how your nominee handles these questions?

The President. No, but I have confidence my nominee will handle it properly. Look, the man is a judge on appeals court. He knows how to treat with this. And the Senate is a free Senate, and they know how to treat with it. I'm not going to get into that. I think it's inappropriate for a President to do that kind of thing.

Q. If I could follow up: Do you think it's appropriate for a nominee to answer specific questions about how he might rule on cases?

The President. I would leave that to the nominee and let the Senate make the final determination.

Q. Were there one or two aspects of the judge's background, his qualifications, that particularly brought him to the top of the list?

The President. Being bright—extraordinarily bright—and then a record for fairness—extraordinarily fair.

Q. Surely—[*inaudible*]—who were bright and fair, though.

The President. Well, I've made my judgment based—you've asked me what I decided it on, and these are some of the qualifications that I think are essential. Plus I gave you the underpinning, which I want somebody that is not going to be a legislator sitting on the Supreme Court.

Q. Did you meet Judge Souter before you made this decision within the last couple of days?

The President. Yes. Just within the last couple of days.

Q. Is this the first time you had seen him?

The President. First time I had met him. And who knows? The amount of time I've spent in New Hampshire, I might well have seen him. [*Laughter*] We've been—as I have indicated—been talking to our Attorney General and Boyden Gray on resumes or on records for a long, long time. And the man is very highly regarded. I just had a short visit with Judge Souter today and obviously was quite impressed.

Q. You had already decided at that point?

The President. No, I had not decided, and that's the truth, as is everything else I've said here.

Q. In speaking to your advisers about resumes and records, as you say, did you ask your advisers to produce only nominees who had no extensive written record on the abortion issue, that is, Trojan Horse candidates who would not provoke a large debate over——

The President. No.

Q. Can you tell me how is it possible to make the selection without reviewing the judge's record or a summary of his record that dealt with specific cases—if not abortion, affirmative action, civil rights issues, free speech, a lot of the emotional issues that the country is very concerned about?

The President. Most of his writings have been at the State level, and I made the decision based on the criteria that I gave you.

Q. So, you're telling us that you have no idea what his judicial opinions are on abortion, affirmative action, civil rights, flag burning?

The President. I'm telling you that you should stay tuned and let the testimony before the United States Senate determine whether he's confirmed or not and that that will bring out all the questions that you are asking here. And the answers—that's up to the judge to see how he should handle that, as one who is going to have to deal with a lot of issues in the future.

Q. Mr. President, has Governor Sununu, who is well-acquainted with the nominee, given you his reading on the judge's views on controversial issues such as——

The President. No.

Way in the back. One, two, three, and then I'm leaving.

Q. Am I back far enough?

The President. One, two, three, four—you're in the middle.

Q. Mr. President, I wonder if you can tell me, sir—you extolled the judge's virtues and pointed out more than once that he was unanimously confirmed by the Senate for his present position. Can you think of any reason, any possibility, the Senate would not confirm the judge for this post, other than ideological grounds?

The President. No. I can think of none why they would not confirm him. None. Period.

Q. And would you object strenuously to a confirmation battle over ideological grounds?

The President. Look, I have nothing to say about that. This is a separate body. I don't control the Senate. I would hope they would accept the—when they've had a chance to ask questions and they've had a chance to review his record—would conclude, as I have, that he is outstandingly well-qualified for the Federal bench, a judgment that was given to him not too long ago by the ABA [American Bar Association] itself—well-qualified, which I gather is the highest rating a judge can have.

Q. You have said you're not interested in making a Bush imprint on the Court. But you may also——

The President. I have to, I guess, but I'm not interested in having this known as a Bush Court or something of that nature.

Q. Well, you may be called upon throughout your term to actually name one or two others. Do you have those in mind?

The President. Yes.

Q. And also, if by——

The President. Yes, right there.

Q. Who are they?

Q. ——by having those names in mind of who you would appoint, are you doing the same thing like in foreign policy, saying that you want to choose a prudent man, or that the imprint would be something peculiar to you?

The President. Look, I'll tell you how I look at this—not in terms of some specific imprint but I want it said when I'm about 90, 24 years from now, that I made a superb choice. And I think it will be so writ.

Q. Mr. President, I'd like to ask you about the phrase you're using—you're opposed to somebody who would legislate from the bench. You're on record as wanting *Roe* versus *Wade* overturned. You're on record as favoring a flag burning amendment to the Constitution. Aren't those sorts of issues tantamount to legislating from the bench as well?

The President. You'd have to tell me the case and advise me as to how—I don't think so. I don't think when called upon to answer a constitutional question that that has to be legislating from the bench.

Q. You would not be upset if the Court overturned *Roe* v. *Wade,* or if the courts upheld the flag burning law?

The President. No, and a lot of other things, too. I believe in the separation of powers, and I happen to think that there's been many, many things that trouble me—encroachment of micromanagement by the United States Congress on the Presidency. But I haven't asked this able judge about those things. But I could cite—you cite two—you cite one that's been on everybody's lips ever since Justice Brennan retired. Listen, I never heard such coverage on the television. You might think the

whole nomination had something to do with abortion. And it's far broader than that. I have too much respect for the Supreme Court than to look at one specific issue and one alone.

I've got time for one. Yes, Kathy [Kathy Lewis, Houston Post]?

Q. Mr. President, there had been some speculation you might name an Hispanic this time and make history in doing so. You went a different route. What do you say to those who might be disappointed that didn't happen, and what is the likelihood you might name a Hispanic should another vacancy develop?

The President. First, I say to whoever it is that inquires: I've made the best choice I possibly could make in terms of qualifications, ability, background, and temperament to serve on this Court. And then I say: look, the great thing about this country is you can achieve anything. There's a lot of time down the road in which I'm sure you'll see a different makeup on the Court. But I'm not going to deal in any one specific group vis-a-vis another one. That's what I would say.

I just would ask the American people to understand I looked at a wide array of names prior to my getting into it in as much depth as I have very recently. The Attorney General, his staff, Boyden Gray, and his staff went through this process. It's a process that's been going on for some time, and the excellence was just there at the top. And so, I would not cite this as something discouraging for anybody that aspires to the Supreme Court or any group that would aspire to have representation on the Supreme Court.

Listen, I really do have to go.

Q. What did you ask him when you interviewed him?

Q. Did he win in the interviews?

The President. He did very, very well. Let me get one. I failed to——

Q. Two or three of the candidates that were mentioned were from your home State, and there was talk that you perhaps would choose somebody from the South because you felt the South had been underrepresented since Justice Powell resigned. Wasn't anybody qualified in the

South, or——

The President. Plenty of people qualified. And you raise a good point, because there is nobody from what I would call the Southeast Conference South, but the South excluding Texas, that is on the bench now. And there's about a quarter of the people from there. So, this is a consideration and was a consideration that was forcefully brought home to me by key Members of Congress. And yet I determined that Judge Souter, given the qualifications I've tried to extol here, the virtues, is the choice for the Supreme Court at this time. But, no, these calls are not easy. And Kathy asked about different ethnic groups. You asked about regional distribution. And I think one considers all these criteria. I think it's fair to say that New England, which is not represented on the bench now that Justice Brennan is retired, might look at it if I had gone with

another nominee as, why were they excluded. So, I can understand regionalism. But please believe me, as a proud Texan I tried to look at it in a national sense. And I think I've come up with the best nominee.

Jessie [Jessica Lee, USA Today], I'm sorry to disappoint you.

Q. A very quick followup if I could: Senator Simpson suggested that you follow the counsel of Mrs. Bush. Did you in any way on this decision?

The President. How did he know? He doesn't even know who I nominated. How could he have said that?

Q. He said that he hoped that that would be what you would do.

The President. Oh, I see. Wonderful fellow, Al. [*Laughter*]

Note: The President spoke at 5:04 p.m. in the Briefing Room at the White House.

Designation of Robert Elsner as Chairman of the Marine Mammal Commission
July 23, 1990

The President today designated Robert Elsner to be Chairman of the Marine Mammal Commission. He would succeed William W. Fox, Jr.

Dr. Elsner has been a professor emeritus at the Institute of Marine Science at the University of Alaska in Fairbanks, AK. Prior to this he was a professor of marine science

at the Institute of Marine Science at the University of Alaska.

Dr. Elsner graduated from New York University (B.A., 1950) and the University of Washington (M.S., 1955; Ph.D., 1959). He was born June 3, 1920, in Boston, MA. He is married, has two children, and resides in Ester, AK.

Remarks at a Republican Party Fundraising Luncheon in Philadelphia, Pennsylvania
July 24, 1990

The President. Thank you, Elsie. For heaven's sakes, you talk about somebody that really gives of herself to help others, I think our national committeewoman, Elsie Hillman, fits that description to a tee. And I'll tell you, we Bushes love her, and we're very grateful to her. I want to salute Sena-

tor Arlen Specter, who came up with me on Air Force One today, and also Congressman Larry Coughlin, who was here—said he had to go back. I don't see him right now. Both of them fantastic Republicans, leading in the Senate and in the House, and I'm delighted to be with them both. I mentioned

Elsie Hillman, and I want to also say to Herb Barness, our new committeeman, we're proud of you, sir. And of course, my friend of longstanding, Anne Anstine, our State chairperson, chairwoman, who is doing a superb job—and a tough, but terribly important job. And I salute them all, the party leadership. And I hope you'll forgive me if I single out one who is priority, particularly this year, and I'm talking about the person that should be our next Governor for Pennsylvania: Barbara Hafer. Please get in there and work hard for her.

And to Matt and to Senator Jubelirer and the leaders of the legislature, let me assure you I want to do whatever I can to help your party leadership and all of you in strengthening our numbers at that legislative level. I still believe in federalism. I still believe that the answers that are best for all America are those that are closest to the people. And that argues, then, not just for the election of a Governor but argues for the need to have a Republican control of the houses of both legislative bodies in this State and in many other States as well. So, please do your best after August and the campaign heats up to help our outstanding candidates that have been recruited this year.

You know, we live in a remarkable age. Isn't it wonderful how everywhere you look in the world you see centralized bureaucracies crumbling—the removal of discredited, monolithic leadership and the inevitable rejection of the stagnant, tired dogma of the past.

Audience member. So, why are we funding death squads in El Salvador?

The President. Enough about the Democrats. [*Laughter*]

Audience member. Why are we funding death squads in El Salvador if monolithic leaderships are crumbling? We're paying $1 million a day to fund death squads in El Salvador.

The Audience. Boo!

The President. May I continue here? It's a wonderful thing about our system. You have an elected democracy in El Salvador—certifiably free elections—and then you have people come here to express their opinion. I think it's a wonderful thing. However, I would like to have a little—please—I

haven't even said anything yet, and I'm lying. [*Laughter*]

You know, it really is a wonderful deal. When you look around the world and see the move towards democracy and free elections and freedom, it is a wonderful thing. So, I used to get all uptight when I'd hear these little protests that would come up. And I'd say, no, these people feel strongly about it; let them have their say. And then a little politeness should prevail, and the guy that's up here speaking ought to be given his day in court. So, don't get all upset about it. I run into this all the time.

I'm sorry to hit and run, but two reasons. As Herb said, I'm off to an inspiring neighborhood action program. And then they did tell me that broccoli was on the menu, and I am staying with my position. [*Laughter*] You know I never change my position on anything. [*Laughter*]

It is easy to understand why the Republican Party held its very first national convention here in Philadelphia and why this was once the Nation's Capital. For three centuries now, Philadelphia has shown the world the true meaning in the measure of freedom. It was here that William Penn founded a colony—considered an unusual, even impossible experiment back then—where people of diverse ethnic and religious backgrounds could live peacefully together, free to work and worship as they chose. And here, just over a mile from where I stand, the Declaration of Independence and the American Constitution were signed—documents the free world has always revered, that now inspire people newly free, from Managua to Gdansk in Poland.

And those documents find meaning in the spirit of the people that sustain them. So, the appointment of a Supreme Court Justice becomes one of the most serious responsibilities facing any President. The Supreme Court must be guided by independent minds. Its members are appointed for life, largely to keep them above the flames of political passion. So, in my nomination of Judge David Souter for Senate confirmation, to fill the seat vacated by Justice William Brennan, there was no single issue, no litmus test or standard, dominating my decision to nominate. And I will add: There should be no litmus test in the process of confirmation. My sole priority was to appoint a Justice true to the life and the spirit of the Constitution, a priority that I'm confident will also guide the Congress in the confirmation process.

America has a longstanding tradition of judicial restraint, going all the way back to the convictions held by a Philadelphian named James Wilson, one of the first Justices of the American Supreme Court, whose writings spoke against adventurous pronouncements on policy by the Court. I believe I'm recommending an individual with a strong, incisive, independent devotion to interpreting the Constitution. He's a quiet man of enormous intellectual strength, a tough trial court judge with a great legal mind and an impartial quality that will serve the Court well. I've nominated this man, David Souter, because I believe his combination of education, experience, and integrity are second to none. And he's a man of great judgment, and I firmly believe that he will be a great Justice on our Supreme Court.

In that light, let me just say a word about the key role that our Attorney General, Dick Thornburgh, has played not only in this search but in working so hard for other things we all believe in. What an outstanding job he's doing for the Nation and, I would also say, for the people of Pennsylvania. And every once in a while, the flak gets pretty heavy down there. But I wanted you, his friends, to know that this President is proud of him, stands by him, and I think we have an outstanding Attorney General.

This city and State have always stood as a focal point of freedom, a center of intellectual, economic, and humanitarian development through three centuries of revolutionary ideas. Today, in this room, that spirit continues, carried on by those who believe in limited government and the accountability of leaders. You're showing the people of Pennsylvania that there is a Republican alternative, a new American independence from big government, from burgeoning bureaucracies—free from these things—from the invasive experiments of the big spenders.

There is room in the Republican Party for differences on some issues, but on principles we stand united, because there is work to be done. And we Republicans know what works. We believe that power has only one purpose—to help people. We believe that America transcends adversity and finds her greatest strength in diversity. And we are, as we always have been, a nation of quiet strength, tolerance, faith, freedom. So, we seek this new American independence for the sake of limited government that spends within its means and a new agenda of unlimited empowerment for the individual.

Right now, the Congress and I are working hard to put America's fiscal house in order, to put the spending policies that brought us to this point behind us. For all of the appropriation bills that have passed the House, our Federal budget called for just under $188 billion. Well, Congress has appropriated over $202 billion. In fact, seven out of eight of those Democrat-controlled House appropriations bills have already surpassed the budget authority that we requested. As long as spending runs out of control in Congress, the American people will pay the price.

There's nothing compassionate about building ever-larger, ineffective, centralized bureaucracies and then adding to the deficit to pay for them. All of us, on both sides of the aisle, in all branches and levels of government, need to stop looking for new ways to spend the people's money and stop measuring success by dollars spent and bureaucracies built and start measuring our actions by how well they empower people. We have to stop asking, "How much are we spending?" and start asking, "Is it working?" And all of us, Republicans and Democrats, deserve and should demand real budget reform—through enhanced rescission or a line-item veto or a balanced budget amendment—some discipline on the process.

Last Tuesday only seven votes stood between victory and defeat in the House for that balanced budget amendment, an amendment that would have disciplined the executive branch and certainly disciplined the legislative branch. Well, this budget charade, these fiscal follies, must end. And I salute those Democrats in the leadership who are now working with me—and several of them were in the Oval Office before I left to come up here—trying to achieve a bipartisan agreement that we all can live with, that would be good for our country, good for everybody around the world who are affected by these ever-increasing deficits.

In the hope for a better future, let me tell you just a little about the recent past. We believe that nothing is more precious than America's children, and so, we put together child-care legislation to put choice in the hands of all families, whether low- or middle-income. We want to help families get the kind of child care they want, whether at home or at church or a synagogue or from a local child-care provider.

Well, the Senate passed a more restrictive child-care bill that takes choice out of the hands of parents, piles more redtape on providers, and builds a bigger day-care bureaucracy at double the cost of our bill—from $9 billion to $18 billion. And then the House, deciding spending equals compassion, outdid the Senate by tripling my request to $29 billion. And there you have a classic budget-busting bidding war—another $20 billion added to the deficit over the next 5 years.

But that wild spending habit is hard to break. Our emergency assistance to Panama and Nicaragua—after 3 long months, our $800 million package had doubled in cost not with emergency aid but with over $1 billion of new, unrequested, unrelated domestic spending. Our Educational Excellence Act—designed to advance educational reform, reward achievement, and encourage accountability and choice—started at a cost of $400 million, but increased to $1.4 billion as costly and unrelated changes were piled on, more than tripling my original request. And it's time we left the tradition of runaway spending behind.

In the budget negotiations now underway, I'm encouraged by the kind of cooperation that we're seeing from both sides of the aisle. I'm hopeful we can break this spending spiral, reach a real budget agreement, and bring about meaningful reform.

But there are clear differences between the parties, and when the voters understand those differences, I think our side wins. Do the voters want a party that rewards excellence in education and empowers local school boards and parents, or the Democrats who've empowered the Washington bureaucracy to limit parental control in the lives of their children? We say the Republicans. Do they want the empowerment of a million new private homeowners or the same old Democratic welfare handouts that stifle hope and devastate our cities? Again, we say the Republicans. And do they want the empowerment of choice in child care—private centers, churches, consortiums, in homes—or do they want government designed day-care centers to warehouse the kids, all run out of Washington? And the answer again is clear—the Republicans.

So, here in Pennsylvania and across the country, we need Republican leadership that understands the value of limited government and the power of the people themselves. You've already got two Republican U.S. Senators who are, in my view, doing an outstanding job. And now, if you believe in this philosophy that I've tried to articulate here today, Pennsylvania needs a Republican Governor—for education reform, for mass transit and better highways, and for better government, government that wouldn't take a $348 million surplus inherited from Dick Thornburgh's administration and turn it into a projected $1 billion deficit. So, the bottom line: Pennsylvania needs Barbara Hafer, needs her bad.

And we need to keep the State senate in Republican hands under Bob Jubelirer's leadership, and we need State senators like Joe Rocks right here in Philadelphia and outstanding new Republican challengers here and across the State. And this year we have a chance to give Republican leadership back to the State house of representatives and make Matt Ryan the next speaker, and believe me, that would help in getting Pennsylvania under control.

Matt and John Perzel have been all over the State recruiting outstanding candidates. And the candidates for both houses are letting Pennsylvania know that there is an alternative to the invasive and destructive tax-and-spend policies of the past. Some may define empowerment as giving government more power to control the people, but we in the party of Lincoln understand that empowerment means individual freedom, and that government exists to serve.

Those who still struggle in this society want opportunity, not paternalism; a hand up, not a handout; not the servitude of welfare and public warehousing but jobs, private property, prosperity. Nobody wants to be dependent; they want a new declaration of independence.

So, keep fighting for it here in Philadelphia. Keep reminding the people of Pennsylvania that we stand for good government. They deserve nothing less.

Thank you for this wonderful support for our party, for our ticket. Thank you all. And may God bless you, and may God bless the Commonwealth of Pennsylvania. Thank you very, very much.

Note: The President spoke at 12:32 p.m. in the Windham Ballroom at the Franklin Plaza Hotel. In his remarks, he referred to Matthew Ryan and John Perzel, State representatives.

Nomination of Ryan Clark Crocker To Be United States Ambassador to Lebanon
July 24, 1990

The President today announced his intention to nominate Ryan Clark Crocker to be Ambassador Extraordinary and Plenipotentiary of the United States of America to the Republic of Lebanon. He would succeed Thomas McCarthy.

Since 1987 Mr. Crocker has served as political counsel at the U.S. Embassy in Cairo, Egypt. Prior to this, he served as Deputy Director of the Office of Israel and Arab-Israeli Affairs at the State Department,

1985–1987. Mr. Crocker served as chief of the political section at the U.S. Embassy in Beirut, Lebanon, 1981–1984. In addition, he served in various capacities in Iran, Qatar, Tunis, and Iraq. Mr. Crocker joined the Foreign Service in 1971.

Mr. Crocker graduated from Whitman College (B.A., 1971) and attended University College in Dublin, Ireland. He was born June 19, 1949, in Spokane, WA. Mr. Crocker is married and resides in Cairo, Egypt.

Statement by Press Secretary Fitzwater on the Appointment of the United States Representatives to the Board of Trustees of the Regional Environmental Center for Central and Eastern Europe
July 24, 1990

The administration today named Frank Loy, John Schmitz, and Helen Petrauskas as the three U.S. representatives to the Board of Trustees of the Regional Environmental Center for Central and Eastern Europe being established in Budapest, Hungary. All 3 have agreed to serve as part of a 15-member board that will oversee the operations of the Center. President Bush first proposed the Regional Center last year during his visit to Budapest.

At the President's request, Congress authorized $5 million for the Regional Environmental Center as part of the Support for Eastern European Democracy (SEED) Act of 1989. The United States and the Republic of Hungary signed an initial agreement in January outlining the goals and structures of the Center. Since then, the U.S. Environmental Protection Agency has been at work laying the operational groundwork for the Center. Today's appointments are effective immediately, although the Center's official opening will not take place until September 6, 1990, when EPA Administrator William K. Reilly will represent the President at the opening ceremony.

The Hungarian Government has committed approximately $800,000 for the Center's operations. When the Center's charter was signed on June 20, 1990, the European Community and The Netherlands joined as cofounders, offering financial support of $2.5 million and $250,000 respectively. The Governments of Austria and Norway have also indicated they will support the Center. Indeed, the list of founders is expected to grow as other governments sign the Center's charter before the official September opening.

Establishment of the Center comes as nations around the world look for ways to assist the Governments of Eastern Europe to institute economic and political reforms. The region is faced, in particular, with critical problems of air and water pollution due in large part to the region's dependency on soft coal, its lack of adequate waste treatment facilities, and the failure of centrally planned economies to give adequate priority to environmental protection.

Although the Regional Environmental Center is being funded initially by government contributions, it will be a nonprofit, independent organization dedicated to finding regional solutions to the environmental challenges common to Central and Eastern Europe. It will draw on business and other private resources. As a source of information and assistance to the citizens and governments of the region, the Center will place special emphasis on the role of nongovernment environmental organizations in

addressing these problems. The Center's charter outlines its mission in four categories: data collection and dissemination, development of institutional capabilities, education, and matching available resources with the needs in the region via a clearinghouse. The Center will focus initially on three major areas of concern: the impact of environmental degradation on health, energy efficiency, and pollution prevention.

The Center's day-to-day operations will be under the management of the Executive Director, Dr. Peter Hardi, a Hungarian who currently serves as the director of the Hungarian Institute of International Affairs and as a professor of political science at Budapest University of Economics.

Frank Loy, of Washington, DC, is the president of the German Marshall Fund of the United States, which sponsors several exchange programs with Eastern European countries. He is also chairman of the Environmental Defense Board. John Schmitz, of McLean, VA, currently serves as Deputy Counsel to the President for environmental and energy matters. Helen Petrauskas, of Davisburg, MI, is vice president for environment and safety engineering for the Ford Motor Co. The U.S. board members will be joined by representatives selected by the Governments of Hungary and other East European countries, the European Community, and Austria.

Also named today as the Center's first program manager was Stephen Wassersug. Mr. Wassersug is currently the Director of the Hazardous Waste Management Division for EPA Region III in Philadelphia. He has served in a number of Agency programs on air, water, and waste during his tenure with EPA.

Remarks at an Antidrug Rally in Philadelphia, Pennsylvania
July 24, 1990

Thank you, Herman. Thank all of you out there for that—thank you, sir, for that terrific welcome. And let me just say hello to all those that are outside, listening on the loud speakers. We know they're out there.

First, a heartfelt thanks to Herman Wrice, for that introduction and for all he's doing. I want to single out Reds Bagnell and Inspector Durkin and Al Wilson, of course, Herman, for all they're doing in leading this fight against drugs. You know, Mayor Goode was here a minute ago, and I was delighted to be with him and hear right from him firsthand about this fight and about the neighborhood's participation in it. And I also would like to give a hand to Cedrick Ward. What an outstanding job that guy did up here. Where are you, Cedrick? There he is. And I think it's a great thing that Charles Barkley is here, Reggie White, Mark Howe, Lionel Simmons, and so many others showing their support for what you are doing in these neighborhoods. I'm proud of you. You might not realize it, but while you're working away out here, America has been hearing you. It's listening to the tolling of a bright new sound: Philadelphians shouting firmly and defiantly to the terrorists who deal drugs, "We're beating the odds." And you are, and we're proud of you.

I love those teeshirts. I saw a couple of them: "Yes To Sports, No To Drugs." Another good message. I'm sure these four big guys will tell you that they appreciate it, too. You kids have the right idea—no crack in Philadelphia except for the one in the Liberty Bell.

But here's what I learned today. Here's what I learned today. Here in this birthplace of independence, you have another kind of independence. You don't have to depend on drugs or on dealers or on crime. You're free to believe in yourselves. And I love those teeshirts that say, too: "I Believe In Me." Well, I believe in you, too. Keep up that pride.

Let me tell you the two stories that stick in my mind as I learned about this Philadelphia Antidrug Coalition. In one, your neighborhood families, numbed by fear, routinely barricaded themselves inside their homes while the sounds of battle raged outside—the burst of gunfire in these drive-by shootings, the echoing threats of the drug dealers, and the shuffle of the zombie-like procession to the infested crack house next door.

And it was, in those days, a war zone of despair. But listen, that was from the past. And here's a story from today. An 11-year-old boy named James used to hang around the edge of those cleanup projects. And he didn't want to go home to his alcoholic mother. He needed money for shoes, but was too young to earn anything but the $15 that these drug pushers would pay him to be a lookout.

And you might say, well, why do I like this story? Because someone who cared found James. And he was Herman Wrice, the John Wayne of Philadelphia and this towering mountain of a man who started a whole movement by declaring war on a crack house with a sledgehammer. To James, living drug-free in the safety of the Wrice home, he is now "Dad."

My friends, you show that individual neighborhoods can, indeed, work together to restore hope and self-respect. You show that community commitment can extinguish the destructive blaze of crack burning up our streets and our kids. And you speak loudly and clearly. The adults are saying that no more children will be won over by these desperados of death. They're saying: We're not going to surrender to you. We're taking back our kids, and we're taking back our streets. That's the message from Philadelphia to Washington, DC.

And you kids out here, just a word to you guys—you're the ones we're proudest of because you're saying: Hey, I believe in me. I believe I'm worthwhile, and I'm not going to waste my life for the filth of your crack houses. And I'm going to believe in something bigger than that; I'm going to believe in my community and my life and my family and in my future.

You've formed this antidrug olympics I've been hearing about and these after-school activities as an alternative to drugs. You've stood on the streetcorners—I love that. For those who are not from this neighborhood, let me tell you about that. They stand on the streetcorners all night long, bearing witness by your presence to the victory being won. And drug dealers see them coming, and they scatter like cockroaches in a sudden burst of light. In an America that worships heroes, in your own way, you are the real thing.

We're also excited about this Operation PEARL, an unprecedented effort to uncover and destroy the dark, dirty roots of drug corruption one neighborhood at a time. This experiment that I've heard about today in community-government cooperation combines the services of city, State, Federal agencies, all with local volunteers. And it embodies the sort of vision and success that our drug czar [William J. Bennett, Director of National Drug Control Policy] in Washington has encouraged since taking command of our drug war.

You know, America has waited too long. And now we've got to move forward to help in Washington with the crime bill and other pieces of legislation, because you are getting your job done right here—in efforts like the all-night bonfire vigil one rainy night, when 300 of you in white hardhats closed down drug action on Indiana Avenue. When you lit that first bonfire, you were lighting more than just one flame against the cold: you were setting up a beacon of hope against evil, a symbol to other communities in despair.

So, in conclusion, you know, I remember the westerns of my youth—the good guys wore the white hats, and they stood firmly and proudly for morality. I am glad to see that right here in this precious neighborhood in Philadelphia the good guys still wear the white hats, still stand firmly and proudly for those same virtues. Now, Herman put it this way. He said he'll take off his hat on the streets of Philadelphia "only when we win this war." Well, I know that I'll return one day and find you out there bareheaded, with your neighbors—strong, drug-free—at your side.

Thank you for this example that you are setting for the entire United States of America. I leave impressed, inspired, and determined to do my part to help you kids in your fight against drugs. Thank you all very, very much.

Note: The President spoke at 1:58 p.m. in the West Philadelphia Community Center. Prior to his remarks, he visited a preschool class at the center.

Nomination of Jerome H. Powell To Be an Assistant Secretary of the Treasury
July 24, 1990

The President today announced his intention to nominate Jerome H. Powell to be an Assistant Secretary of the Treasury for Domestic Finance. He would succeed David W. Mullins, Jr.

Since 1984 Mr. Powell has served as an investment banker with the firm of Dillion, Read and Co., Inc. Prior to this, he was an attorney with Werbel and McMillin, 1983–1984; an attorney with the firm of Davis Polk and Wardwell, 1981–1983; and a law

clerk for Judge E.A. van Graafeiland of the U.S. Court of Appeals for the Second Circuit, 1979–1980. He was a legislative assistant for Senator Richard Schweiker, 1975–1976.

Mr. Powell graduated from Princeton University (B.A., 1975) and Georgetown University Law Center (J.D., 1979). He was born February 4, 1953, in Washington, DC. He is married, has two children, and resides in Pelham, NY.

Nomination of Edward P. Brynn To Be United States Ambassador to Burkina Faso
July 24, 1990

The President today announced his intention to nominate Edward P. Brynn to be

Ambassador Extraordinary and Plenipotentiary of the United States of America to

Burkina Faso. He would succeed David H. Shinn.

Since 1989 Dr. Brynn has served as a member of the Senior Seminar at the Foreign Service Institute. Prior to this, he was deputy chief of mission in Yaounde, Cameroon, 1987–1989; Chargé d'Affaires in Moroni, Comoros Islands, 1985–1987; and deputy chief of mission in Nouakchott, Mauritania, 1982–1985. He served as a staff member on the Senate Select Committee on Intelligence, 1981–1982. Dr. Brynn served at the Bureau of African Affairs, 1980–1981; political officer in Bamako, Mali, 1978–1980; Foreign Service officer in residence at the U.S. Air Force Academy, 1976–1978; and as a political and economic officer in Sri Lanka, 1973–1975. Dr. Brynn served in the U.S. Air Force, 1968–1972.

Dr. Brynn graduated from Georgetown University (B.A., 1964) and Stanford University (M.A., 1965; Ph.D., 1968). He was born August 1, 1942, in Pittsburgh, PA. Dr. Brynn is married, has five children, and resides in Washington, DC.

Accordance of the Personal Rank of Ambassador to Bradley Gordon While Serving on the Nuclear Non-Proliferation Treaty Review Conference Preparatory Committee
July 24, 1990

The President today accorded the personal rank of Ambassador to Bradley Gordon in his capacity as Alternate Head of Delegation to the 1990 Nuclear Non-Proliferation Treaty Review Conference Preparatory Committee.

Since 1990 Dr. Gordon has served as Assistant Director of the U.S. Arms Control and Disarmament Agency in the Bureau of Nuclear Weapons and Control at the Department of State in Washington, DC. Prior to this he was legislative assistant in the office of Senator Rudy Boschwitz, 1987–1989. He was a professional staff member for the Senate Committee on Foreign Relations, 1985–1987; political analyst for the Central Intelligence Agency in the Office of Near Eastern/South Asian Analysis, 1979–1985; research assistant with the Middle East Institute at Columbia University, 1975–1976; and a research assistant with the Bureau of Applied Social Research at Columbia University, 1975.

Dr. Gordon graduated from Brandeis University (B.A., 1971), University of Vermont (M.A., 1974), and Columbia University (Ph.D., 1979). He was born May 22, 1949, in Burlington, VT. He is married, has three children, and resides in Reston, VA.

Remarks at a Republican Party Fundraising Dinner in New York, New York
July 24, 1990

Thank you all. Thank you so much, Senator. And let me say how very pleased I am to be here. A salute first to Senator D'Amato, who's doing such a superb job in Washington. He and I have to leave before the broccoli to get back to—[*laughter*]—get back down there, so I hope you'll excuse us. But let me salute my old friend, the borough president. Mr. President, we're proud of you—Guy Molinari.

And of course, our senate leader, Ralph Marino—I just met with him, and we talked about the importance of keeping control of this senate, given the significance of redis-

1061

tricting coming up. It is absolutely essential, and thus I want to thank everybody that has helped in this dinner. It is key that Ralph continue to run the senate on the Republican side. We've got to keep control of it.

And I expect, because of his responsibilities as head of this whole campaign for the senate, Guy Velella, over here, knows that he's got some big shoes to fill, too—big responsibilities. Rapp, it's good to see you again—Rapp Rappleyea, the leader over here on our—I wish we had some more troops for him, and maybe we will out of this selection on the assembly. I want to salute our able party chairman, Pat Barrett, a man who's given up an awful lot to lead our troops; and my old friend Dick Rosenbaum, the national committeeman; Comptroller Ned Regan; and Bernard Smith, running here. Is it okay to mention my brother John? Okay. All right. And I'm going to be in real trouble, but Rita—Rita DiMartino, I see her all over the place. She's like Batman—she's everywhere. And Joe Mondello and many other leaders. I'm very pleased to be here. I want to single out two, however, who deserve our support. They have mine, and they are going to surprise a lot of people: Pierre Rinfret for Governor, and Geff Yancey. We need them. They're a good team. They've got great families.

You know, for 2 years, when I was Ambassador to the U.N., Barbara and I lived up here, in this—rough living here in this very hotel, room 42–A. And whenever I complained about anything, the Silver Fox would roll her eyes and say, "Just where do you think we live? The Waldorf Astoria?" Well, here we are back again, and I'm pleased to be here. And I understand that New York has been selected as the site of a very important event in 1992—a convention that will attract thousands of participants from all over the country, people who hope to put their past setbacks behind them and plan a winning strategy for the future. That's right, the first reunion of all the ex-managers of the New York Yankees will be held right here in New York City. [*Laughter*]

Then there's the other future New York convention: the Democrats'. Let me say that my hand is still extended to them

when it comes to working for the good of the Nation. I look forward to the Senate hearings of David Souter. I am sure that they will find him to be tough, but fair. He's a first-rate appellate judge, an outstanding jurist, and a great legal mind. And I am delighted that he is the nominee for the Supreme Court.

Many Democrats in Washington have supported me in meeting this fantastic era of change abroad that Al D'Amato so generously referred to, are working with me now to pass the first revision of the Clean Air Act in more than 13 years—tougher standards to cut down on acid rain and other air pollutants. And they worked with me so I could sign into law a bill ending discrimination against disabled Americans. So, tough negotiations can get results. I see Amory Houghton out here, and he and other Congressmen on the Republican side know this. They're in the minority, but they're working hard. Tough negotiations can get results. But differences between the parties are still broad, and they're still deep, and much remains to be done—too much. With more Republicans in Washington and in Albany, think of how much more we can achieve.

In New York, we face a tremendous opportunity to fight the Democrat gerrymander, an opportunity to end discrimination against voters by race and by party. That is our mission this November. That is our mission, and it is one that transcends mere politics because we're deeply concerned about the future of this great State.

To coin a phrase, we love New York, all of New York, from the oak-lined avenues of Long Island to Yankee Stadium to Broadway. From the city streets of Buffalo to the New York of farm towns and the Adirondacks, New York is a city of lights, a State of grandeur, a place where dreams come true. It certainly is for me. After all, New York is where Barbara Bush was born, and she's doing pretty darn well.

But we are concerned for the future because New York has become something else: It's become a showcase of liberal policies. And after 16 years of dominance by liberal Democrats, it's time to judge the results.

For 92 months, America has enjoyed peacetime economic expansion and the creation of more than 22 million jobs. But not all the benefits of those years were enjoyed by the people of New York State. Throughout the 1980's, while most of America was growing and looking forward to the future, life in New York, especially in the city, was becoming more expensive, more difficult, and more dangerous, regrettably, than ever before.

Liberal Democrats blame every problem on Republican policies, especially Republican economic policies. But in the late seventies, a large airline centered in New York didn't go out of business; it just decided to move south to Texas, taking more than a thousand jobs with it. And in 1987, a large energy corporation based in New York didn't go out of business; it just decided to move south to Virginia, taking 3,600 jobs with it. In fact, since 1983 almost a third of the Fortune 500 corporations based here have chosen to leave.

Now New Yorkers want a change. New Yorkers want the companies and the good jobs they represent to stay right here in New York. And New Yorkers want an end to open-air drug marts and these muggings. And New Yorkers want a government that empowers people, not bureaucracies.

Twenty-nine out of the last 35 years of Democratic dominance in Congress have also taken their toll. Only a President carries a national mandate. But like Republicans before me, I know that to deal with a Democrat Congress is to often face government by gridlock, with spending skyrocketing out of control, good legislation thrown aside for pork, and a budget deficit looming over our children's children.

It is time we asked the American people to end the gridlock—to choose the liberal mindset of the Democratic Party or to choose our path, the Republican path of opportunity and growth; to empower government to run their lives or to empower people to run their lives for themselves. Time to ask America to choose.

Here in New York, you must choose a Governor. And let it be a Republican Governor: Pierre Rinfret. Here's a family man—I hope you've all met his family—a decorated war hero, a successful entrepreneur who pulled himself out of Hell's Kitchen and wants to lead others out of poverty. And some say maybe he's not a politician. Well, he may not be a politician, but maybe New York doesn't need another politician. Maybe New York needs a change right now. So, Pierre, we are all for you—you and your ticket. Best of luck!

You know, New York faces another choice: to keep your outstanding senate leader, Ralph Marino, and his colleagues as your prime line of defense against a liberal Governor and his assembly. Republicans, you see, like what works. And that's why your Republican senate has been, and will remain, your watchdog against big spenders and, more, a sane proponent of what works.

So, be thankful that your Republicans in the senate forced a spending cap, forced baseline budgeting. It is the Republicans in the New York Senate who managed to trim $1½ billion in Democratic spending proposals. They know you can't trust a party that would double the fare of the Staten Island Ferry. [*Laughter*] And kidding aside, think of what these Republicans would achieve if they could work with a Republican Governor and a Republican assembly.

Jobs and spending are important, but safe streets are of equal concern, especially in a city that lives in fear. And that's why New York agrees with us: Those violent criminals deserve nothing less than punishment, swift and sure. So, Republicans are united in wanting to change lenient, blame-the-victim laws; liberal Democrats don't want to change these laws. Republicans want to allow the women of this State to be able to defend themselves with Mace, and liberal Democrats don't. And Republicans—and this is a big one nationally—Republicans want murderers and drug kingpins to pay the ultimate penalty, and liberal Democrats don't.

In Washington, we argue that those who sell drugs are selling death, and we propose that drug kingpins reap what they sow. But our crime bill faces another obstacle. Fifteen months ago, I stood before the U.S. Capitol and announced America's determination to take back the streets. The Senate has now cleared a crime bill—Al D'Amato fighting for it—a major new package, 423 days after I proposed it. It's not a perfect bill. It does nothing to ensure that evidence gathered by good, decent policemen acting in good faith isn't barred by technicalities that let bad people go free. But this bill will go a long way toward toughening sentences for violent crime and reducing repetitive appeals. Now, this legislation is over in the House side now, before the House. And let us tell the Members of the House: 423 days is long enough. Don't keep our men and women in blue waiting. Pass a tough bill, and pass it soon.

Let me give you another example of how a liberal Congress, long in power, jealously clings to the failed policies of the past. In April of last year, our administration asked Congress to pass the Education Excellence Act, reform proposals to reward achievement and allow educational choice. And yet Congress killed many of these sensible and cost-effective proposals, and then they doubled our request with hundreds of millions of dollars' worth of unnecessary, unrelated and costly changes.

If liberal Democrats should have learned anything, it is that you cannot reform an education system by throwing billions of dollars at it. So, when is it going to penetrate liberal thinking that we shouldn't throw money at an ineffective education system that is already the most expensive in the entire industrialized world? When are they going to start demanding results and stop measuring the value of a program by the size of its price tag? And when are they going to stop blocking genuine, much-needed reform?

Where the liberal mindset dominates, the net result has been the same: bad schools, dangerous streets, big deficits. Of course, times can change, and I hope they do. As you know, I met this morning, and will meet every morning this week, with the congressional leadership—the Speaker and the Democratic leader and the minority leader on the House side and the two Senate leaders, one Republican, one Democrat on the Senate—met to work for an agreement to lower our Federal deficit. We all know that the Democrats have a long track record on spending. But if the Berlin Wall could come down in the same year that America goes nuts over the Teenage Mutant Ninja Turtles, who knows what could happen next?

And again, times can change. The leaders of Congress can work with me to break the impasse on reducing the budget deficit, and I think they are trying. I've saluted Dick Gephardt, and I'll do it here again tonight. I believe he's trying hard. He's the one that has to lead this enormously diverse group into trying to get a deal. The spotlight is on both sides to place progress over partisanship and the national interest over special interest. I welcome sincere efforts from both sides of the aisle, and I'm eager to get an agreement with congressional leaders to achieve meaningful budget reform. And this is my hope, but as long as the liberal mindset dominates, we will be forced to measure our successes in catastrophes averted and calamities mitigated.

The genius of the American system is that it allows for checks and balances; but this doesn't mean that the voters must choose political stalemate, year after year, decade after decade. So, let me be blunt: Divided government just isn't good enough for America or for New York. We must have more Republicans up there in Albany and in Washington. And I think it's time to ask the American people to let us show what we can do without the albatross of liberal legislatures. It's time to ask America to choose.

As we go into the 1990 election season, remember an adage from a great Republican Governor of New York and a great President. Theodore Roosevelt said, "In life, as in a football game, the principle to follow is: Hit the line hard." The choice is clear: Republican reform or the Democratic status quo. And when we present the people with this stark choice, rest assured, we will hit the line hard in November.

Thank you for all you have done to help this party. We are pledged to be in there supporting Pierre Rinfret and the rest of the ticket. May God bless you, and God bless the United States of America. Thank you all very, very much.

Note: The President spoke at 7:50 p.m. in the Grand Ballroom at the Waldorf Astoria Hotel. In his remarks, he referred to Clar-

ence D. Rappleyea, State assembly minority leader; Pat Barrett, State Republican Party committee chairman; Dick Rosenbaum, Republican national committeeman; Ned Regan, State comptroller; Bernard Smith, Republican candidate for State attorney general; John Bush, former official of the State Republican Party; Rita DiMartino, State Republican Party committee vice chairwoman; Joe Mondello, Nassau County Republican Party chairman; Geff Yancey, Republican candidate for Lieutenant Governor; Thomas S. Foley, Speaker of the House of Representatives; Richard A. Gephardt, House majority leader; Robert H. Michel, House Republican leader; Robert Dole, Senate Republican leader; and George J. Mitchell, Senate majority leader. A tape was not available for verification of the content of these remarks.

Remarks at a Ceremony Commemorating Captive Nations Week
July 25, 1990

The President. Thank you very much, and welcome—welcome to the Rose Garden. And a special welcome to some of our guests—to all of you—but to some special guests today. Of course, I'm very pleased the Vice President is with me for this special occasion; Secretary Derwinski over here, who's been a leader in all of this for many, many years; and of course, our Deputy Secretary, Larry Eagleburger—Deputy Secretary of State; and Dick Carlson, the head of the Voice. And so many of our friends from Congress, welcome to all of you. And a special, again, salute and welcome to all of you who have been in the forefront of the captive nations cause for so many years.

You know, for the last 32 years, Presidents from Eisenhower to Reagan have commemorated the ongoing struggle of captive nations. And traditionally, this one has been the ceremony to commemorate the ongoing struggle of these nations, to bear witness to the suffering of millions—a ceremony to honor courage, a ceremony to tell everyone still in captivity that they are not forgotten. These previous captive nations ceremonies have not been moments of joy but really, rather, of serious rededication and sadness that so many in our world lived in the throes of tyranny.

The Revolution of 1989 was stunning—thrilling, clearly a historic time. And at this ceremony last year, we told the world that we would keep faith with those who were oppressed; and we did. And then taking their lives into their own hands, the very people who are in our hearts crafted an unforgettable year of triumph—the triumph of brave hearts, the triumph of people declaring they would control their own destinies. And last summer while we were in Eastern Europe, Barbara and I sensed that excitement in the air, that some of you here had been telling me about. In meetings with the people of Poland and Hungary, I pledged America's strong support for their historic struggle. And like most Americans, we watched in joy as the barbed wire on that Austrian-Hungarian border came down. And we were deeply moved as the changes swept across the continent bringing within reach the vision of a Europe truly whole and free.

For four long decades, America and her allies have remained united and strong in our mission for peace and freedom. That strength has at long last borne some fruit. What an amazing year this has been—a year of technicolor glory in lands that had been defined by these black watchtowers and walls, and the drab emptiness of lost dreams.

But we are gathered here today not just to celebrate the joyous change of this past year but to celebrate it in a very special way. With us today are some of the young people whose countries were a part of this Revolution of '89. And each is proud of his country. And it's easy to understand why they believe in themselves and in their homelands. For the bold and brilliant light of freedom now illuminates their world. And so, to honor that shining faith in the future, I dedicate this day to this new generation of freedom and to future generations who will never have to bear the burden of tyranny. For some of this new generation this freedom means a whole new world in their own backyard. On that unforgettable morning when the East German borders fell, parents gathered up their kids and brought them to the Brandenburg Gate, the final symbol of tyranny in Berlin. And still in their pajamas, these children on this day of new freedom were passed up from friendly hand to friendly hand to have the thrill of sitting on top of the wall, looking across at the endless horizon of their dreams. And now, a new generation is coming of age in freedom.

In the audience today is a group of young interns from Poland, Hungary, and Czechoslovakia. Supported by funding from private American organizations, they are spending the summer working and learning in our great country. And one is working with the speaker of North Carolina's House of Delegates, another with a television station in Washington, another with the U.S. Chamber of Commerce. And they are here learning how a free society works and will return to build a free Poland, a free Hungary, a free Czechoslovakia.

But while we celebrate for those who are now free, we must also remember those who are not. And I continue to be moved by what I see and hear throughout the rest of the world where unfinished revolutions continue, one heroic story at a time. In the Americas, where a boy with nothing but a board and sail windsurfed to escape the politics of repression. In Asia, where iron tanks were met by the iron will of a courageous lone man. And today, I also want to remember especially the people of Latvia, Lithuania, and Estonia, and renew our unflagging support for their long quest for national self-determination. The road ahead is going to be difficult. But we can now join them in looking forward with hope to the day when their long-cherished dreams will become reality.

Alongside this success story of nations, we also hear quiet stories of individuals who, even in darkness, could see the vision of liberty; those who have risked everything in countries not yet free—the countries we must still remember today; the desperate people we must never forget, boys like Quang Trinh, a young Vietnamese teenager. He almost died escaping from the shattered life of a country where he had seen his mother killed, his father jailed, his brother's spirits broken. Quang fled the only life he had known for freedom. And he jumped into shark-infested waters for freedom. And he starved in delirium for freedom. And after he was finally rescued and told he could enter the United States, he wept all night long.

When did something touch our lives so completely that we cried for joy through the entire night? Quang calls America "freedom country." And how many of us have stopped to think of our homeland in those terms? You know, on my desk inside there in the Oval Office, I have two special mementos with me at all times. One is a small American flag, given to me in an army hospital by a soldier wounded while fighting to free our friends in Panama. It represents America's commitment to freedom and to proud people wherever they may be who seek that freedom. And the other souvenir is a piece of the Berlin Wall, one of the very first chiseled from that horrifying affront to humanity. I keep it as a reminder of the miracle which courage, strength, and unity can achieve. It's sitting right here. And I also wanted to bring with me today this piece of barbed wire which I brought to last year's ceremony—some of you may remember. It came from the Austria-Hungary border. And these two symbols of tyranny should never be forgotten.

Sitting in this peaceful Rose Garden today are several generations of these nations of miracles, including the new generation. But there are also countries that are still waiting to be free. So let us all work together so that next year this dream of freedom extends to all those countries where it is now denied. Let us pray together that the light of liberty will shine across our entire planet and that the next Captive Nations Week will be the last. Thank you all for coming here, and God bless you for your steadfast commitment to freedom around the world.

Thank you all very, very much.

Note: The President spoke at 1:35 p.m. in the Rose Garden at the White House. In his *opening remarks, he referred to Secretary of Veterans Affairs Edward J. Derwinski and Richard W. Carlson, Associate Director for the Voice of America.*

Appointment of Richard W. Porter as Special Assistant to the President and Executive Secretary for the Domestic Policy Council
July 25, 1990

The President today announced the appointment of Richard W. Porter to be Special Assistant to the President and Executive Secretary for the Domestic Policy Council. Mr. Porter succeeds Kenneth P. Yale, who is assuming the position of Chief of Staff in the Office of Science and Technology Policy, Executive Office of the President.

Since February 1989 Mr. Porter has been the Deputy Assistant Secretary for Policy Review and Analysis at the Department of the Treasury. Prior to this he was an analyst and the chief writer on the domestic policy staff of Bush/Quayle '88. Mr. Porter also served as a law clerk to Judge Richard A. Posner on the U.S. Court of Appeals for the Seventh Circuit and worked as a lawyer/economist at Lexecon, Inc., a law and economics consulting firm in Chicago, IL.

Mr. Porter is a Phi Beta Kappa graduate of Middlebury College and received his law degree from the University of Chicago Law School, where he was awarded the John Olin Prize as the outstanding graduate in law and economics. Mr. Porter was born and raised in Mount Kisco, NY. He is married to the former Karen Louise Anderson of Barrington Hills, IL.

Remarks on Signing the Americans with Disabilities Act of 1990
July 26, 1990

Evan, thank you so much. And welcome to every one of you, out there in this splendid scene of hope, spread across the South Lawn of the White House. I want to salute the Members of the United States Congress, the House and the Senate who are with us today—active participants in making this day come true. This is, indeed, an incredible day—especially for the thousands of people across the Nation who have given so much of their time, their vision, and their courage to see this act become a reality.

You know, I started trying to put together a list of all the people who should be mentioned today. But when the list started looking a little longer than the Senate testimony for the bill, I decided I better give up, or that we'd never get out of here before sunset. So, even though so many de- serve credit, I will single out but a tiny handful. And I take those who have guided me personally over the years: of course, my friends Evan Kemp and Justin Dart, up here on the platform with me; and of course—I hope you'll forgive me for also saying a special word of thanks to two from the White House, but again, this is personal, so I don't want to offend those omitted—two from the White House, Boyden Gray and Bill Roper, who labored long and hard. And I want to thank Sandy Parrino, of course, for her leadership. And I again—it is very risky with all these Members of Congress here who worked so hard, but I can say on a very personal basis, Bob Dole has inspired me.

This is an immensely important day, a day that belongs to all of you. Everywhere I look, I see people who have dedicated themselves to making sure that this day would come to pass: my friends from Congress, as I say, who worked so diligently with the best interest of all at heart, Democrats and Republicans; members of this administration—and I'm pleased to see so many top officials and members of my Cabinet here today who brought their caring and expertise to this fight; and then, the organizations—so many dedicated organizations for people with disabilities, who gave their time and their strength; and perhaps most of all, everyone out there and others—across the breadth of this nation are 43 million Americans with disabilities. You have made this happen. All of you have made this happen. To all of you, I just want to say your triumph is that your bill will now be law, and that this day belongs to you. On behalf of our nation, thank you very, very much.

Three weeks ago we celebrated our nation's Independence Day. Today we're here to rejoice in and celebrate another "independence day," one that is long overdue. With today's signing of the landmark Americans for Disabilities Act, every man, woman, and child with a disability can now pass through once-closed doors into a bright new era of equality, independence, and freedom. As I look around at all these joyous faces, I remember clearly how many years of dedicated commitment have gone into making this historic new civil rights act a reality. It's been the work of a true coalition, a strong and inspiring coalition of people who have shared both a dream and a passionate determination to make that dream come true. It's been a coalition in the finest spirit—a joining of Democrats and Republicans, of the legislative and the executive branches, of Federal and State agencies, of public officials and private citizens, of people with disabilities and without.

This historic act is the world's first comprehensive declaration of equality for people with disabilities—the first. Its passage has made the United States the international leader on this human rights issue. Already, leaders of several other countries, including Sweden, Japan, the Soviet Union, and all 12 members of the EEC, have an-

nounced that they hope to enact now similar legislation.

Our success with this act proves that we are keeping faith with the spirit of our courageous forefathers who wrote in the Declaration of Independence: "We hold these truths to be self-evident, that all men are created equal, that they are endowed by their Creator with certain unalienable rights." These words have been our guide for more than two centuries as we've labored to form our more perfect union. But tragically, for too many Americans, the blessings of liberty have been limited or even denied. The Civil Rights Act of '64 took a bold step towards righting that wrong. But the stark fact remained that people with disabilities were still victims of segregation and discrimination, and this was intolerable. Today's legislation brings us closer to that day when no Americans will ever again be deprived of their basic guarantee of life, liberty, and the pursuit of happiness.

This act is powerful in its simplicity. It will ensure that people with disabilities are given the basic guarantees for which they have worked so long and so hard: independence, freedom of choice, control of their lives, the opportunity to blend fully and equally into the rich mosaic of the American mainstream. Legally, it will provide our disabled community with a powerful expansion of protections and then basic civil rights. It will guarantee fair and just access to the fruits of American life which we all must be able to enjoy. And then, specifically, first the ADA ensures that employers covered by the act cannot discriminate against qualified individuals with disabilities. Second, the ADA ensures access to public accommodations such as restaurants, hotels, shopping centers, and offices. And third, the ADA ensures expanded access to transportation services. And fourth, the ADA ensures equivalent telephone services for people with speech or hearing impediments.

These provisions mean so much to so many. To one brave girl in particular, they will mean the world. Lisa Carl, a young Washington State woman with cerebral palsy, who I'm told is with us today, now will always be admitted to her hometown theater. Lisa, you might not have been welcome at your theater, but I'll tell you—welcome to the White House. We're glad you're here. The ADA is a dramatic renewal not only for those with disabilities but for all of us, because along with the precious privilege of being an American comes a sacred duty to ensure that every other American's rights are also guaranteed.

Together, we must remove the physical barriers we have created and the social barriers that we have accepted. For ours will never be a truly prosperous nation until all within it prosper. For inspiration, we need look no further than our own neighbors. With us in that wonderful crowd out there are people representing 18 of the daily Points of Light that I've named for their extraordinary involvement with the disabled community. We applaud you and your shining example. Thank you for your leadership for all that are here today.

Now, let me just tell you a wonderful story, a story about children already working in the spirit of the ADA—a story that really touched me. Across the Nation, some 10,000 youngsters with disabilities are part of Little League's Challenger Division. Their teams play just like others, but—and this is the most remarkable part—as they play, at their sides are volunteer buddies from conventional Little League teams. All of these players work together. They team up to wheel around the bases and to field grounders together and, most of all, just to play and become friends. We must let these children be our guides and inspiration.

I also want to say a special word to our friends in the business community. You have in your hands the key to the success of this act, for you can unlock a splendid resource of untapped human potential that, when freed, will enrich us all. I know there have been concerns that the ADA may be vague or costly, or may lead endlessly to litigation. But I want to reassure you right now that my administration and the United States Congress have carefully crafted this Act. We've all been determined to ensure that it gives flexibility, particularly in terms of the timetable of implementation, and we've been committed to containing the costs that may be incurred.

This act does something important for American business, though—and remember this: You've called for new sources of workers. Well, many of our fellow citizens with disabilities are unemployed. They want to work, and they can work, and this is a tremendous pool of people. And remember, this is a tremendous pool of people who will bring to jobs diversity, loyalty, proven low turnover rate, and only one request: the chance to prove themselves. And when you add together Federal, State, local, and private funds, it costs almost $200 billion annually to support Americans with disabilities—in effect, to keep them dependent. Well, when given the opportunity to be independent, they will move proudly into the economic mainstream of American life, and that's what this legislation is all about.

Our problems are large, but our unified heart is larger. Our challenges are great, but our will is greater. And in our America, the most generous, optimistic nation on the face of the Earth, we must not and will not rest until every man and woman with a dream has the means to achieve it.

And today, America welcomes into the mainstream of life all of our fellow citizens with disabilities. We embrace you for your abilities and for your disabilities, for our similarities and indeed for our differences, for your past courage and your future dreams. Last year, we celebrated a victory of international freedom. Even the strongest person couldn't scale the Berlin Wall to gain the elusive promise of independence that lay just beyond. And so, together we rejoiced when that barrier fell.

And now I sign legislation which takes a sledgehammer to another wall, one which has for too many generations separated Americans with disabilities from the freedom they could glimpse, but not grasp. Once again, we rejoice as this barrier falls for claiming together we will not accept, we will not excuse, we will not tolerate discrimination in America.

With, again, great thanks to the Members of the United States Senate, leaders of whom are here today, and those who worked so tirelessly for this legislation on both sides of the aisles. And to those Members of the House of Representatives with us here today, Democrats and Republicans as well, I salute you. And on your behalf, as well as the behalf of this entire country, I now lift my pen to sign this Americans with Disabilities Act and say: Let the shameful wall of exclusion finally come tumbling down. God bless you all.

Note: The President spoke at 10:11 a.m. on the South Lawn of the White House. In his opening remarks, he referred to Evan Kemp, Chairman of the Equal Opportunity Employment Commission; Justin Dart, Chairman of the President's Committee for Employment of People With Disabilities; C. Boyden Gray, Counsel to the President; William L. Roper, Deputy Assistant to the President for Domestic Policy and Director of the Office of Policy Development; Sandy Parrino, chairperson of the National Council of Disabilities; and Robert Dole, Senate Republican leader. S. 933, approved July 26, was assigned Public Law No. 101–336.

Statement on Signing the Americans with Disabilities Act of 1990
July 26, 1990

Today, I am signing S. 933, the "Americans with Disabilities Act of 1990." In this extraordinary year, we have seen our own Declaration of Independence inspire the march of freedom throughout Eastern Europe. It is altogether fitting that the American people have once again given clear expression to our most basic ideals of freedom and equality. The Americans with Disabilities Act represents the full flowering of our democratic principles, and it gives me great pleasure to sign it into law today.

In 1986, on behalf of President Reagan, I personally accepted a report from the National Council on Disability entitled "Toward Independence." In that report, the National Council recommended the enactment of comprehensive legislation to ban discrimination against persons with disabilities. The Americans with Disabilities Act (ADA) is such legislation. It promises to open up all aspects of American life to individuals with disabilities—employment opportunities, government services, public accommodations, transportation, and telecommunications.

This legislation is comprehensive because the barriers faced by individuals with disabilities are wide-ranging. Existing laws and regulations under the Rehabilitation Act of 1973 have been effective with respect to the Federal Government, its contractors, and the recipients of Federal funds. However, they have left broad areas of American life untouched or inadequately addressed. Many of our young people, who have benefited from the equal educational opportunity guaranteed under the Rehabilitation Act and the Education of the Handicapped Act, have found themselves on graduation day still shut out of the mainstream of American life. They have faced persistent discrimination in the workplace and barriers posed by inaccessible public transportation, public accommodations, and telecommunications.

Fears that the ADA is too vague or too costly and will lead to an explosion of litigation are misplaced. The Administration worked closely with the Congress to ensure that, wherever possible, existing language and standards from the Rehabilitation Act were incorporated into the ADA. The Rehabilitation Act standards are already familiar to large segments of the private sector that are either Federal contractors or recipients of Federal funds. Because the Rehabilitation Act was enacted 17 years ago, there is already an extensive body of law interpreting the requirements of that Act. Employers can turn to these interpretations for guidance on how to meet their obligations under the ADA.

The Administration and the Congress have carefully crafted the ADA to give the business community the flexibility to meet the requirements of the Act without incurring undue costs. Cost may be taken into account in determining how an employee is "reasonably accommodated," whether the removal of a barrier is "readily achievable," or whether the provision of a particular auxiliary aid would result in an "undue burden." The ADA's most rigorous access requirements are reserved for new construction where the added costs of accessible features are minimal in relation to overall construction costs. An elevator exemption is provided for many buildings.

The careful balance struck between the rights of individuals with disabilities and the legitimate interests of business is shown in the various phase-in provisions in the ADA. For example, the employment provisions take effect 2 years from today for employers of 25 or more employees. Four years from today that coverage will be extended to employers with 15–24 employees. These phase-in periods and effective dates will permit adequate time for businesses to become acquainted with the ADA's requirements and to take the necessary steps to achieve compliance.

The ADA recognizes the necessity of educating the public about its rights and responsibilities under the Act. Under the ADA, the Attorney General will oversee Government-wide technical assistance activities. The Department of Justice will consult with the Architectural and Transportation Barriers Compliance Board, the Equal Employment Opportunity Commission, the Department of Transportation, the Federal Communications Commission, the National Council on Disability, and the President's

Committee on Employment of People with Disabilities, among others, in the effort. We will involve trade associations, advocacy groups, and other similar organizations that have existing lines of communications with covered entities and persons with disabilities. The participation of these organizations is a key element in assuring the success of the technical assistance effort.

In signing this landmark bill, I pledge the full support of my Administration for the Americans with Disabilities Act. It is a great honor to preside over the implementation of the responsibilities conferred on the executive branch by this Act. I pledge that we will fulfill those responsibilities efficiently and vigorously.

The Americans with Disabilities Act presents us all with an historic opportunity. It signals the end to the unjustified segregation and exclusion of persons with disabilities from the mainstream of American life. As the Declaration of Independence has been a beacon for people all over the world seeking freedom, it is my hope that the Americans with Disabilities Act will likewise come to be a model for the choices and opportunities of future generations around the world.

GEORGE BUSH

The White House,
July 26, 1990.

Note: S. 933, approved July 26, was assigned Public Law No. 101–336.

Appointment of Michael P. Jackson as Special Assistant to the President and Executive Secretary for Cabinet Liaison
July 26, 1990

The President today announced the appointment of Michael P. Jackson to be Special Assistant to the President and Executive Secretary for Cabinet Liaison.

Since January 1990 Mr. Jackson has served as Executive Secretary for Cabinet Liaison at the White House. From January 1989 to December 1989, he served as Associate Director in the White House Office of

Cabinet Affairs. From 1986 to 1988, Mr. Jackson worked in the Office of the Secretary at the Department of Education, first as Special Assistant for Public Affairs and later as Special Assistant to the Secretary. Mr. Jackson has worked for the White House Conference on Small Business and the American Enterprise Institute and has taught political science at the University of

Georgia and Georgetown University.

Mr. Jackson graduated from the University of Houston (B.A.) and Georgetown University (Ph.D.). He is married and resides in Alexandria, VA.

Letter to Congressional Leaders Transmitting the Report of the Test of Television Broadcasting Into Cuba
July 27, 1990

Dear _____:

Enclosed please find the report on the findings of the test of television broadcasting to Cuba required by section 247(b)(2) of Public Law 101–246.

Sincerely,

GEORGE BUSH

Note: Identical letters were sent to Claiborne Pell and Jesse Helms, chairman and ranking member of the Senate Foreign Relations Committee; Dante B. Fascell and William S. Broomfield, chairman and ranking member of the House Foreign Affairs Committee; and John D. Dingell and Norman F. Lent, chairman and ranking member of the House Energy and Commerce Committee.

Exchange With Reporters Aboard Air Force One
July 27, 1990

The President. Well, this is not yet another news conference, but I just want to welcome everybody. We're looking forward to this weekend. Thank you very much.

Supreme Court Nomination of David H. Souter

Q. How do you gauge the initial reaction of the Senate to your nominating——

The President. Very favorable, so far. It's hard to tell about the Senate because a lot have not expressed their views. But nationally, I'm very pleased, and there seems to be a well-deserved support for Judge Souter. So, we'll see.

Q. Do you expect any difficulty with the confirmation?

The President. Well, I don't really think so. I hope not. I talked yesterday to Senator Thurmond, who is our ranking man on Judiciary, and he was giving me a little across-the-board assessment. And then Senator Rudman, I think, has a positive feeling.

Q. Think he'll sail through? No——

The President. Well, I don't know. I mean, I hope so. I think it deserves to. But I've been very pleased with the initial response; and then the second wave, I think, is very positive because the more people that know him and speak up—it seems to be broad support.

Q. About the only complaint seems to be that nobody knows—people seem to be not sure where he stands. Marshall [Supreme Court Associate Justice] said he'd never heard of him.

The President. Well, I think he's not the most well-known figure in the country, but that's not why I selected him. So, he'll be plenty well-known when he gets testifying and gets through this process, which I think he'll do with flying colors.

Q. Did you see Thurgood Marshall's interview last night?

The President. No, I didn't.

Q. Did you hear about it?

The President. Yes.

Q. Would you respond to it?

The President. My response is: I have great respect for the Supreme Court, and I have no comment at all on it—none.

Q. He says Mr. Sununu [Chief of Staff to the President] is calling the shots on this.

The President. I have no comments at all on this incident. I have a very high regard for separation of powers and for the Supreme Court, and thus I think people can get along without a comment from me on this interview.

Federal Budget Negotiations

Q. How about the budget, Mr. President? Are the Democrats dragging their feet, or——

The President. Well, we're going to have more meetings next week. And I think we're narrowing some differences, Sandy [Sandy Gilmour, NBC News], but it's not dramatic progress at all. So, I'm still sticking by our agreement, and we'll see where we go here next week.

Q. Will you keep them in town, if necessary, in order to——

The President. Well, part of the agreement is not to discuss details of what we're talking about. And that subject is, as you know, being widely discussed.

Q. Details of your plan, and whether your plan will have them out?

The President. Well, on both sides, yes.

Q. What's been the reaction to the plan?

The President. Well, you know, I'm not locked into any specific proposal. And it would be bad faith for me to start taking one part or another out of a proposal. But again, I think both Dick Darman [Director of the Office of Management and Budget], who is really kind of the lead for the White House—he and Brady [Secretary of the Treasury]—and then Dick Gephardt [House majority leader] are dealing in very good faith here. And so, let's see where we come out on it. But I'm not going into any specifics on any plan.

Supreme Court Nomination of David H. Souter

Q. Going back to Judge Souter, is there a precondition that he had expressed that he would not come to Washington unless you promised not to ask him his specific opinions on some of these controversial issues?

The President. No, no.

Q. Senator Rudman sort of indicated that he had expressed that view to him.

The President. I think he's going to come back and chat, but nothing on my side on that.

Gasoline Prices

Q. Mr. President, is there anything you can do about OPEC raising the price by 5 cents or 10 cents a gallon on gasoline?

The President. No, there's not a thing in the world we can do about it. The market forces, as always, will determine what the ultimate prices are, though. You know, they make these agreements, and then markets have a funny way of dominating. But there's nothing we can do on an OPEC decision.

Roseanne Barr

Q. The national anthem—should there be a constitutional amendment to protect—desecration of the national anthem?

Q. Yes, how about Roseanne Barr? What was your reaction to the song?

The President. My reaction is: It was disgraceful. That's the way I feel about it, and I think a lot of the San Diego fans said the same thing. But anyway, that's——

Q. Does this mean that Roseanne Barr won't be coming to the White House real soon?

The President. There's no change of plans in that. [*Laughter*]

Q. You mean, you're going to stop watching her show?

The President. Which show?

Note: The exchange occurred while the President was en route from Washington, DC, to his home in Kennebunkport, ME. In his remarks, the President referred to comedienne Roseanne Barr's performance of the national anthem at a San Diego Padres baseball game. A tape was not available for verification of the content of this exchange.

Remarks to the National Governors' Association
July 30, 1990

The President. Terry, can you hear me?

Governor Branstad. Yes, Mr. President?

The President. How are you doing?

Governor Branstad. We're not hearing you very well.

The President. Well, do you want to try another connection or can you hear it now better?

Governor Branstad. It's better. Mr. President, we appreciate your call, and I think we can hear you a little better now. Can you hear us okay?

The President. Loud and clear. Yes, it sounds like a loudspeaker. But listen, I just wanted to check in. I understand you're having a lunch there with the Governors, and I just wanted to report in and say that I understand from others that you're having a good conference. I'm sorry I'm not down there with you. And also it might be appropriate, but let me just pay my respects to Governor Guy Hunt. He told me about the enthusiasm in his State for this, and I just want to thank him for hosting the conference. Is he right there with you?

Governor Branstad. He's sitting right next to me.

The President. All right. Well, pass along a warm *abbracio* [embrace] to him. And, Terry, to you and all of you, let me just thank you for what you've accomplished this past year. I still feel that the education summit in Charlottesville last September was historic, and I want to continue the partnership that we announced when we announced those six national education goals. I have the report here, your report, on State strategies for achieving the national education goals. And I'm pleased that you've got our two reports on the actions that we're taking at the Federal level to support the goals and on the changes that we're making to give you a greater flexibility in the use of the Federal funds.

Also I want to commend your executive committee for recommending the establishment of a bipartisan panel that will determine how to measure progress. I think it is essential that there be some definitive way of measuring progress toward these education goals during the nineties, and this decision by the executive committee makes good sense. I think all of these actions reflect the enormous amount of work and effort that's being devoted to improving and strengthening our education system, and I can tell you I'm pleased with the progress. I still talk about the spirit of the Governors' meeting, the summit. I talk about it all over the country.

I recognize there is diversity; and I've made it a point not to get involved in any State, pointing out how a Governor might attempt to do the job better, but mainly to support—from a national standpoint—to support these goals. And I want to thank everyone there for the constructive relationship that we've developed and want to assure you that I want it to continue to work together.

And then lastly, if I might, I want to pass along to Booth Gardner, the incoming chairman of the NGA, my best wishes. And, Booth, both you and Terry have worked well; and I appreciate very much—I mentioned him in the beginning, but let me mention you here at the end—I'm very grateful to you for your continued approach on this matter. And I appreciate your input at the beginning, and now I look forward to working with you in this partnership that I think is going to serve our country very well indeed.

So, that's all I wanted to say. But I'm just delighted to have a chance to check in with you.

Governor Branstad. Mr. President, first of all, I think this is the eighth time since you've been President that you've communicated directly with the leadership of the National Governors' Association, and I really think that's unprecedented. We very much appreciate the personal attention that you've given to this association—working with us—and the cooperation that you and your staff have given us in developing these national goals and now this oversight panel.

And let me tell you, it wasn't easy yesterday. Many of us spent a lot of time locked away in a small room to try and get it resolved. We feel real good about the consensus proposal that was approved by the executive committee yesterday. And I just want to say the cooperation and help from the administration and the Congress is going to be essential for us to achieve these very ambitious goals. I also want to give Guy Hunt a chance to say a few words. This is the first time in the history of the National Governors' Association we've ever met in Alabama, and he has really shown us what southern hospitality is all about.

The President. That's not surprising, but put him on.

Governor Hunt. Mr. President, we wish you were here. We would like to show you some more of this southern hospitality, but we appreciate you staying on the job while all of us are away. And we just appreciate what you've done and just to let you know that you are still very much loved in Mobile, Alabama, and in Alabama. And come to see us when you can.

The President. Well, thank you, sir, and my respects to all the others that are assembled there. Booth, do you want the last word?

Governor Branstad. I want to turn it over to Booth, because at the end of the plenary session tomorrow, he's going to become chair of the National Governors' Association, and he will have the responsibility to appoint those six Governors to the oversight committee. And I can't think of a better person to turn over the chairmanship to than to the great Governor of the State of Washington, Booth Gardner.

The President. Put him on there. Booth.

Governor Gardner. He's on. [*Laughter*] We're switching from youth and energy to wisdom as leadership of the National Governors' Conference. [*Laughter*]

The President. I got you.

Governor Gardner. Terry's done a great job, and I appreciate your recognizing that. I just want to add what I think a lot of us feel, which is we appreciate your partnership in this educational effort. And we recognize that you've got financial difficulties like many of us do, but that the major commitment and the first goal was preparing children to get ready for school. And our goal as States is to make sure that we can fully fund our end of it as quickly as possible. And if the Federal Government can help us with that by fully funding Head Start or early childhood education, by the end of your first term, you'd have a lot of friends here.

The President. Listen, I appreciate it. And of course, that's in keeping with one of our major goals, so we'll see what we can do in that regard. But listen, good luck to you and my respects to all. And tell those on the new committee I look forward to working with them. And I'll see you, Booth and Terry, when you come east next. And thanks a lot.

Governor Branstad. Thank you.

The President. All right. Good luck.

Governor Branstad. Thank you, Mr. President.

The President. Over and out.

Note: The President spoke at 1:34 p.m. by telephone from the Oval Office at the White House.

Nomination of Stephen H. Rogers To Be United States Ambassador to Swaziland
July 30, 1990

The President today announced his intention to nominate Stephen H. Rogers to be Ambassador Extraordinary and Plenipotentiary of the United States of America to the Kingdom of Swaziland. He would succeed

Mary A. Ryan.

Since 1986 Mr. Rogers has served as counselor for economic and commercial affairs and officer-in-charge at the U.S. Embassy in Pretoria, South Africa. Prior to this he was a senior policy adviser for oceans and international environmental and scientific affairs at the Department of State, 1985–1986. He was international affairs adviser at the Industrial College of the Armed Forces at the National Defense University, 1984–1985, and a professor of international economic policy at the Industrial College of the Armed Forces, 1982–1984. Mr. Rogers served as Counselor for economic affairs at the U.S. Embassy in Mexico City, 1978–1982; Director of the Office of Regional Economic Policy at the Bureau of Inter-American Affairs at the Department of State, 1975–1978; and Counselor to the U.S.

delegation to the Organization for Economic Cooperation and Development in Paris, France, 1972–1975. He has served as Counselor for economic affairs at the U.S. Embassy in London, United Kingdom, 1970–1972. In addition, Mr. Rogers has served in several capacities in the U.S. Embassies in Paris and New Delhi.

Mr. Rogers graduated from Princeton University (B.A., 1952), Columbia University (M.A., 1956), and Harvard University (M.P.A., 1962). He was born June 21, 1930, in Flushing, NY. He served in the U.S. Navy, 1952–1955. He is married, has three children, and resides in Brooklyn, Pretoria.

Nomination of Mary Sterling To Be Inspector General of the Department of Transportation
July 30, 1990

The President today announced his intention to nominate Mary Sterling to be the Inspector General at the Department of Transportation. She would succeed John W. Melchner.

Since 1989 Mrs. Sterling has served as Assistant Secretary of Labor for Labor Management Standards at the Department of Labor in Washington, DC, and a Special Assistant, 1989. Prior to this she was an attorney with the law firm of McDowell, Rice and Smith in Kansas City, MO, 1989. Mrs. Sterling has served as a White House fellow and Special Assistant to the Attorney Gen-

eral at the Department of Justice, Washington, DC, 1987–1988. Mrs. Sterling was in the private practice of law, 1986–1987, and an organized crime prosecutor at the Department of Justice for the organized crime and racketeering section of the Kansas City Strike Force, 1985–1986.

Mrs. Sterling graduated from Harvard University (A.B., 1976), Ohio State University (M.A., 1977), and New York University School of Law (J.D., 1980). She was born September 4, 1955, in Pioneer, OH, and resides in Arlington, VA.

Remarks to the Youth Leadership Coalition
July 30, 1990

Thank you very, very much. It's good to see you guys. I think this is the darnedest group we've had to the White House. [*Laughter*] I'll tell you, I was looking at the list walking over and a wide array of interests from all over the country. The matrix is youth. And then I guess another possible matrix might be love of country, determination to lead. And so, I wanted to come over

and salute you, each and every one of you. And it's great to be here.

I was talking to Lisa, and she said that when she told one of you that the most powerful man in America would be stopping by to say hello, the wise guy said, "Yeah, when is Arnold Schwarzenegger coming in?" [*Laughter*]

I was not too thrilled with the unceremonious way that we interrupted Lew Crampton here. But he's doing a great job over there. And I hope you'll come back onto the scene after I blow this place. [*Laughter*] And, of course, Reg Walton, the Judge, is doing a superb job not just here in Washington but all across the country, as Bill Bennett's number two in this all-out fight against drugs. And I want to thank all of you in this room who have actively engaged yourselves in this struggle one way or another.

You know, what I wanted to do is come over and just say a word about a recent happening to this group that has the optimism and the energy and the vision to shape our country into the 21st century. And that's a big challenge, incidentally. I also might say it's a tremendous responsibility because one of our greatest obligations ought to be to leave a legacy of excellence to the children and grandchildren. But what I really wanted to mention was, in that context, my decision to nominate Judge David Souter to the Supreme Court.

I'm sure a lot of you have been reading about that. I view this as one of the most critical, crucial decisions that any President can make. And I'll tell you what was on my mind; and it was this nation's absolutely crucial demand for dedication, intelligence, and integrity in its leaders.

And you know, nominating a Supreme Court Justice is a responsibility. I felt that to live up to that responsibility, that trust that the American placed in me back in election time, I had to ensure that my nominee would bring these kinds of values of commitment to the service of our country. And I'm convinced that Judge Souter, the man whom I have named, will do exactly that.

You know, America's going to change tremendously over the coming decades, and technology may really make this world unrecognizable from today's standards. So, we can't even imagine the variety and the complexity of the decisions that the next Supreme Court is going to be called on to make. And that's why we can't choose a Justice based on some simplistic—they call it—litmus test on one issue or another. It's a much broader responsibility, and I tried to have that in mind in this nomination.

We have to choose the next Supreme Court Justice on the basis of his inner core as a human being; on the strength of character that informs his decisions; and then, I would also say, the depth of his intellect and his caring and his thoughtfulness and fairness and his faithfulness to the Constitution.

You know, you are the ones, obviously, who are going to be inheriting this country; and so, I want to make you a promise and a pledge. And I do this with total confidence and candor. Judge Souter will serve us all fairly and wisely and well as our generation turns the reigns of the administration over to yours; and he will bring to this country experience, informed impartiality, and an admirable moral compass that will guide us through the changes and crises that lie ahead.

I am very happy with the way this choice has been received across the country—really in a nonpartisan manner. I'm proud of him, and I know that when the country gets to know him, the country will be very proud of David Souter as well.

So, I wanted to come and put that in focus, not asking anything of you in terms of activism on this. The matter is now going to be before the United States Senate. Everyone here who has studied our system knows that the Senate has a responsibility to advise and to consent. And now they'll be taking a look at it in hearings that start before the Judiciary Committee in mid-September. But it's moving in the proper direction. I probably won't have too much more to say about it. But knowing this group and looking at whence you've cometh and seeing the degrees of excellence that you all have, I wanted to at least come over and put this in proper perspective for all of you.

I'm delighted to have had a chance to pop in. I hope you're finding these briefings and these seminars worthwhile. I don't want to sound gratuitous, but I am one who has great confidence in the young people of this country. And I'm just delighted that you took the time, what for some I'm sure was a nice summer vacation, to come to hot Washington and to hear from some of our very top people.

But thank you for coming, and bless all of you. Thank you very, very much.

Note: The President spoke at 1:51 p.m. in Room 450 of the Old Executive Office Building. In his remarks, he referred to Elisabeth Battaglia, Executive Assistant for the Office of Public Relations at the White House; Lewis S.W. Crampton, Associate Administrator of the Office of Communications and Public Affairs at the Environmental Protection Agency; and William J. Bennett and Reggie B. Walton, Director and Associate Director of National Drug Control Policy. A tape was not available for verification of the content of these remarks.

Joint Statement by the President and the Governors on a Process for Measuring and Reporting on Progress Toward the National Education Goals
July 31, 1990

At the historic Education Summit, the President and the Nation's Governors, as elected chief executives, made a commitment to be held accountable for progress in achieving the national education goals. To fulfill this commitment, this Joint Statement establishes the process for identifying measures of performance and reporting on progress toward the goals, and reaffirms the decade-long partnership toward realizing the goals.

In order to provide the direction and support needed to instill public confidence and the full cooperation of Federal and state officials, the President and Governors agree to establish the National Education Goals Panel to oversee the development and implementation of a national education progress reporting system. The process for developing and establishing appropriate measures and reporting annually on progress will build on the constructive, bipartisan partnership between the President and the Governors initiated at the Charlottesville Summit.

National Education Goals Panel

The National Education Goals Panel will be composed of:
- Four senior-level Federal Executive Branch officials appointed by the President;
- Six Governors appointed by the Chairman of the National Governors' Association in consultation with the Vice-Chairman, with no more than three of the Governors being from the same party; and
- Four Congressional Leaders (Senate Majority and Minority Leaders, the Speaker of the House or his designee and House Minority Leader) invited to serve as ex officio non-voting members.
- The Chairman of the Panel will be appointed annually by the Chairman of the National Governor's Association.

The Executive Branch officials will serve at the pleasure of the President. Governors will be appointed to the Panel for a two-year term, except that two of the initial appointments, equally divided between the two parties, shall be for a three-year term.

The Panel will be responsible for determining the indicators used to measure the national education goals and reporting progress toward their achievement. Its responsibilities shall include:
- Selecting interim and final measures and appropriate measurement tools to be developed as necessary in each goal area;
- Determining baselines and benchmarks against which progress may be evaluated;
- Determining the format for an annual report to the Nation; and
- Reporting on the Federal government's action to fulfill those responsibilities set forth in the Federal-state partnership at Charlottesville, including funding the Federal financial role, providing more flexibility in spending under existing Federal programs, and

controlling mandates that limit the states' ability to fund education, as defined in the Joint Statement issued at the Charlottesville Summit.

In addition, the Panel will review proposed changes in national and international measurement systems as appropriate and make recommendations to the President, the Congress, and the Governors for needed improvements.

The Panel will not be limited by availability of current data and measurements in its decisions. It will seek to identify fair, constructive measures that will boost the performance of students at all levels.

In making final decisions, the Panel will operate on the principle of consensus among the Governors, the Executive Branch, and the Congress. In the event that a vote must be taken, a decision will require 75 percent of the voting members.

Expert Advisers

The process for developing and establishing appropriate measures shall benefit from the experiences and expertise of the education research and measurement communities and other interested parties.

The Panel, in carrying out its responsibilities, will consult broadly with experts in the field of research and measurement, as well as with other interested parties, in order to:

- Identify and evaluate existing indicators; and
- Prepare specific options and recommendations for the Panel concerning: the selection of appropriate indicators; baselines and benchmarks against which performance may be evaluated; and the format for an annual report.

Report to the Nation

The President and the Governors agree that beginning in 1991, the Panel will issue a report card to the Nation on the anniversary of the Education Summit (September 27–28) on progress toward the national education goals. The Governors reaffirm their commitment made in Charlottesville to report individually on restructuring efforts in their states on the first anniversary of the Education Summit.

In developing the report card, the Panel will be guided by the following principles:

- The measurements and benchmarks should be consistent with the intent of the Charlottesville Joint Statement and the comprehensive statement of national education goals adopted by the President and the Governors.
- The measurement of benchmarks should not discriminate in favor of or against any state based on its current performance or the degree of improvement needed to reach the goals. The main focus of the national report card will be measuring each state's progress toward achieving the goals based on each state's baseline.

Following the release of the annual report card, each Governor shall issue a report on progress in his or her state related to the goals.

Extending the Partnership

Although the immediate task relates to national, state, and international assessments, the President and the Governors encourage the creation of similar systems of accountability in every school in America.

The President and Governors agree to begin work immediately to fulfill the commitments made in this Joint Statement.

Statement on the Establishment of the National Education Goals Panel
July 31, 1990

I am pleased by the agreement reached with the Nation's Governors to establish a National Education Goals Panel to measure and monitor progress toward these goals. This is an important step in the process which began last September at the education summit in Charlottesville, VA.

As administration representatives on the panel, I have designated Secretary of Education Lauro F. Cavazos, Gov. John H. Sununu [Chief of Staff to the President], Director of the Office of Management and Budget Richard G. Darman, and Assistant to the President for Economic and Domestic Policy Roger B. Porter.

I look forward to working with the members of the panel in the important task of identifying and implementing a fair, constructive way to report to the Nation on the education goals.

Remarks Following Discussions With President Gnassingbé Eyadéma of Togo
July 31, 1990

President Bush. With your permission, Mr. President. First, it has been a privilege to welcome you to the White House on this historic visit to our country. From the first days of Togo's independence 30 years ago, ties between our two nations have been very strong, and today's meetings are proof that Togo and the United States build on firm foundations, proof that we share a commitment to work together in what can be a decade of great promise for all of Africa.

In the past year, we have seen a narrowing of many of the great differences that divide nations, a growing consensus on the principles and policies that secure peace and progress. As our meetings today made clear, there is no more potent engine of economic progress than the free market.

Mr. President, I was very interested to learn more about the reforms that the Togolese Government is taking to open trade, encourage investment, and improve overall economic growth. And I am pleased that the United States has been able to assist Togo in this time of transition, pleased that AID and OPIC are now working with your government to create a duty-free industrial zone near the port of Lome, the point of entry for so many of the goods bound not only for Togo but for the neighboring nations of Mali and Burkina Faso and Niger. With each of these steps, Togo moves steadily toward a more prosperous future for its people and a leading role in the development of west Africa.

The U.S. is ready to do what it can in order to build on the encouraging economic changes already taking place in Togo. Our aim is to provide expanded trade opportunities and help Togo attract new capital to fuel lasting economic growth. But in the great revolution of ideas the world is now witnessing, the free market is only one half of the equation. What we have seen in country after country in every continent is the universal desire to live, work, and worship freely; a universal desire that finds its political expression in democracy. As in Europe, Asia, and right here in the Americas, the love of freedom is alive in Africa. And people the world over are discovering that, in the deepest sense, the path to development and the path to democracy are one and the same.

Mr. President, I'm encouraged by your recent statements in favor of a more open political system and on the value of the free flow of ideas. Mr. President, we share the view that Togo, like so many of its African neighbors, is a land of tremendous potential. And our talks today, proof of the strong and stable relationship between our two countries, point the way to a future of progress and prosperity.

So, once again, welcome to Washington. And with your permission, and at great risk, I would like to just say a few words in my very bad French to the Togolese people.

[*At this point, President Bush spoke in French, but a translation was not provided.*]

God bless you, sir, and God bless the people of Togo.

President Eyadéma. Mr. President, it is a great pleasure for us to be in your great and charming country on this official and working visit at Your Excellency's kind invitation. This visit has given us a good opportunity to exchange views on problems concerning relations of friendship, cooperation, and ever-broadening solidarity which unites the American and the Togolese people. Taking place at a time when serious changes are happening throughout the world, this visit has also given us the opportunity to go over a wide range of matters which concern the international community, and especially the Third World.

Seven years ago, when I visited your country for the first time, nobody could imagine that our world would become today the scene of social, economic, and political changes which, in so short a time, have thoroughly shattered the well-known facts of contemporary history. In less than 3 years, rivalries between ideological blocs have diminished and have removed the barriers of prejudice, thus favoring the negotiated settlements of several regional conflicts and the process of a nuclear disarmament which has become a reality today. This climate of eased tensions, trust, and tolerance, as a token of balance of mankind, is the result of the pragmatic, realistic, and perfected policy that you have instituted— and which quite recently opened right here in Washington, DC, a new era of cooperation between your country and the Soviet Union.

Yet the positive evolution which marked international relations in recent months and which gave rise to rightful feelings of hope within people who love peace, freedom, and justice will only be fruitful if appropriate remedies are found for the serious development problems facing Third World countries in general and Africa in particular.

Our continent, victim of starvation, widespread diseases, and all kinds of calamities, relies only on an economy which is still at a preindustrial stage. The considerable decrease of export revenues resulting from the constant fall of the prices of the raw materials is at the origin of our shaky economies as well as the burden of the African debts, which according to estimates will rise from $250 billion in 1990 to $600 billion in the year 200 [2000]. That is the

reason why we are instantly calling on industrialized countries that supplies the market of raw materials to eliminate obstacles that hinder the North-South trade and to set up resources in favor of Africa in order to enable her to promote a sustained and lasting development.

I would like to take this solemn opportunity to once again appeal to the friendly nations of Africa, such as the United States, so that, like the aid granted to the Eastern countries, they set up a real Marshall plan in favor of the African Continent. Just as in the past, I'm quite sure that Togo can rely on your country, to which it is bound by links of friendship and cooperation covering not only agricultural, social, and political sectors but cultural ones as well.

This American-Togolese cooperation, which grows stronger and stronger every day thanks to the contribution of the U.S. AID and of the Peace Corps volunteers, recently found a new inspiration through the position of your government and that of the OPIC to set up an industrial free zone in the Togolese territory. Allow me to acknowledge to you, Mr. President, how the Togolese people are so much touched and honored by this invaluable gift you offer them and which is particularly meant for our young people, whose hopes lie in that industrial free zone as a source of prospect and job opportunities. Our country, which has already chosen the way of private initiative, economic liberalism, protection and defense of human rights, and which continues its step-by-step democratization processes, enjoys all the necessary conditions that guarantee the success of that industrial free zone.

I, therefore, wish to invite American investors to come in numbers and settle in Togo where, within the framework of that industrial-free zone, they could enjoy a climate of peace, security, and freedom, a necessary condition for the development of their businesses, including the best attracting conditions of investments.

Our country has a strong belief in the future of the close cooperation which links our two nations, and there is no doubt on my mind that this official visit will further consolidate the friendship and the solidarity which bind the people of both nations and strengthen our thoughtful and sincere relations in any field.

Long live the United States of America. Long live the friendship and the cooperation between America and Togo.

Note: President Bush spoke at 1:16 p.m. at the South Portico of the White House. President Eyadéma spoke in French, and his remarks were translated by an interpreter. Prior to their remarks, the two Presidents met privately in the Oval Office and with U.S. and Togolese officials in the Cabinet Room, and then attended a luncheon in the Old Family Dining Room.

Nomination of Thomas F. Kranz To Be an Associate Director of the Federal Emergency Management Agency
August 1, 1990

The President today announced his intention to nominate Thomas F. Kranz to be an Associate Director of the Federal Emergency Management Agency for External Affairs. He would succeed James P. McNeill.

Since 1989 Mr. Kranz has served as Associate Director of the White House Office of Presidential Personnel for National Security Affairs. Prior to this, he served as Principal Deputy General Counsel in the Office of the Secretary of Army at the Department of Defense in Washington, DC, 1985–1988; member and then partner with the law firm of Alexander, Inman, Taner and Wede-

meyer in Los Angeles, CA, 1977–1985 and 1969–1974; special counsel to the Los Angeles County district attorney for superior court hearings, 1975–1977; and deputy public defender in the Los Angeles County public defender's office, 1965–1968.

Mr. Kranz graduated from Stanford University (B.A., 1959), University of California at Berkeley (LL.D., 1964), and University of California at Los Angeles (M.A., 1973). He was born March 18, 1938, in Los Angeles, CA. Mr. Kranz served in the U.S. Navy, 1959–1961. He is married, has two children, and resides in McLean, VA.

Statement by Deputy Press Secretary Popadiuk on the Iraqi Invasion of Kuwait
August 1, 1990

The United States strongly condemns the Iraqi military invasion of Kuwait and calls for the immediate and unconditional withdrawal of all Iraqi forces. We have conveyed this message to the Iraqi Ambassador in Washington and to the Iraqi Government

through our Embassy in Baghdad. We deplore this blatant use of military aggression and violation of the U.N. Charter. Together with Kuwait, we are calling for an emergency session of the U.N. Security Council.

Statement by Deputy Press Secretary Popadiuk on the Iraqi Invasion of Kuwait
August 2, 1990

National Security Adviser Brent Scowcroft has been chairing an interagency task force in the Situation Room monitoring the Iraqi invasion of Kuwait. The President was informed of the initial signs of the Iraqi action at approximately 9 p.m. yesterday by National Security Adviser Scowcroft and has been receiving periodic updates since.

The United States is deeply concerned about this blatant act of aggression and demands the immediate and unconditional withdrawal of all Iraqi forces. We do not have exact details at this time concerning the extent of the Iraqi action, although it is clearly extensive. We have no reports of any harm to American citizens. The State Department is in constant contact with our Embassy in Kuwait concerning the status of U.S. citizens.

At the urging of Kuwait and the United States, the United Nations Security Council will be meeting early this morning to consider this matter. In addition, we have been informed that the Arab League and the Organization of the Islamic Conference will be convening to review the situation. We are urging the entire international community to condemn this outrageous act of aggression.

The United States is reviewing all options in its response to the Iraqi aggression.

Remarks and an Exchange With Reporters on the Iraqi Invasion of Kuwait
August 2, 1990

The President. Let me make a brief statement here about recent events. The United States strongly condemns the Iraqi military invasion of Kuwait. We call for the immediate and unconditional withdrawal of all the Iraqi forces. There is no place for this sort of naked aggression in today's world, and I've taken a number of steps to indicate the deep concern that I feel over the events that have taken place.

Last night I instructed our Ambassador at the United Nations, Tom Pickering, to work with Kuwait in convening an emergency meeting of the Security Council. It was convened, and I am grateful for that quick, overwhelming vote condemning the Iraqi action and calling for immediate and unconditional withdrawal. Tom Pickering will be here in a bit, and we are contemplating with him further United Nations action.

Second, consistent with my authority under the International Emergency Economic Powers Act, I've signed an Executive order early this morning freezing Iraqi assets in this country and prohibiting transactions with Iraq. I've also signed an Executive order freezing Kuwaiti assets. That's to ensure that those assets are not interfered with by the illegitimate authority that is now occupying Kuwait. We call upon other governments to take similar action.

Third, the Department of State has been in touch with governments around the world urging that they, too, condemn the Iraqi aggression and consult to determine what measures should be taken to bring an end to this totally unjustified act. It is important that the international community act together to ensure that Iraqi forces depart Kuwait immediately.

Needless to say, we view the situation with the utmost gravity. We remain committed to take whatever steps are necessary to defend our longstanding, vital interests in the Gulf, and I'm meeting this morning with my senior advisers here to consider all possible options available to us. I've talked to Secretary Baker just now; General Scowcroft and I were on the phone with him. And after this meeting, I will proceed to deliver a longstanding speech. I will have consultations—short ones—there in Aspen with Prime Minister Thatcher, and I will be returning home this evening, and I'll be here in Washington tomorrow.

I might say on a much more pleasant note, I just hung up from talking to Mr. and Mrs. Swanson, the parents of Tim Swanson, the Peace Corps volunteer who has been held against his will—held hostage or kidnaped—there in the Philippines. And I want to thank everybody in the U.S. Government that was so instrumental in working for his release. And, Bob, I hope you'll convey that to the Ambassador and others in our Philippines country team.

Q. Mr. President?

The President. Yes, Helen [Helen Thomas, United Press International]?

Q. Do you contemplate intervention as one of your options?

The President. We're not discussing intervention. I would not discuss any military options even if we'd agreed upon them. But one of the things I want to do at this meeting is hear from our Secretary of Defense, our Chairman, and others. But I'm not contemplating such action.

Q. You're not contemplating any intervention or sending troops?

The President. I'm not contemplating such action, and I again would not discuss it if I were.

Q. What is the likely impact on U.S. oil supplies and prices?

The President. This is a matter that concerns us, and I don't know yet. Again, I'm going to hear from our experts now. Our Secretary of Energy is here, if you'll note, and others who understand this situation very well indeed—our Secretary of Defense. And we'll be discussing that. But this is a matter of considerable concern, and not just to the United States, I might add.

Q. Are you planning to break relations?

The President. You've heard me say over and over again, however, that we are dependent for close to 50 percent of our energy requirements on the Middle East. And this is one of the reasons I felt that we have to not let our guard down around the world.

Q. Are you contemplating breaking diplomatic relations?

The President. I'm discussing this matter with our top advisers here in just a minute.

Q. Is this action in your view limited to Kuwait?

The President. There's no evidence to the contrary. But what I want to do is have it limited back to Iraq and have this invasion be reversed and have them get out of Kuwait.

Q. Do you think Saudi Arabia is threatened or any of the other Emirates?

The President. I think Saudi Arabia is very concerned; and I want to hear from our top officials here, our Director of Intelligence and others, as to the worldwide implications of this illegal action that has been condemned by the United Nations.

Q. And you were taken by surprise?

The President. Not totally by surprise because we have good intelligence, and our intelligence has had me concerned for some time here about what action might be taken.

Thank you all very much. And I expect I will say something further because I'm having a joint press meeting with Margaret Thatcher and, at that time, I might be able to take a few more questions on this subject. But the main thing I want to do now is hear from our advisers, and then we will go forth from this meeting all on the same wavelength. I'm sure there will be a lot of frenzied diplomatic activity. I plan to participate in some of that myself, because at this time, it is important to stay in touch with our many friends around the world, and it's important that we work in concert with our friends around the world.

Q. Gorbachev?

The President. Thank you very much.

Obviously—Helen, you might be interested—this matter has been discussed at very high level between Secretary Baker and the Foreign Minister of the Soviet Union. And so far I've been pleased with the Soviet reaction.

Q. Well, do you expect to make decisions?

The President. That's all I've got to say

right now. We've got to go on with this meeting.

Note: The President spoke at 8:05 a.m. in the Cabinet Room at the White House. In his remarks, the President referred to Brent Scowcroft, Assistant to the President for National Security Affairs; Prime Minister Margaret Thatcher of the United Kingdom; Robert M. Gates, Assistant to the President and Deputy for National Security Affairs; Colin L. Powell, Chairman of the Joint Chiefs of Staff; William H. Webster, Director of Central Intelligence; and Soviet Foreign Minister Eduard A. Shevardnadze.

Remarks and a Question-and-Answer Session With Reporters in Aspen, Colorado, Following a Meeting With Prime Minister Margaret Thatcher of the United Kingdom
August 2, 1990

The President. Let me first welcome Prime Minister Thatcher back to the United States. It's a very timely visit, and as you can well imagine, we have been exchanging views on the Iraq-Kuwait situation. Not surprisingly, I find myself very much in accord with the views of the Prime Minister. I reported to her on contacts that I've had since I left Washington: personal contacts with King Hussein [of Jordan]; Mr. Mubarak of Egypt, President Mubarak; President Salih of Yemen—a long conversation just now. I can tell you that [Secretary of State] Jim Baker has been in close touch with the Soviet leadership, and indeed, the last plan was for him to stop in Moscow on his way back here.

We are concerned about the situation, but I find that Prime Minister Thatcher and I are looking at it on exactly the same wavelength: concerned about this naked aggression, condemning it, and hoping that a peaceful solution will be found that will result in the restoration of the Kuwaiti leaders to their rightful place and, prior to that, a withdrawal of Iraqi forces.

Prime Minister, welcome to Colorado and to the United States. And if you care to say a word on that, then we can take the questions.

The Prime Minister. Thank you, Mr. President, and thank you for the welcome.

We have, of course, been discussing the main question as the President indicated. Iraq has violated and taken over the territory of a country which is a full member of the United Nations. That is totally unacceptable, and if it were allowed to endure, then there would be many other small countries that could never feel safe.

The Security Council acted swiftly last night under the United States leadership, well-supported by the votes of 14 members of the Security Council, and rightly demanded the withdrawal of Iraqi troops. If that withdrawal is not swiftly forthcoming, we have to consider the next step. The next step would be further consideration by the Security Council of possible measures under chapter VII.

The fundamental question is this: whether the nations of the world have the collective will effectively to see the Security Council resolution is upheld; whether they have the collective will effectively to do anything, which the Security Council further agrees, to see that Iraq withdraws and that the government of Kuwait is restored to Kuwait. None of us can do it separately. We need a collective and effective will of the nations belonging to the United Nations—first the Security Council and then the support of all the others to make it effective.

Iraqi Invasion of Kuwait

Q. Mr. President, when Kuwaiti shipping was in danger in the Gulf war, you put those ships under American flags. Now Kuwait itself has been invaded. The Kuwaiti Ambassador says that they're desperate for help and that American intervention is of paramount importance. Will you answer that call, and how will you?

The President. I answer that we're considering what the next steps by the United States should be, just as we strongly support what Prime Minister Thatcher said about collective action in the United Nations.

Q. Are you still not contemplating military intervention?

The President. No. I mentioned at the time we were going to discuss different options, which I did after that first press conference this morning. And we're not ruling any options in, but we're not ruling any options out. And so, that is about where we are right now. We had thorough briefings—you know who was at the meeting today—by General Powell [Chairman of the Joint Chiefs of Staff], General Schwarzkopf [Commander of the U.S. forces in the Persian Gulf] and others. But I think it would be inappropriate to discuss options.

Q. What are the chances of U.S.-Soviet cooperation in restoring peace to the Gulf?

The President. I would say they're very good. I reported to Prime Minister Thatcher on a conversation that I had with Jim Baker on the plane flying out here. And I think you could say that he would not be stopping in Moscow unless there would be a good degree of cooperation between the Soviet Union and the United States. But again, the Soviet Union is a member of the United Nations. They voted with the United Kingdom and with the United States. And so, I think there is a good level of cooperation with the Soviets and, hopefully, with other permanent members and, hopefully, with the rest of the members of the Security Council.

Q. We understand that the Soviets have announced that they are cutting off arm shipments to the Iraqis. Are the French, which is the other big arms supplier to Baghdad, also planning to cut off arms shipments?

The President. I've not talked today—I believe you had contact, Prime Minister, at some level with the French Government, but I can't answer that question.

The Prime Minister. We had contact. Douglas Hurd [British Foreign Secretary], I believe, had contact with Mr. Dumas [French Foreign Minister]. This was about the Security Council resolution which France, of course, fully supported.

Q. Mr. President, isn't Saddam Hussein [President of Iraq] at the root of this problem? Hasn't he replaced Qadhafi [leader of Libya] as sort of the bad boy of the region? Would you like to see him removed? And what can you do about him?

The President. I would like to see him withdraw his troops and the restoration of the legal government in Kuwait to the rightful place, and that's the step that should be taken. I might say that I am somewhat heartened by the conversations I had with Mubarak and with King Hussein, Mr. Salih—all of whom I consider friends of the United States—and all of them are trying to engage in what they call an Arab answer to the question, working diligently behind the scenes to come to an agreement that would satisfy the United Nations and the rest of the world. So, there are collective efforts beginning to be undertaken by these worthy countries, and let's hope that they result in a satisfactory resolution of this international crisis.

Q. But, Mr. President, Saddam Hussein has been the source of the most recent mischief in the region—nuclear triggers, missiles, the big gun—as Prime Minister Thatcher knows about. Is he going to be a constant source of problems there in that region?

The President. If he behaves this way, he's going to be a constant source. We find his behavior intolerable in this instance, and so do the rest of the United Nations countries that met last night. And reaction from around the world is unanimous in being condemnatory. So, that speaks for itself.

The Prime Minister. Did I hear someone say Prime Minister?

The President. You hope you did. [*Laughter*] Please.

The Prime Minister. I'm sorry. I told you I'd finished. [*Laughter*] But so, I thought that that guy shouldn't have it all. [*Laughter*]

Q. Prime Minister, is there any action short of military intervention that Britain or the other United Nations countries could take——

The Prime Minister. Yes, of course.

Q. ——that would be effective against Iraq?

The Prime Minister. Yes, of course. Yes, of course there is—you know, the whole chapter VII measures. And that, of course—obviously we're in consultation now as to which measures we could all agree on so the Security Council would vote them. And then they'd become mandatory. The question then is whether you can make them effective over the rest of the nations. And obviously, the 14 couldn't do it on their own. And so, there will be a good deal of negotiation as to what to put in the next Security Council resolution if Iraq does not withdraw.

Q. But are you confident that you'd be able to mobilize that kind of international support?

The Prime Minister. I believe that further chapter VII measures would have a good chance of getting through. We certainly would support them.

The President. May I add to that, that the United States has demonstrated its interest in that by the action that I took this morning by Executive order: cutting off imports from Iraq to this country.

Q. Mr. President, can I ask both of you to answer this? How does the fact that they apparently have chemical weapons now affect your decisionmaking and narrow your options?

The Prime Minister. I don't figure it affects it at all. What has happened is a total violation of international law. You cannot have a situation where one country marches in and takes over another country which is a member of the United Nations. I don't think the particular weapons they have affects that fundamental position.

Q. But doesn't it affect what actions we can take? And doesn't it make military action——

The Prime Minister. No, I do not think it necessarily affects what actions we can take.

The President. I would agree with that assessment.

Q. What did the Arab leaders that you talked to ask the United States to do? Did they ask you to either restrain yourself or to become militarily involved? And have you contacted Israel?

The President. We've had contact with Israel, yes. I have not personally, but we have. And they asked for restraint. They

asked for a short period of time in which to have this Arab solution evolve and be placed into effect. And they are concerned, obviously, with this naked aggression. But it was more along that line: Let us try now, as neighbors and Arabs, to resolve this. And I made clear to them that it had gone beyond simply a regional dispute because of the naked aggression that violates the United Nations Charter.

Q. What did Israel say it would do at this point?

The President. I would have to think back to the details of it; but offering cooperation, I think, was about where I would leave it there.

Q. Mr. President, we're hearing reports now that some of the Americans, particularly in the oil fields, may have been rounded up by Iraqi troops. Do you have anything to that? How does that affect your reaction?

The President. Well, I don't have anything on that right now. And secondly, it would affect the United States in a very dramatic way, because I view a fundamental responsibility of my Presidency as protecting American citizens, and if they're threatened or harmed or put into harm's way, I have certain responsibilities. But I hadn't heard that, Charles [Charles Bierbauer, Cable News Network], and I hope that that is not correct.

Q. May I also ask about British citizens? Any word? Are they safe?

The Prime Minister. We have some British citizens in Kuwait. You probably know that there was a British Airways flight there on its way to Africa, and the passengers there are now in a hotel in Kuwait. So, we have some there, and of course, we have a number of other British citizens in Kuwait. And we, too, are concerned for their safety.

Q. Mr. President, some of the smaller nations in the Persian Gulf—Bahrain, the Emirates, and the others—obviously have reason to worry about what has happened here. What can the United States and Great Britain say to those countries and those people who are feeling very concerned today?

The President. Well, the United States can say that we are very much concerned for your safety. And this naked aggression would understandably shake them to the core. And so, what we are trying to do is have collective action that will reverse this action out and to make very clear that we are totally in accord with their desire to see the Iraqis withdraw—cease-fire, withdraw, and restitution of the Kuwaiti government. And that would be the most reassuring thing of all for these countries who, whether it's true or not, feel threatened by this action.

Q. At the risk of being hypothetical, if Iraq does not move out quickly and has gained a foothold among the smaller Gulf nations, what can the United States and other nations do militarily?

The President. We have many options, and it is too hypothetical, indeed, for me to comment on them. And I'd refer that also to the Prime Minister.

The Prime Minister. That's precisely why you're looking at the next stage in the Security Council; second, what other measures can be put into action mandatorily; and why the very nations to whom you refer— we should also need their cooperation in putting other actions into effect.

Q. Mr. President, have you dispatched the U.S.S. *Independence* to the region, and have you heard from Saudi Arabia?

The President. Well, I would not discuss movement of any U.S. forces. And what was the second part of your question?

Q. Have you heard from Saudi Arabia?

The President. No, but I have a call to King Fahd, and I was supposed to have taken that call before now, but it's been delayed by a few minutes. And so, I hope before I leave here I will talk to him. I think it is very important I do talk to him. And I'd leave it there.

Q. What do you expect him to say?

The President. Well, that's too hypothetical, too. I know he'll be expressing the same kind of concern that we feel.

Q. Prime Minister, if I could, the President's Executive order this morning established a U.S. embargo on trade with Iraq. When you mentioned chapter VII measures, would you support in the Security Council a call for an international embargo on Iraqi oil?

The Prime Minister. We are prepared to support in the Security Council those measures which collectively we can agree to and which collectively we can make effective. Those are the two tests. We have already frozen all Kuwaiti assets. Kuwaitis have very considerable assets, and it's important that those do not fall into Iraqi hands. Iraq, we believe, has only very, very small assets and rather a lot of debts, so the position is rather different with her.

Note: The question-and-answer session began at 2:10 p.m. outside the residence of Henry Catto, U.S. Ambassador to the United Kingdom.

Memorandum on the Withholding of Assistance to Iraq
August 2, 1990

Memorandum for Heads of All Departments and Agencies

Subject: Withholding of Assistance to Iraq

Effective immediately, you are instructed not to provide any form of assistance to Iraq, including, but not limited to, financial assistance, loan guarantees, and export licenses.

GEORGE BUSH

Statement by Press Secretary Fitzwater on the President's Telephone Conversation With King Fahd bin 'Abd al-'Aziz Al Sa'ud of Saudi Arabia
August 2, 1990

President Bush and King Fahd of Saudi Arabia discussed the Iraq attack on Kuwait in a telephone call at approximately 4:45 p.m. MDT. The two leaders spoke for nearly one-half hour. They agreed that the attack on Kuwait was absolutely unacceptable, and they discussed possible options for dealing with the situation. President Bush described the conversations he had earlier in the day with other Arab leaders and with Prime Minister Thatcher [of the United Kingdom]. The President emphasized the United States demand for the immediate and unconditional withdrawal of Iraqi forces.

Statement by Press Secretary Fitzwater on Secretary of Health and Human Services Louis W. Sullivan
August 2, 1990

Louis Sullivan, Secretary of Health and Human Services, is an outstanding Cabinet officer who has forcefully and effectively spoken out for the public's health and welfare. His courage is exemplary. President Bush and Chief of Staff Sununu commend his work on behalf of health and social issues, including his leadership for civil rights. He is a role model for black and white youth in America who aspire to high achievement.

Congressman Fortney Stark's bigoted assault on the integrity and ability of Secretary Sullivan is an affront to the Congress and the Democratic Party. We trust the Democratic Party and its chairman, Ron Brown, will disassociate themselves from Congressman Stark's ill-tempered and shameful remarks.

Remarks at the Aspen Institute Symposium in Aspen, Colorado
August 2, 1990

Thank you. Lod Cook, thank you so very much for that genuinely warm welcome. I've really been looking forward to coming here. To David McLaughlin, our president, and John Phelan, the chairman, I salute you for what you are doing, what you have done. To Henry Catto, our distinguished Ambassador to the Court of Saint James, I salute him and Jessica and thank them for their hospitality. I'm honored that the Governor of the State of Colorado, Governor Romer, is here today. Thank you, sir, for being with us. And to all the Aspen alumni and all our distinguished guests, many, many thanks for this warm welcome.

And of course, I've saved the piece de resistance to the very end, our very special guest, our friend, the distinguished world leader, Margaret Thatcher. It was very, very comforting to me today when I went out to try to represent you, the people of the United States, in expressing our views on the current emergency, I would say, in the Persian Gulf—naked aggression by the State of Iraq. I felt very comforted by the fact that as I spoke Prime Minister Thatcher was there with me answering the tougher questions and standing shoulder to shoulder with the United States. Madame Prime Minister, let me say that for more than a decade now America has known no better friend of freedom anywhere in the world than you, and it's an honor to join you today.

Kind of ironic, isn't it? Washington is getting more like a three-ring circus—and here I am—[*laughter*]—under the big tent. [*Laughter*] Of course, it's a special pleasure to experience the splendor of Aspen in August. The climate in Washington's tough this time of year. Lots of heat and temperatures rising. Everyone's hot under the collar. The weather's fine, but I'm talking about the budget summit. [*Laughter*]

I am delighted to celebrate with all of you the 40th anniversary of this most illustrious Aspen Institute. In those 40 years, the spirit of Aspen has come to signify the attempt to bridge the worlds of thought and action and, of course, to understand the tremendous changes taking place around us. Think back to the headlines 40 years ago, the time of that first Aspen conference, in 1950. North Korea roared across the 38th parallel. Klaus Fuchs was caught and convicted for revealing the secrets of the atom bomb to the Soviets. The "cold war"—a term introduced into our political vocabulary by Bernard Baruch—had come into its own as the shorthand to describe the halfway house of an armed and uneasy peace, a world divided, East from West. That was the world as Aspen came into being, the world Aspen sought to study, analyze, and to shape.

The 40 years since then have been a time of tremendous progress for the nations of the West, an era of unparalleled prosperity, peace, and freedom. But at the same time, we lived in a constant condition of tension, cold war and, indeed, conflict.

That world is now changing. The decades-old division of Europe is ending, and the era of democracy-building has begun. In Germany, the divided nation in the heart of a divided continent, unity is now assured as a free and full member of the NATO alliance. The Soviet Union itself is in the midst of a political and economic transformation that has brought unprecedented openness—

a process that is at once full of hope but, let's face it, still full of uncertainty.

We've entered a remarkable stage in our relationship with the Soviet Union. Just today I talked to Jim Baker in Ulan Bator. He'd just left Irkutsk. And he had very positive talks with Foreign Minister Shevardnadze. And my discussions with President Gorbachev have been open and honest. All the issues are on the table; we don't dodge the tough ones. That's been the secret to our success so far, and over time, that's how we are going to narrow our differences and seize this historic opportunity to help create lasting peace.

The changes that I'm talking about have transformed our security environment. We're entering a new era: the defense strategy and military structure needed to ensure peace can and must be different. The threat of a Soviet invasion of Western Europe launched with little or no warning is today more remote than at any other point in the postwar period. And with the emergence of democracy in Eastern Europe, the Warsaw Pact has lost its military meaning. And after more than four decades of dominance, Soviet troops are withdrawing from Central and Eastern Europe.

Our task today is to shape our defense capabilities to these changing strategic circumstances. In a world less driven by an immediate threat to Europe and the danger of global war, in a world where the size of our forces will increasingly be shaped by the needs of regional contingencies and peacetime presence, we know that our forces can be smaller. Secretary Cheney and General Powell are hard at work determining the precise combination of forces that we need. But I can tell you now, we calculate that by 1995 our security needs can be met by an active force 25 percent smaller than today's. America's Armed Forces will be at their lowest level since the year 1950.

What matters now, then, is how we reshape the forces that remain. Our new strategy must provide the framework to guide our deliberate reductions to no more than the forces we need to guard our enduring interests—the forces to exercise forward presence in key areas, to respond effectively to crisis, to retain the national capacity to rebuild our forces should this be needed.

The United States would be ill-served by forces that represent nothing more than a scaled-back or a shrunken-down version of the forces that we possess right now. If we simply prorate our reductions, cut equally across the board, we could easily end up with more than we need for contingencies that are no longer likely, and less than we must have to meet emerging challenges. What we need are not merely reductions but restructuring.

And what we require now is a defense policy that adapts to the significant changes we are witnessing without neglecting the enduring realities that will continue to shape our security strategy, a policy of peacetime engagement every bit as constant and committed to the defense of our interests and ideals in today's world as in the time of conflict and cold war.

And in this world, America remains a pivotal factor for peaceful change. Important American interests in Europe and the Pacific, in the Mediterranean and in the Persian Gulf—all are key reasons why maintaining a forward presence will remain an indispensable element of our strategy.

We all remember when the Soviet Union viewed our presence, that forward presence, as a threat. Indeed, when we met at Malta, at the seasick summit—[*laughter*]—President Gorbachev handed me a map—I still have it, I still have it on display in my library—a map purporting to show American encirclement of the Soviet Union. And we talked about this in depth. And I think he understands now that we have no intention of threatening his country. And I happen to think that it's those kinds of conversations, frankly, that we had up there at Camp David that help make such progress.

I was candid with him, and I told him that for all the positive changes we have seen, the Soviet Union remains a world-class military power. Even after the conventional arms reductions that we're now negotiating, the Soviets will continue to maintain 2 to 3 million men under arms. And of course, our number one concern: the Soviets continue to maintain and modernize their arsenal of strategic weapons.

We and our allies welcome this new course, this clearly new course that the Soviet Union has chosen. But prudence demands that we maintain an effective deterrent, one that secures the peace not only in today's climate of reduced tensions but that ensures that renewed confrontation is not a feasible option for any Soviet leadership.

The Soviets will enter a START treaty with a fully modernized, highly capable, and very large strategic force. To maintain clear and confident strategic deterrence into the next century, we need the B-2. Secretary Cheney has already scaled back the program. Seventy-five aircraft makes strategic sense. Further delays will only increase the costs. And we need to complete the Trident program. Those 18 submarines will ensure a survivable, submarine-based deterrent. And we can defer final decisions on our land-based ICBM's [intercontinental ballistic missiles] as we see how the START talks proceed but we must keep our options open. And that means completing the development of the small ICBM and the rail-based Peacekeeper.

And finally, I am convinced that a defensive—and I reemphasize that word—a defensive strategic deterrent makes more sense in the nineties than ever before. What better means of defense than a system that destroys only missiles launched against us without threatening one single human life. We must push forward the great promise of SDI [Strategic Defense Initiative] and deploy it when ready.

And the United States will keep a force in Europe as long as our allies want and need us there. Prime Minister Thatcher and I have discussed this at length. We will keep forces there as long as we are wanted and needed. As we and our allies adapt NATO to a changing world, the size and shape of our forces is destined to change to suit new and less threatening circumstances. But we will remain in Europe to deter any new dangers, to be a force for stability, and to reassure all of Europe—East and West—that the European balance will remain secure.

Outside of Europe, America must possess forces able to respond to threats in whatever corner of the globe they may occur.

Even in a world where democracy and freedom have made great gains, threats remain. Terrorism, hostagetaking, renegade regimes and unpredictable rulers, new sources of instability—all require a strong and an engaged America.

The brutal aggression launched last night against Kuwait illustrates my central thesis: Notwithstanding the alteration in the Soviet threat, the world remains a dangerous place with serious threats to important U.S. interests wholly unrelated to the earlier patterns of the U.S.-Soviet relationship. These threats, as we've seen just in the last 24 hours, can arise suddenly, unpredictably, and from unexpected quarters. U.S. interests can be protected only with capability which is in existence and which is ready to act without delay. The events of the past day underscore also the vital need for a defense structure which not only preserves our security but provides the resources for supporting the legitimate self-defense needs of our friends and of our allies. This will be an enduring commitment as we continue with our force restructuring. Let no one, friend or foe, question this commitment.

In spite of our best efforts to control the spread of chemical and nuclear weapons and ballistic missile technologies, more nations—more, not less—are acquiring weapons of mass destruction and the means to deliver them. Right now, 20 countries have the capacity to produce chemical weapons. And by the year 2000, as many as 15 developing nations could have their own ballistic missiles. In the future, even conflicts we once thought of as limited or local may carry far-reaching consequences.

To cope with the full range of challenges that we may have to confront, we must focus on readiness and on rapid response. And to prepare to meet the challenges we may face in the future, we must focus on research—an active and inventive program of defense R&D.

Let me begin with the component with great long-range consequences: research. Time and again, we have seen technology revolutionize the battlefield. The U.S. has always relied upon its technological edge to offset the need to match potential adversaries' strength in numbers—cruise missiles, Stealth fighters and bombers, today's

"smart" weapons with the state-of-the-art guidance systems, and tomorrow's "brilliant" ones. The men and women in our Armed Forces deserve the best technology America has to offer.

And we must realize the heavy price that we will pay if we look for false economies in research and development for defense. Most modern weapons systems take a minimum of 10 years to move from the drawing board to the battlefield. The nature of national defense demands that we plan now for threats on the distant horizon. The decisions we make today, the programs we push forward or push aside will dictate the kind of military forces we have at our disposal in the year 2000 and beyond.

Second, we must focus on rapid response. As we saw in Panama, the U.S. may be called on to respond to a variety of challenges from various points on the compass. In an era when threats may emerge with little or no warning, our ability to defend our interests will depend on our speed and our agility. And we will need forces that give us a global reach. No amount of political change will alter the geographic fact that we are separated from many of our most important allies and interests by thousands of miles of water. And in many of the conflicts we could face, we may not have the luxury of matching manpower with pre-positioned material. We'll have to have air- and sea-lift capacities to get our forces where they are needed, when they are needed. A new emphasis on flexibility and versatility must guide our efforts.

And finally, as we restructure, we must put a premium on readiness. For those active forces we'll rely on to respond to crises, readiness must be our highest priority. True military capability never exists on paper; it's measured in the hours spent, experience gained on the training ground, under sail, and in the cockpit. Nothing is more shortsighted than cutting back on training time to cut costs; and nothing, I might add, is more demoralizing to our troops. Our soldiers, sailors, our airmen, our marines must be well-trained, tried and tested, ready to perform every mission we ask of them.

In our restructured forces, reserves will

be important, but in new ways. The need to be prepared for massive, short-term mobilization has diminished; and we can now adjust the size, structure, and readiness of our reserve forces to help us deal with the more likely challenges we will face.

Our strategy will guard against a major reversal in Soviet intentions by incorporating into our planning the concept of reconstitution of our forces. By the mid-nineties the time it would take the Soviets to return to the levels of confrontation that marked the depths of the cold war will be sufficient to allow us to rely not solely on existing forces but to generate wholly new forces. The readiness to rebuild, made explicit in our defense policy, will be an important element in our ability to deter aggression.

A rational restructuring of the kind that I've tried to outline here will take 5 years. I am confident we can meet the challenges that I've outlined today provided we proceed with an orderly reduction, not a fire sale. Any reduction of this magnitude must be managed carefully to minimize dislocations not just to the military balance but, in my view, equally as important, to the morale. And I can say right now as Commander in Chief that we will take every step possible to minimize the turbulence of these changes. The turbulence that will be created for our soldiers, sailors, airmen, and marines. I simply will not break faith with the young men and women who have freely chosen to serve their country.

And frankly, any parents who might be under this tent, you talk to any one of the general officers, and they'll tell you that we have the finest group of young people serving at any time in the history of this country. They are absolutely superb. And they are all volunteers, every single one of them.

All of us know the challenges we face are fiscal as well as military. The budget constraints we face are very real; but so, too, is the need to protect the gains that 40 years of peace through strength have earned us. The simple fact is this: When it comes to national security, America can never afford to fail or fall short.

Let me say once again how very pleased I am to appear here today—especially with our honored friend, Margaret Thatcher. Today, of course, is not the only time Amer-

ican and British leaders have shared the stage. The world remembers that day 44 years ago in Fulton, Missouri, when Churchill delivered what history calls now the Iron Curtain speech. But that wasn't what he called it. He titled it "The Sinews of Peace." And by that he meant to summon up a vision, a vision of strength of free nations united in defense of democracy.

At long last we are writing the final chapter of the 20th century's third great conflict. The cold war is now drawing to a close, and after four decades of division and discord, our challenge today is to fulfill the great dream of all democracies: a true commonwealth of free nations. To marshal the growing forces of the free world, to work together, to bring within reach for all men and nations the liberty that belongs by right to all.

Thank you very much for all you do to contribute to the deliberations that, frankly, have helped lead to a more peaceful world. It is a great honor for me to be here; and I might say, with some special pride, I brought with me one of the movers and shakers of this institute, who I'm proud to have at my right hand every day. I wished I hadn't seen him at 5 o'clock this morning. I'm talking about Brent Scowcroft, who's done such a great job for this institution—hiding in the trees over here. But now I see firsthand what the people here at Aspen saw long ago: just how decent and honorable he is and how strong and knowledgeable. So, I would end by saluting him.

I'm sorry that the Silver Fox is not here. [*Laughter*] At this time of year, we're heavily in the grandchild business, and we have a sick dog. [*Laughter*] So, our priorities are such that she asked me to send you her love and affection and to tell you she's very sorry she's not here. And if I might say parenthetically, I'm proud of Brent, but I'm even prouder of Barbara Bush.

And I would also say—we were faced with a lot of problems here, budget problems, problems with Iraq and Kuwait, problems of restructuring the best defense force in the entire world—but I can't think of a more exciting time in the history of the United States to be your President. And I'm grateful. Thank you very, very much, and

God bless you.

Note: The President spoke at 3:35 p.m. in the Music Tent at the Aspen Institute. In his remarks, the President referred to Lodwrick M. Cook, David McLaughlin, and John Phelan, trustee, president, and chairman of the institute; Jessica Catto, wife of Ambassador Catto; James A. Baker III, Secretary of State; Colin L. Powell, Chairman of the Joint Chiefs of Staff; and Brent Scowcroft, Assistant to the President for National Security Affairs.

Message to the Congress Transmitting the "Regulatory Program of the United States Government"
August 3, 1990

To the Congress of the United States:

The annual *Regulatory Program of the United States Government* sets forth the Administration's regulatory priorities for the coming year. This is my Administration's first *Regulatory Program* published pursuant to Executive Order No. 12498. it represents my long-standing commitment to prudent and cost-effective Federal regulation.

The decade of the nineties will demand governmental action to meet a broad range of challenges and opportunities. Cleaning up the environment, encouraging the use of new technologies, maintaining America's global competitiveness—these are just a few of the issues that will vitally affect the quality of life of all Americans.

My Administration is committed to using necessary Federal regulation, reasonably applied, as an effective tool for positive change. At the same time, imprudent and unnecessary regulation can create greater cost than benefit. Further, many regulations burden the economy by staying on the books long after their useful life is over. Federal regulations impose estimated direct costs on the economy as high as $175 billion annually—more than $1,700 for every taxpayer in the United States. These costs are in effect indirect "taxes" on the American public—taxes that should only be levied when the benefits clearly exceed the costs.

I strongly believe in the commonsense regulatory principles that I helped develop and implement when as Vice President I chaired the Task Force on Regulatory Relief. These principles provide that regulations should be issued only when they are necessary, economically sensible, responsive to public comments and concerns, and understandable. Except where prevented by law, agencies should not take regulatory actions unless the benefits outweigh the costs. Regulations should also improve the quality of life for all Americans, rather than benefit a narrow special interest.

Agencies need to consider the effect of new regulations in the context of existing ones. The overall regulatory structure should be coherent, and obsolete regulations should be eliminated or revised. After considering all of these factors, agencies should select the best regulatory options from among the available alternatives. In doing so, they should select alternatives that minimize paperwork burdens on the public. Agencies should, where appropriate, establish performance standards that allow American businesses (and the marketplace) to choose the most cost-effective way to reach those standards; they should avoid command-and-control regulations that dictate specific solutions. I count on our Cabinet Secretaries and agency heads to use these principles of prudence and cost-effectiveness in developing regulations consistent with law.

To ensure that this Administration continues to remove unnecessary regulatory burdens from the American people, I have asked the Council on Competitiveness, chaired by Vice President Quayle, in conjunction with the Office of Information and Regulatory Affairs, to oversee the regulatory review process established by Executive Orders Nos. 12291 and 12498. Such review should bolster our Nation's competitiveness and strengthen the economy.

Regulatory reform is a continual, dynamic process. In the coming months, agencies within the executive branch will propose, under the guidance of the Council on Competitiveness, new and revised regulatory reforms to reflect the priorities and policies of this Administration. I expect our agency heads to report to me on their progress in these areas. I also expect our regulatory review process will continue to lead to important improvements in the regulatory program of the United States.

GEORGE BUSH

The White House,
August 3, 1990.

Nomination of Paula J. Dobriansky To Be an Associate Director of the United States Information Agency
August 3, 1990

The President today announced his intention to nominate Paula J. Dobriansky, of Virginia, to be an Associate Director of the United States Information Agency for Programs. She would succeed Charles Edward Horner.

Currently Ms. Dobriansky serves as Deputy Assistant Secretary of State for the Bureau of Human Rights and Humanitarian Affairs in Washington, DC. Prior to this, she served as Director of European and Soviet Affairs for the National Security Council at the White House, and Deputy Director of European and Soviet Affairs for the National Security Council, 1983–1984.

Ms. Dobriansky graduated from Georgetown University (B.S.F.S., 1977) and Harvard University (M.A., 1980). She was born September 14, 1955, in Alexandria, VA. Ms. Dobriansky resides in Washington, DC.

Message to the Congress on the Declaration of a National Emergency With Respect to Iraq
August 3, 1990

To the Congress of the United States:

Pursuant to section 204(b) of the International Emergency Economic Powers Act, 50 U.S.C. section 1703(b), and section 201 of the National Emergencies Act, 50 U.S.C. section 1621, I hereby report that I have exercised my statutory authority to declare a national emergency and to issue two Executive orders that:

—prohibit exports and imports of goods and services between the United States and Iraq and the purchase of Iraqi goods by U.S. persons for sale in third countries;

—prohibit transactions related to travel to or from Iraq, except for transactions necessary for journalistic travel or prompt departure from Iraq;

—prohibit transactions related to transportation to or from Iraq, or the use of vessels or aircraft registered in Iraq by U.S. persons;

—prohibit the performance of any contract in support of Government of Iraq projects;

—ban all extensions of credit and loans by U.S. persons to the Government of Iraq;

—block all property of the Government of Iraq now or hereafter located in the United States or in the possession or control of U.S. persons, including their foreign branches; and

—prohibit all transfers or other transactions involving assets belonging to the Government of Kuwait now or hereafter located in the United States or in the possession or control of U.S. persons, including their foreign branches.

The Secretary of the Treasury is authorized to issue regulations implementing these prohibitions. These two orders were effective 5:00 a.m. e.d.t., August 2, 1990.

I am enclosing a copy of each Executive order that I have issued making these declarations and exercising these authorities.

I have authorized these measures in response to the Iraqi invasion of Kuwait, which clearly constitutes an act of aggression and a flagrant violation of international law. This action is in clear violation of the national sovereignty and independence of Kuwait and the Charter of the United Nations. It threatens the entire structure of peaceful relations among nations in this critical region. It constitutes an unusual and extraordinary threat to the national security, foreign policy, and economy of the United States.

The measures we are taking to block Iraqi assets will have the effect of expressing our outrage at Iraq's actions, and will prevent that government from drawing on monies and properties within U.S. control to support its campaign of military aggression against a neighboring state. Our ban on exports to Iraq will prevent the Iraqi government from profiting from the receipt of U.S. goods and technology. Our ban on imports, while not preventing sales of Iraqi oil to third countries, denies Iraq access to the lucrative U.S. market for its most important product.

At the same time, in order to protect the property of the legitimate Government of Kuwait from possible seizure, diversion, or misuse by Iraq, and with the approval of the Kuwaiti government, we are blocking Kuwaiti assets within the jurisdiction of the United States or in the possession or control of U.S. persons.

We are calling upon our friends and allies, and all members of the world community who share our interest in the peaceful resolution of international disputes, to join us in similar actions against Iraq and for the protection of Kuwait.

GEORGE BUSH

The White House,
August 3, 1990.

Note: The Executive orders are listed in Appendix E at the end of this volume.

Nomination of Arlene Render To Be United States Ambassador to The Gambia
August 3, 1990

The President today announced his intention to nominate Arlene Render to be Ambassador Extraordinary and Plenipotentiary of the United States of America to the Republic of The Gambia. She would succeed Ruth V. Washington.

Currently Ms. Render serves as a member of the senior seminar in the Foreign Service Institute in Rosslyn, VA. Prior to this she served as Deputy Chief of Mission in Accra, Ghana. In addition, Ms.

Render has served as a career Foreign Service officer in Cote d'Ivoire, Iran, Italy, the People's Republic of the Congo, Jamaica, and Ghana.

Ms. Render received her bachelor of science degree from West Virginia State College and her masters degree in public health from the University of Michigan. She was born August 16, 1943, in Cleveland, OH. Ms. Render resides in Alexandria, VA.

Nomination of Gordon L. Streeb To Be United States Ambassador to Zambia
August 3, 1990

The President today announced his intention to nominate Gordon L. Streeb, of Colorado, a career member of the Senior Foreign Service, Class of Minister-Counselor, to be Ambassador Extraordinary and Plenipotentiary of the United States of America to the Republic of Zambia. He would succeed Jeffrey Davidow.

Since 1988 Dr. Streeb has served as Senior Inspector in the Office of the Inspector General at the Department of State. Prior to this, he served as Deputy Chief of Mission for the United States Embassy in New Delhi, India, 1984–1988; Deputy Assistant Secretary for Economic and Social Affairs at the Bureau of International Organization Affairs at the Department of State, 1981–1984; executive assistant for the Under Secretary for Economic Affairs at the Department of State, 1980–1981; economic Counselor for the United States Mission to the European Office of the United Nations and other International Organizations in Geneva, 1977–1980; instructor in economics, 1974–1975; international economist in the Office of Trade Agreements for the Bureau of Economic and Business Affairs at the Department of State, 1973–1977; examiner for the Board of Examiners for the Foreign Service at the Department of State, 1972–1973; and as an instructor in economics, 1969–1972.

Dr. Streeb graduated from the University of Colorado (B.S., 1959) and the University of Minnesota (Ph.D., 1978). He served in the United States Air Force Reserve, 1961–1966. Dr. Streeb was born December 24, 1935, in Windsor, CO. He is married, has three children, and resides in Centreville, VA.

Nomination of Donna M. Owens To Be Director of the Bureau of Justice Assistance
August 3, 1990

The President today announced his intention to nominate Donna M. Owens to be Director of the Bureau of Justice Assistance at the Department of Justice. This is a new position.

Ms. Owens has been the mayor of the City of Toledo in Ohio, 1983–1989. Prior to this, she served as a city councilwoman in Toledo, 1979–1983. In addition, Ms. Owens served as vice president of the Lucas County Board of Education, 1976–1979.

Ms. Owens attended Stautzenberger Business College, 1955. She was born August 24, 1936, in Toledo, OH. She has three children and resides in Toledo, OH.

Remarks and an Exchange With Reporters on the Iraqi Invasion of Kuwait
August 3, 1990

The President. I listened to Marlin's briefing, and I know most of your questions have been handled. And I don't intend to have a major question and answer period here; but I wanted you to know that, first off, we view this situation with gravity. We view it as a matter of grave concern to this country, and internationally as well. What Iraq has done violates every norm of international law.

I have been meeting this morning with my top security experts from the defense side, the economic side; and I'll have another such meeting tomorrow at Camp David. I've been talking to some of the world leaders, and one of the reasons for the delay is I've just hung up from talking again to Margaret Thatcher, informing me of steps that the United Kingdom has taken. We are moving with them and many other countries in terms of how we view these international sanctions—tightening that up along the way.

I talked also to another staunch friend of the United States just a few minutes ago: President Özal of Turkey. Turkey, as you know, is in a very strategic location of geographical importance—importance as a steadfast member of NATO. I think it's fair to say that President Özal and I look at this matter with the same sense of urgency and concern.

So, we're following it closely. We've got many diplomatic channels open. I will be making several other calls to world leaders before I go to bed tonight, and I expect over the weekend. But before I left here, I wanted to make very clear to everybody how strongly I feel about the nature of this uncalled-for invasion and our determination to see the matter resolved.

Q. They're only 5 miles from the Saudi border.

The President. Helen [Helen Thomas, United Press International]?

Q. What can you do if Iraq decides to expand into Saudi Arabia?

The President. I'm not discussing options, but I would simply say the status quo is unacceptable, and further expansion would be even more unacceptable. There are a lot of options. I'm not going to discuss what they are. We've already taken economic steps, and all options are open—economic and otherwise.

Q. Mr. President, do you feel your hands are tied until these Arab meetings conclude and they decide what they're going to do?

The President. No. I support the fact that Foreign Ministers have met in Cairo. I am very pleased that there is active diplomacy going on in Saudi Arabia—high-level official from Iraq meeting today, as I understand it, with the top officials in Saudi Arabia. All that is good. But my hands aren't tied in terms of having to wait for somebody else in any way. But there's a certain complication to all of this that requires a certain amount of time. It's not an easy matter in any sense—economically, militarily, anything else.

But I want to just make clear here how strongly we all feel about it. And I'm not just talking about the United States; I'm talking to every leader I've talked to.

Q. Mr. President, it's been reported that Saddam Hussein [President of Iraq] has informed the Soviets that he was going to pull his troops out of Kuwait in a few days.

The President. Well, let's see him haul them out right now, then. I saw that report. And very candidly, let me say something about the Soviet Union. I am very, very pleased with the cooperation that we're having with the Soviet Union on this important question. If you go back a few years, that would have been a very different ingredient, a different part of the equation. So, because the Soviet Union has had in the past reasonably good relations, let us hope that Saddam Hussein will do what that report indicated. But I can't comment, Jim [Jim Miklaszewski, NBC News]. I don't know how accurate it is.

Q. Mr. President, economic sanctions have not had a very good history of effectiveness. Why do you think they will work in this case?

The President. I didn't say I thought they would work. But we're putting them on there, and we're going to go and do everything we can to see that they do work. But, yes, you're right, there's been a spotty record of economic sanctions working. Iraq, in spite of its underground wealth, has some big economic problems. We have taken the lead, and I think properly so, in slapping an embargo on those. And then we're also talking at the United Nations about chapter VII action. But you're right; you put a finger on what's happened to some of them in the past, and I think we have to consider that as I review all options.

Brit [Brit Hume, ABC News]?

Q. Mr. President, you said yesterday morning in the Cabinet Room that you would not discuss intervention. Now you're saying, and have been saying since yesterday afternoon, that all options are open. What, if anything, has changed, sir?

The President. Nothing has really changed. I perhaps was inaccurate in answering the question. What I thought I was doing was waiting until the briefing was over.

Q. Are you committed to defending Saudi Arabia if the Iraqis cross the border?

The President. The integrity of Saudi Arabia, its freedom, are very, very important to the United States; and I've made that clear to King Fahd in a very long conversation with him yesterday. General Scowcroft met with the Saudi Ambassador today, and I think he's had other meetings with government officials. And we're making sure that the Saudis know that. When you look at vital interests of the United States, the relationship with Saudi Arabia and its independence and its freedom come under the heading of very, very important.

Q. Did the Saudis ask for anything specifically? And I'd like to ask you about the Turks as well.

The President. I can't divulge the details of the conversations I've had with King Fahd; but if they ask for specific help, it depends, obviously, what it is. But I would be inclined to help in any way we possibly can. It's that serious. All you have to do is look at the energy requirements of the world plus the direct violation of international law by Saddam Hussein to understand why I feel so strongly about it.

What was the second part?

Q. Will the Turks cut off the Iraqi pipeline? Did you ask them to?

The President. I'm again not going to go into details. But clearly, a good deal of that oil goes out through Turkey. And that will be an option I'm certain.

Q. But if he's in accord with you, doesn't he need to do this?

The President. I'm not discussing the details of these conversations. One of the difficulties is there's a lot of questions that the American people would like to have the answers to. But I have got to go forward with a reasonable degree of confidentiality so that I work in concert with our allies. And then, sometimes, maybe we'll have to work on our own. In this question, clearly, we need to have cooperation of allies.

Q. They just asked mine.

The President. Did they? Good. Well then I'll go to Camp David. Thank you all very much. Thank you.

Q. Mr. President, there's some talk of a meeting in Jedda. Do you see the diplomatic efforts getting better at all within the Arab League?

The President. I'm encouraged when I see diplomatic efforts. But, no, I can't tell you I see the results of those any better today than I did yesterday.

Q. What about the effect on our energy supply, sir?

Q. What about the missing Americans, Mr. President? How concerned are you about them?

The President. We have no reports of Americans being held against their will, because as I indicated yesterday, that is a matter of importance to us.

Q. What about the effect on our energy supply, sir, and the ramifications about the price situation and the supply situation?

The President. The economic aspects of this are well-known to the American people. And fortunately, right now there's a bit of an overhang of surplus crude, but that's short-run. And long-run economic effects on the free world could be devastating, and that's one of the reasons I'm as concerned as I am. And that's one of the reasons, incidentally, I've been talking about having a strong defense in this country. And it's time some of our Congressmen wake up to the need to have a strong defense.

Thank you all very much.

Note: The exchange began at 3:15 p.m. on the South Lawn at the White House, prior to the President's departure for Camp David, MD. In his remarks, the President referred to Marlin Fitzwater, Press Secretary to the President; King Fahd bin 'Abd al-

'Aziz Al Sa'ud of Saudi Arabia; Brent Scow-croft, Assistant to the President for Nation- *al Security Affairs; and Prince Bandar bin Sultan, Ambassador from Saudi Arabia.*

Statement by Press Secretary Fitzwater on the Evacuation of United States Citizens From Liberia
August 5, 1990

We have been advised that the initial stages of this morning's Liberia operation have been successfully completed. A total of 59 people were flown to U.S. Navy ships offshore by U.S. Marine Corps helicopters. The U.S. Marine Corps reinforced rifle company is in place providing protection for U.S. citizens. The initial operation went well, and we are unaware of any shots being fired or resistance encountered.

Statement by Press Secretary Fitzwater on Japanese Economic Sanctions Against Iraq
August 5, 1990

Prime Minister Kaifu of Japan called the President this morning to inform the President of Japan's decision to impose various sanctions against Iraq. These unprecedented measures undertaken by Japan are in step with those that the United States and other countries have put in place against Iraq for its blatant aggression against Kuwait. The President welcomed Prime Minister Kaifu and the Japanese Cabinet's decision and expressed confidence that such measures will help intensify international pressures aimed at achieving the immediate, complete, and unconditional withdrawal of Iraq from Kuwait.

Remarks and an Exchange With Reporters on the Iraqi Invasion of Kuwait
August 5, 1990

The President. Hello, everybody. I just wanted to fill you all in on the diplomatic activity that is taking place—intensive diplomatic activity around the world. I've got to go in now. I'm getting another call from President Özal of Turkey, with whom I have been in previous conversation. Yesterday I talked to him.

I talked this morning to Prime Minister Kaifu, and I applaud Japan's stance: cracking down on the imports from Iraq. I just hung up, up there in Camp David, talking with Prime Minister Mulroney. We're all in the same accord—he and President Mitter- rand, with whom I've spoken, Chancellor Kohl, Margaret Thatcher. I think the alliance, the NATO alliance, is thinking exactly the same way on this. I also talked yesterday to Kuwait's Amir and gave him certain assurances.

What's emerging is nobody seems to be showing up as willing to accept anything less than total withdrawal from Kuwait of the Iraqi forces, and no puppet regime. We've been down that road, and there will be no puppet regime that will be accepted by any countries that I'm familiar with. And there seems to be a united front out there that says Iraq, having committed brutal, naked aggression, ought to get out, and that this concept of their installing some puppet—leaving behind—will not be acceptable.

So, we're pushing forward on diplomacy. Tomorrow I'll meet here in Washington with the Secretary General of NATO. And Margaret Thatcher will be coming in here tomorrow, and I will be continuing this diplomatic effort. And I'm sure you know of the meeting I had in Camp David with some of our top military people, and I will continue that kind of consultation as well.

Q. How are you going to keep the puppet government from being accepted and installed? And are you going to move militarily?

The President. There is no intention on the part of any of these countries to accept a puppet government, and that signal is going out loud and clear to Iraq. I will not discuss with you what my options are or might be, but they're wide open, I can assure you of that.

Q. Have you talked to Saudi Arabia and the Turks about turning off the oil pipeline to their countries to——

The President. All options are open. There is a strong feeling on the part of the NATO countries to whom I've talked, Turkey being one of them, that we must have concerted and, I'd say—well, concerted action to isolate Iraq economically. And you can just assume from there that those matters are being considered.

Q. Are the Saudis inclined to cut off the pipeline, Mr. President?

The President. I can't tell you the state of play. I've discussed this with King Fahd and I—whether I'll be talking to him again today, I don't know. But I'm not going to characterize their position on this. Let them speak for themselves.

Q. Mr. President, what is the situation on the ground? Do the Iraqis appear to be dug in, or are they readying for——

The President. Iraqi lied once again. They said they were going to start moving out today, and we have no evidence of their moving out.

Q. Do we have evidence that there's 18 new divisions coming in as——

The President. I'm not going to discuss the intelligence situation on the ground right now, but I've not heard a figure of 18 new divisions going in.

Q. Have you given any time of ultimatum——

Q. Are Americans in danger in Kuwait or other areas down there? And you said——

The President. I wouldn't want to say they're in danger, but you know how I feel about the protection of American life and willingness to do whatever is necessary to protect it. But I don't have the feeling that they're in imminent danger right now.

Q. And the people who are now in control in Kuwait are saying they may close some of the Embassies in Kuwait City, that they will regard any reaction against them as, "You should take care if you have your nationals in our country." Isn't that a threat?

The President. I'm not trying to characterize threats. The threat is a vicious aggression against Kuwait, and that speaks for itself. And anything collaterally is just simply more indication that these are outlaws, international outlaws and renegades. And I want to see the United Nations move soon with chapter VII sanctions; and I want to see the rest of the world join us, as they are in overwhelming numbers, to isolate Saddam Hussein.

Q. Mr. President, how can you and other world leaders prevent the installation of what you term a puppet government?

The President. Just wait. Watch and learn.

Q. Mr. President, have you, in fact, tried to reach Saddam Hussein to tell him all these other things?

The President. No. No, I have not.

Q. But King Hussein has embraced him.

Q. Mr. President, have we asked the Saudi Arabians for the use of their military bases?

The President. I'm not going to discuss what I'm talking to the Saudis about. I'm not going to discuss anything to do about military options at all.

Q. Mr. President, have you talked to King Hussein of Jordan, because he indicated his support for——

The President. I talked to him once, and that's all.

Q. Are you disappointed in what he said?

Q. But he's embraced Saddam Hussein. He went to Baghdad and embraced him.

The President. What's your question? I can read.

Q. Are you disappointed in what King Hussein has said?

The President. I want to see the Arab States join the rest of the world in condemning this outrage, in doing what they can to get Saddam Hussein out. Now, he was talking—King Hussein—about an Arab solution. But I am disappointed to find any comment by anyone that apologizes or appears to condone what's taken place.

Q. Is Secretary Cheney going to Saudi Arabia, sir?

The President. I'm not going to comment on anything that we're doing of that nature.

Q. Mr. President, are you disappointed in the failure of the Arab nations——

The President. Well, I was told by one leader that I respect enormously—I believe this was back on Friday—that they needed 48 hours to find what was called an Arab solution. That obviously has failed. And of course, I'm disappointed that the matter hasn't been resolved before now. It's a very serious matter.

I'll take one more, and then I've got to go to work over here.

Q. Have you already taken steps to protect Americans over there? Have you——

The President. I'm not going to discuss what we're doing in terms of moving of forces, anything of that nature. But I view it very seriously, not just that but any threat to any other countries, as well as I view very seriously our determination to reverse out this aggression. And please believe me, there are an awful lot of countries that are in total accord with what I've just said, and I salute them. They are staunch friends and allies, and we will be working with them all for collective action. This will not stand. This will not stand, this aggression against Kuwait.

I've got to go. I have to go to work. I've got to go to work.

Note: President Bush spoke at 3:05 p.m. on the South Lawn of the White House upon returning from a weekend stay at Camp David, MD. In his remarks, he referred to Prime Minister Brian Mulroney of Canada, President François Mitterrand of France, Chancellor Helmut Kohl of the Federal Republic of Germany, Prime Minister Margaret Thatcher of the United Kingdom, Amir Jabir al-Ahmad al-Jabir Al Sabah of Kuwait, NATO Secretary General Manfred Woerner, and President Saddam Hussein of Iraq.

Remarks at the Presentation Ceremony for the All-American Cities Awards
August 6, 1990

The President. Thank you very much. Excuse the little delay here. Welcome to the White House. I want to single out an old friend of mine, Henry Cisneros, the chair of the National Civic League. Wayne Hedien of Allstate, Members of Congress who are here, State representatives, mayors and, above all, some friends of the finest cities in America, it's an honor and, indeed, a pleasure to have you here at the White House.

The event is special. It's special because too often it seems the function of the Federal Government is to make laws and set limits. But the cities and citizens we honor today are reminders that America's potential is truly unlimited. The All-American Cities are all-American success stories. At a time when so many mourn what's wrong with American cities, you have quietly gone to work to make them right. You've refused to surrender to crime and to drug dealers and to natural disaster, to despair. You refuse to see the problems of the homeless and the jobless as somehow impossible to solve. Instead, you've set out to unleash the infinitive range of what is possible when Americans really put their minds to it.

Along the way, you've reaffirmed the American ideal of empowerment. Empowerment sounds like a new idea, but it's something President Teddy Roosevelt well understood and wanted to promote when he founded the National Civic League back in 1894. "There are many different ways," he once wrote, "in which a man or a woman can work for the higher life of American cities."

Well, the men and women with us are proving Teddy Roosevelt right. So, we've gathered to celebrate the spirit of empowerment and the potential of partnerships perhaps unique in America, the spirit that in an earlier time could have built a meetinghouse or raised a barn on a windswept field.

Today the All-America Cities are forming partnership for challenges of every kind. In small industrial towns, in urban canyons, citizens, businesses, government, and volunteers are joining forces for the future of their communities. In some cases, they've mobilized after an accident, like Flight 232 in Sioux City, Iowa, whose citizens had planned and acted on an outstanding emergency response system. Or, they've responded to a natural disaster the way the people of Charlotte-Mecklenburg, North Carolina, did after Hurricane Hugo.

All Americans are uplifted by stories of courage and compassion that emerged during those difficult times. No hand was idle and, certainly, no heart was untouched. But these cities and others have been just as notable, I think, for their courage and creativity in meeting the longer term challenges.

When the schools of South Gate in Los Angeles faced an enrollment explosion, young kids—many of them immigrant and at-risk in overcrowded classrooms—civic volunteers, and local businesses volunteered money and time and talent to turn the tide against drugs and gangs. The kids, 15,000 of them, got involved in marches and posters and essay contests and assemblies and anti-gang, antidrug pledges. Test scores improved. Attendance went from among the lowest to among the highest in the Los Angeles School District, and the dropout rate is now the lowest in the L.A. Unified School District—an outstanding case study in how

to save our schools.

The same vision for a better future has driven the city of South St. Paul as they deal with the challenges and the change. Rather than mourning the loss of a key industry, citizens began to plan a public walkway and trail system on old industrial land along the river. And volunteers work tirelessly at town meetings to convince their neighbors that urban renewal means an improved city, economic growth, and new jobs. Stock certificates for Mississippi Miles were sold for $1 each, enlisting even the kids. Now the center of South St. Paul is coming back to life. One high school senior even told a local historian, "I just have to thank you for giving me back my hometown."

For 41 years the National Civic League has recognized community excellence through these awards. Success stories like these—as in Bakersfield, California, and Tampa, Florida; Coeur D'Alene, Idaho; Hamlet, North Carolina; Harrisburg, Pennsylvania; Abilene, Texas—all are a hopeful reminder that the success of democracy depends on the resilience and capacity of citizens for self-governance, education, civic responsibility, and economic development.

We single out all 10 of these cities not because they claim to be the best cities in America—I think they're too smart or, in some instances, too modest for that—but because they represent what's best about American cities. Rather than looking for an outside solution or a quick fix, they're looking within for the answers and they're finding them. By recognizing and unleashing the power and potential of the people themselves, they're proving that big cities can meet enormous challenges, small towns can do very big things.

So, congratulations to all of you. You've earned the admiration of the Nation because when people say, "It can never be done," you're doing it. And when they say, "You can't get there from here," you've proved that you can. So, I'm very grateful, and now if I could ask Henry and Wayne to join me up here, we'd like to present this year's awards. Congratulations to all of you.

Note: The President spoke at 10:15 a.m. in

Room 450 of the Old Executive Office Building. In his remarks, he referred to Wayne Hedien, chairman and chief executive officer of Allstate Insurance Co.

Nomination of Herbert Donald Gelber To Be United States Ambassador to Mali
August 6, 1990

The President has nominated Herbert Donald Gelber, of Florida, to be Ambassador Extraordinary and Plenipotentiary of the United States of America to the Republic of Mali. He would succeed Robert Maxwell Pringle.

Since 1986 Mr. Gelber has served as Special Assistant for International Affairs to the Supreme Allied Commander in Europe. Prior to this, he served as Chargé d'Affaires in Lagos, Nigeria, 1985–1986; Deputy Chief of Mission in Lagos, Nigeria, 1982–1984; Director of the Office of Research and Analysis for Western Europe, 1980–1982; counselor for political-military affairs in Ankara, Turkey, 1978–1980; legislative management officer in the Bureau of Congressional Relations, 1976–1978; foreign policy adviser to the Commander in Chief for the U.S. Naval Forces in Europe, 1973–1976; Special Assistant for International Affairs to the Chief of Naval Operations, 1971–1973; and Special Assistant to the Assistant Secretary for Political-Military Affairs, 1969–1971. In addition, Mr. Gelber was assigned to the consulate general at Calcutta, India, 1965–1969; the Embassy in Pakistan, 1961–1965; and assigned as a junior officer to the Embassy in Greece, 1958–1960. He joined the Foreign Service in 1957.

Mr. Gelber graduated from City College of New York (B.A., 1954) and Columbia University (M.A., 1956). He was born July 20, 1932, in Brooklyn, NY. Mr. Gelber is married and has two children.

Nomination of Scott M. Spangler To Be an Assistant Administrator of the Agency for International Development
August 6, 1990

The President has nominated Scott M. Spangler, of Arizona, to be an Assistant Administrator of the Agency for International Development, U.S. International Development Cooperation Agency, for the Bureau for Africa. He would succeed Charles L. Gladson.

Currently Mr. Spangler serves as president of First Phoenix Capitol, Inc., in Scottsdale, AZ. Prior to this, he served as president, chief executive officer, and director of AZL Resources, Inc., 1973–1984; president of Spangler and Co., in Houston, TX, 1970–1973; vice president of finance for the industrial group at White Motor Co., in Houston, TX, 1968–1970; assistant controller and assistant treasurer for Cooper Industries, Inc., in Mount Vernon, OH, 1966–1968; and an MIT fellow in Africa, 1963–1966.

Mr. Spangler graduated as a mechanical engineer from the University of Cincinnati in 1961, and he received a master's in business administration from Harvard Business School in 1963. He was born August 4, 1938, in Toledo, OH. Mr. Spangler is married, has three children, and resides in Paradise Valley, AZ.

Nomination of Charles B. DeWitt To Be Director of the National Institute of Justice
August 6, 1990

The President has nominated Charles B. DeWitt, of the District of Columbia, to be Director of the National Institute of Justice, Department of Justice. He would succeed James K. Stewart.

Currently Mr. DeWitt serves as an independent consultant for the Department of Justice and as a research fellow for the National Institute of Justice for the Department of Justice in Washington, DC. Prior to this he served as director of the justice division for Santa Clara County, CA, 1978–1984; program manager in the office of the county executive in Santa Clara County,

CA, 1978; criminal justice specialist for the criminal justice planning board in Santa Clara County, CA, 1974–1978; staff analyst for community development study at Stanford University, 1970–1972; and deputy sheriff in the office of the sheriff in Santa Clara County, CA, 1971–1974.

Mr. DeWitt graduated from Stanford University (B.A., 1972). He was born March 13, 1950, in Los Angeles, CA. Mr. DeWitt served in the U.S. Marine Corps, 1968–1971. He is married and resides in Washington, DC.

Appointment of Charles E.M. Kolb as Deputy Assistant to the President for Domestic Policy
August 6, 1990

The President today announced the appointment of Charles E.M. Kolb to be Deputy Assistant to the President for Domestic Policy. He would succeed William Roper.

Since 1988 Mr. Kolb has served as Deputy Under Secretary for Planning, Budget, and Evaluation at the Department of Education. Prior to this, he served as Deputy General Counsel for Regulations and Legislation at the Department of Edu-

cation, 1986–1988; Assistant General Counsel in the Office of Management and Budget, 1983–1986; and a lawyer with the law firm of Covington and Burling and with the law firm of Foreman and Dyess.

Mr. Kolb graduated from Princeton University (A.B., 1973), Oxford University (M.A., 1980), and the University of Virginia (J.D., 1978). He is married and resides in Alexandria, VA.

Remarks and an Exchange With Reporters Following a Meeting With Prime Minister Margaret Thatcher of the United Kingdom and Secretary General Manfred Woerner of the North Atlantic Treaty Organization
August 6, 1990

The President. We better get Manfred Woerner. But listen, it's raining out here. This was basically a chance to have a photo to show that we were having these very

important consultations. I might say that we are very encouraged, all of us, by the action taken in the United Nations—a strong resolution up there that shows, I think, that the world is united against the kind of aggression that we've witnessed.

But I'd like to ask our guest, the Prime Minister, to say a word, and then the Secretary General, who's just arrived. We were going to do this differently, but now we're out here. Go ahead, please, Margaret.

The Prime Minister. May I support the President of the United States in saying that the news from the United Nations and the strength of the vote—13 votes in favor of mandatory, comprehensive sanctions and no votes against—is very good. That means that it becomes law in all the countries of the world. That is extremely good. It also follows the strong support that has been given by the European countries in their condemnation of the action of Saddam Hussein in invading Kuwait. Japan also condemned strongly, and so did the Soviet Union. So, really, the world is condemning the action, and the United Nations resolution will become mandatory and mean that those sanctions must be enforceable.

I cannot remember a time when we had the world so strongly together against an action as now, and I hope that those sanctions will be properly and effectively enforced as a positive action against what we all totally and utterly condemn.

The President. Manfred, are you prepared to say a word?

The Secretary General. I just arrived. Just a few thoughts which we have exchanged. My impression is that this is the moment for the West to show cohesion, determination and to make it clear what cannot be accepted in this world and to safeguard its own security interests.

The President. Thank you all.

Iraqi Invasion of Kuwait

Q. Mr. President, have you received any assurances from Saddam Hussein that he won't invade Saudi Arabia?

Q. Mr. President, did you hear from Saddam today?

The President. I have had no such assurances directly to me.

And what was the last question? We really have to get in. You all are getting——

Q. Did you get a message, a personal message, from Saddam?

The President. No, I have not had a personal——

Q. Do you hope that, in light of these sanctions, that you can forgo a blockade?

The President. These sanctions—we need to discuss full and total implementation of these sanctions, ruling out nothing at all. These sanctions must be enforced. I think the will of the nations around the world—not just the NATO countries, not just the EC, not just one area or another—the will of the nations around the world will be to enforce these sanctions. So, we'll leave the details of how we implement it to the future. But we'll begin working on that immediately, working—one of the consultations that's going on right now in the Oval Office is just exactly how we go about encouraging others to do that and what we ourselves should be doing.

Q. Mr. President, the oil pipeline in Saudi Arabia——

Q. Well, what did Saddam tell the U.S. Counselor—Chargé?

The President. These things will be enforced, whatever it takes.

Note: The President spoke at 3:57 p.m. in the Colonnade at the White House. Saddam Hussein was President of Iraq.

Statement by Press Secretary Fitzwater on the Cease-Fire Between the African National Congress and the Government of South Africa
August 6, 1990

We welcome the report of a cease-fire in South Africa. We are very encouraged and congratulate both parties for having made this important step forward. The United

States has urged dialog for bringing an end to apartheid. We hope this step facilitates this process.

Statement by Press Secretary Fitzwater on the Anniversary of the Central American Peace Plan
August 7, 1990

August 7th commemorates a decisive anniversary in the history of Central America: the third anniversary of the signing in Guatemala City of Esquipulas II, the Central American peace plan. On this date 3 years ago, farsighted and courageous Central American leaders decided to forge a destiny of peace by constructing a framework for democracy. Enshrined as the central pillar of this agreement was the promise to "make dialog prevail over violence and reason over rancor."

Three years later, Central Americans can proudly claim progress. Fair and honest elections were held in Nicaragua, a coalition committed to the consolidation of democratic institutions has been elected, and the civil war has ended. President Chamorro [of Nicaragua] is courageously rebuilding her country. Although irregular forces still conduct campaigns of violence against democratically elected governments in El Salvador and Guatemala, a serious process of dialog has begun in both countries which we hope will lead to an end to the war and a strengthening of democracy.

We salute the work of Presidents Calderon [of Costa Rica], Callejas [of Honduras], Cerezo [of Guatemala], Chamorro, and Cristiani [of El Salvador] and the work of their predecessors. On this day, we join with them in recommitting the United States to work with them and all Central Americans for democracy, development, and peace in the spirit of Esquipulas.

Address to the Nation Announcing the Deployment of United States Armed Forces to Saudi Arabia
August 8, 1990

In the life of a nation, we're called upon to define who we are and what we believe. Sometimes these choices are not easy. But today as President, I ask for your support in a decision I've made to stand up for what's right and condemn what's wrong, all in the cause of peace.

At my direction, elements of the 82d Airborne Division as well as key units of the United States Air Force are arriving today to take up defensive positions in Saudi Arabia. I took this action to assist the Saudi Arabian Government in the defense of its homeland. No one commits America's Armed Forces to a dangerous mission lightly, but after perhaps unparalleled international consultation and exhausting every alternative, it became necessary to take this action. Let me tell you why.

Less than a week ago, in the early morning hours of August 2d, Iraqi Armed Forces, without provocation or warning, invaded a peaceful Kuwait. Facing negligible resistance from its much smaller neighbor, Iraq's tanks stormed in blitzkrieg fashion through Kuwait in a few short hours. With more than 100,000 troops, along with tanks, artillery, and surface-to-surface missiles, Iraq now occupies Kuwait. This aggression came just hours after Saddam Hussein specifically assured numerous countries in the area that there would be no invasion. There is no justification whatsoever for this outrageous and brutal act of aggression.

A puppet regime imposed from the outside is unacceptable. The acquisition of territory by force is unacceptable. No one, friend or foe, should doubt our desire for peace; and no one should underestimate our determination to confront aggression.

Four simple principles guide our policy. First, we seek the immediate, unconditional, and complete withdrawal of all Iraqi forces from Kuwait. Second, Kuwait's legitimate government must be restored to replace the puppet regime. And third, my administration, as has been the case with every President from President Roosevelt to President Reagan, is committed to the security and stability of the Persian Gulf. And fourth, I am determined to protect the lives of American citizens abroad.

Immediately after the Iraqi invasion, I ordered an embargo of all trade with Iraq and, together with many other nations, announced sanctions that both freeze all Iraqi assets in this country and protected Kuwait's assets. The stakes are high. Iraq is already a rich and powerful country that possesses the world's second largest reserves of oil and over a million men under arms. It's the fourth largest military in the world. Our country now imports nearly half the oil it consumes and could face a major threat to its economic independence. Much of the world is even more dependent upon imported oil and is even more vulnerable to Iraqi threats.

We succeeded in the struggle for freedom in Europe because we and our allies remain stalwart. Keeping the peace in the Middle East will require no less. We're beginning a new era. This new era can be full of promise, an age of freedom, a time of peace for all peoples. But if history teaches us anything, it is that we must resist aggression or it will destroy our freedoms. Appeasement does not work. As was the case in the 1930's, we see in Saddam Hussein an aggressive dictator threatening his neighbors. Only 14 days ago, Saddam Hussein promised his friends he would not invade Kuwait. And 4 days ago, he promised the world he would withdraw. And twice we have seen what his promises mean: His promises mean nothing.

In the last few days, I've spoken with political leaders from the Middle East, Europe, Asia, and the Americas; and I've met with Prime Minister Thatcher, Prime Minister Mulroney, and NATO Secretary General Woerner. And all agree that Iraq cannot be allowed to benefit from its invasion of Kuwait.

We agree that this is not an American problem or a European problem or a Middle East problem: It is the world's problem. And that's why, soon after the Iraqi invasion, the United Nations Security Council, without dissent, condemned Iraq, calling for the immediate and unconditional withdrawal of its troops from Kuwait. The Arab world, through both the Arab League and the Gulf Cooperation Council, courageously announced its opposition to Iraqi aggression. Japan, the United Kingdom, and France, and other governments around the world have imposed severe sanctions. The Soviet Union and China ended all arms sales to Iraq.

And this past Monday, the United Nations Security Council approved for the first time in 23 years mandatory sanctions under chapter VII of the United Nations Charter. These sanctions, now enshrined in international law, have the potential to deny Iraq the fruits of aggression while sharply limiting its ability to either import or export anything of value, especially oil.

I pledge here today that the United States will do its part to see that these sanctions are effective and to induce Iraq to withdraw without delay from Kuwait.

But we must recognize that Iraq may not stop using force to advance its ambitions. Iraq has massed an enormous war machine on the Saudi border capable of initiating hostilities with little or no additional preparation. Given the Iraqi government's history of aggression against its own citizens as well as its neighbors, to assume Iraq will not attack again would be unwise and unrealistic.

And therefore, after consulting with King Fahd, I sent Secretary of Defense Dick Cheney to discuss cooperative measures we could take. Following those meetings, the Saudi Government requested our help, and I responded to that request by ordering U.S. air and ground forces to deploy to the Kingdom of Saudi Arabia.

Let me be clear: The sovereign independence of Saudi Arabia is of vital interest to the United States. This decision, which I shared with the congressional leadership, grows out of the longstanding friendship and security relationship between the United States and Saudi Arabia. U.S. forces will work together with those of Saudi Arabia and other nations to preserve the integrity of Saudi Arabia and to deter further Iraqi aggression. Through their presence, as well as through training and exercises, these multinational forces will enhance the overall capability of Saudi Armed Forces to defend the Kingdom.

I want to be clear about what we are doing and why. America does not seek conflict, nor do we seek to chart the destiny of other nations. But America will stand by her friends. The mission of our troops is wholly defensive. Hopefully, they will not be needed long. They will not initiate hostilities, but they will defend themselves, the Kingdom of Saudi Arabia, and other friends in the Persian Gulf.

We are working around the clock to deter Iraqi aggression and to enforce U.N. sanctions. I'm continuing my conversations with world leaders. Secretary of Defense Cheney has just returned from valuable consultations with President Mubarak of Egypt and King Hassan of Morocco. Secretary of State Baker has consulted with his counterparts in many nations, including the Soviet Union, and today he heads for Europe to consult with President Özal of Turkey, a staunch friend of the United States. And he'll then consult with the NATO Foreign Ministers.

I will ask oil-producing nations to do what they can to increase production in order to minimize any impact that oil flow reduc- tions will have on the world economy. And I will explore whether we and our allies should draw down our strategic petroleum reserves. Conservation measures can also help; Americans everywhere must do their part. And one more thing: I'm asking the oil companies to do their fair share. They should show restraint and not abuse today's uncertainties to raise prices.

Standing up for our principles will not come easy. It may take time and possibly cost a great deal. But we are asking no more of anyone than of the brave young men and women of our Armed Forces and their families. And I ask that in the churches around the country prayers be said for those who are committed to protect and defend America's interests.

Standing up for our principle is an American tradition. As it has so many times before, it may take time and tremendous effort, but most of all, it will take unity of purpose. As I've witnessed throughout my life in both war and peace, America has never wavered when her purpose is driven by principle. And in this August day, at home and abroad, I know she will do no less.

Thank you, and God bless the United States of America.

Note: The President spoke at 9 a.m. from the Oval Office at the White House. In his remarks, he referred to President Saddam Hussein of Iraq, Prime Minister Margaret Thatcher of the United Kingdom, Prime Minister Brian Mulroney of Canada, and King Fahd bin 'Abd al-'Aziz Al Sa'ud of Saudi Arabia. The address was broadcast live on nationwide radio and television.

The President's News Conference
August 8, 1990

The President. Terry [Terence Hunt, Associated Press]?

Persian Gulf Crisis

Q. Mr. President, how many American troops have you sent to Saudi Arabia? How long are you committed to keeping them there? And why not use them to drive Iraqi forces out of Kuwait?

The President. There will be a military briefing at the Pentagon—I think it's within an hour—and so, I'll leave the numbers to them. I would expect there would be some reluctance to give out specific numbers at this point for very obvious reasons.——

What was the last part of your——

Q. The other parts, sir, were: How long will you keep American forces in Saudi Arabia, and why not use them to drive the Iraqi troops out of Kuwait?

The President. Well, as you know from what I said, they're there in a defensive mode right now, and therefore, that is not the mission to drive the Iraqis out of Kuwait. We have economic sanctions that I hope will be effective to that end. And I don't know how long they'll be there. They just got there or are just getting there.

Q. Is this an open-ended commitment? I mean, could this drag on for years?

The President. Nothing is open-ended, but I'm not worrying about that there at all. I'm worrying about getting them there and doing what I indicated in our speech in there is necessary: the defense of the Saudis and trying through concerted international means to reverse out this aggression.

Q. Mr. President, are we in a war? And what other nations have agreed to join our forces in defending Saudi Arabia? And I take it you also have included other Gulf nations in that umbrella.

The President. We're not in a war. We have sent forces to defend Saudi Arabia. I will leave announcements about what other nations will be participating to the Saudis. But I believe Margaret Thatcher, after talking to King Fahd [of Saudi Arabia], has announced that forces will be going in; and then I think you'll see other such actions. But I'd much prefer to leave that to Saudi Arabia, who indeed—it's their country.

Q. But was [Secretary of Defense] Cheney's mission successful in rallying support with Egypt and Morocco?

The President. Well, I, having talked to Mubarak [President of Egypt] a couple of times myself, feel that we are in very close agreement with him.

Who was your other country you asked about?

Q. Morocco, Yemen.

The President. Morocco—very, very supportive of the Saudis and of our overall position on the Mideast. So, I was very pleased with the Cheney mission in that regard.

Brit [Brit Hume, ABC News]?

Q. Mr. President, there are several dozen Americans in Baghdad apparently not able to leave at this point, and perhaps hundreds more in Kuwait—perhaps elsewhere in Iraq as well. In view of the extreme political sensitivity of Americans toward this whole question of hostages, why should not Saddam Hussein feel that he holds very high cards now in dealing with the United States?

The President. I've been encouraged that there have been actually announcements, I believe, saying people were free to leave. So, I'm not going to speculate or hypothecate beyond that. I want to see them out of there, obviously. But what he does—that's a bit unpredictable. But I'm not going to try to heighten tensions in this regard by responding to hypothetical questions that might go beyond your question.

Q. Well, I just wonder what assurances you might be able to provide, sir, that our policy in this instance will not become, as it has in the past, hostage taking.

The President. I can provide only the assurance that I consider the protection of American life fundamental to my job and responsibilities as President.

Q. Mr. President, the question of chemical weapons—there are reports that the Iraqis were seen loading airplanes with chemical weapons. How concerned are you that he would use these over our troops that are there now?

The President. I think anytime you deal with somebody who has used chemical weapons on the battlefield you are concerned about it. I would think that he'd know, given the way the world views the use of chemical weapons, that it would be intolerable and that it would be dealt with very, very severely. So, I would hope that there would be no use of chemical weapons.

Q. Mr. President, I'm being told in my ear that there is a report or a rumor out of Jedda that Saddam Hussein is dead. Have you heard anything of this?

The President. I have not heard anything of that.

Q. Do you know if the Saudis are going to follow the Turks' lead in shutting off an

Iraqi pipeline, the one to the south? Have you had any promises from the Saudis or any other oil-producing countries that they will increase production to make up for this shortfall?

The President. I believe that the Venezuelans have announced a significant increase, and I expect you'd find others to follow.

And what was the first part, John [John Cochran, NBC News]?

Q. The Saudis cutting off the pipeline.

The President. That matter will be discussed, I'm sure. And I know that the Saudis are fully in accord with the action taken by the United Nations in terms of chapter VII sanctions. But we have no deal with them in that regard.

Q. Sir, it's difficult for us to get information from Saudi Arabia, one reason being the American news media were not permitted to accompany American troops into Saudi Arabia. Was that your decision or King Fahd's?

The President. That decision didn't come to me, but there's plenty of reporters in Saudi Arabia right now.

Q. Well, do you think there should be a Pentagon pool as there was, for example, in Panama?

The President. I'd have to discuss that with the Secretary of Defense. I'm glad that that many forces could be moved with not too much advance warning and with not too much, therefore, risk to Saudi Arabia or to these troops.

Q. Mr. President, was there any one single thing that tipped your hand into deciding to send U.S. troops and aircraft into Saudi Arabia? And secondly, how supportive have the Soviets been of your decision?

The President. There was no one single thing that I can think of, but when King Fahd requested such support, we were prompt to respond. But I can't think of an individual, specific thing. If there was one, it would perhaps be the Saudis moving south when they said they were withdrawing.

Q. You mean the Iraqis, sir?

The President. I mean the Iraqis. Thank you very much. It's been a long night. The Iraqis moving down to the Kuwait-Saudi border when, indeed, they had given their word that they were withdrawing. That

heightened our concern.

Q. How supportive have the Soviets been of your decision, sir?

The President. The Soviets have been very responsible, in my view. They have joined the United Nations on that resolution; and [Secretary of State] Jim Baker, as recently as yesterday afternoon or evening, was in touch with Shevardnadze [Soviet Foreign Minister] again. And you know, I can't ask for a more favorable response than he received.

Yes, Gerry [Gerald Seib, Wall Street Journal]?

Q. Mr. President, is it your intention to let economic pressure alone provide the force that drives Iraq out of Kuwait? And are you prepared to wait several months, which is how long it might take for the economic sanctions to really bite?

The President. Well, we've taken this first significant step to defend Saudi Arabia. The economic sanctions should begin to bite pretty soon. There will be further steps taken to ensure that they are fully effective. And then we'll wait and see where we go from there. But I'm not beyond that in my thinking. There obviously is a lot of contingency planning that always goes on and, prudently, should go on.

Charles [Charles Bierbauer, Cable News Network], then Ann [Ann Devroy, Washington Post].

Q. Mr. President, I can understand the need for individual countries to announce their own intentions with regards to the multinational force, but it's our understanding that the Saudis wanted an Arab component in that force. Is that, in fact, the case, and will there be one?

The President. They didn't tell us that, but it would not be at all surprising if there was an Arab component in that force, not at all.

Q. But you do not have one at this point?

The President. Well, I'm not going to comment on—because I think announcement of all components really should come from the participating countries.

Yes, Ann?

Q. Not even broadly to define it as Arab, if not by nation?

The President. No. I told you I wouldn't

be surprised if that happened but I'd much prefer to have the announcements of that come from others. I think it is important that the focus be on Saudi requests and on defensive nature of the move we've made with these forces.

Yes, Ann?

Q. Mr. President, you've told us several times of Saddam Hussein's lies in his dealings with other leaders and with the United States on his intentions. Why do you now believe the Iraqi Government's statements that they will let Americans go if there is no evidence of an American being let go?

The President. I'm not sure I totally believe them. I hope they're telling the truth.

Q. Do you have assurances from any intelligence source, any other source that indicates movement by those Americans or any——

The President. Well, I've had a source of movement by some foreigners. So, I would hope that this would then apply to Americans.

Q. Which foreigners?

Q. Mr. President, you said in your speech this morning that the puppet regime in Kuwait was unacceptable, and so was the acquisition of territory. At the same time, though, you said that the deployments are wholly defensive. The question is: How do you actually expect to force Hussein to withdraw from Kuwait?

The President. Economic sanctions, in this instance, if fully enforced, can be very, very effective. It's a rich country in terms of oil resources. They're a poor country, in a sense, because he squandered much of the resource on military might. And there are some indications that he's already beginning to feel the pinch, and nobody can stand up forever to total economic deprivation.

Q. Can I just follow: Will you rule out preemptive strikes against Iraq as a way of forcing——

The President. I am not going to go into hypothetical situations. We've been very careful not to do that, and I simply am not going to respond.

Maureen [Maureen Santini, New York Daily News]? Then we'll go to the aisle.

Q. Mr. President, could you share with us the precise military objective of this mission? Will the American troops remain there only until Saddam Hussein removes his troops from the Saudi border?

The President. I can't answer that because we have a major objective with those troops, which is the defense of the Soviet Union, so I think it's beyond——

Q. Saudi Arabia. [*Laughter*]

The President. A defense of Saudi Arabia. So, I think it's beyond just the question of the tanks along the border.

Q. Sir, are you prepared for a prolonged ground war?

The President. They have a lot of air power, for example.

Q. Are you prepared for a prolonged ground war in the Persian Gulf?

The President. I'm not preparing for a long ground war in the Persian Gulf. There's not a war going on there right now.

Q. But I'm just saying, could you just tell the American people what your specific military objective is?

The President. My military objective is to see Saudi Arabia defended. That's the military objective. Our overall objective is to see Saddam Hussein get out and go back and to have the rightful regime of Kuwait back in place.

Q. Mr. President, can you tell us what U.S. and Saudi forces will be up against? You mentioned surface-to-surface missiles. You've spoken previously of the chemical warfare capability of the Saudis. What are they up against? And the second part of the question is: Did we misread Saddam Hussein? A couple of months ago the administration was up on the Hill deflecting a move to put sanctions on Iraq.

The President. Let me ask you—I'm not going to take the question on the exact military problem there because we're going to have a thorough briefing at the Pentagon. I think they're much better equipped to handle that kind of detail.

On Saddam Hussein, look, we've tried very hard to see if there wasn't a way to have somewhat improved relations. There's no question about that. And I have no regret about having tried to have discussions that might have led to a better relationship. But that had to stop the minute you have this kind of aggression. But I think, having tried tentatively to have a little better relationship with the person over the last couple of years, we've still been very, very wary all along of his intentions.

Q. Did our intelligence let us down, or did you know that what has happened— when did you get an indication it would be, as far as moving into Kuwait and that sort of thing?

The President. No, I don't feel let down by the intelligence at all. When you plan a blitzkrieg-like attack that is launched at 2 o'clock in the morning, it's pretty hard to stop, particularly when you have just been given the word of the people involved that there wouldn't be any such attack. And I think the intelligence community deserves certain credit for picking up what was a substantial buildup and then reporting it to us. This information was relayed properly to interested parties, but the move was so swift that it was pretty hard for them to stop it. I really can't blame our intelligence in any way—fault them in this particular go-around.

Yes, Ellen [Ellen Warren, Knight-Ridder Newspapers]?

Q. Mr. President, you said this morning that our troops would also defend our other friends in the Gulf. Do we view the American troops there as peacekeepers throughout the Gulf?

The President. We view them there to defend Saudi Arabia, and hopefully, their presence there will deter adventurism against any of the other Gulf countries.

Q. What other countries, sir, are we prepared to defend in the Gulf region?

The President. I'm not going to give you a list, but we're certainly interested in the freedom and the independence of all those countries in the GCC [Gulf Cooperation Council], just for openers.

Q. Mr. President, do you see any domestic impact on the budget talks or deficit from this situation in the Middle East— impact on the gasoline tax possibility, or in any other way?

The President. An operation of this nature has considerable expense associated with it. But I've asked for some estimates now as to what that price may be. But whatever it is, we're going to have to pay it, but I don't

have the exact figures yet.

John [John Mashek, Boston Globe]?

Q. Mr. President, national security analysts say that this crisis demonstrates once again the constant vulnerability of the oil fields in the Middle East. Doesn't this suggest that this force that you've sent over there may be there for some time or at least fragments of it will be there to make sure that there is a steady flow?

The President. You might interpret it that way. I'm not prepared to say that I think that's what the outcome will be because I think if there is this pullback that the world is calling for, and if the sanctions are effective, I think you would reduce the risk of future adventurism.

Q. In your call to the producing countries to pick up the slack, do you expect that to begin immediately?

The President. Well, I think it will start very, very soon. I don't know about today by way of——

Gerry [Gerald Seib, Wall Street Journal]?

Federal Budget Negotiations

Q. Mr. President, with the economy tipping or close to the edge of recession, do you think you still can afford to raise taxes and cut spending, or won't that increase the risk of a deep recession?

The President. I still think it's absolutely essential to get a budget agreement. And that's going to require a lot of compromise, and it's going to require a lot of principle. But you know, what I want to do is separate out my feelings about the budget now that I feel uninhibited by an agreement not to say anything, because I want to tell you exactly how strongly I feel about it, but I don't want to do it here today. I don't want to mix it into this briefing that is largely dominated by the world concern about the Middle East. But I feel like a liberated human being now. I don't feel bound by——

Q. Why not?

The President. May I finish what I'm saying here? I don't feel—[*laughter*]—I don't feel bound by an agreement that I've told the congressional leaders is no longer in effect. We've been getting one side of that, mainly from the Democrats in the

Congress, and now you're fixing to get the other. But not this minute; you have to stay tuned.

Persian Gulf Crisis

Q. Mr. President, to follow up. Do you think the spike in oil prices, if that occurs significantly at home as a result of the Persian Gulf problems, could edge the economy into a recession?

The President. I have not been advised of that. I hope that is not the case. What I hope to do is see a reduction in oil prices once it becomes clear that there will not be shortage. There's an overhang now of oil in the marketplace—thank God. We have a Strategic Petroleum Reserve that we can draw from. Other countries have the same—a couple of other countries have SPR's themselves. And I hope that this rapid spike on oil prices will not be permanent. And I think if the world begins to see assurances that there will not be a dramatic cutoff or cut-down on oil, that then things will return much more to normal in the market.

Q. Mr. President, assuming——

The President. One more after this.

Q. Assuming that you achieve your withdrawal of Iraqi forces out of Kuwait, Saddam Hussein is still going to be sitting there on top of a million-man army that he's shown an inclination to use. What happens in the long run after that? And can you contain that, short of removing Saddam Hussein from power?

The President. I would think that if this international lesson is taught well that Saddam Hussein would behave differently in the future. And that's what has been so very important about this concerted United Nations effort—unprecedented, you might say, or certainly not enacted since 19—what was it—23 years ago, 23 years ago. So, I don't think we can see that clearly down the road. But a line has been drawn in the sand. The United States has taken a firm position. And I might say we're getting strong support from around the world for

what we've done. I've been very, very pleased about that. Large countries and small countries—the world reaction has been excellent. And I would hope that all of this would result in Saddam Hussein or some calmer heads in Iraq understanding that this kind of international behavior is simply unacceptable. We see where we go.

Yes, Sarah [Sarah McClendon, McClendon News]?

Q. Sir, would you please——

The President. This is the last question.

Q. I understand that we provide most of the food for Iraq and have done so on the long term and short term, and subsidies, payments—credit systems—for some time. That means that we've been letting them have a lot of food and a lot of other products from our farmers at probably low rates, arranged by the Department of Agriculture. Now, would you please discuss the effect of your embargo, and how much do you think that the Iraqis already owe us for food?

The President. I don't know what they owe us for food. But I know that this embargo, to be successful, has got to encompass everything. And if there's a humanitarian concern, pockets of starving children or something of this nature, why, we would take a look. But other than that, this embargo is going to be all-encompassing, and it will include food. And I don't know what Iraq owes us now for food. Generally speaking, in normal times, we have felt that food might be separated out from—you know, grain, wheat—might be separated out from other economic sanctions. But this one is all-encompassing, and the language is pretty clear in the United Nations resolution.

Thank you all very much. And let me just say this on a personal basis: I've screwed up a couple of times here, and I'm very grateful for your assistance in straightening it out. God, I'd hate to have some of those answers stand. Thank you.

Note: The President's 55th news conference began at noon in the Briefing Room at the White House.

Statement by Press Secretary Fitzwater on the President's Meeting With the United States-Mexican Binational Commission
August 8, 1990

President Bush met today with the U.S.-Mexican Binational Commission, whose annual meeting is taking place today in Washington. President Bush praised the work of the Commission, noting that the high-level attention given to its work is a sign of the importance both countries attach to managing their special relationship in a coordinated and amicable manner based on mutual respect.

Secretary of Commerce Robert Mosbacher and Mexican Secretary of Foreign Affairs Fernando Solana reported on the Commission's discussions of bilateral and international issues. These included trade and investment, antinarcotics cooperation, border relations, environmental issues, education, and agriculture.

President Bush heard from U.S. Trade Representative Carla A. Hills and Mexican Secretary of Commerce and Industrial Development Dr. Jaime Serra Puche, who jointly recommended to him and Mexican President Salinas the formal initiation of negotiations on a comprehensive bilateral free trade agreement (FTA). President Bush was pleased to learn that the Ministers agree that an FTA could create a more prosperous trade and investment relationship between Mexico and the United States and that they found substantial support in both countries for this view.

President Bush announced that, if President Salinas agrees, he expects to notify Congress formally when it reconvenes in September of the intent of the United States and Mexico to negotiate an FTA.

President Bush lauded Mexico's aggressive drug enforcement policy, which has given Mexico the world lead in cocaine seizures. The United States will continue to support these efforts through law enforcement cooperation and material assistance.

President Bush reiterated his admiration for President Salinas' dynamic leadership. He said he looked forward to his state visit to Mexico later this year in Monterrey, in President Salinas' home state, where the two Presidents will continue discussions on the issues dealt with in the Binational Commission.

Appointment of Frances McMurtray Norris as Special Assistant to the President for Legislative Affairs
August 8, 1990

The President today announced the appointment of Frances McMurtray Norris as Special Assistant to the President for Legislative Affairs. She would succeed Nancy Dorn.

Since 1989 Mrs. Norris has served as Director of Congressional Relations for the Office of National Drug Control Policy. Prior to this, she served as Assistant Secretary of Education for Legislation; assistant to Representative Trent Lott, the Republican whip, on the House Rules Committee; and legislative assistant to Representative G.V. Montgomery.

Mrs. Norris graduated from the University of Mississippi (B.S., 1968) and the University of Kentucky (M.S.L.S., 1970). She is a native of Jackson, MS, and resides in McLean, VA, with her husband, Stephen.

Nomination of Jeanne S. Archibald To Be General Counsel of the Department of the Treasury
August 9, 1990

The President today announced his intention to nominate Jeanne S. Archibald, of Virginia, to be General Counsel of the Department of the Treasury. She would succeed Edith E. Holiday.

Since 1988 Mrs. Archibald has served as Deputy General Counsel of the Department of the Treasury. Prior to this, she served as Deputy Assistant General Counsel of the Department of the Treasury, 1986–1988; Associate General Counsel and Chairman of the Section 301 Committee at the Office of the U.S. Trade Representative, 1980–1986; and a professional staff member on the trade subcommittee for the Committee on Ways and Means, 1975–1980.

Mrs. Archibald graduated from State University of New York at Stony Brook (B.A., 1973) and Georgetown University Law Center (J.D., 1977). She was born January 30, 1951, in Copiague, NY. Mrs. Archibald is married, has one child, and resides in Reston, VA.

Letter to Congressional Leaders on the Deployment of United States Armed Forces to Saudi Arabia and the Middle East
August 9, 1990

Dear Mr. Speaker: (Dear Mr. President:)

On August 2, 1990, Iraq invaded and occupied the sovereign state of Kuwait in flagrant violation of the Charter of the United Nations. In the period since August 2, Iraq has massed an enormous and sophisticated war machine on the Kuwaiti-Saudi Arabian border and in southern Iraq, capable of initiating further hostilities with little or no additional preparation. Iraq's actions pose a direct threat to neighboring countries and to vital U.S. interests in the Persian Gulf region.

In response to this threat and after receiving the request of the Government of Saudi Arabia, I ordered the forward deployment of substantial elements of the United States Armed Forces into the region. I am providing this report on the deployment and mission of our Armed Forces in accordance with my desire that Congress be fully informed and consistent with the War Powers Resolution.

Two squadrons of F–15 aircraft, one brigade of the 82nd Airborne Division, and other elements of the Armed Forces began arriving in Saudi Arabia at approximately 9:00 a.m. (EDT) on August 8, 1990. Additional U.S. air, naval, and ground Forces also will be deployed. The Forces are equipped for combat, and their mission is defensive. They are prepared to take action in concert with Saudi forces, friendly regional forces, and others to deter Iraqi aggression and to preserve the integrity of Saudi Arabia.

I do not believe involvement in hostilities is imminent; to the contrary, it is my belief that this deployment will facilitate a peaceful resolution of the crisis. If necessary, however, the Forces are fully prepared to defend themselves. Although it is not possible to predict the precise scope and duration of this deployment, our Armed Forces will remain so long as their presence is required to contribute to the security of the region and desired by the Saudi government to enhance the capability of Saudi armed forces to defend the Kingdom.

I have taken these actions pursuant to my constitutional authority to conduct our foreign relations and as Commander in Chief. These actions are in exercise of our inherent right of individual and collective self-defense. I look forward to cooperation with

the Congress in helping to restore peace and stability to the Persian Gulf region.
Sincerely,

GEORGE BUSH

Note: Identical letters were sent to Thomas

S. Foley, Speaker of the House of Representatives, and Robert C. Byrd, President pro tempore of the Senate. The letter was released by the Office of the Press Secretary on August 10.

Letter to Congressional Leaders on Additional Economic Measures Taken With Respect to Iraq and Kuwait
August 9, 1990

Dear Mr. Speaker: (Dear Mr. President:)

On August 2, 1990, I reported to the Congress that, pursuant to section 204(b) of the International Emergency Economic Powers Act, 50 U.S.C. section 1703(b), and section 201 of the National Emergencies Act, 50 U.S.C. section 1621, I exercised my statutory authority to declare a national emergency and to issue two Executive orders that imposed a comprehensive economic embargo against Iraq and blocked both Iraqi and Kuwaiti government property within the jurisdiction of the United States or under the control of U.S. persons.

In the days after the imposition of U.S. economic sanctions, the Iraqi government has tightened its unlawful grip over the territory of Kuwait and has installed a puppet regime that in no way represents the people or legitimate Government of Kuwait. On August 6, the United Nations Security Council, to bring the invasion and occupation of Kuwait to an end and to restore the sovereignty, independence, and territorial integrity of Kuwait, decided that all nations shall impose sweeping economic sanctions against both Iraq and Kuwait.

Today, I have taken additional steps to respond to these developments and to ensure that the economic measures we are taking with respect to Iraq and Kuwait conform to United Nations Security Council Resolution 661 of August 6, 1990. Specifically, pursuant to section 204(b) of the International Emergency Economic Powers Act, 50 U.S.C. section 1703(b), section 201 of the National Emergencies Act, 50 U.S.C. section 1621, and the United Nations Participation Act, 22 U.S.C. section 287(c), I have issued two new Executive orders.

The order I have issued with respect to Iraq:

—prohibits exports and imports of goods and services between the United States and Iraq, and any activity that promotes or is intended to promote such exportation and importation;

—prohibits any dealing by a U.S. person in connection with property of Iraqi origin exported from Iraq after August 6, 1990, or intended for exportation to or from Iraq to any country, and related activities;

—prohibits transactions related to travel to or from Iraq or to activities by any such person within Iraq, except for transactions necessary for prompt departure from Iraq, the conduct of official business of the United States Government or of the United Nations, or journalistic travel;

—prohibits transactions related to transportation to or from Iraq, or the use of vessels or aircraft registered in Iraq by U.S. persons;

—prohibits the performance by any U.S. person of any contract in support of certain categories of projects in Iraq;

—prohibits the commitment or transfer of funds or other financial or economic resources by any U.S. person to the Government of Iraq, or any other person in Iraq;

—blocks all property of the Government of Iraq now or hereafter located in the United States or in the possession or control of U.S. persons, including their foreign branches; and

—clarifies that the definition of U.S. persons includes vessels of U.S. registry.

In a separate order, I have extended to Kuwait all economic sanctions currently in effect against Iraq. Specifically, that order:

—prohibits exports and imports of goods and services between the United States and Kuwait, and any activity that promotes or is intended to promote such exportation or importation;

—prohibits any dealing by a U.S. person in connection with property of Kuwaiti origin exported from Kuwait after August 6, 1990, or intended for exportation to or from Kuwait to any country, and related activities;

—prohibits transactions related to travel to or from Kuwait or to activities by any such person within Kuwait, except for transactions necessary for prompt departure from Kuwait, the conduct of official business of the United States Government or of the United Nations, or journalistic travel;

—prohibits transactions related to transportation to or from Kuwait, or the use of vessels or aircraft registered in Kuwait by U.S. persons;

—prohibits the performance by any U.S. person of any contract in support of certain categories of projects in Kuwait;

—prohibits the commitment or transfer of funds or other financial or economic resources by any U.S. person to the Government of Kuwait, or any other person in Kuwait;

—blocks all property of the Government of Kuwait now or hereafter located in the United States or in the possession or control of U.S. persons, including their foreign branches; and

—clarifies that definition of U.S. persons includes vessels of U.S. registry.

Today's orders provide that the Secretary of the Treasury, in consultation with the Secretary of State, is authorized to take such actions, including the promulgation of rules and regulations, as may be necessary to carry out the purposes of those orders. The orders were effective at 8:55 pm e.d.t., August 9, 1990.

The declarations of national emergency made by Executive Orders 12722 and 12723, and any other provision of those orders not inconsistent with today's orders, remain in force and are unaffected by today's orders.

I am enclosing a copy of each of today's orders.

Sincerely,

GEORGE BUSH

Note: Identical letters were sent to Thomas S. Foley, Speaker of the House of Representatives, and Robert C. Byrd, President pro tempore of the Senate. The Executive orders are listed in Appendix E at the end of this volume. The letter was released by the Office of the Press Secretary on August 10.

Appointment of Condoleezza Rice as a Special Assistant to the President for National Security Affairs
August 10, 1990

The President today announced the appointment of Dr. Condoleezza Rice as a Special Assistant to the President for National Security Affairs.

Since February 1989 Dr. Rice has served on the staff of the National Security Council as the principal Soviet specialist. She became Senior Director for Soviet Affairs in May 1990. She is on leave from her post as associate professor of political science at Stanford University, where she was a member of the Center for International Security and Arms Control. In 1986–87, Dr. Rice was the recipient of a 1-year Council on Foreign Relations fellowship during which she acted as Special Assistant to the Director of the Joint Chiefs of Staff assigned to strategic nuclear policy. She is the author of "The Soviet Union and the Czechoslovak

Army" and, with Alexander Dallin, "The Gorbachev Era," as well as numerous articles on Soviet and East European military policy. In 1984 Dr. Rice was awarded the Walter J. Gores Award for excellence in teaching at Stanford. She was a Hoover Institution national fellow in 1985–86. Dr. Rice has also served as a consultant to ABC News on Soviet affairs.

Dr. Rice graduated from the University of Denver (B.A., 1974; Ph.D., 1981) and the University of Notre Dame (M.A., 1975).

Exchange With Reporters Aboard Air Force One on the Persian Gulf Crisis
August 10, 1990

Q. What's your reaction to Saddam Hussein's declaration of war against the United States——

The President. It's not unexpected. He is so isolated in the world, so much backed into a corner by world opinion, which is almost 100 percent against him, that he has to find some mechanism to rally support. And it won't work. His problem is in the Arab world and the Moslem world as well as it is in the rest of the world, so it's a rather frantic ploy to try to gather some support. But it's going to be ineffective; it will not work.

Q. Mr. President, are you hearing anything out of the Arab summit that encourages you?

The President. Haven't got any reports yet from the Arab summit, one way or another.

Q. Mr. President, are you confident there are enough American troops already in Saudi Arabia to be able to withstand any sort of an assault? Basically, do you think American troops can—would be able to win?

The President. To be able to withstand an assault on Saudi Arabia? Well, I think——

Q. Immediately, if it happens now.

The President. Well, there's no evidence as of right now that Saddam Hussein would be foolish enough to cross that border. But we have implemented the air power out there, air forces. Saudi has strong air power. Some of the Kuwaiti air force is there in Saudi Arabia. Other elements will be there. We have a carrier there. So, I think that our fighting men that are on the ground there will be safe. But I don't want to heighten

concern because I've seen—they have not presented me with any evidence that the troops that have already been moved forward are being reinforced, or that they are preparing to move across the Saudi border.

Q. [*Inaudible*]—obviously now leaving the United States to go over there. Can you please give us more of an idea of the size of the force you're sending and how long you're going to need to ask the American people to keep them there?

The President. No. They haven't even gotten there yet, so I can't estimate how long it will be. I might say, since you mention the American people and asking them how long they should be supported, I am very pleased with the strong support for what we've done from the American people—indeed, from around the world. I think it's been very gratifying and I think it means that people understand that this aggression cannot go unchallenged.

So, in terms of the numbers, I'd prefer not to go into that. I never believe that it's good to pinpoint numbers of forces. And that's, of course, the way [Secretary of Defense] Dick Cheney and General Powell [Chairman, Joint Chiefs of Staff] conducted themselves. So, I can't give you any help on that right now, and I'm not going to even give you any estimates on it right now. But it will be a substantial force, and others will be coming in with more forces, too.

Q. The numbers of ground troops that we obviously see leaving along with their equipment suggest some preparation for extensive capabilities on the ground. Can you enlighten us—is that your plan? They would suggest that you're preparing for something other than——

The President. Listen, I'd love to see the economic sanctions be so successful that the forces could be withdrawn. And I think they will be successful. But I just can't—my problem is, I just can't estimate the time right now, how long it will take. But there will be substantial force. There will be enough force so that Americans are protected from unwarranted attack, and it won't be just U.S. forces and Saudi forces.

Q. [*Inaudible*]—foreigners are being taken out of Kuwait into Baghdad——

The President. Well, I view that as a prime responsibility. But you're right, there have been very disturbing reports of violence against the citizens of several countries. And there was a report of a British airline stewardess having been violated and humiliated by Iraq soldiers. There are scattered reports, but I will say that it's not just against Americans. But I think all countries are concerned about the safety of their citizens, and part of any planning has to be about how to protect citizens. Now, we all know the difficulties of that if somebody does violence like has already taken place, as a matter of fact. So, it worries me because I do view it as a prime responsibility. But I would say—I'm not going to go beyond that and I'm not going to invite further harassment by elevating the value of any citizen.

Q. [*Inaudible*]

The President. We're not helpless, no. But as we've seen with hostage situations—and I don't think this is one—sometimes it's very difficult.

Q. Mr. President, how do you read Saddam's—[*inaudible*]—is this just rhetoric?

The President. Yes, rhetorical, because he's backed into a corner. He's been isolated by the rest of the world. Nobody supports him. And so, he's trying to rally Arab support generally. The problem he's got is that most of the Arab countries violently disapprove of what he's done. But he doesn't have many options, so he's resorting to radical rhetoric trying to mobilize opinion. But his problem is everybody sees through this. Everybody around the world will see through this rhetoric.

Q. ——the Arab leaders——

The President. No. No, I think it's going well, and my talks with Arab leaders have been very supportive. It's the right thing that you have an Arab meeting of this kind. I salute [Egyptian] President Mubarak for having stayed with the idea. The more such meetings, the better. Maybe, just maybe—and I'm not too optimistic—somebody can talk some sense into this man who has been thoroughly censured by the rest of the world.

Q. You say that Saddam—[*inaudible*]—rhetoric, but is there no danger to that kind of rhetoric——

The President. No, I don't see any danger.

Q. [*Inaudible*]—holy places being turned over to foreigners?

The President. I think it's so extreme that people that are in Saudi Arabia, loyal to the King—they're not going to rise up when a cornered radical tries to mobilize support when he has none. I mean, people see this so clearly that I wouldn't worry about that.

Q. Mr. President, speaking of the safety of Americans, what about the safety of Americans outside of Iraq and Kuwait? What are you being told about the possibility of terrorist attacks as a result——

The President. Well, you always worry about that. As you know, I've worried about that for a long time, long before this incident. And, indeed, Americans are still being held against their will, probably in Lebanon, and this will continue to concern me, wherever they are—whether it's in the Middle East or elsewhere. So, I do worry about extremists taking extreme action.

Q. Do you have reason to believe that it's more likely?

The President. No specific reason on this case, and no intelligence that has me alarmed. But I continue to worry about it. And we, of course, take the proper warning procedures in our various embassies. But all you can do is make clear to people that there are these dangers.

Q. What's your best assessment——

The President. The best assessment is that I'm very encouraged by the worldwide support for sanctions in the United Nations. I am very encouraged by King Fahd's determination to stand up against this reckless action taken by Saddam Hussein. I am pleased the way the Alliance—our allies are coming through, and I am determined that the economic sanctions that are already beginning to bite against Iraq can be tightened up even more. So, at this juncture, I've got a lot to be grateful for. I'm very pleased with the way our defense forces on short notice answered the call to mobilization that I put out, and the way—the professional manner in which they moved these forces without incident. And so, there's a lot of good things out there.

The troubling thing is we're up against a man who is known for his brutality and irrationality and who has taken a step that, though widely condemned, has still not been reversed.

Q. [*Inaudible*]—a blockade—[*inaudible*]

The President. The United Nations has already moved for chapter VII sanctions, which are all-encompassing. I'm not prepared to use the word "blockade," but I am prepared to say that we will do whatever is necessary to see that the exports from Iran referred to under the U.N. resolution do not go forward. And that means pipelines and that means seeing that the product does not get to market that might attempt to. But I'm not prepared to go further than that for several reasons. But I would just leave it right there right now.

But we're moving ships; the British and the French are moving ships; others will be moving ships. Right at this very minute Canada is announcing that they are joining with some ships. So, we'll just let those signals go out that there is a determination on the part of a lot of countries to implement the U.N. action.

Q. ——bottled up right now?

The President. Less of it is getting to market, but I cannot tell you that it is totally out of the market.

Q. Mr. President, are you saying that you're going to—if an Iraqi oil ship went out today, U.S. ships would stop it or some ship would stop it?

The President. I didn't say that.

Q. [*Inaudible*]

The President. What is your question?

Q. If an Iraqi ship went out today, would a U.S. ship or another ship——

The President. Put it this way: I would advise Iraqi ships not to go out with oil.

Q. Could you tell us a little more——

The President. No, I'll just leave it right there because there are a lot of things going on right now that I don't feel like commenting on.

Q. Mr. President, you mentioned earlier about terrorism that all you can say is that there is—[*inaudible*]—because this man is known for his brutality and his irrationality. Is there any kind of warning you would give to the American people?

The President. Yes, I'd say don't go to Iraq right now. How's that?

Q. How about other kind of——

The President. Don't go to Kuwait. You'll find it difficult to land. No, but it's a very good question, and certainly I'd say to Americans be careful about travel to certain areas right now. There's been concerns about terrorism for many years. And those concerns have been there long before this irrational action by Saddam Hussein, and they are ongoing. Because, you know, you could well see terrorist groups try to capitalize on this.

Q. Do you think Americans need to be careful in travel to other places in the Middle East?

The President. Well, I think they've always been advised to be careful of travel. I'm not prepared to say nobody should travel anyplace in the Middle East. I'm not prepared to say that at all.

Q. What about outside the Middle East?

The President. I'd be careful wherever you go these days.

Q. Do you have any concern about your own trip to Kennebunkport? Will you be able to stay on top of the game while you're up here?

The President. I think we're going to have a safe trip. Are you referring to the safety of the trip?

Q. No—stay on top——

The President. No, I can easily stay here. We have highly complex and highly efficient communications. I have some of my top advisers here. Others will be coming up there from time to time. I expect to see [Secretary of State] Jim Baker up there very soon. And I am in very close—I will be in very close touch with Pentagon officials or whoever is behind the National Security Council. Right now, it'll be General Scowcroft [Assistant to the President for National Security Affairs]. So, I'm determined that life goes on.

I will have a busy schedule, busier than I'd like to have had, of contacts. In fact, I've got a list of calls that I'll be making over the next couple of days—not all to the Middle East, incidentally. So, it will be a little different than I had hoped, but I think I'm doing the right thing. I think the American people want to see life go on, so long as they understand that their President and his top officials are on top of a troubled situation.

So, that's the way I looked at it. And if I find matters seem to require my going back, it's an hour and a half to go back. So, I think we're in pretty good shape on that.

Q. [Inaudible]

The President. Yes. Haven't you seen the telephone in my golf cart? Or boat? Word of honor. Well, I talked, you know—where was it? We talked to—where was it when we were out in the *Fidelity* the last time?

Q. [Inaudible]

The President. No, no. Well, that was one. Yes, that was one. But, no, the other day we were out and talked overseas, I believe it was. But in any event, I think I should reassure the American people that the communications is extraordinarily good. And if I found that I needed meetings with these top officials or with foreign officials and it would be more convenient to do it in Washington, it's very easy to go back.

Q. [Inaudible]

The President. No. I think the American people will support what I'm—you mean on this?

Q. ——going on a vacation at the same time——

The President. No, not at all. Because I'm going to be working—normally, you know, what I've said is, look, if I'm on vacation I want to have a vacation. And I don't want to try to kid the American people that I'm working. Play and play hard, and then work like hell the rest of the time when you're in Washington. And I think I've done that—go to work early in the morning, go home late at night. This one will be different because there are some tasks that I must undertake up here, so it will be a little—it will be legitimately a combination of work and play. But I don't want to deceive the American people—just tell them what you think and ask for their support. And I think people will understand that. So, that's the way I approach this.

You know, what you don't want to do is appear to be held hostage in the White House to events. And I'm not going to do that. That's why we have all this sophisticated intelligence. So, I feel all right about it.

Q. [Inaudible]

The President. I don't think you weigh your vital national security interests and then say, well, we can't undertake these because there are other pressing problems. There are other pressing problems, but this is so fundamental to the security of the United States and to the free world and, indeed, to the whole integrity of a lot of free countries around the world that when I went to do this I didn't say, listen, please give me a cost estimate to do it. This is what we have to do. And so——

Q. [Inaudible]

The President. Probably will. But as you look at some of the forces—you know, we've not had to enhance the Armed Force units there; they're all there. It's not like a mobilization where you bring in a lot of people that are not on the payroll. So, you have a lot of costs that are ongoing that can apply here to the forces in Saudi Arabia just as they'd apply to them if they were sitting in a base in the United States. Having said that, there will be additional costs—a lot of it logistical support, getting the materials there. But we're beginning now to get some hard estimates on this.

But regrettably, this is just something that we have to do. And you're faced with decisions where you can't say, I'm not going to do this because of the arts, or education, or the drug fight, or whatever. This is something that is in the national interest, and it is essential that we do it. And I am very gratified that the American people seem to understand that. And I would cite the strong support for what I've done as something that makes me feel they do understand it.

Q. Mr. President, any suggestion that the Saudis would be able to defray any of the cost——

The President. Well, I think that they more than likely would. And I think the Kuwaitis have already made clear that they want to help with some of the expenses involved to the Turks, for example. So there's a—I think you'll see a rather cooperative effort, those that have military forces and those who mainly have funds. But I don't know exactly on the Saudis. We haven't gone into that that I know of.

Thank you all. I hope you get a little relaxation.

Q. What are you going to do tonight?

The President. I don't know. I'm debating. I've got to wait and see what the weather's like. Might go fishing—test the communications—or might tee it up. But I've got to wait and see what's happening up there. We haven't—it's not set yet. But I'll do something. I'm not going to sit idly by.

Q. You wouldn't want to do that.

Q. Will Baker come in tonight?

The President. No. I think he's going to Washington and then come up over the weekend, either tomorrow or the next day. Pretty well locked in. But he won't—unless there's a last-minute change, he won't. I think he gets back—what—9:30, 10:30 tonight. And so I think it will be over the weekend. But it will give us some interesting stuff to talk about. I'm very interested to see how it went with our NATO consultations.

Q. Are you going out tonight?

The President. Tonight? No, no. You guys are free.

Note: The exchange took place at approximately 1:35 p.m. en route from Andrews Air Force Base to Kennebunkport, ME.

Statement by Press Secretary Fitzwater on the Arab League's Statement on the Persian Gulf Crisis
August 10, 1990

We welcome the Arab League statement as a positive and significant statement.

We are pleased with the very strong condemnation of Iraqi behavior and the equally strong support for Kuwaiti sovereignty and the return of the legitimate government. We are gratified to see the explicit statement of support for the measures taken by Saudi Arabia as regards its right to self-de-fense. We see as positive the fact that the Arab summit resolution provides a basis for individual governments to send forces to support Saudi Arabia and other Arab States of the Gulf.

National security adviser Brent Scowcroft called the President aboard the *Fidelity* this afternoon to discuss the Arab League statement.

Excerpts of a Statement by Press Secretary Fitzwater on the Persian Gulf Crisis
August 11, 1990

President Bush called President Mubarak of Egypt at 5:45 a.m. this morning to congratulate him on the successful outcome of the Arab League meeting. President Bush praised President Mubarak's constructive role in securing passage of the resolution to send Arab troops to participate in a multinational force. The President said the Arab League action was very favorable and gives us significant optimism for the future of the mission.

President Bush this morning also telephoned Amir 'Isa bin Salman Al Khalifa of Bahrain to thank him for his efforts on behalf of the resolution and to discuss the situation generally. President Bush plans to call Amir Khalifa bin Hamad Al Thani of Qatar.

The United States welcomes the participation of forces from so many countries in our joint efforts to fight the aggression of Saddam Hussein. Military participation by Canada, Australia, West Germany, France, Belgium, and the United Kingdom signal a high degree of unity. We expect others to join this group as well. The NATO pledge of support was also important with so many individual countries bringing their resources to bear on the situation.

We are pleased to confirm that 11 Americans, including Penelope Nabokov, have been able to leave Iraq and cross the border into Jordan. We do not have details on their departure, but it is encouraging that this group has been able to join other Americans in leaving Iraq and Kuwait. Our Embassy is in contact almost hourly with Iraqi officials concerning the safety of U.S. citizens.

There are news reports this morning in three different publications showing three different levels of eventual troop strength in Saudi Arabia. We will not comment on these stories nor provide any numbers on troop strength for obvious national security reasons. Similarly, we will have no comment on the stories today about a possible blockade. We have said in the past that planning for a blockade is underway, should it be necessary.

Right now the United Nations sanctions are being widely implemented, and there is no Iraqi oil leaving Turkey or Saudi Arabia. The embargo appears to be having a considerable effect. We are pleased that Venezuela, Iran, and other countries have indicated ability to make up for oil shortfalls. Fortunately, oil stocks in the United States are quite high, and the surge capacity around the world is also high. America is in a very positive situation in terms of its ability to withstand existing oil disruptions.

Note: The statement referred to President Saddam Hussein of Iraq and to Penelope Nabokov, a 10-year-old girl from Albany, CA, who was taken into custody by Iraqi troops on August 2, when her commercial air flight was grounded in Kuwait City during the Iraqi invasion of Kuwait.

Material from the statement that pertained to the President's stay at his home in Kennebunkport, ME, has been included in Appendix A at the end of this volume.

Remarks and an Exchange With Reporters on the Persian Gulf Crisis
August 11, 1990

The President. Well, let me just say that we've had a very good briefing, update, from the Secretary of State. I thanked him for the success of his diplomatic mission, a very important trip to our good friend President Özal of Turkey. And Jim filled me in on the details of the Turkish leg. And then, of course, I'm so pleased that the NATO alliance is together and that we're in accord on how to look at the problems in the Middle East; and I think every single member of NATO is in accord with our economic plan. And so, it was a good trip, and I'm very grateful to Secretary Baker, just on the heels of this long swing, to come back up here and brief us.

I filled him in on four phone calls I had today: President Mubarak [of Egypt], King Fahd [of Saudi Arabia], and then two other countries. And I think things are moving in the right direction, and we're pleased so far with the solidarity, cohesiveness of the economic actions that have been taken.

So, I'll be glad to take one or two questions. And then I know the Secretary would, too. Yes?

Q. Mr. President, did President Mubarak say that Egyptian troops would stand shoulder to shoulder with American troops in Saudi Arabia?

The President. Well, he—did who say that?

Q. Did President Mubarak tell you Egyptian troops will be on the ground next to ours in Saudi Arabia?

The President. Well, he made clear that they're willing to do their share and, yes, that they will be there.

Q. When will they be there?

The President. I don't have the exact time on that. But they will do their share, and so will other Arab countries. And I think we've been saying all along, or indicating all along, that, indeed, this would be a multilateral force and it would be a multilateral force with some Arab components. And that's exactly the way it's working out, and I think that sends a very good signal.

Q. Mr. President, did you—or can you tell us, please, the state of play on the thinking of an international naval quarantine of Iraq at this time?

The President. The good news is that no shipping from Iraq is coming through the Strait of Hormuz. And we are in consultation—active consultation—with other powers who have naval vessels there or underway to be sure that no oil goes out. But we aren't prepared to announce anything more than that. But I think, in terms of the world market and in terms of the effectiveness of the sanctions, I can tell you that, with the exception of one small tanker, I believe it was, no vessels from Iraq or Kuwaiti ports are trying to get out of there with cargo, with oil cargo.

Q. Sir, if I may follow up: Haven't you made the decision in principle anyway to impose this kind of quarantine?

The President. I've made the decision in principle—and I think most other leaders have—that the sanctions will be fully enforced and that exports from Iraq will not get into the market.

Q. Let me ask you, at this point, with all of the diplomatic efforts that you've constructed, what exactly is your strategy now? If not simply just patience—is that it?

The President. No. Well, the goal is to get Iraq out, obviously, of Kuwait and have the legitimate rulers return. That is the goal. And the strategy is to use economic sanc-

tions, fully effective, to see that that happens. And there's another part of our strategy, and that is to show a willingness on the part of the United States and other countries to tell Saddam Hussein [President of Iraq] that aggression will not be successful and that friends will be protected.

Q. Is it part of your thinking, sir, that with all of these sanctions in place and the effective encirclement that you have going, that there will be forces inside Iraq who will rise up against Hussein?

The President. That sometimes happens when leaders get so out of touch with reality that they commit their country to outrageous acts. That does happen. And I know that some countries around the world are hoping that that will happen in this situation. But we'll wait and see.

Q. Is the United States one of them?

The President. My feeling is that whatever it takes to have our objectives met is what should take place.

Q. Mr. President, who is in command of the multinational force that is on the ground in Saudi Arabia now? And who will take the lead——

The President. Well, General Schwarzkopf is in command of the United States forces, and then arrangements are being worked out as these other countries send components to have a more detailed structure. And clearly, we're in Saudi Arabia at the invitation of the King. The Saudis have forces on the ground, so we will be very sensitive to the requirements of the Saudi Government.

Q. But is it the Saudis who are actually in control of——

The President. Well, as I say, the arrangements—I don't believe—you could ask General Scowcroft——

General Scowcroft. Still working on it.

The President. Still being worked out.

Q. Mr. President, yesterday you said that maybe, just maybe, somebody could talk some sense into Saddam so he'll retreat and back off. But you said you weren't optimistic. Following the events of the past 24 hours with the Arab League and whatnot, are you any more optimistic that——

The President. Well, I don't know about being optimistic or pessimistic, but I must say that the forthright position taken by the Arab summit is very, very positive, and it must make Saddam Hussein realize how isolated he is in terms of world opinion. There have been many manifestations of that before the Arab summit; but now with the Arab countries weighing in, in spite of Saddam's outrageous rhetoric and outrageous military action against Kuwait, I'd say that's very promising.

Q. Mr. President, you just said a moment ago you supported doing whatever it takes to meet your objective. Does that include overthrowing Saddam Hussein?

The President. I'll just leave it sit out there, and everybody can figure it out. And they can see the mobilization of forces and they can see the determination on the part of the whole world to make these economic sanctions be successful.

Q. Mr. President, can you give us any optimistic report on efforts to get out non-diplomatic citizens who are trapped there?

The President. Well, I might ask Secretary Baker to comment on that. But some Americans have come out today. But, Jim, can you add anything to that?

Secretary Baker. Simply repeat what I said yesterday in Brussels, and that is that we are still discussing this matter with representatives of the Government of Iraq. We're hopeful that we'll be able to resolve the situation, because it does, after all, run against all international norms—the fact that American citizens and other foreign nationals as well are not permitted to leave Iraq or to leave Kuwait.

Q. Why do you not believe this constitutes a hostage situation, since they are, in fact, detained there?

Secretary Baker. Well, nothing has been demanded or asked in connection with permitting them to leave the country, for one thing. And we think it would be a mistake to characterize it as a hostage situation and to use a word like that since we are in discussion with respect to the matter. And as far as we know, no American citizens have as yet been mistreated.

Q. Will you keep the Kuwaiti Embassy open, Mr. Secretary, unless the Iraqis force it closed? Is that what it would take to close the Embassy in Kuwait City?

Secretary Baker. That's a matter that,

frankly, we are discussing today; and we will continue to discuss it. The European Community, the ASEAN nations, and others have all told Iraq that they are going to maintain their Embassies because they do not want to give credence to the suggestion that Iraq has somehow annexed Kuwait. I think it's important to remember that not only do we have these loyal government officials there, but we have 3,800 American citizens in Kuwait as well.

Q. Mr. President, there are now reports there may be as many as a quarter million American troops going to Saudi Arabia——

The President. Again, I'm not prepared to comment on troop numbers. I've tried to make that clear. I believe that [Secretary of Defense] Cheney and Powell [Chairman of the Joint Chiefs of Staff] have taken that same position, and as long as forces are moving, we're just going to leave it there.

Q. But, sir, is a quarter million out of the realm of possibility?

The President. You must have misunderstood me. I said I'm not going to comment.

Q. Mr. President, did you talk to King Hussein [of Jordan]?

Q. Mr. President, on the subject of—why don't you go over there. I'll come back.

The President. Okay. No, I did not speak to King Hussein. The two other Arab leaders that I talked to today were the rulers of Qatar and Bahrain [Amir Khalifa bin Hamad Al Thani and Amir 'Isa bin Salman Al Khalifa, respectively].

Q. There seems to be some concern that Jordan is something of a back door for Iraq, both in terms of being able to provide a supply line and also perhaps further military exercises. What are you saying or trying to do to convince Hussein that he should perhaps go along with the rest of his Arab neighbors?

The President. Well, you know, it was interesting at the Arab summit that Jordan did not vote against the resolution. I believe they abstained. But in any event, they were not against. We all recognize the difficult position that King Hussein is in; there's no question to that. And in my view, he has been a friend of the United States for a long time, and I'd like to see that friendship be reinstated or be reinvigorated in the future.

He's in a difficult position, and I was pleased that he did not vote against that resolution yesterday. But let's face it, we have had some differences with Jordan over what initially appeared to be a little bit of a strong backing for Saddam Hussein.

So, we respect the territorial integrity of Jordan. We respect its sovereignty. And I will not—not inclined to go into hypothetical situations as what might happen to Jordan. But it is a relationship that Presidents for years have valued; and it's one that I hope we can restore, through a lot of contact, to its vitality in the future. I think I spoke quite candidly the other day when I said there was a certain disappointment factor there. But now, with what the King was able to do yesterday, perhaps we can find ways to move forward—and would like to do that when all of this calms down.

Q. What's your next step, Mr. President, now?

The President. My next step is to stay in touch with the situation over there and to implement the plan that is already in effect. And that is to do what we can to guarantee the total effectiveness of the chapter VII sanctions and then take further steps—that I'm not prepared to discuss in detail—that will guarantee the integrity of Saudi Arabia for openers and, by being there, offer some moral support at least for countries in the area who could be threatened in the future from this Saddam Hussein.

Q. Mr. President, some said yesterday's Arab summit effectively exhausted the diplomatic solution. Do you feel that as well? Is the next step military?

The President. No, I think we've still got plenty of diplomacy ahead of us with lots of countries and in lots of different avenues. So, I wouldn't say that.

Q. How do you get to Saddam Hussein? He's not listening to anybody, it would seem, right——

The President. Well, we have these economic sanctions. They haven't been in effect very long. Already, as I've indicated, there are some signs that they are going to have an effect; and we'll just have to wait and see. These kinds of actions cannot be judged 48 hours after they're put into place—or 72 or whatever. I think we've just got to wait and see how all of this develops.

But I think he does see today more clearly than he saw yesterday at this time that the world is united against him. And by that I mean the action of the Arab summit was very, very important in this regard. So, these things are happening as we go along now—different countries taking strong positions. And so, I'd say there's still room for more diplomacy, but we'll just have to wait and see whether it makes an impact on him.

Q. Mr. President, would you like to see a United Nations military force? And can you tell us specifically what other countries you expect to put troops on the ground in Saudi Arabia?

The President. No, I can't tell you what others. But I think you'll see others and—I know you'll see others. And I cannot prematurely say who they will be. And in terms of the United Nations, I think that there could be a role in the naval side for some U.N. role. But I don't think that our plans are contingent upon a U.N. flag flying over the effort, as was the case in Korea, for example.

Q. How critical is it that there be other troops besides Americans? So that this does not look just like an American effort?

The President. Well, they are there, and that's very important.

Q. Mr. President, is the United States prepared in any way to support the overthrow of Saddam?

The President. No, we're not prepared to support the overthrow. But I hope that these actions that have been taken result in an Iraq that is prepared to live peacefully in the community of nations. And if that means Saddam Hussein changes his spots, so be it. And if he doesn't, I hope the Iraqi people do something about it so that their leader will live by the norms of international behavior that will be acceptable to other nations.

This is the last one.

Q. Mr. President, we all noticed yesterday that you didn't want to use the word "blockade." Is that because, in your own mind right now, you consider that the chapter VII sanctions enable you legally to stop an Iraqi ship at sea?

The President. I think we have the authority to stop a ship at sea under chapter VII. There may be some difference of opinion on that. But there's no use using words that may have different connotations in different countries, and this one does in terms of legality. And so, why do that? What we want to do is see that no oil comes out through the Strait of Hormuz. And if it requires naval vessels to see that that happens, fine. But I just am not one who flamboyantly believes in throwing a lot of words around. I'm more interested in action. And so far I've been very pleased that the Iraqis recognize that the export of oil is almost an impossibility now. But we've got some more diplomacy to make sure that it's a total impossibility.

Thank you all very much. I'm glad it's cleared up.

Q. Have the oil companies stopped gouging?

The President. Well, I think there's been a lightening up on the pricing. And there's a lot of efforts underway to see that there's plenty of supply in the international market. For those who are familiar with the availability of production that isn't on the market, one would conclude that other countries can be helpful in making up the loss in Kuwait and loss from Iraq.

So, to the American people I would say: We are using every diplomatic channel we can to be sure that there are no shortages and there is no gouging and there isn't some profit windfall out of these most unfortunate events.

But I'm confident that there can be stability in the international oil market because there is excess capacity around the world. And some countries have stepped up and said they want to help, and we salute them for that. And I'm encouraged by how the diplomacy is working there. And yet we still have more to do to guarantee that there not be a lot of hardship for countries around the world.

Thank you all very, very much. Thank you.

Note: The President spoke at 1:35 p.m. at Walker's Point, his home in Kennebunkport, ME. In his remarks, he referred to Gen. H. Norman Schwarzkopf, USA, commander in chief of the U.S. Central Command, who was in charge of the Persian Gulf deployment. A tape was not available for verification of the content of these remarks.

Statement by Press Secretary Fitzwater on the Persian Gulf Crisis
August 12, 1990

This morning the President received a letter from His Highness, Sheik Jabir al-Ahmad al-Jabir Al Sabah, the Amir of Kuwait, requesting on behalf of the Government of Kuwait and in accordance with article 51 of the U.N. Charter and the right of individual and collective self-defense that the United States Government take appropriate steps as necessary to ensure that the U.N.-mandated economic sanctions against Iraq and Kuwait are immediately and effectively implemented.

In view of the Amir's request, the President has decided that the United States will do whatever is necessary to see that relevant U.N. sanctions are enforced. The President stressed that these efforts will comple-

ment, not substitute, for individual and collective compliance that has been highly successful thus far. The United States will coordinate its efforts with the Governments of other nations to whom the Kuwaiti Government has made similar requests.

Regarding Saddam Hussein's proposals announced today, the United States categorically rejects them. We join the rest of the U.N. Security Council in unanimously calling for the immediate, complete, and unconditional withdrawal of Iraqi forces from Kuwait and the restoration of Kuwait's legitimate government. These latest conditions and threats are another attempt at distracting from Iraq's isolation and at imposing a new status quo. Iraq continues to act in defiance of U.N. Resolutions 660, 661, and 662, the basis for resolving Iraq's occupation. The United States will continue to pursue the application of those resolutions in all their parts.

Note: The statement referred to President Saddam Hussein of Iraq.

Statement Announcing the Lifting of Restrictions on Soviet Businesspeople in the United States
August 13, 1990

I have today lifted our longstanding ceiling on the total number of Soviet businesspeople who are permitted to work and reside in the United States. This action is taken as an expression of our policy to build a more normal economic relationship with the Soviets. It is also consistent with our interest in expanding business contacts and trade with the U.S.S.R. At the Malta summit last December, I proposed a work program for closer economic cooperation between our two countries. At the June summit in Washington, we signed four landmark economic agreements, including a trade agreement to expand and deepen our economic relationship. Our work continues, and as I stressed at Houston, we now place special emphasis on technical economic cooperation to help institutionalize lasting, market-oriented economic reforms in the U.S.S.R.

Our businesspeople in the U.S.S.R. and Soviet businesspeople here play an important role in this process. The time has come to eliminate obstacles to commercial presence in both of our countries and to allow the number of resident businesspeople to grow in tandem with the expansion of our economic relations.

We have made clear to the Soviets that we retain the right to reconsider our decision should there be evidence that this opportunity is being misused for intelligence gathering or other inappropriate activities.

The step taken today will of course be important to establish overall equality of opportunity for American businesspeople resident in the Soviet Union. I believe President Gorbachev shares my view and will ensure that our efforts are matched with reciprocal improvements in the climate for American business in the U.S.S.R.

Statement by Press Secretary Fitzwater on United States Interdiction of Iraqi Shipping
August 13, 1990

There seems to be some confusion about what is covered in terms of our interdiction efforts. When the President said "everything," he obviously meant everything that is included in the U.N. resolution. We do not intend to go beyond the resolution. Specifically, the resolution lists those items covered and says, "but not including supplies intended strictly for medical purposes. . . ."

The President's News Conference
August 14, 1990

The President. Excuse the slight delay on the timing. I was just on the phone with Mr. Mandela [African National Congress leader].

Let me just say—I have a statement here on the—[*laughter*]—it's that kind of world, I'll tell you. And with your forbearance, I will make a statement here at the beginning. Bear with me. It may be a tad longer than we're used to in this press room, but I want to get in focus the question of the budget.

I know that the focus of the media attention today, and understandably, is on a crisis 6,000 miles away. But there's another important, well-known, longstanding crisis at home, and that's the failure of the budget process to produce a solution to this nation's terrible deficit. Even while we address our critical international obligations, we must address that persistent, real need. Therefore, I want to just take a few minutes to talk about that.

Our current budget, or lack thereof, constitutes a real threat to the economic well-being of this country. In this case, the problem is a lack of action on the part of the Congress, an abdication of responsibility that endangers our economic vitality and the jobs that go with it.

It is no secret to the American people that the congressional budget process has broken down. Over the last couple of decades, we've seen the real problems of overspending. We've seen the stalemate in budgeting which is the result of internal congressional conflicts and a committee system that is so complex that not only have the hard decisions been postponed or avoided but today nearly all budget decisions are being finessed.

Previous Presidents have urged fundamental budget reform. We can all remember President Reagan slamming down that massive continuing resolution. And yet Congress has failed to straighten out this procedural monstrosity. As a result, the deficit continues to grow.

With the growing threat such deficit spending poses, I took the initiative in May in calling on the Democratic congressional leaders to join me in a bipartisan summit on the budget. The success of this summit is essential to ensure the economic health of the Nation; to resolve once and for all the deficit dilemma; and in doing so, to avoid the painful sequester cuts which will occur without an agreement.

As the talks flagged, I acted to jump-start them, and you're all familiar with that. When the Democrats sought to hold the talks hostage over new revenues, I made a very difficult decision to put everything, including taxes, on the table to make those budget talks succeed. To keep those budget talks going, I feel I kept my share of the bargain. The administration refrained from divisive rhetoric. We worked in earnest. We held meeting after meeting without any preconditions and emphasized the need, above all, for progress to put a budget package together. We offered billions in additional spending cuts even as congressional committees were voting out spending bills that would bust the budget.

On July 26th, both sides agreed to put budget plans on the table. We again had a complete proposal ready for negotiation. After weeks of good faith negotiating, we honestly believed there would be a specific Democratic plan in exchange.

While the summit failed to move forward with specific solutions, the Congress continued with counterproductive legislation. For example, the House has already passed 10 appropriations bills, 8 of which exceed my request for discretionary spending by $14 billion and are $25 billion higher than the budget for last year. And the Senate is asking that the taxpayer now put up another $150 million to finance election campaigns of Congress. And let me be clear on that one: I oppose adding this kind of taxpayer financing of congressional elections, and I'm going to veto any such bill that appears on my desk.

Congress is now on recess; and 100 days after I called on Democrats and Republicans in the Congress to work with me toward a bipartisan solution, I note, frankly in sadness, that after 3 full months the Democrats have yet to offer one single proposal at the budget summit.

I've been reluctant to go public in this manner. We've dealt in good faith with the leaders. We have played by the rules. Now it is up to the Democrats who control Congress—it is up to the Democrats in Congress.

I stand ready to work on this process as long as it takes to get a 5-year package which solves the problem. I've postponed what I think was a very important September trip to Latin America so as to focus on this issue. There are, however, a number of specific realities to be noted.

First, it's the Congress that has the responsibility to pass a budget. While they have the power of the purse, like any President, I've got the power of the veto pen; and I will use that pen to veto any and every spending bill that busts the budget.

Second, if no agreement is reached, that means a sequester on October 1st of about $100 billion. As painful as such deep cuts would be, I must uphold the law. I'm determined to manage them as best I can, knowing I've done all in my power to avoid them. So, the Democrats in Congress should know that if it comes to sequester they will bear a heavy responsibility for the consequences.

Third, if the Congress really wants economic growth and increased government revenues, the place to start is not with tax increases but with incentives for growth, investment, and jobs. And again, I cite the capital gains area as one that would stimulate and be investment-oriented.

Fourthly, the Congress must recognize the utter failure of their budget process to control spending. It's got to be reformed; the process has to be reformed.

Fifth, our budget must maintain a defense posture consistent with the demands on American leadership in the world and in the dangers we face.

And finally, the Democratic leadership of Congress must understand that the American people expect them to get that job done—to come forward with concrete proposals to cut the deficit. I and the members of my administration stand ready to work with them in meeting these obligations.

And I know that it's a complicated time for our country, but it is essential that the American people focus—as they are now on international matters—also focus on the domestic problems we face in terms of budget. That's why I'm doing this today. Congress will be back soon. I hope we can rejoin these talks and get this budget deficit under control once and for all.

Now, I'll be glad to take some questions. Who is the first? Helen [Helen Thomas, United Press International]?

Persian Gulf Crisis

Q. Mr. President, I have a two-part question. After successfully internationalizing opposition to the Iraqi aggression through the U.N., why did you jump the gun and unilaterally order a blockade, upsetting other members? And two, is the U.S. policy against the annexation of captured lands in the Middle East an across-the-board policy with the U.S.?

The President. Upsetting—I don't think we've upset members on our policy of interdiction. We are acting within our legal rights. And I think the world wants to see these chapter 51 sanctions carried out, and that's the role that the United States is trying to do.

Q. We didn't go through the step-by-step of chapter VII.

The President. Well, we're doing it the way our attorneys and others around the world recommend. And I think we're doing it properly, and I hope we're doing it to the degree that all ships will turn back if they are in contravention of the U.N. action.

Q. How about the last——

The President. Last? What was that?

Q. Opposition to annexation of conquered lands—is that our policy?

The President. I can only address myself in the current—currently. I don't know whether there are any exceptions or not; but I know that annexation, if this is what one calls this invasion of Kuwait, is unacceptable and that it won't stand.

Q. Mr. President, Jordan says that it's abiding by the U.N. sanctions, yet truckloads of goods are rolling through Jordan into Iraq, coming from the port of Aqaba. Do you think that Jordan is subverting the sanctions? And what will you do about it?

The President. Before I answer your question, I ought to let King Hussein [of Jordan] tell me what is happening. And if a country is permitting a flow of commerce, it would be in violation of the sanctions. But he's coming here, and I'll have a chance to talk to him and explain the U.S. view, though I'm pretty sure he understands it clearly.

Q. Let me ask you: What do you think about King Hussein's charges that the American forces in the Persian Gulf have created an explosive situation?

The President. I don't know what he means by that, but I don't agree with that. I think we are there not to have the situation explosive but to supplement fully what the United Nations has done in condemning this outrageous aggression. So, we'll discuss that one, too. It's going to be an interesting conversation, I see, if you're writing his agenda for him.

Q. Why is King Hussein coming? When he called to ask you that he'd like to come—his brother has told reporters in Jordan that one of Jordan's problems is it would suffer so economically if it abided by the sanctions, that they complained that they had no guarantees or assurances from the West that Jordan—what can you offer——

The President. Maybe that's what he wants to talk about. I hope it is because, clearly, we've always been a friend of Jordan. We've helped them in the past; we'd help them in the future if they fulfill their obligations here. Ann [Ann Compton, ABC News], I can just tell you what he told me on the telephone yesterday. When he called, he said he'd like to come over and talk about the whole situation. There was no agenda. There was no discussion of any support for action of that kind.

Q. But you are willing to support him economically or have other countries in the region help him?

The President. I think we would, provided Jordan joined these other countries in fulfilling these obligations under the sanctions.

Q. Mr. President, is there any hope at all of a diplomatic solution to this crisis?

The President. I don't see it right now. But as the sanctions begin to take effect—and it's going to take a while—I would hope there would be a diplomatic solution to this crisis.

Q. But, sir, the other day when Saddam Hussein [President of Iraq] offered his proposal, which I realize was totally unacceptable to you—I mean, could that serve as a basis for perhaps some type of negotiation?

The President. I don't think just any proposal serves as a basis for negotiation. No, I don't see enough positive elements there to think that that would be a basis for a negotiation at all. It was bringing in extraneous problems, and it did not address itself to the fundamental problem, which is that they took over Kuwait and that they've got to get out of Kuwait and they've got to let the rightful rulers return to Kuwait. So, I don't see that as a possibility to negotiate from those proposals at all.

Q. Mr. President, you have ambassadors coming to the State Department, presumably to discuss a U.N. multinational quarantine, or interdiction, whatever word you want. Is it now the policy of the United States to potentially submit to a joint U.N. command or to reflag U.S. ships under a U.N. command?

The President. That is not the plan right now, but we are talking to see how we can make this naval presence most effective. What you've said there is not the policy of the United States.

Q. Well, sir, may I ask: Do you consider in any way—there are reports out of the U.N. that there is some criticism that you have acted unilaterally and perhaps outside your legal authority in the de facto blockade that's going on. Do you consider that you've had your hand slapped, or do you think——

The President. No, I don't think so at all. And I think we're acting legally. So, this little meeting that was called by Cuba yesterday—it doesn't disturb me in the least. I mean, there can be differences, people can discuss them. But I'm convinced we're acting properly, and we are determined to continue to act in that manner.

You see, Perez de Cuellar [U.N. Secretary-General] apparently talked about only the U.N. through resolutions can decide about a blockade. But he also said every country has the right to bring up article 51, and the Secretary-General had nothing to say against it. And we have good opinions that we are acting properly. And I have no intention to change at all. I think it's important that others join in and do their part, which most of them are doing in their determination to see that commerce does not continue.

Q. Mr. President, given the staggering number in the deficit and the cost of the military operation in the Gulf and in Saudi Arabia, doesn't it make sense that some of the countries that are relying on us will pay some of the cost? I'm thinking, of course, of Japan, Germany, France, Italy. Shouldn't they pay some of the cost of our troops over there?

The President. I think that we will find a very cooperative spirit in that regard from countries. I am convinced, from a good talk I had—I think it was yesterday—with Prime Minister Kaifu that the Japanese are more than ready to entertain proposals along those lines. I've not talked to Kohl [Chancellor of the Federal Republic of Germany] about that recently. France, of course, has vessels and are spending funds on their own right now. I think we'll have a cooperative effort here—some on the financial side, some on the military and shipping side.

Q. What about the Saudis themselves, the most direct beneficiaries?

The President. Yes, I think the Saudis will do their part in helping out along the way. I'm confident of that. I also would say—the question hasn't yet been asked—that I am also confident that other countries will make up the shortfall in production that comes about from Iraqi oil and Kuwaiti oil not going to market. I can't give you the details on that, but I've had enough conversations with people around the world—[Secretary of State] Jim Baker has as well, General Scowcroft [Assistant to the President for National Security Affairs]—to feel that things are moving in the right direction there.

Q. Sir, I'm a little confused about the King Hussein invitation. When it was first announced, there was a flurry of excitement. Now it seems to be treated rather

casually. He's getting in here about 1 o'clock in the morning Washington time. You're not going to meet with him until Thursday morning at Kennebunkport. He's supposed to have a letter from Saddam. Why the casual nature of this?

The President. One, he mentioned no letter from Saddam to me. He may well have it. Secondly, he told me he wanted to come over and see me. I said: Okay, how about tomorrow? And he said: Well, I'll let you know. So, I said: Well, call Brent, will you? Because I didn't want to get called at 2 in the morning or whatever it was. So, he called Scowcroft, and they agreed that they would meet the soonest. But I think what he indicated—and I don't think I'm violating a confidence—that he would like some time to rest before we head into the meeting.

So, that was all there was to it, because I would have been prepared to meet with him now or tomorrow. I think it's important to talk with him. But there was no—I think you're right. The way it was presented to me by His Majesty was, I want to come talk to you about the situation over here, with no specific—not as a specific emissary of some kind or another. So, I made myself available.

I have a longstanding relationship with King Hussein. Some of us have brought out the differences here that are on the table now between Jordan and the United States, and I'd like to see if we can't reduce those differences and eliminate them if possible. So, I'm looking forward to seeing him.

Q. Can I just ask you about Saddam and this offer he made on Sunday? You rejected it out of hand. But do you feel he blinked a little bit? Are you encouraged at all?

The President. One might say that the fact that he took some step, even though I wasn't particularly impressed with his steps, is encouraging. But it seemed to me like a replay of old positions. So, I don't want to mislead the American people by saying that I'm heartened in any way by Saddam Hussein's proposals, John [John Cochran, NBC News].

Q. As you assess your budget situation, are you now able to put a cost figure on the operation in the Middle East?

The President. Not yet. And I'm going over to the Pentagon—maybe I'll get a better idea of the numbers there tomorrow, but I don't have any figures for you on that right now.

Federal Budget Deficit

Q. Have you, though, inevitably lowered your estimates on what you're going to be able to do in terms of reducing the deficit?

The President. I don't want to lower the estimates in what we can do in reducing the deficit at all. We still stay with $50 billion and $500 billion as the targets—$50 billion for the first year and $500 billion over the five. But it may cause for a rearrangement in how money is spent, because this is not a freebie out there in terms of the expenditure. But I just don't have the figures to give you. But I don't want to move away from those targets now.

Persian Gulf Crisis

Q. Are you pleased with the support that you've been getting from the Soviet Union——

The President. Well, let me put it this way: Suppose we set the clock back 5 years, say nothing of 10 or 20, and we had an event of this nature in the Middle East. The major unknown and the major area of concern would have been: How would the Soviets react? How would the Soviets view this? What actions are the Soviets apt to take? Now, today we don't have that concern because they have joined in in the United Nations in condemning this aggression. That's a significant difference from the way it used to be. It makes the equation much easier to solve.

So far, I am very pleased with the Soviets' reactions. Jim Baker, I believe, talked to Mr. Shevardnadze [Soviet Foreign Minister] as recently as yesterday, and I know he shares this assessment. I'm not saying we have no differences with them, but it is much, much different, Jessie [Jessica Lee, USA Today], than it would have been 5, 10 years ago.

South Africa

Q. What did you talk with Nelson Mandela about?

The President. Well, what I talked to him about was the apparent breakthrough over there between the ANC [African National Congress], Mandela, and De Klerk [President of South Africa] and the Government in terms of the peaceful resolution to the problem of how you eliminate apartheid. I talked to him a little bit about the joy we felt and the progress that's been made on releasing prisoners. That was about it—congratulating him, and Mr. de Klerk yesterday, on the same progress. It's very exciting what's taking place there.

Persian Gulf Crisis

Q. Mr. President, the Iraqis have now held Americans for 12 to 13 days. Are you willing to sacrifice those Americans should it come to direct military action?

The President. I'm never willing to sacrifice the life of any American. Sacrifice—no.

Q. Do you believe the Iraqis are using those Americans as a shield against potential American——

The President. I don't have that feeling now, and I hope I never come to that. Because you see difficulty of others getting out, but it's a troubling situation when people are held against their will or delayed from leaving. It troubles me.

Q. What's the status, in your view?

The President. The status is inconvenienced people who want to get out. And it's not only them but a lot of others. I hope that it doesn't become more than that. I have no reason to think at this juncture that it will. But the more we talk about it and the more we speculate about it, the less helpful it is, I think. But I'd like to feel that all foreigners who want to leave Kuwait or want to leave Iraq would be free to do so. And there have been some encouraging statements—you heard from their Ambassador this morning—that make me say, well, let's wait and see on that one.

Federal Budget Negotiations

Q. Mr. President, your June 26th statement specifically said there were points in it that were jointly agreed by Democrats and Republicans. Why do you suppose the Democrats have not made any proposals other than that, and what other proposals have the Republicans offered?

The President. We had a proposal that happened to ease into the public domain there against my best judgment. I'd like to say I have no control over those leakers—they got out there. We were still prepared to hand over that proposal in all its detail to the Democrats in accord with their handing us one. But that didn't materialize.

I think there was some politics in it. I'm not going to accuse Tom Foley [Speaker of the House of Representatives] of this, or Dick Gephardt [House majority leader] of this. But I think there was some saying: Hey, we think we've got the President over a barrel here. We've made him back away and give and give and give and get nothing. My view is: Well, fine, if that's the game that some up there want to play. But I think the American people understand it is the Congress that has to pass this budget. They're the ones that have the power of the purse. I sat there and played by the rules, didn't comment on this proposal or that proposal, just as I said. Others did, and frankly, some Republicans as well as Democrats did.

But I think what I'm trying to do now is to put it in focus so the American people will understand that it is the Congress that must move now to bring this deficit under control.

A followup?

Q. Yes, sir. Other than sequestration, do you have any tools at your disposal to get anything done on this?

The President. Well, sequestration is a pretty strong one, and veto is a helpful one.

Q. ——pan out publicly?

The President. No, not now. I still have hopes that we can resume this kind of summitry that is essential if you're going to get a deal. I felt that way when we entered into the deal, and I still feel that way, in spite of the fact that I do think there has been some politics rearing its head.

Persian Gulf Crisis

Q. Assuming that Saddam Hussein were to work out some face-saving way to withdraw from Kuwait, he would still be there with a very large army, still presumably intimidating to his neighbors, having invaded once. Given all that, do you think it is possible for this crisis ultimately to be resolved without removing Saddam Hussein from power, and if so, how?

The President. All I want to do is see it resolved the way the world opinion wants it resolved, and then we will worry about the rest of that later on. But the main thing is to have the withdrawal and the restoration of the rulers to their responsibilities. So, it's too hypothetical for me to go into what happens beyond that. But, yes, I'd like to feel that that can still happen. The economic sanctions are just beginning to—Marlin [Marlin Fitzwater, Press Secretary to the President] says pinch, I'd say bite—and I think that they're going to be quite effective, more so than in the past—I certainly hope so. So, let's just see how all that works.

Q. Mr. President, if I could go back to the naval interdiction effort for a second. The Soviets apparently are proposing some kind of a joint security council command to control the naval interdiction effort. Are you pursuing that in any way with the Soviets? Are you interested in the idea at all?

The President. There was originally a—I think that was raised to Jim Baker by Shevardnadze. And I don't have any problem talking to the Soviets about that. I think it would be a very good thing to have an active Soviet presence to enforce these U.N. resolutions. All I'm saying is that I don't think it is essential that you have a U.N. flag in order for countries to carry out their responsibilities. But I'd be somewhat open-minded to talk further along those lines.

Q. Do you think it will be necessary at some point to stop ships going into Aqaba because that is a potential lifeline——

The President. I think at some point it might well be. If it's a hole through which commerce flows in an otherwise tight net, I would certainly think that Aqaba should be closed to Iraqi commerce.

Federal Budget Negotiations

Q. I have a question about the budget, Mr. President. After 100 days of negotiating, don't you think the I'll-show-you-mine, you-show-me-yours strategy is getting a bit silly? And why not just as President show some leadership and put your proposal on the table and say, here's where I want to go?

The President. No, we got one out there. And it wasn't totally on the table; it was kind of oozed out on the side. And all we did was have a bunch of Democrats going after me, going to every special interest, raising hell. And now it is time that the Congress, who have to pass the budget—must pass the budget—get going. I'm still here in a nice, tranquil mood wanting to discuss it with them. [*Laughter*] And I will discuss it with them.

But I'm using this—you see we had—there's kind of a truce on this abiding by the Marquis of Queensberry's no-comment rules. And so, during this period of truce, I'm going to put the focus where it belongs and where the American people year after year know it belongs, and that is on the party that controls the United States Congress. And then I'll be here in a reasonable mode come September, saying: Well, here, here's our proposals. What's yours? Let's go. But it doesn't do any good. They've been laughing all the way to what they think is the electoral bank saying—every time we throw up a proposal, they gun it down and rush off and tell the special interest of one kind or another, We're going to protect you. Ha ha. Now it's time for them to come forward. And we will be more statesmanlike and try to resolve this national problem. [*Laughter*]

Q. Is it also true that when that proposal oozed out, as you say, it was Republicans who were involved in the——

The President. That's why I was very careful how I said who leaked it.

Q. They led the fight for that plan in revolt, I think.

The President. Which one?

Q. The proposal that oozed out, as you said.

The President. Listen, if you're ever—I can't find anybody elated over any facet of taxes, Democrat or Republican. They want to stick it to the other guy a little bit. But what I'm saying is: We had a proposal. People know what was in it. We had an original proposal with detail. They've had none. And the deal was they were to have a proposal. Now let's come forward with it and set aside politics. It's getting tough now. It's getting right down to the crunch. And the American people know that the

Congress appropriates every single dime and tells us how to spend every single dime. Now, they ought to get on with doing something about budget reform, process reform. Nobody's interested in the jurisdiction of this committee or another. The American people want the deficit down, and they don't want to have these delaying arguments about, Well, I can't move because the chairman of this committee hasn't passed a continuing previous resolution and seconded the motion. Nobody cares about that. They want the deficit—

I can't hear you, Sarah [Sarah McClendon, McClendon News Service]. You're right in the middle. [*Laughter*]

Persian Gulf Crisis

Q. Mr. President, should the American people look forward to an ongoing American presence in Saudi Arabia over a period of years?

The President. I don't know about a period of years, but certainly we're going to be there long enough to get the job done. But I'd like to give you a timeframe, and I can't.

Q. Mr. President, you called the President of Venezuela [Carlos Andrés Pérez] to ask him for some help with the oil. Did you talk numbers with him at all?

The President. No, I called him to thank him for what I understood was a Venezuelan willingness to step up and increase production—they can still do it at a reasonably efficient rate, I am told—and to thank him for his approach on this. He told me that he'd sent his Foreign Minister [Reinaldo Figueredo Planchart] to various capitals to coordinate all of this. And I had a couple of other matters to discuss with him, too, that were unrelated to the Persian Gulf. Mainly—I can give you a little hint—on Central America, an area where he and I stay in very close consultation and touch on this. But I didn't have a—if your question was, did I have a specific request of him, no, I didn't.

Last one.

Q. To follow up, just a second: Are you satisfied with the offer of Mexico as far as oil—100,000 barrels a day?

The President. I haven't the slightest way

of knowing whether it ought to be more or less, but I am very, very pleased with Mexico's cooperation on all of this. President Salinas, a courageous man, and I am very pleased that he is willing to pitch in and help. I can't help you with the exact numbers—whether it ought to be 100,000 or something else. But when we heard that, I said that's good. We've got a good relationship now with Mexico.

Thank you. All right, here's the last. This is—I really do have to run.

Q. Thank you, Mr. President. Just very briefly: You have called repeatedly for the Iraqis to be out of Kuwait, to withdraw unconditionally and completely, and you've helped put sanctions in place to try to force them to do that. How important is that withdrawal? Is it important enough that if the sanctions don't seem to work after a short period then you will promise to use military force to force Saddam Hussein out?

The President. It is too hypothetical a question. We have a plan, and the plan is to implement fully the United Nations sanctions. And also part of our arrangement with King Fahd [of Saudi Arabia] is to help protect Saudi Arabia, in a part of a multinational force now of quite a few countries, against aggression from Saddam Hussein—the same kind of aggression that took over Kuwait. So, that's where we are. That's the plan, and I just can't help you by going in a hypothetical sense any further.

Listen, I hate to run, but I do have an appointment in here. And thank you very much.

Note: The President's 56th news conference began at 4:19 p.m. in the Briefing Room at the White House.

Presidential Determination No. 90–30—Memorandum on Trade With the German Democratic Republic
August 15, 1990

Memorandum for the Secretary of State

Subject: Determination under Section 402(c)(2) of the Trade Act of 1974—German Democratic Republic

Pursuant to section 402(c)(2) of the Trade Act of 1974 (the "Act"), 19 U.S.C. 2432(c)(2), I determine that a waiver by Executive order of the application of subsections (a) and (b) of section 402 of the Act with respect to the German Democratic Republic will substantially promote the objec-

tives of section 402.

You are authorized and directed to publish this determination in the *Federal Register.*

GEORGE BUSH

[*Filed with the Office of the Federal Register, 3:55 p.m., August 28, 1990*]

Note: The Executive order is listed in Appendix E at the end of this volume.

Letter to Congressional Leaders on Trade With the German Democratic Republic
August 15, 1990

Dear Mr. Speaker: (Dear Mr. President:)

Pursuant to subsection 402(c)(2) of the Trade Act of 1974 (the Act) (19 U.S.C. 2432(c)(2)), I have determined that a waiver

of the application of subsections (a) and (b) of section 402 with respect to the German Democratic Republic will substantially promote the objectives of section 402. A copy of that determination is enclosed. I have also received the assurances with respect to the emigration practices of the German Democratic Republic required by section 402(c)(2)(B) of the Act.

Pursuant to section 402(c)(2), I shall issue an Executive order waiving the application of subsections (a) and (b) of section 402 of the Act with respect to the German Democratic Republic.

Sincerely,

GEORGE BUSH

Note: Identical letters were sent to Thomas S. Foley, Speaker of the House of Representatives, and Dan Quayle, President of the Senate. The Executive order is listed in Appendix E at the end of this volume.

Remarks to Department of Defense Employees
August 15, 1990

Thank you, Secretary Cheney and General Powell and distinguished members of the Joint Chiefs, General Schwarzkopf, and all of you who do all the work. Thank all of you for joining us today and, really most of all, for your hard work in defense of freedom and America every day.

Over the past 10 days you've launched what history will judge as one of the most important deployments of allied military power since the Second World War. As I told the American people last week, let no one underestimate our determination to confront aggression. It is you, the men and women of the Department of Defense, who turn these words into deeds that transform hope and promise into reality.

I've just received a wonderful briefing from Secretary Cheney and General Powell and others here at the Pentagon. Our objectives remain clear: the immediate, complete, and unconditional withdrawal of all Iraqi forces from Kuwait; the restoration of Kuwait's legitimate government; security and stability of Saudi Arabia and the Persian Gulf; and protection of the lives of American citizens abroad. We will achieve these honorable goals.

We've worked for decades to develop an international order, a common code and rule of law that promotes cooperation in place of conflict. This order is imperfect; we know that. But without it, peace and freedom are impossible. The rule of law gives way to the law of the jungle. And so, when the question is asked: Where does America stand? I answer: America stands where it always has—against aggression.

Today, the brave American and allied forces are keeping watch along the sands and off the shores of Saudi Arabia. They're there for a purpose: to serve the cause of justice and freedom, a cause the world supports. But Saddam Hussein would have us believe that his unprovoked invasion of a friendly Arab nation is a struggle between Arabs and Americans. And that is clearly false. It is Saddam who lied to his Arab neighbors. It is Saddam who invaded an Arab State. And it is he who now threatens the Arab nation. We, by contrast, seek to assist our Arab friends in their hour of need.

Saddam has claimed that this is a holy war of Arab against infidel—this from the man who has used poison gas against the men, women, and children of his own country; who invaded Iran in a war that cost the lives of more than half a million Moslems; and who now plunders Kuwait. Atrocities have been committed by Saddam's soldiers and henchmen. The reports out of Kuwait tell a sordid tale of brutality.

Saddam would also have us believe that this is a struggle between the haves and the have-nots. But Iraq is one of the haves, for you see, next to Saudi Arabia, Iraq has the largest oil reserves in the world. But thanks to his ruinous policies of war against other Moslems, he—Saddam Hussein—has transferred wealth into poverty. Sadly, it is the Iraqi people who suffer today because of the raw territorial ambition of Saddam Hussein.

Our action in the Gulf is not about religion, greed, or cultural differences, as Iraq's leader would have us believe. What is at stake is truly vital. Our action in the Gulf is about fighting aggression and preserving the sovereignty of nations. It is about keeping our word, our solemn word of honor, and standing by old friends. It is about our own national security interests and ensuring the peace and stability of the entire world. We are also talking about maintaining access to energy resources that are key, not just to the functioning of this country but to the entire world. Our jobs, our way of life, our own freedom, and the freedom of friendly countries around the world would all suffer if control of the world's great oil reserves fell into the hands of that one man, Saddam Hussein.

So, we've made our stand not simply to protect resources or real estate but to protect the freedom of nations. We're making good on longstanding assurances to protect and defend our friends who have the courage to stand up to evil and are asking for our help. We are striking a blow for the principle that might does not make right. Kuwait is small. But one conquered nation is one too many.

A half a century ago our nation and the world paid dearly for appeasing an aggressor who should and could have been stopped. We're not about to make that same mistake twice. Today Saddam Hussein's Iraq has been cut off by the Arab and Islamic nations that surround it. The Arab League itself has condemned Iraq's aggression. We stand with them, and we are not alone. Sanctions are working. The armies and air forces of Egypt, Morocco, the United Kingdom, and the Gulf Cooperation Council States are shoulder to shoulder with us in Saudi Arabia's defense. Ships of numerous countries are sailing with ours to see that the United Nations sanctions, approved without dissent, are enforced. Together we must ensure that no goods get in and that not one drop of oil gets out.

I am very grateful for the support all of us here are receiving from the American people. The American people are with us. Congress is with us. Our allies are with us. And the vast majority of the Arab people are with us. No one should doubt our staying power or our determination. We are in a new era, one full of promise. But events of the past 2 weeks remind us that there is no substitute for American leadership, and American leadership cannot be effective in the absence of America's strength. I know that this strength does not come cheaply or easily. You pay for it every day in the work you do, in the sacrifices you make, in the time you spend away from your families. I am relying on you to shape the forces of the future, to preserve peace and freedom in the face of new threats and new dangers.

General Powell told me today that it's a great honor, during these dangerous times, to serve as an American soldier. I know it's a great honor for me to serve as your Commander in Chief. I thank you. And I join people everywhere in praying for you, for those in the field, and for the United States of America. God bless you all. And thank you for what you're doing for your country.

Note: The President spoke at 11:40 a.m. at the River Entrance of the Pentagon. In his remarks, he referred to Secretary of Defense Richard B. Cheney; Gen. Colin L. Powell, Chairman of the Joint Chiefs of Staff; Gen. H. Norman Schwarzkopf, USA, commander in chief of the U.S. Central Command, who was in charge of the Persian Gulf deployment; and President Saddam Hussein of Iraq. Prior to his remarks, the President received several briefings on the situation in the Middle East and toured the Logistics Readiness Center at the Pentagon. Following his remarks, he traveled to his home in Kennebunkport, ME.

The President's News Conference on the Persian Gulf Crisis
August 16, 1990

The President. We've had some good meetings here today—two good meetings—one with King Hussein of Jordan, the other with the Foreign Minister, His Highness Prince Sa'ud of Saudi Arabia. In addition, I was on the phone earlier to President Özal of Turkey. He reported in on some conversations he's had and, I must say, was somewhat optimistic about the effectiveness of these international sanctions in which most countries around the world have joined. So, it's been a very illuminating day.

I, of course, was very pleased that King Hussein, who previously had announced his support for sanctions, his willingness to go with sanctions, reiterated that to me, making clear that this was a decision that Jordan had taken some time ago. But nevertheless, I put this under the heading of very encouraging developments.

In terms of the Saudis, Prince Sa'ud very kindly thanked me for the strong support from the United States, and I told him that we were determined and wanted to do everything in our power to enforce the United Nations resolution which calls for Iraq to get out of Kuwait and calls for the restoration of rulers to Kuwait. So, we're in sync with the Saudis.

I feel that the differences that possibly existed with Jordan have been narrowed, and I cited one extremely important point there. But I was pleased to see them both here at our home.

I'll be glad to take some questions.

Q. Mr. President, what kind of report did King Hussein give you on his trip to Baghdad, and did he offer any kind of hope that Saddam Hussein would pull his troops out of Kuwait and let the Amir return to power?

The President. He didn't go into any details of his trip to Baghdad, and I did not come away from that conversation with a feeling of hope that Saddam Hussein would do that which he's been called upon to do under international law.

Q. Mr. President, what can you tell us about reports—or what do you know about

reports that foreign nationals in both Iraq and Kuwait have been ordered segregated and been reported to report to one place, including some 2,500 Americans? Are you concerned that their lives may be in danger at this point?

The President. I'm concerned that any coercion on foreign nationals in some other country is a violation of international norms, and I must say that I did see a report. We've discussed it. They've checked with one of the hotels to which people were encouraged to go, and the hotel had no knowledge of an influx of people coming there. So, it's a little vague right now, Jim [Jim Miklaszewski, NBC News], but anything that compels individuals to do something against their will would of course concern me.

I don't want to overstate it, because we continue to get statements out of these various representatives of Iraq—the Ambassador to the U.N., for example—that these people in all countries will be permitted free passage or will not be harassed. But I saw the report, and thus, I must say I was concerned.

Q. Following up on that: The Americans who are in Baghdad, I believe, are the ones who were taken from Kuwait. Today the American Embassy personnel were, for the first time, not allowed to go in and see them, and news people were thrown out. Isn't it getting more dangerous for those Americans, and would there be anything that would——

The President. It gets more dangerous, I think, if I heighten the concern that I've already expressed. I have said that the other day, and I'll repeat it here. On the other hand, when you get reports of this nature, of course you're concerned about them.

Q. Mr. President, may I ask your reaction to the rather bellicose speech we heard today from Saddam Hussein in which, as you probably know, he called you a liar and vowed to send Americans home in body bags?

The President. I really haven't seen the

speech. I've seen some excerpts—or the open letter, I think it was. I think it's clear that what we need to do at this point is to enforce the international law. The statements at the United Nations from many countries really say it all, so there's no point in me responding to the letter. Nobody has at least presented, so far, to me from that letter any concrete proposals to which I feel a necessity to respond.

Q. Mr. President, what is the situation on the ground in Iraq and Kuwait? What's going on with the sanctions? How are they working today compared to how they were working 2 days ago, say?

The President. The sanctions against Iraq and Kuwait? I get the feeling that the sanctions just put into effect and just being put into effect are beginning to take hold. I would cite a very upbeat statement from President Özal of Turkey in this regard.

And so, there doesn't appear to be any shipments of oil coming out of Iraq, and that is very positive because I think 90 percent of their foreign exchange—I'm looking for help here—is based on petroleum. And so, I'd say that is a very encouraging step. And the other part of it has to be arms being interdicted, and everything, all across the board—foodstuffs, whatever it is. They have been penalized by the United Nations. Chapter VII is seldom used, but it has been used now to bring these people to do what's right. And I must say I'm encouraged with this concept of the world staying together and making these sanctions fully effective.

Q. But is there evidence of their feeling it, though?

The President. I can't cite specific evidence. There was one little tidbit that we saw saying that—and again, I probably shouldn't even go into the details of it at all—but anyway, it was a report that some of the bakers had been ordered to stop making confectionery goods, whatever it is, sweets and these things, and concentrate on the fundamentals, the staples. But knowing the economic situation in Iraq, I don't think one can sustain true international isolation for long, especially when you depend on the outside world for a lot of your goods.

Q. Did you call up or sign the order calling up the Reserves, and is that something you think you may have to call upon?

The President. I've not signed anything on that. There's some consideration. We have a Ready Reserve. We have a Reserve that I've been told by a couple of proponents of the Reserves they're very eager to do their part. But no decision has been made in that regard.

Q. Mr. President, your feeling now of the situation: Do you think the situation is stabilizing, or do you think the United States and Iraq are getting closer to war?

The President. I don't know that I can choose between the two options. But I do know that there is a determination on the part of so many countries to do something about redressing the grievances that I think it's going to work. But I can't say that it's stabilized totally. I hope that the American presence and the presence of Arab forces and the presence of others—many others— in Saudi Arabia and in those areas has lessened the risk of further adventure on the part of Saddam Hussein.

Q. Is King Hussein in any way a go-between the United States and Iraq?

The President. I didn't get the feeling. I read some reports, and now I'm wondering where they all came from because I'd read some previous reports indicating that the man was coming with a letter from Saddam Hussein. Some maybe printed it here, which I find hard to believe without any evidence. And so, I was wondering where all this was coming from. And I think I addressed myself to that question at the press conference—when was it, yesterday or the day before—where I said I didn't know of that and that I—and I felt to myself—and whether I said it—is I think he might have mentioned to me if there was such a letter.

But back to your question. There was no intermediary mission that I detected at all. I think he'd like to find some way to be helpful, and he reiterated his interest of making everything in an Arab context. But I had an opportunity to tell him my views on the situation and to tell him that in spite of the differences that may have appeared to be grievous a week or so ago that, on the part of this President and I think of the United States entirely, we'd like to see better relations. And I do think that his expressed willingness—again, expressed before he came here and then reiterated—to go forward on this international sanctions is something that will be widely appreciated here in the United States and, indeed, around the world.

Q. Mr. President, did King Hussein give you assurances that Jordan would not allow Iraqi goods in and out of the port of Aqaba?

The President. Yes.

Q. Mr. President, Iraq made some pretty significant peace overtures to Iran. Were you surprised by that? What do you know about it? How do you think it will affect the overall equation there? Are you concerned by it?

The President. No, I'm not concerned at all by it, and I—surprised only in the fact that it seems to be acquiescing to all of Iran's terms, something that Saddam Hussein has been unwilling to accept—not totally all of them. But I don't know the effect of it. And I do know that Iran has expressed their indignation about the takeover of Kuwait by Iraq, and I see nothing that has changed that. I don't know of any statement that leads me to be concerned that they're going to reverse their position on that point.

Q. You're not concerned that Iran may throw in with Iraq? Or what does it tell you about Saddam Hussein's position right now?

The President. Well, I'm not concerned about the former, and I would simply let the facts and the evolution of events answer the last part because, you see, I don't know that there's been an agreement on all these points. I don't think there has, that I know of. I don't think it's been fully, finally agreed—has it?

Q. But if it comes to that, don't you think he's desperate, sir?

The President. Well, that's what you think. I'd rather just not speculate on that and just keep my eye on the ball, which is to just isolate—in conjunction with others—to isolate Iraq.

Q. Back to King Hussein, Mr. President: You said that he agreed to cut off shipments to Iraq to the port of Aqaba, but he told us that he's exploring with the United Nations what the sanctions mean. Did he tell you that everything would be cut off, including

food, oil?

The President. Let me ask Jim because I think he'd—let me ask the Secretary—lawyer, fine lawyer that he is, in addition to being a good Secretary of State—to answer that because he was the one that engaged the King in that particular discussion.

Secretary Baker. I think what the King meant was that there is a provision in the sanctions that permits food for humanitarian purposes, or some such language. And there's really been no definition of exactly when that triggers and what that means, and the Government of Jordan is seeking some guidance from the United Nations on the subject.

Q. Is that a loophole?

Secretary Baker. No, it's not a loophole; it's the way the sanctions were written by the United Nations when they voted 13–0 to impose them.

The President. Last one.

Q. Are you satisfied that goods will no longer go through Jordan to Iraq? Are you——

The President. I'm not satisfied to total satisfaction on any point regarding the sanctions. I'm very encouraged that they look like they'll be effective. We've got to guard against cheaters. You've got to guard against people who, for economic gain, will try to violate these sanctions from whatever part of the world they come from, whatever country they come from. So, I can't say I am satisfied. But what I am is encouraged that Jordan, prior to the King's coming here, took this position. And I think that is something that is encouraging, and I think it might send a message to some around the world who need a little leadership in that regard.

Thank you all very much. I know you have a deadline. It's been a full day.

Note: The President's 57th news conference began at 5:08 p.m. at his home in Kennebunkport, ME. In his remarks, he referred to President Saddam Hussein of Iraq. President Bush met at his home with King Hussein I of Jordan at noon and with Foreign Minister Sa'ud al-Faysal Al Sa'ud of Saudi Arabia at approximately 3 p.m.

Presidential Determination No. 90–31—Memorandum on Export-Import Bank Services for the German Democratic Republic
August 17, 1990

Memorandum for the Secretary of State

Subject: Determination Under Section 2(b)(2) of the Export-Import Bank Act of 1945, as Amended—German Democratic Republic

Pursuant to section 2(b)(2) of the Export-Import Bank Act of 1945, as amended, 12 U.S.C. 635(b)(2), I hereby determine that it is in the national interest for the Export-Import Bank of the United States to guarantee, insure, extend credit and participate in the extension of credit in connection with the purchase or lease of any eligible product or service of U.S. origin by, for use in, or for sale or lease to the German Democratic Republic.

You are authorized and directed to report this determination to the Congress and to publish it in the *Federal Register.*

GEORGE BUSH

[Filed with the Office of the Federal Register, 3:56 p.m., August 28, 1990]

Statement by Press Secretary Fitzwater on the Treatment of Foreign Nationals in Iraq and Kuwait
August 18, 1990

On several occasions since the Iraqi invasion and subsequent occupation of Kuwait, the President has stated publicly his interest in the well-being of American citizens and all foreign nationals in both Iraq and Kuwait. The President thus views yesterday's statement by the Speaker of Iraq's National Assembly [Sadi Mahdi], that Iraq will "play host to the citizens of these aggressive nations as long as Iraq remains threatened with an aggressive war," to be totally unacceptable. He is deeply troubled by the indication that Iraqi authorities intend to relocate these individuals within Iraq against their will. The President is also deeply concerned about today's announcement by the Government of Iraq that foreign nationals may not have access to adequate quantities of food.

The use of innocent civilians as pawns to promote what Iraq sees to be its self-interest is contrary to international law and, indeed, to all accepted norms of international conduct. We urge that Iraq immediately reconsider its refusal to allow any foreign national desiring to leave to do so without delay or condition. We would also hope that Iraq would take note of yesterday's statement by the U.N. Security Council President expressing the Council's concern and anxiety over the situation of foreign nationals in Iraq and Kuwait and calling upon the Secretary-General to take all appropriate steps. The United States intends to consult with other governments with citizens being held in Iraq and Kuwait to determine what additional measures ought to be taken.

Statement on Signing the Oil Pollution Act of 1990
August 18, 1990

I am today signing into law H.R. 1465, the "Oil Pollution Act of 1990." In May 1989 the Administration sent its comprehensive oil pollution liability and compensation legislation to the Congress in the wake of the worst marine environmental disaster this Nation has ever experienced. During this disaster 11 million gallons of oil spilled into the waters of Prince William Sound, Alaska. Since then, California, the Gulf of Mexico, the Mid-Atlantic, and New England have suffered serious oil spills.

In most respects, the Oil Pollution Act of 1990 is a responsible piece of legislation. Most important, the prevention, response, liability, and compensation components fit together into a compatible and workable system that strengthens the protection of our environment.

The Act addresses the wide-ranging problems associated with preventing, responding to, and paying for oil spills. It does so by creating a comprehensive regime for dealing with vessel and facility-caused oil pollution. It provides for greater environmental safeguards in oil transportation by: setting new standards for vessel construction, crew licensing, and manning; providing for contingency planning; enhancing Federal response capability; broadening enforcement authority; increasing penalties; and authorizing multi-agency research and development. A one billion dollar trust fund will be available to cover cleanup costs and damages not compensated by the spiller, whose financial responsibility requirements are significantly increased.

Although I am approving this legislation, I deeply regret the Act's inclusion of an unrelated provision that would place a moratorium on exploration for oil and natural gas off the coast of North Carolina. This area, located over 38 miles offshore, is the largest potential natural gas field east of the Mississippi and could be used to offset our dependence on foreign energy sources. Much work has been done to address my environmental concerns related to exploration in this area—and it should be noted

that exploration for gas this far offshore carries little environmental risk. It is shortsighted to restrict exploration for this relatively clean energy source, especially in light of our recent efforts to accommodate national and State concerns regarding the environmental effects of energy exploration and development. Such a moratorium is ill-advised in view of recent events in the Persian Gulf, where I have found it necessary to deploy American soldiers 7,000 miles from home to protect our vital national interests. The moratorium contained in H.R. 1465 is highly objectionable, and my Administration will seek to repeal it.

In addition, H.R. 1465 does not implement the 1984 Protocols to the 1969 Civil Liability Convention and the 1971 Fund Convention. These oil spill treaties, if ratified, would provide our Nation with swift and assured compensation for foreign tanker oil spills and access to up to $260 million per spill from an international fund. Our failure to ratify the Protocols may weaken long-standing U.S. leadership in the development of international maritime standards.

Ultimately, the threat of oil pollution is a global challenge, and the solutions we devise must be broad enough to address the needs of all nations. Therefore, I urge the Senate to give immediate consideration to the international Protocols and give its advice and consent to ratification of these treaties.

I am concerned about another consequence of the failure to ratify the Protocols. We must work to ensure that, in response to the provisions of this Act, a situation is not created in which larger oil shippers seeking to avoid risk are replaced by smaller companies with limited assets and a reduced ability to pay for the cleanup of oil spills. We will need to monitor developments in order to protect against such undesirable consequences.

The oil industry faces many new requirements as a result of this legislation. These requirements include substantially increased financial responsibility; preparation of contingency plans; and the replacement of fleets with safer oil tankers. A balance has been sought to give the industry the flexibility to meet the requirements of the Act without incurring excessive costs.

Finally, I note that section 3004 of the bill could be construed to infringe on my constitutional authority over the conduct of diplomacy by requiring me to take certain actions with respect to international organizations. I shall construe this section consistently with the Constitution and therefore shall regard it as advisory.

In signing this landmark Act, I pledge the support of the Administration for the Oil Pollution Act of 1990, notwithstanding the concerns that I have addressed. This represents a continuation of my Administration's efforts to work with the Congress and other nations to protect the Earth's environment.

GEORGE BUSH

The White House,
August 18, 1990.

Note: H.R. 1465, approved August 18, was assigned Public Law No. 101–380.

Statement on Signing the Customs and Trade Act of 1990
August 20, 1990

I am pleased to sign into law H.R. 1594, the "Customs and Trade Act of 1990." This legislation is the culmination of many long hours of work. It was worth the effort, for the Act accomplishes a number of important goals shared by both my Administration and the Congress:

—The extension and enhancement of the Caribbean Basin Initiative, which will continue to promote economic growth and democracy in that region;

—The amendment of Jackson-Vanik procedures, which will facilitate cooperation between the Executive and the Congress to encourage reform in the Soviet Union and assist the emerging democracies of Eastern Europe; and

—A new structure for U.S. customs user fees, which demonstrates our unfaltering commitment to the General Agreement on Tariffs and Trade (GATT).

Furthermore, the spirit of bipartisan cooperation that this Act represents bodes well for the coming months. We head into the fall facing the challenging tasks of completing the vital Uruguay Round of global trade talks by December and then drafting implementing legislation in 1991.

The results of this Round of negotiations, held under the auspices of the GATT, can be the engine that drives the United States and world economies into the 21st century.

The agreement we reach will be the ultimate competitiveness initiative. It will open new markets for American business, help reduce prices and increase choices for consumers, and secure rigorous rules of fair play in international trade.

The Customs and Trade Act of 1990, therefore, is part of the cooperative process that ultimately will result in growth, jobs, and prosperity, not only for America, but also for the world.

Let me give special mention to three vital provisions of the legislation I am signing today.

First, this legislation makes permanent and enhances the Caribbean Basin Initiative, or CBI.

Since its inception in 1983, CBI has promoted stability, security, and the movement to democracy and free markets that we now celebrate not only in this hemisphere but around the world. This legislation will foster continued economic growth and opportunity in the region.

By enacting this bill we assure investors in the Caribbean and Central America that their investments will continue to earn returns on duty-free exports indefinitely. It further extends the range of products that receive preferential duty treatment under CBI.

Because of the success of the CBI example, I announced on July 23 that I would seek legislation for limited-duration CBI-like trade preferences for the Andean countries of Bolivia, Colombia, Ecuador, and Peru. This measure would assist these countries in eliminating the production of illegal drugs and promoting competitive activity in world markets. I hope that my proposal will be given rapid, favorable consideration once it is presented to the Congress.

America's security and prosperity depend in large measure on continued progress toward democracy and economic development in the Caribbean Basin.

Second, the Act will help the United States support the emerging democracies of Eastern Europe and encourage change within the Soviet Union.

It does so by amending Jackson-Vanik procedures for approval of the historic trade agreements the United States has signed with the Soviet Union and Czechoslovakia. These agreements provide for improved access to each country's markets; facilitate business by easing restrictions on commercial activities; and offer strong intellectual property protections.

By working together to gain approval for these accords, the way is paved for continued cooperation between the Administration and the Congress on future agreements with other countries subject to the Jackson-Vanik Amendment.

Third, the Act is another demonstration of our Nation's abiding commitment to the GATT, the international constitution of trade.

A GATT panel in 1988 adopted a finding that the structure of U.S. customs user fees violated GATT rules. This Act authorizes a new fee structure that brings us into compliance with GATT rules.

This demonstration of our dedication to GATT comes at a critical point in the Uruguay Round of global trade talks. The great trading nations of the world can choose either to open their markets so that trade can expand, and thereby create global prosperity; or, they can choose to close their markets, splinter into exclusionary trading blocs, and thereby cause dangerously diminished prosperity for all.

The United States has chosen the first path. With the cooperation and support of the Congress and the private sector, we stand committed to the successful conclusion of the negotiations by December and prompt implementation of the results in 1991.

H.R. 1594 also contains a set of provisions that will be helpful both to our environment and our economy. The Act makes permanent the current ban on the export of unprocessed logs taken from Federal lands west of the 100th meridian and would sharply restrict the export of such logs taken from State lands. On June 23, the U.S. Fish and Wildlife Service listed the Northern Spotted Owl as a threatened species under the terms of the Endangered Species Act. There can be no doubt that high levels of export of unprocessed timber have contributed to the decline in habitat that has caused this species to be listed. This legislation will help to address problems related to this listing decision. While I am supporting this provision because it assists in the preservation of critical habitat, I also note that it will ease the economic transition in areas affected by the listing of the spotted owl.

Finally, I note that one of the provisions of H.R. 1594 warrants careful construction to avoid constitutional concerns. Under Article II, section 3 of the Constitution, the President has the discretion to determine what legislative proposals he will present to the Congress, as well as the discretion to determine the procedure he will follow in formulating a legislative proposal. Section 223(b) of this Act purports to require the President, in exercising his discretion to prepare legislative proposals on "rules of origin," to take into account a particular report and obtain the advice of various entities, including committees of the Congress. In light of the President's constitutional discretion with regard to preparing and submitting legislative proposals, I will construe this provision to be precatory rather than mandatory. As always, I will endeavor to consult with the Congress about our policy on such matters.

GEORGE BUSH

The White House,
August 20, 1990.

Note: H.R. 1594, approved August 20, was assigned Public Law No. 101–382.

Remarks at the Annual Conference of the Veterans of Foreign Wars in Baltimore, Maryland
August 20, 1990

Thank you so much. Please be seated. And it's a privilege to join you and a deep personal pleasure to renew old ties, greet new friends. My thanks to all of you, but especially to you, Walter Hogan—doing a great job as commander in chief. Following the likes of Larry Rivers isn't easy—we all know that—but Walter's done the VFW proud. I also know we're looking forward to the same kind of strong leadership from James Kimery. And let me offer my thanks again to another old friend, Cooper Holt, a real legend who gave so many years of service to the VFW. Cooper, we welcome you.

Next I want to thank my outstanding Veterans Secretary, fellow VFW member, Ed Derwinski. Ed's got so much going on, but I'm especially happy to see the work he's doing to improve these veterans hospitals. His Department is intent on serving you, much as you have served America.

I'm glad to see the Secretary of the Army with us today, an old friend of mine, a friend of yours, Mike Stone. And let us remember those who could not be with us. Our administration will not forget our POW's and MIA's as well as those brave men and women who gave what Lincoln termed "the last full measure of devotion."

Again, my acknowledgement to Mike Stone and also Baltimore's mayor, who courteously came to greet me, Kurt Schmoke. Glad to see you here, sir. And finally, also let me single out today's honorees, Budd Dudley and our own United Nations Ambassador, Tom Pickering, who is doing an outstanding job up there in the United Nations for the United States of America. Both Budd and Tom are being honored appropriately by you tonight.

Apologies for keeping you waiting. There are some events going on around the world. And I was on the telephone to a good friend of the United States, President Özal

of Turkey, and also to another great friend of the United States, Prime Minister Thatcher of the United Kingdom. And I must say, I'm proud of the support that we are all getting around the world.

You know, as a veteran, I want to salute this organization on its 91st year. By supporting our nation's veterans, the VFW has enriched America. And I'd like to take a moment to ask your support for a man whom I'm convinced will also enrich America—I want to work in a strong plug—and I'm talking about our Supreme Court nominee, Judge David Souter. [*Applause*] I see the New Hampshire delegation is here. [*Laughter*] Well, they know something we all know, and that is that he is an exceptional jurist and a brilliant legal mind. He will be a voice of excellence on the Nation's highest court, and I call on the Senate to confirm him without delay.

But this morning I'm also grateful to have this special opportunity to discuss an issue of great concern to all Americans: the crisis in the Persian Gulf—a crisis that will require American planning, patience, and yes, personal sacrifice; but a crisis that we must and will meet if we are to stop aggression, help our friends, and protect our own interests and the peace and stability of countries around the globe.

Eighteen days ago, these beliefs prompted me to take action in the Middle East to restore the sovereignty of Kuwait and deter those who threaten friendly countries and the vital interests of America. I acted knowing that our cause would not be easy but that our cause is right. And that while one should not underestimate those who endanger peace, an even greater mistake would be to underestimate America's commitment to our friends when our friends are imperiled or our commitment to international order when that, too, is imperiled.

Today, the outcome is not yet decided. Hard choices remain, but of this we are certain: America will not be intimidated. When some ask: Where does America stand? our answer is: America stands where it always has—against aggression, against those who would use force to replace the rule of law.

And who better than this group know? Throughout history, we have learned that we must stand up to evil. It's a truth which the past 18 days have reaffirmed, and its lessons speak to America and to the world.

The first lesson is as vivid as the memories of Normandy, Khe Sanh, Pork Chop Hill. We have been reminded again that aggression must and will be checked. So, at the request of our friends, we have sent U.S. forces to the Middle East—reluctantly, but decisively—knowing, as Teddy Roosevelt said, that America "means many things, among them, equality of rights and, therefore, equality of duty and obligation."

Yet we are not acting alone but in concert, helping to protect our own national security interests as well as those of the broader community of nations, which brings me to the second lesson reaffirmed by the past 18 days. By itself, America can do much. Together with its friends and allies, America can do much more—for peace and for justice.

Think back with me to World War II, when together allies confronted a horror which embodied hell on Earth, or Korea, where United Nations forces opposed totalitarianism. Today, once again, many nations—many of them Moslem—have joined to counter aggression and, thus, to restore the peace.

Our Saudi friends, under the wise leadership of King Fahd, asked for our help in deterring further aggression by Iraq. I salute the many countries who have courageously responded to Saudi Arabia's request. I also salute those governments who were responding to the Amir of Kuwait's call for the full enforcement of United Nations sanctions.

We must not delude ourselves: Iraq's invasion was more than a military attack on tiny Kuwait; it was a ruthless assault on the very essence of international order and civilized ideals. And now, in a further offense against all norms of international behavior, Iraq has imposed restrictions on innocent civilians from many countries. This is unacceptable. And that's why the United Nations Security Council voted unanimously Saturday night to condemn Iraq's action, just as it earlier voted to condemn the invasion itself. They know, as we do, that leaders who use citizens as pawns deserve and will receive the scorn and condemnation of the entire world.

And so, to the leaders of Iraq, I will now make two points clear: In moving foreign citizens against their will, you are violating the norms of your own religion. You are going against the age-old Arab tradition of showing kindness and hospitality to visitors. And so, my message is: Release all foreigners now! Give them the right to come and go as they wish. Adhere to international law and U.N. Security Council Resolution 664.

We've been reluctant to use the term "hostage." But when Saddam Hussein specifically offers to trade the freedom of those citizens of many nations he holds against their will in return for concessions, there can be little doubt that whatever these innocent people are called, they are, in fact, hostages. And I want there to be no misunderstanding. I will hold the Government of Iraq responsible for the safety and well-being of American citizens held against their will.

Let me also take a moment to thank President Gorbachev for his recent words condemning the Iraqi invasion. He has shown—if anyone doubted it—that nations which joined to fight aggression in World War II can work together to stop the aggressors of today.

A third lesson has also been reaffirmed by the last 18 days—as veterans, it won't surprise you: the steadfast character of the American will. Look to the sands of Saudi Arabia and the waters offshore, where brave Americans are doing their duty, just as you did at Anzio and Inchon and Hamburger Hill. And think of the men and women aboard our planes and ships—young, alone, and so very far from home. They make us humble; they make us proud. And I salute the finest soldiers, sailors, airmen, and marines that any nation could possibly have. And moreover, I pledge to you: We will do whatever it takes to help them complete their mission.

This means realizing the fourth lesson reaffirmed by the past 18 days. Although the size of America's Armed Forces in the years ahead will be smaller because the threat to our security is changing, future American defense capacity must be even more "a lean, mean fighting machine." And by 1995, we estimate that our security needs can be met by an active force 25 percent smaller than today's, the lowest level since 1950. And yet we must ensure that a reduction of numbers does not mean a reduction in American strength.

Operation Desert Shield proves vividly that instead of relieving past contingencies we must prepare for the challenges of the 1990's and beyond. By ensuring that our troops are ready and trained, we can exert our presence in key areas and respond effectively to crisis. And this is readiness measured in days and hours, not weeks and months. And Operation Desert Shield has underscored the need to be able to get our soldiers where they are needed and when they are needed. This kind of responsiveness will be critical in the crises of the future.

Recently, our outstanding Chairman of the Joint Chiefs, General Colin Powell, spoke to this when he praised "the finest peacetime military in the history of America." We will be smaller in troop strength and restructured, but we will remain purposeful, proud, and effective. Just look at the last 18 days. Desert Shield has been a classic case of America's military at its best.

I think, for instance, of Airman First Class Wade West, home on leave to be married. On August 7th, he was called up, and within an hour he had the ceremony performed and left for the Middle East. And he's now stationed over in Saudi Arabia. You talk about a guy that gets things done. [*Laughter*] But I would like to empathize with his bride wherever she may be. [*Laughter*] And another example: 7 years ago, Diana Kroptavich worried at home while her husband, Walter, steamed off the Lebanon coast on the U.S.S. *New Jersey* defending the marines. Today their roles are reversed. Retired, Walter is at home with their 6-year-old son, and Diana serves aboard the destroyer U.S.S. *Yellowstone*. [*Laughter*] Here's an Army couple: today paratrooper Joseph Hudert of the 82d Airborne Division is serving in Saudi Arabia, and his wife, nurse Dominique Allen, of the 44th Medical Brigade, will be deployed there within the next 2 weeks. Finally, recall the 8-year-old who, watching her dad leave for the Mediterranean, spoke truth from the mouths of babes. "I just think," she said, "that they shouldn't let daddies go away this long. But they still have to, to keep the world safe."

These profiles show the true caliber of America and the vital essence of our mission. What's more, they remind us of the fifth and final lesson reaffirmed by the past 18 days: the need for a continued strong defense budget to support American troops, or as George Washington said in his first inaugural address, "To be prepared for war is one of the most effectual means of preserving the peace." History has shown the wisdom of his words—especially in our century. What Desert Shield has shown is that America can ensure the peace by remaining militarily strong.

Now, I know that we're operating in a time of budget restraint. We have limited resources; we must use them wisely. The budget deficit is a threat to our vital interests at home and won't be made easier by today's threat abroad. Everyone realizes that the deficit is too large, that it's got to be brought down, and that Congress must act courageously and immediately when it returns from recess. But here's the point: We cannot attack the deficit by attacking the very heart of our Armed Forces—committed men and women who are motivated and ready.

Last week I asked Congress to do what we have done: produce a budget proposal, including defense, that is both responsive and responsible and, most of all, fair. When they do, I will listen—listen, but not break faith with the troops who are defending our nation. Make no mistake: To prevent aggression, to keep America militarily prepared, I will oppose the defense-budget slashers who are out of tune with what America needs to keep freedom secure and safe.

You know, most Americans know that when it comes to national defense, finishing second means finishing last. So, they reject what the House Armed Services Committee recently suggested: unacceptable cuts from our defense budget for fiscal year 1991. Most Americans know, too, that giving peace a chance does not mean taking a chance on peace. So, they endorse giving the military the tools to do its job: the Peacekeeper, the Midgetman, B–2 bomber, and the Strategic Defense Initiative. Americans want arms negotiations to succeed, but they know that even a START treaty will not help our security if we disarm unilaterally.

Let us never forget that our strong national defense policies have helped us gain the peace. We need a strong defense today to maintain that peace. I will fight for that defense, and I need your help. So, help me convince the Congress, given recent events, to take another look and to adequately fund our defense budget.

Let me tell you a little story about why I feel so strongly. I was talking to some of the young soldiers who liberated Panama. We invited them to come with General Thurman and others to the Cabinet Room for a briefing for me. I asked one of them—a medic—about the operation. Corporal Roderick Ringstaff spoke of combat, and he spoke of the heroics of others, but not of his own. Next to him was his commanding officer, and so his commanding officer filled in the rest. This medic had been wounded, but repeatedly braved fire to rescue others wounded, pulling soldier after soldier to safety. For that he was awarded the Silver Star for bravery. Listening, I thought to myself: I will never send young men and women into battle with less than the very best that this nation can provide them. I will never—I will never, ever—let Americans like this down.

August 1990 has witnessed what history will judge one of the most crucial deployments of allied power since World War II. Two weeks ago, I called for the complete, immediate, and unconditional withdrawal

of all Iraqi forces from Kuwait; second, the restoration of Kuwait's legitimate government; third, the security and the stability of Saudi Arabia and the Persian Gulf; and fourth, the safety and protection of American citizens abroad. Today, I say, those objectives are and will remain unchanged.

Will it take time? Of course. For we're engaged in a cause larger than ourselves, a cause perhaps best shown by words many of you remember—words spoken by one of the greatest Americans of our time to allied soldiers and sailors and airmen. "The eyes of the world are upon you," he told them. "The hopes and prayers of liberty-loving people everywhere march with you." And then he concluded with this moving prayer: "Let us all beseech the blessing of almighty God upon this great and noble undertaking."

Fellow veterans, more than half of all VFW members fought in World War II, many of you serving under the man who spoke those words, Dwight David Eisenhower. You know how America remains the hope of "liberty-loving people everywhere." Half a century ago, the world had the chance to stop a ruthless aggressor and missed it. I pledge to you: We will not make that mistake again. For you see, together we can successfully oppose tyranny and help those nations who look to us for leadership and vision.

Thank you for your support and your prayers. And may God bless the land we so deeply love, the United States of America. Thank you all, and God bless you.

Note: The President spoke at 10:39 a.m. at the Baltimore Arena. In his remarks, he referred to Walter G. Hogan, Larry W. Rivers, James Kimery, and Cooper Holt, commander in chief, assistant adjutant general and executive director, vice commander in chief, and former commander in chief of the Veterans of Foreign Wars, respectively; Budd Dudley, executive director of the Liberty Bowl Festival Association; President Saddam Hussein of Iraq; and Gen. Maxwell R. Thurman, commander in chief of the U.S. Southern Command.

Exchange With Reporters Aboard Air Force One
August 20, 1990

Persian Gulf Crisis

Q. ——turn up the heat today by, in fact, calling these Americans held against their will hostages. What's the strategy behind that?

The President. I don't think it was any turning up the heat. It's a recognition of the fact that now demands are being made for the release of people. And that, I think, is the definition of hostages.

Q. But there was some reluctance on the part of the administration earlier because now it will require some kind of response, would it not, from Saddam Hussein?

The President. Well, it's only in the last couple of days that these demands have been made—obviously, demands that are totally unsatisfactory to most countries in the world—demands that these multilateral forces and U.S. forces, of course, included, get out and return to the status of Saddam Hussein's having invaded Kuwait. And that can't stand. So, he linked a demand to it. But it's a semantical thing. The situation is about the same as it was a few days ago.

Q. Are we prepared to stop the tankers, actually stop the tankers that——

The President. Well, just watch. You just watch and see. Please don't ask hypothetical questions because there's a lot going on there, and we're just going to——

Q. We've been shadowing them, though, for a day.

The President. You said it.

Lee Atwater

Q. Mr. President, let me switch gears. How is Lee Atwater? What do you hear?

The President. Well, I haven't heard anything in the last few days. I've been concerned, but I haven't heard anything in the last few days about him. He's still in the hospital, so I've got to get a report from our doctor here.

Presidential Campaigning

Q. Mr. President, can I ask you, on the front, is there anything incongruous about going and doing political fundraisers and bashing Democrats at a time of national crisis like this? Are you at all uneasy about it?

The President. I don't feel I've bashed Democrats too much. But life goes on, so I'm not uneasy about going to political fundraisers, no. I have to do that. Reelections are coming up in a couple of weeks, and I want to help Republicans. I want to help people that look at these problems the way I do.

Relations With the Press

Q. So, you're back talking to us again now? The silent period is over or——

The President. How long did the silent period last? What silent period? Which one?

Persian Gulf Crisis

Q. Mr. President, in your speech, when you talked about personal sacrifice, were you making a specific reference to those Americans being detained? Are you concerned, sir, that this may require a sacrifice on their part, that we may in fact lose some of these——

The President. I'm just going to let the words stand just exactly for what they say here. I'm not going to go beyond what I've said on it. There's no point in heightening all this. We'll just leave it there.

Defense Budget

Q. On the budget talks, are Pentagon cuts now off the table, but taxes still on the table?

The President. No, as I said, Pentagon cuts are not. But reckless Pentagon cuts are—we just can't tolerate them. And I think that most Members of Congress will return and understand this now.

Persian Gulf Crisis

Q. When did you decide to call them hostages? Last night we were told that you did not regard them as hostages.

The President. Well, I think that when we had a meeting there last night, and then this morning I decided: Look, as long as these demands are being made, why, it's semantical. Why not just say that?

Q. What about them asking us to close our Embassies?

The President. What?

Q. In 5 days they want all the outside Embassies closed—foreign——

The President. For all over, yes. That's unacceptable.

Q. Calling up Reserves?

Q. Are we going to stay?

The President. Well, I'll have something to say on that later on.

Q. Today? Later on today?

Q. Are you trying to get more of an international and United Nations leadership——

The President. We're in the United Nations right now, and the United Nations has

performed very, very well. And it's important because that keeps world opinion strongly with us. I found out today—talking to Margaret Thatcher reiterated that.

Thank you all.

Note: The exchange took place approximately at noon en route from Andrews Air Force Base, MD, to Providence, RI. In his remarks, President Bush referred to President Saddam Hussein of Iraq; Prime Minister Margaret Thatcher of the United Kingdom; and H. Lee Atwater, chairman of the Republican National Committee, who was undergoing treatment for cancer. A tape was not available for verification of the content of this exchange.

Remarks at a Republican Party Fundraising Luncheon in North Kingstown, Rhode Island
August 20, 1990

Thank you all very much. Thank you for that warm welcome back. Ed, thank you especially. This may have escaped some, but it has not escaped Barbara and me: Ed DiPrete was perhaps my earliest supporter, or certainly one of them, when I started the quest for the Presidency.

I'm delighted to be here. Slightly—only slightly—disappointed. I kind of expected to be driven up here in Winnebago One. [*Laughter*] And though Nick Janikies tells me that the club's chef makes terrific broccoli—[*laughter*]—I understand that the Winnebago is the best place around to get a homemade bologna sandwich. [*Laughter*] But really, it is a pleasure to be here and to see so many of our other good Rhode Island friends.

You know, I was asked, I think, an appropriate question—not all questions are appropriate, but this one was—by the press coming up. And they said, "Well, don't you feel a little funny going to a political event at this time?" And I knew exactly why the question was asked, and I certainly respect it. But life goes on, and we have an election coming up in the fall. And I think it's important that I conduct my duties of the

Presidency in the best way I possibly can. But you can't exclude the fact that there's a lot of things happening. And a lot of it gets right back to the kind of elected officials that we're going to have in the future. And so, I didn't think about changing this event.

And I'm delighted to be here and see so many friends. Of course, Senator Chafee and I go back longer than either of us would like to admit, I'm sure. Claudine Schneider—more later. Ron Machtley, who's doing such an outstanding job as a member of the Armed Services Committee and a great Member of the United States Congress, and Norma and Elinor and Ned Grace, who's done such a great job chairing this event. And I might also mention another. If she can save the bay, she ought to be able to save Congress—I'm talking about Trudy Cox, sitting over here, and wish her well. But you know, with a strong leadership team like this, elected officials and party leaders, Rhode Island's party, I believe, is headed for victory in November; and it's very important.

I want to give a special thanks to Traf— mayor, my old friend Mayor Traficante—for letting us play through, so to speak. He's got his own golf tournament working, and two things worried my Secret Service agents about that tournament. First, that it's a "shotgun" start. [*Laughter*] And second, that Jerry Ford might be teeing off on the 18th while we're here. [*Laughter*] But we're safe. And, Traf, good to see you.

What a great sight it was as we came in. I must say I was very moved by the response from your fellow Rhode Islanders. And to see the bay, the clean beauty of that bay, as we came in—a sight that we must not and cannot take for granted. And I remember, as you do, last year's oilspill and how Ed, the man on my right, immediately leaped into action and tapped into Federal resources and, indeed, many say, prevented a catastrophe. And that kind of sums up Ed DiPrete: committed to the environment, a take-charge leader.

I've seen his leadership first-hand. I saw it at our education summit with the Governors last year—the first such summit ever held—the one in Charlottesville. He had a tremendous impact with his innovative public-private partnership, the Children's Crusade for Higher Education. And he has a great record in other areas of urgent priorities, where he stands shoulder to shoulder with me, and I'm thinking of our battle that we must win in the war on drugs. One of the most aggressive fighters in the anti-narcotics field is Ed DiPrete. His national leadership for the rights of the people with disabilities is well-known. And I might say parenthetically, I was delighted to have worked for and then the other day signed the ADA bill [Americans with Disabilities Act of 1990]—long overdue, but a wonderful bill to help those with disabilities in this country.

And all of us familiar with the area know that New England has had a tough time in a lot of ways economically. But I'm proud of the way that he's revitalized economic growth in this State where the American Industrial Revolution began and, in the process, has restored Rhode Island's bond rating, which is a good indication of how others, how the markets, feel about this State. And so, after all, if you want to talk business in Rhode Island, talk to a businessman, talk to the Governor. And I want him there, reelected, strong, at my side as we

face the problems coming up for the rest of the nineties.

And now I turn to another Rhode Islander because, very candidly, we need Claudine Schneider in the United States Senate. She's a special friend of mine and of Barbara's and, I'd say, of Rhode Island's. She's one of your best exports. In Washington we're amazed by her vitality, her passionate enthusiasm, and that astounding, almost frustrating energy level of hers that leaves others in the dust. I think I work hard. And I try to. Sometimes play hard. But try to keep up with Claudine, it's impossible. Try to overtake her in a 3K or a 10K or a marathon, it can't be done.

But it's not just in a road race that she's leading the pack. She's a principled, independent leader in the finest tradition of John Chafee, the finest tradition of Rhode Island—tenacious, fierce individualism. She's setting the pace in areas like education and like fighting crime and especially in the worldwide struggle to preserve and protect the environment.

Claudine has been a great Member of the United States Congress. She'll be a great Senator. Rhode Island needs her voice and leadership, and I really do need her in the Senate. The difference between the Senate today and the Senate when it was controlled by the Republicans for a Republican President is night and day. And so, we need her for her own merit, but we also need her to get us back in control of the United States Senate. So, get the message out. Go on and have some more debates, Claudine. You did just great in the debate, and I hope you have more.

Today I want to just mention a couple of challenges. We've been talking about them here, challenges that our able Members face—Members of Congress. But today two of them—really two of the most critical issues that our nation has faced in decades—I'm talking about our own fiscal affairs, our own budget deficit; and then, of course, the subject that's on everybody's minds, the question of the Middle East.

I have stated here the frustrations of dealing with a Congress that's controlled by the other party and controls the purse strings. And I'll work with the Congress. I have tried to work cooperatively and with compromise with the United States Congress, and I will continue to do that. But we were working towards a budget summit, an economic summit, a summit that would solve once and for all the budget deficit. And that broke up when Congress decided it was time to go on and have the recess. But the Congress comes back soon. And what I want to say to you is: I have not lost my interest in seeing us get a budget agreement that is going to reform the budget process, get the deficit down, and get it under control once and for all. We owe that to the younger generations here today.

This is a national problem, and it isn't going to go away. And sure, it's been affected by events that are happening halfway around the world. But we must not let those events reduce the urgency that we all feel about getting the Federal deficit under control.

I don't intend to dwell on it here, but let me just point out that the House has passed appropriations bills this year exceeding my request by $14 billion in spending. And the Senate Budget Committee voted a new legislation weakening the budget process. In my view, this is going in the wrong direction. I think we've got to turn around now, get an agreement, and get some reform and get some incentive built into the system.

I know some people think I'm a broken record. But if there ever was a time that you need to stimulate economic growth it's now, and one of the best ways to do that is to reduce the tax on capital gains. It will bring in revenue, and it will create jobs.

You know, I've been blessed by a steadfast group in the House and in the Senate, and I'm very grateful to them. But I must say that if the spending bills continue like this, I have to say, as I've said before in Washington a few weeks ago, that I will veto every single spending bill that busts the budget. We're in that tough a shape now, and I'm going to do it. So, they can mark it down and put it in the bank.

So, I think cooperation is still possible. As I said down there in Washington a couple of weeks ago, I've been pleased with the way some of the Democratic leadership has approached this process. I think Senator Chafee would agree with me, and I think

Claudine would agree with me and Ron would agree with me: that there's been some good faith effort in terms of negotiation. But it is essential now when the Congress comes back that this cooperation be renewed and that it continue because it is our country that's at stake.

Every day now, we're witnessing an extraordinary unity of individuals and of parties and of nations, showing what can happen when people put personal goals aside in pursuit of something bigger. So, even while we're here in this extraordinarily tranquil setting, our thoughts are, indeed, over in the Middle East, where other Americans are seeing not this serene beauty of Narragansett Bay but an arid landscape where the hot desert winds carry, regrettably, the threat of conflict. No sane person likes the specter of confrontations, and yet as we try to chart the course of our existence, we must be guided by the imperatives of a strong moral compass.

It was not with passionate haste but really with a heavy heart that I had to commit our troops to Saudi Arabia. I took this action not out of some national hunger for conflict but out of the moral responsibility, shared by so many committed nations around the world, to protect our world from fundamental evil. We cannot remain silent, for peace is more than just the absence of war. And its preservation really exacts on great countries like ours a certain obligation.

It is this obligation that the finest troops—if you talk to the Joint Chiefs, they'll tell you, every one of them, whatever their service, that we have the finest young men and women that the service has ever had, an all-volunteer Army, all-volunteer force, if you will, and the finest young kids ever, suited up and serving. So, it is this obligation that brave men and women are shouldering today in Saudi Arabia—the finest—finest men and women.

But they don't act alone. And this is another key point; Ed and Claudine both referred to it. Nations of every language, of every religion, size, and form of government have joined in renouncing the aggression against Kuwait. It is also important to note that 12 Arab countries condemned Iraq—12 condemned Iraq at the Arab summit and at the United Nations Security Council. And I want to commend Ambassador Pickering and the fine work that our delegation is doing at the United Nations, because it is important that we bring along and lead our friends around the world in this regard. The United Nations Security Council approved chapter VII sanctions on Iraq because of its aggression. It was the first time that's happened in, I think, something like 23 years. We've seen an extraordinary expression of world unity, and I am hopeful that together the United States and the many other peace-loving nations committed to this noble effort will prevail.

I wanted to talk about this because of your State's own history: commitment to individual rights. Your State may be small—Kuwait is small—but your ideals loom large. And you've always responded to the call of moral responsibility. In the early days of this country, Rhode Island answered threats upon individuals by fiercely defending each person's right to believe what he wanted and worship as he or she wished. Just a few minutes ago, in here, I met with leaders of the Touro Synagogue—an impressive, moving story—the oldest synagogue in continental America, a symbol of your State's lifelong affirmation of the inalienable rights of all people. And Rhode Island also responded to the moral obligation to defend these rights when the world was called upon to confront staggering aggression during World War II. Your State answered by sending 58,000 of its finest sons and daughters into battle.

The world is now called upon to confront another aggressor, another threat made by a person who has no values when it comes to respecting international law, a man of evil standing against human life itself. I am convinced that the same moral underpinnings that have underpinned this State for years and underpin our great country is the compass that's going to guide us. And I believe that our presence in the Middle East sends a great signal of commitment around the world.

I must tell you that I'm troubled by Americans that now seem to be held against their will and other foreigners held against their will.

I'm grateful for our friends. This morning,

I had a long talk with President Özal of Turkey on the telephone. If you'll look at the map and then see the courageous stand taken by President Özal and the Turks, you will understand what it means to work cooperatively with other countries, and you'll understand why I am grateful for the full cooperation of this strategically placed ally.

Another talk I had this morning—and one of the reasons I was a little late on this trip—was with Margaret Thatcher. You talk about somebody that stands tall when the going gets tough, and you talk about somebody that knows what it is to have a moral compass. Thank God for allies and friends like Margaret Thatcher when the going gets tough. And right now, it could get fairly tough over there.

I might say parenthetically, I feel blessed as your President by the quality and the character of the leadership in our own government. I can do my job knowing that options come my way; knowing that our team stays together; and knowing I'm relying, perhaps, on the finest Cabinet and the finest people in the Pentagon that any President could have to work with. And I am very grateful to each and every one of them as we approach some very tough decisions that lie ahead.

The bottom line is life goes on. And so, we're here today talking some politics. We're here today talking some fiscal sanity. We're here today to say a prayer for the United States and all the people around the world that are supporting us in our bid to provide a moral compass for the rest of the world.

I am grateful. I am privileged. Even though this time may be a little difficult, I am privileged to be your President in one of the most fascinating times in history. I'll do my best I possibly can. And thank you for your warm hospitality.

Note: The President spoke at 1:45 p.m. on the grounds of the Quidnessett Country Club. In his remarks, he referred to Nicholas Janikies, president of the country club; Norma Willis, State Republican Party chairwoman; Elinor Clapp, Republican national committeewoman; Ned Grace, the luncheon chairman; Trudy Cox, candidate for the House of Representatives and former executive director of Save the Bay; Michael Traficante, mayor of Cranston, RI; former President Gerald Ford; and Prime Minister *Margaret Thatcher of the United Kingdom. Following his remarks, the President traveled to his home in Kennebunkport, ME.*

Statement by Press Secretary Fitzwater on President Bush's Conversations With President François Mitterrand of France and Senator Robert Byrd on the Persian Gulf Crisis
August 20, 1990

President Bush this afternoon telephoned President Mitterrand of France. They spoke for about 30 minutes. President Bush said he appreciated the firm response and leadership that France has taken in this crisis. The two Presidents also discussed their concern about foreign nationals being held hostage in Kuwait and Iraq.

The President also called Senator Robert Byrd, who was in Amsterdam on his way to Turkey. The President discussed the situation in the Gulf with the Senator and certain other matters that might be raised during his trip to Turkey.

Letter to Congressional Leaders on the Mobilization of United States Reserves
August 22, 1990

Dear Mr. Speaker: (Dear Mr. President:)
I have today, pursuant to section 673b of title 10, United States Code, authorized the Secretary of Defense, and the Secretary of Transportation with respect to the Coast Guard when it is not operating as a service within the Department of the Navy, to order to active duty units and individual members not assigned to units of the Selected Reserve to perform such missions the Secretary of Defense may determine necessary. The deployment of United States forces to conduct operational missions in and around the Arabian Peninsula necessitates this action.

A copy of the Executive order implementing this action is attached.

Sincerely,

GEORGE BUSH

Note: Identical letters were sent to Thomas S. Foley, Speaker of the House of Representatives, and Dan Quayle, President of the Senate. The Executive order is listed in Appendix E at the end of this volume.

Statement by Press Secretary Fitzwater on the Mobilization of United States Reserves
August 22, 1990

The President today authorized the Secretary of Defense to call Reserve units of the Armed Forces to active duty. The order permits the Secretary of Defense to call to duty selected members and units of the Reserve components of the Army, Navy, Air

Force, and Marine Corps as needed to support United States and multinational operations now underway. The President signed the order after the Secretary of Defense advised him that the effective conduct of military operations in and around the Arabian Peninsula may require augmentation of Active components of the Armed Forces. The actual number of Reserve personnel to be called to active duty will depend upon the operational needs of the Armed Forces, but at this time, we do not anticipate approaching the full 200,000 authority provided by law.

The Total Force Policy, which was established in 1973, allocates various military capabilities among the Active, Reserve, and National Guard components that together make up the Armed Forces of the United States. Under this policy, the capability to perform certain critical military activities has been concentrated in the Reserve component. Activating reservists to support operations such as those now underway has been a central feature of this approach.

The skills concentrated in the Reserve component include airlift, food and water handling, surface transportation, cargo handling, medical services, construction, and intelligence. By making judicious use of the President's authorization, the Secretary of Defense will be able to ensure that essential capabilities such as these and others are available to support our operational requirements.

The President issued the order authorizing the Secretary of Defense to call Reserve units to active duty in accordance with section 673b of title 10 of the United States Code. The order also authorizes the Secretary of Transportation to call to active duty elements of the Coast Guard Reserve. Another order signed by the President permits the Secretary of Defense greater flexibility in military personnel management actions.

Note: The Executive orders are listed in Appendix E at the end of this volume.

The President's News Conference on the Persian Gulf Crisis
August 22, 1990

The President. Let me make a brief opening statement, and then I'll be glad to take any questions.

First, Secretary Cheney and General Powell have just given me a very full and, I would say, encouraging briefing on the status of our deployment to the Persian Gulf. This has been a very complicated mission calling for precision, calling for maximum coordination with Saudi Arabia and the other nations providing forces. The process has gone smoothly, and we've now moved what amounts to a medium-sized American city, completely capable of sustaining itself, all the way over to the Middle East.

And the Secretary reports that the men and women in the Armed Forces have performed with extraordinary ability, their morale is high, and they've accepted the challenge of their mission with extraordinary dedication to duty. And I'm very proud of each and every single one of them, and I want them to know that the American people are behind them 100 percent, supporting them strongly.

And it's also crucial that everyone understand that we are not in this alone. We stand shoulder to shoulder right there in the Middle East with the armed forces of 22 other nations from the Middle East, from Europe, and around the world.

Secretary Dick Cheney reports an impressive alliance of multinational forces that stands behind the United Nations resolve that Iraq completely and unconditionally withdraw from Kuwait with the restoration of the legitimate government in that country. The United Nations has provided enormous leadership to the whole world community in pursuing this objective and voting the sanctions necessary to carrying it out. And let's be clear: As the deployment of the forces of the many nations shows and as the votes in the United Nations show, this is not a matter between Iraq and the United States of America; it is between Iraq and the entire world community, Arab and non-Arab alike. All the nations of the world lined up to oppose aggression.

And as our forces continue to arrive, they can look forward to the support of the finest Reserve components in the world. We are activating those special categories of reservists that are essential to completing our mission. The United States considers its Reserve forces to be an integral part of the total military command. These essential personnel will soon be joining the cohesive organization required to support the military operations in and around the Arabian Peninsula, and I have the highest confidence in their ability to augment the Active forces in this operation.

We continue to pursue our objectives with absolute determination. I might add that I talked to the four leaders of Congress today, and I am very pleased that they are giving us the strong support they have been—the Speaker, Senator Mitchell [majority leader], Senator Dole [minority leader], Congressman Michel [Republican leader]. And the world simply cannot waiver in its opposition to the threat that Iraq has placed on the doorstep of all nations who cherish freedom and the rule of law.

Now what I plan to do is take some questions, and then I know you'll have more questions for Secretary Cheney and General Powell. And then the discussions that we've had with these two gentlemen and with Secretary Eagleburger and General Scowcroft, our Chief of Staff, and Bob Gates will continue for a little while this afternoon before they return to Washington.

But Dick, I am very grateful to you for your successful mission. And, both to you and Colin, my sincere thanks for the superb leadership you are giving the United States military, the superb leadership you are showing in working with other countries as we pursue these high moral objectives.

Q. Mr. President, the Soviets have voted with us in the Security Council for the economic sanctions, but we learned today that they have 193 military advisers still advising the Iraqi army on how to use Soviet-built

weapons against the allied forces. Do you call upon them to pull those people out?

The President. Frankly, I'd like to see Iraq do what is civilized and permit foreigners who want to leave, leave. But I'm not going to comment on that because I don't have this information that you're telling me about. Maybe Dick Cheney can comment on it later.

Q. Can I just follow, sir?

The President. Yes.

Q. You've talked to at least a dozen world leaders right from here in the past week and a half. Have you called President Gorbachev, and will you call President Gorbachev for his help in the crisis?

The President. Secretary Baker talked to Foreign Minister Shevardnadze less than 2 hours ago. And we are in close touch with the Soviets. At this point, I can say we are getting superb cooperation from the Soviets. There may be some differences. In fact, I think it's fair to say we've been discussing some of them regarding the timing of certain further U.N. action. But I have no argument with the way in which they have cooperated, and I would expect that Secretary Cheney would agree on that point.

Q. Could I follow on that, sir—talking about the U.N., the action that you would hope to have. The U.S. forces fired across the bow of a ship that then was allowed to continue on, is now in Yemen. Why did they not pursue that farther? Do you want to wait until you now have that U.N. authority?

The President. Well, you know, we feel we have all the authority we need; and the world leaders I've talked to, particularly François Mitterrand [President of France] and Margaret Thatcher [Prime Minister of the United Kingdom], agree that we have all the authority we need. We have been trying, and I think prudently so, to work with other countries around the world; and the more unanimity we get out of the United Nations, for example, the better. So, we're prepared to intercept shipping. But where I stand now is: I'm talking to my top advisers here and been on the phone to Secretary Baker a couple of times in the last 2 hours, talking about should the United Nations—should we give the United Nations more time to take more productive action. And it has taken productive action, obviously; the chapter VII was a significant step. So, I think we've made clear to the shipping that they can be stopped and that we have the forces to stop them right now. And I believe that General Powell would back me up on what I've just said.

So, my question is: How much more United Nations action is required? And so, I'm going to continue the discussion, asking for the advice of my officials here. But at this juncture, I'm not prepared to say whether we're going to insist on U.N. action before we go further. But I think the signal must go out to the world that many countries are prepared to fully enforce these sanctions. And if there's some U.N. action that will help, so much the better.

Q. How long would you wait for that U.N. action?

The President. We haven't made a determination. I think the signal is out there—as we pursue certain vessels and clearly have the demonstrated ability to board these vessels—that we can do it. So, now the question is: How much more U.N. action benefits this idea of the world staying more closely together? And I might be prepared to give a little time, speaking just for the U.S.—we're only one country there, important one though it may be—in order to get more collective action. But on the other hand, I need more advice in terms of the logistics: where these ships are, what the signal would be if we go ahead and take action to stop them, which we could confidently do.

Q. Mr. President, despite demands from the Iraqis that the U.S. and other countries close their Embassies in Kuwait and remove all their diplomatic personnel, the State Department announced today that the U.S. would not do that. Why have you decided to take that course of action, and how can you possibly enforce that?

The President. Because the occupation of Iraq is illegal under international law, and other countries agree totally that we must not take the position that this illegal regime can shut down legitimate Embassies as a result of their aggression. That's why.

Q. But with Iraq in military control of Kuwait, how can you possibly hope to en-

force that?

The President. My view is let's wait and see what happens. I don't go into these hypothetical questions. I'd like to explain this because I know there's a lot of them out there—as to what I might not or might do under certain circumstances. But here, I think most countries that I'm aware of, and I defer to Secretary Eagleburger, would agree that they will not go along with agreeing to this kind of affirmation of Iraq aggression—aggression that has been thoroughly condemned by the United Nations.

Q. I'd like to ask, please, about your hostage policy. You were very firm the other day in warning Saddam [Saddam Hussein, President of Iraq] not to harm the Americans. But I wonder: As Commander in Chief, sir, do you consider the U.S. has been provoked right now?

The President. Consider what?

Q. Has been provoked. Has the United States been provoked now by—

The President. I don't think it's a question of the United States; I think it's a question of the world is being provoked by this illegal action—outrageous action.

Q. Do you have a plan for getting them, sir?

The President. I don't discuss hypothetical contingencies. But I would reiterate, it is a grave concern to all the countries whose leaders I've talked to.

Q. Mr. President, will the United States give safe haven to our citizens in Kuwait and Iraq in the Embassies if——

The President. If citizens came to the Embassies seeking support and help, clearly we would do that.

Q. Do you have plans to draw down the number of Americans in our Embassy in Kuwait?

The President. I'd like to defer that question to Secretary Eagleburger when I continue this. There has been talk of it. Indeed, I think we're talking about taking down some personnel. But I'd like to ask him to be a little more definitive.

Q. Mr. President, how constrained do you feel by the Americans trapped in Kuwait as you make your decisions?

The President. I think any decisionmaker in the United States or in any of these countries is concerned about the lives of innocent civilians, innocent people. And so, you weigh that very thoroughly against your actions. Having said that, international law, in this case the chapter VII sanctions, must be enforced.

Q. Mr. President, you said last Wednesday at the Pentagon that part of what we're fighting for, or standing for, in the desert is our way of life. Part of our way of life is heavy usage of energy, much more so than any other industrialized country. We haven't really heard you call upon Americans to conserve as part of this crisis. Will you do so now?

The President. I call upon Americans to conserve.

Q. You won't elaborate?

The President. No. I think we ought to conserve in times like this. On the other hand, we're doing everything we can to guarantee that we don't panic Americans and that there will be an adequate supply of hydrocarbons. But I think it is a good time to conserve. So, I'm glad you reminded me of that, and I would call upon Americans to conserve. And I think that doesn't mean that life screeches to a halt. And, therefore, I would say that. But I also think that we're going to be able to guarantee an adequate supply of petroleum.

Q. Mr. President, how many Reserves are going to be called up as a first step in the next few weeks?

The President. I will defer that question to Secretary Cheney.

Q. Mr. President, do you sense any frustration or even desperation in the recent statements we've been hearing out of Iraq?

The President. I certainly sense a sense of isolation. I think the urgency in these statements and the high immoderate tone is due to worldwide isolation, and I think that's very clear. And I think he's trying to whip up support and make this Iraq versus the United States. Indeed, it is Iraq versus the rest of the world. I talked to leader after leader after leader—talked at length to Helmut Kohl [Chancellor of the Federal Republic of Germany] today, and he's been making just that point and will continue to make that point. But, yes, I think there is some of that feeling: that as they become isolated from their Arab brothers—and they

are—and as they become isolated from traditional trading partners—and they are—there is a sense of irrational urgency there.

Q. How seriously do you take his public threats?

The President. The United States won't be threatened.

Q. Mr. President, the other day you called on Americans for personal sacrifice, but you didn't really elaborate. Were you talking about economic deprivation or were you perhaps——

The President. No, I was not particularly talking about economic deprivation. I'm thinking of families whose plans have been severely altered by this. I'm thinking more of that kind of thing when I made the statement.

Q. Are you preparing Americans for the possibility of war and American deaths?

The President. I think anytime you move American forces and anytime you are up against what most of the world now considers to be an outrageous violator of international law that the best thing is to be prepared.

Yes, Charles [Charles Bierbauer, Cable News Network]?

Q. Mr. President, King Hussein today in Jordan suggested that perhaps you moved too precipitously, in his words, that if there had not been this buildup that we might not be in the situation we're in and that Saddam Hussein might have withdrawn. Was there ever any signal, anything that was suggested that that might have been the case?

The President. No. And the King regrettably did not have much support in the Arab world for that position. You recall the vote at the Arab summit. He certainly had no support for that position in the United Nations and as the United Nations moved toward chapter VII. I would simply remind people who hear that allegation that it isn't just the United States, it's the rest of the world.

But when we are invited by a friend to help defend it against aggression that has recently taken place and that threatens to take place again, we're going to respond. And that's a good signal to send to friends around the world. And I might say the request for support was not taken without reason. The Saudis were very much concerned. And let me just recite the history for the American people here.

Saddam Hussein had said, "We're withdrawing." I believe it was on a Sunday. And they had a picture of one truck, people frantically waving goodbye to the beloved brothers in Kuwait as they went north. And at the same time, there was truckload after truckload of armor and mechanized equipment moving south. Now, we're not dumb when we see that, nor are the Saudis, nor are the other countries that are rejoicing, as Dick Cheney will tell you, in the fact that we moved. But I think it's important to keep reminding people of why the Saudis felt threatened and probably today still feel threatened.

Q. If I could follow up, sir——

The President. Let Charles follow up, and I'll be right over, Ann [Ann Devroy, Washington Post].

Q. ——just to get another sense of the enormity of this buildup. The reports have come during the Secretary's visit that the Saudis wanted—and we're preparing to send them—the most advanced fighter, the F–15E. Is that, in fact, the case? And isn't there a political problem with that?

The President. I will let Secretary Cheney address himself to it. But the Saudis have been threatened; a neighboring country has been aggressed against. International law has condemned it. We should do all we can to help the Saudis arm themselves against aggression. So, he can talk about 15E's or some other weapon system; I want to do everything I can. And I hope there would be no political problem because the world clearly sees that the Saudis have been strongly threatened, Charles.

Q. Prince Bandar [Saudi Ambassador to the United States] is on his way into Moscow. King Hussein says he's going back to Baghdad. Is there a new stage of diplomacy that's beginning now?

The President. There's a lot of activity, Ann, going on, a lot of diplomatic activity. I'm continuing to conduct a good deal of it; Secretary Baker is. I mentioned his recent call with Shevardnadze. Other countries are reaching out to friends, trying to be sure that we all stay together in this; and indeed,

the Japanese, I might say, have a very big diplomatic initiative going now. And I must say once again that I think Prime Minister Kaifu's [of Japan] willingness to help some of these countries that might be victimized by a full enactment of the sanctions is very good. The Turks, as I've told you, have been heavily involved. I talked to Mr. Mitsotakis [Prime Minister] in Greece today, who have been cooperative. So, there's an awful lot of diplomatic activity behind the scenes.

Q. And does it help to have King Hussein going back to Baghdad?

The President. I have no feelings about that. I——

Q. ——a message?

The President. No, there was no message or anything of that nature. As you remember, there was a lot of speculation that the King was coming here bearing a message, and I can tell you unequivocally there was no request on my part for a message to go back—other than one: our determination to stay joined up with others to see that this aggression is reversed and that the rightful rulers of Kuwait are returned.

Yes, Jim [Jim Miklaszewski, NBC News]?

Q. Mr. President, you mentioned concern for the families here in the United States a few minutes ago. Traditionally, those families have been able to rely on open press coverage of young men and women who are sent into the breach, such as they've been now. Despite their earlier hospitality, the Saudis are now restricting press coverage and are saying that they will probably order foreign press out of that country, perhaps by the end of this week. Is there anything you can do to ensure that Americans will have free, complete, and open press coverage of their young men and women abroad?

The President. We are the guests of Saudi Arabia, in their country. I think Dick can address himself to that question because it has been discussed. And the more coverage the better, as far as we're concerned. However, when people travel to countries like Iraq and countries of that nature, I hope the press coverage will be totally objective, just as it is right here in this marvelous setting.

Q. Are you saying then that we're at the total mercy of Saudi Arabia, that there's nothing we can do to ensure——

The President. No, I'm not saying that. I'm saying I'll let the Secretary address himself to this question.

Q. Has the coverage not been——

The President. I'm saying I hope the same tough questions are asked in every country as they are in this country. And I'm speaking of Iraq particularly.

Q. Are you saying they were not?

Q. Is that a criticism of the press coverage, Mr. President?

The President. No, that's not criticism, Jim. I've learned long ago that you've got the loudest mike, and I just am standing here. So, I'm not criticizing. Don't be so sensitive about it. [*Laughter*]

Q. How was the coverage?

The President. The American people know what the American people see. And so, all I'm simply saying is: Don't be sensitive. It's not a criticism; it is an objective statement.

Q. Mr. President, why is Iraq still being allowed to receive supplies through Jordan?

The President. I'm not sure they are, and I hope they're not. And very little is going into the Gulf of Aqaba these days—don't be sensitive—and so it is a question, though, that if it is going in it clearly violates not only the sanctions but what King Hussein told me.

Q. Is it your understanding that it's been stopped? I mean, many of our colleagues at the border say——

The President. Yes, there's a difference of view on it. And I'm not sure I know the total facts on that because we were discussing it a few minutes ago.

Yeah, Mike [Michael Gelb, Reuters]?

Q. Mr. President, when you made the announcement that you were sending U.S. troops to Saudi Arabia, you said their mission was not to kick the Iraqis out of Kuwait. Do you still rule out the use of U.S. military force to evict the Iraqis?

The President. I don't rule in or rule out the use of military force. And I learned long ago not to tie oneself down by stating what I will or will not do in that regard.

These two last, and then I'll go peacefully, Marlin [Marlin Fitzwater, Press Secre-

tary to the President]. One and two.

Q. Mr. President, we asked you last week if you saw any hope of a diplomatic solution. You said, "I don't see it right now." Do these statements from Baghdad that they are willing to put their cards on the table increase the hopes there will be a diplomatic solution?

The President. If they're willing to put all their cards on the table, that's good. I didn't hear that; but if they're willing to put them all out there, including complying with international law, that would be good. And in terms of readiness to talk, we've got a very able person [Joseph C. Wilson IV, U.S. Chargé d'Affaires] there in Baghdad who is prepared to talk. And they came in the other day and said they'd like to talk. Well, there he is, available to talk. But please, don't tell us that they're going to talk with conditions that are unacceptable under international law, because that is not the way it would work. And the world community has made a strong statement, a very strong statement, and I don't sense any view in the world community that it's going to back away from that statement. And that statement included removal of Iraqi forces from Kuwait and the restoration of the rulers.

Yeah, Charles? Last one.

Q. Mr. President, somebody's got to ask the tough question. You've talked about conservation. Does that include *Fidelity?*

The President. I'm going to keep using my boat, and I hope the rest of America will prudently recreate. I don't think we've reached the point where I want to call on everybody in the recreation industry to shut it down or everybody that's taking a vacation in America to shut it down. So, it's not a tough question; it's a very fair question. And I would simply say that there's a lot of industry, a lot of people that have been looking forward to vacations in this country; and I would not suggest that the situation at home requires they stay at home now or that they don't use their recreational facilities.

Q. We're not in any energy——

The President. No, now, we are not.

Q. In what condition are those 54 missing Americans? Have you been told? And is the number still 54?

The President. I can't answer the question about the condition. Maybe Larry can expand on this later on. He says we don't know.

Thank you all very much. And now I will turn it over, again with a vote of thanks, to Dick Cheney and to Colin, who are doing a superb job, and to both of whom the American people owe a strong vote of thanks, and people around the world, too.

It's all yours. Good luck.

Note: The President's 58th news conference began at 2:07 p.m. at his home in Kennebunkport, ME. In his opening remarks, he referred to Secretary of Defense Richard B. Cheney; Gen. Colin L. Powell, USA, Chairman of the Joint Chiefs of Staff; Deputy Secretary of State Lawrence S. Eagleburger; Brent Scowcroft, Assistant to the President for National Security Affairs; John H. Sununu, Chief of Staff to the President; and Robert M. Gates, Assistant to the President and Deputy for National Security Affairs.

Statement by Press Secretary Fitzwater on the United States Commercial Space Launch Policy
August 22, 1990

The United States seeks a free and fair international commercial space launch market to further the use of outer space for the betterment of mankind. At the same time, because space launch technologies have significant military applications, important U.S. national security considerations must be addressed by our commercial space launch policy.

Over the past several weeks, the President has had detailed discussions with the Vice President and other senior advisers on U.S. commercial space launch policy developed by the National Space Council. The President has authorized the Secretary of State to approve a license application for participation by a U.S. firm in Australia's Cape York space launch project, provided certain agreements necessary to ensure U.S. national security interests are reached.

Specifically, the U.S. will seek agreements to ensure that:

(1) The U.S.S.R. will provide launch services (boosters, equipment, technology, or training) only from Cape York or any other single location,

(2) The U.S.S.R. and Australia will observe the Missile Technology Control Regime, and

(3) U.S. regulations on technology transfer to the Soviet Union will be observed.

The United States hopes and expects that these agreements can be concluded quickly so that the license can be granted. To permit continued U.S. participation, the United States in the coming months will also be seeking agreements to ensure free and fair trade in the international commercial space launch market. Details of the U.S. commercial space launch policy will be announced in the near future.

Letter to Congressional Leaders Transmitting an Alternate Federal Civilian Pay Plan
August 24, 1990

Dear Mr. Speaker: (Dear Mr. President:)

Under the Federal Pay Comparability Act of 1970, the President is required to make a decision each year on what, if any, pay adjustment should be provided for Federal employees under the General Schedule and the related statutory pay systems.

My pay advisors have reported to me that the following increases in pay rates, to be effective in October 1990, would be required under existing procedures to raise Federal pay rates to comparability with private sector pay rates for the same levels of work:

	Percent
GS–1	22.32
GS–2	22.78
GS–3	23.29
GS–4	23.86
GS–5	24.48
GS–6	25.16
GS–7	25.89
GS–8	26.68
GS–9	27.54
GS–10	28.45
GS–11	29.42
GS–12	31.55
GS–13	33.94
GS–14	36.60
GS–15	39.55
GS–16	39.55
GS–17	39.55
GS–18	39.55

However, the law also empowers me to prepare and transmit to the Congress an alternative plan for the pay adjustment if I consider such an alternative plan appropriate because of "national emergency or economic conditions affecting the general welfare."

Pay raises of this magnitude are clearly unacceptable. They would be detrimental to our efforts to set Government spending at levels that promote noninflationary growth. Further, if a fully responsible deficit reduction program is not enacted by the Congress, we will face a massive across-the-board cut in Federal spending that will adversely affect almost every Federal program. Excessive Federal pay raises would only exacerbate these effects.

Accordingly, upon consideration of the reports of my Pay Agent and the Advisory Committee on Federal Pay, I have determined that the fiscal year 1991 Federal civilian pay raise will be made in accordance with the following alternative plan:

> In accordance with section 5305(c)(1) of title 5, United States Code, the pay rates of the General Schedule and the related statutory pay schedules shall be increased by an overall percentage of 3.5 percent for each schedule, with such increase to become effective on the first day of the first applicable pay period beginning on or after January 1, 1991.

Accompanying this report and made a part hereof are the pay schedules that will result from this alternative plan. I am also including, as required by section 5382(c) of title 5, United States Code, the rates of basic pay for the Senior Executive Service that will take effect at the same time, assuming implementation of changes made to Executive Level pay by the Ethics Reform Act of 1989.

Sincerely,

GEORGE BUSH

Note: Identical letters were sent to Thomas S. Foley, Speaker of the House of Representatives, and Dan Quayle, President of the Senate.

Statement by Press Secretary Fitzwater on United Nations Authorization of Enforcement of Economic Sanctions Against Iraq
August 25, 1990

The United Nations Security Council has passed Resolution 665 calling for enforcement measures to maintain the comprehensive sanctions against Iraq. The unanimous vote further underlines the deep concern of the world community regarding the blatant aggression by Iraq against Kuwait. The resolve of the international community is strong. The vote exhibits the commitment of the world to act effectively to achieve the complete, immediate, and unconditional withdrawal of Iraq from Kuwait. The United States pledges its complete support of the United Nations action.

Excerpt of a Statement by Press Secretary Fitzwater on Soviet President Mikhail Gorbachev's Endorsement of United Nations Economic Sanctions Against Iraq
August 25, 1990

President Gorbachev's statement yesterday supporting the United Nations sanctions was a very important development. We welcome his voice to the world condemnation of the aggression by Saddam Hussein. The United Nations resolution passed last night further strengthens the world resolve to force Iraq out of Kuwait. We are encouraged by the progress of events at the United Nations and by President Gorbachev's strong support.

Note: The statement referred to President Saddam Hussein of Iraq. It also provided additional information on President Bush's stay at his home in Kennebunkport, ME, which has been included in Appendix A at the end of this volume.

Initial Order for Emergency Deficit Control Measures for Fiscal Year 1991
August 25, 1990

By the authority vested in me as President by the laws of the United States of America, including section 252 of the Balanced Budget and Emergency Deficit Control Act of 1985 (Public Law No. 99–177), as amended by the Balanced Budget and Emergency Deficit Control Reaffirmation Act of 1987 (Public Law 100–119) (hereafter referred to as "the Act"), and in accordance with the report of the Director of the Office of Management and Budget issued August 25, 1990, pursuant to section 251(a)(2) of the Act, I hereby order, pursuant to section 252(a), that the following actions be taken effective October 1, 1990, to implement the sequestrations and reductions determined by the Director in that report:

(1) Each automatic spending increase that would, but for the provisions of the Act, take effect during fiscal year 1991 is suspended as provided in section 252. The programs with such automatic spending increases subject to reduction in this manner, specified by account title, are National Wool Act, Special Milk Program, and Vocational Rehabilitation.

(2) The following are sequestered as provided in section 252: new budget authority; unobligated balances; new loan guarantee commitments or limitations; new direct loan obligations, commitments, or limitations; spending authority as defined in section 401(c)(2) of the Congressional Budget Act of 1974, as amended; and obligation limitations.

(3) For accounts making payments otherwise required by substantive law, the head of each Department or agency is directed to modify the calculation of each such payment to the extent necessary to reduce the estimate of total required payments for the fiscal year by the amount specified in the Director's report.

(4) For accounts making commitments for guaranteed loans and obligations for direct loans as authorized by substantive law, the head of each Department or agency is directed to reduce the level of such commitments or obligations to the extent necessary to conform to the limitations established by the Act and specified in the Director's determination of August 25, 1990.

In accordance with section 252(a)(4)(A), amounts suspended or sequestered under this order shall be withheld from obligation or expenditure pending the issuance of a final order under section 252(b).

This order shall be reported to the Congress and shall be published in the *Federal Register.*

GEORGE BUSH

The White House,
August 25, 1990.

[Filed with the Office of the Federal Register, 10:25 a.m., August 25, 1990]

Note: The report of the Director of the Office of Management and Budget issued August 25 was printed in the "Federal Register" of August 27.

Statement by Press Secretary Fitzwater on the Continuation of United States Television Broadcasting to Cuba
August 27, 1990

The President signed on Sunday, August 26, a Presidential determination that the tests of TV Marti have demonstrated that television broadcasting to Cuba is feasible and will not cause objectionable interference with the broadcasts of domestic television licensees. Our international telecommunications commitments have been observed throughout the test period.

The President has determined that TV Marti broadcasts will continue in a manner which is consistent with our international obligations. TV Marti is an integral part of U.S. policy to provide free access to information for people who are denied that right. We regret the Cuban regime's decision to attempt to deny the free flow of information by jamming. But we recall the experience of Radio Free Europe and Radio Liberty in which the broadcasts were jammed for years, yet people were able to listen.

Note: The Presidential determination was printed in the "Federal Register" of September 20.

Remarks and a Question-and-Answer Session With Reporters in Kennebunkport, Maine, Following a Meeting With Prime Minister Brian Mulroney of Canada
August 27, 1990

The President. Let me simply say that, once again, Prime Minister Mulroney and I have had a very good discussion—talked about bilateral matters, but also, obviously, about the situation regarding Iraq.

And Canada, a member of the Security Council, has been not only in a role of leadership there but side by side with the United States and others. I told the Prime Minister that I'm very grateful for Canada's position. As we all know, they've contributed to this—I believe it's now 22-nation—international force, both on the land and Canada's participation on the sea—ours also—as well as land. And so, we're very grateful to them.

And once again, as I say, we've had very fruitful discussions. And Prime Minister, welcome back to what—when this was divined—was to be a purely social event because we want to once again welcome Brian Mulroney and his wonderful family here. But we have some of that, but we also have had an opportunity to discuss in-depth world events.

Welcome, sir, and the floor is yours until we go to the questions.

The Prime Minister. Thank you, Mr. President. We've had, and will continue a little later on, some excellent discussions, both in regard to bilateral problems which are in the process of clearing up—somewhat like the weather, although we have some important matters on our plate—but also, principally, the matter in Iraq.

I, along with all members of the government of Canada and the people of Canada, were pleased—very pleased—with the decision of the United Nations Security Council to provide what I believe is quite unprecedented leadership. Certainly one of the most important days of the United Nations since its foundation have been the series of resolutions in respect of Iraq, where the United Nations as one—Security Council—dealt effectively and well with a rogue leader who sought to annex another nation and believed that he could conduct himself with impunity, both vis-a-vis his Arab neighbors and the world.

And the world turned against him in a quite extraordinary manner. And that is to the credit of the United Nations and those who—pursuant to the lead of the United States under President Bush—like-minded nations who participated in what we believe is a very important initiative to curb aggression in the Middle East.

And so, I'm happy to have this opportunity to review some very important matters with the President, thank him again for his hospitality. And I would be happy to take whatever questions come my way.

The President. Maybe we could set some ground rules here. What we did last time was to alternate the questions, and if that's agreeable with everybody, as it seems to be, why, we'll go ahead.

You're the guest.

Persian Gulf Crisis

Q. Prime Minister, if I could start by asking you whether there was some discussion of the conditions under which Canada's military presence in the Middle East might be enlarged?

The Prime Minister. No. We believe that our contribution for the moment is adequate, but as the Minister of Defense has indicated in the past, we haven't ruled out or ruled in anything else either. We are firmly resolved to resist the aggression and to join with our friends and allies in pursuit of that objective. But we seek, obviously, a peaceful resolution of this; and we're very pleased with the initiatives that may hold some promise from the Secretary-General of the United Nations [Javier Perez de Cuellar de la Guerra]. And the President and I have had an opportunity to touch on that briefly.

Q. Mr. President, aren't you concerned, by the action that you took today against the Iraqi Embassy [expulsion of Iraqi diplomats from the United States], that you're increasing the tension and lessening the possibilities for a diplomatic solution and you're also possibly giving the Iraqis more of a rationale to take harsher action against our own diplomats and the hostages?

The President. No, I'm not concerned about that at all. This is an action that others are taking. Nobody will be held against their will. They're all free to go. In essence, we're kind of keeping some reasonable parallelism in terms of numbers. So, I don't think there's any chance for any misunderstanding on that account.

Q. Can I ask you, just to follow up, Mr. President: You said a couple of weeks ago that you didn't really see much prospect at the time for a diplomatic solution. Has that changed? Do you see more hope now?

The President. Well, I don't particularly see more hope now because it's so clear what the world is demanding of Saddam Hussein [President of Iraq]. Clearly the objectives remain the same: Get out of Kuwait and restore the rightful leaders to their place. But the Secretary-General, I understand, will be meeting with Foreign Minister of Iraq [Tariq 'Aziz]—I think it's in Amman, Jordan. I haven't talked to him yet. I have a call in to him and will probably get him. But the U.N. mandate is so clear and, on the other hand, Saddam Hussein has been so resistant to complying with international law that I don't yet see fruitful negotiations.

But the Secretary-General, knowing the U.N. mandate, is a very good man. And I might add, parenthetically, the Prime Minister and I both did talk about this, and we both agree that the U.N. has perhaps demonstrated its finest in recent actions. So, if Perez de Cuellar, an old friend of mine, wants to go forward and try to find some way to get the U.N. action complied with, so much the better.

Q. Mr. Prime Minister, in light of the U.S. decision today, would Canada consider similar action in expelling Iraqi diplomats or nationals from Canada or taking any sort of action against them?

The Prime Minister. We are going to—this is a time-honored diplomatic practice, and if it applies to Canada, we won't hesitate to take remedial action. What you have is an abuse of—one of the most fundamental privileges of democratic and civilized nations is, namely, to be represented in another's country without our representatives being harassed or intimidated or assaulted. Those assaults can take place in many ways, and we have to make sure that the fundamental rule of international law is respected. So, if there is a requirement for us to do so in Canada with our own Ambassadors and our own representatives, we will exercise reciprocity.

Q. Mr. President, do you have any assurances or will you seek any assurances from Perez de Cuellar not to try to negotiate something beyond the U.N. sanctions—cut a deal that may undercut the sanctions themselves?

The President. It's inconceivable to me that the Secretary-General, an experienced diplomat, a good leader, would do that. I think it would be gratuitous for me to discuss that with him. He knows what the United Nations has done. He knows how unanimous the support has been for resolution after resolution. So, it's inconceivable to me that he would not have that message. He's a very sound man. Actually, as Brian Mulroney reminded me, he had a very

useful role, I believe, in between Iran and Iraq. But, no, I wouldn't give any gratuitous advice of that nature. It's so clear; it's so obvious.

Q. Is there a danger once you go down this path of negotiations on one day and small peace offerings the next that this thing could be dragged out and world resolve will crumble?

The President. No. I've never seen the world community so closely aligned against this man. Somebody asked me the other day at a press conference here—Saddam Hussein said he'd like to talk. We have a Chargé there [Joseph C. Wilson IV, U.S. Chargé d'Affaires in Baghdad, Iraq], a very able person. He could go talk to him, have his people talk to him.

So, I'm not saying we're not going to talk. But what, clearly, world opinion is saying and what the United Nations has said and what is now codified in international law is: Out, Saddam Hussein, Iraqi, out of Kuwait, and restore the leaders! But you have to talk to get there. But that doesn't mean there is to be compromise. Clearly, we would oppose any compromise on these fundamental principles that have been laid down by the United Nations.

Conflict Between the Mohawks and the Canadian Governments

[*At this point, a question was asked and answered in French, and a translation was not provided.*]

Q. Aren't you afraid, sir, there could be a bloodbath if the army goes in to take down the barricades?

The Prime Minister. The laws of Canada have to apply to all citizens equally. I indicated yesterday that the Government of Canada and the Government of the Province of Quebec had demonstrated what I thought was quite exceptional patience. And yet, in the end, the laws of a civilized nation must apply to us all. There can't be a double standard. They apply to all of us.

Persian Gulf Conflict

Q. Mr. President, President Gorbachev of the Soviet Union called on Arabs today to display their ability to consolidate very quickly to increase their presence in this conflict to avoid actual armed confrontation. He said it would be necessary for them to do that. Do you agree with that? is the first question—do you agree that they have to interject themselves more forcefully into this?

The President. I think the Arab world has been responsibly united in opposition to Saddam Hussein's aggression. I did not see that particular comment by President Gorbachev; but since you've invoked his name, let me simply say I've been very pleased with the way the Soviets, for their part, have conducted themselves at the United Nations and elsewhere. But I didn't see that, so I can't comment. But I would simply say that I think both the Prime Minister and I are very pleased that a number of Arab countries have joined in the position that we've talked about here. And indeed, it's only a tiny minority that is in opposition.

And so, I keep coming back—it is not as Saddam Hussein is trying to make it: the Arab world against the United States. It is the United States and most of the Arab world and Canada and other countries against this outrageous aggression. We've got to keep saying that so there will be no erosion—the erosion that Jim [Jim Miklaszewski, NBC News] asked about. But it's true, and everyone knows it's true.

Q. Have you talked with President Gorbachev or do you plan to, if not?

The President. I haven't talked to him recently. As you know, the Secretary of State has been in very close contact with [Soviet] Foreign Minister Shevardnadze.

Q. Mr. Mulroney, can you say exactly how many Canadians are trapped in Iraq and Kuwait, and why you won't call them hostages, as George Bush does?

The Prime Minister. Well, I've indicated that President Bush has information and circumstances that quite appropriately allow him to describe American citizens held the way they are in the manner in which he has. There are large numbers of Canadian nationals being held—I think the third largest number of foreigners held in Kuwait and in and around Baghdad. And we have not yet the kind of information that would allow me to apply that word to the Canadian citizens being detained. Which is not to

suggest that it couldn't happen tomorrow, and it certainly is not to suggest that it shouldn't have happened at all.

It's quite an achievement when a leader of a state in 1990 can make himself a pariah not only with leaders around the world but with his immediate Arab neighbors. That's quite a piece of work to be able to do that all in a short period of time. And to provoke what is an extraordinary response of leadership by the United Nations and the allies in such a short period of time is in itself another good piece of work—among the finest in the United Nations since its foundation.

President's Schedule

Q. President Bush, you've decided this morning to go back to Washington for 2½ days. Some people consider that some kind of concession to the need to be in Washington during the crisis. Why shouldn't they think that?

The President. Think what?

Q. That the need to go back to Washington for 2½ days, a need to be in Washington—why shouldn't people believe that's some kind of concession on your part, to be in Washington at a time you need to handle a crisis instead of here?

The President. Well, I was in Washington—what was it—a week ago——

Q. Why are you going back to Washington for 2½ days?

The President. Well, we've got—wait until you see the schedule we've got back there.

Q. Well, tell us about it.

The President. A wide array of meetings. And they're all—some of them have nothing to do with the Iraq situation. We've got budget discussions that are going to take place. I'll be talking about our energy requirements there. And it just seemed easier to accommodate others than rather bring all the people with whom I'll be meeting up here. So, you'll see as the schedule develops that it's, in my view, good; and I expect to get back here as soon as possible.

Q. The stories say that you're not enjoying this vacation. You don't look like it's any fun.

The President. Well, Ann [Ann Compton, ABC News], that's not true. Tied into four enormous bluefish today, having struck out earlier this morning, starting at 5:15 a.m. I've been able to keep in very close touch, and of course, we're making a lot of international phone calls that you wouldn't normally expect at the time of a vacation. But I've got a good team, and they've been supportive. A lot of them have been up here. And then I've been able to conduct international meetings of some importance up here. And again, I'm grateful, very grateful, that a meeting that was scheduled as pure R and R with Prime Minister Mulroney has turned out to be extraordinarily substantive.

So, I see people making these comments, but we're on top of the situation. I think the American people understand that. And when you see the schedule that works out over the next 2½ days, I think it will be clear that it is wise to conduct that business there. I might have encouraged everyone to come here, but it seemed to be better to go down there, as we did last week. It's a mixture. But have I enjoyed this vacation? A lot of things about it I have, yes.

Persian Gulf Crisis

Q. Mr. President, how would you describe your policy for ousting Saddam Hussein right now, as of this moment? Would it be fair to describe it as wait and see?

The President. No. My policy is to do everything we can, working with other nations, to enforce the sanctions. We have moved forces, considerable forces, and I hope that that has safeguarded Saudi Arabia, which in my view was clearly threatened when Saddam Hussein moved his forces south from Kuwait City. So, I think it is now: Get plenty of force in place—we're still doing that. Enforce the United Nations sanctions rigorously—and for the U.S., we will do that and encourage others to do it. And that's about where we are right now.

Q. You were very effective, sir, in getting the U.N. to join in on this sea blockade. Are you now considering doing the same thing on an air interdiction policy?

The President. Well, I don't think there have been many examples of this net being penetrated, broken through, by air. But we have been talking to countries about not permitting overflight and tightening up in every way, all aspects of the economic sanctions that were called for by the United Nations.

Q. Prime Minister, have you discussed, the two of you, under what circumstances Canada could play a larger role in this? And, Mr. President, would you welcome a larger Canadian role?

The Prime Minister. We haven't discussed it, but I've indicated earlier that Canada hasn't added anything in or added it out. We will play it as circumstances develop. We think that our contribution is appropriate. As I said when I announced it, Canada is not a superpower. But we believe that we—along with countries, for example, all the way to Australia—have an obligation to stand with our friends and allies and resist aggression. And if more is required, the Government of Canada will consider that and make an appropriate decision. But for the moment, we're pleased with the leadership of the United Nations, very pleased with the skill of the President of the United States and the manner in which he has brought about quite a remarkable display of solidarity, both from our European partners and around the world.

I think that the achievement of the President, if I may say, in respect to the Arab world is certainly unprecedented in my memory. That this kind of action would be contemplated with the results of approval coming as strongly as they have from so many Arab nations is in itself a remarkable achievement of political leadership, and I think it's important to note that.

The President. Charles and Norm [Charles Bierbauer, Cable News Network, and Norman Sandler, United Press International], I've recognized both. So, if we can do, with your permission, those two; and then you take as many as you want. But I should do those. Marlin [Marlin Fitzwater, Press Secretary to the President] is getting a little restless.

The Prime Minister. And I'm going for a swim.

Q. This is really a question for both of you, sir. For all this talk of unanimity, there seems to be divergences on tactics. You are content to use force. The Soviets say they won't use force to stop the blockade. You have hostages; Prime Minister Mulroney does not have hostages. Mrs. Thatcher doesn't think talking is such a good idea. Is there a divergence, and is it potentially undermining?

The President. I think any nuances of difference are so overwhelmed by the common ground that they are almost meaningless, is the way I view it. I mean, I think the thing of note is how together everybody is, not that there might be nuances of difference.

I don't know whether you want to——

The Prime Minister. Well, I've noticed the points that you make. If somebody had told you 2 years ago that this kind of crisis would emerge and the Soviet Union would repudiate Iraq and that the United Nations Security Council would stand in unanimous support of five resolutions and that you would see this kind of support emerge, as I say, from Canada to Australia, you would have bought him a ticket to the funny farm right away.

This is an historic achievement by the United Nations, by members of the alliance, and by the President of the United States. This is a remarkable achievement. There are few parallels for it, certainly, in modern history. But there are differences of opinion. Sure there are. You better believe it; they happen all the time. The story is not that. It's that there are so few of them and so modest in nature, given the profound dimensions of the challenge. There will be others ahead of us, and it's going to require this kind of cooperation and consultation to make sure that they all mesh together and that we try and bring about the end that is sought.

The President. Norm?

Q. Mr. President, if Saddam Hussein is in a box, as General Scowcroft [Assistant to the President for National Security Affairs] said yesterday, are you willing to give him any way out short of unconditional surrender? Which is to say, if there are going to be negotiations, what's negotiable here?

The President. Well, certainly not the U.N. position. The position of the international law is not negotiable. I think that's what Prime Minister Thatcher was addressing herself to. I would agree with that. The United Nations has spoken—country after country supporting the action taken by the

Security Council. So, there's no room for compromise or negotiation on that point. But I don't think you should ever say you'll never talk about anything. But I'm not saying that there's any flexibility, is what your question is. And there is no flexibility on Iraq getting out of Kuwait and the rulers being permitted to come back to Kuwait.

Q. But is there any flexibility on the future composition of the Kuwait Government, which is to say——

The President. No.

Q. ——is the United States firmly committed now to restoring the Al Sabah family, to keeping that family in power?

The President. That's a matter for the Kuwaitis to decide. Of course, they should be restored. I suppose that you might say that's true of any country—leadership, whether it's the United States or Iraq or Kuwait or anyplace else. But there's no compromise on the question of getting legitimate government back and getting the illegitimate invaders out. And so, that's where we stand. And I haven't heard one single country that has been supportive at the outset suggest that we should back off from the principle so clearly stated, certainly, by the United Nations and, hopefully, by the United States and Canada and many others.

Q. Mr. President, you've been pretty fortunate in that Congress has been on vacation all this time. Tomorrow aren't you opening a Pandora's box by meeting with 150 of them?

The President. Is that all that will be there, only 150 out of 450, 465, is it? No, what is it, 450? Look, the Congress, I think, has stayed in close touch. I'm very grateful to the leadership for the almost Vandenbergian support for the actions that we have taken. Indeed, in this case, differences have seemed to end at the water's edge. And so, if this briefing is helpful to them, and I hope it will be, so much the better. And I again might just take this opportunity to thank the leaders on both sides of the aisle for the support they've given us.

But I don't think there's any Pandora's box involved in briefing the Congress. They'll have an extensive briefing period, because not only will I brief them and tell them what's on my mind but I believe the

Secretary of Defense, Secretary of State—and, Brent, I don't know if you're scheduled to brief or not—but they'll have adequate briefing. And it is most understandable that they want to know what is going on and get up to speed on things. Some, indeed, will be going there. So, I welcome this, and I don't worry about any Pandora's box aspect of it at all.

You can always dig around and find somebody that will want to fine-tune it or have some little criticism. But look, the support has been overwhelming, and I think the American people see that. They know that this isn't a Republican or a Democrat policy, but it's the policy of their country. And to the credit of the Members of Congress, I think they have helped convey that.

Meeting of the Canadian Parliament

Q. Prime Minister Mulroney, why do you not see any need to recall Parliament, facing the situation in Oka and also in the Persian Gulf?

The Prime Minister. Well, I'd indicated that I'd be happy to recall Parliament if the government were of the view that it would be helpful and appropriate. We haven't arrived at that view yet, but should that change, I'll be happy to call the House back. Wouldn't hesitate at all.

Conflict Between the Mohawks and the Canadian Governments

Q. Prime Minister, is military intervention now the sole option of resolving the Oka situation?

The Prime Minister. Pardon me?

Q. Do you consider further military intervention as the sole option now to resolve the Oka situation?

The Prime Minister. All I've said is that we have negotiated now for some 46 or 47 days, demonstrated, I think, quite remarkable patience. And we've sought a negotiated settlement of this. And if the settlement is elusive and we are getting these demands at the table which can only be construed as bizarre, then obviously the law of Canada must be applied to all of us and will be applied to all of us in exactly the same way.

Thank you very much.

President's Dogs

The President. I'd like to just clear up one thing. And this is just if the Canadian press would drop all notebooks and not write this down and consider this off the record. This is just for the American press.

The other day our dog Ranger appeared at the press conference, and he was called "Millie." He's a strong male dog here, as you can see, and his feelings were slightly hurt. And some decreed that because Ranger looked so frisky that Millie was well—calling Ranger "Millie." So, I'd like to clear it up as best I can. Knowing my way with the English language, I hope that's got it all clear for you guys. [*Laughter*]

Note: The President spoke at 3:33 p.m. outside his home. In his remarks, the Prime Minister referred to a conflict between Mohawk Indians and the Quebec and Canadian Governments that began when police tried to remove barricades erected by the Indians to prevent commercial development of land they considered to be sacred. Prime Minister Mulroney and his family arrived in Kennebunkport at noon and returned to Canada the following day.

Remarks at a White House Briefing for Members of Congress on the Persian Gulf Crisis
August 28, 1990

Let me just start off by thanking all of the Members of Congress who were able to get back here to discuss this situation of deep concern to every American. What we will do is, I'll make a few remarks here and then we'll go into executive session. And I will be glad to respond to your questions as best I can, backed up ably by the team that's here with me.

But meeting the challenge in the Persian

Gulf is not something that I or this administration can do by ourselves. We can only succeed if all of us—executive and legislative, Republican and Democrats—work together. And that was one of the reasons I wanted you to come here today. Let no one at home doubt my commitment to work with the Congress, and let no one abroad doubt our national unity or our staying power.

Let me begin by providing some background to the unfolding drama in the Gulf; and then later, I want to hear from you and, as I say, respond to questions.

First, the background. When this administration began, we sought to strengthen the cease-fire between Iran and Iraq and to improve relations with Iraq. We held no illusions about that. We hoped, along with many in the Congress, that Iraqi behavior might be moderated. But even before the current crisis, though, Iraq was moving at odds to our interests and to the interests of many around the world. So, we suspended the provisions of the CCC [Commodity Credit Corporation] agricultural credits, stopped the export of furnaces that had the potential to contribute to Iraq's nuclear capabilities.

You all know the events of the last several weeks. Iraq threatened Kuwait, lied about its intentions, and finally invaded. In 3 days, Iraq had 120,000 troops and 850 tanks in Kuwait, moving south toward the Saudi border. And it was this clear and rapidly escalating threat that led King Fahd of Saudi Arabia to ask for our assistance. We knew that an Iraq that had the most powerful military machine in the Gulf and controlled 20 percent of the world's proven reserves of oil would pose a threat to the Persian Gulf, to the Middle East, and to the entire world. We responded to this quickly, without hesitation. Our objectives were obvious from the start: the immediate, complete, and unconditional withdrawal of all Iraqi forces from Kuwait; the restoration of Kuwait's legitimate government; security and stability of Saudi Arabia and the Persian Gulf; and the protection of American citizens abroad.

Our actions to achieve these objectives have been equally clear. Within hours of

the assault, the United States moved to freeze Iraq's assets in this country and to protect those of Kuwait. I asked Dick Cheney, Secretary Cheney, to go to Saudi Arabia, Egypt, and Morocco to arrange for military cooperation between us and key Arab States. And I asked Jim Baker, Secretary Baker, to go to Turkey and to Brussels to rally the support of our NATO allies. Both of these missions were extraordinarily successful. The world response to Iraq was a near-unanimous chorus of condemnation.

With great speed, the United Nations Security Council passed five resolutions. These resolutions condemned Iraq's invasion of Kuwait, demanded Iraq's immediate and unconditional withdrawal, and rejected Iraq's annexation of Kuwait. The U.N. has also mandated sanctions against Iraq, those chapter VII sanctions, and endorsed all measures that may be necessary to enforce these sanctions. And the United Nations has demanded that Iraq release all foreign nationals being held against their will without delay.

The United Nations sanctions are in effect and have been working remarkably well, even on a voluntary basis. Iraqi oil no longer flows through pipelines to ports in Turkey and Saudi Arabia. And again, I want to thank both the Saudis and the Turks for their lead role in all of this. And today reports indicate that traffic through Aqaba has come virtually to a halt.

U.S. military forces stand shoulder to shoulder with forces of many Arab and European States to deter and, if need be, defend Saudi Arabia against attack. And U.S. naval forces sail with the navies of many other states to make the sanctions as watertight as possible. This is not, as Saddam Hussein claims, the United States against Iraq. It is truly Iraq against the majority in the Arab world, Iraq against the rest of the world.

And so, the basic elements of our strategy are now in place. And where do we want to go? Well, our intention, and indeed the intention of almost every country in the world, is to persuade Iraq to withdraw, that it cannot benefit from this illegal occupation, that it will pay a stiff price by trying to hold on and an even stiffer price by widening the conflict. And of course, we seek to achieve these goals without further violence. The United States supports the U.N. Secretary-General and other leaders working to promote a peaceful resolution of this crisis on the basis of Security Council Resolution 660.

I also remain deeply concerned about the American and other foreign nationals held hostage by Iraq. As I've said before, when it comes to the safety and well-being of American citizens held against their will, I will hold Baghdad responsible.

That's the general comments I wanted to make for public consumption. And then I'd now like to suggest that we all remain, if we could, and excuse our friends from the press and go into executive session here so I can just make one or two more comments and then respond to the questions that may come to me or any of the others here. But thank you all very much for attending.

Note: The President spoke at 3:19 p.m. in Room 450 of the Old Executive Office Building. In his remarks, he referred to President Saddam Hussein of Iraq and United Nations Secretary-General Javier Perez de Cuellar de la Guerra. Prior to the briefing, he met in the Cabinet Room at the White House with congressional leaders to discuss the Persian Gulf crisis.

Radio Address to United States Armed Forces Stationed in the Persian Gulf Region
August 29, 1990

Of the many duties and responsibilities I've worked to fulfill as President, there can be no greater honor than to offer a few words to the brave men and women serving in our Armed Forces—especially now, to those who stand ready to repel aggression in Saudi Arabia and the Gulf region, because you represent America's best, and the world's best hope for peace.

Last week I reminded the American people that this nation stands where she has always stood: against aggression. And today, with a tradition of two centuries behind you, you stand on the front line against aggression and international lawlessness. We've never sought conflict, nor do we hope to chart a course for other nations. But at the hands of injustice, in the face of aggression, ours is a once-reluctant fist now clenched resolutely.

To preserve the peace, America will always stand for what's right. To preserve her commitments, America will always stand by her friends. Together with allies, old and new, we've seen a nearly unanimous condemnation of Iraq's injustices in the Persian Gulf region, and we've been a part of a remarkable international commitment to peace and the rule of law.

And from the beginning we've been guided by four straightforward principles. One, we seek the unconditional and complete withdrawal of Iraqi forces from Kuwait. Two, that nation's legitimate government must be restored. Three, we are committed to the security and stability of the Persian Gulf. And four, we are determined to protect the lives of American citizens abroad. Those are the principles that drive us. But it's your presence, your skills, your talents, your judgment that bring America's principles to life and give them strength and meaning.

You're now in the middle of one of the toughest military missions in modern memory, enduring the long, hot days of the Gulf region's cruelest month. As one young soldier in the 82d Airborne Division put it: "You never get climatized; you just learn to tolerate it." Well, as tough as it is, know this: Thanks to you, nobody's feeling the heat more than the government in Baghdad.

And while all of you should know that what you're doing is just, a few of you have already gotten a glimpse of the gratitude of the Kuwaiti people. Like one lieutenant colonel in the AWACS control center in

Saudi Arabia who was approached by a Kuwaiti refugee in the lobby. The man spoke almost no English, but he handed the colonel a note for their commanding officer, a note that included the letter "I" and a heart and "U.S.A."

So, to the sailors who have kissed their wives or husbands goodbye for now, to the soldiers and marines protecting peace in the desert heat, to the flyers in the air, to the reservists committed and ready, to the men behind the guns: Stand strong. Our troops around the world are providing the kind of strength and security that makes this mission possible. And with the support of friends and family and the admiration of this great nation, you're proving you'll do what it takes at any hour, anywhere, to contain aggression and keep freedom's light alive.

We have an important advantage in the Persian Gulf, because in the air, at sea, and on land, soldiers of peace will always be more than a match for a tyrant bent on aggression. With your strength, we have the will; together with our allies, we will find the way to peace.

May God bless you and bring you home safely and soon.

Note: The President spoke at 8:47 a.m. from the Oval Office at the White House.

Statement by Deputy Press Secretary Popadiuk on Consultations on the Persian Gulf Crisis
August 29, 1990

General Scowcroft met recently with a former official of a previous administration in which that official relayed ideas concerning the Persian Gulf situation. The administration has received many such proposals and ideas, as it does at any time during a crisis, from various individuals. There was nothing in this particular proposal that merited its pursuit. As is customary, at the time of this particular message, General Scowcroft informed Secretary Baker of the suggestions he had received.

Note: The statement referred to Brent Scowcroft, Assistant to the President for National Security Affairs, and Secretary of State James A. Baker III.

Letter to Congressional Leaders Reporting on the Cyprus Conflict
August 30, 1990

Dear Mr. Speaker: (Dear Mr. Chairman:)
In accordance with Public Law 95–384 (92 Stat. 739; 22 U.S.C. 2373(c)), I am submitting to you this bimonthly report on progress toward a negotiated settlement of the Cyprus question.

This report covers the period from mid-May through July 1990, a time in which American efforts with respect to Cyprus were concentrated on finding a means to restart the U.N.-sponsored intercommunal negotiations. These negotiations had come to an abrupt and unsatisfactory end in early March.

I discussed the Cyprus issue personally with President Gorbachev during the U.S.-Soviet summit at the end of May, and we both agreed to do whatever we could to support the efforts of the United Nations Secretary General. Then on June 4 and 6, respectively, Secretary Baker and I reaffirmed directly to Greek Prime Minister Mitsotakis during his visit in Washington the United States strong interest in progress toward a Cyprus settlement. While we expressed our willingness to discuss ideas about Cyprus with all interested parties, we emphasized as well that a Cyprus solution could not be provided by the United States but had to be reached through direct negotiations between the two Cyprus communities in the context of U.N.-sponsored talks.

In late May and early June the U.S. Special Coordinator for Cyprus, Ambassador Nelson Ledsky, visited Athens, Ankara, and Nicosia. During his trip he met with the Prime Minister and Foreign Minister of Greece, the Foreign Minister of Turkey, and President George Vassiliou and Mr. Rauf Denktash in Cyprus. In all his discussions Ambassador Ledsky emphasized the importance of resuming intercommunal negotiations in accordance with U.N. Security Council Resolution 649 of March 12, 1990. He also stressed the need for confidence-building measures as a means of creating trust between the two communities and, in turn, enhancing prospects for a durable political settlement. He urged leaders of both communities to take the initiative in proposing confidence-building measures of this type.

On May 31, the United Nations Secretary General reported to the Security Council on U.N. operations in Cyprus for the period December 1, 1989–May 31, 1990 (report attached).

The report concluded that the continued presence of the U.N. Forces in Cyprus (UNFICYP) "remains indispensable to achieve the objectives set by the Security Council," and recommended extension of the UNFICYP mandate for a further 6-month period. The Secretary General also underlined that UNFICYP faced "a chronic and ever-deepening financial crisis, which imposes an inordinately heavy burden on the countries contributing troops to the force."

In mid-June, both President Vassiliou and Mr. Denktash provided assurances to representatives of the Secretary General that they endorsed all the provisions of U.N. Security Council Resolution 649. This was of particular significance, given the Resolution's call "to co-operate, on an equal footing, with the Secretary General in completing, in the first instance and on an urgent basis, an outline of an overall agreement . . . [and] to refrain from any action that could aggravate the situation." On June 22,

Mr. Denktash reaffirmed publicly Turkish Cypriot acceptance of "all aspects" of Resolution 649 and pledged that "the Turkish Cypriots are ready to cooperate with the Secretary General . . . with the aim of completing the basic lines of a comprehensive solution."

Progress toward reconvening U.N.-sponsored intercommunal talks was interrupted by two developments in July. Each in its own way was viewed by one community or the other as cause for concern, and as a step that soured the atmosphere for productive negotiations.

First, on July 4, the Government of Cyprus submitted an application for membership in the European Community (EC). The mere filing of the document angered the Government of Turkey and the Turkish Cypriot community. Both viewed the application as a unilateral effort on the part of the Cyprus Government to arrange the island's political and economic future without consulting directly the Turkish Cypriot community.

Second, in mid-July the Turkish army completed a transfer of responsibility for the security of the fenced, uninhabited area of the city of Varosha to Turkish Cypriot security forces. This area had been under the control of the Turkish army since 1974. The Government of Cyprus feared that this action could constitute a first step in the eventual movement of Turkish and Turkish Cypriot settlers into Varosha. The United States expressed its concerns on this matter directly to the Government of Turkey.

As required by U.N. Security Council Resolution 649, the U.N. Secretary General submitted to the Security Council on July 12 a further report on his mission of good offices (report attached). The report referred to "a general deterioration" of the atmosphere and went on to urge both sides to show moderation and compromise. The report then outlined "a plan of action" that would begin with separate discussions in Nicosia—designed to begin preparation of an outline for a Cyprus settlement—between U.N. authorities and each of the two Cypriot communities. The Secretary General envisioned that as work progressed on this outline it would be possible late this year to call for a meeting between him and the two community leaders.

On July 19 the U.N. Security Council, responding to the U.N. Secretary General's report of July 12 unanimously adopted a statement that was read by the President of the Security Council, as follows:

"The members of the Security Council have considered the Secretary General's report on his mission of good offices in Cyprus (S/21393). They are unanimous in giving their full support to the Secretary General's current effort to assist the two communities to reach a just and lasting solution. They agree with his assessment of recent developments, share his concern about the lack of progress, and endorse his plan of action.

"The members of the Council reaffirm their Resolution 649 (1990) of 12 March, 1990 which was accepted by both sides, and reiterate the importance they attach to an early negotiated settlement of the Cyprus Problem.

"The members of the Council call on the leaders of the two communities to cooperate fully with the Secretary General on the basis of his plan of action and to arrive, on an urgent basis, at an agreed outline of an overall agreement. In line with Resolution 649 (1990), they request the Secretary General to make suggestions as necessary, to assist the two communities in arriving at an agreed outline.

"The members of the Council again call on the parties concerned to refrain, especially at this sensitive stage in the process, from any action or statement that could aggravate the situation. They express their concern over any action which contravenes paragraph 5 of UNSC Res 550 (1984) and paragraph 5 of UNSC Res 649 (1990). They call upon both communities to concentrate their efforts on promoting mutual confidence and reconciliation.

"The members of the Council request the Secretary General to inform the Council by 31 October, 1990 about the implementation of his plan of action."

Sincerely,

GEORGE BUSH

Note: Identical letters were sent to Thomas S. Foley, Speaker of the House of Representatives, and Claiborne Pell, chairman of the Senate Foreign Relations Committee.

The President's News Conference on the Persian Gulf Crisis
August 30, 1990

The President. I have a brief statement, and then I'll be glad to take some questions.

The United States is engaged in a collective effort, involving the overwhelming majority of the member states of the United Nations, to reverse the consequences of Iraqi aggression. Our goals, enshrined in five Security Council resolutions, are clear: the immediate and unconditional withdrawal of Iraqi forces from Kuwait, the restoration of Kuwait's legitimate government, the stability of Saudi Arabia and the Persian Gulf, and the protection of American citizens.

What is at stake here is truly significant: the dependability of America's commitments to its friends and allies, the shape of the post-postwar world, opposition to aggression, the potential domination of the energy resources that are crucial to the entire world. This effort has been truly international from the very outset. Many other countries are contributing. At last count, 22 countries have either responded to a request from Saudi Arabia to help deter further aggression or are contributing maritime forces pursuant to United Nations Security Council Resolution 665. Still others are providing other forms of financial and material support to these defense efforts or to countries whose economies are affected adversely by sanctions or by higher oil prices. Still others are paying a heavy economic price at home for complying with the United Nations sanctions. It is important that the considerable burden of the effort be shared by those being defended and those who benefit from the free flow of oil. Indeed, anyone with a stake in international order has an interest in ensuring that all of us succeed.

The United States has large interests in the balance and has undertaken commitments commensurate with them. We're more than willing to bear our fair share of the burden. This includes, above all, the thousands of men and women in our Armed Forces who are now in the Gulf. But we also expect others to bear their fair share.

A number of countries already have announced their willingness to help those adversely affected economically by this endeavor. It's essential, though, that this be a concerted and coordinated one and that all affected countries participate. It is important to get the priorities right and make sure that those most deserving of assistance receive it and that those most able to contribute do so.

For that reason, I directed an interagency effort to develop a strategy to accomplish this objective. The group's report was presented at yesterday's National Security Council meeting here, and this morning I approved an action plan. Our approach calls for substantial economic assistance to those states—in particular I'd single out Turkey and Egypt—who are bearing a great part of the burden of sanctions and higher oil prices. The plan also targets additional countries, including Jordan, the countries of Eastern Europe, and others, for special assistance. The United States will also seek burden-sharing for part of our own effort.

At the same time, we will be asking other governments, including Japan, the Republic of Korea, the Federal Republic of Germany, Saudi Arabia, the Emirates, free Kuwait, and others, to join us in making available financial and, where appropriate, energy resources to countries that have been most affected by the current situation. To facilitate this undertaking, I've asked Secretary of State Jim Baker and Secretary of the Treasury Nick Brady to lead high-level delegations to the Persian Gulf, Europe, and Asia. And I'll be getting directly in touch with the leaders of these countries before Secretaries Baker and Brady arrive to spell out our general objectives.

Let me close by repeating what I said the other day in meeting with the congressional leaders. The basic pieces of our policy are in place. The Iraqi regime stands in opposition to the entire world and to the interest of the Iraqi people. It is truly Iraq against the world. But I want to make this point clear: We have no argument with the people of Iraq.

The sanctions are beginning to take hold. In the meantime, we want to ensure that countries contributing to this unprecedented collective response do not suffer for doing so. And what I've announced today and what I expect will be implemented in the coming days should help create a context in which sanctions against Iraq can be sustained with the intended effect.

Another area where there has been unprecedented international solidarity is OPEC's willingness to take up the slack in oil production created by the embargo on Iraqi and Kuwait's oil. In this connection, I met this morning with our energy advisers, who are watching the oil production situation very, very closely. And we are pleased with OPEC's decision to help take up the slack in crude oil production.

And although we're in what I would see as a transition period, the situation appears manageable. At the present time, we don't anticipate major imbalances in the oil market, but we do have the strategic petroleum reserve tested and available if it is truly needed. Our energy policy is resulting in increased oil production and fuel switching to natural gas and to other fuels.

I also repeat my previous request for Americans to conserve and for all parties to act responsibly. Right now the situation, I would say, is relatively stable, and I am very pleased by the coordination that is taking place with so many countries in maintaining adequate fuel levels.

And now I would be glad to take some questions. Who's first? Terry [Terence Hunt, Associated Press]?

Q. Mr. President, Saddam Hussein [President of Iraq] has rejected demands that he pull his troops out of Kuwait, and he's holding several thousand foreigners hostage to keep the world at bay. You say you don't see much chance for diplomacy to work.

How long can the West allow this impasse to go on? And would you take any action that might endanger the lives of those hostages?

The President. It will go on as long as it takes to have these United Nations sanctions fully implemented. And I'm glad that these diplomatic efforts are taking place. Perhaps one will hit pay dirt. But as of now, I must say I'm not optimistic because the man keeps reiterating terms that simply fly in the face of the United Nations action.

And on the second question, look, I feel very concerned about Americans that are held against their will. But we cannot permit hostage-taking to shape the foreign policy of this country, and I won't permit it to do that.

Q. Sir, does that mean that their lives would be expendable if you judge in the national interest——

The President. That's too hypothetical a question. It means I will not change the policy of the United States—and I don't think other leaders whose foreign nationals are in the same predicament will change their policies—to pay homage or to give credibility to this brutal move of staking out citizens and a brutal move of holding people against their will.

Q. Mr. President, there are reports that there's a split in your administration—some who want to expand the goals to include the eventual ouster of Saddam. And also, there are many, many suggestions for a Middle East conference that would include in what you would call the post-postwar shape of the world, the perennial problems of the Middle East. What do you think on both——

The President. Well, I think on the second part of the question that we ought to get on with the business at hand, the shorter run business, which is the solution to this question: the making right the situation in Kuwait, meaning the pulling out of forces, obviously, and the restoration of the rulers. As I look at the countries that are chipping in here now, I think we do have a chance at a new world order, and I'd like to think that out of this dreary performance by Saddam Hussein there could be now an opportunity for peace all through the Middle East. But we have to be sure that what's

been undertaken so far is successful before we can move to that other agenda, it seems to me.

Q. Well, would you support then a conference afterwards? I mean, this may be premature, but the question is: Are you shooting for that?

The President. I haven't—that's not an objective, a conference. Peace through the Middle East is an objective. And as you know, we have never ruled out a conference of any nature. In fact, it was part of our diplomacy just several years ago. But I don't want to get out ahead of where we are right now on this. The question right now is: What do we do to get Saddam Hussein to comply with international law?

I left out—you had another part of it.

Q. And you want to get him out of his job? You want to get him out of——

The President. Well, it wouldn't disappoint me if the Iraqis got up and said, look, this man is our problem. I've said right here the problem is not with the people in Iraq—simply isn't. But I've spelled out our objectives here, and I've stopped short of adding to them what—the answer that you were seeking from me on the President——

Q. Mr. President, some have expressed the fear that Saddam Hussein might seek to inflame the Arab world against the United States by drawing Israel into the conflict here, perhaps by a strike against Jordan. Can you tell us if you're prepared for such a contingency, and if so, how?

The President. Well, that's, again, hypothetical. I can't predict what he's going to do. But I can tell you that we are continuing to implement our forces and we are continuing to take all the diplomatic moves that are necessary to prepare for any eventuality.

Q. Let me just follow up by asking a question about Jordan's participation in the U.N. sanctions. There are numerous reports coming out of the East, some quoting Israeli intelligence, to the effect that Jordan is a highway, really, for supplies still reaching Iraq. Are you aware of those reports, and what do you——

The President. I'm aware of some. But, Brit [Brit Hume, ABC News], it is my view, based on what I've seen most recently, that commerce has come down to a bit of a trickle there. There are reports of enormous numbers of trucks being laid up with no goods to transport. So, I don't know how effective it is right now. I do know that King Hussein [of Jordan] told me, looking me right in the eye, that they were going to comply with the sanctions. But I've seen reports that indicate there's some leakage there, but I just can't give you the quantity. I just don't know.

It's my feeling that commerce through Aqaba, the port of Aqaba, and, indeed, through Jordan going to Iraq and vice versa has slowed down. Regrettably, there's a lot of refugee traffic, and I think that's hurting the Saddam Hussein image because people see the humblest being brutalized the most. And they see a lot of refugees out there, and I think that's sending not a very good signal as far as he's concerned.

Q. Sir, you're going to return to Kennebunkport this afternoon. May I ask how bothered you may have been by the opinion of many Americans, many of whom think you're doing a great job in this crisis, who nonetheless are bothered by you going out and fishing and golfing while in command of the troops in the Gulf?

The President. No, I'm not bothered by it. I've expressed myself on that. If I were bothered, I wouldn't be going back there for the Labor Day weekend with my family. And I think the American people are supporting strongly what I'm doing. And I would repeat: I am in very close touch, done a lot of the diplomatic work that has gone into this project from my house there, received a couple of foreign visitors there, have had many briefings there. And I think the American people are fundamentally fair, and I think they see that. So, I'm not troubled by it. If I were, I expect I wouldn't be going back again.

Q. Marlin Fitzwater at one point said that you were pretty adamant or stubborn about it, saying to him at one point that you needed the rest. [*Laughter*] Is that what it boiled down to? [*Laughter*]

Mr. Fitzwater. I beg your pardon. [*Laughter*]

The President. I need to rest, and I haven't gotten as much as I'd like. But I wouldn't call it adamant or stubborn be-

cause I refuse to——

Mr. Fitzwater. Neither would I. [*Laughter*]

The President. He better not have, either. [*Laughter*] Marlin's going through kind of a downer, though, because the Iraqi spokesman has the matching tie and hankie, you know, so he's been a little—[*laughter*]——

Q. You were about to answer the question about the rest.

The President. No, I think I do. I'm getting some—not as much as I'd like. But it's been very pleasant there, and yet I've managed to accomplish my objectives in terms of work, too.

Q. Mr. President, on the question of burden-sharing, since you're sending your envoys out, it sounds like you have not gotten the voluntary contributions you might have liked to have gotten. Can you give us a sense of how much you're looking for and where you expect to find it?

The President. No, I don't think it's a question of doing this because we haven't gotten what we think is fair for other countries and for burden-sharing generally.

What we're talking about here, Charles [Charles Bierbauer, Cable News Network], is a consulting and coordinating effort, and we've had strong indications of support. But now we're moving up a little bit and trying to take the lead here—leadership in helping sort out who should help whom. Somebody has to do that. And we've made a significant commitment in various ways. And so, it seemed appropriate that we take the lead in working with our friends and allies.

But look, Prime Minister Kaifu [of Japan] called me last night—no, he didn't need a mission for this—and made a significant contribution and then pledged to do more in terms of support for other countries. Now, that is very good, and that was voluntary. But it needs to be coordinated. Somebody needs to take the lead on saying: Look, we don't put all the money to this one country. Several countries are involved here, and let's see that these generous responses are fairly allocated.

Q. If I could follow up: There have been concerns expressed about the Japanese not making any military contribution. They could send minesweepers or something like that. Is money not enough in the Japanese case? And what has happened to your good friend Helmut Kohl [Chancellor of the Federal Republic of Germany], who seems extraordinarily silent?

The President. I wouldn't say money is not enough. I'm fully aware of the constraints on the Japanese, and I've not pressed him to go beyond what his Constitution provides. Helmut Kohl—I think they'll be very responsive. And part of what we're talking about here is to follow up on comments like the ones Helmut Kohl made to me about, we want to be a part of this—we want to help. So, I have no argument with the Germans at all.

Q. Is the United States doing anything to help the Kuwaiti underground, the Kuwaiti rebels, in training, supplies—anything?

The President. One, I wouldn't comment on it. Two, but in a broad way, I support the Kuwaiti underground. I support anybody that can add a hand in restoring legitimacy there to Kuwait and to getting the Iraqis out of Kuwait.

Q. How do you justify it legally under the U.N. resolution—for any support activity for the underground?

The President. I'm just encouraging people who are patriots and feel that their country has been pillaged and aggressed against.

Q. Would you draw the line at sending the Green Berets or some sort of American military force in cross-border raids? And do you——

The President. That's too hypothetical. I've given you the principle. If there were some quiet support, which I wouldn't ever confirm or deny—we never comment on those matters—I would simply leave it out there. But you say, well, am I supportive of—I think what you said was resistance. And I'd be supportive of anybody that wants to try to fulfill the statements that the world has made through the United Nations.

Q. You didn't rule out cross-border raids by American military personnel either.

The President. Well, if they're going to happen—let me be clear on this—if it were going to happen, I wouldn't comment on it. It would be the dumbest thing I could possibly do, in my view, to tip your hat. But I

have no plans for that right now.

Q. Mr. President, a related question about this. There are some Iraqi opposition groups in London and elsewhere, and the Kurds, and they have all said in recent weeks they've heard nothing from your administration. If anything, they've been encouraged just to—that the United States only wants covert contacts with them. Why not, if, as you say, you want the Iraqi people to rise up, why has this administration not done anything with the opposition groups?

The President. We've got a plan, and the plan is to work diplomatically, and the plan is to put on the ground a significant military force. And if these comments I made today about anybody who wants to help the United Nations and those of us who want to see Iraq out of Kuwait succeed, so much the better.

Q. If I could just follow up: You said also today, you don't want to hurt the Iraqi people. But isn't this embargo and these sanctions only hurting them and hurting them first before they hurt Saddam?

The President. There's nothing that's painless, David [David Hoffman, Washington Post], when you get into a situation like this and when you have a leader that could brutalize his own people. There's nothing that's painless in all of this.

Q. On the question of negotiations, Mr. President, are all channels still open? Specifically, have there been any back-channel contact or proposals to White House officials that are worth pursuing?

The President. None that I know of.

Q. If I could follow on that, sir: Saddam Hussein has suggested that you and he and Margaret Thatcher [Prime Minister of the United Kingdom] go on TV to debate this. What do you say to that?

The President. I say he can put an empty chair there as far as I'm concerned. [*Laughter*]

Q. Mr. President, in your peptalk to the armed services yesterday, you mentioned the difficulty of the mission, citing the weather. Isn't boredom even a bigger factor as weeks slip into months over in the desert?

The President. Well, I would hope not, but I'm not sure it's the world's most exciting assignment, if that's what you mean. But I think there will be programs to keep morale high. Right now it's extraordinarily high.

Q. A suggestion has been made that some reduction in the troops might be made in the days ahead to give a more international tinge to the force over there. Would you entertain such—or support such a move?

The President. I'm more interested in seeing the fulfillment of commitments made.

Q. Mr. President, you're about to begin a new round of budget negotiations. Federal employees are facing furloughs because of the Gramm-Rudman law. And this operation is costing over $1 billion a month. How do you assess the impact of the cost of Operation Desert Shield on your budget problem?

The President. It's difficult at this juncture to know fully what the impact will be. Clearly, it will have some budget implication. I have not moved off of my view that we must get a budget agreement with Congress as soon as they get back, and I'll have more to say about that in the weeks ahead. But I really haven't changed my view on that. And I think it will be very clear to Members of Congress that the deficit problem has gotten worse as a result of the action that we have had to take.

Q. If I could follow that up: Senator Leahy has suggested a sort of war tax to pay for this. How do you feel about that concept?

The President. I don't feel that the answer is a war tax.

Q. Mr. President, do you have any problem with the live TV coverage of Saddam Hussein's media events, which a lot of people complain just gives him a propaganda platform?

The President. No, I have no complaints about it. I think that it hasn't helped him very much with world opinion. I don't know what it's done at home; maybe it's been reassuring to the people there. But I don't think that it is cutting into the desire to see the U.N. sanctions fulfilled. I must say, I haven't seen the last couple of interviews with the man, but I think the one with the—what he calls guests and what we call hostages was really so brutal and so

totally unacceptable that it worked against him—was manipulative and cynical. So, I haven't been concerned that he's got a shot there. He's had a real opportunity to present his case to the American people. I'd like to have a similar opportunity to present our case to the people in Iraq. But I have no complaints about that at all, Rita [Rita Beamish, Associated Press].

Q. Mr. President, could you accept a situation where Iraq withdraws from Kuwait but keeps its military power intact, regardless of who's in charge?

The President. Well, again, that's too hypothetical. I want to see the goals that I stated fulfilled. And of course, I think part of that would be—I think the world would demand that there be no chance of another invasion the minute this ended.

Q. If I could follow, sir: Senator Lugar and some others have said that this is something that we should discuss now.

The President. Well, we are discussing it now. I had dinner with him last night, as a matter of fact, because I knew he felt that way. It was a very good evening, as a matter of fact. I had about 11, 12 Members of Congress over there, and it was helpful to me to get these diverse views. I got some of the feeling of that from briefing the Congress. But I have great respect for Dick Lugar, and so we'll be talking more. But I have not changed the objectives, you'll notice, in the publicly stated objectives here.

Q. What is the total amount of money you are expecting from the allies?

The President. There is no total price tag that I have in mind.

I do have to go, in a couple of questions—after two.

Q. Has Israel served as a strategic ally in this crisis? And is there anything you can do to help protect Israel and Saudi Arabia against a chemical attack as was threatened today?

The President. Israel has behaved very well, and Israel has never had difficulty defending itself. In terms of Saudi Arabia, we are committed to the defense of Saudi Arabia, and I believe that we have a major stake in protecting them against that kind of further aggression.

Q. May I follow? Of the countries you're asking for assistance, have you asked South Africa to contribute anything to this?

The President. I don't think we've asked any of these—well, we may have asked some of them so far, but I don't know that there's been a request made of South Africa or not.

Last one.

Q. Mr. President, some of the Members of Congress who attended the meeting with you the other day left here with the feeling that the longer the situation drags on, the less the chance there is of outright fighting involving U.S. troops. At the moment, what is your assessment of the risk of fighting involving our forces?

The President. Well, it's so hard to answer that question because of the unpredictable nature of Saddam Hussein himself. And so, I think it's almost impossible. I've had meetings today with some of our top analysts and specialists on the Arab world. I don't want to put words in their mouth, but that was one of the questions that I asked. It's very hard to predict; it's very hard to measure intentions. But I think the answer is to have the forces in place to be ready. I would think that the defense of Saudi Arabia is far more assured today than it was 2 weeks ago because the United States and others have moved substantial forces there. And they're ready, and they're strong, and they're able, and their morale is high. Similarly, there's a lot of naval power and, of course, air power that's there. I would think that that would be a deterrent to anybody with any degree of rationality. Having said that, I don't know what is in this man's mind.

Q. To follow on, sir: What actions by Iraq, sir, would trigger a U.S. response?

The President. That is too broad a question to get a response from. But we're ready, and if there's some provocative action, why, then we'd have to make a determination at that time. But I just can't help you. Your question is too broad.

Last one from Texas. Cragg [Cragg Hines, Houston Chronicle]? And then I've got to go. I really do.

Q. Mr. President, are you concerned that this burden-sharing, as you call it, is going to make American forces look like mercenaries in the Middle East?

The President. I wouldn't want to have anything done that would make them look like mercenaries. But I don't think so. In fact, we would be very careful that that conclusion could not be drawn.

I raised that question—one of the Members of Congress asked me that—said I don't want mercenary forces. But there are ways that burden-sharing can be accomplished without making the forces mercenary. And I'm thinking of the enormous fuel bills that are involved and transportation and these kinds of things that are involved in moves of this nature.

But I'm glad you raised it, because U.S. forces should never appear to be mercenary forces. And that will not be the outcome of this, I can guarantee you.

Thank you all very much. Thank you so much.

Note: The President's 59th news conference began at 2:02 p.m. in the Briefing Room at the White House. Marlin Fitzwater was Press Secretary to the President.

Remarks Announcing the Upcoming Meeting With President Mikhail Gorbachev of the Soviet Union and an Exchange With Reporters in Kennebunkport, Maine
September 1, 1990

The President. I have a brief announcement that I'd like to make, and that is that President Gorbachev and I will meet on Sunday, September 9th, in Helsinki, to discuss international and bilateral matters.

I spoke with President Koivisto of Finland this morning, and I believe the Soviets made a similar approach to President Koivisto to secure the final arrangements. Secretary Baker and [Soviet] Foreign Minister Shevardnadze have been working out the details of this meeting over the last few days. And we got word this morning that an announcement at this time would be agreeable to the Soviets, so I wanted to get that out.

And I'm looking forward very much to seeing Mr. Gorbachev again. We have many matters to discuss. There is no special agenda relating to the Middle East. Nobody is doing any negotiating or anything of that nature. When President Gorbachev was here, he and I agreed that it would be useful to have periodic meetings without casting them in the vein of a summit, and that's exactly what this meeting is about. And I will be delighted to see him again, and we have many subjects to discuss.

Q. Mr. President, this is a little bit sudden. Can you tell us what you hope to accomplish? I mean, it seems sudden, on such short notice. What do you hope to accomplish? And also, was this your initiative or his?

The President. It's not overly sudden. We just haven't been discussing it. I believe, in this case, I made the suggestion that we have this meeting at this time and at this place.

Q. What do you hope to accomplish?

The President. Being sure we're together. As you know, I've been very pleased with the cooperation we've been getting from the Soviet Union on a wide array of questions and subjects, and I think it is important at this juncture that we discuss issues not just as they relate to Europe—and try to update where we can on these arms negotiations—but also to discuss the Middle East.

Q. Is this at all motivated by concern that the Soviets either don't understand or don't agree with U.S. actions in the Gulf region, specifically, the military deployment that they've expressed some doubt about?

The President. No, I'm very pleased, as I think I've said before publicly, that we seem to be in general agreement on a lot of issues, a lot of questions that relate to the Middle East. But it is my view that it is just

important that we have good, free-flowing discussions about this. So, it wasn't driven by any worry that we might be apart, rather that there's a wide array of questions that could use consultation at this time.

Q. Can you tell us why you haven't talked to President Gorbachev until now, since this crisis erupted a month ago?

The President. Because I had anticipated seeing him.

Q. Have you talked to him about the summit meeting?

The President. No, but I've been in direct contact with him about the summit meeting personally.

Q. Mr. President, will you be asking Mr. Gorbachev to pull his military advisers out of Iraq?

The President. We have no agenda, no issues of that nature that have been agreed on to discuss.

Q. Is it a concern here, though—doesn't that help the Iraqi military?

The President. I'm not sure of the status of those military advisers right now, Sandy [Sandy Gilmour, NBC News].

Q. Can you say what you will be talking about other than the Middle East? Will you be discussing, for example, START talks, CSCE, or any other possible meetings later in the year?

The President. Other meetings?

Q. With Mr. Gorbachev.

The President. Well, I hadn't—I mean, we've just set these meetings up, and the way I've described it from our side to him was that we'd have no agenda and that it would be free-flowing discussions. But I know that we'll have discussions of, as I mentioned, CFE; and a CFE agreement would lead to the CSCE meeting. So, I think we'll be talking about all these things, Sandy.

Persian Gulf Crisis

Q. Mr. President, what role would you like to see the Soviets play in the burden-sharing campaign that the administration has started for the Persian Gulf?

The President. I don't know that they have a role to play in burden-sharing at all.

Q. Why?

The President. The Soviet Union has a lot

of responsibilities around the world. If they want to help in the burden-sharing, that's fine. But I don't go there with a specific burden-sharing role in mind. It should be disconnected from the mission that Secretary Baker and Secretary Brady are undertaking. It has just—put it this way—this meeting, in my view, is not about burden-sharing. We may get a better idea of all of this because I think Jim Baker will be in Moscow very soon.

Q. Mr. President, given the Soviet relationship with Iraq, do you see Moscow playing a mediating role in the crisis in the Gulf?

The President. I don't see a mediating role at all, and I don't think the Soviets see themselves having a mediating role. There are a lot of mediators out there trying hard, [United Nations] Secretary-General de Cuellar being in the forefront of this. I talked today to the President of Yemen from up here, who thinks there's some chance for some mediation. And so, it's fine for them to go forward, but I don't think the Soviets see themselves in a mediating role, and I don't intend to ask them to see themselves in a mediating role, nor do I expect him to ask the United States to be in a mediating role.

Q. You said last week when you didn't foresee at that point a diplomatic settlement of this problem. Has your view of that changed?

The President. Well, I haven't seen any flexibility on the key point, which is the operating within the United Nations mandate. I've listened carefully and follow up as carefully as we can on various conversations that Saddam Hussein has, and what the world community has said is to get out of Kuwait and to restore the rulers. And now you see the Arab League acting and calling for reparations, for Saddam Hussein to make good on reparations. But I don't see any willingness on his part to undertake what the world community is looking for.

So, I'd like to be optimistic, and I think it's fine to have these talks going on. I encouraged Javier Perez de Cuellar and told him I wished him great success. But I don't want to mislead the American people by saying I think that there's some breakthrough at hand or some flexibility that is clearly going to be required on his part to live within the mandate of the United Nations.

Q. Sir, what do you make of the piecemeal approach that Saddam has been taking in releasing a few women and children at a time?

The President. I don't like that. Yes, I don't like it. I don't like it. I don't think the world likes it. I'm glad when any American comes out of there, but there's a certain brutality, a certain tawdry performance in all of this.

Q. What do you think his motive is in handling it that way?

The President. I can't anticipate his motive. But it's just turning off world opinion. It is so base and so outrageous that I think most people in the Arab world are very embarrassed by this, and I think that's certainly true of others around the world. I've talked to so many leaders, and they all agree that this is just a despicable performance.

Q. How long can you let it go on, sir?

The President. Well, I don't—I'm not one on deadline—I don't deal in deadlines.

Upcoming Meeting With President Gorbachev

Q. Mr. President, can you tell us when you first broached this idea of a meeting with Mr. Gorbachev?

The President. Over a week ago, maybe, or something like that.

Q. And why have you opted for what seems to be a fairly—just kind of a hit-and-run brief encounter in Helsinki as opposed to talks over a couple of days?

The President. I think we can get done what we need to do in one day, and that's what he feels also.

Egyptian Debt

Q. Mr. President, there were reports that you're going to recommend forgiving $7 billion in Egyptian debt. Can you comment on those reports? Are you going to——

The President. No, I have no comment on it. But Egypt, in my view, has been stalwart in this Middle East situation, and they do have grave financial problems, and I want very much to work with President Mubarak to alleviate these problems. But the steps that I'd have to take is to make any recommendations along that line to the United States Congress. And my gut instinct is to do that, but I'm just not prepared to say where we stand on it.

Upcoming Meeting With President Gorbachev

Q. Mr. President, just to clarify, you said there is no special agenda relating to the Middle East, and you seem to be telling us that, well, you were going to have this meeting on other topics. But yet, you brought it up just a week ago. Is it that the timing of it was spurred by the Middle East crisis?

The President. It's a subject that certainly will be discussed. But what I'm trying not to do is say this meeting is about the Middle East. I've already gotten a question here, is there some negotiating role or is there some agenda about the Middle East? And there isn't; but, yes, it will be a subject that we discuss. But we have a wide array of other issues, is all I'm trying to say. I mention CFE because I do want to see that lead to a CSCE summit, but I can't say that the Middle East has nothing to do with this meeting at all. I just don't want to mislead you. But it is not the whole thing. But I'm very anxious to discuss that subject, but please add a wide array of other subjects.

And so, I've had in mind, as I think I've mentioned to you all, more frequent meetings. I think I said that, and I think he agreed with this when he left, that we would have more frequent meetings. We both agreed up at Camp David that this kind of informal, unstructured format might be very good in a world where there are so many changes, so it's a good chance to test

that now. And it's reported to me that he is very enthusiastic about this, Jim Baker having been handling the modalities of it all and making the overtures, although the original one was a proposal by me direct to Mr. Gorbachev. But Jim's been working the details of this out, and I expect he'll have something to say about that.

Persian Gulf Crisis

Q. Mr. President, there was a report on the wires this morning that U.S. marines have moved to positions—at least a unit of them has moved to a position within 25 miles of the Kuwaiti border, whereas before they were well over 100 miles behind the scenes. Anything going on——

The President. I have no comment on it, Sandy, because I'm not aware of that. It's a tactical matter. It gives me a great opportunity to repeat the enormous confidence I have in our CINC, General Schwarzkopf, and also in our Chairman and others involved in this enormous movement of troops, the logistical support for them, and the deployment of them. I just have full confidence in our military that they will take the proper action to achieve our objectives.

Thank you all very much.

Note: The President spoke at 1:03 p.m. at his home. In his remarks, he referred to United Nations Secretary-General Javier Perez de Cuellar de la Guerra; President 'Ali 'Abdallah Salih of Yemen; President Saddam Hussein of Iraq; Gen. H. Norman Schwarzkopf, USA, commander in chief of the U.S. Central Command and commander of the U.S. forces in the Persian Gulf; and Gen. Colin L. Powell, Chairman of the Joint Chiefs of Staff.

Message on the Observance of Labor Day, 1990
September 1, 1990

This year, we celebrate Labor Day at a time of both change and challenge for the United States and its workers. However, trial and change are nothing new to Amer-

ica or to the working men and women who have done so much to make this Nation a source of hope and inspiration for people throughout the world.

When the Industrial Revolution transformed the United States from an agrarian society into an industrialized power, millions of Americans moved from the farm to the factory and helped to forge the most productive economy the world has ever known. When World War II threatened the lives and liberty of millions of people, American workers converted their assembly lines into a pillar of our national defense, helping to make the United States a strong and effective guardian of freedom and human rights. More recently, when we attempted to conquer Space, our highly skilled work force built machines that have not only enabled us to travel safely to the Moon but also allowed us to send unmanned missions far beyond Earth's orbit. Dauntless and determined, American workers have risen to every challenge and opportunity to come before us.

Today, our economic strength and our competitive instincts are also being tested in a swiftly changing global marketplace, one that demands flexibility and rewards technological excellence. We must continue to emphasize education. We must continue to provide our work force with the training and tools needed for success in a highly competitive global economy. I am confident that America's working men and women will respond as they always have—with courage, ingenuity, and the will to succeed.

On this Labor Day, we take special pride in the rights and opportunities that our system of government and innate sense of fairness ensure all American workers. As long as we cherish these rights and opportunities that are uniquely ours, this Nation will continue to be blessed with prosperity and progress.

At a time when our commitment to freedom and justice and our resolve to defend these cherished principles are being tested in the Middle East, let us remember that keeping the United States free, strong, and prosperous is the responsibility of all Americans—and it is a job that is never finished. As we look to the future, we can take great confidence in the capabilities and the indomitable spirit of the American worker.

GEORGE BUSH

Remarks at a White House Briefing on National Drug Control Strategy
September 5, 1990

I wanted to come over here today just to make a brief statement prior to Bill Bennett's presentation. One year ago today, I announced one of the most important initiatives of our administration: the National Drug Control Strategy, a blueprint—a clear blueprint—for the war on drugs. We've devoted unprecedented new resources to the fight—new material, new money, new management, new manpower. And this is true virtually across the board: for law enforcement; for treatment; for school, community, and workplace prevention; and for our friends in Latin America. We've pulled the entire Federal effort together. We've given every participating Department a clear antidrug mission. And we've joined hands with State and local governments—and of course, private citizens—all across the country. Never before has so much effort, involving so many people, been applied to the scourge of drugs.

In a moment, as I say, our very able drug czar, Bill Bennett, will give you a more detailed assessment of the progress that the Nation's already made, what we've done and, of course, what is left to be done. But I'm here because I wanted to tell you personally that I think America is making progress against drugs and will continue to do so. The crisis is far from over, but there are clear signs of progress. So-called "casual drug use" is continuing to decline. There are early promising signs that even the problem of hardcore addiction has taken a turn for the better. Today in America, cocaine is harder to find, more expensive, less pure than it was just one year ago.

Statistics like these help put perspective in the very real progress that we've made in this war on drugs. Too often, public attention focuses only on the face of the battle—the drive-by shootings and the horrible individual tragedies. The other side might not make good television. But many of you in the press have traveled with me this past year. We've seen the recovering drug addicts who are getting help, seen the families, the neighborhoods, the whole communities that are being restored to health and safety.

I think back to Erma Scales who took back a part of Acres Homes, a big park there—part of my old congressional district in Houston. Heroes like Al Brooks in that Baptist church basement in Kansas City—he just had enough and decided to do something on his own and mobilize the spirit of that community. The rallying cry of Father George Clemens in Chicago—here's the way he put it: "There are more of us than there are of them." Just those few words, and mobilized opinion and got community action going.

So, while the statistics are good, progress can't be measured only by statistics. The past year has also seen a fundamental change in attitude, a growing awareness that drugs can take away your family, your job, your health, your freedom and, yes, even your life. We've also seen stunning new successes in law enforcement in both this country and Latin America that are difficult to measure by statistics alone. There are drug lords who—arrogant and free only a year ago—are today behind bars or on the run, or have already paid the ultimate price for a life of crime and violence.

Today's good news that Bill is going to share with you is welcome. We've made important progress. But clearly, that's not enough. There is still too much violence, too much destruction, too many innocent victims. Drugs are still an international menace. So, we're going to stick to this comprehensive drug strategy. We're going to renew our call for Congress to pass a true crime bill—one that's tough on the criminals and not on the police. My administration will remain on the front lines until this scourge is licked for good. Block by block, school by school, child by child, we will take back the streets. We will never surrender. I know that other subjects are preoccupying all of us these days. But this one remains number one. It will continue to remain number one when the international situation has calmed down—an entirely different climate.

I want to thank all of those here who have been laboring, sometimes without identity or without acclaim, on the front lines. I am proud of the work of Judge Walton and, of course, Bill Bennett and all of you, and I want to thank you for what you're doing, and keep it up. I now will turn the podium over to our able drug czar, Bill Bennett. Thank you all very much. Good luck.

Note. The President spoke at 11:11 a.m. in Room 450 of the Old Executive Office Building. In his remarks, he referred to Reggie Walton, Associate Director for State and Local Affairs in the Office of National Drug Control Policy.

Statement by Press Secretary Fitzwater on the United States Commercial Space Launch Policy
September 5, 1990

The President has approved a new National Space Policy Directive providing important guidance which will further encourage the growth of U.S. private sector space activities. This policy, developed by the Vice President and the National Space Council, is completely consistent with and provided the policy framework for the President's August 22, 1990, decision regarding participation by a U.S. firm in Australia's Cape York space launch project. The policy supplements the National Space Policy which the President approved on November 2, 1989.

The commercial space launch policy recognizes the many benefits which a commercial space launch industry provides to the United States. It balances launch industry needs with those of other industries and with important national security interests, and establishes the long term goal of a free and fair market in which U.S. industry can compete. The policy specifies a coordinated set of actions for the next 10 years aimed at achieving this goal.

White House Fact Sheet on the United States Commercial Space Launch Policy
September 5, 1990

Policy Findings

A commercial space launch industry can provide many benefits to the U.S. including indirect benefits to U.S. national security.

The long-term goal of the United States is a free and fair market in which U.S. industry can compete. To achieve this, a set of coordinated actions is needed for dealing with international competition in launch goods and services in a manner that is consistent with our nonproliferation and technology transfer objectives. These actions must address both the short term (actions which will affect competitiveness over approximately the next 10 years) and those which will have their principal effect in the longer term (i.e. after approximately the year 2000).

— In the near term, this includes trade agreements and enforcement of those agreements to limit unfair competition. It also includes the continued use of U.S.-manufactured launch vehicles for launching U.S. Government satellites.

— For the longer term, the United States should take actions to encourage technical improvements to reduce the cost and increase the reliability of U.S. space launch vehicles.

Implementing Actions

U.S. Government satellites will be launched on U.S.-manufactured launch vehicles unless specifically exempted by the President.

Consistent with guidelines to be developed by the National Space Council, U.S. Government agencies will actively consider commercial space launch needs and factor them into their decisions on improvements in launch infrastructure and launch vehicles aimed at reducing cost and increasing responsiveness and reliability of space launch vehicles.

The U.S. Government will enter into negotiations to achieve agreement with the European Space Agency (ESA), ESA member states, and others as appropriate, which defines principles of free and fair trade.

Nonmarket launch providers of space launch goods and services create a special case because of the absence of market-oriented pricing and cost structures. To deal with their entry into the market there needs to be a transition period during which special conditions may be required.

There also must be an effective means of enforcing international agreements related to space launch goods and services.

Appointment of Shawn Smeallie as a Special Assistant to the President for Legislative Affairs
September 5, 1990

The President today announced the appointment of Shawn Smeallie as Special Assistant to the President for Legislative Affairs (Senate) at the White House.

Since February of 1989 Mr. Smeallie has been in charge of Senate Relations in the Office of Legislative Affairs at the Office of Management and Budget. Prior to this, he served as a legislative assistant to United States Senator Alfonse D'Amato, 1984–1989.

Mr. Smeallie graduated from St. Lawrence University (B.A., 1981) and Georgetown University (M.A., 1990). He currently resides in Washington, DC.

Remarks at a Fundraising Luncheon for Governor Mike Hayden in Topeka, Kansas
September 6, 1990

Mike, thank you for that very kind and very generous introduction. It's great to be here with you and Patti. And, of course, always a pleasure to be with—glad to see today your distinguished Senator, Nancy Kassebaum. What a job she's doing for this State and for the entire country. Your re-election is crucial not just to Kansas, but to the entire Nation. You know, Nancy is part of Kansas' superb Republican team in Washington. Let me salute another part of that team, a man who could not be with us today—our outstanding Republican leader in the Senate, Bob Dole. As President—and I mean this from the bottom of a grateful heart—I could not possibly have a finer leader with whom to work in the United States Senate than Bob Dole. He has been outstanding and superb and supportive. And I wanted to congratulate him in front of his friends from his State, but he's not here, so give him that message. I hope he knows I feel that way anyway.

Jan Meyers, Congresswoman Jan Meyers, is here. I salute her and I know she will continue to represent her Third District with style. And she's been magnificent in Washington. And also, let me put in a plug for two fine candidates who will make an important contribution to the Congress: Scott Morgan and Dick Nicholls. To Harland and Wynn Priddle, thank you for cohosting this luncheon. Also, thanks to Lieutenant Governor Jack Walker and Harold [Howard] Wilkins, my old friend and our Ambassador there in The Netherlands. We're proud of him and the job he's doing for our country in helping one of our important NATO allies in staunch step with us. He's done a great job over there.

I'm pleased—I heard her announced just before Patti and Mike and I walked in—to have Jeanie Austin with us today. She is, as you know, the cochairman of the Republican National Committee. And I salute her along with the national committee members from this State: Mary Alice, Jack Ranson, Rochelle Chronister, who's our chairwoman. And it's great to see all of them and John Peterson, who did such a magnificent job of running our campaign here in 1988, as well as Don and Adele Hall. And a special hello to a friend of Mike's, Lacey Cook of Dodge City. This brave young girl won her battle for a liver transplant, and she'll be 3 years old next Tuesday. All Kansans can take pride in the courage evidenced by this wonderful child.

Today, I'm privileged to be back in the very heartland of America—and to speak on behalf of a friend. He is a Vietnam veteran; he's an environmentalist and a businessman. Most of all, he is a great Governor of a truly great State. Ladies and gentlemen, Governor Mike Hayden.

As you may have read, I had some mishaps on my way here. First, I was fishing with the Canadian Prime Minister on my boat when it broke down. I crunched a rock, I think. But anyway, the next day we went back out, and I got hooked in the ear while fishing with the Prime Minister and my son Jeb. The barb from one of these hooks went all the way through the ear. We refer to our son as Captain Hook now. [*Laughter*] Talk about adding insult to injury—after they unhooked me, Jeb tried to throw me back. [*Laughter*] Luckily, he was dissuaded.

But it's wonderful to be here now, back to work—discuss how far the last 4 years Mike has come. Mike's compass, Mike Hayden's compass, has helped chart the future—not just for now but the future of Kansas. It's a compass of integrity, embodying the Kansas of hard work and character. And if I wasn't aware of that, you should have heard Mike telling me about that on the way in from the airport as we saw the citizens lining the street with that warm, warm Kansas welcome. Man of family— think of Mike's wife, Patti, and the two girls who were out there to greet us at the airport. A compass of what I like to think of as traditional values. And plain common sense—he keeps things in perspective. It's like Mike—never a man of failing to say what he thinks—he tells me: "It's fine that you're here, Mr. President. But if you really want to help out, bring Barbara." [*Laughter*]

These qualities have endeared Mike to Kansas' good and quiet and decent people. And it's no surprise that "Kansas Likes Mike." And just look at this background: Kansas State graduate; member, then Speaker, of the Kansas House of Representatives. He's living proof of the words spoken by that great Kansan to whom he referred, Dwight Eisenhower. Ike said, "Our best protection against bigger government in Washington is better government in the States." And today we meet to help Mike keep making government better in the State of Kansas. And so, let's reelect him to a second term in the Governor's mansion.

Take a look at the numbers. Today, more Kansans are working than at any time in

our history. Unemployment is the lowest in 11 years. And no wonder "Kansas Likes Mike." Here's more: Think of the increase in net farm income—up $4 billion since '87. And we realize some farmers are hurting because those wheat prices are down. Four billion dollars since '87 and a $2.6 billion construction program to modernize the highways. Affection stems from achievements like these. And how did they happen? Not from Washington, DC, doing for Kansas but through Kansans doing for themselves. Not expanding the budget of the bureaucracy; rather, expanding the horizons of Kansans young and old.

And now, you may have heard—I hope you haven't heard too much about it—but we have a budget, too, in Washington, DC. And back in June, when the budget talks were at an impasse, I decided that the time had come to put it all on the table, lay it right out there for all to see, whatever it was—revenues, spending cuts, budget reform. And I did that as an act of good faith. And I believe I've tried hard, and I believe I have kept the faith. And, yes, took some heat, understandably—I expected that—through 5 long months of budget talks. But today—and I really feel strongly about this when I see the young people that are here today and that were out to greet us when we arrived—time is running out.

And here's a fact: October 1st begins a new fiscal year for the Federal Government, and still no agreement on getting our deficit under control. Another fact: We've got to draw the line on spending—break free once and for all from the tired old mindset that says for every new problem we must create a new bureaucracy. And the budget I've asked for—$1.5 trillion—is not exactly miserly. It is certainly enough to do the vital work of government. And so I say, Congress, let's get with it.

I pledge again to work with the leaders in Congress on both sides of the aisle to get an agreement that makes real cuts in the deficit now and eliminates the deficit within 5 years. The time for partisanship, in my view, is past; and the time for avoiding the tough decisions is gone. They're not going to do it exactly the way I want, and I understand that. And I can't do it exactly the way one element or another in the Congress wants, and I think they must understand that. But the time is now for decision. And I say let's fix this Federal budget mess once and for all—get it done.

All of you remember Nancy's dad, another great Kansan, Alf Landon. And perhaps you don't recall how once he said, "There are some intelligent people in Washington. There are more of them in Kansas." Well, Mike Hayden encapsules Kansas' thinking. So, let me briefly talk about how he and you can help meet America's challenges. Challenges at home—the budget among them; also, challenges abroad.

At home, we begin with education, where Mike has launched a campaign to make Kansas number one in the whole country. And your support can help him convince the Congress to pass our National Educational Excellence Act. And then, comes the environment. Here, too, I need Mike; I need his commitment. I need, Mike, for you to help support me in Washington. Your support can help convince Congress to grant the Environmental Protection Agency cabinet status and pass clean air legislation that I can sign. I want to do that. I think it's important for our country. But we also have to remember the job base in this country. So, we've got to get a bill that the President can sign. And finally, I need Mike to keep Kansas our nation's breadbasket. Look, you produce more wheat than any other State. You know how vital agriculture is to America and to the entire world.

Mike grew up in a farm family. You get strong support coming out of the farm families across this State. And I'm sure he's heard the tale—old—most have heard it—of how a city person bought a chicken farm. A friend was astonished. "Do you know anything about breeding chickens?" he asked. "No," said the city person, "but the chickens do." Well, in Kansas, even chickens realize that when it comes to farming, Washington does not know best, Kansans do. So, I ask you to back a new farm bill that emphasizes market-oriented policies. Bob Dole understands this; Nancy Kassebaum understands it; Jan Meyers understands it. Our new farm bill must be even-handed and level-headed, enhancing America's competi-

tiveness. I know winter wheat goes in the ground this month, and I hear from Mike of your concerns about the wheat market, and I understand that. We must help lower interest rates and the deficit while increasing choice for farmers and consumers.

We also need to get the most from the grain agreement that President Gorbachev and I signed at our recent summit, a deal calling for at least 50 million metric tons of grain to be purchased by the Soviets in the next 5 years. Our ongoing Uruguay round of negotiations can continue this movement toward cooperation and free trade. Here's one more way to keep agriculture strong. I ask you to support our capital gains tax cut proposal which will create new investment. And I will again call on the United States Congress to take action on this proposal now.

So far I've discussed a little about how we can keep America proud at home. So, let me close by talking about what we can do to serve the principles we hold dear abroad. I refer to the issue, of course, that's central to our minds and hearts, the crisis in the Persian Gulf. As you know, the events are still unfolding. Hard choices remain. But of this we are certain: When some ask, where does America stand, our answer is, America stands where it always has—against aggression. And America will not be intimidated.

You know, 5 weeks ago, these beliefs prompted me to take action in the Middle East toward restoring the sovereignty of Kuwait and deterring those who threaten—who threaten friendly countries and the vital interests of America. Those objectives are unchanged today, and they will remain unchanged. And we will not stand by while one country devours another unthreatening country. We will stand firm against the aggression now condemned around the entire world.

Our cause may not be easy, but it will always be right. So, we will do whatever it takes to help our men and women restore peace and, thus, complete their mission. We're doing this with the cooperation of the United Nations—22 countries involved in the Persian Gulf effort—22. I'm proud that a substantial majority of Arab nations support our efforts. Saddam Hussein is trying to make it America against the Arabs—couldn't be more untrue. It is the rest of the world, including most of the Arabs, against Saddam Hussein—most standing with us against this brutal aggression. The world is united for stability and security, and we will remain united. In that spirit, I look forward to Sunday's meeting with President Gorbachev in Helsinki.

When he and I met last June, I mentioned the hope then that we could meet more frequently. The better we understand each other, the closer, I believe, that we can work. The past year has seen new levels of cooperation between our two nations. The Persian Gulf shows what this cooperation can achieve. So, on Sunday, President Gorbachev and I will talk of the Gulf crisis and other regional issues as well—arms control issues, a wide array of issues. I also hope to also discuss the progress of Soviet reform. And I will continue to press for a prompt resolution of a START treaty. This meeting can further expand cooperation between the United States and the Soviet Union.

Yet to complete our Persian Gulf mission will also require what Chairman of the Joint Chiefs of Staff Colin Powell called "the finest peacetime military in the history of America." As long as I am President, that military will remain purposeful and proud. They are the finest young kids that have ever served the United States Government.

Today, those finest soldiers, sailors, airmen, and marines that any nation could have are showing how the best way to keep the peace is to keep America militarily strong. Here are just a handful of examples, all now on active duty in Saudi Arabia with the Air National Guard's 190th Air Refueling Group from Topeka's Forbes Field. Sergeant Johnnie Keller is a graduate of Osage City High School, who last March joined the Guard. Today, he's standing shoulder to shoulder for what is right and good with colleagues like Theresa Boyd of Lawrence, a jet engine mechanic and 11-year Guard veteran, and technical sergeant Bill Hortenstine, a Highland Park grad who helps maintain these KC–135 tankers that refuel planes all the way on their way over to faraway Saudi Arabia.

These Kansans reflect the true caliber of America and the vital essence of our mission, a mission embodied by a short note received by Lieutenant Colonel Don Fowler in the Saudi Arabian control center. And the note came from a Kuwaiti refugee who didn't speak English well, but whose words had a simple eloquence: a capital "I" and then a small heart and the letters "USA." And the letters "USA" aren't merely part of the alphabet. They stand for something called freedom and justice—qualities that Kansans have upheld for decades. And they express the belief that America could not be the land of the free if it were not the home of the brave—a belief that Kansans are courageously defending right now on the sands and the waters offshore of Saudi Arabia.

For more than half a century, generations have marveled at a movie—wonderful movie—set here in Kansas. And ask anyone from Warsaw to Wichita; they know what Dorothy said: "There's no place like home." And there is nothing I want more than for our American servicemen and women to come home—and they will—and once we've completed a mission that does right by America and does right by the entire world. Abroad, let us raise the flag of peace and justice. And at home, let's show that Kansas does like Mike. On November 6th, ours is the chance to show what we think of the past 4 great years. And let's seize it— and by reelecting Mike Hayden Governor, help make the next 4 years the greatest in Kansas' history.

Thank you for this wonderful reception. And may God bless the United States of America and those fine men and women serving her today. Thank you all very much.

Note: The President spoke at 11:56 a.m. in Landon Arena at the Kansas ExpoCentre. In his remarks, he referred to Donald J. Hall, chairman of Hallmark Cards, Inc. Following his remarks, the President traveled to Tallahassee, FL.

Remarks at a Fundraising Barbecue for Representative Bill Grant in Tallahassee, Florida
September 6, 1990

Bill Grant, thank you, Congressman, thank you for that warm introduction. If I was about to be hung, I believe I'd listen to the man. [*Laughter*] Bobby, Coach Bowden, thank you, sir, for being with us. To Janet, Janet Grant, who greeted us at the airport here, my respects and glad to see you—what a campaigner she is. Jeanie Austin is with us, who is a former Florida chairman, now doing a great job as cochairman of the Republican National Committee. And our State chairman, Van Poole, is with us. Finance chairman, Alec Courtelis, an old friend of the Bushes. And then, of course, the man who's going to take Florida forward into the nineties, who's earned the right to a second term, a great friend, an early supporter of mine, a leader among the Nation's Governors, and I mean your own, Bob Martinez. We must see him elected. And, Mary Jane, the same goes for you.

And I want to salute Congressman Bill McCollum. Congressman Bill Young was to be here; I'm not sure he's made it yet. And, of course, an old friend of mine and a man that's served Florida with great distinction, former Congressman Bob Sykes, over here. Bob, it's great to see you here.

Well, it's a pleasure to be with you—Jim, Tom, so many others, too—but it's a pleasure to be with all of you here to share the summer's last cookout together—[*laughter*]—and, of course, to be standing at the side of north Florida's pride, Congressman Bill Grant.

Bill told me everyone in Tallahassee's been looking forward to this week, getting ready for the main event. Coming in today, I could see the excitement on people's faces. I'll bet there's not a person within 50 miles of here who doesn't know the Seminoles play this Saturday. Good luck! If you're for Bill Grant, okay, we're for you.

Well, look, I'm here really today to show my support for one of Florida State University's favorite sons. Eighteen months ago, Bill made a decision of principle. He joined the ranks of the Republican Party, and he

became a valuable member of my team up there on Capitol Hill. I remember the talk we had when I called and invited Bill and Janet down to the White House to make the announcement. Bill knew that because of some traditions in this part of the State, for a lot of reasons, that he'd be opening himself up to an all-out challenge in the upcoming election. But he made this switch with the complete confidence that he had the support of the people of this district because here in north Florida, when someone stands by his convictions and is motivated by principle, you stand by him. And that's why I believe he's going to win.

And there's never been a question, never been a question of party label. Bill Grant stands on the side of every hard-working family in northern Florida. He's been a key player in the United States Congress, backing a tough, no-nonsense strategy in the war on drugs. He knows that drugs and the violence that drugs breed aren't confined to the cities; they're not simply confined to urban America. Smalltown America faces the same threat. And every community must take steps to defend itself against the deadly scourge of drugs.

Bill Grant stands with me in his unshakable commitment to our environment. He can take great pride in being named Forest Conservationist of the Year by the Florida Wildlife Federation—no small honor. Through Bill's efforts, Florida has added 25,000 prime acres of black bear country to the Osceola National Forest.

And he's been a leader in the crusade to restore fiscal restraint in Congress. Today, I want to just mention a few words about the key challenge in this crusade. I'm talking about the budget talks up there. You know how I feel about raising taxes: I'd rather eat broccoli for breakfast. [*Laughter*]

But back in June when the budget talks were at an impasse, I decided that more important than anything is the future of these kids, kids that are here today. We cannot continue to mortgage the future of the young people by keeping these deficits. And so, I put it out on the table—all of it—and said, let's talk in order to fix this budget mess once and for all. I did it as an act of good faith, and I hope I've kept the faith; I've tried hard. And I took a little heat, through 5 long months of these budget talks.

But now time's running out. October 1st begins the new fiscal year; there's still no agreement. Congress is back now. When I leave here I'll go tomorrow to bipartisan budget talks that resume tomorrow. I want a budget agreement. I think it is in the interest of every family here that we get a budget agreement. The country needs it. And I'll approach these talks, I pledge to you, in good faith—work with the leadership to get a sound deficit-cutting agreement. In my view, it's no longer time—Republican or Democrat, liberal or conservative, the time for action is now, and we've got to succeed. And, thank God, we have people like Bill Grant in the Congress that understand this. I believe one of the reasons I'm here is that Bill has been one of the tough people holding the line on spending—cost-cutters, you might say—a real bulldog in the battle against government waste. I pledge to you and to every American taxpayer that I will not accept a budget agreement that isn't fiscally sound and fundamentally fair.

These are challenging times here at home and, of course, as Bill mentioned, abroad. And so, let me just speak for a moment about the situation in the Persian Gulf. So many people—we had a small reception here and—coming up and saying, "Well, I've got a son in Saudi Arabia," or "My kid is ready to go," or something of this nature. No President, no President is quick to order American troops abroad. But there are times when this nation, when any nation that values its own independence, must confront aggression. What's at stake is a matter of vital interest. Beyond the very real threat of our economic independence—and that is at stake—there is a larger issue, there's a more fundamental issue. There's an issue of principle that the people of northern Florida will understand, an issue with lasting implications for peace and security.

Just as we suffer here at home when lawbreakers walk our streets and plague our communities, the world suffers when outlaws assault the international order. Every use of force unchecked is an invitation to further aggression. Every act of aggression unpunished strikes a blow against the rule of law and strengthens the forces of chaos and lawlessness that, ultimately, if unchecked, threaten us all. Nothing strikes with greater force at the very heart of the international order than the act of naked aggression perpetrated by [President] Saddam Hussein of Iraq.

I'm confident our response is the correct one. I believe that these economic sanctions, enforced by almost the entire world, are beginning to bite. The squeeze is on, and Saddam Hussein is up against a united front—forces from 25 nations stand side by side in the Gulf region—and a strong mandate—5 resolutions overwhelmingly supported by the United Nations Security Council. Strong international support for what your sons and daughters are doing halfway around the world. It is vital that that support remain. So, tomorrow I depart for Helsinki, Finland, where I've asked President Gorbachev to meet me to talk about a wide array of issues including, of course, the situation in the Gulf and the world's response—its overwhelming response—to Iraq aggression. Never before have we seen the kind of cooperation between nations, proof that the world community will not stand aside and watch one nation swallow up another. The world is united against this aggression. And I am glad the Soviet Union is on our side on this one.

Let me be very clear: We seek a peaceful solution to this crisis. And let me be clear on another point: There can be no compromise when it comes to the sovereignty for Kuwait and the removal of all Iraqi forces. And that removal must be complete, it must be immediate, and it must be unconditional.

And this crisis has taught us that there is no substitute for American resolve, American strength in the service of the rule of law. And there is no substitute for the support of the American people. Under our system, you're the ones with the power. You've got it in your hands. And I need your support, and I hope I have it as we continue to stand up against aggression in the Middle East. I am very grateful. And I thank Congressman Bill Grant and the people here. I am confident that with your support and the continued, concerted action of the world community, justice will prevail over the forces of aggression.

And one more thing. You know, I think we Americans should make something very clear. Our argument is not with the people of Iraq. Rather, it is with Iraq's dictator, who uses innocent travelers as shields; who now, in direct contravention of international law, holds hostage civilians from many countries, using them as shields—a vital violation of international law, no matter how you look at it. But he must know that our policy and the policies of the many countries that stand with us will not be altered by this brazen blackmail. I will not change the policy of the United States Government in standing up against aggression in order to submit to this international blackmail.

So, let me close with a few words of appreciation for the young people in our armed services from the cities and towns of northern Florida—Bill and the Governor telling me in the short time we've had to visit of the patriotism and the support of the people here, many of them on duty right now, half a world away: servicemen like Ensign Les Pulley and his brother, Charles, a marine corporal who grew up in Tallahassee. Charles is a veteran of Operation Just Cause in Panama, and Les now shipped out for the Middle East. Or Sergeant Roy Land of the 82d Airborne, who went to school right here at Godby High, served—[*applause*]—some of his fellow students over here—served 2 years ago as a NATO peacekeeper out in the Sinai Desert, and serves today with our proud peacekeepers in the sand and the heat of Saudi Arabia.

As Commander in Chief of the Armed Forces, let me tell you: With men like these, with all the brave young men and women of our Armed Forces, rests America's spirit of pride and sense of purpose.

Every single member of the Joint Chiefs of Staff has told me—from the Chairman, General Colin Powell, right through the Services—that never in their lives have they seen finer young men and women in the service of the country than they have today. And never have they seen more people properly motivated in operation than they're seeing right now in this operation halfway around the world. It is a tribute to the sons and daughters of northern Florida and to the rest of the United States.

And as I said a moment ago, these are challenging times when we draw on the very best America has to offer. We are a country, one nation under God. And I like what Bill said about the faith of the people in northern Florida, always respectful of the denomination of another. But one nation under God. And I'm here for Bill Grant because Florida and the Nation needs public servants like him that understand that point and need public servants that are motivated by principle.

It is not easy. It is not easy to leave a party, but he did it based on principle. And he's brought with him many, many people—many who are here today—that say, "I'm a Democrat," and that's fine. But I want to ask you to vote for Bill Grant because we need public servants of principle in Washington, DC.

It's been a wonderful sendoff for me, coming here to northern Florida before heading for Helsinki and meeting the President of the Soviet Union. It will be a little cooler in Helsinki, I expect—[*laughter*]—but I hope that the spirit over there is about half as warm as this, and the United States will do just fine, thank you.

Thank you all, and God bless you.

Note: The President spoke at 6:14 p.m. at Tom Brown Park. In his remarks, he referred to Bobby Bowden, coach of the Florida State University football team, the Seminoles; Janet Grant, wife of Representative Grant; Mary Jane Martinez, wife of Governor Martinez; Jim Smith, secretary of state of Florida; and Tom Gallagher, secretary of the treasury and insurance commissioner of Florida.

Memorandum on Trade With Czechoslovakia
September 6, 1990

Memorandum for the Secretary of State

Subject: Determination under section 405(a) of the Trade Act of 1974, as amended—the Czech and Slovak Federal Republic

Pursuant to the authority vested in me under the Trade Act of 1974 (P.L. 93–618, January 3, 1975; 88 Stat. 1978), as amended (the "Trade Act"), I determine, pursuant to section 405(a) of the Trade Act, that the "Agreement on Trade Relations Between the Government of the United States of America and the Government of the Czechoslovakia Federative Republic" will promote the purposes of the Trade Act and is in the national interest.

You are authorized and directed to transmit copies of this determination to appropriate members of Congress and to publish it in the *Federal Register.*

GEORGE BUSH

[Filed with the Office of the Federal Register, 3:29 p.m., September 24, 1990]

Letter to Congressional Leaders on Trade With Czechoslovakia
September 6, 1990

Dear Mr. Speaker: (Dear Mr. President:)

In accordance with section 407 of the Trade Act of 1974 (P.L. 93–618, January 3, 1975; 88 Stat. 1978), as amended (the "Trade Act"), I am transmitting a copy of a proclamation that extends nondiscriminatory treatment to the products of the Czech and Slovak Federal Republic. I also enclose the text of the "Agreement on Trade Relations Between the Government of the United States of America and the Government of the Czechoslovak Federative Republic," including exchanges of letters that form an integral part of the Agreement, which was signed on April 12, 1990, and which is included as an annex to the proclamation.

The Agreement will provide a nondiscriminatory framework for our bilateral trade relations, and thus strengthen both economic and political relations between the United States and the Czech and Slovak Federal Republic. Conclusion of this Agreement is an important step we can take to provide greater economic benefits to both countries from this relationship. It will also give further impetus to the progress we have made in our overall relationship since the general improvement in our diplomatic relations last year.

I believe that the Agreement is consistent with both the letter and the spirit of the Trade Act. It provides for mutual extension of nondiscriminatory tariff treatment, while seeking to ensure overall reciprocity of economic benefits. It includes safeguard arrangements to ensure that our trade with the Czech and Slovak Federal Republic will grow without causing disruption to the U.S. market and consequent injury to domestic firms or loss of jobs for American workers.

The Agreement also confirms and expands for American businesses certain basic rights in conducting commercial transactions both within the Czech and Slovak Federal Republic and with Czechoslovak nationals and business entities. Other provisions include those dealing with settlement of commercial disputes, financial transactions, and government commercial offices. Through this Agreement, Czechoslovakia also undertakes obligations to modernize and upgrade very substantially its protection of all forms of intellectual property rights. Once fully implemented, the new Czechoslovak intellectual property regime will be on a par with that of our principal industrialized trading partners.

On February 20, 1990, I waived application of subsections (a) and (b) of section 402 of the Trade Act to the Czech and Slovak Federal Republic. On June 3, 1990, I determined that continuation of this waiver will substantially promote the objectives of section 402 and, pursuant to section 402(d)(5) of the Trade Act, submitted a report to the Congress outlining the reasons for my determination.

I urge that the Congress act as soon as possible to approve the "Agreement on Trade Relations Between the Government of the United States of America and the Government of the Czechoslovak Federative Republic."

Sincerely,

GEORGE BUSH

Note: Identical letters were sent to Thomas S. Foley, Speaker of the House of Representatives, and Dan Quayle, President of the Senate.

Remarks and an Exchange With Reporters on the Federal Budget Negotiations
September 7, 1990

The President. I just wanted to say a quick word on the budget. We're going out now with Dick Darman and with Scowcroft. We're going to try to insist that—working with the leaders of Congress on both sides of the aisle to get these budget talks moving. I'm pleased with what Dick Darman told me about the cooperative attitude that exists up there now. I think there's a new opportunity to do what this country desperately needs, and that is to have a budget agreement that will get these deficits under control.

And I am very hopeful that this spirit of cooperation that I'm told by Dick exists across both sides of the aisle will be the catalyst in getting a budget agreement which, in my view, is long overdue and is absolutely essential in terms of the well-being of our economy. So, that's what this trip is about. Then we'll head on back.

Q. Why are you taking Scowcroft? Does that mean the Gulf is going to have a part of this——

The President. Well, it means that the defense component and the domestic component are together as far as the administration goes. That's why Brent's going out. I've got to run.

Note: The President spoke at 10 a.m. on the South Lawn at the White House. In his remarks, he referred to Richard G. Darman, Director of the Office of Management and Budget, and Brent Scowcroft, Assistant to the President for National Security Affairs.

Exchange With Reporters Prior to a Meeting With Federal Budget Negotiators
September 7, 1990

Q. Are we going to get an agreement here, Mr. President?

The President. Let's walk over and talk about that for 1 minute. I just want to say at the outset here that I'm very pleased to be out here at the kickoff of these very important budget meetings. Dick Darman has filled me in on preliminary talks that have started since the recess ended. I think there is a new spirit of optimism that we can get an agreement. It's going to take compromise. But I want to thank the leaders on both sides of the aisle for what I understand is a good mood, now, towards getting final agreement. If big differences remain, I will tell them that I remain committed to a budget agreement. We haven't changed our focus or objectives as to the size of that agreement, and I will reiterate there that nothing has transpired anywhere that makes me less interested in getting a budget agreement that gets this deficit under control once and for all.

So, I won't take any questions here, but I'm now going in to tell the leaders essentially what I've said here, go into a little more detail on it. And then I look forward to meeting with them when we come back from our important visit with Mr. Gorba-chev [President of the Soviet Union] in Helsinki. But that's about where we are. Our people are, I'd say, somewhat optimistic that this can be hammered out in a very short period of time. And then again, the Congressmen have committed to staying with this, and I think that's good. So, let's see what we can do. But it is still vitally important to our country that this deficit get under control once and for all.

Q. Fifty billion carved in stone?

The President. Yes.

Note: The President spoke at 10:26 a.m. on the tarmac at Andrews Air Force Base.

Statement by Press Secretary Fitzwater on the Presidential Mission to the Soviet Union
September 7, 1990

The President today announced a Presidential mission to the Soviet Union to demonstrate his commitment to expanding U.S.-Soviet trade and economic cooperation. Secretary of State James A. Baker III and Secretary of Commerce Robert A. Mosbacher will lead a group of 15 U.S. business executives to Moscow and Leningrad September 10–14 for meetings with senior Soviet officials. The mission is part of the administration's continuing efforts to expand trade and investment and strengthen U.S.-Soviet economic relations. The mission's efforts will focus particularly on energy, housing, transportation, food processing and distribution. The mission members will report their findings to the President on their return.

Mission participants will meet with the President in Helsinki on September 9 after the conclusion of his meeting with President Gorbachev. In the U.S.S.R., mission members will meet with a wide variety of Soviet officials, including President Gorbachev; Prime Minister Ryzhkov; Russian Republic President Yeltsin and other republic leaders; the mayor of Moscow, Gavril Popov; and the mayor of Leningrad, Anatoly Sobchak. The mission will provide an opportunity for the business executives to ex-change views freely with the Soviets on how trade and investment can work to further Soviet economic reforms. The business executives will also discuss a number of projects with their appropriate counterparts in the Soviet industrial ministries to explore possible trade and investment opportunities.

Following up on proposals made by President Bush at Malta, Secretaries Baker and Mosbacher will announce several new and expanded economic cooperation programs. These programs are designed to help the Soviets make the transition to a market economy.

The private-sector members of the delegation are:

Dwayne O. Andreas, chairman and chief executive officer, Archer-Daniels-Midland Company, Decatur, IL.

Lodwrick M. Cook, chairman and chief executive officer, Atlantic Richfield Company, Los Angeles, CA.

Kenneth T. Derr, chairman and chief executive officer, Chevron Corp., San Francisco, CA.

John J. Murphy, chairman, president and chief executive officer, Dresser Industries, Inc., Dallas, TX.

James B. Hayes, publisher, Fortune magazine, New York, NY.

James D. Jameson, chairman, Glenair International, Del Mar, CA.

H. Leighton Steward, chairman, president, and chief executive officer, The Louisiana Land and Exploration Co., New Orleans, LA.

Donald B. Marron, chairman and chief executive officer, Paine Webber Group, Inc., New York, NY.

Donald M. Kendall, chairman of the executive committee, Pepsico, Inc., Purchase, NY.

Chesley Pruet, president, Pruet Oil Co., El Dorado, AR.

Leonard Sylk, chairman and chief executive officer, Shelter Systems Group, Hainesport, NJ.

Alex J. Mandl, chairman and chief executive officer, Sea-Land Service, Inc., Edison, NJ.

James W. Kinnear, president and chief executive officer, Texaco, Inc., White Plains, NY.

Mark C. Hungerford, chairman and chief executive officer, Transcisco Industries, Inc., San Francisco, CA.

William T. Esrey, chairman, United Telecommunications, Inc., Westwood, KS.

Statement by Press Secretary Fitzwater on Emergency Assistance for Persian Gulf Refugees
September 7, 1990

The plight of innocent people turned refugees by the current situation in Iraq and especially Kuwait, caused by the Iraqi invasion and occupation of Kuwait, demands immediate and effective international response. The President has, therefore, authorized the use of $10 million from the Emergency and Migration Assistance Fund for emergency assistance to the tens of thousands of people fleeing Iraq and Kuwait who are in Jordan and Turkey. This authorization brings total U.S. assistance for this humanitarian purpose to $28 million.

The $10 million approved today by the President will go for food, water, and shelter and for transporting persons back to their countries of origin. Earlier U.S. help consisted of $13 million in food assistance and $5 million for tents, water, and other emergency items.

We are pleased to note that the other governments are also contributing to this urgently needed relief effort. In particular, Saudi Arabia, many countries of Europe, and Japan are providing generous levels of assistance. Secretaries Baker and Brady are urging potential donor governments to provide transportation and additional humanitarian aid. We call upon governments, and especially those whose citizens are among the refugees, to make available transportation that would facilitate their rapid return home. We are also working closely with the United Nations and private voluntary organizations in the United States to ensure that the services and supplies required by the refugees are provided as quickly as is possible.

Note: Presidential Determination No. 90–39 of September 7, which authorized the emergency assistance, was printed in the "Federal Register" of December 14.

Remarks at the Arrival Ceremony in Helsinki, Finland
September 8, 1990

President Koivisto, Mrs. Koivisto, and members of the Finnish Government: The city of Helsinki has often been a meeting place for nations seeking to advance the cause of peace. And my thanks to the people of Finland first for hosting this meeting and for setting an example for all the world in your resolute commitment to liberty and independence.

When President Gorbachev and I met in Washington, we discussed the possibility of meetings such as the ones we'll hold here tomorrow. We agreed that the United States and the Soviet Union had reached a stage in our relations where meetings should occur more frequently—less fanfare, working meetings, held as circumstances might dictate. And our aim was that these meetings be unstructured and informal, with an open agenda and a maximum opportunity to exchange views on issues of mutual importance.

Well, in keeping with that aim, here in Helsinki President Gorbachev and I will focus on a full range of issues. We seek continued movement towards a new Europe, whole and free. We seek to advance the pace of arms control, strategic and conventional. And I want to hear about the progress of the Soviet reform and explore other issues of interest to our two countries. And, of course, I expect that we will devote a large part of our time together to the situation in the Persian Gulf.

I've said many times this past year that we have entered a new era in world affairs. This meeting comes at a critical time, at a moment when the actions we take can shape this new world for years to come. In the past, many regional conflicts have played themselves out against the background of the larger conflict of the cold war. Renegade regimes and unpredictable rulers resorted to force, counting on superpower stalemate to frustrate a united response. International law and international organizations were often paralyzed, powerless to prevent conflict or restore the peace. But the international response to Iraq's invasion proves how much has changed. Here in Helsinki, President Gorbachev and I meet hopefully to strengthen our common approach to this unjustifiable act of aggression.

Much is at stake, and there is much the world stands to gain if we succeed. If the nations of the world, acting together, continue, as they have been, to isolate Iraq and deny Saddam the fruits of aggression, we will set in place the cornerstone of an international order more peaceful, stable, and secure than any that we have known.

To our Finnish hosts, let me simply say that I intend to take full advantage of this very brief but welcome opportunity to renew America's warm friendship with Finland. I meet today with President Koivisto, whose counsel I have valued over the years. Barbara and I often talk about our visit here in the early eighties—1983. And it was then that I first met your President, President Koivisto. We've stayed in very close touch since then. And I look forward to hearing his views on the many issues that I've just mentioned and others as well.

Finland has long been a voice of peace and stability between nations in the councils of the CSCE, as a member of the United Nations peacekeeping forces. And today at this time of challenge, Finland once again stands with the forces of peace. I thank the Government of Finland for its staunch support as a member of the United Nations Security Council, upholding international law in face of Iraq's unwarranted aggression.

Together with the nations of the world, I am confident that we can reverse the dangerous course of events brought on by the actions of Saddam Hussein and restore peace, stability, and respect for the rule of law.

Thank you, Mr. President. And may God bless the people of Finland. Thank you. In his remarks, he referred to President Saddam Hussein of Iraq.

Note: The President spoke at 11:24 a.m. on the tarmac at Helsinki-Vantas Airport. In his remarks, he referred to President Saddam Hussein of Iraq.

Remarks to Members of the American Embassy Community in Helsinki, Finland
September 8, 1990

Well, I'm delighted to be here. And what I really want to do is to shake hands and say hello, cut these ropes down if we can, and just have a quick visit before we go off to accept more of this fabulous Finnish hospitality staying at the Guest House.

I want to pay my respects to the Finnish business people that are here and their families, and thank them very much for adding to what's been a wonderful welcome so far. Of course, I'm very proud of our Ambassador. He and Virginia have been our friends for a long time. And I knew they would do a superb job in Finland, and sure enough, they have. And I'm delighted, and I thank them for welcoming this invasion squad from the United States.

And to your new DCM, and to your admin officer, and to everybody else who has anything in the world with the planning on this visit, we make a solemn promise. And that promise is that we will leave on time—[*laughter*]—and you won't have to put up with us for long.

But, you see, I have a little inkling of what this Embassy has gone through because—as I said, I think, when I was here 5 years ago—I was on the receiving end of a visit like this when Barbara and I had the mission in China. And we survived one visit from President Ford and two visits from Henry Kissinger. [*Laughter*] So, if you think you have it rough, you ought to have been where we were. [*Laughter*]

But in all seriousness, I know the logistics and the communications and all of these things are very complex, and I am grateful to you, the Ambassador telling me that you all have pitched in. And it's gone, from our standpoint anyway, very well.

I must say, I don't know how an American feels living here and working in the Embassy exactly, but if it's anything like the feeling Barbara and I got when we came in in separate cars and saw all those people and the warm welcome for the United States, why, it really is very touching and very moving. And we are very grateful.

We're in tough times. Finland is an important player in all of this international action. As a member of the Security Council, the Finns have been in a very out-front position. And I am very pleased that we are side by side with Finland as we try to stand up against aggression down in the Persian Gulf.

I know that we have several Finnish employees or workers or coworkers in our Embassy. And to you I would simply say: You enrich our staff by your knowledge of and love of your own country, and it's good. You know, I think some countries don't permit foreign nationals in their embassies, and they miss something. We get a lot from that all around the world. And I know it's true here just as it is in so many other embassies. So, to those from Finland who have worked here—and I talked to some of them inside—those out here I want to simply say: We appreciate what you do working with us. We respect your country, and we think we're enriched by your being a part of all of this.

I'll simply say one last word, and that is that this meeting tomorrow with Mr. Gorbachev is indeed an important meeting. We are very fortunate to be trying to coordinate and, in a sense, lead in an international effort here to stop aggression in the Persian Gulf—fortunate to have the Soviet Union very much in accord with what we're trying to do and what Finland is trying to do. And if you wanted to think of a complicated situation, shift the clock back several years and think about how difficult it would be to work this equation now, get the international support that has been gotten, but try to do it without the Soviet Union being a part of it.

So, tomorrow we'll be speaking not to some adversary but to a leader of a country with whom I think we're going to have increasingly productive relations. And clearly, I hope that we'll come out of this meeting tomorrow not with every difference ironed out but with the common purpose so that

Finland and the United States and the Soviet Union will all be seen by others around the world to be in accord in our determination to stop this ugly aggression, this brutal treatment of civilians that's being put into effect by Saddam Hussein of Iraq.

We've got a major national challenge, but I'm very proud of the way countries around the world have come together. And I view it as a very important part of my responsibility to see that we keep this cohesion and that the aggression against Iraq [Kuwait] be rectified and that the rightful rulers of Kuwait be restored to their place. And I can tell you the United States is determined.

And for those of you who might have relatives—brothers, cousins, sisters, whatever it might be—in Saudi Arabia, let me simply tell you what the Joint Chiefs have told me, and what General Colin Powell, our distinguished Chief Chairman has said, and that is that never in the history of the United States—and perhaps our military attachés would agree—have we had finer men and women serving in the Armed Forces.

So, when you take a large force like this, send it on a mission of peace halfway around the world, and see the way it all came together, it is phenomenal what our military has done. And I am grateful to them every single day. And it's not just the United States, it's not just the President

that's grateful, it's many, many other countries that don't have the forces and don't have the ability to stand up who are counting on us and counting on those kids that are over in Saudi Arabia.

So, I think we—wherever we are, if it's Helsinki or Washington, DC—I think we can be grateful to these young men and women who are serving over there—135-degree heat and all of that, 120 or whatever, and downing gallons of water—but they're doing a first-class job. And I just want you to know how proud I am, as Commander in Chief of the Armed Forces, of these young people. What a marvelous signal it sent around the world.

So, with no further ado except, once again, to say thank you to you, I'd love to come out there, and maybe we can get some pictures with the families. And Barbara—Bar is suggesting we get the kids, all children, all you guys under—let's see, how old are you? Twelve and under, all come here, and we're going to get a family picture with all the children. And then we'll get a chance to visit with everybody.

Note: President Bush spoke at 1:57 p.m. in front of the U.S. Ambassador's residence. In his remarks, he referred to U.S. Ambassador John G. Weinmann and his wife, Virginia; Max Robinson and William J. Burke, deputy chief of mission and administrative officer at the Embassy; and President Saddam Hussein of Iraq.

Soviet Union-United States Joint Statement on the Persian Gulf Crisis
September 9, 1990

With regard to Iraq's invasion and continued military occupation of Kuwait, President Bush and President Gorbachev issue the following joint statement:

We are united in the belief that Iraq's aggression must not be tolerated. No peaceful international order is possible if larger states can devour their smaller neighbors.

We reaffirm the joint statement of our Foreign Ministers of August 3, 1990 and our

support for United Nations Security Council Resolutions 660, 661, 662, 664 and 665. Today, we once again call upon the Government of Iraq to withdraw unconditionally from Kuwait, to allow the restoration of Kuwait's legitimate government, and to free all hostages now held in Iraq and Kuwait.

Nothing short of the complete implementation of the United Nations Security Council Resolutions is acceptable.

Nothing short of a return to the pre-August 2 status of Kuwait can end Iraq's isolation.

We call upon the entire world community to adhere to the sanctions mandated by the United Nations, and we pledge to work, individually and in concert, to ensure full compliance with the sanctions. At the same time, the United States and the Soviet Union recognize that UN Security Council Resolution 661 permits, in humanitarian circumstances, the importation into Iraq and Kuwait of food. The Sanctions Committee will make recommendations to the Security Council on what would constitute humanitarian circumstances. The United States and the Soviet Union further agree that any such imports must be strictly monitored by the appropriate international agencies to ensure that food reaches only those for whom it is intended, with special priority being given to meeting the needs of children.

Our preference is to resolve the crisis peacefully, and we will be united against Iraq's aggression as long as the crisis exists. However, we are determined to see this aggression end, and if the current steps fail to end it, we are prepared to consider additional ones consistent with the UN Charter. We must demonstrate beyond any doubt that aggression cannot and will not pay.

As soon as the objectives mandated by the UN Security Council resolutions mentioned above have been achieved, and we have demonstrated that aggression does not pay, the Presidents direct their Foreign Ministers to work with countries in the region and outside it to develop regional security structures and measures to promote peace and stability. It is essential to work actively to resolve all remaining conflicts in the Middle East and Persian Gulf. Both sides will continue to consult each other and initiate measures to pursue these broader objectives at the proper time.

Note: The joint statement was made available by the Office of the Press Secretary but was not issued as a White House press release.

Joint News Conference of President Bush and Soviet President Mikhail Gorbachev in Helsinki, Finland
September 9, 1990

President Bush. I've been advised that I'm to take the first question. And if so, I would identify Helen Thomas, of the UP [United Press International].

Persian Gulf Crisis

Q. I'd like to ask both Presidents whether we are going to have a war in the Persian Gulf. And I'd like to follow up.

President Bush. Well, with your permission, Mr. President, I hope that we can achieve a peaceful solution, and the way to do that is to have Iraq comply with the United Nations resolutions. And I think the part of our joint statement, two short lines, said it most clearly: Nothing short of the complete implementation of the United Nations Security Council resolutions is acceptable. As soon as Saddam Hussein realizes that, then there certainly will be a peaceful resolution to this question.

Q. How about President Gorbachev— what do you think?

President Gorbachev. In replying to your question I should like to say that the whole of our 7 hours of meeting today were devoted to the quest for a political resolution of that conflict. And I believe that we're on the right road.

Q. Mr. President, if I may follow up with you, President Bush. You are indicating that hostilities could break out if this is not resolved peacefully.

President Bush. The question is what?

Q. I said, you are indicating that there could be hostilities.

President Bush. No, the United States is determined to see these resolutions enforced, and I'd like to feel that they will be enforced and that that will result in a peaceful resolution.

Middle East Peace Efforts

Q. Do you think, Mr. President, that the conflict of the Gulf gives the opportunity to solve the Palestinian problem through an international peace conference for the Middle East? And my second question is, was this problem discussed today with Mr. Gorbachev?

President Bush. Well, let me say that I see the implementation of the United Nations resolutions separate and apart for the need to solve the other question. That question has been on the agenda of many countries for many years, and it is very important that that question be resolved. The Secretary of State said the other day, and I strongly support that, that under certain circumstances the consideration of a conference of that nature would be acceptable. Indeed, it's been a part of our policy from time to time. But the thing that I feel strongly about is that these issues are not linked. And any effort to link them is an effort to dilute the resolutions of the United Nations.

Persian Gulf Crisis

Q. This question to President Bush from Soviet radio and television. How long will the United States troops be present in the Persian Gulf area?

President Bush. They will be present in the area until we are satisfied that the security needs of the area have been met and that these resolutions have been complied with. And the sooner they are out of there, as far as I'm concerned, the better. I made very clear to President Gorbachev, as I think he will confirm, that we have no intention keeping them a day longer than is required. So, I'd leave it right there.

President Gorbachev. I'd like to add something and to confirm what the President of the United States has just said to me in our conversation—that the United States of America does not intend to leave their forces in the zone. And in connection with the change or the normalization of the situation, the United States administration and, personally, the President will do everything

possible to ensure that the forces are withdrawn from the region, from the zone. And that is a very important statement.

Economic Assistance for the Soviet Union and Soviet Military Advisers in Iraq

Q. I have a question for both Presidents. The unity that you're expressing doesn't ignore the fact that there is still some irritants between the two countries. President Bush, are you more sympathetic to suggestions of Western economic aid to the Soviet Union? And President Gorbachev, would you be willing to withdraw the Soviet military advisers from Iraq?

President Bush. For my part, I am very much interested in assisting to be sure that *perestroika* is successful. We, indeed, have a mission of high-level businessmen on their way to the Soviet Union—right now they happen to be in Helsinki. This is but one manifestation of the fact that we are trying to encourage economic cooperation in as many ways as possible. And we had a good, long discussion in our expanded meeting this afternoon about that. And I am—given the common stand that the Soviet Union and the United States have taken at the United Nations, it seems to me that we should be as forthcoming as we possibly can in terms of economics, and I plan to do that. There are certain constraints, as you say. There are certain nuances of difference; there are certain differences—real differences.

But on the other hand, I have said before—and I'll repeat it here in front of all these journalists from all around the world—we, of course, want *perestroika* to succeed. It is an internal matter of the Soviet Union. But I think this remarkable cooperation that has been demonstrated by the Soviet Union at the United Nations gets me inclined to recommend as close cooperation in the economic field as possible. And I will be saying this to the Congress when I get back. We still have problems. Look, we've got some big problems ourselves in our economy, and we are not in the position, operating at the enormous deficits, to write out large checks. Having said that, there are many ways that we can endeavor to be of assistance to the emerging economy in the Soviet Union.

President Gorbachev. There was a question also addressed to me. I would like, nevertheless, on the question which did appear also to be addressed to me—the Western assistance to the Soviet—I would like to continue. The conversation with President Bush is continuing on the Western assistance to the Soviet Union. I see that there is an attempt being made to link, to establish a link between this and disagreements or the lack of disagreements. In response to that, I would say the following:

We began our conversation today together by reviewing the situation and realizing that the whole of world society and our two great states are undergoing a trial. This is a test of the durability of the new approach to resolving world problems. And as we enter upon a new peaceful period and as we emerge from the cold war, we see that no less efforts are necessary in order to find ways and means in this period of peace to meet the new situation and to tackle all problems that may arise. I think if it hadn't been for Malta it would have been very difficult for us to act in the very difficult situation which arose in Eastern Europe—in Europe and in the situation connected with the unification of Germany.

I think that if, following that, there hadn't been Washington and Camp David and the other meetings on this level with other partners in international relations, we would now be in a difficult situation facing the crisis in the Persian Gulf. And the fact that today we have taken a common approach to such difficult problems—problems which may well have tragic consequences for the whole world, not just for the peoples of that region—demonstrates that we still are moving forward in the right direction and that we are capable of resolving the most difficult and the most acute problems and to find appropriate responses to the challenges of our time. And the greater part of our conversation together was devoted to this. I believe that this is the most important point to bear in mind. Differences, nuances in the differences of view, arguments, these can be—these are natural. It's natural those should arise. But what we have seen today is that we have confirmed the most important progress of recent time.

Now I should like to say something about the Iraqi question—but, in fact, I haven't quite finished on the first subject. I wouldn't want President Bush's reply to give rise to the opinion that the Soviet Union is going to align a certain sum with a certain behavior. We are acting in a difficult situation. We are finding a solution. We shall find a solution which will be satisfactory and, above all, which will remove the danger of an explosion. And this is becoming a normal element of the new kind of cooperation—in trade, in technology, in human exchange. All of these elements characterize the new peaceful period upon which we are just now embarked, which we have to get used to.

It would be very oversimplified and very superficial to judge that the Soviet Union could be bought for dollars because, although we do look forward to cooperation in this very serious time of far-reaching changes in our economy—and that's normal—let's remember the reforms of recent years in a number of states. They always, in addition to the principal efforts made by the peoples concerned themselves, they always involved also the participation of the world community in one form or another. So if anybody wants to try to impose a different view, that's unacceptable to us. It's unacceptable to the United States, it's unacceptable to the Soviet Union, and it would be unacceptable to any other state.

Now, to move on the second part of your question concerning our experts in Iraq. They are not so much advisers as specialists or experts who are working under contract. And their number is being reduced. Whereas at the beginning of the conflict I think there was still 196 of them, there are now some 150 of them. And the Iraqi leadership looks upon the matter thus: that if they haven't completed their work, their normal work under contract, even though it may be a matter of weapons, then they are nevertheless leaving Iraq and the process is going forward. So, I don't really think there's a problem.

Persian Gulf Crisis

Q. A question to both. Did you discuss

any possible military options for curbing Iraqi aggression? And what would be the conditions, and what would be the point where you would consider that the political options were exhausted and it was time to go to the Security Council and talk about—through the Security Council—demanding an Iraqi withdrawal from Kuwait?

President Bush. The answer to your question is, no, we did not discuss military options. And your question is too hypothetical. And I would like to see this matter peacefully resolved.

President Gorbachev. I would like to support what was said by President Bush. And I stress once more that the whole of our time together was spent on talking about this conflict in a mutual search for a political solution. And I think we can look with optimism, in the final analysis, on the efforts being taken by the international community working together within the Security Council of the U.N.

Q. You were just saying that if Iraq doesn't withdraw its forces peacefully, then it will be necessary to take military steps. What kind of Soviet contribution will there be to those military steps? And what will happen then to the Soviet citizens who are in Iraq now? And what will the Arab factor be?

President Gorbachev. Firstly, I did not say that if Iraq does not withdraw peacefully we're going to have recourse to military methods. I did not state that. I do not state that. And moreover, in my view, that would draw us into consequences which we can't at this stage forecast. Therefore, our country and the United Nations as a whole has a whole range of possibilities of finding a political solution to this problem. Therefore, I would limit ourselves to that and, therefore, the second part of your question is irrelevant.

Q. If I could ask President Gorbachev, specifically: Iraq had been your ally. What directly have you done in contact with Saddam Hussein to reverse the situation there? And, President Bush, what specifically have you asked Mr. Gorbachev to do directly? Have you asked him to make a direct contact with Saddam Hussein?

President Gorbachev. I should say that from the start of the crisis we've been ac-

tively exchanging views and carrying forth dialog, not only within the Security Council, not only with the administration of the U.S.A. These types of contacts have great importance to us, but we are also holding active dialog with the leadership of China, of India, of all the other European states, especially those which are members of the Security Council. And in my view, it's this dialog which has helped us towards the Security Council resolution which was passed.

On top of that, we're also actively cooperating with the Arab States, the countries of the Arab world. And here our dialog is no less intensive than with our partners in the countries I previously mentioned, including dialog with President Hussein. And I can state that what we have announced publicly is also being said to President Hussein in our dialog with him. Which all means that the President and the leadership of Iraq are expected to show a reasonable approach, to stop and to understand what is implied by the position taken by the Security Council on this issue. This is the dialog which we have undertaken with him. And we are trying to make sure that our arguments are convincing. We discussed various options for ending the situation with him. And we are also attempting, as I already said, to make it quite clear to Saddam Hussein that if Iraq were to provoke military action then the result would be a tragedy first and foremost for the Iraqi people themselves, for the whole of the region, and for the whole of the world.

You know, this is, of course, a dialog in a very difficult situation; but we consider it's a very useful dialog. And we don't exclude the possibility of establishing new contacts, of having new meetings at various levels. And the type of communication which we have had up until now with the Iraqis gives us hope that those links we have with them can be used positively for the sake of all of us, for the sake of finding a peaceful solution to this problem and especially of preventing the situation turning into aggression in the situation.

President Bush. My answer would simply be that there is no need to ask President Gorbachev to contact Saddam Hussein. Clearly, from his answer you can see that

President Gorbachev answered the question about the contact with Saddam Hussein. And clearly, your question to me is if I asked him to contact Saddam Hussein? The answer is no.

The Soviet Union is in contact. He, himself, received the Foreign Minister, 'Aziz. But I would just simply sum it up by saying the best answer to Saddam Hussein—or the best contact is the contact that took place at the United Nations when there was worldwide condemnation of the aggression. And I happen to feel that this statement showing the Soviet Union and the United States in essential agreement here is another good statement for Saddam Hussein. And hopefully, he will see that he is not going to divide us and divide other countries and that he will do what he should have done sometime ago, and that is comply with the United Nations' sanctions. But I did not ask him to do that because they're way ahead of us on that. They are having contacts and trying to be helpful in that regard.

Arms Control Negotiations

Q. I have a question to Mr. Bush. Mr. President, what is your position on the question of signing a treaty limiting strategic offensive weapons? And when do you think that such a treaty will, in fact, be signed?

President Bush. We still remain committed to a strategic arms treaty. We vowed that we would encourage our negotiators to move forward more rapidly on both the strategic arms treaty and the conventional force agreement. And I'm still hopeful that by the end of the year we will have such an agreement.

President Gorbachev. I'd like to confirm what President Bush has just said: that we really have agreed to make fresh efforts to give further instructions because we see that there is a possibility successfully to complete the negotiating process in those two fora and to come up with positive results in the course of this year.

Middle East Peace Efforts

Q. My question is for President Bush. And I would also like to hear President Gorbachev's comment on that. President Bush mentioned that you fail to see the link between the Palestinian question and the present situation. I would like to know how come it is so important to implement U.N. resolutions in this particular instance when other standing ones have been frozen and overlooked and disregarded for so long? So I'd like to know how come this situation is so different from other ones. And I would also like to add that I personally feel that the Palestinian dilemma and question needs the attention of the superpowers more than ever. Thank you very much.

President Bush. I agree that it needs it, and we are very much interested in implementing Resolution 242 of the United Nations. We've been zealously trying to do that, as have many other powers for many years. But the fact that that resolution hasn't been fulfilled when it calls for withdrawal to secure and recognized boundaries—and it should be, and hopefully we can be catalytic in seeing that happen—does not mean that you sit idly by in the face of a naked aggression against Kuwait. And the United Nations has moved, and the United Nations resolutions should be implemented on their face without trying to tie it in to some other unresolved dispute. But I couldn't agree more that it is important. It is very important that that question eventually, and hopefully sooner than later, be resolved.

President Gorbachev. I think that everything that is taking place in the Middle East is a matter of concern to us—of equal concern. And even more than in the case of the Persian Gulf, we need to act more energetically in order to resolve the complex of problems in the Middle East and to come up with decisions and to devise a system to devise guarantees that would ensure the interests of all peoples and of the whole world community because it's a matter which is of vital concern to all of us.

And it seems to me that there is a link here because the failure to find a solution in the Middle East at large also has a bearing on the acuteness of the particular conflict we've been talking about here.

Persian Gulf Crisis

Q. A question for both Presidents, please. In your statement, you pledged to work individually and in concert to ensure full compliance with the U.N. sanctions against Iraq. May I inquire what, if any, specific and concrete steps you have agreed to take in furtherance of that?

President Bush. We didn't agree to specific and concrete steps. I think President Gorbachev in the contacts he's had with Saddam Hussein—I mean with the Iraqis—and if they continue, will be a step in that direction. Clearly, this message itself will be a step in the right direction. But we did not sit at this meeting and try to assign each other or ask each other to undertake specific measures in keeping with that particular paragraph.

President Gorbachev. I'd like to add to that that the emphasis here is on the significance of the political fact that we feel necessary to reflect in this statement and which testifies to our political will to act jointly, or in parallel, independently really, in search of these new steps toward a peaceful resolution of the problem.

I think that, therefore, the meeting and the document that we've just adopted is more important than our enumerating various steps that might have been taken here. That forms the basis for the further active quest for solutions.

Soviet-U.S. Relations

Q. I also have a question to the Presidents of both countries—Mr. President, Mr. Gorbachev, first of all. Since the last meeting, it seems to be that you've had a good mutual understanding. Have you succeeded in deepening that mutual understanding in the course of today's meeting? And how, in general—what bearing, in general, is that factor having on the results of your negotiations?

President Bush. I think clearly there has been a developing mutual understanding over the years. I like to feel, and I think President Gorbachev agrees, that our meeting in Malta had something to do with furthering that understanding. I'm convinced that our meeting in the United States, at Camp David particularly, furthered that understanding. I think the world sees clearly that if this had occurred 20 years ago, there wouldn't have been this cooperative feeling at the United Nations. And I think it's very

important.

So, I don't know how one quantifies mutual understanding, but I feel we're moving on the right track. Neither of us, when we talk, try to hide our differences. Neither of us try to indicate that we look at exactly every problem exactly the same way. But the very fact we can talk with that degree of frankness without rancor, I think, enhances mutual understanding. And then, when we see us on a question of this nature, standing shoulder to shoulder with many other countries at the United Nations, I think it is obvious manifestation of this developing mutual understanding.

It's a very broad philosophical question. But differences still remain. But the common ground, in my view at least, surges ahead of these differences. And we will continue to cooperate with President Gorbachev.

President Gorbachev. I don't know if I would be allowed to tell you a secret here. I haven't asked President Bush if he'll let me. But I must admit that I'm dying to take the risk and tell you. [*Laughter*] But it's too important to give you an answer to this particular question. But that last sentence does really give me the hope that we'll get by. In our talks, the President said, "You know, there was a long time when our view was that the Soviet Union had nothing to do in the Middle East—had no business being there." This was something that we had to talk through during this meeting here in Helsinki. And what was said here is that it's very important for us to cooperate in the Middle East, just as it is on other issues of world politics.

So, that is—in answer to your question, it is very important that at each meeting we move forward, we enrich our relationship, and I think I should say that we increase our trust. If trust is engendered between the leaders of two such nations during meetings of this kind—then I'm sure you'll agree with me—that that is for the good of all of us, whether we want it or not. History dictates that a lot is going to depend on whether the two countries can work together. That's not our ambition, it's just the way that history has gone. So, far from excluding such a possibility, we intend to cooperate with all sorts of other countries as well, more and more. That's how we see our role in the world developing.

And my last comment is also very important. It seems to me that the way the world is, the way the world is changing, in today's world no single country, however powerful, will be able to provide the leadership which individual countries formerly tried to provide, including some countries which are represented here. We can only succeed if we work together and solve our problems together. That is what is emerging from these negotiations, and that we consider the most important aspect.

Persian Gulf Crisis

Q. I'm going to speak French, if I may. Could I ask Mr. Gorbachev whether the Soviet Union is still Iraq's friend, as Minister Tariq Aziz declared in Moscow last week? Are you still the friend of Saddam Hussein? And another question also directed to Mr. Gorbachev—President Saddam Hussein stated yesterday that the Soviet Union would demonstrate that it is a great power by resisting George Bush's pressure and by supporting the Baghdad regime. Could you indicate to me, if you would, what your reply would be to Saddam Hussein?

President Gorbachev. I want to reply to you and so to repeat it also to Saddam Hussein—the same reply that I've given to previous questions—my position is unchanged. We see our role and our responsibility, and within the framework of that responsibility we shall act in cooperation with the other members of the Security Council. And, in this instance, I can once again say since we are sitting here, two Presidents together, I should interact and cooperate with the President of the United States.

I'd very much like to express the hope that President Saddam Hussein will display—I really hope that he will display sobriety, will look carefully at the whole situation and will respond to the appeals and the demands of the world community, and that he will take steps that are suitable to the situation, that are carefully weighed in their worldwide implications and in their implications for the Arab world, too. No one has any intention of trying to exclude Iraq from the community of nations, but what the present Iraqi leadership is doing is driving it into a dead end. And I hope that President Saddam Hussein will heed this appeal to him.

Q. As a neighboring country of the conflict—we're from Turkish press.

Q. I think I'm next. I'd like to ask Mr. Gorbachev if you have ruled out the possibility of a Soviet military participation in this effort in any sense, either as part of the naval blockade or as part of some future peacekeeping force in the region? And I would follow up with a question to Mr. Bush—to what degree that would be a disappointment to you if that's Mr. Gorbachev's position?

President Gorbachev. I don't see the point of doing that now. And we shall continue to act in cooperation within the Security Council and in strict compliance with all of its decisions.

President Bush. I'm not disappointed in that answer. [*Laughter*]

Q. I mean, you said you're determined to see this aggression end and current steps are being considered. What does this mean? What comes next?

President Bush. It's too hypothetical. We want to see the message get through to Saddam Hussein. We want to see him do what the United Nations calls on him to do. And that statement can be interpreted any way you want to interpret it, but it's out there. And I would simply not go into any hypothetical questions that would lead me beyond what that statement says.

President Gorbachev. Could I add a couple of words? Please, if you would excuse me, I'll add a couple of words just to what Mr. Bush has already said. You know, in my view, I have the impression that both the press and public opinion in some countries is in some ways saying that there's a lack of decision on somebody's part, that we're withdrawing in the face of those who are trampling on international law. I cannot agree with that view. In fact, it's a view which causes a certain amount of embarrassment to the leadership of nations which are acting through the Security Council in this respect.

What has been done up until now in answer to Iraqi aggression is very important because action has been taken not only within the framework of the Security Council, but there has been unanimous world opinion, a kind of solidarity which has never been expressed before in the history of the world. And we have prevented the aggression going any further. We have preserved the functioning of the structures which are of economic importance which would affect so many other countries as well.

And finally, the resolution has been taken on an embargo, which is a very stiff measure, in reaction to the aggression. In my view, this is a strategic way of tackling the question which has been tackled successfully at the first stages. And we are convinced that the next stage of a political solution, achieved politically, to put an end to this acute international crisis and make sure that a political sentiment should be possible—that in this situation, decisiveness, willpower, and responsibility, and political faith in the possibility of a political solution to this very difficult issue shows that the political leaders of the world are being responsible to their own nations and to the world. And we do not want to get caught up in arguments about prestige and so on.

Q. Concerning the humanitarian aid, does your joint statement mean in practice that you consider that food should be now allowed to Iraq?

President Gorbachev. The Presidents felt it necessary to reflect in our joint declaration that we see the need to uphold what was decided by the Security Council on this subject. And the Security Council was prepared to admit, for humanitarian purposes, the supply of medicines and of foodstuffs required first and foremost for children. We've actually stated this quite plainly in our statement. And so, we've taken a very clear-cut position on that. But we've also made it clear that this mistake is within the framework of certain international organizations and being monitored by them at all stages of the operations. So I think that this is being stated in the correct terms.

President Bush. I agree with President Gorbachev on that point and that the language is very good because it does express the concern that both countries feel in the event there actually are children and others

who are suffering because of lack of food. I hope that nobody around the world interprets this as our view that now there should be wholesale food shipments to Iraq. Because I can speak only here for the United States when I would call attention to the fact that we need some kind of international agencies to see that there is this humanitarian concern, as expressed, this exception in the United Nations embargo for humanitarian purposes—and not only is it required for this humanitarian circumstance but that the food gets where it is supposed to go. So, this should not be, from the U.S. standpoint, interpreted as a wholesale big hole in this embargo. It was not our intention, and I think the language is very clear on that point.

Q. A few things if you could clear up for us. First of all, you seem to disagree on the military option when you talk about further steps being taken to implement the U.S. sanctions. President Bush, you seem to be saying the military option is still out there. President Gorbachev seems to disagree. Do you disagree on that? Did you ask President Gorbachev to pull his experts out of Iraq? And did you ask him to send troops into the Gulf region?

President Bush. I did not ask him to send troops in. If the Soviets decided to do that at the invitation of the Saudis, that would be fine with us. But I did not ask him to do that. I believe with the 23 countries that are participating on the ground—23 countries that are participating on the ground and at sea—that the security of Saudi Arabia is close to safeguarded.

What were the other two points?

Q. Did you ask him to pull the experts out of Iraq? And do you disagree on the use of military force? You seem to say it's still an option. He seems to say it's not an option ever.

President Bush. We may have a difference on that. As I think I've answered over and over again at home, I'm not going to discuss what I will or won't do. And President Gorbachev made an eloquent appeal, to which I agree, that a peaceful solution is the best. So I've left it open. He can comment on the other.

Again, John [John Cochran, NBC News],

I'm sorry—the second point.

Q. The experts, pulling the experts out.

President Bush. Well, I think it would facilitate things. But on the other hand, he's given his answer here. And that is not a major irritant. You've said that—I think he said that he is reducing the numbers there. But I think I tried to make clear that this was a question that was widely being raised in the United States, and it would facilitate things if they were out of there in terms of total understanding. But I heard his answer, listened to it very, very carefully, and must say that I would let it stand at that. If I was just saying, would I like to see them all out of there, I think I'd say, absolutely. But I'd let him add to that.

President Gorbachev. In answer to all these questions which you gave us such a clear list of, I've already given answers. I really don't have anything to add to the answers I've already given.

Q. A question to the two Presidents, please. You mentioned something about the security arrangements. Is the Soviet Union going to participate in any kind of security arrangements, and what is the role of the region and the countries of that region of the Middle East?

President Gorbachev. To the first question, as we began, we intend to continue to cooperate closely and actively in the framework of the Security Council. And on the basis of the decisions that have been adopted we shall act accordingly. That's the first point.

Secondly, as concerns the role of the countries of the region, yes, I think that, generally speaking, I would stress the importance of the Arab factor not yet really having been brought to bear in efforts to help resolve this crisis situation. I don't want to offer you an analysis right now as to why that's the case, but nevertheless, I am convinced that there is an obvious activation of the quest on the part of Arab States to find the response to the urgent situation which faces us all here. We cooperate with all the Arab countries and I might say, not unusefully. The outlines of possible steps are beginning to emerge, but it is too soon to be specific. We are continuing our cooperation with Arab countries, and at a certain stage when the situation has changed

and when the tension has been reduced, then perhaps we might carry this further. But we shall continue in the Security Council, the United Nations Security Council, to guarantee security.

I have no doubt that we shall succeed in resolving the problem by political means.

President Bush. May I comment on that one, please? I am very glad that the Arab States—the Arab League, and in other ways—have stated their condemnation of Saddam Hussein. He is trying to make this a contest between the Arab world and the United States. And it is no such thing—if you will look at how the United Nations has overwhelmingly condemned him. So the Arab States have a very key role in this. Many Arab States have responded in the defense of Saudi Arabia—Syria, Morocco, Egypt, say nothing of the GCC countries. So, it is not Saddam Hussein and the Arab world against the United States; it is Saddam Hussein against the United Nations and against a majority of the Arab League. And that is a very important point that I will continue to make, because the Arab League itself has stood up to him and urged his compliance with the sanctions and condemned his aggression.

So, in this case, I see the Arab States as having a very important role to play in the resolution of this question. And they have not been taken in by his attempt to make this the Arab world versus the United States of America when it is nothing of the kind.

Mr. Fitzwater. Thank you very much.

President Gorbachev. I want, the President and myself, to conclude this press conference by stressing our deep sympathies and feelings for the people of Finland, for the hospitalities extended to us on this soil, and to appreciate highly the contribution made by the President of this country and his wife to make these excellent arrangements for these meetings.

President Bush. May I simply add that President Koivisto and Mrs. Koivisto have been most hospitable. And I agree with this. We owe them a great debt of gratitude, and the people of Finland.

Note: President Bush's 60th news conference began at 5:52 p.m. in Finlandia Hall.

President Gorbachev spoke in Russian, and his remarks were translated by an interpreter. Marlin Fitzwater was Press Secretary to *President Bush. Following the news conference, President Bush returned to Washington, DC.*

White House Statement on Reform of the Federal Financial Accounting System
September 10, 1990

The President today approved and sent to Congress requests for fiscal year 1991 budget amendments that reallocate funds to reform the Federal financial accounting system. This reform is part of an effort to improve financial control and to bring greater attention to claims on future Federal financial resources.

Because reform of Federal financial management systems and operations is a key component of the President's commitment to improving management in the Government, the Office of Management and Budget has initiated improvements in several areas of financial management. One of these is a policy that calls for developing and auditing agency financial statements. The current accounting system lacks an adequate balance sheet, satisfactory controls or audits, and the capability to provide an accurate picture of the Government's assets, liabilities, or financial risks.

Audits of these agency financial statements are especially important because they would help to ensure the accuracy of agency financial reports. At present, the Federal Government and most of its component agencies are not capable of producing annual general-purpose financial statements that can be audited. This initiative calls for the 14 Cabinet Departments, the Environmental Protection Agency, and the National Aeronautics and Space Administration to have agency financial statements developed and audits conducted by fiscal year 1994.

Preparation and audit of financial statements for all or part of 10 of the 16 targeted agencies would be conducted in fiscal year 1991. Five of the agencies will proceed without further congressional action. These amendments would permit 5 of the 10 agencies to reallocate funds to provide for audits.

Message to the Congress Transmitting the Report on the Fiscal Year 1991 Federal Budget Sequestration
September 10, 1990

To the Congress of the United States:
In accordance with the Balanced Budget and Emergency Deficit Control Act of 1985 (Public Law 99–177), as amended, I transmit herewith the program, project, and activity information required by section 252(a)(5) of the act.

The attachment provides information on both base and sequester amounts for each program, project, and activity in each budget account subject to the sequester.

GEORGE BUSH

The White House,
September 10, 1990.

Nomination of Richard A. Claytor To Be an Assistant Secretary of Energy
September 10, 1990

The President today announced his intention to nominate Richard A. Claytor to be an Assistant Secretary of Energy for Defense Programs. He would succeed Sylvester R. Foley, Jr.

Currently Mr. Claytor serves as Principal Deputy Assistant Secretary for Nuclear Energy at the Department of Energy. Prior to this he served with Burns and Roe Enterprises, Inc., in several capacities, including president, 1981–1989; president of Humphreys and Glasgow Synthetic Fuels, Inc., a joint venture company formed by Burns and Roe, 1979–1981; and vice president, 1973–1979. In addition, Mr. Claytor served in the U.S. Navy in several capacities from 1949 to 1973, including project manager for the Nuclear Power Division, Bureau of Ships, and assistant manager for the Pittsburgh Naval Reactors Office for the U.S. Atomic Energy Commission.

Mr. Claytor graduated from the U.S. Naval Academy (B.S., 1949) and the Webb Institute of Naval Architecture (B.S., 1956; M.S., 1956). He was born September 4, 1927, in Roanoke, VA. Mr. Claytor served in the U.S. Navy as a captain, 1949–1973. He is married, has three children, and resides in Bethesda, MD.

Nomination of Frederick P. Hitz To Be Inspector General of the Central Intelligence Agency
September 10, 1990

The President today announced his intention to nominate Frederick Porter Hitz, of Virginia, to be Inspector General of the Central Intelligence Agency in Washington, DC. This is a new position.

Currently Mr. Hitz serves as managing partner with the law firm of Schwabe, Williamson and Wyatt in Washington, DC. Prior to this, he served as legislative counsel to the Director of the Central Intelligence Agency, 1978–1982, and Deputy Assistant Secretary of Defense for Legislative Affairs, 1975–1977. He served in the Central Intelligence Agency from 1967 to 1973.

Mr. Hitz graduated from Princeton University (A.B., 1961) and Harvard Law School (J.D., 1964). He was born October 14, 1939, in Washington, DC. Mr. Hitz is married, has one child, and resides in Alexandria, VA.

Statement by Press Secretary Fitzwater on the President's Telephone Conversations With Foreign Leaders on the Persian Gulf Crisis
September 10, 1990

President Bush called Presidents Mitterrand [of France], Mubarak [of Egypt], and Özal [of Turkey], King Fahd [of Saudi Arabia], and Prime Minister Mulroney [of Canada] today. President Bush noted the historic nature of the joint statement on the Persian Gulf issued at the conclusion of his meetings with President Gorbachev [of the Soviet Union], and pointed out how this underscores the world community's determination to oppose Iraq's aggression against Kuwait. All the leaders expressed satisfaction on their concerted efforts against Iraq and pledged continued cooperation in this endeavor.

Remarks at the Presentation Ceremony for the National Medal of the Arts
September 10, 1990

First, a greeting to the members of the President's Cabinet that are here today. I want to welcome all of you. And I'm very happy to have John Frohnmayer here. As a matter of fact, I'm very happy to have him heading the National Endowment for the Arts. And, of course, Barbara, awake now, after—[*laughter*]—a kind of rather hectic trip. And I want to welcome the new Chairman of our Committee on the Arts and Humanities, Don Hall, whom I have not seen, but is here someplace—right over here. Don, thank you for undertaking this.

And thanks, especially, to our honored guests, the artists and the patrons of a special American tradition who grace us with their presence here today. Welcome to the White House. Welcome to the sixth annual presentation of the National Medal of the Arts.

Last year—I'll never forget it—this luncheon was held a week before Thanksgiving and was delayed when I got held up in the Rose Garden doing a photo opportunity with the national turkey. [*Laughter*] We awarded medals that day to some of the artistic giants of our time: Alfred Eisenstaedt and John Updike, Katherine Dunham, Dizzy Gillespie, among others. And with all that assembled talent, guess which one was pictured standing next to the President on the news that night? The national turkey. [*Laughter*] So, we've done a little better on the scheduling this year, Helsinki notwithstanding.

The people we honor today who have earned a collection of awards with names that have become the world's touchstones of excellence—names like Grammy and Oscar and Tony and the Pulitzer Prize and the Kennedy Center Honors—a collection of awards that would just about fill its own Smithsonian. But where most of these awards were aimed at honoring individual works, today we gather to salute the full body of their work—their contributions to the arts, to the Nation, and really to life in the 20th century. Embracing an era that reaches back as far as George Abbott's birth in 1887 and representing many generations of American talent, our artists stand alongside the artists who helped define America, no longer just another sprawling industrial nation but one of the cultural giants of the world.

Most had humble beginnings. I think of Jessica Tandy, sewing her own costumes in a backroom theater in Soho. B.B. King, touring backstreet bars and dancehalls—somebody had to do that—and on the road for over 20 years before most Americans would ever even hear his name. Even their hometown names read like the very tapestry of America itself: Forestville, New York; Centralia, Washington; Itta Bena, Mississippi; Brooklyn; and Atlantic City. Three were foreign-born, drawn here by freedom and opportunity, seeking not to enrich themselves but to enrich our culture. And today, they are Americans all, striving in the creation of beauty.

Taken together, today's honorees represent an apparently inexhaustible reserve of creativity, one that's often defied categorization. But there are at least two characteristics, I believe, that can apply to each. Each is a trailblazer, an authentic pioneer who literally helped to shape his or her art form. And each is an artist who pressed the very limits of his or her particular art form, often crossing over to combine distinct mediums in new and very different ways. Sometimes that cross-fertilization is self-evident, such as with the multidisciplinary approach of landscape architect Ian McHarg; with New York legends like George Abbott and Beverly Sills, who've thrilled audiences with their performances onstage and with their leadership behind the scenes; or with the love and magic of Hume Cronyn and Jessica Tandy, whose creations seem to float effortlessly from stage to screen and back again.

I probably shouldn't do this, but I might tell you of a frustration—not an overwhelming frustration but a frustration that I have. I think Barbara Bush is secretly in love with Hume Cronyn. [*Laughter*] There they go again.

But you also see it in painter Jasper Johns' collaborative efforts with choreographer Merce Cunningham; and the visual arts, where Frederick Douglass was brought to new life beneath the brush of Jacob Lawrence; and in the cries and hollers and work songs of field hands who labored in another time, once again heard rising on the wind through the guitar of B.B. King.

Speaking at Wellesley College back in June, Barbara urged young Americans to go out and seek their own true colors. And that's, of course, exactly what our honorees have done. You've created sights and sounds and characters, crafted anew within the human imagination, and in doing so, enriched the colors on the canvas of our national life. And that's why America continues to need and want and appreciate your creativity, your talent, and your diversity. Indeed, it is your efforts in the arts and humanities and the realm of the spirit that distinguish America as a world leader rather than as merely a world power.

And I'm proud that as a people and as a nation we continue to support the arts, both through public agencies and through private champions of the arts—patrons like our old friends Harris and Carol Masterson from Houston, Texas; a Southwestern Bell company in the forefront of all of this, St. Louis; and Washington's own David Lloyd Kreeger. We salute you for the joy you have given to Americans of many ages.

Thank you. Congratulations to all of you. And now I'd like to ask John Frohnmayer to assist me in presenting the awards. Well done, each and every one of you. Thank you very much.

Note: The President spoke at noon in the East Room at the White House.

Statement by Press Secretary Fitzwater on the Iraqi Offer To Give Oil to Developing Countries
September 10, 1990

Iraqi President Saddam Hussein's latest statement is a transparent attempt to deflect the focus of world attention from his blatant aggression against another country. Such maneuvers have not worked in the past and will not work this time. The international community is united in its strong determination to overcome the Iraqi aggression. U.N. Security Council Resolution 661 makes quite clear that all commodities and products originating in Iraq or Kuwait are prohibited from importation anywhere. It does not delineate between free exchanges or those paid for. Sanctions are complete, comprehensive, and binding on all nations. In addition, U.N. Security Council Resolution 665, which calls upon states to use measures as may be necessary to enforce sanctions, would still apply.

It is an affront to all countries for Saddam to think that they would sacrifice the principles of freedom and nonaggression for the Iraqi oil or the oil that he has taken through his naked aggression against Kuwait. Saddam's isolation in the world is complete, and the world community will not be deterred from its determination to have sanctions achieve the complete, immediate, and unconditional withdrawal of Iraq from Kuwait.

Memorandum on the Combined Federal Campaign
September 10, 1990

Memorandum for the Heads of Executive Departments and Agencies

Americans who make serving others central to their life and work are part of our kinder, gentler Nation. This commitment is displayed through no better example than Federal employees contributing every year to the Combined Federal Campaign. Public servants working in nearly every corner of the globe not only contribute to the campaign, but many spend countless hours in leadership roles each year to assure that the campaign is a huge success. I am asking you to become part of the team of Federal employees who, voluntarily, give a part of themselves through their leadership of the Combined Federal Campaign.

Secretary of the Interior Manuel Lujan, Jr., has agreed to serve as Chairman of the 1990 Combined Federal Campaign of the National Capital Area. I am asking that you support Secretary Lujan by personally serving as Chairman of the campaign in your agency and appointing a top official as your Vice Chairman. Please confirm with Secretary Lujan your willingness to serve and provide him with the name of your designated Vice Chairman.

Your involvement and visible support are essential to a successful 1990 campaign. Please join me in encouraging Federal employees everywhere to become a part of this important effort.

GEORGE BUSH

Message to the Congress Transmitting the Annual Report of the Railroad Retirement Board
September 11, 1990

To the Congress of the United States:

I hereby submit to the Congress the Annual Report of the Railroad Retirement Board for Fiscal Year 1989, pursuant to the provisions of section 7(b)(6) of the Railroad Retirement Act, enacted October 16, 1974, and section 12(l) of the Railroad Unemployment Insurance Act, enacted June 25, 1938.

The Railroad Retirement Board (RRB) serves over 900,000 railroad retirees and their families and 290,000 railroad employees who rely on the system for retirement, unemployment, disability, and sickness insurance benefits. Beneficiaries depend on the financial integrity of the pension fund for payment of their benefits.

Unfortunately, the long-term financial outlook for the rail pension system remains bleak, primarily because of steady drops in rail employment. Time and again, refinancing legislation has been enacted to address the Board's chronic solvency crises, yet the trust funds still have a $34 billion unfunded liability.

In 1987, the Congress acknowledged the problems faced by the system, and the rail sector was given a chance to address them with the creation of the seven-member legislative advisory Commission on Railroad Retirement Reform. The Commission was directed to examine different ways to resolve the long-term stability of the railroad pension system that do not include continued general fund subsidies. I urge the Commission to adhere to the Congress' wishes and propose ways to put the total cost of current and future rail pensions on a sound basis financed solely with rail sector resources.

In 1983, the rail sector was granted a limited rail pension subsidy by a diversion of Federal income tax payments to the rail fund. The temporary subsidy expires at the end of fiscal year 1990. Extending the subsidy would set an undesirable and threatening precedent. In the long run, *railroad workers will be served best by stable rail sector funding.* The condition of our budget calls for restraint on Federal spending. I therefore strongly oppose renewal of the diversion of Federal income taxes to the rail pension.

While the Commission has been examining the financial solvency of the Railroad Retirement Board, the Office of Management and Budget (OMB) has been scrutinizing its operations and recently completed a Management Review of programs run by the Board. Based on that review, OMB and the Board are developing a joint plan to address RRB's management weaknesses. I am particularly pleased that the Board's Inspector General has in recent weeks identified $73 million owed the Government. This good management work will benefit both railroad retirees and taxpayers generally. The Congress has also shown an interest in this review, and we would like to work with its Members on solutions to problem areas that could be improved with legislative changes.

GEORGE BUSH

The White House,
September 11, 1990.

Address Before a Joint Session of the Congress on the Persian Gulf Crisis and the Federal Budget Deficit
September 11, 1990

Mr. President and Mr. Speaker and Members of the United States Congress, distinguished guests, fellow Americans, thank you very much for that warm welcome. We gather tonight, witness to events in the Persian Gulf as significant as they are tragic. In the early morning hours of August 2d, following negotiations and promises by Iraq's dictator Saddam Hussein not to use force, a powerful Iraqi army invaded its trusting and much weaker neighbor, Kuwait. Within 3 days, 120,000 Iraqi troops with 850 tanks had poured into Kuwait and moved south to threaten Saudi Arabia. It was then that I decided to act to check that aggression.

At this moment, our brave servicemen and women stand watch in that distant desert and on distant seas, side by side with the forces of more than 20 other nations. They are some of the finest men and women of the United States of America. And they're doing one terrific job. These valiant Americans were ready at a moment's notice to leave their spouses and their children, to serve on the front line halfway around the world. They remind us who keeps America strong: they do. In the trying circumstances of the Gulf, the morale of our service men and women is excellent. In the face of danger, they're brave, they're well-trained, and dedicated.

A soldier, Private First Class Wade Merritt of Knoxville, Tennessee, now stationed in Saudi Arabia, wrote his parents of his worries, his love of family, and his hope for peace. But Wade also wrote, "I am proud of my country and its firm stance against inhumane aggression. I am proud of my army and its men. I am proud to serve my country." Well, let me just say, Wade, America is proud of you and is grateful to every soldier, sailor, marine, and airman serving the cause of peace in the Persian Gulf. I also want to thank the Chairman of the Joint Chiefs of Staff, General Powell; the Chiefs here tonight; our commander in the Persian Gulf, General Schwartzkopf; and the men and women of the Department of Defense. What a magnificent job you all are doing. And thank you very, very much from a grateful people. I wish I could say that their work is done. But we all know it's not.

So, if there ever was a time to put country before self and patriotism before party, the time is now. And let me thank all Americans, especially those here in this Chamber tonight, for your support for our armed forces and for their mission. That support will be even more important in the days to come. So, tonight I want to talk to you about what's at stake—what we must do together to defend civilized values around the world and maintain our economic strength at home.

Our objectives in the Persian Gulf are clear, our goals defined and familiar: Iraq must withdraw from Kuwait completely, immediately, and without condition. Kuwait's legitimate government must be restored. The security and stability of the Persian Gulf must be assured. And American citizens abroad must be protected. These goals are not ours alone. They've been endorsed by the United Nations Security Council five times in as many weeks. Most countries share our concern for principle. And many have a stake in the stability of the Persian Gulf. This is not, as Saddam Hussein would have it, the United States against Iraq. It is Iraq against the world.

As you know, I've just returned from a very productive meeting with Soviet President Gorbachev. And I am pleased that we are working together to build a new relationship. In Helsinki, our joint statement affirmed to the world our shared resolve to counter Iraq's threat to peace. Let me quote: "We are united in the belief that Iraq's aggression must not be tolerated. No peaceful international order is possible if larger states can devour their smaller neighbors." Clearly, no longer can a dictator count on East-West confrontation to stymie concerted United Nations action against aggression. A new partnership of nations has begun.

We stand today at a unique and extraordinary moment. The crisis in the Persian Gulf, as grave as it is, also offers a rare opportunity to move toward an historic period of cooperation. Out of these troubled times, our fifth objective—a new world order—can emerge: a new era—freer from the threat of terror, stronger in the pursuit of justice, and more secure in the quest for peace. An era in which the nations of the world, East and West, North and South, can prosper and live in harmony. A hundred generations have searched for this elusive path to peace, while a thousand wars raged across the span of human endeavor. Today that new world is struggling to be born, a world quite different from the one we've known. A world where the rule of law sup-

plants the rule of the jungle. A world in which nations recognize the shared responsibility for freedom and justice. A world where the strong respect the rights of the weak. This is the vision that I shared with President Gorbachev in Helsinki. He and other leaders from Europe, the Gulf, and around the world understand that how we manage this crisis today could shape the future for generations to come.

The test we face is great, and so are the stakes. This is the first assault on the new world that we seek, the first test of our mettle. Had we not responded to this first provocation with clarity of purpose, if we do not continue to demonstrate our determination, it would be a signal to actual and potential despots around the world. America and the world must defend common vital interests—and we will. America and the world must support the rule of law—and we will. America and the world must stand up to aggression—and we will. And one thing more: In the pursuit of these goals America will not be intimidated.

Vital issues of principle are at stake. Saddam Hussein is literally trying to wipe a country off the face of the Earth. We do not exaggerate. Nor do we exaggerate when we say Saddam Hussein will fail. Vital economic interests are at risk as well. Iraq itself controls some 10 percent of the world's proven oil reserves. Iraq plus Kuwait controls twice that. An Iraq permitted to swallow Kuwait would have the economic and military power, as well as the arrogance, to intimidate and coerce its neighbors—neighbors who control the lion's share of the world's remaining oil reserves. We cannot permit a resource so vital to be dominated by one so ruthless. And we won't.

Recent events have surely proven that there is no substitute for American leadership. In the face of tyranny, let no one doubt American credibility and reliability. Let no one doubt our staying power. We will stand by our friends. One way or another, the leader of Iraq must learn this fundamental truth. From the outset, acting hand in hand with others, we've sought to fashion the broadest possible international response to Iraq's aggression. The level of world cooperation and condemnation of

Iraq is unprecedented. Armed forces from countries spanning four continents are there at the request of King Fahd of Saudi Arabia to deter and, if need be, to defend against attack. Moslems and non-Moslems, Arabs and non-Arabs, soldiers from many nations stand shoulder to shoulder, resolute against Saddam Hussein's ambitions.

We can now point to five United Nations Security Council resolutions that condemn Iraq's aggression. They call for Iraq's immediate and unconditional withdrawal, the restoration of Kuwait's legitimate government, and categorically reject Iraq's cynical and self-serving attempt to annex Kuwait. Finally, the United Nations has demanded the release of all foreign nationals held hostage against their will and in contravention of international law. It is a mockery of human decency to call these people "guests." They are hostages, and the whole world knows it.

Prime Minister Margaret Thatcher, a dependable ally, said it all: "We do not bargain over hostages. We will not stoop to the level of using human beings as bargaining chips ever." Of course, of course, our hearts go out to the hostages and to their families. But our policy cannot change, and it will not change. America and the world will not be blackmailed by this ruthless policy.

We're now in sight of a United Nations that performs as envisioned by its founders. We owe much to the outstanding leadership of Secretary-General Javier Perez de Cuellar. The United Nations is backing up its words with action. The Security Council has imposed mandatory economic sanctions on Iraq, designed to force Iraq to relinquish the spoils of its illegal conquest. The Security Council has also taken the decisive step of authorizing the use of all means necessary to ensure compliance with these sanctions. Together with our friends and allies, ships of the United States Navy are today patrolling Mideast waters. They've already intercepted more than 700 ships to enforce the sanctions. Three regional leaders I spoke with just yesterday told me that these sanctions are working. Iraq is feeling the heat. We continue to hope that Iraq's leaders will recalculate just what their aggression has cost them. They are cut off from world trade, unable to sell their oil. And only a tiny fraction of goods gets through.

The communique with President Gorbachev made mention of what happens when the embargo is so effective that children of Iraq literally need milk or the sick truly need medicine. Then, under strict international supervision that guarantees the proper destination, then food will be permitted.

At home, the material cost of our leadership can be steep. That's why Secretary of State Baker and Treasury Secretary Brady have met with many world leaders to underscore that the burden of this collective effort must be shared. We are prepared to do our share and more to help carry that load; we insist that others do their share as well.

The response of most of our friends and allies has been good. To help defray costs, the leaders of Saudi Arabia, Kuwait, and the UAE—the United Arab Emirates—have pledged to provide our deployed troops with all the food and fuel they need. Generous assistance will also be provided to stalwart front-line nations, such as Turkey and Egypt. I am also heartened to report that this international response extends to the neediest victims of this conflict—those refugees. For our part, we've contributed $28 million for relief efforts. This is but a portion of what is needed. I commend, in particular, Saudi Arabia, Japan, and several European nations who have joined us in this purely humanitarian effort.

There's an energy-related cost to be borne as well. Oil-producing nations are already replacing lost Iraqi and Kuwaiti output. More than half of what was lost has been made up. And we're getting superb cooperation. If producers, including the United States, continue steps to expand oil and gas production, we can stabilize prices and guarantee against hardship. Additionally, we and several of our allies always have the option to extract oil from our strategic petroleum reserves if conditions warrant. As I've pointed out before, conservation efforts are essential to keep our energy needs as low as possible. And we must then take advantage of our energy sources across the board: coal, natural gas, hydro, and nuclear. Our failure to do these things has made us more dependent on foreign oil than ever before. Finally, let no one even contemplate profiteering from this crisis. We will not have it.

I cannot predict just how long it will take to convince Iraq to withdraw from Kuwait. Sanctions will take time to have their full intended effect. We will continue to review all options with our allies, but let it be clear: we will not let this aggression stand.

Our interest, our involvement in the Gulf is not transitory. It predated Saddam Hussein's aggression and will survive it. Long after all our troops come home—and we all hope it's soon, very soon—there will be a lasting role for the United States in assisting the nations of the Persian Gulf. Our role then: to deter future aggression. Our role is to help our friends in their own self-defense. And something else: to curb the proliferation of chemical, biological, ballistic missile and, above all, nuclear technologies.

Let me also make clear that the United States has no quarrel with the Iraqi people. Our quarrel is with Iraq's dictator and with his aggression. Iraq will not be permitted to annex Kuwait. That's not a threat, that's not a boast, that's just the way it's going to be.

Our ability to function effectively as a great power abroad depends on how we conduct ourselves at home. Our economy, our Armed Forces, our energy dependence, and our cohesion all determine whether we can help our friends and stand up to our foes. For America to lead, America must remain strong and vital. Our world leadership and domestic strength are mutual and reinforcing; a woven piece, strongly bound as Old Glory. To revitalize our leadership, our leadership capacity, we must address our budget deficit—not after election day, or next year, but now.

Higher oil prices slow our growth, and higher defense costs would only make our fiscal deficit problem worse. That deficit was already greater than it should have been—a projected $232 billion for the coming year. It must—it will—be reduced.

To my friends in Congress, together we must act this very month—before the next fiscal year begins on October 1st—to get America's economic house in order. The Gulf situation helps us realize we are more economically vulnerable than we ever should be. Americans must never again enter any crisis, economic or military, with an excessive dependence on foreign oil and an excessive burden of Federal debt.

Most Americans are sick and tired of endless battles in the Congress and between the branches over budget matters. It is high time we pulled together and get the job done right. It's up to us to straighten this out. This job has four basic parts. First, the Congress should, this month, within a budget agreement, enact growth-oriented tax measures—to help avoid recession in the short term and to increase savings, investment, productivity, and competitiveness for the longer term. These measures include extending incentives for research and experimentation; expanding the use of IRA's for new homeowners; establishing tax-deferred family savings accounts; creating incentives for the creation of enterprise zones and initiatives to encourage more domestic drilling; and, yes, reducing the tax rate on capital gains.

And second, the Congress should, this month, enact a prudent multiyear defense program, one that reflects not only the improvement in East-West relations but our broader responsibilities to deal with the continuing risks of outlaw action and regional conflict. Even with our obligations in the Gulf, a sound defense budget can have some reduction in real terms; and we're prepared to accept that. But to go beyond such levels, where cutting defense would threaten our vital margin of safety, is something I will never accept. The world is still dangerous. And surely, that is now clear. Stability's not secure. American interests are far reaching. Interdependence has increased. The consequences of regional instability can be global. This is no time to risk America's capacity to protect her vital interests.

And third, the Congress should, this month, enact measures to increase domestic energy production and energy conservation in order to reduce dependence on foreign oil. These measures should include my proposals to increase incentives for domestic oil and gas exploration, fuel-switching, and to accelerate the development of the Alaskan energy resources without damage to wildlife. As you know, when the oil embargo was imposed in the early 1970's, the United States imported almost 6 million barrels of oil a day. This year, before the Iraqi invasion, U.S. imports had risen to nearly 8 million barrels per day. And we'd moved in the wrong direction. And now we must act to correct that trend.

And fourth, the Congress should, this month, enact a 5-year program to reduce the projected debt and deficits by $500 billion—that's by half a trillion dollars. And if, with the Congress, we can develop a satisfactory program by the end of the month, we can avoid the ax of sequester—deep across-the-board cuts that would threaten our military capacity and risk substantial domestic disruption. I want to be able to tell the American people that we have truly solved the deficit problem. And for me to do that, a budget agreement must meet these tests: It must include the measures I've recommended to increase economic growth and reduce dependence on foreign oil. It must be fair. All should contribute, but the burden should not be excessive for any one group of programs or people. It must address the growth of government's hidden liabilities. It must reform the budget process and, further, it must be real.

I urge Congress to provide a comprehensive 5-year deficit reduction program to me as a complete legislative package, with measures to assure that it can be fully enforced. America is tired of phony deficit reduction or promise-now, save-later plans. It is time for a program that is credible and real. And finally, to the extent that the deficit reduction program includes new revenue measures, it must avoid any measure that would threaten economic growth or turn us back toward the days of punishing income tax rates. That is one path we should not head down again.

I have been pleased with recent progress, although it has not always seemed so smooth. But now it's time to produce. I hope we can work out a responsible plan. But with or without agreement from the budget summit, I ask both Houses of the Congress to allow a straight up-or-down vote on a complete $500-billion deficit reduction package not later than September 28. If the Congress cannot get me a budget, then Americans will have to face a tough, mandated sequester. I'm hopeful, in fact, I'm confident that the Congress will do what it should. And I can assure you that we in the executive branch will do our part.

In the final analysis, our ability to meet our responsibilities abroad depends upon political will and consensus at home. This is never easy in democracies, for we govern only with the consent of the governed. And although free people in a free society are bound to have their differences, Americans traditionally come together in times of adversity and challenge.

Once again, Americans have stepped forward to share a tearful goodbye with their families before leaving for a strange and distant shore. At this very moment, they serve together with Arabs, Europeans, Asians, and Africans in defense of principle and the dream of a new world order. That's why they sweat and toil in the sand and the heat and the sun. If they can come together under such adversity, if old adversaries like the Soviet Union and the United States can work in common cause, then surely we who are so fortunate to be in this great Chamber—Democrats, Republicans, liberals, conservatives—can come together to fulfill our responsibilities here. Thank you. Good night. And God bless the United States of America.

Note: The President spoke at 9:09 p.m. in the House Chamber at the Capitol. He was introduced by Thomas S. Foley, Speaker of the House of Representatives. The address was broadcast live on nationwide television and radio.

Remarks to Federal, State, and Local Prosecutors
September 12, 1990

Please be seated. And please take off your coats. I mean, it's a little warm out here in the Rose Garden. Well, thank you, Attorney General Thornburgh, and U.S. attorneys, State attorneys general. I see our Director of the FBI here, and local district attorneys and other law enforcement officials. I am just delighted to have this opportunity to welcome our nation's prosecutors to the White House. I know that you spent the morning over at Justice with Dick Thornburgh. I just got briefed on that—discussing the legal changes that we need to help you do your jobs more effectively. And I know that other subjects are preoccupying all of us these days, but I repeat today what I said last week: Drugs and violent crime remain a top priority.

And on behalf of all the American people, I want to thank you, all of you, for working to help us take back the streets. We know full well that the life of a prosecutor is not easy. For gifted, hard-working lawyers like yourselves, the financial sacrifice is immense. And more importantly, over the past 30 years America's criminal justice system has become bogged down with technicalities that stymie our prosecutors' simple goals—to see the truth come out, the guilty punished, the law upheld, and justice done. Too many times, in too many cases, too many criminals go free because the scales of justice are unfairly loaded against dedicated law men and women like you.

Since taking office, we've worked with many of you to try to steady the scales of justice, to seek a fair balance between the legitimate rights of criminals and criminal suspects, and society's right to protect itself from evil predators. And America took an important step towards balancing these scales when I had the chance to name a tough, a fair-minded, intellectually brilliant judge as my first nominee to the Supreme Court—New Hampshire's Judge David Souter. With a decade of law enforcement experience prior to being elevated to the bench, Judge Souter comes from your own ranks. The Senate starts these confirmation

hearings tomorrow, and I call on them to act swiftly so that he can take his place as the only career prosecutor on the Court in time for the Court's first sitting. And, of course, I am very pleased—all of us are pleased—that the American Bar Association gave him their highest rating by a unanimous vote. And we're especially pleased that the National District Attorneys Association endorsed Judge Souter for the Supreme Court, praising him as a tough anticrime judge. This is a group that knows all too well the problems with the criminal justice system that all too often simply doesn't work.

And that's why I stood before the Capitol on a rainy day in May last year—and many of you were there—calling on Congress to pass legislation to give our prosecutors and police the tools they need to fight back against the epidemic of violent crime still raging in America. That was over a year ago. And despite the urgency of the problem, the Congress has failed to act on key aspects of my proposal. What's worse, several measures receiving serious consideration in the House this week would actually weaken law enforcement and hamper your efforts to protect the citizens of this nation. But your presence here today sends a powerful warning to Congress, a shot across the bow of a ship that is moving in the wrong direction. We will not accept a crime bill that is tougher on law enforcement than it is on criminals.

We need a crime bill that will stop the endless abuse of habeas corpus, that guarantees that criminals who use serious weapons face serious weapon charges and serious time, and that ensures that evidence gathered by good cops acting in good faith isn't barred by technicalities that let bad people go free. And for the most unspeakable of crimes, we do need a workable death penalty, which is to say a real death penalty. I simply will not accept anything that rolls back the clock on America's ability to fight crime and punish wrongdoers. The bottom line is really this: I will not sign a crime bill that handcuffs the police. I will not sign a bill that overturns recent Supreme Court decisions limiting frivolous habeas corpus petitions, that expands the coverage of the exclusionary rule, or that creates a racial quota system for capital punishment.

You know the difference between my proposals, which give you the legal tools you need to win this fight, and the anti-law-enforcement proposals that some in the Congress are attempting to peddle as a crime bill. For the past 2 weeks America's been gripped by chilling headlines that tell of kids going back to school in bulletproof coats; and a visiting Utah man, a kid really, sports lover, killed while defending his mother from a New York subway gang said to be after pocket money so they could go dancing. The American people really are fed up. You know this perhaps better than I because you're on the front lines, but they're fed up. And I urge the Congress to heed the voices of our people, our police, and our prosecutors, and send me a crime bill that will help take back the streets.

I want to thank you. I really wanted to have this meeting, and so did Dick, so that both of us here, in the majesty of the Rose Garden and the shadow of the White House, we could tell you that we are grateful to you. And we know it's not easy, but keep up your dedicated efforts to make our community safe. We're lucky—America is lucky—to have men and women of your quality and your character out doing the job for all of us.

Thank you and God bless you. And God bless our great country. Thank you very much.

Note: The President spoke at 2:05 p.m. in the Rose Garden at the White House. In his opening remarks, he referred to William Sessions, Director of the Federal Bureau of Investigation.

Nomination of Harmon Elwood Kirby To Be United States Ambassador to Togo
September 12, 1990

The President today announced his intention to nominate Harmon Elwood Kirby, of Ohio, to be Ambassador Extraordinary and Plenipotentiary of the United States of America to the Republic of Togo. He would succeed Rush Walker Taylor, Jr.

Currently Dr. Kirby serves as Director of the Office of Performance Evaluation at the Department of State. Prior to this he has served as Director of United Nations Political Affairs at the Department of State. He has been a Foreign Service officer for the Department of State in Geneva, Madras, New Delhi, Brussels, Khartoum, Rabat, and Washington, 1961 to present. In addition, Mr. Kirby has served as an executive assistant to the executive vice president of Hudson Pulp and Paper Corp. in New York City, 1960–1961, and in personnel and labor relations for the Diamond National Corp. in Middletown, OH, 1959–1960.

Mr. Kirby received his bachelor of arts degree from Harvard University and his master of arts degree from George Washington University. He was born January 27, 1934, in Hamilton, OH. Mr. Kirby served in the U.S. Army, 1956–1958. He is married, has two children, and resides in Bethesda, MD.

Statement by Press Secretary Fitzwater on the Treaty on the Final Settlement With Respect to Germany
September 12, 1990

The President welcomes the historic signing in Moscow this morning of the Treaty on the Final Settlement With Respect to Germany. Today's agreement settles the external aspects of the establishment of German unity and makes the achievement of a unified, free, and democratic Germany just a short step away. With formal unification scheduled for October 3, the way is now clear for creation of a united Germany, enjoying full sovereignty and remaining a full member of the North Atlantic alliance and the Western community of nations.

The treaty provides for the termination of the historic rights and responsibilities of the four wartime allies—the United States, Great Britain, France, and the Soviet Union—for Berlin and for Germany as a whole, dating from wartime and early postwar agreements. It restores full sovereignty to Germany over all its territory, including Berlin, and confirms that the borders of the united Germany will be the frontiers of the current Federal Republic of Germany and German Democratic Republic. The Government of Poland has expressed its satisfaction with the treaty's resolution of the border issue.

Last October, before the dramatic opening of the Berlin Wall on November 9, the President expressed his strong support for German unification and his full confidence in Germany's commitment to the Western alliance. The President is gratified that the United States was able to play a leading role in supporting the aspirations we have long shared with the German people for a Germany united in peace and freedom. Last February, the United States proposed that negotiations to resolve the external aspects of German unification be held among the Two Plus Four, the two Germanys together with the United States, Great Britain, France, and the Soviet Union. Those negotiations are now complete, and we join the German people in looking forward to the unification of Germany and a continued close and fruitful relationship between our countries and peoples. The United States and Germany will be, as the President put it in his speech in Mainz of May of last year, "partners in leadership."

Statement by Press Secretary Fitzwater on the President's Taped Address to the People of Iraq
September 13, 1990

In his meeting with Acting Secretary [of State] Eagleburger this morning the Iraqi Ambassador stated that the President's taped message to the Iraqi people would be broadcast in its entirety in prime time. We are disappointed, however, that he declined to take personal possession of the tape for transmittal to Baghdad. The State Department will be transmitting the tape to our Embassy in Baghdad for delivery to the Iraqi Government. We expect that this will take place within the next day or two.

Remarks on Transmitting the Enterprise for the Americas Initiative Act of 1990
September 14, 1990

Please be seated. Thank you all very much for being with us today. A most distinguished gathering here this morning. And I want to thank the Vice President, Secretary Brady, Secretary Eagleburger, and Ambassador Hills, and Bill Reilly for being with us today. I'd also like to welcome the OAS Secretary General Baena Soares, and the IDB President Enrique Iglesias. It's very good to have you all here.

In Latin America and the Caribbean, a new generation of leaders, with the support of their citizens, has turned increasingly to market forces as they pursue economic reforms designed to encourage growth. And we've welcomed these developments. And that's why in June we announced the Enterprise for the Americas, a major new initiative to help forge a genuine partnership of free market reform that will sustain both growth and political stability in Latin America and the Caribbean. I consider this one of the most important initiatives of my administration. It opens a bold new chapter in hemispheric relations—one based on trade, not aid.

Since announcing this initiative, I've been extremely grateful for the warm response that it's received from leaders in the hemisphere. Prime Ministers and Presidents from Jamaica to Uruguay, from Brazil to Honduras have either written or called me to express their support. And as I said back in June, I know there's been some concern in the Americas that with so many things going on in the world that our focus will shift away. But I've assured the leaders throughout our hemisphere that the United States will not lose sight of the tremendous challenges and opportunities right here in what we hope will soon be the first fully democratic hemisphere in the world.

For the first time, the three economic issues of greatest importance to Latin America—trade, investment, and debt—have been joined in a single endeavor. On trade, we've set forth clearly our long-term objective—a hemispheric free trade zone from Alaska to Argentina. As a step in that direction, we offer to negotiate framework agreements and will address specific Latin American trade concerns within the Uruguay round. We've already signed framework agreements with Mexico, Bolivia, Colombia, and Ecuador, and others are in progress. On investment, we want to increase the incentives for countries to adopt policies that will attract capital. And on debt, we're supplementing the Brady Plan with a new proposal to reduce official debt.

The legislation that we're transmitting to Congress today advances both the investment and debt portions of the initiative and contains an innovative approach to the environment. I ask for prompt action this session by the Congress. Without congressional authority we cannot get underway on some of the most important elements of the initiative.

To cite two examples: Our initiative includes a $1.5 billion multidonor investment fund administered through the Inter-American Development Bank to provide support and technical assistance to carry out investment reforms. And we want to thank the IDB President Iglesias for his strong support of this initiative. And congressional action is also necessary to authorize reduction of the debt owed by our Latin American neighbors to the United States Government. We will also pursue debt-for-equity and debt-for-nature swaps to improve the hemisphere's environment.

We believe these measures together will boost trade, investment, and growth in our hemisphere. This legislation is good for our neighbors. It's good for the hemisphere. And I believe it is very good for the United States of America. It has my full backing and my support. The Western Hemisphere is our common homeland, and its political and economic well-being will always be of the utmost importance to us. That's why we need to move forward. Let's pass this important legislation soon. And so, now I would like to invite our two distinguished guests here, if you would, to join me while I sign this. Please come forward, if you will. Might I express my appreciation to everybody here that worked on all of this. I know David and the others here—John, everybody—thank you all very much. I think it's very, very important, and I will assure you, those in the departments that have worked on it, I will push it in every way I can.

And thank you all for being with us.

Note: The President spoke at 10:36 a.m. in the Roosevelt Room at the White House. In his remarks, he referred to Deputy Secretary of State Lawrence S. Eagleburger; Carla A. Hills, U.S. Trade Representative; William K. Reilly, Administrator of the Environmental Protection Agency; and David Mulford and John Robson, Assistant Secretaries of the Treasury.

Message to the Congress Transmitting the Enterprise for the Americas Initiative Act of 1990
September 14, 1990

To the Congress of the United States:

I am pleased to transmit a legislative proposal entitled the "Enterprise for the Americas Initiative Act of 1990." This proposal sets forward key measures to implement the investment, debt, and environmental components of my "Enterprise for the Americas" initiative announced on June 27, 1990. It will build more constructive relations in the Western Hemisphere and a more hopeful future.

The last 14 months have been a remarkable time for the world. Yet the rapid changes at which we have marveled in Eastern Europe are not unique. Freedom has made great gains in our hemisphere, as a resurgence of democratic rule has swept through the Americas.

Parallel to this political shift has come a realignment of policies in the economic sphere. As the people of Latin America and the Caribbean search for prosperity following a difficult decade of painful economic adjustment, their governments are focusing on economic growth and the free market policies needed to nourish it.

For the benefit of all people of this hemisphere, the United States needs to reach out to support the efforts of these countries as each undertakes its own approach to economic reform. My new Enterprise for the Americas initiative aims to build a broad-based partnership for the 1990s that will strengthen our economic ties and encourage economic growth and development throughout the Western Hemisphere.

This initiative rests on three pillars—actions on trade, investment, and debt—through which we can reach out to our neighbors and support economic reform and sustained growth. *First,* we want to expand trade both by cooperating closely with the nations of Latin America and the Caribbean as the Uruguay Round comes to a close and by entering into free trade agreements with the ultimate goal of a hemisphere-wide free trade system. *Second,* we want to encourage investment and help countries compete for capital by reforming broad economic policies and specific regulatory systems. *Third,* we want to build on our successful efforts to ease debt burdens and to increase the incentives for countries to reform their economies by offering additional measures in the debt area. As part of our efforts on debt, we want to support the environment by promoting sustainable natural resource management as a key element of building a strong future for the hemisphere.

The proposal I am transmitting to the Congress today focuses on the investment, debt, and environment components of the Enterprise for the Americas initiative.

The proposal provides for contributions by the United States to a multilateral investment fund to be established by the Inter-American Development Bank (IDB) to foster a climate favorable to investment in Latin American and Caribbean countries.

This Enterprise for the Americas Investment Fund will provide additional support for reforms undertaken as part of the new IDB investment sector lending program. It will do so by advancing specific, market-oriented investment policy initiatives and reforms and financing technical assistance.

The proposal establishes the Enterprise for the Americas Facility to support the objectives of the initiative through administration of debt reduction operations for those nations that meet the investment reform and other policy conditions. Latin American and Caribbean countries can qualify for benefits under the Facility if they:

- have in effect International Monetary Fund/World Bank reform programs;
- have in place major investment reforms in conjunction with an IDB loan or are otherwise implementing an open investment regime; and
- for countries that owe a substantial part of their debt to commercial banks, have negotiated a satisfactory financing program with commercial banks, including debt and debt service reduction if appropriate.

The proposal authorizes the reduction of concessional obligations extended under the Foreign Assistance Act of 1961 and credits extended pursuant to title I of the Agricultural Trade Development and Assistance Act of 1954. The agency whose loans or credits are affected will exchange—at the direction of the Facility—new obligations for obligations outstanding as of January 1, 1990. Principal on the new obligation will be paid in U.S. dollars. Interest will be at a concessional rate and paid in local currency if an eligible country has entered into a framework agreement establishing an Environmental Fund; otherwise, interest will be paid in U.S. dollars.

The Environmental Fund into which local currency interest payments are deposited will be owned by the debtor country but be subject to joint programming by the debtor country and the United States Government. An environmental framework agreement will establish joint programming requirements and will also specify the use of the Environmental Fund to support environmental projects and programs. It is envi-

sioned that local committees in each eligible country will include strong representation of local private environmental groups, as well as the United States Government and the host government, and will initiate overall country plans and carry out a fundamental review of proposed projects. In setting up this broad framework and establishing relationships in each eligible country, we will consult closely with nongovernmental organizations with expertise in natural resource management and conservation.

The proposal also authorizes the sale, reduction, or cancellation of loans made to eligible countries under the Export-Import Bank Act of 1945, as amended, and assets acquired under export credit guarantee programs authorized pursuant to the Commodity Credit Corporation Charter Act or section 4(b) of the Food for Peace Act of 1966. These sales, reductions, or cancellations will be undertaken only when purchasers confirm that they will be used to carry out debt-for-equity or debt-for-nature swaps in eligible countries.

We believe that these investment, debt, and environment measures will provide significant support to the efforts of Latin America and the Caribbean to build strong economies.

The United States has not gone untouched by the economic crisis faced by Latin America and the Caribbean over the last decade. As countries in the region cut imports, postponed investment, and struggled to service their foreign debt, we too were affected. We lost trade, markets, and opportunities.

Latin American and Caribbean leaders have made a great deal of progress in coping with this crisis. A new generation of democratically elected leaders is turning the tide away from economic decline. Enactment of the Enterprise for the Americas Initiative Act of 1990 will permit the United States to support the efforts of these leaders, increasing the prospects for economic growth and prosperity throughout the hemisphere.

GEORGE BUSH

The White House,
September 14, 1990.

White House Fact Sheet on the Enterprise for the Americas Initiative Act of 1990

September 14, 1990

The President will transmit to the Congress a legislative proposal to implement the investment, debt, and environmental elements of his Enterprise for the Americas Initiative. The purpose of this legislation is to encourage and support market-oriented reform and economic growth in Latin America and the Caribbean through interrelated actions that will promote investment reforms, debt reduction, and environmental protection.

In the investment area, the proposed legislation will provide for contribution by the United States to the Enterprise for the Americas Investment Fund, a multilateral investment fund to be established at the Inter-American Development Bank. Authorization for contributions of $500 million to the Fund and authorization of appropriations for the contribution will be sought. The President will seek $100 million a year over 5 years for the Fund. The Fund is designed to foster a climate favorable to investment in Latin American and Caribbean countries and would support efforts in these countries to facilitate investment and the reflow of flight capital. It would advance specific, market-oriented investment policy initiatives and reforms and finance technical assistance for privatization efforts, business infrastructure, and worker-training and education programs. The Secretary of the Treasury will seek contributions from other countries to the Fund.

The proposed legislation will also establish the Enterprise for the Americas Facility in the Department of the Treasury to support the objectives through administration of debt reduction operations for nations that meet certain investment reform and other policy conditions.

The legislation would establish criteria to govern eligibility to participate in the debt reduction operations under the Facility. These criteria will aim to encourage economic reform, including measures to liberalize investment regimes. An eligible country should:

- have in effect an International Monetary Fund (IMF) standby arrangement, extended fund arrangement, or an arrangement under the structural adjustment facility or enhanced structural adjustment facility, or, in exceptional circumstances, an IMF-monitored program or its equivalent;
- as appropriate, have received structural or sectoral adjustment loans under the International Bank for Reconstruction and Development (World Bank) or the International Development Association (IDA);
- have in place major investment reforms in conjunction with an IDB loan or otherwise be implementing open investment regimes; and
- as appropriate, have agreed on a satisfactory financing program with commercial banks including, if appropriate, debt and debt service reduction.

Clear authority will be necessary to undertake the actions proposed in the debt element of the Initiative. The administration will seek authority to reduce concessional loans extended under the Foreign Assistance Act of 1961 (FAA) and credits extended under title I of the Agricultural Trade Development and Assistance Act of 1954, as amended (P.L. 480). This reduction would be accomplished through an exchange of new obligations for obligations outstanding as of January 1, 1990. Once agreed by the President, the responsibility for executing an exchange of obligations that will result in the debt reduction rests with the agency that holds loans or credits to be affected. Such agency will act at the direction of the Facility.

Once an exchange is undertaken, principal payments on new obligations will be paid in U.S. dollars and credited to the accounts established to receive principal payments on the old debt obligations. Interest payments will be at a concessional rate and will be made in local currency if the debtor country has reached an environmental agreement with the United States establishing an Environmental Fund. Under such an agreement, interest payments would be deposited in an Environmental Fund and jointly programmed by the U.S. and debtor country government. In the absence of such an environmental agreement, interest would be paid in U.S. dollars into the account established for interest payments of the obligations exchanged therefor.

The President would be authorized to enter into agreements with countries receiving debt reduction under the Initiative which, in addition to establishing Environmental Funds and providing for joint programming, could specify the uses of monies in the Funds. The President intends to encourage the involvement of local private environmental groups in decisions on the use of grant funds and to consult with nongovernmental organizations in the United States and abroad regarding the establishment, structure, and operation of the Environmental Fund program.

In addition to the authority to reduce concessional debts, the President would be authorized to sell, reduce, or cancel loans made to an eligible country under the Export-Import Bank Act of 1945, as amended, and assets acquired as a result of credit guarantees made in connection with export sales to eligible countries under programs authorized pursuant to the Commodity Credit Corporation (CCC) Charter Act, as amended, or section 4(b) of the Food for Peace Act of 1966, as amended. Such sale, reduction, or cancellation would only be undertaken for those loans made or assets acquired prior to January 1, 1990 and would be consistent with terms or conditions of prior agreements relating to the loans or assets.

Eligible purchasers for Eximbank loans and CCC assets would depend on the presentation of satisfactory plans for engaging in debt-for-equity or debt-for-nature swaps. Once an eligible purchaser is identified, the Facility will notify the agency that holds the loans or assets to be affected, and that agency will carry out the sale, reduction, or cancellation. Prior to such a transaction, consultations would be undertaken with the eligible country regarding the amounts to

be affected and their uses for debt-for-equity or debt-for-nature swaps. The proceeds of any sale, reduction, or cancellation of a loan or asset would be credited to the account established for the repayment of that loan or those assets.

Such sales, reductions, or cancellations of loans or assets would be carried out in a way to maximize return to the U.S. Government. These transactions would not be required to be registered pursuant to the Securities Act of 1933 and, for the purposes of that Act, neither Eximbank nor CCC would be deemed an issuer or underwriter with respect to any subsequent sale or other disposition of such loan or asset pursuant to a debt-for-equity or debt-for-nature swap.

The President would transmit an annual report to Congress on the operation of the Facility.

Implementation of the Initiative

The key investment, debt, and environment components of the "Enterprise for the Americas" initiative are as follows:

(1) Contributions to the Enterprise for the Americas Investment Fund to be administered by the Inter-American Development Bank (IDB).

(2) Development of an investment sector lending program in the IDB to provide loans in support of investment reforms.

(3) Creation of the Enterprise for the Americas Facility within the Treasury Department to support the objectives of the Initiative through debt reduction operations for eligible nations.

(4) Reduction of concessional (AID and P.L. 480) debts owed by eligible countries.

(5) Use of interest payments on reduced concessional obligations to support environmental programs in the debtor country.

(6) The sale, reduction, or cancellation of Eximbank loans and CCC assets to facilitate debt/equity or debt-for-nature swaps.

The following provides further detail on

the expected operation of these elements.

Enterprise for the Americas Investment Fund

This fund is expected to be multilateral in nature, although it could commence operations based initially on U.S. contributions if other contributions are not available. The administration will be seeking authority to contribute (as grants) $100 million annually to this Fund over five years beginning in FY 1992.

The Fund is expected to provide support for investment policy initiatives and reforms and to finance technical assistance for privatization, development of business infrastructure, and worker training and education programs.

The administration discussed this proposal with other G–7 industrial countries at the Houston economic summit and will continue to seek contributions from European countries, Japan, and Canada.

Although the IDB would manage the Fund, contributing countries would be expected to provide guidelines for disbursement of grants to eligible countries.

IDB Investment Sector Loan Program

The President has proposed the establishment of an IDB sector lending program to provide fundamental support for investment reforms. Liberalization of investment regimes is particularly important as a means of attracting the scarce capital critical to sustained growth. The objective for Latin America and the Caribbean must be to compete effectively for investment in a world of limited resources and to attract the capital of their nationals back home.

The U.S. Government will work with the Inter-American Development Bank to develop an investment sector lending program consistent with these goals.

Enterprise for the Americas Facility

The Enterprise for the Americas Facility will support the objectives of market-oriented reform and economic growth, investment reform, and environmental protection through the administration of debt reduction operations for eligible countries.

To be eligible for debt reduction, Latin American and Caribbean countries must:

- have in effect International Monetary Fund/World Bank economic reform programs;
- have in place major investment reforms in conjunction with an IDB loan, or otherwise be implementing an open investment regime; and
- for countries that owe a substantial part of their debt to commercial banks, have negotiated a satisfactory financing program with commercial banks, including debt and debt service reduction if appropriate.

Decisions on country eligibility, based on these criteria, will be made through an interagency process chaired by the Secretary of the Treasury. The Enterprise for the Americas Facility will issue instructions to the appropriate Federal agencies to effect the debt reduction, sale, or cancellation which has been negotiated with eligible countries (see below). It will also provide technical support for an interagency team, to include relevant agencies, which will negotiate the terms of debt reduction with individual countries.

Reduction of Concessional Debts

Decisions on the extent of debt reduction on Agency for International Development and P.L. 480 obligations of individual eligible countries will be made through an interagency process chaired by the Secretary of the Treasury.

Debt reduction will be effected through the exchange of outstanding obligations for new, reduced AID and P.L. 480 obligations bearing concessional interest rates (see environmental support discussion below).

Reduction, Sale, or Cancellation of Eximbank and CCC Obligations

Decisions on the amount of Eximbank loans (and loans acquired pursuant to its guarantee and insurance programs) and the amount of CCC assets acquired as a result of its export sales guarantees which will be available for reduction, sale, or cancellation for eligible countries will be made through an interagency process chaired by the Secretary of the Treasury.

Such reductions, sales, or cancellations will be made solely to facilitate debt/equity swaps or debt-for-nature swaps. Specific mechanisms will be developed to assure that this objective is realized.

Enterprise for the Americas Environmental Funds

The administration will seek to negotiate an environmental agreement with each country determined eligible for debt reduction. Conclusion of such an agreement would allow the eligible country to make interest payments on new obligations resulting from debt reduction in local currency. The agreement would establish an Environmental Fund to receive interest payments and would determine the operation of the Fund and the use of its resources to provide grants for environmental projects and programs.

The local currency interest payments would be deposited in an eligible country's Environmental Fund and would be jointly-programmed by the United States and that country. It is contemplated that local committees—composed of U.S. Government representatives, eligible country representatives, and representatives of local private environmental groups—would have a significant role in formulating programs and projects funded by each country's Environmental Fund.

The administration is committed to encouraging the involvement of local nongovernmental environmental groups in the decision-making process. We have heard preliminary views from nongovernmental organizations in Washington and believe it will be important to consult with these groups regarding the establishment, structure, and operation of the Environmental Fund program.

We anticipate that annual programs for individual countries would be formulated at the local committee level, as would proposals for specific projects to be funded. Annual programs would be subject to the joint approval of the U.S. Government and the debtor government.

Remarks to Participants in the International Appellate Judges Conference
September 14, 1990

Welcome to the White House, everybody. I'm delighted that you all are here and very pleased to be sharing this platform, this stage, with two people for whom I have very high regard: Justice Sandra Day O'Connor, Justice of our Supreme Court, and then my own legal counsel in whom I have great confidence, Boyden Gray.

I wanted to single out for special commendation Judge Cynthia Hall, for all the work that you have done, ma'am, on making this a highly successful event and making this conference possible.

And, of course, someone else I think we all should thank for his role in the conference, and, of course, I'm talking about our Chief Justice William Rehnquist, Chief Justice of the Supreme Court, who regrettably could not be with us today. He wanted to be here.

Rarely has the White House been graced by such distinguished talent. More than 100 chief judicial officers from around the world, chief justices representing most of America's 50 States and territories, and practically the entire leadership of the Judicial Conference of the United States.

I heard that Judge Souter might invite some friends to Washington for his hearing, but I never dreamed it would get out of control like this. [*Laughter*] Truly it is a great honor to welcome this extraordinary assembly to Washington and a great honor to welcome you here at the White House.

It's an historic visit for many reasons, yours. Your Washington gathering marks the first time this conference has been held in the United States. But even more historic than the place are the times. And your visit comes as the capstone of America's celebration of 200 years of the world's oldest continuous constitution and independent judiciary. And with what I call the Revolution of '89 just behind us, your conference also serves to commemorate the emergence of some of the world's newest democracies. And so, I'm especially pleased to welcome and congratulate those justices representing the new and more independent judiciaries of Central Europe and Central America and, yes, also our new friends from the Soviet Union.

More than 200 years ago, 55 Americans met late into the night during a sweltering hot Philadelphia summer, debating a document that would be adopted by the American people as the supreme law of the land. By common agreement, Americans chose to live not under individual dictate but according to the rule of law. Its greatest innovation, an independent judiciary that protects constitutional principles through judicial review of executive and legislative actions. And truly, the U.S. Constitution stands as one of the world's great experiments in freedom and diversity and one of the world's great milestones in the effort to be free of tyranny, to be just, and to be civilized.

The American experience is a continuing one, and our success as a nation that is ruled by law and not by men depends upon our continuing commitment to an independent judiciary, a judiciary that is not subject to the political whims, to the nation's changing political climate, but that will interpret fairly and impartially our Constitution and the statutes as adopted by the elected representatives of our people.

And in the American tradition, the key to preserving a truly independent judiciary is ensuring that the role of the judiciary, like the role of the government itself, remains true to its constitutional function. The role of our judiciary is not to set policy but to apply the law of the land as found in our Constitution and in our statutes. Our Supreme Court plays a role of referee; it does not make up the rules but rather applies the rules to the situation that comes before it. And thus, our judiciary is not a substitute, you see, is not a substitute for representative government; rather, it's a limitation on it.

I mention the historic times, and of course, it's also an historic week right here

in Washington. Even as we speak, our constitutional experiment is unfolding up the street in the United States Senate, where America is engaged in the solemn process of the confirmation of a very fine and decent judge—a judge who I hope and believe will be our next, our newest Supreme Court Justice.

My old friend and neighbor, and one who I think Sandra Day O'Connor admires as well, was the late and beloved Justice Potter Stewart. He was once asked to name the most important attributes in a judge. And he fired back without hesitating, "Quality and competence, temperament and character, and diligence." Well, those attributes are exactly the qualities that I believe describe Judge Souter, my nominee to the Supreme Court. He's strong, incisive, has an independent devotion to the Constitution that was demonstrated during 12 years of distinguished service on the trial court, the U.S. Court of Appeals, and in particular, on the supreme court of his State, the New Hampshire Supreme Court. And I understand that after the conference ends today many of you are going to go out to observe our State supreme courts in action. They are America's judicial laboratories, the court of last resort for most of our citizens' cases, the proving grounds for some of our most distinguished U.S. Supreme Court Justices: New York's great jurist, Benjamin Cardozo; William Brennan, who has just stepped down after 34 years on the Supreme Court; and of course, Oliver Wendell Holmes.

But as we gather to talk about the rule of law this week, there's another subject that I'm sure is on everybody's mind, and I've said many times in the past year that we've entered into a new era in world affairs. And the international response to Iraq's naked aggression against a tiny neighbor proves just how true that is. As I said in Helsinki, just 6 days ago when I was over there to meet with President Gorbachev, if the nations of the world acting together continue to isolate Iraq and deny Saddam the fruits of aggression, we will set in place the cornerstone of an international order more peaceful, stable, and secure than any we have known.

One of the leaders of the world's last great unified alliance before the chilly descent of the cold war was Dwight David Eisenhower, a man that occupied this House as President of the United States. And Ike understood the stakes when he said: "The clearest way to show what the rule of law means to us in everyday life is to recall what has happened when there is no rule of law."

And as we stand here today commemorating more than 200 years of constitutional government in America, we look back with pride on the justice that we've achieved as a nation and the promise that has been offered the world through this one simple, magnificent idea: the idea known as the rule of law. Because like many of the principal nations you represent, all today who embrace the rule of law stand as a powerful force for justice at home and as a powerful example for justice abroad. I salute this great tradition, its rich heritage, and all the fine men and women gathered here who are dedicated to justice and the rule of law.

I want to thank you all once again for coming to the White House. Congratulations on what I'm told has been a highly successful conference. And Godspeed, all of you, in your service in the cause of justice around the world. Thank you all very, very much.

Note: The President spoke at 11:35 a.m. in the East Room at the White House. In his remarks, he referred to C. Boyden Gray, Counsel to the President, and Cynthia Hall, U.S. Circuit Judge for the Ninth Circuit and chairman of the Committee on the International Appellate Judges Conference.

Appointment of Teresa A. Gorman as Special Assistant to the President for Policy Development
September 14, 1990

The President today announced the appointment of Teresa A. Gorman as Special Assistant to the President for Policy Development at the White House.

Before joining the White House, Ms. Gorman was a professional staff member with the House Energy and Commerce Committee for over 5 years. She was responsible for the assessment and evaluation of environmental issues, including the Clean Air Act, Superfund, and global climate change. In addition, Ms. Gorman served as a policy analyst in the Environmental Protection Agency's Office of Policy, 1982–1984, and as a policy analyst at the Department of Energy, 1981–1982.

Ms. Gorman graduated from Cornell University (B.A., 1979) and George Washington University (M.A., 1982).

Nomination of Walter E. Massey To Be Director of the National Science Foundation
September 14, 1990

The President today announced his intention to nominate Walter E. Massey, of Illinois, to be Director of the National Science Foundation for a term of 6 years. He would succeed Erich Bloch.

Currently, Dr. Massey serves as vice president for research for the Argonne National Laboratory and a professor of physics at the University of Chicago in Chicago, IL. In addition, Dr. Massey has served as chairman of the board of the Argonne National Laboratory for the University of Chicago Development Corp. Prior to this, he served as a professor of physics at the University of Chicago, 1979–1982, and laboratory director for the Argonne National Laboratory, 1979–1984. He was an associate professor, 1970–1975, and a professor of physics and dean of the college at Brown University, 1975–1979. Dr. Massey was an assistant professor of physics at the University of Illinois, 1968–1970; staff physicist, 1968; postdoctoral fellow for the Argonne National Laboratory, 1966–1968; a postdoctoral research associate at Washington University, 1966; and a teaching assistant at Washington Uni-

versity, 1960–1961. In addition, Dr. Massey has served as an instructor of physics at Howard University, 1960; instructor of physics at Atlanta University, 1959; and an instructor of physics at Morehouse College, 1958–1959.

Dr. Massey graduated from Morehouse College (B.S., 1958) and Washington University (M.A., 1966; Ph.D., 1966). He was born April 5, 1938, in Hattiesburg, MS. Dr. Massey is married, has two children, and resides in Chicago, IL.

Nomination of Leonard H.O. Spearman, Sr., To Be United States Ambassador to Lesotho
September 14, 1990

The President today announced his intention to nominate Leonard H.O. Spearman, Sr., of Texas, to be Ambassador Extraordinary and Plenipotentiary of the United States of America to the Kingdom of Lesotho. He would succeed Robert M. Smalley.

Since 1988 Dr. Spearman has served as U.S. Ambassador to the Republic of Rwanda. Prior to 1980 he served in various positions at the Department of Health, Education, and Welfare in the Office of Education in Washington, DC: Associate Deputy Commissioner for Higher and Continuing Education, 1978–1980; Acting Deputy Commissioner for Higher and Continuing Education, 1976–1978; Associate Commissioner for Student Assistance, 1975–1978; Director of the Division of Student Financial Assistance, 1972–1975; and Director of the Division of Student Special Services, 1970–1972. In addition Dr. Spearman has served as a

distinguished professor of educational psychology at Texas Southern University, 1986–1988; president of Texas Southern University in Houston, TX, 1980–1986; professor of psychology at Southern University in Baton Rouge, LA, 1960–1970; associate professor of psychology at Florida A&M University, 1957–1960; teaching fellow in the School of Education at the University of Michigan Hospital Children's Psychiatric Institute, 1954–1957; instructor for the School of Education at Florida A&M, 1950–1954; science instructor at Lincoln High School in Tallahassee, 1948–1949; and a laboratory assistant at Florida A&M University, 1947–1948.

Dr. Spearman graduated from Florida A&M University (B.S., 1947) and the University of Michigan (M.A., 1950; Ph.D., 1960). He was born July 8, 1929, in Tallahassee, FL. Dr. Spearman is married and has three children.

Remarks on the Persian Gulf Crisis and an Exchange With Reporters
September 14, 1990

The President. Well, I just want to say a couple of things here, and be glad to take

just a handful of questions.

First, I want to publicly acknowledge and

express my appreciation for the decision by the Japanese Government to make additional contributions to the effort that we're all making in the Gulf. Specifically, Japan will be providing significant economic assistance to key countries in the region that are most severely affected by the sanctions and higher energy prices. Japan is also increasing its support for the multinational forces involved in the collective defense effort. And I gave my personal thanks to Prime Minister Kaifu last night when he called me to tell me about this news. And we are grateful to the Japanese—significant contribution.

And second, and in a similar vein, I want to say that early this morning Prime Minister Thatcher phoned to give me the additional good news of her country's latest contribution. She informed me that the United Kingdom would be sending a full armored brigade along with the additional helicopters and aircraft to Saudi Arabia. Some Americans may remember the name, the Desert Rats. And that's who will be going. As I told the Prime Minister over the phone, given all that the United Kingdom is already doing, this truly comes as the icing on the cake, a significant move by the Brits.

And I also called President Mitterrand a few minutes ago to consult with him on the outrageous Iraqi break-in at the French Embassy residence in Kuwait. These developments not only underscore the brutal behavior of Iraq but also the international support that exists and is marshaled against Iraq's occupation of Kuwait. I've often said that it is not the United States against Iraq but Iraq against the world. And for our part, we will continue to do everything possible to ensure that the sanctions work as intended and to deter and, if need be, defend Saudi Arabia against armed attack.

And here I just want to reiterate what I said when I first ordered the U.S. forces to Saudi Arabia—namely, that the United States forces were sent to Saudi Arabia at the request of the Saudi Government. And those same U.S. forces will depart as soon as they are no longer needed or wanted. And they will remain not one day longer than is absolutely necessary.

Q. Are we any closer to armed combat

because of what has happened at the French Embassy and also because a U.S. warship apparently has now fired across the bow of an Iraqi tanker? What do you know about that, sir?

The President. I wouldn't put it closer to a war situation. I still hope that this matter can be peacefully resolved. And the way for that to happen is for Iraq to comply with the sanctions. Yes, an American vessel did, in accordance with United Nations resolutions and in accordance with the sanctions, cause another Iraqi vessel to heave to, and it has been boarded. And I expect confidently that if it indeed is not carrying any contraband or anything that will violate the sanctions, it will be permitted to go on its way. But it did require a bit of a warning before the captain pulled over and permitted the boarding party to have a look.

Q. Mr. President, what can you tell us about the U.S. consul that was detained in the Canadian Ambassador's house? Any protest or any action about that?

The President. I don't have all the details on that one. But again, I would lump that into the unacceptable action category. I don't have the facts on that.

Mr. Scowcroft. They've been released, Mr. President.

The President. They have been released. But any of these incidents—all of them add up to clear violations of international law. And I think they do raise tensions; they clearly do.

Q. Mr. President, how is Ambassador Howell [U.S. Ambassador to Kuwait], and would the U.S. have to respond militarily if Iraq entered the United States compound in Kuwait City?

The President. That's too hypothetical, the last part of the question. But I have no reason to believe that Ambassador Howell is not in good shape. I haven't heard anything to the contrary.

Q. How long are you going to keep him there, sir?

The President. I've not made a determination on that.

Q. Mr. President, gasoline prices are up dramatically, and heating oil is at a record level in today's wholesale price report.

What kind of warning signals does that send to you about the overall economic situation related to the Gulf crisis?

The President. Well, I think anytime you have price inflation, sudden inflation, it is a matter of concern, given the state of the economy. What it does is make me argue even more vociferously for a budget agreement. But the shortages—this speculation—we're talking about future market prices. We're talking about futures. That speculative atmosphere belies the reality, which is that there are sufficient petroleum products so that the market should not be going for higher prices. In other words, it's speculation. It's futures speculation.

Q. What's your reading on——

The President. I believe you're talking about October prices that are quoted on the crude market.

Yes.

Federal Budget Negotiations

Q. What's your reading on the budget negotiations as the clock ticks out?

The President. Well, kind of up and down like a roller coaster. This morning, there was the feeling—Dick Darman and John Sununu, Secretary Brady felt that they were closing the gap. Last night it was a little more pessimistic. So, I can't tell you; I haven't talked to our negotiators in the last 2 hours.

Persian Gulf Crisis

Q. Is France going to take action as a result of the Embassy incursion? Will the United States take action as a result of that?

The President. I don't know what France is going to do. But clearly, I will continue close consultation with Mr. Mitterrand because I told him I view this as a matter that is of grave concern to the United States. It happens to be the French Ambassador's residence, but it is a matter that we look at as—it concerns everybody, and told him that I would do anything I could to support whatever he decides to do. And he will be back—I found him in Czechoslovakia, and he will be back, and I believe he has a Cabinet meeting tomorrow. So, we'll simply wait and see what they recommend.

Q. Does that include help militarily?

Q. Mr. President, you're suggesting that

the Iraqis are, in fact, tightening the screws in a number of areas. Is there an escalation now required from you and your allies?

The President. When an escalation is required from me, Saddam Hussein will know it.

Q. What about the tape, Mr. President?

The President. The tape? Haven't heard. I think it's there now. Do we know if the tape has arrived?

Mr. Fitzwater. It should be there tonight.

The President. It got off to a slow start with that Eagleburger handoff, but it should be there tonight. [*Laughter*] One of the classic scenes. [*Laughter*]

Supreme Court Nominee

Q. Mr. President, have you had a chance to see any of Judge Souter's testimony, and do you have any kind of a feeling for how it's going?

The President. I have seen it, and I think it has been magnificent. I haven't seen it all, but I must confess, slight confession—and maybe it's because our budgeteers were out at the summit doing all the heavy lifting—I watched it for about an hour and a half yesterday, and I watched it for about 20 minutes today. And my admiration for Judge Souter, respect for him is even higher. I really think he's conducted himself extraordinarily well.

Q. Do you believe the questioning has been fair?

The President. What I've seen so far, yes. And a Senator has the right to ask any question he wants. And what I think has been masterful is the way Judge Souter has gone as far as he possibly can and yet has handled it with such intellect, in such a knowledgeable manner. I don't think anybody gets the feeling that he is improperly avoiding things.

Federal Budget Negotiations

Q. Senator Dole this morning said that if you can't get the capital gains issue resolved, maybe you shouldn't continue with the budget talks. Is it fair to hold the budget talks hostage to the capital gains differential?

The President. Listen, Senator Dole is doing a magnificent job out there. I don't know in what context he placed that. I think everybody in the summit knows of my commitment to it. I am absolutely convinced that it would not even be a revenue loser, although it's scored that way, and it is something that is fundamentally important to the continued growth in the economy, a growth that, frankly, is far too slow right now. So, I hope it's put into effect. But I'm not going to kind of go beyond that.

Q. But last November, on November 2d, you issued a statement to the effect that if you were ever going to get a deficit cut deal arranged, you should pursue capital gains as a separate vehicle. Why don't you do that now if you're serious about——

The President. Because we've got a strategy. And I think it's working, and I think all our people are on the same side on this issue.

Rita [Rita Beamish, Associated Press], and then I've got to go——

Persian Gulf Crisis

Q. Mr. President, I couldn't hear what Charles [Charles Bierbauer, Cable News Network] asked, but did you tell Mitterrand that you would back him with military retaliation if that's the way he wants to go?

The President. We didn't go into the details of the backing, but I just told him he has the full support of the United States. And he does.

Q. Have you talked to Ambassador Howell about what he should do if Iraqi forces——

The President. I haven't talked to Howell in the last week.

Last one, John [John Cochran, NBC News], and then I've really——

Q. Mr. President, is it different, sir, from the American Embassy being invaded, however?

The President. I'm not sure I'd make that distinction.

Q. Well, are you rattling at least one saber? You talk about——

The President. No, I'm not rattling sabers.

You're trying to get me to sound like I'm rattling sabers. When I rattle a saber, the man will know it.

Q. But you talked about grave concern, but you also talked about the fact that you'll pull the troops back as soon as you can. So, we saw a mixed signal there.

The President. Oh, no, there should be no connection between those at all. I mean, what I was trying to do is there's been some speculation, some of it mischievous, in the Middle East that the United States wants to remain there. And so, what I want to do is just reiterate what I think I said in the meeting to the Joint Session, and that is that we want those people, all of them, out as soon as possible. And so, that should be separated from anything I'm saying here. I'm glad you asked. Let me clarify that.

Q. Are the Saudis getting anxious about having so many American troops there?

The President. I haven't heard that at all, and I don't think so. I know I would have heard it if that were the case. They're totally clued in on what our plans are. So, there's no disquiet on that at all.

Thank you all.

Federal Budget Negotiations

Q. Do you expect a budget agreement this weekend?

The President. Expected one a week ago.

Note: President Bush spoke at 1:31 p.m. on the South Lawn of the White House prior to his departure for Camp David, MD. In his remarks, he referred to President François Mitterrand of France; John H. Sununu, Chief of Staff to President Bush; President Saddam Hussein of Iraq; and Lawrence S. Eagleburger, Deputy Secretary of State. Brent Scowcroft was Assistant to the President for National Security Affairs, and Marlin Fitzwater was Press Secretary to the President. A reporter referred to an address that President Bush taped for broadcast to the Iraqi people.

Address to the People of Iraq on the Persian Gulf Crisis
September 16, 1990

I'm here today to explain to the people of Iraq why the United States and the world community has responded the way it has to Iraq's occupation of Kuwait. My purpose is not to trade accusations, not to escalate the war of words, but to speak with candor about what has caused this crisis that confronts us. Let there be no misunderstanding: We have no quarrel with the people of Iraq. I've said many times, and I will repeat right now, our only object is to oppose the invasion ordered by Saddam Hussein.

On August 2d, your leadership made its decision to invade, an unprovoked attack on a small nation that posed no threat to your own. Kuwait was the victim; Iraq, the aggressor.

And the world met Iraq's invasion with a chorus of condemnation: unanimous resolutions in the United Nations. Twenty-seven States—rich and poor, Arab, Moslem, Asian, and African—have answered the call of Saudi Arabia and free Kuwait and sent forces to the Gulf region to defend against Iraq. For the first time in history, 13 States of the Arab League, representing 80 percent of the Arab nation, have condemned a brother Arab State. Today, opposed by world opinion, Iraq stands isolated and alone.

I do not believe that you, the people of Iraq, want war. You've borne untold suffering and hardship during 8 long years of war with Iran—a war that touched the life of every single Iraqi citizen; a war that took the lives of hundreds of thousands of young men, the bright promise of an entire generation. No one knows better than you the incalculable costs of war, the ultimate cost when a nation's vast potential and vital energies are consumed by conflict. No one knows what Iraq might be today, what prosperity and peace you might now enjoy, had your leaders not plunged you into war. Now, once again, Iraq finds itself on the brink of war. Once again, the same Iraqi leadership has miscalculated. Once again, the Iraqi people face tragedy.

Saddam Hussein has told you that Iraqi troops were invited into Kuwait. That's not true. In fact, in the face of far superior force, the people of Kuwait are bravely resisting this occupation. Your own returning soldiers will tell you the Kuwaitis are fighting valiantly in any way they can.

Saddam Hussein tells you that this crisis is a struggle between Iraq and America. In fact, it is Iraq against the world. When President Gorbachev and I met at Helsinki [September 9], we agreed that no peaceful international order is possible if larger states can devour their neighbors. Never before has world opinion been so solidly united against aggression.

Nor, until the invasion of Kuwait, has the United States been opposed to Iraq. In the past, the United States has helped Iraq import billions of dollars worth of food and other commodities. And the war with Iran would not have ended 2 years ago without U.S. support and sponsorship in the United Nations.

Saddam Hussein tells you the occupation of Kuwait will benefit the poorer nations of the world. In fact, the occupation of Kuwait is helping no one and is now hurting you, the Iraqi people, and countless others of the world's poor. Instead of acquiring new oil wealth by annexing Kuwait, this misguided act of aggression will cost Iraq over $20 billion a year in lost oil revenues. Because of Iraq's aggression, hundreds of thousands of innocent foreign workers are fleeing Kuwait and Iraq. They are stranded on Iraq's borders, without shelter, without food, without medicine, with no way home. These refugees are suffering, and this is shameful.

But even worse, others are being held hostage in Iraq and Kuwait. Hostage-taking punishes the innocent and separates families. It is barbaric. It will not work, and it will not affect my ability to make tough decisions.

I do not want to add to the suffering of the people of Iraq. The United Nations has put binding sanctions in place not to punish the Iraqi people but as a peaceful means to convince your leadership to withdraw from Kuwait. That decision is in the hands of Saddam Hussein.

The pain you now experience is a direct result of the path your leadership has chosen. When Iraq returns to the path of peace, when Iraqi troops withdraw from Kuwait, when that country's rightful government is restored, when all foreigners held against their will are released, then, and then alone, will the world end the sanctions.

Perhaps your leaders do not appreciate the strength of the forces united against them. Let me say clearly: There is no way Iraq can win. Ultimately, Iraq must withdraw from Kuwait.

No one—not the American people, not this President—wants war. But there are times when a country—when all countries who value the principles of sovereignty and independence—must stand against aggression. As Americans, we're slow to raise our hand in anger and eager to explore every peaceful means of settling our disputes; but when we have exhausted every alternative, when conflict is thrust upon us, there is no nation on Earth with greater resolve or stronger steadiness of purpose.

The actions of your leadership have put Iraq at odds with the world community. But while those actions have brought us to the brink of conflict, war is not inevitable. It is still possible to bring this crisis to a peaceful end.

When we stand with Kuwait against aggression, we stand for a principle well understood in the Arab world. Let me quote the words of one Arab leader, Saddam Hussein himself: "An Arab country does not have the right to occupy another Arab country. God forbid, if Iraq should deviate from the right path, we would want Arabs to send their armies to put things right. If Iraq should become intoxicated by its power and move to overwhelm another Arab State, the Arabs would be right to deploy their armies to check it."

Those are the words of your leader, Saddam Hussein, spoken on November 28, 1988, in a speech to Arab lawyers. Today, 2 years later, Saddam has invaded and occupied a member of the United Nations and the Arab League. The world will not allow this aggression to stand. Iraq must get out of Kuwait for the sake of principle, for the sake of peace, and for the sake of the Iraqi people.

Note: The President recorded this address in the Oval Office at the White House on September 12, and it was broadcast unedited on Iraqi television on September 16.

Remarks and a Question-and-Answer Session With Members of the Regional News Media
September 17, 1990

The President. Let me just make a few opening comments, and then I'll be glad to respond to your questions. I've been talking to him, and I understand from [Secretary of Defense] Dick Cheney, who's left, and also Roger Porter [Assistant to the President for Economic and Domestic Policy], who was with me, that you've been discussing both the international situation and the domestic budget scene. And if I may, I just want to add one or two comments and then take questions. As I told the American people and the Congress on Tuesday night in that address to the Joint Session, the level of world cooperation in opposing Iraqi aggression is simply unprecedented. More than 20 nations have joined us. Now, armed forces from countries spanning four continents have taken up defensive positions at the request of King Fahd of Saudi Arabia.

Over the last several days we've seen Great Britain announce that it will send a full armored brigade—the famous Desert Rats. And France has announced that it'll also be sending a significant ground force. Japan and Germany have also said that they will contribute billions to the cost of the multinational effort and to the related effort of easing the economic hardship of those nations that are hardest hit—those supporting sanctions. Just this weekend the United Nations Security Council has once again strongly condemned Saddam Hussein [President of Iraq] for those outrageous break-ins at the diplomatic premises in Kuwait.

For America to maintain its responsibilities abroad, America must remain strong and vital. Again, as I said last week, our world leadership and domestic strength are mutual, and they are reinforcing. That's why I am very interested in these negotiations going on on the budget and, again, calling on the budget negotiators from the Congress and the administration to redouble their efforts to get a budget agreement. I want to see one that is oriented toward growth—a point I made in last week's address to the Joint Session—one which contains incentives like the capital gains tax cut, which I am absolutely convinced will create jobs. The Congress must also enact real spending cuts, not these smoke-and-mirror cuts that simply don't cut spending as advertised. Congress must ensure that the budget process reform takes place. And its 5-year plan absolutely must be enforceable.

Finally, Congress must enact a multiyear defense budget that meets the needs of this country not only in terms of the improvement of East-West relations but also our broader responsibilities in other parts of the world—responsibilities that the crisis with Iraq has once again brought home to us.

Earlier, I asked for an up-or-down vote on a complete $500 billion deficit reduction package, with or without a budget summit agreement, by September 28th at the latest. The Nation stands only 13 days away from the drastic consequences of what's known as a mandated sequester, required if Congress is unable to get me a budget by then. We in the administration stand ready to do our part. I am confident that Congress will do its part. I've been happy to see that we've made some headway recently in budget talks, but it really is time now to get an agreement now. I think we owe that to the American people.

So, on both these fronts there's a lot going on. I wanted to get those comments on the record, and I'll be glad to take a few questions.

Persian Gulf Crisis

Q. Sir, going back to the Iraqi matter again—the raid on the residence of the French Ambassador on Friday—French President Mitterrand was quoted as saying, "There is no sign coming from Iraq about avoiding an armed conflict." The French President seems to be saying our chances of talking our way out of a shooting war are diminishing. Could I have your comments, please?

The President. I talked to him yesterday from Camp David, had a good conversation with him. As I indicated, we are together on how we look at most aspects of this problem. We were very grateful that France took the action. I had called him a few days before to express empathy with him on what had happened to their Embassy. I must say that I didn't get the feeling that he has given up on any kind of a peaceful solution from the two contacts I've had with him personally within the last 2 weeks. But I think when you see actions like this that the French Embassy went through take place, you wonder what motivates this. France, historically, has been reasonably close to Iraq. They have never condoned the terrorism or some of the happenings in the Iran-Iraq war, even, but they've had a long relationship there. And I think the French Government and the French President wonder: Why in the world is he behaving like this? So, there's an uncertainty that perhaps he was reflecting there. But I didn't get the feeling that he feels that there is no chance for a peaceful solution.

Dismissal of the Air Force Chief of Staff

Q. Mr. President, thank you. Has General Dugan's actions put you in a difficult bargaining position in Iraq, and how much damage has that done?

The President. No, it hasn't. I'll have nothing to say about that, except I strongly support our Secretary of Defense. And he'll have more to say on the details of that in a few minutes at a press conference. But I don't think that we can possibly assess that at this juncture to give you a real answer.

Q. Just a quick followup. Are our troops in any more jeopardy now today than they have been in the past because of those remarks?

The President. Well, I wouldn't want to say that we are less able to protect our troops in Saudi Arabia. We're going to do that, and I am not—that is not the concern I have.

Economic Incentives

Q. Sir, in New England as elsewhere around the country, thousands of people have been laid off in their defense jobs. What initiative should the Government take to help these people or help them find new work?

The President. Well, it's a very difficult situation for many families in New England. Other areas of the country have gone through similar regional downturns. I think of the Southwest, particularly in Texas not so many years ago, my hometown of Houston. I think the best thing the Federal Government can do is to get these interest rates down and to adopt growth incentives so that people will continue to create jobs. And that's the major responsibility, it seems to me, of the Federal Government—fiscal discipline and a budget agreement that will incentivize the economies. You may recall what Alan Greenspan [Chairman of the Board of Governors of the Federal Reserve System] said recently about if you get an agreement, the Fed would then feel inclined to move quickly to significant interest rates.

So, I really think that job creation is the best thing we can do, and I think private sector job creation is the answer, not government programs in that sense.

Q. Mr. President, are you adamant about a capital gains tax reduction in the budget talks?

The President. I've indicated all along that this is something to which I am—I really believe is necessary to stimulate the economy. And I have not changed my view on that.

Urban Crime

Q. You have acted decisively in the Iran crisis. But many in New York City, for example, feel that efforts to control the flow of drugs and crime is not working. Why are you doing not more to meet the challenge?

The President. I think we are doing as much as we can to meet the challenge. Perhaps there's more, and I would welcome any constructive criticism. But we are doing pretty well in terms of interdiction——

Q. A followup.

The President. I'm not quite finished with the beginning, but then you can follow up when I finish with it. We want you to do that. [*Laughter*] But I'd like to see our crime bill pass. I think that would send a good message to the policemen on the streets of New York that we plan to back them up more. I favor the ultimate penalty for these drug traffickers, these major traffickers, and we've got a difference with some in New York on that one. So, we've put forward an anticrime proposal last year that, if enacted, I think would have already been of benefit. But in terms of the interdiction, I think we're getting reasonably good cooperation from abroad. It can be better. And we're working on more initiatives with those Andean countries.

What was the followup?

Q. What do you say to the folks on the street that we talk to every day who just see it getting worse? They can't walk outside without somebody getting shot by a stray bullet. What do you tell those people?

The President. I tell them that I'd like to get more anti—in the Federal level. I don't know how the States—let the city and the States do their job; that's their responsibility. But at the Federal level, please support me. Please get all your Congressmen to support the anticrime legislation that we have called for. And I really believe that will help. And in some of these areas where people are—they just feel that they're up against enormous odds. And the condonation of crime that comes through soft treatment of the criminal I think sends exactly the wrong signal to those embattled citizens.

Economic Incentives

Q. Mr. President, the economy is showing some troubling signs that Americans can see with the rising gas prices and the stock market condition, the budget negotiators holed up at the Air Force base and the talk about the teetering on the brink of a recession. How would you characterize the condition of the economy? And do you think there's a financial crisis in America?

The President. I don't think there's a financial crisis. I think the economy's growth is slow. I do not think that nationally we're in a recession. I heard the Secretary of the Treasury yesterday. I agree with what he said. I agree with what the conference board says. I agree with what the Chairman of the Fed says on that. But I do think that a budget agreement is the best antidote to further economic slowdown because I think it'll result in lower interest rates and a renewed sense of confidence in investment in America, both of which are necessary to guarantee a more robust growth.

Q. Do you think that pessimism among consumers could create a snowballing effect with this—it could get worse, people see the economy getting worse, and therefore it becomes worse?

The President. Certainly I don't want to contribute to that psychology by making a comment that goes beyond what I've just said. So, I don't want to answer it in a way that that is a concern I really have. I think all of that—the psychology of the market—can be turned around by a good budget agreement that has some growth incentives in it.

Persian Gulf Crisis

Q. Mr. President, do you think the American people would support the Persian Gulf policy as much as they have been if we started to take thousands and thousands of casualties, which is a likelihood if there is fighting?

The President. I don't know. But I am inclined to feel that we're off to a very good start. I think your hypothesis alluded to that. But I don't want to make a prediction as to how the American people would respond under that. I'm old enough to remember a clear-cut case—different circumstances, different times—World War II. Many here are too young to actually remember the effect that had on American public opinion and all of that. But there was

a lot of sorrow; there was a lot of regret. Everyone identified with the families who lost loved ones. But the country stayed fairly well together. Now, at this juncture, I think the American people are magnificently united in terms of standing up against this aggression. But I think it's a little too hypothetical for me to feel comfortable going beyond that.

Q. There is the thought, too, that the American public traditionally doesn't support stalemates that last a long, long time. If this gets bogged down in a nonshooting stalemate, will that support erode?

The President. I don't know. I read lots of predictions from people that say it would, and I would hope not. But, again, it's a little hypothetical because I think you have to know what else is going on at the time. But how long is too long? How much—I think about those questions, but I can't define it for you. I want those soldiers out as soon as possible. I want them all out. All out, period. And yet, I can't say when that will be.

What we are trying is this all-out, full-court international press on the diplomatic side. And I want to see that work. Interestingly enough, you have different interlocutors, heads of government that'll tell you in varying degrees how effective they think the sanctions will be—some absolutely convinced that these economic sanctions not only are working but will be very, very effective in a short run; others thinking it's going to take longer. But I don't think it would be good for me to get into that debate because I'm not clear in my own mind how long this kind of support holds up.

AIDS

Q. Mr. President, but we have had thousands and thousands of casualties in the AIDS crisis in the San Francisco area where we have been particularly hard hit. And there are many there who feel that the Federal Government has not done enough and you've sort of drug your feet a bit on this issue. I'd like to know first of all what you think when you see in the papers every day the escalating number of casualties, and secondly, what you could say to the people of the bay area who are fighting AIDS?

The President. Breaks my heart when I see it. And I think of the families. I think of the loved ones. I think of the personal tragedy. I also think of the fact that when you're wrestling with an enormous medical problem of this nature, it is very difficult to have a snappy answer that will allay the fears of all the people. I also think of the fact that we are spending a considerable amount of money, through NIH [National Institutes of Health] and other ways, to beat this dreaded disease.

I think some groups do not give proper credit to the fact that a lot of people are laboring night and day doing just that. And a lot of people are—I think of some of the nurses and doctors, particularly—really giving of themselves around the clock to take care of these people. So, I wish there was some quick and easy cure. I wish somebody could convince me that if you could only spend a quarter of a billion dollars more, we would have the answer. I have been listening to what I think are the finest research people and doctors in the country, and I think they feel that we've done pretty well in funding levels at the Federal level. And then there's an awful lot going on across private hospitals and private research labs all across the country.

So, I can understand the agony. I must say some of the excesses of those groups does not help the cause. When Secretary Sullivan, a dedicated doctor and the head of HHS, goes to California and isn't even permitted the courtesy to get his message out because of people shouting throughout it, I don't think that helps the so-called activists in the movement. And I had a lot of mail saying people were quite embarrassed by that. But, again, I have to say I feel very sad and can identify with those families whose kids are suffering or older people who are afflicted by this disease. And I just hope we have a breakthrough.

Q. But, meanwhile, while we're waiting for a cure, the hospitals are overcrowded. Is there anything that you could suggest for people who are not getting the proper care?

The President. No, not anything beyond what Secretary Sullivan suggested out there, which was pretty good.

Persian Gulf Crisis

Q. Not long ago, the Wall Street Journal reported that as recently as the day before the Iraqi invasion of Kuwait, members of your administration were quietly lobbying against a bill by Representative Howard Berman that would have essentially slapped Kuwait [Iraq] on the knuckles—proposed sanctions for their increasingly aggressive behavior. That bill and other examples of administration support for Iraq—do you now regret those things in light of the invasion?

The President. Absolutely, in light of the invasion. However, there was some reason to believe that perhaps improved relations with the West would modify the behavior. But given the invasion, absolutely. I think if everybody had the benefit of total hindsight, why, you'd go back and say, hey, this didn't make much sense. I'm not sure, having said that, that that would have changed Saddam Hussein's intention to take over Kuwait.

Q. Where was the miscalculation in U.S. policy?

The President. I don't think this is caused by miscalculation in the United States policy. I think it's caused by a miscalculation by Saddam Hussein. And I think the American people understand that to a fare-thee-well.

Q. Mr. President, if Saddam Hussein is a loose cannon, is he going to respond to any logic or rational—in any logical or rational way to this—to the embargo?

The President. That's a good question. And I don't know how one responds to it, because what he has done is clearly irrational if he felt it would bring down the wrath of the United States and 20 other countries and, indeed, the entire world at the United Nations.

But I am convinced that the sanctions are working to some degree. I can't tell you definitively how effective they are at this minute. But they are working. And what we want to do is tighten them up every way we can, joining other countries in doing that, to give that approach the maximum attempt at success, and then we'll see. But it may be beyond his control because nobody wants to see their whole economy screech to a total halt. And you got to remember, 90 percent of his funds from abroad came from oil, and that is tightened way down. In fact, I don't think there are any exceptions to that at all.

Q. Mr. President, do you——

The President. Coming over.

Q. Do you think that perhaps an air embargo might encourage Saddam Hussein to react more rationally to the sanctions?

The President. I can't certify to you how much is going in by air. What we want to do is tighten up the United Nations sanctions so nothing is going in. And that's hard to do in terms of overflights and some countries that seem to be more willing than others to avoid the sanctions. But I know that François Mitterrand has talked to this point, and I understand it. And I would be prepared to work with anybody to tie that additional knot in the sanctions.

Q. I have a followup. Do you think that your message to the Iraqi people had any impact on public opinion there? I think there was a report that said that the cartoon ratings did a little better.

The President. It got a good exercise for the demonstrators who had been notified to demonstrate before they had even heard what I had to say. So, it kept them hustling around, jumping up and down, screaming about the United States. And if that helped them vent their frustrations, fine. [*Laughter*]

What I do think it will do is to send a word, very objectively, to other Arab countries that it isn't Saddam Hussein and the rest of the Arab world against the United States, but it's something quite different. And if two Iraqi citizens heard that, it would be worth the effort. And who knows? Those things—the truth is a good thing. It's a good thing to put into Iraq—getting very little of it now. And so, I think it was worthwhile. And I'm told that the response in other areas has been pretty good. So, we'll have to—I think it's a little early to evaluate it all. But I think they must have been a little concerned about it because the demonstrators with their signs already printed—at least from one report I read—were already heading to the demonstration point before they knew what I said. How did they know what I was going to say?

Medicare

Q. Mr. President, on this, the 25th anniversary of Medicare, we have the budget coming down to the wire again, and again Medicare is taking it on the chin, very hard. It seems to be getting worse every year. The providers are complaining. Hospitals are closing. Certainly, the elderly are complaining, and their organizations are getting very vocal. What do you have to say to these people? Why Medicare?

The President. I'm saying that no decisions have been made. And I've tried to avoid discussing details of this budget agreement while these details are being hammered out. I think the American people are very much concerned about the escalating costs of hospital care. There's no question about that. That shows up as something that's very much on their minds. But beyond that I don't feel like going at this point because there's some negotiations going on. But I'm not sure that I've seen anything in print that accurately reflects a consensus out there at Andrews.

Persian Gulf Crisis

Q. Mr. President, with regard to the question of national unity in response to the Gulf crisis, do you have any worries that the political battles over the economic summit—some of the things that have been said—are tearing away at that?

The President. No. And that's a very important point. And I don't see any evidence of that whatsoever. And I think that's very good. And it transcends liberal, conservative, Republican, Democrat. The support is there, and I have seen no evidence that any of the deliberations about the summit, at the summit or outside of the summit meetings, have eroded support in Congress, for example, or amongst the American people. But I think it's important that that not happen.

Q. Mr. President, what are your concerns about Iran's apparently warming relations with Iraq and how that might affect the equation in the Gulf crisis?

The President. Iran got almost everything they wanted from Iraq. This has not enhanced Saddam Hussein's standing in Iraq. Hundreds of thousands of lives were lost on both sides. And now, the victory has been handed to Saddam Hussein. We have had indirect assurances from Iran that they want to see these sanctions complied with and enacted. Until I am shown that Iran is violating the sanctions, I'm not going to buy into the argument that they've made some secret deal to violate the sanctions.

Q. Even with the statements by the Iranian clergy, the fundamentalist clergy, that this is time for a holy war against the United States?

The President. Nobody has suggested that out of this there's going to be a harmony and sweetness between some of those factions in Iran and the United States. But read carefully what he said. I'm told by some experts that he did not call for a jihad. But you've got to analyze it very carefully. But there will be factions inside Iran that will continue to resist any improvement in relations between Iran and the United States, and we understand that.

But the main thing is, I think the important thing is right now is that Iran do what Iran has publicly said it would do, and that is to comply with the international sanctions. And they have said that publicly.

Q. You've been reporting with some pleasure on the fact that our allies and friends around the world have been joining us in the Gulf, and even those countries that are constitutionally restrained, like Germany and Japan, from sending troops have been sending money. At the same time as this is happening, the cost estimates for our presence there have been jumping just as much as the troop counts have, and earlier Secretary Cheney mentioned that the deployment isn't even finished. Should we be concerned as taxpayers that the Persian Gulf crisis has been written a blank check for the duration?

The President. You know what I think about that one? I think the American people want me to do exactly what we ought to do to fulfill our four objectives over there. And if that means that we have to ask others to support certain aspects of this in a burden-sharing way, we're going to continue to do that. But I believe that the American people have confidence in the decisions that we've taken, and I don't think they would want to shortchange the

effort, no matter how serious the budget complications are right now.

Q. Does this scotch any hope for—big-city mayors, for instance, have talked about a peace dividend. It may have been a phantom all along.

The President. I've always felt that that was a phantom because I don't think you can declare a dividend when you're operating at a loss. And we're operating at a tremendous deficit. So, I hope that they have been disabused of the fact that there would be enormous money to spread around. But I think a big-city mayor would stand right up next to me, no matter how serious the problems in his or her city, and would say, we don't want to shortchange the military effort. If we're going to have those people over there, we ought to do what is necessary to give them full support. I think that's the way they'd all react.

Energy Policy

Q. Mr. President, at the beginning of the crisis, there were some calls for you to use the strategic petroleum reserve to hold down gas prices. What do you consider a proper use of the strategic petroleum reserve, and are you satisfied with the level at which it is right now?

The President. I think that when you have a real shortage of a product or you see an external event that is going to guarantee that there be shortage, then would be the time when you most certainly should use the SPR. It is my judgment that there isn't such a shortage at this time. There is some feeling that a demonstrative, albeit not large, drawdown would calm a fluctuating market. We'd say, now, wait a minute, you speculators that are speculating on the price of oil out into October sometime do so at your own risk. You could make a case—and I'm listening to those in the administration and on the Hill that make the case—that such a drawdown of a small amount perhaps at the beginning might argue against or guarantee against speculation in the futures market. That's an intellectual and economic argument that has some appeal.

But the reason we haven't drawn down the SPR is, in my judgment, I have not felt that there was a shortage. Fortunately, if this had to occur, it occurred at a time when there was reasonable amounts of stock. So, you're seeing the fluctuation driven not by market forces, not by supply and demand today, but by speculation as to what it might be in the future, and I just don't think that that would entirely be offset by a SPR drawdown.

So, there are other circumstances under which you would clearly have to draw down. I mean, if we had left Saudi Arabia undefended and if, when Saddam Hussein sent the tanks and the armor south from Kuwait City down to the border, they had gone across, cut off Dhahran or something like that, then you would have had a situation where you might have short-range stocks overhanging the market that would last for a few days, but clearly you would have had an emergency. You would have had something that any President would have, I think, instantly called for a drawdown of the SPR.

Q. Mr. President, can you address the question down the road about the tradeoffs in environmental concerns with regard to the current oil situation, and in particular if you could address what's going on in California right now? You banned offshore oil drilling for 10 years. But there are a lot of environmentalists in California who are afraid that you're going to go back on your word.

The President. I have no plans to revisit the decisions I have taken. But what I do want to do—and I may run into conflict with some groups—is to more vigorously go forward with incentives for domestic drilling. I mentioned Alaska, I mentioned tax incentives that I proposed a year ago—over a year ago—and I want to press for those.

When I met with the California delegation, I said to them: We simply cannot have it prevail that we don't want any drilling here, and she doesn't want any drilling there, and he doesn't want any drilling there. Everybody do some drilling, but do it in somebody else's area. That is not good enough. And I said someday we're going to realize that we are becoming too dependent on foreign oil. You can ask the California delegation with whom I met just prior to my decision. I don't believe that the

supply situation is such that I have to revisit the decisions I did make that affect Florida and affect those certain areas in California.

Q. A followup. You're going to be going to California tomorrow to do some campaigning for Senator Wilson. He is currently opposed to an initiative in California that would ban offshore oil drilling. Will you be saying anything about that when you are there?

The President. I doubt it. I've got enough problems right here in Washington without going out and commenting on a provision out there. [*Laughter*] But if the question is put to me at a press conference, "Do you want to ban offshore drilling?" the answer will be no. If the question is put to me as you put it, "Do you feel you need to change the decisions you've already made?" I'll say no, I don't think I need to do that. I'm not familiar with that proposition, but this is the point: I mean, I don't think these regions can have it. Some never want a refinery. Some never want a drilling rig anywhere near their place. And yet, they see clearly the adverse economic effect on their citizens that comes from a dislocation of this nature.

The bottom line is: It's going to have to be conservation. It's going to have to be alternative sources. It's going to have to be more hydrocarbon drilling. I think we can accomplish those objectives through incentives and through sounder practice and through new technology and—for example, clean coal technology—without having to do damage to the highly sensitive environmental areas.

I've got time—28:40—and I said to answer questions for 30—so I don't want to get in trouble with Kristen [Kristen Taylor, Director of Media Relations at the White House]. But it's 28:47.

Q. Mr. President, you won't hear many people in Houston or in Texas saying, "We don't want drilling here."

The President. No, I haven't heard that.

Q. What are your Houston oil men and women friends telling you they want by incentives? And what are you telling them?

The President. I haven't been in personal touch with the Houston oil people, though [Secretary of Commerce] Bob Mosbacher, unrecused now from giving advice to the President, feels that the incentives that we put forward last year should be vigorously pushed to stimulate domestic drilling. There are also things that we had in there that would give an exemption—you'd understand—maybe not all of us here today—on secondary oil, a break to permit some of this secondary—these stripper-well productions from going offstream. The oil is there, but—produce so little, the option is, do I get some incentive to do this, or do I shut the well down?

So, I think there are things we can do in that. I think there are things we can do in R&D in terms of tertiary production that would be of benefit. But the major incentive would be to give a tax incentive to domestic drillers for future drilling. It won't detract from current income, current revenues in the tax situation. I think that is the place where we'd push hard. Now, there's all kind—you're hearing other ideas around that would have an effect on the constituency that you ask about: import fees or taxes on petroleum products or whatever. And I just don't want to comment on those as long as this summit is going on.

I've got time for the last one. Here it is, right in the middle.

Persian Gulf Crisis

Q. Mr. President, who makes the decision on how troops from foreign nations are deployed in Saudi Arabia—where the Syrians are deployed, the Egyptians, French, the British? And is there going to be an overall command?

The President. Because of the overall magnitude of the United States force there, there is an active consultation with General Schwarzkopf, our CINC, our commander in chief, in the area. And we have not forsworn the right of that general officer to control American troops, nor have the French—who aren't quite there yet in force—or the Brits, or others, done that. But it is a matter of close coordination, particularly with the host country.

But I don't want to diminish the importance of General Schwarzkopf in the deployment of forces. Clearly, he can't order the Desert Rats to a certain deployment. But in working very closely with his counterpart in the British forces, or the one that controls the British forces, those matters have all been worked out through really fundamental consultation and in accordance with an overall plan that we've worked on with the various—the commanders that have forces in the area. So, it's a coordinated effort. And I have no hesitancy at all to say to the parents of the kids over there, or families: Should something happen that required combat, the command structure will function very, very smoothly. And we're not going to have to stand around waiting for someone else to decide if there is some provocation, either.

Thank you all very, very much.

Note: The President spoke at 2:02 p.m. in Room 450 of the Old Executive Office Building.

Remarks to Participants in the Elementary School Recognition Program
September 17, 1990

Thank you, and welcome to the White House lawn on this beautiful fall day. We're delighted to have you all here. And thank you, Secretary Cavazos, and thank you especially for your leadership in keeping education at the very top of our national agenda. A special welcome to the Governors who are with us today and those who participated in last year's economic [education] summit. I'm so glad that this many are here. And I want to greet Governor Campbell and Governor Casey, Governor Perpich, Governor Schaefer, and I'm just delighted they are here. Will you all stand up, please, and have a welcome from the crowd here? [*Applause*]

And also with us today is Gil Grosvenor, a great friend of ours, friend of education, president of the National Geographic Society, to whom we are indebted for the distribution of this pro-education poster. Gil, thank you very much to you and your associates. And a special welcome to all of you, our special guests.

You know, Barbara's here. I happen to think with some husbandly pride that she's doing a remarkable job for education. She's just finished a reception inside for her new radio program, "Barbara Bush Story Time." It's going to be kind of like Fiorello LaGuardia for you oldtimers—[*laughter*]—used to do this. There's a slight complication on this, however, because attending that reception, and with us today, is Bob Saggett of "America's Funniest Home Videos." Is he over there somewhere? Bob, you're welcome to stay, but your act is over there in the press room; that's where you ought to be to get your material. [*Laughter*] Thank you very much for joining us today.

I'm honored to welcome the representatives of 221 elementary schools chosen this year as winners in our school recognition program. Each of your schools is as diverse as this great country: They are public and private; they range in size from 170 to 1,400 pupils; they serve children from scarcely populated rural areas to some of our largest cities. But you all have something important in common: your success and achievement, ideals to which the other schools across the breadth of this nation can look for inspiration.

This year's winners were judged on the quality of the education they provide, their students' achievements and attitude, and their teachers' and administrators' leadership. But perhaps the most important criteria was a sense of shared purpose among faculty, students, parents, and then the entire community. These schools share a vision of hope that they can foster the full potential and development of each child and, by doing that, help make this a better nation and a better world.

However, those higher goals may have been lost on some of the youngest winners. I understand that when one first grader from Colwyn Elementary School told her parents about her principal being honored, she exclaimed: "Sister Mary won the Academy Award?" [*Laughter*]

We're here today not only to salute these individual schools but also to restate our commitment as a nation to education. For our democracy can remain vital only if our people continue to grow in knowledge and wisdom, facing each new choice with an increased understanding of the complex and competitive world in which we live. And we must realize that education is the key to our future, to our identity as a nation, and to our very soul as a people. I came to this job believing that America can and must have a restructured and revitalized education system to enable us to compete successfully in the world and to empower each citizen to achieve his or her fullest potential. After all, education is our most enduring legacy, vital to everything we are and everything we can become.

We're celebrating an important anniversary here. One year ago this month, we held the President's education summit with the Governors. In fact, my first stop after the summit was right here, where I spoke to last year's winner of this prestigious award. And the summit itself grew out of our pledge to lead a national effort toward a renaissance of excellence in American schools. As a result of this historic event, involving the Nation's Governors and our Cabinet, we emerged with a sense of direction for individual and collective efforts to improve the quality of education for all. For the first time, Americans now have a clear sense of direction toward national education. With the invaluable cooperation of teachers and parents and community leaders and a variety of educators, and working with the Governors at the beginning of this year, I announced our six education goals to be met by the year 2000—absolutely essential goals that recognize education as a life-long enterprise. And I want to repeat them now because they must become so familiar that they seem woven into the fabric of our lives.

First, by the year 2000, all children in America must start school ready to learn. And second, the high school graduation rate must increase to at least 90 percent. And third, American students must be competent in 5 critical subjects with their progress measured in grades 4, 8, and 12. Fourth, our students must be first in the world in science and math. And fifth, every adult American must be able to read. And finally, every one of our schools must be safe, disciplined, and drug-free.

I am very pleased today to be able to unveil a wonderful poster displaying these important goals that have been produced, as I said earlier, by the National Geographic Society, and it will be sent to every single school in the Nation. National Geographic has joined the fight to ensure a first-class education for every American child. And once again, Gil Grosvenor, we are very, very grateful to you and your associates over there. And I'm grateful to you two for holding that up in the wind. [*Laughter*] You're doing a first-class job there, Marcus and Jennifer.

You know, in this past year since our summit, as we've turned our attention to the formidable task of ensuring that these goals are attained, we've seen an extraordinary response as reform took off across our nation. And one of the most important reforms sweeping our great country is educational choice, empowering parents to get involved in their children's education. Today, with us—and I spot her right down here—is Polly Williams, a courageous leader who brought choice to Milwaukee, Wisconsin, school. Polly, would you please stand up, too?

And it's teamwork that's engendering this inspiring success, an extraordinarily constructive partnership between the Federal level, the Governors of our States and territories. Showing our administration-wide commitment to educational excellence,

we've also begun exciting programs involving all of the Cabinet Departments.

Today, I issue a challenge to every American to join us. Step forward in your own way to respond to one of the most crucial issues that we face. And students, set your sights and your personal goals high, so that your future can match your finest dreams. Educators, you're engaged in noble, terribly important work. And we congratulate you and look forward to your continuing dedication to American educational excellence. And then to parents, we urge you to become more involved, more involved in your children's education. And lastly, to the communities, we've made great leaps in getting communities more engaged. The Governors have done a sensational job going to the communities getting them more engaged in local-level action, too. But we need more.

All of us must commit ourselves fully now—right now. And America, really on this one, can't afford to wait, or waste, an entire generation. To all of you, as we look ahead to our goals and to the year 2000, let's answer the call: Let tomorrow begin today.

Congratulations to all of you. Thank you for your interest in education. Thank you for caring about our kids. Thank you very, very much.

Note: The President spoke at 3:36 p.m. on the South Lawn at the White House. In his remarks, he referred to Governors Carroll A. Campbell of South Carolina, Robert Casey of Pennsylvania, Rudy Perpich of Minnesota, and William D. Schaefer of Maryland; Wisconsin State legislator Polly Williams; and students Marcus Laruex and Jennifer Abreo.

Letter to Congressional Leaders on Textile, Apparel, and Footwear Trade Legislation
September 17, 1990

Dear Tom: (Dear Bob:)

I am writing to express my strong opposition to the textile, apparel, and footwear

quota bill (H.R. 4328) which the House is scheduled to consider tomorrow. The bill is a threat to the stability of the world trading system and is completely contrary to the economic, commercial, and political interests of the United States. If the bill passes, I will veto it.

This legislation would seriously restrict textile and footwear imports and violate international trade rules. It represents the worst form of economic policy for America, one based upon the mistaken belief that less trade throughout the world will somehow save American jobs and enhance our prosperity. In reality, the bill would cause slower growth, result in fewer jobs, and create far higher costs for all American consumers. We are enjoying the greatest export boom in our history. This bill will place at risk our $400 billion in exports and the millions of American jobs that depend on world trade.

Ironically, this vote comes at a time when the world is adopting the American model of free enterprise, open markets, and greater competition. It would send the wrong message to retreat now from the world economy and build protectionist walls just when the reform governments of Eastern Europe, Latin America, and Asia need our leadership in forging a more open international economy.

Furthermore, this legislation would close the U.S. market to countries that, despite economic hardship for them, have stood firm with us against Saddam Hussein's brutal aggression. Passage of the textile and footwear quota bill would violate 38 agreements, including agreements with Turkey and Egypt, countries indispensable to our efforts to forge an historic alliance to resist Saddam's aggression against Kuwait.

A vote in the House tomorrow approving the textile and footwear quota bill would be a negative statement about Congress' vision for our economic future and about the value of America's word in international relations.

I urge your support in defeating this damaging piece of legislation.

Sincerely,

GEORGE BUSH

Note: Identical letters were sent to Thomas S. Foley, Speaker of the House of Representatives, and Robert H. Michel, Republican leader of the House of Representatives.

Remarks at a Republican Party Fundraising Luncheon in Denver, Colorado
September 18, 1990

Thank you very much, Natalie. Thank you for that very, very generous introduction. What a job she's doing as Colorado's top elected Republican official—outstanding—and I am confident she'll win big in the fall. It's great to see so many friends out there and to be back in Denver—be with our family, Neil and Sharon.

When Bruce Benson, the State chairman, called and said it would be a big boost if our party's number one asset came out to Colorado, I said, "Sure. What time do you want Barbara to be there?" [*Laughter*] I bring you greetings. I am flying solo today. She sends her regrets. She and our dog are doing a number in the bookstores, but nevertheless—[*laughter*]—I'm pleased, very pleased, to be back in Denver to show my support, to express my appreciation to Bruce and to Barb and everybody else that worked to make this luncheon so successful.

It is great to be in the Mile-High City. Today there's another city that's feeling a mile high, and that's Atlanta. And I want to say congratulations to them. We know they're going to host a terrific Olympics, and I'm proud the Olympic games will be back in the United States.

This tremendous ticket that we're here to support shows the great strength of the Colorado GOP. We've got a strong team of congressional challengers, ready to contribute, ready to fight for what's best for Colorado and for this country: Bob Ellis, Gloria Gonzales Roemer, Jason Lewis, Wayne

Allard—all good. And Colorado's got Capitol Hill veterans like my friend Joel Hefley and Dan Schaefer—back at work in Washington, represented here today by their wives, Lynne and Mary. So, we've got a good team, and we need your support to get them elected. Then there's a well-known voice here in Colorado and Chairman of my Advisory Council on Education, Colorado's candidate for Governor, John Andrews.

And also I want to single out another. I'm talking about our nation's drug czar, who flew out here today with me on Air Force One, Bill Bennett. A year ago we announced a national drug strategy, and a few days ago, Bill and I gave a 1-year update to the Nation. In his view and mine, we are making significant progress on the war on drugs. And Bill has been waging a tireless fight, and he deserves a heartfelt vote of thanks from all Americans for what he's doing to help our kids.

And of course, there's another—not with us today—but my good friend and your great Senator, Bill Armstrong. And I think, like all his friends here, we regretted his decision to leave the Senate. Bill's been Colorado's articulate voice for lower taxes and balanced budget and a strong national defense and cleaner air. I would only say that Colorado, however, is very fortunate to have a strong successor waiting in the wings, a man who's made his mark as a proven leader on Capitol Hill—and I'm talking about Hank Brown.

As you may know, he was scheduled to fly out here with us today, but congressional business kept him back in Washington, on the job—and that's exactly where Hank Brown belongs. And it's great to have Nan with us today. But we need Hank elected to the Senate. All of us who've seen him work there in Washington know he's one of a rare breed. President Reagan and I learned in the eighties that we could rely on Hank in the Congress. And now we're moving briskly into this new decade, in the nineties, and we really do need him. We've got to hold that seat, and I need his excellence in the United States Senate.

Now that Congress is back in session, we've got a lot of work to do. We've got to preserve this precious natural legacy of ours and pass the first package of comprehensive amendments to strengthen the Clean Air Act, the first in a dozen years. And the Congress ought to move now and give the Nation that legislation. I'm convinced the people are coming to realize that this party, our party, is a strong advocate for clean environment. That's an issue that matters to us—every one of us—an issue championed by Hank Brown, a man whose roots in the Rocky Mountain State go back five generations, and the other members of this Colorado ticket that I've talked about here today.

We've got work to do to enhance in all our cities and towns a strong and saving sense of community. That means keeping our streets safe so that young and old alike are free from fear. You have my word: I will not sign a so-called crime bill that makes life tougher for the police than it does for the criminals. We must have strong crime legislation.

And above all, for the sake of our communities and our children, we must draw the line against drugs. No more free ride for drug users. No more freedom, period, for the illegal drug merchants who deal death right on our streets—literally, sometimes on your doorsteps.

But for all of America, the key issue here at home remains, I think, the health of our national economy and the challenge we face to keep this recordsetting economic expansion alive. We can't meet this fundamental challenge until we break free of the spend-now-save-later mentality that has done so much to drive up the national debt.

Just 12 days from now, the fiscal year ends, and the automatic sequester begins. The clock is ticking. That's why I issued my challenge to Congress 1 week ago and why I will renew that challenge today. I've set out a budget agenda that goes beyond the quick fix and gets to the heart of real fiscal reform.

First, I've called on Congress to enact a package of growth-oriented tax incentives, everything from expanded IRA's and family savings accounts to enterprise zones and, yes, a cut in the capital gains tax. Once again, this is not a tax break for the rich. The Treasury estimates that my proposal will not lose revenue—this is the United

States Treasury—not lose revenue. In fact, it will increase revenues to the Federal Government, and it will create jobs. And these are the steps we must take to spur savings, encourage investment, expand jobs for the men and women of America, increase competitiveness—to give this national economy of ours more of what it needs to keep on growing.

And that's just one reason I'm counting on this talented Colorado team, because I need the support of people of Colorado and the votes up on the Capitol Hill to put this progrowth program into effect.

And second, I've called on the Congress to take forward-looking measures to encourage additional energy production here in the United States. [*Applause*] I'm glad there's a few oil men left here in Denver. [*Laughter*] No, but we've indulged a dangerous habit as a nation far too long. And so, today we must move now to end America's excessive dependence on foreign oil. And that means alternate sources; that means more incentives to increase domestic drilling; and, yes, that means more conservation.

Third, I've made clear to Congress it's time to reach a binding budget agreement that shows the American people that we are serious about real deficit reduction. We all know the danger that high deficits can, indeed, drag our economy down. It's time to put ourselves to the test as a nation, as political leaders. Whether we've reached a budget summit agreement or not, I call again on the Congress to allow a straight up-or-down vote on a 5-year, $500 billion deficit reduction package no later than September 28th. I think the Congress owes that to the American people.

This is a critical time. There are challenges we face now in Washington and around the world, challenges that will affect each and every American. I want to speak for just a moment about the most momentous challenge of all—Natalie so generously referred to, talking about me and introducing me—and I'm talking, of course, about the situation in the Persian Gulf.

Never before has the world community been so united—never, anyway, since World War II. Never since the invasion began has Iraq stood so isolated and alone.

The key is collective action: sharing the responsibilities and the risks, the challenges and the costs; meeting Saddam Hussein's outlaw act with a common front against aggression. And that is why forces from over 20 nations—rich and poor, Arab, Moslem, Asian, African—now serve side by side in the Gulf. And that is why Britain and France are sending a substantial group of forces to Saudi Arabia. That's why our Arab friends, together with Japan and Germany, will contribute almost $20 billion towards the costs of operations and to offset the effects of both sanctions and higher oil prices. The message is steady, strong, and certain: The world will not look the other way; Iraq's act of aggression will not stand.

Saddam's illegal act has meant misery and suffering for millions: the brave people of Kuwait, victimized but not vanquished; the hostages held against their will; and those pitiful refugees fleeing Iraq and Kuwait, flooding into neighboring nations ill-equipped to deal with this human tidal wave of tragedy—the poorest of the poor being brutalized by that dictator's inhumanity. For the Iraqi people themselves, the pain that they now experience is a direct consequence of the path that Saddam has chosen.

Let me make clear about any humanitarian and emergency food and medical supplies we might send to the people of Iraq in the future: Should aid become necessary, it must be distributed under strict international supervision to make certain that emergency aid reaches those Iraqis who need it the most, because we cannot allow Saddam Hussein to divert needed humanitarian aid in order to sustain his army of occupation.

We mean to keep the sanctions in place, to keep the pressure on, and prove to Saddam Hussein that aggression does not pay.

You know there's a lot at stake. Much is at stake. And there's much the world stands to gain if we succeed. Even in the midst of the current crisis, I believe that we can all see the outlines emerging of a stronger, more peaceful world order, one where old animosities give way to a new partnership of nations acting to uphold international order and the rule of law. And let me be clear: With all that's at stake, the world will not allow one dictator's aggressive ambitions to stand in the way.

Let me close this afternoon by thanking the young men and women of Colorado who are doing their part out in the sand and hot sun halfway around the world, soldiers like the ones from Fitzsimons Army Medical Center in Aurora, Colorado—like Major Carmelo Otero, Dr. Otero, who's shipping out in the next few days. In the busy final days before his departure, Major Otero's spent most of his time with his wife and two kids. And he even found time to tape-record bedtime stories for his kids to listen to until he's back home again. Or Sergeant Clifton Gordon, an x-ray technician, who's been serving in Saudi Arabia since the end of August and who missed his son's first three football games—three wins—as a freshman quarterback.

And I want to pass along a request made by Sgt. Gordon's wife, Robin, who's here with us today. She's noticed how many support groups there are for spouses and parents; and she thinks maybe its time to spread the word that we've got to do all we can, as individuals and organizations, to help the kids out there whose moms and dads are on duty in the Persian Gulf. You know, she's right. Robin's right. And even as I ask, I know that that support is there in Aurora and here in Denver and in every community all across this country. Let's not wait until our servicemen come home to show our appreciation. Let's start right now

by doing something special for their kids.

One final message today as we focus on November 6th. From the revolutions that changed the face of Eastern Europe from Budapest to Berlin, to the young men and women in our armed services serving now in Saudi Arabia, the world around us reminds us every day that there is nothing more precious than freedom. And so, I urge every citizen of Colorado and every American to get out and vote. Don't take democracy for granted.

Once again, it's a great pleasure to be here today to show my support for this party; to show my support for this strong ticket, for candidates who have so much to contribute to Colorado and to their country. And I thank all of you for this very, very warm welcome. And may God bless this great State and those young men and women serving overseas. Thank you, and God bless you all.

Note: The President spoke at 12:35 p.m. at the Colorado Convention Center. In his remarks, he referred to Natalie Meyer, Colorado secretary of state; Neil and Sharon Bush, the President's son and daughter-in-law; Bruce Benson, chairman of the State Republican Party; Barbara Card, chairperson of the fundraising luncheon; Representative Brown's wife, Nan; and President Saddam Hussein of Iraq. The President also referred to Mrs. Bush's promotion of "Millie's Book as Dictated to Barbara Bush." Following his remarks, the President traveled to Los Angeles, CA.

Remarks at a Fundraising Dinner for Gubernatorial Candidate Pete Wilson in Los Angeles, California
September 18, 1990

Thank you very much, Pete and Gayle. Pete, thank you for that welcome. And all of you, and to Assemblyman Ross and Diane Johnson; Senator Marian Bergeson and Garth; Councilwoman Joan Milke-Flores; Matt and Paula Fong down here; and our State chairman, Frank Visco; of course, Dan and Bobby Lundgren; and Chuck Heston,

my friend here; Tom and Mary Hayes; and Johnny Grant—what a wonderful turnout—thank all of you. Robby Britt, that was an inspiring rendition of the national anthem. Thank you very, very much.

Let me convey the apologies of a very close member of my family who couldn't make it tonight. As it turns out, Millie is back East, promoting her new book. [*Laughter*] Her celebrity status has gone to her head. [*Laughter*] I gave her a bowl of Alpo, and she asked to see the wine list. [*Laughter*]

I'm sorry that our national fitness czar, Arnold Schwarzenegger, could not be with us tonight. You know, he wanted to entertain the troops in Saudi Arabia, but we had to put him down, say no. It turned out they didn't think it was very entertaining to watch a guy bench-press an M–1 tank. [*Laughter*]

But we do have another czar with us tonight, and that is our drug czar, Bill Bennett, who flew in with me today on Air Force One. Bill's bringing his tough and fearless leadership to our national war against the scourge of drugs. A few days ago, there at the White House, he and I gave a 1-year update on our national drug strategy; and we both feel that in many ways we are, indeed, making significant progress. And that's due to the tireless fight that Bill and so many communities and so many police forces—including the one right here, the LAPD—are making, waging against drugs. And we're grateful to you, Bill, and we're grateful to the citizens out here from whatever walk of life that are participating in this war against drugs. We owe him a vote of thanks and, again, all of the volunteers that are pitching in.

Let me say it is great to be back with so many good friends, back here in this Golden State. You know, the people who came to California wouldn't stop looking for gold and glory until the trail stopped at the edge of the Pacific. That's why this State is a place where the dreamers are the doers and why California is leading America into the future. And I can't think of anyone better qualified to lead California into that future than your next Governor, Pete Wilson.

I will say I am very sorry that Barbara's not with us tonight, but she thinks the world of Gayle, just as I do. And both of us are strongly in your corner as you go down to the stretch.

I'll have a lot to say tonight about Pete and the Republican future in California, but first, let me just speak of two matters that are critical to the future of America and the world. A week ago tonight, I went before the Congress and the American people to discuss two urgent yet interrelated matters: the aggression in the Middle East—and, Rabbi, thank you for your overly generous comments, sir—and the Federal budget deficit.

Even before the Persian Gulf crisis, we were already more economically vulnerable than we should ever be, especially with a projected Federal deficit of $232 billion. So, I told the Congress—and I know that Pete Wilson agrees—that we must address our budget deficit not in 1991 or '92 but right now.

We need a budget agreement that meets four basic tests. It must include measures to increase economic growth and cut our national dependence on foreign oil. It must be fair—everyone should be called upon to make a sacrifice, but no one should bear the burden alone. A budget agreement should address the growth of the Government's hidden liabilities, and it must reform the budget process. And one thing more: We can cut this budget without hurting the economy; without another phony-baloney plan; with an agreement that is credible, real, and enforceable—one that will save America half a trillion dollars in 5 years.

I also told the Congress that if America remains strong at home, America can continue and will continue to lead abroad. But there's another component of American leadership that has no price tag, none at all, and I'm talking about the men and women who are serving this country in the Persian Gulf. America is a mighty nation, but we are a great nation only because of those who are ready to leave the comfort of their homes in Oceanside or San Bernardino to serve on the front line halfway around the world in defense of freedom. America is great because its courage is great.

And we all wish their job was done, but we know that it's not. Certain objectives must be met: Iraq must withdraw from Kuwait without condition. Kuwait's legitimate government must be restored. The security and stability of the Persian Gulf must be assured. And American citizens abroad must be protected. These objectives are not ours alone. They've been endorsed by the

United Nations Security Council six times in 7 weeks.

And let me note the good news from our allies. West Germany has pledged to support the mission with almost $2 billion and provide transport ships and planes. Japan has now pledged a package worth $4 billion. France has added another 4,000 troops. And Great Britain has sent 120 tanks, 6,000 troops—the famous Desert Rats that some of us remember from World War II. It is truly, then, Iraq against the world.

We've also put tight sanctions into effect while working with the United Nations Security Council to allow food to reach innocent children, mothers, the sick, and the elderly. And we've been working with many nations to get relief to the most pitiful victims of this conflict—I'm talking about those thousands and hundreds of thousands of refugees, those that can afford it the least, humbled in the desert off the Iraq border.

I spoke of our four objectives. But we have another, final objective; and that is to create a new partnership of nations, a new world order—freer from the threat of terror, stronger in the pursuit of justice, more secure in the quest for peace. The international community has already taken a giant step toward that day. Together with our friends and allies, ships of the United States Navy are patrolling the Mideast waters—already intercepted more than 700 ships to enforce these sanctions against Iraq. And the world is simply telling Saddam Hussein, we will not give in to intimidation.

On matters like these, we are called upon to put country before self and patriotism before party. And so, it's good that politics now are stopping at the water's edge, but that still leaves a lot of America in between. And from Long Beach to Long Island, we should and we will vigorously campaign right up to the November election. And for those of us at home, we can serve our country by being the best candidates, the best citizens and, yes, the best Republicans and Democrats we can be.

I am sure every Democrat agrees: We will not allow our political life to be held hostage to a crisis. When Californians go to the polls, absentee ballots will be coming in from Americans in uniform, including those stationed in the Persian Gulf region. And if our soldiers, sailors, airmen, and marines can find time to vote under such difficult circumstances, surely those of us at home will do our civic duty as well.

Just a few moments ago I spoke of international intimidation. Well, it does Americans no good to stop aggression abroad if bullies take over the streets at home. As a former U.S. marine, as a Senate leader in foreign policy and defense, Pete Wilson understands the need to repel, stand up against aggression abroad. But he also understands the need to repel aggression at home.

Let me tell you a story that means a lot to him, about an immigrant from Ireland named Michael Callahan, who came to these shores to find peace and prosperity. Michael Callahan moved to Chicago, started a family, worked hard, and rose to the rank of detective sergeant on the city police force. And then one evening, while on duty, Sergeant Callahan tried to arrest two cocaine dealers. They drew their guns first. And although Callahan managed to shoot one of the dealers, the other one shot him. Sergeant Callahan died in Chicago at the age of 30, fighting the first wave of cocaine to sweep America. But that was not in 1990 or 1980. Michael Callahan died fighting cocaine in 1908. And his grandson Pete Wilson is with us tonight. So, when your Senator says we need to protect the public and the police from cop killers and kingpins, and when he says that those who deal in death should reap what they sow, you can be sure Pete Wilson means business.

And I share his sense of mission. On a rain-soaked morning in May of 1989, surrounded by hundreds of law-enforcement officers at the foot of the Capitol, I called on Congress to pass a tough crime bill to build on what our Attorney General here tonight, William French Smith, worked on, to build on what my predecessor Ronald Reagan worked on and tried to accomplish. We put forward a new program, and now 16 months have now gone by. And despite the leadership of Pete Wilson and others in the Senate, the House Democratic leadership has gone off into deep left field. And even worse, several measures receiving serious consideration in the House last week would actually weaken law enforcement, would actually make our cities and our streets less safe than they are now. And such a bill will stop at my desk. It will not become law. I'll guarantee you that.

Pete Wilson and I want a crime bill that will stop the abuse of habeas corpus, a bill that guarantees that criminals who use serious weapons will face serious weapons charges and serious time, a bill that guarantees that evidence gathered by good cops acting in good faith isn't barred by technicalities that let bad people go free. I cannot sign a bill that overturns Supreme Court decisions limiting frivolous habeas corpus petitions, expands the coverage of the exclusionary rule, and weakens capital punishment. And I will not sign a bill that handcuffs the police officers all across the United States of America.

But if some in the House have been an obstacle to tougher laws, Pete Wilson has been an advantage in the Senate. He played a key role in passing the death penalty provisions of the 1988 antidrug act, one that allows capital punishment for the murder of a law enforcement officer working on a drug-related case. And Pete says, "I will not have California under siege to rapists and thugs and drug dealers." He wants to govern a California where women need no longer fear the night because drug dealers and criminals will instead fear the law. And he would start by extending capital punishment in California to major drug traffickers, the same as my proposals before the United States Congress.

And so thus, I have to ask: Is it any wonder that the endorsement of a dozen law enforcement organizations has gone to the grandson of Michael Callahan? Pete, we need you to continue the work in this anti-crime field.

Tomorrow in San Francisco, I'll speak of Pete Wilson's fiscal philosophy and especially of his longstanding environmental leadership. He is and always has been a conserva-

tive, but Pete Wilson also is and always has been an activist who wants to use government creatively to improve our quality of life. And this balanced approach is the key to his success as a legislator in Washington and Sacramento and as mayor of San Diego.

It was as mayor that Pete first showed a flair for executive leadership, and now he seeks the largest executive job in America, second only to my own. And he faces a California skeptical of all rhetoric, impressed only by action. But he's faced the voters before, retaining a Senate seat that six predecessors lost. He broke the jinx and made history because he delivers on his promises.

And now Pete says, "If the voters think I'll be more useful as a Governor than as a Member of the U.S. Senate, then that's what I'll be." Well, all of us here know that filling the Governorship after George Deukmejian is not going to be easy, but all of us here know that if there's anyone that can do it, it is Pete Wilson. And I am very proud to be here for him. He should be the Governor. And that is what he must be: Governor Pete Wilson of California.

Thank you for your support. Keep it up. And God bless the United States.

Note: The President spoke at 7:46 p.m. in the San Francisco Ballroom of the Westin Bonaventure Hotel. In his remarks, he referred to Senator Wilson's wife, Gayle; Matt Fong, candidate for State comptroller; Dan Lungren, candidate for State attorney general; Charlton Heston, actor and political supporter; Tom Hayes, candidate for State treasurer; Johnny Grant, master of ceremonies for the dinner; Arnold Schwarzenegger, Chairman of the President's Council on Physical Fitness and Sports; William J. Bennett, Director of National Drug Control Policy; Rabbi Isaiah Zeldin, who gave the invocation; and President Saddam Hussein of Iraq. A tape was not available for verification of the content of these remarks.

Remarks at a Fundraising Luncheon for Gubernatorial Candidate Pete Wilson in San Francisco, California
September 19, 1990

Thank you, Pete, and thank all of you. It really is great to be back in California, united with all of you for such a good cause.

You know, when they called about this fundraiser, they said to me, "It would be a big boost if this country's most famous Republican came here to help out." I replied, "Fine. What time do you want Millie to be there?" [*Laughter*]

Which brings me to the fact that Barbara is not here. And she sends her love. She is as committed as I am to seeing Pete and Gayle Wilson be the first family—succeeding a wonderful first family—but to be the first family of this great State. She sends her love and affection. And I expect she'll be out here campaigning for you.

To my friend—our friend—George Deukmejian, thanks for another welcome here to your State. I can think of a handful of people to whom I especially owe this challenge of being President of the United States, and certainly George Deukmejian, who helped me early on—his name comes to mind. It's great that you're here once again, unselfishly helping the man that now you want to see be your successor. I'm proud of you. What a record you've set for this State. What a terrific act to follow.

I want to echo what both George and Pete said. Looking around, I see lots of reasons why the California GOP is going to be so strong in November—the whole ticket concept, the rest of the ticket—Thomas Hayes, your current treasurer; Marian Bergeson, right here, candidate for Lieutenant Governor; Joan Flores for secretary of state; and Matt Fong for controller; as well as our congressional candidate who's with us today, Alan Nichols. And a special thanks to Frank Visco, our State chairman, who's doing an outstanding job for the State party—a thankless job, but he's doing it very, very well.

And then those who have done and continue to do the heavy lifting around here on making these events so successful: Katie Boyd, Gene Trefethen, and my old friend Ben Biaggini. What a wonderful job you all have done pulling this marvelous event together—twice, I might say.

You have to agree, there's a very great and formidable woman involved in this gubernatorial race, but of course, Gayle Wilson is too modest to admit it. And I know it's true. And, Gayle, good luck to you, and thanks for all you're doing on the campaign trail.

And one other with me here today and traveling with me through southern California and here is our brilliant and hard-working leader in the fierce war—national war—against drugs. And I'm talking about our drug czar down here, Bill Bennett. He and I, a year after the national drug strategy was announced, made a report to the American people a few days ago. And I think it is fair to say that there is reason now to be optimistic about this war on drugs. A lot of that stems from the dedication of Bill Bennett and his able team.

And also—I'm remiss here—I should thank the reverend. Father, thank you for that prayer at the outset of this meeting. And of course, to see my old friend, a true hero, Admiral Jim Stockdale—I'm just delighted to see you again, sir. Your patriotism, your love of country shines through today just as it did when you were held as a prisoner those many years ago.

I had some doubts about coming back to California. Our latest Agriculture Department figures show that your State is the leading producer of broccoli. [*Laughter*] And that sort of gives new meaning to this Big Green movement that we're hearing all about, you know. [*Laughter*]

But here in San Francisco, you've got some fantastic champions—your 49ers. But we're all here today to show the respect and friendship and confidence that we feel for another champion—a champion of the environment, a champion for the victims of crime, a champion for the hard-working taxpayer, a champion of the American vision. The champ: Pete Wilson.

Here's what some say about him. President Reagan calls him principled. George Deukmejian calls him experienced. Congressman Campbell calls him dedicated. Congressman Lewis calls him thoughtful. And even his opponents call him wonderful. [*Laughter*] And as for me, I plan to call him Governor.

Because as we look ahead to the year 2010, when your State's population could soar from 30 to 40 million, we realize that this State needs a Governor committed to the quality of life issues: protecting our natural heritage, fighting crime and drugs, ensuring economic security, creating more jobs and opportunities. That person is, of course, the one we're all here to support: Pete Wilson.

It was important to have Pete in the Senate, and it's now vitally important to have him in Sacramento. To begin with, his brand of environmental activism is the kind California needs. You know, in this area, as in all areas of his commitment, he holds a position of conviction, not convenience. He wrote the first coastal protection act before the environmental movement even began, and he's long fought for clean air—to remove toxic emissions and smog and acid rain from our skies.

Clean air has been one of our administration's top priorities, as he said a minute ago. And so, let me take this opportunity to urge the Congress to send me a clean air bill I can sign. You know, I sent Congress a comprehensive bill more than a year ago, and I negotiated an agreement with Pete's colleagues in the Senate. But I'm still waiting for Congress to send me a solid clean air bill. We must see balanced, rational clean air legislation enacted this year because it's one of the most important endowments we can make to protect the ecology of our nation and, indeed, of the entire world.

I think of how the late photographer Ansel Adams described California beauty: "It's always a sunrise, a glitter of green and golden wonder in a vast edifice of stone and space." Well, Pete will preserve that for our children and our children's children.

These future generations also need the legacy of a strong economy led by a Governor with a truly exceptional fiscal record. Pete will give them that. After all, not only

did he balance 11 straight budgets as mayor, he also received the Watchdog of the Treasury award in Washington for his antispending role every single year that he has been in the United States Senate.

No domestic issue has been on our minds of late more than our economy. And it remains an absolutely critical imperative that we reach a bipartisan agreement on this budget deficit and reach it immediately.

When I spoke last week to the Congress, I said I wanted to be able to tell the American people that we've truly solved our deficit problem. But I added, in order for me to do that, there were several tests that the budget agreement would have to meet.

First, it must include the measures that I spelled out to increase economic growth and reduce dependence on foreign oil. And second, it must be fair to all programs and all people. And third, it must address the growth of government's hidden liabilities. And fourth, it must reform the budget process itself, and it must be real. And finally, it must avoid anything that would threaten economic growth or return us to the days of punishing income tax rates.

And I want very much to stand in front of the American people and tell you that the negotiators have come up with an agreement that meets these tests. And I want to tell you that the agreement reflects not only the improvement in East-West relations but also our broader responsibilities to deal with the continuing risks of outlaw actions and regional conflict. And I really hope we will see this agreement soon. I look forward to saying to America: Together, let us all work for the promise of an exciting and strong new future that's now within our grasp.

And there's one other subject, of course, that's on everyone's mind today that I want to talk about: our commitment to the situation in the Persian Gulf. And this is something Pete, a former military man, understands firsthand. Time and circumstances have proven him farsighted. Pete Wilson has always eloquently supported the utterly essential need for a strong defense.

Six weeks ago we sent our troops half a world away because we were compelled by the moral compass that guides our nation.

As Americans, we could not ignore this brutally aggressive act against international law and order, and nor could the rest of the civilized world. The unity of outrage across the globe, the depth of support in the Gulf, and the ferocity of condemnation in the United Nations are unprecedented.

And now Saddam Hussein has been given notice by the extraordinary joint declaration that President Gorbachev and I signed in Helsinki [September 9]. It is an absolutely unparalleled message of solidarity, a clarion call for Iraq to comply immediately and completely with the five resolutions that had been so urgently ordered by the United Nations Security Council. And it heralds a new era for our world: the Soviet Union and the United States, standing together in vigorous condemnation of an outrageous aggression.

What a dramatic legacy for our children to inherit, this stunning new partnership of nations. Ours is a generation to finally see the emergence of promising, exciting new world order which we've sought for generations. And we are witness to the first demonstration of this new partnership for peace: a united world response to Iraq's aggressive ambition.

And so, the U.N. and the United States and the Soviet Union and countries across the globe have issued with one voice these unequivocal demands: One, Iraq must withdraw totally and immediately from Kuwait. Two, Iraq must restore Kuwait's legitimate government. And three, Iraq must free all hostages in both countries. Humanity itself will tolerate nothing less.

If Iraq does not meet these nonnegotiable conditions, then its isolation will not end. And we are, as I have said before, prepared to take additional steps if sanctions and the quest for a political resolution do not work.

In the meantime, action through diplomatic channels continues. Just this past weekend, the U.N. Security Council passed its seventh resolution—in this case, condemning Iraq for its illegal treatment of foreign diplomats. And last Thursday the United Nations, with our support, passed Security Council Resolution 667, establishing a framework so that food can be delivered under close supervision to Iraq and Kuwait, for humanitarian reasons require

this. And this will provide a fair procedure for allowing food to reach civilians in need—innocent children, mothers, the sick, and the elderly.

And on Friday, I sent to Congress a request that will provide the legal mechanism for the United States to share the extraordinary burden of our presence in the Gulf with our friends and allies. It is important that a considerable part of this effort be borne by those being defended and by those benefiting from the free flow of oil. I am gratified at the international willingness to help. You know, the Arab response has been extraordinary. And last week alone, Prime Minister Kaifu pledged $4 billion on behalf of Japan, and Germany agreed to contribute $2 billion plus transport ships and planes.

But we can't think about the Persian Gulf just on these statistics. We can't think about it without remembering our young men and women there, joined by brave compatriots of armed forces from countries spanning four continents, all standing firm and unyielding in the distant desert sands.

Young Americans like 18-year-old Michael Pigeon, of Detroit, who wanted to join the Marines here in California in order to serve his country in the Gulf. But he wasn't accepted because he was over the weight limit. Here was a young man who yearned so desperately to defend American values that mean everything to him that he trekked the 2,500 miles from his home in order to reach his dream and his goal. And not only did he make it to the San Diego boot camp but he lost the weight along the way. [*Laughter*] And today he's on his way to making a proud marine. And he points out now that marching in combat boots will be no problem for him. [*Laughter*] Gives a new meaning to "I'd walk a mile for a camel." [*Laughter*] Mike, I knew it was risky. [*Laughter*] No, but his kind of— [*laughter*]—but Mike's kind of patriotic self-sacrifice reflects the incredible spirit of the American people, splendid Americans from children to great-grandmothers. And they give our brave young service men and women loving support and proud resolve.

It's touching to hear of the grassroots efforts swelling from coast to coast. Radio stations volunteering to tape family messages to send to the soldiers. Enough cookie airlifts to fill Candlestick Park. A pen pal network to mail greetings to service men and women. Army mothers encouraging everyone to fly their flags in honor of our young people so far from home. Yellow ribbons waving their bright, silent tribute from Maine to California, Washington State to Florida. I even heard of a group of women—some of you've heard of it too, I'm sure—who have formed a group called MASH: Mothers Against Saddam Hussein. [*Laughter*]

Once again, our people, the people of our country, have come together to show the world our finest strengths: American optimism, unity, unselfishness, the wonderful values of family, and the will to stand up for what's right and good—strengths that form the very heart of America and that make possible the freedoms our brave service men and women are striving to defend.

And let's not forget one of these freedoms, approaching—the right to vote, to choose our form of government. And I can't think of anything that better guarantees our own freedom than to exercise that privilege.

I know that every American looks forward to the day when our extraordinary young men and women will return home to a nation proud of its ideals of freedom, integrity, and honor; a nation committed to its tradition of preserving, protecting, and defending those precious beliefs which have always made America a beacon of hope and freedom to the entire world.

I want to thank you, once again, for your warm welcome and for the support that you're giving to the next Governor of this great State, Pete Wilson. God bless you and the United States of America. Thank you all very, very much.

Note: The President spoke at 12:35 p.m. in the Grand Ballroom at the Fairmont Hotel. In his remarks, he referred to Millie, the First Family's dog; Katie Boyd, cohost of the dinner; Gene Trefethen, owner of Trefethen Winery; Ben Biaggini, cohost and master of ceremonies of the dinner; William J. Bennett, Director of National Drug Control Policy; Rev. John Bakas, director of the Valley Children's Hospital Foundation, who gave the invocation; and President Saddam Hussein of Iraq. He also referred to Big Green, the environmental protection initiative on the November ballot in California. Following his remarks, the President returned to Washington, DC.

Nomination of Mary Shannon Brunette To Be an Assistant Secretary of Housing and Urban Development
September 20, 1990

The President today announced his intention to nominate Mary Shannon Brunette, of Virginia, to be an Assistant Secretary of Housing and Urban Development for Public Affairs. She would succeed Sherrie Sandy Rollins.

Since 1989 Ms. Brunette has served as Assistant to the Secretary for Policy and Communications at the Department of Housing and Urban Development in Washington, DC. Prior to this she served as legislative director/press secretary to Representative Jack Kemp, 1988–1989; press secretary to Representative Jim Courter, 1988; senior adviser for Jack Kemp for President, 1987–1988; legislative director for Representative Jack Kemp, 1985–1987; legislative assistant to Representative Jack Kemp, 1982–1984; and staff assistant to the House Republican Conference, 1982.

Ms. Brunette graduated from Le Moyne College (B.A., 1982). She was born September 12, 1960, in Rochester, NY, and currently resides in Falls Church, VA.

Nomination of John P. Leonard To Be United States Ambassador to Suriname
September 20, 1990

The President today announced his intention to nominate John P. Leonard, of Virginia, a career member of the Senior Foreign Service, Class of Counselor, as Ambassador Extraordinary and Plenipotentiary of the United States of America to the Republic of Suriname. He would succeed Richard C. Howland.

Since 1988 Mr. Leonard has served as Deputy Chief of Mission for the U.S. Embassy in Managua. Prior to this, he served with the State Department, 1987–1988; Counselor of the U.S. Embassy in Montevideo, Uruguay, 1985–1987; and Counselor of the U.S. Embassy in Asuncion, Paraguay,

1983–1985. In addition, Mr. Leonard served in the Arms Control and Disarmament Agency, 1981–1983; a politico-military officer in Madrid, Spain, 1978–1981; and in the Department of State, 1973–1978. He also served in Seoul, Republic of Korea, as a political officer, 1970–1973, and as vice consul, 1969–1970; and third secretary and vice consul at the U.S. Embassy in Luxembourg, 1966–1968.

Mr. Leonard graduated from Harvard University (B.A., 1962). He was born July 16, 1940, in New York, NY. Mr. Leonard served in the U.S. Army, 1962–1965. He is married and has two children.

Statement by Deputy Press Secretary Popadiuk on the President's Meeting With the Administrator and Deputy Administrator of the Panama Canal Commission
September 21, 1990

The President met today in the Oval Office with Gilberto Guardia and Raymond Laverty to congratulate them upon their installation as Administrator and Deputy Administrator of the Panama Canal. They were sworn in on September 20, 1990, in a ceremony at the Department of State. Mr. Guardia is the first Panamanian citizen to head the Canal and the first non-U.S. citizen to head a U.S. Government Agency. Panamanian Vice President Guillermo Ford also attended the meeting.

The President noted that the assumption of the offices of Administrator and Deputy Administrator, according to the procedures agreed to by the United States and Panama in the Panama Canal Treaty, is a demonstration that the two countries can work together on the basis of equality and mutual respect to ensure a safe and efficient canal.

Vice President Ford's presence is a fitting reminder of the vitality of the new democratic government in Panama and the strength of the ties between our two countries.

The Panama Canal Treaties provide a sound framework for the common interests of the United States and Panama in seeing the canal continue as a secure and efficient link for world trade. The United States is committed to preparing for a smooth and trouble-free transfer of the canal to Panama at the end of the century. The President asked that Mr. Guardia and Mr. Laverty convey to the American and Panamanian employees of the Panama Canal Commission the thanks and appreciation of the U.S. Government for their skilled and dedicated service.

Nomination of Merrill A. McPeak To Be Chief of Staff of the Air Force
September 21, 1990

The President today nominated General Merrill A. McPeak, U.S. Air Force, to be Chief of Staff of the Air Force. He will succeed General Michael J. Dugan.

General McPeak is presently serving as commander in chief, Pacific Air Forces; air component commander for U.S. Pacific Command; and executive director, Pacific Air Combat Operations Staff. General McPeak was born January 9, 1936, in Santa Rosa, CA.

Nomination of Roscoe Burton Starek III To Be a Member of the Federal Trade Commission
September 21, 1990

The President today announced his intention to nominate Roscoe Burton Starek III, of Illinois, to be a Federal Trade Commissioner for the term of 7 years from September 26, 1990. He would succeed Terry Calvani.

Since January 1989 Mr. Starek has served as Deputy Assistant to the President and Deputy Director of Presidential Personnel at the White House. Prior to this he served as deputy director of presidential personnel for the Bush transition team. In addition, Mr. Starek has served in several positions with the Department of State over a period of 7 years, including Deputy Assistant Secretary for Policy and Counterterrorism; Legislative Counsel to the Undersecretary for Management, 1985–1986; deputy chief negotiator for transportation and telecommunications, 1984; and State Department-White House liaison, 1982–1983. In addi-

tion, he has served as chief minority counsel to the Select Committee on Narcotics Abuse and Control of the House of Representatives, 1979; associate counsel to the House Judiciary Committee, 1976–1979; counsel to the minority of the House Select Committee on Intelligence, 1975; Assistant General Counsel to the Presidential Clemency Board at the White House; counsel to the impeachment inquiry, 1974; legislative assistant and then as a professional staff member for United States Senator Charles Percy, 1972–1973.

Mr. Starek graduated from Syracuse University (A.B., 1969) and the American University, Washington College of Law (J.D., 1973). He was born November 17, 1947, in Minneapolis, MN. Mr. Starek served in the U.S. Army Reserve, 1969–1975. He is married, has one child, and resides in Alexandria, VA.

Nomination of Charles L. Cragin To Be Chairman of the Board of Veterans Appeals
September 21, 1990

The President today announced his intention to nominate Charles L. Cragin, of Maine, to be Chairman of the Board of Veterans Appeals for a term of 6 years. This is a new position.

Currently Mr. Cragin serves as a partner with the law firm of Verrill and Dana in Portland, ME. Mr. Cragin graduated from the University of Maine (B.S., 1967) and the University of Maine School of Law (J.D., 1970). He was born October 9, 1943, in Portland, ME. Mr. Cragin is married, has two children, and currently resides in Raymond, ME.

Appointment of Leigh Ann Metzger as Special Assistant to the President for Public Liaison
September 21, 1990

The President today announced the appointment of Leigh Ann Metzger to be Special Assistant to the President for Public Liaison.

Since 1987 Ms. Metzger has been coalitions and organization director at the National Republican Congressional Committee. Prior to this she served as legislative director for the Eagle Forum in Washington, DC.

Ms. Metzger graduated from Samford University (B.A., 1984) in Birmingham, AL. She is a native of Decatur, GA, and resides in Alexandria, VA.

The President's News Conference
September 21, 1990

The President. I have just a few brief remarks before departing. First, I had a very good and useful meeting this morning with the congressional leaders. We talked about the situation in the Gulf. I made clear that sanctions remain our strategy for resolving this crisis. At the same time, I pointed out my deep and growing concern over what Iraq is doing to Kuwait and to the Kuwaiti people, and to American citizens and foreign nationals, more generally. And I also pointed out that Iraqi support for terrorism would indeed have serious consequences.

I also asked the congressional leaders for the prompt approval of key aspects of our policy; in particular, I urged that the supplemental funds needed to cover defense operations be passed quickly. Similarly, I emphasized just how critical it is that Congress agree to forgive the FMS [foreign military sales] debt of our stalwart ally Egypt. And I also informed the congressional leaders that it is essential that we continue to meet Saudi Arabia's legitimate defense requirements.

Let me just say that I appreciate the support that Congress is giving to the administration during this situation. It's good, and it's strong. And for my part, I pledge to continue to consult fully, consult regularly with the Congress. The United States stands determined and united in its quest to see the Iraqi forces withdraw from Kuwait fully and unconditionally.

On the domestic scene, as the budget negotiators continue their meeting this afternoon, I want to just make it clear to the American people that the goal of these negotiations remains unchanged. We must fix the Federal budget mess and the Federal budget process once and for all. A budget deficit agreement is necessary to help maintain our economic vitality, our competitiveness, and our growth in job opportunities.

And there are several tests that this agreement must meet. I will insist on an agreement that really does promote economic growth. And I will insist on an agreement that is fair, credible, and real. And it must contain real spending cuts. And I will insist on an agreement that addresses reform of the budget process itself. I cannot accept a temporary quick fix that sweeps this problem under the rug, and I will not accept a deal that fails to address in a foolproof way the Government's deficit. We must have a 5-year, $500 billion plan that keeps our country strong, competitive, and puts us on the path to long-term economic health.

In the absence of a budget agreement, the law requires that the sequester will begin in just over a week. We are now 9 days and counting. And so, I hope some progress is made today.

Persian Gulf Crisis

Q. Mr. President, does your warning today of serious consequences about Iraqi terrorism and your statement of concern about what's happening in Kuwait mean that the United States is moving any closer toward a conflict with Iraq? And how do you describe the situation in the Gulf today?

The President. No, I don't want to send that signal. I indicated to the Congressmen that I want to see a peaceful resolution. Obviously, these economic sanctions are going to take some time to work. I don't know how long that is, but we want to see them be effective. In the meantime, I must continue to emphasize to people in this country and around the world that there are certain principles here—right and wrong—moral principles, and that's what I was talking about when I was talking about Iraq pulling out of Kuwait unconditionally, for example. But I don't intend to be sending a signal that I'm shifting more towards the military, if that was your question.

Q. But generally, how do you describe the situation?

The President. Generally? Pleased with the cooperation, concerned about anybody held against his or her will there. But I think the coalition is holding together. Others are pitching in and doing their part. So, I think things are moving forward. I had a good meeting this morning, by way of example, with a Defense Minister from the United Kingdom [Thomas King]; and I believe that after his talks at the Pentagon, we are all on the same wavelength in terms of how our forces interact and will interact when the Desert Rats get down there, for example. So, I think there's a lot of coordinative work going on. And I must say that a lot of this depends on support from Congress and the American people, and so far

I'm very pleased with that.

Q. Mr. President, Saddam [President Saddam Hussein of Iraq] has said that he would not be the first to strike the first blow for a shooting war. Do you believe him? And would the U.S. and the U.N. make that kind of commitment also?

The President. I'm not making any commitments. There are so many contingencies. I've spelled them out. The treatment of American citizens is one thing that concerns me greatly. Possible use of terror is another thing that concerns me greatly. So, we'll just have to leave it. I've tried to spell it out very, very clearly, and I believe I'm in total synchronization with other powers that have forces in the Gulf or moving towards the Gulf.

Q. Do you think that he is ready for a war?

The President. I don't know the answer to that. We watch the deployment of their forces. But I would like to see him comply with the sanctions, is the way I'd phrase that.

Q. ——saying, sir, that sanctions continue to be the policy for bringing about these changes, and yet your expressions of concern in these various areas raise the question of whether further deterioration along the lines you've described might cause you to change that policy. Is that what you're saying?

The President. No, I'm just putting down several universally heralded markers, for example, in terms of the treatment of hostages and the terror. I was very much concerned, out of that meeting in Jordan the other day, when a lot of radicals gathered and they were talking about terroristic acts. We hold Saddam Hussein responsible if there is any terrorist act against us. We just want to be clear, that's all.

Q. Well, Mr. President, if I may follow up, sir, it would appear that there are not a lot of diplomatic or economic arrows left in the quiver of this coalition; and I wonder, if you're going to hold him responsible, what exactly do you mean by that, sir?

The President. I'm saying that the fundamental diplomatic arrow is not fully in the air yet, and I'm talking about the full effect of the economic sanctions. That's going to take a little time for that arrow, which is the major thrust of our policy, to be effective. Again, I can't tell you how long it is, but there are signs that those sanctions are taking hold.

Let me go, one, two, three, then I got to get over here.

Q. Mr. President, how far are you willing to go within the context of the United Nations in enforcing an air embargo? Are you willing to allow airplanes to be shot down, and are you willing to have the U.S. participate?

The President. We haven't crossed that. I'm listening to the discussion in our own administration, and we're in close consultation with other countries, so I'd prefer to not go into that. But if the sanctions specifically include forcing planes down that could be carrying contraband or carrying cargo that violates the sanctions, obviously, the United States would do its part.

Terrorism

Q. Mr. President, you have mentioned terrorism now three times. What has happened that has prompted this heightened concern about that?

The President. Nothing. It's just on my mind because I know irrational people sometimes behave in—regarding terrorism—and the only thing that's fairly new was that outrageous conference in Jordan the other day. That was the only new thing. And then we follow it very, very closely, as best one can through intelligence channels.

Q. Is intelligence showing you heightened activity?

The President. No, I would never discuss what intelligence is showing me. But I would say that I am concerned about this. All you have to do is look at that public conference over there and listen to some of those outrageous radical statements; and that gives me reason to say, hey, you're going to be responsible.

Q. Do you blame King Hussein [of Jordan] for that?

The President. No, I blame Saddam Hussein for that. Everything to do with it that affects our forces—that's where the blame will be and should be.

Q. On the budget?

The President. One, two, three.

Arms Sale to Saudi Arabia

Q. Mr. President, some of the Congressmen came away from the meeting today saying they wanted to see the size of the Saudi arms package scaled back. Are you willing to do that?

The President. We're going to just—I don't want to answer your question directly. I want to stay in close touch with Congress on that. I think there's a universal feeling that we should go forward. We're willing to discuss the details of the package with them. But whatever we send up, I'll stand behind that, is what we think is necessary. But there are some discussions that I think will be taking place on the details of the package, but I don't want to go beyond that right now.

Egyptian Debt Relief

Q. Do you think your reassurances on Egyptian debt forgiveness plan—that this would not open the floodgates to other countries making similar requests for being heeded by Congress?

The President. It could. But what I made clear to the Congressmen, I hope, is the unique importance of taking care of the Egyptian situation right now.

Persian Gulf Crisis

Q. Mr. President, we've talked several times today about the treatment of Americans in Iraq and Kuwait. Do you have any evidence, sir, that they're being more mistreated than they have heretofore?

The President. Not in the last couple of days, Ellen [Ellen Warren, Knight-Ridder Newspapers]. Not in the last couple of days.

Q. But prior to that, did you get reports, sir, that the mistreatment level had increased somehow?

The President. Well, I'll tell you what concerns me—and I really think it concerns all the American people—are the debriefings from these people coming out of Kuwait. Now, that's been within the last 2 or 3 days. And those reports evoke enormous outrage.

Q. Sir, to follow up: Members of Congress who came out of the meeting today felt that the prospect of war really had increased, some of them told us. Have they misinterpreted your remarks?

The President. Well, I don't know, because, certainly, I didn't tell them that. But we're going to continue to move forces—others, the British, the French, moving forces—and maybe that's what they're talking about. But I wouldn't necessarily view that as a step closer to war. It certainly is putting us in a much stronger position, and that will take a while.

Q. Mr. President, last night Saddam called the U.S. a dwarf, among other things. Last Sunday, he called you a liar. He's apparently getting ready to release a 90-minute tape. Do you feel like you're getting involved——

The President. That will finish him off in the United States. I can't speak for the rest of the world—[*laughter*]——

Q. Do you feel like you're getting involved in a global communications war? Do you feel like you have to respond——

The President. No, I don't.

Q. ——in order to keep up U.S. support——

The President. No.

Q. Do you care if the networks broadcast it, or would you——

The President. No, I'd welcome it. Nobody could stay awake through that, honestly. He's had plenty of exposure here. Networks have been extraordinarily fair in giving him a lot of coverage. I have no problem with that. But what he has to understand is, under our system—and who better than you all know it—government can't mandate television time for him. But I have no problem with that. The American people know that the world has acted in concert against this man, so there is very little he can say. He reiterated his view yesterday, and then somebody here, I think, referred to an escalated statement by him. So, I have no problems with that.

And you'll notice I'm not heightening the rhetorical output. And I'm just kind of saying this is the way it is, and not try to elevate it. People ought to analyze carefully the statement that I made to the Iraqi people, which was preceded by about 20 minutes, I am told, on Iraqi television of people downgrading it before it was even played. And then afterward, the mobs that had been rented for the occasion were dancing around in the street criticizing on

their way to their destinations before they even heard what I had to say.

So, we've got a different approach. All I'm doing is reiterating the goals here, and I'm going to continue to do that. And I think it's important that people around the world know we are not shifting our position here. It's steady. It's not highly rhetorical. And the tape that I ask that you look at was very measured in the message to the Iraqi people, and I like to feel that it made some impression. We've had a couple of reports that were right favorable on that, and then some that said it didn't get much mileage.

Q. Mr. President, also in that speech last night, Saddam Hussein said Iraq would not retreat from Kuwait, that Iraq was prepared to fight a long war to a final victory. You say that the U.S. cannot let the Iraqi aggression stand. Isn't that a formula for armed conflict? Isn't that inevitable at this point?

The President. It's not I that says it, Jim [Jim Miklaszewski, NBC News]. It's the United Nations. It's every country on the Security Council. It is steadfast world opinion that says it. See, I don't want to make it Saddam Hussein versus the United States. You've asked a question——

Q. Well, that's——

The President. Wait, may I finish? You've asked a question that puts it in his context. That's not the context. It is the whole world versus Saddam Hussein. And so, he can reiterate his views. He can say what he thinks. And every time he says, it he puts himself in direct contravention of international law.

Q. But given the allied commitment not to let the Iraqi aggression stand and his commitment not to retreat, doesn't that make armed conflict inevitable at this point?

The President. No, because, as I said, the first major pressure to get him out will come from a tight economic embargo. Now, my goal is to see that it's very tight, and I know everybody that's a part of it will do the same thing. So, we have to see how effective that can be.

You know, the man's changed position. We saw, after losing hundreds of thousands of lives, a total retreat and withdrawal, giving the Iranians everything that the

Iraqis fought for. And so, maybe he'll sober up here.

But he's standing against—I just keep wanting to make the point when the question is put that it's me versus Saddam Hussein: Wait a minute, it's the whole world. It is the Security Council of the U.N. and all that. I don't mean to be contentious here, but I have to keep making that point because he's trying to make the point that it is simply the United States versus the Arab world, when the whole majority of the Arab League supports us.

Q. Mr. President, on the sanctions and embargo: There are reports today that a number of heavily loaded oil tankers have left port in Iraq, presumably heading for Iran. Is Iran going to abide by the U.N. embargo, or have they struck a secret deal?

The President. One, as of 8 this morning, I had no evidence that these three tankers—and there were three, I believe—were heading for Iran. There were some rumors that they were. Two, on your broader part of your question, so far it appears to me that Iran is doing what Iran said it would do—supporting the sanctions. There may be some leakage in terms of food across the border, but generally speaking, it looks like Iran is doing what Iran has represented to a lot of countries that they would do, and that is to apply the sanctions. They also have taken an open position that they would not permit shipping, albeit from any country, to use their territorial waters. So, I saw some speculation earlier that those tankers might do that, but I still believe—reserving the right to change my opinion—but I still believe that Iran is doing what it has indicated to the world community it would do.

Federal Budget Negotiations

Q. On the budget, you spelled out several tests that any budget agreement should reach. In your opinion, does Senator Dole's proposal to separate capital gains out of any final budget package pass or fail your test?

The President. Look, we're down to the wire, and I believe that's all being discussed right now, so I would just leave you with the broad principles. Bob Dole was trying to be helpful and trying to get this impasse broken. And I'd rather not, while we have our three negotiators sitting with the con-

gressional negotiating team, go into more specifics than I made in that opening general statement.

Q. But you issued something last November very similar, calling for capital gains to be taken up separately from the budget reconciliation process. Why shouldn't you pursue that separate track system now?

The President. Well, I want to get a capital gains—nobody thinks I'm "soft" on capital gains.

Q. But he's calling for it to be taken up separately.

The President. Well, I want to get capital gains. I'm not endorsing the Dole suggestion, nor would it be appropriate for me to criticize it.

Q. But are you ready to compromise?

The President. Hey, you got to go talk to my negotiators. If I were negotiating with you, why, I'd tell you. But I'm not; I'm negotiating with the Hill.

Last one, Lesley [Lesley Stahl, CBS News], then I've got to go.

Persian Gulf Crisis

Q. Saddam Hussein's speech last night—he was in his military uniform for the first time since this began, and he was more militaristic. How concerned are you—you've been talking about terrorism—that he has shifted now; that he is, in fact, in a more militaristic mood and that he might miscalculate? You seem to be suggesting that he's changed, he's ratcheting up.

The President. I'm glad you phrased it that way. I don't think he's ratcheting up; I think he's hunkering down. And I say that from the way his forces are deployed. But if you're suggesting ratcheting up to attack the allied forces there, I don't believe so.

Q. Terrorism?

The President. Terrorism concerns me, and it will continue to concern me. And I will hold him, as will our allies, directly responsible for terrorist acts. But I'm glad you raised that, because I don't have the intention of suggesting that he is getting more bellicose. You know, Jim asked about his comments, and we analyze all those things, but it's really a reiteration of a very unpopular position. But as these economic sanctions work, I expect you might see more heated rhetoric from him. As the sanctions start grabbing ahold, it would not surprise me if he had to resort to this kind of flamboyant rhetoric in order to keep his public opinion behind him. And public opinion could shift. I don't know where it really is in Iraq, but it could certainly dramatically shift if they see that his policy of invading a neighboring country has brought hardship on every citizen in Iraq. So, I am watching that very carefully, and I think it is something we ought to—I got to go.

Q. World financial leaders are meeting here this weekend, and over the next week——

Q. The question is time. Can the——

The President. Let me just finish this one. I can't help you on time. I've said that over and over again. I just can't help you.

Q. But, Mr. President, do you think the embargo will have effect before Saddam destroys Kuwait and——

The President. That worries me—the dismantling of Kuwait. But we're watching that carefully, and again, I can't give you an answer to that question, nor can anybody else. But you've raised a good point, because there seems to be a systematic dismantling of Kuwait that does violence to the rights of every single Kuwaiti, but also sends a signal that he is trying to incorporate Kuwait into a kind of a piece of territory of Iraq, which he's already stated. He claims it, but now he's trying to do this. This is another ingredient that we're weighing.

Q. So, who blinks?

Q. Please, Mr. President.

The President. Yes.

Federal Budget Negotiations

Q. World financial leaders are meeting here this weekend and——

The President. True. This weekend.

Q. ——and next week to decide the course of interest-rate policy and inflation policy and dollar outlook amidst the crisis. What would you want to steer them towards—growth or anti-inflation—as they try to decide——

The President. I'd want to tell them that we're getting a budget agreement. We're going to have a sound budget agreement. And I'd like to say—before they leave town, I'd love to think we had such a budget agreement that every financial leader from around the world would see was serious and real in terms of getting the budget deficit down. And that is the very best thing that the United States can do. It's the best signal it can send to the Third World, to every country that's plagued by interest rates that are higher than they ought to be because of the interest rates in the United States.

So, my message, I think, would be: We're working hard to get this budget deficit down. And I think if we're successful when they're here it would make a very successful visit by these financial leaders to the IMF and World Bank.

Thank you all very much.

Note: The President's 61st news conference began at 3:03 p.m. at the South Portico of the White House.

Statement by Deputy Press Secretary Popadiuk on United States Military Assistance to Saudi Arabia
September 21, 1990

The United States has a close and valued relationship with its longtime friend Saudi Arabia. It was in the spirit of this relationship that the United States responded favorably to King Fahd's request that we send troops to the Kingdom to deter and, if need be, help defend Saudi Arabia against an attack by Iraq.

Providing Saudi Arabia with improved ability to defend itself is another important element of this relationship. For more than a decade, the United States has made available to the Kingdom defense articles and services. Consistent with this policy and in response to the current threat, the administration recently provided Saudi Arabia equipment on an emergency basis.

Following consultations with the Saudi Government and the Congress, the administration has determined that it is in the interest of the United States to provide Saudi Arabia with additional means to protect itself. Following our consultation with Congress, we will provide this assistance in phases. The specific items to be provided in the first phase are still being determined and will encompass equipment and training requiring early action. This request will be sent to the Congress early next week. Those items that do not require expedited review will be submitted to the Congress early in the new year.

In both cases, we believe that it is essential that the United States be able and willing to provide the Saudi Arabian Armed Forces with the weapons and training it needs to deter and defend itself against aggression. Such support constitutes a key dimension of our overall strategy toward the Persian Gulf and could serve as well to protect American lives.

Remarks at a Fundraising Breakfast for District of Columbia Mayoral Candidate Maurice Turner
September 24, 1990

Thank you all very much. I am delighted to be here with all of you. What a magnificent turnout in support of Chief Turner.

I first want to say that I'm proud to be back, side by side, with Wally Ganzi, a tireless worker for things he believes in and people he believes in. He is the finance chairman of this campaign. And I expect, Chief, that we agree on this and many other things, but we couldn't have a better man in our corner than Wally Ganzi. Thank you.

I want to thank Pastor Brown for his comments and opening prayer. Of course, I believe the Chief is very lucky to have such a distinguished lady as Florence Booker as his campaign chairman. I think it sends a wonderful signal. And to Harry Singleton here, our candidate for DC Delegate, my very best wishes to you. Best of luck in the race coming up. And to Julie Finley, the same—running hard for a seat on the city council. Julie, good luck to you.

Chief, I bring you greetings from People magazine's cover girl this week, Barbara Bush. [*Laughter*] She'd have been here in an instant, but she's getting ready to head up to New York. But she sends her love and her warm, best wishes. And she is with you all the way, too.

I wanted to come over here today and tell you that for me—and I go back with the Chief some time—it is a distinct pleasure to be with you to join in supporting a candidate who can do so much for the District of Columbia; and he is my friend, the Chief, Maurice Turner. We're here this morning to show our support for a man who has given all his adult life to a particular phase—a very important one—of public service: as a proud member of the United States Marines, as a 32-year veteran who worked his way up through the ranks of the DC police force to serve 8 years as chief of police. And now he's going to be the next Mayor of Washington, DC.

You heard what he said about the precincts, and that's the truth: He's been out on the streets of Washington, walking the beat, if you will, speaking to the people of this city, and listening to them talk about the kind of leadership that they're looking for. He tells me that since April he's walked about half the city, from Anacostia to Wisconsin Avenue, and in the process, he's lost 35 pounds. [*Laughter*] But he's gained the fighting edge that he needs to boost this underdog over the top and into the Mayor's office. He'll do anything to get this job done in terms of hard work.

I'd like to ask the voters here to listen to the cops that he's worked with—those that are protecting us every single day—the neighbors who know him, those who know his family. They call him tough, honest, concerned, committed, competent. Well, come November 6th, that's just one thing more I'd like to call him, and that is Mayor.

Maurice has been a fighter from the early days back on Girard Street—a boy his father nicknamed "Little Joe Louis," whose friends and family still call him Joe today. And just like Joe Louis, he's got a strong message for the criminals who create a climate of fear and the drug dealers who prey on our kids: You can run, but you cannot hide. That's his message, and that's one we need to hear over and over again.

No one's tougher on crime and drugs. Then, on the other hand, no one is more concerned about our children—their safety and their schools. And no one's more dead set on getting the deadwood out of city government and providing leadership to help heal Washington, to help this city hope again.

You know, Maurice Turner knows what it is to take pride in being a citizen of our Nation's Capital. He knows how much it hurts to see a city pulled down—from the plague of crime and crack on the streets right up to the crisis of confidence that grips the District Building. That's why it is time for a change: time to put Chief Turner in charge of the whole city.

Maurice Turner knows this city inside out, not just the Washington of monuments and marble, not the cruel Washington the world sees on the 6 o'clock news, but the Washington of neighborhoods, of communities, of churches, of solid citizens and strong values—a Washington full of life and hope and opportunity for everyone who calls this city home. That's the Washington that Maurice Turner comes from, and it's the Washington he'll fight to keep alive and flourishing. So, I ask every one of you to keep working hard for him, and I ask hard-working Washingtonians to give him your vote. Help Maurice Turner turn this city around.

One thing more—a message to all Washingtonians as you get ready to go to the polls on November 6th. This past year, everywhere from streets and squares of Eastern Europe now to the sands of Saudi Arabia, we've learned a powerful lesson about the risks people are willing to take to win freedom and keep it. I urge every citizen in the District of Columbia to get out and vote. Do not take democracy for granted. Go to the polls and exercise your precious right and vote for the candidate of your choice. If you take a little advice from all of us here today, vote for Maurice Turner. He's going to get the job done.

I know these are very trying times for our country. They're trying times internationally. They're trying times certainly on the many domestic fronts that come together to represent the entirety of the United States of America. I mentioned this out campaigning the other day across the country. I am proud that the country has come together in the spirit of former Senator Vandenberg, certainly when it comes to support for what we are trying to do in rolling back aggression in the Middle East. The country is united, transcending political ideology, liberal or conservative; transcending party, Republican, Democrat, or even independent—everybody pulling together. But we must not neglect the domestic agenda. We're coming up into an election cycle. I think it is beholden on those who hold office to get out and say what they think.

So, when Maurice Turner invited me to come here today, I accepted before he could change his mind—[laughter]—because I want to see this good, decent, honorable man the next Mayor of Washington, DC. Thank you all for what you're doing to support him. Good luck, and God bless you all.

Note: The President spoke at 8:26 a.m. in the Grand Ballroom at the Mayflower Hotel.

Remarks Following Discussions With State President F.W. de Klerk of South Africa
September 24, 1990

President Bush. To our friends from South Africa, once again, welcome to the White House. We've just come from an extraordinarily useful meeting. President de Klerk and I have conversed on the phone several times in the past, but it was a great pleasure to hold this face-to-face meeting with the first South African leader to visit the United States in more than 40 years.

President de Klerk described for me in detail what he is trying to accomplish in South Africa: the process of ending apartheid and negotiating a new political reality for all. We talked of this very promising, sometimes difficult situation, especially the recent violence. And I think all Americans recognize that President de Klerk is courageously trying to change things. After all, we have seen in other parts of the world the culture of political violence overwhelm the culture of dialog, and this must not happen to South Africa. The Government has a special responsibility to maintain order, but all political parties and groups have a special responsibility to support the process of peaceful transition.

One thing is apparent in this process of change: The move away from apartheid toward a new political reality is indeed irreversible. And much has already happened. Leading political figures, including Nelson Mandela, have been released from prison. The Government and the ANC, the African National Congress, have reached an agreement on a plan for the release of the remaining political prisoners. Political organizations banned for years are now free to conduct peaceful political activities, and restraints on the media have largely been removed. A framework has been agreed to, between the ANC and the Government, to lead to negotiations over the political future of the country. Other groups are invited to join in. Except for the beleaguered Natal, the nationwide state of emergency has been lifted through the country.

Who among us only a year ago would have anticipated these remarkable developments? Clearly, the time has come to encourage and assist the emerging new South Africa. The United States clearly endorses the principle of constitutional democratic government in South Africa, and I'm here to tell you that I have enormous respect for what President de Klerk and Nelson Mandela are trying to achieve together in pursuit of this principle. And it is not simply this President—I believe, sir, it's the entire American people that feel that way.

South Africa needs a constitutional system based on regular and free elections with universal suffrage, a civil society where authority is responsible in every sense of the word. South Africa needs an unvarying respect for human rights and equal opportunity for all its citizens. And we also would like to see an economic system that's based on freedom and individual initiative and market forces. We believe that only a society that opens equal opportunity to all can remedy the social and economic deprivations inflicted on so many people for so many years by apartheid. And President de Klerk agrees with this principle of equal opportunity for all.

And it is in such a context that the issue of sanctions often arises. Although our meetings today were not about sanctions, obviously, we discussed it; the topic did come up. And let me just say a quick word. As I stated, we believe the process of change in South Africa is irreversible, a fact that we'll bear squarely in mind as we consider specific issues in the future. Our goal must be to support the process of change, and of course, I will consult fully with the Congress on these issues. And as you know, all the conditions set in our legislation have not yet been made, in spite of the dramatic progress that we salute here today. But let me emphasize that these conditions are clear-cut and are not open to reinterpretation, and I do not believe in moving the goalposts.

Finally, we will be in touch with our traditional allies in Western Europe and elsewhere on what we can do to help build democracy in South Africa. It is only in this way that South Africa can again be fully accepted into the wider international community.

Apartheid has long hindered South Africa from within, depriving it of the talent and very dreams of millions of men and women. Little wonder then that the end of apartheid holds the promise of unleashing the creative energies of the restless millions, and that's why the end of apartheid can really mean the beginning of a greater South Africa.

Mr. President, if you're successful in this effort, South Africa around the world will become a beloved country not for one people but for all. And for that—your efforts, your courage—you leave with our gratitude, our appreciation, and a hearty Godspeed. Good luck to you, sir, in this wonderful endeavor. We're pleased you're here, very pleased, indeed.

President de Klerk. Mr. President, ladies and gentlemen, may I, at the outset, also say publicly how appreciative we are of the very kind reception which we have had here in the United States of America. For us it is, indeed, an historical occasion for me to be the first State President ever to visit the shores of America from South Africa.

From the moment we set foot here, we've been overwhelmed with friendliness. And in particular, Mr. President, I want to thank you for the very frank, very open, and very fruitful discussions which we were able to have today for over 2 hours.

I want to say, Mr. President, that from the people of South Africa I bring a message, a message of recognition for the awesome responsibility which rests upon your shoulders in the handling of the very difficult situation in the Gulf. We admire you for the strong leadership which you have shown, and South Africa has fully identified itself with that leadership. You can count on us, as we have publicly stated, to support the steps you have taken to assure that democracy and that the political process of dialog and the political process of keeping all channels open will also be maintained in that part of the world. We will support you, sir, in the very definite steps you have taken to assure that the unacceptable form

of aggression which manifested itself there will be withstood; and South Africa will play its part in that regard. We wish you well in handling this awesome and tremendous responsibility.

Mr. President, I want to thank you for the acknowledgment of the new reality which exists in South Africa. There is, indeed, as you have stated, sir, a new reality; and the process in South Africa is indeed an irreversible one. There will be negotiations, and from those negotiations there will come about a new constitutional situation, a new constitution which will offer full political rights within the framework of internationally acceptable definitions of what democracy really is.

There will be a vote of equal value to all South Africans. There will be effective protection of the very values which you in the United States of America hold so dearly: values such as an independent judiciary; such as effective protection of the rights of the individual in the form of a bill of rights, of checks and balances to prevent the abuse of majority power to the detriment or suppression of minorities and smaller communities. There will be in South Africa the protection of fundamental values with regard to the assurance of an economic system which will create sufficient growth to meet the tremendous challenges which we face in the field of addressing the problems of poverty and illiteracy and housing and urbanization.

There will be in South Africa—the process is irreversible—through negotiation a new constitutional and economic dispensation which will offer equal opportunities and full democratic rights to all its people. In that sense of the word, the international community can rely on us. We will not turn back. The fact, sir, that you have today given recognition to this fact will serve as inspiration to us. We stand on the threshold of a tremendously exciting period in the history of our country. We are adamant to use the window of opportunity which history has given us to assure that we will bring about a new and just South Africa.

In that process, the Government of South Africa won't be acting unilaterally. Our goal is to bring about this fundamental change, to bring about this new and just South Africa, on the basis of building and achieving a broad consensus between all the leaders with proven constituencies, whether they be large or small, in South Africa.

We are making headway with that. There are some stumbling blocks in the way. We have a problem of volatility to deal with which sometimes erupts into violent situations which are totally unacceptable. We've taken steps in an impartial manner, through the use of our security forces, curbed the violence. We are as anxious as you are, sir, that we should move as soon as possible to a situation where also in the Province of Natal the state of emergency can be lifted and where the political process in South Africa can be fully normalized. We've already taken great steps in that direction.

I view, Mr. President, today as an important moment where real progress has been attained in normalizing our country's situation with regard to the international community. You, sir—as leader of the strongest country in the world, economically speaking and militarily speaking—your acknowledgment of the progress which we have made and your encouragement with regard to the progress which we are committed to make in the future is, for us, extremely important.

I thank you for the warm reception. And I look beyond the immediate problems and the historical problems, forward also to the day when South Africa, the new South Africa, with a new constitution and a new government, will, together with the United States of America and other important powers—being one of the strongest regional powers in the Southern Hemisphere, being

the hope of the rebuilding of prosperity and opportunity for almost the whole continent of Africa—where South Africa will, by taking hands as we are now already doing with you and with others, will play a constructive role in ensuring stability on the globe, in ensuring that the vision which we share with you of peace between all countries—where we can make a contribution to ensure that that vision will also become reality.

We wish you, sir, and the American people everything of the best. We invite you to play the constructive role which you have spelled out here today. South Africa is going to overcome its problems. South Africa will become once again a proud member of the international community. And South Africa will be a trustworthy friend of the United States of America in maintaining the very values on which your system is built.

My country, ladies and gentlemen, today finds itself in step, in step with the basic value systems of this great country, the United States of America. And we say to you, sir, thank you for a kind reception. Everything of the best in your endeavors to assure global peace. You will not find South Africa lacking in support when you need it.

Note: President Bush spoke at 1:30 p.m. at the South Portico of the White House. In his remarks, he referred to Nelson Mandela, African National Congress leader. Prior to their remarks, the two Presidents met privately in the Oval Office and with U.S. and South African officials in the Cabinet Room, and then attended a luncheon in the Old Family Dining Room.

Remarks and a Question-and-Answer Session at a White House Briefing for Representatives of the Arab-American Community
September 24, 1990

The President. Welcome to the White House. Thank you very, very much. First, let me thank Richard and Paul. I've been doing a little homework listening—hey, Bill—listening to your questions and saying,

thank God I don't have to answer any of them, because I'm—[*laughter*]—but I'm here to just make a few comments. And I want to start by thanking both the gentlemen that are behind me here, and those with whom they work—in Richard's case, Brent Scowcroft; in Paul's case, Secretary Cheney—and all the team that we have. But these two individuals have worked night and day during this series of events that are called on the evening news, and properly so, the Gulf crisis. So, to both of you, my sincere thanks. And this one over, too, here that some of you know, John Sununu. He's been concentrating a lot on trying to do something about the budget deficit, and the same time being at my side as we cope with the problems in the Gulf. So, all three have been extraordinarily busy, as I know you have. But I want to welcome you to the White House—a pleasure to see so many distinguished leaders of the Arab-American community here.

I'm told that Congressman Nick Rahall is here. Nick, where are you? Oops, way back there—modestly sitting in the back. I don't understand that, but he ought to be in the front row because he's of good conscience and he helps me understand the heartbeat in some of these Arab communities, and certainly in the Arab-American community. And I'm grateful to him that he took the time to be with us today.

I'm going to keep my remarks brief because in the words of the famous Arab-American poet, Kahlil Gibran, "We shall never understand one another until we reduce the language to seven words." Well, I've got a few more than seven words, so please indulge me. But I won't keep you too long.

I am honored that you could be with us to discuss the vital issue of our collective security, both abroad and at home. And I understand that you've had a good briefing. I heard a couple, and I don't know whether you've had others as well, but those were good on the situation in the Gulf. I've never seen an issue, certainly since I've been President, that just pervaded the thoughts of everybody in our country. You, more than most, I think, understand what's at stake here. And our action in the Gulf is not about religion, nor is it about greed or culture or imperialist ambitions, as Saddam Hussein would have the world believe. Our action in the Gulf is about our determination to stand up with other nations against aggression, and to preserve the sovereignty

of nations. It is about keeping our word and standing by our friends. It is about our vital national security interests and ensuring peace and stability in the world. So, to sum it up: It is about principle.

Our objectives remain clear: Iraq must withdraw from Kuwait completely, immediately, and without condition; Kuwait's legitimate government must be restored; the security and stability of the Persian Gulf assured; and American citizens abroad must be protected. And finally, a fifth objective can emerge from these: a new world order in which the nations of the world, East and West, North and South, can prosper and live together.

The extent of world cooperation in condemning Saddam Hussein is literally unprecedented. The concept of burden-sharing is gaining acceptance with our allies and with our friends—from Britain and France to Germany, Japan, and the Arab world—contributing troops and supplies and economic assistance to those countries affected by the economic blockade. In fact, since Saddam Hussein's unprovoked attack on Kuwait, more than 20 countries have answered the call for help from the Gulf nations to provide defensive assistance against Iraq. And indeed, Iraq stands alone against the world community. Over and over again, Saddam Hussein has attempted to make this the Arab world against the United States. You've heard it over and over and over again. And that lie is not going to be perpetuated. It simply is not true. We are joined with many others around the world. Iraq stands alone against the world community. The United Nations Security Council has strongly condemned Saddam Hussein's actions no less than seven times. Active consideration going on for another resolution right now. United against aggression, the world community is working to resolve the crisis peacefully.

We must also resist his attempt—Saddam Hussein's attempt—to link the Iraqi invasion with other conflicts. There are other regional conflicts, and they're serious, and they've got to be solved. And we've got to do our level best to be catalysts for the solution. But we are going to resist his attempts to justify what he did based on other regional concerns. So, I think these are merely, on his part, an effort to create additional pretexts so that he can stay in Kuwait. And I'll guarantee I'm not going to be distracted by this. Once the Gulf crisis is on its way to resolution, of course, we want to go forward with the peace process. And our position is clear and consistent, calling—I heard your questions and I understand where you're coming from. And I agree with much of what I thought was being said here—certainly agree with what our people here have told you. But our position is clear, calling for negotiations based on these two resolutions. And these negotiations have got to involve territory for peace, security, recognition for Israel, and legitimate political rights for the Palestinians.

As I said before, we have no quarrel with the people of Iraq either. Our mission is to oppose the invasion ordered by Saddam Hussein. As you well know, love of justice and respect and dignity are principles as deeply embedded in the Arab tradition as they are in the whole Western tradition—no question about that. And these are qualities embodied in the 2½ million Americans of Arab descent, with origins from Morocco to the Arabian Peninsula. Just like so many who have come to America, Arab immigrants pursued new beginnings. And they came in search of freedom and justice and equality. Unfortunately, today—I'm glad the media are here because I want this message to go out beyond this room—today some Americans are the victims of appalling acts of hatred. And this is a sad irony that while our brave soldiers fight aggression overseas, a few hatemongers here at home are perpetrating their own brand of cowardly aggression. Death threats, physical attacks, vandalism, religious violence, and discrimination against Arab-Americans must end.

These hate crimes have no place in a free society and we're not going to stand for them. I've been appalled by reports from some of you, friends of mine, here in this room—by reports of discrimination against Arab-Americans. And I condemn such acts, and I will continue to condemn them. This administration has supported enactment of the hate crimes legislation because bigotry and hate still do exist in this country. And hate breeds violence, threatening the secu-

rity of our entire society. As I said when I signed the bill, all Americans must join together to rid our communities of the poison of prejudice, bias, and discrimination.

America is home to millions of Moslems who are free to live, work, and worship in accord with the traditions and teachings of Islam. Similarly, America is also home to the millions of Christians and Jews, also free to live, work, and worship. And surely the multinational troops—men and women of every religion and color—who are now on duty in the glare of the desert sun are an example to us right here at home. They prove that a crisis abroad is no excuse for discrimination at home. As we reflect on our ongoing commitment in the Gulf, we should remember an old Arab proverb: God is with those who persevere. With God's help, we shall persevere, and we shall prevail. And I'm very proud to have all of you here today. Thank you.

I have a signing ceremony out there on the South Lawn at 3:30. Let me just take a couple of questions here to get a random feel of what's on you all's mind. [*Laughter*]

Persian Gulf Crisis

Q. I'm Dr. Mansour. I'm with the American Iraqi Foundation. Mr. President, you are a strong and successful advocate of direct dialog between parties in conflict in crisis situations. We saw your skill in influencing President Gorbachev to abandon plans for economic sanctions and military actions against the Lithuanian people during their struggle for independence earlier this year. You were instrumental in bringing about a peaceful resolution to that crisis by encouraging Mr. Gorbachev to have direct negotiations with the Lithuanian leadership. Mr. President, why don't we apply this same successful strategy to the current conflict and have a direct dialog with the Iraq leadership in order to bring about a peaceful resolution to this crisis?

The President. Dr. Mansour, it's a good point, and I think the United States should always be willing to talk. But the United Nations has acted in concert. There can be no negotiation in terms of the criteria set down. We can't talk about dividing up Kuwait, or elections not restoring the leaders, or occupying—permitting this aggression to stand in any way. Eventually, we may do this. But what you've heard is reiteration over and over again from this dictator that they'll never withdraw and all of that. So, I think it's going to take a little time before there can be any fruitful and serious negotiations. Others have tried. You've seen people calling for "an Arab solution," and that's fine. But they have failed, because each time they've tried to do that, whether it's King Hussein [of Jordan] or whether it's [President] Salih of Yemen or whoever else has stepped up to the plate, they have struck out because of this man's insistence on remaining in Kuwait. So, maybe it will come about.

I appreciate what you've said about the fact that sometimes negotiations can bring things forward. We want a peaceful solution, but we don't want to do it and undermine—and I won't do it and undermine the solid consensus that exists in the world. We're not going to yield 1 inch on those provisions that I spelled out, sir.

Q. We are the foundation, and we are ready to have our offices extend—to have a direct dialog between the administration here and the leadership in Iraq. We are ready to take this opportunity with your approval.

The President. You've got my approval if you can succeed without giving on these important points. I mean, that is the thing. I think the Iraqi people would welcome that. I know the American people would welcome it. I know all other 19 countries in the Gulf would welcome it. And I know a hundred jillion members of the United Nations would welcome it. But we cannot give at this junction. We're not going to do that.

Right here, and then over here. Thank you, Dr. Mansour.

Q. In the name of God, I thank you very much that you allow me to speak, Mr. President. I just want to bring four points to your notice. One is, as—[*inaudible*]—we condemn the aggression and annexation of Kuwait in no uncertain terms. And number two, as Moslems, we also object to Saudi Arabia inviting the foreign troops to our land. Number three is, what are you defending now? The oil interest has already been defended, the Saudi Arabia has al-

ready been defended, and if you are defending to put a sultan on the throne, I think it is not comparable to the high ideals of democracy elsewhere in the world.

In Eastern Europe you wanted democracy. We want democracy in Russia. But according to Random House, as of today, 60 percent of all population enjoys the freedom to elect their own governments. Only 40 percent of the people of the world do not enjoy the freedom. And who are those 2 billion people? One billion are Chinese, and the other billion are Moslems from Morocco to Malaysia, because they are under the thumb of their monarchs and dictators because they rule by their fear and fraud, conceit and coercion, and tyranny and terror. So, if they object to put the Sultan back to the throne, I think it is not ideal for a big office like the President of the United States.

The President. The objective is to see that naked aggression does not pay off, sir. That's what the objective is, and that's why we are going to stay with that position and we're not going to permit this. Iraq is no model of democracy, nor was Kuwait. That isn't the question here. The question is international law and respect for one's neighbor.

Q. What I urge you, Mr. President, is to have justice and equality and peace. There should be no double standard there.

The President. That's what I'm for.

Q. There has to be a negotiated settlement——

The President. No negotiations. Withdrawal totally from Kuwait.

Q. But the Palestinians should also have a right——

The President. Yeah, two over here, and I've got to go. I've got a meeting out there on the South Lawn at 3:30. I'm going to be in serious trouble. Right here. Yes, sir.

Q. Mr. President, I'm Woodward W. Woody, from Detroit. I have a proposal that will be a blessing to mankind and solve the Middle East problem.

The President. Let's hear it. Quick. [*Laughter*] We need it.

Q. Solve the Arab-Israeli conflict tenaciously by implementing pressure on both Israel and Iraq to relinquish their occupied territories in exchange for a trade and defense treaty with the United States. Then offer the same trade and defense treaty to other deserving Arab States. Since there would be no remaining cause for belligerency from either side, hopefully peaceful coexistence may be accomplished permanently. Israel knows that time and 150 million Arabs are against them. I have a letter to you——

The President. Send it over, yes. It's got some interesting points. But first, we've got to take care of the situation that exists right now because of naked aggression, one country against another. That cannot be permitted to stand. We have been trying to be involved in the other process. You know that some territory has been given up. We want to see [United Nations Security Council Resolution] 242 implemented. But to permit Saddam Hussein to link these two questions and approve of his aggression that way—I simply can't do that.

Q. Mr. President, my name is Saif Abdullah, and I'm from Kuwait. I thank you very much, sir. In response to this gentleman here, it is up to the Kuwaiti people to choose whether they want an amir or a sultan, and nobody impose anybody upon them.

The President. Good statement. Thank you, sir.

Last one. Listen, you guys are going to get me in trouble. [*Laughter*] One, two.

Q. My name is Donna Nassor——

The President. Donna.

Q. ——from the National Association of Arab Americans.

The President. Yes, ma'am.

Q. We thank you very much for inviting us here today and we hope—and my question, really is to you—will this be the first in a number of briefings that we will be able to have as Arab-Americans? Because we can help you, as you can help us——

The President. Donna, this isn't the first. Maybe for the first the organization. But I see people in this room that I have met with before. And I want to continue to do that. We've tried hard to do this. But I'd like to assure you that it will not be the last. We can argue whether it's the first, because I don't know how—but no, I think you raise a very good point. I meant what I said in

these prepared remarks about what I feel in my heart about what some of you all are going through because you happen to be Arab-Americans. It is simply not fair to lump the outrageous behavior of a dictator halfway around the world into how people are treated here at home.

There are plenty of other reasons to have meetings with you, but that's a good one right there. Sure, hand it over. Now, last one. Thank you.

Q. God bless you, Mr. President.

The President. Thank you, sir. Last word here. Thank you. Go ahead.

Q. Mr. President, my name is Abraham Lutfi, from Los Angeles. I'm from Iraq. I was born in Iraq. Mr. President, I am very concerned about the next President of Iraq who today is a child and today is cutting the food from him. If this young fellow is going to be malnourished and one day he has to sit down with the next President of the United States who will take your office, how he is going to deal with him? Can you please, from humanitarian point of view, let go with the food emergency? It is needed. And I do appreciate it. Thank you, Mr. President.

The President. Absolutely. But let me tell you this. The United Nations—it's a very important point. This is a very important point. It includes Kuwait, it includes Iraq, it includes wherever food and little kids are going without nourishment. But the United Nations has addressed itself to this. And do you know what the response so far has been? The response has been that you cannot—they will not permit any kind of distribution supervision to see that the food gets to the—particularly a lot of Asians stranded there. I talked to one of the most distinguished citizens of the world who has devoted a lot of his life to the refugee business. And he's just back, on behalf of Perez de Cuellar, from surveying the situation. And what he was told is that the Asians particularly who are suffering the most— I'm talking about Filipinos, I'm talking about Bangladeshis and Indians and people—they're the ones who are hurting the most because of Saddam Hussein's refusal to permit what the United Nations has called for.

But look, every American, all of us here, must have our concerns out there for the women and the children and all these others. I am much less interested in feeding Saddam Hussein's army at this point. But we want to get the food to those that need it. And that includes refugees that aren't Iraqi citizens. They're hurting the most. These were the poorest of the poor that had jobs there in Kuwait. And now they're being thrown out with—and the message is coming through—well, you people in Pakistan, you people in India, you people in Bangladesh, feed your own people. We're going to take care of Iraq.

All he has to do is agree to what the world has called for—international supervision. And the United States and others would stand at the ready to help. We're standing at the ready to help anyway. But this is a matter of international law now under the sanctions. So, he can't violate that. You must use your influence, if anyone has any with him.

Q. ——the American Iraqi Foundation. Can we supervise it?

The President. That would be great if we can get that done, yes.

Lebanon

Q. One question about Lebanon, please.

The President. Shoot.

Q. Very short. [*Laughter*] We in the National Alliance of Lebanese Americans applaud and support the lead our government has taken in responding to the Iraqi aggression against Kuwait. In fact, our government has taken every action against Iraq that we have been urging should be taken against Syria for its similar action in Lebanon. Syria is now apparently allied with our government and others against Iraq. This disturbs us greatly, unless our government has some plan to use its newfound leverage on Syria to cause Hafiz Assad to conform to the norms of civilized behavior that we are attempting to enforce against Saddam Hussein.

This is the question: What is our plan to make Syria conform? And if there is no plan, doesn't our alliance with Syria compromise our moral position in the worldwide effort against Iraq?

The President. This thing is so complex over there that it's pretty hard to give you a definitive answer. Out of this, though, there could well be a new world order. And part of that must be the peaceful resolution of the division of Lebanon. I've been there; I've worked there years ago. And I'm old enough—you're too young, but I'm old enough—no, you're not too young, but she is—[*laughter*]—no, seriously, to remember Lebanon as the peaceful crossroad. It didn't matter what was going on in the rest of the world; commerce survived, people got along one with the other, different religions and different ways of life all thriving there.

We want to help on that. I've been frustrated. One of the great frustrations of my job, as John Sununu can tell you from sitting there and listening to me wring my hands all the time, is my inability to have helped bring peace to the Lebanon. And Syria does have a key role. And I hope out of this that we can use this new world order, if you will, that might emerge if we all stay together to be catalysts for peace in the Lebanon. That's why I came back here, because you struck a chord that I really feel strongly about. And so, I would hope that that and many other things that are happening over there would result in the solution to these problems that have escaped us for so many years.

Listen, I do have to go. And thank you all very, very much.

Note: President Bush spoke at 3:11 p.m. in Room 450 of the Old Executive Office Building. In his remarks, he referred to Richard N. Haass, Special Assistant to the President for National Security Affairs; Under Secretary of Defense Paul B. Wolfowitz; Brent Scowcroft, Assistant to the President for National Security Affairs; Secretary of Defense Richard B. Cheney; John H. Sununu, Chief of Staff to the President; President Saddam Hussein of Iraq; Javier Perez de Cuellar de la Guerra, United Nations Secretary-General; and President Hafiz al-Assad of Syria.

Remarks on Signing the National Hispanic Heritage Month Proclamation and the Educational Excellence for Hispanic Americans Executive Order
September 24, 1990

Thank you all, and welcome to the White House Lawn on this spectacular fall day. It is wonderful to have Secretary Lauro Cavazos standing here next to me, a man who is bringing purpose and dedication to one of the toughest and most vital jobs in our administration and in our country, Secretary of Education. And welcome also to another you know well, the Secretary of the Interior, Manuel Lujan, who's doing a great job heading a Department which is crucial to both the economic growth and the beauty of this nation. Thank you, Manuel, for what you're doing. And I'd like to honor all of the Hispanic American appointees of my administration who are here with us today. Congratulations and my thanks to all of you for what you're doing. We appreciate it very, very much.

And I want to salute the Members of Congress who are with us today and ask them to stand if they would—honored—the delegation right over here. Thank you guys for being with us—appreciate it very much. Chairman, thank you.

I was going to salute our own son and his wife, Columba, but I don't see them here. So—oops, they're missing in action somewhere.

And, well, all of our special guests, and especially so many Hispanic leaders who have given me their guidance and valued input on so many critical issues, thank you for your generosity and that true, true friendship of your greeting here today. There's one other I've got to single out, and that is my old friend Governor Don Luis Ferre, over here, from Puerto Rico. Stand up. What a guy; what a man! [*Applause*]

The one in our family who gets that kind of reception, Luis, is our author, Millie, the dog. [*Laughter*] But I told them out there in California that she's impossible to live with now that she's sold so many books. I gave her Alpo last night and she asked to see the wine list up there. [*Laughter*]

My friends, I'm delighted you're here.

This is special, the chance to celebrate Hispanic Heritage Month. You know, America is often called a melting pot, but that doesn't mean that everyone and everything merge into some bland sameness. Rather, our country is a living tapestry. And to this rich identity, Hispanic Americans contribute the bright culture and vital traditions, making this nation a stronger nation and a better nation.

When Barbara and I were spending all of our time in Texas, we saw the wonderful Hispanic communities which gave that State, the vibrant State, so much of its character. And you know, Jeb's wife, Columba, many of you know, is a Hispanic American. Just became a citizen of our country last year. And we cherish the wonderful richness that she and those grandchildren bring to our family. And I remember how very proud Barbara and I were when little Noelle and her mariachi group sang at the First Lady's luncheon during our inauguration. We thought we could never get them off stage; they went on and on and on. But it was our grandkid, and we were proud of her.

The Hispanic dedication to the dignity of life and to faith and to family and to freedom is an inspiration. These are the very principles on which this country was founded. And they're the ideals which have been interwoven into the strong, bright fabric of your traditions for generations. And they're ideals which enrich Hispanic lives today.

Over the past few months I've named many Hispanic individuals and groups as what I call the daily Points of Light, stars of strength and hope shining brightly in the American sky. And with us today are three of these recipients: Jesse Berain, of Boise, Idaho—and where is he? Right here. Jess, good to see you. Representative from San Antonio's Project Amigos—where are you all? Right over here. Thank you very much. And the Hispanic Employees Association of the Pacific Gas and Electric in Fresno, California, right here. Thank you for coming all that way, sir. But I single these out at the risk of embarrassment because they are doing so much to help in their communities. And that, of course, is an example to all of us.

One of the most important jobs any of us can do in our communities is reflected in the theme of this year's Hispanic Heritage Month: "Education Excellence—Key to Our Future." "Education Excellence—Key to Our Future." And you couldn't have made a better nor a more timely choice. It was Simon Bolivar who said, "Nations move toward the pinnacle of their greatness in proportion to their education progress." We must see that education is the key to our future, to our identity as a nation, and to our very soul as a people.

Tragically, too many Hispanic Americans are not getting the kind of first-rate education they need and they deserve. And that must change. And we must work together. And we must start now.

Within 5 years, Hispanics will make up more than half the high school population in some major cities, such as Los Angeles. Within 10 years, 12 percent of all school-age children will be Hispanic. The group's median age is now 26. And in the next century, Hispanics will become the largest ethnic minority of our population.

And this means that youth is the key to the flourishing Hispanic community. Today, though, less than two-thirds of Hispanic young adults earn a high school diploma. We must find new strategies to boost graduation and literacy rates, strategies that really do get the job done, strategies that really work. We must figure out how to help these young people, how to equip them with the tools to enter a nation and a world where technology advances so rapidly that literacy and analytical and technical skills are not luxuries but essentials.

We must help education to help Hispanic children enter the 21st century prepared to take their rightful place at the American table of opportunity. After all, yours is a history strong in education. In 1551, your Hispanic ancestors founded the first universities in the New World, 85 years before Harvard.

To ensure that Hispanic educational needs are met, last December I directed Secretary Cavazos to create this Hispanic Education Task Force. As a result of this task force's hearings, assessment, and reflections, I am pleased to announce that I will sign today the Executive order on educational excellence for Hispanic Americans. It is my fervent hope that this will ensure that Hispanic education is the priority it must be and will be.

This Executive order will create the President's Advisory Commission on Educational Excellence for Hispanic Americans. This group, made up of representatives of business, educational, and community organizations, will advise on how to improve efforts for quality education for Hispanic Americans. The order directs the Cabinet agencies to be actively involved in helping to advance educational opportunities for Hispanic Americans working with those serving the Hispanic community.

Secretary Cavazos will also join with the Governors from key States to develop criteria for a high school diploma for migrant workers, and Federal education programs will work to strengthen the involvement of parents and community groups in education.

But to be effective, we must make sure that at-risk Hispanic American children start school ready to learn. So, our Head Start program will intensify efforts to increase language development for preschool children.

I am excited about these and the other efforts we at the Federal level will be undertaking to give Hispanic Americans the kind of first-rate education they deserve. It's about time. There is much to do, and we must do it together. We can't afford to wait; we can't afford to waste a whole generation. And together let's answer the call: "Let tomorrow begin today."

And so, it is with great pride and, I want to say, a sense of optimism that I proclaim this Hispanic Heritage Month and lift my pen to sign this Executive order.

God bless you all. And thank you very much for being part of this significant day. Thank you.

Note: The President spoke at 3:40 p.m. on the South Lawn of the White House. In his opening remarks, he referred to Representative E. de la Garza, chairman of the House

Agriculture Committee. The proclamation and Executive order are listed in Appendix E at the end of this volume.

Nomination of Robert A. Flaten To Be United States Ambassador to Rwanda
September 24, 1990

The President today announced his intention to nominate Robert A. Flaten, of Minnesota, a career member of the Senior Foreign Service, Class of Minister-Counselor, as Ambassador Extraordinary and Plenipotentiary of the United States of America to the Republic of Rwanda. He would succeed Leonard H.O. Spearman, Sr.

Currently Mr. Flaten serves as the Director of the Office of Pakistan, Afghanistan, and Bangladesh Affairs at the Department of State of Washington, DC. Prior to this, he served as Deputy Chief of Mission at the U.S. Embassy in Tel Aviv, Israel, 1982–1986; Director of the Office of North African Affairs; and Deputy Assistant Secretary in the Bureau of Congressional Relations at the Department of State. In addition, Mr. Flaten has served in France, Pakistan, and Israel; and as a Foreign Service inspector and a legislative management officer at the Department of State.

Mr. Flaten received a bachelor of arts degree from St. Olaf College and a master's degree from George Washington University. He was born May 21, 1934, in Minneapolis, MN. Mr. Flaten served in the U.S. Air Force, 1956–1959. He is married, has four children, and resides in Arlington, VA.

Remarks on Signing the Message to the Senate Transmitting the Treaty on the Reunification of Germany
September 25, 1990

Mr. Ambassador, welcome to the White House, once again, sir. And, Secretary Baker, distinguished visitors here, I'm delighted to welcome all for this historic occasion.

In a few minutes I'll be signing a letter to the United States Senate asking its advice and consent to the ratification of the Treaty on the Final Settlement with Respect to Germany. This treaty is the culmination of 6 months of negotiation among its six signatories: two German states, along with the United States, Great Britain, France, and the Soviet Union. More than that, it is a culmination of more than four decades of Western resolve and determination, from the darkest hours of the cold war to the bright, new horizons that now stretch before us.

This agreement will end the artificial division of Germany and Berlin, and it will restore to Germany sovereignty over all its territory and end all remaining Four Power rights and responsibilities. This agreement clears the way to achievement of the goal we Americans have long shared with the German people: a united, democratic, and sovereign Germany.

I congratulate Chancellor Kohl and the German people in both East and West Germany and in Berlin, so long divided, for keeping their dream of national self-determination ever alive. Together with our other partners in the Atlantic alliance, we Americans are proud to have stood beside you during your long vigil, and proud especially during this past year to have worked with you in common cause toward the goal of German unity.

Our policy, our commitment, never wavered as this goal drew nearer. Today Germans and Americans share the fruit of our friendship, and we join our German friends in looking to the future with hope and confidence to the new beginning this treaty will make possible.

On behalf of the American people and the American Presidents before me who sustained our joint resolve, I am pleased to sign this letter transmitting this historic document to the Senate for its advice and consent.

I want to express my appreciation to Secretary Baker, who worked so hard on this, and once again say that it has been a pleasure for me to work with Chancellor Kohl and others from Germany on this very important question.

And now for the signing.

Note: The President spoke at 9:33 a.m. in the Rose Garden at the White House. In his remarks, he referred to Ambassador Juergen Ruhfus and Chancellor Helmut Kohl of the Federal Republic of Germany and Secretary of State James A. Baker III.

Message to the Senate Transmitting the Treaty on the Reunification of Germany
September 25, 1990

To the Senate of the United States:

I submit herewith, for Senate advice and consent to ratification, the Treaty on the Final Settlement with Respect to Germany and a Related Agreed Minute, signed by the United States, the Federal Republic of Germany, the German Democratic Republic, the French Republic, the Union of Soviet Socialist Republics, and the United Kingdom of Great Britain and Northern Ireland in Moscow on September 12, 1990. I transmit also, for the information of the Senate, a report of the Department of State with respect to this Treaty.

The Treaty that I am submitting today is the culmination of 6 months' negotiation among its six signatories in what has come to be called the "Two-plus-Four" forum, established for this purpose at Ottawa in February 1990. This agreement will end the artificial division of Germany and Berlin; it provides for the full withdrawal of all Soviet forces over the next 4 years; and it terminates all remaining Four-Power rights and responsibilities for Berlin and for Germany as a whole. It thus creates the basis for the emergence of a united, democratic, and sovereign Federal Republic of Germany, capable and ready to assume a full and active partnership in the North Atlantic Alliance, the European Community, and in the many other fora for international cooperation to which the Federal Republic of Germany has already contributed significantly.

The Treaty makes clear that the current borders of the Federal Republic of Germany and German Democratic Republic shall be the final and definitive borders of a united Germany. All the provisions relating to Germany's border with Poland were worked out with the participation and approval of the Government of Poland.

The Treaty specifies that the right of a united Germany to belong to alliances with all the rights and responsibilities arising therefrom shall not be affected by any of its provisions.

The Treaty provides for the withdrawal of all Soviet troops from the territory of a united Germany by the end of 1994. The Treaty also provides for the continued presence of British, French, and American troops in Berlin during the interim period at the request of the German government. During this period the German government shall have complete freedom regarding the stationing of territorial defense units of its own armed forces within the territory of the former German Democratic Republic, and these armed forces shall remain outside the integrated NATO military command structure. Following the departure of Soviet troops by 1994, there shall be no remaining limitations regarding the location of German armed forces throughout Germany and their integration with NATO structures. Non-German Allied forces and nuclear weapons systems shall not be stationed or deployed within the territory of the present German Democratic Republic. The Agreed Minute, for which I am also seeking your advice and consent, provides a special rule for application of the term "deployed."

The Treaty contains a number of assurances provided by the Federal Republic of Germany and the German Democratic Republic on behalf of a united Germany. Among these are a reaffirmation of their renunciation of nuclear, biological, and chemical weapons, and their stated undertaking to reduce the personnel strength of the German armed forces to 370,000 within 3 to 4 years.

Finally, the Treaty provides for the termination of all remaining Four-Power rights and responsibilities for Berlin and Germany as a whole.

I would also like to draw to the attention of the Senate the texts of three letters that were exchanged on issues arising in the context of the unification of Germany (enclosed as attachments to the report of the Department of State). The first is a letter from Secretary of State Baker to Foreign Minister Genscher of the Federal Republic of Germany dated September 11, 1990; the second is a letter from Foreign Minister Genscher and Prime Minister and Foreign Minister de Maiziere of the German Democratic Republic to their counterparts in the Two-plus-Four negotiations dated September 12, 1990; and the third is a letter dated September 18, 1990, from Foreign Minister Genscher to Secretary Baker.

In their letter of September 12 to their counterparts in the Two-plus-Four negotiations, Foreign Minister Genscher of the Federal Republic of Germany and Prime Minister and Foreign Minister de Maiziere of the German Democratic Republic formally convey several additional assurances. Among these are their declaration that the constitution of a united Germany will protect the free democratic order and provide

the continuing basis for prohibiting parties and associations with National Socialist aims. In his letter of September 18 to Secretary Baker, Foreign Minister Genscher also makes clear that the Government of a united Germany accepts responsibility for the resolution of unresolved claims against the German Democratic Republic, both of American citizens, and of Jewish victims of the Nazi regime. In this letter he commits his government to seek, shortly after unification, to provide expeditious and satisfactory resolution of claims of Jewish victims of the Nazi regime against the German Democratic Republic. In this same letter he states that the Federal Republic of Germany will, shortly after unification, resolve through negotiations with the United States Government the claims of U.S. nationals that were previously under discussion with the German Democratic Republic. The commitments contained in these two letters are further evidence that the Government of the united Germany will sustain and build on the exemplary record of the Federal Republic of Germany in promoting democratic values.

The Treaty represents a major achievement for our German allies, who have not forgotten the past or the role Germany once played in the horrors of 1933–45, but who have demonstrated over 4 decades of steadfast support for democracy and the Western alliance what the world can expect from the united Germany.

The Treaty is also a tribute to the courage and the determination of the people of Germany to achieve unity in peace, freedom, and concord with their neighbors.

The emergence of a free, united, and democratic Germany, linked to the United States and to its European neighbors by indissoluble ties of friendship, common values, and mutual interests, and ready to act as a full partner within a broader community of democratic nations, has been an enduring goal of American foreign policy for over 40 years. Seldom has any President had the privilege of submitting for the Senate's advice and consent an agreement which so fully realizes our national purposes. This agreement is the result of decades of steadfast effort and resolve on the part of past Presidents and Congresses, and our Allies. It is an achievement of which we can all be proud.

It is wholly fitting that Germany formally and irrevocably achieve its unified status at the earliest possible moment, unfettered by Four-Power rights, shared by the Soviet Union, which are now outmoded and un-

necessary. I therefore ask the Senate to act expeditiously in giving its advice and consent to ratification of the Treaty and the Related Agreed Minute.

GEORGE BUSH

The White House,
September 25, 1990.

Nomination of Elsie V. Vartanian To Be Director of the Women's Bureau
September 25, 1990

The President today announced his intention to nominate Elsie V. Vartanian, of New Hampshire, to be Director of the Women's Bureau at the Department of Labor. She would succeed Jill Houghton Emery.

Mrs. Vartanian currently serves as founder and president of Elsie V. Vartanian, Inc.,

in Salem, NH. In addition she has been a member of the New Hampshire House of Representatives from 1979 to the present, serving as assistant majority leader from 1987 to 1988. She was born July 19, 1930, in Haverhill, MA. Mrs. Vartanian is married, has one child, and resides in Salem, NH.

Remarks Following Discussions With President Turgut Özal of Turkey
September 25, 1990

President Bush. It has been a very great pleasure for me, and all of us—American side—to welcome President Özal to the White House. And on behalf of every American, Mr. President, I salute your leadership and your courage.

Our talks today have been most cordial and constructive, as befits good friends, and marked by respect and total candor, as befits allies and equal partners. Our two nations have been faithful to each other in war and in peace for more than 40 years. And we in the United States have always valued Turkey's vital contribution to NATO. We've stood together to defend the bedrock principles that unite us: freedom and democracy.

Our solidarity has never been more apparent than since Saddam Hussein marched ruthlessly into a peaceful Kuwait 8 weeks ago, violating all norms of international order. And since then, many nations have

worked together to contain and repel Iraq's brutal aggression—not America alone but the United Nations and staunch allies like Turkey who have told the world: We will not tolerate this invasion; it will not stand.

From the earliest stages of this struggle, Turkey has been in the forefront of the international condemnation of Iraq, thanks in large part to President Özal's leadership. Turkey promptly shut off the pipeline of Iraqi oil and closed its border to trade with Iraq. And Turkey was among the first to endorse the U.N. embargo of Iraqi goods. Turkey has stood firm and steadfast despite the heavy burden the Iraqi invasion has placed on its own economy.

Throughout this crisis, President Özal has been a decisive leader and a true friend. We've been in touch often since August 2d, and I look forward to continued close consultation with him in the period ahead.

In short, Turkey has served as a protector of peace, rallying to its friends when those friends are imperiled. And so, recently Secretary of State Baker and Secretary of Treasury Brady went to 13 nations, securing over $20 billion in international assistance. Many allied governments gladly offered aid in recognition of Turkey's generous contribution in defending our mutual interests. And we stand by those who stand up for civilized values around the world.

In that spirit, President Özal and I discussed today how we might expand the ties—political, economic, cultural, and military—which link Turkey and America. We agreed to work together to invigorate our economic relationship and pledged, as a first step, to initiate negotiations next month toward a new agreement on textiles.

I also told President Özal that the United States continues to support Turkey's application for membership in the European Community. As events in the Gulf have demonstrated the indisputable strategic importance of Turkey to NATO and the United States, we also agreed to maintain our close security and military relationship.

The administration will work with the Congress to make sure that Turkey receives its fair share of security assistance in fiscal year 1991. We will also work to help modernize the Turkish Armed Forces by the future sale of F–16's and provision of other military equipment.

Finally, President Özal and I discussed the importance and desirability of improved relations among all countries of the eastern Mediterranean, including Turkey and Greece.

Mr. President, ties have never been stronger, our friendship never deeper. And for now, I bid you an affectionate farewell. I wish you well up there at the United Nations. And I hope and believe we will see much of each other in the months and the years ahead. Thank you for coming our way.

President Özal. Thank you, Mr. President. I am very grateful to President Bush for his kind words about my country and myself. I was here in January, and we had a similar meeting, but then we didn't have this Gulf crisis in our hands. Today—along with bilateral relations, which are satisfactorily gaining scope and reflect the longstanding friendship between Turkey and the United States—the Gulf crisis, of course, was the top issue.

President Bush has shown exceptional leadership not only for his country but for the whole community of nations since the outbreak of this crisis. His firm stand against aggression and immediate reaction based on the correct assessment of the implications of Iraq's invasion of Kuwait have been instrumental in the mobilization of a united front against the aggression.

I think I am one of the few to know best the invaluable efforts of President Bush since I have been in close and constant contact with him from the very first days of the crisis. For your sagacious and determined stand, Mr. President, you deserve the appreciation of the civilized world all over.

Turkey, on her part, has not only become the key to the successful implementation of the sanctions but by her actions has also been instrumental in encouraging several other countries to follow suit. It is preferable that this crisis is resolved through peaceful means. The effective implementation of the economic embargo may be the only hope for achieving this objective. Therefore, each and every country has a collective duty to strictly observe the mandatory U.N. sanctions and make them work.

During our talk, President Bush and I had the opportunity to discuss extensively our bilateral relations. I am gratified to say that both countries have the political will to promote these relations in every field. Our relations recently began to diversify, and our economic cooperation started to gain momentum.

I emphasized to President Bush today that our motto remains unchanged: Turkey wants more trade than aid. I believe it's a valid object since we should be partners not only in security cooperation but, perhaps even more so, in such other areas as increased trade and economic cooperation. In view of our desire to enter into a closer relationship in this field with the United States, the rapid elimination of trade barriers will be in conformity with the spirit of such a partnership.

I would like to conclude by stating that

our discussions were very satisfactory, reflecting the close friendship that exists between our two countries since many, many years.

Thank you.

Note: President Bush spoke at 1:38 p.m. at the South Portico of the White House. In his remarks, he referred to President Saddam Hussein of Iraq. Prior to their remarks, the two Presidents met privately in the Oval Office and with U.S. and Turkish officials in the Cabinet Room, and then attended a luncheon in the Old Family Dining Room.

Remarks at the Annual Meeting of the Boards of Governors of the International Monetary Fund and World Bank Group
September 25, 1990

Thank you very much, and my special thanks to my good friend, our Secretary of the Treasury, Nick Brady, for those kind words and for the outstanding job that he's doing as our Secretary. To Chairman Saitoti and Mr. Camdessus and my old friend and former seatmate on the Ways and Means Committee, Barber Conable, it really is a pleasure to be back with you this year to welcome you all to Washington for this very important work. And it's a particular pleasure today to welcome the new members here from Bulgaria, the Czech and Slovak Republic, and Namibia, and of course, the special invitees from the Soviet Union. Your presence here reminds us all of how events of the past year are producing a new partnership of nations—a fundamental, indeed, inspiring change in the world's political and economic order.

The movement toward democratic rule, already strong throughout the 1980's, accelerated during what I call the Revolution of '89. The rights of the individual have been reaffirmed with greater adherence to the rule of law. The freedom to choose political leaders, and even political systems, has triumphed in countries that only a year ago were ruled by single-party regimes. And hand in hand, new economic freedom has begun to emerge as well. Today leaders around the world are turning to market forces to meet the needs of their people, and of course—and I understand this—change has not come easily. But as I said last year at this same meeting, the jury is no longer out—history has decided.

And today the results of that global experiment are unmistakable. Today the consensus is this: Governments by themselves cannot deliver prosperity. Rather, the key to economic growth is setting individuals free—free to take risks, free to make choices, free to use their initiative and their abilities in the marketplace. We are seeing this, for example, in the restoration of private ownership in countries where the state once controlled every single aspect of economic life. And for efficient production, private ownership is still the most powerful incentive known to man.

Matched by the rejuvenation of markets, the ability to make individual economic choices is the fastest, most effective way to achieve and sustain broad-based economic growth. And that is why leaders everywhere are undertaking difficult economic reforms; building stronger, more versatile private sectors; improving efficiency; and making government decisionmaking much more rational.

That process takes time. Economic adjustment is often difficult. And in recent months, a new challenge has arisen which could hinder this process of change, and of course, I'm talking about Iraq's illegal and unprovoked aggression against the sovereign nation of Kuwait. Clearly, the greatest harm is to Kuwait and its people. When the Saudi border was opened, Kuwait's newest refugees brought fresh tales of cruelty and horror inflicted on the Kuwaiti people and foreign nationals as well by the occupying forces of Saddam Hussein.

And today other countries, already facing painful economic and political transformations, must now deal with additional hardships. Serious challenges have emerged for countries rocked by unpredictable tides in the flow of oil, trade, displaced workers, and—God bless them—the refugees. This staggering burden, which is pressing upon these most seriously affected countries, calls for a generous response from the world community. Toward that end, we have already begun to mobilize financial resources for the frontline states to ensure responsible sharing among creditors.

The initial response to that effort has been impressive. Now, in order to transform commitments into concrete contributions, I am pleased to announce the formation of a Gulf crisis financial coordination group under the chairmanship of Secretary Nicholas Brady, our Secretary of the Treasury, with the aim of achieving effective, timely, and sustained financial support to these most seriously affected countries.

But let us not forget an even larger group of countries represented here will suffer from higher oil prices and other economic dislocations. While world attention has rightly focused on those countries closest to the situation and bearing the heaviest economic burden, I can tell you that the rest of the world is certainly not forgotten and never will be.

This gathering here of world financial leaders gives us an opportunity to discuss how we can work together to address the special financial burden of this crisis, and do so in a way that will sustain the dramatic worldwide transition to free markets. The IMF and World Bank, given their central role in the world economy, are key to helping all of us through this situation by providing a combination of policy advice and financial assistance. The political leadership of the U.N. must be matched by the economic leadership of the IMF and the World Bank.

Secretary Brady will be making some specific suggestions in his remarks for possible means of utilizing current IMF and World Bank programs more effectively. But let me say it again: We are determined not to allow the brutal behavior of one aggressor to undermine the historic process of democratic change or to derail the movement towards market-oriented economic systems.

Let me continue more broadly with a vision of the role of the United States and of a world economy we can all share.

First, we believe that the United States should contribute to economic stability and growth. And perhaps the greatest contribution that the United States can make to the health of the international economy is to get our own house in order. Our budget deficit must be brought under control and reduced.

And second, the United States is strongly committed to promoting development and growth in the newly emerging democracies of Latin America, Central and Eastern Europe, Africa, and Asia. We're working in all four regions to ease debt burdens under the Brady plan. In this hemisphere, where debt overhang holds back progress—impedes progress—we announced the Enterprise for the Americas Initiative to promote economic growth by expanding trade and investment, to reduce debt owed to the United States Government, and to provide funds for needed local environmental projects. In Eastern Europe, where massive restructuring is needed, we are working with other nations to provide billions of dollars in assistance to the newly emerging democracies. And in Africa, where undevelopment hangs on so stubbornly, many of the lowest income countries have already benefited from reductions in debt owed to the United States.

Third, the United States is committed to the central role of the IMF and World Bank in helping bring about economic reforms. Reform efforts can only be successful if countries carry through on their responsibilities; and that means regulatory reform and privatization, sound macroeconomic and structural policies, and open borders for trade and investment.

This is why your work here in Washington this week is so important. For more than 40 years, the Fund and the Bank have quietly been enlisting the talents and the energies of the developed and developing world in a global struggle against poverty. And today, in a world where ideology no longer confronts and big-power blocs no longer divide, the Bank and the Fund have become paradigms of international cooperation. Indeed, we especially appreciate your efforts in carrying out a study of the Soviet economy that is unprecedented in its scope. This study will produce recommendations for economic, financial, and structural reform.

As the coming week unfolds, part of your task will also be to plan for the future of your two great institutions. And I pledge the continued support of the United States for a World Bank and IMF which so clearly advance our common struggle to improve the quality of life for all people everywhere. For this reason, we strongly support the IMF quota increase and the strengthening of the IMF arrears policy. And we would also like to challenge both institutions to intensify their focus on building dynamic private sectors in member countries, one of the most important stimulants for energizing these new market economies.

And we would also ask the World Bank to place a high priority in three other issues vital to sustain growth. First is protecting the environment. As I said here last year, environmental destruction knows no borders. Second, eradicating poverty must continue to be a central mission of the Bank. And third, we strongly support greater efforts to integrate women into the development process.

Finally, as we plan for the future, we must work together for success in another important international economic institution: the GATT. As we meet today, less than 70 days remain in the 4-year Uruguay round of global trade talks. Lasting reform is essential for developed and developing countries alike, and it's the key to a successful round which establishes new rules and opportunities for all countries. These negotiations are one of the world's greatest economic opportunities of the decade, but much remains to be done.

The round is not just a trade issue: it is a growth issue. And it's not just an exercise for bureaucrats in Geneva. The trade talks are the last train leaving the station, and countries throughout the world must jump aboard. It can be the engine of economic growth that carries us into the 21st century.

The round promises to remove barriers in four crucial areas, areas untouched in previous rounds: services, investment, intellectu-

al property, and agriculture. As a matter of fact, agriculture reform remains a major stumbling block. Indeed, it threatens to bring down the rest of the round. We must let farmers compete with farmers, instead of farmers competing with the deep pockets of government treasuries. We need a successful resolution of the agricultural issues if we are to have an agreement.

If countries around the globe don't muster the political courage to face these tough issues in the time remaining, we will forfeit new markets for our businesses, impose higher prices on our consumers, and forgo new jobs and higher incomes for workers in all countries. Worst of all, we will endanger a vital, proven framework of international cooperation. A collapse of the round will inevitably encourage increased protectionist pressure and political instability; and that, frankly, is something that we can ill afford as we forge a new partnership of nations against aggression in the Persian Gulf.

I urge you to work actively within your governments to ensure success, and I urge my counterparts around the world—as we did at the Houston economic summit—to instruct your negotiators to bring all the components of the Uruguay round to a successful conclusion by December.

In all these efforts, there is so much at stake. Almost 35 years ago, President Eisenhower first appeared at an IMF-World Bank meeting, and he spoke of the lessons that he learned while waging a war that brought together so many different soldiers from so many different lands. Ike noted, as I do now, that there were people in the audience who were our allies in that grand effort. And he said: "We early found one thing. Without the heart, without the enthusiasm for the cause in which we were working, no cooperation was possible. With that enthusiasm, subordinating all else to the advancement of the cause, cooperation was easy."

As the unity of the nations has demonstrated in the past 2 months, the worldwide enthusiasm for today's noble cause, the cause I've described as a new partnership of nations, is not only unprecedented but truly remarkable. And I urge you to seize that enthusiasm in your meetings this week, to forge the new levels of cooperation needed to succeed.

Thank you very much for coming to Washington, DC. I hope you feel welcome, because you are. Good luck this week in the meetings ahead, and God speed you in your travels home. Thank you all very, very much.

Note: President Bush spoke at 3:06 p.m. in the ballroom of the Sheraton Washington Hotel. In his remarks, he referred to George Saitoti, Chairman of the International Monetary Fund and the World Bank Group; Michel Camdessus, Managing Director and Chairman of the Executive Board of the International Monetary Fund; Barber B. Conable, President of the World Bank Group; and President Saddam Hussein of Iraq.

Remarks on the Federal Budget Negotiations
September 25, 1990

Let me just make a comment, if you all are ready, on this deficit problem. Frankly, I had a good report from the Hill, and I want to commend the Republican members of the House Appropriations Committee for voting to deal with the budget problem forthrightly.

The Democrats in the House wanted to avoid fiscal responsibility and keep government spending growing and deficit growing. And the Republicans said: Look, no more business as usual. No more dodging responsibility. It is time to get the budget agreement done. Without an agreement, the deficit gets worse, the economy gets worse, and clearly it's the American people that will suffer.

So, if there is no budget agreement with real spending reduction and real process reform by the end of the week, I will have to veto it—I will veto any continuing resolution that suspends Gramm-Rudman and budget discipline and thereby destroys our best chance of bringing this deficit under control once and for all.

So, I want to thank the Republicans who have stood firm on this. I do not want to see further delays and kicking this problem on down the road. Enough is enough! The American people want a deal, and they want it now. They want to get the deficit down, and that's what I want.

That's it. Thank you.

Note: The President spoke at approximately 3:40 p.m. on the South Lawn of the White House, upon returning from the annual meeting of the Boards of Governors of the International Monetary Fund and the World Bank Group.

Statement on Signing the Carl D. Perkins Vocational and Applied Technology Education Act Amendments of 1990
September 25, 1990

Today, I am signing H.R. 7, the "Carl D. Perkins Vocational and Applied Technology Education Act Amendments of 1990." This legislation amends and extends the Carl D. Perkins Vocational Education Act. It reauthorizes one of the Federal programs that supports State and local efforts to develop a work force that will keep this country competitive in the world market.

This Act creates a more effective vocational education program through its emphasis on accountability and program improvement. The Act requires that each State develop a system of performance standards and measures for secondary and post-secondary vocational education programs. It requires that State leadership activities include teacher training, curriculum development, and program assessment. It places a greater emphasis on programs that combine academic and vocational instruction and on programs that develop a coherent sequence of courses beginning in high school and continuing through community college. The Act encourages cooperative academic links between secondary and post-secondary institutions, with the goal of providing students with higher levels of technical competency.

In addition, H.R. 7 continues the important emphasis on providing access to quality vocational education programs to our least advantaged populations. It focuses on students with disabilities, students with limited English proficiency, and students who are educationally disadvantaged.

In signing this legislation, however, I must take note of two provisions that raise constitutional concerns. First, the Act requires that each State receiving funds must set aside a certain percentage for "Sex Equity Programs" that can be used, among other purposes, for educational activities for girls and women aged 14 through 25. Such activities would, on their face, discriminate on the basis of gender. Since the funding for "Sex Equity Programs" also can be used for other, nondiscriminatory programs, these nondiscriminatory programs will be preferred in administering the legislation.

The discriminatory programs will be implemented only if there is a sufficiently strong justification to withstand judicial scrutiny.

Second, the Act requires the Secretary of Education to submit directly to the Congress two reports prepared by the Department of Education's Office of Educational Research and Improvement. According to subsection 403(c)(3), these reports "shall not be subject to any review outside the Office of Educational Research and Improvement before their transmittal to Congress . . . ." This provision is unconstitutional because it purports to preclude me from exercising my constitutional duty to supervise the executive branch. Because I cannot abandon my oversight responsibility, I shall treat the unconstitutional portion of the Act as severable from the rest of this legislation.

In conclusion, H.R. 7 excludes many of the changes proposed by my Administration and includes certain constitutionally troublesome provisions. However, it does reflect progress over current law. My Administration, particularly Secretaries Cavazos and Dole, will continue to work with the next Congress to make more improvements in the overall systems for financing and delivering training.

GEORGE BUSH

The White House,
September 25, 1990.

Note: H.R. 7, approved September 25, was assigned Public Law No. 101–392.

Message to the Congress Transmitting the South Pacific Environmental Protection Convention and Protocols
September 25, 1990

To the Senate of the United States:

I transmit herewith, for the advice and consent of the Senate to ratification, the Convention for the Protection of the Natural Resources and Environment of the South Pacific Region, with Annex, and the Protocol for the Prevention of Pollution of the South Pacific Region by Dumping, with Annexes, done at Noumea, New Caledonia,

on November 24, 1986. The report of the Department of State in respect of the Convention and Protocol is attached for the information of the Senate. I also transmit to the Senate, for its information, the Protocol Concerning Cooperation in Combating Pollution Emergencies in the South Pacific Region.

The Convention for the Protection of the

Natural Resources and Environment of the South Pacific Region will create general legal obligations designed to protect the marine environment of the region from a variety of sources of marine pollution. In so doing, the Convention provides new environmental protection for American Samoa, Guam and the Northern Mariana Islands, as well as for the Convention area generally.

The Convention and its Protocols on dumping and pollution emergencies entered into force on August 22, 1990. Ten countries have ratified or acceded to the Convention. These are: France, Australia, New Zealand, Papua New Guinea, Solomon Islands, Fiji, the Marshall Islands, the Federated States of Micronesia, Western Samoa, and the Cook Islands. Expeditious U.S. ratification of the Convention and Protocol

would demonstrate not only our commitment to the protection of the marine environment of the South Pacific but our continuing political commitment to the region as well. It would also allow the United States to participate fully at the first meeting of Parties, which will likely establish the financial and institutional arrangements for implementing the Convention.

I recommend that the Senate give early and favorable consideration to the Convention and Protocol and give its advice and consent to ratification, subject to the two understandings described in the accompanying report of the Secretary of State.

GEORGE BUSH

The White House,
September 25, 1990.

Letter to Congressional Leaders on Mexico-United States Free Trade Negotiations
September 25, 1990

Dear Mr. Chairman:

In a letter to me of August 21, President Salinas formally proposed initiation of negotiations for a free trade agreement between the United States and Mexico (copy enclosed). As you know, President Salinas and I had endorsed the objective of a free trade agreement at a meeting in June, and our respective Trade Ministers, Secretary Serra and United States Trade Representative Hills, had so recommended in a joint report of August 8 (copy enclosed).

Mexico is our third largest trading partner, and you are aware of the dynamic, market-oriented reforms undertaken by President Salinas. We see substantial opportunities for mutual benefit in further lowering impediments to bilateral trade in goods and services and to investment.

Accordingly, I welcome the recommendations in the joint report and President Salinas' proposal. Negotiation of a comprehensive free trade agreement is consistent with the efforts of both my Administration and the Congress to eliminate barriers to the flow of goods, services and investment, and

to protect intellectual property rights.

Therefore, pursuant to Section 1102(c) of the Omnibus Trade and Competitiveness Act of 1988, I am hereby notifying the Senate Committee on Finance [House Committee on Ways and Means] of trade negotiations with Mexico.

I also want to inform you that the Government of Canada has recently expressed a desire to participate in the negotiations, with a view to negotiating an agreement or agreements among all three countries. I welcome the opportunity to work with our two neighbors towards this end. We, with the Canadian and Mexican Governments together, will be consulting in the coming months to explore the possibilities in this regard, which we will also discuss with your Committee. I will send a further or revised notice to your Committee as appropriate, depending on the outcome of our consultations.

I want to emphasize that such trilateral consultations will not affect the continued validity of the existing free trade agreement with Canada. Further, in all these discussions, we expect to build on our multilateral negotiating efforts in the Uruguay Round, which is scheduled to conclude at the end of this year.

Ambassador Hills has already begun consultations with your Committee, and the Administration will continue that process throughout the negotiations.

Sincerely,

GEORGE BUSH

Note: Identical letters were sent to Lloyd Bentsen, chairman of the Senate Finance Committee, and Dan Rostenkowski, chairman of the House Ways and Means Committee. The letters were released by the Office of the Press Secretary on September 26.

Message to the Senate Transmitting the Soviet Union-United States Maritime Boundary Agreement
September 26, 1990

To the Senate of the United States:

I transmit herewith, for the advice and consent of the Senate to ratification, the Agreement Between the United States of America and the Union of Soviet Socialist Republics on the Maritime Boundary, with Annex, signed at Washington, June 1, 1990. I also enclose for the information of the Senate the report of the Department of State with respect to this agreement and an illustrative chart of the maritime boundary.

In the agreement, the Parties agree that the line described in Article 1 of the Convention Ceding Alaska, signed March 30, 1867 (the 1867 Convention Line), is, as defined in the agreement, the maritime boundary between the United States and the Soviet Union. As such, it defines the limits within which each Party may exercise territorial sea jurisdiction or exclusive economic zone jurisdiction in those areas where their claimed 12 nautical mile territorial seas or 200 nautical mile exclusive economic zones would otherwise overlap or were otherwise in dispute. It also delimits, as between the Parties, such continental shelf jurisdiction beyond 200 nautical miles from their coasts as they may exercise in accordance with international law in the Arctic Ocean, Bering and Chukchi Seas, and a portion of the North Pacific Ocean.

I believe the agreement to be fully in the United States interest. It reflects the view of the United States that the maritime boundary should follow the 1867 Convention Line. The agreement resolves differences over where each Party has the right to manage fisheries and oil and gas exploration and development, as well as exercise other sovereign rights and jurisdiction, in these marine areas. Through its transfer of jurisdiction provisions, it also ensures that coastal state jurisdiction, in accordance with international law, is exercised by one or the other Party in all marine areas within 200 nautical miles of either or both coasts. Therefore, the agreement will permit more effective regulation of marine resource activities and other ocean uses and removes a significant potential source of dispute between the United States and the Soviet Union.

I recommend that the Senate give early and favorable consideration to this agreement and advise and consent to ratification.

GEORGE BUSH

The White House,
September 26, 1990.

Exchange With Reporters Aboard Air Force One on the Federal Budget Negotiations
September 26, 1990

Q. Did you have a good flight?

The President. Big political day today.

Q. How did the discussions this morning go, sir?

The President. Good. Good. Republicans are staying solid.

Q. Are you concerned that you've lost Mr. Michel's support on your——

The President. I always like to talk to the people involved.

Q. Are you flexible on capital gains at all, sir?

Q. What did he tell you, Mr. President?

The President. He told me that they're working hard to get a deal. And we are. And the Republicans know what I want when I talk about growth. I'm not interested in raising the tax rates on the American people. And our team is fighting very hard. So, we'll see where we go.

Q. Can a sequester be avoided, or do you think it will go right up until the deadline?

The President. It can be avoided if they get doing what they should. It's the Congress—and I would say now the Democrats in the Congress that are in charge of the Congress that have not come forward with a package. And we're still working hard in a good, bipartisan spirit there, they told me today. We're getting right down to the wire.

Q. Are you concerned that you might look too inflexible on the capital gains issue?

The President. No, I'm not concerned about that at all because there's an awful lot of issues that are still out there, like spending and trying to tax the American people excessively and things where the American people are on our side. So, we'll just see how we go. But I want to see the Democrats now get into a spirit of compromise. I started early on. You all wrote about it; everybody talked about it. We talked about the revenue side. Now I want to see some flexibility on their part, and I'm going to take our case to the American people. The American people don't need this. They don't need it all. They don't want it. I don't think they yet realize how serious sequester is.

But this concept that they tried yesterday—the Democrats did—to just move it on down the road, kick the can down the road, is not fair to the American people nor to the economy. So, we're going to stay with what I said yesterday. And I was very proud that the Republicans stayed together and would not permit the Democrats in the House of Representatives to simply delay the day of reckoning. That's what they tried to do. Everybody knows that. I think the American people know it—loud and clear.

Q. Are you going to join the talks at some point this week, sir?

The President. They know—both Democrats and Republicans—that if my presence there would be helpful, I'm available.

Note: The exchange occurred in the morning while the President was en route from Washington, DC, to Akron, OH. In his remarks, he referred to Robert H. Michel, Republican leader of the House of Representatives. A tape was not available for verification of the content of this exchange.

Remarks at a Fundraising Luncheon for Gubernatorial Candidate George Voinovich in Akron, Ohio
September 26, 1990

Alex, thank you. Thank you all. What a great welcome back to Akron—same place, a couple years later. Thank you all very, very much. Thank you, Mayor—soon to be

Governor—Voinovich. And Janet, Barbara sends her love. She looks forward to being with you. I don't know whether it's next week or when it is, but she'll be out here to show not only support for the ticket but to show the affection that she and I have for you and George.

To Mike and Fran DeWine, we wish you well. I can't wait for the day that you are Lieutenant Governor, but I'm going to be disappointed to have you leave the House of Representatives that you served so very well, indeed.

And of course, it's like old home week here with Alex—your Alex, mine. [*Laughter*] One of the great political leaders—and I mean this—is a former national chairman who himself studied under Ray Bliss of Akron and still has great affection in his heart for Ray Bliss. They don't have many political leaders like Alex around this country. And he's good, and he's honest, and he's decent, and I get fired up every time I'm around him. Alex, thank you for this wonderful event here today—Alex Arshinkoff.

And while we're at it, I want to salute our State chairman, Bob Bennett, over here. The State party has never been more vibrant or supportive of these candidates. Bob, stand up there.

And Senator Roy Ray is here, 1 of 10 Republican State legislators out of 3,000 in the country to win the prestigious Legislator of the Year Award—Roy. There he is, right there.

And I want to put in a plug right at the beginning for the strong State ticket we've got, and one of those members is with us today—I think the only one. If I'm wrong, somebody holler, but Jim Petro, who's running for auditor, standing right here. And it's a very important position because it has a lot to do with the redistricting. And we want a fair redistricting not just in Ohio but all the way across this country, and his election can contribute to that.

As for Paul Mifsud, over here, who's running the Voinovich campaign, he's the guy that suggested I meet Gorbachev in Malta. [*Laughter*] He's from Malta, you may know. And people are still throwing up over there because of the weather. [*Laughter*]

You know, there's a handful of people across the country to whom Barbara and I always will be indebted for the marvelous opportunity to serve in this office that I have now, and one of them is Paul. And he's worked very, very hard, always helpful to me and, of course, always at George Voinovich's side. So, you've got a good team.

I want to apologize for a very close member of my family who couldn't make it today. As it turns out, Millie is on the road, promoting her new book—[*laughter*]—our springer spaniel. I told them last night that her celebrity status has gone to her head. I gave her a bowl of Alpo, and she asked to see the wine list there at the White House last night. [*Laughter*]

But look, enough of this. If I seem a little relaxed, it's because you have a wonderful way here in Akron of making a person feel at home. And I really am delighted to be back here in a State that Barbara and I feel we know very well, indeed. For us, Ohio means Dayton, where Barbara's parents lived; Miami, where both Bar's mother and dad went to college. For me, Columbus, where my father was born and where he grew up. It also means many other things, having campaigned extensively in this State: smalltown boulevards of Lima, busy streets of Cincinnati—I've probably been in Hamilton County as much as everybody in this room put together; it seems like it—and then of course the vibrance and the factory yards of Akron and the farms nestled in the Appalachian foothills along the Ohio River.

So I mention all this because to know the diversity we call America you really just have to get a feeling for the State of Ohio. So it should come as no surprise that I've been looking forward to coming out here to say a few words about an Ohio leader who revitalized your neighboring city of Cleveland, taking it from the gloomy and dark days of ridicule and despair and bringing it into the bright light of achievement and respect. I didn't come out here to talk about Bernie Kosar, incidentally. [*Laughter*] I'm here today to show my support for an Ohio leader, a great mayor, soon to be a great Governor; and I'm talking about George Voinovich.

I think all Ohioans, regardless of party,

agree that he's already demonstrated this uncommon ability we're talking about in his three terms as mayor of Cleveland. Little wonder, then, that George often says that Cleveland "is off the rocks and on a roll." Now he wants to do the same for all of Ohio. And make no mistake, after 8 years, Ohio needs this Voinovich leadership and this Voinovich integrity in the Governor's office.

For years now, you, as Ohioans, and some of us from outside have been reading the investigative journalists' reports detailing the cronyism, the political favoritism, the taxpayer rip-offs that have taken place in this State. And at least one candidate for Governor has had enough. Here's what George Voinovich says: "State government needs a thorough housecleaning, a gust of fresh air." And I can guarantee you he'll do that for the State.

So, this campaign is about the future of Ohio—an Ohio whose natural beauty is preserved for future generations, an Ohio that empowers people and not the bureaucrats, an Ohio that leads this country—and you heard him commit to this—to education reform to keep America competitive and to give our children a better future.

Both George and I believe that when we ask more of our kids, they'll respond; so will our teachers and our schools and our parents and, yes, our elected public officials. With his "schools first" policy, George would upgrade the entire Ohio educational system while rewarding outstanding teachers and excellent schools. And he has embraced fully the goals of the Charlottesville educational summit that I convened last year because, he says, "these goals are right for the entire Nation and for Ohio."

And the first goal of all is that George and I want our schools to be free of violence and drugs, and we must work towards that end. There's also the heartfelt goals of our Congressman here, Congressman Mike DeWine, who's been a leader in shaping the antidrug laws for the Nation as a Member of the United States Congress. And I'm going to miss his advice, as I said, in Washington. Not only has he distinguished himself fighting this whole concept of illegal drugs and crime but he's earned recognition from Watchdogs of the Treasury and the National Taxpayers Union—both—as a fighter for fiscal responsibility. This outstanding record of service to the people of Ohio at county and State and national levels makes Mike DeWine the right choice for Lieutenant Governor of Ohio, and we urge your strong support for the ticket.

Let me just take a minute to address a couple of other matters important to the people of Ohio, but also to the people of our entire country and, indeed, to the world. This is, indeed, as George pointed out, an extraordinary moment, a moment when our national will is being tested both at home and abroad.

We can meet the test at home—I'm confident we can meet it—but what we must do is first put our fiscal house in order. And right now, at this very minute, we are coming down to the wire in Washington, the final few days of the fiscal year. You remember, the new fiscal year starts October 1st, the way the Federal Government keeps its books. So, we're right down at the end of the old fiscal year, coming to the new one, final few days; and still we do not have an agreement in hand to bring this deficit down. It's up there in the Congress right now. We sent a proposal there months ago.

Five days from now the ax falls, an automatic, mandated sequester that will cut $100 billion from the Federal budget. A cutback of this scope is going to hit hard, and it's going to hit home, and it's going to hit many, many people.

Let me give you a couple of examples so you'll understand when you hear that word what sequester means. For air travelers, it means big cutbacks in air traffic control and substantial increases in flight delays and outright cancellations. For farmers, it will mean that ASCS [Agricultural Stabilization and Conservation Service] offices will close during harvest time. For meatpackers, plants may close when inspectors fail to show up. For college students, it means an end to 1.2 million Pell grants—1.2 million eliminated outright. Add to that a 22-percent cutback in grants to another 2 million students. In this very city, this means that the poor students, the poor kids, will not be able to attend Akron University.

And let me tell you, the sequester is strong medicine, but it's medicine patented by the Congress itself. It represents the last attempt by Congress to cure itself of its feverish spending habits, and without an agreement, it is the only way for Congress to force itself to make the very necessary tough choices. It is the law of the land. And I took an oath to the Constitution to uphold the law of the land. And we've tried to do our part to solve this difficult problem, and I made a good-faith effort to reach a sound and sensible budget agreement.

Let me go back to the beginning, back to February 1st, when I sent a complete budget up to Capitol Hill, and back to April 1st, when Democrats who controlled both Houses of the United States Congress missed the deadline to take action on that budget—their own deadline, spelled out in their own rules for the Congress. A month later, in May, I convened a budget summit, recognizing we only had a few months to go to this October 1st that's now a few days away. We wanted to jump-start the process.

And at the end of June, when the talks bogged down, I made a concession demanded by the Democrat leaders to get Congress off dead center. And I put it all on the table, even taxes, and I took a lot of political heat coming out of the Democratic Party and the Democratic leaders. They had a great bunch of joy out of all of that. And then in July, when both sides pledged to exchange comprehensive budget plans, the Democrats delayed while we delivered.

And all through the talks, for 135 long days, time and again I've gone the extra mile, and I think the Republicans in the Congress have gone the extra mile. And each time, the other side says: It's still your move. It's still your move.

Well, that's not just our move anymore. And if and when the ax falls, the Democratic Congress knows that it will be held accountable, and I will take that message to every State in the Union. It is their fault for holding up getting a budget agreement. I've sat on my hands; I've suffered the slings and arrows that I expect from the political process. But I have a podium, too. I have a bully pulpit, too. And I'm going to see that it is not printed one side of this story, one Democrat after another knocking my socks off on Capitol Hill. The American people want a budget agreement. They know who controls the Congress, and they want them to deliver a budget agreement to get this deficit down.

Let me come again to you. It goes well beyond political rhetoric. It's one of the great economic challenges that our country has faced. It is important to get a solution. But the threat of sequester doesn't change the fact that the fundamental test of any agreement is whether it sustains conditions for continued economic growth and job creation. And that's why I've called on Congress to build a package of progrowth incentives into a budget agreement, incentives that create jobs and encourage aggressive, competitive R&D that sustain growth and steer this economy clear of recession.

And, yes, that's why I will continue to push hard for incentives for capital investment. In this global environment, many of our fiercest competitors are way ahead of us in promoting the savings and essential investment opportunity to success in the international marketplace.

And contrary to what you may have heard, the hangup is not capital gains; the hangup is with the Democrats on Capitol Hill. And we're still waiting for the Congress to come up with enough real spending cuts—cuts that are enforceable, not just another empty promise of future savings, a promise waiting to be broken. And we're still waiting for Congress to commit to meaningful budget-process reform—reform that builds real discipline into the budget process. The American people are not dumb. They know, as they watch the Congress, that the budget process is a mess and it must be fixed once and for all.

We're going to bear the heat here. The last thing we want is for the year's budget fiasco to become next year's instant replay. So today I say this to the United States Congress: Keep those lights burning on Capitol Hill if you have to, but before that deadline passes 5 days from now, let's reach the agreement that the American people are waiting for. No quick fix. No deal to delay these difficult budget decisions until after the election.

Yesterday, one of the powerful committees controlled by the Democrats voted on party line to delay the solution. Kick it on down the road. Don't make the tough decision today. Well, I'm going to stand in the way of that plan, if using every ounce of pressure I have, including the veto, to see that that does not happen. No quick fix. No delays.

October 1st is the zero hour, and it's real. We've got to prove to the American people once and for all that we can come together to deal with this deficit. There have been times when the cooperation has been good. And frankly, I'll be honest with you, I think the leaders—the two or three top leaders on the Democratic side—have tried pretty hard on this matter. But that's not enough. That is not enough. The control lies there, and the responsibility to come forth with an agreement lies there.

Congress should listen to men like Mike DeWine, Members like he; Lynn Martin, who is with us here today, who is running over in Illinois; and others, who say it's simply outrageous that important government services be jeopardized because Congress cannot do its job and pass a budget with the necessary reductions.

Reaching an agreement is critical. It really is. And we simply cannot fail to put our fiscal house in order, especially now with the challenge that we're facing over there, halfway around the world, in the Persian Gulf.

Emotions in the budget debate, as I report to you today, I can tell you, are running high—they're running very high. You haven't heard much out of me on this. I've waited in the wings and tried to conciliate, and as I told you, I think I've given a great deal. But no matter how heated the exchange of words may be over the budget, we need to—and I will do this—continue to maintain a bipartisan spirit in support of America's response to Iraqi aggression. I would be remiss if I didn't tell you I am grateful, in this Vandenberg concept of partisanship ending at the water's edge, that the Democrats and the Republicans in the House and the Senate are pulling together. And I'm grateful to the Democratic leadership for the support that they have publicly given—what this country is trying to do in the Middle East.

I am often asked when we can bring our kids home—some still arriving. But I can understand that from parents and loved ones here in this country—the concern they feel about our men and women that are serving over there. The answer has got to be general: It's got to be as soon as possible—every single one of them—but when the job is done.

Certain objectives have to be met. Iraq must withdraw from Kuwait, without condition. Aggression unchecked today will rear its ugly head tomorrow. Kuwait's legitimate government must be restored. The security and the stability of this vital area, an area that affects the lives of every American, must be assured. And American citizens abroad, those held hostage in this brutal shielding technique that Saddam Hussein is using, must be protected.

But we have another, final objective: to create a new partnership of nations; a new world order that is free from the threat of terror, stronger in the pursuit of justice, more secure in the quest for peace.

These are our objectives and those of the United Nations Security Council and our allies. There are many, many countries to whom I am extraordinarily grateful for this tremendous cooperation. West Germany has pledged to support the mission with almost $2 billion and provide ships and planes, while Japan has pledged a package worth more than $4 billion. France added another 4,000 troops, and Great Britain is sending 120 tanks, 6,000 troops, the famous Desert Rats those of us who are old enough to remember World War II will recall. And we're side by side in the soil there with Egyptian troops and Syrian troops and other Arab troops. It's truly Iraq, then, against the world. The world is simply standing up and telling Saddam Hussein: We will not give in to intimidation.

Americans are showing their determination right here in Ohio. Look no further than Ashland University, to the father of a marine stationed in the Gulf region, Professor Charles Brereton. Dr. Brereton published in the school newspaper a list of soldiers in his son Jim's Alpha Company weapons platoon. That one appeal led to a massive outpouring, a flood, of letters and hometown papers and care packages.

This is just one way—tiny way, perhaps—but it's one way that Ohio is sending a message to the Americans stationed in the Middle East. That message is a simple one: We're with you all the way. And another thing, support for our mission is strong, bipartisan in the sense of what Senator Vandenberg meant. For those of us at home, we believe that the best way we can serve our country is to debate and campaign and be the best Republicans and Democrats we can be. But we cannot allow our political life to be held hostage to a foreign crisis.

When Ohioans go out to the polls, absentee ballots will be streaming in from Americans in uniform, including those stationed in the Persian Gulf. If our soldiers, sailors, and airmen, and marines can find the time to vote under such difficult circumstances, I hope America can count on all Ohioans to get out there and vote. And when you do—

let me end it this way—when you do, I hope you and thousands like you around this great State will make George Voinovich the next Governor of Ohio.

Thank you. God bless the United States of America. Thank you all.

Note: President Bush spoke at 12:07 p.m. at the Tangier Restaurant. In his remarks, he referred to Mayor Voinovich's wife, Janet; Representative Michael DeWine and his wife, Fran; Ray C. Bliss, former State and national Republican Party chairman; Alex Arshinkoff, executive committee chairman of the Summit County Republican Party; Bernie Kosar, quarterback for the Cleveland Browns football team; and President Saddam Hussein of Iraq. He also referred to Millie, the First Family's dog, and "Millie's Book as Dictated to Barbara Bush." Following his remarks, President Bush attended a private reception and then traveled to Chicago, IL.

Remarks at a Rally for Senatorial Candidate Lynn Martin in Chicago, Illinois
September 26, 1990

The President. Thank you very, very much for that warm introduction.

Audience members. Four more years! Four more years! Four more years!

The President. Thank you, thank you. Thank you all. Lynn, thank you. Thank you, all of you. And, Lynn, thank you for that warm and wonderful introduction, and thank all of you for making me feel so at home.

We were in Ohio earlier today, and the crowds there were almost as enthusiastic. One exception: I saw a lady holding up a sign—true story—that read, "Where's Millie?" [*Laughter*] Which reminds me to bring you greetings from Barbara Bush. She salutes Lynn, as I do.

And like Lynn, I was thrilled to see that wonderful turnout from the Bears, those great linemen. I was thrilled to be with my friends the Gatlins once again and, of course, thrilled to feel this enthusiasm here.

I saw Jim Edgar a little earlier, and I don't know if he's still here, but I want you to know how strongly I support him for Governor. There he is. And marvelous support for our next Governor. And then the next Lieutenant Governor I believe is with us, Bob Kustra. And the rest of our statewide ticket is also here: George Ryan for secretary of state, Jim Ryan for attorney general, Gregg Baise for treasurer, and Sue Suter for comptroller. We've got a first-class ticket.

And I want to make a special notice of two that are with us who are running for the Congress, who flew with me today from Akron—two—back here to Chicago. And of course, I'm talking to two outstanding candidates, both of whom have an excellent shot to win, Walter Dudycz and Manny Hoffman. We've got to get them in the Congress. I need their support.

And I understand my old friend Pate

Phillip is here, and Bill Weiss. And I want to thank them for putting on this magnificent event.

It's great to be here, back in the Chicago area. And it is a particular joy to speak on behalf of this close friend and a national cochairman of my 1988 campaign, five-term Congresswoman, and the next Senator from Illinois, Lynn Martin. And I wouldn't say it's ironic but it's appropriate that we're here at the home of the great DePaul Blue Demons, because come November, Lynn Martin is going to give the opposition one devil of a surprise.

And really, you heard it. You heard a little taste—what's this bug doing here? [*Laughter*] Making it very difficult. You heard it tonight, and really what it's about—it's because Lynn is someone that people believe in. She began as a working mother and schoolteacher and State senator, and then became a nationally prominent Member of the United States Congress, the first freshman ever to serve on the prestigious Budget Committee. She won the respect of her colleagues simply by outsmarting her opponents, speaking out against injustice and unfairness, and always standing up for the people of this great State. I believe and Lynn believes, as we all do, that power should be in the hands of people, not government. Empowerment is at the heart of Lynn's campaign, and it is a cornerstone of our administration's domestic policy.

[*At this point, audience members interrupted the President's remarks.*]

There's something about me. Why do I attract—I don't know what it is. [*Laughter*] Thank you, thank you very much. I don't know whether it's me or Lynn. [*Laughter*] This happens sort of deja vu, as Yogi Berra would say, all over again. It happened downtown here. But in any event, they're entitled to their say, and it doesn't hurt a thing. Thank God we live in a country where they can pay 25 bucks and have their say.

But the point—back to the subject at hand—the point is we do stand for opportunity and empowerment for all Americans. You know, the Democrats believe that every time a new problem arises in America it's time to create a new bureaucracy—turn to the Federal Government. Republicans don't. We prefer not to expand the budget of the bureaucracy. But like this sign behind me says—"Victory on the Horizon"—we seek to expand the horizons of Illinoisans, young and old, from offering more options to parents seeking child care to giving students and parents more choice in education, from allowing tenant management for residents of public housing. And we believe in a clean environment, and we believe in creating free-market answers to environmental problems—and taking back our streets, incidentally, from the drug dealers and the murderers. In short, we are working hard to build a better America, and that's why I need Lynn Martin in the Senate. We need a change.

And I'm here not to speak against her opponent, but for her. But I have to say in all candor, I'd love to have someone in the Senate in this seat who would vote with me every once in a while. [*Laughter*]

Lynn will help us accomplish these goals by helping us first keep the economy moving forward. You know, over the last 8 years, we've seen the longest peacetime economic expansion in history. Twenty-two million jobs have been created. But to build the best America we can, we've got to get our own fiscal house in order. We must bring down this overwhelming Federal budget deficit. And that means we've got to do it now. And that means we must first have a budget agreement—one that maintains our economic strength, bolsters our international competitiveness, and spurs continued job growth. The reason we don't have an agreement is simple: Congress—both Houses controlled by the Democrats—hasn't acted on our proposals. Let me give you a little history, because this is on the minds of the American people tonight.

On January 29th, we sent a complete Federal budget to Capitol Hill. By April 1st, Congress was supposed to act under the rules. One hundred seventy-eight days later, we're still waiting. On May 15th, I took the initiative and called on the Democratic congressional leaders to join me in a bipartisan summit on the budget. That was 134 days ago.

On June 26th, with the budget summit going nowhere, I was asked by the Democratic leaders to make a sacrifice, to allow everything to be put on the table, to allow taxes to be put on the table. Not my first choice. Not my second. But in a good-faith effort to get Congress off dead center, it was a concession that I felt had to be made. A month later, our administration prepared another comprehensive budget plan with the understanding that it would be considered side by side with the Democratic offer, but the other side arrived emptyhanded. And that was 62 days ago, and we're still waiting.

Now, I do want to clarify one point because at this very moment the budgeteers are meeting again—the leaders are meeting. And Secretary [Speaker] Foley and Leader Mitchell raised a point that I want to clarify. Earlier today I said the Democrats had not come forward with a package. And they have put a series of proposals on the table in these private negotiations. I accept that in the private negotiations there have been such proposals. And if my statement on Air Force One confused things and if I can clarify it here, I want to do that. I apologize for misspeaking on that technical point. However, my concern remains that we have yet to see from the Democrats a comprehensive plan that contains serious spending cuts, necessary budget process reform and enforcement, growth incentives, and a sound approach to defense. And I do hope that in the negotiations taking place as I speak that we can see the progress that will finally bring this process to a conclusion.

We have proposed several 5-year, $500 billion deficit reduction packages. The American people are not dumb. You've seen the headlines about these negotiations and the arguments over which party is "on the side of the working people." I'm talking, though, about incentives for job growth, capital investment, and credits for research and development because I want to continue economic growth, I want to avoid a recession, and I want to produce more jobs for the people of Illinois. And that's what this debate is about.

We are keeping our eyes on the goal that does the most good for everyone, and we want to keep creating jobs for all the American people. But without a budget agreement, 5 short days from now we'll have tough decisions. We'll face a $100 billion mandated sequester: multibillion-dollar across-the-board budget cuts that will have a damaging effect on Americans young and old, rural and urban. It is the law of the land. And I took an oath to uphold the law, and that's what I'm going to do. We know these cuts will be tough.

Let me just give you some examples of what life will be like when this sequester hits. For college students, Pell grants for 1.2 million college students would be eliminated outright. For young children, approximately a million would not be vaccinated for polio, measles, and rubella. For air travelers here at O'Hare Airport, flights will be canceled; in fact, each day, up to 58 arrivals and departures would be canceled per hour because there won't be enough air traffic controllers to ensure safe operations.

Sequester will be painful, but it can still be avoided if Congress will make the tough choices. And as I said this morning, the hangup isn't capital gains; the hangup is with the Democrats on Capitol Hill.

And on this subject, you might say Lynn Martin sounds like a broken record, but I'm glad she does. We are still waiting for the Congress to come up with enough real spending cuts, cuts that are enforceable, not just another empty promise of future savings waiting to be broken. We're still waiting for the Democrats in Congress to commit to meaningful budget reform—reform that builds real discipline into the budget process. The last thing we want is for this year's budget fiasco that worries the American people to become next year's instant replay. Clearly, the budget system cannot work if Congress will not act.

Just yesterday, in a straight party line vote, House Democrats once again moved to dodge the budget deadline and reach into America's wallet and keep Government spending growth and the deficit ballooning. Only a unified Republican response was able to sidetrack this effort, at least temporarily. And while the rest of the Nation faces across-the-board cuts, with Head Start programs sitting empty without teachers and Social Security offices closing early, we simply cannot afford business as usual. It's time we then sent a message to the Congress: Time has run out. Congress must act because America deserves better.

And today it is especially important that America is economically healthy and militarily strong, at home and abroad. Let me caution those who might take advantage of the current crisis in the Persian Gulf; those who might seek profit by subverting the sanctions; or here at home, those speculators who might try to drive up the price of oil. While the oil market is very tight with little spare capacity, there is sufficient oil to meet current needs. The oil markets have simply not taken into account the additional production coming onstream from a variety of sources nor the available commercial stocks. There is no justification for intensive and unwarranted speculation in oil futures.

However, should the oil supply situation deteriorate, the United States, in concert with our partners in the International Energy Agency, is prepared to bring additional oil to the market. And we must make sure that we can act quickly, if necessary. And, therefore, I have today directed the Secretary of Energy to conduct an immediate test to the Strategic Petroleum Reserve, which contains 590 million barrels, by selling 5 million barrels of SPR reserve oil. And I'm prepared to take additional steps, if necessary, to ensure that America stays strong right here at home.

We all know who's keeping America strong right now halfway around the world: those brave soldiers who left their spouses and children to serve in the front lines in the Persian Gulf. And they are some of America's finest men and women, and we're proud of them—proud of every single one of them that's serving their country. I've said it before: Our service men and women are proving that America could not be the land of the free if it were not the home of the brave.

As I mentioned before—or you may have detected—I have major difference with the Democrats in the Congress on the tax-and-spend issue. But in the finest tradition of bipartisanship, support for our effort in the Middle East is strong. And I'm grateful to the Democratic leaders of the House and the Senate for this steadfast support. That's what Senator Vandenberg meant years ago when he said: "Politics stops at the water's edge." And again, I am grateful to the Democrat leaders and the Members for their strong bipartisan support in the Middle East. Our effort is not Republican or Democrat or liberal or conservative; it is truly American—all American.

You know, each one of these kids, each one of our soldiers in the Gulf is a story of America at its best. For example, last week I read in the Chicago Tribune about Lorraine Kuryla, a 63-year-old grandmother from nearby Hillside who volunteered for active duty with the Air Force Reserve Unit out of O'Hare. Her kids called her Grambo. [*Laughter*] After hearing about her tenacity, her courage, and her toughness, all I can say is: "Move over, Mike Ditka." [*Laughter*]

Master Sergeant Kuryla and other reservists alongside her are standing up to aggression and preserving the sovereignty of nations. But our G.I.'s are in good company. Not only do we have 22 nations now, including many Arab States and the Soviet Union, on our side—well over half the Arab League, a vast majority—we have freedom and justice on our side. Our goals have been endorsed by the United Nations Security Council eight times. For as I told the joint session of Congress 2 weeks ago: America and the world must defend our common vital interests. America and the world must support the rule of law. America and the world must stand up to aggression. And we will not be intimidated by Saddam Hussein.

Recent events prove that there is no substitute for our American leadership in the shaping of a new partnership of nations. Lynn Martin's known that from day one. Unlike others, she has consistently voted for a strong defense. She knows you can't stand up to tyranny and despotism while recklessly slashing military levels. Her opponent called for bombing Iraqi pipelines, on one hand, and, on the other hand, cut defense spending by 50 percent. Not logical. People know Lynn stands for a strong America, economically and militarily. That's another reason why we need Lynn Martin in the United States Senate.

So many in this room have done so much for her campaign, and I thank you for it. But another important task lies ahead. On election day our G.I.'s, in the searing heat of the desert dunes and the hot glare of the Persian Gulf, will send in their absentee ballots. We owe it to those brave men and women, laying their lives on the line for peace and stability in the world, to exercise the precious right to vote.

I am grateful for this tremendous rally, for all the work you've done for Lynn Martin. And now, go out and vote, each and every single one of you. Drag any unsuspecting customer to the polls with you. Let's be sure we make Lynn Martin the next Republican Senator from this great State because Illinois deserves the best.

Thank you, and God bless you all.

Note: President Bush spoke at 8:23 p.m. in the Rosemont Horizon Arena. In his remarks, he referred to Millie, the First Family's dog; the Gatlin Brothers, country music entertainers; DePaul University's Blue Demon basketball team; State Senators Walter Dudycz, Manny Hoffman, and Pate Phillip; Thomas S. Foley, Speaker of the House of Representatives; George Mitchell, majority leader of the Senate; Mike Ditka, head coach of the Chicago Bears football team; and President Saddam Hussein of Iraq. A tape was not available for verification of the content of these remarks. Following his remarks, President Bush traveled to Minneapolis, MN.

Letter to Congressional Leaders on Legislation To Amend the Clean Air Act
September 26, 1990

Dear _____:

It has now been more than a year since I sent to Congress legislation to reauthorize and strengthen the Clean Air Act. As you know, my proposal would have permanently reduced sulfur dioxide emissions by 10 million tons below 1980 levels, cut smog-causing emissions by over 40%, brought virtually all of the 100 cities now in violation of our air quality standards into attainment with those standards by the year 2000, and cut by more than three-quarters the amount of toxic emissions into America's air.

As the current session of Congress draws to a close, I am concerned that the House-Senate conference committee still has not completed its work and that its direction has strayed significantly from that of my proposal and of the bipartisan Administration-Senate agreement announced in March of this year. In short, I fear that the slow progress and apparent course of the conference committee may jeopardize enactment of this critically important legislation.

It is particularly important that any bill presented to me for signature abide by certain principles:

• It must not contain extraneous and costly provisions that are unrelated to clean air and set highly adverse precedents for other environmental legislation;

• It must achieve, at a minimum, the environmental benefits I have set forth in my bill, and it must do so in an efficient manner, that is, for the lowest possible cost to American jobs, consumers, and businesses; and

• It must be capable of being administered in a straightforward and sensible manner, one that minimizes the kind of time-consuming litigation that could prevent the law from being implemented on schedule.

There are several pending features of both bills which are not in accord with these principles. The conference committee must act quickly to produce a bill that is environmentally strong and economically sound. All Americans deserve clean air, but they also deserve the good jobs and rising living standards that only a competitive economy can provide. Unless the committee produces such a bill, Congress will not have time to make any necessary adjustments, and the substantial progress made in the past 21 months will be undone.

To help avoid that outcome, I have instructed my staff to make available a comprehensive proposal to the conference committee to help break the logjam that has once again appeared. This comprehensive proposal will achieve the same environmental benefits as either the House or Senate bills—and in fact it draws on the best features of each proposal. By employing the most cost-effective approaches contained in each, and avoiding those provisions which add gratuitous burdens, this compromise will achieve those benefits at a cost to America's economy of several billion dollars per year less than either bill.

It has been 13 years since the Clean Air Act was reauthorized. By developing a comprehensive proposal and reaching an historic agreement with you and your colleagues, I have worked actively to break the legislative stalemate which has precluded earlier action on clean air. I offer the enclosed comprehensive proposal to help finish the job before time runs out in the current session of Congress.

It would be a terrible shame, and a disservice to the American people, if the prospects for cleaner air were to be scuttled because of a continuing impasse in the conference, or because of the addition by the conference of restrictive and inefficient provisions that saddle the American people with additional costs but yield no additional environmental benefits.

Sincerely,

GEORGE BUSH

Note: Identical letters were sent to Senators Max Baucus and John H. Chafee and Representatives John D. Dingell and Norman F. Lent.

COMPREHENSIVE PROPOSAL

Acid Rain

- Senate acid rain provisions.
- Modify House and Senate provisions on WEPCO (and related modification pro-

visions in other titles) to parallel Administration proposal.

The Senate acid rain provisions will provide utilities and independent power producers with greater certainty and can be administered in a clear and efficient manner. The Senate acid rain provisions do not include extraneous provisions, such as the restrictions on clean coal technology funding found in the House bill. The administration's proposed solution to WEPCO addresses the serious uncertainties created by the WEPCO decision in a balanced manner that protects the operation of the allowance trading program.

Air Toxics

- House provisions on MACT and utility emissions.
- Senate provisions on residual risk, the NAS study, voluntary risk reduction, and NRC regulation.

The House provisions requiring the maximum achievable control technology coupled with the Senate provisions on residual risk and voluntary risk reduction will provide for a 75- to 90-percent reduction in air toxics exposure in a cost-effective manner. The Senate National Academy of Sciences study and the House provision on toxic emissions from utility plants will allow for scientifically sound regulatory decisions that are based on the public health risks posed by those emissions.

Nonattainment

- Senate title I provisions.

The Senate provisions on stationary source controls would not saddle smaller businesses with excessive controls and would provide emissions reductions in a cost-effective and administratively superior way. The Senate title I does not include extraneous and potentially costly provisions, such as the Wise amendment on labor protection which is unacceptable.

Mobile Sources

- House Tier I and Tier II tailpipe standards.
- Senate approach to mobile source toxics.

The House provisions for Tier I and Tier II standards for tailpipe emissions, modified by substituting the Senate study on mobile source toxics, ensure progress in reducing tailpipe emissions in a rational way that reflects cost, need, and feasibility of controls.

Fuels

- Modified Senate reformulated gasoline program to include: (1) a 15 percent reduction in VOC and toxic emissions, as defined in the Senate bill; (2) a minimum 2 percent oxygenate requirement; and (3) a general equivalency program starting in 1993, with full phase-in by 1995.
- Modified House oxygenated fuels program in all 44 CO nonattainment areas with a 2.7 percent oxygenate requirement; and new provisions to permit opt-out or opt-down from the 2.7 percent requirement based on modeling attainment demonstrations.
- Senate nine city alternative fuels program with a composite standard of .75 gpm in 1995 and .66 gpm in 2000. States would have the flexibility to opt-in to the nine city program or opt-up to the California program.

This combination of Senate and House provisions builds upon the administration's clean fuels program by achieving environmental benefits in a cost effective way. It will allow for the phase-in of the most promising low-emitting fuels in a way that avoids market dislocations and supply problems.

Permits and Enforcement

- The permit program as recently agreed to by the conferees, striking the permit requirements in all other titles.
- Maintain core of Senate enforcement provisions with House citizen suit provisions and safe harbor for firms who initially discover potential violations while conducting internal audits.

The permit provisions found in the air toxics, nonattainment, and acid rain titles of the Senate bill are unnecessary and potentially conflicting.

CFC's

- The CFC provisions as agreed to by the conferees.

Remarks at a Fundraising Breakfast for Gubernatorial Candidate Jon Grunseth in Minneapolis, Minnesota
September 27, 1990

Thank you all very, very much. Thank you for that warm welcome. Jon, thank you for that generous introduction. Vicki, great to be with you. Also, my old friend Senator Dave Durenberger, delighted you're here, sir. And it's good to see our wonderful emcee, another friend of some time, State Auditor Arnie Carlson; and our State chairpeople, Bob Weinholzer and Barb Sykora; and our national committee man and woman, Frank Graves, Evie Axdahl. What a team we've got. And then our next Republican in Congress, Republican taking Bill Frenzel's place, Jim Ramstad. He's got to win. We want him to win. I think he will win.

And let me give a special hello to my friend and outstanding United States Sena-

tor, Rudy Boschwitz. Rudy is up for reelection this year, and I feel good about it. But I can't think of a Senator anywhere in this great country more deserving of another term than Rudy Boschwitz. He has done an outstanding job for the State, and he has been a strong supporter of this President when I've needed him, and I'm very, very grateful to him. I seldom speak for the Silver Fox, but, Rudy, Barbara and I wish you the very best. Good luck! [*Laughter*]

And now to Jon's talented runningmate, Sharon Clark. Let me pose a question of the hour: Isn't it about time we had a hog farmer on the ticket? [*Laughter*] Talk about rooting for a candidate. Whoops! [*Laughter*] I knew I shouldn't have done it; I'm sorry.

Well, in any event, moving onward, it is

an honor to be here, to root for Jon Grunseth. His talents as a leader have been noted already at the Federal level several years now. One example: After Minnesota experienced the worst pipeline explosions in history, it was Jon who was called upon by his current opponent to cochair the Commission on Pipeline Safety. So, President Reagan appointed him to the National Board. And I personally looked to the entire Grunseth family during the last Presidential campaign when they served on this State's steering committee. So, I am very proud to be here today to support a great candidate.

You know, I was talking just as we walked in here a few minutes ago with someone involved in planning this event. She told me that, of all the details and decisions, what concerned her most was the speaker. I said I imagined she wanted someone influential, a world leader, a charismatic speaker. And she said, "No, Mr. Gorbachev has already been here." [*Laughter*] In any event, President Gorbachev came to Minnesota to see some of the leading-edge technology being produced by your private sector, the kind of technology and aggressive economic enterprise Jon Grunseth understands because he's made it happen himself.

Today I've come here to affirm the kind of leadership that can make sure Minnesota moves forward with fresh ideas, new leadership and, indeed, new hope for the future. But before I focus on change in Minnesota, I'd like to make note of a significant change in our relations with Moscow.

Over the last year, if anyone were to ask me what is the most meaningful and really hopeful sign of change in the world, I'd point to the quality of real cooperation now shared by the United States and the Soviet Union as we work to face down aggression in the Persian Gulf. It is amazing what's happened, and it is strongly in our interest that it continue. Our two nations haven't shared such unity of purpose for 45 years, but now in the heat of crisis in the Middle East, we forge reason for real hope—hope for a more peaceful, more stable world order. Through uncommon cooperation, we have made peace our common cause. That is reason for celebration.

Still, while that kind of cooperation is new, there's one thing we've been able to rely on: that is the commitment of the American service men and women to contain aggression and the American people's support of our men and women in uniform. We've seen no greater proof of that commitment than right here among the people of Minnesota: Minnesota radio stations sending tapes of local news, Park Center High School students tracking down names of earlier graduates now in the Gulf and writing them to let them know how the football team's doing. And among so many others, I heard about a group here in Minneapolis, newly established, called S.O.C.M., Support Our Country's Military. They're a volunteer group providing financial and emotional support for people with family members in the military. Writing letters and sending board games to the troops—even arranging for child care to help the grandmother of two girls who was worried her son and daughter-in-law might both be called up. That kind of collective spirit, that kind of shared commitment, is important. And it is those actions, large and small, celebrated or little noticed, that make possible American leadership around the entire world.

But leadership abroad—shifting back—demands good leadership here at home. Minnesotans are great people, and they deserve a great Governor, and that's just exactly what Jon Grunseth will be. You've got a lot to be proud of. Nestled in this fertile land of 10,000 lakes, of forests and rolling farmland, the Twin Cities are vibrant, prosperous examples of urban life the way it ought to be. You've got a diverse economy—building the world's largest and fastest computers and producing more turkeys than almost any other State. [*Laughter*] I hope your political opponents don't take that the wrong way. [*Laughter*]

But as one who first was exposed to Minnesota in the fall of 1943, when I came out here as an 18-year-old kid to learn to fly airplanes at Wold-Chamberlain as a naval aviation cadet, I understand—because I saw it then and I've seen it every time I've come back here—that Minnesota's greatest strength has always been its people. And so, today I'm here to give my whole-hearted support to a candidate for Governor who understands the power of the people themselves, a candidate for change who wants to unleash the full potential of the great State of Minnesota. And once again, Jon Grunseth understands that and is determined to empower the people.

Jon knows—we've talked about this—he knows that a bright future for Minnesota, industrial and agricultural, won't be built by a burgeoning bureaucracy. It will be built by the people, empowered and encouraged to make a difference for themselves and their communities.

He arranged for me to meet with some rural educators from Minnesota today, and you can just feel that sense—not Federal Government do more but empower the people to help solve, in this case, the problems of rural education. I was most impressed, Jon, by that wonderful turnout from these dedicated teachers that came to rally support for you and to tell me of their concerns about rural Minnesota.

That's why Jon's devoted himself to reforming of education, also protecting the environment and controlling State spending.

Minnesota has always had a strong bipartisan tradition in education. But now education has captured national attention, and that says something about America because the importance of a well-educated citizenry transcends partisanship and politics. Real education reform demands that all of us work together to improve our schools. And that's why this candidate isn't interested in who's taking credit for what program. He cares about what works—results. Results are what we're after. And working together with Jon Grunseth, results are what we are going to get.

But along with this deeply held conviction on the importance of education, Jon shares the environmental ethic that is so crucial to preserving the grandeur of the great North Woods. He believes, as I do, that we can and must recapture the heritage of Teddy Roosevelt. And he understands the importance of community involvement in preservation efforts, to carefully manage our wild lands and our wildlife.

But Minnesota's outstanding record on air and drinking water quality, conservation, and recreation reflects a community effort and a special volunteer ethic that Jon Grunseth will promote and expand. And he knows what he's talking about. He helped build a billion-dollar business, applying new ideas and new technology in environmental sanitation. As Governor, he will be a leader for the environment right here in Minnesota.

And he'll also be a leader in managing fiscal resources. You heard just the tip of the iceberg here this morning. He's proved his prowess in the private sector, and he'll apply the same financial fortitude that he's demonstrated there—he'll apply that as Governor. He's called for a cap on State spending and real, honest property-tax reform. He has said, as this party believes, that the answer is not to spend as much as you can tax, but to tax only as much as you need to spend. And you know, there's a good lesson there for all of us. He's absolutely right about that.

Which brings me to my line of work. As you all know, we've been trying to reach an agreement on the Federal budget for months. Four days from today—and I listened carefully to what Rudy said, and I had a chance to talk to Dave on Air Force One when Jon and he and I flew up here last night—4 days from today America, under the law, faces serious automatic, indiscriminate, across-the-board cuts in services of every kind. Why? Because Congress and that Democratic leadership there could not get serious about making real cuts in spending, enforceable cuts in spending, and they wouldn't get serious about real budget reform. No point going through this dance every year; we need budget reform in Washington, DC. Lacking discipline of their own, they've delayed so long that that Gramm-Rudman meat ax is about to do it for them.

And you might say: Well, what does that mean to me? What does that mean to Minnesota? What does that mean to my family or to the schools? What does it mean to you? It means many—and this is not a worst case or what they call in Washington the Washington Monument syndrome—it means many of Minnesota's spectacular parks, recreation, wildlife management programs will be shut down; they'll be closed. Funds to curb demand for illegal drugs through prevention and treatment will be cut by one third—Federal programs. Air traffic controller cutbacks will lead to delays and cancellations. And nearly 1.5 million college students will lose their Pell grants because the Congress could not do its homework.

These cuts—the figure is $100 billion in all, total—will be hard for everyone to take. And there may be teachers who can't go to work in Head Start programs. There may be senior citizens wondering why their Social Security checks are late. We can't afford business as usual. The American people deserve better, and the people of Minnesota deserve better.

Let me give you a little history. Back in January I sent a complete budget up to the Hill. There was a deadline set by themselves, as Rudy and Dave know. The leadership there missed the deadline—it was in April—they missed the deadline to respond. And in May I then convened a budget summit—some of you may remember that—to get things moving. In June they still weren't moving. And the Democrats, seeking political gain because they know how I feel about taxes and they know how I feel about spending, demanded that I put everything on the table, including taxes, to get Congress off dead center. And I had to make a decision. It was a tough decision. But to put our fiscal house in order, I did what had to be done to get Congress to act.

And they acted, all right—they acted like they had all the time in the world. And so, in July I offered up another budget plan that would save half a trillion dollars over 5 years, and again I extended a hand to the Members of Congress, asking them to work together in good faith. And again, they did not respond. We talked about the summer recess, and I said: Would it help to keep the Congress in? The Democratic leadership said: No, don't do that. That will be counterproductive. That will make it more difficult to get a job. So, I complied there with that request—my gut instinct being we ought to have kept Congress there in August to get the job done.

Now, 2 months have passed since I made that proposal, and they have still offered no

serious comprehensive plan with the needed budget reforms to reduce the deficit. And 4 days from now, sequestration will become a tragic fact of life. So, I call on the Congress again: Deal with this deficit through real, enforceable spending cuts and meaningful budget reform now.

Talks are going on probably now—well, probably within a few minutes, the clock ticking. And I'm very hopeful that the Congress will get the message and that there will be the compromise that's needed to keep this country from screeching to a halt at this critical time.

You know, everything I read, everyone I talk to tells me that they are fed up with the Federal lawmakers' evasion of responsibility. You hear this new thrust there. And thank heavens we have people like Rudy Boschwitz in the Congress, in the Senate—this year up for election—who sets an example that sends a strong message to the Democratic leadership and the Democratic opposition.

We need leaders who are going to fight for fiscal discipline in every branch of government and at all levels, from the White House to the Minnesota statehouse. And that's reason enough to be here this morning, because I do believe that here in Minnesota Jon Grunseth will make sure that spending stays under control. It has to happen at the Federal level, and it must happen at the State level. I honestly know in my heart that he'll make a great Governor.

It's been a genuine pleasure to come back here and join you today. But before I go, there's one more thing: Let me ask each one of you to make an effort to get out the vote this fall. On the farms and fields, in the suburbs and cities, make sure that the people of Minnesota know what's at stake here. In an era that celebrates the dawning of democratic freedoms around the world, when so many who have struggled so long have at last found their voice, those who live in freedom should never rob themselves of the priceless power of the ballot. Encourage people to exercise that power, to confirm the kind of leadership they're after, and to preserve the enduring glow of the North Star State.

By electing Jon Grunseth and by electing a Republican majority in the State legislature, you can unleash new ideas and bring about a change for an even greater Minnesota.

Thank you for what you're doing. God bless you, and God bless the United States of America. Thank you all very much.

Note: The President spoke at 8:27 a.m. in the Nicollet Ballroom at the Hyatt Regency Hotel. In his remarks, he referred to Jon Grunseth's wife, Vicki. Prior to the breakfast, the President met with educators at the hotel. Following his remarks, he traveled to Cleveland, OH.

Remarks at a Fundraising Luncheon for Gubernatorial Candidate George Voinovich in Cleveland, Ohio
September 27, 1990

Thank you, George, for those kind words. Janet, what a pleasure it is to see you again.

Before we begin, I just got some good news from Washington. Just moments ago, the Senate Judiciary Committee strongly endorsed my outstanding nominee for the United States Supreme Court, Judge David Souter. It was a 13-to-1 vote, and they recommended Judge Souter to the Senate. And I called and thanked Senator Biden just now and Senator Thurmond, two ranking Members on that important committee. I now would urge the full Senate to act as quickly as possible to confirm this man. He is an outstanding jurist, and I want to see him join his colleagues on the Nation's highest court, as the Court's new session begins next week. But I think that is good news for all of us who are committed to the Constitution of the United States. He'll be a superb Justice for the Supreme Court.

I understand now that—back to the business at hand—Wayne, you say you were in charge of the budget for the Cavs [Cavaliers]? If so, come with me on Air Force One. We have a mission to do. [*Laughter*] In Texas, as they say, we could use a man of your "big" over there. [*Laughter*] But thank you, sir, for being here and emceeing this. To Rabbi Rube, thank you, sir. We heard outside your very generous blessing.

I understand that most of our statewide ticket is here. I know Bob Taft is. Bob, where are you? Would you please stand up? [*Applause*] It's very important that Bob win as secretary of state—that race. And then the next one, Jim Petro—Jim, are you out

here someplace? I can't see too well. But in any event, that's the State auditor's job Jim's running for, and that one's a key race because between the Governor and these two races it has an awful lot to say about fair, nongerrymandering redistricting. And also, another old friend of mine running statewide, Judith Brachman for State treasurer. I know she's here, because I saw her. Judith, please stand up wherever you may be. Maybe she fled.

Then, the ones who couldn't join us today: Mike DeWine, who was with me yesterday—but his wife, Fran, is here, and want to wish her well—a wonderful candidate for Lieutenant Governor. And then, the other is an old friend of mine, Paul Pfeifer, who we want to see elected attorney general. So, we have an outstanding ticket this year for the whole statewide offices in Ohio.

Of course, there's another that I want to pay tribute to, a person that makes it all possible. That is Bob Bennett, the chair of the Ohio State party. And then, of course, my old friend and compadre in the political wars from—I don't want to date him or me, but he goes back a long time—Bob Hughes up here. And Paul Mifsud. These are political operators, and good ones.

I'd be remiss if I didn't single out my old friend who gives me lots of free advice about the caribou and how to run the country, and I mean Jim Rhodes, who served this State with such distinction.

Now, with Wayne Embry, the general manager of the Cavs; Dick Jacobs, owner of the Indians; and Art Modell, my old friend, the owner of the Cleveland Browns—Art, I don't know how the Browns are going to do this year—[*laughter*]—but I can tell you one thing: The way the fans throw the dog biscuits out onto the field, the Browns are Millie's favorite team. [*Laughter*]

But look, I mean this, it is great to be back here, and I look around this room out there, and then others up here, and I see so many to whom Barbara and I are indebted for your having given us the support that was required, the support that we needed when we were running for office, and now, most recently, when I ran for President of the United States. So, it is great to be back here, the capital city of the North Coast, to show my support now for one of the real standouts on Capitol Hill, a man who has been strong and effective in Washington. And again, I want to refer to him, because he's not here today. He's now ready to serve this State as Lieutenant Governor; I mean Mike DeWine. I wish he were here. You've got to know him. He's going to be a superb Lieutenant Governor.

And now to the piece de resistance. Center stage there's the man who led this city's comeback, the man who's served with distinction in a career that spans 3 decades in elective office. And I'm talking about the next Governor of the Buckeye State, Cleveland's own George Voinovich. Please give him a round of strong endorsement. [*Applause*] I want to again say hello to a woman who will make a great first lady, one that Barbara Bush loves, Janet Voinovich. Janet, good luck to you on the campaign trail.

I'm always a little leery about having George and me at the same event. You don't want the audience to suffer from a charisma overdose. [*Laughter*] We agreed not to speak too long because we realize you can only stand so much excitement, you know, here in Cleveland. [*Laughter*]

Cleveland may be the home to the Rock and Roll Hall of Fame; but let me tell you, come November 6th, George Voinovich is going to make the opposition shake, rattle, and roll. You can count on him to lead the way, to make Ohio one of the great pathbreaking States in the nineties—in Ohio's cities and towns, where crime and drugs

breed fear and violence and threaten our whole fabric of society, our sense of community. In Ohio's schools, he knows as well as I do that the key to competitiveness tomorrow is our classrooms of today.

He will bring the same drive and determination, the same intelligence and integrity to the Ohio statehouse that he brought to Cleveland's city hall. The people of Ohio can count on George Voinovich—Governor Voinovich—to create a climate for growth; to work with the business community to help the Ohio economy adapt and advance, attract new businesses, and—you heard him—create new jobs; to help the Ohio entrepreneur realize his dreams.

Take a look at this man's track record right here in Cleveland, the way he retooled this proud smokestack city to meet the high-tech challenges of the 1990's. The bottom line is beyond doubt: George Voinovich has developed a formula for success that can work statewide, right down from Cleveland to Cincinnati and in every city in between. George knows what it takes to keep this economy on the upswing. And rest assured, we're going to do our part in Washington to help this State prosper and grow.

And it starts with a sound Federal budget. Unfortunately, we're running out of time to put our fiscal house in order. Four short days from now the fiscal year ends, and there's still no budget agreement in hand.

You've seen the headlines about these negotiations, and you've heard the arguments over which party is on the side of the working people. Well, let me tell you—let me tell you what Americans want. They want to keep on working. Ohioans want to keep on working. And the last thing they need is a budget breakdown that puts us on the road to recession.

We need a budget agreement to help maintain our economic vitality, our competitiveness, and our job creation. And that's why I continue to push the Congress to enact incentives for job growth; incentives that promote savings and investment, research and development; incentives that will help us sustain economic expansion and steer clear of recession. We need an agreement that contains real spending cuts and the means to enforce these real spending cuts. No more promises to spend now and save later. And finally, I insist on agreement that will reform the budget process itself. Let this be the last time that the American taxpayer is forced to witness a fiscal fiasco.

And I don't want to sound defensive, but I made a good-faith effort to reach agreement. Let me review a little history. In January I sent a complete budget to Congress, and under the rules, Congress was due to respond on April 1st. And Congress, with both Houses controlled by the Democrats, failed to respond. So, in mid-May—you may remember this one—we began this budget summit process—135 days ago. A month later, when the talks were at an impasse, I was asked by the Democratic leadership to allow taxes to be put on the table—it's like making me eat broccoli—[*laughter*]—put them on the table. They called on me to make a sacrifice. It wasn't my first choice, it wasn't my second choice, but it's a concession I made to get Congress moving. And that was over 3 months ago, and still, no agreement. In late July, after both sides pledged to put forward a comprehensive budget plan, we delivered. Congress delayed. And since then, we've advanced a number of serious proposals built around a 5-year, $500-billion deficit reduction package; and still Congress has failed to offer a comprehensive plan with serious spending cuts, real budget-process reform and enforcement, incentives for growth, and a sound approach to the defense of this country.

Because of congressional inaction, the Nation is now 4 days away from mandated sequestration—$100 billion in across-the-board budget cuts that will hit hard all across America. The sequester will—it will cause real pain, and no one wants to see it take effect. But without an agreement, the lever of sequestration is the only way to force the Congress to make tough choices.

Take a look—let me just give you some examples—take a look at what sequestration will mean. For air travelers, it will mean cutbacks in air traffic control. And this will mean untold hours of flight delays and, in many cases, flight cancellations. For anyone living near a toxic waste site, it means no

new cleanups, a complete stop in all the new Superfund projects. For college students, it means the loss of 1.2 million Pell grants. And with over 130,000 college students in the Cleveland area alone, that's bound to take its toll.

Of course, there are 4 more days now until the ax falls, and it isn't too late to act. So, today I say again to the United States Congress: Don't delay 1 day longer. Prove to the American taxpayer once and for all that we can deal with this impossible deficit. Let's get it down once and for all.

And another point: reaching a sound budget agreement is critical. We simply cannot fail to put our fiscal house in order, especially now, with the challenge that we face halfway around the world in the Persian Gulf.

Let me speak for a moment about what this crisis is all about. When Iraq crossed over the Kuwaiti border—when Saddam Hussein set out to erase the existence of a sovereign nation that posed no threat to his own, he set in motion what is really the first test of this new postwar era. The stakes are clear. The world community must act to draw the line against Saddam's outlaw act. Failure is an invitation to further aggression. Success is a step into a new partnership of nations, more peaceful, stable, and secure than we've ever known before. And I am confident that we can succeed. World response, as George referred to it, has been swift and certain; and Saddam Hussein must know now that the world will not allow his outlaw aggression to stand.

As I mentioned before, I have major differences with the more liberal elements of the Democratic Party and with some of the leaders in this Congress on this budget question—I don't hide that—and, yes, on other issues like our crime bill and on our education bill and—but let me just say this in fairness. In the finest tradition of partnership, support for our Middle East effort is strong; and that is what, you remember, Senator Vandenberg meant years ago when he said that politics stops at the water's edge. I am proud of our country. And I am very proud of the way the Democrat and Republican leadership as well as Members of Congress have pulled together, for our support effort is not Republican or Democrat or liberal or conservative—it is truly American.

And I can sense this when you meet with or interact with the American people. And I wish you could have been in the car riding in from the airport with George Voinovich and me and the mayor of Cleveland today. You could feel the support for what America is trying to do in leading all around the world. You could feel it from the hardhats in the construction projects or those working around that airport or those that—more white-collar jobs—when we came in here. It was for me a very emotional experience knowing that the American people stand steadfast in support of the principles I've outlined all the way around there in the Middle East. It is a wonderful thing. And I will do my level best to keep our country out front and to hold this fantastic international coalition together.

Now, let me close with a word of recognition for the young men and women in our Armed Forces, on duty now over there, halfway around the world, servicemen like Private First Class John Brickley—known as the Brick to his old teammates on the Orange High School football team—now serving with the 82d Airborne; like Air Force Staff Sergeant John Kinton—a three-sport athlete from Cleveland's Collinwood High—or as he's now called, Tiffany, as in "Breakfast at Tiffany's." And Sergeant Kinton's tent kitchen serves up some of the best pancakes and scrambled eggs in Saudi Arabia—[laughter]—a little bit of home out in the sand and hot sun.

These two men—all our soldiers, sailors, airmen, and marines deserve every ounce of our support. And with them in mind, I want to add just one more thing—and, incidentally, I might tell you, every member of the Joint Chiefs I've talked to has told me, as they looked back over their shoulders in history of military service in this country, that never have we had more motivated, better educated, or more dedicated troops than the men and women that are serving in Saudi Arabia right now. It is a great tribute to the young people in this country.

But I'd like to just add one more thing, a message to all Ohioans as November 6th draws near. Right now, in the sands of Saudi Arabia, the young men and women of our armed services are teaching us a lesson about what it means to love liberty, the precious freedom that gives America its meaning. And I urge every citizen in Cleveland and all across this great State to get out and vote. Do not take democracy for granted. And so, that's the message. Please participate. And all of you here are doing that in this magnificent support for our outstanding candidate for Governor.

Once again, let me thank you for this warm welcome back to Cleveland. I'm proud to be here to show my support for Mike DeWine, and for the man I am sure is well on his way to the statehouse, your next Governor, George Voinovich.

May God bless the State of Ohio, and God bless the United States of America. Thank you all very, very much.

Note: President Bush spoke at 1:40 p.m. in the Grand Ballroom at Stouffer's Tower City Hotel. In his remarks, he referred to Robert Hughes, Cuyahoga County Republican Party chairman; Paul Mifsud, manager of the George Voinovich for Governor campaign; Jim Rhodes, former Governor of Ohio; Michael White, mayor of Cleveland; and President Saddam Hussein of Iraq. He also referred to Millie, the First Family's dog. Following the luncheon, President Bush met with Eastern European-American community leaders at the hotel and then traveled to Detroit, MI.

Remarks at a Fundraising Dinner for Senatorial Candidate Bill Schuette in Detroit, Michigan
September 27, 1990

I was going to say it's nice to be back where I started; but I think back to that Republican Convention right here in Detroit, 1980, and maybe that's not an overstatement. But in any event, thank you for the warm welcome. And to my dear friend, close friend Max Fisher, thank you for that most generous introduction. And I'm proud, once again, sir, to be back at your side.

To Bill Laimbeer, it's amazing—[*laughter*]—how one of the "bad boys" can do such a good job as master of ceremonies. [*Laughter*]

And of course, I want to salute another old friend, a man that helped me enormously in 1988, a man who is going to be the next Governor of this great State, John Engler. John, good luck to you. Best of luck.

And one who next January will become a sorely needed Republican Congressman, Jim Dingeman. Jim, where are you? Somewhere—right back in the middle. Good luck to you. And I also want to single out another traveler with me on Air Force One, a member of my Cabinet, doing an outstanding job, my superb Secretary of Veterans Affairs, Ed Derwinski. Where is Ed? Anyway, he's here. Oh, right here. There he is. How could I miss him?

And also I want to extend a warm welcome to your State party leadership—our chairman, Spence Abraham, over here. Spence, good to see you again. And Detroit city councilman Reverend Keith Butler, welcome. Down there. And Larry Patrick, school board chairman. And finally, Jermaine Davis, who did such a great job of going with the Pledge of Allegiance. And that's it. You've got a lot of big shots out there.

So, thank you all. And ladies and gentlemen and honored guests, I appreciate the chance to be with you and, what's more, the chance to support a man who can provide "the change we need" and that Michigan needs; and that is the next Senator from the State of Michigan, Bill Schuette.

Now, I was told that Bill wanted a speaker who is beloved in Michigan, a man known for his popularity, quick reaction, grace under pressure. Unfortunately, Isiah Thomas could not make it—[*laughter*]—and so I'm here instead.

This past summer, Isiah, Bill, and the rest of Chuck Daly's team visited the White House after winning the NBA title. And we saluted that winning team, and today we salute another winning team: the entire Michigan Republican ticket. And I want to salute all of you who've worked so hard and long at the grassroots level.

You know that support has never been more crucial than in this election year of 1990. Together we must maintain our majority in the State senate and gain a majority of the house of representatives. Together we must elect a Governor who ensures fair reapportionment. No more gerrymandering! We need a Governor to guarantee fair reapportionment, and of course, that's John Engler once again. And together, we must bring change and new ideas to Michigan by electing the Man from Midland, Bill Schuette.

You all know him, but let me just recite a little background: educated at Georgetown University and the University of San Francisco Law School; became a practicing attorney up in the Saginaw Valley and then, at 30, the energetic, outstanding Congressman from the 10th District. The Detroit News calls him an unusually fine candidate. Bob Dole calls him the clear candidate. And Guy Vander Jagt calls him a natural. For my part, I plan to call him Senator.

Let me tell you why I support him. He's a friend, first. When he was managing my Michigan campaign in 1980, he drove me around the State in his car and in his mother's jeep. We spent more time on the road together than Hope and Crosby. [*Laughter*] So, if anyone tries to tell you that he's not a man of character, that Bill Schuette is not the candidate who can do more for Michigan's future, then tell them to ask somebody who knows him. Tell them to ask

George Bush.

Without going into great detail, let me mention several issues where he can be "the change we need." The first is education. He knows that excellence in our schools comes from accountability, flexibility, and more parental choice in their children's education. I need Senators like him to help pass our administration's Educational Excellence Act that for 17 months has sat on the Congressman's desk without any movement at all. The American people voted for that kind of education program when they elected me in 1988, and they've got no action on it because it's been stymied by the old thinkers who want to continue to have the Federal Government figure out all the answers from back there. I want the Michigan input into the educational excellence, and the way to get it is to get more like Bill Schuette in the Senate.

And the second issue—and it's of great concern to everybody in this beautiful State—is the environment. And here, too, Bill is what we need. He backed legislation to protect the Great Lakes from the oilspills, and yet he also believes we don't have to throw people out of work to protect these resources. For 14 months, Congress has delayed our administration's bill to rewrite the Clean Air Act, and I need Bill Schuette and Senators like him to help pass a Clean Air Act that I can sign.

And next, the third issue, where the needed change Bill can bring will help America—and I don't know whether they're number one issues or two, but this is right up at the top—and I'm talking about crime and drugs. Bill supports our Comprehensive Violent Crime Control Act. And he and I want a crime bill with a workable death penalty for the killers of Federal law enforcement officers. And we want a bill that gets tougher on the criminals and cares more about the victims of crime, not one that slaps the handcuffs on the police officers. And we've got such a bill, and it's gone nowhere because of the liberal control of the Congress.

So far, I've talked about Bill's views— some of his views and achievements. And if that isn't enough for you, think about this one: Last month he won the celebrity cow milking contest at the Michigan State Fair.

[*Laughter*] But even without that experience, Bill Schuette knows it's the cows who should be milked, not the taxpayers. [*Laughter*]

Which leads to a final domestic issue where change is needed. And of course, I refer to what he mentioned, the Federal budget negotiations, and to this twilight zone of sequestration, now just 4 days from now—4 days away.

Let me take a moment—not to bore you to death—but I just want—it's important. We're going right down to the wire, this nation is, towards sequestration. So, let me take a moment to briefly sketch the history of these negotiations.

Last February I proposed a budget for the coming fiscal year, and Congress by its own rules needed to respond by April. It did not. In May, in order to get Congress off the dime, I called for a budget summit, bringing together the leaders of the Republicans and the Democrats in both Houses of the Congress. And by the end of June, the talks were going nowhere. To jump-start the budget process, I agreed to the demand of the Democratic leadership to put everything on the table, including revenues, including taxes. I didn't want to, but felt I had to, to get this deficit down and get the Democrats off of dead center. And 1 month later, we prepared another revised comprehensive budget plan—we did, and again, the Democrats came up emptyhanded. And that was 2 months ago. I thought about keeping Congress in session in August. I talked to the leaders and they asked me not to do that. They felt it would be counterproductive and that if I didn't do that we'd have a better chance to get a budget agreement early in September. So once again, I compromised and went along, hoping that this would be the approach to use to get a deficit reduction deal early in September.

And here we are, 4 days from sequestration, and today Congress still refuses to make real spending cuts, enforceable cuts, or enact real budget-process reform that we've got to have. And the result? Under Gramm-Rudman-Hollings, we face a mandated sequestration that will cause $100 billion—$100 billion—in automatic spending cuts. Need this occur? Of course not. If it occurs, there will be no doubt whatsoever about who is responsible: a Congress addicted to tax and spend.

And here are just a few examples of what would happen—and this isn't what we call in Washington the Washington Monument syndrome, when you cite all the things that ought to go on in order to get your way with the Congress or something of that nature. Let me tell you what would happen under sequestration. Here in Detroit, the Social Security office will be closed on Fridays. Hundreds of young children will be cut off from Head Start funding. And investigations of white-collar criminals will drop by 25 percent. All of this and more will happen—much, much more—unless Congress does what it was elected to do: serve the American people.

And so, today I call on the Congress to do exactly that—to avoid sequestration and, instead, help fix the budget problem. We need the Congress, particularly the Democrats, to support growth incentives—growth incentives that promote savings, job creation, and capital investment. Congress has got to stop being manic-depressive: manic on spending, depressive for the economy. [*Laughter*]

And one more thing: If Congress doesn't see the light, on November 6th the voters will make it feel the heat, because they know where the blame for this delay stands.

Bill Schuette, of course, has always seen the light at home, as a member of the Budget Committee, receiving the Golden Bulldogs award from the Watchdogs of the Treasury. That's an organization that's trying to keep spending down. Watchdogs of the Treasury—the Golden Bulldog award—our dog Millie liked that award. [*Laughter*] Incidentally, I bring you—because I talked to her this morning at 5 a.m. I woke up at 5 a.m., and I was on the next time zone over. And I thought, well, Barbara is always up at 6 a.m., so I called. Regrettably, she was in Texas, and it was also 5 a.m., and I did not get an overly warm welcome. But I did tell her I was going to be here this evening. She shares my affection for Bill Schuette and for Max Fisher and for so many people in the room. So I bring you warm regards from the Silver Fox, who in my view is doing an outstanding job for education all across this country.

But look, in all seriousness, Bill knows that we've got to meet this budget challenge to keep us economically strong; Max, an experienced businessman, once again driving that point home to me this evening. And as I look around the room, I am sure there is unanimous agreement that we've got to get a deal that's going to bring this deficit down once and for all. So, I hope that the negotiations that are going on right now—right this minute—that the Congress will result finally in the kind of budget agreement that I can accept and bring to you, the American people, for approval.

Bill also knows that we've got to meet our challenges abroad. You heard him refer to that. So in closing, let me just discuss an area where change is especially urgent. And I refer to the need for more Senators who understand, like Bill, that when it comes to national defense, preparedness is not something to rest upon. Preparedness is something to build upon. And all of us know that we must defend civilized values around the world. So, we are resolved that aggression in the Persian Gulf cannot stand.

Our four objectives in the Gulf reflect a multinational resolve. Iraq must withdraw from Kuwait immediately and completely. Kuwait's legitimate government must be restored. The security and the stability of the Persian Gulf must be maintained. And American citizens and others must be protected abroad. Those are our four objectives, and I will see that those four objectives are fulfilled.

I hope I don't need to repeat it, but let me say those objectives are unchanged. And we can't say how long it will take to reach these objectives. We don't know what sacrifice will be demanded, but this we do know: America will not stay in the Persian Gulf 1 day longer than necessary, but we will remain for as long as we need to complete our mission.

This means that our friends and allies must be with us, and they are. Think of what Max referred to: the unprecedented support in the United Nations, or aid—economic or military—from a variety of countries. Think of the support of the American people. They know that no country should mug another and get away with it. And finally, especially think of how our service men and women are standing for us, reflecting America at her finest. What wonderful young kids we have in the Armed Forces, all volunteers, every single one of them proudly serving with an unprecedented morale. The greatest soldiers, sailors, airmen, and marines that any country could have are showing that the best way to keep the peace is to keep America militarily strong.

Just a couple of examples—all sons and daughters of Michigan now on active duty in Saudi Arabia. Navy Petty Officer Leslie Rogers is a medic from Williamston. He's standing shoulder to shoulder for what is right and good with colleagues like Lansing's Enrico Arquisola, serving aboard the U.S.S. *Independence,* or Army Engineer Todd Dimock of Mount Morris or First Lieutenant Stacey Miller—she's from Kalamazoo—of the Air Force's 379th Combat Support Group. These men and women reflect the true caliber of America and the vital essence of our mission. They show that America would not be the land of the free if it were not also the home of the brave.

Now, I think you may have detected that I have some disagreements with the Congress—liberal Democrats, particularly—on the budget issue—and I do—and, quite frankly, on a number of other issues as well, where Bill Schuette and I stand in one place on education, crime, child care, and those that control the Congress on the other party stand exactly 180 degrees opposite. But there's one thing we do agree on, and we agree strongly on it, and that is support for our service men and women in the Gulf. I am proud of them, and I am proud of the congressional leadership—Democrat and Republican—as well as individual Members for the way that they've pulled together to stand up against aggression. This is exactly what Senator Arthur Vandenberg meant years ago when he said that politics stops at the water's edge. We should all be grateful for this kind of bipartisan support because our effort isn't Republican or Democrat, liberal and conservative: it is an American effort, and it's gained the respect of everybody around the world.

And lastly, Bill Schuette knows that, while our forces are defending us around the world, we must provide leadership here at home and that a Senate sharing this belief can help build a truly better America. So, now let's go out and get out the vote. Let's win the statehouse. Let's win the Senate. Let's win both houses of the State legislature. Let's pick up seats in the U.S. Senate and the U.S. House of Representatives. Let's elect Republican Congressmen and John Engler as Governor. And let's roll up our sleeve and elect a superb United States Senator.

Thank you for this evening. God bless the United States. And let's make Bill Schuette the next Senator from the great State of Michigan. Thank you all very, very much.

Note: The President spoke at 6:42 p.m. in the Renaissance Ballroom at the Westin Hotel. In his remarks, he referred to Max Fisher, honorary dinner chairman; and Bill Laimbeer, Isiah Thomas, and Chuck Daly, players and head coach of the Detroit Pistons basketball team, respectively. Prior to the dinner, the President met with Eastern European-American community leaders and major campaign contributors. Following the dinner, he returned to Washington, DC.

Remarks and an Exchange With Reporters Prior to Discussions With President Zhelyu Zhelev of Bulgaria
September 28, 1990

President Zhelev. Mr. President, I'm very grateful for the time you spare to receive us, considering your busy schedule. It's a great support for our young democracy indeed.

President Bush. We're wishing that young

democracy all the best. The American people are very excited about the changes.

Q. Are you pleased with the way things are going at home in this democratic change?

President Zhelev. Generally, yes. Our country has embarked firmly upon the road of democracy. And for our nation, this is a symbolic visit because the greatest democracy in the world is extending a helpful hand to the youngest democracy in Europe.

President Bush. We're very anxious to see this democratic change solidified and continuing in a lot of countries. But we have great respect for what you're trying to do, a great respect for that.

Just wanted to have a chance to wish you well and to say in front of the press here in our country and around the world that the changes in Eastern Europe have really captured the imagination of the American people. Every place you go, people are talking about it. I've been meeting the last couple of days in our Midwest with ethnic Americans from different heritage groups, and the excitement is still very high, very high.

Q. Mr. President, would you convey some words for the Bulgarian television?

President Zhelev. The processes in Bulgaria are irreversible. Mr. President, this country's no longer a Communist, a totalitarian state. We have a multiparty system, for instance, independent trade unions, free press, independent radio and television, a democratically elected parliament, and a democratically elected President in my capacity.

President Bush. It is this kind of exciting change that has the full support of the American people. I hope you feel that in your visit now.

Q. Mr. President, some words for the Bulgarians?

President Bush. I just said that we support strongly the democratic change all across Eastern Europe. Thank you all very much.

Note: President Zhelev spoke at 10:06 a.m. in the Oval Office at the White House. A tape was not available for verification of the content of these remarks.

Remarks Following Discussions With Amir Jabir al-Ahmad al-Jabir Al Sabah of Kuwait
September 28, 1990

The President. Well, it is my great pleasure to welcome His Highness Sheik Jabir Sabah to the United States. His Highness is visiting Washington for the first time. What normally would be a pleasurable occasion instead is a time for sobriety and sorrow. Our meeting has taken place with the backdrop of the tragedy that has been vested on Kuwait and its people by a ruthless and ambitious dictator.

Iraqi aggression has ransacked and pillaged a once peaceful and secure country, its population assaulted, incarcerated, intimidated, and even murdered. Iraq's leaders are trying to wipe an internationally recognized sovereign state, a member of the Arab League and the United Nations, off the face of the map.

To them and to the world, I will state what I told His Highness, the Amir. Iraq will fail. Kuwait—free Kuwait—will endure. And I have reaffirmed to the Amir that America's resolve to end this aggression against Kuwait remains firm and undiminished. Kuwait's sovereignty and territorial integrity will be restored, the stability and security of the Persian Gulf region is assured, and the safety of all innocent citizens is secured. And this is consistent with our longstanding interests endorsed by all my predecessors since Harry Truman. And this is consistent with the will of the world community, endorsed by the United Nations in eight Security Council resolutions. And just yesterday, the standing ovation that greeted the Amir's moving address to the U.N. General Assembly was one more powerful expression of international support for a free Kuwait.

His Highness and I reaffirmed our support for the U.N. Security Council resolutions as the means to bring about a peaceful end to the crisis. But ultimately, that is up to Saddam Hussein. I reiterated our strong belief that we just continue to stand on the principles by which the United States and the rest of the civilized world are governed. And that means that no nation should be allowed to conduct its relations with another on the basis of threats or the use of brute force. And finally, His Highness and I agreed that we must keep all our options open to ensure that Iraq's unlawful occupation of Kuwait is ended and Kuwait's legitimate government restored. We also discussed the key role that His Highness, his government, and the Kuwaiti people are playing and will continue to play in the international effort to achieve these efforts.

I want to thank the Amir for his generous support for those who are being asked to make sacrifices. And I also want to single out the valiant efforts of the Kuwaiti resistance who are continuing to fight vigorously for their country. Despite incalculable risks, many are willing to pay the highest price to rid their country of foreign occupation and to protect innocent citizens, including Americans, from harm. And many have already paid the ultimate price.

His Highness and I will continue to stay in close touch and to work together to find a solution to this tragedy. As I stated in my address to the Nation earlier this month, we will stand by our friends.

And to my guest, let me, sir, say one more thing, sir. I look forward to the day that I can visit you and the Kuwaiti people in your rightful home Kuwait.

Thank you for coming.

The Amir. Mr. President, I am pleased to have visited the capital of your great nation. And I wish I could have had the pleasure of receiving you in Kuwait City, the capital of my country, were it not for the Iraqi aggression which has denied us that opportunity temporarily, God willing. Nevertheless, the people of Kuwait, as well as myself, look forward to receiving you, Mr. President, in liberated, independent Kuwait.

I take pleasure in expressing to you once again, Mr. President, and to your great people the deep feelings of friendship and appreciation Kuwait feels for you. Our stand together in the face of treachery and aggression is proof that relations between our two countries are based on the solid foundation of common values and principles that, in turn, provides guidance for the fruitful cooperation that evolved and developed in various fields between the United States and Kuwait.

Your principled, courageous, and decisive position in face of the Iraqi aggression on Kuwait is a true expression of the unabated faith and commitment of the American people to the humanitarian morals on which and for which the United States of America was founded. The unity of the international community in support of our position against aggression and occupation, the two most flagrant violations of human rights, conclusively indicates the determination of all nations and peoples of the world to put a definitive end to armed aggression as any country's foreign policy tool. This unity takes on added relevance given the world's entrance to an era dominated by an atmosphere of peace, rapprochement, cooperation, and optimism.

We look with admiration to the role you, Mr. President, and your nation have played in inaugurating and enhancing the foundation of this era. Mr. President, your just position by the side of Kuwait in this ordeal represents a categorical rejection of aggression in all its forms and manifestations, whatever its source or pretext. The unity and support shown by the friendly American people towards the position and measures taken by you, Mr. President, against Iraq's aggression, whose first and foremost victims are the human rights of the Kuwaiti people, are perfectly compatible with the unflinching faith in the standards of justice and fairness for which the American people stand. This is the faith that brings together the nations and peoples of the civilized world.

I am fully satisfied by the identical views we hold on issues covered in our talks this morning with you. Truly, this mutual agreement reflects the advanced stage in relations our two friendly countries and peoples have reached.

Thank you, Mr. President.

Note: President Bush spoke at 1:45 p.m. at the South Portico of the White House. In his remarks, he referred to President Saddam Hussein of Iraq. The Amir spoke in Arabic, and his remarks were translated by an interpreter. Prior to their remarks, the two leaders met privately in the Oval Office and with U.S. and Kuwaiti officials in the Cabinet Room, and then attended a luncheon in the Old Family Dinning Room.

Statement by Press Secretary Fitzwater on the Cancellation of the State Visit of President Wojciech Jaruzelski of Poland
September 28, 1990

President Wojciech Jaruzelski of Poland has written President Bush to decline his invitation to pay a state visit to the United States this fall. President Jaruzelski explained that because of the forthcoming Presidential elections in Poland and his decision to step down before the expiration of his term he did not feel it appropriate to proceed as planned with his visit to the United States.

President Bush accepts President Jaruzelski's decision with full understanding. It is in keeping with President Jaruzelski's contribution to the process of democratic change in Poland since the historic Roundtable Agreement of April 1989. President Jaruzelski deserves great credit for the role he has played, together with the government of Prime Minister Mazowiecki, in working toward Poland's economic recovery and democratic consolidation.

President Bush regrets that President Jaruzelski will not be able to accept this long-standing invitation for a state visit but looks forward to receiving President Jaruzelski at the White House in a private capacity at some time in the future.

Remarks at the Washington National Cathedral Dedication Ceremony
September 29, 1990

Thank you all, ladies and gentlemen. Thank you, Bishop Browning, and it's a great pleasure to be with you again. And a special thanks to Bishop Haines, and special thanks to Colonel Bourgeois and our wonderful Marine Band. Thank you, ladies and gentlemen. And a warm welcome to all of you out there, standing and seated, in this splendid scene of bright unity across these gorgeous grounds—the clergy and other interfaith leaders, members of this great Washington National Cathedral, representatives of our government and other countries, and the men and women who have worked on this magnificent structure, and all our friends.

Barbara and I feel privileged, privileged to be with you on this day of ecumenical thanksgiving. There's one man, mentioned by Bishop Browning, who has gone before us, yet who is in so many of our hearts today, the late Episcopal Bishop of Washington, John Walker. Like many of you here, I treasured his friendship, and I valued his counsel. And were he still with us, the stone setting would be the culmination of his life's work and his life's dream. But tomorrow, on the first anniversary of his death, the very first service will be held in the completed cathedral. I'd like to dedicate these remarks to his memory.

What an extraordinary moment this is.

Eighty-three years ago this day, this hour, our predecessors here laid a cornerstone. Now, eight decades later, we look at Mount St. Alban and say: Here we have built our church—not just a church, a house of prayer for a nation built on the rock of religious faith, a nation we celebrate as "one nation under God," a nation whose founding President, George Washington, said: "No people can be bound to acknowledge and adore the invisible hand which conducts the affairs of men more than the people of the United States."

And so, we have constructed here this symbol of our nation's spiritual life, overlooking the center of our nation's secular life, a symbol which combines the permanence of stone and of God—both of which will outlast men and memories—a symbol that carries with it a constant reminder of our moral obligations. You know, whenever I look up at this hill and see the cathedral keeping watch over us, I feel the challenge is reaffirmed.

Woodrow Wilson's last public words, inscribed here on the wall next to his tomb, say it best: "Our civilization cannot survive materially unless it be redeemed spiritually." To do that, we must govern by the imperatives of a strong moral compass; a compass based on the kind of purity and vision and values that inspired our early founders; a compass that would lead us to enter this building through its oldest door, "The Way of Peace"; and a compass oriented to the words of St. Paul, who gazes down from our left: "And now abideth faith, hope, and love, these three; but the greatest of these is love."

Our personal family compass has for many years led us here for public and private worship. We were neighbors when we lived in the Vice President's residence, and before that, our children went to school at St. Alban's. I was a board member at National Cathedral School, and Canon Martin baptized one of our grandchildren, and two sons were confirmed here. And Barbara's even read "The Christmas Story." I'll stop in case each of you want to tell me of your family connection with this wonderful institution. [*Laughter*]

One of the high points of our inaugural weekend was the prayer service here, part of a national day of prayer across the country. I want to take a moment to say goodbye to Provost Perry, Charles Perry, who so beautifully organized that service and who is leaving tomorrow after a dozen years of devoted work.

I'd like to share with you some thoughts on why we find this cathedral so moving. To begin with, there is profound meaning in the physical beauty. The devout say they can see here the invisible hand of God in the visible handiwork of man. We all can see in this astonishing place of stone and light a massive 300-million-pound mountain of Indiana limestone created as an act of worship.

I want my grandchildren to come here. I want them to feel reassured that there always will be comfort here in the presence of God, and I want them to delight in the colors and the sounds and the tapestries and mosaics to the fine old hymns. And I want them to know a very special way of understanding this wondrous place—studying the brilliant stained-glass windows. From where we now stand, the rose window high above seems black and formless to some, perhaps; but when we enter and see it backlit by the sun, it dazzles in astonishing splendor and reminds us that without faith we too are but stained-glass windows in the dark.

But the magnificent story of this place, then, is human as well as spiritual. The greatness of this masterpiece comes from the loving and sometimes lifelong dedication of the finest craftsmen. For some, it has been a multigenerational work, son following son throughout the birth of this house of worship. Many of these workers are now gone. For their memorial, simply look around you.

But most of the gifts that made this great American dream a reality—gifts of funds, work, love, spirit, and prayer—were from the people who were its congregation: the millions across America. They caught the exhilaration of the dream that seized those who envisioned this cathedral and yet didn't live to see it a reality, men like Pierre L'Enfant, whose 1791 plan for Washington included "a great church for national purposes," or Henry Satterlee, this city's first Episcopal Bishop, who yearned for a place "forever open and free," and the Members of Congress who voted the 1893 Charter of Foundation.

There are some here who share that dream in a unique way. They were also here 83 years ago today for the laying of the cornerstone, and they remember sunlight shining through the rain while 10,000 watched and cheered. For instance, Elsie Brown is now 90, but was 7 when her mother took her to that event. Ninety-five-year-old Taylor Eiker was 12 when he donned his cassock to sing in the boys choir that noon. And Ruth Oliphant, now 98, walked over with her other 15-year-old Cathedral School classmates.

It was a very American ceremony. President Teddy Roosevelt spoke, and Bishop Satterlee tapped the stone with the gavel which George Washington had used to set the cornerstone of the United States Capitol. That was only right for a cathedral whose style is 14th-century Gothic and yet also very much American, a cathedral that's not just about faith but was also about a nation and its people: a cathedral where mosaics of the Great Seal of the United States and the State seals are set into the floors; where bays honor Washington, Lincoln, Stonewall Jackson, and Robert E. Lee; where you can find an eagle, a bison, and even a stained-glass codfish; where needlepoint memorials are to Herman Melville, Alexander Graham Bell, Harriet Tubman, and John Fitzgerald Kennedy; where lie the graves of President Wilson, Admiral George Dewey, and Helen Keller; where the mesmerizing stained-glass Space Window includes a Moon rock given by astronaut Michael Collins, who went to school on these very grounds at St. Alban's; and where an unexpected shaft of sun can leave a stunning memory—the statue of George Washington, strong and solid and earthbound, suddenly dappled by the brilliance of stained-glass light. It's a place where the history of the cathedral and of the country have been interwoven.

When we need to grieve, we come here. We held funerals for Presidents Truman and Eisenhower and Vice President Humphrey, the burial of President Wilson, and a fantastic memorial service for Winston Churchill.

When we want to understand, we come here. Over a 3-day period, at the dedication of the Vietnam Memorial, the names of 57,939 lost Americans were read in chapels. Other times, we listened to Bishop Tutu or Billy Graham or Martin Luther King.

When we want to celebrate, we come here. When the hostages were freed from our Embassy in Tehran, there was a service of thanksgiving. Later, a national prayer service for the 50th Presidential inauguration. And bells peal out on the national holidays.

When we want to express our concern, we come here: to hold a memorial for victims of the American Embassy bombing in Beirut; a service of reflection on the 40th anniversary of Hiroshima; and even now, prayers for our brave young service men and women in the harsh, distant deserts.

And so, today, we prepare to raise that final 1,008-pound grand finial to its spot on one of the great pinnacles of St. Paul's Tower, the last step in an eight-decade-long journey.

Now that our national treasure is complete, how will it fit into our lives? I would love to see the entire country discover this cathedral as America's resource, refuge, and reminder, somewhere to strengthen the Nation's heart. We should consecrate this place in the words of Isaiah: "For mine house shall be called a house of prayer for all people." All people. All America. And we should come here to pledge ourselves to the work of Martin Luther King, envisioned from the splendid Canterbury pulpit in his last sermon, 3 days before he died. And he said: "We will bring about a new day of justice and brotherhood and peace. And on that day, morning stars will sing together, and the sons of God will shout for joy."

For eight decades, the dream of a completed cathedral dominated this hill, and now Dr. King's words should become our new vision. Eighty-three years ago on this spot, President Teddy Roosevelt said: "God speed the work begun this noon." And today I say: God speed the work completed this noon and the new work yet to begin.

God bless all of you, this magnificent cathedral, and the United States of America. Thank you all very much.

Statement by Press Secretary Fitzwater on President Bush's Meeting in New York City With President Cesar Gaviria of Colombia
September 29, 1990

President Bush met with President Gaviria of Colombia at approximately 4:15 this afternoon and discussed a number of bilateral issues of interest to both countries. President Bush advised President Gaviria that he will include Colombia in legislation that he will soon send to the Congress on a CBI [Caribbean Basin Initiative]-like trade preference system for four Andean countries. One product of special interest to Colombia, cut flowers, will be included in this legislation. The two countries have discussed tariffs on cut flowers for a number of months, and President Bush has promised to seek relief.

President Gaviria expressed his concern about a new wave of terrorism in Colombia and the need for both countries to deal forthrightly with the drug situation. The two Presidents discussed possible trade benefits that could accrue to Colombia to make up for adverse economic impacts due to the drug war.

President Bush raised the issue of "consensual" boarding of ships suspected of carrying drugs. President Gaviria indicated he would look into the process of getting approval for U.S. coastguardsmen to inspect ships at sea. President Bush reiterated that the United States wants to cooperate with Colombia in drug interdiction and would not act without Colombian approval.

The two Presidents discussed the situation in the Persian Gulf, including its impact on oil prices in the United States and Colombia. President Bush thanked President Gaviria for his decision to increase oil production in Colombia. President Bush repeated his concerns about market speculators driving up the price of oil. President Bush thanked President Gaviria for his support in the United Nations on the resolutions related to Iraq.

Statement by Press Secretary Fitzwater on the President's Meeting in New York City With Prime Minister Salim al-Huss of Lebanon
September 29, 1990

The President met with the Prime Minister of Lebanon, Salim al-Huss, at 5 p.m. The President assured the Prime Minister of continued U.S. support for the Government of Lebanon. He said the United States supports Lebanon's independence, unity, sovereignty, and territorial integrity. The President also advised the Prime Minister that the United States seeks the withdrawal of all foreign forces from Lebanon. The President emphasized that the U.S. contacts with Syria would in no way be detrimental to Lebanon.

The two leaders discussed the situation in the Persian Gulf at some length.

The President raised the issue of American hostages in Lebanon, pointing out that we continue to seek all information that could be helpful in securing the release of our hostages. The Prime Minister assured the President that he would provide any information that might possibly be helpful in securing their release.

Statement by Press Secretary Fitzwater on the President's Meeting in New York City With Prime Minister Brian Mulroney of Canada
September 29, 1990

The President met with Prime Minister Mulroney of Canada at 6 p.m. to discuss the United Nations World Summit for Children. Prime Minister Mulroney is one of the sponsors of the World Summit for Children. The Prime Minister discussed the major themes of the summit and the scenario for tomorrow's meeting. The Prime Minister said there were 15 million children in the world under 5 years old who die every year from disease. He said we must work to improve the world environment.

The President and the Prime Minister also discussed the situation in the Persian Gulf and the status of the multinational force there.

Statement by Press Secretary Fitzwater on the President's Meeting in New York City With Prime Minister Tadeusz Mazowiecki of Poland
September 29, 1990

The President and Prime Minister Mazowiecki met at 6:30 p.m. to discuss the status of Poland's move toward the development of a private economy and democratic reforms. The Prime Minister said his country is making considerable progress in building democracy and has undertaken several specific efforts to privatize their economy. He indicated an initial emphasis on moving smaller companies into the private sector.

The President congratulated the Prime Minister on the success they have had so far. He said the United States supports Poland in its reform efforts. "America wants you to succeed," the President said. "We will help in every way we can." The President outlined the U.S. economic assistance program for Poland.

The President thanked the Prime Minister for Poland's contributions to the Persian Gulf. Poland is sending a hospital ship and a field hospital to the region. The Prime Minister said his country is considering other helpful measures as well.

Remarks at the Opening Ceremony of the United Nations World Summit for Children in New York City
September 30, 1990

Mr. Secretary-General and President Traoré, Prime Minister Mulroney, and my distinguished colleagues from around the world, thank you all, and welcome to the United States.

I'm proud to address you here today as

the President of this country, in which this special summit is being held. And at the outset, let me join all in expressing our appreciation to UNICEF and then to the kids here with us today.

President Traoré, our thanks to you, sir. And may I extend my special respects and special thanks to the Prime Minister of Canada. It was largely his foresight and persistence that resulted in this impressive turnout.

In recent days, the world community has acted decisively in defense of a principle: that small states shall not become souvenirs of conquest. It was just 3 weeks ago that I spoke to the American people about a new world order, a new partnership of nations—freer from the threat of terror, stronger in the pursuit of justice, more secure in the quest for peace. Today we are holding this unprecedented world summit to work for the well-being of those who will live in and lead this new world. Their voices are still faint and unheard. So, we've come together, more than 70 strong—heads of state, chiefs of government—chiefs of state and heads of government—to speak for the children of the Earth.

But first, we should acknowledge that for many children the only blessing they will ever know is their innocence. The facts are as stark as they are oppressive: There are almost 3 billion young people on Earth today, and more than 14 million of them will die this year. In the next hour alone, 1,000 babies will perish. But I think we're all gathered here to defy these statistics. We've seen children—swollen bellies. We've seen the pleading eyes of starvation. We've heard the cries of children dying of disease. So, let us affirm in this historic summit that these children can be saved. They can be saved when we live up to our responsibilities not just as an assembly of governments but as a world community of adults, of parents.

In my time as President, I've heard the heart-rending cries of AIDS babies. I've stood helpless over infants born addicted to cocaine, their tiny bodies trembling with pain. But I've also been to many classrooms across America where the influence of love and well-being can be seen instantly in bright faces and wondering eyes. From all these experiences and many more, I've learned that our children are a mirror, an honest reflection, of their parents and their world. Sometimes, the reflection is flattering. At other times, we simply don't like what we see. So, we must never turn away.

So, let me tell you what the American people intend to do. This month, our Secretary of Health and Human Services, Dr. Sullivan, announced ambitious new health objectives that we as a nation—citizens, families, business, and government—hope to reach by the year 2000. We seek to reduce infant mortality and low-weight births, to increase child-immunization levels and improve the health of both mothers and children. And we want to see the day when every American child is a part of a strong and stable family.

We're working in partnership with other governments and international organizations to eliminate child-killing diseases. Of course, many diseases are but a manifestation of an even more basic disorder: malnutrition. And to combat world starvation, the United States will continue to help food production in many countries, and we will send almost 150 million metric tons of food abroad this year.

And sadly, there is another child-killer loose in the world that knows no cure: AIDS. And nowhere is this killer taking more lives than in Africa. So, I've asked Dr. Sullivan and Dr. Ronald Roskens, the Administrator of AID, to go to Africa to see what else America and the world can do to advance child survival across that continent and across the world.

So far, I've spoken here just briefly of the most urgent issues of survival, but simple survival is not enough for a child lacking in health or learning, or denied the love of family and time for play. One year and two days ago, I met with the Governors of our 50 States on a single topic of national importance. We agreed to set ambitious education goals for the year 2000. For America, this is a stiff challenge, self-imposed. I see among us today many leaders who should take pride in giving the world examples of educational excellence, examples the next generation of Americans will not leave unchallenged.

But of course, education is a mystery to the 100 million children not in school. It's an outrage that so many spend their childhood in mines, in factories, in the twilight world of the streets. The United States outlawed most forms of child labor decades ago. Let us strive together to make education the primary work of all children.

So, all children must be given the chance to lead happy, healthy, and productive lives. Let me be the first to say that the United States can learn from many of the nations represented here today, but what my countrymen have learned from hard experience is that progress begins when we empower people, not bureaucracies. Programs can best enhance the welfare of children by strengthening the mutual responsibilities of public institutions and individual families. We should also look to the private sector as an essential partner. Public efforts on behalf of children should encourage ex-perimentation among neighborhoods and local governments, not stifle it. So, when it comes to improving the welfare of children, empowerment should begin first with their parents, as President Salinas a minute ago so eloquently stated.

Saving one child is a miracle. As world leaders, we can realize such miracles, and then we can count them in millions.

My friends and colleagues, thank you very much. And may God bless the children of this world. Thank you very much.

Note: President Bush spoke at 10 a.m. in the General Assembly Hall at the United Nations. He referred to United Nations Secretary-General Javier Perez de Cuellar de la Guerra; President Moussa Traoré of Mali and Prime Minister Brian Mulroney of Canada, cochairmen of the summit; and President Carlos Salinas de Gortari of Mexico. Following his remarks, President Bush returned to Washington, DC.

Message to the Congress on the Continuation of Export Control Regulations
September 30, 1990

To the Congress of the United States:

Pursuant to section 204(b) of the International Emergency Economic Powers Act, 50 U.S.C. 1703(b), I hereby report to the Congress that I have today exercised the authority granted by this Act to continue in effect the system of controls contained in 15 C.F.R., Parts 768–799, including restrictions on participation by U.S. persons in certain foreign boycott activities, which heretofore have been maintained under the authority of the Export Administration Act of 1979, as amended, 50 U.S.C. App. 2401 *et seq.* In addition, I have made provision for the administration of section 38(e) of the Arms Export Control Act, 22 U.S.C. 2778(e).

The exercise of this authority is necessitated by the expiration of the Export Administration Act on September 30, 1990, and the resulting lapse of the system of controls maintained under that Act.

In the absence of controls, foreign parties would have unrestricted access to U.S. commercial products, technology, and technical data, posing an unusual and extraordinary threat to national security, foreign policy, and economic objectives critical to the United States. In addition, U.S. persons would not be prohibited from complying with certain foreign boycott requests. This would seriously harm our foreign policy interests, particularly in the Middle East.

Controls established in 15 C.F.R. 768–799, and continued by this action, include the following:

—National security export controls aimed at restricting the export of goods and technologies which would make a significant contribution to the military potential of certain other countries and which would prove detrimental to the national security of the United States.
—Foreign policy controls that further the foreign policy objectives of the United

States or its declared international obligations in such widely recognized areas as human rights, antiterrorism, regional stability, missile technology nonproliferation, and chemical and biological weapons nonproliferation.

—Nuclear nonproliferation controls that are maintained for both national security and foreign policy reasons, and which support the objectives of the Nuclear Nonproliferation Act.

—Short supply controls that protect domestic supplies, and antiboycott regulations that prohibit compliance with foreign boycotts aimed at countries friendly to the United States.

Consequently, I have issued an Executive order (a copy of which is attached) to continue in effect all rules and regulations issued or continued in effect by the Secretary of Commerce under the authority of the Export Administration Act of 1979, as amended, and all orders, regulations, licenses, and other forms of administrative actions under the Act, except where they are inconsistent with sections 203(b) and 206 of the International Emergency Economic Powers Act.

The Congress and the Executive have not permitted export controls to lapse since they were enacted under the Export Control Act of 1949. Any termination of controls could permit transactions to occur that would be seriously detrimental to the na-

tional interests we have heretofore sought to protect through export controls and restrictions on compliance by U.S. persons with certain foreign boycotts. I believe that even a temporary lapse in this system of controls would seriously damage our national security, foreign policy, and economic interests and undermine our credibility in meeting our international obligations.

The countries affected by this action vary depending on the objectives sought to be achieved by the system of controls instituted under the Export Administration Act. Potential adversaries may seek to acquire sensitive U.S. goods and technologies. Other countries serve as conduits for the diversion of such items. Still other countries have policies that are contrary to U.S. foreign policy or nuclear nonproliferation objectives, or foster boycotts against friendly countries. For some goods or technologies, controls could apply even to our closest allies in order to safeguard against diversion to potential adversaries.

It is my intention to terminate the Executive order upon enactment into law of a bill reauthorizing the authorities contained in the Export Administration Act.

GEORGE BUSH

The White House,
September 30, 1990.

Note: The Executive order is listed in Appendix E at the end of this volume.

Remarks Announcing a Federal Budget Agreement
September 30, 1990

The President. I am joined here today by the bipartisan leadership of the Congress— the Speaker of the House, the Senate majority leader, the Senate Republican leader, the President pro tem of the Senate, the House majority leader, and the House Republican leader—and other members of the budget summit negotiating group. The bipartisan leaders and I have reached agreement on the Federal budget. Over 5 years, it would reduce the projected deficit by

$500 billion; that is half a trillion dollars.

The agreement has five basic parts. First, it would save $119 billion in entitlement and mandatory programs.

Second, it would produce 182 billion in discretionary program savings. These savings would come principally from defense. In the next 3 years, defense outlays would be reduced by $67 billion, relative to the projected baseline. All other discretionary programs would be firmly capped at the projected baseline levels; that is, for the next 3 years they would in total be allowed to grow at no more than the inflation rate.

Third, the agreement would increase tax revenues by $134 billion. The largest single increase, single contributor, would be a phased-in increase in the gasoline tax of 5 cents per gallon in the first year and another 5 cents in the following years. I do not welcome any such tax measure, nor do I expect anybody up here does. However, this one does have the virtue not only of contributing to deficit reduction but also, over time, of decreasing America's dependence on foreign oil, an objective whose importance has become increasingly evident in the face of the Iraqi invasion of Kuwait. I am pleased to be able to note that the budget agreement also includes several new incentives to increase domestic exploration and development of oil and gas resources. The combination of these measures should help reduce America's vulnerability to the interruption of supplies of foreign oil imports.

Fourth, the agreement extends the Gramm-Rudman budget discipline for 5 years. In addition, it improves the budget process and substantially strengthens the enforceability of the 5-year budget plan to which we have agreed.

Fifth, this agreement includes important new initiatives to stimulate economic growth: it authorizes new tax incentives for the development of enterprise zones; extends the R&D tax credit; it provides powerful new incentives for productive investment in the kinds of companies that account for most of America's job growth. These incentives include: a new 30-percent credit for R&D; 25-percent deduction for the purchase of new equity; indexing of the basis of new stock in such companies; expansion of expensing of investment in tangible equipment and scientific equipment; a minimum basis rule that encourages investment in new ventures and in companies with high growth potential; and other such incentives.

In addition to these targeted growth incentives I would note that prompt enactment of this entire 5-year deficit reduction package would itself help stimulate long-term economic growth with a half a trillion

dollars in real deficit reduction. And let me repeat: The leaders here and I think that these are real deficit reduction figures. Long-term interest rates should be able to come down.

This package should be a strong component of a positive, responsible fiscal and monetary policy. I heartily thank the negotiators who have worked so long and so hard to develop this package. The bipartisan congressional leadership and I have pledged our very best to get this entire package signed into law by October 19th. As any such plan would have to, ours requires that virtually everyone contribute in some way. It is balanced, it is fair, and in my view it is what the United States of America needs at this point in its history. And we are united in our firm determination to see this program enacted.

I do not want to imply that some who have not been in the final negotiations are for every part of this. But I can only speak for my part, and then the top leadership here will speak. But I will simply say: This is priority. This is priority for our nation. This is something that the country is calling out for and world markets are looking for. And so, there will be some tough fights ahead; but I have pledged to the Speaker, to Congressman Gephardt, to Bob Michel on our side, to George Mitchell and Bob Dole and the Senate pro tem leader, Senator Byrd, that I will do everything I can to lay aside partisanship here and to take the case for this deal to the American people in every way I can. Sometimes you don't get it just the way you want, and this is such a time for me, and I expect it's such a time for everybody standing here. But it's time we put the interest of the United States of America first and get this deficit under control.

Mr. Speaker, I am grateful to you, the Democrats, and the Republicans that have seen that the interest of this country come first. Thank you for what you've been doing, and I'd appreciate it if you want to say a few words.

Speaker Foley. Thank you very much, Mr. President. I'll be brief in just echoing what you, yourself, just said, sir, that this is a package that your negotiators and the bipartisan participating negotiators from the House and the Senate—ranking Republican Members, chairmen, and the leadership on both sides—have sought to achieve. It's not going to be easy or simple to obtain the votes that are necessary in both the House and the Senate, the majority of both parties and both bodies, that will have to be found to enact this package—and within the next 3 weeks. But we pledge our efforts with yours to convince our colleagues in the country that this is a strong undergirding of our economic future, our national prosperity, and joint national interest. And in that spirit, we are going to begin today to present to you legislation which will allow the orderly functioning of the Federal Government for the continuation of this next week, in preparing to take the first step to implement this program.

I want to pay a word, if I can, of special thanks to all of my colleagues who have participated in this, and especially to Dick Gephardt, the chairman of these budget negotiations, who, all sides—Republicans and Democrats, Senators and House Members, and you, yourself—have spoken eloquently to his patience and leadership. Thank you, sir, for your involvement and your determination to aid in the process of bringing this package and the interests of the country to final achievement.

The President. Now if I might ask Senator Mitchell and then Senator Dole, Congressman Gephardt, and Congressman Michel to speak.

Senator Mitchell. Thank you, Mr. President. Now comes the hard part. It's one thing to get a budget agreement among ourselves for which all involved should be commended. It's another thing to get the votes to pass it through the House and the Senate. That is a task to which we must now commit ourselves.

This agreement is a compromise. Both sides can accurately say that the agreement includes provisions they don't like. Both sides can also accurately say the agreement doesn't include some provisions they think should be included. Cutting the deficit requires difficult choices. But our nation's economic future requires that we make those choices. We have already debated too long. Now we must act decisively.

Senator Dole. Mr. President, thank you very much. And I want to thank my colleagues and again, particularly Dick Gephardt. The nay-sayers and the nitpickers may have a field day because the easy vote in this case is to find something you don't like and vote no. But in my view, we owe more to the American people than finding fault with what I consider to be a good, positive, solid agreement that, in my view, will help the American economy and demonstrate to the American people, who are sometimes somewhat cynical, that the Congress and the President of the United States can work together, and we can look ahead and we can do the right thing for our country. And so, I would hope that my colleagues—and I speak now to my colleagues—certainly will study this document very carefully, will give it their best effort, and when the role is called that we'll have a majority of Republicans and Democrats for this outstanding package.

Thank you, Mr. President.

The President. Thank you. Dick?

Representative Gephardt. Thank you, Mr. President. Forty years ago a mountaineer who joined in the first successful climb of Mount Everest explained the success by saying no expedition enjoyed better teamwork. To the Speaker of the House, Congressman Foley; the Senate majority leader, George Mitchell; to the Members of Congress who are here with us on the stage; to the administration and their representatives and the great staffs of all sides who worked so long and so hard with us: You have been heroic as we've made this climb together.

The American people are today asking: Why was this summit necessary, why did it take so long, and what did it achieve? If we are to enact this agreement—and I think we must—these questions must be answered persuasively and honestly. For 10 years we have chosen a course together that has created large deficits and limited our capacity to meet the needs of our people and the demands of a very challenging age. Today, we face a weakened economy and high rates of interest and inflation. Tomorrow, in absence of an agreement, massive across-the-board budget cuts would occur.

The alternative to this agreement is fiscal chaos. To meet our responsibility to America's working families, this summit simply had to succeed. What delayed us for months is what has divided us for a decade. The parties to these talks had—and continue to have—deep disagreements over values, the role of government, and the fairness of our taxes. But we all made compromise in the national interest.

To bring this process to a successful conclusion, all of us—the American people and our national leaders—must accept the responsibilities of the day. And as this debate unfolds I hope this will be said: that we achieved the largest deficit reduction package in our history, that we focused the national debate on whether the tax code will be based on everybody's individual ability to pay. The vital issues—investing in our people, making our nation competitive, and realizing social justice—will rise again on the national agenda, and then enactment of this measure will enable us to confront these important issues successfully in the years to come.

I thank you, Mr. President, and I thank all the members of the summit.

The President. Bob?

Representative Michel. Well, thank you, Mr. President, and my colleagues. I support the package wholeheartedly because I was one of the narrower group that, within the last 10 days or so, made some of the final decisions.

There may be some reservations with respect to some of our other summiteers on the platform. I think probably rightly so because we're making decisions that will reach far out, to 5 years. Everyone is entitled to know exactly what we have wrought in the printed word. As a matter of fact, I wasn't privy to the last few lines that were written early this morning.

But, on balance, when I look at what we were originally faced with—and here we are refraining from increasing marginal rates and not touching the unmentionable out there, Social Security—and then to have the incentives for growth that I see here and the expenditure caps over the next several years that are real and enforceable, it seems to me that in the alternative so much

better that we've done what we've done, and hopefully that in the ensuing days we'll be able to sell a majority of the Members on both sides of the aisle in both Houses to give us the affirmative vote that I think is so imperative that we have before we adjourn.

Thank you, Mr. President.

The President. Well, thank you all very much. And let me conclude by singling out the White House team by name: Secretary Brady and Dick Darman, John Sununu, who stayed in there day in and day out with the Members of Congress. In my view they did an outstanding job, too.

You know, Senator Bentsen said in this meeting—I hope it's not betraying a confidence—that he hoped that I would do my level-best to take this case to the American people. And I told him inside what I want to repeat here: I will do everything I can to generate support from the American people for this compromise.

I am convinced that the American people do not want to see us continue to mortgage the futures of their children and their grandchildren. And as I say, compromise is the word here. All of us have had to do that. But to Senator Bentsen I said in there, and I would say it here publicly: I want the American people to understand how important we feel this is. I want them to understand this is real. It is not a phony smoke-and-mirrors deficit-cutting program. And I will do everything in my power to help the leadership, Republican and Democrat, get this passed in the United States Congress.

Thank you all very much for coming.

Note: The President spoke at 1:45 p.m. in the Rose Garden at the White House. In his remarks, the President referred to George J. Mitchell, Senate majority leader; Robert Dole, Senate Republican leader; Richard A. Gephardt, House majority leader; Robert H. Michel, House Republican leader; Secretary of the Treasury Nicholas F. Brady; Richard G. Darman, Director of the Office of Management and Budget; and John H. Sununu, Chief of Staff to the President. Later in the afternoon, the President returned to New York, NY.

Statement by Press Secretary Fitzwater on President Bush's Meeting in New York, New York, With President Václav Havel of Czechoslovakia
September 30, 1990

At 6:10 p.m. President Bush met with President Havel of Czechoslovakia. President Havel discussed the status of his country's economic reform measures. He indicated that considerable progress is being made.

President Bush thanked President Havel for their early support of the U.N. sanctions against Iraq, saying, "We understand your sacrifices in supporting the U.N. embargo, and we are grateful."

President Bush informed President Havel that the United States will lift travel restrictions on Czechoslovakia's diplomats in the United States. These restrictions were imposed before Czechoslovakia's moves toward democracy.

President Bush said the U.S. interest in Czechoslovakia's success is very strong: "We want to see you succeed."

Address Before the 45th Session of the United Nations General Assembly in New York, New York
October 1, 1990

Mr. President, thank you very much. Mr. Secretary-General, distinguished delegates to the United Nations, it is really a great privilege to greet you today as we begin what marks a new and historic session of the General Assembly. My congratulations to the Honorable Guido De Marco on your election, sir, as President of the General Assembly. And on a personal note, I want to say that, having witnessed the unprecedented unity and cooperation of the past 2 months, that I have never been prouder to have once served within your ranks and never been prouder that the United States is the host country for the United Nations.

Forty-five years ago, while the fires of an epic war still raged across two oceans and two continents, a small group of men and women began a search for hope amid the ruins. And they gathered in San Francisco, stepping back from the haze and horror, to try to shape a new structure that might support an ancient dream. Intensely idealistic and yet tempered by war, they sought to build a new kind of bridge: a bridge between nations, a bridge that might help carry humankind from its darkest hour to its brightest day.

The founding of the United Nations embodied our deepest hopes for a peaceful world, and during the past year, we've come closer than ever before to realizing those hopes. We've seen a century sundered by barbed threats and barbed wire give way to a new era of peace and competition and freedom.

The Revolution of '89 swept the world almost with a life of its own, carried by a new breeze of freedom. It transformed the political climate from Central Europe to Central America and touched almost every corner of the globe. That breeze has been sustained by a now almost universal recognition of a simple, fundamental truth: The human spirit cannot be locked up forever. The truth is, people everywhere are motivated in much the same ways. And people everywhere want much the same things: the chance to live a life of purpose; the chance to choose a life in which they and their children can learn and grow healthy, worship freely, and prosper through the work of their hands and their hearts and their minds. We're not talking about the power of nations but the power of individuals, the power to choose, the power to risk, the power to succeed.

This is a new and different world. Not since 1945 have we seen the real possibility of using the United Nations as it was designed: as a center for international collective security.

The changes in the Soviet Union have been critical to the emergence of a stronger United Nations. The U.S.-Soviet relationship is finally beyond containment and confrontation, and now we seek to fulfill the promise of mutually shared understanding. The long twilight struggle that for 45 years has divided Europe, our two nations, and much of the world has come to an end.

Much has changed over the last 2 years. The Soviet Union has taken many dramatic and important steps to participate fully in the community of nations. And when the Soviet Union agreed with so many of us here in the United Nations to condemn the aggression of Iraq, there could be no doubt—no doubt then—that we had, indeed, put four decades of history behind us.

We are hopeful that the machinery of the United Nations will no longer be frozen by the divisions that plagued us during the cold war, that at last—long last—we can build new bridges and tear down old walls, that at long last we will be able to build a new world based on an event for which we have all hoped: an end to the cold war.

Two days from now, the world will be watching when the cold war is formally buried in Berlin. And in this time of testing, a fundamental question must be asked, a question not for any one nation but for the United Nations. And the question is this: Can we work together in a new partnership of nations? Can the collective strength of the world community, expressed by the United Nations, unite to deter and defeat aggression? Because the cold war's battle of ideas is not the last epic battle of this century.

Two months ago, in the waning weeks of one of history's most hopeful summers, the vast, still beauty of the peaceful Kuwaiti desert was fouled by the stench of diesel and the roar of steel tanks. Once again the sound of distant thunder echoed across a cloudless sky, and once again the world awoke to face the guns of August.

But this time, the world was ready. The United Nations Security Council's resolute response to Iraq's unprovoked aggression has been without precedent. Since the invasion on August 2d, the Council has passed eight major resolutions setting the terms for a solution to the crisis.

The Iraqi regime has yet to face the facts, but as I said last month, the annexation of Kuwait will not be permitted to stand. And this is not simply the view of the United States; it is the view of every Kuwaiti, the Arab League, the United Nations. Iraq's leaders should listen: It is Iraq against the world.

Let me take this opportunity to make the policy of my government clear. The United States supports the use of sanctions to compel Iraq's leaders to withdraw immediately and without condition from Kuwait. We also support the provision of medicine and food for humanitarian purposes, so long as distribution can be properly monitored. Our quarrel is not with the people of Iraq. We do not wish for them to suffer. The world's quarrel is with the dictator who ordered that invasion.

Along with others, we have dispatched military forces to the region to enforce sanctions, to deter and, if need be, defend against further aggression. And we seek no advantage for ourselves, nor do we seek to maintain our military forces in Saudi Arabia for 1 day longer than is necessary. U.S. forces were sent at the request of the Saudi Government, and the American people and this President want every single American soldier brought home as soon as this mission is completed.

Let me also emphasize that all of us here at the U.N. hope that military force will never be used. We seek a peaceful outcome, a diplomatic outcome. And one more thing: In the aftermath of Iraq's unconditional departure from Kuwait, I truly believe there may be opportunities for Iraq and Kuwait to settle their differences permanently, for the states of the Gulf themselves to build new arrangements for stability, and for all the states and the peoples of the region to settle the conflicts that divide the Arabs from Israel.

But the world's key task—now, first and

always—must be to demonstrate that aggression will not be tolerated or rewarded. Through the U.N. Security Council, Iraq has been fairly judged by a jury of its peers, the very nations of the Earth. Today the regime stands isolated and out of step with the times, separated from the civilized world not by space but by centuries.

Iraq's unprovoked aggression is a throwback to another era, a dark relic from a dark time. It has plundered Kuwait. It has terrorized innocent civilians. It has held even diplomats hostage. Iraq and its leaders must be held liable for these crimes of abuse and destruction. But this outrageous disregard for basic human rights does not come as a total surprise. Thousands of Iraqis have been executed on political and religious grounds, and even more through a genocidal poison gas war waged against Iraq's own Kurdish villagers.

As a world community, we must act not only to deter the use of inhumane weapons like mustard and nerve gas but to eliminate the weapons entirely. And that is why, 1 year ago, I came to the General Assembly with new proposals to banish these terrible weapons from the face of the Earth. I promised that the United States would destroy over 98 percent of its stockpile in the first 8 years of a chemical weapons ban treaty, and 100 percent—all of them—in 10 years, if all nations with chemical capabilities, chemical weapons, signed the treaty. We've stood by those promises. In June the United States and the Soviet Union signed a landmark agreement to halt production and to destroy the vast majority of our stockpiles. Today U.S. chemical weapons are being destroyed.

But time is running out. This isn't merely a bilateral concern. The Gulf crisis proves how important it is to act together, and to act now, to conclude an absolute, worldwide ban on these weapons. We must also redouble our efforts to stem the spread of nuclear weapons, biological weapons, and the ballistic missiles that can rain destruction upon distant peoples.

The United Nations can help bring about a new day, a day when these kinds of terrible weapons and the terrible despots who would use them are both a thing of the past. It is in our hands to leave these dark machines behind, in the Dark Ages where they belong, and to press forward to cap a historic movement towards a new world order and a long era of peace.

We have a vision of a new partnership of nations that transcends the Cold War: a partnership based on consultation, cooperation, and collective action, especially through international and regional organizations; a partnership united by principle and the rule of law and supported by an equitable sharing of both cost and commitment; a partnership whose goals are to increase democracy, increase prosperity, increase the peace, and reduce arms.

And as we look to the future, the calendar offers up a convenient milestone, a signpost, by which to measure our progress as a community of nations. The year 2000 marks a turning point, beginning not only the turn of the decade, not only the turn of the century, but also the turn of the millennium. And 10 years from now, as the 55th session of the General Assembly begins, you will again find many of us in this hall, hair a bit more gray perhaps, maybe a little less spring in our walk; but you will not find us with any less hope or idealism or any less confidence in the ultimate triumph of mankind.

I see a world of open borders, open trade and, most importantly, open minds; a world that celebrates the common heritage that belongs to all the world's people, taking pride not just in hometown or homeland but in humanity itself. I see a world touched by a spirit like that of the Olympics, based not on competition that's driven by fear but sought out of joy and exhilaration and a true quest for excellence. And I see a world where democracy continues to win new friends and convert old foes and where the Americas—North, Central, and South—can provide a model for the future of all humankind: the world's first completely democratic hemisphere. And I see a world building on the emerging new model of European unity, not just Europe but the whole world whole and free.

This is precisely why the present aggression in the Gulf is a menace not only to one region's security but to the entire world's vision of our future. It threatens to turn the dream of a new international order into a grim nightmare of anarchy in which the law of the jungle supplants the law of nations. And that's why the United Nations reacted with such historic unity and resolve. And that's why this challenge is a test that we cannot afford to fail. I am confident we will prevail. Success, too, will have lasting consequences: reinforcing civilized standards of international conduct, setting a new precedent in international cooperation, brightening the prospects for our vision of the future.

There are 10 more years until this century is out, 10 more years to put the struggles of the 20th century permanently behind us, 10 more years to help launch a new partnership of nations. And throughout those 10 years, and beginning now, the United Nations has a new and vital role in building towards that partnership. Last year's General Assembly showed how we can make greater progress toward a more pragmatic and successful United Nations. And for the first time, the U.N. Security Council is beginning to work as it was designed to work. And now is the time to set aside old and counterproductive debates and procedures and controversies and resolutions. It's time to replace polemic attacks with pragmatic action.

And we've shown that the U.N. can count on the collective strength of the international community. We've shown that the U.N. can rise to the challenge of aggression just as its founders hoped that it would. And now is the time of testing. And we must also show that the United Nations is the place to build international support and consensus for meeting the other challenges we face.

The world remains a dangerous place; and our security and well-being often depends, in part, on events occurring far away. We need serious international cooperative efforts to make headway on the threats to the environment, on terrorism, on managing the debt burden, on fighting the scourge of international drug trafficking, and on refugees, and peacekeeping efforts around the world.

But the world also remains a hopeful place. Calls for democracy and human rights are being reborn everywhere, and these calls are an expression of support for the values enshrined in the United Nations Charter. They encourage our hopes for a more stable, more peaceful, more prosperous world.

Free elections are the foundation of democratic government and can produce dramatic successes, as we have seen in Namibia and Nicaragua. And the time has come to structure the U.N. role in such efforts more formally. And so, today I propose that the U.N. establish a Special Coordinator for Electoral Assistance, to be assisted by a U.N. Electoral Commission comprised of distinguished experts from around the world.

As with free elections, we also believe that universal U.N. membership for all states is central to the future of this organization and to this new partnership we've discussed. In support of this principle and in conjunction with U.N. efforts to reduce regional tensions, the United States fully supports U.N. membership for the Republic of Korea. We do so without prejudice to the ultimate objective of reunification of the Korean Peninsula and without opposition to simultaneous membership for the Democratic People's Republic of Korea.

Building on these and other initiatives, we must join together in a new compact—all of us—to bring the United Nations into the 21st century, and I call today for a major long-term effort to do so. We should build on the success—the admirable success—of our distinguished Secretary-General, my longtime friend and yours, my longtime colleague I might also say, Javier Perez de Cuellar. We should strive for greater effectiveness and efficiency of the United Nations.

The United States is committed to playing its part, helping to maintain global security, promoting democracy and prosperity. And my administration is fully committed to supporting the United Nations and to paying what we are obliged to pay by our commitment to the Charter. International peace and security, and international freedom and prosperity, require no less.

The world must know and understand: From this hour, from this day, from this hall, we step forth with a new sense of purpose, a new sense of possibilities. We stand together, prepared to swim upstream, to march uphill, to tackle the tough challenges as they come not only as the United Nations but as the nations of the world united.

And so, let it be said of the final decade of the 20th century: This was a time when humankind came into its own, when we emerged from the grit and the smoke of the industrial age to bring about a revolution of the spirit and the mind and began a journey into a new day, a new age, and a new partnership of nations.

The U.N. is now fulfilling its promise as the world's parliament of peace. And I congratulate you. I support you. And I wish you Godspeed in the challenges ahead.

Thank you very, very much.

Note: The President spoke at 11:44 a.m. in the General Assembly Hall at the United Nations.

Statement by Press Secretary Fitzwater on United States Emergency Military Assistance for Israel
October 1, 1990

On September 30, the President decided to provide two Patriot air defense fire units to Israel on an urgent basis under provisions of the law that allow for emergency military assistance from U.S. military stocks. The President's decision followed notification of Congress on September 29. The Patriot system will help Israel to upgrade its air defenses, including against an increased threat from ballistic missiles in the Iraqi inventory. In making this decision, the President reaffirmed his strong commitment to U.S.-Israel friendship and to the security of Israel.

Note: Presidential Determination No. 90–40 of September 30, which authorized the emergency military assistance, was printed in the "Federal Register" of October 24.

Statement by Press Secretary Fitzwater on the Release of Shiite Moslem Prisoners in Lebanon
October 1, 1990

We welcome the release of the 40 Shiite Moslem prisoners in Lebanon. It is consistent with our position that, for humanitarian reasons, all persons being detained without legal basis in the Middle East should be released immediately. Our particular concern is, quite naturally, the Americans being held hostage in Lebanon; and we call upon all parties to use their influence to effect their immediate and unconditional release. As President Bush has indicated, the release of American hostages would help improve our relations with countries contributing to that release.

Remarks on Signing a Resolution Providing Funding for Continued Government Operation and a Question-and-Answer Session With Reporters in New York, New York
October 1, 1990

The President. The bill that I'm signing here today will keep the Government operating through October 5th, pending passage by Congress of a budget resolution which reflects the summit agreement. It also provides the important supplemental funds for Operation Desert Shield.

This bill represents the first step in implementing the budget summit agreement. And now it's up to Congress. The budget agreement we've reached is a good package. This budget is the right package at the right time. It is important to our nation. And it represents our best chance to get the deficit under control.

To the American people, I would say this agreement is balanced, it is fair, and it is absolutely critical to our country that we get an agreement through the Congress. We cannot keep mortgaging the futures of our children and our grandchildren, and we will not.

To the Congress, I would say that this is a time for leadership. We must put aside partisanship for the sake of our nation. We must act now to solve this budget problem.

I would also say this to Congress: Many of us in the political leadership have spoken for years about the need to deal with the deficit. As is usually the case in politics, many different approaches have been urged. We now have a deficit reduction package. It is a good package. It is a compromise. Certainly, I didn't get everything I wanted, and the Democrat leadership didn't get everything they wanted. But like most compromises, it's certainly not going to satisfy everyone. But this is the time to move beyond these individual concerns and exercise leadership for the good of the country.

The deficit reduction package is a balanced package. It cuts spending. It provides incentives for jobs and economic growth. It cleans up the budget-process mess. And it raises needed revenues without raising personal tax rates. And most important, these deficit measures are real; they have real teeth. It's time to end the talk about the deficit. It is time for action on the deficit. And it's time—I think past time—to put the interest of the country first.

And so, I will now sign this joint resolution and keep things moving.

[*At this point, the President signed the resolution.*]

I'd be glad to take a couple of questions on this or any other subject before I go on—at the United Nations. It's been a busy one, and I'll be glad to take a few, and then have to go.

Federal Budget Agreement

Q. Is there a planned attack to sell those conservative Republicans, who are already saying they're not going to vote for this?

The President. Well, I want to sell the Democrats who are saying they won't vote for it, and I want to sell the Republicans who are saying they won't—absolutely. When I go back, I'll do my best. I'll take the case, as I'm doing to some degree here, to the American people. I've already been on the telephone. And I think back to what President Reagan had to do in the early eighties. And I heard the hue and cry from Democrats and Republicans, and I could understand it. I mean, if I were in the Congress, maybe I'd be screaming about something I wanted the most. But the time for this is passed. This is too serious now. And the leadership have worked hard. And so, you bet I'll be selling to everybody I can get to listen to me.

Q. But does it concern you, sir, that the loudest voices come from within your own party——

The President. I don't think——

Q. ——especially on the issue of taxes?

The President. I don't think it's the loudest. Depends who you—I was watching on the tube last night, and I put down a few of the Democrats as unenthused. But look, expect that. What you've got to do is explain the country's at stake here, and that's what I plan to do.

Persian Gulf Crisis

Q. Mr. President, your speech today is being interpreted as having a little bit of a conciliatory tone. And you also brought in the Arab-Israeli conflict that would seem to be along Mitterrand's [President of France] pattern. Is there something new you were offering?

The President. No.

Q. Is there some sort of an olive branch in all of this that——

The President. No.

Q. What do you mean, no?

The President. I mean, no, there's no change in my position.

Q. But you did offer negotiations, and you seem to be holding out——

The President. Let me—I thought I might get this question, so I've underlined it in this yellow pen here. [*Laughter*] "In the aftermath of Iraq's unconditional departure from Kuwait, there may be opportunities." Now, unconditional is what the United Nations is calling for, and that's what the United States—so there's no flexibility here. And I was surprised when I heard that some were interpreting it as such.

We've got to keep together. The thing that I've garnered through many, many talks up here is almost that—well, it's totally solid support for the U.N. position and the U.S. position. So, there isn't flexibility. And I'm glad to get a chance to clear that up.

Q. But you don't think there's solid support for military action, do you?

The President. I don't know. As I've said, I want to see a peaceful resolution if at all possible. We'll cross that bridge when we get to it. But I have heard rather encouraging words on two points: one, that Saddam Hussein [President of Iraq] is beginning to understand that it is he against the world; and secondly, there's more optimism in various quarters that the sanctions are really beginning to bite hard.

So, both of those have been reinforced for me. And so, we'll just have to wait and see. But this was not designed to convey flexibility or shift in position.

Q. But, Mr. President, your words were

that after this unconditional withdrawal there may be opportunities for Iraq and Kuwait to settle their differences permanently. We were told, you were told last week by the Amir [Amir Jabir al-Ahmad al-Jabir Al Sabah of Kuwait] that Kuwait is being dismantled by Iraq.

The President. They are, and that's why they have to get out now.

Q. They're taking away everything that can be moved. Are you suggesting that perhaps Iraq can get these disputed islands if they pull out now?

The President. No.

Q. What are you suggesting?

The President. No, let me be very clear. I'm just suggesting that you've got to make whole Kuwait the way it was—and absolutely not that there can be any giving away by the United States or the United Nations of anything. The restoration of Kuwait, its leaders, is a terribly important part of this. They should go back there. And Iraq should unilaterally and unconditionally withdraw.

Q. And if I could follow: You mentioned today the eight major resolutions. Do you want a ninth major resolution clearly stating that the U.N. multilateral force is authorized to go in and do combat with Iraq?

The President. We have not been pressing for that at this point. You heard Prime Minister Thatcher [of the United Kingdom] on that, I guess, this morning. But we're still pursuing the road that let's get these sanctions to work, let's get the forces in place. And let's hope that the little optimism I'm picking up around here about the sanctions will prevail.

There's also another theme that this man, if you look at his record, will do a 180. You look at the history with Iran, and he's done a 180-degree turn and done exactly what he said he wouldn't do. So, some people are basing their hopes on that, some of the diplomats I've talked to.

Q. Mr. President, you don't come to the United Nations very often, and certainly, you were trying to emphasize something here that you haven't said in the past. I wondered what it might have been, if anything.

The President. Now, Saul [Saul Friedman, Newsday], why would you say I would want to emphasize something? I want to keep emphasizing what I have been saying in the past, and that is that the United Nations has done a superb job. These resolutions are unprecedented. We have the broadest possible support to stand up against this aggression, and we want to see the unilateral withdrawal, unconditional withdrawal from Kuwait. It's a question of emphasis, but I'm not trying to convey something new in that. I know you're a foreign affairs—you love the nuance. [*Laughter*] But seriously, you're reading too much into this. There's not any nuance to this that you think you might be missing.

Q. Do you agree with Mrs. Thatcher, who also said on television this morning that the United States or the allies would not need any further permission from the United Nations in the use of military force?

The President. Well, we felt that under article 51 that authorization was there. And I think she was talking about 51. However, you may remember that we waited until we got a resolution before interdicting ships that more directly confirmed the right to do that. But, no, I agree with her on that point.

Q. Mr. President, given the brutality of the Iraqi occupation and their efforts to develop the germ warfare capability, how long can we afford to wait for Saddam to do a 180?

The President. Well, it's a very good question to which I don't have the answer; I don't know the answer to that question. And it goes back to this question about what the Amir told me about the dismantling, rape, pillage, and plunder of that country. So, I can't put a timeframe on that for you. I wish I had a clearer answer for the American people. I don't.

Q. Mr. President, do you believe that Saddam Hussein is capable of a 180 at this point? And if he does pull a 180, doesn't that still leave him as an irritant in the region, a major military threat?

The President. The answer is: I'm just taking on board what I've been told by people that have studied it carefully—that he is capable of that. I should tell you this, though. That's the one hand. On the other hand, there are those who say that if he withdraws from Kuwait that is the end of

him because of having had to withdraw from Iran. So, you have to weigh the two.

But I don't have to act on these opinions. I have to just keep this consensus together; keep getting the sanctions as tight as possible; and hope that that makes him understand that, alone against the rest of the world, he has to do what the United Nations called for.

What was the second part, Mick [Jim Miklaszewski, NBC News]?

Q. Well, doesn't that leave him—a 180—wouldn't that leave him an irritant, a potential military threat in the area?

The President. You mean just if he went back to the status quo ante? Yes, it would be a problem, and it would have to be resolved in some way.

Q. If I may follow up——

The President. That's the third followup. Go ahead. What's the second followup?

Q. Was that your reference to chemical weapons in today's speech? In other words, after Iraq pulls out of Kuwait, if that happens, was that what you were referring to in terms of eliminating chemical weapons in the region?

The President. No, I wasn't specifically referring to that. But this is a very troublesome capability he has, and it does worry us. But I think there would be great unease about the simple status quo ante. But we've been talking here about the dismantling of Kuwait. I'm sure there would be claims in that regard. The international community would have to have something to say about that. I'm sure that neighbors would want to know that there was not a risk of another reckless invasion of this nature. And then that would lead you to say, Well, what kind of security provisions would be put into effect?

So, it's not a clear withdrawal to the status quo ante that would solve everything, but it is what's called for under these resolutions.

Federal Budget Agreement

Q. This budget agreement that you have, Mr. President, is it one that's likely to look better in '92 when you're running for reelection than it does to Republicans now?

The President. I think what matters at

this juncture is not who's running in the fall of '90 and not who's running in the fall in '92 but what's best for the country in the fall of 1990, what is essential for the country. And I think getting this deficit down with a realistic program is essential for our country.

I've said—and I'm not looking at this in a political way—we've got to get it done. I've had to compromise; the Democrats have had to compromise. And I hope that other voices who are troubled by one aspect or another of this or something that wasn't in it that they wanted would also compromise. Every once in a while, you come to a position, come to a time, when you have to do that to get something done.

I don't control the Congress. I don't control either House of the Congress as the President. My party doesn't control it. But I was elected to govern. And I can stand; I can veto; I can do a lot of things. But the time, in my view, has come, because of the seriousness of the deficit, to lay aside getting it done exactly the way I want; to make a compromise, which I think is a good one, to preserve many of the things I want; and to go forward and get it put into effect.

So, it's in that spirit and not in the spirit of elections. And I would refer those on either side who worry about their election to look at the debate around the two tax increases that President Reagan had to go forward with. And there wasn't a political fallout because I think the country understands when the President concludes that a deal is necessary; they're inclined to give him the benefit of the doubt.

Q. What then does it say about campaign promises, such as "cut capital gains tax" and "read my lips"?

The President. It says you need more Republicans, and then we'll do it exactly my way. But we don't have that right now, so you have to do the best you can, Charles [Charles Bierbauer, Cable News Network]. It's funny, but that's the way it works. I'll be glad to take my case out there. I'll say: If you want all these things, give me some more Republicans. That comes after we get a deal. And then we go right through the election cycle again. I've tried that.

We don't control the Congress. They're not going to do it exactly my way. So, I've

had to compromise, and the Republican leadership has compromised, and so have the Democrat leaders. So, I'm not about to start flailing away on that. I want this deal through. It would be unproductive to start unleashing a fall of '90 campaign during these critical days here.

Q. You haven't broken your promises?

The President. I'm not interested in talking about that. I'm interested in governing. But let me tell you this. I expect others will be talking about that. Fine. Take the heat, take the hit. There have been changed times. It didn't work the way I want. I don't have the horses in the Congress to do it exactly my way. So, you have to govern, you have to lead, and that's what I'm trying to do.

Persian Gulf Crisis

Q. You say you are not pressing for an additional sanction now for military action. Is it because you don't have support for that kind——

The President. No, because we're still giving sanctions the time to work, the time to be effective. And I'm a little encouraged that perhaps they are having a strong effect. But so, we're not pressing for that right now.

Federal Budget Agreement

Q. When you made the big concessions, sir, especially on taxes and on capital gains, how motivated were you at that point about the fear of recession?

The President. I've been concerned about the fear of a recession. I'm concerned about a slow economy. And I believe a good budget agreement will result in lower interest rates. I would look to the Federal Reserve to lower the rates. I hope they would once they see that a sound budget agreement has been put into effect. And I would hope they think this is a sound budget agreement. So, I am concerned, but I don't want to talk ourselves into recession. The President has to be very careful in commenting on prices, on markets. But I believe—and I must say the initial market response just today—I don't know how it's going to play out over the days—has been rather encouraging, saying, well, markets are looking for a deal.

Q. I'm going to ask you a long question so the camera has time to put in fresh videotape because I think we've run out.

The President. You want me to come back?

Soviet-U.S. Relations

Q. No, no. I wanted to ask you: Mr. Shevardnadze [Soviet Foreign Minister] came downstairs sounding very encouraged about both CFE and the possibility of a START agreement by the end of the year. He even said it's at the point of talking about a time for you coming to Moscow. Do you think that you could finish this year with both those treaties signed, and will you go to Moscow by the end of the year?

The President. I don't think by the end of the year. However, I told Mr. Gorbachev in Helsinki and repeated it here to Shevardnadze that I'm looking forward to it. That would be a return summit, you see, as opposed to the Helsinki, which we tried to point out was an exceptional meeting.

And he was very confident that CFE would be ready for a Paris agreement late this fall. And he did mention to me that he hoped that the START agreement would be done and that we could have an early—I thought he said early next year. Maybe he said end of this year. But in any event, I'd like to see it finished—the agreement—before the first of the year. I'm a little more optimistic about CFE getting done than START right now. But I came out of the meeting encouraged also and asking for flexibility so that these negotiators can polish off the remaining differences.

German Reunification

Q. Are you sorry you missed the celebration in Berlin?

The President. Yes. I can understand the excitement. I can understand the pride that the Germans feel in a unified Germany. We've tried to be an integral part. I remember there were some skeptics around when we talked about a unified Germany being full members of NATO. And I remember some of the difficulties about whether this could even happen before there were agreements signed with Poland on the borders. There have been a lot of problems along the way. So, I think our

diplomacy has been helpful. But I think much more important, obviously, is the dream fulfilled, the dream of the German people of having one country again. And it is very, very moving.

And I can say this—not in a big "I" sense or an egotistical sense—but every German that I encounter along the way, in the field of diplomacy or their leaders from business or whatever it is, express their gratitude to the American people. It is a very moving thing. And it's not just for recent events; it's for the way that we help Germany and have stood with Germany and understand Germany and recognize that a new and unified Germany has an enormously constructive role to play in the world. It is very emotional. So, yes, I wish I could have been a part there, but I just couldn't be there—been on the road quite a bit.

Oil Prices

Q. Mr. President, several of the leaders that——

Mr. Fitzwater. Last question.

Q. ——you met with came out of your parlor here saying that you had expressed concern to them that speculators were driving up the price of oil. Do you have a plan to combat or bring that speculation down or end it?

The President. Well, I'd like to see market forces determine it rather than excessive speculation. And I'm confident in the long run that supply and demand will set the price, not speculations in some futures market. I have no plan to intervene in the markets or anything of that nature.

Q. What do you think is a reasonable price for a barrel of oil—$25?

The President. It's not for me to decide. It's for the market to set the price. But the best analysis I've seen on supply and demand points out that on this day there are no shortages. There are no shortages. Certainly there is no fear of shortage that should drive the market in the $40 range. Somebody told me it came off about $3 today. And we have the Strategic Petroleum Reserve that could be drawn down. Other countries are endeavoring to step up their oil production, including the Saudis.

I talked at length to some in our own hemisphere about increased production—

1339

Mexico and Venezuela. So, I would caution the high-flying speculator: Hey, be careful. Because most of the estimates that I've seen on what supply and demand would do to the market would have the market price significantly below current October future levels—significantly below it. So, it's not for me to try to price oil. I've got enough problems out here.

Q. Where would you be comfortable with it?

The President. Let the market set it. But I'm just telling you that the analysts all say that the supply and demand situation cannot support a price where the October futures have been selling.

Q. But perhaps the market fears war.

The President. I think you're right, Saul. I think there is speculative fever. And anytime there's some bellicose statement it will slip back up. I can understand that. That's a different point than the one I'm making.

Q. Any less bellicose today than usual?

The President. I'm the same gentler and kinder self. What are you talking about?

Q. How can you stop it then? How can you stop this?

Q. But your budget assumes $21, Mr. President. Is that where you think it should be?

Q. How can you stop it?

The President. Talk sense out there. What?

Q. Twenty-one dollars is what your budget assumes. Is that where you think it should be?

The President. What budget? This agreement?

Q. Mr. Darman's [Director of the Office of Management and Budget] budget.

Q. Projection.

Q. It's based on a $21-a-barrel oil price.

The President. He's entitled to his opinion. It's like telling what level the stock market ought to be or how much the dollar ought to be worth against the yen or the deutsche mark. I've got enough difficulties without getting into that business, and I shouldn't do it. I've already done that. You heard me out there. You didn't make the trip to the middle west the other day. [*Laughter*] You missed the substance and reported only on the politics. [*Laughter*]

Q. I'm sorry about that. [*Laughter*]

Persian Gulf Crisis

Q. Are you more optimistic, sir, after the 21 or 22 one-on-ones [bilateral meetings held in New York City] or whatever it is?

The President. On the Middle East?

Q. On the Persian Gulf.

The President. Well, what I'm optimistic about is that there isn't one single breach in the armor. I didn't hear one single voice. And I haven't listened to all the speeches, but some respected diplomats over there tell me nobody rose to the podium to defend Saddam Hussein. They said they've never seen it quite this united on any question of any kind. And let's hope then that he'll understand that he stands alone. And let's hope that that, coupled with the economic sanctions, will cause him to do what he's done in the past: do a 180 and get out.

Federal Budget Agreement

Q. Speaking of a breach, Mr. President, what about Newt [Representative Newt Gingrich]?

The President. I just told you, I understand the Republicans that don't like certain aspects of this deal. I understand Democrats that don't like certain aspects of this deal. And I'm going to be encouraging all those Republicans and all those Democrats to vote for it. And I don't like some aspects of it, and I don't expect George Mitchell and Tom Foley do, or Bob Dole and Bob Michel. Every once in a while in your country's history you've got to lay aside what you feel the most strongly about and come together. And I'm going to urge as many Democrats and Republicans as possible to come together.

Q. But wouldn't you at least expect one of the Republican budget negotiators to support the package?

The President. I'd expect all Republicans and all Democrats to support me, but that's not the way it works in real life.

I'd like to raffle—[*laughter*]. No——

Q. What happened to Gingrich and [Senator] Packwood?

Bill-Signing Pen

The President. Helen [Helen Thomas, United Press International], you be the start here. Are you the senior representative of the press corps?

Q. Yes.

The President. You get the pen that shows the signing of—would you like this memorialized——

Q. Great. A 5-day pen. [*Laughter*]

The President. Thank you. This counts on Marlin's books as a full press conference, the equivalent of an East Room press conference. He said if I made it for 10 minutes that we'd rack it up as the 71st. As long as we've survived for 25, it's the equivalent of one of those that we used to do with everybody all dressed up, you know. [*Laughter*]

Trip to Saudi Arabia

Q. Are you going to Saudi Arabia?

The President. Hey, listen, I'm tired. I've got to go. What?

Q. Are you going to Saudi Arabia for Thanksgiving?

The President. Not set, not settled. I've been reading in the paper that I'm going.

Address to the Nation

Q. ——about the budget? Do you think that's needed?

The President. Not set yet, but if it would help, I would be glad to do it. In fact, some of the Democrats raised that and others too, some of the Republicans. I'm going to get home now, and then we'll try to figure out what's the best way to get this message across.

Note: The President spoke at 2:07 p.m. at the Waldorf-Astoria Hotel. In his remarks, he referred to George J. Mitchell, Senate majority leader; Thomas S. Foley, Speaker of the House of Representatives; Robert Dole, Senate minority leader; and Robert H. Michel, Republican leader in the House of Representatives. Marlin Fitzwater is Press Secretary to the President. H.J. Res. 655, approved October 1, was assigned Public Law No. 101–403.

Remarks at the Ministerial Meeting in New York, New York, of the Conference on Security and Cooperation in Europe
October 1, 1990

On behalf of the American people, it is my great pleasure to welcome all of you to the United States. It's especially fitting that this meeting of the Conference on Security and Cooperation in Europe, the first ever on American soil, comes at this time of momentous change. For just as Europe enters a new and promising era, so, too, do America's relations with Europe.

We Americans are bound to Europe by a shared heritage and history and the common bonds of culture. Through the Atlantic alliance and the broader partnership that bind our two continents and peoples together, we have brought about the end of Europe's division and set our eyes on a new Europe, whole and free. Together we can forge a new transatlantic partnership at the CSCE, a commonwealth of free nations that spans the oceans between us.

In this past year, we would all agree, we've witnessed a world of change. Mo-

ments ago, right here in this building, the Foreign Ministers of France and Great Britain, the Soviet Union and the United States signed the document suspending all remaining Four Power rights and responsibilities in Germany, effective at the moment of German unification. I must say that just before I left from the hotel I saw that on television. And for me, and I think for many of the American people, it was a very moving moment, because with those final strokes of the pen really ends an era of discord and division. The way is now open for a united, sovereign, and democratic Germany. We rejoice with the German people that their nation is unified once more, and we will soon welcome a united Germany into the CSCE's community of states.

Germany's long-awaited day of celebration is the culmination of a year of change that, indeed, transformed a continent. This transformation is testimony to the power of the principles in the founding charter of the CSCE, the Helsinki Final Act. There, in the human rights and fundamental freedoms set down in Helsinki 15 years ago, we find the cause and catalyst of what I refer to as the Revolution of '89.

In the darkest days of dictatorship, those principles blazed forth a bright star, inspiring ordinary people to extraordinary acts. Think of Walesa, the father of Solidarity; of Sakharov and his unflinching humanity in the face of repression; of Havel, Mazowiecki, and Antall, not so very long ago political prisoners, now President and Prime Ministers of three of the world's newest democracies, and Zhelev, another ex-political prisoner, now President of Bulgaria. Think of all the millions of ordinary men and women at long last free to speak their minds, free to live, work, and worship as they wish.

CSCE shares in this monumental triumph of the human spirit. Our challenge now is to keep pace with the tremendous political transformations that have changed the face of Europe, to create a CSCE that consolidates these great gains for freedom and bring East and West together—in eastern and central Europe, a CSCE capable of helping hard-won democratic principles take root and draw strength; a CSCE that can help secure a firm foundation for freedom in the new Europe now emerging.

In July, at the London summit, the leaders of the Atlantic alliance put forward a series of proposals aimed at strengthening the CSCE and channeling its energies in new directions. We urge the member nations of the CSCE: to create a Center for Prevention of Conflict, to build on the CSCE's success in establishing confidence- and security-building measures that have done so much to reduce the risk of war by accident or miscalculation and to conciliate disputes; to establish a small permanent secretariat to serve the CSCE, one that could support an accelerated schedule of the CSCE consultations and review conferences; to create a CSCE elections office to foster free and fair elections, the fundamental democratic principle from which all others follow. And on behalf of the United States, let me say that I hope that these new institutions can be situated wherever possible in the new democracies of central and eastern Europe.

And finally, at the London summit, we issued an invitation to member nations to convene an assembly of Europe, a parliament where the growing family of democracies, old and new, can chart a common course towards this new Europe, whole and free.

Today, as we prepare for a summit of the CSCE nations, I urge the ministers to make this meeting a milestone in the history of the CSCE. And to this end, let me mention one more area where rapid progress is critical: the ongoing negotiations of conventional forces in Europe.

An agreement to reduce conventional forces remains the cornerstone of a new security architecture for Europe. And for that reason, the United States believes a conventional arms accord is an essential prerequisite to a CSCE summit. And today I now call on the negotiators now working in Vienna to redouble their efforts in the weeks ahead. And I can pledge you the United States will cooperate in every way possible. We must resolve outstanding issues and reach agreement so that a summit can be held this year.

Fifteen years ago, in a Europe divided East from West, the CSCE offered a vision of a Europe united, whole and free. Today, with that new Europe within our reach, the CSCE remains central to all that Europe can become.

So, once again, welcome to the United States. And may the spirit that has carried Europe forward guide your discussions, and may you meet with every success. Thank you all very, very much.

Note: President Bush spoke at 3:07 p.m. at the Jacob Javits Center. He referred to President Václav Havel of Czechoslovakia, Prime Minister Tadeusz Mazowiecki of Poland, and Prime Minister Jozsef Antall of Hungary. A tape was not available for verification of the content of these remarks. Following his remarks, President Bush returned to Washington, DC.

Statement by Press Secretary Fitzwater on the President's Meeting With General Mikhail A. Moiseyev, Chief of the General Staff of the Soviet Union
October 2, 1990

The President met with Soviet Chief of Staff Gen. Mikhail Moiseyev for approximately one-half hour this morning in the Oval Office. General Moiseyev is participating in the military contacts program with the Department of Defense and is in the United States at the invitation of the Chairman of the Joint Chiefs of Staff, Gen. Colin Powell. He arrived in Washington on September 30 and will remain in the United States through October 6, during which time he will also visit New York, Detroit, San Francisco, San Diego, and Colorado. The President noted the need for continued progress on both CFE and START negotiations.

The President noted his very fruitful meeting with President Gorbachev in Helsinki and requested that General Moiseyev pass on his regards to President Gorbachev. The President stated that the status of U.S.-Soviet relations is excellent, and he appreciates the Soviet cooperation in the Persian Gulf.

Statement by Press Secretary Fitzwater on President Bush's Meeting With President Patricio Aylwin Azocar of Chile
October 2, 1990

President Bush met in the Oval Office today with Chilean President Patricio Aylwin. This was the first meeting between the two leaders. President Bush told President Aylwin that he is looking forward to his visit to Chile during his South America trip later this fall. He expressed the United States strong support for Chile's return to democracy and our commitment to close and cooperative relations with Chile.

The President informed President Aylwin that the Overseas Private Investment Corporation (OPIC) can now resume its investment guarantee programs in Chile. This OPIC activity had been revoked under the previous government because of concerns over worker rights. Following a review process, it has been determined that these abuses have been eliminated.

President Bush also congratulated President Aylwin on the completion of a bilateral framework agreement on trade and investment between our two countries. This is the third such agreement since the Enterprise for the Americas initiative was announced on June 27. Other agreements have been signed with Colombia and Ecuador. We welcome the opportunity to strengthen this aspect of our economic cooperation with Chile.

The two Presidents reviewed other economic issues in the relationship, such as GSP, and the Letelier case. President Bush told President Aylwin that we look forward to the completion of Chilean legislative action which will insure that justice is done.

Remarks to Business Leaders on the Federal Budget Agreement
October 2, 1990

Thank you very, very much for coming over. I met this morning with the Republican Members of the Congress to underscore the necessity for quick and decisive action on the budget agreement through the bipartisan leadership in both Houses. And I again am calling on the Congress to act, and act soon, on this vital legislation. Tonight I'm going to take the case for this budget agreement to the American people on a national television address at 9 p.m.

But to you all I want to say I appreciate the past support. I know that there are provisions in this that cause different people different problems, and I understand all that. And I will say, in achieving this agreement, everybody has had to compromise. I did it because the country, frankly, is at stake here. And every once in a while in one's Presidency, I think it dawns on the incumbent of the Oval Office that you're not going to get it exactly your own way. In this case, my party does not control both Houses of the Congress. But as I look at the ever-increasing deficits, I think it is time we do something and do something serious.

And with that philosophy has emerged this budget agreement. And I don't want to sound sanctimonious about this, but I was elected to govern. I was elected to make things happen. And we're trying to do that in the international scene, and where now it's time to come and do something on the domestic scene that will benefit all Americans.

I think—respecting the differences that do exist not only in this room but in the Congress—I think we all realize the time has come to get America's fiscal house in order. And I honestly believe—and this is what I came over to tell you—that this compromise is a major step towards this goal. By 1955 [1995] it will bring government spending as a percentage of gross national product to its lowest level since 1966.

And let me tell you what the budget agreement will do. Overview: The 5-year bipartisan budget compromise will boost our economic vitality in the long run. It will give small- and medium-sized business a shot in the arm and create jobs. It will reduce the deficit by $500 billion, the single biggest cut ever agreed to, and that is the prerequisite for bringing real interest rates down. I believe firmly that if we get this agreement through without watering it down that interest rates will come down.

The budget agreement raises the prospect of a long-term healthy economy. It raises the potential for growth. It raises America's ability to compete. But it does not raise personal income tax rates. I was able, with the help of the negotiators—or put it this way: They did all the heavy lifting on it but held the line on tax rates, which is something that I feel strongly about.

On the growth incentive side, the agreement includes incentives for oil and gas development. If there ever was a time when we needed to become less dependent on foreign oil, it's now, and I think these incentives can help in that direction. Incentives for the development of enterprise zones to create jobs and opportunity and, specifically, to keep small business competitive.

So, there are small business incentives that I'd like to ask you to look at very carefully: a 30-percent research and experimentation credit, tax indexing for individuals who buy stock in small corporations, a tax deduction for investment in small corporations, and an expanded ability for small businesses to expense certain scientific equipment.

On the domestic cuts—and here I think everybody in this room, whether you agree with me or not, knows that I wanted to get a capital gains cut. I also wanted to hold the line on tax rates. We're half successful, but we have some incentives here that I think will accomplish some of what I had in mind when I spoke about the growth in jobs and opportunity that would come from capital gains. So, look hard at these incentives.

Domestic cuts: The agreement will cut the projected Federal deficit by half a trillion dollars, with nearly $120 billion in real and enforceable spending cuts on entitlement and mandatory programs. And I'll ask—John and the others here are well equipped to give you the details on this. But we feel these are real and enforceable spending cuts, and they do have teeth. For the first time, they will be guaranteed in law. No smoke or mirrors in this category here.

Now, let me just say, if we do not reform entitlements to bring their growth under control, as this agreement does, we'll never be able to solve the whole problem of the deficit. America's going to be unable to invest in the future because the entire budget would be gobbled up by entitlements and also interest on this ever-increasing debt.

On military cuts: Although the defense budget is cut by $67 billion over 3 years, and then more over 5, the Persian Gulf forces will still get the backing that they deserve to accomplish their mission. And frankly, I am one who happens to believe we need a strong defense and have always supported defense spending. I think everyone in this room is realistic in that defense was going to take a hit, but it comes out better than I thought it would. And of course, this is causing strains on some who disagree as to whether we ought to have a strong defense spending or not. But here's one where these negotiators have done an extraordinarily good job.

On budget reform: The budget discipline of Gramm-Rudman will be extended for 5 years, and the agreement includes substantial budget-process reform. Once again, I didn't get everything I wanted. I've gone around calling for a line-item veto. That one never got out of the chutes, frankly. But I still would like to have it. It's not part of it, but we do have some substantial budget-process reform.

Now, if Congress spends the money it doesn't have, then a minisequester will come into effect and will cut it for them. So, for the next 5 years, all discretionary spending by Congress is capped.

And for the first time, mandatory entitlements, which have been the biggest source of spending growth, will be subject to a sequester to keep their growth under control. New entitlements will be subject to a pay-as-you-go system; they can't grow without offsetting cuts or revenues to cover their cost.

The budget is tough; it really is. It is fair, and again, it really is. It is a solid package to boost economic growth and solve long-term problems without having the burden fall entirely on any one group. The time has come to move beyond the narrow interests and put the broad interests of the United States first.

Most importantly, this budget agreement is our last, best chance to get the Federal budget deficit under control. To all the people that disagree and the people on the sidelines that are rushing out and having their press conferences and the critics, let me say this: You can pick the package apart, but you cannot realistically put a better package together.

Again, the philosophy that I was elected on runs out of gas in terms of votes in the United States Congress. And I think everybody here—and I've had enormous support for the various men and women in this room, strong support, who support me on difficult calls on veto overrides. But to get something done, to have something positive happen and have it happen in anything like timely fashion, I will say once again, there's been some compromise here. But we've tried in many ways, through single pieces of legislation, to get some of my philosophical underpinning for the economy put into effect. And we've tried hard, with the help, as I say, of people here. And we've simply failed because the votes aren't there. But here's a package that I think preserves much of what I believe. I've had to give some. We've taken some. And I just came over to strongly urge your support.

I'm grateful to the Vice President for his advocacy of this program up on the Hill. He did a superb job yesterday. I want to give a vote of confidence to all sitting up at the head table here—the dais or whatever we call it—who worked so hard on this. But John Sununu and Nick Brady and Dick Darman spent endless hours, endless hours, trying to hammer out the best possible deal; and I think they've done exactly that.

So, it has my enthusiastic support. Again I would like those who have reservations to look hard at it, to study it, to consider the fact that alternatives have been tried and we weren't able to get them through. And then I would like to ask your strong support for this package. The country is at stake here, and we need you. We need you bad.

So, thank you all very much. And now for the experts. Thank you.

Note: The President spoke at 1:16 p.m. in Room 450 of the Old Executive Office Building. In his remarks, he referred to John H. Sununu, Chief of Staff to the President; Secretary of the Treasury Nicholas F. Brady; and Richard G. Darman, Director of the Office of Management and Budget.

Remarks at the Presentation Ceremony for the Presidential Awards for Excellence in Science and Mathematics Teaching
October 2, 1990

To our Secretary of Energy, Jim Watkins, delighted to see you sir; and Ted Sanders, the Under Secretary of Education; Fred Bernthal; Dr. Bill Phillips; and all of you here in the Rose Garden.

I am very pleased to have this opportunity to join you today and add my congratulations to those that you have already received. Presidential Awards for Excellence in Science and Math Teaching have been presented for the past 8 years to secondary schoolteachers, but this is the first year that elementary schoolteachers have also received these awards. So, you are the pioneers in what will be a continuing effort to honor the achievement of this nation's many outstanding schoolteachers.

You are a very select group—107 teachers from the more than 1½ million elementary school instructors in this country. For many students, you represent their very first exposure to science and math, which gives you a vital responsibility. Most kids who go on to become scientists or engineers first became interested in those subjects in elementary school or junior high. And most often, the reason they do is because they are exposed to a teacher like you—like each one of you—someone who can speak their language, communicate with them, spark their imagination, and evoke the sense of wonder that is inherent in science and math.

Kids are natural-born scientists, but too many of them lose interest when their only exposure to science is through long lists of facts. And you've discovered how to bring out the fun in science and math, and in so doing, you provide a model and an inspiration for elementary schoolteachers everywhere.

You're also helping to meet a crucial national need. We live in an increasingly complex and competitive world, and the link between science and technology and our standard of living is stronger today than ever before. At a time when our international position in certain key industries is being challenged, we face impending shortfalls of qualified scientists and engineers. The students who can fill those shortfalls are in the classrooms right now, and we must ensure that they are given the education and the encouragement that they need.

Just a little over a year ago, I met with the Nation's Governors at Charlottesville for the first education summit, a first step towards building a strong partnership among this administration, the Governors, educators, parents and, indeed, community leaders. And this historic event resulted in a sense of direction and national goals for individual and collective efforts to improve the quality of education for all Americans.

Well, three of those goals directly involve science and math. By the year 2000, American students must demonstrate competency in five critical subjects, including science and math, with their progress measured in grades 4 and 8 and 12. We must also make American students the first in the world in science and math by the year 2000. And we must ensure that every adult American must be able to read and have the skills, including technological skills, to compete in a global economy.

So, these are ambitious goals, but they are faithful to the ambitions of this country. And as a people, we've set tough goals before: to send men to the Moon or to serve the cause of freedom abroad. And we know that when the challenge is great, great things happen in America.

Already, a great many things are happening at the Federal, State, and local level. The Department of Energy and NASA are opening up their research labs to students and teachers so that they can experience cutting-edge science firsthand. And the Department of Education and the National Science Foundation are working together and with the States on strengthening research, assessment, and curricula. Equally exciting are things that are happening in the States themselves.

But achieving the goals that I announced last January will require that everyone get involved. That means parents; it means teachers, school administrators, businesses, and universities.

Parents really are especially important. And it is very difficult for you as teachers to go out and do your job if you don't get help from parents, and that's why we want to see parental empowerment in education. We must make American education the best it can be, and that takes two things: greater parental involvement and, in my view, greater choice in education.

Reading about your accomplishments makes me confident that we will succeed. The letters of recommendation that helped bring you to Washington are really spectac-

ular; and they give ample testimony to your ingenuity, your determination and, indeed, enthusiasm. In one letter, the parents of a kid named Woody write: "When we used to ask Woody what happened in school, he would tell us about recess. And now he tells us about science." You know, that really is a wonderful, wonderful statement about Woody's teacher, it seems to me. Another one, another letter, writes of a teacher who "studies with the mind of a scholar; perceives through the eyes of a child; and communicates with the voice of an understanding, compassionate, and energetic motivator." And all of the letters are unanimous about one thing: the enthusiasm that each one of you bring to the classroom, an enthusiasm that goes beyond the classroom, that touches everyone that you know.

You are truly remarkable people, and you're able to take children and lift them up and inspire them and broaden their horizons and then aim them off in new directions. So, the country owes you an immense debt of gratitude. But your real rewards can't be printed on some scroll, one piece of paper. The real rewards are the students who will remember you and what you have done for them for the rest of their lives.

Thank you all very much for being here today, and God bless each and every one of you for your wonderful commitment to the young people of this country. Thank you.

Note: The President spoke at 1:35 p.m. in the Rose Garden at the White House. In his remarks, he referred to Frederick M. Bernthal, Acting Director of the National Science Foundation, and William D. Phillips, Associate Director of the Office of Science and Technology Policy.

Statement by Press Secretary Fitzwater on the President's Meeting With Jonas Savimbi of the National Union for the Total Independence of Angola
October 2, 1990

The President met for 30 minutes today with UNITA leader Jonas Savimbi. The President pledged our continued support

for Dr. Savimbi and his movement. The President believes that the steadfastness of that support is a key factor in pushing the current negotiations to a successful conclusion. The President expressed the hope that these negotiations will lead to peace and national reconciliation in Angola. The President pledged that we are prepared to do what we can to promote this goal.

Address to the German People on the Reunification of Germany
October 2, 1990

It is with great pleasure that I congratulate Chancellor Kohl and the German people at this historic moment. And it is my distinct honor to address the people of the united Germany.

In Berlin and Bonn, from Leipzig in the east to western towns along the Rhine, people are celebrating the day that all of Germany has been waiting for, for 45 long years. For the world, those 45 years were a time of tension and turmoil. For your nation, fate was particularly cruel. For 45 years, at the heart of a divided continent stood a divided Germany, on the fault line of the East-West conflict, one people split between two worlds.

No more. Today begins a new chapter in the history of your nation. Forty-five years of conflict and confrontation between East and West are now behind us. At long last the day has come: Germany is united; Germany is fully free.

The United States is proud to have built with you the foundations of freedom; proud to have been a steady partner in the quest for one Germany, whole and free. America is proud to count itself among the friends and allies of free Germany, now and in the future. Our peoples are united by the common bonds of culture, by a shared heritage in history. Never before have these common bonds been more evident than in this past year as we worked in common cause toward the goal of German unity. Today, together, we share the fruits of our friendship.

In this past year, we've witnessed a world of change for the United States, for the united Germany, for the Atlantic alliance of which we are a part. Even as Germany celebrates this new beginning, there is no doubt that the future holds new challenges, new responsibilities. I'm certain that our two nations will meet these challenges, as we have in the past, united by a common love of freedom. Together, building on the values we share, we will be partners in leadership.

This day, so full of meaning for Germany, is full of meaning for the world. Meters away from the walls of the Reichstadt, scene of the first session of the newly united German Parliament, stood the Berlin Wall, the stark and searing symbol of conflict and cold war. For years, free men and women everywhere dreamed of the day the Berlin Wall would cease to exist, when a world without the Wall would mean a Germany made whole once more—when Germany, united and sovereign, would contribute in full measure as a force for peace and stability in world affairs.

Today the Wall lies in ruins, and our eyes open on a new world of hope. Now Germany is once more united. Now the Wall no longer divides a nation and a world in two. The last remnants of the Wall remain there at the heart of a free Berlin, a ragged monument in brick and barbed wire, proof that no wall is ever strong enough to strangle the human spirit, that no wall can ever crush a nation's soul.

Today the German nation enters a new era; an era, in the words of your national anthem, of "unity and justice and freedom." At this moment of celebration, as we look forward with you to a future of hope and promise, let me say, on behalf of all Americans, may God bless the people of Germany.

Note: The President's remarks were videotaped in the Oval Office at the White House for broadcast by German television.

Address to the Nation on the Federal Budget Agreement
October 2, 1990

Tonight I want to talk to you about a problem that has lingered and dogged and vexed this country for far too long: the Federal budget deficit. Thomas Paine said many years ago, "These are the times that try men's souls." As we speak, our nation is standing together against Saddam Hussein's aggression. But here at home there's another threat, a cancer gnawing away at our nation's health. That cancer is the budget deficit.

Year after year, it mortgages the future of our children. No family, no nation can continue to do business the way the Federal Government has been operating and survive. When you get a bill, that bill must be paid. And when you write a check, you're supposed to have money in the bank. But if you don't obey these simple rules of common sense, there's a price to pay.

But for too long, the Nation's business in Washington has been conducted as if these basic rules did not apply. Well, these rules do apply. And if we fail to act, next year alone we will face a Federal budget deficit of more than $300 billion, a deficit that could weaken our economy further and cost us thousands of precious jobs. If what goes up must come down, then the way down could be very hard.

But it doesn't have to be that way. We can do something. In fact, we have started to do something. But we must act this week, when Congress will hold the first of two crucial up-or-down votes. These votes will be on a deficit reduction agreement worked out between the administration and the bipartisan leaders of Congress. This budget agreement is the result of 8 months of blood, sweat, and fears—fears of the economic chaos that would follow if we fail to reduce the deficit.

Of course, I cannot claim it's the best deficit reduction plan possible. It's not. Any one of us alone might have written a better plan. But it is the best agreement that can be legislated now. It is the biggest deficit reduction agreement ever—half a trillion dollars. It's the toughest deficit reduction package ever, with new enforcement rules to make sure that what we fix now stays fixed. And it has the largest spending savings ever—more than $300 billion. For the first time, a Republican President and leaders of a Democratic Congress have agreed to real cuts that will be enforced by law, not promises—no smoke, no mirrors, no magic act, but real and lasting spending cuts.

This agreement will also raise revenue. I'm not, and I know you're not, a fan of tax increases. But if there have to be tax measures, they should allow the economy to grow, they should not turn us back to higher income tax rates, and they should be fair. Everyone who can should contribute something, and no one should have to contribute beyond their fair share. Our bipartisan agreement meets these tests. And through specific new incentives, it will help create more jobs.

It's a little-known fact, but America's best job creators and greatest innovators tend to be our smaller companies. So, our budget plan will give small and medium-size companies a needed shot in the arm. Just as important, I am convinced that this agreement will help lower interest rates. And lower interest rates mean savings for consumers, lower mortgage payments for new homeowners, and more investment to produce more jobs. And that's what this agreement will do.

Now, let me tell you what this agreement will not do. It will not raise income tax rates, personal or corporate. It will not mess with Social Security in any way. It will not put America's national security at risk. And most of all, it will not let our economy slip out of control.

Clearly, each and every one of us can find fault with something in this agreement. In fact, that is a burden that any truly fair solution must carry. Any workable solution must be judged as a whole, not piece by piece. Those who dislike one part or another may pick our agreement apart. But if they do, believe me, the political reality is, no one can put a better one back together again. Everyone will bear a small burden. But if we succeed, every American will have a large burden lifted. If we fail to enact this agreement, our economy will falter, markets may tumble, and recession will follow.

In just a moment, the Democratic majority leader, Senator Mitchell, will offer what is known as the Democratic response, often a rebuttal. But not tonight. Tonight the Democratic and Republican leadership and I all speak with one voice in support of this agreement. Tonight we ask you to help us move this agreement forward. The congressional leadership and I both have a job to do in getting it enacted. And tonight I ask for your help.

First, I ask you to understand how important—and for some, how difficult—this vote is for your Congressmen and Senators. Many worry about your reaction to one part or another. But I know you know the importance of the whole. And so, second, I ask you to take this initiative: Tell your Congressmen and Senators you support this deficit reduction agreement. If they are Republicans, urge them to stand with the President. Urge them to do what the bipartisan leadership has done: come together in the spirit of compromise to solve this national problem. If they're Democrats, urge them to stand with their congressional lead-ers. Ask them to fight for the future of your kids by supporting this budget agreement.

Now is the time for you, the American people, to have a real impact. Your Senators and Congressmen need to know that you want this deficit brought down, that the time for politics and posturing is over, and the time to come together is now.

This deficit reduction agreement is tough, and so are the times. The agreement is fair, and so is the American spirit. The agreement is bipartisan, and so is the vote. The agreement is real, and so is this crisis.

This is the first time in my Presidency that I've made an appeal like this to you, the American people. With your help, we can at last put this budget crisis behind us and face the other challenges that lie ahead. If we do, the long-term result will be a healthier nation and something more: We will have once again put ourselves on the path of economic growth, and we will have demonstrated that no challenge is greater than the determination of the American people.

Thank you. God bless you, and good night.

Note: The President spoke at 9 p.m. from the Oval Office at the White House. In his address, he referred to President Saddam Hussein of Iraq. The address was broadcast live on nationwide radio and television.

Remarks and a Question-and-Answer Session With Regional Newspaper Editors
October 3, 1990

The President. Well, thank you all very much, and welcome to the White House. I've asked Dick Darman and Secretary Brady to be with us, though I know they've responded to many of your questions. And I want to take this opportunity to thank them and also Governor Sununu. These were our three top negotiators. They lived through every agonizing minute of the discussions that led up to an agreement that I am strongly recommending to this country.

And so, last night you heard me suggest that passing a bipartisan budget agreement is absolutely essential for this country. We have a lot of people telling us: If you could only get this provision or that provision it would be a better deal. And I would readily concede that, from my standpoint, the things I believe, I could craft a better deal. But I'm convinced that at this juncture I can't craft a better deal that can have the approval of both sides of the aisle in the Congress. And there comes a time when you have to simply make tough decisions, give a little to get what is best for the country. And what is best for the country now is a solid budget agreement. And it's a good deal. I think it's balanced. I think it's fair. I think the burden is spread, and the agreement delivers the biggest deficit cuts ever. We're talking about, in 5 years, half a trillion dollars.

I am convinced—and some of this is highly technical—but that the enforcement provisions are good; and Dick Darman, I'm sure, has discussed that with you, and Nick Brady as well. But there was quite a bit of concession in order to get enforcement provision. The entitlement savings—120 billion between now and '95—they're real. I know plenty of people are going to say: Well, we've heard all this before. I know the American people are going to say: Well, we heard this before in other deals. But again, these are the toughest enforcement mechanisms ever—some of the most skeptical Members of Congress I think recognizing that now. So, for every new program or added expenditure, the enforcement says you've got to make up for it somewhere else. And if at some time in the future the old bad habits get the upper hand and the urge to overspend returns, there's a surprise in store: automatic cuts kick in to bring the budget back into line.

So, everyone knows that this is a product of 8 long months of difficult negotiation and compromise. And no one was in a position to dictate the terms, and no one got everything that he or she wanted. But the plan again that was hammered out in my view is balanced; it is fair; and frankly, it is our last, best chance to try to get this Federal deficit under control. I said last night to the cynics and the critics—and there are plenty of them around—you can pick this package apart, but you cannot put a better package together that can pass both Houses in the Congress.

Tomorrow, Congress meets. So, today I strongly urge and call upon the Congress, both House and Senate, to cast their vote for this plan and to prove to the American people that we can solve problems, that we can go out and get something done and put this nation back on the path to long-term economic growth.

So, with no further ado, I'll be glad to take a few questions. This is going to be difficult.

Federal Budget Agreement

Q. Mr. President, Larry Lipman, of the Palm Beach Post. You say that this package is balanced and it's fair, yet half of the entitlement comes from cuts in Medicare. How can you say that that is fair to the elderly?

The President. A lot of it comes in constraints on defense spending. We're trying to contain the growth of medical care. We do not feel that these cuts are onerous to the elderly. I would ask them to look at options, look at what did not happen. The biggest part of the expenditures in the Federal budget are due to entitlements, generally. You have Social Security. And we did not mess with Social Security; we protected Social Security. Some of it is what is being done, and I think that's fair, and some of it is what didn't happen, and we tried to be very fair there. But to get the deficit down, you have to deal with where the major growth in spending is; it's just that clear, unless they want to support extraordinarily higher income taxes. Another thing that's not in this budget is increasing income tax rates.

Q. I'm Tom Smith, from the Bonneville News. You just stated a second ago that this is the last and best effort to get the deficit under control. The emphasis so far has been on this end of the 5-year package. Let me ask about the other end. Will there be a pay-as-you-go budget format for the Government at that time? And if Americans are asked to bite the bullet now to see this package pass, what benefits will they enjoy at the end of the 5-year period?

The President. The major benefit will be a more vigorous economy. Major benefit is, I think, short-run, staving off economic catastrophe. The Secretary of Treasury pointed out to us yesterday that $8 billion failed to come into the markets from abroad on financing this incredible debt that is mortgaging the future of our kids. So, we think we've got that now moving in the right direction, and therein lies the benefits: a vigorous economy.

You know, even after TEFRA [Tax Equity and Fiscal Reform Act]—which was a flawed deal because it had so much more on the revenue side and less on the spending side—even after that deal was passed, interest rates came down, short-run, real fast.

I'm inclined to feel that—just from a lot of talks up in New York recently, as well as my own conviction—that the people are looking at us and wondering: Can we get this deficit under control? And I think if we get it under control we send a signal to world markets that is very encouraging. And that stimulates the economic growth that is projected in these 5-year projections. And it's real, and it'll happen. But if we linger along and don't get a deal, I'll tell you, we are courting disaster in this country.

Q. What does deficit reduction under control mean? Does it mean——

The President. It means getting down to a balanced budget. That's what it means—longer run. And I think Nick can give—I don't know if you—how many years that takes, but that's what we're courting. We don't want to spend more than we take in. I tried to make that one clear last night.

Sarah [Sarah McClendon, McClendon News]?

Q. Thank you, sir.

The President. I'm in for trouble.

Q. It looks like with this great gasoline tax that you're going to have a total tax, ultimately, on a gallon of gas that's 21 cents?

The President. Sarah——

Q. That's going to keep a lot of men who have to drive a long distance to jobs—that's going to make a lot of people be out of jobs, doesn't it?

The President. I don't think it'll be out of jobs. What will get them out of jobs is if we don't get this deficit under control and this economy goes into recession. That's what'll get them out of jobs. I don't think that that particular proposed tax is overly onerous. You're talking to a guy that doesn't want to do anything about taxes at all. I mean, I can't get enthusiastic about a tax on the American people, nor can I get enthusiastic about the relentless spending that is going on. We are not dealing with the best of all worlds. We're trying to solve an enormous problem. So, I think the tax is fair. I think when you look around at world prices on gasoline—I mean, we're still substantially below world markets. So, I would simply say that it is a tax that everybody has to pick up, as I said last night, some share of the burden. And that's where it hits. And I hope that also in this case we can have these incentives passed that will make us less dependent on foreign oil. I keep making that pitch.

Energy Policy

Q. Is that your energy policy?

The President. No, we've got an overall energy policy. I might make a pitch for part of it now. I think, you know, we've gotten to a phase in nuclear policy that it's almost impossible to go forward with that clean fuel. We're talking about alternate—more use of natural gas. We're talking about clean coal technology. We're talking about all kinds of planks that fit into a national energy policy. But, yes, that's part of it—is less dependence on foreign oil by more hydrocarbon production in this country.

Q. Mr. President, I'm David Lightman, from the Hartford Courant. Do you agree that the 2-cent tax on petroleum products should also be a tax on home heating oil?

The President. Well, I'd like to ask Dick to tell you about the debate on home heating oil because—[*laughter*]—it's highly technical. And nobody is without pain here. Nothing is without pain. You're talking about a small incident here. You're talking about, as Sarah was saying, those who drive the most—and that's out West—picking up what some would say is an unfair share of the burden. There's nothing that is without pain. I'll tell you what is without pain. I mean, I'll tell you what does concern me is a lot of people around this country say: No drilling; we don't want to have any drilling here. Don't want to have any refineries. Don't want to go with nuclear power. But please send me plenty of energy. It doesn't work that way anymore. So, now we've got to have a policy that expands the uses of alternate sources of energy, and thus hopefully will bring the price down.

Incidentally, I—you know, this gets you off into the Middle East, but some are pointing out to the fact that we've got some dangers there, and I think they are correct.

We're not there simply because of the oil fields in Saudi Arabia and the GCC countries. We're there for a fundamental principle about aggression. But the world is fairly small; and our fortunes, when we are becoming 50 percent dependent on other countries, are linked to our success in that part of the world, which will impact directly on fuel—home heating oil or on the price of gasoline.

Q. Mr. President——

The President. One, two.

Economic Policy

Q. I'm James Brosnan, with the Memphis Commercial Appeal. You claim that your package will spur economic development in the poorest regions of the country: the inner cities and the rural areas, like the Mississippi Delta. And if not, would you favor targeting assistance to some of those areas?

The President. I favor bringing interest rates down, which will indeed help those areas. And that is the biggest thing you can do is to have an economy where people are willing to start new businesses, to employ people, to keep economic growth going, and to keep this country—falling into recession. That policy alone will benefit the people who are hardest hit in this country.

Presidential Crisis

Q. Mr. President, Tom Brazaitis, from the Cleveland Plain Dealer. This morning's New York Times has a headline on the front page that says: "A Presidency on the Line." And with an oil crisis and a hostage crisis and a budget crisis, some people are making comparisons to former President Carter. How do you respond to that? *[Laughter]*

The President. Look, nobody said it would be easy. *[Laughter]* And we're getting good support for our policy in the Middle East. Incidentally, I was—overwhelming—the support at the United Nations when I was up there was just so apparent and very, very good. But every once in a while, the going gets a little tough. And I'm pleased that we have been able to hammer out a bipartisan agreement to get over an enormous problem that has been growing for years, and that is the Government simply

spending more than it takes in and the ever-increasing deficits. And so, put it this way: I don't feel embattled at all. I don't feel embattled.

Q. Is your Presidency on the line?

The President. I don't know what that means. Please refine it, and I'll——

Q. It means it's a make-or-break period in your tenure as President.

The President. Put it this way: It's, I guess, about as complicated as a period as we've had since I've been President. But I'm not looking at it in terms of reelection or—I mean, I think there were some connotations in one story I saw—maybe it wasn't the same one—about all of that. The American people are entitled to something a little bit more broader gauged than that. I haven't thought about it in those terms.

But I look back over my shoulder at some of the challenges we've had and some of the comments that we're not doing something properly. I try not to sound egotistical, but we've been right on German unification. And yet, I remember many people saying: It's impossible; the Soviets aren't going to permit a unified Germany to be in NATO. It isn't going to happen. You can't have a unified Germany before you have two peace treaties with Poland.

The reason this is on my mind is I just called—in the middle of a hard-sell session to Members of the Congress—Helmut Kohl [Chancellor of Germany]. I was very moved when I saw what happened at the Brandenburg Gate and the feeling there, and I just felt I had to call him on this very special day to congratulate him. But that brought back to mind some—somewhat—I wouldn't say difficult time in my Presidency, but questioning whether our objective and the German objective could be fulfilled. So, there are difficult times along the way.

We've got two big things coming together now. One is the deficit, and one is this crisis halfway around the world. But I'm telling you honestly, I don't look at it in terms of whether it's good for a Bush Presidency or popular politically. And that's why last night I tried to give cover to Members of Congress, Democrat and Republican, and say: You don't have to support crossing every t and dotting every i, but say the

President encouraged you to do it. Blame me. Because I know what's best for our country, but I don't suspect it's politically popular.

Federal Budget Agreement

Q. Mr. President, I'm Bobbie Ulrich, the Oregonian. Will future campaign visits by yourself and members of your Cabinet be affected by how Republican Members in the House or Senate vote on this package?

The President. I'm going to use every means at my disposal to convince Republicans and Democrats that they ought to vote for this. But I can't tell you that I will change the rhetorical output or the number of campaign stops if somebody is not with me on a specific issue.

We've been able to hold the line on vetoes. The only way we've been able to make good things happen is because of vetoing lousy legislation. Sometimes we lose Republican votes on vetoes that are very important to me, and I get the same question. But I'm approaching this with no rancor in my heart, but trying at this juncture to use every weapon in my arsenal to get people to do it our way. But I'm not going to go into that or suggest that I would do that.

I must say, sometimes you neglect your friends, and I don't want to do that anymore. But I don't have any plans to do what your question properly asks about.

Q. Mr. President, Alice Lipowich, from the Bridgeport Post. For the Northeast region, which is one of the first regions to be experiencing a real estate slump and the beginnings of a recession, how can you explain that the combination of defense cuts, higher taxes on gasoline, and the home heating oil tax won't hurt that economy more?

The President. I'm not sure there won't be any adverse effects by one provision or another. I am totally sure that failure to get a deficit deal will adversely affect every region of the country.

Q. Mr. President, this is the biggest solution to the debt problems in the 10 years that we've been living with it, but the problem is growing even faster than the solutions. Could you explain why you think that this first $40 billion in the first year will

avert a financial catastrophe, as you saw it?

The President. Because I think what it'll do is send a signal to the international markets that this is serious. And you say for the first time I'd be glad to—I think, given the enforcement provisions, I accept your hypothesis. I think what it'll do is send a signal not only to the international financial markets but to the domestic financial markets that this is serious business and that $500 billion of reductions over this period of 5 years is the medicine that a sluggish economy needs to go forward to have more growth.

I go back and—we did some research—and you go back and look at the political rhetoric on both sides of the aisle at the time of the TEFRA, which was in the Reagan-Bush administration. That was not a very popular piece of legislation. It didn't have the enforcement provisions here. The spending cuts were not solidified. And yet on that one, right after TEFRA was passed the interest rates started down, and within 4 months they were down by about 3 points. Admittedly, they were reasonably high because, you remember, that period was a recession period. But we're in a sluggish economy—I don't want to say recession here—and I think the best answer is this kind of formulation where each Congressman has to give a little bit. Nobody gets it just the way he wants or campaigned; certainly, that's true for a President. But the best answer to these regional questions—I mean, to your question—is the fact that the world markets will see that we're serious about the deficit, and thus the economies will respond.

Let him finish. He has a follow-on.

Q. Many people in the markets were hoping for a sequester as opposed to this smaller package. Could you explain why the sequester was not preferable since it was so much larger?

The President. I don't think anybody—I don't know who is hoping—you mean for a lasting sequester? I can't think of anyone in his right mind that would want to see a lasting sequester of $90 billion in 1 year. The American people would properly be up in arms.

Now, if this thing bogs down and we have

to enforce the law of the land, which I swore to do, we have to revert to sequester. And it would be extraordinarily painful. So, I honestly—I'm not being argumentative—I never heard anyone suggest that a sequester for a year was a remedy that this country could sustain for a long period of time.

Crime

Q. On another regional question, you've been to New York a number of times and suggested that the city ought to gets its crime problem under control. The Governor [Mario Cuomo], the mayor [David Dinkins] continue to argue that by limiting the deductibility of State and local taxes you make it tough for them to put cops on the street and that the Feds are talking out of their mouth but not willing to come with any money. Could you comment on that notion—this part of the package?

The President. Yes. What I want is the support from those politicians up there for a crime bill. That's what I want, and that's the comment I'd make. I went up there to New York a while back, and one very prominent politician there jumped all over me for suggesting that we needed to support the police more. Now, I understand that there's quite a bit more interest in support for that.

My overall response would be, Please—Republican or Democrat in New York and all the rest of the States—help us get our anticrime package through, which is provided for in terms of its spending levels. So, again, nobody wants to pay any taxes. Everybody can say if the money goes to a tax, whether it's for gasoline or for whatever deduction it might be, that money won't be there to fight crime or it won't be there to clean up the environment or it won't be there to educate our kids. So, I understand that, but I just don't happen to agree with it.

Now, let me do this—because I do have a signing ceremony over there—let me take three more. I don't know how to be fair about this. Way in the back. We haven't worked the back here.

Federal Budget Agreement

Q. Mr. President, John E. Mulligan, from the Providence Journal. You say that you

use words like "catastrophe" that need to be averted here. But yet you compare this issue to vetoes that you've sustained, and you say: Well, I won't withhold my visits from people running for election this year. Are you giving a free ride to the Claudine Schneiders, the Tom Taukes, the Lynn Martins—a free no vote on this?

The President. Look, I've got to understand—and I said this last night—I've got to understand that there is a lack of enthusiasm on Democrats and Republicans for certain provisions of this, and I have to be realistic. If we had—let me make a partisan statement—if we had control of both Houses of the United States Congress, there would be things in this package that are extraordinarily different than what we see now.

I have to understand the passions of people standing out there for election. I will continue to urge every single Republican, in office and out, to support this package. But I can't bring myself to be recriminatory. I think we've got enough credibility that we can get this thing passed. It isn't easy. But if I might use this opportunity—your having raised the question—I wish all of them would support me strongly and lay aside some of the passions that one or the other of them have on a specific issue. That probably isn't going to happen, if I believe what I'm hearing on the television. So, now what I've got to do is get 50.1 percent, and then we're home.

Yeah, on the aisle back here, yes, sir; and then one over here. Persistence pays up.

Q. Mr. President, John Nestor, with Newslink. Why do you suppose this package is so unpopular? If that vote was held today, who would win, and can you turn it around?

The President. The American people would win if we pass it. It is tough, and the reason is because there's a lot of people that have long been advocating specific things that they're not going to get out of this package. You're looking at one of them. But I think that's where the difficulty stems.

I mean, there are broad philosophical differences. Some want to raise income tax rates and increase spending. Dick Darman and Nick Brady can tell you they fended off in the negotiations some significant increases in domestic spending. Others, on the other hand, want to have certain bigger tax cuts and want to curtail more spending. Most know that the biggest part of the budget increases come from COLA's, entitlements. But entitlement freezes or entitlement cuts on Social Security, for example, aren't in there because it's politically impossible to get those things through. So, we've protected the senior citizens in this regard.

So, I think what's happening is we have people who have been out front advocating certain positions—coming out of the left, coming out of the right, coming out of the broad center. And I'm having to say to them: Now, look, lay aside that passion for that specific issue or that specific spending program or that specific approach, and put the national interest first. And I can do that; I know I can do it with conviction. I hope I can do it persuasively, because I feel that the best antidote for all the problems is an economy that grows with lower interest rates and more jobs.

So, that's the argument I'm making to those on the left and those on the right and those on the center who, for constituent reasons, have extraordinarily difficult problems. And I'm saying to a Democrat that's openminded: Blame the President. Say I rallied to support the President. He was elected, and I don't like this, but I'm going to support him. To a Republican, I'd say the same thing. I happen to like it because I think it's a good deal, but you're hitting the right notes here because individuals have made commitments on one specific or another. And so, I'm asking them: Look, please accept the view that this is serious business. We've got to get this deficit down. We've got to move now credibly to get it down, and this in spite of your differences with this part or another, or my differences with this part or another—the overall good things outweigh the negative. And besides, the country has got to be governed. We have to move.

Last one.

Q. Mr. President, Roger Renningen, of the Small Newspaper Group of Illinois. Agriculture subsidies have gone from 26 billion in '85 down to more than—they've been cut in more than half now. Your budget package calls for $13 billion in cuts over the next 5 years. On top of that, agriculture will be dealing with the gas tax and other energy taxes. How can that be fair?

The President. It is fair because if we're correct—and I'm happy to say the ag economy for the most part has increased and farmers' income is at a—I don't know about an all-time high, but a significantly good level—we're talking about $13 billion of program over 5 years. You've got a $5½ trillion economy. That means that—you put it in percentage of the total economy—it isn't that high. And I believe if we are successful in our trade round—and we're fighting like mad to do it—that alone offsets in one fell swoop all the programs you possibly have.

So, I don't think it's burdensome. And I think people ought to look carefully at the details. And again, any time a subsidy or a support program is cut, I can understand people being critical. But I think they also know that an economy that is in recession, for example, would wipe out instantly or offset instantly the individual amounts of money that one gets from program A, B, C.

And it isn't just agriculture. It isn't just agriculture. It's in some of the entitlements areas as well. So, I'd ask the farmers: Look at what we're trying to do. Look at the success of the market-oriented approach we took to agriculture. Look at how—where agriculture—the per capita income to farmers stands. And help us preserve the kind of markets that guarantee continued prosperity to the farmer. So, that's the approach.

Hey, listen, I really have to go. We got German Unification Day across the way.

Voter Initiatives

Q. Mr. President, what do you think of all the voter initiatives in California and Colorado?

The President. Let them worry about that. [*Laughter*] I've got one right here I can worry about.

Thank you very much.

Note: The President spoke at 10:31 a.m. in Room 450 of the Old Executive Office Building. In his remarks, he referred to Richard G. Darman, Director of the Office of Management and Budget; Secretary of the Treasury Nicholas F. Brady; and John H. Sununu, Chief of Staff to the President.

Remarks on Signing the German-American Day Proclamation at a White House Ceremony Celebrating the Reunification of Germany
October 3, 1990

Thank you very, very much. And to Ambassador Ruhfus and Bruce Gelb, Elsbeth Seewald, Mr. Theune, Mr. Kruger, Senators Biden and Lugar and Pressler, and all of you, welcome to the White House.

I want to especially thank the German Army Band for their stirring rendition of our national anthem. Thank you, gentlemen. Thank you all. And I don't want to leave out the Marines, either. They're back here, and I thought they did a good job on the German national anthem.

And of course, I think we would all agree that this special event is all the richer for the participation of these kids here today. Thank you, guys. Both of you, men and women.

I just hung up from talking to Chancellor Helmut Kohl, and I told him that on this very special day the people of America send their heartiest congratulations to all Germans. Even as we meet here in our Rose Garden, Germans are celebrating their new unity from Berlin to Bonn, from Munich to Bremen, from the urban plazas of Leipzig to the golden vineyards along the hills of the Rhine.

And throughout this newly united nation, Germans celebrate a wonderful moment, delayed for almost half a century. And as part of that celebration, I've sent a video address to the people of Germany—sentiments that I'd like to just share with you here today briefly.

For 45 years, at the heart of a divided continent lived a divided people. A cruel wall of concrete literally cut off neighbor from neighbor, husband from wife, child from parent, a nation from itself. And on this fault line on the East-West conflict, one people split literally between two worlds. And as the German people suffered through this long ordeal, Americans were much more than sympathetic observers. After all, we are united by bonds of culture that reach back to the early colonial times, when Germans first became German-Americans.

And at the invitation of William Penn, Germans arrived in America to start a new life. And life was tough. Their first homes were caves hollowed out in the ground. And their determination, though, was harder. And they built a community—Germantown, Pennsylvania—inspiring millions more to follow and to continue to build.

German-Americans founded Hagerstown and Frederick, Maryland; Mecklenburg County, North Carolina; New Braunfels in my State, Texas; Frankfort, Kentucky; Berlin, Wisconsin; Anaheim, California. And they went on to help build some of the great cities of America: Philadelphia, Cincinnati, St. Louis, Milwaukee.

And the 60 million American sons and daughters of these German pioneers, like all Americans, felt a deep tie to both Germanys—one, a new democracy in the heart of Europe; the other struggling to be free.

And after all, our own country once lived under oppression. We remember John Peter Zenger, a young German-American newspaper editor who dared to challenge authority way back in 1734. And it was this same German immigrant who helped America established our most cherished tradition, freedom of speech.

And so, now, Ambassador Ruhfus, when East Germans were punished for dissent, we shared your spirit of defiance. And when German people were shot for attempting to flee to freedom, we shared your outrage. And when West German leaders dared to hope for a Germany united in freedom, we shared your dream.

And so, I guess what we're here to do is

to affirm that dreams sometimes do come true. Germany is united; Germany is free. This day was very clearly envisioned by Konrad Adenauer, who said that a solution to a divided Germany is only possible with the help of our friends. And over the decades, Adenauer's vision of a friendship between Germany and the United States, between Germany and the free peoples of the world, has indeed been realized. And this moment has come because Americans stood by the people of Berlin, from the daredevil pilots of the airlift to a young President who made his bold declaration before the Wall.

This moment has also come because of the determination of West German leaders to make Germany whole and free—not only Adenauer but Ernst Reuter and Ludwig Erhard, Willy Brandt, Helmut Schmidt and, of course, today's Chancellor Helmut Kohl. And this day has come because in 1989 the people of Germany stood their ground for freedom.

The United States is proud to have joined your countrymen in building the foundations of freedom, proud to have been a steady partner in your quest. America is also proud to count itself among the friends and allies of a free Germany now and forevermore.

This has been a year of change for America; for a united Germany; for the Atlantic alliance, of which we are both a part. And I'm certain that our two nations will meet the challenges of the future as we have in the past: as partners in leadership. This day, so meaningful for Germany, also inspires the world. Meters away from the walls of the Reichstadt, scene of the first session of the newly reunited German Parliament, stood the Berlin Wall. For years free men and women everywhere dreamed of the day that the Berlin Wall would cease to exist, when a world without the Wall would mean a Germany made whole once more, and when Germany, united and sovereign, would contribute in full measure as a force for peace and stability in world affairs.

Well, today it is the Wall that lies in ruins, and our eyes open on a new world of hope. The last remnants of the Wall remain there at the heart of a free Berlin, a ragged monument in brick and barbed wire; proof that no wall is ever strong enough to strangle the human spirit, that no wall can ever crush a nation's soul. And this is my message to the German people, and that is the heartfelt sentiment of the American people.

But before I sign this document proclaiming this very special German-American Day, let me just add one more thing. Last Sunday I attended the World Summit for Children up there at the United Nations. More than 70 heads of state, heads of government, and chiefs of state were there. And we discussed many critical issues: health care, education—many others. But we were profoundly touched by the knowledge that we must entrust the future of our nations to another generation. And looking at these kids here today, I believe I can see the future of the new Germany—a future of liberty and leadership, good will, and greatness.

So, once again, my heartfelt congratulations to the people of this united Germany. I know I confidently speak for all Americans. Thank you very much for coming.

Note: The President spoke at 11:09 a.m. in the Rose Garden at the White House. In his remarks, he referred to Ambassador Juergen Ruhfus of Germany; Bruce S. Gelb, Director of the U.S. Information Agency; Elsbeth Seewald, national president of the German-American National Congress; Adalbert Theune, national chairman of the Steuben Society of America; Helmut Kruger, president of the United German-American Committee of the U.S.A.; Chancellor Helmut Kohl of Germany; and Konrad Adenauer, former Chancellor of the Federal Republic of Germany. The proclamation is listed in Appendix E at the end of this volume.

Message to the Congress on the Continuation of Naval Petroleum Reserves Production
October 3, 1990

To the Congress of the United States:

In accordance with section 201(3) of the Naval Petroleum Reserves Production Act of 1976 (10 U.S.C. 7422(c)(2)), I wish to inform you of my decision to extend the period of maximum efficient rate production of the naval petroleum reserves for a period of 3 years from April 5, 1991, the expiration date of the currently authorized period of production.

I am transmitting herewith a copy of the report investigating the necessity of contin-ued production of the reserves as required by section 201(3)(c)(2)(B) of the Naval Petroleum Reserves Production Act of 1976. In light of the findings contained in that report, I hereby certify that continued production from the naval petroleum reserves is in the national interest.

GEORGE BUSH

The White House,
October 3, 1990.

Remarks on Signing the Proclamation Commemorating the Designation of Atlanta as Olympic Host City
October 3, 1990

Thank you all very, very much. First, look, it's a great pleasure to have you all here. I want to pay my respects to the Members of the Congress that are down to salute this event—Senators, Congressmen. And I can feel this Atlanta spirit that you've made famous.

I thought for a minute Maynard Jackson was taking over here. But nevertheless—[*laughter*]—I want to particularly welcome and pay my respects to Billy Payne; also to Maynard and Andy Young; the Governor of the great State, Governor Joe Frank Harris—these people who committed themselves, heart and soul, to bringing the games to Atlanta. And they'd kill me because it includes so many that are here today. I can't single you all out, though. The administration's own Georgia contingent is here—Secretary Lou Sullivan and Paul Coverdell, the head of the Peace Corps—along with, as I say, Members of the Congress. And I particularly salute the members of the Georgia delegation. And of course, Bob Helmick is with us, the president of the USOC [U.S. Olympic Committee]; Harvey Schiller, the executive director, to join in this national celebration.

Before going further, I'm pleased to have just signed, inside, H.R. 4962, which authorizes the minting of commemorative coins to support the American athletes training for the '92 Olympics. And this afternoon, our thoughts are not only on the '92 Olympics but the '96 as well. And it's an honor to be here today to celebrate the selection of the host city for the '96 summer Olympics, the next great international city, Atlanta, Georgia.

Nearly a century ago, in April of 1896, the King of Greece opened the first modern Olympic games in Athens, a revival of the ancient games that were held in honor of the Greek god Zeus. And the architect of those modern Olympic games was a Frenchman, Baron de Coubertin, who envisioned a new era in international sports. We all remember the baron—[*laughter*]. But anyway, here's what the guy said—[*laughter*]—"Let us export our oarsmen, our runners, our fencers into other lands. That is the true free trade of the future, and the day it is introduced into Europe, the cause of peace will have received a new and strong ally."

Well, as we approach the 100th anniversary of the first modern Olympics, we still dream of an open and peaceful world—open to the free trade of ideas, the free movement of peoples. And as the approach, we look forward to the free competition of athletes from the nations of the world under the Olympic motto, "Swifter, higher, stronger."

Those three words might as well have been the motto for the city of Atlanta, where the Old South has become the new South, with Atlantans leading the way. And they'll continue to lead the way because the Olympics will bring an estimated $3.5 billion into Georgia's economy in the next 6 years and create, predictably, 84,000 jobs. And that's not just good news for Atlanta; I believe that's good for all of America.

When Maynard Jackson heard the news, he said: "I feel like an exclamation point has just been placed on the life of our city. We won't let the world down." And I'm absolutely certain that he's right and that Atlanta will not let the world down. This great city of yours has already made history as the cradle of the American civil rights movement—home to Martin Luther King, Jr., Whitney Young, Maynard Jackson, Andy Young. And the 1996 games will give Atlanta the chance to make new history.

You know, Justice White, who we all know—a Supreme Court Justice—we all remember as a Heisman Trophy winner from Colorado University. He once said sports constantly makes demands on the participant for top performance; and they develop integrity, self-reliance, and initiative. And he said that in addition to teaching loyalty to yourself, sports teaches loyalty to your team. And that's what the Olympics are all about: initiative, self-reliance, integrity, and loyalty.

Those very same qualities are the ones that brought the Olympics to Atlanta. On top of your sports facilities and worldwide name recognition, you won the competition because Atlanta's had tremendous leadership and community which united behind it. The community spirit and enthusiasm shown by the people of Atlanta has been nothing short of remarkable, and you are America at her best.

And my thanks to all the volunteers, incidentally—the volunteers who made such a difference in this herculean effort. I congratulate each and every one of you. And I join all Americans in anticipation of those four magic words, "Let the games begin."

And now I will sign this proclamation proudly, designating today as Atlanta: Olympic Host City Day.

Thank you all, and God bless you. Thank you for being with us.

Note: The President spoke at 2:08 p.m. in the Rose Garden at the White House. In his opening remarks, he referred to Maynard Jackson, mayor of Atlanta; Billy Payne, organizer of the Olympic games; Andrew Young, former mayor of Atlanta; and Secretary of Health and Human Services Louis W. Sullivan. The proclamation is listed in Appendix E at the end of this volume.

Message to the Congress Reporting Budget Deferrals
October 4, 1990

To the Congress of the United States:

In accordance with the Impoundment Control Act of 1974, I herewith report seven deferrals of budget authority now totalling $1,120,243,863.

The deferrals affect the International Security Assistance program, as well as programs of the Departments of Agriculture, Defense, Health and Human Services, State, and Transportation. The details of the deferrals are contained in the attached report.

GEORGE BUSH

The White House,
October 4, 1990.

Note: The attachment detailing the defer-   *of October 11.*
rals was printed in the "Federal Register"

Nomination of Michael Joseph Bayer To Be Federal Inspector of the Alaska Natural Gas Transportation System
October 4, 1990

The President today announced his intention to nominate Michael Joseph Bayer, of Ohio, to be Federal Inspector of the Alaska Natural Gas Transportation System. He would succeed Theodore J. Garrish.

Since 1985 Mr. Bayer has served as manager of operations for the Panhandle Eastern Corp. in Washington, DC. Prior to this, he served as counselor for the U.S. Synthetic Fuels Corp. in Washington, DC, 1984–1985; consultant for Reagan-Bush 1984 campaign and the Republican National Committee, 1983–1984; Associate Deputy Secretary of Commerce, 1982–1983;

Deputy Assistant Secretary of Energy for Congressional Affairs, 1981–1982; executive assistant to the Honorable Clarence J. Brown, 1979–1981; and counsel to the Honorable Clarence J. Brown, 1977–1979.

Mr. Bayer graduated from Ohio State University (B.S., 1973; M.B.A., 1974) and Capital University School of Law (J.D., 1977). He was born August 2, 1947, in Dayton, OH. Mr. Bayer served in the U.S. Army, 1967–1970, and the Army National Guard, 1971 to present. He is married, has two children, and resides in Potomac, MD.

Remarks on the Conventional Armed Forces in Europe Negotiations
October 4, 1990

Yesterday in the Rose Garden, we celebrated the dawn of a new era for Germany and welcome the prospect of a Europe whole and free. But despite these dramatic political events, Europe is still the site of the greatest concentration of armed strength in the world. As Europe is transformed politically, we must also redraw the military map of the Continent and lift some of the shadows and fears that we and our allies have lived with for nearly half a century.

Today Secretary Baker will describe our latest efforts to ensure that the political transformation of Europe is matched in the military field in our negotiations to reduce and limit conventional armed forces in Europe, the so-called CFE talks.

Some of you here will remember when, in May of 1989 at the NATO summit, I proposed a series of initiatives to quicken the pace in CFE. I pledged then to devote our full effort to the speedy conclusion of a

CFE agreement, a treaty that would decisively improve the balance of military power on the Continent and back our hopes for lasting stability. We followed through on that commitment, and there is still—let's face it—more work to do. I want to remind you that CFE is not an accord between the United States and the Soviet Union; it'll be a treaty among 22 states, East and West. All must be satisfied with the treaty's provisions.

We've consulted repeatedly with our allies about our efforts, both before New York and then during the many talks up there. We believe our allies are pleased with the progress being made. Pending further consultation with our NATO partners, we have agreed in principle with the Soviet Union on resolution of all the major remaining issues in CFE and on many of the essential details as well. Along with our allies, we will continue to push to complete this treaty next month so that the way is clear for convening a CSCE summit in Paris.

In conclusion, I want to thank the Secretary of State and the people that have been working with him during these negotiations, and let me just say how pleased I am with the progress that we have achieved here. And I would like to now turn to Sec-retary Baker who has a statement, and then he'll be glad to take your questions.

Well done.

Note: The President spoke at 2:14 p.m. in the Briefing Room at the White House.

Appointment of Jeffrey R. Holmstead as an Associate Counsel to the President
October 5, 1990

The President today announced the appointment of Jeffrey R. Holmstead to be Associate Counsel to the President at the White House.

Since September 1989 Mr. Holmstead has served as Assistant Counsel to the President. Prior to this, he served as an associate with the law firm of Davis Polk and Wardwell, 1988–1989; a law clerk to the Honorable Douglas H. Ginsburg on the DC Circuit Court of Appeals, 1987–1988; and a summer associate with the law firm of Cravath, Swaine and Moore, 1987.

Mr. Holmstead graduated from Brigham Young University (B.A., 1984) and Yale Law School (J.D., 1987). He was born June 20, 1960, in American Fork, Utah. Mr. Holmstead is married, has one daughter, and resides in Washington, DC.

Remarks on Transmitting to the Congress Proposed Legislation on Trade Preference for Andean Countries
October 5, 1990

Let me greet Secretary Yeutter and Secretary Aronson and the Deputy USTR, Mr. Katz; and thank Ambassador Mosquera and Minister Crespo—Ambassador Crespo, Chargé Valdes of Peru, and Minister Zuquilanda of Ecuador for joining us here today.

This legislation we're sending up follows through on our Cartagena summit agreement to offer special measures of assistance to the Andean countries. And it provides trade preferences patterned along the lines of the extremely successful Caribbean Basin Initiative—CBI legislation. It's the second piece of legislation affecting our hemisphere that we're sending to Congress in a month. And as you will recall on September 14th, I sent to the Congress the Enterprise for the Americas Act of 1990. We're working hard for passage of that legislation in this session. And I know Secretary Brady and Under Secretary Mulford have been working very hard on that. And I'd like to see the Congress act favorably this session.

The idea behind this legislation is to give the countries an extra boost. It's designed to complement our proposals on trade, investment, and debt under the Enterprise for the Americas Initiative by providing a special 10-year access to the U.S. market. When this legislation comes into force along with the Enterprise legislation, our arsenal against drugs will expand to include the following: economic development assistance; police and military assistance for interdiction; investment in debt measures; and finally, trade preferences. And now, if I could invite the four distinguished Ambassadors and DCM to join me here, while I sign this transmittal to the Congress. Please, come forth.

[*At this point, the President signed the transmittal.*]

Thank you all very much for coming to the White House. Work lies ahead, but this is a beginning. Well, I guess we'll go back to work. Thank you all.

Note: The President spoke at 1:52 p.m. in the Roosevelt Room at the White House. In his remarks, he referred to Secretary of Ag- *riculture Clayton K. Yeutter; Bernard W. Aronson, Assistant Secretary of State for Inter-American Affairs; Julius L. Katz, Deputy U.S. Trade Representative; Ambassador Victor Mosquera of Colombia; Ambassador Jorge Crespo of Bolivia; Chargé d'Affaires Jorge Valdes of Peru; Minister Patricio Zuquilanda of Ecuador; Secretary of the Treasury Nicholas F. Brady; and Under Secretary of the Treasury David C. Mulford.*

Message to the Congress Transmitting Proposed Legislation on Trade Preference for Andean Countries
October 5, 1990

To the Congress of the United States:

I am pleased to transmit a legislative proposal entitled the "Andean Trade Preference Act of 1990" and a section-by-section analysis. The Andean nations are engaged in a serious struggle to combat illegal narcotics trafficking. It is incumbent upon the United States to aid them in their efforts to develop legitimate trading opportunities for their people. Their struggle is our struggle as well.

This proposal would implement my Andean Trade Preference Initiative of July 23, 1990. It would create a trade preference program patterned after the Caribbean Basin Initiative (CBI) for four Andean countries—Bolivia, Colombia, Ecuador, and Peru.

The Andean Trade Preference Initiative is intended to:

- fulfill, in part, my commitment at the Cartagena Summit to expand economic alternatives for these four Andean countries;
- complement the program of economic assistance, drug control, and the economic reforms agreed on with the Andean countries; and
- provide U.S. economic support to those Andean countries that are fighting to eliminate the production, processing, and shipment of drugs.

Just as CBI did for the countries of the Caribbean Basin, the Andean Trade Prefer- ence Act of 1990 will provide the authority to establish duty-free treatment of imports from the four Andean countries. These trade preferences would be granted for a period of 10 years.

The legislation outlines the rule-of-origin requirements for duty-free entry. Articles must be imported directly from a beneficiary country. These imports must consist of at least 35 percent value-added in one or more of the beneficiary countries, or one or more of the CBI countries, to which 15 percent of the total value from U.S.-made components may be applied. If foreign components are used to produce an article, the final product must be substantially transformed into a "new and different article of commerce" in one or more of the beneficiary countries. Products not qualifying under these three requirements will be dutiable.

Products that are particularly sensitive to import competition will still be dutiable. These products include textiles and apparel; footwear; canned tuna; petroleum and petroleum products; and watches and watch parts. Handbags, luggage, flat goods, work gloves, and leather wearing apparel also will continue to be dutiable, but will be subject to the same duty reduction program as has been made available to products from the Caribbean Basin. Duty-free entry of sugars, syrups, and molasses is provided consistent with the tariff-rate quotas on these products.

The proposal includes provisions for general import relief and emergency relief to safeguard domestic industries. Specific relief provisions are also included to safeguard domestic industries producing perishable products (i.e., live plants and fresh cut flowers, certain fresh or chilled vegetables, certain fresh fruit, and concentrated citrus fruit juice).

To assess the effects of the legislation on the U.S. economy and on particular industries producing like or directly competitive articles, the U.S. International Trade Commission would be required to issue reports to the Congress. The first such study will assess the effectiveness of the Act during its first 2 years, with annual reports thereafter. The proposal also requires the Secretary of Labor to report to the Congress annually on the impact of the Act on U.S. labor.

Enactment of the Andean Trade Preference Act of 1990 will permit the United States to support the efforts of the Andean countries to eliminate the production, processing, and shipment of illicit drugs. In conjunction with other Andean trade measures announced on July 23 and the Enterprise for the Americas Initiative announced on June 27, it will also increase the prospects for economic growth and prosperity in the Andean countries and throughout the hemisphere. I look forward to working closely with the Congress to enact this vital initiative.

GEORGE BUSH

The White House,
October 5, 1990.

Message to the House of Representatives Returning Without Approval the Textile, Apparel, and Footwear Trade Act of 1990
October 5, 1990

To the House of Representatives:

I am returning herewith without my approval H.R. 4328, the "Textile, Apparel, and Footwear Trade Act of 1990," which imposes import quotas on textiles, textile products, and nonrubber footwear. This highly protectionist bill would damage the national economy, increase already artificially high costs to consumers of several basic goods, and abrogate our international agreements. It would also reverse the tremendous progress we are making to generate a global economic renaissance.

Economic indicators illustrate that the problems this bill is intended to address do not exist. Despite assertions to the contrary, the textile industry has done well. Domestic production has been up slightly since 1987. Unemployment in major textile-producing States is currently lower than the national average. Since 1989, the textile industry has continued to operate at a higher rate of capacity than the average for all U.S. manufacturing industries.

All consumers, and particularly those at lower income levels, would be adversely affected if this legislation were to become law. The consumer costs of all restrictions on textile and apparel imports are conservatively estimated to increase to a total of $160 billion over the next 5 years—that amounts to an onerous $2,600 for a family of four over that same period. These costs would continue to rise annually. In essence, this legislation picks the pockets of U.S. consumers in order to subsidize the textile industry at a cost of $70,000 annually per job saved.

Furthermore, U.S. merchandise exports, which have increased by more than 9 percent in the first half of this year, would be jeopardized. We could anticipate swift retaliation by countries exporting textiles and footwear if this bill became law. These countries have large and rapidly growing markets for U.S. exports, which would be placed at risk by the new restrictions required under H.R. 4328. They would retaliate against our most competitive exports, such as agriculture, aerospace, high technology, capital goods, and services, to the detriment of domestic employment in these industries.

All of these economic costs to consumers and American industry would be incurred without eliminating a single "unfair" trade practice or opening even one closed market abroad. Rather than address the industry's competitive problems constructively, this legislation merely closes our markets and insulates the textile, apparel, and footwear industries from international competition.

We already have very effective laws that provide remedies to unfair competition from abroad, which various sectors of the textile and apparel industries have used when necessary. Our best hope for opening new markets overseas and for sustaining our textile and apparel industries is not this legislation, but the Uruguay Round of global trade talks, now in its critical final weeks.

We are working in the Uruguay Round to negotiate a means for the textile and apparel industries to:

—Enhance their international competitiveness in the long term and to open foreign markets to our exports.

—Ensure that the current special quota protection for the industry is not terminated abruptly, but is phased in over a reasonable period of time to protect those parts of the industry that require more time to adjust to import competition.

—Provide sufficient stability so that our textile and apparel industries, as well as our importers and retailers, have a smooth, gradual path of adjustment to the regular rules of the General Agreement on Tariffs and Trade (GATT), as they are strengthened in the Round.

H.R. 4328 would eliminate any hope we have of achieving a successful Uruguay Round agreement in December that accomplishes these objectives. The bill would do this by taking a sector of considerable importance in international trade off the negotiating table. Furthermore, it would be an egregious violation of GATT rules, our commitments under the Multifiber Arrangement (MFA), and the numerous bilateral agreements we have negotiated under the MFA's auspices. This protectionist bill unquestionably would result in a mass exodus of perhaps half the 100 nations participating in the Round. All that we hope to achieve for the textile and apparel industries would be lost, as would all of our efforts for American businesses, consumers, and workers.

Beyond this economic calamity, H.R. 4328 is reprehensible at a time when the United States' highest international priority is to strengthen international cooperation. Many of the countries whose interests would be damaged by H.R. 4328, such as Turkey and Egypt, are ones that have cooperated effectively in resisting Iraqi aggression in the Persian Gulf. In addition, this bill would undercut our attempts to rebuild economies on free-market principles and to build a strengthened global trading system that will permit trade to expand and thereby increase world prosperity and stability.

Additionally, while the Congress holds the authority to regulate commerce with foreign nations, several provisions of H.R. 4328 interfere with the President's constitutional prerogatives in conducting international negotiations and in proposing legislation.

The Textile, Apparel, and Footwear Trade Act of 1990 is simply not the panacea advertised by its proponents. Instead, it is blatantly protectionist, unwarranted, economically harmful, and internationally unviable.

Accordingly, I am disapproving H.R. 4328.

GEORGE BUSH

The White House,
October 5, 1990.

Statement on the Intention To Veto a Resolution Providing Funding for Continued Government Operation
October 5, 1990

The hour of reckoning is at hand. At midnight tonight, the Congress of the United States must face up to the shutdown of government services and resulting confusion that will be strewn across this land because we could not produce a budget. It is deeply discouraging that the governing bodies of this country would wrangle with the Nation's fiscal affairs for nearly a year and fail.

Tonight, because there is no budget, the United States Government, under existing law, does not have the authority to continue operations. And I will not be a party to the process that would once again put off meeting this responsibility for a few more days. I will not sign the continuing resolution passed by the House and Senate tonight, which simply delays once again the most serious constitutional responsibility of government: to manage the people's money.

At midnight tonight, our national parks and monuments will close. Cleanup at hazardous waste sites will cease. Social Security offices will accept no new applications. Border inspections will be delayed. In one government agency after another, thousands of Federal employees will no longer be able to serve public tasks necessary for the public good. The people of America did not send their representatives to Washington to produce these consequences.

As I said in my Inaugural Address, they did not send us here to bicker. And tonight I challenge the Congress to act as quickly as possible to produce an acceptable budget. Don't wait for people to lose confidence in their government. Act now, tomorrow, as soon as possible to produce a budget that reduces the deficit, avoids recession, and puts our economy on the path of sustained growth.

I stand ready to work with the Members of Congress to produce a responsible plan. After months of hard work, we produced a budget agreement that would have cut a real $500 billion off our deficit over the next 5 years. The White House and the congressional leadership of the Democratic and Republican Parties worked hard to put together that agreement and put in place the largest deficit reduction in history. It's a sad commentary that the full House did not have the courage of those convictions. But surely the reality of a government closedown will convince everyone that a solution must be found. It is time to act responsibly on this problem and produce a fiscal year 1991 budget.

Note: The President returned H.J. Res. 660 without approval on October 6.

The President's News Conference on the Federal Budget Crisis
October 6, 1990

The President. I just wanted to comment. I know the leaders have been speaking. And I have not yet signed but, within the next couple of minutes, will veto the continuing resolution. We've had good cooperation from the Democrat and Republican leaders. The Congress has got to get on with the people's business. I'd like them to do that business—get a budget resolution—and get it done in the next 24 hours or 48 hours.

But as President, I cannot let the people's business be postponed over and over again. I've jotted down the numbers. There have been three dozen in the last decade—three dozen continuing resolutions—business as usual. And we can't have it. The President can only do this one thing: send that message back and say this is not a time for business as usual. The deficit is too important to the American people.

So, I expressed my appreciation to the Speaker, the majority leader in the Senate, the majority leader in the House, two Republican leaders—thanked them for coming together in a spirit of compromise to get an agreement that I strongly supported. It didn't have everything I wanted in there, but now I'm calling on those who did not vote for it on the Republican side and on the Democratic side to get up with the leadership and send down something that will take care of the people's business once and for all.

I am sorry that I have to do this, but I made very clear that I am not going to be a part of business as usual when we have one deficit after another piling up. Had enough of it, and I think the American people have had enough of it.

Q. What changed your mind, sir?

Q. Mr. Mitchell [House majority leader] came out here a minute ago and said that this served no useful purpose. What useful purpose?

The President. We have a disagreement with him. I think it disciplines the United States Congress, Democrats and Republicans. They're the ones that have to pass this budget, and they ought to get on with it. And the leaders, to their credit, tried. But a lot of Members think they can get a free shot, right and left. What this message says is: No more business as usual. So, we did have a difference on that particular point. I think both the Speaker and the majority leader did not want me to do this.

But look, let me take you guys back a while. In August I wanted to keep the Congress in. That story was written. And I've listened to the leadership, both Republicans and Democrats; said no, we'll acquiesce—because they said that to keep the Congress here in August will be counterproductive: "Everybody will be angry with you. But the way to get it done is with the discipline of the calendar running after the summer recess."

And so, I acquiesced. I compromised. I gave. I'm not going to do it anymore. I'm very sorry if people are inconvenienced, but I am not going to be a part of business as usual by the United States Congress.

Q. Mr. President, Senator Dole [Republi-

can leader] said that you had agreed to send up a new short-term spending bill that would include spending cuts—a sequester. Could you tell us something about that?

The President. I'm going to stay out of exactly what we're going to do and let the leaders handle the details of this now. It's in the Congress, and I still strongly support the agreement that both Democrat leaders and Republican leaders came down on. And I'll say this: I do think that there's a lot of agreement and good will still existing for that. It's not going to be passed exactly that way. It was defeated. But let's leave the details of negotiation on that to the Congress—starting back in right now. They're going to have to contend with this veto I sent up—and obviously, I want to see that veto sustained.

Q. You say no more business as usual—in one breath you say no more CR's [continuing resolutions], and in the next breath, Dole says there's some CR which is——

The President. Well, if it has some discipline—what I'm saying is, I want to see the system disciplined. If what Bob Dole said is correct—I'll sign one if it puts some discipline on the system. And if it doesn't discipline the system, then I stay with my current position. No, excuse me, I'm glad you brought that up, because I would strongly support that.

Q. Mr. President, the leadership made a strong point in saying that it's the average Americans who are going to be hurt, the Federal workers and so forth. It's not Congressmen but average Americans who are going to be strongly hurt by this.

The President. The average American is smart. The average American knows what's going on, I think. And I think they know that the Congress will continue to kick this can down the road and that they've got to act. I am very sorry for people that are inconvenienced by this or hurt by this. But this is the only device one has for making something happen, and that is to get the Congress to act, to do its business.

Q. Mr. President, you seem to be blaming Congress, but in fact, a lot of their constituents are the ones that urged them to vote against this. They say it's unfair—the burden is unfairly divided, that the poor and the middle class are paying too much. Is it possible that maybe this program that you proposed with the leaders just was not acceptable to the American public?

The President. Well, certain aspects of it might well not have been acceptable to the American public on both the right or the left. But when you're trying to do the country's business, I've discovered you have to compromise from time to time, and that's exactly what I did. Took a few shots in the process, but it doesn't matter. What matters is, let's move this process ahead now.

But, yes, you're right—some people didn't like one aspect or another. We had Republicans jumping up on our side of the aisle and saying, "I'll vote for it if you change this," or "I don't like this part of it, but if you change that—" And similarly, you've got people that you were quoting that were on the other side.

But at times, one has to come together to do the country's business for the overall good. And these outrageous deficits cannot be permitted to go on and on and on and on. I'm worried about international markets. I'm worried about this country—the opinion that it can't take care of its fiscal business.

And to their leaders' credit, Democrat and Republican, they tried very hard. They failed to get a majority on the Democratic side. And Republican leaders, with the help from this President and all I could bring to bear on it—we failed, because we had people—were looking at one narrow part of the package and not at the overall good. And I am hopeful now that with the urgency this veto brings to bear on the situation, that reasonable people, men and women in the Congress, can come together.

Q. Mr. President, what kind of progress is being made on a new budget resolution? And sources on the Hill are saying that there is growing support for raising the tax rates of the wealthy in exchange, perhaps, for the cuts on premiums for Medicare. But you have opposed that in the past. Are you willing to give on tax rates for the wealthy?

The President. I don't know the answer to your question. They're just going back up now to try. I like the parameters of the other deal wherein I compromise. We've got people—your question reflects the

views on the more liberal or left side of the political spectrum—who raised those questions. We have some on the right side of the political spectrum coming at the process from another way.

Now, I say: Let them go up and negotiate it. This is the business of the Congress. And our people will stay in touch. I won't mislead them. If there's something that's so outrageous I can't accept it, I'll let them know at the beginning so they don't waste their time. But we're flexible. I've already compromised. And I'm not saying that I can't take a look at new proposals. But you've got to put together a majority in the Congress, and that's where the leaders are having great difficulty.

Q. Following up on that, members of your own party dislike the deal so much, how could you and your advisers have misjudged the sentiments of members of your own party?

The President. Because it's easy when you don't have to be responsible for something. It's easy to just get up and say, hey, I've got an election in 3 weeks, and I'm going to stand up against this particular package— Medicare, the taxes, the home heating oil, or the fact there's not enough growth or not enough incentive. Any individual Member can do that. Maybe it plays well at home. The President and the leadership of both Houses have to be responsible for the overall good of the country, have to make something happen. I can't get it done just my way. I don't control both Houses of Congress. I'd love to think that that luxury would come by way someday, but it hasn't. Therefore, we've had to compromise. So, I will keep trying in that spirit—that cooperative, positive spirit.

But when it comes to the discipline that comes from saying, "I'm sorry, no more business as usual," that's where I can stand up. I don't need a consultation to do that. I've got plenty of advice on one side of that question and the other. But I am absolutely convinced this is right.

Even those who are inconvenienced by this are going to say, thank God, we'll get the American people's business of getting this deficit under control done. That's my objective. I think every parent out there who sees his kid's future being mortgaged by the outrageous deficit, sees a shaky economy that's being affected by prolonging these deliberations, will be grateful in the long run. In the meantime, we've got to take a little heat.

Q. Mr. President, the budget resolution that failed is one that you worked hard for. Despite the fact that you gave a national televised speech, despite the fact that your popularity is very high—and you failed to sway even a majority of votes in your own party. Does that concern you, and do you think this is a major setback for your Presidency?

The President. No, I don't think that at all. But I do think—yes, it concerns me. I'd like everybody to do it exactly the way I want, but it doesn't work that way. So, now we have to use a little discipline——

Q. Mr. President——

The President. ——nice guy stuff, and we'll try. It's a tough decision, it's not an easy decision I've made, but it is the right decision. So, I'm disappointed they didn't do it my way. But I'm in here to do what is best for the country; and what is best for the country is to get this deficit under control, to get this economy moving again, and to see people at jobs, not out on some welfare line. And that's what's at stake here—economic soundness of the United States.

We've got a lot of things going on in the world, and a strong economy is vital to what I want to see achieved in this country. So, you have to take some hits. I mean, you don't get it done exactly your own way.

But I read these speculative stories. Tomorrow, there's going to be another vote. Tomorrow, somebody else will move the previous question or second the motion, or some committee chairman will jump up and say, hey, what about me—my little empire is being invaded here. And I'll say, hey, the President's the guy that has to look at the overall picture.

I can understand Congressmen doing that. But we came together on a deal. We worked for it. Everybody had a chance to posture that didn't like it. They have no responsibility. But I feel a certain responsibility to the American people to move something forward here—want a compromise. Now we're going to say: We'll try it

this way. No more business as usual. Do not just keep putting off the day of reckoning. And I don't want to be a part of that, and that's why I've had to veto this resolution.

Q. Mr. President, you've talked a lot about discipline today. Do you think the American people on average are willing to accept the discipline of a tough budget?

The President. That's a very good question. And if you look at the vote in the House of Representatives, you might say no. But I think in the final analysis the answer will be yes, because I think we sometimes underestimate the intelligence of the American people. I can see where a Congressman can jump up on a specific spending program that'll help him in his district. I can see when somebody will give you the broad tax speech or help him in his district.

But in the final analysis, what the American people look at is: Do we have an economy in which I can feed my family, where I can have opportunity to work for a living, and where I can put a little aside to educate my kids? And therein lies the problem, because that's what we're working for—is we're trying to get this Federal deficit down.

But I think you raise a good point. I think a lot of these Congressmen can jump up without any responsibility for running the country, or even cooperating with their leaders, and make a point that's very happy for the home folks. But I think that view underestimates the overall intelligence of the American people, whether conservative, whether a guy's working on a factory line someplace, whether he's an investor someplace.

That's why I think this is very important that the Congress now finally come to grips with this.

Q. There's some talk about this special challenge to Civiletti.

Q. Mr. President, it sounds like you're now saying: Hands off. It's up to the congressional leaders to do the negotiating.

The President. They've already started up the road there to go to Congress and start negotiating. But, no, we've made very clear that we're continuing to help. I don't want to mislead them. There are certain things I can accept. There are certain things I can't.

So, I think it's very important that our able team, in whom I have total confidence, stay in touch with them.

Q. But not sit at the negotiating table with them?

The President. Oh, I think they'll be there. I think it all depends on what forum. I think there is some feeling, Ann [Ann Devroy, Washington Post], that on the part of Members, both Democrat and Republicans—hey, you summiteers handed us a deal. Well, what the heck? I mean, how do you expect to get as far along toward an agreement as we did get? But what I want to do is facilitate it. And if they want to know where the White House is, fine. If they want the ideas that largely led to an agreement, fine, and I think they will. But we're not going to force our way in. This is the business of the Congress. The American people know that. They know that the President doesn't pass the budget and doesn't vote on all this stuff. It's the Congress who does it.

So, I'm not trying to assign blame. I'm simply saying, we're available. We want to talk—fine. I think both leaders have indicated they wanted to stay in fairly close touch with the White House.

Q. Mr. President, there is some talk of a constitutional challenge to Civiletti on the bill that the Attorney General's opinion is not sufficient to run the Government, and that violates section 7 of the Constitution.

The President. I haven't heard anything about that.

Q. Mr. President, are you going to cancel your campaign schedule next week if this impasse is not resolved?

The President. I don't know. I've got to cancel everything that has to do with government, I guess. Maybe that's a good chance to get out there in the political process.

Q. How long can you hold out? How long can you let the Government stay shut down before you decide to toss——

The President. Watch and learn.

Q. How long do you think the Government can stay shut before——

The President. It's not a question of how long I can take it; it's how long the Congress can take it. But Congress is where the action is. It's the Congress that has to pass this in the House and in the Senate. That's where the action is. They've postponed this tough decision as I've mentioned—how many—30-some times. And we just can't have it. The American people are saying, "I want something done about this." That's where the focus will be.

So, I don't think it's a question of taking heat here or these guys marching out here about honking their horns on taxes. They know I don't like taxes. You get some other guy in Washington out here with a little placard, demonstrating—something about the government employees—we've been supporters of the government employees. But we cannot have business as usual.

The American people—I don't know about inside the beltway, but outside they are fed up with business as usual, and so am I. I wish I had total control so we could do it exactly my way, but we don't. So, I've compromised. Now we're prepared to say, I'm not going to accept a resolution that just postpones it. I've told you I tried that approach.

I tried it in August. Let everybody go home on vacation when I had some good, sound advice I probably should have taken: Make the Congress stay in August. And I listened to the leaders, and they said: "Oh, please don't do that. It will be counterproductive." Now they're saying to me: "Please don't veto this. It will be counterproductive." When do the American people have a say? They want to see this deficit under control. And I don't have many weapons here as President, but one is the veto. When I do it, cast it on principle, I hope it is supported.

Q. What's happened to the prestige——

Q. If Dole sends up another CR, if the Congress sends up a CR with sequestration, when could that happen? Do you have some timeframe?

The President. I don't know.

Q. Could it happen the next couple of days, sir?

The President. Oh, yes, absolutely. It could happen this afternoon.

Q. It could happen this afternoon?

The President. Sure. Whether we—together? I'm not that certain. Perhaps it's a little oversimplification because they're telling me there are some difficult problems right and left, both sides. But, no, they're going right back to negotiating. Let's hope it does. That's the way to serve the constituents.

Q. If it came up this afternoon, sir, would you sign it this afternoon?

The President. It depends what it is. I'll be around.

Q. You have vetoed the CR?

The President. Yes—well, I haven't actually signed it, but I've got to rush right in there now and do that and send it up to the Hill. They know that they've——

Last question.

Q. Why did you change your mind?

Q. What's all this done to the prestige and influence of you and your office?

The President. Well, I think it will demonstrate that there is some power in the Presidency to compel the Congress to do something, and I think that's good.

Q. You are vetoing, though?

The President. Oh, yes. It hasn't been vetoed yet, but I need a typewriter in there to get it done. By the time we finish this press conference that has gone longer than I thought, it'll—probably all typed up.

Q. Might you trade the bubble for capital gains now? Do you foresee that as a compromise?

The President. The negotiators in the Congress have a lot of flexibility. I remain in a flexible frame of mind. Certain things I can accept and can't. But I'd like to think that now those who postured on one side or another with no responsibility will join the leaders, Republican and Democrat, and say: Hey, we've got a responsibility to the overall good here. We can no longer just give a speech. We've got to pitch in and come together. And that's what my pitch is.

And that's why I'm doing it and doing this veto—saying, hey, no more business as usual. And I think people understand that sometimes a President has to make a difficult decision. So, I don't worry about the prestige. I was elected to do what—in a case like this—what I think is best and in the national interest. And that's exactly what I'm doing.

Thank you all very much.

Q. Are you going to type those up yourself?

The President. Yes, but I didn't give you the full load.

Note: The President's 62d news conference began at 11:30 a.m. on the West Driveway of the White House. A tape was not available for verification of the content of this news conference.

Message to the House of Representatives Returning Without Approval a Resolution Providing Funding for Continued Government Operation
October 6, 1990

To the House of Representatives:

I am returning herewith without my approval H.J. Res. 660—a resolution making continuing appropriations—which would extend funding for the Federal Government through October 12, 1990. In providing for such funding, H.J. Res. 660 would also suspend the sequester that is required by the Gramm-Rudman-Hollings law. The sequester would be suspended even though the Congress has failed repeatedly to act in any meaningful way to reduce the Federal deficit. Under these circumstances, I simply

cannot approve H.J. Res. 660.

When the Budget Summit Agreement was announced by the Bipartisan Leadership on September 30th, I indicated that I would not sign a continuing resolution until a satisfactory budget resolution was passed. The Congress failed to pass such a budget resolution during the past week. I have made the difficult political decisions that are required to achieve a meaningful reduction in the Federal deficit. Responsible congressional action to reduce the deficit can be delayed no longer. It is time for the Congress to act responsibly on a budget resolution—not time for business as usual.

I urge the Congress to concentrate its energies on passing a satisfactory budget resolution to clear the way for approval of another short-term continuing resolution, and the enactment of meaningful deficit reduction legislation no later than October 19th.

I note that H.J. Res. 660 would also increase the Federal debt limit until October 12th. If it becomes clear that the Congress cannot pass a satisfactory budget resolution

by October 9th, I urge that it enact a clean bill extending the debt limit so that the U.S. Government will not default on its obligations on October 11th. The latest date by which action on a debt limit extension is needed to avoid default is October 9th, so that the Treasury can auction securities on October 10th and settle them on October 11th.

GEORGE BUSH

The White House,
October 6, 1990.

Remarks at the Swearing-In Ceremony for David H. Souter as an Associate Justice of the Supreme Court of the United States
October 8, 1990

The President. Thank you all, and good afternoon. Mr. Chief Justice, and members of the Court; Members of the United States Congress that are here today, Senate and House; members of the Cabinet; Mr. Vice President: It is truly an honor to greet you all here at the White House and particularly to welcome the friends of this extraordinary Justice to Washington.

Today's ceremony is historic for many reasons. It is, of course, the first Supreme Court appointment of this Presidency. More importantly, it serves as another occasion to celebrate the 200 years of the Constitution of the United States and the independent judiciary it launched.

We meet on Columbus Day, birthplace of a modern hemisphere and an auspicious date for any new beginning. Elsewhere around the world, the origins of many countries are almost lost in time, their roots unclear, unknown. Not so in America. We know exactly where and exactly when our modern history began. But we often forget that back in 1492, Christopher Columbus was searching not for a new world but a new way—a passage to the riches of the Far East. In fact, Columbus was so confident he carried a letter from Queen Isabella to be delivered to the Emperor of China. This marked history's first known case of mail getting lost on its way—[*laughter*]—across

America.

But if our modern history began with a search for earthly treasure, it was a search for something more elusive that actually gave birth to the United States: a search for freedom, a search for justice and self-government, a search that produced the Constitution of the United States.

In ancient China, the word "wisdom" was formed by a combination of the ideograms for wind and lightning—wind and lightning. And years before the American Revolution, Benjamin Franklin lofted a kite upon the wind and seized lightning from the sky. And at age 81, he did it again. For 4 sweltering months in the summer of 1787, 55 delegates met in Philadelphia, debating a wonderful, audacious, unsettling idea. Washington called the Constitution "little short of a miracle." It was—with wind and lightning—a nation inventing itself.

One of those 55 delegates was James Wilson, the son of a Scottish farmer and the Pennsylvania lawyer who shared responsibility for writing the Constitution's first draft. A fervent advocate of the sovereignty of the people, Wilson fought for a strong national judiciary and was one of the first to envision the principles of judicial review. Today Wilson's idea stands as one of the cornerstones of our republic and one of America's greatest gifts to the world.

Tomorrow morning, Justice David Souter—sounds good, doesn't it, David—[*laughter*]—assumes a distinguished seat on the Supreme Court. It was first held by that very same James Wilson, one of the five men that President George Washington first appointed to the Supreme Court in 1789. His successor was Bushrod Washington, a nephew of the President, soldier in the Revolutionary War, and a founding member of one of the many organizations that has recognized David Souter for his intellect—namely, Phi Beta Kappa.

Thirty-four years ago this distinguished seat became open during the Presidency of one of my personal heroes, Dwight D. Eisenhower. And Ike filled that seat with a jurist who was to become one of the most personally beloved and respected members of the Court, Justice Brennan. Will you stand up? [*Applause*] I guess you can tell that all of us wish you a most pleasant and active retirement. And thank you for your service, sir.

Like his predecessor, Justice Souter comes to the Court with a distinguished record of judicial service. And I'm grateful that many of the fine judges with whom he has served are able to be with us today. During the recent hearings, Justice Souter clearly demonstrated the superb education, training, and experience that grace his record. But even more important, he once again demonstrated his lifelong devotion to principle—a simple, straightforward, and enduring principle, a principle quite familiar to Justice James Wilson and the other framers of the Constitution. And the principle is this: The role assigned to judges in our system is to interpret the Constitution and lesser laws, and not to make them.

And on this issue of principle I also want to congratulate and thank the Judiciary Committee and the full Senate for the prompt and faithful exercise of their own constitutional responsibilities. Chairman Biden is with us and Senator Thurmond and others, and we are grateful to you for your role in this procedure.

Like many Americans, I was particularly moved by Justice Souter's opening comments at his hearings. "The first lesson," he said, "simple as it is, is that whatever court we're in, whatever we are doing, at the end

of our task some human being is going to be affected. Some human life is going to be changed by what we do." And he added, "And so we had better use every power of our minds and our hearts and our beings to get those rulings right." Now, those are the sentiments of a very thoughtful and caring man.

And just down the street, as the autumn twilight descends on Washington, an underground vault holds America's founding papers, the birth certificate of a nation. The paper is a deep yellow, but the writing is still strong and distinct: "We the People of the United States." And the Constitution is not just a symbol but a living idea, the world's greatest experiment in freedom and self-government, four handwritten pages that promise freedom and justice before the law. Unlike other nations, Americans cannot look to a common heritage of culture or blood. Americans come from every corner of the world, linked only by this—an idea—a nation that invented itself.

In just a few moments we will all bear solemn witness to the oath of office of America's newest Supreme Court Justice. And so, let me conclude with Justice Souter's own description of the task ahead: "It is the responsibility to join with eight other people to make the promises of the Constitution a reality of our time, and to preserve that Constitution for the generations that will follow us after we are gone from here."

And now I would invite the Chief Justice, William Rehnquist, with the assistance of Erin Rath, to administer the constitutional oath of office to Justice David Souter. And I also understand that Judge Souter would like Senator Rudman and Tom Rath to join us up here also. So, Mr. Chief Justice, if you will do it, sir.

[*At this point, Justice Souter was sworn in.*]

Justice Souter. Mr. President, Mr. Vice President, Mr. Chief Justice and members of the Court, members of the leadership, Chairman Biden, Senator Thurmond, and members of the Judiciary Committee, all Members of the Congress, and my friends—new and old.

It is exactly 11 weeks to the hour since I

stood next to the President in another room in this house, facing about the same number of people. I'm sure that you remember, if you saw films of that afternoon, that I was in a state of virtual shock. And I'm glad that I can say that in the 11 weeks since then I've at least advanced in the direction of some degree of composure. I have not, however, in the 11 weeks, got myself to the point this afternoon where I really am capable of saying what is on my mind. What I would like to try to say something about—I think I can explain to you if I tell you a story about what happened later that afternoon 11 weeks ago.

After the President's news conference, I was immediately taken into Governor Sununu's office and the planning process began. And this went on for I guess about an hour. And at the end of that hour the Governor came in, and he said that the President believed I could probably stand some refurbishing. And I thought, well, the President finally got it right this afternoon. [*Laughter*] So, I was taken upstairs to where the President and Mrs. Bush were watching the news, and the President gave me a drink to compose myself. And after a couple of minutes of conversation, Mrs. Bush said to me, "How is your mother taking this?" I told her that I called my mother on the phone and I could report that the mother was taking things a lot better than the son was. And the President said, "What's her phone number?" So, I gave him her phone number, and he called my mother on the phone.

And he said—as best I can recall the conversation, he said, "Now, look, Mrs. Souter," he said, "I want you to know he's okay." [*Laughter*] He said, "We've got him up here, and we're watching the news, and he's having a drink. And we'll look after him, and he's going to be all right." [*Laughter*]

That is a phone call, although it did not come to me, that I will never forget and no one in my family will ever forget. And it epitomizes for me the reason why my sense of gratitude to the President goes so far beyond anything that could be called simply "official." And that same sense of gratitude extends not only, of course, to my mother, who took the call that afternoon,

but to virtually everyone who has dealt with me in those 11 weeks.

It certainly extends to the Judiciary Committee of the Senate, which used me with consummate fairness, and to all the Members of the Senate who reviewed their recommendation. It extends to the members of the Supreme Court, who, even before today, have done their best to make me feel welcome and have repeated their efforts to me this afternoon. It extends to the ABA [American Bar Association] committee, the standing committee on the judiciary, which reviewed my credentials; and most particularly, to the subcommittee which worked so long on me.

And I wish I could also thank adequately the counselors that I've had, right from that first bit of advice from Governor Sununu so shortly after the nomination to Kenneth Duberstein and to Frederick McClure, who have counseled me in extraordinary ways these last couple of months, to Boyden Gray and to the members of his office, particularly to Fred Nelson, who was sort of my guide through these weeks and proved a wonderful guide.

My thanks certainly go to the Attorney General and to the members of his office who helped me on research chores and were fastidious in drawing a line between what was appropriate for the Justice Department and what was appropriate for the nominee. And my thanks certainly extend to the attorney general of New Hampshire and to his office, which but for their competence would have been rendered dysfunctional by the efforts to construct a paper trail and a biography for me, which— [*laughter*]—did not seem as apparent on July 23d as it later seemed to be.

And, of course, if I could, I would thank the people who have supported me and shored me up and given me the spirit for the race that I have had to run these past 11 weeks, to my neighbors and to my friends both old and new.

And I stand here saying to you, or asking to you, how can I thank you? And I think everyone in this room knows that I cannot really. We can never recompense the people who do us good. What we can do, and what we try to do instead, is pass it on and to make the gifts and kindnesses that come to us a kind of human currency that goes on traveling.

And I think the most that I can say this afternoon is that that is what I will try to do. I will try to pass on what I have received. Most importantly, I will try to pass on the constitutional authority that I have received this afternoon. I will try to use it as best I can according to the light that God gives me. And in due course I will try to pass it to another in as vigorous condition as I have received it this afternoon, as it were, from Justice Brennan. I will try to preserve it. And I will try to transmit it—I hope refreshed—to another generation of the American republic which is the inheritance of us all.

The President. It is not because Mr. Justice Souter is from strict Yankee tradition in New Hampshire that the reception will be without a lot of largess in there. [*Laughter*] But I think we all know the circumstances.

But I would like to ask the members of the Court and the Vice President and members of the Cabinet and members of the Judiciary Committee and other Members of Congress and then everybody else to join us just in a receiving line so we can all tell Justice Souter how happy we are. So, let's go. We'll meet you out here.

Note: The President spoke at 5 p.m. in the East Room at the White House. In his remarks, he referred to Erin Rath, the daughter of Tom Rath, a friend of Justice Souter. Justice Souter referred to John H. Sununu, Chief of Staff to President Bush; Kenneth M. Duberstein, former Chief of Staff to President Reagan; Frederick McClure, Assistant to the President for Legislative Affairs; C. Boyden Gray, Counsel to the President; Frederick D. Nelson, Associate Counsel to the President; Attorney General Dick Thornburgh; and John Arnold, New Hampshire attorney general.

Statement on Signing a Resolution Providing Funding for Continued Government Operation
October 9, 1990

I am today signing H.J. Res. 666, a temporary continuing resolution, providing funds for the Government to operate through October 19, 1990.

In vetoing the previous continuing resolution, I said I would not sign any such resolution until the Congress had passed a budget resolution. I want to thank the Members of the Congress who voted to sustain my veto.

The Congress has now passed a budget resolution which, if fully implemented, would reduce the Federal deficit by $500 billion over the next 5 years. If achieved, this would be the largest deficit reduction program in history. While I am not fully satisfied with the budget resolution, it does provide a framework within which the committees of the Congress can now work to provide substantive law that comes close to fulfilling the letter—and that does fulfill the spirit—of the Bipartisan Budget Summit Agreement announced on September 30,

1990.

The next step in implementing the budget resolution is the passage of a budget reconciliation bill. Its component parts are to be submitted to the budget committees of the Congress by October 12th.

There is, unfortunately, no assurance that the congressional committees will, in fact, produce a fully satisfactory reconciliation bill. But I repeat: I will not accept business as usual.

I am obliged to make clear that the reconciliation bill now called for:

—must be largely consistent with the Bipartisan Budget Summit Agreement;

—must achieve the intended savings from each of the specified committees on a basis that is scored by both the Office of Management and Budget and the Congressional Budget Office as "real"— no smoke, no mirrors;

—must include mutually agreeable, growth-oriented tax incentives;

—must include the process reform measures announced in the Bipartisan Budget Summit Agreement;

—must be fully and satisfactorily enforceable on a continuing basis;

—must be produced on a bipartisan basis—with full and fair opportunities for constructive participation by both parties and both branches; and

—must be passed by both Houses of the Congress in satisfactory form by October 19th.

As the responsibility for action now shifts to the committees of the Congress, I will be following the work of the committees closely. And if, by October 19th, the Congress has failed to pass a budget reconciliation bill that meets the tests I have outlined, I will again have to withhold my signature from any continuing resolution.

GEORGE BUSH

The White House,
October 9, 1990.

Note: H.J. Res. 666, approved October 9, was assigned Public Law No. 101–412. The statement also referred to H.J. Res. 660, which was returned without approval on October 6.

The President's News Conference
October 9, 1990

The President. Let me just go with an opening statement, and then be glad to respond to questions.

First, on the budget, the committees of Congress now take up the arduous task of implementing the budget resolution that they just passed. We've been pulling and tugging at this framework agreement for nearly 5 months, and it's been difficult because that whole underlying problem is difficult. And we're trying to reduce the Federal deficit by $500 billion over the next 5 years—$40 billion of it in the first year. And this would be the largest such cut in history.

So, while it's easy to get caught up in the maneuvers and the countermaneuvers of the legislative process, I want to assure the American people this morning that I will do everything in my power to encourage Congress as it struggles to bring forth the most comprehensive and significant deficit-cutting plan ever.

This morning I outlined several conditions for a budget reconciliation bill. As the committees of Congress begin to fill in the blanks in determining how we raise the revenues and cut the spending, we must be mindful not to let the hard-won goals of the budget resolution dissipate or lose direction.

The budget reconciliation bill due on October 12th must measure up to the savings Congress has outlined, without smoke and mirrors, with growth-oriented tax incentives, with process reform, with enforceability, with bipartisan support, and with passages by both Houses of Congress by October 19th. These are the objectives that we fought for since the beginning of the long budget struggle. But they're worthy of our effort.

In any undertaking of this size, there is bound to be anguish, and I want to recognize the valiant Federal work force that had to suffer through some uncertainty of this period.

On Saturday morning, I said we cannot have business as usual. But the Congress has finally acted and we are back on course. And there can be no letup in our attention to detail, in our commitment to purpose. We must fulfill the requirements of the budget resolution.

Now I'd be glad to take some questions. Terry [Terence Hunt, Associated Press]?

Federal Budget Negotiations

Q. Mr. President, a week ago you asked Americans to help get a budget passed, and they gave you the back of the hand. Then, despite a government shutdown, Congress still hasn't been able to produce a budget. How can Americans fail to have anything except grave questions about your ability and that of Congress to govern?

The President. Well, I think there probably are some questions. I don't feel the American people gave the back of the hand to the budget agreement. If you look at the surveys that carried in the magazines and all of this, they show that, I think, more people wanted the agreements than not. So, we've just got to do a better job of getting it through. But listen, I can understand the frustration. I feel it myself at times. And when you have a government with one party controlling the Congress, where the action is and where the action will remain now for a while, and then you have a President of a different party—nobody thought it would be easy, and it isn't.

So, I think there's some frustration, but I notice that there was strong support for the package. The problem was that you ask on individual categories of the package—oh, no, we don't want this; we don't want that; we don't—no. A lot of special interest. But people seem to want the deal. I think the deal—though not keeping me happy in every way—was a good one, and I was proud to join in with the Republican and Democratic leaders in supporting that original budget agreement.

Now we've got some of the main ingredients of it—broad instruction to these committees that were contained within the original agreement—and let's see if the Congress can get moving and come up with a deal that I can accept. And we'll be working with them. I'm not up here to assign blame.

Q. Mr. President, no matter what you say, there was a lot of feeling in the country that the package was not fair. Are you willing to accept a higher tax rate for the wealthy, perhaps in exchange for a capital gains cut, but even so, a higher tax rate?

The President. I haven't seen great sentiment for raising people's income tax rates. And I'm not for that. Now, during the budget process—and this was little noted—there was discussion about getting capital gains for straightening out the bubble, which means raising some rates. We were quite openminded. There was some negoti-

ation. So, let me say this: That's on the table. That's been talked about. And if it's proper, if it can be worked in the proper balance between the capital gains rate and the income tax changes, fine. But I don't think it's fruitful here to negotiate the details or try to.

What we've got to do is get up now with, particularly, Ways and Means and Finance—Danny Rostenkowski [chairman of the House Ways and Means Committee], Lloyd Bentsen [chairman of the Senate Finance Committee], Bill Archer [senior Republican member of the House Ways and Means Committee], and Bob Packwood [senior Republican member of the Senate Finance Committee]—and discuss with them quietly what we can accept. I want them to know it. But I don't think I can stand here and kind of negotiate or mandate exactly what will happen.

Q. Sir, don't you think, though, the secrecy was an impediment? It felt like a lead balloon. The senior citizens in this country do not consider themselves a special interest; they're a quarter of the population.

The President. Right.

Q. People who drive to work 50 miles every day or less certainly did consider it a hardship. Had you not negotiated more in public, more public dialog, more debate, don't you think you would have been better off?

The President. Well, I don't know that any person who is opposed to raising gasoline taxes would have been more inclined to accept them if the negotiations between Democrats and Republicans on these committees had been done in public. But I think now the positions are clearer. And what I want to do is to see us go forward now. I mean, those are all out there now. And so, the committees know where the opposition's coming from.

But, Helen [Helen Thomas, United Press International], the basic problem is this: Nobody wants to do anything in terms of where they're affected. I mean, they just don't want that, and yet they want the deficit down. And that's what makes it difficult. But that's why I was very pleased to see the agreement. Everyone had to give a little bit. But we'll go back now and see if we can't, in that spirit, get a deal by the 19th that I can sign.

Q. Mr. President, House Republicans by the end of last week were being accused of behaving like Democrats. There seemed to be fairly deep divisions within their ranks. You and the leaders did not carry a majority of House Republicans on the budget deal. What hope do you now have, and what reason do you have for holding that hope, that you can do that the next time on a program that will, in effect, be written by the Democratic Party?

The President. Brit [Brit Hume, ABC News], you only stated it, if I could—I don't want to be argumentative, but the Democrats didn't have their troops behind them. They didn't have what they needed to get it through. So, it isn't just the Republicans. I think the hope is that people see more clearly now that it isn't easy. And as people go with their own alternatives now, they find that they can't get the support. So, I think what we'll end up doing is staying very close to the agreement that I reached with the Republican and Democratic leaders. The last couple of few days have been like a catharsis; there's been a clearing of the air. People—[*inaudible*]—here's what I'd do, here's what I'd like to do. And then they find, well, there's no votes to do exactly what they'd like to do.

So, I think we just have to work the process now and hope that the Congress will come up with a reasonable deal. The action is in the Congress—I keep pointing out—but we'll work with them.

Q. There seem to be considerable bitter feeling among Republicans towards some members of your team who felt they had been dealt with in a ham-handed or high-handed way. Has anything been done to patch this up, sir? And have you talked to members about that?

The President. I've talked to the leaders, our leaders—Dole [Senate Republican leader] and Michel [House Republican leader] and others, Bill Archer yesterday—over the weekend—Al Simpson [assistant Senate Republican leader] and others. But any time you have a difficult road like this, there's bound to be griping about it. I have total confidence in our team. And I think they did a first-class job. And I don't think

we would ever have gotten the agreement out if they hadn't done a first-class job.

But also, you need a little time to calm things down, cool things off, and let's try to go forward. I think it's my responsibility to say, look, it's not easy. All of us have had to compromise. Now let's move the country forward to what really everybody wants, and that is getting these deficits under control.

President's Support for Republican Candidates

Q. Mr. President, getting back to the lack of support from Republicans: Tomorrow you're going to be campaigning in North Carolina for Senator Jesse Helms, who was one of your opponents on the budget. What is your message to the voters? Vote blindly Republican, or vote for legislators who support your policies?

The President. If we'd had more people on fiscal policy like Jesse Helms—and by that I mean control of the Senate—we wouldn't be in this mess. People—[*inaudible*]—been doing it more the way I want it done. So, I can't confine my support to somebody who agrees with me on a deficit deal today or some bill tomorrow. We're talking about the broad approach to saving money. And I think Senator Helms has been very good about trying to contain the growth of Federal spending.

So, I would be talking about the common themes. Everybody will be saying, hey, what about that—he was against you on the budget deal. Tomorrow it will be something else. So, we're talking about the broad principles that unite us and urge you vote not just for Jesse but for others who—let's see how I get this properly with the grammar—if we had more of whom we had—[*laughter*]—we wouldn't be in such a problem.

Q. But if there's no threat of retribution, what is to keep your fellow Republicans on the Hill from defying you with impunity on other issues?

The President. Reason.

Federal Budget Negotiations

Q. Mr. President, sort of back to Terry's question. You had unprecedentedly high levels of popularity for a very long period of time. My question is, what do you suppose, sir, that popularity is good for if you can't use it to persuade the American people on an issue you yourself described as one that was critical to the country?

The President. I'm not—I've been the one around here that if—you always ask me on these polls, up or down, what do I think? Every Monday there's some new poll, by some new combination of a magazine and a television studio, and every week somebody wants me to comment on these. And I've been rather consistent in saying, look, I don't believe in these polls. But what it says is, we're not doing too bad. Like to be doing better. And I think there's still pretty strong support. But I guess I learned that you can't do it exactly my way when we get down on something like the deficit. I do think internationally the support is still very, very strong. So, when you get into somebody's pocketbook, or you're worrying about a tax or a spending cut that affects someone, I've learned that it's just not going to be done the way I want it, especially if you don't control the Senate or you don't control the House. So, I can't worry too much about it. I just have to try to get this process moved forward. And that's what we've done. I've had to compromise, but I think it will come out all right.

Q. Sir, if I might, I wonder if you think, though, that you're paying the price now in asking the American people for sacrifice and having them rebuff it the way it happened—paying the price for all those years in the Reagan-Bush administration that you sold supply-side economics.

The President. No, I don't think so. I think that when you see Democratic votes against the leadership, we're talking about something a little shorter term here. I think you're looking at something that—when people have analyzed a package and don't like parts of it. Because they're still saying, hey, we want you to vote for the overall package. So, the problem comes from some specific part of the package. That's the way I analyze it.

Q. Sir, you say you've learned that you just can't have things the way you want it on the budget. But earlier this year you raised the stakes when you said the budget crisis would be the biggest test domestically

of your Presidency. So far, have you failed the test, given the fiasco of last week?

The President. Give me a couple of weeks here. I want to see if we can't get this deal through. I thought we did pretty well when we got an agreement with the Republican leadership and the House leadership, Democrat and Republican. To me, that's getting something done. And we couldn't get it through the Congress yet, so we'll try again. So, I think the jury is still out on that, John [John Cochran, NBC News].

Q. Do you suddenly feel politically a bit more vulnerable now? The Democrats smell blood. They're looking to '92 now. George Bush has slipped. What do you think?

The President. Well, without referring to the polls that I don't like to refer to, have them take a look. [*Laughter*]

Congressional Term Limits

Q. Considering the movement to limit terms in Congress that's been spreading around the country, would you support, either because of your current problems with Congress or because of the philosophy, term limitations?

The President. You know, that was in the Republican platform. So, I may go public on that. Certainly not opposed to it. I haven't decided exactly. But I think people want a change against the incumbents up there on the Hill. And you saw what happened in Oklahoma. I don't know what's going to happen. There's two of those State—what do they call them, on the ballot—referendums on the ballot in California. Both of them are different slightly in terms of how they're put into effect. But I expect they have a good chance. And as I say, we are committed in our platform to some limitation. But whether I make that a prime mover in the political campaign that lies ahead in the next few weeks, I don't know. But I will remind people that it's in there.

Federal Budget Negotiations

Q. Can we clarify something that we talked about earlier? Many of the lawmakers say that the repudiation of the budget package reflects the fact that people feel that economic policy in this country over the last 10 years was fundamentally unfair, that it redistributed income too much to the wealthy and too little to the poor. Do you think that that is part of the reason that your package was rejected?

The President. Might have been part of the reason, but I don't think the entire reason, because I don't think that's why Republicans rejected it at all.

Q. Could you also clarify your statement on the bubble? You said that it was talked about. Is that one of your positions, that you would support an exchange at the top——

The President. Sure, at some level.

Q. What rate would you——

The President. I've told you I'm not going to try to negotiate it here. I want to get something done in these committees. So, what we've got to do is get with the Senate leaders, House leaders, Finance, and Ways and Means, and see if we can reach a formula. I don't think it would be helpful to draw a line in the sand on what percentage of the exclusion on capital gains and then what we'd give in terms of leveling out the bubble or getting rid of the bubble.

Q. Mr. President, during the campaign, when you took the position that you absolutely, positively would not raise taxes under any circumstance, and then a lot of your fellow Republicans, as you know, were encouraged to follow suit by taking this anti-tax pledge—do you think that that now is part of the reason that you're having——

The President. Yes?

Q. ——so much trouble?

The President. I think that makes it more difficult for people.

Q. Do you regret that you took that position?

The President. No, because what I do is take a look at the situation at the time—see the changed economics and say, I've got to go forward here.

Q. Except that the deficit was very large then also.

The President. Well, I know, but I thought we could get into effect the program that I ran on. Ran up against a lot of Democratic opposition—sent a budget up that didn't gain the support we wanted, and have done that twice. But I think you raise a good point, and some have told me that when I was talking to them.

Q. Mr. President, a question about the process. The budget now being back in the hands of the congressional committees, where it was envisioned in the first place, do you have second thoughts about all this summitry that led up to this situation?

The President. No, I don't, because what we did is to get a deal that I think has support from the American people overall. And we've gotten out a lot of the underbrush. We've moved out a lot of the debate and moved it into a package that was supported by the President, by the Republican leader in the House and the Senate, and by the Democratic leaders in the House and the Senate.

So, I think we've made some progress, even though, obviously, it didn't get through either House. But now we're going to have to keep working this week. And some of the Members who would like to do it exactly his or her way are going to see that it doesn't work quite that way. So, I don't think it's been time wasted at all.

Q. Well, how badly does it undercut you politically in terms of some of the antagonism between your staff, your budget director [Richard G. Darman, Director of the Office of Management and Budget], your Chief of Staff [John H. Sununu], people on the Hill, and within the Republican Party?

The President. I don't worry about that at all. I really don't. I've been campaigning for, and will continue to campaign for, people that might agree with me on this or might disagree with me on this; and we have broad principles that unite us. And when people get tired and stay up until 3 in the morning, every morning, why, there's bound to be tensions. Calm it down, and try to go forward—that's my approach to it.

Palestinian Demonstrators Killed in Jerusalem

Q. Mr. President, yesterday Israeli forces used the live ammunition to put down demonstrations in Israel, killing 19 Palestinians. Today Saddam Hussein [President of Iraq] is using that incident in an attempt to rally Arab support against Israel and, essentially, against the United States in the region. Do you think this incident could create a crack in the alliance against Iraq? And what's your reaction to the incident?

The President. Well, I don't think it could do that. But, look, let me just express my strong feelings about this. First, my sorrow at this tragedy. It is particularly saddening, given the sanctity of the holy places and observances there, that violence shattered all of this. And I want to echo what [Secretary of State] Jim Baker said earlier: that Israeli security forces need to be better prepared for such situations, need to act with greater restraint, particularly when it comes to the use of deadly force. And at this point, what is needed most of all is calm on all sides.

I don't think I need to say this, but let me just state that we want to see the longstanding policy of maintaining open access to the holy places preserved, tempered only by mutual respect for people of other faiths. So, I am very, very saddened by this needless loss of life, and I would call on all for restraint. The action will shift to the United Nations now.

To the other part of your question, Jim [Jim Miklaszewski, NBC News], there's no relationship here. Saddam Hussein has tried to, from the very beginning, justify the illegal invasion of Kuwait by trying to tie it in to the Palestine question. And that is not working. The Arab world is almost united against him. If he tries now to use this unfortunate incident to link the two questions, I don't think that will be successful. And certainly, I will be doing what I can to see that it is not successful.

Having said that, I hope nobody questions our interest in seeing a solution to the Palestine question, to the implementation of the Security Council resolutions. And that's what Jim Baker has been working so hard on for such a long time. But let's separate out this violence and say: We deplore it, and it must not happen, and regret it—the loss of life—for everybody.

Persian Gulf Crisis

Q. Also a followup, please: Saddam Hussein also indicated today that the Iraqis have a new sort of missile that can reach into Israel and can reach the U.S. troops, and he's threatening to use that force.

The President. I noticed that, and I notice he's getting a little more bellicose. Once in

a while you see a conciliatory statement, and then you hear a lot of heightened rhetoric about what he is going to do and what he's not going to do. Now, I'm satisfied that we can defend our interests now, and I'm satisfied that these threats of his are counterproductive in terms of solving any peaceful resolution of the question. They don't help a thing; they just polarize.

So, I don't want to overreact to it. I keep reading statements like this, ever since this illegal annexation, illegal aggression took place. There's not too good a pattern. We watch it very carefully, and it's pretty hard to detect a pattern. Now there's a theme, and that is trying to link the Palestine question into his—kind of giving justification for what he did against Kuwait. And yet the logic falls totally flat.

Palestinian Demonstrators Killed in Jerusalem

Q. Mr. President, on that subject, you said the action now shifts on this one to the United Nations. Having just been to the United Nations and talked about its increased relevance and role, how far are you prepared to go as far as the United States is concerned in meeting some of the Arab efforts to partially condemn Israel's action and pass a resolution in that regard?

The President. I think it all depends what the resolution is. And so, that's just starting up there now, and we're not sure exactly what direction it all will take. So, I'd want to stop short of saying exactly what the U.S. Government could support or what it couldn't support.

Persian Gulf Crisis

Q. If I may, sir, on a related topic: When the Amir of Kuwait [Jabir al-Ahmad al-Jabir Al Sabah] was here, you expressed grave concern about the dismantling of Kuwait.

The President. Yes, I did.

Q. Your advisers said that that could affect the timetable for permitting sanctions to work. What is your feeling on that now, and is the dismantling continuing?

The President. I thought General Scowcroft [Assistant to the President for National Security Affairs] put it very well after the Amir left here. And I am very much concerned, not just about the physical dismantling but of the brutality that has now been written on by Amnesty International confirming some of the tales told us by the Amir of brutality. It's just unbelievable, some of the things at least he reflected. I mean, people on a dialysis machine cut off, the machine sent to Baghdad; babies in incubators heaved out of the incubators and the incubators themselves sent to Baghdad. Now, I don't know how many of these tales can be authenticated, but I do know that when the Amir was here he was speaking from the heart. And after that came Amnesty International, who were debriefing many of the people at the border. And it's sickening.

And so, if your question was how long, I can't give you an answer in days or months, but it is a new equation in the last 3 weeks—the systematic dismantling of Kuwait that concerns us enormously. And I think the more people understand it, the more Saddam Hussein will be condemned. But I have to stop short of telling you where that leads me to in terms of recommending action by the allied forces there.

Q. It does sound like your patience is wearing thin on the sanctions.

The President. It's wearing very thin on that account, yes.

Foreign and Domestic Policy

Q. Mr. President, a couple of minutes ago, you said that public opinion seemed to support your handling of foreign affairs better than domestic affairs. Why do you think you're so much more comfortable with or better at foreign matters than domestic? To some people, it seems like almost two Presidents here.

The President. Well, I've read that sophisticated analysis. [*Laughter*] And I'm troubled because I don't really know the answer to it. Perhaps it has to do with the fact that in one, I think the Vandenberg theory applies. People really basically want to support the President on foreign affairs, and partisanship does, in a sense, stop at the water's edge. Whereas on domestic policy, here I am, with Democratic majorities in the Senate and Democratic majorities in the House, having to try to persuade them to do what I think is best. It is complicated.

I mean, I think that's part of it. Well, I don't want to get stretched out on the couch too far in terms of analysis. [*Laughter*]

But when you get a problem with the complexities that the Middle East has now and the Gulf has now, I enjoy trying to put the coalition together and keep it together and work towards what I think is a proper end, seeing that this aggression doesn't succeed. I can't say I just rejoice every time I go up and talk to Danny Rostenkowski, my dear friend, about what he's going to do on taxes. Does that help you? [*Laughter*]

Have you got a followup?

Q. It doesn't sound like you have as much fun at it as you do at the other.

The President. That's about right. [*Laughter*]

Mr. Fitzwater. Final question, please.

Federal Budget Negotiations

Q. Mr. President, you pulled out all the stops on this budget deal, and it just flopped. Are you concerned, sir, that your leadership on other domestic issues now will be eroded since you couldn't carry even half your own party in the House? You talk about clean air. You talk about crime. Are you worried that you're just going to—the honeymoon is entirely over?

The President. No, because I want to talk to Speaker Foley about this and [Senate majority] leader Mitchell, because they pulled out all the stops and they didn't get the votes they needed. So, I don't think they feel that they can't conduct their business in the House or in the Senate. And certainly, I don't feel that I can't conduct my business here. So, I don't think there is erosion. In fact, you saw the House side come together in terms of a veto right quick, like that. And I think there's a certain maturity there. And we go on to the next event—I mean—and stay with it. You can't stay there forever and mope about it. I don't worry about that.

Q. In terms of the disdain up on the Hill from both Republicans and Democrats for some members of your staff—some of them in this room—have you taken any of your staff to the woodshed, sir?

The President. Absolutely not. I have full

confidence in them. And when the passions get high, I understand that there's bound to be a little broken china up there. But, hey, look, if I got outraged every time I watched C–SPAN and heard some outrageous Democrat go after me, and I sulked about it and I fretted about it, and I called Tom Foley about it and said why do you permit this, I wouldn't be able to do anything. So, I don't worry about that.

In terms of my team, they did an outstanding job. And I've had more Members tell me that. So, what you hear is the squeaking wheel. You hear those that aren't particularly happy. Maybe they didn't get it exactly their way. The news, of course, is man bites dog. Republican goes after Republican. So, I don't think we've got a problem at all. We've got three bright people working hard to move my objectives forward—and I think they happen to be the country's objectives—forward.

Q. Who, sir, are these Members of Congress who are hailing the work of your team?

The President. Plenty of them. Go talk to the leadership. Talk to Bob Michel. Talk to Bob Dole. They're the leaders. They're the key leaders of the Congress. You want to talk about a squeaking wheel from time to time. I want to talk about those that have a broader view of things.

Two more. One, two—and that's the second in the middle. [*Laughter*]

Q. You forgot the back row.

The President. That's the way we counted the votes on the deal. Go ahead. [*Laughter*]

Q. Following on Ellen's [Ellen Warren, Knight-Ridder Newspapers] question, do you think anyone on your staff—or do you think, in general, not—without naming names, which I'm certain you won't want to do in any case—didn't the White House end of this handle anything wrong? Is it all——

The President. I probably made some mistakes. I thought, frankly, that we had a deal that would get support from a majority of the Republicans. And I tried very hard. I made, golly, I can't remember how many phone calls. So, if we're trying to assign blame, lay it right here. But I'm not going to go into trying to analyze the performance of each staff member, because I have confidence in the constructive role they

played in bringing the deal as far as it was brought.

Sat there night after night, day after day, trying to make something positive happen. The time we had of what seemed to be a harmonious meeting in the Cabinet Room, those leaders that were there spoke very proudly and positively about the role of the White House negotiators—with great awe of some of them because of the totality of their knowledge on the details of this. So, I can't get all caught up because there's now a new wave of stories trying to get inside the White House as to who's winning, who's losing. I mean, that's endless, and we can't do it.

Once and then twice. Sorry, we really do have to go.

Q. Mr. President, you've correctly noted that the Democrats and the Republican majority voted against the deal last week, but you've omitted mentioning that only the Democrats voted in both Houses—a majority of the Democrats voted for it in the new deal. And a majority of the Republicans feel that's because you met the objections of Democrats and that you signed onto that this morning. Could you explain why you agree——

The President. The budget resolution was passed with Republican votes. We provided a majority of our people to vote for it up there.

Q. Yes, but not the majority in the House, sir, by far, and only a bare majority of four in the Senate.

The President. But they voted, I thought, overwhelmingly and on the record for the continuing resolution.

Q. You don't feel you have any opposition among Republicans in the House?

The President. Oh, yes. Absolutely.

Q. What are you going to do to fix that?

The President. Work with the committees, try to point out what we're working towards—and towards $500 billion in serious, real budget cuts. And then ask them, here's what you want, now we've tried that one. How will you get it done? Listen intently, reach out to heal. Get everybody in the room and say, now wait a minute, how are we going to get something done? It's easy to be against something, but what are we going to be for? How are we going to solve the problem so we don't mortgage the future of the kids, and so we move forward and get interest rates down, and so we create more jobs? And I've got to do quite a bit of that myself, and the staff will be working with that approach. But that's the way I do it.

Last one. Yes?

Q. As you pointed out a lot of the hard work really remains ahead. Are you determined, as you were before, to keep Congress to the October 19th deadline? Will you veto another CR [continuing resolution] if they haven't finished the job by then?

The President. I think the fact that I vetoed that last one resulted in the new budget resolution and a continuing resolution that we could accept, because the budget resolution was passed, both Houses. I'm absolutely convinced that if I had not vetoed that CR and that had not been sustained, everybody would have gone home, they'd all marched in the parades for Columbus Day holding the signs up, and started negotiating today. So, once in a while the President, using the veto, can indeed move the process forward. And that's exactly what happened. And I would do it again if I felt that it would constructively lead to getting the problem solved.

Let me make this point again. Last summer, it was my gut instinct to ask the Congress to stay here and not go off for a vacation. And I talked to the leaders and they convinced me, for better or for worse, that that would be counterproductive. Looking over my shoulder—somebody here—what mistakes have I made, or did we make—that may have been one of them because I think maybe we could have had a lot of this underbrush out of the way well before now if I had done that. But I didn't do it. And they told me, they assured me it would be a much more cooperative environment after Labor Day.

Now, they asked me the other day not to veto this continuing resolution—the Democratic leaders did. And I said, look, I hope you don't think I've been under any false colors with you people, because I've made very clear that I'm going to veto it. And they agreed with that, but they just thought I made the wrong call on it. I don't think

so. I think I made the right call, and I think there's one of the times when a President's veto can discipline the process. And so, I reserve the option to use whatever constitutional weapons I have to move things forward.

Q. Sir, will you veto the civil rights bill now?

The President. I think that's the last question, we said, by agreement there. And so, thank you very much.

Q. What about the civil rights bill?

The President. Mary [Mary McGrory, Washington Post], you haven't been here in a long time. I run the risk of getting into trouble here because you haven't been too understanding of my programs, but what is it? [*Laughter*]

Q. Will you veto the civil rights bill?

The President. Is your name Mary?

President's Support for Republican Candidates

Q. Last week your Chief of Staff said that you would go into Members' districts who opposed you on the budget resolution. This morning you have said you will go into their districts. Is this a thought-out strategy of bad cop-good cop? And if it's just a routine, don't you think people would feel cynical?

The President. Why don't I let the Chief of Staff say what it was he said exactly. You heard what I said. And he and I are in total agreement on what I will do in terms of campaigning. Would it be useful to have him repeat what he said?

Q. Yes.

Mr. Sununu. I said the President will be out there campaigning for them and might look them in the eye and ask for their support on the budget. That's what I said.

Q. You didn't say that he would go into their districts and campaign against them?

Mr. Sununu. No, I didn't. And nobody has said I said that. What I said was: The President could go into your district, campaign for you. If he wants your support on the budget, he's going to look you in the eye sometime and ask you to do it, and I hope that you've supported him because if he looks you in the eye and asks you to do it on the campaign, it might be a little embarrassing.

Q. Did you go too far, Governor?

Mr. Sununu. I don't think so. We got a budget passed, didn't we?

Note: The President's 63d news conference began at 10:30 a.m. in the Briefing Room at the White House. Marlin Fitzwater is Press Secretary to the President.

Remarks at a White House Briefing on Drugs in the Workplace
October 9, 1990

I'm sorry to have missed the briefings, but I first wanted to thank Jim Burke, my old friend, and Bill Moss, Bob Allen for co-hosting this event today. And of course, thank Bob Mosbacher and our czar, Bill Bennett, for participating today as well.

You know, I am very pleased to be over here. A lot going on in other quarters, as we all know. [*Laughter*] But we've got to keep the focus on your important work here, and I think we are endeavoring to do that. So, I really wanted to come here to just demonstrate my determination to do everything in my power to see that the scourge of drugs is banished from this country.

It may not always be on the front pages, but let me assure you that it's on our minds every day. Bill Bennett is doing an outstanding job in this fight, coordinating a lot of strong-willed Cabinet officers in the process—Bob Mosbacher, Jim Baker fully involved because of the international aspects of this. So I can tell you, it does have the attention and concern of all our top administration officials.

By strengthening our interdiction efforts and then supporting law enforcement and expanding our treatment opportunities, I think we're doing our part. You can't say we can't do more. But we've got a good national drug strategy that I'm sure you've heard about and that's been spelled out so clearly by Bill Bennett.

But I keep coming back to what Jim Burke and I first talked about. And that is simply that this war is not going to be won by government alone. It simply cannot be. And so, we have to enlist the aid of every corporation. Seventy percent of all illegal drug users are employed. One in twelve full-time employees report current use of illicit drugs. But day by day—and you've heard the numbers—we are winning the fight against drug abuse in the workplace, due in large part to the corporate Points of Light which are shining brightly all across this country, many of which are represented right here today.

There are countless ways in which corporate America can make a real difference in the communities in helping them be drug-free. There are counseling and treatment programs in the workplace for drug-dependent workers, and then also for the families of these drug-dependent workers. Education programs show employees how to avoid the temptation of drugs. Many companies are going way beyond the workplace to fight drugs and their ravaging effects in their surrounding communities. It's almost like some of you all are adopting the communities in which you live, and it's a wonderful thing.

Many corporations fighting to make the workplace and the larger community drug-free are exactly what we talk about when we talk about this concept, Points of Light. You know, when that slogan or those words were put together and we started in talking about them—I see Gregg Petersmeyer, who's our lead in the White House on this—when that all started, it passed the laugh test, but people weren't quite sure whether we'd follow up. And I'll tell you, it is wonderful when you go out around the country and meet some who have been designated Points of Light. It doesn't make the front page of the Washington Post or the evening news on the networks. But I'll tell you, it really spreads out through communities and then to neighboring communities across the States.

And so, I think the Points of Light concept is being understood. And I think it fits right in, Jim, to what you were talking to me about when I first became President—individuals, corporations, unions, schools, places of worship, groups, organizations of every type recognizing that drugs are, indeed, everyone's problem. So, being a corporate Point of Light in the fight against drugs is not some do-good concept. It's smart business, and it is indeed, in many instances, the key to our economic survival.

To maintain our edge in an increasingly sophisticated international economy, our workers have got to be literate and well-trained and, indeed, drug-free. So, when I talk about competitiveness now, I talk about the workplace being drug-free. Thanks to your efforts and those of the other Points of Light there's been a sea change in the attitude of a special group of Americans about substance abuse, and I'm talking about our young people.

Doing drugs is no longer—and I'm sure Bill's talked to you—perceived as "cool." It's come to be seen for what it is: a dead-end street, a dark tunnel with no light at the end. Those advertisements that Jim and others have been responsible for are really powerful—powerful message. I think they're getting through to the American people.

So, I wanted to thank you because you're helping me convey to the young people the message that there is no place for them in the work force of tomorrow if they're hooked on drugs today.

So, thank you very much for what you're already accomplishing, and I want to urge you to sally forth and enlist other corporations in this movement against drugs in the workplace. Every corporation can make elimination of drugs in the workplace its personal mission. We're on the right road; I'm confident we're heading in the right direction.

There is a light at the end of this tunnel. The figures back this up. It's not just our emotion—Bill Bennett's and mine, Bill Moss' and mine—the figures back this up, a direct and consequential result of your efforts beginning to pay off.

So, thank you very much for what you've done. Please keep it up. Thanks for coming to the White House, taking out busy schedules and taking your mind off of all of the problems that are out there. But I can't think of anything that gets more fundamentally to the fabric of our society than this question of illegal drug use and our challenge of trying to get rid of it. So, thank you all very, very much. I appreciate it.

Note: The President spoke at 11:22 a.m. in Room 450 of the Old Executive Office Building. In his remarks, he referred to James E. Burke, chairman of the Partnership for a Drug-Free America; William Moss, Chairman of the President's Drug Advisory Council; Robert E. Allen, chairman of American Telephone and Telegraph Co.; Secretary of Commerce Robert A. Mosbacher; William J. Bennett, Director of National Drug Control Policy; Secretary of State James A. Baker III; and C. Gregg Petersmeyer, Deputy Assistant to the President and Director of the Office of National Service.

Statement by Press Secretary Fitzwater on the President's Meeting With Prime Minister A.N.R. Robinson of Trinidad and Tobago
October 9, 1990

The President met today with Prime Minister A.N.R. Robinson of Trinidad and Tobago in the Oval Office. The President expressed his sorrow over the loss of life in the coup attempt in late July, and he congratulated the Prime Minister and his government for the bravery shown in confronting the terrorists and in defending their democratic institutions. The Prime Minister thanked the President for U.S. support of democracy in his country. He said that the situation had returned to normal.

The United States and Trinidad and Tobago have closely cooperated on a number of issues of mutual concern. The President commended the Prime Minister for his market-oriented economic policies, his commitment to the war on drugs, and for his strong statement of support for U.N. measures against Iraqi aggression. The recent extension of the Caribbean Basin Initiative is a sign of our firm commitment to the economic well-being of the Caribbean, and we are confident that the Enterprise for the Americas Initiative will support Caribbean integration.

Statement by Press Secretary Fitzwater on the President's Meeting With Foreign Minister Sa'ud al-Faysal Al Sa'ud of Saudi Arabia
October 9, 1990

The President met this afternoon in the Oval Office with His Royal Highness, Prince Sa'ud al-Faysal, the Foreign Minister of the Kingdom of Saudi Arabia. The President asked the Prince to convey to His Majesty, King Fahd, assurances of the United States continued commitment to ending Iraq's occupation of Kuwait and the restoration of the legitimate government of Kuwait. The Prince said that Saudi Arabia is pleased by the support it has received from the United States and the international community in opposing Iraqi aggression. The President and Prince Sa'ud both agreed on the importance of economic sanctions as a means of achieving a peaceful solution to the crisis. They also shared their concern over Iraq's brutal behavior against Kuwait and the Kuwaiti people. They also discussed other matters, including the recent violence in Jerusalem, deploring it and calling upon all parties to exercise restraint.

Remarks at a Fundraising Breakfast for Senator Jesse Helms in Raleigh, North Carolina
October 10, 1990

Thank you for that welcome. And let me say at the outset, I'm very, very pleased to be back. It's always good to see Governor Jim Martin, Dottie. He hasn't lightened up any, but nevertheless—[*laughter*]—I'm glad to see him. Of course, Jim Gardner, my old classmate in the House, and his wife, Marie, and to Bill Graham, our State banking commissioner, who did a fabulous job as the Bush-Quayle chairman for the State, and of course, to our present State chairman, Jack Hawke, who's doing a superb job for the State party—thanks to each and every one of you.

If recent events have shown anything at all, it is that we need more Republicans in the Congress. There are two here today who you must support, should support, will win: Ted Blanton and John Carrington, both running for the House—and we need them. We also have some State legislative candidates: State Rep Art Pope and Skip Stam—both are needed back in the Statehouse. Don't forget that level of government. And we should send Bill Boyd to the State senate to join them. Also, a big thank you to those who made this special event possible: Jim Johnson, the chairman of RJR, and to Jim and Dave and so many others that have been so instrumental in the success of this important event.

I'd be remiss if I didn't mention two who flew down with Jesse and me today on Air Force One. First, someone who this crowd is particularly proud of, and I'm talking about our Secretary of Labor, Elizabeth Dole. She has done an outstanding job for us. And then another who has roots in this State and has done a superior job, a superb job, of heading up our battle against narcotics—designed our national drug strategy that is beginning to work—and I'm, of course, talking about Bill Bennett, the drug czar, down here.

And again, it's great to be back in Raleigh. I bring you greetings from Barbara. Dot—where's Dot? She sends you her special love. They're very good friends. To brag just a little bit, I'd like to point out what a great job my Barbara is doing to combat illiteracy in the United States.

When we first arrived in Washington, the words of Harry Truman and advice stuck in my head. He said, "If you want a friend in Washington, get a dog." [*Laughter*] Well, times have gotten a little hectic up there. Who would have thought that our own dog, Millie, would write a book that was the number one on the bestseller list last week of the New York Times? [*Laughter*] Give her Alpo and she wants to see the wine list. [*Laughter*]

But it is a pleasure to be here after this momentous week: the unification of Germany, the bipartisan budget agreement, and of course—particularly here in the Tarheel State—the 30th anniversary of "The Andy Griffith Show." [*Laughter*]

But I am very proud and privileged to again be at the side of my friend, this champion of conviction, Senator Jesse Helms.

As a public servant who's given 18 years to the U.S. Senate, Jesse has become one of its most effective leaders as a watchdog of taxpayer money and a defender of family values. And he's earned a reputation—well-earned reputation—of independence and candor. And occasionally, of course, there are going to be differences. And yesterday we had a national press conference there, and they tried to point out, well, Jesse wasn't with us on one issue or another. That's not the point. The point, I told them, is that if we had more Senators like him we wouldn't be trying to solve some of these problems. They should have been solved months ago—years ago.

But we've got a budget problem, and we are standing together. And the fact that the Democrats control the Congress is all the more reason for Republicans to stand firm to make this the best budget deal possible.

Pressures caused by the deficit have been boiling for years. This year, they've reached the boiling point. For 8 long months, we've wrestled with this problem. For 8 long months, I've tried to negotiate in good faith and laid it on the table, even revenues. Took the heat, pushed hard for the bipartisan agreement not because it was the best plan ever but because it was the best plan possible. And I will continue now to press hard for a budget that fulfills the spirit of that bipartisan plan and proves to the American people once and for all that we can deal with this deficit that is mortgaging the future of those young children over there. We've got to turn it around now and get the deficit under control.

So, my objective now—and that's what Jesse and I and other leaders were talking about yesterday—is to put together a better package, one that meets our target of $500 billion of deficit reduction over the next 5 years. As the Congress works on this new agreement, let me be clear that any package I sign must meet the following criteria: It must be consistent with the themes of the bipartisan budget summit agreement. It must be produced on a bipartisan basis. And it must have full and fair opportunities for all voices to be heard. It must deliver real spending cuts with real savings.

The American people, I think, are sick and tired of this smoke-and-mirrors approach to the fiscal policy of the United States. So, I think it is time for the Congress to rise to the occasion, to make the hard choices and real reductions.

The budget must include progrowth incentives to create jobs and to keep the economy moving forward. And the spending cuts we agree on must be fully enforceable. And the budget I sign must include significant budget process reforms, just as those that were hammered out in that bipartisan agreement. Someday I would like to have—and I expect I can confidently speak for Jim Martin—what he'd like to have in the State, I'd like to have at the Federal level—if the Congress can't do these cuts, the cuts that Jesse's been recommending for years, give the President the line-item veto. Give him a shot at it.

And I'm also still in favor of the balanced budget amendment. I think it would discipline the Congress, and I think it would discipline the Federal Government as well. I think the American people have every right to expect more from their elected representatives. So, let's not let them down. If this is the best the system can do, then it's time to build a better budget system.

And Jesse knows exactly what I'm talking about because he is one of the toughest fighters in Washington for lower government spending. He's out there on the point day in and day out. And ironically, he practices what he preaches. He's never taken a so-called junket. He doesn't send out mass mailings at taxpayers' expense. And he's returned $3 million to the United States Treasury in unused office funds.

This is an interesting statistic: He ranks number one in the Senate for cutting wasteful spending and opposing massive spending bills, according to the National Taxpayers Union. In fact, that group said: "If every Member of Congress cast spending votes as carefully as Senator Jesse Helms, we would have a balanced Federal budget, lower taxes, and a healthier economy." And I agree with that, and the people of North Carolina agree with that, too.

And he has always been a clear and a strong voice for this State. Ask the more than 43,000 North Carolinians who got their Social Security checks after Jesse cleared away the redtape for them, or the serviceman Jesse helped get home from the Philippines and into Walter Reed Hospital up there for malaria treatment, or the dying little boy whose dream of attending a Redskins football game and meeting players came true, thanks to this Senator. And that's the kind of compassion and commitment that North Carolina needs, and that's what Jesse Helms stands for. He's never forgotten who sent him to the United States Senate, and he never will.

And he is known as a tough fighter, a man of tenacity. Senator Sam Ervin once said, "I admire Senator Helms very much because he's one of the few men in public life who's got the courage to stand up for what he honestly believes. Courage," he

went on, "is the rarest trait among public men. Many of them are intelligent, but there are very few of them that are courageous." What a wonderful tribute to your Senator.

True grit. Speaking of true grit, it was John Wayne who once said, "Jesse, we need a hundred like you." And I'll tell you, the liberals must be thanking their lucky stars they've only got one Jesse Helms. But if we did have a hundred, here's where it would have made a difference—one place—and that's on the crime bill I'm fighting for.

Jesse's father was a police chief. And he's supported 45 different bills to crack down on crimes and drugs. And Jesse, like me, believes that cop killers do deserve the ultimate penalty. And so, in May of '89, after consultation with Senator Helms and other leaders in the Senate, I sent our Violent Crime Control Act to Capitol Hill, with a real, workable death penalty for criminals who kill Federal law enforcement officers, right at the heart of the legislation. Last week, the House finally passed its version of our crime bill, after nearly 16 months of delay. Now it goes to the House-Senate conference committee for deliberations. Well, if we had a Republican majority, that crime bill would have been passed 16 months ago. That's a disgrace, and that's why we need more Republicans in Congress—both Senate and House.

I think the voters are beginning to understand that our crime legislation seeks to eliminate these liberal loopholes that allow the worst criminals to escape punishment. And the message voters send to criminals in North Carolina will be determined by the Senator the voters send to Washington in November. And that Senator will, of course, be Senator Jesse Helms.

I've said it before here in the State and in Washington: The Jesse Helms I know is a man of conviction, a man who embodies the values of North Carolina's quiet and decent people—God-fearing good citizens who believe, for instance, as I do, in returning voluntary prayer to our nation's classrooms; people with the kind of mainstream values that gave them the nickname Tarheels—famous for sticking to their principles.

A reporter once asked Jesse what he would most like to be remembered for. Perhaps, thought the reporter, it would be Jesse's plan for choice in education or his tireless work on behalf of so many charities or even his magnificent family—five kids and six grandchildren. But the Senator replied this: "Not once have I bent a principle."

And that's the Jesse Helms who, for the last 18 years, has stood for one very important principle, a strong defense, even when it meant standing up against the odds. In the 1970's, Jesse was a lone voice crying out against the cuts in defense that nearly brought America to her knees. And he was one of President Reagan's strongest supporters in rebuilding our vital defense needs. Today freedom is on the march from Moscow to Managua, and it really is because America is strong again. And a strong America is helping build a more democratic world, offering the hope of freedom that could never have been offered if people saw this country as weak.

And now, as we face this new challenge in the Persian Gulf, we realize the importance of the decisions that were taken in the past years, by leaders like Jesse Helms, to keep our forces ready, mobile, in first-class condition. As they say, you've got to go with what you've got. And thank God the 82d Airborne, proudly stationed here in North Carolina, the All American Division, was at the ready when Saddam Hussein launched his unprovoked attack on Kuwait. Our service men and women at Fort Bragg, Camp LeJeune, and Cherry Point understand the need for a strong defense, and so does Jesse.

And the people of this State, perhaps disproportionately so, understand it. I've gotten long letters from many North Carolinians telling me of the wonderful community support in the State for our troops overseas. Thousands of families with loved ones far away in the desert sun have learned the hard way that—as one woman from Lexington, North Carolina, wrote me—"They also serve who only stand and wait." I thank each and every one of you for your service and support to those brave men and women.

Our GI's have left spouses and children behind and headed for the Persian Gulf, and on election day they will be sending in their absentee ballots from their posts. In a year that has seen so much encouraging movement toward democracy, the least we can do is exercise our own right to vote. We owe it to the millions of freedom fighters around the world working for democracy, and to troops defending democracy as well, to take the time to cast our ballots. So, let's make our country proud and get out the vote on November 6th.

North Carolina has this wonderful, proud heritage from the heart of the Smokey Mountains to the farms of the Piedmont to the barrier islands of the Outer Banks. In fact, on Kitty Hawk stands a granite memorial to the Fathers of Flight, the Wright brothers. The inscription commemorates their conquest of the air, their victory over gravity, "achieved by dauntless resolution and unconquerable faith." This November, those same qualities—dauntless resolution and unconquerable faith—will bring Jesse Helms to victory.

I think I would conclude by saying that this is perhaps the most challenging time to be President of the United States, certainly in anytime in the Nuclear Age, anytime since World War II. The challenges are enormous. And it's exciting to be there. And I am grateful, I might say, as I look around this room—and met some people earlier—for those who were so instrumental in my having a chance to serve in this way. And Barbara feels exactly the same way about it. But I want to put it in this perspective as we honor Jesse Helms: It is very important to a President that he has people in the United States Senate who will tell it as it is—in whom he has trust, in whom he has confidence. And I came here today to say I have trust and I have confidence in your Senator. Send him back to Washington!

Thank you, and God bless this State.

Note: President Bush spoke at 9:30 a.m. at the Raleigh Civic Center. In his remarks, he referred to Governor Martin's wife, Dottie; James Johnson, chief executive officer of R.J. Reynolds Tobacco Co.; James Peden, Jr., member of the State board of transporta-

tion; David Flaherty, State secretary of human resources; William J. Bennett, Director of National Drug Control Policy; and President Saddam Hussein of Iraq. He also

referred to "Millie's Book as Dictated to Barbara Bush." Following his remarks, President Bush traveled to St. Petersburg, FL.

Remarks at a Rally for Governor Bob Martinez in St. Petersburg, Florida
October 10, 1990

The President. Thank you very, very much. I'll get to that in a minute. [*Laughter*] Listen, Governor Martinez, and to Mary Jane, thank you both for greeting us. And thank all of you for that welcome. I want to pay my respects to all of you and thank you for being here. And I guarantee to get out of here before Marco gets in here—or whatever the name of that hurricane is—and I'm taking off my coat because it feels like it's coming.

My respects to Sheriff Allison DeFoor, the next Lieutenant Governor of this State. We need him. And inasmuch as this area of Florida has been right out in the forefront of the fight against drugs, I want to single out a member of my top echelon in government, the man that is leading the fight nationally against drugs, our drug czar, Bill Bennett. What a job he's doing. And to Congressman Ireland and Congressman Young, thank you for your support in being with us today. I'm particularly glad—whoops, he's not here. I was going to welcome another Floridian from this area who flew down with us on Air Force One, Mel Sembler, our Florida guy who's now our Ambassador in Australia. But forget him, he didn't make it. [*Laughter*] And of course, an old friend of mine, Van Poole, our State chairman—great to see you, Van, and thanks for what you're doing to get out the vote on election day. And I also want to single out the Governor's able, terrific, fantastic campaign chairman—that's my boy, our son Jeb, over here. And I want to put in a plug for John McKay and Don Sullivan. Next month let's elect them to the State senate and help Florida claim the first Republican legislative body in the entire South.

And lastly, but first in importance, I do want to say what a privilege it is to be back here on behalf of my friend of longstanding, your great Governor, Bob Martinez. His first term has been magnificent, and now we're going to ensure a second term that's even better—better for the people of Florida.

You know, this visit arose from a phone call. Jeb told the Governor, he said, "We've got a surprise for St. Petersburg which will really excite people." Bob said, "You mean big league baseball's finally coming to St. Pete?" But I'm not taking any sides in that fight. I know Tampa wants a team, Miami, Orlando—they're all in the expansion running, and they're running to win. And that's the whole purpose of my being here: I want to be standing next to a guy who is also running to win, and will win—Bob Martinez.

Most of you know the background, but let me give it to you once again: grandson of Spanish immigrants; son of a waiter; worked his way through school; became a teacher, then a businessman, then mayor of Tampa. Bob Dole calls him "Florida's distinguished and dynamic Governor." Ronald Reagan calls him "the embodiment of the American Dream." For my part, I just plan to call him Governor for the next 4 years.

Audience. Four more years! Four more years! Four more years!

The President. Okay, you guys are committed. That's good. So am I. [*Laughter*] Let me explain why I support him. First, he's a man of ingenuity. Who else but Bob would buy a little possum at Wausau's annual Possum Festival and then name it his campaign mascot? You see, he knows the difference between possums and liberal

Democrats. Possums only pretend to be asleep. [*Laughter*]

The Bob Martinez that I know also has conviction. He's not been a follower who gets lost in the current. He's a profile in character who alters the tide. We need a leader with that kind of courage in Tallahassee in the 1990's. He has not been afraid to make the tough decisions, and that is the kind of Governor we need.

He's strong on traditional values, keeping things in perspective. It's like Bob tells me, "It's fine that you're here, but if you really want to wow the crowd, bring Barbara." She's doing pretty well, isn't she? Best wishes, too, for the most charismatic figure in our family, the noted author Millie, our dog. [*Laughter*] Seriously, our dog wrote a book that was bestseller on the New York Times best-seller list a week ago.

You can see why this is the third trip then that I've made to Florida for Bob. We've probably spent more time on the road together than Hope and Crosby. But I'm back again because folks always respect him, even when they disagree with him. And so, I think the way to sum it up is that he is taking a strong stand for a better tomorrow.

Just a couple of the issues—look first at the environment. Every time I fish along the flats off Islamorada, I'm reminded how special Florida is. We want to protect those natural resources. So, Governor Martinez created the East Everglades Land Acquisition Task Force. And because Florida set aside part of this land, I was able to sign a bill increasing the size of the Everglades National Park by more than 100,000 acres. I hear the alligators are so pleased they're wearing Polo shirts with a picture of Bob Martinez on their chests up here. [*Laughter*] But also, I'm very pleased and grateful for his support for our rewriting of the Clean Air Act. The problem is that for 14 months the United States Congress has refused to act. Here's a solution: On November 6, elect Bob Martinez, who then will help convince the Congress to pass a clean air bill that I can sign.

And another area that unites us—and certainly one that Bill Bennett understands— I'm talking about crime and drugs. Bob knows that drugs threaten every single community in the United States. So, he set a precedent by appointing a State drug czar. And he also has another conviction that goes with the law enforcement side: He believes that cop-killers ought to get what they deserve. And so do I. And that's what we're trying to do in changing the Federal law. And so, he stiffened the Florida criminal code, doubling the prison space to enforce it—backs our administration's Crime Control Act to enact a workable death penalty—a real penalty—for those who kill our Federal law enforcement officers.

And last week, after 16 months of delay, the House of Representatives up there finally passed its version of the Crime Act. And now it goes to the Senate-House conference committee. And so, please help me. Join with me in sending them a message to draft a tough bill that takes the shackles off of the policemen, the courts, and the law of this land.

This past summer, Bob has taken his message to all 67 of Florida's counties. You get to know a State that way, understand its heartbeat, its priorities; get to learn what the voters want—policies which empower people, not the bureaucrats.

And perhaps the best example of this is a comprehensive budget agreement to cut the Federal budget deficit by $500 billion over the next 5 years. And I want the Congress to send me a plan which spurs growth, opportunity, and prosperity. Growth, opportunity, and prosperity— GOP—that has a nice ring.

So, let me tell you what needs to be done now in the next 10 days to get a final agreement on the Federal deficit that is mortgaging the future of these kids here. And let me be candid. There's no doubt that with Republicans in control of Capitol Hill—good ones, like the two that are sitting with me here today—there would be a different story to tell—something to keep in mind on November 6th. But the fact that Democrats control the Congress is all the more reason for Republicans to stand firm for the best budget deal possible.

Pressures caused by the deficit have been building for years, and this year, they reached the boiling point. For 8 long months, we've wrestled with this problem. And for 8 long months, I have tried to negotiate in good faith with the liberals in the Congress. And I believe the American people didn't send me as President to play cheap politics; they sent me up there to govern. And so, I put it all on the table, even the revenue side, even taxes. And I took plenty of political heat and then pushed hard for a bipartisan budget agreement not because it was the best plan ever but because it was the best plan possible. And now I will continue to press hard for a budget that proves to the American people that we can and that we will—in real terms—bring this ghastly Federal budget deficit to its knees.

And let me just say to the Members of Congress that might be listening: Here's things it's got to achieve. It must be consistent with that bipartisan budget agreement on the bipartisan basis it was produced. It must include progrowth incentives to stimulate the economy. It must deliver real savings through real spending cuts—cuts with teeth, cuts that are enforceable. And any budget I sign must include the significant budget process reforms hammered out in that bipartisan agreement. There is no point going into an agreement and then having the same congressional dance take place year in and year out at getting nothing done.

The test comes 9 days from now. And Congress' budget must still be passed by both Houses no later than October 19th. And let me make clear to Congress just how serious I am about this deadline. Last Friday night, with no budget agreement, I vetoed that thing—they call it the continuing resolution. And that keeps the government—to go—if they signed that and I had signed it, that would have just kept the operating of the government just day in and day out the same old way. Well, I vetoed that. The veto was sustained. And I kept the pressure on, and to make the point: No more business as usual. Let's get the job done, Members of Congress.

I didn't come down here to assign blame. But you know, I've seen those surveys. The American people are pretty smart. They know where the action is, and they know that Congress has the responsibility to pass

a budget. And it's about time that they met that responsibility.

And I might say parenthetically, I got a little heat for closing the Washington Monument. And I would apologize if there are any of those Boy Scouts or Girl Scouts here from Florida that went up there. But I know that if I hadn't taken that action Congressmen would have all headed home, marched out in the front of the Columbus Day parade all over the country, telling people what good they were doing, instead of staying in Washington and solving the deficit problem.

A sound budget deficit agreement will defend our vital interests at home, and all of us know that we must also defend our vital interests and our civilized values around the world. So, in the Persian Gulf, we have, and we will, take a strong, unalterable stand against the outrageous aggression of Saddam Hussein.

I read a lot of the letters from parents and relatives of those who have family over there, and I can't tell them—I wish I could—how long it will take to reach our objectives. And I can't tell exactly what sacrifices will be demanded. But this we do know: American troops will not remain in the Persian Gulf a day longer than we are wanted or needed by our friends. But we will stay for as long as it takes to complete our mission. We're going to keep up the pressure, and we're going to keep the faith—faith with our friends and allies and the U.N. and the American people—faith, finally, with the finest soldiers, sailors, airmen, and marines any nation could possibly have.

You want a couple Florida examples: Daniel Rich, an Air Force tech sergeant from Daytona Beach. And today he's standing shoulder to shoulder with colleagues like Army Lieutenant Colonel Robert Tippete, of Tallahassee, or the Marines First Lieutenant Helen Pratt, of Satellite Beach. And then there's Brenda Spriggs. And she wrote me from Fort Lauderdale to say how proud she is of her son Jeff, currently serving out there in Saudi Arabia. Mrs. Spriggs, let me tell you, I share your pride. And to you I pledge: America will never, ever, let our service men and women down. We will stand with them in every single way possible.

These kids show that America would not be the land of the free if it were not also the home of the brave. And Bob knows this—Bob Martinez. He knows that while our forces are defending us abroad we must defend them here at home. And so, on November 6th, let's take a strong stand for what America is and what America stands for, what we embody in the world: Let's get out the vote. Let's win the State senate and the house of representatives. And let's roll up our sleeves and reelect this outstanding Governor.

Thank you for this occasion. God bless the United States of America. And let's keep Bob Martinez our great Governor.

Note: President Bush spoke at 1:30 p.m. in Vinoy Park. In his remarks, he referred to Governor Martinez' wife, Mary Jane; William J. Bennett, Director of National Drug Control Policy; Robert Dole, Senate Republican leader; and President Saddam Hussein of Iraq. He also referred to "Millie's Book as Dictated to Barbara Bush." Following his remarks, President Bush traveled to Atlanta, GA.

Remarks at a Fundraising Reception for Gubernatorial Candidate Johnny Isakson in Atlanta, Georgia
October 10, 1990

Be seated, at least some of you. [*Laughter*] Johnny, thank you very much. And to you and Dianne, Barbara and I send our warmest best wishes for a big victory in November.

And I want to thank Chairman Poitevint, who is doing such a good job for our party; former chairman and my great friend and longtime supporter, without whom I expect I wouldn't be standing here, Fred Coopert. And with him in those early days was Paul Coverdell, now doing an outstanding job for the Peace Corps, right here. And then, I know something from having been in politics a long time about the movers and shakers and the volunteers that make things happen. I want to pay my respects to Saye Sutton, over here—she is terrific; to finance chairman Joe Rogers, who's doing a great job.

Also with me is another one. I don't know that they were introduced. But I'll tell you something: If you look at the recent facts coming out on our national battle against drugs, we are making progress. And if there is one man that deserves the credit for our national drug strategy—that it's working— it's Bill Bennett, who is with me today. Where is the man? There he is.

And also sitting up here with me is the Deputy Secretary, the number two man in the Department of the Treasury, John Robson, well and favorably known to everybody. But he also is doing a superb job in Washington.

I'm glad to see our former Senator Mack Mattingly here—Barbara and my dear friend. Ann and John Parker, whom I go back with a long, long time. I think it was the Peanut Festival somewhere down the southern part of the State. [*Laughter*] But that's how I got started. John, thank you. Like my line of work now. [*Laughter*] And I want to single out John Lender, who is with us, I think, who is the candidate for the Fourth Congressional District—a winnable race. And we want to see him elected.

And I'm going to take all night doing this. But another friend, the guy that I served with in the Pacific—and he's been a strong supporter of me and of Johnny Isakson and others—Jack Guy was a torpedo bomber pilot. I'll give you a little war story. VT–51, back in 1944, and he's a winner of the Navy Cross and a close friend of mine and a longtime citizen of Atlanta, Jack Guy, right back here.

And last, but certainly not least, the guy that's been at my side in the campaign when the going was tough—and you heard him tonight—my dear friend, one of country's music's greatest stars, Lee Greenwood. Lee, thank you so much for being here.

And I've got to pay tribute to Atlanta for a lot of reasons, but it's great to be here in the proud home of the 1996 Olympics. You know, the other day—and I love the volunteer spirit on all of that—several of you were up there in the Rose Garden. And to you I apologize, because when you have that kind of enthusiastic group there, I just wish that Barbara and I could have made you feel a little more at home. But I had a chance there to congratulate another friend, your mayor, Maynard Jackson; Billy Payne, who Johnny talked about, who's done an outstanding job. I guess he really deserves the credit for their work. And especially had a chance to say what I think of the volunteer work—the volunteers, the Thousand Points of Light that went into this concept of bringing the Olympics to Atlanta. And so, I think it's going to be a fantastic group of Olympic games, and I am very, very pleased that it's going to be here. And I look forward to coming here.

Now, you're no stranger to spectacles, however. There's the Super Bowl coming in 1994. And of course, you remember the summer of 1988—the Democratic Convention. [*Laughter*] Atlanta has been a feat to some remarkable rhetorical gymnastics. [*Laughter*] And they kept asking—one lady's voice—"Where's George? Where's George?" Well, here I am, supporting Johnny Isakson to be the next Governor of the State of Georgia. And the "silver foot in my mouth" has melted, and everything's okay. Now—[*laughter*]——

I remember the call, "Where's George?" Today I was brought down to Earth, though, because I went in there campaigning for a guy and felt so good in St. Petersburg. A couple of signs saying, "Where's Millie?" That's our dog. I mean, they really know—[*laughter*]—if they really knew the truth, Millie—Barbara, you know, wrote this book, she and Millie together. It was number one on the best-seller list in the New York Times—number two this week, number one the week before. You say, "Where's Millie?" She's eating her Alpo and looking at the wine list back there at the White House. [*Laughter*]

But I've come to the capital of the new South, this great international city, with a message for the status quo: Georgia has potential unrealized, dreams yet unfulfilled. This State stands at the threshold of a new era, a bright new era with great possibilities. Everyone here is here because you understand that Georgia won't get there with the old ideas. It is time for new leadership. So, I came here today to lend my wholehearted support to the man who can bring Georgia out of the past with a brilliant future, Johnny Isakson. If they can do it in Czechoslovakia and if they can do it in Hungary and if they can do it in Romania, Johnny Isakson can bring two-party politics to the top of the ticket here in the State of Georgia.

He's been called Mr. Cobb County. The Jaycees call him outstanding. His fellow legislators call him effective and fair. And come the 6th of November, I'm going to call him Governor of the State of Georgia.

The new Georgia it is. Johnny has called for a "new partnership for Georgia's future." He wants to make the government—you heard it here—open to all citizens. He said it's time to "unshackle the limits of one party rule." And that means he needs the support of thinking Democrats and of Republicans and of independents to bring that new day to this State.

There may be some in the other party who think that they've got it locked up because of the way it used to be—a lock on the Georgia electorate. And we say to them, you may be in for a great big surprise in November. There may be some who take Georgia's vote for granted, who think people will settle for the policies of the past. We know those policies haven't worked and that the people of this State are ready for leadership that they can trust. Trust is the key word—leadership that uses its head, feels with its heart, and extends an offered hand to all Georgians, regardless of whatever walk of life they come from. And so, as I look at this race, having known Johnny Isakson and watched him and being his friend, I'd say that Georgia is now ready for Johnny Isakson to be Governor.

You know, he's devoted himself to the Governor's race as the "candidate for the children" because he understands that the future begins and ends with these kids—their education, their safety, their future. So, he's really committed himself to real school reform, beginning with the classroom—and you heard it—not the bureaucracy, beginning with the classroom. And because no kid can be safe as long as drug dealers wander the streets peddling poison, Johnny has already written tougher State laws for these merchants of death. As Governor, he wants to enlist every public institution, business, school, and campus, joining us in this national war against drugs that we're going to win.

And there's another thing. For all the people of Georgia, he understands the importance of partnerships for economic growth. He's built them himself in business, and he knows how to bring new business to Georgia.

And he also knows how to keep government spending under control, unlike his liberal opponent. For over a decade, he's fought for changes that would have prevented the fiscal problems of Georgia. And he's still asking, with good reason, how a State government could run out of money a year after the largest tax increase in State history.

He may never get an answer, but he knows how to make sure it never happens again. That's by getting at the root of the problem, by reforming the process—reforming the budget process. And I might say that that's what I'm working for at the Federal level. And believe me, when you don't control either House of the United States Congress, it ain't easy. [*Laughter*] And right now, the Federal budget process is like a huge Rube Goldberg machine: out of control—noise-producing, smoke, light, heat—I mean heat and no light at all. It is an outrage what's happening up there—and sucking up more and more tax dollars on one end and churning them into spending programs without end. And frankly, if we had more Republicans in Congress, we wouldn't be in this mess.

But I have got to work with the Democrats in Congress because I was sent there to govern, not to give speeches about it. And I want to tell you something: I've tried. For 8 long months, we've wrestled to get this deficit down. I do not want to be a legacy of my Presidency mortgaging the future again of these young kids here today. And so for 8 long months, we've tried. And I put it all on the table, and I've compromised. And I took plenty of heat for that politically. And I pushed hard for a bipartisan budget agreement because you can't get it done if you don't have the votes. We're outnumbered. We've got to get the Democrats to come with us not because—and incidentally, this plan, I'm for it not because it was the best plan ever, because it was the best plan possible that would reduce the budget by $500 billion over 5 years and we need it. And now I'm going to continue to press hard for a budget that fulfills the spirit of that plan—there are things wrong with that—and proves to the American people once and for all that we can deal with this deficit.

We've had a few days now for the smoke to clear, and now I think it's time for the country to move forward. We've got many thousands of men and women halfway around the world. We've got enormous problems facing this country in terms of a slow economy. You've got a Chairman of the Fed that says if you get a good deficit deal—the one that we had—that the interest rates will come down. So, now is the time to pull together and keep the pressure on the Congress until we get a budget deficit deal.

And you can't just get any deal. It's got to be one that ensures that four crucial tests are met—consistent with the budget summit agreement, full and fair opportunity for all voices to be heard. And it's got to include progrowth incentives, to create new jobs and keep the economy moving. The spending cuts that we agree on—and we must have them—must be fully enforceable spending cuts. And then, with those significant budget-process reforms hammered out in the bipartisan agreement. And finally, as I say, the deal must have real spending cuts—with real savings—because the American people are fed up with the Rube Goldberg budget machine in Washington, DC.

They gave me a little grief out there once in a while over the weekend there for shutting down the Government. Well, my feeling was it's no time for business as usual. And, yes, I vetoed that piece of—that, uh—[*laughter*]—that stuff that came down there. And everyone was saying: This is going to be a disaster. The Congress will be up and—both the Democratic leaders said: You can't do this. They're going to be all upset. I know what they want to do. They want to go home and march in the head of the Columbus Day parade. And so, we kept them there, and now we got a budget resolution. And the clock is running, and it's going to keep on running. And I'll veto it again if we don't get a satisfactory deal.

And the budget has got to be passed by both Houses no later than October 19th. And I'm confident that Congress can complete its vital work. I'm not just down on all the Democrats. Frankly, I think their leadership tried very hard to be cooperative in this. But there's got to be a sound budget passed that puts the Nation on the path to long-term economic growth.

And that's our problem in Washington. But here in Georgia, you're also approaching a deadline, a referendum, if you will, on the kind of leadership you want in the coming decade. And so, this race for governorship should rightly be understood as a choice between what has been, what was, and what should be. And we know how bright Georgia's future can be. If a journey of a thousand miles begins with a single step, Georgia's journey toward the future begins with a single vote. Every vote is going to count this fall.

So, let me ask all of you, irrespective of party, and all that aren't here tonight, irrespective of party: Get out and vote. Do all you can to get the people to the polls. It is a part of our heritage, and we ought to exercise our right to vote. Please urge your neighbors to vote. They're filling out absentee ballots halfway across the world now over in Saudi Arabia. And if they can do it and take the time in those adverse conditions, why, surely, all of us here tonight and those others across this great country of ours can do the same thing.

I might tell you that, as I climbed off Air Force One out there, there was a group of young soldiers—airmen, perhaps—from a Guard unit out here at the air base where we landed. And they had just come back from Saudi Arabia. And their kids were there, and they'd been touring planes, or taking people over, whatever it was they were doing—a transport unit of some kind. They're fine-looking young men. And I thought to myself what every member of the Joint Chiefs has told me about these kids—said these are the finest soldiers, sailors, airmen, marines—men and women—that the United States has ever had in uniform.

And I know that there are parents here probably tonight who have kids over there. And I want to tell you how strongly I feel about trying to do what is right to hold that fantastic international coalition together to lead and then to fulfill our mission. And our mission is to see that naked aggression will never pay off and international law will be respected and adhered to.

And so, when I saw those kids, I said to myself, I am going to do everything in my power in working with leaders around the world to protect them, to give them strength, to help them, and to see that we have a satisfactory conclusion. Never again is the United States going to cut and run from our responsibilities. And that message ought to be loud and clear for Saddam Hussein as well as to the people of America.

You've got a good man running for Georgia's Governor. You've got an outstanding man. You've got a family man and a wonderful guy. And so, my appeal to you now is help move this great State into the next century by bringing this outstanding man here as your next Governor. He's good. He's real. He's compassionate. He's strong. He's your friend, and he's mine. He's Johnny Isakson, the next Governor of Georgia.

Thank you all very, very much.

Note: President Bush spoke at 7:12 p.m. in the Grand Ballroom at the Waverly Stouffer Hotel. In his remarks, he referred to Johnny Isakson's wife, Dianne; Paul D. Coverdell, Director of the Peace Corps; Saye Sutton, chairman of the Governor's Host Committee; Joseph Rogers, finance chairman of the Johnny Isakson gubernatorial campaign; William J. Bennett, Director of National Drug Control Policy; Billy Payne, chairman of the Atlanta Organizing Committee for the Olympics; and President Saddam Hussein of Iraq. He also referred to "Millie's Book as Dictated to Barbara Bush." Following his remarks, President Bush returned to Washington, DC. A tape was not available for verification of the content of these remarks.

Appointment of David C. Gompert as Special Assistant to the President for National Security Affairs
October 11, 1990

The President today announced the appointment of David C. Gompert as Special Assistant to the President for National Security Affairs at the White House. He will also serve as Senior Director for European and Soviet Affairs.

Mr. Gompert's career has encompassed both government service and business. Most recently, he served as president of Systems Management Group for the Unisys Corp. He has also been a vice president with AT&T. From 1973 to 1983, Mr. Gompert held a number of positions in the U.S. Government, with responsibilities in European,

East-West, and national security affairs. He served in several positions at the Department of State, including Deputy to the Under Secretary for Political Affairs, Deputy Assistant Secretary for NATO and Southern Europe, Deputy Director of the Bureau of Political-Military Affairs, and Special Assistant to the Secretary. In addition, he has served on the national security staff.

Mr. Gompert graduated from the U.S. Naval Academy (B.S., 1967) and the Woodrow Wilson School, Princeton University (M.P.A., 1973).

Nomination of Marion Clifton Blakey To Be an Assistant Secretary of Transportation
October 11, 1990

The President today announced his intention to nominate Marion Clifton Blakey to be an Assistant Secretary of Transportation for Public Affairs. She would succeed David Philip Prosperi.

Since 1989 Ms. Blakey has served as Director of Public Affairs at the Department of Commerce in Washington, DC. Prior to this, she was Deputy Assistant to the President for Public Affairs and Communications Planning, 1988–1989, and Special Assistant to the President and Director of Public Affairs, 1987–1988. Ms. Blakey was Director of Public Affairs at the Department of Education, 1986–1987, and Special Assistant to the Secretary at the Department of Education, 1985–1986. Ms. Blakey served in several capacities at the National Endowment

for the Humanities, including Director of Public Affairs, 1982–1984; Assistant Director of the Division of Special Programs, 1980–1982; Director of Youth Programs, 1975–1980; program specialist for the research division, 1972–1974; and program assistant for the research division, 1970–1972.

Ms. Blakey graduated from Mary Washington College of the University of Virginia (B.S., 1970). In addition, she attended Johns Hopkins University, School of Advanced International Studies, in 1973 and the Universita di Firenza in Florence, Italy, 1969. She was born March 26, 1948, in Gadsden, AL. Ms. Blakey is married to William Ryan Dooley. They have one child and reside in Washington, DC.

Statement by Press Secretary Fitzwater on the President's Meeting With House Republican Leaders
October 11, 1990

The President met for nearly an hour and a half this morning with Republican congressional leaders of the committees of the House of Representatives to discuss the budget. This group parallels the Senate Republican ranking committee members that the President met with on Tuesday.

The President said: "The country needs a 5-year, $500 billion deficit reduction program to be enacted this month. The largest portion of that deficit reduction program must come from spending less, not taxing more. The savings must be real—no smoke, no mirrors—and the savings must be enforceable. And in signing the short-term continuing resolution, I stated these and other tests that a reconciliation bill must meet. I will not sign a reconciliation bill that fails these tests."

The President addressed the issue of tax rates, the bubble, and capital gains:

"We have been willing to explore a compromise if it were balanced and fair; that is, if the capital gains incentive were really strong and the rate change helped those in the bubble.

"Over a month ago, I authorized my negotiators at Andrews to explore such an option—up to 31 percent on the rate in trade for a 15-percent capital gains tax—if it could be part of an otherwise satisfactory $500 billion package. They were unable to negotiate such a compromise. Indeed, the idea was opposed not only by Democrats but also by some of the same Republicans who now favor it.

"I do not believe such a compromise is now possible. Indeed, I'm quite concerned that pursuing it in the current context may not only fail, it may legitimize something farther to the left that we cannot accept.

"In any case, I will not tolerate 'bursting the bubble' by raising rates to 33 percent. I believe that would mean far more than just 'taxing the rich.' It would start us back on the path toward higher income tax rates for everyone. I cannot accept that."

The President pointed out that the administration supported the bipartisan budget agreement, and he still feels it is a sound basis for agreement.

The President said the ball is now in Congress' court. He said that if Congress fails to pass a satisfactory reconciliation bill by October 19th, he will withhold his signature from any business-as-usual continuing resolution.

Remarks at a White House Briefing for Representatives of Veterans Organizations
October 11, 1990

Thank you very much for coming to the White House. And I want to single out and thank my fellow Cabinet member here, Ed Derwinski, who's doing an outstanding job for the American veterans, in my view. And I understand also that our Chairman of our Joint Chiefs was over here, Colin Powell. And then I think you heard from another right-hand man of mine who's the number two guy on our National Security Council, Bob Gates—extraordinarily knowledgeable about what's happening halfway around the world. And so, I hope you feel that it's been worth your time; from my standpoint, it is certainly worth mine to get to come over here and to greet this distinguished group.

I'm glad to see Bob Turner, Joe Andry, and Jim Kimery from three of our major veterans organizations. I just met with some others—important leaders—in the hall. I want to recognize Mr. Orval M. Hooten, over here, national commander of the Veterans of World War I. What I want to do is find out the kind of youth pills he's taking—[*laughter*]—because he was born in October 1895. Happy birthday, this month, thank you. And thanks for being with us, Orval.

We are pleased to welcome all of you here and to tell you how much that I personally—and all of us at the White House—appreciate your efforts, your organizations. And we support you, and we appreciate your support.

During the past 10 weeks, the events in the Gulf have reminded us of the importance of a strong America. And the world is still a dangerous place, and America must be ready. In World War II, the world paid dearly for appeasing an aggressor who could have been stopped early on. And we're not going to make that same mistake again.

Exactly 50 years ago today, America awoke to headlines of another massive air raid in London. The Battle of Britain was in full rage then. And true, the democracies were battered, but their resolve was never more clear. And they did, indeed, stand up to tyranny. And a day later, on October 12th, Operation Sea Lion, the invasion of England, was canceled. As Churchill said, it was truly Britain's finest hour. Such courage inspired America and, indeed, the world, which rallied to the cause of freedom and defeated the dark forces which threatened to engulf us all.

Since World War II, allied strength and resolve have been tested over and over again, but when we look back on that history of valor and sacrifice, it is clear that the strength of our arms and the strength of our will is up to the challenge in the Gulf. We're ready for that, and we're not alone. Thanks to the efforts of our U.N. Ambassador, Tom Pickering, and others, the U.N. Security Council has passed eight major resolutions setting the terms for solving the crisis.

And the Iraqi regime, in my view, has yet to fully face up to the facts. But as I've said, the annexation of Kuwait will not be permitted to stand. And the regime is up against not only the law of nations but also the law of mathematics. The numbers are against them. Today it's not Iraq versus Kuwait; it's not Iraq versus the United States; it's Iraq against the entire world.

By waging a war of aggression, plundering a peaceful neighbor, and holding these innocents hostage, Iraq has violated every standard of international behavior. And we're not talking about international etiquette here; we're talking about international law. And outlaw nations and outlaw leaders simply have got to understand that.

Here at home, the efforts of you in this room to improve the lot of veterans has been an important component in the success of America's all-volunteer forces. Colin Powell—maybe he told you about this—but he recently returned from a visit with our troops in the Gulf. And your support is evident in the pride and high morale found today in the young American heroes serving overseas.

It reminds me of another hero. And it was this very week in 1918 that Tennessee's Sergeant York captured 132 enemy prisoners and 35 machineguns singlehandedly. And when asked how he did it, he answered simply, "I surrounded 'em." [*Laughter*] And that's about what we've come to expect from an American soldier. And that kind of spirit is going to carry us to victory in whatever challenges we face.

Tonight, as evening falls across America, there will be candles in our windows and prayers in our hearts. The Empire State Building will be awash in lights—red, white, and blue—lights to honor the men and women now standing watch in the Persian Gulf. And like your presence here today—and like your good works every day—these gestures show that the folks at home have not forgotten the sacrifice of our soldiers and our sailors and our airmen and our marines—and I might add, also, our coastguardsmen, many on duty tonight many miles from home.

So, I really wanted to come over to thank you for the important work in defending our nation's freedom. You've been in the forefront. You've seen it clearly when others were suggesting that—given the relaxation of tensions with the Soviet Union and other countries in Eastern Europe—that the defense mission was over. Well, as we've seen clearly, it is not over. And I wanted to thank you all for the support that you have given to reasonable levels of defense spending, because you've seen so clearly the need to keep our country strong.

Thanks for coming to the White House, and God bless the United States of America. Thank you all very, very much.

Note: The President spoke at 11:45 a.m. in Room 450 of the Old Executive Office Building. In his remarks, he referred to Secretary of Veterans Affairs Edward J. Derwinski; Robert M. Gates, Assistant to the President and Deputy for National Security Affairs; Robert S. Turner, national commander of the American Legion; Joseph E. Andry, national commander of the Disabled American Veterans; and James L. Kimery, commander in chief of the Veterans of Foreign Wars.

Remarks and an Exchange With Reporters on the Federal Budget Negotiations
October 11, 1990

The President. This is what we call a modified——

Q. Photo opportunity.

The President. ——photo opportunity. Maybe take a couple of questions.

Q. No kidding. Yea!

The President. Which I haven't done since—in 48 hours. What do you mean, yea?

No, but let me just—I know there's a lot of interest in you all being here, and I'm very pleased to be meeting with the members of the Ways and Means Committee Republicans on the House side.

There have been a lot of different plans floating around. I'm strongly in favor of what's known as the Andrews summit or the Rose Garden summit agreement, and I'm very grateful to those here that did support us on that, particularly the leadership of the Republican side, Bob Michel and Bob Dole. It was a good plan. It got done what I wanted done, which was a $500 billion reduction over 5 years—real enforcement. Didn't get everything I wanted. Had to compromise.

But today Marlin put out a statement that demonstrated that we have tried other approaches. One of them included a certain flexibility on the question of capital gains. But I'm not very flexible on that. We tried at 31 percent and—15 percent on capital gains and income rates at 31. I will not go beyond that. But some in the House feel that there's room to maneuver there. My view is, it's going to be very difficult be-

cause our leadership tried very hard to get that, and the Democrats would not yield on that.

But nevertheless, 2 days ago I said there was certain flexibility, and that's what it is. My view is that it's not going to happen, and we're going to try to move forward in another approach. I notice with interest the bill—that the leadership role in Ways and Means coming out with a program—I don't know. I want to hear from you—this is consultation—as to how you read that. But it does seem to preserve some of the aspects of the bipartisan agreement, and thus, it will give us something to build around.

But I want to hear from you all when we get into the privacy of our talk. But it's coming forward, and we will get a deal, I'm convinced. Nobody is going to get it exactly the way they want.

Q. Well, are you going to tell the committee to go ahead and try to negotiate up to the 31——

The President. I think a lot of the people on the committee felt that they weren't—I was told this morning—I don't know about this group here—that maybe didn't have enough input. So, now let some try. I've told what I want. I've billed out the broad definition of what we need, and I've said that there's certain flexibility. But I'm not going to vary from the terms that I've just spelled out. If they can get that done, fine. I think it's a waste of time because I just don't think it can get through both Houses of Congress.

Q. Why not? Why not?

The President. Because it's just not going to get through both Houses of Congress.

Q. Well, why not just drop it then? Take it off the table instead of having——

The President. Because I'm not going to deny House Members an opportunity to do something that they think can be done. That's not my role.

Q. But what about those who are concerned that it will take up Members' time when they don't have a great deal before the next deadline is coming up?

The President. No. We've got to—everybody's looking at the time certain, which is the 19th. And that's where the President does have some say, because I'm going to insist that we have a package that fits this description. So, the meter is running.

But look, I can't dictate to the Congress—Republicans or Democrats—what to take up and when to take it up. I can say what we're for. And I stood out here in the Rose Garden and said what I'm for. I'm still for it. Now, if there's some modifications, I want to hear from ranking Member Bill Archer and from Bob Michel as to where they see us going. But the broad parameters must be met.

Q. Mr. President, you said repeatedly you like the original budget agreement. But that agreement raised taxes less on the wealthiest Americans than on middle-class Americans. Why aren't you——

The President. I don't buy the argument of the liberal Democrats. I fought that battle in the campaign. I don't buy the argument that our proposals favor the wealthy.

Q. These are figures from the nonpartisan Joint Committee on Taxation. [*Laughter*] You're saying, sir—you're saying, sir, that——

The President. ——answer. I hope it's played in full. [*Laughter*] I will say one

thing: A lot of these figures talk about tax rates, but they don't talk about the benefits that go into the whole equation. So, that's another very important part of it that's left out when people accuse us—me and all our colleagues around this table—of favoring the rich against the poor. It isn't true. In every campaign any of us has been in, that battle was taken to the American people, and they came down at least on the side of all of us that are sitting here around the table, or we wouldn't have been elected. That's the age-old Democrat cry of favoring the rich. The American people want to favor growth, and they want to favor jobs, and they don't believe all this handout mentality. So, we have a big difference, frankly.

Q. Do you think you've been damaged politically by this and called wishy-washy and flip-flopping——

The President. No, I don't think so. These things come and go. The best thing—we get a good deal. If we get a good deal, people forget the name calling, and they'll forget the little rancor and the tension at the time.

But the other thing—I'm elected to try to get something done here. Nobody thinks you can be popular by standing up and having to take, in a compromise, ingredients that you wouldn't necessarily want. So, I'll do what I think is best and take the slings and the arrows that go with it. I haven't felt too much pressure.

Note: The President spoke at 1:40 p.m. in the Cabinet Room at the White House, prior to a meeting with Republican members of the House Ways and Means Committee. In his remarks, he referred to Robert H. Michel, House Republican leader; Robert Dole, Senate Republican leader; Marlin Fitzwater, Press Secretary to the President; and Bill Archer, senior Republican member of the committee.

Remarks on Signing the Fire Prevention Week Proclamation
October 11, 1990

Let me just first greet the members of the fire-service community, Members of Congress who are here, officials from FEMA, Fire Marshal Bernard Johnson, Fire Chief Rayfield Alfred, my own firefighters—call them my own—Engine Company 13 and Tower 10—welcome to the White House. We've got a few fires to put out around here, and that's why I've been late. [*Laughter*] Thank you very much.

More than 2,100,000 fires broke out in the U.S. this year, claiming 6,000 lives. Fires strike at the most vulnerable among us, especially children and the elderly. And it also strikes the most valiant among us; many casualties are, indeed, the firefighters who lose their lives in a last-ditch struggle to save someone else's life.

Then, after the cost in lives, we've got to count the enormous property losses in excess of $8 billion. Now, these dollars cannot adequately represent the tragedy of so many beloved homes, churches, and businesses literally going up in smoke.

There is an army of dedicated Americans who stand ready to fight these fires, anytime, anyplace: the more than 1 million firefighters. The organizations involved in fire prevention efforts are too numerous to mention. But all are true heroes, and their heroic role is on display here today for National Fire Prevention Week.

At the Federal level, the U.S. Fire Administration, part of FEMA, is the national leader in firefighting and emergency response. These men and women from the Fire Administration are dedicated to the development of effective programs to help fire departments, State and local governments, private business and organizations, and educators promote fire safety and awareness in communities across the country. At the State level, many dedicated agencies labor to provide training courses for firefighters and emergency medical technicians, arson investigation services, and research. And of course, in virtually every community across this great country are the men and women who make up the

front lines in the battle, the firefighters, both career and volunteers, who continue a long and distinguished tradition of firefighting that goes back all the way to the first volunteer fire company founded by Benjamin Franklin in 1736.

Congress also has a role to play through the Congressional Fire Services Caucus, whose cochairmen are Senator McCain and Congressman Curt Weldon. The caucus boasts 370 Congressmen and Senators—370—making it the largest on Capitol Hill. Most of all, Congress recently updated our safety laws in the Hotel-Motel Fire Safety Act, authored by Congressman Sherry Boehlert.

All of these groups, from volunteers to Members of Congress, can tell you that the best way to fight fire is not with fire but with prevention. The National Fire Protection Association does a great job in this endeavor, working with young people such as Shanta Jones, the 1990 NFPA national fire safety poster contest child winner. In this and in so many other ways, they are getting the word out on fire prevention.

As you know, Tuesday marked the anniversary of a key event in American history, the great Chicago fire, a sweeping conflagration that destroyed most of that great city back in 1871. Years later, outrage over devastating citywide fires led to a national effort to prevent fires.

To focus this national campaign, President Wilson proclaimed October 9, 1920, National Fire Prevention Day. In 1922 President Harding made it Fire Prevention Week, saying that fire prevention should be practiced "by every man, woman, and child not only during the week designated in this pronouncement but throughout every hour of every day of the year."

That's true today. Every hour of every day, we can help save a life by preventing a fire. And we can keep these brave men and women with us today from having to risk their lives to save ours.

So, I am again very pleased to be with you all and to sign the proclamation declaring this week as National Fire Prevention Week. Thank you all for coming down.

Note: The President spoke at 2:45 p.m. in Room 450 of the Old Executive Office Building. In his remarks, he referred to Bernard C. Johnson and Rayfield Alfred, fire marshal and fire chief of the District of Columbia Fire Department. The proclamation is listed in Appendix E at the end of this volume.

Nomination of David A. Kessler To Be Commissioner of Food and Drugs
October 11, 1990

The President today announced his intention to nominate David A. Kessler, of New York, to be Commissioner of Food and Drugs for the Food and Drug Administration at the Department of Health and Human Services. He would succeed Frank E. Young.

Currently Dr. Kessler serves as medical director of the Einstein-Montefiore Hospital in New York and on the Advisory Commission on the Food and Drug Administration at the Department of Health and Human Services. In addition, he teaches food and drug law at Columbia University School of Law and has written extensively on FDA issues.

Dr. Kessler graduated from Amherst College (B.A., 1973), University of Chicago Law School (J.D., 1978), and Harvard Medical School (M.D., 1979). He was born May 31, 1951, in New York, NY. Dr. Kessler is married, has two children, and resides in Scarsdale, NY.

Statement by Press Secretary Fitzwater on President Bush's Telephone Conversation With President Mohammed Hosni Mubarak of Egypt
October 12, 1990

President Bush called President Mubarak to convey his condolences over the assassination of the Speaker of the People's Assembly, Rifaat el-Mahgoub. President Bush asked that his condolences be conveyed to the family, as well as to the families of the bodyguards who were slain. President Bush was shocked by this blatant and senseless act of violence. President Mubarak expressed appreciation for President Bush's call and concern.

The two Presidents briefly discussed the status of the current United Nations Security Council debate. They reaffirmed their commitment to work for a resolution that will enjoy the support of a majority.

Statement on Signing the Bill Establishing a National Policy on Permanent Records
October 12, 1990

Today, I have signed S.J. Res. 57, a joint resolution "To establish a national policy on permanent papers." S.J. Res. 57 brings to public attention the fact that future generations of Americans will lose access to documents of enduring value unless we take action.

A significant portion of our intellectual and cultural legacy is rapidly disintegrating in libraries, archives, museums, historical societies, and other repositories across the country. Millions of books, serials, manuscripts, and documents are decaying because of the acidic content of their paper. S.J. Res. 57 will help institutions and organizations responsible for these endangered materials to confront this problem by promoting the use of acid-free paper.

GEORGE BUSH

The White House,
October 12, 1990.

Note: S.J. Res. 57, approved October 12, was assigned Public Law No. 101–423.

Presidential Determination No. 91–3—Memorandum on Refugee Admissions
October 12, 1990

*Memorandum for the United States
Coordinator for Refugee Affairs*

Subject: Determination of FY 1991 Refugee Admissions Numbers and Authorization of In-country Refugee Status Pursuant to Sections 207 and 101(a)(42), Respectively, of the Immigration and Nationality Act

In accordance with section 207 of the Immigration and Nationality Act ("the Act") (8 U.S.C. 1157), and after appropriate consultation with the Congress, I hereby make the following determinations and authorize the following actions:

a. The admission of up to 131,000 refugees to the United States during FY 1991 is justified by humanitarian concerns or is otherwise in the national interest; provided, however, that this number shall be understood as including persons admitted to the United States during FY 1991 with Federal refugee resettlement assistance under the Amerasian admissions program, as provided in paragraph (b) below.

Ten thousand of these admissions numbers shall be set aside for private sector admissions initiatives, and may be used for any region. The admission of refugees using these numbers shall be contingent upon the availability of private sector funding sufficient to cover the reasonable costs of such admissions.

b. The 131,000 admissions shall be allocated among refugees of special humanitarian concern to the United States as described in the documentation presented to the Congress during the consultations that preceded this determination and in accordance with the following regional allocations; provided, however, that the number allocated to the East Asia region shall include the number of persons admitted to the United States during FY 1991 with Federal refugee resettlement assistance under section 584 of the Foreign Operations, Export Financing, and Related Programs Appropriations Act of 1988, as contained in section 101(e) of Public Law 100–202 (Amerasians and their family members):

Africa	4,900
East Asia	52,000
Soviet Union	50,000
Eastern Europe	5,000
Near East/South Asia	6,000
Latin America/Caribbean	3,100
Not Designated	[1] 10,000

[1] Funded by the private sector.

Utilization of the 121,000 federally funded admissions numbers shall be limited by such public and private funds as shall be available to the Department of State and the Department of Health and Human Services for refugee and Amerasian admissions in FY 1991. You are hereby authorized and directed to so advise the judiciary committees of the Congress.

Unused admissions numbers allocated to a particular region within the 121,000 federally funded ceiling may be transferred to one or more other regions if there is an overriding need for greater numbers for the region or regions to which the numbers are being transferred. You are hereby authorized and directed to consult with the judiciary committees of the Congress prior to any such reallocation.

The 10,000 privately funded admissions not designated for any country or region may be used for refugees of special humanitarian concern to the United States in any region of the world at any time during the fiscal year. You are hereby authorized and directed to notify the judiciary committees of the Congress in advance of the intended use of these numbers.

An additional 5,000 refugee admissions numbers shall be made available during FY 1991 for the adjustment to permanent resident status under section 209(b) of the Act (8 U.S.C. 1159[b]) of aliens who have been granted asylum in the United States under section 208 of the Act (8 U.S.C. 1158), as this is justified by humanitarian concerns or is otherwise in the national interest.

In accordance with section 101(a)(42) of the Act (8 U.S.C. 1101(a)(42)), I also specify, after appropriate consultation with the Congress, that the following persons may, if otherwise qualified, be considered refugees for the purpose of admission to the United States while still within their countries of nationality or habitual residence:

a. Persons in Vietnam and Laos who have past or present ties to the United States or who have been or currently are in reeducation camps in Vietnam or seminar camps in Laos, and their accompanying family members.

b. Present and former political prisoners, persons in imminent danger of loss of life, and other persons of compelling concern to the United States in countries of Latin America and the Caribbean, and their accompanying family members.

c. Persons in Cuba who are (1) in immediate danger of loss of life and for whom there appears to be no alternative to resettlement in the United States, or (2) are of compelling concern to the United States, such as former or present political prisoners, dissidents, or human rights and religious activists, or (3) were employed by the United States Government for at least 1 year prior to the claim for refugee status; and their accompanying family members.

d. Persons in the Soviet Union and Romania.

You are hereby authorized and directed to report this determination to the Congress immediately and to arrange for its publication in the *Federal Register.*

GEORGE BUSH

cc: The Secretary of State
The Attorney General
The Secretary of Health and Human Services

[Filed with the Office of the Federal Register, 12:45 p.m., October 15, 1990]

Note: The memorandum was released by the Office of the Press Secretary on October 15.

Nomination of Robert William Gambino To Be Director of Selective Service
October 15, 1990

The President announced his intention to nominate Robert William Gambino, of Virginia, to be Director of Selective Service. He would succeed Samuel K. Lessey, Jr.

Currently Mr. Gambino serves as vice president of the Petite Research Group, Inc., in Falls Church, VA. Prior to this, he served as project manager for the System

Planning Corp., 1987–1988; self-employed consultant, 1987; vice president of Kaiser Steel Corp., 1985–1987; deputy inspector general and then group vice president for the U.S. Synthetic Fuels Corp., 1982–1985; self-employed attorney, 1981; vice president of international development for Guardsmark, Inc., 1981; and operations and issues officer for the Reagan-Bush campaigns, 1980. In addition, Mr. Gambino worked for the Central Intelligence Agency, 1960–1980.

Mr. Gambino graduated from the University of Virginia (B.A., 1951) and George Washington University (J.D., 1958; M.S., 1968). He was born November 11, 1926, in Martinsburg, WV. Mr. Gambino served in the U.S. Army Reserve, 1951–1980. He is married, has three children, and resides in Vienna, VA.

Final Order for Emergency Deficit Control Measures for Fiscal Year 1991
October 15, 1990

By the authority vested in me as President by the statutes of the United States of America, including section 252 of the Balanced Budget and Emergency Deficit Control Act of 1985 (Public Law 99–177), as amended by the Balanced Budget and Emergency Deficit Control Reaffirmation Act of 1987 (Public Law 100–119) (hereafter referred to as "the Act"), I hereby order that the following actions shall be taken to implement the sequestrations and reductions determined by the Director of the Office of Management and Budget as set forth in his report dated October 15, 1990, under section 251 of the Act:

(1) Each automatic spending increase that would, but for the provisions of the Act, take effect during fiscal year 1991 is permanently sequestered or reduced as provided in section 252.

(2) The following are sequestered as provided in section 252: new budget authority; unobligated balances; new loan guarantee commitments or limitations; new direct loan obligations, commitments, or limitations; spending authority as defined in section 401(c)(2) of the Congressional Budget Act of 1974, as amended; and obligation limitations.

(3) For accounts making payments otherwise required by substantive law, the head of each Department or agency is directed to modify the calculation of each such payment to the extent necessary to reduce the estimate of total required payments for the fiscal year by the amount specified by the Director of the Office of Management and Budget in his report of October 15, 1990.

(4) For accounts making commitments for guaranteed loans as authorized by substantive law, the head of each Department or agency is directed to reduce the level of such commitments or obligations to the extent necessary to conform to the limitations established by the Act and specified by the Director of the Office of Management and Budget in his report of October 15, 1990.

All reductions and sequestrations shall be made in strict accordance with the specifications of the October 15th report of the Director of the Office of Management and Budget and the requirements of section 252(b).

This order supersedes the Initial Order issued on August 25, 1990.

This order shall be published in the *Federal Register*.

GEORGE BUSH

The White House,
October 15, 1990.

[Filed with the Office of the Federal Register, 1:21 p.m., October 15, 1990]

Statement on Signing the Radiation Exposure Compensation Act
October 15, 1990

I am today signing into law H.R. 2372, the "Radiation Exposure Compensation Act." This bill establishes new entitlement programs for persons physically present in areas near the Nevada Nuclear Test Site during atomic testing at the site.

Atmospheric testing of atomic devices— important to national security during the darkest days of the "cold war"—ended in 1963 when, under President Kennedy, the United States signed and ratified the Limited Test Ban Treaty. Prior to the Treaty, the United States detonated over 200 atomic devices in the open air, in both the South Pacific and in Nevada.

The bill provides compassionate payments to persons with specified diseases who fear that their health was harmed because of fallout from atmospheric atomic testing at the Nevada test site, regardless of whether causation can be scientifically established. The bill entitles each person meeting specific criteria to a payment of $50,000. Uranium miners meeting separate criteria will be entitled to compassionate payments in the amount of $100,000. These payments fairly resolve the claims of persons present at the test site and of downwind residents, as well as claims of uranium miners.

The bill, which is fiscally responsible, establishes a trust fund, and $100,000,000 is authorized to be appropriated to be paid into the fund.

H.R. 2372 is the result of close cooperation between the Administration and the Congress. As a result of the Administration's initial concerns, many earlier objections have been addressed, and the bill has been vastly improved. This legislation establishes a compensation system in the executive branch that can be administered efficiently and permit eligible claimants to receive compensation without the expense and delay of traditional litigation.

GEORGE BUSH

The White House,
October 15, 1990.

Note: H.R. 2372, approved October 15, was assigned Public Law No. 101–426.

Remarks at a Fundraising Luncheon for Gubernatorial Candidate Clayton Williams in Dallas, Texas
October 15, 1990

Thank you all very much. Thank you so very much, Claytie, for those generous and very kind words. And of course, my special thanks to all of you for that warm welcome. Let me just simply say it is great to be back home again. And it's always a pleasure for me to set my silver foot back on Texas soil. [*Laughter*] Uh-huh. [*Laughter*]

It is, as Claytie said, an honor to share this podium up here with so many of Texas' leading lights: my mentor, in a way, in Texas politics, my dear friend John Tower, over here. Governor Bill Clements, former business partner and great Governor of this State, and Rita—I'm just so glad to see you all. Texas will long remember, I believe, your courage and your commitment to our great State. So, thank you, sir, for your leadership.

And on the end down here, another well-known to Dallas, Bill Moss, who is giving of his time as, you might say, one of our main Points of Light, heading the President's Drug Advisory Council and doing a first-class job in the battle against drugs. Bill, I'm glad you're with us today.

And of course, I'm delighted to be here to show my support for my friend from Midland, my old stomping grounds, the next Governor of this great State: Claytie

Williams. Claytie, you've got to win it. You've got to win.

And when I finish up here, I'm going to be going to a reception for Texas' next Lieutenant Governor, Rob Mosbacher. What a team they will make in Austin. And I believe they're going to do it.

And of course, Barbara asked me to give Modesta a hug; glad to see you. Claytie, glad to see your great mom here. She shared with me a story about Clayton and his father: the time little Claytie—if you can picture it—[*laughter*]—went to break his first bronco. The horse broke free and began to buck. Claytie's dad rushed in to separate the horse and his son and did all he could to keep this wild horse in front of him and Claytie right behind him. That's when Claytie said, "Daddy, if you won't run, get out of the way for someone who will." And here he is. [*Laughter*]

But he's always run hard. Those of us who have followed his career in business, watched him in this election—Modesta told me exactly how many months and days and minutes it's been since they've been on the campaign trail. He runs hard, and today he's running to win. His victory will be a triumph for the old-fashioned virtues that made Texas what it is, and the new spirit of enterprise that will take this State forward into the nineties.

He's a Texan, born and bred—steady, strong, calls them as he sees them, straight-forward, a tireless advocate for every hard-working Texan.

And I've watched the issues unfold. He's tough on crime. He knows that the hand-cuffs belong on the criminals and not on the cops and the courts committed to uphold the law. This position that he has staked out—this position meshes perfectly with the no-nonsense anticrime package that I sent up to the United States Congress almost a year and a half ago. So, let me take advantage of you all to put a little heat on the Congress to act now and make life a little bit tougher on the criminals.

Claytie is ready to wage a statewide war on drugs. And we in Washington want to be at his side every step of the way. And again, our positions mesh perfectly with our national drug strategy that has resulted—and I can report this accurately—our national drug strategy has resulted in significant progress on the nationwide war on drugs. Claytie knows that the best way to win this war is to stop drug use before it begins. That means education; that means drug awareness. And he knows from a painful personal experience when it's time for compassion, time to help drug users battle back, break free from addiction, and rejoin society. And he knows when it's time to draw the line for drug kingpins, who deal death right out on our street corners. And he does, as I do, support the ultimate penalty, the death penalty, for those drug kingpins.

He is a friend to the Texas taxpayer, champion for fiscal integrity and fiscal sanity, for a government that is lean and limited. I know he'll fight for that when he gets to Austin.

With Claytie there, business men and women will have another Governor who knows what it means to meet a payroll. He knows what it means to start with nothing more than a dream and build a business from the ground up. The secret to his success as a businessman is plain, old-fashioned hard work. I can guarantee that, as Governor, no one will work harder for the State of Texas than Clayton Williams.

We had a chance to talk about this on the way down on Air Force One; and I agree with Clayton that what the States need is not more programs mandated, directed from Washington, DC, but more confidence and trust in people and in the power of the local communities. After all, Texas doesn't just have problems; Texas and Texans have the solutions.

The single most important factor for what the future will hold here in Texas and across the entire country is economic growth. That's why I want to speak to you for just a minute about the work that remains to be done back in Washington to reach final agreement on the Federal budget.

I pushed hard, as you all know, for a bipartisan budget agreement not because it was the best plan ever but because it was the best plan possible that would get the Federal deficit down by $500 billion over 5 years—real significant enforcement provisions.

And I am grateful—very grateful—to Senator Phil Gramm, who couldn't be with us today, and also to your Congressman, Steve Bartlett, for their strong leadership and their support. And I will continue to press hard for a budget that fulfills the spirit of that bipartisan plan and proves to the American people once and for all that we can deal with this budget deficit.

Now, let me speak from my own experience. I'm—I hate to confess—66. And that's a time in life when you begin to spend as much time thinking of the next generations as you do of your own. And our children deserve to inherit more than an avalanche of unpaid bills mounting up year after year.

We get some amazing mail at the White House, but let me share with you a letter sent to me at the White House from a little girl named Courtney—no last name, no return address. And it's short, and it's simple. She says: "Dear Mr. President: I don't want to owe when I grow up. I don't want to owe when I grow up."

Well, I would say to Courtney, since I can't write her back: I got your letter, and I'm going to do my level best to make sure that the Democrat-controlled United States Congress gets that message. We owe it to these kids that they not be mortgaged over and over again.

Time is short. The meter's ticking up there. Four days from now, on October 19th, the clock on all these procedural things runs out. And the American people have every right to expect more from their elected representative. Congress has a responsibility. And if this is the best that the system can do, then it's time to build a better budget system.

One of the problems is that much of the political debate on the budget has been based on that inside-the-Washington-DC-beltway jargon. And the jargon just hides the basic issues. Let me try to simplify it. America must have a real and significant deficit-reduction budget to get the economy moving. And that deficit reduction will bring down interest rates on home purchases and car loans and help create new jobs. You heard the testimony of the Chairman of the Federal Reserve Board about the budget agreement we worked out with the leadership. He said those interest rates

will come down. And that will help in creating new jobs. And to get these results, the budget cannot be smoke or mirrors or phony estimates—business as usual—can't be that. It must be real, it's got to be enforceable, and it's got to have incentives for growth.

And as always, the real problem has been the unwillingness in Congress to vote for holding down spending. I'm sure you're confused: the House now doing what they should, trying to come up with their agreement, and the Senate now working its will. And one thing that appeals to me about the current Senate package is that it holds the line on income tax rates. One of my biggest fears has always been that the Congress will continue to pay for its spending habits by raising income taxes on everybody. And in fact, the budget summit has moved us in the right direction and has brought us now to the final countdown week.

In the next 5 days, Congress has the chance—and in my view, Congress has an obligation—to act once and for all. And lest there be any doubt, let me make clear to Congress just how serious I am about meeting that Friday deadline. Thirty-seven times—John Tower will remember some of these—in the last 10 years, Congress has missed its own budget deadline. Twice now this year, I've signed emergency legislation to add more time to the clock. Well, this Friday, time's up. The American people deserve more than this stopgap government. And I'm confident now that Congress can meet this deadline, can complete its vital work, and pass the sound budget that puts this nation on the path to a long-term economic growth.

Getting that deficit under control is essential not just from the standpoint of the American economy but, as I look at the big picture, I'd say especially now, with the challenge that we face in the Persian Gulf. We all know the grave economic consequences of Iraq's occupation of Kuwait. But as serious as these consequences may be, what is ultimately at stake is far more than a matter of economics or oil. What is at stake is whether the nations of the world can take a common stand against aggression or whether Iraq's aggression will go unanswered, whether we will live in a world governed by the rule of law or by the law of the jungle. And that is why America and the world cannot allow this outlaw act to stand. That is why Saddam Hussein will fail.

Every day now, new word filters out about the ghastly atrocities perpetrated by Saddam's forces: eyewitness accounts of the cruel and senseless suffering endured by the people of Kuwait, of a systematic assault on the soul of a nation, summary executions, routine torture. Under the forces of Iraqi occupation, we are told that mere possession of the Kuwaiti flag or a photograph of the Kuwait's Amir are crimes punishable by death.

And last month at the White House, I met with the Amir of Kuwait. And I heard horrible tales: Newborn babies thrown out of incubators and the incubators then shipped off to Baghdad. Dialysis patients ripped from their machines, and those machines then, too, sent off to Baghdad. The story of two young kids passing out leaflets: Iraqi troops rounded up their parents and made them watch while those two kids were shot to death—executed before their eyes. Hitler revisited. But remember, when Hitler's war ended, there were the Nuremberg trials.

America will not stand aside. The world will not allow the strong to swallow up the weak. Not a day goes by that we don't think of the young men and women of our Armed Forces, side by side out there in the sands of Saudi Arabia. Today, with those young men and women in mind, let me just add one final note. Right now, our service men and women are teaching all of us a lesson about what it means to love liberty, as they prove once more to all the world that America means freedom. So, as November 6th draws near, I urge every Texan to do what some of those kids are doing by absentee ballot: Get out and vote. We must never take democracy for granted.

Once again, I am delighted to be here. I can't tell you what a pleasure it is to be out of Washington. [*Laughter*] And it is always nice to come home, but it's a special pleasure to come home to support somebody I believe in, somebody who will be our next Governor: Clayton Williams.

Thank you all very much. Now go out and work and vote and get this man elected to the governorship. Thank you very much.

Note: President Bush spoke at 12:35 p.m. in the Reunion Ballroom of the Hyatt Regency Hotel. In his remarks, he referred to former Senator John Tower; Governor Clements' wife, Rita; Clayton Williams' wife, Modesta; Alan Greenspan, Chairman of the Board of Governors of the Federal Reserve System; President Saddam Hussein of Iraq; and Amir Jabir al-Ahmad al-Jabir al-Sabah of Kuwait. Following his remarks, President Bush attended a reception at the hotel for Rob Mosbacher, candidate for Lieutenant Governor, and then traveled to Omaha, NE.

Remarks at a Republican Fundraising Reception in Omaha, Nebraska
October 15, 1990

Oh, how nice it is to be out where the real people are—outside of Washington, DC. Gosh, what a wonderful welcome. Thank you so much.

Kay, thank you. Please be seated, audience. [*Laughter*] Thank you. What is it about Nebraska that just gives you this warm feeling of welcome? Barbara was here not so long ago and came home raving. It was at that point that our dog wrote a book. [*Laughter*] But she does send her love, and she is so interested in this Governor's race and in this Senate race and this congressional race. And so, I bring you her best wishes.

I want to thank Duane Acklie and Sallie Folsom—I'm not sure Sallie is here—our national committeewoman; my old friend and campaign mate and a former Governor, Charlie Thone. And of course, it's great to be here at the Red Lion. I heard that you Cornhusker fans were enthusiastic, but do you name all the inns after the Big Red? [*Laughter*]

Look, I'm delighted to be here on behalf of this ticket: Kay Orr, Hal Daub, Ally Milder. They say that good luck comes in threes, and I think this may be a very lucky year for the people of this State. And if it's lucky for you, it is going to be fantastic for me as President of the United States.

We've got a good, strong Nebraska delegation in Washington. I want to improve on it. Virginia Smith, as you know, has done a remarkable job for this State. Doug Bereuter continues to do a phenomenal job. But they wouldn't hesitate to tell you that we need more support in the Congress. So, on November 6th, let's make our Nebraska delegation a solid Republican delegation in the House; and that means let's elect Ally Milder to the United States Congress.

I was looking over the voting records, and I tell you, it would be very nice to have a Congressman from this district that would support me as much as Ted Kennedy. [*Laughter*] And that's what the numbers—and with Ally, it would be one heck of a lot better than that, I'll guarantee you. [*Laughter*] You look at the record, look at the voting records.

And then, of course, our candidate for the United States Senate, a man of integrity, Hal Daub. I've known Hal for about 20 years, and I know this: He's made a difference as a lawyer, as a businessman, when he was in Congress 4 terms. And he'll make an even bigger difference as the next Senator for the State of Nebraska. I believe everyone here knows that we need to move up and get control of the United States Senate if we're going to bring Nebraska values to Washington. [*Applause*]

And then that brings me to my old friend, your great Governor, Kay Orr. She made the record books as the first woman Governor in Nebraska history and the first Republican woman Governor in American history. She's made the tough decisions. She's faced the difficult choices over the last 4 years. And she came down on the right side—not always the easy or popular one—but on the right side of the issues. And I've looked at her record and what

she believes, and we've had many opportunities to talk about it. And we agree on our approach to crime. And we agree on approach to education. She was one of the movers and shakers of the National Governors Conference as we set those national goals for this country, goals that we must meet by the end of this decade. And we agree on the approach to child care: to give parents more choice and to permit the communities to remain involved. And another point where we agree is, she's told me she doesn't like to have her hands tied—your hands, that means the people of Nebraska—by more and more mandated programs out of the liberal Congress in Washington. Give Nebraskans a chance to solve the problems.

And these are the issues that are at stake. And I need Kay Orr. And that's why I think this State needs Kay Orr.

In fact, these three candidates—Ally Milder, Hal Daub, and Kay—they stand for growth, opportunity, and prosperity for all Americans—GOP. That's because all three of them are sound, sensible Republicans.

Ally mentioned that we needed more Republicans in Washington right now, and I honestly believe that if we had had more Republicans in control of Capitol Hill over the last couple of decades, this budget mess that we're in right now would never have happened. We had a little reception earlier, and over and over again, citizens of this State told me that they understand this and brought it up to me. It is the Congress that has the responsibility to pass a budget. And year after year, they go down to the wire, and they fail to do so. And when the Democratic-controlled Congress fails to meet its own timetables, it continues this business-as-usual by what's known as a CR. It's awful high-tech word—it's a continuing resolution. There have been 37 of these emergency measures since 1981—7 in 1 year alone—just to keep the Government's door open. I am sickened by such mortgaging of our children's future, and that's what I am fighting about in Washington right now.

I say we need more Republicans. But right now, as you know, the Democrats control both the Houses of the Congress; and they control every single committee of the

United States Congress. And that's all the more reason for Republicans to work to make this budget now the best possible. We're fighting against the odds. We're fighting against the majorities—the liberal majorities—that control both Houses. We're fighting the entrenched tax-and-spend philosophy on Capitol Hill.

And you know, much of the political debate we hear in Washington is tired, and it's old. And it's all this "inside the beltway" jargon, and it's jargon that just gets in the way of what's really at stake. So, let me try to simplify it. America must have a real and significant deficit-reduction budget to get this economy moving. And that deficit reduction will bring down interest rates on home purchases and car loans, and it will create new jobs. And to get these results, the budget cannot be the same old political shell game. We must not tolerate business as usual. The budget must be real, enforceable, and preserve incentives for growth in this country.

And you know what the problem has always been: It's the unwillingness in Congress to vote to hold down Federal spending. And you know, with higher spending, higher taxes are usually not far behind. And that said, let me mention here that one thing that appeals to me about what's going on now, appeals to me about the current Senate package, is that it holds the line on income tax rates. And that is worth fighting for, in my view.

I have this concern that's always been that Congress will continue to pay for its spending habits by raising income tax rates on everybody. After concessions by both the Democratic and the Republican leaders—the budget summit—nobody liked every part of it. It did move us in the right direction, and it has brought us to the final countdown week. And in the next 5 days, Congress has the chance—in fact, I'd put it this way—Congress has the obligation to act. And I believe the American people have every right to expect the United States Congress to act responsibly.

And so, my message—and I expect it would be your message—to the Congress is simple and straightforward: Complete your work, meet Friday's deadline, and pass a sensible budget. We've got to put this nation back on the path to long-term economic growth, and the way to do that is to get a budget through. And that will bring the interest rates down, and that will put more and more Americans back to work where they belong.

Well, you can see why I need a Republican majority in Congress and in our statehouses, because at no time in recent history has an economically healthy and militarily strong America been more important. And Nebraskans know it more than most. I am proud to see the people of Nebraska supporting our brave men and women overseas. You could sense it when we landed there at Offutt. And you should have seen those kids that have just come back from Operation Desert Shield. And I've read of your community efforts: the students at Omaha's Westside Middle School sending more than 400 letters to the troops in Saudi Arabia, the wives of the Nebraska Army National Guard shipping over nearly 200 pounds of sugar cookies. I'm sure I could stand it or some of you guys out here could stand it, but nevertheless, that's what they've done. And I'm afraid that that beats C-rations any day for our GI's in the hot desert sun.

And they've left spouses, children, and even Big Red football to defend our cause. And they're doing a fantastic job. And every single member of the Joint Chiefs will tell you that never in the history of this country have we had finer young men and women better trained, more highly motivated than we do today.

Now, we've got a major challenge over there. I'm concerned at the systematic dismantling of the country of Kuwait. The aggression itself was bad enough: one dictator bully taking over a neighboring country. And then the United Nations and the United States joining in—all countries—almost every country in the world condemning this aggression. And in spite of that condemnation, there is this systematic dismantling of Kuwait, which is accompanied by unprecedented brutality. It's an ugly scene. Amnesty International has reported on it, and I'll spare you the details of the brutality. But all that does is make me convinced even more than ever that this aggression by Saddam Hussein will not stand. We are not going to pull out short of our obligations.

And you know, from these posts out there in the deserts of Saudi Arabia, in the glare of the Persian Gulf, our GI's are beginning to send in the absentee ballots. In the year that's seen the promise of democracy grow from Moscow to Managua, the least we can do is exercise our own right to vote. So, let's make our country proud, and let's get that vote out on November 6th.

And so, I wanted to just pop in here again. I don't want to overstay my welcome in this marvelous State that gave me more votes than any other State in the country on a proportionate basis, I believe. But you have a class-act Governor. You've got a quality Governor of character. And you've got a man running for the United States Senate that can make a difference and will support the President. And you've got a woman running for this congressional district, Ally Milder, who will be with me instead of opposing me every inch of the way.

And so, in the 21 days, 12 hours that remain before the polls open, do your best. You've already given some money or you

wouldn't be standing out here. Do that. Help each one of these people win. We've got to do it.

And I remain optimistic about our country. I think we're just on the threshold of a fantastic decade of opportunity and growth. We can do better in education and fighting crime and battling drugs, but we need the people in the Congress that are going to stand for the values that you expressed when you elected me your President in 1988. And that's why I'm here.

Vote for Kay Orr. Vote for Ally Milder. And vote for Hal Daub. And thank you all very, very much.

Note: The President spoke at 7:02 p.m. in the Red Lion Ballroom of the Omaha Red Lion Inn. In his remarks, he referred to Duane Acklie, Republican national committeeman; Representatives Virginia Smith and Doug Bereuter; and President Saddam Hussein of Iraq. The President also referred to "Millie's Book as Dictated to Barbara Bush." Following his remarks, the President attended a reception for Governor Orr and then traveled to Des Moines, IA, where he stayed overnight.

Statement Congratulating President Mikhail Gorbachev of the Soviet Union as the Recipient of the Nobel Peace Prize
October 15, 1990

President Mikhail Gorbachev of the Soviet Union has been a courageous force for peaceful change in the world. I want to offer my congratulations on behalf of the American people for his selection to receive the Nobel Peace Prize. He has brought historically significant change, both political and economic, to the Soviet Union and to Eastern Europe. East-West relations hold

greater promise for peace and world stability today than at any time in the last 45 years. The United States continues to work with the Soviet Union to promote regional and international peace. Barbara and I send our warmest regards to President and Mrs. Gorbachev in receiving this international honor.

Remarks at a Republican Fundraising Breakfast in Des Moines, Iowa
October 16, 1990

Thank you so much for that welcome. Please—thank you very much. What a mag-

nificent turnout for Governor Branstad and Senator-to-be Tom Tauke. I'm delighted to be here. Let me first pay my respects to my former runningmates—kids from Dowling here. I still have my T-shirt that I ran on the track out there with some of you all. And I'm very pleased, really, to be back here in Des Moines.

Last December, I spoke here on behalf of your next Senator, Tom Tauke. And then in June, I returned for your current and future Governor, Terry Branstad. And since I was here, things have really moved for both of them—moved in the right direction in terms of the electorate. Now we only have 20 days to go, and I can't think of a single State that has two more important races for the future of this country than the State of Iowa 20 days from now.

You've got my warmest memories and great sentiments in this State. I've had wonderful times in so many towns and so many cities here. And it was in those visits——

[*At this point, audience members interrupted the President's remarks.*]

I'll have a little say about that in a minute. You know, some people never get the word: The fight isn't about oil; the fight is about naked aggression that will not stand. Where were we? [*Laughter*]

You know, we were talking about the qualities that we need in the United States Senate and that we need to keep in the Governor's mansion here. Let me first single out our statewide candidates who I want to see elected to help Terry Branstad run this State. They are outstanding men and women, and you have the very finest in compassionate, committed public servants in these people right over here. So, please work hard for them in the last 20 days. They prove what Alf Landon meant when he said, "There are some intelligent people in Washington. There are more of them in the Middle West."

But back to Senator-to-be Tauke and to Governor Branstad. Both have fought for the family, for the taxpayer, and for the farmer. They fought for the working people of this State. And as a result, I think we are seeing—and I've been proud to be at their side—and I think we are seeing an agricultural economy that's rebounded from its recent lows.

And now we are in a battle in Washington to keep the economy moving forward, to get it revitalized. And the best thing we can do to revitalize it is to get a budget-deficit agreement that gets the deficit down by $500 billion over 5 years and does it in an enforceable way. And that's what I'm fighting for in Washington, and that's why I need the support of people like Tom Tauke.

But the battle isn't only about fiscal sanity. It's about things like education, where Terry Branstad has been in the lead nationally, supported ably—I am—in the Congress by Tom Tauke. This excellence record in Iowa is well-known nationally: Iowa students ranking fifth in high school graduations all across the country, first in SAT and ACT scores—an outstanding record. So, I want to do nationally that which you have done locally. So, 18 months ago, we proposed our National Educational Excellence Act to encourage flexibility, accountability, increased educational choice for parents and students. And Terry Branstad is a leader in the Governors' Association, was a leader as we set these national goals for this decade. He took the bastion of leadership, the symbol of leadership, and carried it forward to hammer out these national goals. He's well-known in the State of Iowa. He deserves reelection here. But I'll tell you, he has shown himself to be a national leader in the field of education.

I've sent an educational bill up there—I think it embodies the values of Iowans—sent it up to the Congress, and Tom Tauke is giving it strong support. We need some straight talk—that's what Tom—his motto, "Talking Straight." He's right, he is. And he's strong. And that straight talk is what we need to help elect Republicans who are going to end this delay and pass an educational bill which will help make American education number one—not the old thinking of the tired liberals in the United States Senate but the new thinking of Tom Tauke in the House, moving into the Senate, and of Terry Branstad right here at the Governor's level.

A major national question is crime and drugs. And for 16 months, the liberal Democrats who control all the committees in the United States Congress—the national Democrats—have sabotaged our violent crime bill. Evidently they think they can soft-pedal the need to be hard on crime. And Tom and Terry both disagree with that. They back a workable and a real death penalty for those who kill Federal law enforcement officers. And I back that. I support it, and I believe the country supports it overwhelmingly.

I hope some of you will have an opportunity—and maybe you're working with them—the victims of crime groups. I think it's time in the country that we showed a little more sympathy for the victims of crime and a little less for the criminals themselves.

And just one more word about agriculture. Five years ago, Tom Tauke helped pass—and Terry backed strongly—a farm bill to help a community in crisis. And it's no coincidence that farm income has hit near-record levels or that Terry Branstad has created over 300,000 new jobs, many of them agricultural, since 1983. And our job is to make that progress still better. And how? By recalling that when it comes to farming, Washington does not know best. Iowans know best. And we want to keep the control in the marketplace.

As we're drafting this new farm legislation, let's see that it emphasizes market-oriented policies. We don't need more government in Middle America—we need more Middle America thinking in the Washington Government. And that goes double when it comes to passing a sensible Federal budget.

It's no secret that I could use more Republicans in the United States Senate and in the United States House right now. Frankly, it would be a luxury to have a Senator in this Iowa seat that would vote with me at least as much as Teddy Kennedy has done. Take a look at the record. Take a look at the Congressional Quarterly. And in Tom Tauke we'd have somebody that would support our ideas much, much more than that. So, send him to Washington to be our Senator.

Republicans know: It's our heartbeat that we need to control Government spending and keep the taxes down. But unfortunately, the simple fact is the Democrats do control both Houses of Congress, and they control every single congressional committee. The American people know that they have control of both Houses and control all these committees. And it's also a fact that, year after year, Congress fails to meet its own timetable for producing the budget.

Year after year, the Congress has to pass emergency measures—it's all Washington jargon called continuing resolutions; after you've been there a month or two, you call them CR's—just to keep the government operating. Enough is enough. I think we've had something like 37 of these CR's in the last decade because Congress can't meet its own deadlines. Enough is enough. And this Friday, the Congress must face the budget deadline once again. But this time let them face up to their responsibilities as well.

I know that the Americans are fed up with much of the political debate coming out of Washington. It's the same old inside-the-beltway hogwash that obscures what's really at issue, so let me try to clarify it.

America must have a real and significant deficit reduction—real and significant deficit reduction—to get the economy moving. And that deficit reduction will, indeed—and almost instantly—bring down the interest rates that are holding back new job creation and holding back job opportunity. The deficit rate is going to bring those interest rates down. You're going to have more home purchases, more car loans, create new jobs.

And to get these results, Congress simply cannot play with the numbers in order to get phony savings. We can't afford business as usual in Washington anymore. So the budget must be real, it must be enforceable, and it must preserve our incentives for growth. I want to see this economy grow, not shrink from higher taxes and more government spending.

And I told you, Terry Branstad's right, and he's sure right when he says that the President ought to have the line-item veto. If Congress can't control the spending, give the President a shot at it.

We're not dumb in this country. Most people know that the failure to hold down spending is inevitably followed by higher taxes. They might be just around the corner. And that said, let me reiterate right here that the one thing that appeals to me about the current Senate package—you've got a House bill that looks like it's going through: raise the rates, index the taxes that's on the middle class and on the lower middle class. That's every taxpayer in this country. Nobody understands it, but that's what indexing means. So, they're saying it's a "soak the rich" bill. But inevitably, it gets into your pocket. It gets in the pocket of every working man and woman. And that's exactly what's coming out of the House.

But the Senate bill has some merit to it. It holds the line on income tax rates. And I've always been concerned—and I think the American people share this concern—that the Congress will continue to pay for its spending habits by going back and starting to raise the income tax rates on everyone. And I want to hold the line on the tax rates.

So, we're in a countdown. We're in another countdown. The next 4 days Congress has the responsibility and the obligation to act. And the American people have every right to see this Congress act responsibly.

You know, I have a difference, I think, on some of this with Speaker Foley. We had good cooperation with the Speaker on trying to hammer out a budget agreement—frankly, one in which I had to compromise and he had to compromise and the Senate had to compromise. But in my view, even though there were things in it I didn't like, I think it was a good deal. But where I've got a difference with the Speaker, it appears, is that he doesn't think it's useful to keep Congress in. He doesn't think it's useful to hold their nose to the grindstone by refusing to go along with business as usual by signing yet the 38th continuing resolution. So, we have an honest difference of opinion of that. But I think, in spite of the inconvenience to the American people, that there is support for this concept, whether it hurts the President or not, that the Congress ought to finish the job it was sent to Washington to do. And if we had more like Tauke in the Senate it would be getting done because we'd control the United States Senate.

One of the interesting parts of this job is some of the mail you get. And it gives you a certain trust in the American people. It's a way a President can get a feeling for what people are thinking. Some of it isn't particularly complimentary; and some of it, fortunately, is. But the people are smart. They want a budget that makes sense. And let me give you the wisdom from the mouths of babes.

It's a letter from Lisa Lilla, a 10-year-old from Clearwater, Florida. She writes that she wants us to solve our budget problem so that she "won't have to pay $5 million when she grows up." Then she adds this P.S.: "I really think you should not enlarge the taxes because when I'm 18 I'll have to pay $500 tax on a can of peas." [*Laughter*]

Well, she may be off slightly—[*laughter*]—but her logic is sound. Her logic is very, very sound. And even 10-year-olds know fiscal insanity when they see it, and they know where it starts. And they know that the Congress, controlled by the Democrats, appropriate every dime and tell us how to spend every single dime.

And it's not going to get better until we do something special on November 6th. We've got to send Congress a wake-up call, if you will. And so, let's reject the tax-and-spend policies that created the problem in the first place, and let's tell the Congress to remember kids like little Lisa. She does not want to pay $500 tax on a can of peas when she's 18 years old.

I think of Iowa as an international State, and I was interested in the opinion of these individuals here who wanted to make their statement. But I think of Iowa as an international State. I think you've always been out front in the terms of being engaged and being involved in foreign policy, whether it's through farsighted policies on international trade, whether it's through the earliest support and strong support for the United Nations that has now been revitalized, or whatever.

So, let me simply say—and I have to tell you, I understand where these kids are coming from. I understand that. I went through World War II. We've been through a couple of agonizing periods with the Korean war and the Vietnam war. So, their view shouldn't be entirely written off, but they've got it wrong. They've got the facts wrong. They're looking introspectively in a bit of an isolationistic way. We can't do that. We have the responsibility to lead—the United States does.

If we don't stand up against aggression around the world when it's naked and brutal, who will? The United States has the responsibility to lead and to put together this coalition that says to Saddam Hussein very simply: You cannot bully your neighbor; you cannot wipe him out—a member of the Arab League, a member of the United Nations. And that's what the issue is about.

Let me try to put it in perspective for those three kids that left—and I mean this in all seriousness, because this affects my thinking very much—what's happening. We've got to stand up for civilized values. But what's happening is unprecedented acts of brutality inflicted by Iraq.

I want to mention—and I don't mean to be overly shocking here—but let me just mention some reports, firsthand reports. At a hospital, Iraqi soldiers unplugged the oxygen to incubators supporting 22 premature babies. They all died. And then they shot the hospital employees. At another hospital, troops reportedly cut off oxygen supporting the 75-year-old mother of a Kuwaiti Cabinet Minister. Iraqi aggression. Iraqi naked aggression—taking dialysis machines, taking the patients off them, shipping the machines to Baghdad—systematically dismantling a member of the United Nations, a member of the Arab League.

And so, the bottom line for us is that Iraqi aggression will not be allowed to stand. Saddam Hussein will be held accountable. And the legitimate government of Kuwait

will be restored. And America will remain in the Persian Gulf not one single day longer than necessary. I look forward to the day that every single man and woman serving there now with pride—and beautifully trained—every single one of them comes home. But we must stay for as long as it takes to complete our mission.

Now, in your great State, common sense has never gone out of style. You know that while our forces—and there's a unit from Mason City on the way—you know that while our forces are defending us abroad, we must defend them here at home. And I know that Iowans want policies which empower people and bring prosperity and opportunity to communities all over this State.

So to sum it up, Tom Tauke, whom I've known for years and with whom I have worked for years and whose record I have admired for years, must be elected to the United States Senate. And Terry Branstad, who has served this State with such distinction, and now a high official in the National Governors' Association because of the way his fellow Governors look at him—look at his record of achievement, look at his leadership—must be reelected as well.

And so, I came out here to enthusiastically stand with you Iowans in support of these two fine men. We can send the rest of the country a signal by reelecting Terry Branstad overwhelmingly and by sending Tom Tauke to the United States Senate.

Thank you, and God bless the people of Iowa. Thank you very much.

Note: The President spoke at 9:04 a.m. in the atrium of the State Historical Museum.

Remarks at a Campaign Rally for Gubernatorial Candidate Jim Edgar in Chicago, Illinois
October 16, 1990

Thank you, Jim, and thank you all. What a thrill to be introduced by the next Governor of the State of Illinois. Thank you, Jim. And to you and your wonderful family, Barbara and I send our love.

To Bob Kustra and Jim Ryan and George

Ryan and Greg Baise, Sue Suter, Pate Philip—we've got a first-class team running for statewide office in Illinois, and I am out here to enthusiastically endorse each and every one of them.

And of course, to Governor Jim Thompson, who this January concludes his fourth term—14 great years for the State of Illinois—what a job Jim's done! Thank you, Jim, for that warm introduction, too.

And let me pay my respects to another friend of mine, a man who came up here from Tennessee—I saw him on Nashville Network the other night, and I wrote him a letter about "American Boy"—and I'm talking about Eddie Rabbitt, great patriot and a wonderful musician. Eddie, thank you very, very much, and all you guys, too. And besides that, I never saw anybody sign so beautifully in country music as Donna Brandwine right here—had that rhythm going.

You know, there's some real excitement here today—the balloons, the marching bands, the thousands of cheering people. And I haven't seen anything like it since Millie had her last book-signing party. All of which reminds me, I bring the love and affection of Barbara Bush, who feels as strongly about Jim Edgar as I do.

This State, this great State of Illinois, made the difference in the 1988 Presidential election; and you're about to make a crucial difference in this race next month. That's because this county, Du Page County, is Republican country. So, get out the vote. Get out the vote. Let Du Page say who's going to run this State for 4 more years.

Let me put in an enthusiastic second for another great daughter of Illinois, and I'm talking about Lynn Martin. We need her in the United States Senate, and we need her bad.

And so, here we are in this field house of dreams, sharing the vision of a brighter future for this great State. It's a vision that pulses right through the heartland of America, the deep-running mainstream, the full, big-hearted center that says we want leadership to be direct, we want it to be honest, we want it to be candid, we want it to be purposeful and principled.

So, we are meeting here today in support of a candidate whose record lives up to his rhetoric, whose deeds are worthy of his words—who says what he means and does what he says. And I'm talking about Jim Edgar, the next Governor of Illinois.

I was talking to some of my friends before we walked in here, and they tell me that there's a lot of opposition posing as Republican look-alikes these days. Well, come November 6th, the opposition will learn what Jim Edgar already knows: It's not enough to play for the prime time and deliver the lines; you've got to deliver the results. That's what Jim Edgar has done as your secretary of state, and that's what he's going to continue to do as Governor of this State.

You've already got—after Jim and your State's assets—you already have a lot to be proud of. You've got a vital manufacturing base. You've got world-class business and financial centers. You've got agriculture that feeds the world. In fact, they say that Illinois produces everything from bulldozers to turkeys. I'm not here to talk about your political opponents, but I am here with a message for the people of Illinois: As much as you've got to be proud of, you'll have a lot more to look forward to with Jim Edgar.

You know, he knows that education is crucial for these kids, and he's pledged to make Illinois the very first State to reach those national education goals that we set out for America. Jim Thompson, 49 other Governors, and I spelled these goals out after last year's successful education summit. And he has spelled out—Jim has—where he'll get the financial resources to improve the schools. And even more important, he understands that you've got to empower the people, not the bureaucrats. Because when it comes to the kids, we are all accountable, and we must be accountable.

So, Jim has already marshaled what I would call a real partnership between business and labor leaders and local officials and educators and community groups that's made it possible for over 40,000 adults to learn to read. Jim Edgar doesn't just talk about progress in education; he makes it happen.

And Jim also knows that no kid can be safe as long as drug dealers wander the streets peddling poison. So, he's called for tougher penalties for gang leaders and gang crimes. And incidentally, he and I agree 100 percent on another issue: Both of us want to stand up against drunk driving. And those who try to penalize him on this issue must not have things their way.

Now, may I address myself to this opinion here [*audience interruption*]. What we are for is peace in the Middle East. What we are also for—[*applause*]—but what we are also for is principle. And that's why I have put together the strongest international co-operation that we've ever seen in modern times. And with all respect, we will stand up against this aggression in the Middle East. No big nation can bully a small one, and that is the principle that I stand for.

It is only the United States that can stand for principle. And I'm so glad we have free speech here, but once in a while, you know, we ought to get on with our business.

I can report to you that we're making some progress now in the war against drugs. Our national strategy is working. And Jim believes, as I do, that these drug kingpins, these mass merchants of death, deserve the ultimate penalty—and I am talking about the death penalty for these drug kingpins.

I might add parenthetically that Jim and I care about the victims of crime a little more than we do about the criminals themselves. And that is the Du Page way, too.

Jim Edgar is calling, with his belief in fiscal sanity, for an amendment to strengthen the Governor's budget-cutting powers. And he will control State spending. And speaking of that, I wish I had what 43 Governors have, and that is the line-item veto. If the Democrat Congress can't do it, give the President a chance to cut this spending under control.

You know, we had a good package—it was a compromise—up there that would get the deficit down by $500 billion, not the best of all possible worlds but the best plan possible. And I'm grateful to the legislators that stood with me—Illinois' own Bob Michel right out there in front. And they worked to build consensus, not controversy.

Sometimes the rhetoric back there gets pretty thick inside that Washington beltway. So, let me just put it in perspective for you. I heard Jim Thompson talking about it. We must have a significant and real deficit-reduction budget to get this economy moving. And when we get that kind of a deal, it will bring down the interest rates on home purchases and car loans. It will bring

them down and create new jobs. So the time for Democratic rhetoric is over, and the time to move ahead is to get the Congress moving now, to get us that kind of an agreement. I guess what I'm saying is we can't afford business as usual. The budget's got to be real, it's got to be enforceable, and it's got to preserve our incentives for growth.

You know, I'll take my share of the hits, but I believe the American people really know that the problem has always been the failure of this one-party-controlled Congress to hold down spending. We're not taxing you too little; we're spending too much. And so, make no mistake about it: When you hear this liberal crowd that runs the Congress in Washington talking about taxing the rich, they're going to be after you the next thing you know, because that's the way it works—tax and spend, tax and spend. And I want to end that once and for all.

So, today they're marking up a big budget plan back in Washington. It's a Democratic tax plan. If it reaches my desk, the one that comes out of the House of Representatives, I will veto it because it raises the income taxes of the working men and women of this country. And I am not going to do that.

One thing, incidentally, that appeals to me on this Senate package is that it holds the line on income tax rates. Republicans have always feared that Congress will continue to pay for its spending habits by raising the income tax rates on everybody. So clearly, the budget summit moved us in the right direction, brought us to this final countdown week. And now we're down to 4 days back there in Washington. And Congress has the opportunity and the obligation to act. And the American people have every right to expect the Congress to finally act responsibly for the taxpayers' interest in this country.

Well, when we get back to the Governor's race here, I know what you're looking for in any leader. You're looking for principle—statesmanship, not gamesmanship. And that's what Jim Edgar embodies in mind and spirit. I really believe—I believe this deep in my heart—that he will be a great

Governor for the State of Illinois.

And what you're about here is setting the fundamental direction for Illinois politics in the nineties, in the next century. So, let me close by asking all of you to get out the vote. Go out and work to get out the vote. It's a time of great hope and enormous challenge around the world, particularly over there in the Persian Gulf. And let us all remember and none relinquish the priceless power of the vote that we have here at home.

It was the great son of Illinois, Abraham Lincoln, who said that "Ballots are the rightful and peaceful successors of bullets. And such will be a great lesson of peace: teaching men that they cannot take by an election, neither can they take by war."

This fall, reach out to those around you.

Get them to the polls. Make the meaning of democracy read loud and clear here in America's heartland. And make Jim Edgar and this outstanding ticket elected to office. Send them to Springfield to do the people's work.

Thank you, and God bless the State of Illinois. Thank you very, very much.

Note: The President spoke at 1:23 p.m. at the field house at the College of Du Page. In his opening remarks, he referred to the following Republican candidates for State office: Bob Kustra, Lieutenant Governor; Jim Ryan, attorney general; George Ryan, secretary of state; Greg Baise, treasurer; Sue Suter, comptroller; and James Pate Philip, senate minority leader. The President also referred to "Millie's Book as Dictated to Barbara Bush."

Statement on Signing the Market Reform Act of 1990
October 16, 1990

I am today signing H.R. 3657, the "Market Reform Act of 1990." This bill addresses concerns with regard to the stability of U.S. securities markets as a result of many factors, including the extraordinary volatility that transpired in the market break in 1987 and the less severe break in 1989. The bill provides a number of worthwhile measures to enhance financial market stability that have been strongly recommended by the Securities and Exchange Commission (SEC). Many of these measures were also suggested in the 1988 report of President Reagan's Task Force on Market Mechanisms.

Overall, H.R. 3657 is consistent with recommendations the Administration has made to the Congress over the last 2 years. In particular, I welcome the following features of the bill:

• the authorization for increased monitoring of risks that are posed to SEC-regulated firms by their holding company and other affiliates;

• the provision for the institution of a large trader reporting system by the

SEC that could facilitate analysis of market developments; and

• the authorization for the SEC to facilitate the establishment of a coordinated national system for safe and accurate clearance and settlement.

One provision of this legislation to enhance market stability was of significant concern in its original formulation, and is still troubling. Under certain limited circumstances, the bill permits the SEC during "periods of extraordinary volatility" to "prohibit or constrain" certain trading practices. The final language of the bill gives the SEC only carefully limited and narrow authority to control trading practices and is an improvement over earlier versions of the legislation. However, it is still important that this authority be carefully and judiciously exercised to prevent any interference with technological innovations in financial markets that can enhance market liquidity. We must be careful not to damage the vitality of America's markets at the same time that we protect market stability.

I have one more observation to make regarding the financial markets. Earlier this year the Administration transmitted to the Congress the "Capital Markets Competition, Stability, and Fairness Act of 1990." This important legislation would mandate badly needed reform of the stock index futures market by clarifying the jurisdictions of the Commodity Futures Trading Commission and the SEC. I strongly support this legislation and urge the Congress to complete the job of market reform by passing the Administration's bill.

I am particularly pleased to sign H.R. 3657 into law and thereby to improve the stability of America's vital securities markets and the protection of tens of millions of investors.

GEORGE BUSH

The White House,
October 16, 1990.

Note: H.R. 3657, approved October 16, was assigned Public Law No. 101–432.

Remarks at a Campaign Rally for Gubernatorial Candidate John Engler in Grand Rapids, Michigan
October 16, 1990

Thank you all very much, and I'm very pleased to be back here. And what a great ticket we have heading up to run the State of Michigan. We need the change. We need John Engler to be the next Governor. We need Connie Binsfeld to be the Lieutenant Governor.

And so, I just came out here to do what Barbara did last week, and that is to wish John and Connie and all the rest of them— I'm going to be going into a few omissions here, but I see way down on the end a guy running for the university trustees, Marv Esch. He and I were elected to the Congress the same time, and he's been a good friend ever since. And so, you have outstanding quality running to serve Michigan. And that's why I'm here. Thank you for giving us such a welcome.

I want to pay my respects to Brooks Patterson, who is the Bush-Quayle cochairman, and Ronna Romney, the national committeewoman, and Rich and Betsy DeVos; and so many others.

But let me begin by stating what I said in Detroit about 3 weeks ago on behalf of a good friend, and I'm talking about Congressman Bill Schuette, who I want to see Senator Bill Schuette. He's in a tough fight, but we're right in the period when these people start moving in the polls, and moving up. And we need him. We need him—the change we need—and we need

him in real leadership. So, let's elect the man from Midland. Let's elect Bill Schuette to the Senate.

[*At this point, audience members interrupted the President's remarks.*]

May I address myself to the question that has been raised. We are not in the Middle East to protect oil; we are there to stand up against aggression. And we will stay there as long as it takes.

And now what we need is something in Michigan that we do not have in Washington, and I'm talking about a Republican State senate. We need to get control here so Governor Engler can run this State the way you and I want him to run the State. So, let's maintain our majority in the senate and gain a majority in the house. And then, of course, that brings me to the man of the hour. You know who I'm talking about. He's the right man to do the job, my friend and your next Governor, John Engler.

It's a question that all boils down to a question of leadership. And when the going was tough for me back in 1988 and in earlier days, this man stood up and led, and I'll never forget it. And that's why I'm here, because I know what he can do as a leader for this great State.

You know the story better than I: from a family farm in Beal City to a graduate of Michigan State, a State representative, and then one of the most respected members of the Michigan State Senate. And some say it's impossible to beat an incumbent. Well, you tell that to John Engler. He's already beaten three. And I'm here to help him make it number four—the cleanup hitter.

Twenty-one days from now, just about now actually, the polls will be closing in Michigan, so please get out the vote. Get your neighbors to the polls. Do not fail to exercise your democratic franchise. If we do it, if we turn our vote out, this man and Connie and others will be elected, I can guarantee you.

The issues are not so unlike the issues in Washington. This election is going to decide whether Michigan chooses the bankrupt policies of tax and spend or, on the other hand, whether it chooses Republican policies that put Michiganers back to work. It is not right that this industrial State trails behind all the others in terms of employment.

I am fighting with our national drug strategy in place now, fighting to win this battle against narcotics. And I can tell you, nationally, we're making progress. But I want to see John Engler here who does not softpedal the need to be tough on crime. We share each other's philosophies on that. And I happen to believe that it is time to care more about the victims of crime and a little less sympathy for the criminals that are causing the crimes.

And there's another key ingredient here. This race will have a lot to say about whether or not Michigan has fair reapportionment. And let's face it, Michigan needs its reapportionment map drawn by the Democrats like the Spartans need their playbook written by Ohio State. We don't need that at all.

And so, what it means then is getting people that believe, as John does, that the challenges are met through the human heart and through the mind, and not through the heavy hand of Washington, DC. Over and over again, he has told me to cut back if I can on the mandated programs, the programs from Washington dictated by the liberal Democrats that tell everybody in Michigan exactly how you have to solve their problems. I want to put the action where it belongs—right here in the

hands of the Governor, not back there in Washington, DC.

And there's another field where we totally agree, and that's the field of education. And the Governors do have a special role. John Engler knows that excellence is obtained through higher standards, through more accountability, through empowering the parents with more choice in where their kids go to school. And so, we unveiled the Educational Excellence Act in Washington—Excellence Act of 1990. And we worked with the Governors to develop this country's first-ever national education goals. So, what I say is: Let's back men like John Engler who will work with me to make those goals a reality and to make our great country the number one in education around the entire world.

I mentioned the fight on narcotics. Sixteen months ago I sent a violent crime bill to Congress. It's a tough one. It supports the police; it's tough on the criminals. And here's the problem: The liberal Democrats have made every effort to water down the bill. The solution: electing candidates who support toughening laws at both the Federal and State level. And so, join with me in telling Congress to take the shackles off policemen, the courts, and the law. We need a guy like Bill Schuette in the Senate. We need John Engler in the Governor's mansion, who will help our police take back the streets.

I hate to ruin this wonderful evening, but let me just say a word about the Federal budget deficit. The American people have watched with growing frustration as this process drags on and on. And it hasn't been pretty, and it hasn't been nice. Year after year, Congress fails to meet its budget deadlines on time. And it resorts to passing emergency bills just to keep the Government operating. It has happened 37 times in the last 10 years. And if this is the best that the system can do, the system controlled—House and Senate—by the liberal Democrats, then it's time to build a better system.

So, let me tell you what we must have and what I'm fighting for on your behalf in Washington. We must have real and significant deficit reduction to get this economy moving again. When we get this deal—listen to the Chairman of the Federal Reserve—when we get a budget agreement, that will bring down interest rates on home purchases and car loans. That will create jobs. And to get this deficit down, Congress cannot resort to the old political shell game, and America cannot afford business as usual. And so, the budget—it must be real, it must be enforceable, and it must preserve our incentives for growth. And I will keep the Congress there as long as it takes to get that kind of budget for the American people.

Right this very minute, right this very minute back in Washington, the House is taking up—the House of Representatives—the House Democratic budget plan. It is a big Democratic tax plan. And if it reaches my desk, I will veto it because it raises the income taxes of the working men and women in this country. And that is simply unacceptable. And the best shot we've got is the Senate package. At least it holds the line on income tax rates. So, I'm interested in seeing that one move forward.

You know, all Americans are concerned that Congress will continue to pay for its spending habits by raising the income taxes on everybody. And the budget summit did move us in the right direction. It's brought us to this final countdown week, and it's down to 4 days. And Congress has the responsibility and it has the obligation to act, and the American people have a right to expect the United States Congress to act reasonably.

And so, on November 6th, let's send Congress a message. Let's reject the Democrats' tax-and-spend policies that got us here in the first place and tell Congress that America's kids, the young ones here, deserve to inherit more than an avalanche of unpaid bills in a mortgaged future.

You know, when I was here—on another subject—when I was here 3 weeks ago, I spoke to Michigan's sons and daughters in another context, one that's on the minds of all Americans. And I spoke of those young men and women now on active duty in Saudi Arabia, saying these men and women show that America would not be the land of the free if it were not also the home of the brave. And we intend to stand by those who stand up for what is right and good. And so, we will remain in the Persian Gulf for as long as it takes to complete our mission. And above all, we will keep faith with the greatest service men and women any nation could possibly have.

So, we're down to the wire; 20 days from now we've got to keep faith with America. So, let's get to the polls. Let's show our will and our resolution, and let's keep a Republican majority in this State's senate and win a majority in the house. And let's elect Bill Schuette as Senator. And let's send the right man to Lansing: Let's elect John Engler the Governor of the State of Michigan. You can do it. You hold it in the palm of your hands to get this job done. So, take a friend. Go to the polls. Vote for John Engler.

And God bless the State of Michigan, and God bless the United States of America. Thank you very much.

Note: The President spoke at 6:33 p.m. in the Grand Hall of the Amway Grand Center. In his remarks, he referred to Richard DeVos, Republican candidate for the State board of education, and his wife, Betsy, Republican chairman for the Fifth Congressional District; and Alan Greenspan, Chairman of the Board of Governors of the Federal Reserve System. Following his remarks, the President attended a reception at the Amway Grand Plaza Hotel and then returned to Washington, DC.

Statement on the Federal Budget
October 16, 1990

Tonight the Democrats in Congress have turned back the clock. By a partisan vote in the House of Representatives, the Democrats pushed through a tax increase on working men and women.

The hidden tax is back. By removing the indexing of tax rates, the Democrats have resurrected an inequity most Americans thought was a thing of the past: bracket creep. Also, I find unacceptable surcharges and other hidden mechanisms that increase income taxes on all Americans.

I am determined that the budget deficit-reduction package be fair. I am determined that the budget not be balanced on the backs of working Americans. That's why I will veto the Democratic plan passed by the House should it reach my desk.

I am hopeful that it will not come to that. The bipartisan plan now being considered in the Senate does not raise income tax rates. Its approach is therefore much more in keeping with our efforts to ensure that the final budget plan is fair to all Americans.

Statement on the Children's Television Act of 1990
October 17, 1990

I have decided to withhold my approval from H.R. 1677, the "Children's Television Act of 1990," which will result in its becoming law without my signature. This bill is intended to increase the amount and quality of children's television programming and to diminish the commercialization of programming for children.

I wholeheartedly support these goals, but regret that the Congress has chosen inappropriate means of serving them. In an effort to improve children's television, this legislation imposes content-based restrictions on programming. The legislation limits the amount of advertising that broadcasters may air during children's programming, and the Federal Communications Commission is charged with policing the adequacy of broadcasters' efforts to serve the educational and informational needs of children. The First Amendment, however, does not contemplate that government will dictate the quality or quantity of what Americans should hear—rather, it leaves this to be decided by free media responding to the free choices of individual consumers.

I recognize that the Supreme Court has upheld the application of certain content-based regulations to broadcast licensees, on the theory that the "scarcity of broadcast frequencies" makes government involvement inevitable. *Red Lion Broadcasting Co. v. FCC*, 395 U.S. 367 (1969). Whatever validity this analysis may have been thought to have some 2 decades ago, its factual premise has been eroded by the proliferation of new video services that supplement those provided by traditional broadcasters. Accordingly, a constitutional challenge to this legislation may provide the Supreme Court with an occasion to reconsider its decision in *Red Lion*.

I also have very strong reservations about the legislation's application of quantitative advertising restrictions to cable operators. *Red Lion*'s "technological scarcity" theory does not apply to cable service, which should be considered analogous to the print media under the First Amendment. Even under the commercial speech doctrine, I do not believe that quantitative restrictions on advertising should be considered permissible when applied either to newspapers or to cable operators.

Finally, the advertising limits imposed by this legislation cannot reasonably be expected to advance their intended purpose. To the extent that children's programming is financed by the revenue from advertising during such programming, restrictions on the amount of advertising will tend to *diminish*, rather than enhance, the quantity and quality of children's programming.

GEORGE BUSH

The White House,
October 17, 1990.

Note: H.R. 1677 became law on October 18, upon the expiration of the 10-day period   *allowed for Presidential action, and was assigned Public Law No. 101–437.*

Remarks at the Welcoming Ceremony for Prime Minister Jozsef Antall of Hungary
October 18, 1990

The President. Mr. Prime Minister, it's a tremendous pleasure to welcome you and your wife, Klara, to the White House today.

Seven years ago, I became the highest ranking American official to visit Hungary and, last year, the first American President to journey there. Even though it was pouring rain when we arrived in Kossuth Square, the people of Hungary gave us a very warm welcome. Barbara and I have seen few cities more lovely than Budapest; and we've seldom seen a city more alive— alive with commerce, change, and above all, hope; alive with a people who believe that, like a lamp lighting the darkest night, liberty can light the globe.

The arrival at the White House of the first democratically elected Prime Minister of Hungary in over 40 years is, indeed, sir, an historic event; and it brings to mind the arrival 138 years ago of another Hungarian patriot at another house which embodies freedom, the Congress of the United States. That man was Lajos Kossuth. His statue stood behind us that day in the rain in Budapest, in the square that bears his name. And in today's historic meeting, his memory lifts us and teaches us. For his life was a celebration of bravery and of dreams. He knew that a courageous people would not bow to bayonets and barbed wire, and he knew that the light of liberty would shine forever.

Today in your homeland, from the streets of Budapest to the great plains to the waters of the Danube and the gentle towns that grace its banks, Hungary's new patriots believe that all things are possible for a nation and for a people; and they proclaim the individual, not the state, as the voice of tomorrow. Today in Hungary that voice is being heard. Hungary is no longer an emerging democracy; Hungary is a democ-

racy. The government you head is a sovereign, pluralistic, democratic European state. The dream of Hungarians has been fulfilled and carried beyond their own borders to others in Central Europe. And now, in 1990, Hungary has taken its natural place as a valued member of the commonwealth of free nations.

During our visit to Budapest, we saw the Hungarian love of excellence in careful craftsmanship, in bountiful harvests from family farms, in the pride of scientists in their work. And American companies have already demonstrated their faith in Hungary's economic potential by committing well over half a billion dollars in new investments. General Electric is making lightbulbs in a joint venture with Hungarian firm Tungsram. General Motors is producing auto parts there. And I encourage more American businesses to find out what Hungary has to offer.

Prime Minister Antall's government has demonstrated its determination to integrate Hungary into the global market by developing an ambitious economic reform program, and we pledge our continuing support for your courageous efforts. The Hungarian-American Enterprise Fund has announced its first investment in a joint venture to market high-tech equipment. For the new fiscal year, our administration has asked Congress for a $300 million economic aid package for Eastern Europe. Our Regional Environmental Center in Budapest commenced operations last month. And we are offering $47.5 million in credits for the purchase of about 500,000 tons of feed grains to compensate for the effects of the severe drought that Hungary has experienced this year.

And we also know that, like all of us, Hungary and the other new democracies of

Central Europe are paying a high price for resolutely supporting the United Nations sanctions against Iraq. And we understand that the loss of export markets and rising energy costs complicate your historic effort to transform a centrally planned economic system to a free-market economy. And so, to help ease this burden, I am announcing today that the United States is asking the International Monetary Fund to increase its lending to the countries of the region by as much as $5 billion, modifying its lending policies as appropriate. And we also asked the World Bank to accelerate its assistance in the energy field, drawing on the $9 billion now committed to Central and Eastern Europe.

The United States has been a partner of Europe for most of this century and will remain so. And we welcome Hungary and the other new democracies into a new partnership in a new Europe—a Europe whole and free. The United States is committed to helping you find a secure place in the new Europe and is building with you a new era of U.S.-Hungary relations. In that regard, I am pleased to announce the lifting of the travel restrictions for Hungarian diplomats and our agreement to your request to establish an Hungarian consulate general in Los Angeles.

And so, Mr. Prime Minister, we welcome you amid dramatic times. We welcome you amid a feeling of hope and promise. And as old friends and as new partners, we welcome you amid a spirit of cooperation, looking forward to these conversations that lie ahead.

And when Kossuth came to America, his reception showed how our two peoples share a common love of liberty. And in New York harbor, an armada of ships sounded horns to celebrate his arrival. Thousands rushed his open carriage. Perhaps no visitor since Lafayette had been greeted so emotionally.

Like Hungarians, the Americans of that time believed in helping individuals and nations who understood that real freedom makes all progress possible. For they, like Hungarians and Americans today, were determined to ensure that the light of liberty will shine forever.

So, welcome to America, Mr. Prime Min-

ister, and God bless the friendship between our two nations. Thank you.

The Prime Minister. Mr. President, Mrs. Bush, ladies and gentlemen, I feel sincerely moved when standing here in the garden of the White House on this occasion when you are receiving here the Prime Minister of Hungary, the first freely elected Prime Minister of our free government.

We are proud of the fact that all the American ideals of liberty, those ideals that used to be the constitutional treatise and credo of Washington, Jefferson, and all the other famous American statesmen, belong also to us.

We are proud of the fact that whenever you remember the wars, the battles you came out as the triumphant party of, you had Hungarians taking side with you, in support of you, who were there with you at those triumphant battles and wars.

We are also proud of the fact that a soldier of Hungarian origin, Milahy Kovacs, who fought in your War of Independence, sacrificed his life to gain your independence. Yesterday we also felt very much moved when paying tribute at the memory of your heroes in the cemetery and, at the same time, we could also salute the memory of Hungarian heroes there.

We also take pride in the fact that there were also many Hungarians contributing to building up your country. Whatever has been done in order to make your country, the United States, be a great power had contribution on behalf of Hungarian military men, Hungarian workers, Hungarian farmers, as well as from Hungarian scientists.

Mr. President, you have just spoken about Lajos Kossuth, and you also recalled your visit in Budapest. When standing in front of the statue of Lajos Kossuth, you delivered your speech there. Lajos Kossuth represents freedom and liberty for everyone. It happens not by chance that it is exactly the personality of Lajos Kossuth that binds us together, because that is a token and symbol of freedom for both Hungarians and Americans.

The era that created Lajos Kossuth, in fact, forms part of the Hungarian historic mythology. Therefore, should there be any matter related to any war of liberation or revolution, we always return to that particular period of our history. It happened like that also in the year of 1956, when Hungary, as one nation, took arms and started to fight the Soviets and made an attempt on that occasion to establish the independent Hungarian democracy. It was that which has brought us the spirituality, during which we, after a period of more than three decades, set out in our country to demolish the building of dictatorship.

On this occasion, I would like to express my thanks to you because ever since the time when America recognized that Soviet power had been extended onto the regions of Eastern and Central Europe and through all the peoples living in that region, has been very persistent in trying to defend the grounds of the free world.

I would like to thank you for having elevated the issue of human rights onto governmental level. And you have been representing that important issue in the last decades at that very high level.

I would also like to express my thanks to you for having forced the Soviet power to enter into fierce competition of technology, military, and economic nature. By doing so, you have contributed to helping reform politician in the personality of Gorbachev to make an attempt to change the Soviet Union. And also the peoples living in East and Central Europe have been given more opportunities to make use of their freedom.

We started the transformation of the political institution system, and Hungary today is a parliamentary republic. We have also laid down the grounds for a free-market economy. At the same time, we do not want to hide the fact that to implement an economic change in a country is far more difficult than execute a political one.

You, Mr. President, have spoken about all those matters that I could have also mentioned here when presenting my request or when speaking in form of complaints. Well, I think this is an indication of the fact that we have come here as friends. And we are seeing friends here. We are being received by friends who can perhaps read our thoughts.

All those that you have just spoken about and all of those that you were very gracious and kind to promise us as future prospective potentialities will help us to survive this very severe crisis.

May I say thank you for receiving me and for receiving the members of my delegation representing the Government of Hungary. And may I assure you that Hungary is a faithful friend of yours and will remain so until the very end of times. Without you, the system of dictatorships would have never been collapsed in East and Central Europe.

And people were able to realize that all those that had been preached and declared by Marxism-Leninism was nothing else but a series of lies.

Twenty-five years ago I could cite in one of my articles that I wrote about Lincoln one of the sayings of his: It is possible to cheat many people for a short time. During a long time, it is possible to cheat one person. However, it is impossible to cheat many people during a long time.

Thank you very much for receiving me, and thank you very much for the benevolence of America. Thank you very much, Mr. President.

Note: The President spoke at 10:11 a.m. at the South Portico of the White House, where the Prime Minister was accorded a formal welcome with full military honors. The Prime Minister spoke in Hungarian, and his remarks were translated by an interpreter. Following the ceremony, the President and the Prime Minister met in the Oval Office.

Statement by Press Secretary Fitzwater on the Lifting of the State of Emergency in Natal
October 18, 1990

We warmly welcome the announcement today by the South African Government that they are lifting the state of emergency in Natal. We see this as yet another important landmark on the road toward full normalization of political activity in South Africa.

We believe that President de Klerk deserves credit for his political courage and leadership. We would reaffirm our full support for the historic process in which he and Mr. Mandela [leader of the African National Congress] are currently engaged.

As President Bush said on the occasion of President de Klerk's visit to Washington, we believe that the process of change in South Africa has become irreversible. The lifting of the state of emergency in Natal reflects that reality.

Remarks to White House Interns
October 18, 1990

I understand what we're going to do here in just a second is: I retreat, we divide up into two groups—given the weather—and get some pictures taken. But really I'm glad to have this opportunity to come over here and meet with you all today because I do know what a contribution you've made to the workings of this White House. Sometimes the chores assigned might seem a little ordinary, might seem somewhat removed from the weighty processes of government that you may be studying in school or are more interested in, but I'm sure that you've learned that little things do add up to the greatness of this whole system of our democracy. And so, I really did want to come over and say thank you very much for these internships.

And I also want to take a moment just to share a few ideas with you about the issues that you're hearing so much about today, and mainly I'm talking about the big budget debate that's going on on Capitol Hill. Now, let me venture a guess that you've learned a great deal about how Washington works here in what we lovingly call "inside the beltway." And you've learned some of the jargon: continuing resolutions and sequestration and conference committees. And it's a good thing. But many people hear this technical talk, and they think that it's all so complicated that it couldn't mean anything to them. Well, when you return home, maybe you can let these folks know that decisions in Washington do make a difference in the lives of everyday Americans for better or for worse.

You've also recently heard a lot coming out of Capitol Hill about soaking the rich. And let me translate this bit of Washington doublespeak for you. When some Members of the Congress talk about "soaking the rich," they really do mean raising taxes on everybody. Their talk about progressivity and regressivity is just a smokescreen, in my view, to try and hide their effort to raise the income taxes of ordinary working Americans.

Let me tell you about another word, and this one's a little complex. But again, I expect many people here do understand it. I'm talking about indexing. You were all perhaps kids—I don't want to put you in a time warp here—but when indexing was established, that was back in 1981. And you may not know that there was a time when inflation simply pushed the middle-class Americans into higher and higher tax brackets. Inflation was so rapid that people were moving fast into higher brackets, brackets that were once designed to soak the rich.

In other words, the Federal Government really was a silent partner in inflation, profiting from higher prices even as families suffered. I say profiting because more and more money came in under inflation and under no indexing. Elimination of indexing does not affect the rich because they are already in the top bracket. Indexing is a protective shield for the middle class. And tell your parents and families that I am not going to permit this shield, this protective shield for working Americans, to be pierced, to be broken.

We must reduce this deficit so that interest rates can come down. Many of you have heard what Alan Greenspan said: If we get a good package, they will come down. We have got to enable people, then, to buy homes and cars so that business can invest in new jobs. And that's what lower interest rates will do. And they won't come down unless we get this deficit under control.

Now, let me tell you about another word I'm sure you're hearing about: incentive. When tax rates get too high, and they did this before indexing came in, then people didn't save because the Government tax takes so much that there is no incentive to save or to invest. And that's the reason why, as I look at what's going on up on Capitol Hill today, I prefer the Senate version of the budget because it keeps the 28-percent rate and it doesn't raise the income tax on any middle class or lower income Americans—not because I want to help the rich but because I want to help everyone.

And once they start changing anybody's income tax rates, they cannot resist changing everyone's tax rates. And you don't have to be an expert in Federal fiscal policy to understand the real issue here. As I said, I am determined to reduce this deficit, but I'm even more determined to continue economic growth so that all of you can enjoy a better future. And I'm talking here about jobs, willingness to invest in new businesses and to employ more people. And I'm not going to let the politicians who speak so passionately about soaking the rich get away with killing the indexing, the very indexing which preserves incentives and protects the family budget from the attack of a Federal Government which spends so much that it simply cannot balance its own budget.

So, I will hold everyone's feet to the fire and make them up there, to the best of my ability, do the right thing. I really do believe in what I'm doing, and I believe that the national interest is more important than my own personal interest and certainly more important than the special interest. And I'm going to fight the taxers and the spenders because it is right.

And in the coming weeks, I plan to take this message to the American people. And I really believe in my heart that as the voters learn more about what the real issues are, issues like indexing—and again, what that does to the working men and women in this country when you tamper with it—incentive—what that means in terms of creating new jobs and growth to get this economy moving. It's sluggish, and I want to see it move forward so more people have hope and opportunity. And when people understand this, I think they're going to join me in demanding that Congress be responsible and that it reduce the deficit by controlling taxes and spending.

And when I look at all of you, I'm reminded of the young men and women of my generation who had the opportunity to live the American dream. And I firmly believe that it's still alive, but that we all must always work to preserve it and to protect it in a way. And I feel I have an obligation to my own kids and to my own grandchildren in this regard and to all of you.

And so, that's what this battle is about up there—getting the deficit under control; having a firm 5-year program that has real reductions, not phony reductions, real reductions that result in $500 billion real reduction deficit, but do it in a way that you don't sock it to the middle class or the working people of this country. And that's where the battle is. And the opposition is trying to say favoring the rich. And I'm saying I'm favoring jobs, incentive, investment; and through battling against what the House has done on indexing, protecting the working men and women of this country.

I really didn't mean to unload on you like this, but—[*laughter*]—we're getting down to the wire here, and I feel very, very strongly about it. And I am grateful to the leaders up there in the Congress—and I'd say both Democrat and Republican—for the way they're working as we go down to tomorrow night's deadline. We're getting good cooperation from the leadership there. And now I just want to see that what I've spelled out for you here is what prevails, so when Congress adjourns we can start to see this economy recover and every single American will have more hope and better opportunity.

Now, with no further ado, let me simply say, once again, thank you, each and every

one of you. And I will go until the cruise director gets in here and figures out how we can get at least two pictures that we'll send over your way as soon as we get them done. And thank you all very, very much for what you're doing. Appreciate it.

Note: The President spoke at 3:20 p.m. in Room 450 of the Old Executive Office Building. In his remarks, he referred to Alan Greenspan, Chairman of the Board of Governors of the Federal Reserve System.

Toasts at the State Dinner for Prime Minister Jozsef Antall of Hungary
October 18, 1990

The President. Mr. Prime Minister and Mrs. Antall and to our Hungarian and American friends, I am glad you are all here, especially those from out of town, because so many are grounded or circling at this very moment trying to get here. [*Laughter*]

But it is a great pleasure for Barbara and me to welcome you both to the White House tonight. There's a great poet of Hungary's 1848 Revolution, Sándor Petöfi, once wrote: "Let me address you in the name of millions." And so, tonight, Mr. Prime Minister, let me greet you in the name of millions who convey their warmest welcome, the people of the United States.

And as I look around this room, I see why Americans feel so enriched by our long friendship with the Hungarian people. We see the kinship in the nearly 2 million Americans of Hungarian descent: in giants like nuclear scientist Edward Teller—we're honored to have here with us tonight—or conductor Eugene Ormandy, who proved that music is the universal language, or Colonel Kovacs, who gave his life for America's struggle for freedom way back during our own Revolutionary War.

But this kinship isn't just one way. Americans admire Hungarians whose deeds so inspire us, heroes like the great founder of the Hungarian state, St. Stephen, and great

composers like Liszt and Bartók, or Hungary's many winners of Nobel prizes or Olympic medals, or that great patriot Janos Hunyadi, who more than five centuries ago stopped foreign invasion. In his honor, the Pope ordered each Catholic church in Europe to ring its bell at midday. And since then, Catholic church bells all over the world ring precisely at noon. Heroes, yes—American, Hungarian.

Today, more than ever, this kinship binds the people of the United States and Hungary. And our nations are linked by many things: hard work, the role of community, religious devotion, and of course a fierce love of freedom. And especially during the past 2 years, your gallantry has evoked our admiration. Your example has been our inspiration.

When we were in Budapest last year, I was given a piece of the Iron Curtain. And I keep it there in my office that you visited today, sir, as a stark symbol of Hungary's courageous decision to open its borders, unleashing a force that helped transform Europe and eventually brought down the Berlin Wall.

If Kossuth could be with us here tonight, he would see that his dream of a free and democratic Hungary had been fulfilled, and he would see that this new day in Hungary's history is the result of the Hungarian people's determination to live in freedom. Your presence here tonight, Mr. Prime Minister, bears testimony to Hungary's new role as a sovereign member of the new and growing partnership of nations.

The darkness lifts, the bell resounds, and the light grows brighter by the day. And so, Mr. Prime Minister, let us raise our glasses, and let us raise what Kossuth called the morning star of liberty. God bless you, and as your national anthem proclaims so unforgettably, "God Bless the Hungarians." We are very pleased you're here, sir. To your health.

The Prime Minister. I consider this day a great day in the life of the Hungarians and to all of us. We feel that you have done a lot for our freedom, because you have been determined, because you have stuck to all those moral principles that your forefathers and the Founding Fathers have brought home in this country.

And this past also binds both you and ourselves. We are proud that Hungarians were able to do a lot for America. It is a special, very good feeling to be able to be here. And it is also a good feeling that, with your national flag, the Stars and Stripes, the humble Hungarian tricolor is also on the same level with you.

We have restored the old Hungarian coat of arms and the holy crown—according to tradition, the crown of King Stephen the Saint was preserved by you. And sometime in the future, historian may find that the return of the crown played a very important role to once again being able to identi-

fy ourselves within our own self. Thousands and thousands of people pay tribute in front of it when the party state still was operating and was in function. We at home, we once again felt we were Hungarians, and we also felt the great pressure of this old traditional symbol. Afterwards, Hungarians came back to visit Hungary who had not been to Hungary before.

Your visit last year, Mr. President, took place at a time when the opposition carried out with the first negotiations in the framework of the opposition in roundtable talks. Your presence has once again encouraged us. And I am sure that you may also have felt the feeling that the United States of America, and personally you, are so popular. And please accept my apologies for this exaggeration that, perhaps, not so popular anywhere else in the world. [*Laughter*]

Well, Mr. President, suppose you don't have a chance to be a third-time President of the United States. I am sure the Hungarian nation would willingly elect you as President. [*Laughter*]

I raise my glass to eternal friendship of the United States of America and Hungary and to you, personally, Mr. President and Mrs. Bush.

Note: The President spoke at 8:15 p.m. in the State Dining Room at the White House. In his opening remarks, he referred to the interruption of commercial air service caused by inclement weather. The Prime Minister spoke in Hungarian, and his remarks were translated by an interpreter.

Remarks to the National Italian American Foundation
October 19, 1990

What I really want to do is get this distinguished group to ask you to file through into the Oval Office. Take a look at that and maybe get individual pictures.

But let me just tell you where we stand as we're getting near the end of this Congress, the end of this session. Last night the Senate passed a bill that offers, I think, some real hope for getting this budget defi-

cit matter under control. I have stood against raising these individual income tax rates, and I think I'm on the right track in that. And I'm going to try to hold the line.

The Senate did a very good job on that compromise on one side or another. But I congratulate the leaders. I just had Bob Dole in here and got to thank him personally for his steadfast leadership. And then I think certain credit goes to George Mitchell, who held the line on the Democratic side. So, now they go to conference. They're starting at 11 o'clock. I expect it will start off with a photo opportunity—all life does these days—[*laughter*]—and then they'll get down to some serious work.

It is a question now that could be solved in a very short period of time. But I think they have been serious—the Senate—working until all hours to bring it this far. There are big differences between the Senate and the House legislation, but I'd prefer not to go into what I think the details of the final bill will be. But I will say I, for the first time, feel optimistic that we can get this job done for the American people, and it needs to be done. I've found that if you want to make something happen, if you want to govern rather than just give speeches, you have to sit and work very hard and give a little and take a little. And it's in that spirit now that the White House is going to approach this conference. I hope that we can finally demonstrate to the American people that this deficit that is plaguing the generations to come can be managed. So, that's where we are on that one.

On the Middle East, you've, I'm sure, all followed that. And we've got a lot of kids over there—wonderful, highly motivated, well-trained men and women. I'm as determined as I was the day that the first troop left that Saddam Hussein's aggression not be rewarded by some compromise, not be rewarded by our failing to get him totally out of Kuwait or restore the legitimate rulers.

And it's been a fascinating experience as we've pulled together the largest coalition of this nature perhaps since World War II— I'm sure since World War II. And it's disparate: It's Arabs as well as other countries. Saddam Hussein's still trying to make people believe this is the Arab world against the United States of America. And he couldn't be more wrong. We have a majority in the Arab League—strong majority. We've got strong support, both on the ground and in diplomatic forums, for what we're doing from Arab countries.

So, I think we've sent a very strong signal, but I think the bottom line is he can't prevail. So, we're going to stay with this, stay the course, and send a strong moral message out there, and a simple one: One big country can't bully its neighbor and take it over. That's the principle that we're fighting for. We also have national security interests which relate to the energy out there. So, it's been a fascinating experience.

With Pete Secchia here, I will simply say that—I want to thank him for the job he's doing—but say that I can't think of anybody who has been more cooperative in all of this than the Italian Government. You know, I've had a chance now to work with the Italian Prime Ministers in NATO, for example, and in the G–7 meetings [economic summits of industrialized nations], and I can report to you what I think most of you already know, and that is that the relationship between Italy and the United States probably has never been better. We don't get in and choose up on some of the domestic political issues over there, of course. I mean, that's their business. We deal with whoever the Prime Minister is, whoever the government is. But whether it's one party or another, they've been steadfast friends of the United States, constructive in debate and in discussion, and we always end up kind of on the same wavelength. And I think that's a very, very important thing. And at times, I feel that, for reasons that escape me, people don't fully understand how well this relationship is set up and how well it's going.

I think, Pete—I expect you'd agree with those comments, but—and I will say that this Ambassador has done a very good job of getting out around the country, getting the feel for the people themselves, and making clear to them in every way possible—through papers, through appearances and different groups around the country— that we are their friends. Not that they doubt it. It doesn't hurt sometimes, when you have the turmoil around the world, to let your friends know you're not neglecting them and you're not forgetting the importance of them.

Besides that, we have an awful lot to learn from the Italian experts over there in matters that relate to neighboring countries. I'm thinking of the turmoil in Yugoslavia today, and I'm thinking of the evolution of change all through Eastern Europe. And I've found Mr. Andreotti and company to be extraordinarily helpful as I've had many, many discussions with them.

So, I think that part of our business is in fair shape. I've dwelled only on one domestic issue here, and that is the necessity of getting the budget deficit down. Congress is running out of time now to act on our Educational Excellence Act, which I think fits into some of the work of the foundation on education. And I regret that very, very much because we've got a good, sound program.

We are making progress, as Bill Bennett—I don't know whether he's talked to you all today or not—but anyway, making significant progress on this all-out war against drugs. Some of the statistics are very, very encouraging. I know, Paul, you know Jim Burke, who used to be head of Johnson and Johnson, and some of the rest of you probably know him as well. And he's headed up what we call a Points of Light approach, in this instance bringing media advertising to bear on this question of antinarcotics. And part of the work is staying in very close touch statistically through polls and surveys on this. And he shares Bill Bennett's optimism about the fact that the country is finally making progress, with dramatic use of heroin down, use of cocaine down—use of all these heavy drugs down. And so, there's a light at the end of that tunnel, and we're going to stay with that one.

And on the national drug strategy, I think in fairness, we are getting pretty good support from Congress. We're not getting the support I want on the crime bill. We've had a different approach to it. Ours is hard-line. Ours is tough. And I think it's proper. And I regret very much that they have not come through and given us a crime bill that I can sign. And I don't think that we're going to get it before the end of this session.

Clean air—I'm disappointed that we haven't finalized a clean air bill that is reasonable and one that does do what we started out to do, and that is make dramatic improvements in the clean air amendments. And I had one up there that we had to get agreement with on some of the Sena-

tors. And then we go to the House, and it gets caught up in a lot of extremes over there—people wanting to drive industry totally to its knees. And I'm still convinced that we can find a sound balance between growth and jobs and sound environmental practice. And so, we're not home yet on the clean air amendments, but I'm hoping that we will be because I think it's very important for our country and for the generations to come. So, we're going to keep working.

A lot of these issues will carry over, obviously, until the brand new Congress—they've got to start over, but headway will not be totally lost on some of these key questions. But I'm not handing out grades to Congress. They're grading me every single day. Some of it very flattering, and some of it not so pleasant. [*Laughter*] But that goes with the territory. And what I'm trying to do in the last—back to where we started—in the last few hours of this Congress is say: Look, let's put the people's business first. Let's lay aside this political rhetoric and get a job done that should have been done long ago, because it simply isn't right to mortgage the future of these kids anymore.

And with an economy that is sluggish, it is just exactly the time to demonstrate to the world that we can get the deficit down. You've all heard what Greenspan said about interest rates, provided we get a sound budget agreement. And I think better than a speech on the floor of the House would be a sound agreement that brings these interest rates down and starts growth and job opportunity for the American people. So, that's where I'm spending my time at the end of this session.

Thank you all very much for coming. And now if those who have the time—I'd love to have you just file through and see the majestic Oval Office, and we'll get pictures. Thank you all very much.

Note: President Bush spoke at 10:16 a.m. in the Roosevelt Room at the White House. In his remarks, he referred to Robert Dole, Senate Republican leader; George Mitchell, Senate majority leader; President Saddam Hussein of Iraq; Prime Minister Giulio Andreotti of Italy; William J. Bennett, Director of National Drug Control Policy; Paul Oreffice, chairman of Dow Chemical Corp.; James E. Burke, chairman of the Partner- *ship for a Drug-Free America; and Alan Greenspan, Chairman of the Board of Governors of the Federal Reserve System.*

Excerpt of a Statement by Press Secretary Fitzwater on the Citizens Democracy Corps
October 19, 1990

The President launched the Citizens Democracy Corps in May as a new initiative to support the voluntary efforts of American citizens to help strengthen the emerging democratic institutions and market economies of Central and Eastern Europe. It is today being expanded to include activities in the Soviet Union as well.

The President is pleased to announce the names of the Chairman and Executive Committee of the Board of Directors of the Citizens Democracy Corps. He is gratified that these distinguished American leaders, representing a cross section of our society have agreed to serve. They are as follows:

Chairman of the Board

The Honorable Drew Lewis, chairman of the board, Union Pacific Corp.; former Secretary of Transportation

Executive Committee

The Honorable John R. Block, president, National American Wholesale Grocers' Association; former Secretary of Agriculture

The Honorable Derek Bok, president, Harvard University

Mr. Lodwrick M. Cook, chairman and chief executive officer, ARCO

The Honorable William A. Hewitt, former

chairman, John Deere & Co.; former U.S. Ambassador to Jamaica

The Honorable Barbara Jordan, the Lyndon B. Johnson chair in national policy, University of Texas; former Member of Congress

The Honorable Nancy Kassebaum, U.S. Senate

The Honorable Lane Kirkland, president, AFL–CIO

The Honorable Henry A. Kissinger, chairman, Kissinger Associates, Inc.; former Secretary of State.

Mr. Robert H. Krieble, president, Krieble Associates

The Honorable Frederic V. Malek, vice chairman, Northwest Airlines; cochairman, Coldwell Banker Commercial Groups

Mr. Frank N. Piasecki, president and chief executive officer, Piasecki Aircraft

The Honorable Robert S. Strauss, partner, Akin, Gump, Strauss, Hauer & Feld; former chairman, Democratic National Committee; former U.S. Trade Representative

Mr. William T. Ylvisaker, president and chief executive officer, Corporate Focus, Inc.

A Board of Directors will be announced later.

Statement on Civil Rights Legislation
October 20, 1990

Today I received S. 2104, the Kennedy-Hawkins "Civil Rights Act of 1990." As I have said before, in its current form, this bill is a quota bill. Throughout congressional consideration of this bill, I have said repeatedly that I want to sign a civil rights bill this year that addresses certain Supreme Court decisions regarding employment discrimination. There are reasonable compromises that I would support that address legitimate issues raised in these cases without resulting in employers adopting quotas.

The legislation as enacted by Congress fails to cure several critical defects I find in the bill. In its present form, the measure remains a quota bill because inescapably it will have the effect of forcing businesses to adopt quotas in hiring and promotion. Throughout congressional consideration of this bill, I have emphasized my support for legislation to strengthen our employment discrimination laws, and have already signed the most sweeping civil rights bill in 25 years: the Americans with Disabilities Act. With regard to S. 2104, I want to sign a civil rights bill; but I will not sign a quota bill. Instead of solving problems, quotas foster divisiveness and litigation, set group against group, minority against minority, and in so doing, do more to promote legal fees then civil rights. S. 2104 undermines the basic principles of fairness on which our system of laws is based. The administration has tried to work with Congress in good faith on these issues, but I cannot accept legislation that is unfair and turns back the clock on progress that has occurred since passage of the Civil Rights Act of 1964.

Because I believe Congress shares my commitment to civil rights and my opposition to quotas—an opposition that is shared by most Americans—I believe together we *can* enact good legislation. During House and Senate consideration of this measure, the administration supported bipartisan alternatives to S. 2104.

On Monday I will veto S. 2104 and return it to Congress with my objections. I believe legislation *can* be enacted that I can sign before Congress leaves. The bill I am today forwarding to Congress includes those specific changes to the Civil Rights Act of 1990 that will make it acceptable. My proposal contains a number of compromises designed to accommodate the concerns of the proponents of S. 2104. It overrules several Supreme Court decisions from last year, and it addresses the so-called "*Wards Cove* issue" by shifting the burden of proof to the defendant to justify "business necessity" in disparate impact cases. I urge Congress to enact my proposal before adjournment.

Congress has the opportunity to cure the defects that necessitate my rejection of S. 2104. With the changes I am forwarding to the Congress, together we can produce legislation that will strike a blow against racial bias without institutionalizing quotas.

Note: S. 2104 was returned without approval on October 22.

Message to the Congress Transmitting Proposed Civil Rights Legislation
October 20, 1990

To the Congress of the United States:

I am pleased to transmit a legislative proposal that if adopted would cure critical defects in the Civil Rights Act of 1990, a bill which, in its current form, S. 2104, I am compelled to veto.

As presented to me, S. 2104 would lead employers to adopt quotas for hiring and promotion, and it would prevent or discourage some victims of illegal quotas from seeking legal redress. The harm this would do to the cause of civil rights is potentially profound. Any measure that causes employ-

ment decisions to turn on factors of race, sex, ethnicity, or religion—rather than on qualifications—is fundamentally unfair, and is at odds with our civil rights tradition. Our war against discrimination is impeded, not advanced, by a bill that encourages the adoption of quotas.

On Monday, I will return S. 2104 to the Senate, along with my objections. It is my hope that the Congress will immediately forward to me a corrected bill for consideration. We cannot shrink from our national commitment to equal protection under the

Photographic
Portfolio

erleaf: Speaking at the
ristening of the U.S.S. *George*
ashington in Newport News, VA,
y 21. **Above left:** Meeting with
e Cabinet on the Federal budget
the Cabinet Room, October 5.
ft: On the Colonnade,
ptember 11. **Above:** Meeting
th President Mohammed Hosni
ubarak of Egypt in Cairo,
vember 22. **Right:** Signing the
mericans with Disabilities Act on
e South Lawn, July 26.

Left: Walking with economic summit leaders in Houston, TX, July 10. *Below left:* Meeting with Colin Powell, Chairman of the Joint Chiefs of Staff; Secretary of Defense Dick Cheney; Brent Scowcroft, Assistant to the President for National Security Affairs; and Chief of Staff John Sununu in the Oval Office, September 24. *Right:* With Prime Minister John Major of the United Kingdom at the North Portico, December 21. *Below:* Sharing a Thanksgiving meal with U.S. troops in Saudi Arabia, November 22.

Left: Meeting with Supreme Court nominee David Souter in the Oval Office, September 12. **Below:** At the Vice President's Residence, December 13. **Right:** Toast with President Václav Havel of Czechoslovakia in Prague, November 17. **Below right:** Visiting a preschool class at the West Philadelphia Community Center in Philadelphia, PA, July 24. **Overleaf:** Meeting with President Carlos Salinas de Gortari of Mexico in Monterrey, November 27.

law and equal opportunity for all. Unaltered, S. 2104 would violate that pledge. With the changes that I propose, the Civil Rights Act of 1990 would no longer result in the imposition of quotas, but would be made a true civil rights bill that I would like to see become law.

With the legislative proposal, I also transmit a section-by-section analysis explaining the need for these changes and describing

the Civil Rights Act of 1990 as amended by my proposal. I urge speedy action on this measure and hope that it will be adopted so that we may take another step in defending the civil rights of all Americans.

GEORGE BUSH

The White House,
October 20, 1990.

Message to the Senate Returning Without Approval the Civil Rights Act of 1990
October 22, 1990

To the Senate of the United States:

I am today returning without my approval S. 2104, the "Civil Rights Act of 1990." I deeply regret having to take this action with respect to a bill bearing such a title, especially since it contains certain provisions that I strongly endorse.

Discrimination, whether on the basis of race, national origin, sex, religion, or disability, is worse than wrong. It is a fundamental evil that tears at the fabric of our society, and one that all Americans should and must oppose. That requires rigorous enforcement of existing antidiscrimination laws. It also requires vigorously promoting new measures such as this year's Americans with Disabilities Act, which for the first time adequately protects persons with disabilities against invidious discrimination.

One step that the Congress can take to fight discrimination right now is to act promptly on the civil rights bill that I transmitted on October 20, 1990. This accomplishes the stated purpose of S. 2104 in strengthening our Nation's laws against employment discrimination. Indeed, this bill contains several important provisions that are similar to provisions in S. 2104:

- Both shift the burden of proof to the employer on the issue of "business necessity" in disparate impact cases.
- Both create expanded protections against on-the-job racial discrimination by extending 42 U.S.C. 1981 to the performance as well as the making of

contracts.
- Both expand the right to challenge discriminatory seniority systems by providing that suit may be brought when they cause harm to plaintiffs.
- Both have provisions creating new monetary remedies for the victims of practices such as sexual harassment. (The Administration bill allows equitable awards up to $150,000.00 under this new monetary provision, in addition to existing remedies under Title VII.)
- Both have provisions ensuring that employers can be held liable if invidious discrimination was a motivating factor in an employment decision.
- Both provide for plaintiffs in civil rights cases to receive expert witness fees under the same standards that apply to attorneys fees.
- Both provide that the Federal Government, when it is a defendant under Title VII, will have the same obligation to pay interest to compensate for delay in payment as a nonpublic party. The filing period in such actions is also lengthened.
- Both contain a provision encouraging the use of alternative dispute resolution mechanisms.

The congressional majority and I are on common ground regarding these important provisions. Disputes about other, controversial provisions in S. 2104 should not be allowed to impede the enactment of these proposals.

Along with the significant similarities between my Administration's bill and S. 2104, however, there are crucial differences. Despite the use of the term "civil rights" in the title of S. 2104, the bill actually employs a maze of highly legalistic language to introduce the destructive force of quotas into our Nation's employment system. Primarily through provisions governing cases in which employment practices are alleged to have *unintentionally* caused the disproportionate exclusion of members of certain groups, S. 2104 creates powerful incentives for employers to adopt hiring and promotion quotas. These incentives are created by the bill's new and very technical rules of litigation, which will make it difficult for employers to defend legitimate employment practices. In many cases, a defense against unfounded allegations will be impossible. Among other problems, the plaintiff often need not even show that any of the employer's practices caused a significant statistical disparity. In other cases, the employer's defense is confined to an unduly narrow definition of "business necessity" that is significantly more restrictive than that established by the Supreme Court in *Griggs* and in two decades of subsequent decisions. Thus, unable to defend legitimate practices in court, employers will be driven to adopt quotas in order to avoid liability.

Proponents of S. 2104 assert that it is needed to overturn the Supreme Court's *Wards Cove* decision and restore the law that had existed since the *Griggs* case in 1971. S. 2104, however, does not in fact codify *Griggs* or the Court's subsequent decisions prior to *Wards Cove*. Instead, S. 2104 engages in a sweeping rewrite of two decades of Supreme Court jurisprudence, using language that appears in no decision of the Court and that is contrary to principles acknowledged even by Justice Stevens' *dissent* in *Wards Cove*: "The opinion in *Griggs* made it clear that a neutral practice that operates to exclude minorities is nevertheless lawful if it serves a valid business purpose."

I am aware of the dispute among lawyers about the proper interpretation of certain critical language used in this portion of S. 2104. The very fact of this dispute suggests that the bill is not codifying the law developed by the Supreme Court in *Griggs* and subsequent cases. This debate, moreover, is a sure sign that S. 2104 will lead to years—perhaps decades—of uncertainty and expensive litigation. It is neither fair nor sensible to give the employers of our country a difficult choice between using quotas and seeking a clarification of the law through costly and very risky litigation.

S. 2104 contains several other unacceptable provisions as well. One section unfairly closes the courts, in many instances, to individuals victimized by agreements, to which they were not a party, involving the use of quotas. Another section radically alters the remedial provisions in Title VII of the Civil Rights Act of 1964, replacing measures designed to foster conciliation and settlement with a new scheme modeled on a tort system widely acknowledged to be in a state of crisis. The bill also contains a number of provisions that will create unnecessary and inappropriate incentives for litigation. These include unfair retroactivity rules; attorneys fee provisions that will discourage settlements; unreasonable new statutes of limitation; and a "rule of construction" that will make it extremely difficult to know how courts can be expected to apply the law. In order to assist the Congress regarding legislation in this area, I enclose herewith a memorandum from the Attorney General explaining in detail the defects that make S. 2104 unacceptable.

Our goal and our promise has been equal opportunity and equal protection under the law. That is a bedrock principle from which we cannot retreat. The temptation to support a bill—any bill—simply because its title includes the words "civil rights" is very strong. This impulse is not entirely bad. Presumptions have too often run the other way, and our Nation's history on racial questions cautions against complacency. But when our efforts, however well intentioned, result in quotas, equal opportunity is not advanced but thwarted. The very commitment to justice and equality that is offered as the reason why this bill should be signed requires me to veto it.

Again, I urge the Congress to act on my

legislation before adjournment. In order truly to enhance equal opportunity, however, the Congress must also take action in several related areas. The elimination of employment discrimination is a vital element in achieving the American dream, but it is not enough. The absence of discrimination will have little concrete meaning unless jobs are available and the members of all groups have the skills and education needed to qualify for those jobs. Nor can we expect that our young people will work hard to prepare for the future if they grow up in a climate of violence, drugs, and hopelessness.

In order to address these problems, attention must be given to measures that promote accountability and parental choice in the schools; that strengthen the fight against violent criminals and drug dealers in our inner cities; and that help to combat poverty and inadequate housing. We need initiatives that will empower individual Americans and enable them to reclaim control of their lives, thus helping to make our country's promise of opportunity a reality for all. Enactment of such initiatives, along with my Administration's civil rights bill, will achieve real advances for the cause of equal opportunity.

GEORGE BUSH

The White House,
October 22, 1990.

Statement on Signing the San Carlos Mineral Strip Act of 1990
October 22, 1990

I am today signing H.R. 4593, the "San Carlos Mineral Strip Act of 1990."

H.R. 4593 is intended to resolve the status of an area of the San Carlos Apache Mineral Strip that has long been administered by the United States Forest Service as part of the Coronado National Forest in Arizona. The bill would resolve the issue by transferring to the Secretary of the Interior the administration of the surface rights in the land at issue. Title to the land is to be held by the Secretary in trust for the San Carlos Apache Indian Tribe.

While I support the change in land status that would be effected by H.R. 4593, I am concerned that the bill does not contain an express description of the lands it will affect. I am signing this bill with the understanding that these lands consist of, and are limited to, approximately 10,650 acres of the Mineral Strip that the Forest Service has been administering as part of the Coronado National Forest, as recognized in the congressional committee reports on this legislation. Finally, it is my understanding that H.R. 4593 is not intended to affect any other existing boundary between federally managed lands and the San Carlos Apache Indian Reservation.

GEORGE BUSH

The White House,
October 22, 1990.

Note: H.R. 4593, approved October 22, was assigned Public Law 101–447.

Statement by Press Secretary Fitzwater on Violence in the Middle East
October 22, 1990

The President deplores the tragic killing of three Israeli citizens in West Jerusalem yesterday. The President offers his condolences to the families of the victims. These killings make it all the more imperative that the cycle of violence be ended. We urge all parties to act to reenforce peace and calm in the region.

Similarly, another tragedy is the assassination of Dany Chamoun and his family in Lebanon. And we reiterate our call for all Lebanese to unite behind the government of President Harawi. As we have said, it is now time for national reconciliation in Lebanon and for the creation of a free, independent, and sovereign nation—free of foreign forces and armed militia. We hope that the reunited army and the Lebanese people will support President Harawi in the effort to implement the Taif agreement.

Note: Press Secretary Fitzwater read the statement during his daily press briefing, which began at 11:15 a.m. Dany Chamoun was the head of one of the principal Christian families in Lebanon.

Memorandum on the Kaho'olawe, Hawaii, Weapons Range
October 22, 1990

Memorandum for the Secretary of Defense

Subject: Use of the Island of Kaho'olawe, Hawaii, as a Weapons Range

You are directed to discontinue use of Kaho'olawe as a weapons range effective immediately. This directive extends to use of the island for small arms, artillery, naval gunfire support, and aerial ordnance training. In addition, you are directed to establish a joint Department of Defense-State of Hawaii commission to examine the future status of Kaho'olawe and related issues.

GEORGE BUSH

Message to the Congress Transmitting the Annual Report on the State of Small Business
October 22, 1990

To the Congress of the United States:

I am pleased to submit my first annual report on the state of small business, which documents the progress of small firms in 1989. Over the record-breaking past almost 8 years of economic expansion, the economic environment for small business growth has been remarkable. Entrepreneurs have seized the opportunity to create millions of new enterprises, innovative products, and jobs.

In 1989, the number of business tax returns filed in the United States topped 20 million—an increase of more than 50 percent over a decade ago. Most of these businesses are very small ventures, but their importance cannot be overstated: by testing thousands of new ideas, products, and processes in the marketplace, they are inventing America's future.

Small firms have had good earnings growth over the years of the expansion, and they continue to generate income for an increasing number of America's workers and entrepreneurs. Our economy experienced unemployment rates of only 5.3 percent in 1989, its lowest level since 1973. Small firms created a more than proportional share of new jobs relative to large businesses, as they have throughout the decade. Even when the pace of economic activity slowed, small firms often cushioned adverse effects on the labor force, laying off workers only as a last resort.

More women became small business owners during the 1980s than at any other time in America's history; the number of women proprietors almost doubled from 2.5 million in 1980 to 4.4 million in 1987. Minorities, too, started businesses in growing numbers during the 1980s. Women and minorities can be expected to continue making great strides in business ownership over the coming decade.

Small firms grew rapidly in the 1980s and contributed immeasurably to the diversity of the American economy. It was not easy. New companies often must struggle to enter competitive new markets with limited resources, vie with more established businesses for a trained labor force, and face increasing international competition.

While the 1980s were a decade of great achievement for America's entrepreneurial small businesses, the 1990s promise great opportunity and great challenge. We must invest in America—in human, intellectual,

and physical capital. We must continue to find the means to educate and empower young people, new immigrants, women, minorities, and all who aspire to be entrepreneurs.

In a time of great economic opportunity around the world, we must equip ourselves, not only to meet new international competition, but to take the lead in a global economy. I am confident that, with the strength and spirit of American enterprise, we will be able to build an even stronger economy in the last decade of the 20th century.

GEORGE BUSH

The White House,
October 22, 1990.

Remarks at the Presentation Ceremony for the Theodore Roosevelt Conservation Award
October 22, 1990

Well, first, welcome to so many Members of Congress. Delighted to see you all here. And to all others, welcome to the White House. Of course, it's a great pleasure to be with Bill Reilly—he's doing such an outstanding job at EPA—and then, Mike Deland of the CEQ, right here in the White House—the same. And they're both, I think, leading a really fine, renewed effort to protect America's environment. I'm delighted to see Duncan and Porter here—Duncan Hunter and Porter Goss—who, in a sense, organized this whole concept of these awards. And I want to thank all that have been involved in launching the Theodore Roosevelt Conservation Awards. All of you here today, thank you for coming—those of you who worked so diligently to protect the environment and make conservation more than just a word, but really, in a sense, a way of life.

You may remember a couple of years back when Time magazine named Earth the "planet of the year." And Jay Leno said, "What do you expect? All the judges came from Earth." [*Laughter*] Well, it was almost exactly 1 year ago that I met here at the White House with many of you all, many of

the same Congress men and women, joining together to develop a program in the spirit of Teddy Roosevelt's historic commitment to conservation. And today it's a great honor to stand with you as we commemorate the great strides that these individual Americans have made towards preserving a clean environment for all Americans.

You represent a whole new breed of American heroes, people that are making investments in our environment today that are bound to pay dividends for the kids tomorrow—people like Charles Caniff from Porter Goss's own district in Florida. Charles helped found the Port Charlotte Harbor Environmental Center, a unique partnership between the private sector, local government, and public schools.

And, Charles—where is Charles? Right here. Congratulations, sir. People like you do represent the power of voluntarism, the power of those that might be physically challenged and the power of an idea whose time has come—the grassroots effort to build a better America, where the quality of our environment matches the quality of our dreams.

Already we've come a long way, not only

as a planet but as a people. And in the not so distant past, the skies of our cities were being blanketed with clouds of pollution and American rivers were being filled with sewage and industrial waste, and we were squandering our vital natural heritage. But in recent years, we have seen a new attitude—a return, if you will, to the conservation ethic of Teddy Roosevelt and the birth of a worldwide environmental movement that started right here in the United States.

The change has been both fundamental and pervasive. And many of you, in Congress and out, have been leaders in rekindling the flame of conservation in the hearts and the minds of the American people—people like Bill Rutherford, Bob Michel's honoree from Illinois, who helps run the Wildlife Prairie Park without one single penny of tax support; or David Woodside, who we learned from Pat Saiki, who has helped save—learned about from Pat—he's helped save the endangered species in Hawaii; Mary Lou Ryan, a New York grade school teacher, who's cultivating character in her kids by cultivating concern about the environment.

Americans like you help keep our conservation ethic strong. And that enduring commitment requires sustained action from each of us. We've taken a series of actions to protect America's environment: planting trees and preserving wetlands; developing cleaner domestic sources of energy; working with our global neighbors to fight pollution that knows no boundaries, especially in the emerging democracies.

Bill Reilly, just back, wrote me a fascinating letter, and I'd hope that you'll share those views with all the Members of Congress about this new Budapest Center that we've helped set up. Americans, again, like you, have provided an extraordinary foundation for the efforts of our administration. The clean air initiative, just to cite an example, that we launched in the Grand Tetons over a year ago is a very ambitious and very aggressive piece of legislation. And it will sharply cut air pollution's big three: acid rain, smog, and toxic pollutants. And it re-

spects another kind of delicate ecology: the ecology of jobs and opportunity. The bill has been 13 years in coming, but no American should have to wait another day for clean air. This Congress this week should send me a clean air bill that I can sign.

Our nation really has made great headway, but our mission is not just to defend what's left but to take the offense, to improve our environment all across the board. And some of today's winners, veteran foresters like California's Charles Colver or tree-planting teachers like Wisconsin's Ed Dietz, are doing just exactly that. And I've said this before: Trees can reduce the heat of a summer's day, quiet a highway's noise, help feed the hungry, provide shelter from wind and cold and habitat for wildlife. And every tree planted is a compact between generations.

Many challenges do remain, but thanks to you and to your congressional partners with you here the future holds great promise for our environment. All of you personify the selfless acts of thousands of concerned Americans who strive every day to leave a better world for our kids. And when I look out at the faces of Americans like those that we honor here today, I realize we've hardly begun to discover what God put on Earth and what God put in man.

Congratulations to all of you winners. Congratulations to each of you leaders from the United States Congress who are making this possible. Again, Porter, to you and Duncan, a special congratulations for bringing all this to fruition. And again, thank you, and good luck to each and every one of you. And God bless you.

Note: The President spoke at 3:07 p.m. in Room 450 of the Old Executive Office Building. In his opening remarks, he referred to William K. Reilly, Administrator of the Environmental Protection Agency; Michael R. Deland, Chairman of the Council on Environmental Quality; Representatives Duncan Hunter and Porter Goss; and comedian Jay Leno.

Remarks at a Republican Fundraising Breakfast in Burlington, Vermont

October 23, 1990

Thank you, Vermonters, for that warm welcome. This is magnificent music today from Norwich. Thank you all for being with us today and for that stirring music.

To Dick Snelling and Senator Jeffords, old friend Jack Lindley, Walt Freed, Madeline Harwood—we go back a long time, Madeline, to those early days in the seventies—and to Walt Page, all of whom are doing such a great job, thank you. Let me salute the statewide candidates that are here in the audience today.

And really it is wonderful to be here. Cold and drizzly day out there; but then, I think that some of you drove 2 or 3 hours to get here, getting up at 4 a.m. in the morning. And I think this shows fantastic support for our present and future Congressman Peter Smith.

It's easy to have a very special feeling for this place. It's not just, I guess, the beauty of the Green Mountains. Maybe it's the fact that Vermont, as I was reminded by Messrs. Jeffords and Smith, has voted for more Republican Presidential candidates than any other State in the history of this country. Why wouldn't a Republican President love Vermont? [*Laughter*]

But I think it's something more, and we talked about this coming up here today. This State is known for its independent state of mind—making up its own mind on problems—a place that values the individual voice, believes, of course, in self-reliance and opportunity, and understands how government ought to be accountable, above all, to people.

And that's really why I came up here today: to lend my support to candidates that represent the kind of leadership Vermont has known and valued in the past and that is an absolutely essential necessity for the future of this State.

First, there's a champion for the environment, an effective voice for reform in education—educator himself—who knows how to make Vermont's vote count in the U.S. House of Representatives. And of course,

I'm talking about our friend Peter Smith. Like all Vermonters, he is a man of independent mind. I wish he'd stop reminding me that we do have a few differences out there. [*Laughter*] But hey, listen, nobody is going to do it exactly my way; I've found that out. There are 435 of these people in the United States Congress—[*laughter*]—but this one votes his conscience. He's earned an unusual degree of respect in the House.

Jim Jeffords was right on that, because he knows how to work with the leadership on both sides of the aisle. He wants to make something happen, not just give a little rhetoric out there. He wants to reach a solution. And he understands bipartisanship, because he's made it happen.

We need more of that spirit on Capitol Hill. Every once in a while, a Congressman comes along who is willing to look at the big picture, who recognizes that he is 1/435th of the House of Representatives. A problem can't be solved just exactly the way I want it solved or the way Pete Smith wants it solved or Jim Jeffords wants it solved. That's particularly true for a President when he doesn't control either House of the United States Congress. So, Peter puts the good of the country first.

And it's so easy for an opponent to sit on the sideline, carping, criticizing, offering a lot of heated political rhetoric, making speeches about things that will never happen. Peter wants this deficit down. He wants to stop mortgaging the future of the young people of Vermont, and so do I. We need him in the Congress. When he voted for that early compromise, it wasn't an easy vote. He knew he was going to get sniped at from people way on the right or way on the left or wherever, but he did what he felt he had to do. I, perhaps in a different perspective, had to do exactly the same thing, and I'll get to that in a minute.

Now, back here at the State. Vermont needs leadership that knows what it takes to bring new growth and create new jobs while protecting the environment, and leadership that won't spend beyond its means. I'm talking about experienced leadership, tested leadership. That's why I'm so enthusiastic about Dick Snelling's coming back as Governor of this State again.

We've got a sluggish economy out there nationally. That's one of the reasons I favor this deficit so much and want the interest rates down. But after a record—what was it—four terms as Governor, Dick knows how to create opportunity. And he also knows the balance that's needed: that environmental protection and economic growth have got to complement each other. That's why he's built this proven record of public-private partnerships for the environment.

But above all, after 30 years of experience at the State and local level, he knows how to balance a budget. He's proved it, controlling spending every term that he's been in office. He understands good government. I just asked him if he had a line-item veto. Give a tough guy like this a line-item veto and watch things happen in this State, I'll guarantee you. [Laughter] I'd like to have it, as a matter of fact, as President, because if Congress can't control the spending, I think I could do it with the line-item veto, frankly.

But really, Dick, as I said over in our neighboring State of Maine, it's time for you to return as yet another great Governor, a repeat performance. And I'm confident you will.

To help Dick push through his programs through the legislature, creating this climate for growth that I think Vermonters want—business vitality, jobs—and also to help him control spending, I want to see Mike Bernhardt Lieutenant Governor. We need him. I think Dick needs this good team.

So, these are all candidates—our state-wide level—that Vermont can count on, the kind of leaders that will do what's right for this State and, of course, for our country. That means, first and foremost, bolstering the economic strength of our nation. And that's why I want to speak to you just a moment about the issue that we've been wrestling with back in Washington for more than 8 long months now. I'm talking about reaching final agreement on the Federal budget.

When it comes to the roles and responsibilities of government, the days of tax-and-spend and damn-the-deficit must come to an end. I share the frustration of the people. No American family could afford to run its household the way the Congress runs the Federal budget. Our children deserve to inherit more than an avalanche of unpaid bills. There's no doubt in my mind, Congress wouldn't be in this mess today if we had more Republicans in the Congress.

But the fact that the Democrats control both Houses means compromise. I've found as President if you want to make something happen, you have to have the votes to make it happen. You can't do it just the way you want to do it. So, it means compromise. And that means a budget that isn't the best ever, but the best possible. We're hanging tough for a good agreement, one that shows we're serious about driving this deficit down, a serious $500 billion reduction in 5 years that has the enforcement that the American people should be demanding. There's no point passing a deal and then having it overruled the next day. This agreement that I hope is about to be forthcoming here has strong enforcement provisions in it.

The reason I feel so strongly about the deficit is that I believe real deficit reduction will help bring these interest rates down and make it easier for American families to buy a new home or buy a car, make it easier for the American entrepreneurs to create more jobs—more jobs for American workers. That is a goal of this deficit reduction. Now it's time—past time—that Congress proves to the American people that it can learn to live within its means and that it can pass a budget that puts the Nation on the path to long-term economic growth.

To come up with any budget at all this year, I had to work with the Democrats who control the Congress. You remember 1982. President Reagan found in 1982, in spite of his own historic aversion to taxes, that the only way to govern was to accept a compromise that included raising revenue. Peter mentioned that. You know my feeling on taxes. I like new taxes about as much as I like broccoli. [Laughter]

President Reagan had to swallow hard back then. The rhetoric was almost identical. Go back and take a look at the Congressional Record. The rhetoric was almost identical. I had to swallow hard; but the long-term health of the United States of America, of our economy, has to come before self-interest.

There are a few leaders on both sides of the aisle who understand that. At the risk of repeating it, I'll say it again: Peter Smith is one of them. He has shown that kind of political courage that we need on Capitol Hill. Laid aside what he believes is just the best way to do it, because he knows that we must get the job done. And I salute him. I think that alone should recommend him to the people of this great State for reelection.

So, my message before the election is going to be this: Only Congress has the power to tax. Only Congress has the power to spend. But Congress may have forgotten one thing—the people have the power to choose who sits in the Congress. That's a message I am going to take all over this country. We need more people who are going to lay aside their own small desire to do what's best for the United States of America. If America wants economic growth, if we want to hold the line on taxes and cut spending, and if we want to get serious about reducing the deficit, then America needs to elect more Republicans to the United States Congress.

You know, putting our fiscal house in order is critical not just from the standpoint of the American economy but especially now, in the light of the big picture: the challenge that we face in the Persian Gulf. The Gulf is a reminder of how intricately the interests of nations are interwoven. What happens in Baghdad matters in Burlington because our concern, far beyond the price of oil, is the fate of sovereign nations and peoples. There's a moral underpinning, a strong moral underpinning, to what's happened in the United Nations as we've stood up unanimously against Saddam Hussein's aggression: a world order free from unlawful aggression, free from violence, free from plunder.

I saw some signs coming in: "No War for Oil." I can understand the sentiment by some of those young people. But I would simply say that the rape and the systematic dismantling of Kuwait defies description. The holding of hostages, innocent men and women whose only mistake was to be in Kuwait or be in Iraq when the invader took over Kuwait—holding them goes against the conscience of the entire world. The starving of embassies—good God, this is 1990. And you see this man starving out small embassies in Kuwait. These are crimes against humanity.

There can never be compromise—any compromise—with this kind of aggression. The U.N. has lived up to its promise, and we're not alone there. We have 23 countries on sea and on the land with us, standing side by side with our kids in Saudi Arabia, on the seas of the Straits of Hormuz or the Gulf. We're not alone. We're a part of a magnificent coalition, perhaps the grandest coalition ever put together in times of crisis.

I'm reading a book, and it's a book of history—great, big, thick history about World War II. And there's a parallel between what Hitler did to Poland and what Saddam Hussein has done to Kuwait. Hitler rolled his tanks and troops into Poland. Some of us are old enough, Madeline, to remember this. [*Laughter*] Sorry about that. [*Laughter*] She's a friend. I can get away with anything. No, but some of us do remember when those troops went in. And do you know what followed the troops? It was the Death's Head regiment. Do you know what the Death's Head regiments of the SS were? They were the ones that went in and lined up the kids that were passing out leaflets.

Do you know what happened in Kuwait the other day? Two young kids, mid-teens, passing out leaflets—Iraqi soldiers came, got their parents out and watched as they killed them. They had people on dialysis machines, and they ripped them off of the machines and sent the dialysis machines to Baghdad. And they had kids in incubators, and they were thrown out of the incubators so that Kuwait could be systematically dismantled. So, it isn't oil that we're concerned about. It is aggression. And this aggression is not going to stand.

I recently got a letter from two parents

right here in Burlington, saying their son had decided to have his wedding early when he heard that he would be headed for the Gulf. And he wrote them, saying: "I know this whole situation was unexpected, but I'm ready to do anything necessary to help our country. Mom and Dad, try not to worry, because I'm going to come home, and I'll make you proud."

Well, Second Lieutenant Matthew Campbell, like so many others, is making his nation proud. And he sent his parents those thoughts on their 39th wedding anniversary. And I was told that they might be with us today. If they are, I don't want to embarrass you, but I'd like you to stand up. There they are. [*Applause*]

So, my appeal today is to let us reward the commitment of all of these best trained, highly motivated kids out there, all of those in uniform with the same resolve here at home. Here in Vermont you've got a chain of drug stores setting out greeting cards for people to walk up to write special messages to the troops; a country-western station taping broadcasts, sending them over. Burlington Electric adopted an entire company in the 82d Airborne. They're gathering gifts and personal items to send to let the soldiers know that Vermonters care. It's those actions—multiply them by a great country—large and small, celebrated or little noticed, that make possible American strength and stability around the world.

So, let me thank you and the thousands of Americans like you who are doing something extra to support our outstanding men and women in uniform. Let me just ask one more thing in honor of them, if you will. As democratic freedoms are dawning in once darkened corners around the world—and what an exciting time this has been to be President—the evolution of democracy in Eastern Europe and the evolution of democracy in our own hemisphere—but as these freedoms are dawning, let us keep the flame of democracy burning brightly here at home by reaffirming our own power of the vote. And get people to the polls this fall, because less than—I don't know how many weeks it is now—but a few days from now, Americans will choose their leadership for the next 2 years.

Here in Vermont, the choice is very, very clear, with leaders who can give this great State an even greater future. We've got a good statewide ticket. We have an outstanding candidate for Governor of Vermont, Dick Snelling. And of course, we have an outstanding Congressman in place who must be reelected, Peter Smith.

I'm delighted to be with you today. God bless Vermont, and God bless the United States of America.

Note: President Bush spoke at 9:14 a.m. in the Champlain Exhibition Hall at the Sheraton Burlington Hotel. In his remarks, he referred to Jack Lindley, former State manager for the Bush-Quayle campaign; Walter Freed, State Republican Party chairman; Madeline Harwood, Republican national committeewoman; Walter Page, Republican national committeeman; and President Saddam Hussein of Iraq. Following his remarks, President Bush attended a reception at the hotel for Republican Party supporters. He then traveled to Manchester, NH.

Remarks at a Republican Campaign Rally in Manchester, New Hampshire
October 23, 1990

Thank you, Mary Jo. With that enthusiasm, I'd say about 73 percent for Bob Smith, next Senator from the State of New Hampshire. And thank all of you for that greeting. A little trouble parking out here— we were trying to get the 18-wheeler parked on the side. [*Laughter*]

I am delighted to be back here. I came to salute this outstanding ticket—Judd Gregg, of course, having served this State so well. I feel confident that he will be reelected Governor of the State. He deserves it, and we need him. And Chuck Douglas isn't with us, but I want to pay my respects to him—looking solid and strong in that congressional district. Of course, Warren Rudman is not here, but I've seen a great deal of him lately. [*Laughter*] He is marvelous, and you're well-represented. And of course, Gordon Humphrey, also not with us, but having elected on his own to keep his pledge to not stay too long; and he's coming on back to the State. And I just want to pay my respects to him and say we have an outstanding congressional delegation from New Hampshire in Washington, DC.

And that brings me to the First District, where Bob, having left it to move—hopefully and, I'd say, confidently—to the Senate. I want to pay my respects to an old friend, a man that helped me early on. Steadfast—snow, rain, whatever it was, didn't deter him. And I am enthusiastically and strongly for Bill Zelliff for the United States Congress. He's an outstanding individual.

And I'm very sorry that Barbara's not here. If I might be permitted a word of husbandly pride, she is doing an outstanding job for education in this country, and I am very proud of what she's doing in helping as one of the brightest Thousand Points of Light in the United States. And I bring you her greetings.

We're having a little trouble with our best-selling author, Millie, our dog. [*Laughter*] Give her the Alpo, and she asks to see the wine list these days. [*Laughter*]

But in any event, we've spent a lot of time up here, as Mary Jo said, going way back to the '78–'79, during my first campaign. And 1978, I think, was a turning point in New Hampshire politics because that was the year that you sent a clear story to Washington, DC. The messenger was Gordon Humphrey; and the message, which still is a sound message, was limited government and trying to hold the line on the growth of Federal Government.

And 1978 really marked the first wave of what became known as the Reagan Revolution, a set of new ideas that are really as old as the Republic itself: that people, not government, know what's best for themselves and their families; that a strong—and I would reemphasize—a strong, diverse economy, not a strong, centralized government, is the true source of prosperity; that a firm defense does not threaten peace but promotes it. And the bottom line is this: We seek to protect family, empower the poor, and reward the creative and the risktakers. These are what I would say are the values of New Hampshire, the values of America, and certainly the values of our next Senator, my friend Bob Smith.

For 6 years, Bob has been New Hampshire's trusted friend in Congress. The people here know him, not just in this room but across this State. They know him as a man of principle, and he isn't running for office to satisfy his ego. And so, I'm convinced that New Hampshire is going to send a new Senator to Washington this year. And today, more than ever, the Senate needs leaders in the New Hampshire conservative tradition, leaders like Bob Smith.

Let me just say a word about the mess in Washington. Congress wouldn't, in my view—and I really mean this—would not be in the mess that it is in today if we had more Republicans in the United States Congress. The Democrats control both Houses, and that means if a President is going to make something happen—and I'm determined to do it—you've got to reach out.

And I want to get the best possible budget because I do not want to see us continue to mortgage the future of the young people in this country, year after year, with triple-digit deficits. And so, we are hanging tough for a good agreement. Right now it's in turmoil down there.

And I want to see it be an agreement that is serious about driving the deficit down. The fundamental reason is, real deficit reduction is going to bring the interest rates down. Make no mistake about it. And if we do nothing, they will not come down. It's that clear. So, more important to the economy than any program, some new program, or any single provision in a bill is the need to get the interest rates down and get America back to work again, get jobs for the American people. And the way to do that is to bring the interest rates down. And the way to do that is to get the Federal deficit down.

And now it is time—it's past time—that

Congress proves to the American people that it can learn to live within its means and that it can pass a budget that puts this nation on the path to long-term economic growth.

I went to the bargaining table, assisted by a very tough, a very principled negotiator, New Hampshire's John Sununu. But let's face it, no Democratic Congress is going to send me a Republican dream package. That's simply not the way it works when you're outnumbered in both Houses of Congress. So, to come up with any budget at all this year, I had to work with the Democrats who controlled Congress.

And President Reagan found the same thing—1982. Go back and look at the record. The rhetoric was about the same— that in spite of his aversion to taxes, the only way to govern was to accept a compromise. You know my feelings on taxes. I like taxes about as much as I like broccoli—and that ain't much. [*Laughter*] But Reagan swallowed hard, and the economy moved, and interest rates came down—from 15 percent to 11 percent—when he did what he had to do, not as a Congressman but as President of the United States. And the longtime health of the economy has to come before any political self-interest.

Only Congress has the power to tax, and only Congress has the power to spend. But Congress may have forgotten one thing: The people have the power to choose who sits in the United States Congress. And that's the message I'm going to take all over this country. We need more Republicans like Bob Smith and Bill Zelliff.

And if America wants economic growth and if America wants to hold the line on taxes and cut spending and if America wants to get serious about reducing the deficit, then we must send Republicans like Bob Smith to the United States Senate. We only lack a handful of votes. If we can get control of the Senate, you'd see an entirely different agenda for the American people.

Deficit reduction is not the only challenge that requires tough Republican leadership in Congress. Another priority for this new decade has to be the environment. Bob Smith really cares about protecting the environment and the marvelous scenic beauty of this State. And as the yellows and

reds and golds tinge the leaves of the White Mountains, I only wish I had time to drive across the highway and see the beauty. But I don't expect the tourists would like to see yet another Presidential motorcade driving across the State.

But nevertheless, as chairman of the House Republican task force on acid rain, Bob and I worked closely to put together the first improvement in the Clean Air Act in a dozen years. Launched last year with bipartisan support, the Clean Air Act has been bogged down until very, very recently on Capitol Hill. We can balance—and this point is essential—we can balance the need for economic growth with the need to preserve and enhance the Earth that we live on. We can clean up the air, and we can rid our lakes of acid rain. But we can't do it unless we get final action today or tomorrow from the Congress on the clean air bill that I sent up there months ago. It is time for them to act, and I think they will now do it.

I might say that Judd Gregg feels the same way that Bob and I do on this question of the environment and of New Hampshire's precious national heritage.

You know, one of New Hampshire's most famous nature-lovers, I'm proud to say, is also America's newest member of the Supreme Court. And I'm talking, of course, about Weare's own Justice—Mr. Justice to me—Mr. Justice David Souter. What a fantastic choice that he is for the Court. There's something marvelously understated about David. They said to him a while back—ask him, "How do you feel about leaving for Washington?" And he said, "Well, I don't know anyone that would want to leave New Hampshire." And that made a profound impression on a lot of us, I'll tell you.

Anyway, Congress could use some of that famous New Hampshire common sense. It's always a sacrifice, I know, leaving this State; but when Mr. Smith goes to Washington, the whole country is going to benefit from his brand of hard work, intelligence, common sense, and integrity. You've got to win this race, Mary Jo. I'm sure you will.

Bob served in the Naval Reserve, and today a whole new generation of this State's finest young men and women are continuing the New Hampshire tradition of patriotism and courage. From New Hampshire's own National Guard, the Air Guard, the men and women of the 157th Air Refueling Group have flown over 200 missions in support of Operation Desert Shield—airmen like Lieutenant Colonel Everett Bramhall, of Manchester, who flew 14 missions in 30 days, refueling other planes en route to the Persian Gulf; or Sgt. Mark Joyce, of Portsmouth, who, on top of his regular work as a civilian helicopter mechanic, has been volunteering for the evening shift with his Guard unit. This uncommon sacrifice by service men and women and their families has been a common virtue in New Hampshire and all across this magnificent country of ours.

So, putting our fiscal house in order is critical not just from the standpoint of the American economy but especially now, in the light of the big picture: this enormous challenge that we face in the Persian Gulf. The Gulf is a reminder of how intricately the interests of our nations are interwoven. What happens in Baghdad does matter in Manchester because our concern, far beyond the price of oil, is the fate of sovereign nations and peoples and a world order free from unlawful aggression, violence, and plunder. The rape and the dismantling of Kuwait that's going on right today defies description. The holding of hostages, the starving out of embassies—that cries out against the human decency that we ought to be experiencing. There can be no compromise—there can be none—with this type of brutal aggression where a bully can move in and take over an entire country.

The United Nations has lived up now, at last, to its promise. And we've got strong support in the United Nations with resolutions that people wouldn't even believe possible 2 or 3 years ago all because of the naked aggression of Saddam Hussein. So, the world is united. And I must tell you that I am more determined than ever to see that this invading dictator gets out of Kuwait with no compromise of any kind whatsoever.

There is a fundamental moral principle involved here, and of course, that principle is: One country won't take over another.

But there's also some moral principles involved in the manner in which this dictator is treating Kuwait. I'm not sure that Americans fully understand how deep the rape and the pillage and the plunder has been. Over in Vermont I gave them a few examples.

I am reading this great history of World War II. And I read the other night just about how Hitler, unchallenged—the U.S. locked in its isolation in those days, the late thirties—marched into Poland. Behind him—some of you will remember this—came the Death's Head regiments of the SS. Their role was to go in and dissemble the country. Just as it happened in the past, the other day in Kuwait, two young kids were passing out leaflets in opposition. They were taken, their families made to watch, and they were shot to death—15- and 16-year-old. Older people on dialysis machines taken off the machines, and the machines shipped to Baghdad. Kids in incubators thrown out so that the machinery, the incubators themselves, could be shipped to Baghdad.

And that's what we're dealing with. We're dealing with Hitler revisited, a totalitarianism and a brutality that is naked and unprecedented in modern times. And that must not stand. We cannot talk about compromise when you have that kind of behavior going on this very minute. Embassies being starved, people being shot, women being raped—it is brutal. And I will continue to remind the rest of the world that this must not stand.

Lastly, let me just say that all these months from the ships in the Red Sea, from air bases and these tank battalions in Saudi Arabia, these absentee ballots will be mailed back to our GI's home States from them. And if they can take the trouble to vote halfway around the world, can't every one of us, from Dover to Dixville Notch, get down to the firehouse or the schoolhouse to vote, taking people with you? It really does make a difference. We should never take this privilege, this right, for granted. I believe that you can make a difference, each and every single one of you, as we have these races unfold for just a couple of weeks from now.

Bob Smith is going to make a difference when he is elected, and Bill Zelliff the same—make a difference when he is elected. I want to say that I am very pleased to be back here with this message: to send us sound conservatives, help us get control of the United States Senate, and pick up seats in the House of Representatives. And then, I believe, we can fulfill our pledge to the people of New Hampshire to get this country moving again, put it back to work, bring the interest rates down, and get prosperity back to every working man and woman in the State of New Hampshire.

Thank you all, and God bless you for what you're doing. Thank you very much.

Note: President Bush spoke at 12:36 p.m. in the Armory at the Holiday Inn-The Center of New Hampshire. In his remarks, he referred to Representative Bob Smith's wife, Mary Jo; Representative Chuck Douglas; Senators Warren B. Rudman and Gordon J. Humphrey; John H. Sununu, Chief of Staff to the President; and President Saddam Hussein of Iraq. Following his remarks, President Bush attended a reception at the hotel for Republican Party supporters. He then traveled to Waterbury, CT.

Exchange With Reporters Following a Fundraising Reception for Congressional Candidate Gary Franks in Waterbury, Connecticut
October 23, 1990

Federal Budget Crisis

Q. Mr. President, Congress seems to be hung up on the budget again. Will you sign another continuing resolution, number what—38 or 39? [*Laughter*]

The President. Jim [Jim Miklaszewski, NBC News], I don't know. I'm so frustrated by Congress' inability to do anything, I don't know what I'm going to do. And I really don't know where it stands. I'm not dodging it. I was just on the phone, and I don't think Congress knows. So, when I get back, why, I'll be talking to our leadership. And this morning, I talked to the Speaker about 6:15 a.m., and I had been somewhat encouraged that they would be able to move. But I gather they had a raucous caucus on the Democratic side, where they couldn't agree on anything.

And so, we'll have to wait and see what happens before I can make a decision on what I'm going to do. But I feel the frustration that I think people all across this country feels about Congress' inability to move. They control both Houses of the Congress. And I am frustrated, but we'll wait and see.

Q. You've come down to 31 percent. Do you feel you've given enough?

The President. I'm not going to talk negotiations; my position is known. And I think

they've got to get their act together, is about the way I see it. And I feel free to campaign for a good man at the Governor's level, congressional level here; and our candidates—men and women all across this country—are, I think, going to do all right. I think they share the same frustration I feel about the Congress' inability to move. But it doesn't seem to be interfering with what real life is out here in these districts and across this State, I'll tell you from——

Civil Rights Legislation

Q. Mr. President, the civil rights bill—do you think there's a chance that Congress will pass the compromise version this session? And if so, why haven't you bothered to utter a word about it today to give it a push?

The President. Well, because I was hoping that the Congress would do what I asked them to do: pass a civil rights bill—because I am for civil rights—that is not a quota bill. I'm opposed to quotas. And I'm glad to have an opportunity to do it here, but I hope they'll get on and do it.

Mr. Franks. And I, too, would be opposed to the original version of the Civil Rights Act of 1990. I do see a quota element to that bill. Whenever a company can be deemed guilty of discrimination due largely to not having the proper number of minorities and females in certain job classifications, it smells like a quota. And I worked for 10 years in labor relations personnel, and I know that goals and timetables do work, but quotas do not work.

Q. Mr. President——

The President. I hope we'll get a bill tomorrow. But I don't see any inkling on their part to go ahead and to do this. We've sent one up that is a strong civil rights bill. Marlin [Marlin Fitzwater, Press Secretary to the President] read to you the other day all the similarities between these two bills and pointed out the significant difference.

Q. Mr. President, despite what the candidate says, his position is a minority among blacks and any other minorities. What kind of a signal do you think your veto sends to the minority groups that the Republicans and yourself are trying to draw into the party?

The President. I think it sends a signal that we are for civil rights and we are opposed to quotas. And I think most citizens, when they understand that, regardless of race, will be appreciative of that. But the problem is, I heard one of the leading civil rights activists—a white man in Washington—criticizing us on something that's not even in the bill. And I thought Marlin Fitzwater did pretty well on that.

And so—this customer relations provision—not in there. And yet he jumped us on that provision. So, I do what I think is right, and I believe I'll have strong support from the American people across the racial lines when they understand that I strongly am for civil rights. And I'm going to continue to oppose something that will inevitably lead to quotas.

Q. Is there any movement to pass that bill, though, in the next couple of days?

The President. I can't tell you. I think the first step would be to see if they can override my veto. Then I would hope that those who are really for civil rights would stand up and say, let's vote for this civil rights bill.

Q. What's your best count? Do you think your veto will hold?

The President. I don't know. I don't know the answer to that. I think we'll sustain it.

Q. Are you making any efforts on that

front today?

The President. I think we'll sustain—no, I feel pretty good about—you mean about sustaining the veto?

Q. Yes.

The President. I think we're in good shape on that.

Q. Have you called anyone?

The President. Not today. No, I feel the issue is clear enough that I think we'll be all right.

Palestinian Demonstrators Killed in Jerusalem

Q. Mr. President, are you prepared to call on Israel to accept a U.N. fact-finding mission?

The President. We've already made clear in the United Nations that we feel that it would be good to have that mission go there, yes.

Q. Is it a mistake, though, that they're refusing?

The President. I've said that we want them to accept it.

Israeli Travel Ban

Q. Mr. President, Israel today closed off the borders of the occupied territories and is prohibiting Palestinians from leaving the occupied territories into Israel. What do you think of that action?

The President. I need to know more about it. I haven't seen that, Tom [Tom Raum, Associated Press]. I don't like to comment on something until I know exactly what happened.

Persian Gulf Crisis

Q. Mr. President, your reaction to the Saudi comments yesterday—were they too conciliatory in your mind?

The President. They repudiated the first report that came—that Prince Abdullah [Prince Sultan bin 'Abd al-'Aziz Al Sa'ud, Defense Minister of Saudi Arabia] clarified his own statement. And he was not talking about any compromise, a territorial compromise at all. And that is my position. There is no give on it. If you reward the man with one iota of territory, you've rewarded aggression, and that is not the position of the United States nor of our coalition partners.

Federal Budget Crisis

Q. And just to be clear, last time Congress approached a deadline for the budget, you said time's up, and you threatened to shut down the Government. You sound much more conciliatory this time.

The President. If I sound conciliatory, I don't quite understand that, because I sound frustrated, not conciliatory. I don't know what's happening down there. I thought we'd have a deal this morning, a reasonable deal to get this nation on the road to more jobs and lower interest rates. And I've approached these talks in the spirit of compromise. But now is all kind of action in the Congress. It was in the House of Representatives, and I don't know what they've done today. So, I can't comment on a conciliatory mood or hostile mood——

Q. But are you willing to shut down the Government——

The President. ——or anything other than a confused mood.

Q. ——at midnight tomorrow?

The President. I'm going to wait until I get back and talk to the leaders and see exactly what can be done.

Mr. Franks. I'd like to make this presentation, the first of many for Franks for Congress effort.

The President. That's great.

Mr. Franks. And once again, thank you, Mr. President, for coming to Waterbury.

The President. Thank you. Am I being thrown out? [*Laughter*] Glad to see you all.

Thank you very much. Well, an elephant. Thank you.

Iraqi Release of American Hostages

Q. Any reaction to the release of the Americans, Mr. President?

The President. What?

Q. Any reaction to the release of the Americans today?

The President. Well, I'm always pleased when Americans might be released, or anybody is released. But it just reminds me of the total brutality of holding people against their will and then parceling them out as though to look generous. It is brutal. It is unacceptable. But any life that's spared, fine. But it just brings me back to the genesis, and the genesis is it is wrong to be holding people against their will in contravention of all international law.

Mr. Franks' Income Tax Records

Q. Mr. President, have you asked Mr. Gary Franks to release his income tax?

The President. Proponent ploy—yes, I've seen that. [*Laughter*]

Q. What did you think about it?

The President. Don't get me started. [*Laughter*]

Note: The exchange began at 5:10 p.m. at the Sheraton Waterbury Hotel. At the end of the exchange, Mr. Franks gave the President a black ceramic elephant. A tape was not available for verification of the content of these remarks.

Remarks at a Fundraising Dinner for Gubernatorial Candidate John Rowland in Stamford, Connecticut
October 23, 1990

Thank you all very, very much. John, thank you. Thank you very, very much, all of you, for that warm welcome back to the place in which I grew up. I've got a lot of home States, but—[*laughter*]—as I just said in Vermont, this place is near and dear to my heart. No, I'm really—[*laughter*]—no, but it was fun. We had a little reception earlier, and I saw many friends that have

been in the political scene here for a long time and have been very friendly to and supportive of my dad. So, we Bushes do consider this a very special place, both Barbara and me. I'm delighted to be here.

If I'm not mistaken, that magnificent music was from the Greenwich High School Band. I don't want to insult them if they weren't, but you do much better than Roseanne Barr, I'll tell you. [*Laughter*] I apologize for keeping you waiting, and I know that it's a bore, but we have been on the road a lot. One thing I've been picking up on the Connecticut part of this swing is this magnificent enthusiasm for our next Governor, John Rowland. You can feel it. You can feel it in the air. You can feel the campaign moving. I give him a lot of the credit, but those who have seen Deb swing into action—his great wife—know that she's a big part of this, a magnificent campaigner, out there all the time.

And of course, it's wonderful to be with my indefatigable friends Midge Baldrige and Betsy Heminway up here, who do so much for all of us in the Republican Party. Father Devine, my respects, sir, and thank you for being with us. To our State chairman, Dick Foley, who is tough as nails and strong. And that's who we need as a chairman, and he's doing a great job.

And of course, to our committee people, John Miller and Jo McKenzie, the Republican national committee man and woman, my respects. And then, of course, the only person that could go head-on-head with "60 Minutes" and emerge victorious—[*laughter*]—the mayor of Bridgeport, Mary Moran. I don't know how she did it. Barbara Bush was up here, and she saw Mary, and she chased her down the hall to shake the hand of somebody that had prevailed in that very difficult arena. [*Laughter*]

And, of course, I just want to single out Tom Scott, who is running for Congress in the Third District. I'll tell you, we need him. He's an outstanding guy. And another man I was with—fellow Yalie—I guess we can say that in Connecticut without being stoned. [*Laughter*] But nevertheless, I'm talking about Gary Franks, the man who's going to take John Rowland's place, is with us here someplace.

And I want to single out Bob Jaekle. You know, he is recognized on the merits as the number one legislator in the State, and he will now be our Lieutenant Governor, and I want to salute him right here. Good to be with you.

Now, back to the man of the hour. People who know John Rowland—they know he's got politics in his blood. John's granddad, Sherwood Rowland, comptroller for the city

of Waterbury back in the thirties, is still remembered in western Connecticut for fighting and battling and rooting out corruption. John followed in those footsteps early on, just out of college, winning a seat in the Connecticut State Legislature, where he worked his way up to minority whip; and then, at the tender age of 27, going on to become the youngest Member of the U.S. Congress.

And John tells me that he would have made it to Congress earlier, but his mother said he couldn't leave the table until he finished his broccoli. So, that took him 3 or 4 years. [*Laughter*] But he's still got that youthful vigor, and he's ready now to put that energy and that expertise that he's displayed right there on Capitol Hill back to work right here in this State that he loves so much.

You know where he stands. I know where he stands. We're in some tough times now, and I'm delighted that these changes towards democracy have taken place in Eastern Europe. And I'm very pleased that we're working the problems of the Middle East with the Soviet Union on our side in terms of opposition. Having said all that, it is essential that the United States remain strong. John is strong on our national security and defense; he's been a mainstay on the Armed Services Committee, making sure that our nation is strong enough to uphold our interest in our ideals. That commitment will now come back to work for the State on the State issues.

One of the issues that plagues this State and all the States is the question of crime. He's tough on crime. He's been a strong supporter of our comprehensive crime bill, a bill that's been stalled and sabotaged by the liberal Democrats in the Congress for the past 16 months. He and I agree that it's time to break that logjam, and we can't put criminals behind bars if we handcuff our law enforcement officers. He has been strong for that, and that commitment to back up the law enforcement officers and be a little tougher on the criminals and a little more compassionate about the victims of crime is the kind of philosophy that I believe we need in Hartford running this State.

I know the concern in this State and all States about the narcotics battle. I am very pleased that our national drug strategy, under our drug czar, Bill Bennett, is doing pretty well. We've got marvelous support in the private sector and all across this country. The statistical evidence is, we're beginning to win this battle. But John is now ready to bring his commitment to a statewide battle against illegal drugs. No more free ride for the so-called casual drug users. No more freedom for the drug dealers. And for the drug kingpins who sell poison for profit, he and I agree that the ultimate penalty—the death penalty—is essential if we are going to back up these people and get this under control.

I've seen him battle in Washington for lean and limited government. He's a champion, therefore, for every Connecticut taxpayer. And this is one candidate who doesn't think that the answer to every problem is a new mandated program from Washington, DC. With John in the statehouse, we won't need a State income tax to deliver the kind of government the citizens of this State want and deserve.

He is the kind of Governor I know I can work with to do what's right for this State and for our country. And that means—first and foremost—bolstering the economic strength of our nation. And I want to talk just a minute tonight about the issue that's been going back and forth that we've been wrestling with in Washington for more than 8 long months now: reaching some agreement on the Federal budget.

When it comes to the roles and responsibilities of government, John and I both know that the days of tax-and-spend and damn-the-deficit must end. I share your frustration about this. No American family could afford to run its household the way Congress—the Democrats that control Congress, I might say—run the Federal budget. Our children deserve to inherit more than an avalanche of unpaid bills, and I am trying to do something by getting a $500 billion, 5-year deficit reduction program that is enforceable. The Democrats are out there saying: "Tax the rich. We're going to soak the rich. And what that means—be careful. Every working man and woman in Connecticut, we're after what's in your

pocket." And we know it. We've seen it. They're done this over and over again, and we are not going to permit them to get further into the pockets of the taxpayers in this country under the guise of soaking the rich.

As the old Democratic legacy, it's failed in the past and it's going to fail in the future. The reason I am interested in getting this deficit down for the short run is, I am absolutely convinced—and some of you have heard Chairman Greenspan on this— that as soon as we get a real deficit reduction package, interest rates will come down. And that makes it easier for the American family to buy that new home or car. It makes it easier for American entrepreneurs—those that create the jobs—to build new businesses. It makes it easier for more jobs to be created. And I still believe that far better than a welfare program is a job with dignity in the private sector. And that's why I want to get this deficit down.

So, I believe that it is past time that Congress proves to the American people that it can learn to live within its means and that it can pass a budget that puts this nation on the path to long-term economic growth. And to come up with any budget at all this year, I had to work with the Democrats who control the Congress. You remember the dilemma President Reagan found in 1982: in spite to his aversion to taxes, the only way to govern, to make something happen—it's different when you're President than if you're one Member in the Congress—the only way to govern was to accept a compromise that included raising the revenues.

You know my feeling on taxes. I like taxes just about as much as I like broccoli. [*Laughter*] And President Reagan had to swallow hard, and so did I. But the long-term health of our economy has to come before self-interest. Only the Congress has the power to tax, and only the Congress has the power to spend. Congress may have forgotten one thing. The people have the power to choose who sits in the Congress. That's a message that I will take all over this country. I believe the people are fed up with this philosophy of tax and spend, and I think they're going to see a change on that

Democratic side of the aisle. The bottom line is that if we want economic growth and if we want to hold the line on taxes and spending and if we want to get serious about reducing the deficit, then America needs to elect more Republicans to Congress. And I mentioned two here tonight that I'm dying to see elected down there, because I know exactly how they'd behave on these issues of protecting the taxpayers' money.

Putting our fiscal house in order is critical, not just from the standpoint of the American economy but I think especially now in light of the challenges in the big picture, the challenges that we face in the Persian Gulf.

You know, we all know the grave economic consequences of Iraq's outlaw act of aggression. But as serious as these consequences may be, what is at stake is not a matter of economics or oil. What is at stake is whether aggression pays or whether aggression is punished, whether we live in a world governed by the rule of law or in a world which is the law of the jungle.

Make no mistake: America will not waver. The world will not allow Saddam Hussein's act of aggression to stand. There can be no compromise on the territorial integrity of a neighboring nation.

When this ordeal is over, and when Kuwait is once again a sovereign and free member of the family of nations, Saddam Hussein must pay for the pain and the hardship that he has caused. The world will hold him accountable, just as it held Adolph Hitler accountable in the wake of the destruction of World War II.

So, our staying power, and ultimately our success, is a matter of the strength of the forces that we send to Saudi Arabia. But it's also a measure of our support back here at home. That support is strong and deep—across the country, right here in Connecticut, where Darien's VFW Post 6933 became one of the first in the Nation to adopt an Army unit now stationed in Saudi Arabia. It's spearheaded by veterans of Vietnam and Korea, like Robert Hornlein and James Sparrow, who remember what it's like to serve overseas and how much it means to get a package from home. Whether it's extra pens and paper, or high-demand items like sunglasses and flyswatters, every package is a reminder to every member of our armed services that America cares.

And with the young men and women of our Armed Forces in our minds, I want to add one more thing. Right now, in the sands of Saudi Arabia half a world away, those brave young men and women are teaching all of us a lesson about what it means to love liberty, the precious freedom that gives America its meaning. I expect everybody here has a contact one way or another—maybe a son, maybe a daughter, maybe a nephew, maybe a friend—who is in some way or other touched by this mobilization and deployment. But let me tell you what the Joint Chiefs of Staff tell me—every single one of them. Never, in their view, never in this history of this country have we had more motivated, more better trained, or more fine troops, men and women, than we have today—never in our history. Every one of them a volunteer. Every one serving and knowing why he or she is serving. They're motivated, and they are well-trained, and they believe.

So as November 6th draws near, I want to just urge every citizen in Connecticut to do what a lot of those kids are doing, filling out the absentee ballots and getting in—but they're voting. I want to urge every citizen of Connecticut: Get out and vote; do not take democracy for granted.

We've got a lot at stake in these elections. We have an outstanding candidate for Governor, outstanding candidate for Lieutenant Governor sitting up here. The State is at the crossroads. But here, we have a high-energy, well-trained—great experience—candidate for Governor in John Rowland. And my thanks again for this warm welcome. As John knows, in the 1990's a lot of ideas that shape government and a lot of action—if you believe in federalism as we do—won't originate in Washington. They're going to be generated right here at the grassroots and at the State and local level.

That's why it is critical to have the strongest possible link between the White House and the statehouse, and that's why I was so very proud to accept John's invitation to come here in the homestretch to support him. And so, please—I know you've been hit pretty hard for this one. [*Laughter*] But I would simply urge that now let's get into that mode of getting out the vote. Talk to your neighbors. Talk to your friends. Go out and ask them to support the next Governor of the State of Connecticut: John Rowland. Thank you all, and good night, and God bless each and every one of you.

Note: President Bush spoke at 6:40 p.m. in the International Ballroom of the Tara Stamford Hotel. In his remarks, he referred

to Midge Baldrige, widow of former Secretary of Commerce Malcolm Baldrige; Betsy Heminway, a friend of the Bushes; Father Joseph A. Devine, who gave the invocation; comedienne Roseanne Barr, who sang the national anthem at a San Diego Padres baseball game; William J. Bennett, Director of National Drug Control Policy; Alan Greenspan, Chairman of the Board of Directors of the Federal Reserve System; and President Saddam Hussein of Iraq. Following the event, President Bush returned to Washington, DC.

Remarks on Presenting the Congressional Gold Medal to Andrew Wyeth
October 24, 1990

The President. Welcome, welcome.

Mr. Wyeth. What a day!

The President. We're so proud to have you here. Please be seated. Well, apologies for keeping you standing and waiting. But first, just a warm White House welcome to Andrew Wyeth, I'd say; to John Frohnmayer; and of course, to our distinguished Members of the Congress, Senators Heinz and Specter and, of course, Dick Schulze, who did so much to make this day possible. Welcome to all of you members of the family. We are very pleased, sir, to welcome you to the White House, and we're pleased to be honoring this man who has so honored his country with his art.

As the legislative citation reads: We act today in recognition of Andrew Wyeth's outstanding and invaluable contributions to American art and culture. His detail-loving paintings of his native Pennsylvania and of Maine magnificently evoke homes and landscapes and friends, somehow familiar and dear to us all.

He is, of course, one of America's foremost artists. He is known for his mastery of difficult technique and, especially, for the realism of his work. And I, too, have been trying locally—though not yet with Mr. Wyeth's success—to encourage a certain realism among the congressional budget artists. [*Laughter*] And I wish I had Dick

Schulze's mastery, where he could get something passed unanimously—[*laughter*]—in the House of Representatives like he did this tribute to Mr. Wyeth.

But you, sir, are no stranger to this place. In 1963 President Kennedy chose to award Mr. Wyeth the Presidential Medal of Freedom—the first artist to be so honored. Saying that this man had caught the heart of America in 1970, President Nixon sponsored an unprecedented exhibition of Andrew Wyeth's paintings at the White House.

Today it is evident that Andrew Wyeth has caught the heart not only of America; internationally he has, for example, been honored by the French Academy of Fine Arts and the Soviet Academy of the Arts. His works have been exhibited and admired from England to Japan.

I am delighted to present yet another first: the first Congressional Gold Medal awarded to an artist. The Treasury Department's medal itself is quite simple and beautiful. It features a profile of Andrew Wyeth from a portrait by his son Jamie. Jamie, like Andrew, has learned much from a talented father.

So, sir, your family, your friends, your admirers everywhere join Barbara and me in extending sincere best wishes and congratulations as you receive the Andrew Wyeth

Congressional Gold Medal. Congratulations, and we're so proud to have you.

Note: The President spoke at 11:11 a.m. in the Roosevelt Room at the White House. In *his opening remarks, he referred to John Frohnmayer, Chairman of the National Endowment for the Arts, and Representative Richard T. Schulze.*

Remarks Announcing the Resignation of Secretary of Labor Elizabeth Dole
October 24, 1990

The President. Let me say at the outset here that I have an announcement to make. I will not take questions, but I will have this statement and then ask Secretary Dole to say a few words. And then keep the focus on this subject. She will be glad to respond to questions.

This morning, Secretary Elizabeth Dole offered me her resignation. And it is with real, deep regret that I accept this resignation. But let me hasten to say I understand her desire to continue her public service as president of the American Red Cross.

After a quarter-century of service to this country, Elizabeth Dole has earned the respect of the American people. And as Secretary of Labor, she's made the workplace safer, healthier, and more secure. She's reached out to Americans on the job, youth at risk, workers in retirement.

Secretary Dole, you really have changed the way America looks at education and training, retraining in the workplace. And you've built better labor-management relations; you've kept collective bargaining a vital American institution. And no one has been a stronger voice for job opportunity for young people.

I couldn't help but notice this morning some very supportive comments about Secretary Dole by the Nation's number one labor leader, Lane Kirkland. They were supportive, and they almost said it all. And I was very pleased because, for me, that was just one more important testimony to the job that she has done as Secretary of Labor.

So, Barbara joins me in wishing you nothing but the best in this big, new challenge at the Red Cross. Bob, the Senator, tells me your first project is disaster relief. Capitol Hill maybe or—[*laughter*]. But anyway, good luck, and thank you so very much. It's been a joy serving with you in the Cabinet, and I look forward to staying in very close touch. You have done a superb job for this country.

Secretary Dole. Thank you, Mr. President. Thank you so very much.

Reporter. Are you going to have a budget tonight, Mr. President? Budget?

Q. Will there be business as usual?

Secretary Dole. Ladies and gentlemen, I have some comments to make. First of all, Mr. President, I want to thank you so very much for the opportunity you've given me to serve as your Secretary of Labor. I'll always be extremely proud of the fact that I had an opportunity to serve the American people under your strong leadership, and I appreciate the faith that you have shown in me. I'm grateful for that faith and confidence.

And you know, as I leave the Department of Labor, I take with me a strong inspiration which has been fired in me in that particular post; and that's the fact that the American working men and women are the greatest engines of productivity that this world has ever known. And if we're going to continue to be competitive in a complex global market, then we must realize that our most precious resources are our human resources.

And you know, Mr. President, I remember so well when you and I first talked about the Labor Department position. It was just about 2 years ago. It was before Christmas. And we were talking about the kinder, gentler Nation that you want to bring about. And I mentioned that I felt a calling to join with those who wanted to increase charitable giving in this country. And you said, "Elizabeth, the Labor Department offers many opportunities to make a difference, a positive difference, for people." And how right you were.

The Labor Department is the people's department. And what we've tried to do there is use the power of the Labor Department to empower people with the skills they need, the safety on the job, and with security of their pensions in their retirement years.

And I consider it just a great honor to have had this opportunity to work on issues that mean so much to me in making a difference in people's lives. But this does make my 25th year in government service, and I plan to continue my public service now from a different organization.

As president of the American Red Cross, I'll have the opportunity to work with about 1,200,000 volunteers all across America, 250 million volunteers around the world, Mr. President. And the sole purpose of these individuals and the 23,000 staff members—

the sole mission is to make that positive difference for people, to meet dire human needs and to improve the quality of human life.

Now, it's occurred to me that since the Congress has chartered the Red Cross and you're the honorary chairman and it's located just across the street here—I wonder if we couldn't just regard this as a transfer, Mr. President. What do you think about that? Do you think that would work?

The President. It's fine with me. Fine with me.

Secretary Dole. But in any case, you will still be the boss, and a wonderful boss, a strong boss. And I look forward to continuing to work with you. And again, I thank you for your support. I thank you for your trust in me and for your friendship.

The President. Well done.

Note: The President spoke at 11:37 a.m. in the Briefing Room at the White House. In his remarks, he referred to Lane Kirkland, president of the American Federation of Labor-Congress of Industrial Organizations, and Senator Robert Dole, the Secretary's husband.

Statement by Press Secretary Fitzwater on the Federal Budget Crisis
October 24, 1990

We continue to have discussions with House and Senate conferees concerning an agreement on the budget. Although there are several areas of disagreement that remain to be worked out, sufficient progress has been made for the President to sign the continuing resolution expected to be passed by Congress tonight. This 3-day continuing resolution includes budget savings that approximate those envisioned in the first year of the bipartisan budget agreement.

We expect the President to sign this continuing resolution tomorrow morning. All

Federal employees should report to work as scheduled. The Government will continue to function without interruption.

Tomorrow's travel to New Mexico and Arizona by the President has been canceled. On Thursday the President will continue to monitor the budget situation through his negotiators, who will be working out details of a budget agreement.

Note: H.J. Res. 681, approved October 25, was assigned Public Law No. 101–461.

Exchange With Reporters on the Federal Budget Crisis
October 25, 1990

The President. Last picture.

Q. Got a budget?

Q. One big, happy family?

The President. Exactly. They got the message.

Q. How did you convert Mr. Gingrich, Mr. President?

Q. Are you all voting for the package?

The President. Some will, and some won't. But the point is we're unified and trying to win these elections, and that's what this is about. And we're going to do all right. And speaking for myself, I want to see this budget matter behind us. The leaders are going to meet outside with some of you all, and they can answer your individual questions. But I think all of us are totally united in our determination to take a sound, strong Republican message across this country. And if you got the symbolism, so be it.

Q. Is Rollins fired?

Q. What is the message, Mr. President?

Q. How about Rollins?

The President. Stay tuned. You'll start hearing that tomorrow morning, as you've been hearing it.

Q. What about a capital gains cut next year?

The President. Look, we're going to cross a lot of bridges next year, I'll guarantee you. I haven't given up my interest in incentives to get this economy moving, but we will see. We're working now to try to finish up the deal. And I will defer to the leaders; they'll speak to you about that out on the steps. But there are different views as to how quickly this will be done. But that's just one matter. It's a very important one. But we've got a lot of other problems, and we're coming together now to take our case for sound fiscal policy.

We have to keep the taxes down, get the spending down, and get this message out across the country. We've been bludgeoned by a bunch of demagogic attacks from the Democrats for months. And I've been relatively sanguine in the face of that because we've been trying to get something done; but as soon as we get this finished with, why, I will then be free—as will everybody here who's been working on this—to have our say.

Q. Are you going to bludgeon them now?

The President. Stay tuned, John [John Cochran, NBC News].

Q. What did you win, Mr. President?

Q. What did you get out of it?

Q. What do you think you won?

The President. Wait until we see what happens. Wait until you see the result.

Q. But what's all this unity based on?

The President. The fact that we're Republicans and that we all share the same values. We're the party that's trying to keep the taxes down. When they talk about taxing the rich, they're talking about taxing the working men and women of this country. We all agree on that, no matter how you feel on the budget deficit. We talk about the spending side—we believe, and always have, people aren't taxed too little, the Government's spending too much. These broad themes are still strong, and they're still valid.

We happen to believe that we don't need a lot of mandated government programs from Washington, DC. Further, if you look at the way the Congress seems to be operating and the other party seems to think: Well, let's tell the States exactly how they ought to do it, whether it's child care or whatever the issue is. And education— we've made some great progress here because of this Republican unity. And so, the message is strong, but it's been masked by the "inside the beltway" attention to a very important issue of one where the Democrats seemed to have carried the play with some of you all.

Q. Well, why did you go along?

The President. So, we're going to try to change all that. We're going to try to change it.

Q. "Outside the beltway"——

Q. ——the Albuquerque speech or the Phoenix speech?

The President. I feel if we had more Republicans, like everyone of them standing here, we wouldn't be in this fiscal mess.

That's what I feel.

Q. What about Ed Rollins?

Q. Have you made a deal?

Q. Do you want Ed Rollins fired because of that memo that he wrote? [*Laughter*]

Q. ——raising taxes. Can you get away with that?

The President. You got out of there just in time, gang.

Note: The exchange began at 1:58 p.m. in the Rose Garden at the White House. Newt Gingrich is a Member of the House of Representatives. Edward J. Rollins, cochairman of the National Republican Congressional Committee, had sent a memo to Republican candidates advising them not to hesitate "to oppose either the President or proposals being advanced in Congress."

Remarks to a Fundraising Luncheon for New Mexico Gubernatorial Candidate Frank Bond
October 25, 1990

Well, Frank, thank you very, very much; and thank all of you for that warm response. As you know, and as Frank so generously said, there is business here keeping me in Washington; it relates to the Federal budget and my determination to get this deficit down so we will no longer continue to mortgage the future of our kids. And I can assure you that no one willingly ever misses a chance to visit New Mexico. Having spent 12 years of my life right next to Eunice and Hobbs, I feel I know the State well. But I wanted to say that it's a pleasure to have this opportunity to speak by this satellite—here I am, I'm not quite sure whether I'm on the telephone or on the television. [*Laughter*]

But, nevertheless, I'm delighted to be talking to you. And, Frank, once again, a thousand apologies for not being with you today. But we've got some very able proponents: Jack Kemp, an outstanding Secretary of Housing. What a job he's done taking the message of hope and opportunity to all America.

And of course, the same is true of my old, dear friend, with whom I served in Congress, Manuel Lujan. Manuel knows the West. He knows how New Mexico has this terribly important part of the West. He's advancing our fight against drug use on public lands. And he's doing an outstanding job for his country, and I'm proud to have him in our Cabinet.

And that brings me to one of my earliest advisers in my quest for the Presidency in

'88, Garrey Carruthers, your able Governor. Came to Maine and sat down with me and told me exactly the line and the approach we should take to help solve the problems of education and crime. And he gave me the same sound advice that he's given the people of New Mexico over the years, putting the State on the path to progress and prosperity. And Garrey, I'll always be grateful to you. Thank you for your wonderful service to that State and, indeed, to your country.

And now for the man of the hour, Frank Bond. Twelve short days from now, New Mexico is going to come to a crossroads. And New Mexico doesn't have to retrace its steps. You can reach forward; you can keep on the forward path that Garrey has set out. You can reach forward to the future, and you can make New Mexico of the 1990's a land of progress and possibility for all. You know, there's no doubt in my mind about the man who can lead the way. New Mexico will move forward with Frank Bond.

Let's just take a quick look, because I've been reviewing Frank's record and following with keen interest—education to start with. He knows that the key to competitiveness tomorrow is in our classrooms today. He's sure of that. And he favors choice, and he favors the same approach as we do. And I want to see fewer mandated educational programs from Washington and more control in the hands of Governors like Frank

Bond will be.

On the environment—I'm hoping, incidentally, to have on my desk very soon a clean air bill that's a good one. And I look forward to signing it. But I can take a lesson from Frank. He's a fourth generation New Mexican. The love of the land comes just as natural to him as breathing. And again, you can count on him to help New Mexico pursue wise wildlife and water and land use policies, to help preserve New Mexico's national treasures for generations to come. He's a sound environmentalist. He knows that growth and a sound environmental policy can come together to benefit all people of New Mexico.

And then on the economy—it is the key issue this year, I think, for New Mexico and, I believe, for all America. And Frank knows what works, how to generate new opportunities and new incentives for investment in new markets. And all that adds up to one thing—incentives, opportunities, investment, new markets—it all adds up to new jobs for New Mexico.

We've got to do our part to promote economic growth right here in Washington. And that starts with the budget and an end to this long and frustrating fiscal fiasco. And I can tell you right now, Congress wouldn't be in this mess if we had more Republicans in the Congress, and electing Republicans is what this November 6th is all about.

And nothing's changed. The question is: Do we want to continue the Democratic policies of tax and spend, or do we want a Congress that knows that cutting spending and a strong economy is the way to go? It is critical that we get a budget in place, put our house in order here at home, especially now with the challenge that we face in the Persian Gulf.

You know, let me just say a word about this, and I put this in a very much of bipartisan spirit because—as Jack Kemp can tell you, as Manuel Lujan can tell you—we have had strong bipartisan support, crossing the party aisle all the time, for our policy in the Gulf. We all know that Saddam Hussein's outlaw act threatens grave consequences. What is at stake is far more than a matter of economics or oil. What is at stake is the principle at the very heart of international order and whether aggression pays or whether aggression is punished. Our position is that a bully of a neighbor must not be permitted to take over a smaller country—a member of the United Nations, a member of the Arab League—and I am determined that that aggression will not stand.

You know, I've talked to all the Joint Chiefs, and every single one of them has told me that we have never had finer young men and women—more highly motivated, better trained—than we have right now serving in Armed Forces both at home and abroad. And so, I would say that the brave young men and women are teaching us a lesson, in some ways, about what it means to love liberty, the precious freedom that gives America its meaning. They are filling out their absentee ballots and sending them in from the sands of Saudi Arabia to the 50 States inside the United States.

And thus, I would urge not all of you there alone but everybody in the State of New Mexico, every citizen, to get out and vote. And simply put it this way: Do not take democracy for granted. You know, this November 6th is critical, and I need you to send New Mexico's strong Republican team back here to Washington.

[Senator] Pete Domenici—what a fantastic job he's doing for the country as well as the State of New Mexico. And both Joe Skeen and Steve Schiff are superb Members of the United States Congress. You've got to send them back here. And then, again, to the man of the hour. New Mexico really needs a leader for the nineties that it can count on. You've been spoiled, in my view, with Garrey Carruthers there at the helm. He's proven over and over again what strong leadership can do. But now we're in a new decade, we're moving into the nineties, and it is absolutely essential that New Mexico's next governor be Frank Bond.

Once again, my thanks to Jack Kemp and to Manuel Lujan and to the Governor. And my respects, Frank, to you. My apologies for missing what I know is an exciting event. Give my precious Columba a big hug when she comes there to campaign for you on behalf of our entire family. And now back to you. And to all of you, my most sincere thanks.

Note: President Bush spoke at 2:17 p.m. in Room 450 of the Old Executive Office Building, and his remarks were broadcast via satellite to the Pavilion of the Hyatt Regency Hotel in Albuquerque, NM. In his remarks, he referred to President Saddam Hussein of Iraq; Senator Pete V. Domenici; and Columba Bush, his daughter-in-law.

Remarks at a Fundraising Breakfast for Gubernatorial Candidate Pete Wilson in Irvine, California
October 26, 1990

Don, thank you so very much for that very, very generous introduction. If I began to try to express my gratitude to Don for all he's done for me, it would be impossible. So, I just want to say thank you—thank you for what you and George have done for this wonderful event in support of Pete Wilson, for all that you both do in support of this party. And I am very, very pleased to be here.

I'm delighted to see our able State chairman down here. He's done a remarkable job pulling this party together, getting it unified so we will win these statewide elections in about 11 days from now. Frank Visco, thank you, sir, for your great leadership for the party. I know out here somewhere is Tom Fuentes, the Orange County chairman. Where is—[*applause*]. If Tom ever needs a campaign chairman for national office, all he has to do is call the White House and ask for Barbara Bush. That's his biggest admirer, and she feels about him just the same way I do. What a job he's done.

And I also want to congratulate in advance, hopefully, the rest of this ticket here: your own Marion Bergeson, who's—I love what Pete Wilson said about her—is yours, who's now going on to be the State's Lieutenant Governor; Matt Fong for comptroller down here; and of course, Thomas Hayes, who we know will remain as State treasurer.

So, I think we've got an outstanding team. And I also want to put in a plug for one who was just here, had to go on to that campaign trail—and I'm talking about the next Congressman from one of these districts right here, Bob Hammock. He's in a tough race, but I believe he's going to make

it. And boy, do we need him in that seat.

Well, I'm delighted to be here. And it was very generous of Pete to get on that telephone and give me those warm words of welcome. He is doing exactly what he should do as this Congress wraps up. I wish they'd been out of business long before now, frankly. But he's got to be there to protect the interests of the people of California, and I believe he'll do just that.

But I'm here this morning because the stakes are high. And we all know that out on the trail right now there's a strong, vibrant woman involved in this race. People say she's a winner, the one woman who's finally a match for Pete. But Gayle is much too modest to admit that. [*Laughter*] What a job Gayle Wilson is doing for her husband across this State. It is unbelievable. And Barbara and I salute you, and we admire you, and we are just grateful that you are with us here today.

You know, it's good to be back. And I start by saying thank you. Thank you to all those in Orange County—and I thought Don put it pretty well—all of you for giving me and, I'd say, Barbara, too, the opportunity to serve the greatest country on the face of the Earth as President. And I must say, last night when I arrived at El Toro and landed at the Marine base and saw the dedication of those families, many of them with their husbands halfway around the world—those marines out there—I must say it really moved me as I went down and shook hands with each and every one of them. And transcending the partisan politics that bring us this morning, I just want you to know this: we are not going to fail in our mission halfway around the world.

Some think that the differences between

the parties are blurred. And to that I say, nonsense. Republicans believe that power should be in the hands of people, not in the Government in Washington, DC. Republicans want to reform Washington so we can expand the opportunity for all Americans instead of expanding the budget year in after year out. In education, Republicans want reform to empower parents to choose their children's schools. In child care, we're the ones that want reform to empower parents to choose who will watch over their children. In the most desolate inner city, we want reform, so we strive to create enterprise zones, zones of opportunity, to remove barriers to mobility and remove barriers to success, to empower people with the spirit of enterprise.

In short, we do want to build a better America. That is why I need more Republicans in the United States Congress. And that's why I want to see Pete Wilson as Governor of this great State, so that we are going to have a fair shake in redistricting in a couple of years from now. We've been gerrymandered out of it, and the time has come for fairplay.

In addition, Pete's been there in Washington; he's seen it. He's seen what 40 years of Democratic control of the Congress have given us: bigger and bigger government with more and more spending. And remember, it is Congress that appropriates every dime and tells us how to spend every dime. And the American people know this in overwhelming numbers: that it is the United States Congress that must be changed if this country is going to move ahead.

I met yesterday with the Republican leadership in the House and Senate, and one thing is clear: We are united in the opposition to the tax-and-spend policies of the Democrats. Now, after 8 long months of negotiations, we may be on the verge of a budget agreement. This morning, in a major newspaper, I was challenged by one of the House Democratic leaders who now puts the budget negotiations into the context of the Presidential politics of 1992.

Well, let me tell you something. Let me say, first off, that the number of Democratic leaders—and I'm talking about the leadership in the House and the Senate—have

been working cooperatively. And I think they have been working very hard to get a budget agreement. For that I salute them, because I firmly believe that we must get an agreement to start getting these deficits under control—with real enforcement, 500 billion dollars' worth of cuts over 5 years that cannot be changed by the next Congress or the next one after that.

But in criticizing me today and in justifying the higher taxes that their party has long been proposed, one was quoted in the paper as follows: "The President needs to explain to the American people why they are being asked to swallow strong medicine"—that's what Democrats call taxes— "but he didn't do it." He says, "The President didn't do this." Well, let me try once more.

For 36 years, his party, the Democratic Party, have controlled the House of Representatives. And year after year after year, they have presided over these budget deficits. They appropriate every dime, and they tell me how to spend every dime. And yes, we need a deficit agreement. And yes, I have had to compromise. Haven't liked that a bit, but I've done it because the President must, at certain times, put the overall good of the country first. You have to give a little from time to time.

But the American people know all too well that strong medicine—I refer back to that quote—is required because the Democratically controlled Congress simply has been on an uncontrolled spending binge for years. You don't have to be a rocket scientist to know that Congress has been spending more than we take in for far too long. And that's got to stop.

For the sake of the Nation, we have to reduce the deficit now. I was determined to do it by a careful balance of spending cuts. Predictably, the Democrats wanted to slash defense and raise income taxes for all Americans. Take a look at that House-passed bill. Don't let them tell you that was a tax package to hit the rich. That was going after the working men and women in this country, through the deferring of index. And everybody out there is smart enough to see it.

The agreement that we get won't be the

best deal possible, but in my judgment, it will be the best deal possible with this Congress. And the best way for America to stand against more spending and more taxes is to elect more Republicans to the House and to the Senate of the United States.

The budget, regrettably, isn't the only thing we've waited for. We've waited for action on the environment. We all want a safe and healthy world, preserved and protected for our kids. In fact, when I think of Gayle's husband, Pete, he wrote the first Coastal Protection Act. He's been fighting for clean air for years, long before it became the cause. His brand of environmental activism is what California really needs because he proves that a leader can be green without being "Big Green."

I hope you know this, but clean air at the Federal level has been one of my administration's top priorities as well. It's been 13 years since the Clean Air Act has been successfully amended and improved. And so, on July 21st, 1989, we sent to the Congress new comprehensive clean air legislation to cut acid rain, urban smog, and air toxics. Not 5, not 10, but over 100 amendments were added; and it took Congress 6 weeks to appoint the members of the conference committee. And then 150 congressional negotiators squabbled for 15 weeks. Now, 462 days after we sent that legislation, it looks like a bill finally—thank heavens—might arrive on my desk. You see, I believe the American people do deserve clean air. And I believe Californians deserve clean air. And what they don't deserve is a Congress that is hamstrung by special interests wrangling over our nation's priorities.

Here's another thing that can't wait—and again, I admire Pete Wilson for being out front, both in California and in Washington, on these questions. Another thing that can't wait: safe streets and schools. Here in California, Pete Wilson has worked for harsher penalties for those convicted of rape and assault. Back in Washington, he supported the tough crime bill that we sent to Capitol Hill nearly 16 months ago. And when liberal Democrats tried to gut the death penalty, it was Republicans who stopped them. Republicans demanded a real, workable death penalty for those who kill Federal law en-

forcement officers. That's my position; that's Pete's position; that is the position of the people of California.

Well, that crime legislation is still in a conference committee. If Congress sends me a weak bill here in the final hours, I'm going to veto it. And if Congress sends me a strong bill, it's because of Republicans like Pete Wilson, who insist that these people that murder our police officers get the kind of punishment they deserve. Innocent Americans are waiting for a criminal justice system that is tougher on criminals than it is on law enforcement and one that cares a little bit more about the victims of crime and a little less about the criminals themselves. And if you do that, take the message across this State—heavily laden, heavily rich in congressional seats—that the best way to get that done is by voting for a new Congress, a Republican Congress, on November 6th.

You know, congressional Democrats are upset because they know that the Republicans are on the right side of the issues. We just need more Republicans on the right side of the aisle. The voters are fed up. They know where the blame lies. And that's why Californians are supporting Proposition 140, the one Pete endorsed. For those who may have straggled in from inside the Washington beltway, let me say that that's the one that limits the terms of permanent politicians and puts the power back into the hands of the people. The 1988 Republican platform supports limitation on terms for Members of Congress. In 1988—I'm not just jumping on the bandwagon—that was in our platform. And that is one way to correct the abuse of power and the unbridled influence of an entrenched Congressional staff. And I say, it's an idea whose time has come.

There's another point—Pete's been in the forefront on this one: our party has always stood for strength at home and strength abroad. And today it's no different. But partisanship, as Senator Vandenberg said, stops at the water's edge. We got away from that a little bit in the Vietnam days—subsequently related to South America. But I respect that. I like that concept that when it comes to foreign affairs, the partisanship should, indeed, stop at the water's edge.

And so, I think in a spirit of fairplay—given what we're facing halfway around the world—I ought to say, and I say it proudly, that I am very grateful for the bipartisan support for our stand against aggression in the Persian Gulf.

Our ability to build a worldwide consensus condemning Iraq and its brutality proves that there is no substitute for American leadership in the community of nations. We and the world are determined that Saddam Hussein's aggression and his brutality will not stand.

Here at home, we can, indeed, fulfill our party's mission of creating opportunity and empowering people, set forth so long ago— the mission begun by Abraham Lincoln and Teddy Roosevelt and continued by our last President, a great son of California, Ronald Reagan. The time has come to fulfill that mission now. But to do it, we need more Republicans in Washington and, indeed, in Sacramento.

So, my appeal to you is—you in this county who hold so much of the fate of all these statewide candidates in your hand— let's get out our vote on November 6th. And let's make Pete Wilson the next great Republican Governor of the State of California. Go to work. Get out there now with 11 days to go and elect this man Governor.

Thank you very, very much.

Note: President Bush spoke at 9 a.m. in the International Ballroom of the Hyatt Hotel. In his remarks, he referred to longtime friend Don Bren; Gov. George Deukmejian of California; and President Saddam Hussein of Iraq. President Bush also referred to "Big Green," the environmental protection initiative on the November ballot in California.

Message to the Congress Transmitting the Annual Report on Agricultural Trade Goals
October 26, 1990

To the Congress of the United States:

In accordance with section 4201 of the Omnibus Trade and Competitiveness Act of 1988 (Public Law 100–418; 7 U.S.C. 5211), I herewith transmit the second annual U.S. Long-Term Agricultural Trade Goals and Strategy Report for Fiscal Year 1991. This report provides recommended policy goals for U.S. agricultural trade and exports, and recommended levels of spending on international activities of the Department of Agriculture, for 1-, 5-, and 10-fiscal year periods.

GEORGE BUSH

The White House,
October 26, 1990.

Remarks at a Campaign Rally for Gubernatorial Candidate Pete Wilson in Los Angeles, California
October 26, 1990

Let me say to our next Governor, thank you very much for that warm introduction and those generous comments. I might say, Gayle, Pete can't be here, but I'm delighted to be at your side. Gayle Wilson continues to amaze. She finds all the time in the world to be compassionate and work with these drug babies, engaged in the battle against narcotics; and yet she's Pete's secret weapon out on the campaign trail every single day. He's lucky, and it's going to make a tremendous difference.

I, too, want to pay my respects to my old friend George Deukmejian, to Gloria, too.

I'll tell you, the State has been well served by his decency, his honor, his sense of commitment. George, thank you for what you've done for this State and for the country. I, too, want to thank our State chairman, Frank Visco, and our statewide slate. Marion Bergeson is here with us, the candidate for Lieutenant Governor; Thomas Hayes for treasurer; and Matt Fong for comptroller—all with us here today. And I want to thank the marvelous talent, the Velvet Fog, Mel Torme. Nobody can do "The Star-Spangled Banner" any better than that. If you give lessons, you might try Roseanne Barr on for size. [*Laughter*]

I want to say thanks to my friends Andy Williams and Buddy Ebsen, Donald O'Connor and, of course, Scott Baio, the youngest of us all. It's great to be with you all, and I'm so appreciative. And then, my special and profound thanks to two old friends that have been really sweet to Barbara and me over the years; and I mean Barbara and Frank Sinatra. Thank you all for being with us, too.

I bring you all greetings from Barbara Bush. If I might say so—as I said about Gayle—I think Barbara is doing an outstanding job on behalf of literacy across this country. That first pitch she threw out at the Reds' catcher there probably screwed up the Oakland team, but nevertheless—[*laughter*]—she sends her very best regards.

I want to just get back out here—this morning in Orange County, and now here, and then Monday in San Francisco—to just say a few words of support for our next Governor, Pete Wilson.

You know, Pete understands California. He knows that Californians want a government that is responsible and, in short, a government worthy of respect. That's why he endorsed this Proposition 140 to reform our government by limiting the terms for the lawmakers.

You know, some don't know this, but our 1988 Republican national platform called for limiting terms for Members of Congress. Now momentum is building all across this country. But the Democrats, including Pete's opponent, don't understand the mood of the country. They truly believe that they deserve to be reelected from now

until kingdom come. I believe in citizen legislators returning to live under the laws they've made. I believe term limitation is an idea whose time has come.

This system, gerrymandered to perpetuate incumbency, reminds me of the Michael Keaton character in "Pacific Heights": Once they move into your basement, they never move out. [*Laughter*] But Pete Wilson has said enough is enough, and so do I. And we don't need perpetual legislators. We need more Republicans like Pete Wilson, and we need a Congress in Washington that works. We need a Congress that works for the national interest, not the special interest.

In education—Pete touched on it—we want reform to empower parents, give the parents the right to choose their children's schools. In child care, we want reform to empower parents to choose who will watch over their children. We don't want the Government telling them that that's the way it's got to be in child care.

And in the most desolate, the most poverty-stricken inner cities, we want reform. And so, we strive to create job zones of opportunity, to remove barriers to mobility and success, to empower people with the spirit of enterprise.

In civil rights, we want expanded guarantees of equal opportunities for all. We want to eliminate prejudice in the workplace, but we do not want quotas. And that is why I vetoed that civil rights bill. And the very day I did that, I sent a—I've been for civil rights all my life, and I sent a civil rights bill up to the Hill that will guarantee against discrimination in the workplace, but it will not establish quotas. And I ask the Congress—they're sitting around up there now—they could pass it in 20 minutes if there was a genuine interest in civil rights and less interest in trying to embarrass the President of the United States.

And in housing, we want to empower public-housing tenants to take charge of their own lives, to be able to control the places in which they live.

But this is a Congress that I have to live with. I'm now much more empathetic with the Duke—what he's put up with over these last couple of terms. This is a Congress that would rather proclaim National Home Care Week than give me a housing bill. This is a Congress that would rather issue feel-good proclamations than address the fundamental problems of this country. And this is a Congress that is just now delivering a budget almost a full month into the new fiscal year and after 8 months of negotiations.

You know, almost 40 times in the last 10 years—just in the last 10 years—Congress has had to pass emergency measures just to keep the Government operating. They did it again just last Wednesday for the third time this month. I believe that the American people have had enough. And there is an alternative. And I met yesterday at the White House with the Republican leadership from the House and the Senate, and I made clear to the leadership and to our negotiators from the White House how much we owe to their untiring efforts these past 8 months—efforts to fight the Democrats' determination to tax and spend.

It is my deeply held conviction that I must do all I can to get a $500-billion deficit reduction that can't be turned over next year or the year after—get that 5-year deficit reduction and get it in place. And that has meant that I've had to do some compromising. I don't control the Senate, and I don't control the House. But I will not do one that reverts back to raising the income tax rates on everybody in the name of "soaking the rich." What they're really doing is trying to get into the pocket of the working man and woman of this country by that indexing that the Democrats ran through the House with.

God, it's nice to be out of Washington, I'll tell you. [*Laughter*] Getting warmed up here. But we are united by a certain bunch of principles, group of principles. And we stand against the age-old failed tax-and-spend policies of the Democrats who control both Houses of the Congress. We're working to turn things around in Washington. Right here in California, back here, reform starts now with Pete Wilson.

In our war on crime and drugs, Pete, as George Deukmejian said, has been absolutely outstanding. As your next Governor, here's what he says: "I will not have California under siege to rapists and thugs and drug dealers." And is it, therefore, any surprise that he, and not his opponent, is endorsed by the women prosecutors of California? They know that Pete wants to govern a California where women no longer fear the night, because drug dealers and criminals will fear the law. They know he would make your streets safer by extending capital punishment in California to those major drug traffickers—the same as my proposal, exactly the same as my proposal before the Congress.

The first time I called on Congress to pass a tough, comprehensive crime bill, I was surrounded there by hundreds of law enforcement officers at the foot of the Capitol on a rain-soaked morning in May of 1989. Now, after a year and a half, the Democrat Congress still has not passed our crime bill. The only crime bill the Democrats have ever talked about passing is one that would leave our courts, our cops, and ultimately, our citizens weaker than the criminals who plague our cities. And I will not accept that kind of legislation. When the Democrats tried to push through an exclusionary rule that would have handcuffed law enforcement officers, it was Republicans—in the minority—but it was Republicans that held the line. And when they tried to assure criminals a process of endless appeals, Republicans held the line. And when they tried to cut the death penalty, Republicans held the line.

The hour is late. And if Congress sends me a bill now—even now at this last minute—that is tougher on criminals than it is on the cops, then I'll sign it the instant it lands on my desk. It troubles me, it troubles me that our Democratic Congress doesn't bother to listen to the most vulnerable of our society: those families living in fear in West L.A. or in Watts, in neighborhoods where just going to school or the corner store requires an act of courage.

If the Democrats in Congress want real justice, if they want peace in our neighborhoods, they would have protected Americans—all Americans—with the tough laws that we proposed so very long ago. If we had had more people like Pete Wilson in the United States Senate and more like him in the House, we would have done much better sooner to protect the average man and woman of this country.

Well, now California can do something about the arrogance of the liberal State legislature. You can do something because you, the voters, are the true incumbents. You can elect more Republicans, and you can elect a Governor who will never waver in fighting crime, standing firm for fiscal sanity, protecting the environment. You can elect Pete Wilson.

November 6th is just 11 days away, and already the absentee ballots are coming in from the Gulf, thousands of votes from our men and women in uniform. If they can find the time to do their civic duty under demanding circumstances, I know that Californians at home will turn out as well. So we need you to get out the vote. That's what a lot of this luncheon is about today—helping Frank Visco and the State party get out the vote for our outstanding statewide ticket.

Let me just close with a word relating to what's happening in the Gulf. I was very moved when I landed at El Toro and met the wives and kids of many of those who are serving us right now halfway around the world in Saudi Arabia. It's a very moving thing to see those fantastic young people whose husbands and wives are serving halfway around the world.

You know, Arthur Vandenberg talked about partisanship ending at the water's edge. That was a good concept. We got away from it in Vietnam and the post-Vietnam era. But I'm very pleased—and I want to say it right here in front of what I suspect is a bit of a partisan audience when it comes to George Deukmejian and Pete Wilson—but we've had good support across the aisle from the Democratic leadership and from the Democratic Members of Congress and the Democratic Members of the Senate for what I'm trying to do halfway around the world.

But I come to these meetings, and you see some signs out there, and it says: "No war for oil." Let me tell you that that's not what the question is. The question is: Will the United States, the only country in the world that has the power to effect this unprecedented coalition and put it together, will the United States insist—and I think the answer is yes—will we insist that Saddam Hussein get out of Kuwait, that the Government of Kuwait be restored, that the rape and the pillage and the plunder of Kuwait stop, and that aggression not be rewarded? It isn't oil, it is aggression—naked, brutal aggression.

So, I can assure you that when this is over the world will say, thank God that the United States made it clear that no country can bully and take over its neighbor. That's what's at stake. And I want to say to the American people and to those in California, regardless of party: I am grateful for the steadfast support—for your steadfast support. And I will not let you down. The United States of America will prevail.

Thank you all, and God bless each and every one of you.

Note: The President spoke at 12:45 p.m. in the ballroom at the Century Plaza Hotel. In his remarks, he referred to Pete Wilson's wife, Gayle; Gov. George Deukmejian and his wife, Gloria; entertainers Andy Williams, Buddy Ebsen, Donald O'Connor, Scott Baio, and Frank Sinatra; and President Saddam Hussein of Iraq. President Bush also referred to comedienne Roseanne Barr's performance of the national anthem at a San Diego Padres baseball game and Barbara Bush's appearance at the second game of the 1990 World Series in Cincinnati, OH.

Remarks at a Fundraising Dinner for Senatorial Candidate Pat Saiki in Honolulu, Hawaii
October 26, 1990

Well, thank you all, really, for that warm welcome back. Frank, thank you. Keep up the good work as campaign chairman. You know, you can get a feeling of these campaigns, and I love the feel of this Saiki campaign for the Senate. I feel we've got a winner out there. And I was privileged to be met at the airport by Senator Hiram Fong, an old friend of my family's and a friend of Barbara's and mine. Mayor Fasi greeted us and Fred Hemmings, our able candidate for Governor. I sure hope he'll get in there. We need a little change in that place.

And then we've got two great candidates for Congress: Mike Liu, we want you to win. Andy Poepoe, we want you to win. So good luck, First and Second Congressional Districts. And to David Kahanu, our Bush-Quayle chairman, my gratitude. To our State chairman, Andy Anderson, my respects and thanks for what you're doing to hold this party and build it. To Governor Peter Coleman, who's here from American Samoa somewhere, my greetings to you. I haven't seen Peter, but an old friend. And of course, flying out with me, the Representative of Guam, an old friend of mine, a former general officer in the Means, Congressman Ben Blaz. I know he's here, but I don't know where he is. But anyway, we want to welcome him—Congressman from Guam. And of course, ones from amongst you are now head of OPIC—Ambassador Fred Zeder is also here. [*Applause*]

Thank you all. I see Zeder's got two friends here. Well—[*laughter*]—thank you all for that warm welcome. I wasn't kidding when I told Pat, because it is nice to get away from Washington to warmer climes and to cooler heads. [*Laughter*] I was hoping to do a little fishing here, but after a lifetime catching fish with names like skate, perch, pike, bass, and trout, somebody told me that Hawaii's State fish is the humuhumunukunukuapua'a. If I can't say it, I'll never catch it, so anyway—[*laughter*].

No, but Hawaii is a wonderfully welcoming place. And you feel it in the warm wind, and you see it in the eyes of the young and the old. Sense it even in your State capitol—not some dark, exclusive dome but a roof open to the sky, to the Sun and the stars, as if to make room for higher aspirations. And Hawaii has taught the world that men and women from Asia, Africa, and the Americas, and Europe can

tie their destinies together in a common cause. And so, we're here to support someone who brings that lesson to life every single day for all people, of any party or persuasion, who want a brighter future for Hawaii; a great teacher; a great lady; a great leader who cares about this State and its people and knows how to serve them well in Washington. And of course, I'm talking about our dear friend Pat Saiki, the next Senator from Hawaii.

She's been one who's been beating the odds. And back when the experts said she had no chance, she won her House seat with 60 percent. And next month, with your help, she's going to defy the odds again as the first Asian American woman in the United States Senate. And it's about time. She can reach out to independents, to Democrats. And over her two terms in Congress, I watched her in action, admired her bipartisan approach to her work, seen her build consensus across the aisle, getting Republicans and Democrats to pull together. And she's smart, and she's effective, and she moves government forward. And she knows that leaders are sent to Washington not to quarrel but to lead. And I know that America needs that spirit of aloha in the United States Senate.

You know, Pat Saiki adds an important voice to this great State's presence in Washington. She was part of a broad coalition concerned about Japanese Americans interned during World War II. And it was Pat who helped convince President Reagan to sign legislation reaffirming us as a nation of integrity and fairness. And just this month, I was proud to personally communicate the Nation's regret to the noble survivors of those camps.

Pat's commitment to justice is just one way that she has helped make America ever stronger and ever more proud. You know, long before it became a national code, Pat has been a leader in the Congress to safeguard Hawaii's precious environment: protecting marine life from drift netting, expanding wildlife refuges, and working to establish oilspill strike teams to protect Hawaii's waters. And very soon I hope to have on my desk in Washington a clean air act that I can sign—the one my administration proposed way back last year to the United States Congress. And if I do get such a bill, I know that part of the reason will be the steadfast support Pat Saiki has given to our environmental initiatives. She's been a champion, a clear-thinking champion for the environment. And that bodes well for all of you when she becomes the next Senator from this great State.

You know, I remember the visit I had when Pat came to see me, urging that the bombing of Kaho'olawe should be halted. And just this week I directed the Secretary of Defense to discontinue the island's use as a weapons range, effective immediately. And if that is good, give some credit to Pat Saiki. She's an effective, compassionate leader—sound judgment—whose voice gets heard, who makes things happen.

You know, when she did come to see me in the Oval Office last spring, she stressed the importance of these environmental issues and also talked about trade with our Pacific Rim neighbors. And she's got a vision of Hawaii as more than a gateway to the Pacific Rim. She's excited about the meeting I'm having tomorrow with these leaders from the islands. And I think it's a good time—and I think it's about time—that an American President sat down with the heads of these countries out there and tell them that we are as one in our respect for and love of the Pacific.

And she sees Hawaii as I do, a future focal point for international trade and new technology. For example, she and I know how important it is to achieve success at these GATT talks—the final part of the Uruguay round. These negotiations, if we're successful—and I was on the phone to some of the foreign leaders, the leaders of Europe, today on this very subject—if these negotiations are successful, they will open up new markets for Hawaii's agricultural products. And I am absolutely convinced that the United States can compete with anyone, anywhere, as long as the playing field is level and the competition is free and fair. And that's what Pat and I are fighting for.

Further, she knows how to harness the power of Hawaiian business by unleashing the power of the people themselves. We'll

have a brighter future with Pat in the Senate. You know, Pat knows the future will always be just out of reach if we follow the failed tradition of taxing and spending, spending and taxing. And that's why she's got the best spending record of anyone in the Hawaiian delegation. In fact, her efforts against waste in government made her a two-time winner of the Golden Bulldog Award. You can just picture it. You've got to be careful when I'm talking about these dogs because Barbara was out here recently and you may recall that our dog, Millie, is now a famous author. [*Laughter*] And if she hears Pat wins the Golden Bulldog Award, our springer spaniel may be jealous. Ever since her book hit the bestseller list, she's been a lot—full of herself. Give her some Alpo and she asks for a wine list around the White House these days. [*Laughter*]

I'm sure you've been watching the news about these budget negotiations with Congress. Put it this way: I hope you haven't been watching the news about the budget negotiations with Congress. [*Laughter*] If you think it hasn't been pretty from 5,000 miles away, you ought to try it close up. [*Laughter*] No, it hasn't been pretty. But I think we are getting closer to an agreement—an agreement that is long, long overdue. Because every time I see a little guy like this one in the front row—and for you in the back, he's about this big—I say to myself, we must stop mortgaging the future of these young kids by deficit after deficit after deficit. And the Congress better get going and get something done about it.

You know, it's different—I've discovered a few things. One is, it's different being President. There's a weighty observation. [*Laughter*] And Harry Truman was right—the buck does stop at my desk. Because as President, I do have to put the national interest first before the parochial interest. And so, I am determined to do my level best, in a spirit of compromise and in a spirit of outreach, to get an agreement that puts a stop to this congressional spending binge. Unless you haven't noticed it, I want a 5-year, $500-billion deficit reduction program that is enforceable—a bill that cannot be overridden the very next year and that will really guarantee these young kids that they will not have their future mortgaged by the big-spending Congress of the United States. And I say this not in a spirit of partisanship, but if we had more people like Pat on our side of the aisle and we had more like her elected to the Senate, I can guarantee you we wouldn't be back year after year in a deficit mode. She is a fiscal conservative, and we need her in the United States Senate.

Some talk about the blending of principles between the Democrat and the Republican Party nationally. But principles like—I think they're clear—principles like the enduring commitment to freedom and justice and individual empowerment—I think of that as a principle that unites us. The constant determination to place our faith in limited Federal Government—one that's got compassion and one that's got conscience, though. And this party and our leadership in Washington continues to fight the failed policies of the past. Look back. Our 1988 platform called for limiting the terms on the Members of Congress. And as you look at the momentum growing across the country, I am convinced that it's an idea whose time has come.

We are the party that empowers people, not an entrenched bureaucracy of 20,000 congressional staffers on Capitol Hill. And we are determined to put the national interest ahead of the special interest. So I'm here at this event on a purely partisan mission—because I believe so strongly in Pat Saiki. I know she can reach out and get voters from both sides of the aisles. I know she can make good things happen for the people of her State. So, I need her as part of our team.

But as Senator Vandenberg said many years ago, partisanship stops at the water's edge. I must tell you, in that spirit of bipartisanship, that I am truly grateful for the bipartisan support not only from the Congress but also from the American people for our efforts to stand up firm against Saddam Hussein's aggression and brutality in the

Persian Gulf. The Democratic leaders in the House and the Republican leaders in the House, and the Democratic leaders in the Senate and the Republican leaders in the Senate came together in a resolution supporting the efforts that I have taken, the moves that I have made as President of the United States. And I think that sends a good, clear symbol of unity to that invading dictator halfway around the world.

On Sunday, I'm going to be putting partisanship aside and head out for Hickam Air Force Base to tell Hawaii's service men and women how much they mean to America and to the cause of peace in the whole world. Our thoughts and prayers are with them and their family every day. And I know that Pat and all of you here join me in saluting the finest young men and women that have ever served in the uniform of the United States of America.

President Eisenhower worried about global conflict in 1959. And he said: "Hawaii cries insistently to a divided world that all our differences of race and origin are less than the grand and indestructible unity of our common brotherhood. The world should take time to listen to Hawaii."

Well, today Washington does listen to Hawaii and to Pat Saiki. And it's been a close race for her. But we're beginning to see the daylight. And that means bright days for this State are ahead. So this November, do absolutely all you can to get out the vote, from Hilo on the Big Island to Maui to Kaneohe—where I flew out of there during World War II for a little bit—to the bustling streets of Honolulu right here on Oahu. Get the people to the polls, and send Pat Saiki to the United States Senate. We need her. She is outstanding.

Thank you, and God bless the United States of America. Thank you all.

Note: The President spoke at 7:20 p.m. in the Coral Ballroom at the Hilton Hawaiian Village Hotel.

Remarks on the Federal Budget Agreement and an Exchange With Reporters in Honolulu, Hawaii
October 27, 1990

The President. Let me start with a statement, and then be glad to take some questions. But I've just been informed that the United States Senate has just passed the House-Senate conference report on the budget. This completes congressional action on an agreement to reduce the Federal deficit by over $490 billion over the next 5 years.

This budget blueprint represents corrective action on a pattern of Federal spending gone out of control. We have put on the brakes, and the process has sometimes been painful. But I will sign this legislation because, for the first time, it makes significant and long-term cuts in Federal spending that should have a positive impact on America's economic future. All political points of view have sacrificed to bring this agreement about. And, needless to say, I don't like raising taxes and never will, but there is a price to divided government, and that means that I have had to compromise on items that I feel strongly about in order to do what I think is best for the country, and that is to reach an agreement.

At the same time, we've cut Federal spending programs and applied some self-discipline, steps that also may not be popular. But the essential ingredient which has produced bipartisan agreement is that we must get the deficit down, get interest rates down, and keep America moving. And I might add, I'm told that the final enforcement provisions are very, very strong, so that we're guarding against more spending—out-of-control spending next year and into the future, covered by this agreement.

In addition, I am pleased that many of my proposals on child care are incorporated in this budget reconciliation bill. The legislation provides tax credits, grants, and vouchers that put choice in the hands of parents rather than in the hands of bureaucrats. So, I'm very pleased about the child-care provision, something I've been fighting for.

I intend to sign the agreement. And I will also review closely the various appropriations bills to make sure that they conform to this new spending agreement. We've made the tough decisions, and now it's time to move on.

And I am pleased that the Congress also has passed historic Clean Air Act amendments which will reduce acid rain, urban smog, and toxic air pollutions. We proposed this far-reaching environmental cleanup legislation some 15 months ago with the hope that this initiative by the administration would break the logjam that had prevented a clean air bill from being passed previously. This is an important milestone in preserving and protecting America's natural resources, and I look forward to signing the bill.

I want to conclude by thanking everyone involved, including the bipartisan leadership in Congress for their tireless efforts in forging and passing the new budget agreement. The Speaker [Thomas S. Foley], Minority Leader Bob Michel, the Majority Leader Dick Gephardt, Senator Mitchell, and Senator Dole have all had to compromise some. And they've stayed with it long, long hours, trying to hammer out this agreement, so I want to take this opportunity to thank them.

I'll be glad to take a few questions, and then we've got to head on.

Budget Agreement

Q. Mr. President, you signed on to this budget agreement and your negotiators negotiated it with Congress, including the tax increases that you vowed you wouldn't do when you ran for office. Are you prepared now to give it a sound endorsement and urge Republican candidates to go out and sell it to the voters as well——

The President. No——

Q. ——or are you going to turn your back on it and blame the Democrats for the tax increases that you agreed with?

The President. I'm going to say, look, I've reluctantly signed this. There are things in it that, if I controlled both Houses of Congress, wouldn't be in it; and I think the Democrats will be saying the same thing. I noticed some of them saying yesterday that they felt we ought to have higher income tax rates. One of the things I'm glad about is that we've held the line on income tax rates.

A handful of the wealthiest went up, and 10 times that many of the upper middle income came down. Some went from 28 to 31; others came down from 33 to 31. There are certain things in it that I can strongly advocate. There are some things in it that I had to gag and digest. And so, that's the approach I'm going to be taking, and expect everyone else will, too.

Q. Mr. President, you said it's time to move on. Do you have any fear or do you think—expectation that the whole fiasco over the last couple of weeks is going to haunt you in the election?

The President. No, I don't think so at all. Sometimes the President has to make a tough call; this is one of them. I'll be right out on the campaign trail advocating the election of more Republicans to the Congress. And we wouldn't have been in this mess if we had that.

Q. Mr. President, how can you go out now and blame Democrats, criticize Democrats, when in fact they, more than Republicans, helped you get this budget package—which you supported—passed?

The President. Hey, listen, that shows that I don't like everything in the package. I mean, if I were all that enthusiastic about it you'd have seen more Republicans voting for it. So, nobody got it exactly the way he or she wanted, but now it's behind us. As soon as I sign it, that's behind us. And I hope it will have the effect of bringing interest rates down. But the philosophy of holding the line on spending and holding the line on taxes is my philosophy. And I will be clearly advocating that.

Taxes

Q. What message will you use now, then, to replace your "no new taxes" pledge? Everybody is very accustomed to that, all the Republicans. And I just want to know what slogan or——

The President. Let me be clear: I'm not in favor of new taxes. I'll repeat that over and over and over again. And this one compromise where we begrudgingly had to accept revenue increases is the exception that proves the rule. That's the way I'll handle it.

Q. The exception that proves what rule?

The President. The rule that I'm strongly opposed to raising taxes on the American people and that we ought to do a better job of controlling spending. And I think we can. So, that's the message, loud and clear.

Q. Will you reinstate today your "no new taxes" pledge, perhaps "no new new taxes"? Do you think—remember after '86 that the Congress passed a resolution saying they wouldn't tamper with it for 5 years. Do you think now the line should be drawn again and, having made this compromise, you should now hold the line on taxes again?

The President. Absolutely going to hold the line on taxes. And hopefully—the big thing is to hold the line on spending so nobody will come up and try to propose new taxes. But I noticed one of the Democratic leaders said yesterday, well, he wants to raise income tax rates. And he's going to have a whale of a fight on it. This was a one-time compromise.

Budget Agreement

Q. You really don't seem very enthusiastic about this budget deal. You don't seem euphoric after all you and the others have been through——

The President. That's right. You got it.

Q. ——and I might note that it doesn't appear to meet your own objectives. You've been insisting on a $500-billion deficit reduction target—now only $490 billion. Plus I understand the deal is based on rosy economic assumptions over which there is much disagreement. How do you feel?

The President. I feel that it's been a long, arduous battle. And I feel that every once in a while the President has to do something he doesn't like, and that is to compromise. And I did that here. So, I'm glad it's over, and I have to say that the hours that the Democratic leaders and the Republican leaders spent working this problem has just been exhausting for everybody, including me, although they did much more of the work. So, I'm glad it's behind us, and I feel good that it's behind us, but I can't be euphoric about every provision in this bill.

I am very encouraged about the enforcement provisions because they are strong. And no guy can go out and put in a new program without the offset. The guarantees of enforcement are strong, and I'm going to do my level best to see that they stay strong.

So, you're trying to describe mood. I am pleased it's behind us, and I will be out vigorously campaigning on the campaign trail for more Republicans who feel as I do about holding the line on taxes and about spending. And we have a difference of opinion. You have more people that wanted to increase, on the Democratic side, these permissive spending programs. So, the philosophy, the fundamental philosophical underpinning—yes, I haven't changed my view on that, and I'm sure the liberal Democrats haven't either. But we'll take that case to the American people.

Q. Can you really show the American people with all your heart that this is a good deal?

The President. Parts of it are good. No, I can't say this is the best thing that's happened to us since sliced bread or the elimination of broccoli. It has got some good things in it, but if we were doing it my way, or the Republican leader in the Senate's way, or the Republican leader in the House's way, it would be very, very different.

But I think it is good that we have a $490 billion—I'd like to have seen $500 billion, but this is a lot of money—$490 billion, enforceable deficit reduction program. And that part, that overall part, I am enthusiastic about. But how we got it—I reserve the right to be as critical as the next person on that.

Republican Campaign Strategy

Q. Mr. President, do you think it was proper for the Republican Congressional Campaign Committee to recommend that the party's candidates distance themselves from the President on this?

The President. No, I want everybody to be right with me on everything I do.

Q. Is the architect of that strategy, Ed Rollins [cochairman of the committee], history as far as you're concerned?

The President. That is inside the beltway—I know how people love that. They thrive on it. I don't. And you know, ever since I got out around the country, not one person has sidled up to me and asked me about that particular incident. And I'm going to keep my sights set on the big picture and not accommodate you when you want me to go back into that. I understand it; I understand it because people thrive—what was that, Lori [Lori Santos, United Press International]?

Q. Does he know?

Q. Is he out?

Q. Is he out?

The President. I'm not discussing it because it would divert me from the major goal, which is to elect more Republicans to agree, as I do—hold the line on taxes and spending, get people back to work in this country by getting interest rates down, and empowering people, not programs and bureaucrats. So, I get diverted if you try to get me into some little staff matter.

Representative Gingrich

Q. Conspicuously missing from that list of leaders that you recited, Mr. President, was the name of Newt Gingrich. Some people have suggested that you could have gotten a better deal if he had not led the Republican revolt a couple of weeks ago. Do you think that he should remain in his leadership position because of his actions?

The President. Remember—what was the give-and-take in the debate when Ronald Reagan said, there you go again trying to get me caught up in something divisive. Newt Gingrich stood out there in the White House—I'm not sure you were there that day—and strongly endorsed Republican unity, and that's exactly what should happen. So, please don't ask me to relive the agony of a budget agreement that I am glad is signed and is now behind us.

Mr. Fitzwater. One final question.

Budget Agreement

Q. Do you feel that the Republican Party has been badly hurt by this——

The President. No.

Q. ——and aren't you sorry that you couldn't have gotten more Republican votes?

The President. Not particularly sorry that not gotten votes because a lot of the Members feel as I do: They were gagging on certain provisions, but glad that it's passed. And I think if this compromise had been perfect from the Republican side, you'd have seen—obviously have many, many more votes. So, I think those that didn't vote against it, on both sides, had problems with it. Some on the Democratic side were saying, we want to raise income tax rates on the American people more. That's literally what they wanted to do. They called it soak the rich, but what they meant was—when that bill that they passed in the Congress, with that indexing—went after every working man and woman in this country. And that's the old tax-and-spend view, and some of them didn't feel it went far enough. Some on our side didn't like anything to do with revenues; that's more along my line of thinking.

So, I think that's history now, but I have no rancor about it. I'm just glad it's passed. I wish it had been passed when we had the summit agreement, and we'd have been much further along.

But I don't—back to the first part of your question—no, I sense strong enthusiasm for Republican candidates. And I think we've been caught up in a bit of an inside smokescreen here. But let's see now how we do. I'm going to be out there, working my heart out for Republican candidates who feel as I do that we ought to hold the line on taxes and that we ought to curtail spending.

The Economy

Q. Are we headed for another recession?

The President. The economy is sluggish, and there's no question about that. And I am convinced, whether I like every paragraph of this or not, that this is good medicine for the economy, particularly if the Federal Reserve Board now follows up with lowering interest rates. You know, that is what's needed, and I'm not here to do anything other than to state that principle. But I listened carefully to [Federal Reserve

Board Chairman] Alan Greenspan's testimony, and I was encouraged that interest rates might come down. Better than any program is getting these rates down so economic growth gets stimulated.

Appropriation Bills

Q. You said that you're going to review the appropriations. Has that process begun? And are you certain that the appropriations bills that have been passed are not raising spending levels at the same time that you're claiming to have cut some for deficit reduction?

The President. No, I'm not sure of that, Jessica [Jessica Lee, USA Today]. The process is underway, of course, but I'm not certain that there's no breaches of the spending goals.

Q. Sir, if I could just switch to the——

The President. A couple of more, and then I've got to go. We've got a very interesting meeting with the Pacific chiefs of state. It's a fascinating and long-overdue meeting. And I'm learning from them, and I am giving them the best I can, right from the shoulder, the American view of the importance of the Pacific. I know that, given the budget summit at home and the interest that that has stimulated, that attention hasn't been focused elsewhere. But this is a very important meeting, and I'd say historic, with these small countries—but all friendly to the United States and all very important to the United States.

I've got to get back down there in just a minute. Did I cut you off?

Q. No, sir.

The President. You've got a followup.

Persian Gulf Crisis

Q. Just to switch to the Gulf crisis for a moment. Secretary Cheney indicates we may send as many as 100,000 new troops in and a lot more tanks. What's the purpose, sir, if it's not to take offensive action and get engaged in combat with Iraq?

The President. Just a minute. Power outage here.

We have not announced what we are going to do in terms of additional troops. We have been still, as everybody around the world knows, still moving forces. The purpose is to make clear to Saddam Hussein [President of Iraq] that his aggression will not stand. What I do in the future will be determined after I have a discussion with Dick Cheney and the Chairman of the Joint Chiefs [Colin L. Powell], General Scowcroft [Brent Scowcroft, Assistant to the President for National Security Affairs], and Secretary Baker, which I expect we'll be doing—looking for help with Brent—when we get back. Maybe we'll have more to say about that then.

But I believe a couple of things on this. One, I think Saddam Hussein really felt that nobody was going to move against his aggression in Kuwait. I also believe that he really intended to threaten Saudi Arabia— or else why did he move all his armor south to the Saudi border? I think as he sees the U.S. forces moving in conjunction with many Arab country forces, in conjunction with many European country forces on land and on the sea, that he's taking another look. Because we are deadly serious. I want to see these economic sanctions work.

I'm not too good at the emotional side of it, but when you talk to the parents and spouses of our kids halfway around the world, it makes a real impact on you. I remember when I got off the plane at the Marine base, and they were saying, "Take care of my husband," and yet, "We back you 100 percent." So, I don't think that's a conflict exactly, but I want to take care of every young man and woman that's serving the United States halfway around the world. But they want, and I want, to see that Saddam's aggression is unrewarded and, indeed, repudiated. So, the moving of U.S. force up to now has sent a strong signal to him. We have the finest, most highly motivated, best trained, best equipped Armed Forces in the world. And they're right there. They're right there in substantial numbers—land, air, and sea.

Now, Mr. Saddam Hussein, get out of Kuwait with no condition. This talk of some condition—that is unacceptable not just to the United States but to the other countries around the world. I just got off the phone talking to President Mubarak [of Egypt]— steadfast friend to the United States. He's made that same message loud and clear. On his travels he's heard it from those who

were side by side with us in the Gulf, and then he's told his visitors that. So, we're staying pretty well together on this end.

Just a couple of more, and then I really have to get going. One, two, three over here, and then I'm—you're history, Jessica—I've got to go.

Q. When you say you think that Saddam Hussein has gotten the message that we are deadly serious, do you think now that chances are better for a negotiated settlement of this situation than they were?

The President. I don't know about a negotiated settlement. There's nothing to negotiate, other than the acceptance of the United Nations-mandated resolutions. So, there's nothing to negotiate. But in terms of a peaceful solution, I'm told that the economic effects are taking hold—effects of the sanctions—and that is encouraging. I'm told that he now sees that he's up against a substantial force that clearly could prevail in any battle. So, I'm hopeful that there will be a peaceful solution to this question. But there can be no preconditions. There can be no rewarding of aggression.

Q. There are two points to my question. There are some people who are saying that the U.S. continues to send in even more troops because the U.S. has underestimated the Iraqi troop strength. That, coupled with yesterday—apparently in Spain, President Gorbachev apparently said he notes a softening on the position of Saddam Hussein. Do you have any reason to believe there has been a softening? Has Mr. Gorbachev told you something you'd like to share with us? Has that softening manifested itself in any way?

The President. I have not noticed a softening, but I've heard more kind of little threads of talk of "negotiation"—that's all. Maybe that's what President Gorbachev is talking about. But he has not shared with me any feeling of a softening of public opinion. But what was the first part?

Q. Has the U.S. underestimated, perhaps, the troop strength of the Iraqis? Is that why we're continuing to send in more troops?

The President. No. I think it's true that Saddam Hussein beefed up his armor and his forces in Kuwait. From the original deployment, he then has stepped that up by pouring more armor in.

I'll never forget the day when he said, well, we're taking our people out of Kuwait, and they had one forlorn-looking soldier in the back of a truck waving goodbye—truck heading north—and then he had all his armor moving south. So, it was a sheer fraud. And he moved a heck of a lot of armor down against the Saudis. So, I'd leave it there, but I think that when you see a lot of force there, why, the free world and those of us that are allied together are going to say: Wait a minute! We're going to do what we've got to do to protect American life or Egyptian life or, in this instance, Syrian life or Saudi life. And that's why you're seeing a substantial movement of U.S. force and forces of other countries.

I keep repeating this because it's a very important point. It is not the United States versus Saddam Hussein; it is the United States, big majorities in the Arab world, and the United Nations versus Saddam Hussein. And that point—I keep making it because he is still trying to divide and weaken this strong coalition. And he's failing, he is failing miserably because all these countries are united against his brutal aggression.

Yes, Rita [Rita Beamish, Associated Press], and then Jessica. I'm recanting because I wasn't very kind. Go ahead.

Budget Agreement

Q. Just back on the budget for a minute. What do you think it says about your leadership and your ability to lead the party that you couldn't get more Republicans to stay with you and vote with you on this very important issue of the budget?

The President. I learned a lot from Ronald Reagan, with whom I worked closely and watched and learned. And in 19—what was it—82, when we had that big tax bill, I think we got fewer votes than we did today, and he went right out and did beautifully what he felt in his heart he should do, and say, look, I'm against increasing taxes and the American people know this. And he went right on about his business. And that agreement brought interest rates down. And we all went forth and said, wait a minute, every once in a while when you don't control Congress you don't get to do it exactly your way.

And so, I understand Republicans defecting from a package that they don't like. But a President, to make something happen, once in a great while has to make a significant compromise. And that's what I did. And I think the American people understand that. They know that I'm trying pretty hard, and they know that I have their interest at stake when I want to see interest rates down and more jobs for the working men and women in this country. And that's the way I'd handle that one.

Now, last one, Jessica, and then I am leaving.

White House Staff

Q. Well, there is conventional wisdom and Periscope and other information from our weeklies that suggest there's a Cabinet shakeup in order: that the Budget Director's going to be going to head a financial firm, that the Chief of Staff will be going to the campaign trail, that [Secretary of Transportation] Skinner will go to the Budget— all kinds of things. Anybody else resign or retiring since [Secretary of Labor] Elizabeth Dole?

The President. Jessica, you know something? I don't know who writes these columns—Periscope—I mean, you talk about sheer mischief. In the ones I've seen—you go back and look at them. Somebody ought to go—not you all, you all do your job, ask the questions. So, I wish I were in a case to ask all the knowledgeable people here, who writes this stuff? I mean, if all that's going on, I don't know about it.

Q. Does that mean it's true?

The President. No.

Q. No shakeup then?

The President. Not that I've ever heard of. And maybe I'd be the last to know, but I don't think so. [*Laughter*] I think I'd be the first to know, and I'd know it way ahead of Periscope, whoever he is, whoever she may be. It is pure unadulterated gossip that comes out of these columns. It is not serious coverage. So, I can't comment; I haven't even seen this. I guess they didn't dare show it to me because I've been a little irritable lately, trying to get this job done.

Budget Agreement

Q. Irritable? Why would you be irritable?

The President. I'm going to finish my diatribe here. What?

Q. Why would you be irritable?

The President. Things aren't going exactly the way I want them done. I wish we could have got this deficit down without touching revenue. I wish that we could have got it done without all this inside-the-beltway furor because it's diverted me from major objectives.

Q. Do you feel—by Republicans in all of this——

The President. No, no, no. I feel happy about Republicans. I'm glad this is behind us, and I wish we had more of them. No matter what little philosophical wing of the party they're from, all of them would be better than what I face when I try to get stuff done from the Democrats. I mean, that's what it's all about.

President's Campaigning and Pacific Island Nations-U.S. Summit

Q. Well, you've got strategists, aides to Clayton Williams [gubernatorial candidate] in Texas, who say he's losing points because you've come to Texas and you're campaigning for him. How do you feel about that?

The President. I feel they're lying. [*Laughter*] Otherwise why has he invited me back? And I feel that my son, who I talked to—who talked to somebody high up—tells me that Williams is doing very well. So, please go to Texas and find out and take a look at whether the President can help a candidate in Texas or not. Please don't get it from some Periscope, if I might——

Now, wait just a minute here. I have a major national announcement here. Linda [Linda Tiara, CBS News], sorry. I'm glad to be in a place from whence you cometh. [*Laughter*] I might say, let me use this seriously to thank the people in Honolulu, your home, I believe, for this wonderful hospitality.

And again, I want to end on a nonpartisan note. I hope that you will record that this is a very important meeting. The United States—we're caught up in Iraq or worries about Saddam Hussein and new developments in Eastern Europe and my desire to help lift the debt off the countries in South and Central America. But we never should neglect our friends. And we are a Pacific power. And this meeting—some of these leaders come from very small countries, but they are properly proud of their sovereignty. They are concerned about the very problems that I fight, whether it's environmental or economic growth or revenues. And for me, it's been a wondrous day. And I think it is very important that a President demonstrate—in this instance to the people of the Pacific—that we are not going to neglect our friends no matter how pressing the business of the world might be from other quarters.

Thank you all.

Q. Can you—no new taxes—read your lips again? [*Laughter*]

The President. Thank you so much. Read my what? [*Laughter*]

Q. Yes, that's right. We can't figure out which part of your anatomy.

Note: The President spoke at 12:15 p.m. at the Center for Cultural Interchange Between East and West. Marlin Fitzwater was Press Secretary to the President, and John H. Sununu was Chief of Staff to the President.

Remarks at the Conclusion of the Pacific Island Nations-United States Summit in Honolulu, Hawaii
October 27, 1990

Distinguished friends, it's been a great pleasure to greet you here in the Pacific, here in the United States. We've just completed an unprecedented dialog on a wide range of mutual interests and concerns. In particular, we emphasize that America shares the islands' vision of the region's future—seeing the Pacific not as a great ocean of small islands and tiny populations, but rather as an aquatic continent—the world's largest—covering a full third of the Earth's surface. Like a string of pearls spread out across the sea, each nation is unique, each is precious, and each has something to contribute to the value of the whole.

The Pacific Islands have a special place in the minds and hearts of the American people. And, on my own visits, starting almost 50 years ago, I witnessed the natural charm of the island peoples and the natural beauty of the islands. Their reputation is well-deserved. With island jurisdictions of our own, we are also proud of America's special place in the extended family of Pacific nations. We enjoy close relations linked by many bonds of friendship and family. Today, we share this great aquatic continent as partners in peace, bound together in an oceanic community pledged to protect both new democracies and worthy old traditions.

During World War II, many Americans journeyed to the Pacific Islands to help protect our shared heritage of freedom and peace. And today we have returned, this time to help protect our shared heritage of beauty and nature. That is why, just last month, I signed the Convention for the Protection of the Natural Resources and Environment of the South Pacific Region and promptly sent it to the Senate for ratification.

Similarly, we have directed our Ambassador in New Zealand to sign the Wellington Convention, a major new step in dealing with the challenge of driftnet fishing. We also described our plan to host the first round of discussions for a framework convention on global climate change beginning in Washington next February 4th. This effort is being bolstered by the world's largest environmental research program—our administration's initiative to commit about $1 billion a year to explore the causes and effects of climate change.

We also shared a valuable discussion on one program of particular concern to the island nations and of particular concern and importance to our global arms control ef-

forts—the destruction of all chemical weapons on Johnston Island. We emphasized our common interest in ridding the world of these terrible weapons and asked for their understanding and support in this significant step towards peace and disarmament.

We assured the leaders that we plan to dispose of only the chemical munitions from the Pacific theater currently stored at Johnston Atoll, any obsolete materials found in the Pacific Islands, and those relatively small quantities shipped from Germany. We confirmed that these munitions will be destroyed safely on a prioritized schedule and that, once the destruction is completed, we have no plans to use Johnston Atoll for any other chemical munitions purpose or as a hazardous waste disposal site.

We also assured the leaders that the safeguards we're employing ensure that there will be no associated environmental damage. And we expressed the hope that they would accept our offer for a technical team, sponsored by the South Pacific Forum, to visit Johnston Atoll to independently monitor the operation. Today the United States has rededicated itself to lasting security in the region—a security which comes not so much from force of arms but through nurturing of free people, free markets, free economies.

In order to strengthen these economies, we were pleased to announce several initiatives. First, we proposed establishing a joint commercial commission with the island nations to meet each year at senior government levels to identify and address commercial opportunities and trade concerns. Second, we announced that the Overseas Private Investment Corporation would establish two new funds, an Asian Pacific growth fund and an environmental investment fund, to respectively assist private sector and natural resource development. In addition, OPIC will lead a 1991 mission of American investors to Pacific island countries. And third, we announced our plan to begin negotiations to extend the South Pacific Regional Fisheries Treaty. And fourth, the addition of AID private sector assistance programs to enhance agricultural and marine resource development. And fifth, three new programs—educational exchanges sponsored by the East-West Center and USIA.

And further, I would also like to announce an extension of our APEC [Asia Pacific Economic Cooperation] Partnership for Education Initiative to include the Pacific island countries. This last initiative will enhance educational links all across the Pacific, through both the public and private sector.

I am very pleased that you all came. Like the early Pacific navigators who braved the seas alone so that others could follow, you have come to Hawaii today to help chart a new course for the children of the Pacific— the children of tomorrow. Together, we are moving forward. And together, we're racing toward a new era in the Century of the Pacific. Together, we and the island nations can ensure it is, indeed, a new era of peace and growth.

Thank you—all of you—for this visit. You've shown us friendship. You've shown leadership in promoting democracy and

economic progress. I simply want to wish each and every one of you the very best. The frankness of the exchange, the chance to exchange ideas has been extraordinarily beneficial to me, and I expect those American officials with me feel exactly the same way. We look forward to working with you as together we face the enormous challenges of the future. So, thank you and God speed you on your journeys home. Thank you all very, very much.

Note: The President spoke at 1:45 p.m. in the Wailana Room at the Center for Cultural Interchange Between East and West. At the summit, the President met with representatives of the Solomon Islands, Tonga, Tuvalu, the Cook Islands, Papua New Guinea, Western Samoa, Fiji, Nauru, Micronesia, the Marshall Islands, and Kiribati. In the morning the President attended a plenary session, and in the afternoon he attended a working luncheon for the summit participants.

Message to the Congress Transmitting a Report on Panamanian Government Assets Held by the United States
October 27, 1990

To the Congress of the United States:

1. I hereby report to the Congress on developments since the last Presidential report of April 30, 1990, concerning the national emergency with respect to Panama. This report is submitted pursuant to section 207(d) of the International Emergency Economic Powers Act, 50 U.S.C. 1706(d).

2. On April 5, 1990, I issued Executive Order No. 12710, terminating the national emergency declared on April 8, 1988, with respect to Panama. While this order terminated the sanctions, the blocking of Panamanian government assets in the United States was continued to permit completion of the orderly unblocking and transfer of funds I directed on December 20, 1989, and to foster the resolution of claims of U.S. creditors involving Panama, pursuant to 50 U.S.C. 1706(a). The termination of the na-

tional emergency did not affect the continuation of compliance audits and enforcement actions with respect to activities taking place during the sanctions period, pursuant to 50 U.S.C. 1622(a).

2. Since March 12, 1990, the Office of Foreign Assets Control ("FAC") has released $39 million of the remaining $169.7 million blocked to the control of the Government of Panama. This $39 million was comprised of $600,000 from blocked accounts at commercial banks, and $38.4 million from blocked reserve accounts established under section 509 of the Panamanian Transactions Regulations, 31 C.F.R. 565.509 ("509 accounts").

The $130.7 million remaining blocked consists of $127.8 million in the Federal Reserve Bank of New York that continues to be held in escrow at the request of the Government of Panama to fund a portion of

Panama's arrearage to international financial institutions, $1.5 million in commercial banks for which the Government of Panama has not requested unblocking, and $1.4 million in 509 accounts. The remaining 509 account balances are subject to bilateral negotiations between the Government of Panama and U.S. firms that have both debts to and obligations owed from the Government of Panama. We will continue to work with the Government of Panama to resolve its outstanding obligations.

4. Representatives of the Department of the Treasury visited Panama to discuss with senior Panamanian officials and representatives of the business community the conclusion of the Panama emergency and the unblocking of funds, and to request their assistance in enforcement and compliance actions that may still occur. The Department of the Treasury is in the process of reviewing potential civil penalty cases involving violations of the Panamanian Transactions Regulations, 31 C.F.R. Part 565, which occurred prior to the end of the economic sanctions program against the Noriega regime. Prepenalty Notices have been issued in two such cases as of this date.

5. I will continue to report periodically to the Congress on the exercise of authorities to prohibit transactions involving property in which the Government of Panama has an interest pursuant to 50 U.S.C. 1706(d).

GEORGE BUSH

The White House,
October 27, 1990.

Nomination of John A. Bushnell To Be United States Ambassador to Costa Rica
October 27, 1990

The President today nominated John A. Bushnell, of Connecticut, a Career Member of the Senior Foreign Service, Class of Minister-Counselor, as Ambassador to the Republic of Costa Rica. He would succeed Deane Roesch Hinton.

Since 1989, Mr. Bushnell has served as Deputy Chief of Mission in the Republic of Panama. Mr. Bushnell entered the Foreign Service in 1960 and has served in the following positions: assigned to the Department of State, 1960–1962; international economist in Bogotá, Colombia, 1962–1964; international economist in Santo Domingo, 1964–1965; program officer for the Agency for International Development, 1965–1969; international economist for the U.S. Mission in Geneva, 1969–1971; National Security Council, 1971–1974; Deputy Assistant Secretary for the Department of the Treasury, 1974–1976; assigned to the Department of State, 1976–1981; member of the Board of the Panama Canal Commission, 1980; Deputy Chief of Mission in Buenos Aires, 1982–1987; and interfunctional officer in the Office of the Director of Management Policy, 1988–1989.

Mr. Bushnell graduated from Yale University (B.A., 1955) and the University of Melbourne (M.A., 1959). He was born July 26, 1933, in New York. Mr. Bushnell is married and resides in Panama.

Statement by Press Secretary Fitzwater on Lebanon
October 27, 1990

The United States believes that order and security should be brought to Lebanon as soon as possible by the legitimate government. We believe that implementation of the Taif Accord should proceed. The United States strongly supports the unity, sovereignty, and territorial integrity of Lebanon and urges the disbandment of all militias and the removal of all foreign forces from Lebanon so that the process of national reconciliation can proceed.

For 15 years we have argued against violence in Lebanon. Now is not the time to settle old scores. Now is the time for healing. The United States has made this point to Syria as well as to the various Lebanese parties.

Remarks to Officers and Troops at Hickam Air Force Base in Pearl Harbor, Hawaii
October 28, 1990

The President. Thank you, Admiral Hardisty. Please be seated. And thank each and every one of you for joining us here today— and for joining in the defense of freedom every day. You know, I'm proud to be back here at Pearl and proud to be back as your Commander in Chief and proud to be back standing up for fighting men and women like you that serve in the Armed Forces of the United States. We have never had a finer group of people. Governor Waihee, the Governor of the State—proud to be in your State, sir. To my dear friend Pat Saiki, the Congresswoman from this district, thank you for joining me and thank you for being at my side coming out here. To Colonel Lyon, my respects, sir. And again, Admiral Hardisty, thank you, sir, for this unforgettable welcome back here to this marvelous Hickam Air Force Base. This is quite a crowd. But I can't help but think of the warning that one soldier gave to comedian Steve Martin last week when Steve Martin began a talk in Saudi Arabia. This is a true story. He said, "You'd better be funny. We've got bullets."

Well, you may recall, there was a slight confusion a couple years ago when I said that Pearl Harbor Day was September 7th. But now I've put an end to all that confusion—and I just want to say I'm very happy to be back here in at Clark Air Force Base. [*Laughter*] The truth is, I will always remember the first time that I saw Pearl Harbor in the early spring of 1944. Our ship and my squadron were en route to Wake Island and out to the rest of the Pacific. Then, as now, it was an impressive sight. The fleet, having been pounded, had

recovered—the naval shipyard here having set the world record for the fastest repair work completed on battle-damaged ships. No member of that generation can ever forget the clarion call that Pearl Harbor represented. Things changed instantly. The country came together and, like you here today, we each knew our duty.

There was a movie a few years back where the actor John Houseman, Paper Chase's Professor Kingsfield, played a World War II veteran now deskbound in Washington. Seizing on a passing reference to the war, a snide young colleague asks, "Do you miss the action of those days, sir?" And Houseman's response was classic. He yanked off his glasses and calmly fired back, "No, I miss the clarity." Well, today in the Persian Gulf, the world is once again faced with the challenge of perfect clarity. Saddam Hussein has given us a whole plateful of clarity, because today, in the Persian Gulf, what we are looking at is good and evil, right and wrong. And day after day, shocking new horrors reveal the true nature of the reign of terror in Kuwait. In one hospital, dialysis patients were ripped from their machines and the machines shipped from Kuwait to Baghdad. Iraq soldiers pulled the plug on incubators supporting 22 premature babies. All 22 died. The hospital employees were shot and the plundered machines were shipped off to Baghdad. But you cannot pull the plug on a nation. The invasion of Kuwait was without provocation. The invasion of Kuwait was without excuse. And the invasion of Kuwait will not stand.

Iraq's invasion marks an outrageous breach of the peace, a broad-faced violation of the United Nations Charter. And by its actions, the Iraqi regime has shown its contempt for the very principles on which the United Nations was founded. Saddam Hussein will be held accountable. Iraq has waged a war of aggression, plundered a peaceful neighbor, held innocents hostage, and gassed its own people. And all four of those crimes are punishable under the principles adopted by the allies in 1945 and unanimously reaffirmed by the United Nations in 1950. Two weeks ago I made mention of the Nuremberg trials. Saddam Hussein must know the stakes are high, the cause is just and, today more than ever, the determination is real.

You know, if you look into history, America never went looking for a war. But in World War II, the world paid dearly for appeasing an aggressor who could have been stopped. Appeasement leads only to further aggression and, ultimately, to war. And we are not going to make the mistake of appeasement again. And one of the other mistakes—one of the other lessons, rather—that America, like it or not, was part of the whole—that was the lesson. And Hitler rejoiced at the news—if you remember your history books—rejoiced at the news from Pearl Harbor. And Adolf Hitler called the attack on Pearl Harbor the turning point of the war. And he was right. But not in the way he thought. Pearl Harbor changed the world and America's role in it for all time.

And you here know that. During the past 3 months, men and women like you from all 50 States have helped to launch what history will judge as one of the most important deployments of allied military power since 1945. But make no mistake: The decision for this deployment was not made in Washington; the decision for this deployment was made by the men in Baghdad. And we are the ones that are standing up for civilized values, standing up for a principle that's almost as old as our Republic.

Franklin Roosevelt put it clearly in a fireside chat, just after Pearl Harbor. He said: "Together with other free people we are now fighting to maintain our right to live among our world neighbors in freedom and in common decency without the fear of assault." And Harry Truman understood this lesson. Almost 10 years after Pearl Harbor

he, too, spoke to the Nation, and he could almost have been talking about Kuwait. "Korea is a small country," he said, "thousands of miles away. But what is happening there," said Truman, "is important to every American." And he called the unprovoked invasion a "direct challenge to the efforts of the free nations to build the kind of world in which men can live in freedom and peace."

And since that time, allied strength and resolve have been tested many, many times. But when we look back on that history of valor and sacrifice, it is clear that the strength of our arms and the strength of our will is up to the challenge that we all face today in the Persian Gulf. And we are not alone—remember this: we are not alone. The United Nations Security Council has passed eight major resolutions setting the terms for solving this crisis. A majority of the Arab League is with us. The Soviet Union and China are with us. And NATO's resolve has never been more firm. And today it is not Iraq against Kuwait, but it is Iraq against the rest of the civilized world. And that message—we must say it over and over again.

And so, this unprecedented unity is a result of hard work and favorable winds—not the winds of war, but the winds of change. And from these magnificent Pacific islands it's easy to see how, with skillful hands at the helm, these winds can carry us towards a future of vast horizons—a dynamic new Asia and a new partnership of nations where free peoples and free markets look to our shore for partnership and security and leadership. The world is still a dangerous place. And those in uniform will always bear the heaviest burden. Perhaps I know something of what you endure—the waiting, the uncertainty, the demands of family and professional life. We want every single American home. No American will be kept in the Gulf a single day longer than necessary, but we will not walk away until our mission is done.

As we meet, it is midday in Hawaii. And soon the Sun will be setting across much of America. An hour of prayer, a day of rest, a nation at peace. And soon many of those prayers will follow the Sun westward across the Pacific and Asia. And soon, like the rays of the Sun itself, those prayers will reach down to carry the light of a new day to the brave men and women standing watch over the sands and shores of the Gulf. Not an hour passes that they are not on my mind. And so, we've come here to thank you for the important work that you—all of you—do in defending our nation's freedom, in keeping our nation strong, and holding high the banner of freedom.

Thank you very much for coming. And

God bless the United States of America. Thank you.

Note: The President spoke at 1:20 p.m. on the tarmac at Hickam Air Force Base. In his opening remarks, he referred to Adm. Huntington Hardisty, commander in chief of the U.S. Pacific Command, and Col. Don A. Lyon, 15th Airbase Wing commander. Following his remarks, the President traveled to San Francisco, CA.

Exchange With Reporters in San Francisco, California
October 29, 1990

The President. Well, let me just say that I'm delighted to be back here. We had a fundraising event for Pete Wilson and I am very encouraged with the support we keep reading about and hearing about for a Senator now about to be Governor. This State is a critical State in the sense of this election coming up. The governorship here is enormously important. It has national importance. And I am enthusiastically for Pete Wilson, and he can give you a little vibration or two as to how he feels it's going. But I like the feel of this campaign.

Senator Wilson. Mr. President, I share your enthusiasm and your optimism. I think it's going well. We are very pleased with the polling numbers that we're seeing and even more pleased with the reaction that we're getting from the crowds. It sure is nice to be back.

The President. Now you don't have to go back there anymore. That's good.

Federal Budget

Q. Can I ask you a question on the budget, Mr. President?

The President. Yes.

Q. Even with this deficit reduction deal the deficit this year is going to go to $250 billion—a record. In over 5 years the debt is going to go from $3 billion to $5 billion—or trillion—excuse me. Doesn't that mean there's a lot more painful medicine out there for the American people?

The President. Well, it means we've had

to swallow some painful medicine. And I'm hopeful that this will have a beneficial effect on the economy, and if we can restore the United States to more reasonable levels of growth, the revenues will pour in. But that means we've got to guard against what I think of as this mentality of taxing and spending.

You know, the minute the budget deal was over, one of the Democratic leaders said, well, now we're going to renew our fight to raise taxes on the rich. That is the old class warfare, tax-and-spend mentality. So, what I'll be doing is taking the message across this country that this resurrecting that tired old philosophy will not get America back to work again. I think we can do better than what these numbers suggest, Terry [Terence Hunt, Associated Press]. But, no, we've taken a major step, and it's a step in the right direction in some ways, but there's plenty of reasons to oppose a lot of it.

Persian Gulf Crisis

Q. Mr. President, now that the Primakov mission in the Middle East has gotten nowhere, is there any chance for anything short of a military solution in the Gulf?

The President. Yes. And I would hope that the economic sanctions, coupled with the worldwide solidarity against Hussein—Saddam Hussein—will convince him that he should, without conditions, get out of

Kuwait.

Q. And negotiations in any form whatsoever?

The President. No—there's no way we're going to have negotiations with conditionality. There's no way to do that. Now, if he gets out of Kuwait and restores the legitimate government, then there's a way to work out difficulties that may have existed. But we're not going to have any preconditions. And so—and the world is holding tight. I think—talking to Mr. Primakov, I think he understands how strongly we feel. I know that he had the same reaction when he talked to President Mubarak [of Egypt]. And I think that President Gorbachev is holding just as firm as he can. And that's good, you see, Ann [Ann Compton, ABC News], because that sends a strong signal that the free world is united against this dictator.

Q. No hope of the Primakov mission coming up with any kind of solution?

The President. I haven't seen anything to convince me that there's anything positive on it.

Q. Mr. President, how do you plan to resupply the Embassy in Kuwait if the U.N. resolution is passed?

The President. Well, I think the best thing is to see that that resolution does pass, and then we'll see. Because this concept of starving embassies is unconscionable and inhumane. And the world reacts angrily against that kind of thing.

Q. But surely you plan to take some action if you're supporting the resolution. How do you plan to carry it out? Do you mean it to be a provocative act?

The President. I plan to see us go forward with the United Nations.

Q. Do you mean it to be a provocative act?

The President. I just will stand with what I've told you. Thank you.

Q. Mr. President, Senator Cohen said this morning that you should not commit troops to action in the Middle East without congressional approval. How do you feel about that?

The President. Well, I'm going to—look forward to having some talks tomorrow with some of the leaders on this question. I know the authorities that a President has.

I'm working to try to get this matter resolved peacefully. We have a lot of force there, and they're well-trained. They're highly motivated, and that alone is sending an enormously strong signal to Saddam Hussein. So, before going into a lot of hypothesis about what I might or might not do, let's take a look at the positive sides and hope that there can be a peaceful resolution. But I'll be talking to the congressional leaders tomorrow.

But history is replete with examples where the President has had to take action. And I've done this in the past and certainly—somebody mentioned provocation—would have no hesitancy at all.

Q. Mr. President, do you object to France trading that planeload of medicine for the 300 hostages they're due to get back today?

The President. No.

Q. You don't see that as a break in the embargo?

The President. No, not medicines—and understand that it's going to be inspected to be sure that medical supplies are what's going there.

Budget Agreement and Upcoming Elections

Q. Will you be to blame if the Republicans sustain big losses a week from now? Will some of that be shouldered by the—blamed by the Presidency and the tax package?

The President. I'm sure somebody will put the blame there. But listen, so what's new? But I'm not looking for defeats; I'm looking for victory. And I'm looking to take this message across the country that this class warfare, tax-the-rich, is really an attack on the working men and women of this country. And so, I'm not trying to make some hypothesis about if things don't go the way I want them to go. But, you know, nobody said it would be easy, so I look for—I'm really getting fired up for the next few days.

Q. Mr. President, why shouldn't Americans feel betrayed that you caved in on raising taxes?

The President. Because I think people know that this Congress is controlled by the taxers, by the liberal Democrats. And they also know that we needed to try to get something done, and they also know that a President is elected to compromise at times—only rarely. But he's also elected to govern. And so I think it's that message that will get—American people are fair. They know I'm against taxes.

The same thing happened to President Reagan in 1982. But when you're up against these enormous majorities, once in a while you've got to reach out. But that's over now. We've got some good things in that deficit package, and we've got some bad things in it. And now I will try to get more Republicans so we don't have to put up with the kind of taxing and spending that we've been through as a country.

Capital Gains Tax

Q. Do you plan to push forth a capital gains tax next year?

The President. I wish we could. I saw George Mitchell [Senate majority leader] go out and say that he wants to raise income tax rates next year. Thank God we held the line on income tax rates, leveled that off at 31 percent. But this idea of as soon as you finish a deficit-reduction package, to say we're going to go out and raise tax rates—I'm going to fight that all the way.

And, of course, I'm for the incentive and the growth and the jobs that go with capital gains. But I don't know whether we're going to—you know, on capital gains, we had a majority in the House and in the Senate for it. But the liberals that controlled it would never let it come to a vote so we could get the action taken. That was amazing, absolutely amazing.

Persian Gulf Crisis

Q. Are you preparing the American public for war?

The President. No.

Q. Do you think it's going to happen?

The President. I'm just doing my job as President of the United States. I'm not preparing anybody for anything. We are going—I am determined as I've ever been that this aggression will not stand. And this coalition is strong, it's diverse, it is holding together. And we're sending a very clear signal to the invader that he's got to get out of Kuwait.

President's Popularity/White House Staff

Q. ——stop the slide in the polls that has stemmed from the budget fight?

The President. Thank God you raised the old polling question. I want you to hear this answer.

Q. We want to hear the question.

The President. The question is about polling, living and dying by polling. Thank God when things were looking pretty good I kept telling every one of you here, these polls don't mean anything. It doesn't mean anything to me. So, what I'll do is get out and say what I believe, work for people that I'm enthusiastic about, and do the very best I can. But I don't live and die by these.

And there's another symbol of all this— it's the inside-the-beltway bickering. God, it's so nice to be out here. You know, about staff. I want to say, I read a story today about the staff—that I am upset with the staff. May I just say to those of you who thrive on the inside-the-beltway chatter, I have never had more confidence in [Chief of Staff] John Sununu, in [Budget Director] Dick Darman, in Secretary Brady—ever. And they are strong, and they are able. And anytime you've got to do some heavy lifting on behalf of the President, you're bound to get caught up in a little crossfire.

So, please don't give any credence to this kind of mischievous, gossipy reporting when we have things like Iraq, budget deficits, enormously important elections. It's just crazy.

Q. But, sir, you have to govern inside the beltway——

Q. ——polls have suggested that perhaps your outfit has been running a little lean and that perhaps you need more political in-house advice.

The President. I've never said that.

Q. Do you think that Governor Sununu is stretched too thin and perhaps you do need more in-house——

The President. I think everybody, including myself, have been stretched thin by these endless negotiations. But I think he's doing an outstanding job. And I don't think that we're short of personnel.

Q. You don't believe Senator Wilson's polls that he's ahead if—you don't believe the polls that show Senator Wilson ahead?

The President. I'll let him speak to that.

Senator Wilson. I believe them. [*Laughter*]

The President. No, I just don't like to comment—live or die on these polls. And I told you, Ann, over and over again when polls were astronomical and "the honeymoon has lasted too long" and—you know, don't let's deal with that. Let's stay on the issues. That's what I'm talking about. And I still feel that way.

Q. But sir, you have to govern inside the beltway. Are you concerned that the "Democrats made me do it" argument might be making you look weak inside the beltway with the people you have to work with?

The President. I don't worry about inside the beltway.

Q. But you have to govern those people, sir.

The President. This is a great American country out here—govern what people? Inside the beltway?

Q. You have to govern with these people. They're the opposition party. They control the Congress.

The President. Oh, the opposition party. Hey, I'm used to that kind of demagoguery. And so, I'm out here on the campaign trail now laying it to rest. They talk about taxing the rich—they want to get into the pocket of every man and woman. The House bill that was passed—let me give you an example. They talked about socking the rich—that indexing provision hit every taxpayer in the United States. And so, I've got to get that in focus, because they've been getting away with this tax-the-rich class warfare kind of garbage that they always resurrect at election time. And we've been under some constraints because I've been trying to get a deficit deal. Now I feel free to go out and take this message across the country.

Q. But my question is, do you think it makes you look weak?

The President. No, I don't think so. I don't think so at all. Everybody knows that the President must govern. Harry Truman was right—the buck does stop there. And every once in a while, you have to do something to make something happen. But I don't think that's a sign of anything other than reality.

Capital Gains Tax

Q. ——go back and seek capital gains, do you then reopen the whole package?

The President. There is a danger to that, and so we've got to be careful how we do that. But I would simply reiterate my conviction about it in saying that it is good for jobs. You know, when you have a slow economy, the more things we can do to stimulate investment and opportunity for working people, it's important. So, there's a big philosophical debate on that, and I am absolutely convinced that it's correct to have a capital gains differential.

Incidentally, there is a small one in this new budget package—very small. So the principle is there, but it's not as much incentive as it should be.

Q. Are we in a recession?

Q. Are you prepared in this case to trade off an increase in rates for a reduction in capital gains? You wouldn't want to trade off a further increase, would you?

The President. Trading—we just got this package, so we'll let that sit for a while. But I'm just saying philosophically I haven't lost my interest in this at all.

Q. Recession?

The President. I don't think so.

Veto of Civil Rights Bill

Q. Mr. President, you are very strong on not wanting to see taxes raised, and you talk about class warfare with the Democrats. Why is it that you're willing to sign this bill, but you vetoed the civil rights bill, when you say you feel strongly about that? Why didn't you not agree to sign this as well?

The President. Let me tell you first about the civil rights bill. I have long stood for civil rights. I think anybody in public life knows that I have long stood for civil rights. But I just don't think it's fair to sign a bill that will result in quotas. The day I vetoed that bill I attached to it a civil rights bill challenging all these proponents of civil rights: Pass a real civil rights bill. And they didn't even permit the House and Senate to vote on it because they wanted to try to embarrass the President. I am for civil rights, and I am against quotas. It is not right to any minority group to pass legislation that is going to result in quotas.

If the leaders of the Congress had been a committed as some say they are to civil rights, why didn't they permit my bill that eliminates discrimination in the workplace to be voted on? It is because they tried to embarrass the President. And they didn't at all, because the American people are fair and they do not want quotas.

Taxes

Q. Mr. President, it sounds like you're willing to veto quotas but not higher taxes. That doesn't sound like a very strong stance.

The President. Give me a chance to veto higher taxes. Send one down there that I can veto, and I will. You're darn right I will, absolutely. I'm glad you raised that. It was a beautiful question, because I am opposed to higher taxes—strongly.

Upcoming Elections

Q. You look like you're going to enjoy this last trip.

The President. I really am looking forward to it.

Q. Are you going to draw blood?

The President. Well, I don't know about blood. I just want to get my message out there, and it's going to be good. We're going to work hard, and we're going to take a positive message across the country: that if we had more Republicans in the United States Congress—Senate and House—I would be able to more easily fulfill the mandate I was given when I was elected President of the United States. I don't like playing defense; I like being on the offense.

Q. Can you beat the odds that—where Presidents usually lose seats?

The President. We're going to wait and see. But I think you raise a point. The party in power normally loses seats, but I'm going to be out there like we're going to win seats and work very hard to do that.

Q. So are these elections now a referendum on you, sir?

The President. I don't know what they're a referendum of. But I want to make them a referendum on the Democrats' taxing and spending and class warfare. I mean, it's absurd. So, we'll see. They have control of both Houses of Congress; they can frustrate the legislative agenda that I want. So, I'd like to see us change that around if we possibly can.

Note: The exchange began at 9:25 a.m. on the tarmac at San Francisco International Airport in San Francisco, CA. A tape was not available for verification of the content of these remarks.

Remarks at a Rally for Gubernatorial Candidate Bill Price in Oklahoma City, Oklahoma
October 29, 1990

I'm delighted to be back here. First, let me pay my respects to a man that campaigned for me way back in the early sixties. He's been my friend and Barbara's friend and your Governor: Henry Bellmon, over here. Henry, delighted to see you, sir. Of course, two who are with us today who are so active in Washington in leadership roles—one in the Senate and one in the House. I'm talking about Senator Don Nickles and, of course, Mickey Edwards, the Congressman. We're delighted to have them with us here today.

Bill, thank you for that introduction. Oh, what a joy it is to be with your wonderful family. Barbara sends her love. It's not that our dog is writing another book, but she, too, is out on the campaign trail. I'm just delighted to bring you her greetings. It's a pleasure to be here for a man who will make a difference—he always has—your next Governor, Bill Price. All of you know his story. Well-qualified man—well-qualified. The son of a doctor. Went to Georgetown U, Ohio U—Ohio—OU—[*laughter*]—Oklahoma University Law School, the Big

Red. Finally, he became, as he referred there to it, U.S. Attorney for western Oklahoma, supporting law and order, battling against the craze of narcotics. He's been a good man, a great servant to this country—and now you've got to elect him Governor of this State.

I have looked at the record. He has conviction. He's not a follower who gets lost in the current. He's a profile in character who alters the tide. Look at how he cracked America's then-largest corruption case back in the early eighties. Or his work for the organization he founded, the Oklahoma Alliance Against Drugs. We need a leader with his vision to follow Henry in Oklahoma City. I'm here to talk for Bill, not against his opponent. And I refuse to take it personally that his opponent was the Dukakis chairman in this State—had nothing to do with my being here.

We could use more of his kind of thinking back East, too. All Americans are asking: What on Earth is wrong with Washington? And I know you've been standing, but let me give you the full load about how I see it, as one who thinks we need to change this Congress out and get more Republicans and fewer of those liberal Democrats.

After what seemed like endless negotiations, we finally have a budget. And the negotiations were tough because the one party that has ruled Congress for almost 40 years is dedicated to perpetual reelection. And that party, the Democratic Party, has a bias for redtape over choice, for Washington solutions over community solutions, and for bureaucracy over people. And you add all of this up, and what do you get? You get a liberal Democratic-controlled Congress that's committed to two things: taxing and spending. We went into negotiation, and the final agreement is an example of how the Democratic Congress works—or doesn't work. For the sake of the Nation, I honestly felt that we had to reduce the deficit now. It is high time that we stop mortgaging the future of these young kids here today. And the Democratic spending binge has got to stop.

I discovered, as Harry Truman did, that the buck does stop there on the desk in the Oval Office, and every once in a while, a President of the opposite party than the one that controls the Congress has got to make a compromise. And I felt really that we had to reach an agreement, and I felt strongly about reducing the deficit with spending cuts, not raising taxes. And in fact, that's exactly the kind of budget that I sent to the Congress last February. Predictably, the Democrats instead wanted to slash defense and then raise your taxes. What we got was a compromise.

And there is some good in it. We've got $492 billion in deficit reduction over 5 years; over $350 billion in spending cuts—the largest cut in history. There are some incentives built in it so that we will become less dependent on foreign oil—incentives to stimulate domestic oil and gas drilling and production. And we also got Congress to reduce the rate of spending growth with the first-ever 5-year curb on spending.

Now, we put Congress on a pay-as-you-go plan so that the liberal Democrats will no longer be able to fund programs with red ink. This agreement has strong enforcement provisions. And if Congress tries to raise spending one dime, they've got to cut other excess spending or find the money for it right there and then.

And finally, we held the line—and this one is very important to me and, I believe, to the people of Oklahoma and the whole country—we held the line against the reckless cuts of our Armed Forces. I will not be the President to provide [preside] over the weakening of this nation's defense.

An enforceable deficit reduction agreement is unprecedented. It is long overdue and it is absolutely necessary, but I cannot join the liberal Democrats in an orgy of self-congratulation. After all, we discussed three kinds of proposals: the good, the bad, and the ugly. And I told you about the good. Now let me tell you about the bad—in a word, the taxes. To get an agreement we had to pay a ransom to get the $350 billion in spending cuts. And the American people have had to pay a price for divided government.

But the price could have been worse. The Democrats' bill that passed the House before this compromise that was enacted—that Democratic bill tried to raise income taxes on all working Americans. And they attacked these indexing provisions of the current tax law in a way that raised taxes on every hardworking citizen. And they called it their bill to soak the rich, and what it really did is go after the paycheck of the working man and woman in this country. And we said, we are going to stop you—and we stopped them cold. And let me say this: that was not—and I am grateful to Mickey Edwards and I'm grateful to Don Nickles for their stand—that was not, as these demagogs would have you believe, Republicans protecting the rich; that was Republicans standing up for the working family in this country.

And now we're hearing it again. Some of us are old enough to remember this. It happens all the time with the Democrats. And let those liberals that control Congress raise their ugly old cry of divisiveness and class warfare and of soaking the rich. And we, the Republicans, are going to continue fighting for the working people by holding the line on taxes. You send me more Republicans for the United States Congress, and we'll get the job done.

I don't want you to get the feeling I'm down on the Democratic Congress—[laughter]—but the budget was due last April. The Democratic Congress came to me 6 months late—so late, in fact, that we are on the brink now of an economic downturn. And it's time to call them as you see them, to tell it like it is. And this agreement could have come together in May, in June, or in August—anytime during the last 6 months. But the Democrats choked the throttle, pulled the throttle back of a slowing economy while they hunted for every last morsel of partisan advantage, all in the name of politics and of higher taxes. And we're not going to let them get away with it.

In April, when the budget was due, unemployment was 5.4 percent—a troubling sign. Unemployment last month was 5.7 percent. And since April, when the budget was due, inflation has accelerated and economic growth has slowed. Even after the economy was threatened by the Persian Gulf crisis, Congress delayed. This Congress was content to stall an agreement and stall the economy. We are not going to let them get away with it. There are Congressmen, thank heavens, there are Congressmen—

and you've got some good ones from this State, men like Jim Inhofe and Mickey Edwards and our distinguished Senator Don Nickles—who reject this failed tradition of tax and spend. But they're outnumbered by the big taxers and the big spenders. These three are the real defenders of working America, and I am grateful indeed that they are fighting for you and for Oklahoma and, I'd say, for America up there on Capitol Hill.

You know, as we got into these negotiations, even in the middle of them, the big spenders were looking for the pork-barrel bonanzas. At the 11th hour, in the midst of the budget crisis, congressional conferees on one panel alone pushed through an almost 19-percent increase for pet projects. At the same time, this President and these Republican Members were doing our level-best to curtail spending, Congress voted to spend a half a million dollars to create a Lawrence Welk tourist attraction. And we all like Lawrence Welk—"dah-dee-dah"—you know how he is. [Laughter] But I cite this as a symptom of the problem.

Audience member. Get the line-item veto.

The President. I'm getting to that. [Laughter] Believe me, the American people know when their Congress asks them to tighten their belts and Congress loosens its own. And I'll tell you what I'd like to do about it. Yes, give me what 43 Governors have: Give me the line-item veto. They've failed to cut spending. Let me have a shot at it. While we're at it, let's have a balanced-budget amendment that would discipline the Executive and darn sure would discipline the Democrats in the House of Representatives and the Senate.

There's one other tool I need even more than the line-item veto and a balanced-budget amendment. And I really mean it: that is more Republicans in Congress that think the way these two do. God, I'm glad to be out of Washington. I am thrilled to be out of Washington. And let me say, I hear that talk back there that people don't know the difference between the Republicans and the liberal Democrats. In education, we are the ones that are fighting for reform to empower parents to choose their children's schools. In child care, Republicans are the ones who demanded reform to empower parents to choose who will watch over their children. And we now have that bill, as a matter of fact. And we're the ones still determined to bring hope and opportunity to the most desolate of the inner cities.

The Democrats are still pushing that old line of liberal programs, more taxes, more bureaucracy, more government control—tell the people of Oklahoma City how to mandate things, tell them what they've got to do. They're still peddling that tired old saw about Republicans and the rich. Well, you and I both know that that is hogwash, and we're not going to let them get away with that anymore. I'm taking this message all across the country: We are for the working people in this country.

This is a Congress that can only act at the last minute when their political feet were held to the fire, a Congress who would rather pass feel-good proclamations than address problems. Look, this is the Congress that passed a resolution called National Crime Prevention Month while it gutted, took the heart right out of our anticrime bill. Bill Price knows that we need strong Federal legislation to back up our prosecutors and our law enforcement officials. And Congress passed that crazy Crime Prevention Month, but did nothing about the toughness of the crime bill that we called for.

This is the Congress that declared Clean Water Month, but bickered for months over the clean air bill. And if you find all this tough to swallow, don't worry—they've also served up National Digestive Disease Awareness Month. [*Laughter*] But I guarantee you one thing: If they send me that bill to make these kids eat their broccoli, I will veto that legislation. No liberal Democrat Congress—and notice I say "liberal Democrat Congress." I know my State next door. And I know the State here, and there's plenty of sound conservative Democrats in the State of Oklahoma that are going to vote for the next Governor standing right here.

But this liberal Democrat Congress has become America's biggest and most entrenched special interest. In 1959, Congress was served by 5,800 staff members. Today it is served by almost 20,000 staff members,

who control the perks and pass out the pork. And the Democratic Congress is a confusion of committees and turf-conscious chaos. The House intended to be closest to the people has become a House of Lords—98 percent who seek reelection and reelection—and it is time to turn the tables. The American people deserve a new Congress—this time a Republican Congress. And they still block my proposals for campaign reform. We want to abolish special interest PAC's. The Democrats want the taxpayer to foot the bill for the reelection. Democrats talk about taxing the rich, but they all want to have every one of us throw in money for congressional elections. America needs a change. America needs a better deal.

You know, maybe I'm a little old-fashioned, but I think that a $1.3 trillion budget gives us ample room to dream again, to advance new ideas, to renew our government, to rethink and to restructure our priorities. But the Democratic Congress would rather raise taxes than raise the issue of reform. The problem isn't with the American people and their dream; the problem is this Democrat Congress that protects its perks and privileges and turns its back on the American dream. And I say we have had enough. That bill 2 weeks ago by the Democratic Congress would have raised the income taxes on every working family in America. They call it soak the rich—every single family, because of the indexing, would have had a tax increase. And we fought it, and we beat it. And America needs a Republican Congress that will balance the budget by cutting spending, not by raising taxes on everybody here.

The Democratic Congress turned its back on our police officers. America needs a Republican Congress that will pass those laws that are necessary to finally get tough on crime. And there's only one way, there is only one way to send this message to Washington, and that is not to send the liberal Democrats back there so they can keep on going down the same tired old road.

You know, last month Oklahoma voters sent politicians a message, and they voted overwhelmingly to restrict State legislative terms to 12 years. Next week voters across this country can follow your lead. Term limitations applying to State officials will be on the ballot in California and in Colorado. But America doesn't have to wait for a ballot initiative to limit the terms of the Democrats in Congress; they can start next Tuesday. I have great confidence in the American people, the American ideals, which is why the remaining days of this campaign, and for the rest of Presidency, I'll take a message out there to the people: America doesn't need a liberal House of Lords. America needs a responsible Congress. America needs a Republican Congress.

Harry Truman reminded us that only a President represents all the people, can stand for the national interest and stand against the special interests. And in this spirit—I think you'll all remember this—I did extend my hand. I worked for a bipartisan solution to this horrible budget mess. And you sent me to Washington to govern, to make something good happen for our country. And I've tried very hard, only to have a parade of liberal Democrats march to the microphone in the well of the House to blame me for their failures. And my good will has been rewarded with business as usual. Well, I'll tell you something: America has had enough of business as usual, and we don't have to take it anymore. I say send me more Members of Congress who will

vote like these two here today. I need them up there. And here in this State, people think straight and they like straight talk. So, do your talking at the polls on November 6th, and roll up your sleeves and elect this good man Governor of the State of Oklahoma because you deserve the best.

And as for me—I know you're glad this is over; it's hot in here. But I'm just getting warmed up. But I'm really not. [*Laughter*] As for me, I'll tell you what I'm going to do. I'm going to crisscross this country from coast to coast and take this message to the American people: More Republican Congressmen means more men and women fighting against raising taxes and against the big spenders, and for the values of faith and family, government close to the people that everybody in the State of Oklahoma believes in. More Republicans means a better deal for America. And it doesn't get any straighter than that. And I can't wait to get out on that campaign trail for the rest of the days before the elections.

Thank you. Elect this good man Governor. And God bless the United States of America. Thank you all very much.

Note: The President spoke at 3:40 p.m. at the Cowboy Hall of Fame. Following his remarks, the President returned to Washington, DC.

Remarks Congratulating the Cincinnati Reds on Winning the World Series
October 30, 1990

Well, please be seated. Great fall day in the Rose Garden. And, Marge, welcome to you and Lou Piniella, the players, the coaches, and the official family of the 1990 Cincinnati Reds. I want to look around at our dignitaries here, but Senator Glenn is here, Congressman Gradison, Congressman Luken, Paul Gillmor from Ohio. And then from across the river—whoops, I don't see him, I thought—there he is, modestly in the second row, Jim Bunning, played good old country hardball in his day. And another one, Vinegar Bend, I did see over here.

Welcome, all of you and all the rest. And I want to welcome our umpires, Larry Barnett, Rocky Roe, Jim Quick, Ted Hendry, Frank Pulli, Randy Marsh, and also Bruce Froemming, who can't be with us today. Seldom do the players and families cheer the umpires, but we're glad you're here. Delighted you're here.

Just a minute. A little dissent—I think I can handle it. [*Laughter*] Listen, I might mention that this is the 40th anniversary of the Babe Ruth Baseball League. And we're lucky to have the four Babe Ruth championship teams of 1990 with us today: Staten Island; Youngstown, Ohio; and yes, two from a city whose team visited here last October—Oakland, California. Why don't you guys all stand up, if you would. Here we go. Welcome. Welcome, all of you. You guys better watch out for your jobs—some of these people. And best wishes we bring you from the most charismatic member of the Bush family, the MVP, the Most Valuable Pooch. Schottzie—tell her Millie sends her love and in a minute we'll bring out the dog so you can at least say hello, because we missed them. Let me welcome all of you to the White House and to this most appropriate salute to the Cincinnati Reds, a team of heart which achieved its impossible dream.

Marge, I know that I risk this because I know Bobby Brown is president of the American League, but let me tell you about a story, how as a player for the Yanks he roomed with one of my favorite philosophers, Yogi Berra. And Bob and Yogi were reading late at night in their hotel room. Bobby was studying a medical journal, and Yogi, a comic book. And finally, Yogi put the magazine down, turned off the light, and said, "Bobby, my book had a happy ending. How did yours come out?" Well, to members of this newest Big Red Machine, the story of the 1990 Reds had the happiest of endings: a world championship for America's oldest baseball franchise, for some of America's best baseball fans, for a team that looked its opponent in the eye and made the opponents blink.

Today we're talking baseball and a team that won 91 games in the regular season, leading wire to wire the first time in league history. We're talking the team that beat a marvelous Pirates club in the playoffs. And they were good. And I hope our guided missiles are as straight as Eric Davis' throw to nab Bobby Bonilla. This is the team that swept the defending champion Oakland A's in an unforgettable World Series. And what moments you have given all of us that love baseball. And what memories we have of one of the greatest bullpens in baseball's tide of times. You know how the Reds spell relief: N-A-S-T-Y. [*Laughter*]

And of the Series' most valuable player—Jose Rijo—yielding all of 1 run in 15-plus innings. Maybe you can help us with the interest rates—you get the ERA [earned run average] down, now it's the interest rates. [*Laughter*] And then Billy Hatcher—seven straight hits. Nine for twelve in the Series. And yes, Eric the Red, whom I wish continued recovery. And when I talk to Mr. Gorbachev about offensive weapons, I'm going to tell him number 44's bat is not negotiable. [*Laughter*]

Go anywhere—they love the Reds. Go to Dayton or Louisville or Des Moines or Siler City, and they'll tell you about heroics too numerous to mention. Glenn Braggs and Barry Larkin fielding brilliantly. Joe Oliver winning game 2 with a memorable base hit. And Chris Sabo, he's off in Japan, but his three home runs are still in orbit someplace. And Paul O'Neill and, yes, Tom Browning, the man who combined a World Series and the birth of a son—batting a thousand along the way. And each of these men and so many others were dedicated to a cause—bringing the world's championship back to the banks of the Ohio. You achieved that goal. And to you, Lou—Lou Piniella—let me say you've been an inspiration to all of us that love the game. All of us you showed why two of the most beautiful words in any language—all of you showed us—play ball!

Reds broadcaster Joe Nuxhall often says that "This is the Old Left-hander rounding third and heading for home." And this year home for one of sports' greatest franchises was the 1990 world championship. So let me leave you by quoting another Reds announcer, Marty Brennaman: "This one belonged to the Reds." And when it comes to baseball, Cincinnati is truly number one. Thank you for coming here, congratulations, and God bless the United States. Thank you all.

Note: The President spoke at 1:33 p.m. in the Rose Garden at the White House. In his remarks, he referred to team owner Marge Schotte, manager Lou Piniella, and Representative Jim Bunning.

Remarks at the Republican National Committee Election Countdown Rally
October 30, 1990

Good to see you all. Thank you very much. Let me just say that it's terrific to see so many good friends of this administration and of this country. Barbara and I are delighted to be with you, and I want to salute the members of my Cabinet who are up here with me. You know, I am blessed as a President to have such an outstanding Cabinet working for this country every single day. They're good, they're strong, they're principled, and I am very, very fortunate.

I'm told that in addition to these Cabinet members, why, our able Administrator, my friend Bill Reilly is here, Bruce Gelb from USIA, Paul Coverdell. And also, of course, I want to single out two or three who are here that have just worked their hearts out on recent events in Washington, and I'm talking about our Chief of Staff John Sununu, Dick Darman, and Secretary Brady, who have done an outstanding job wrestling with the United States Senate and the House.

And, of course, I wanted to come over and express my personal gratitude to Charlie Black and to Jeanie Austin, who are leading our party at this critical time, and to say to other friends of Lee Atwater's—and all of us are—Lee continues to be a great inspiration to both Barbara and to me and all of our family. And I'm sure he is to each and every one of you, too.

I wanted to come over here at this time and talk to you, the faithful, those that are standing there getting the job done day in and day out, because election day is exactly 1 week from today. I look at it as opportunity day, a day when America's voters will have the opportunity to do something: to vote for change and to vent their frustration, their anger, and the betrayal that they have felt at the hands of the unresponsive and irresponsible Democratic Congress.

You know, I read about voter frustration, but America has the opportunity to send that crowd up there on Capitol Hill, that one party that's controlled Congress for year after year after year—the Democrats—

send them a message by sending more Republicans to Congress.

You know, this country faced an enormous challenge here, a challenge of, I'd say, tremendous consequences: a Federal budget deficit spiraling into the hundreds of billions of dollars, and the Democratic philosophy of tax and spend was coming home to roost. And I was elected to make some tough decisions, to govern.

At times, every President finds that he's had to compromise for the good of the country. And I reached out my hand—I think everybody here knows it, and I think people all across the country know that I tried to reach out my hand to work with the Democrats in Congress. They control the House, they control the Senate. And I tried very hard to do that, only to have a parade of liberal Democrats march to the microphone in the well of the House to blame me for their own failures.

Well, I believe we've had enough of that. And now we get to take our case to the American people. You see, we can—we can send a message to every Democratic Congressman or Senator who mortgaged the future of our kids. To every Democrat who tried to raise income taxes, not as they say on the rich but on every working American, and to every Democrat who's part of this Democratic spending binge: Americans say we're not going to take it anymore, because this is our country and it belongs to those who work in the fields and in the factories, who run the small businesses, who teach our kids, who protect the land. And each one is every bit as much a part of the American dream as the privileged few who roam the congressional corridors of power. And I want to abolish, for example, I want to abolish these special interest PAC's, and Democrats don't. Democrats want the taxpayers to underwrite the bill for their own reelection, and I don't. And if we have more Republicans on Capitol Hill, Uncle Sam won't foot the bill for Democratic campaigns.

Democrats may be busy taking care of their special interests and these reelection interests. And they may have forgotten their most basic sacred trust is the common interest. Well, I don't think we have forgotten. And I think Americans are going to remember who stands with these values that we all believe and that I've campaigned on and still feel fervently about. It's the Republicans who were looking out for the working men and women of this country.

And who would have thought that the finest instincts and ideals of Jefferson and Adams would have come down to this: an arrogant majority that uses its power to protect its own prerogative, its own perks, its own privileges, its own pet projects. And it is time that American people say enough is enough. No more Democratic control of the Congress.

You know, they say there are two things you should never watch being made: sausage and laws. [*Laughter*] When it comes to the Democrats in Congress, I'd say this year has been—we've all been taken on a first-class tour of the hot dog factory. [*Laughter*]

I was disappointed but not surprised—the minute that this budget deficit agreement was reached—disappointed but not surprised to hear a Democratic leader say that the Democrats will continue to demand higher taxes, raising the income tax rates next year. Disappointed to hear the distortion of Republican motives, goals, and accomplishments. Disappointed to hear the clumsy explanation of the Democrats' attempt to raise $40 billion—this is the figure from the recent Democrat-passed bill in the House—$40 billion in new income taxes on working Americans. And at the same time they were talking about soaking the rich—there was a $4 billion surtax proposal in there—$4 billion for that, and $40 billion trying to sock it to every working man and woman in this country. The rhetoric is wrong, and their purpose is wrong. And we're not going to let them get away with it.

After 6 endless, 6 endless months of budget negotiations, we finally got a deal. We fought for what's good in the package. I think the spending cuts, when you look at them, are good. The entitlement reform is good. The tough enforcement provisions are better than I thought we could ever get in any way out of this Congress. But for 6 months, the Democrats stalled. For 6 months this Congress stalled the budget agreement and, in my view, risked stalling the economy. They tried to pull back the throttle on this economy, all in the name of politics and higher taxes. And the American people can hold them responsible because we are not going to let them get away with it.

All in all, this budget agreement is unprecedented. It is long overdue, and in my view, it is essential. And every time I see out there across the country some young kid or a class of third graders, I think to myself: We have got to do something to stop mortgaging the future of these young people. It isn't fair, and it isn't right, and the tax and spend mentality has gone too far when you see us with $500 billion added to the deficit over and over again.

We got nearly $350 billion in spending cuts, and almost $500 billion—$492 billion I believe was the figure—in total deficit reduction. But to get an agreement, there was a ransom. And that ransom was taxes. And, after all, the Democrats' chant has always been tax and spend and damn the deficit. And we pushed hard to cut spending, to get the deficit down. And I just simply could not bring myself to leave America's children an avalanche of unpaid bills.

The issue is larger than one budget agreement or one session of Congress or one election. It may sound corny, but it's about the American dream. It's about the differences between the parties and who can best build a better America. It's about America's families and America's values and who represents them. And I think you know the answer: Republicans do.

You know the difference between Republicans and Democrats. We are the ones fighting for family perspective in this year's legislation—in education, in child care, in housing. And we're going to keep right on fighting. And we're the ones determined to bring hope and opportunity to the millions forgotten by the Democrats. And we won't give up on them. We're the ones with more sympathy for the victims of crime than for the criminals. And that was in my bill that got shuttered aside, parts of it passing but the toughest parts held up by the liberal Democrats in the House of Representatives. We're going to keep on supporting our police officers. And we're the ones who understand that the world remains a dangerous place and that American leadership can meet the challenges of an uncertain world. And America will continue to lead because Republicans will not undermine America's strength.

I just came back yesterday from California and Oklahoma, and there, as all around this country, there's a growing momentum for limiting terms of legislators. The biggest, most entrenched special interest in America is right here. And in 1988, the Republican platform called for limiting the terms for Members of Congress. Republicans were the ones out 2 years ago leading the call. Term limitation is an idea whose time has come. And I think its time has come to Capitol Hill, frankly.

Another good thing about getting out in the country, you see what works, see how Governors make things happen. Let me tell you what works. Forty-three Governors already have it; Governor Deukmejian used it 4,000 times. And I'm talking, of course, about the line-item veto. If Congress can't cut spending, give a President a shot. Give me the line-item veto and see what we can do. These ideas work. This is an idea that is working in the States, and most of the States have balanced budget amendments. I'd like to see one of those for the entire country. Let's get out and campaign for it.

We really do need a government of more Republicans from the breadths of this great nation who owe their allegiance to the communities of our 50 States, not to the Democratic tax-and-spend dogma of Capitol Hill; a government led by men and women with a sense of history, with a sense of the potential of this country and of every American, with a willingness to make difficult choices on behalf of the national interest; and men and women who have a genuine vision, the kind of vision that enabled this administration to drag some important legislation out of a gridlocked Democratic Congress. Remember, both Houses, the Senate and the House, in the hands of the Democrats.

We got a good Clean Air Act, and I think that's good for the entire United States of America and internationally as well. We had to pull it out, and it worked. We got a child-care bill out of this deficit agreement, and it's a good one—doesn't give central government control over all child care—it empowers parents.

We got a good, fair, and effective Americans with Disabilities Act—a landmark piece of legislation in terms of fair play long overdue. We got a Defense budget that in my view protects our nation's security. It was under vicious assault and vicious attack from the liberal elements in the Democrats in both the House and the Senate. But thanks to the negotiating of those right here and the work of our Secretary of Defense, we got a reasonably good Defense number, one where I can certify to the American people we can keep our interests wherever they may be. We can keep our commitment. And we built some incentives, finally, into our budget agreement for oil and gas explorations so that we will be less dependent on foreign oil.

And that brings me to another piece of news—I was talking to Secretary Watkins about this—that I want to tell Americans about, all Americans. Thanks to a combination of markedly increased world production and consumption measures, the gap in oil supply created by the loss of Iraq and Kuwait production has been closed. And under current circumstances, consumers can count on adequate supplies of petroleum products. And that is good news for all Americans.

In times of crisis and challenge, the American spirit has been a constant source of strength. It's true now, obviously, in the Persian Gulf, and it's just as true at home today. Because across this land still pulses the generosity and the optimism of the true American spirit, the spirit to which Republicans are responding. We will reform this city in the Capital, revive this institution, renew this nation, and together we can keep this country strong and compassionate and idealistic. And we'll do it by bringing this country what we deserve: a better deal.

And I'm going to be carrying that message to the American people. And today

I'm here in Washington within sight of the Capitol Dome, but I'll go the vineyards of California and the farms of Ohio, to the shores of Massachusetts and out to the oil fields in Texas. And every time I talk to the American people, I'm going to tell them this: More Republicans in Congress means more men and women fighting against raising taxes and against the big spenders. More Republicans means a better deal for America.

And I wanted to thank each and every one of you. And with a week to go before the election, please keep it up. Redouble your efforts. We can make a difference for this, the greatest and freest country on the face of the Earth. God bless you and God bless America. Thank you all very much.

Note: The President spoke at 2:20 p.m. in the Regency Ballroom of the Hyatt Regency Hotel. In his remarks, he referred to William K. Reilly, Administrator of the Environmental Protection Agency; Bruce S. Gelb, Director of the U.S. Information Agency; Paul D. Coverdell, Director of the Peace Corps; Richard G. Darman, Director of the Office of Management and Budget; Charlie Black, Jeanie Austin, and H. Lee Atwater, spokesman, cochairman, and chairman of the Republican National Committee; and Gov. George Deukmejian of California.

Statement on Signing the Bill Reauthorizing Native American Higher Education Assistance
October 30, 1990

Today, I am signing S. 2167, a bill "To reauthorize the Tribally Controlled Community College Assistance Act of 1978 and the Navajo Community College Act." In approving this legislation, I recognize and acknowledge the tribal colleges for the contribution they have made and continue to make in improving the quality of life for many American Indian people. Tribal colleges represent an opportunity for many American Indians to develop academic knowledge and job-related skills and become contributors to the economy both on and off Indian reservations. In addition, the tribal colleges are excellent examples of the Administration's policy of self-determination for Indian tribes.

I note that section 106(b) of the Act purports to require the President, within 1 year of enactment, to submit a report to the Congress containing recommendations for amendments to certain Federal laws. The Constitution grants to the President the power to recommend to the Congress such measures as he judges necessary and expedient. Because of this power, provisions such as the one contained in this bill have been treated as advisory and not mandatory. I will, therefore, interpret section 106(b) accordingly.

I also note that section 105 of the Act provides that the right of Native Americans to express themselves through the use of Native American languages shall not be restricted in any public proceeding. Such proceedings include publicly supported education programs. I construe this provision as a statement of general policy and do not understand it to confer a private right of action on any individual or group.

GEORGE BUSH

The White House,
October 30, 1990.

Note: S. 2167, approved October 30, was assigned Public Law No. 101–477.

Exchange With Reporters in Alexandria, Virginia
October 31, 1990

The President. ——anticrime legislation that I sent up to Congress a long time ago, talking about many issues that I think are of benefit not just to the people of northern Virginia but of the whole country. We need more people like Stan Parris, and I'll be telling them that, too.

Q. Mr. President, are you using the situation at the Kuwaiti Embassy——

The President. Just to say the things I like about it and the things I don't, but we'll be talking about some of that. But the main thing is the positive agenda and the things that he has stood for and fought for. And my view is that if I had more support like that in the Congress, not only would we not have fiscal problems out there—the same ones that we're trying to do something about—but we'd be much better off on a positive agenda for all America.

I think we're on the right track, but we just need to be sure we have this kind of support. We talk about this in family values and the values and incentives, and growth and opportunity. His voting record is the kind we need. We don't need more of where the Government has to do everything—the mandated program. I think they don't work. So, it's a great positive agenda that I'll be discussing in there.

Persian Gulf Crisis

Q. Kuwaiti Embassy, Mr. President? What's the situation this morning, and is this situation——

The President. I haven't talked—this morning—I haven't seen the intelligence. I came right here from the White House.

Q. Well, Mr. President——

Q. Is this situation being used as a pretext for a confrontation?

The President. No, there's no pretext. You don't use pretext when you have force deployed. You don't need any pretext; you just do what's right. I am concerned about the lives of Americans held against their will. So are the American people. When you see the United Nations act in concert, the United Nations is concerned. So, there's no pretext involved. I'm simply trying to have

the American people understand how strongly I feel about the brutality of Saddam Hussein's policy. And it's been condemned by the world, and we ought to do something about it. These are American citizens that are held against their will. There are a lot of other citizens that have been just destroyed in Kuwait as he has dismantled it. I think world opinion is saying he's got to stop it.

Q. Well, Mr. President, yesterday in that meeting with congressional leaders there was some concern that that distress for the hostages, for the Embassy in Kuwait, not provoke the U.S. into a premature military response. Do you feel at all that your hand is being forced at this point?

The President. No. I don't think so at all.

Q. Mr. President, is Secretary Baker going to be discussing, during his trip, scenarios for possible military responses?

The President. He will cover a wide array of issues with these leaders over there. I was trying hard to keep our coalition partners fully informed. I will share with them, through Secretary Baker, the concerns that I feel about Americans that are held hostage and other citizens that are held hostage. We will discuss, obviously, the United Nations resolutions condemning the treatment of embassy personnel. And so, it's going to be a wide array of topics to discuss. I'm very pleased that the coalition is together. So, we just have to stay in close touch. I'll be doing some, I'm sure, by phone myself. But the Baker trip is very important.

Q. What are you going to do about resupplying the Embassy at this point?

The President. Well, I can't tell you exactly what I'm going to do.

Q. Well, how soon? Let's put it that way.

Q. Mr. President, what is the end line? In other words, how do you know you've reached the end?

The President. Well, it's a very difficult—appropriate question and very difficult. But we're still moving force, and we have a significant coalition of armed forces on the ground. We'll just have to wait and see. In the meantime, we will send a steady, strong message to Saddam Hussein that we are not going to tolerate this aggression.

Q. You haven't mentioned sanctions at all.

The President. And when you look at world opinion and statements from world leaders, there is an enormous coalition there still together, unanimous in its condemnation. So, we've just got to keep that in focus and keep doing what we're doing: quietly, but significantly, being prepared.

Q. Do you have a timeframe in mind?

The President. A timeframe for what?

Q. Action in Iraq.

Q. Is time running out for the sanctions?

The President. There's no date of that nature in mind. But we're doing absolutely everything to be sure we safeguard American life, protect Saudi Arabia against aggression, and also to see that we are in a position to help fulfill the United Nations resolution.

Q. Are you becoming impatient, Mr. President? Are you becoming impatient?

The President. I'm not impatient, no. Just going steadily, doing my job.

Q. But, sir——

The President. And so are all our allies.

Q. Because of your concerns, though, sir, can you afford to continue on, waiting for sanctions to take effect?

The President. I am prepared at this juncture to wait to see if economic sanctions will work—at this juncture.

Q. Are you disappointed with the progress today? Marlin said yesterday it was clear they hadn't been successful.

The President. I wouldn't say that they had not been successful at all, but they certainly haven't driven the man to do what he should have done, which is to get out of Kuwait and reverse this aggression. But I think that that's what Marlin was saying—they had not been totally effective.

Q. Did you think they'd have a quicker effect?

The President. Well, Norm [Norman Sandler, United Press International], there's been differences of opinion. I know some of our partners thought that the economic pressure by now would have come close to compelling him to withdraw. I've not had a

view on that because it's such a major undertaking—economic sanctions—that I haven't really been thinking in terms of time lines.

Q. Are the hostages becoming a more important factor in the equation, in what you do?

The President. No more important, but they are tremendously important. Any factor—and I've always said this—anytime an American or anybody else is held against their will in direct contravention of international law, it concerns me. I wouldn't say more, but I am very, very concerned about it. I think any President would have to be. I know that other leaders to whom I've talked around the world feel the same way about their citizens. I mean, the Soviets do; I mean, the Japanese have. And so, it's brutal what he's doing. It is total brutality and in direct contravention of international law. I think it is important that Saddam Hussein know just how seriously we view this matter——

Q. You suggested, sir——

The President. ——so it's worth repeating from time to time.

Q. You suggested early on, I think, that the hostages wouldn't drive U.S. policy. Is that still——

The President. Exactly.

Q. ——is that still your position?

The President. Yes, it is still my firmly held position.

Q. Are you still comfortable with that?

The President. Yes. Very comfortable with it, very comfortable.

Q. But you're elevating the importance of the situation at the Kuwaiti Embassy and the importance of the hostages. Are you, in fact——

The President. The Kuwaiti Embassy is being starved. The people out there are not being resupplied. The American flag is flying over the Kuwaiti Embassy, and our people inside are being starved by a brutal dictator. And do you think I'm concerned about it? You're darn right I am. And what I'm going to do about it? Let's just wait and see. Because I have had it with that kind of treatment of Americans. And I know others feel that way. I know Margaret Thatcher feels that way about the Brits. I think the whole world feels outraged by this. So, of course I'm concerned. As each day goes by and these Americans are isolated, cut off from supplies, who wouldn't be concerned? The American people are concerned—those that understand this have this message. So, you should think very carefully about what he's doing there.

Q. Do you have a plan in mind for resupplying the Embassy, or how are you going to do that?

The President. If I did, I wouldn't discuss it here.

Civil Rights Bill

Q. What was in the civil rights bill that told you it would lead to quotas?

The President. The public—the necessity—part of it. And I sent a civil rights bill up there that they didn't even vote on. And why? Because they didn't want to give the President a chance to continue a strong civil rights record. It was a good piece of legislation, and the Congress wouldn't even permit a vote unless it was done just the way a handful of leaders—civil rights leaders—wanted it done.

I've compromised; I've tried to work it out. We had a deal with Ted Kennedy, and he reneged on the deal. So, I am for civil rights, and I am strongly opposed to quotas.

It's that public necessity part that inevitably would have led to quotas. It's not fair to black Americans; it's not fair to Hispanic Americans; it's not fair to Asian-Americans. So, I am glad to have a chance to set the record straight on that one, and I will push for civil rights legislation that removes discrimination in the workplace, but I will not accept quotas. That message has to get through loud and clear, because there's been a lot of demagoguery on the other side of that now. I am right, and I think the American people will strongly support me.

It's highly technical. It's highly technical. But I'm glad to have the opportunity to say that I will continue to push for strong civil rights legislation, and I will continue to fight against legislation that will result in quotas in the workplace.

Any others? It's been a pleasure—so early, and a beautiful day.

Note: The exchange began at 7:35 a.m. on the lawn of Belle Haven Country Club, prior to a fundraising breakfast for Representative Stan Parris. In his remarks, President Bush referred to President Saddam Hussein of Iraq; Marlin Fitzwater, Press Secretary to the President; Prime Minister Margaret Thatcher of the United Kingdom; and Senator Edward M. Kennedy.

Remarks at a Fundraising Breakfast for Representative Stan Parris in Alexandria, Virginia
October 31, 1990

The President. Thank you very, very much. It's a pleasure to be here. I am simply delighted to be here with Stan. We talked about this a couple of months ago. Given the schedule and the demands on one's time, I haven't been able to do as many campaigns strictly for congressional candidates. But as he said, and I will affirm, we are friends. We go back a long time. When I look for steady, constant, principled support in Congress, I've got it in Stan Parris. I just do not want to contemplate the alternative—having another Massachusetts—[*applause*]—we've got enough Massachu-

chusetts liberals in the Congress as it is, and so we don't need any more. [*Laughter*]

So, it is a pleasure to be here and speak briefly because Stan is on our side. Even when there's a difference of opinion on an issue, he does it in a way where he stands for what you all elected him to do—does it with principle and is most supportive of this President. And I am very, very grateful for that.

I want to single out only one person in addition to the two Parrises, and that's Judy Black, who is the campaign chairman. Her husband, Charlie Black, doing such an outstanding job as our major national party spokesman. And Judy, good luck to you on the last few days of this campaign.

But you know the record. Stan is not only a friend of mine and a friend of Northern Virginia but a friend of sound, conservative fiscal policies of all the American people. He and I have a special bond. I'm the one who taught him everything he knows about charisma. [*Laughter*]

I also trust his honesty and value his perspective on these major issues. He happens to be a big [University of] Virginia Cavaliers football fan—that's the honest part—and you know of his interest in transportation. I think he's overdoing it when he wants to move the University of Virginia to Fairfax County, but nevertheless—[*laughter*]——

There is his record. He mentioned modestly the Korean war; but really he's a man that, as we wrestle with these problems halfway around the world, I think he understands the big picture. Served in the Korean war, returned to attend George Washington University, then practiced law, and then the Virginia House of Delegates, and served as secretary of the Commonwealth. He's been a superb, seven-term United States Congressman. He's on the side of what I think of as family values and traditional values, of every decent American who values growth and opportunity and prosperity. It all adds up to GOP, if you'll think of it. [*Laughter*]

You know, everybody is concerned in every area, municipal or rural, about transportation. Stan was one of the leaders, if not the key leader in the House, on this legislation which will complete this area's Metro system. I think it's long overdue, and I think it's something that you can give him great credit for having done.

He also is instrumental in this Korean War Memorial. I'm sure everybody here has been to the Vietnam Memorial. I've only been there a couple of times, but I can't help but shed a tear when I'm there. It is appropriate that those veterans be honored. Similarly, I think it's long overdue that we do have a similar monument—a monument to those who served and gave their lives in the Korean war.

So, this is a man of broad perspective and great patriotism. We agree on a lot of the issues. I know how some of these newspapers around here feel, but I will continue to oppose statehood for the District. I support Stan's position. I don't think that's right. We've got a Federal city; it's special; it's the people's city for people from all over. And so, I am not a supporter of this statehood. I know that you can get into a lot of arguments about that, but I support Stan's position on that.

He reflects the good in, I'd say, decent, quiet people. He reflects their values. And he believes in government which serves the people, not the other way around. By that I mean he has stood up over and over again against this wealth of mandated programs.

You go across the river and you get up onto Capitol Hill, and all of those that control Congress—these committees—mainly the liberal Democrats, feel that the way to do it is for them to tell the people of Northern Virginia or Iowa or Texas or wherever exactly how they ought to solve the problem of housing or of education, health care, whatever—mandated programs. And Stan has stood up against the mandated approach, believing that people should be free to choose, whether it's in education or in housing, or free to have diversity in something like health care. And so, I need that kind of philosophical support that Stan Parris and a handful of others give in the United States Congress.

I wanted to mention just a word on process and what recently happened: the Democrats trying to claim that it's the Republicans who favored the rich, this whole class warfare, this old divide-and-conquer mentality that we've heard every single campaign year of the Democrats when they talk about we favoring the rich and taxation. Let me just point out one thing that Stan stood up against, loud and clear.

When the Democrats passed a bill—not the one that was finally enacted, a deficit agreement—they passed a bill that they called a soak-the-rich tax bill. And their national chairman was jumping with joy because he thought—and they had all these little ugly ads prepared, and they were claiming "soak the rich."

The part of the tax bill that they passed in the House that would have soaked the rich was $4 billion on a surtax, which I fought against and we got removed, incidentally, in the final version. And there was a $40 billion soak-the-working-man-and-woman through the indexing of income tax rates. And here they were, raising the class warfare charge of divide and conquer, divide and—the ugliest kind of campaigning for America. We're not divided by classes as some other societies that are. We're the ones that represent the working man and woman through opportunity and growth.

But while they raised the surtax $4 billion—something that they shouldn't have done anyway—and in the same legislation, $40 billion on taxes on the working man and woman of this country. So, when you hear them say "soak the rich", if you're poor or middle in terms of income, zip up your wallet because they're coming after you. [*Laughter*] And that's exactly what they'd been doing in all this legislation over there.

I want to say that some good things have happened coming out of this Congress—a lot of it because Stan has been very, very helpful to us. I'm very pleased that we at last have the amendments to the Clean Air Act. They're good; they're strong; they're reasonably well-balanced. And I think it sends a strong environmental message across this country. And I'm proud that we were in the forefront. This was our administration's goal early on.

And now, 18 months later, or whatever, we have the first and most successful amendment to the Clean Air Act in history. We obviously had Democratic support, but it was a Republican initiative. And we can take credit in that. We staved off a bill by the Democrats to make you eat broccoli. [*Laughter*] And I would veto that if it comes my way, you're right. [*Laughter*]

There's another issue that is really near and dear to the hearts of everybody, and it ties into our national drug strategy, which, incidentally, is beginning to work—I'd say is working. Bill Bennett, our drug czar, has done a superb job; and he's managed to get this issue into the consciousness of all Americans. And we're really beginning to make progress, thank heavens. It's long, long overdue. But what we haven't done is back up the national drug strategy and the local

police officers on the beat with strong enough crime legislation.

And Stan has stood for the kind of crime bill that I sent up to the Congress and that has been gutted by the liberal Democrats in the Congress. We don't need more people that are going to continue to have a little more concern about the criminal rather than the victim. We need people to do it the other way: more concern about the victims of crime and less about the criminals themselves. And that's where he is with us.

About a year and a half ago, across the river there, stood before the Capitol with a lot of police men and women to demand Congress pass a crime bill and pass it soon. That was about 18 months ago. And we hoped that this Congress, liberal though the committees that deal with this kind of issue are, would finally pass a workable Federal death penalty to protect America, to protect our police officers, those that are out there on the front line. That didn't happen. We hoped they would end the legal loopholes and technicalities that free the criminals and handcuff the police. That didn't happen. We hoped that we would give our prosecutors the tools they need to keep the criminals off the street and behind bars.

Seventeen months later—eighteen—the Congress passed a crime bill, a tough bill; and then they proceeded to weaken it, later, out of sight, in a back room someplace. And in the crush of final legislation—Congress finally getting out of town—the mutilation to this bill was itself a mugging, a legislative attack on this legislation that could only take place behind closed doors, because the American people have spoken strongly about the need for tough anticrime legislation.

And again, I am very grateful to Members of Congress like Stan Parris who stand up and encourage the passing of strong anticrime legislation. And look at the records on these. Quiz the opponent. See where he stands and whether it's just going to be some more passing of legislation that really doesn't give us the tools that we need. I got a little of what we wanted on our education program, but I'm going to continue to fight for parental choice in education. We got a day care bill that I think we can take great credit in, Stan, because it does preserve this great principle that parents should be free to choose and should be able to shape the destiny of their own kids without having a lot of mandates and decrees from Washington, DC.

So, in terms of my agenda, the thing that I was elected to perform on, we got some of what I wanted. We lost a lot of what I wanted. I had to digest some in the way of compromise that I didn't want. But a President from time to time does have to make the tough decisions, does have to do something that only a President has to do, and that is to govern. And so, I would say that it brings me, halfway through this term as President, to the view that I need more people like Stan Parris in the Congress who will back us—you and me—on what we believe is the best approach to these enormous problems facing the United States of America.

Let me just say a word—and I want to say this, giving credit here at the outset to both parties—I want to just say a word, because it's on everybody's mind, about the Middle East. And it's something that I live with 24 hours a day. And I think Vandenberg was right when he talked about partisanship stopping at the water's edge. And you know, we got away from that a little bit in the deviousness of Vietnam—to some degree, Stan, Korea, but mainly the Vietnam experience. But in all candor and with all fairness, I would say I have been blessed by having strong bipartisan support for this policy in the Middle East; and I am grateful to the leaders, both Democrat and Republican, on this one. And so, I want to be sure, as I just answer a couple of questions here about a subject that's on everyone's mind, that I make this in a very nonpartisan way because it is essential that this country stay together in support of our kids halfway around the world.

I'm not going to dwell on this question, but I was asked by some of our friends in the press coming in here about my concerns in terms of the Embassy in Kuwait. And the answer is, yes, I am very much concerned about that. We have Americans—some diplomats, some nondiplomats—in that little Embassy in Kuwait. The American flag is flying over that Kuwait Embassy. The United Nations has called for resupply. The United Nations has passed yet another resolution of condemnation against this kind of brutal violation of international law; holding people against their will and desecrating embassies by isolating them and starving them.

And so, when I was asked, well, am I concerned or increasingly concerned—I am increasingly concerned each day about this, because any President must have the concern of the safety of American citizens in the foremost position in his mind. And I said early on that one of the major goals of our policy was the concern about the safety of American citizens.

And so, as you look at what's happening halfway around the world, we've moved substantial force there—substantial force. And I bet everybody in this room has some friend, son, daughter, cousin, brother—whatever—that's over there. And these are the finest, most highly motivated, best trained forces that have ever served in the United States armed services. They're all volunteers, and we have every right in the world to be proud of this kind of service to country and this kind of patriotism. So, we cannot let them down. And yet, at the same time, we cannot fail in our goal to wipe out this aggression.

You know, there are some interesting historical parallels here. And I shared with some the other day that I've been reading a book on the history of World War II. And some of you all that are still in school take a look back into history, into what happened when Hitler invaded Poland. There is a direct parallel to what has happened to Kuwait. The Death's Head regiments came in behind the regular armed forces of Germany. And the Death's Head regiments were those SS troops, and they came in and systematically wiped out a lot of Polish people, lined up kids and shot them. And the same things are going on in Kuwait today. It has been brutal. It has been aggressive. It has been totally in contravention of international law.

And I think it's my obligation as President of the United States to be sure that our citizens and the citizens around the world know just how strongly we feel about this naked aggression. And I'm not here to rattle a saber, but I am here to express my pride in the young people that are serving. And I'm here to restate, once again, that this aggression will not succeed. It is the United States' honor that's at stake here. It is the United Nations that is at stake here.

And so, I wanted you to know that I do carry with me in my heart every single day and night concern over these Americans, concern over our kids in the armed services over there, always, however, with great pride in their service. These are not easy times internationally. And again, I'm blessed to be supported by the American people in a support that transcends—thank God—transcends party politics.

Now, back to where we started. Please go out, work hard, and send Congressman Stan Parris back to the Congress of the United States.

Thank you all very much.

Note: The President spoke at 8 a.m. in the ballroom at Belle Haven Country Club.

Exchange With Reporters on the Persian Gulf Crisis
October 31, 1990

The President. We've already had a big, major press conference—I'm sorry you all missed it—about 20 minutes from here.

Q. There are already accusations——

The President. You should have been over there.

Q. Are we going to war?

Q. There are already accusations and some reports out there that a lot of this turning up the heat now is politically motivated to coincide with the election.

The President. Jim [Jim Miklaszewski, NBC News], I don't think there are already many reports to that end. And I don't think even the most cynical would ever suggest that a President would play politics with the lives of American kids halfway around the world. So, I'm sad if you've seen reports like that. I haven't, and I think it is the ultimate of cynicism and indecency.

We're talking two separate things: one, a major crisis halfway around the world where we have strong support—Democrats and Republicans, the American people supporting us, the whole world and the United Nations supporting us. And I don't think any decent, honorable person would ever suggest anything of that nature. So, I would discount it, but I would simply say that you separate that from the political process that's going on. It is so cynical, and I'm sorry to even have that question asked because it is indecent. Nobody would make a decision based on some political—certainly not me. I've been through World War II, and I've been trying to keep our kids from—you know, try to find a peaceful solution to this.

So, you have to raise it, but I'm offended that anybody would even suggest that. I don't think any decent, honorable person would.

Q. Are we closer to war today? I mean, there seems to be an escalation and turning up the heat in general.

The President. I was asked that a minute ago. I don't think so. We're still giving these sanctions a chance to work. We're still moving forces. I'll tell you, I am, I'd say, as concerned, if not increasingly concerned, about the lives of Americans. Take a look at the Embassy in Kuwait. The American flag's still there, and these people are getting starved out. I mean, we still have some supplies there, thank heaven. But it is so brutal and so inhumane and so directly in contravention of international law that I am increasingly concerned about that. You saw some reports—I did—in the morning paper about testimony about the condition under which some of these "guests"—I mean, hostages—are being held. That worries me. Anytime an American citizen is held against his or her will, of course, the President is concerned about that.

Q. Is there any way you can get aid to them short of war?

The President. I don't know. I don't know. And we're looking at every possibility—every possibility.

Q. Now, I understand that there was going to be an attempt by the Americans to convey the U.S. desire to resupply the Embassy. Has that happened yet? Has the Chargé told the Iraqis that we intend to do that?

The President. I'm not sure about that, but I think the loudest signal on that was the action taken at the United Nations. And that gets through to Saddam Hussein. I mean, clearly, he sees his continued isolation. Clearly, he feels the condemnation of the entire world of this kind of inhumane activity. But whether there's been a direct contact from Mr. Howell in our Embassy in Kuwait, I don't know about it, and I'd be inclined to doubt that because of the inhumane way in which our Embassy is isolated.

Q. If the Iraqis refuse to allow the Embassy to be resupplied, would the U.S. then ask that all the Americans, including the civilians, be permitted to evacuate the Embassy?

The President. I'd request that right now. Anybody should have free access to come or go where they want to. Absolutely.

Q. But do you want——

The President. And they ought to be able to come home. They ought not to have to go be marched off as prisoners. And so, clearly, I'd call on them, and so is the United Nations. This is in keeping with the United Nations condemnation.

Q. But what about the diplomats? Are you going to keep them there now that the U.N. has at least given you the right to resupply them?

The President. I think we have to look at that. And the main thing is, at this juncture, there are priorities to be sure people have enough to eat and that they're not put under continued duress there.

Q. Well, have you made your point? Is it necessary to have them there anymore?

The President. There are other Americans there, and always your Embassy has kind of a consular service to try to service the concerns of other citizens. But as others are brutalized and thus sent into hiding, why, that function becomes a little more blurred. So, I just don't know the answer to that.

Q. If they blocked resupply, would that be the sort of provocation you've spoken about earlier?

The President. Either it would be directly contravening a mandate from the United Nations, and we would view that very seriously, yes.

Q. You mean, military——

The President. Too hypothetical.

Q. Mr. President, there is some——

The President. I can't go into hypothesis. I can understand why you want to know that, why the American people would want to, but it would not be good for me to signal what I might or might not do.

Q. How much longer do the diplomats have before you have——

The President. I don't know. There's varying reports. You mean in terms of how long they can——

Q. ——they can hold out.

The President. ——hold out against this inhumane treatment? I don't know. I think we have varying estimates of time. We can talk to them. There is communication. But I think some of that is not yet clear to me as to how long——

Q. Mr. President, some people——

The President. ——what a drop-dead date is, a pullout date it might be.

Q. Some past foreign policy experts who have been at the State Department think you haven't done enough on the diplomatic front, like sending an emissary, a mediator like Jimmy Carter or someone who will—and also that you don't know that in the Middle East they deal.

The President. That what?

Q. Deal. Dealmaking.

The President. There's no compromise. There is no compromise with this aggression. And the allies are together on this. The Arab countries, Soviet Union, France—all of us are together on this. And every time somebody sends an emissary, that gives Saddam Hussein a little bit of hope that there might be some way that he can stop short of doing what he must do: get out of Kuwait unconditionally, free these people that are being held against their will, and have the legitimate government restored. So, there may be critics, but I've been very gratified at the rather overwhelming support we've had for the approach I'm taking.

Q. But why is Baker going? Is he an emissary?

Q. What do you want the Secretary to do?

The President. I want him to discuss all options with the people that are helping us there and with whom we are allied on the ground and at sea in the Persian Gulf. It is very important we stay in very close touch with our coalition partners. I do some of that on the telephone, but I think this Baker mission is very important. We'll be talking about all kinds of alternatives and doing everything we can to see that no stone is left unturned in determining how we implement the United Nations resolutions.

Q. Will he be asking the allies for permission to use military force?

The President. I'd leave that to further discussion, where no stones will be unturned.

Q. Well, on Primakov——

The President. Helen [Helen Thomas, United Press International], I've got to go. This has been a long and exhausting press conference——

Q. Press conference?

The President. And I had not intended to have it because it makes number 84.

Q. Thanks.

The President. Thank you.

Note: The exchange began at 8:50 a.m. on the South Lawn of the White House, following the President's return from a fundraising breakfast for Representative Stan Parris in Alexandria, VA. In his remarks, he referred to President Saddam Hussein of Iraq and W. Nathaniel Howell, U.S. Ambassador to Kuwait.

Statement by Press Secretary Fitzwater on the President's Meeting With Secretary of State Agostino Cardinal Casaroli of the Holy See
October 31, 1990

The President met with the Vatican Secretary of State Agostino Cardinal Casaroli for approximately 40 minutes in the Oval Office this morning.

Cardinal Casaroli came to the United States to receive the Prisoner of Conscience Award from the Appeal of Conscience Foundation in New York. Following his meeting with the President, the Cardinal went on to have a private meeting with the Vice President. Later this afternoon he will be having lunch with [United Nations] Secretary-General Perez de Cuellar in New York.

During the Oval Office meeting, the President and the Cardinal discussed the situation in the Gulf. The President expressed appreciation for the Vatican's support for U.N. sanctions against Iraq and reiterated our position that nothing short of complete implementation of the U.N. Security Council's resolutions is acceptable. Both leaders expressed the hope that a peaceful resolution to the current crisis could be found.

Remarks at a Republican Party Fundraising Breakfast in Burlington, Massachusetts
November 1, 1990

Thank you all so much for that warm welcome. My only hope is that when I had

to stand you up a few weeks ago that you paid again to get in here—[*laughter*]—because it is absolutely essential that Bill Weld be elected the next Governor of this State.

It's great to be back here, not far from where I was born. Great to be back here, very, very close to where my beloved sister votes—Nan Ellis. Glad to see her again. And great to be near Concord.

When John MacGovern is elected to represent the Fifth District, it's going to be the second "shot that was heard round the world." John supported me way back in '78, and we were reminiscing about that as we flew up on Air Force One today. And I do believe he'll be an important new voice for Massachusetts, the kind of voice for change that Bill so articulately called for.

I see many friends here today, people that helped me a lot: Dave Locke and, of course, Ray Shamie and Steve Pierce, who's in there fighting for our ticket; Andy Card, who's doing such a great job in the White House now; Ron Kaufman, your national committeeman. I'm delighted to be with all of them. And Gussy Hornblower, I'm glad to see you, our national committeewoman.

The first thing I want to do is give my congratulations to the terrific team that is going to bring change and a clean house to Massachusetts on Tuesday. It's headed by a man of total integrity and vision. He wants a State without corruption. Bill Weld will turn Massachusetts into a place where strength means strength of character, not strength of old-boy connections. Another leader for the nineties is my friend of long-standing. We go back a long, long time in the political wars. I'm talking about Paul Cellucci. I am grateful for his loyalty, his dedication, and his ability. And along with Bill and Paul, we've got Joe Malone, candidate for State treasurer. He knows what's needed to pull the economy out of tough times, though I myself had an idea for a creative solution to your budget mess: Just start paying the judges by the hour. [*Laughter*] And of course, Paul McCarthy for secretary of state and Doug Murray for auditor, Bill Sawyer for the AG. It's a wonderful team—clean, strong, able.

A few years ago, a Democrat teenager had a summer job working here for the city. When he tried to give back the leftover project money, he was told, No, spend it all, or else we won't get any added on next

year. It was at that moment that our next Senator, Jim Rappaport, decided he'd have nothing more to do with the tax-and-spend politics of the State Democrats. He became a Republican. We're glad he did. And believe me, you look at that Senate, and you can understand why I need him in Washington, DC. Good luck, Jim.

You heard Bill mention this. There is no higher domestic priority for the Republican agenda than America's economy. The economy—we've got to get it going, because the economy is the job-creating engine that every family of this country counts on.

If events that he talked about in Eastern Europe and around the world have reminded us of anything, it's that free markets and enterprise are good for people. And America still does it better than anybody else. Still, in recent months, we've seen some uncertainty and concern about slower economic growth in this country. That's one reason for me getting a budget agreement was critical and why I was willing to go the extra mile to get it.

The negotiations, as we all know, were difficult, and they were tough, but we finally reached an agreement with the Democratic majority that controls the Congress. There were clear differences between the two parties in our approach to solving this spiraling deficit problem facing our country. They simply wanted to raise taxes, including income tax rates. I wanted to reduce the deficit with spending cuts in accord with the budget that I sent up to Congress and couldn't get passed. What we got then was a compromise, and like all compromises, there was some good with the bad.

We got about $500 billion—I think the figure is $492 billion—in real deficit reduction over a 5-year period, close to half a trillion dollars. We got $350 billion in spending cuts out of that—the largest cut in history. We got incentives to try to stimulate economic growth. And we put Congress on the pay-as-you-go plan. The enforcement—one of the key things about this that is good—the enforcement provisions of this budget agreement: They are real, they are strong, and no longer can these Washington programs that are inflicted on the States be funded with red ink. And if they try to raise spending one dime, they've got to cut other excess spending or find the money for it right there and then. The enforcement provisions are good, and I'm going to see they stay that way.

Finally, we did hold the line against reckless cuts of our Armed Forces. I'm determined to ensure that this nation's defense remains strong. We owe that much to our men and women in the Persian Gulf.

But getting our fiscal policy on track is just part of what we've accomplished, as what Bill and Paul and Jim called the party of change. Well over a year ago, I challenged the Congress and people to work with me to break the stalemate that has hindered our progress on clean air for the past decade. We put our best minds to work on both sides of the aisle, both ends of Pennsylvania Avenue, to turn technology and the power of the marketplace to the advantage of the environment; to create; to innovate; to tip the scales in favor of recovery, restoration, and renewal.

A year ago, I said, "Every American expects and deserves to breathe clean air. And as President, it is my mission to guarantee it for this generation and for generations to come." Today, thanks to the innovation and cooperation of industry, government, environmental experts, I can say that I now have a clean air bill that I can sign.

And the legislation will remove 10 million tons of emissions that cause acid rain from the air. It will bring the Nation's 100 most smog-laden cities safe, healthy air. And it encourages the use of alternative fuels that are safer for our environment and make us far less dependent on foreign oil. This bill is good for us; it's good for our kids; and it's good for Canada, our neighbor to the north, and Mexico, our neighbor to the south. And it sends a signal of commitment and leadership to the rest of the world.

The fulfillment of this commitment has broken a 13-year legislative logjam; but most important, it's going to make every man, woman, and child breathe a little easier. Because Republicans care about change, and we've got a clean air bill. We've got it because we were the ones that wanted to effect change. And I think that is something to celebrate.

But of course, there's still work to be done on our national agenda that coincides very closely to Jim Rappaport's agenda and Bill Weld, Paul Cellucci's agenda. See, I think that our country is fed up with crime. And the Republicans know handcuffs belong not on the cops and the courts, they belong on the criminals.

Shortly after taking office, I stood before the Capitol, and I called on Congress to pass new, tough laws to help America take back the streets. Instead, in the final hours of the Congress, as we were moving toward tougher crime legislation, Democratic liberals choked and completely gutted our package to fight back against violent crime.

Republicans fought for the habeas corpus reforms, aimed at stopping convicted criminals from endlessly abusing the appeals process. Republicans fought for reforms of the exclusionary rule, a judge-made law that lets the guilty go free. And Republicans fought for a real Federal death penalty for drug kingpins and terrorists. And the liberal Democrats blocked these provisions, blocked the will of the American people. We need to be tough on crimes and criminals. We want change. Give me more Republicans, and we'll get the kind of change that the Nation deserves.

Republicans want to build a better America, and it's not just Washington. To do it, we need more Republicans. We need a Governor like Bill Weld in the statehouse. And of course, we need more Members of the United States Senate that think as we do on matters of crime and the environment. And again, I repeat my plea for Jim Rappaport. He'll be outstanding.

Now, I know there's an awful lot of interest in what's happening halfway around the world. And I also know that we're standing here at an event that is strong on partisan politics. It's the way the American system ought to be; it's the way it is. And as I was flying in over—making our approach, coming into the field out here at Hanscom, I couldn't help but be struck by not only the beauty of New England but by the importance of what we're all engaged in: participation in the American political process. I'm not a cynic. I believe in it. I look at these candidates, and I think we are fortunate to have such outstanding, dedicated, qualified individuals running for statewide office and congressional office in this State—feel strongly about it.

So, I have no apologies, only pride in being at a partisan political event. But for the minute now, I want to ask you to just set partisan politics aside, because I know that everyone in this country is vitally interested in the situation in the Middle East. So, let me just, in a few minutes, bring you up to date. You see, I believe that Senator Arthur Vandenberg was right when he said: "Politics ends at the water's edge." We got away from that in the turmoil of Vietnam and, to some degree, even in Korea, but mainly out of the Vietnam experience. And I should say right here before commenting that I am grateful to the leaders and other Members of Congress, Democrat and Republican, for their strong bipartisan support.

On August 2d, Iraq invaded Kuwait. They literally raped, pillaged, and plundered this once-peaceful land, this nation that is a member of the Arab League, a member of the United Nations. Iraq began then to brutally and systematically dismantle Kuwait. There is an historical analogy here between what's happened to Kuwait and what happened to Poland when the world stood still, sat on the sidelines, including our country. They began to systematically dismantle it by shipping its medical equipment, its machines, its records, its assets back to Baghdad—brutal, systematic dismantling.

They've tried to silence Kuwaiti dissent and courage with an old way of doing that—I'm talking about the firing squads. In one incident, a 15-year-old boy gunned down, his family forced to watch. His crime: passing out leaflets.

The United States and the rest of the world, united in anger and outrage, determined to force Saddam Hussein out of Kuwait. On August 5th, he announced that he was pulling his forces out of Kuwait. At that very moment, he sent his armor and his troops south to mass along the Saudi Arabian border, threatening yet another member of the United Nations, another member of the Arab League.

Subsequently, the United Nations Security Council passed 10 resolutions of condemnation and disapproval. On August 5th, I said that Saddam Hussein's aggression will not stand. Today I am more determined than ever. This aggression will not stand.

This morning, right now, over 300 innocent Americans—civilians—are held against their will in Iraq, denied the freedoms granted all under international law. Many of them are reportedly staked out as human shields near possible military targets, something that even Adolf Hitler didn't do. Many more Americans are in hiding in Kuwait, hidden by courageous Kuwaitis, their lives at stake. A number imprisoned in an Embassy of the United States right there in Kuwait City, and they are cut off from food and other supplies, and they are surrounded by Iraqi troops. Our flag does still fly, but the rights of these American citizens are, at this very moment, being denied by Iraq's brutal dictator.

So, let me be clear: We have no argument with the Iraqi people, none at all. We bear no hostility to the Iraqi people, nor do any of the other 25 countries represented on land and sea, standing with us shoulder to shoulder in the Gulf. Our problem is with Saddam Hussein alone.

I want desperately to have a peaceful resolution to this crisis. Indeed, we've worked closely with the United Nations in putting sanctions into effect, in passing resolutions, in speaking with one voice against the invader's aggression. We are giving the sanctions the time to work. And I hope that there will never be a shot fired in anger. But let me be very, very clear: There will be no compromise on the stated objectives of the United Nations Security Council resolutions, none at all.

The brutality against innocent civilians will not be tolerated and will not stand. Saddam's clear violations of international law will not stand. And that means, yes, his brutal aggression will not stand. No one wants a peaceful end to this crisis more than I do. But no one is more determined to see this aggression turned back than I am. And I will not change on that fundamental point of morality.

As to our own kids, our own forces in the Gulf, they are the best. They're the best young men and women ever to serve in our Armed Forces. They're all volunteers.

They're all volunteers. They're all well-trained. They are all highly motivated. They are your sons and daughters; they're your neighbors' kids. They're the finest, and we owe them an enormous vote of thanks.

You know, these men and women don't take democracy for granted. Thousands upon thousands of them are going to be sending in absentee ballots from the Saudi desert or upon the seas of the Gulf of Oman and near the Straits of Hormuz. And if they can find the time to vote under such challenging conditions, so can every single American here at home. We have an obligation to show these extraordinary GI's that we don't take democracy for granted either. So, let's make them as proud of us as we are of them.

Now, shifting the gears back 180, I was here to support an outstanding ticket for the statewide offices and congressional offices in the State of Massachusetts. You can be a part of significant change if you'll elect Bill Weld the next Governor and elect Jim Rappaport the next Senator.

Thank you, and God bless you all.

Note: President Bush spoke at 9:41 a.m. in the Grand Ballroom at the Burlington Marriott Hotel. In his remarks, he referred to David Locke, minority leader of the State senate; Ray Shamie, chairman of the State Republican Party; Steve Pierce, minority leader of the State house of representatives and chairman of the Bill Weld campaign; Andrew H. Card, Jr., Assistant to the President and Deputy to the Chief of Staff; Paul Cellucci, candidate for Lieutenant Governor; and President Saddam Hussein of Iraq. Following his remarks, President Bush traveled to Mashpee, MA.

Remarks at a Republican Campaign Rally in Mashpee, Massachusetts
November 1, 1990

Thank all of you for this warm welcome. I'd like to single out all the kids here today from Mashpee Middle School—music to my ears. You were just great!

And now I have the pleasure, if I haven't fouled this thing up, to ask the Falmouth High School Band to play the national anthem for us. I think it's most appropriate on a day like this. And if—are you guys geared up? Let's fire it up.

[At this point, the band played the national anthem.]

Great. Thank you so very much, all of you.

Let me say how great it is to be back on the Cape, to breathe the deep magic of this place. You know, Henry David Thoreau, Massachusetts' native son, once said about the Cape: "A man may stand here and put all America behind him." Way back in 1943, in the fall, just about this time in 1943, I spent some time at the Cape, stationed at the naval air station, then at

Hyannis. I've never forgotten the joy and the wonder of the Cape. It's great to be back, and it's great to be back with these winners.

Let me first say hello to a friend and a candidate I want to see added to the Republican ranks down on Capitol Hill. I'm talking about John Bryan—whoops, here he is. He made it. John Bryan, the right man for the Cape in the 10th District. Good luck to you.

And of course, I want to mention two that are helping me so much in the White House, two of Massachusetts' sons: Andy Card, one of our top staff people there, and Ron Kaufman, the national committeeman for the State.

And now to the team that's ready to run things for the Commonwealth of Massachusetts: your next Senator, Jim Rappaport. We need him in Washington. Another man I've known for years, a Republican of fine standing, a leader—I'm talking about Joe Malone, the next State treasurer.

One of my earliest supporters in politics—and some of you all on the Cape might remember this—is the next Lieutenant Governor of this State, Paul Cellucci, who is with us today. And then, of course, the man of the hour, the man we're counting on to turn this State around, Bill Weld, the next Governor. I am for him 100 percent.

You know, this area, I'm told—doing a little homework for this visit—I'm told that Mashpee has a long independent streak, as long as the winters are out here on the Cape. Here in Mashpee, you know better than most that the time has come for a change. If there's ever been a State in the Union that has been a playground for one-party politics, it's Massachusetts. The Democrats are the ones that have every statewide office, and they are the ones that hold all but one of the congressional seats, and they are the ones holding 8 of 10 seats in statehouse in the senate. And the Massachusetts taxpayers—they're the ones holding the bag. We are going to change that by the election of this outstanding team.

I like the way they are campaigning for change, because I believe that one of the most important things that we can do together is to get more Republicans elected at every level. Because this party is the party with an agenda; the party of change, not the status quo; and the party of new ideas with a finger on the pulse of this nation.

There is no higher domestic Republican agenda item than this nation's economy, because America's economy is the job-creating engine that every family in the country counts on.

You know, in the events in Eastern Europe—and I'm sure some of you kids have been reading about these in schools—and around the world—other changes—if they've reminded us of anything, it is that free markets and free enterprise are good for people. And America still does it better than anybody else. Still, in recent months, we've seen some uncertainty and some concern about slower economic growth. And that's one reason that getting a budget agreement was crucial, why I was willing to go the extra mile.

I couldn't agree more with Jim; there's an awful lot of it I don't like. The negotiations were difficult; they were tough. But we finally reached an agreement with the Democratic majority that controls both Houses of the Congress. And there were clear differences between the parties. They wanted to raise taxes, including income tax rates. I wanted to reduce the deficit in the way my budget called for: reduce it with spending cuts, not by raising taxes on the working man and woman of this country.

We did get a $492 billion, 5-year reduction program, about a half a trillion dollars. And $350 billion of that was in spending cuts—the largest cut in history. And then—this is critical—we did manage, through a lot of hard work by the Republican leaders, to get Congress on a pay-as-you-go plan, the enforcement provision. I'm sure there's a lot of skepticism anytime that Congress takes action. But the enforcement provisions of this agreement are real, they are strong, and no longer will these programs be funded with red ink, mortgaging the future of the young people here in Mashpee today.

And as we landed at Otis, I thought of another thing. We did hold the line against the reckless cuts of our Armed Forces. Defense spending went down, but I can certify to the American people, I think, given the changes in the world, I believe we do have proper levels now to sustain United States interests around the world. And I am determined to ensure that this nation's defense remains strong and prepared. And certainly we owe that much to our men and women now serving with pride in the Persian Gulf.

And there were some other things in there that were good. You know, we're the party that knows nothing is more precious than the well-being of our children. So, that's why we called for a child-care bill, one that would put the choice in the hands of the parents, in the hands of the American family, empowering parents.

Some in Congress tried to build a bigger day-care bureaucracy at double the cost of our bill. Then the House outdid the Senate—Democratic-controlled House—by tripling our request. But we turned the classic, budget-busting bidding war around and gave choice back to the families. And we've got a child-care bill that puts dollars in the pockets of low- and middle-income parents, because we know Americans don't want government-sponsored day-care centers to warehouse our kids, designed and managed by bureaucrats miles away. Keep the child care close to the family. Because—as Bill said and Jim said—because Republicans care about change, American parents will now have increased choice in child care.

There's still more work to be done, lots more on our agenda, the agenda I outlined for you several years ago when I was here. American education has got to be second to none. This party understands that our ability to compete demands that our kids' education is nothing less than the very best. That's why we sent Congress the Education Excellence Act: for fundamental education reform; to reward achievement; to encourage accountability; and to give parents more say, more choice in their kids' education.

Where some called for a bigger bureaucracy, we called for flexibility. Where the liberal Democrats said throw more money at the status quo—we spend more per capita than almost any country in the world on education—we call for reform, finding a way to do it better. We need excellence in education. This party is committed to fundamental change in American education. I know that Jim Rappaport in the Senate and Bill Weld right here in the statehouse in Massachusetts agree with me: Reform and change is what is needed to make education better for these kids.

So, we are at a turning point. There are so many other issues that we are making some progress on. I'll be signing a clean air bill in a few days. We would never have done it if we hadn't had Republicans fighting for that legislation.

We'll be signing—I think there will be some kind of crime legislation. But the kind of crime legislation that I want, the one that defends the police officers and a little tougher on the criminals, never got anywhere because of the liberals in the United States Congress. If we had more people like Jim down there, we would get good, sound anticrime legislation that would make the streets safe in this country.

So, there's an unfulfilled agenda, and I want to fulfill it promptly by getting more Republicans in Washington and by having more Republicans in the statehouses across this country. And in this ticket and in this candidate for the Senate, we have an outstanding chance for reform and for change. Elect Bill Weld, his team, and elect Jim Rappaport to the Senate. That's what you can do to participate in this change.

Now, let me just make a few comments on the Middle East. As I mentioned earlier at a reception outside of Boston, we are at a partisan political event. But I want to ask you now to shift gears. Just for a moment, let me speak to you as President of the United States for all and as Commander in Chief of the Armed Forces. And I want to ask you to put politics aside, because I know that everyone is vitally interested in the situation in the Middle East.

I believe, as Arthur Vandenberg did long ago—Senator Vandenberg—who said that politics ends at the water's edge. That's a noble sentiment. It's strong. It makes sense today. We crept away from that because of the agony of Vietnam. Now we are united.

First, I am very grateful to the Democrats and the Republicans, the leaders and the Members of Congress, for their strong support for what I felt I must do—bipartisan support, bipartisanship at its best.

On August 2d, Iraq invaded Kuwait. They literally—literally, not figuratively—literally raped, pillaged, and plundered this once-peaceful land, this nation that is a member of the Arab League and a member of the United Nations. Iraq began to brutally and systematically dismantle Kuwait—shipping its medical equipment, its machines, its records, its assets all back to Baghdad; taking machines out of the factories and machinery out of the hospitals, sending it back to Baghdad.

They've tried to silence Kuwaiti dissent and courage with firing squads, much as Hitler did when he invaded Poland. They have committed outrageous acts of barbarism. In one hospital, they pulled 22 premature babies from their incubators, sent the machines back to Baghdad, and all those little ones died.

The United States and the rest of the world, united in anger and outrage, determined to force Saddam Hussein out of Kuwait. On August 5th, Saddam Hussein announced that he was pulling his forces out of Kuwait. And at the very moment, there was a picture of a truck with some lonely Iraqi soldier smiling and waving as the truck went north. Saddam Hussein's armor went south to the Saudi Arabia border, threatening yet another member of the United Nations, another member of the Arab League.

Subsequently, the United Nations Security Council passed 10 resolutions of condemnation and disapproval. And on August 5th, I said that Saddam Hussein's aggression will not stand. And today I am more determined than ever in my life: This aggression will not and must not stand.

This morning, this very morning, over 300 Americans, innocent civilians, are held against their will in Iraq. Saddam Hussein calls them guests. They are held in direct contravention of international law, many of them reportedly staked out as human shields near possible military targets. Brutality that—I don't believe Adolf Hitler ever participated in anything of that nature.

Many more Americans are in hiding in Kuwait, their lives at stake. A number imprisoned in the United States Embassy in Kuwait City, the Embassy surrounded by Iraq forces. They're cut off from food. They are cut off from other supplies. They're surrounded. And our flag still flies, but the rights of these American citizens at this very moment are being denied by Iraq's brutal dictator.

So, let me be very clear with you: We have no argument with the people of Iraq. We bear no hostility to the people of Iraq, nor do any of the other 25 countries represented on land and sea in the Gulf area bear hostility to the people of Iraq. Our problem is with Saddam Hussein alone.

And I want desperately to have a peaceful resolution to this crisis. Indeed, we have worked and gone the extra mile, working with the United Nations and putting sanctions into effect, in passing resolutions, in speaking with one voice against the invader's aggression. And we are giving sanctions time to work. I hope there will never be a shot fired in anger. But I owe it to you, the American people, to make this clear, very clear: There will be no compromise on the stated objectives of the United Nations Security Council resolutions, none at all.

The brutality against innocent civilians will not be tolerated and will not stand. Saddam's clear violation of international law will not stand. And that means, yes, Saddam Hussein's brutal aggression of Kuwait will not stand. And that is the message from the United States to the dictator in Iraq. No one wants a peaceful solution to this crisis more than I do. And no one is more determined to see this aggression turned back—more determined than I am.

You know, as our own force is deployed in the Gulf, I think I should tell you, as to them, that they are the best young men and women ever to serve in our Armed Forces. They are volunteers. They are well-trained. They are highly motivated. They are your sons and daughters and your neighbors' kids. And they are the finest, and we owe them a vote of thanks.

Well, I tell you, these men and women don't take democracy for granted. And thousands upon thousands of them will be sending in their ballots from the Saudi desert. And if they can find the time to vote under such challenging conditions, so can every single American here at home. We have an obligation to show these extraordinary GI's that we don't take democracy for granted, either. Let's make them as proud of us as we are of them. Go to the polls and vote. Do it on Tuesday, and vote for our outstanding ticket.

Thank you all, and God bless you.

Note: The President spoke at 12:01 p.m. in the gymnasium of the Mashpee Middle School. In his remarks, he referred to Andrew H. Card, Jr., Assistant to the President and Deputy to the Chief of Staff. Following his remarks, the President traveled to Orlando, FL.

The President's News Conference in Orlando, Florida
November 1, 1990

The President. Good afternoon. Let me just make a brief statement, and then I'll be glad to respond to questions.

I want to begin today by simply restating for the American people some of the key points about our efforts to turn back aggression in the Persian Gulf. I believe that it is essential that the American people fully understand the objectives of the United States and the United Nations as well as the magnitude of the outrage perpetrated by the Government of Iraq.

The United States and the rest of the world are united in the condemnation of Iraq's invasion of Kuwait. We have no quarrel with the Iraqi people. Our problem is with Iraqi's dictator, Saddam Hussein.

I want a peaceful resolution to this crisis. We're giving the United Nations sanctions imposed on Iraq time to work. But let me be very clear: There will be no compromise on the stated objectives of the United Nations Security Council resolutions.

Iraq's brutality against innocent civilians will not be permitted to stand. And Saddam Hussein's violations of international law will not stand. His aggression against Kuwait will not stand.

And now I'd be glad to take questions. I think, Tom, you have the first one.

Persian Gulf Crisis

Q. Yes, Mr. President, you raised the—[*inaudible*]—your comments in recent days have been aimed, at least in part, in preparing the American people for the possibility of war. Is that true, and do you think the American people are ready?

The President. Well, Tom [Tom Raum, Associated Press], I want to have a peaceful resolution to this question, and our dealing through the United Nations and working with them for common objectives, I think, is evidence of that. I've indicated we're prepared to give sanctions time to work, and I'll repeat that here again today. But I am not ruling out further options, and I am not trying to prepare our country for war.

We have had a little bit of a hiatus because of the attention on the budget and other matters from keeping in focus our objectives in Iraq. There's been a little less attention to it in some quarters. And I want to—in a sense, Tom, it's a little bit awkward because here we are, just a few days before an election, and I want to continue to work for Republican candidates. But I must continue to keep our objectives regarding Iraq in focus. And so, what I try to do is separate out the foreign affairs, the Iraq question, from domestic politics.

But it is essential that I do the latter, but in doing that, I am not trying to sound the tocsin of war. But I am trying to point out the concerns that I feel, for example, on the hostage question. And I'll continue to do that.

Q. Do you think the American people are ready for it—ready for war?

The President. Well, I think the American people feel as I do: that they much prefer to have a peaceful resolution to this question. But who can tell what would happen in a situation of this nature? There's a lot of unforeseen things that can take place. And I think I would have to go to the American people with my recommendations if it regarded the safety or defense of our key interests.

Q. Mr. President, today you said that Saddam Hussein was even more brutal than Adolf Hitler. Talking about starving out the Americans in the Embassy in Kuwait City, is there a chance that you might be exaggerating a bit for effect? And coming just 1 week before the elections—I know you said you can keep these separate, but you're making these statements on the bandstand with political flags behind you. If you really wanted to keep these separate, why don't you just address the Nation in some other forum?

The President. Well, I'm addressing it in another forum now, and this is in a nationally covered press conference, I'm sure. I don't think I'm overstating it. I know I'm not overstating the feelings I have about it. The reports coming out of Iraq just today cause even further concern—these reports of the way our innocent civilians are being treated. I think the American people are as outraged as I am about the treatment of the people in our Embassy, for example. And I think it's important that they know my concerns on this subject.

So, I don't—the last question that you raised does concern me some, but it is very important that I keep pointing out the objectives and where I think Iraq stands. All the people we're addressing are extraordinarily interested in that, and I go to great ends to make sure that I give proper credit to the Democrats and the Republicans in Congress—make clear that this is not a partisan effort that we're involved in here. I've been very gratified for the enormous support from both Houses of Congress and from the American people.

But as we continue to move forces and as we see the various events taking place over there, I think it is important that the President continue to spell out for the American people not only our objectives but telling them how I feel about the various events.

Q. Mr. President, are you considering now a reprovisioning mission of some sort?

The President. Well, I'm hopeful still that the United Nations resolutions that call for reprovisioning will be followed. And I'd rather leave it there. But I am very concerned about the people in that Embassy. It's cut off from food. They have enough right now, but the whole ploy of Saddam Hussein is to starve them out. And I think that is unconscionable. And I think the world needs to know how strongly those of us in the United States responsible for this policy feel about it.

Q. Mr. President, apart from the distraction that may have been caused by the budget battle, what other factors have caused you to approach this task of readdressing this issue with such urgency?

The President. The sand is running through the glass. We've got these economic sanctions in play. And I think there's an urgency on the part of people to understand—desire on their part, rather, to understand whether the sanctions are working. We continue to move force. And I think it's important that the American people know why I'm continuing to do this. So, I think it's just rather that there was a

period where I didn't do as much of it, but now I'm going to keep on, now and on past the election as well.

Q. Mr. President, I know you say that you're not trying to prepare the American people for war, but could not your message of today and this week be summed up as that you are seeking a peaceful resolution if possible, but a military one if not?

The President. I think that I've made those statements before. I think I've been rather consistent in pointing out that I would not rule anything out. If you go back and look at the things I've said, I believe I've been on the record before with that kind of comment, Brit [Brit Hume, ABC News]

Q. Mr. President, Saddam Hussein today invited American families to come visit the hostages over the next holiday. A two part question, sir, is: Would you welcome some visits by Americans? And what do you make of that kind offer in general?

The President. I think it's a—well, let me start, I think that those people should come home to visit with their families. I think they should be released from captivity. This canard of calling people that are held hostage—calling them guests when they're hostages is turning off the whole world. And further, the reports that are coming out from some of these French hostages coming home, of their understanding of the way the Americans are being treated, is just terrible. And the whole concept of staking out people next to what might become military targets is also unconscionable. So, I see it as a ploy, but I don't think he'll win the humanitarian of the year award for that. I think that people see it as a rather brutal toying with the emotions of families, frankly.

Q. If I may, sir: Would you blame Americans if they took him up on the offer?

The President. We have a notice out that we are discouraging Americans from going there, and that would hold.

Q. Mr. President, you've said on one occasion that your patience is running out, that you've had it. You're telling us on this occasion that you're willing to wait and see the sanctions work. We've seen your senior staff out today trying to say that there's consistency in your message, but yet there seems to be a variance there. Are you having trouble getting your message across?

The President. No. And I don't think there's any inconsistency. And if you'd like—I don't want to take up your time, but thinking I might get a question of this nature, I wrote down the various things that I've said on this subject for some time. And they are quite consistent. One time you might have a little more emphasis on one point—like yesterday—on the outrage I feel about the hostages. In another, you might have a little more emphasis on having the sanctions work. But I think we have been extraordinarily consistent.

And I think the key point on this, regarding substance, is that our allies understand this. They know exactly where the United States stands in terms of our determination to see the United Nations sanctions fulfilled. So, I'm not worried about it. There was one story today that was just clearly wrong in that regard. But I think we've had a rather consistent approach to this, very consistent. And so, I don't worry about that. And the key point would be if our allies thought that, and they don't, or Saddam Hussein thought that, and he doesn't; he can't.

Q. If I could follow up: Are you concerned about an erosion within your alliance, the fact that Saddam Hussein may be successful in prying some people apart from your position?

The President. I know he's going to continue to try that, Charles [Charles Bierbauer, Cable News Network]. He's doing it every way he can. He did it first—an interesting point—his people contacted a parliamentarian in Canada roughly the same day they contacted the Foreign Minister of Germany [Hans-Dietrich Genscher], roughly the time they contacted a Member of Parliament in the United Kingdom. And the whole concept was: You come; we'll parcel out some hostages. Trying to divide and show a humanitarian side of some sort. He continues to through the Primakov [Soviet Presidential Council member] visit. I think his concept there was to try to find some division, and I don't think that division exists.

But it does concern me that he not be successful. And that's why I think it is im-

portant that the United States continue to reiterate our conviction on seeing that there can be no compromise with this aggression and that these United Nations resolutions must be fulfilled in the entirety.

Q. Mr. President, in the beginning of this crisis you held out little hope for a diplomatic solution. Today——

The President. You say a little hope, or little hope?

Q. Little hope for a diplomatic solution. Today you talk about hoping that there's a peaceful resolution. I'm just wondering are we any closer to possibly having a diplomatic solution?

The President. I don't see that. I don't see that we are. I've said from the very beginning I hope that the sanctions would have an effect that would cause him to comply with the resolutions. I think they're having an effect, but our problem is, and the problem of our allies around the world is, we can't certify for the world how disastrous or strong an effect these sanctions are having. But from the very beginning, I've been saying I would hope that the sanctions would be effective. And we'll give them time. Again, my problem is, and the problem of those with whom I consult very closely is, we can't say how much is enough in terms of the sanctions or how much time it would take.

Q. Well, sir, then, if you're not expecting a diplomatic solution, but you're hoping for a peaceful resolution, does that mean you expect Saddam to just give up?

The President. That's what I'd like to see, yes. That's what the United Nations calls for. It calls for him to withdraw. It calls for the restoration of the rulers. And so, that's exactly what he ought to do. And I think if we hold firm—and we are holding firm in this coalition with some 25 countries in the Gulf or on the sea there, plus the solidarity that the United Nations has demonstrated— the hope is eventually he might do that. But we can't guarantee to the American people how long will it take.

Q. Sir, your wife is campaigning in Omaha today, and perhaps you've seen reports about that. She was asked if you would consider meeting face to face with Saddam Hussein. And she replied, "I think he would consider anything to get the Kuwaitis back in their country and our men out." That is being interpreted as you would consider a one-on-one meeting with Saddam. Would you?

The President. I would consider it if there was an agreement that he would totally withdraw and comply fully, with no conditions to the United Nations sanctions. I mean, I think anybody would do that. But that would mean that he has to do exactly what I've been saying here, with no condition, no negotiation—just leave. But I don't think at that juncture that it would be much of—pleasant meeting. But I never—that's something I guess Barbara was asked on her own. I've not discussed it with her or anybody else. But that's the only way that it would be productive for me to have a meeting, it seems to me, because there is no flexibility on our position. There is no compromise. There is no conditionality. My position—and I think it strongly represents the coalition partners' position—is he must comply. And so, I don't think a meeting short of just acceptance of those terms would be in the national interest or in the interest of the coalition.

Q. If I could just ask about some of the cynicism and skepticism about—[*inaudible*]—about the public speaking out on Iraq. It's not just because of the elections next week. It's also because of—the signals we were getting were that the Embassy in Kuwait had plenty of food and water for the time being; the American Ambassador's wife said Tuesday morning on one of the morning television programs they were growing vegetables there, they had a well there. All seemed to be going well. All of a sudden, within the next 24 hours, you're talking about Saddam starving these people out. What caused this change?

The President. I don't think it is a change. I've been increasingly concerned about it. I'm delighted to know about the vegetables; that's the first time I've heard of that. And I've known that they've had enough tuna fish for some time. There was earlier estimates that the Embassy would have to be closed before now, and they've stretched the timeframe there.

But it's that plus the reports coming out of Iraq that make me feel I must keep this

in focus for the American people. They must know how strongly I feel about an American Embassy, the American flag flying, and these people inside being cut off and, I would say, brutalized by that behavior; and secondly, how strongly I feel about the Americans that are held hostage in Iraq itself. And it is essential that we not lose track of those key points. These people are not guests; they are hostages. And I think you're on to something because I don't think there has been that much discussion lately of these things that really concern me, John [John Cochran, NBC News]. These matters concern me deeply.

Gubernatorial Candidate Clayton Williams

Q. Mr. President, a political question. You're going into Texas to campaign for Clayton Williams. This week he really stumbled because he was asked about the only proposition on the Texas ballot and he didn't know what it was, he didn't know what his position was, and he also wasn't sure how he'd voted on it. Is there any excuse for that at this stage of the game, given the fact it involved gubernatorial appointments?

The President. I'm not familiar with the details of that. I'm strongly in favor of Clayton Williams over his opponent—not just for personal reasons, either. And don't ask me for a review of the ballot items yet. I'll be voting down there Tuesday and take a look at them. And don't ask the people of California, where they don't have one but they have I don't know how many of these referendum items on the ballots. So, I'm not troubled by that because what I see in Clayton Williams is a person that will be a very good, strong Governor for the State. And I am enthusiastically for him. And I'm not even familiar with the details of the ballot item you're talking about.

Persian Gulf Crisis

Q. Mr. President, Vice President Quayle said yesterday that the United States must deal with Iraq's chemical, biological, and nuclear capability. Is this now a fundamental goal of U.S. policy in the Persian Gulf? Is it one of the things on which there is, as you say, no flexibility?

The President. I think from the very beginning we spelled out some objective, but one that I think has been clearly spelled out has been ensuring the security and the stability of the Gulf. And that, obviously, is affected by the possession of these chemical and biological weapons and things of that nature.

So, I don't think that the goalposts are being moved; I think it's just simply a statement of reality. If you're going to have a stable and you're going to have a secure Gulf after Kuwait is freed and the Iraqis have withdrawn their invasion, you're going to have to have some arrangements I'm sure—I think others would agree with this around the world—that guarantee the peace there. And I would hope that—as I've said earlier, I want all United States forces out of there as soon as possible—every single soldier.

And it's important I keep repeating that because there's the allegations by some over in that part of the world that we want to keep forces there. That's not what we want to do. We want to come out. But there has got to be some security arrangements worked out, absolutely.

Q. Mr. President, just to make sure I understand what you're saying, the United States and this international force we have cannot successfully leave the Persian Gulf until we have secured in some manner these weapons the Iraqis now have?

The President. No, I wouldn't say that. But there has to be some security arrangements that guarantee against a future aggression of this nature.

Q. Mr. President, you said today that Saddam Hussein has committed atrocities that were worse than Adolf Hitler. Can you tell us what Saddam Hussein has done that can be compared to the Holocaust?

The President. Worse than—compares with what Hitler has done?

Q. With the Holocaust.

The President. Yes, go back and—well, I didn't say the Holocaust. I mean, that is outrageous. But I think brutalizing young kids in a square in Kuwait is outrageous, too. And I think if you go back and look at what happened when the Death's Head regiments went into Poland, you'll find an awful similarity.

I was told—and we've got to check this carefully—that Hitler did not stake people out against potential military targets and that he did, indeed, respect—not much else, but he did, indeed, respect the legitimacy of the Embassies. So, we've got some differences here. But I'm talking—when I'm talking about—I see many similarities, incidentally. I see many similarities by the way the Iraqi forces behaved in Kuwait and the Death's Head regiments behaved in Poland. Go back and take a look at your history, and you'll see why I'm as concerned as I am.

Q. Mr. President, you've spoken now about the brutality against the hostages in Iraq. However, there's a report today by Amnesty International that there has been some—our own allies, the Saudi Arabians, have been guilty of committing some kind of atrocities, at least torturing some citizens of Yemen who are in their country. What do you say to that? And will you put any pressure on them to change their ways?

The President. Yes, I have not seen that, and I think that violations of individual's rights or torture should not take place. And I'd be glad to represent that.

Q. How do you feel, though, about the United States helping someone who is doing the same sort of things that you're criticizing the Iraqis for?

The President. I feel that I'm delighted that we are there with the Saudi Arabians to stand up against this kind of international aggression in violation of international law. And that is the question. And that's where I'm going to keep my focus, because it is very important, one, that Saudi Arabia be defended—and I think now that we can certify that Iraq does not have the capacity to invade Saudi Arabia—and secondly, we are united with Saudi Arabia in our determination to overthrow this aggression.

Soviet Union–U.S. Relations

Q. Secretary Baker is going to meet Shevardnadze [Soviet Foreign Minister] in Europe in the next few days. Is that because you're concerned that the Soviets are drifting in the Gulf strategy, or is it because there's a deal behind the scenes after the Primakov visit in Baghdad, or is it only because you want to push the START agreement?

The President. Well, we've got a broad agenda of items. We've got to finish up CFE. We want to move START towards conclusion. We have these common interests that you're asking about in the Gulf. And then we have economic problems that we discuss all the time. So, there will be a broad agenda in the meetings with Shevardnadze, and I'm sure that one of them will be a discussion of the Primakov visit to Iraq and the Primakov visit that preceded that to Egypt and the Primakov visit that followed that to Saudi Arabia.

But the mission, if I understand the question, is not simply to focus on this Gulf question because I am anxious to get these other matters resolved. The CFE is all but put to bed, but there's a tiny technical matter that I think—well, hopefully, it's been resolved by now. But it's a broad agenda.

Q. Are you concerned that the Soviet Union is drifting?

The President. No, I don't. And I think one point that we ought to keep reminding the American people of is that we are very fortunate, in wrestling with this problem of international aggression, that the Soviet Union and China have been with us, or we've been with them—however you want to look at it—in the United Nations as we try to bring international pressure to bear—and have brought it to bear.

Campaign Speeches

Q. Mr. President, in your two speeches in Massachusetts this morning, you were a lot softer on the Democrats than you've been in recent days. Why the change of heart?

The President. It's not a change of heart. It's a question of—I think I made my point. But I'll have a shot at them as we get into the—depending on how warmed up I get today, campaigning enthusiastically for Governor Martinez [of Florida]. And I'd like to finish on a positive note in these campaigns. But I think it's a little early to say that there will be no more flamboyant rhetoric about the Democrats, because I'm absolutely convinced if we had more Republicans things would be a lot better.

Persian Gulf Crisis

Q. Mr. President, early in the course of the Persian Gulf crisis, you said that you would not allow hostage-taking to dictate your policy. You said that would endanger every American because every American would then be subject to being held hostage. Your comments today seem to change that: it seems to highlight their situation. Have you changed your mind about the importance of highlighting hostages in this crisis?

The President. I want to be sure I understand your question. I'm not sure I understand it—on highlighting hostages. What I think I said before was hostage-taking punishes the innocent and separates families—back in September. It is barbaric, it will not work—September 16th—and it will not affect my ability to make tough decisions.

Now, there are other quotes here, so I want to be sure I understand. You see, because what I think some are picking up is there's a different emphasis. But I think—is that one in accord with what you're asking about?

Q. Yes, sir. I see you were prepared for the question. [*Laughter*]

The President. It's a good question, but you see, I think some are saying: Hey, there's a shift here. There's a dramatic shift in how we approach hostage-holding. And I don't think so.

I'll tell you what is different, though, Michel [Michel McQueen, Wall Street Journal]. It's the sense of kind of urgency I feel given the reports coming out of Iraq and given the status of the Embassy. So, maybe that's what's being picked up here. But I think there's been a consistency in my outrage about the policy itself.

Ann [Ann Compton, ABC News], and then——

Q. If I could just follow: The concern is that many analysts say that that was the key mistake that President Carter made: that he made the hostages so important that he gave the Iranians at that time more of an incentive to hold on to them. The question is, are you now highlighting their situation to a point where Saddam Hussein has the same incentive?

The President. I don't think so. I don't

think so at all. I think the whole world has spoken out on this. So, I don't think there's a parallel.

Q. In the political speeches today, why have you so carefully now cut the Gulf issue out of the political speeches and appealed for bipartisanship? If it's good, strong leadership to have a strong policy in the Gulf, why not use it to Republican political advantage?

The President. Because I don't think it is a partisan issue, and I worry about that. I know there was a—some Democrat, paid Democratic functionary, made the point that I would likely go out and use Iraq to garner votes. I view this as something much more important than just garnering votes. I think it is important that this policy, which has been supported by Democrats and Republicans, be articulated, but not under even the threat of a cloud of doing this for political advantage. That's why I got a little incensed because somebody raised the question with me yesterday—are you doing this for pure partisan gain or something. And I find when you have servicemen over there and you have an obligation as Commander in Chief and you have an obligation as President that you just have to make very clear you're not trying to make what we do in Iraq partisan.

I need bipartisan support. We've got bipartisan support. One of the reasons I'm consulting with Congress as much as I have is to keep the bipartisan support. And so, I don't want—the reason I'm doing this, Ann, is just to be sure that people know that I am not trying to do what this Democratic functionary suggested I might be doing.

Q. Mr. President, you said that earlier in the press conference the sand is running through the glass now. It sounded like suddenly time is no longer on your side, that you seem to be hinting it may be shifting. Is that the reason why you've begun to emphasize the military option more, or what exactly are you thinking about the clock now?

The President. I'm not sure I've emphasized military option more. I don't recall discussing military option per se except to say I'm not ruling things out. But I do think that in a sense time might be on our side, because if the sanctions are to have any

effect, they should be having more effect now than they did when they started, and hopefully more tomorrow than they do today. But I don't think that the status quo can go on forever and ever. And I don't know how long—as I've tried to be very frank with you all—I don't know how long is long enough. But I've just got to keep putting the focus there and keeping everybody on notice that we are going to be successful. But it's—I'd leave it right there.

Q. Mr. President, sir, my question goes back to the issue of whether to keep the Embassy open. Sir, you do seem to have changed your position. In August, in Kennebunkport, the administration ordered all nonessential personnel home. The Marine guards were ordered home. There are very few people there today. Why is it so important to keep the Embassy open? It sounds as if perhaps an armed conflict might be triggered whether the Embassy gets a resupply of food?

The President. I believe that the Embassy should remain open because I don't believe a dictator should violate international law by starving out or isolating another person's Embassy. I think there's a fundamental principle involved in that. And I view the Embassy as entitled to certain international respect and international protection. And so, I just want to be sure everybody knows that I feel this way.

What was the second part?

Q. Is it worth triggering an armed conflict—whether the Embassy gets a resupply of food?

The President. It's too hypothetical. You're assuming that it would trigger an armed conflict. And I'm not going to discuss what will or won't trigger an armed conflict. But let me simply repeat: This one is one that I believe is of enormous concern to our allies and to the American people. And I can certainly recertify, as I did yesterday, that it is of that kind of concern to me. But I don't want to go into what incident, what provocation would stimulate military action. But I'm very concerned about this.

The last one, he said—Tom, you had your hand up. You didn't have your hand up. [*Laughter*]

White House Staff

Q. Mr. President, some of your closest friends, some senior members of your government, and even a lot of Republican Members of Congress who support you were telling us that your White House staff is simply not strong enough, not heavy enough to serve you well, and that's one of the reasons why you've taken this political beating lately. Are any of these people telling you that? And if they are——

The President. No.

Q. ——how do you react to that?

The President. No, they're not telling me that because they know that I have full confidence in my White House staff and full confidence in my Cabinet. And I have been blessed with good advice, some of which I take, and maybe more of which I should have taken in one thing or another. But nobody has come and presented that to me at all. I've read meaningless speculation about that in certain periodicals, but I'm inclined to discount it because I know what I feel about my top staff and I know whether they have my confidence or not—and they do.

Do you have a followup to that one? [*Laughter*]

Q. Over the next couple of months, do you envision any shakeup at all in the White House staff, either in terms of personnel or in terms of the structure of the operation?

The President. There may be some. I think we'll have an announcement very soon on one of our top people—not one that has been speculated about, incidentally. But there could be. It will be 2 years into an administration, and I think if you look back at history, why, there's been very, very little turnover. So, there could be one or two, but it won't be because of the kind of dissatisfaction with somebody's performance at all. And it damn sure won't be related to any standing in the polls or anything as—am I ever glad that I told you all—[*laughter*]—and I would like to remind you of it—months ago—[*laughter*]—September. [*Laughter*] No, but seriously, I think it's fair to point out I told you, when things were soaring like eagles, don't believe the polls. And I think now I'm entitled to say: Hey, we're going to come on back. Don't worry about it. They'll be all right.

Thank you ever so much. Thank you. Thanks a lot.

Note: The President's 64th news conference began at 4:36 p.m. in Room D at the Marriott World Center Hotel.

Remarks at a Reception for Governor Bob Martinez in Orlando, Florida
November 1, 1990

Thank you all very, very much. You've been standing there a long time. Thank you. I am just delighted to be here. And the minute I got off this airplane, I felt that enthusiasm, the surge that guarantees that Bobby Martinez will be the Governor come election day once again. He deserves it, and he's got it moving. And Mary Jane, you were fantastic. If you want our dog to come down and campaign for you, just invite her. Barbara's already done her thing for Bob. [*Laughter*]

And of course, Allison DeFoor—I mean, here's a sheriff, a man of the law, a man of the people. He'll be an outstanding Lieutenant Governor serving at Bob's side, working against the criminals in this State—law and order, sound fight against narcotics. We're lucky to have a man like this on our ticket, I'll tell you.

Let me pay my respects to the Senator standing next to me here, Connie Mack. Although he's not running, he's out there across this State campaigning hard, giving the Florida Democrats a "Mack attack"—[*laughter*]—and doing a first-class job. And we're delighted you're here today.

And then my old friend Bill McCollum.

He and I have been suited up in the political warfare for years. And you ought to see, you ought to see the job he does on his anticrime legislation and on this whole protection of the rights of the American family. He is superb. And we need another like him, and that's why Bill Tolley has got to be elected. Bill, good luck to you. For those of you in this congressional district, get out the vote and send me another good member of the Florida delegation, someone I can work with to hold down these taxes and keep the government out of your pocket. Bill, we need you.

And, of course, I want to pay my respects to three old friends: Jeanie Austin, who's doing a superb job on the national level as cochairman of the Republican National Party; Van Poole—Mr. Chairman, we now call him—thank you for your extraordinary effort in leading this party to majority status. And then, of course, when you want some heavy lifting done, I'll give you a little advice: get Alec Courtelis to do it. What a superb job he's done as finance chairman.

And so, I'm thrilled to be back here. This election here in Florida is close; it's crucial; it is important. And a few nights ago—I missed it, but I've had the instant replay—you saw it. You saw what was at stake. You saw what it takes to be a great Governor. And you saw a Governor offer the balanced approach that you would expect from a seasoned leader of a city, now a leader of a great and a growing State. You saw Governor Bob Martinez in action win that debate and go on to win the vote—now he'll do it on Tuesday.

And some of what came through there was much of what we've been watching as his admiring friends over the years. We saw one who believes that the people of Florida know what's best for themselves. And he believes in empowering people, empowering communities, tapping into the power that comes when millions work for a common vision. And little surprise, then, that under a Republican Governor Florida is moving forward for a cleaner environment, for better schools for these kids, for streets safe from drugs and crime.

Florida ranks number one in the creation of new businesses and new jobs, especially in high-tech manufacturing. And the credit goes, of course, to the people of Florida and to this man, Governor Bob Martinez.

You're looking at a kindred soul when it comes to one who has respect for the Everglades because I love going down there each year. And you know that I know that every Floridian treasures the Everglades, that unique and irreplaceable resource. And last year, I was able to sign into law a bill increasing the size of the Everglades National Park by more than 100,000 acres—Connie Mack being most instrumental in this, strong supporter of this legislation; Bob Martinez urging that it be done. I need a Governor here with whom I can work in the White House.

And, yes, I think we can say—and this message goes out to other States—that Florida is tough on drugs. Bob is in the lead here—leading Governor on substance abuse and drug trafficking for the National Governors' Association—fighting against these for the good of Florida. And he set a national precedent by appointing a State drug czar. And he's been a leader in making sure that parolees undergo drug testing and counseling to get straight and stay straight. And the credit goes to this man, Governor Bob Martinez.

And so, whether he is standing up for the environment or standing up to the drug dealers, he's completed a remarkable record of achievement that would make any Governor proud. He's never been one to walk away from a job. And for Governor Bob Martinez, even the toughest challenge is just another day at the office. We're lucky to have him. Please reelect him.

I was up in Massachusetts—two stops in Massachusetts—and the theme there is the same as it is here. The Republican Party is the party of change, not the status quo. We are the party of new ideas. And there is no higher domestic priority on the Republican agenda than the Nation's economy because our economy is the job-creating engine that every family in this country counts on.

And I know in recent months there's been some understandable uncertainty about and concern about slower economic growth. And that's one reason getting a budget agreement in my view was important and why I was willing to go the extra mile to get it. The negotiations were tough. And my approach was clear. The Democrats wanted to raise taxes, including income taxes, and I wanted to reduce the Federal budget deficit with spending cuts. And if we had had more Senators like Connie Mack, more Congressmen like Bill McCollum, we would have got it done exactly the way I wanted. Because they don't want to raise taxes on the American people. And they want to cut spending.

But every once in awhile a President has to compromise to make something happen—to govern. And in this one, there was some good news, actually. We got $492 billion in deficit reduction, $350 billion in spending cuts. And then we've got some incentives in there to make America less dependent on foreign oil. And this is critical, and it is very important: We put Congress on a pay-as-you-go basis. The enforcement provisions of this agreement are real, and they are strong, and no longer will new programs be funded with red ink.

And finally, we did do something that I think is vitally important—and these two Members of Congress agree is vitally important—and that is we held the line against reckless cuts in our defense spending. You see, I am determined that given the threats we face around the world, I am determined that this nation's defense remain strong and prepared. And we owe that much, at least, to those fine young men and women who are stationed in the Persian Gulf serving our country with such distinction.

But let me tell you other places where our agenda coincides with what Bob Martinez believes. We fought for a responsible child-care law, one that would put choice into the hands of American families. You see, it is our belief that we ought to empower parents to choose those who will care for their children, not let the Federal Government make a determination how that should work. We fought for this, and these leaders here helped enormously, and we won it.

And we also fought for a responsible clean air bill. And we asked Congress to cut acid rain, to cut smog by harnessing new technology with the power of the marketplace. And we fought for this, and we won it.

And of great concern to me and to Florida is yet another landmark law, a fair and effective law to ensure the civil rights of every disabled American. And so, I was particularly proud in this session to sign into law the Americans with Disabilities Act, historic legislation that protects the civil rights of 43 million men, women, and children with disabilities. And that bill does prohibit discrimination against the disabled in employment and public accommodations and transportation and communications. And all Americans with disabilities can now pass through a once-closed door to a bright new era of equality and independence and freedom and opportunity.

And so, there were some historic achievements: clean air, child care, this ADA bill. The great strides, though, are just beginning to show what Republicans can do for this country. And, of course, there is still much more work to be done on the Republican agenda. And at the top of our agenda—and I report to you with not too much happiness on this one—was crime. America is fed up with crime, whether it's neighborhood crime or crime in somebody else's city. And Republicans know handcuffs belong not on the cops and the courts, handcuffs belong on the criminals. And that was the underpinning of our crime bill.

And shortly after taking office, I stood before the U.S. Capitol and called on Congress to pass tough, new laws to help America take back its streets. And instead, in the final hours of Congress, the Democratic liberals—those in Washington like the ones Bob is running against here—completely gutted our package to fight against violent crime. Republicans—two of them right here—fought for habeas corpus reforms aimed at stopping convicted criminals from endlessly abusing the appeals process. Republicans fought for revision of the so-called exclusionary rule, a judge-made law that lets the guilty go free. And Republicans fought for a real Federal death penalty for drug kingpins and terrorists. And we've got to be tough on crime and criminals. And it's Republicans that want change. Give me more Republicans in the House and in the Senate to get this job done.

And as I make that plea for Bill Tolley to

go to Congress to support Bill McCollum and Connie Mack, as I do that, let me just say that Republicans can look no further than what Bob Martinez has done. With his leadership, it can be done. In other words, with his leadership, Florida has been tough on crime, toughening laws to ensure that the criminals stay behind bars and adding the prison space to enforce it. He picked a no-nonsense sheriff—standing right here—as his running mate. And that tells you something. Bob Martinez and Allison DeFoor will make Florida an even safer place to live, and you can count on it. You can count on their doing just that.

And that's what this election is all about. But, of course, while the election in Florida is crucial, our thoughts are also halfway around the world with the brave young men and women who are teaching us a lesson about what it means to love liberty. And so, my appeal would be this: As November 6th draws near, 5 days from now, I urge every Floridian to get out and vote. Do not take democracy for granted. And when you do vote, I hope you cast your ballot for a Governor who will carefully balance the needs of Florida's abundant and beautiful natural resources with the needs of man.

Bob Martinez—and I've been in his home; I've known him for years; he's been in our home up in Washington—he believes in the Florida dream. We can make the most of economic opportunity while protecting this State's special way of life.

And so, my appeal to you tonight on behalf of your State and nation is to vote for a leader who can take Florida forward. Vote for Governor Bob Martinez.

Thank you for all you have done for our country and for our party. And now go out and give America a better deal. Thank you all very much.

Note: The President spoke at 5:32 p.m. in the Grand Ballroom of the Marriott World Center Hotel. In his remarks, he referred to Governor Martinez' wife, Mary Jane, and Van Poole, State Republican Party chairman. Following his remarks, the President traveled to Cincinnati, OH, where he remained overnight.

Remarks at a Republican Reception in Cincinnati, Ohio
November 2, 1990

The President. Thank you all very, very much. Thank you. How long have you been standing there? I won't say please be seated, but listen, I am delighted to be back here. I'm something a little more than an adopted son. Yesterday, when I was in Massachusetts—I was born there, so I said, "I'm your native son." My dad was born in Columbus, and Barbara's family grew up here, so I claim a little bit of Ohio. I know enough about the State to know that when I say we need change and we need George Voinovich and Mike in the capitol, I'm talking Ohio values. We need them to be elected.

And we have an outstanding ticket that can represent change. I've known Bob Taft for years. He helped me get elected President of the United States. And I want to see him in there—and Judy Brachman and Paul Pfeifer. We need this kind of quality and class act to be elected across this State. It is time for a fundamental change for Ohio.

And you do that, you can take care of State government. But I need a little help in Washington, DC. We've got a couple of great Congressmen sitting up here right now—McEwen and Gradison—outstanding. But I want to have John Boehner in Washington with me, and I want to have David Hobson with me. We've got to strengthen the Ohio delegation. And if we did we would not have to have any compromise with the tax-and-spend Democrats that I'm up against every day in Washington. Good luck to both you guys.

I want to salute our State chairman, Bob Bennett, who's doing an outstanding job in strengthening and building this party. I want to salute Martha Moore. That, of course, brings me to another man of the hour for this area, and I'm talking about Ken Blackwell, who we need desperately in the United States Congress. I love the feel of the Blackwell campaign. Everybody I met with—one of the reasons we kept you waiting is we were talking to some of those that had been over, actively involved, I should say, and doing maybe a disproportionate amount. But the enthusiasm for Ken Blackwell, so well-known here because of his own public service, is infectious. And I know that he will be elected next Congressman from Cincinnati and from Hamilton County.

I'm sorry Barbara's not here.

Audience members. We love Barbara.

The President. Yes, I do, too, but—[*laughter*]—she threw that fastball at the Cincinnati catcher, and she didn't dare come back after the opening pitch [of the World Series]. [*Laughter*]

You know, Pearl Buck, talking about Ohio, said there's no flashiness, nothing fleeting in Ohio's approach to life. One feels in the very atmosphere a combination of stability and progress. And I like that because it makes you think about the traditional old-fashioned values, fundamental values of real America, values that say, we don't need more government in middle America, we need more middle America in government.

And if there ever was a ticket that embodies these values—the first thing that comes to mind when you hear the names George Voinovich or Mike DeWine or Bob Taft or Ken Blackwell are honesty and integrity and experience, too. George has—you've heard the record, but he's brought back the city from the brink of financial collapse. And he's brought back its people from the brink of despair. And he shares my belief that government works best when it draws upon the time and the energy and the expertise and, above all, the commitment of its people.

And I'm going to take George's message to Washington when I ask the Congress to work harder and smarter and do more with less. That's what we have to do when we have tough times. But it can be done. Bill [Gradison] told you the revenues in the Federal Government are up by $80 billion in one year. You're not being taxed too little; they're spending too much in that Congress back in Washington, DC.

I can bring you some news from our drug czar: We're beginning to turn things around in the fight on drugs. But when you vote for George and Mike, you're part of a pledge, a pledge that we will not allow our communities to be held hostage to gangs and drug dealers. And you can count on George and Mike to keep that pledge with the people of Cincinnati.

As to Bob Taft, I remember many sessions with him back in '88 when he was cochairman of my campaign here in Ohio, running for President of the United States. And I don't have to tell you, anybody in this room knows how high the stakes are in this race for secretary of state. It's absolutely critical for the upcoming redistricting process. We have to elect this tough, experienced watchdog, this man with a sparkling clean record as a citizen's advocate and as a leader. Bob Taft must be elected secretary of state.

And back to the man of the moment here for the congressional battle. I don't want to overlook my old friend Bill Gradison, but he doesn't seem to be overly concerned about his reelection. [*Laughter*] And the reason is he's done such a superb job they can't find anybody talented enough to run against him. But really it is great to have Ken on the ticket. A terrific candidate. He's got the new ideas. He's got a commitment to fight for them. And we need this fresh approach. We all know that Congress desperately needs change. And I need this man in Washington. And as I say, I like the feel of the campaign; I believe you're going to send him to Washington as the next Congressman.

You know, there's no higher domestic priority on the Republican agenda than the American economy, the job-creating engine that every family in this country counts on. And in recent months we have seen a slowdown, and we've seen some uncertainty and concern about slower economic growth. And that's why a budget agreement, in my view, was critical and why I was willing to go the extra mile to get it. And despite some tough negotiations, we finally reached an agreement with the Democrats that control the United States Congress.

But let's be clear, there was and always will be a major difference with our approach to a solution. The Democrats wanted to raise taxes, including income taxes, for working Americans. They tried to sneak through a proposal on indexing, automatic tax increases, that would have raised the taxes $40 billion on the working families of this country. And they did it all under that demagogic title, "soak the rich." They weren't soaking the rich; they were coming after every working man and woman in Cincinnati and all across the State of Ohio. And we stopped that. And I'm going to fight it every inch of the way from here on out.

And I would repeat this: If we had more Congressmen like those that are here and challengers elected like those that are here, we would not be in this fix. We would not be in this mess of tax and spend, tax and spend. Once in a while, you do have to compromise. Harry Truman was right: The buck does stop on the desk in the Oval Office. And sometimes when you're dealing with two Houses of Congress controlled by the opposition party, you got to give a little to get something done for the United States.

And though I didn't like a lot of that budget agreement, there's some good things in it. It's cut about $492 billion over 5 years off the deficit; that's progress. And $350 billion of that was in spending cuts. There's some incentives left in it. And we did put Congress—and this is the most important part of it—on a pay-as-you-go plan. The enforcement provisions of that deficit agreement are real, and they are strong. And no longer will these programs be funded with red ink, because I have that veto pen and I will use it over and over again to make this Congress live within its means.

There's another idea whose time has come, and the people understand it, but the Democrats in Congress are fighting against it. Give me what 43 Governors have. You give me that line-item veto, and let's see if

we can't do something about cutting the spending in this government.

And one other thing that is rather serious out of that agreement: We did ensure something essential. The defense account took a big hit in the budget as we know, but I can certify to you that the Nation's defense remains strong. And so, we came out of that deal better than I'd hoped in many categories. But getting our fiscal policy on track is just part of what we've done in this party of change.

There's so many other things. Out of that deficit package came a child-care bill to put choice in the hands of the American families. The Democratic approach: Let Washington figure it out. Let Washington tell you what you've got to do on standards and regulations to have your child looked after in child care. And the Republican approach prevailed: parental choice. Keep that child care close to the family. We don't want any government agency warehousing the kids.

I worry, and so does Barbara, about the family values. I worry about the disintegration of family. And one way to keep it strong is to give parents more choice, not only in child care but in the education of their children. And we are going to continue to fight for it. I'm up against an entrenched liberal Democratic bureaucracy in the House of Representatives that wants to mandate more educational programs. Now you give me Ken Blackwell and these two people and add to that many more around the country, and we will try the new ideas that work and not the old ideas that have failed in the past.

Education, it is absolutely essential. And so, when some were calling for a bigger bureaucracy, we called for flexibility. And I believe that's the heartbeat of the State of Ohio. I think that's what they want in this State, and I think that's what they want in their Representatives in Washington, DC.

Our agenda is not fulfilled, but our ideas are still strong and they're still sound. And all we need is some more troops; all we need is some more quality, young, dynamic people in the Congress to help us fulfill our obligation to the American people. And once again, that's why I want Ken Blackwell elected to the Congress of the United

States.

And now, because of knowing about the interest in what's happening halfway around the world, I want to ask you to shift gears with me. Because I view my responsibilities as President and I view my responsibilities as Commander in Chief as something very sacred. And we're at a partisan political event, but there is keen interest in what's happening halfway around the world in this Gulf crisis. And so, in the spirit of Arthur Vandenberg, who said politics ends at the water's edge, I want to just bring you up to date on how I feel as President about what's happening over there. And I will say at the very outset that regardless of the politics, the Democratic leaders in the House and the Democratic leaders in the Senate have been extraordinarily cooperative. The Republican leaders in the House and the Republican leaders of the Senate and the Republican and Democratic Members in both bodies have been extraordinarily supportive because our nation is together in our determination that Saddam Hussein's aggression will not stand.

Several of you earlier on asked me to make comments on this, or asked me about it, and I said I would. On August 2d, Iraq invaded Kuwait, and its soldiers literally—this isn't figurative—raped, pillaged, and plundered this once-peaceful land, Kuwait, a member of the Arab League, member of the United Nations. And the United States and the rest of the world did unite in anger and outrage and determination to force Saddam Hussein out of Kuwait.

The people outside with those signs—I know—I can share their concern. But they're wrong when they say it, no war for oil. We're not talking here about simply oil or the world economy. We are talking about brutal, naked aggression. We are talking about brutal, naked aggression. We are talking about one country bullying a neighbor. And that's why we are there: to say that will not stand. The United States, and only the United States, can lead this coalition against that kind of aggression.

And so, we did do what George said, we did do what he said: we put together a coalition unequaled in modern history. We revitalized the United Nations process, we and the other members of the Security Council. And indeed, the Security Council has passed 10 resolutions of condemnation and disapproval about Iraq.

On August 5th, I said that Saddam's aggression would not stand, and I'll repeat it today and I'll repeat it tomorrow and I'll repeat it the next day because we have a stake in seeing that one nation not bully a neighbor and take it over by force and then pillage and rape its citizens. Let me be clear: We have no argument with the Iraqi people. None at all. We bear no hostility towards Iraq, nor do any of the 25 countries that are represented with us on land or sea. And we're not alone there: over 25 on the land and the sea feeling exactly as we do. Many Arab countries, along with others—Western Europe and Australia and Belgium and wherever—all of us concerned, all standing against aggression.

Our problem is not with the people of Iraq; our problem is with the dictator of Iraq, Saddam Hussein. And I want, let me assure you, a peaceful resolution to this crisis. We need that. And I've worked, indeed, very closely with the U.N. in putting these sanctions into effect, passing resolutions, speaking with one voice against the invader's aggression. And we are giving these sanctions, unprecedented sanctions, economic sanctions against Iraq—we are giving them time to work. And I hope there will never be a shot fired in anger. Let me be very clear, though. There cannot be any compromise with the stated objectives of the United Nations Security Council and the objectives that I have outlined as President of the United States. No compromise at all. Saddam Hussein must get out, and he must get out totally, and the legitimate rulers must be returned.

And one other point. The brutality against innocent civilians will not be tolerated and will not stand. The clear violation of taking innocent civilians and staking them out in areas that could be targets for military action contravenes every tenet of international law. It is inhumane. It is wrong. And it must not be rewarded.

They asked me at a press conference in Florida yesterday why I was concerned about our Embassy. There are several Americans there, a number of Americans.

The American flag is flying over that place. And this man is systematically trying to drive these Embassies out by starving them out, keeping them from getting resupplies. And, yes, I have that on my mind and my conscience because I don't believe that is acceptable international behavior on the part of anybody, dictator or not. That is not the way you respect international law, and I think he is just as wrong as he can be in holding innocent hostages in Iraq and in trying to circle and starve out the United States Embassy in Kuwait. This must not be rewarded.

We do have the finest young kids in the armed services ever. Every member of the Joint Chiefs has told me this. They are volunteers. They're highly motivated, brilliantly trained. And they're serving us halfway around the world, and they're your sons and your daughters and your neighbors and your friends. And we owe them an enormous vote of thanks. And now, I will do my level best to bring every single one of them home without a shot being fired in anger. But we will not stop short of our stated objectives. We are the United States of America. We are standing for principle, and that principle must prevail.

And now before I head off to Minnesota, let me just shift gears back once again to the real world of politics. I have been very enthusiastic for many years about George Voinovich. I've seen him in action. I've seen what he's done in Cuyahoga County. I've seen what he's done for the great city of Cleveland. And I know him. I know his family's integrity and decency and honor. And so, when I stand up here and suggest as an outsider—the one whose dad was born and whose mother-in-law and father-in-law were born here—[*laughter*]—I think I know what I'm talking about. And when Barbara comes out here and puts her arm around Janet and tells the people of Ohio how strongly she feels as a mother and one who also knows this State—we're talking from the heart.

I want you to go out and work hard in the last days of this campaign to elect George Voinovich and the other statewide office seekers. And then I'd say this: We have a chance to make history in the Ken Blackwell race for Congress. Do not let history pass us by. Let's take this giant step for good government in Ohio and good government in Washington, DC. Get out to the polls 4 days from now and elect these outstanding leaders.

Thank you, and God bless you all.

Note: The President spoke at 8:47 a.m. in the Presidential Ballroom of the Westin Hotel. In his remarks, he referred to gubernatorial candidate George Voinovich and his wife, Janet; Michael DeWine, candidate for Lieutenant Governor; Judy Brachman, candidate for State treasurer; Paul Pfeifer, candidate for State attorney general; Martha Moore, vice chairman of the State Republican Party; and William J. Bennett, Director of National Drug Control Policy. Following his remarks, the President traveled to Rochester, MN.

Remarks Upon Arrival in Rochester, Minnesota
November 2, 1990

I just wanted to say to the people of Minnesota that being here for [Senator] Rudy Boschwitz is something I feel strongly about. Here's a man that had the guts, the courage to stand up and do what was right: getting this deficit down. And he's shown that kind of leadership for Minnesota for a long time. And this is a priority race for us, and I couldn't be more supportive. And I'm just delighted to be here.

Note: The President spoke at approximately 11:30 a.m. on the tarmac at Rochester Municipal Airport.

Remarks at a Republican Party Reception in Rochester, Minnesota
November 2, 1990

Thank you for that welcome to Rochester. Rudy, thank you so very much. However, about the weather—*[laughter]*. Forty-seven years ago, almost to this day, I was sent by the Navy to Minneapolis to learn to fly airplanes, and I never landed a plane on anything other than ice and snow, at least in Minneapolis, for 6 months. Don't tell me it's typical, but it is awful nice.

What a joy it is to be here. And let me first thank my friend of long standing, Wayne Newton, who flew all the way from Las Vegas here for this, and now back tonight. And one other matter of tremendous importance to this area—and now I'm caught up in the fray—is I want to congratulate the girls cross-country team at John Marshall that's going to the State finals and wish that—right over here. Good luck at State.

And now for the business at hand. I am just delighted to show my strong support for a national leader in our party and one of America's greatest United States Senators, Rudy Boschwitz. It is essential he be returned to office.

And I might say I'm enthusiastic about Arne Carlson, the "Rocky Balboa of Minnesota," a seasoned leader. Three days is all that's left, and he's going to defy the odds and become what you need: a new Governor for the State of Minnesota. I heard that this guy was in favor of shortened campaign seasons, but this is ridiculous. *[Laughter]*

And I am excited about the rest of our ticket: Joanelle Dyrstad and Kevin Johnson for attorney general and Dave Jennings and Bob Heinrich, John Burger for State treasurer. We've got good people running, and they need your support, too.

Let me just tell you why it's a pleasure for me to be out here for Rudy. He's a person that Minnesotans trust. I know that. He's one who does embody responsible government. And you know he's a member of the Ag Committee, the Senate Agricultural Committee. That means he's a champion of your dairy farmers and a real believer in the wonders of milk. And so, at Rudy's

Super Duper Milk House at the State fair every year, he serves cherry-, banana-, and root beer-flavored milk. What worries me is, I don't mind cauliflower, but I hope he doesn't throw out that broccoli-flavored milk. That's where we draw the line. *[Laughter]*

And Arne, in introducing Rudy Boschwitz, referred to this, but after 10 years on the Budget Committee he is known in Washington and across this country—Rudy—as a tough fighter for lower taxes, a strong advocate of the spending freeze. And here's a Senator in a tight race who made the tough choice and voted for an essential budget agreement that's going to bring this deficit down $492 billion over the next 5 years. And while others were weeping because they didn't get it just the way they want, Rudy put the United States of America's interest and Minnesota's interest ahead of his own desire for this change or that. And that takes courage; that takes guts and independence. And we need more like him in the Congress.

You know, there's no higher domestic priority than the economy, the job-creating engine that every family in this country counts on. And in recent months, we've seen some uncertainty and concern. I'm concerned about the slower economic growth. And that's why a budget agreement was crucial and why I was willing to go the extra mile to get it. And despite tough negotiations, we finally got an agreement with the Democrats that control both the House and the Senate.

And there were clear differences. The Democrats wanted to do it all by raising taxes, including income tax rate increases for working Americans with that insidious indexing provision. They called it socking the rich, and it would have raised $40 billion out of the working men and women of this country. And thanks to Rudy and others up there, we beat it—beat it to its knees. And that isn't going to happen.

Rudy and I, if we'd had our way, wanted to do it more with spending. You see, I don't feel you're taxed too little; I feel because of the liberal Democrats in Washington, we're spending too much. And that's another reason we need him back.

But the best thing about this agreement was we did get strong enforcement provisions in the law. There was another one that's good, too—we held the line on reckless cuts. Defense spending came down, but we eliminated the reckless cuts that would have cut into the heart of our national security. And that wouldn't have happened if we didn't have farsighted Senators like Rudy Boschwitz that know this world is not a tranquil place. We need people that understand the national security interest of the United States of America back there in the United States Senate.

But this is only part of what the battle is about, this fiscal sanity. Let's start with another issue here: the environment, our sacred trust. Rudy, coming from this land of 10,000 lakes, has been a strong advocate for sound environmental practice. I need his voice for the environment. We've finally gotten a clean air bill that I can sign. And that's good for Minnesota; it's good for the Nation; it's good for Canada and Mexico. And we are again in the lead for environmental purity all across this land of ours and across the Earth, but we've got to have more people that understand you can grow and still have good environmental practice. And that's where Rudy is, and I'm grateful to him.

The legislative logjam was broken. I want to give a little credit not only to Rudy but also to Dave Durenberger, because without them I don't believe I would have had a Clean Air Act that I can confidently and optimistically sign. So, I'm grateful to both Rudy and Dave on that one.

There's still a lot of work to be done on the Republican agenda. America, frankly, is fed up with crime. I hope you're doing a little better in Rochester, Minnesota, than we are as a nation as a whole. But nevertheless, Republicans, wherever they are, know that we need tough legislation. We know that the handcuffs belong not on our able police officers but on the criminals themselves. And that's the kind of legislation we were fighting for. Ever since I met with a couple of victims of crime, family groups, it

occurred to me—and I feel strongly about it—that we need a little less sympathy for the criminal and a little more for the victims of these crimes in this country.

And shortly after I took office, I stood in front of the U.S. Capitol and called on Congress to pass tough new laws to help America take back the streets. And instead, in the final hours of this liberal-controlled Congress back there, Democratic liberals choked up and completely gutted our package to fight back against violent crime. Republicans fought for habeas corpus reform and stopping convicted criminals from endlessly abusing the appeals process. We fought for reforms of the exclusionary rule, a judge-made law that lets the guilty go free. And Republicans fought for a real Federal death penalty for drug kingpins and terrorists and those who kill our police officers. And the Democrats blocked it. And we need more Senators like Rudy to stand up in the next Congress and fight for that.

So, if you get the idea that I'm enthusiastic about Rudy Boschwitz, you're beginning to get the message. He's a class act. He's a class act with a great family. Please send him back to Washington.

And so, my main message here today is one of partisan politics, because I believe with Arne as Governor and Rudy in the Senate you're going to be in good hands—very good hands, indeed. But you know, let me now just ask you to set partisan politics aside for a minute, because I want to talk to you about a subject that is in the hearts and on the minds of every single American. And I know that everyone in this country is vitally interested in the Persian Gulf situation.

And you know, former Senator Vandenberg was absolutely right when he said politics ends at the water's edge. And I'm grateful to the leaders—Democratic leaders, Republican leaders, Democratic Members, Republican Members of the House and Senate—for their strong bipartisan support. But I thought I owe it to the American people to keep affirming and bringing as best I can our message of purpose on the question of why we are there.

Let me first be clear: There will be no compromise on the stated objectives of the

United Nations Security Council resolution, none at all. And the reason is this: We cannot compromise with brutal, naked aggression. We cannot permit one country to bully a neighbor and take it over without making them pay the price.

And let me make another point. Let me make another point. The brutality against innocent civilians will not be tolerated, and that will not stand, either. What's happening to those so-called guests—really hostages—is uncivilized. And the world should rise up and demand that those people be let go. It is outrageous what Saddam Hussein [President of Iraq] is doing.

No one, no one, wants a peaceful solution to this situation more than I do—nobody at all. No one, however, is more determined to see this aggression turned back than I am. We forged together the most fantastic international coalition in history. We've resurrected the Security Council of the United Nations, with 10 resolutions passed condemning this brutal aggression and holding of innocent people hostage. And I will do my level best to hold that coalition together, to see that these international sanctions work, and that Iraq get out of Kuwait—and without condition—and free the people that they are holding in contravention of international law.

Now, we are determined, and the world understands it. And thank God the people of the United States understand that it is only the United States that has the strength and, I would say, total commitment to stay the course and see that this aggression is turned back.

These are not easy times. These are not easy times at all. But I have never been more proud of the young men and women—all volunteers—highly motivated, beautifully trained, who are serving halfway around the world than I am today. These are the finest young men and women that have ever served in the Armed Forces of the United States. And we will not let them down.

And so, let me shift back now 180 degrees. I wanted to get you that message of how strongly I feel and end this way. It is right that we participate in partisan politics. It is right that I as the President go around this country talking about the men and women that I want elected to office, as the Democratic leaders are doing for their candidates. And it is right that I came to Rochester, Minnesota, today to tell you from the bottom of my heart—and I seldom speak for the Silver Fox, that's Barbara, my wife—and this one I confidently do. And even our dog, Millie, agrees with this—[*laughter*]—that we strongly support Arne Carlson for Governor. And we urge you—we cry out: Send Rudy Boschwitz, our friend, your admired Senator, back to Washington, DC, for 6 more years.

Thank you, and God bless all of you.

Note: President Bush spoke at 12:22 p.m. in the gymnasium of John Marshall High School. In his remarks, he referred to entertainer Wayne Newton; Joanelle Dyrstad, candidate for Lieutenant Governor; Dave Jennings, candidate for secretary of state; Bob Heinrich, candidate for State auditor; Senator Dave Durenberger; and President Saddam Hussein of Iraq. Following his remarks, President Bush traveled to Sioux City, IA.

Remarks at a Republican Reception in Sioux City, Iowa
November 2, 1990

Thank you very much. Somehow it seems like I just left. But thank you. I am delighted to be back in the Hawkeye State and in Sioux City, this all-American city whose citizens had planned this marvelous emergency response, a city that was ready for the worst kind of a challenge, a city that opened its hearts to the survivors of a tragedy, a city that inspired the world. Thank you for all you've done.

And I'm delighted to be standing here with a United States Senator who does support me, and, I say, support you, the people of Iowa, for our common objectives. An old friend—and I'm talking about Chuck Grassley who is making such an outstanding record in the United States Senate.

Let me say a word about his former spokeswoman, who is now so outspoken on behalf of her husband. What a fantastic campaigner—she is fantastic. Barbara sends her love. I'm talking about Bev Tauke. She's marvelous.

I see some other party leaders, all of whom have been introduced, and I want to thank them. I want to single out the Congressman from the Fifth District, an early and longtime supporter and friend, Congressman Jim Lightfoot, over here. And of course, your very own, from the Sixth District, Fred Grandy. What a job he's doing for his country. And let me also salute Joy Corning—your next Lieutenant Governor—and the rest of the Iowa ticket.

That brings me to the main course: two great Iowans, a great present Congressman, a great future Senator, Tom Tauke, and a great Governor, Terry Branstad. Oh, how we need them both reelected and elected.

You know, as I looked across the national scene, I can't think of any Governor who faced a stronger challenge than Terry did in his first two terms. But he prevailed because he believed in the ethic that Tom was talking about. He believed in controlling spending and promoting enterprise. And as the Omaha World Herald put it, Branstad gave the State of Iowa sensible leadership through the hard times of the past few years and guided the State into its current recovery. Terry is more than a Governor who withstood the test of hard times. He's fought for one of the best State educational systems in the entire country. He's more than a Governor; he's a leader. And he's leading Iowa into an even greater future. Send this man back to the statehouse.

I might add that it's little surprise that at the Charlottesville education summit, this first national summit on education with the President and all Governors, Terry and I worked closely to reform American education, just as he's worked for better schools right here in Iowa. And in short, he has been good for Iowa. He's won your support the old-fashioned way: He earned it. And

he was also instrumental in formulating these national educational goals for the entire country. And I need him now reelected to be sure those goals are met for the entire Nation.

And now a word about another old friend, a man I've known for many years. We're here on behalf of him. He's also earned the right to represent Iowa. He's a tireless fighter for the family, for the taxpayer, and for the farmer and the working people of the Second District and all of Iowa. And I'm, of course, talking about your next United States Senator, Tom Tauke.

You may not know the whole story of why he decided to run for the Senate. Let me tell you about it. It turns out he was walking right through a field one day, almost lost between towering stalks of corn when he heard a voice—[*laughter*]—and the voice said, "If you run, you will win." [*Laughter*] So, "Field of Dreams" aside, I share your dream that he be elected to the United States Senate on Tuesday. We need him bad.

We need him. We need him. And it is not my habit to speak against anyone's opponent. I haven't done that, and I'm not going to start now. I'm here to be for Tom Tauke. But I want to just say that I would like to have somebody in the United States Senate that supports me and my objectives a little bit more and not less than Ted Kennedy. [*Laughter*] So, you figure it out. What he told you about his opponent's support for the President is true. It's written in the Congressional Quarterly. I urge you to look it up.

You know, ours is a party with a vision. We are the party with new ideas—a vision, a change, a sweep of new thinking that can only come with more Republicans. And we're also a party that's committed to a growing economy, that job-creating engine that every family in America counts on.

And I know in recent months nationally—delighted the Iowa economy is doing well—but nationally, we've seen some uncertainty and concern about slower economic growth. And that's why, as President, I had to make a tough decision on this deficit deal. After difficult negotiations, we finally reached that agreement with the party that controls Congress—both Houses controlled by the liberal elements of the Democratic Party. And the Democrats wanted to raise taxes, including income taxes on working Americans. And they called it—and Tom stood up and knocked this down—they called it soak the rich. But here's the fact: Their proposed surtax on the rich to raise—I think it would have raised $4 billion, was in the very same bill. They were yelling about that. And the liberal Democrats in that same legislation rammed through taxes on the working man and woman of $40 billion—$4 billion to soak the rich and $40 billion to hit the working man and woman of Iowa. We need Tom Tauke, not more of these liberal spenders, in Washington, DC.

And I agree with Tom. I agree if we had more like him and Fred Grandy and Jim and Chuck Grassley we could get the job done by more cuts in spending and less taxes out of your pocket, because it is our theory that we don't tax you too little, Washington and the Democrats spend too much.

You know, Terry Branstad can give us all a good, sound lecture on cutting waste. Forty-three Governors, like him, already use the line-item veto. I believe he told me he's used it 120 times, working for the taxpayers of this State. And this is an example not lost on Tom Tauke, who has sponsored and fought for the line-item veto where it is needed most of all: in Washington, DC. And if we put Tom and more like him in the Senate, we can make that line-item veto the law of the land. And if Congress can't do it, give the President a chance to cut that spending.

I'd also like to ask you to compare the records on our crime legislation, legislation to try to curtail crime at the Federal level. Shortly after I took office, I stood before the United States Capitol and called on the Congress to pass tough new laws to help America take back the streets. And instead, in the final hours of this Congress, Democratic liberals completely gutted our package to fight against violent crime.

Now, let me just tell you what Tom Tauke and I want. We want habeas corpus reform because convicted criminals should not be able to endlessly delay justice. We want to reform the exclusionary rule so this judge-made law won't let the guilty go free. And because we believe in backing up our law enforcement officials, we want something else: We want a Federal death penalty for drug kingpins, for terrorists, and those who wipe out Federal law enforcement officials. Republicans are the ones who have more sympathy for the victims and a little bit less for the criminals. That's the kind of vote we need in the Senate.

I believe we're beginning to win this war against drugs. Our national strategy is beginning to work. And there's some heartening information about this—heartening evidence and statistical evidence. So, I don't want to be here with a message of gloom and doom. I believe the Nation is waking up to the idea that we can no longer tolerate the drug culture. But I would say this: We need people like Tom Tauke in the Senate so justice can be done. I happen to believe that a strong offense against the narcotic traffickers is what we need, not this coddling by the law that the Democrats have put up with.

And there are many, many other reforms. We've also, frankly, achieved a lot. I don't want to be just on the negative side; we've achieved a lot recently—remarkable, considering that we're a minority in the House and a minority in the United States Senate. We fought for a responsible clean air bill. And we asked Congress to cut acid rain, to cut smog by harnessing new technology with the power of the marketplace. We fought for this, and we won it. And one of the ways we can clean the skies of America is, as you know in this State so well, with alternative fuels. So, we can cut our dependence on foreign and give our business to the American farmer.

Another good thing that Tom and his fellow Iowans in the Senate and House Republicans have fought for was a responsible child-care law, one that rejects that old liberal Democrat idea of warehousing children, one that would put choice in the hands of American families. Republicans want to empower parents, not the Government, to choose those who will take care of their children. And we won that battle, thanks to Tom and others.

So, I guess what it boils down to is our vision, a vision based on good, old-fashioned family values. In education, in child care, in protecting the environment, Republicans are the ones that are determined to bring hope and opportunity to millions taken for granted by the Democrats. And if ever you despair about our political process, think that it's not working, remember this is your country. It belongs to those who work in the fields and the factories, and it belongs to those who teach the children of Iowa so well—and God bless our teachers for the job they're doing with our young people.

America belongs to the people, and America's leaders should reflect that simple fact. And so, let's make election day an opportunity day. Let's return, of course, Jim Lightfoot and Fred Grandy to the Congress. That's off to a good start right there. And

let's send our great Governor back to Des Moines: Terry Branstad. And then let's take a look at that Senate and send me some people that I can work with for the values that you believe in, someone to help Chuck Grassley, not just cancel out his vote on every issue. And I'm, of course, talking about Barbara and my friend Tom Tauke. Elect him on Tuesday. Work your heart out. We need him. He can make a difference for Iowa and for the United States of America.

Thank you, and God bless the United States.

Note: The President spoke at 6:16 p.m. in Gallery A of the Sioux City Convention Center. A tape was not available for verification of the content of these remarks. Following his remarks, the President traveled to Thousand Oaks, CA.

Remarks at a Tree-Planting Ceremony in Thousand Oaks, California
November 3, 1990

Thank you all. What a lovely, lovely day. Please be seated, and thank you. And may I salute Governor Deukmejian; Senator Pete Wilson; your own Congressman, Congressman Gallegly; Bob Lagomarsino, neighboring Congressman; the distinguished environmentalist who leads our EPA, Bill Reilly, with us today from Washington. And of course, Dr. Jerry Martin [Miller], we want to thank you for cleaning up the air and affording us such a very special day on your campus.

It is a pleasure to see these trees, spread beneath a broad and peaceful sky like, I'd say, a thousand points of shade. [*Laughter*] And in a few minutes, it's going to be a thousand and one.

I'm told that the people of Thousand Oaks have invested countless hours in urban forestry management, something every community in America can do. Trees save on cooling cost, reduce urban smog. Trees mean greener cities and neighborhoods. And they are God's great filter— noise and air; providers of shade, privacy, and wildlife habitat.

But more than that, trees create a sense of community among the people who plant them and a sense of continuity between generations. And if we had stronger trees, these would not be falling over if we had them tied into the tree. [*Laughter*] And that's why I'm so pleased that this year's budget will begin our ambitious national tree-planting program.

I'm also pleased about something else. I made a commitment as a candidate for President to break the congressional stalemate that has hindered progress for clean air in this country for 13 years. And I continued that commitment beginning a year and a half ago by coming forward with a comprehensive clean air proposal. We worked with the leaders from both parties, local government, environmentalists, representatives of industry because I believed that it was time for a new approach. And I want to thank your Senator for his support. I want to thank the example set by the Governor of this State. I want to thank the Members of Congress on both sides of the aisle who were extraordinarily supportive.

The old tradition of simply regulation was not the answer. And we needed a new kind of environmentalism, driven by the knowledge that a sound ecology and a strong economy can go forward together. And so, I challenged the Congress to work with me to break the logjam of clean air. And while our proposals differed in minor details, Congress has passed a bill that is true to the architecture and spirit of our approach.

Thanks to the persistence of Pete Wilson and other Members of Congress and to our able head of our EPA—Bill Reilly is with us today—we are on the verge of a major domestic achievement for all Americans. And I can now say to Californians that I will sign this landmark clean air legislation as soon as it gets to my desk within the next few days.

Just a couple of details: The bill that I proposed last year and that Congress passed last week is efficient, effective legislation that will pull 56 billion pounds of pollution from the air every year—224 pounds for every man, woman, and child in America. And this legislation is a bold departure from the old Washington-knows-best approach. It achieves unprecedented pollution reductions by using incentives and the power of market forces. And in a phrase, we're cleaning up the air not through overregulation but through smarter regulation.

This clean air legislation will cut in half the emissions that cause acid rain, by 10 million tons, and then cap them at these lower levels. It will cut the emissions that cause smog in our cities, so that by the end of this century more than 100 major U.S. cities will have cleaner, healthier air. And it will cut these dangerous air toxic emissions by 75 percent. And it will encourage broader use of alternative fuels.

Ever since I first joined the Congress more than 25 years ago, I have been committed to using our laws to protect the environment; and so, of course, has our Senator Pete Wilson. We both believe that in its size and scope this clean air act isn't simply the most significant environmental legislation of this administration, it's the most significant air pollution legislation in the history of this country.

This clean air act is sound energy policy as well because it does promote conservation. It encourages the use of cleaner fuels. It strengthens America's energy security. And in a short time since we issued the clean air challenge, we've seen a revolution in thinking about alternative fuels. The time is right, the people are ready, and industry is responding.

We are on the verge of a new era for clean air. And so, to commemorate a milestone in America's environmental history, today we'll plant a tree, because what we celebrate this day has roots running deeper than law. It is potential for new progress, a planting with a daily harvest, a promise lasting far longer than our lifetimes.

And so, thank you all for joining us at this symbolic occasion. I am very grateful that we have a clean air act. And now I would encourage all the citizens in our country to follow the example of today, right on this campus, and assist us in making tree planting a major national objective—not only good for the United States but it benefits the entire world.

Thank you all so much for coming.

Note: The President spoke at 9:50 a.m. in Kingsman Park on the campus of California Lutheran University. In his remarks, he referred to Jerry Miller, president of the university.

Remarks at a Reception for Gubernatorial Candidate Pete Wilson in Thousand Oaks, California
November 3, 1990

Thank you very, very much. Pete, let me give you my impartial view of the situation. [*Laughter*] It is absolutely essential to California and it is absolutely essential, I'd say, for the entire country that this, the biggest State in the Union, have Pete Wilson as the next Governor, following our outstanding Governor George Deukmejian.

And I'm delighted to be in Elton's congressional district. We need him back there and plenty more like him. And the same for Bob Lagomarsino for the next district. And this year in California, we have a class-act, skilled, seasoned ticket of excellence. With us today, Marion Bergeson, the next Lieutenant Governor; Joan Milke Flores, as secretary of state; Tom Hayes, State treasurer—we need him there to watch these guys—and of course, Dan Lungren, my old friend and former Congressman, who will be a great attorney general; and Wes Banister, the insurance commissioner. We've got a great ticket. Now you've got to vote for Pete and the rest of them. And after they've served their term, how about sending Eric Peterson off to be Governor of the State? The guy's tough.

I take great pride as President in the way the Marine Band, the President's own, plays "Hail to the Chief." But if they ever get tired, what about the Thousand Oaks High School Band? They were marvelous. You guys were good, real good.

I am delighted to be back with you. What a reception I had at the airport, Point Mugu: red carpet, 21-gun salute, signs saying, "Welcome back!" "We love you!" And when I went down the stairs, I told someone I was surprised by the big greeting. He said, "Not as surprised as I was. We were expecting Barbara."

Gayle, she sends her love to you. She's your friend, as you know. And we Bushes, our entire family, just wish you and Pete all the best on this very important coming Tuesday.

You know, I won't regale you with the background, but you know the record: the great mayor of San Diego, superb Senator. President Reagan calls him principled. Even his opponents call him wonderful. [*Laughter*] And in January, everyone will call him Governor.

He's a great manager. As mayor, he balanced 11 straight budgets. As an environmentalist, he's playing a great big part in my decision to put a moratorium earlier this year on oil and gas leasing off the coast. An advocate for fiscal sanity, quality education. You know of his record as being tough

on crime and wanting the laws in Washington to do something about it. And the same approach would be brought to bear following up on Duke's magnificent record right here in Sacramento. He deserves your support, so I came out here to say: Let's elect Pete Wilson the next Governor of this State.

You know, in recent months, we've seen some uncertainty and concern about the slower economic growth across our country. And that's why a budget agreement of sorts was crucial. And that's why I had to compromise—found as Harry Truman said, that the buck does stop on the President's desk. And every once in a while, you have to make a tough decision to compromise. And despite tough negotiations, we finally reached a budget agreement with the Democrats that control both Houses of Congress.

And when it came to our approach, though, let me point out three big differences. The Democrats—and Elton and Bob know this well, and Pete as well—wanted to raise taxes, including income tax rates on every working man and woman in this country. And I wanted to reduce the deficit by spending cuts. We did get a $492-billion deficit reduction over 5 years—$350 billion of it in spending cuts, incentives to make us less dependent on foreign oil. So, there were some good things there. But the main thing: Congress now is on a pay-as-you-go plan. There are real enforcement provisions. And finally, although the defense budget was reduced, thanks to Pete Wilson and others like him that know the importance of our national security we held the line against reckless cuts to ensure that this nation's Armed Forces remain strong. We are in a dangerous world, and we better not let down our guard. And thank God for Pete and Congressmen like these two.

That's just part of what we've accomplished as a party of change. For example, when it comes to the environment—Pete mentioned it—but he and I believe that to keep our environment green, we don't have to be Big Green. And in fact, Pete wrote the first coastal protection act, and a driving force for our environmental initiatives, supported our expanded land acquisition for national parks and wildlife refuges and forest and public lands. And all of this explains why I asked Pete to lead our crusade for clean air. And today, as a result—thanks to the innovation and cooperation of the industry; of government; our EPA, under Bill Reilly, who's with me here today; and the environmentalists across the country—we have broken a 13-year legislative logjam. And finally, I have a clean air bill that I will be proud to sign when I go back to Washington, DC.

I wish I could give you a better report on the Congress. If we had more Republicans in the Congress like these two, I could give you a better one. But let me just say this: There's still work to be done on our agenda.

Ask Pete, the grandson of a police officer who gave his life in the line of duty. He knows, I know, George Deukmejian knows, America is fed up with crime. And we want people who have a little more sensitivity to the police officers, and a little less for the criminals themselves.

Shortly after I took office, I stood before the Capitol and I called on the Congress to pass tough, new laws to help America take back the streets. And instead, in the final hours of the Congress—George thinks he's got troubles with Willie Brown [speaker of the State assembly]—[*laughter*]—look, in the final hours of this Congress, the Democratic liberals choked, and they completely gutted our package to fight back against violent crime. We fought for habeas corpus reforms aimed at stopping the convicted criminals from endlessly abusing the appeals process. We fought for reforms of the exclusionary rule, a law that lets the guilty go free far too often. And we fought for a real Federal death penalty for drug kingpins and terrorists and those who gun down our police officers. And the liberals gutted those right out of our package. They blocked them, and we've got to get tough now.

And I think especially of the fine, young police officers like San Bernardino's own Rob Shultis, who was brutally killed last February. We will be tough on crime. And give me more Republicans in Washington, more people like Pete Wilson in Sacramento, and we'll get the job done for the American people and for the American families.

It is simply not fair—I wish you all could see these little kids here—but it is simply not fair that their parents have to worry in some areas of this country when the kids go to school, have to worry about the kids' safety. It is time—not to be brutal about it—but it is time to have more thoughtful people who want to be tough on crime to take back our streets. And that's another reason I'm for Pete Wilson.

There's a lot of wonderful young people here from this great school, and I'm grateful to President Miller—[*applause*]—I am grateful to the president and Eric and the students that are here today. But let me—I saw some signs out here, and I understand them. And the signs—so let me first put the caveat down. I want to shift gears. I want to ask you now to lay aside the partisan politics because this is—it's not often I have a chance to talk to this many people in the State, in the State of California—back in Washington all the time.

But we're at a partisan political event, but I'm asking you to shift gears now because everyone I know is vitally interested in what Pete talked about; that's the situation in the Gulf. And just a few words about our mission there, having said that I am very grateful to the Republican leaders, to the Democratic leaders, liberals, conservatives, whoever, for the support they are giving our policy in the Persian Gulf. It isn't partisan; it is American. And I am very grateful for that support.

So you have it—and particularly the young people—so you have it in your sights: We have no quarrel with the Iraqi people, none at all. We bear no hostility to the people of Iraq, nor do any of the other 25 countries represented on land and sea in the Gulf in the most fantastic coalition put together since World War II, or even including that. We have a magnificent U.N.-based coalition standing up to the aggressor of Iraq. So, our problem is not with the young people there or the man on the street there; our problem is with Saddam Hussein and his determination to be the neighborhood bully. And there's a fundamental moral point here: A neighbor cannot take over another neighbor, bully it, brutalize it, rape, pillage, and plunder in Kuwait, and get away with it. If we permit that to happen, we'll pay the price another day. And I will not let that aggression stand.

Yesterday at Point Mugu, I climbed off the plane and had a chance to at least shake hands with some of the wives of our young people over there. And look, they're your brothers, our neighbors, sons, daughters, friends. These aren't strangers. These are the finest trained American troops in the history of this country. Every single one of them is a volunteer. And they are beautifully motivated. And yet their families are split asunder. And so, my message is this: I will give the sanctions—unprecedented economic sanctions—the chance to work. I will give them the time to work. And I can tell each parent, each brother, each sister, I hope there never is a shot fired in anger. I hope that every single one of those kids will come home without a shot having been fired.

Now, having said that, we are the United States. I see these signs about Hungary and the other countries that now enjoy the freedoms that sometimes we have taken for granted, and I can identify with that. And I can identify with the fantastic changes that are taking place in Eastern Europe, but I also can identify with this principle that one country must not be able to bully its neighbor. And so, I will say this: I don't want a shot fired in anger, but there will be no compromise on the stated objectives of the United Nations Security Council—none at all. The United States will lead, and we will stand, and we will prevail against the evil of that dictator.

Pete mentioned the fact that in a few weeks that the kids over there will be sitting down to Thanksgiving dinner. And Barbara and I are really looking forward to visiting those young people halfway around the world. Each member of the Joint Chiefs has told me—and to you parents, listen carefully because you know this, but listen anyway—each member of the Joint Chiefs has told me that, as far as they know, in the history of the United States there have never been finer, more motivated, better trained soldiers than the men and women over there now. That is a fine tribute to your sons and daughters.

And so, that's the situation as I see it today in the Gulf. I will do my level-best to keep this coalition strong, together, standing always for principle. But you young guys remember: It is only the United States that can lead the entire world for this moral purpose. We're the only ones. Countries look to us, and that's the beautiful thing about the heritage groups represented here today. Every single one of them recognizes that this is the country that stands for freedom, stands against aggression. And as long as I'm President, I'll do my level-best to portray that message to every country in the world.

And now let me shift back to the business at hand—salute all of you, thank the students on this great campus, and encourage you to do this: Do not take democracy for granted. Go out there and vote in this important national election. The elections in California will affect every State in the entire country. So go out and elect Pete Wilson and this distinguished team. Elect him Governor of this State. And do your part to move California ahead.

Thank you all, and God bless you.

Note: President Bush spoke at 10:40 a.m. in the auditorium at California Lutheran University. In his remarks, he referred to Representatives Elton Gallegly and Robert J. Lagomarsino; Eric Peterson, president of the university's Republican students speakers' bureau; Jerry Miller, president of the university; Pete Wilson's wife, Gayle; and President Saddam Hussein of Iraq. He also referred to Big Green, the environmental protection initiative on the November ballot in California. Following his remarks, President Bush traveled to Albuquerque, NM.

Remarks at a Republican Campaign Rally in Albuquerque, New Mexico
November 3, 1990

The President. Frank, thank you very much. Thank you all very, very much. I am just delighted to be here. Thank you, thank you, thank you. Frank, I love this enthusiasm. I think it bodes well for the election of Frank Bond as the next Governor of New Mexico. Get out and get the job done.

Frank, to you and Mary Thompson, your running mate, Barbara and I send our warm, best wishes for a strong and successful finish to this race you've both run so well. And I'm delighted to see one of the great leaders in the United States Senate here, Pete Domenici. What a man he's been for his country. And of course, if we had more Congressmen in Washington like Steve Schiff, we wouldn't be worrying about red ink and too much spending; we'd be doing much, much better. And of course, another great Congressman—who is not here with us today—but Joe Skeen is also the same stripe as Frank. Wonderful people—Steve, Frank Bond. And let me just throw in another name well-known in Washington because he served there, but he's served this State with such distinction, my dear friend Garrey Carruthers. What a job he's done.

And I am very sorry that I had to miss the visit just a few days ago, but look at this magnificent turnout. And besides, our daughter-in-law Columba was up in Santa Fe trying to do a little makeup work. I'm glad she was here to show the flag for the family. Our dog, Millie, sends her love. And Barbara Bush, the Silver Fox, sends her love, too.

You know, in a sense, this is kind of like coming home, because I spent 12 years over in west Texas, right near Eunice and Hobbs and not too far from Roswell. And I feel I know this State. I'm delighted to be back. And I want to just say that we are enthusiastic about this trend to send a good man, Frank Bond, to follow a good man, Garrey Carruthers.

In a sense, next Tuesday marks a turning point for New Mexico. You face a choice: whether to turn the clock back and return to those days of the seventies—we used to call them the malaise days—or to make this election the first step towards a future as bright and broad as the New Mexico sky. And there's not a doubt in my mind about the right choice: Starting November 6th, New Mexico will move forward with Frank Bond.

Frank knows what it takes to make New Mexico even more competitive, and he knows what it is to do that and how to open up markets, national and international. He knows what the move towards a free-trade pact with our good neighbor Mexico can mean for this State's economy: new jobs, new businesses, and new opportunities for New Mexico.

And we are on a glorious new path in our relations with our neighboring country Mexico. I've worked hard with President Salinas, and I think I can say to you, relations are on the way. They've never been better, and I think they're still moving up. And I'd like to have a Governor in this State with whom I could work to continue that great cooperation between the United States and Mexico.

You know, here at home, a growing economy is the job number one for our party. And the economy is the job-creating engine that every family in the country counts on. With the help of State leaders like Frank Bond, I'm going to do my level-best to see that the national economy keeps on growing.

You know, in recent months we've seen some uncertainty. Some areas have had some real slowdown. And that's why, in my judgment, a budget agreement was critical and why I was willing to work with Pete Domenici and others to go the extra mile to get it. And despite tough negotiations, we finally got a budget agreement with the Democrats that controlled both Houses of the United States Congress.

And we had our differences—big differences. But I want to say that we ended up with some things I'll tell you about that are good. And it never would have happened without Pete Domenici's courageous leadership in the United States Senate.

The Democrats have started up their old line again. They wanted to raise taxes, including the income tax rates on every working family in America. They talked about "soak the rich." They had a surtax that would have raised $4 billion from soaking the rich. And at the same time, they were sneaking through a provision to raise $40 billion on the working men and women of this country. And we stopped it with Steve Schiff and Joe Skeen and Pete Domenici.

You see, I sent up a budget that would have reduced the deficit with spending cuts because I believe, as you do, that you're not taxed too little, the Government spends too much. We did get some pretty good events out of that. We had $492 billion in deficit reduction—$350 billion of it was in spending cuts. We built in some incentives to encourage oil and gas drilling that will make America less dependent on foreign oil. And I think that's a good thing and very timely. And the best thing about it is Congress was put on a pay-as-you-go plan—real enforcement provisions in this budget agreement. And lastly, although defense was reduced—and I believe it should have been some—we held the line against the reckless cut. And we ensured that America's defenses and Armed Forces remain second to none anywhere in the world.

But you know, getting a budget agreement behind us is just part of what we've accomplished. Let's start with the environment, our sacred trust. Frank Bond's grown up here, in the shadows of the mountains, amid the grandeur and beauty of the New Mexico desert. So, you New Mexicans want someone committed to preserving New Mexico's rich natural heritage in all its singular splendor. And I know a fourth-generation New Mexican you can count on. He's right here, and his name is Frank Bond.

There's a little good news coming out of Washington, because more than a year ago I challenged the Congress to support my determination to break the stalemate that has hindered progress on tough clean air legislation for the past decade, to turn technology and to power the marketplace to the advantage of the environment. And today, thanks to the innovation and cooperation of industry, government, and environmental experts, we've broken a 13-year legislative logjam. And there will be landmark legislation which will decrease by 10 million tons the emissions caused by acid rain. It will bring to the Nation's 100 most smog-laden cities safer, healthy air. And it will encourage the use of alternative fuels that are safer for our environment and reduce our excessive dependence on foreign energy. And Republicans care about the environment. We have finally got a clean air bill that I will sign when I go back to Washington, DC.

There's still work to be done on the Republican agenda—education, for example. Frank Bond knows America can't have a first-class economy with second-rate schools. And we're determined that every child in America has a fair shot at a quality education. That's why I proposed and, earlier this morning, I signed a substantial increase for Head Start, to serve 690,000 kids across this country. And that's why we sent to the Congress the Educational Excellence Act, our action plan for fundamental education reform—to reward achievement and encourage accountability and to give parents more say in their children's education. I would rather have the parents have more choice about the schools than have some committee in Washington assign how this education ought to work at the State level. Frank Bond and I agree on something fundamental: When it comes to the schooling of our kids, the bureaucracy does not know best; the parents do. And we want to support the good, excellent teachers—thank God for those teachers that sacrifice to educate the young people in this country every single day.

You know, today we're here on a very partisan point of view—proudly. And that's what Americans should do. We ought to participate. We ought to work to elect those candidates we believe in. Now, as I've been doing for a couple of days, I want to put partisan politics aside. And I know that everyone in this country is vitally interested in the situation in the Persian Gulf. So, let me just say a few words about our mission there.

You know, former Senator Vandenberg was right when he said politics ends at the water's edge. And I am very grateful to the leaders in the Congress, both Democrat and Republican, and to the Members of the Congress—all of them—and to the American people for the steadfast support they are giving the policy of the United States of America in the Persian Gulf.

You know, I want to be very clear about this. The United States bears no hostility to the people of Iraq, nor do any of the over 25 countries represented on land and sea in the Gulf area. We have no argument with the people of Iraq. Our problem is with Saddam Hussein and his determination to take over and bully a neighbor. And we are not going to permit that to stand. And let me say this: I want a peaceful resolution to this crisis. Indeed, we have worked closely with the United Nations in putting sanctions into effect. The United Nations has never been more united nor more fulfilling its peacekeeping mission than it is today as it unanimously condemns the aggression of Saddam Hussein, the invading dictator of Iraq.

So, we are giving the sanctions time to work. And I hope there will never ever be a shot fired in anger. But once again, let me be very, very clear: There will be no compromise on the stated objectives of the United Nations Security Council resolutions. The brutality against innocent civilians will not be tolerated. And it will not stand.

Saddam Hussein calls them guests, and I call them hostages. And Americans are being held against their will, and we cannot rest until every single one of them comes home, free to enjoy the liberties of the United States of America. So, let me say simply to those that are concerned, protesting: They've got it wrong. We're not talking about oil. We are talking about standing up against aggression. And if the United States can't do it and cannot lead, nobody can. We do not need another Hitler in this time of

our century. To stake out innocent civilians and to isolate and try to starve out an embassy is unacceptable behavior. And even these friends over here ought to understand that.

New Mexicans seem to understand this. Right now, brave young men and women are serving over there, halfway around the world. And they are the finest forces ever to serve. They're standing ready there in the sand and the heat of the desert sun. In a few weeks, they're going to sit down for a special Thanksgiving, miles from home and family. And Barbara and I have a lot to be thankful for. And we will be with those troops on Thanksgiving Day, and I will give them the thanks of everybody here today and of all the American people.

Yes, these are challenging times for our country. They really are challenging times for a country. But I can think of no more exciting time to be President of the United States than today. It is a tremendous challenge. Our country is united, and we will prevail.

And now back to the partisan business at hand. Next Tuesday think about the liberties we enjoy in this great country. Think about what a privilege it is to walk into a polling booth and vote. Think of the changes in Eastern Europe and the crying out for democracy that has been fulfilled. Think of the changes south of our border in this hemisphere. And do not take democracy for granted; go out and vote. Vote for Frank Bond, for his running mate, for Pete Domenici. Do your duty, and we will have better government in the State of New Mexico for the next decade.

Thank you, and God bless you. And God bless America. Thank you.

Note: The President spoke at 4:05 p.m. in the Durand Hanger at Albuquerque International Airport. In his remarks, he referred to Gov. Garrey Carruthers. Following his remarks, the President traveled to Houston, TX.

Remarks to a Campaign Rally for Senatorial Candidate Hal Daub in Plattsmouth, Nebraska
November 4, 1990

Mr. Daub. Mr. President?

The President. Yes.

Mr. Daub. We're gathered in Plattsmouth, Nebraska, in a Veterans of Foreign War post with lots of friends and supporters. And it's actually a part of the Second District that it was my privilege to represent when you were Vice President.

The President. Well, Hal, let me just say hello to everybody gathered at Plattsmouth. Barbara and I are here in Houston. We vote here day after tomorrow—end up my campaigning—we'll be here tomorrow. But we just wanted to wish you and Cindy the very best as this campaign wraps up.

Obviously, both of us have been there before. But I'd like to once again ask the people in Nebraska to send you, Hal Daub, to the Senate. I need more support. If we're going to get the job done for the people of Nebraska and the country, we need more people that think like you do. And I really am emphasizing the fact that we need change. Somebody told me that you'd visited 93 counties—every single one of Nebraska's counties—at least once in this campaign. And if there's ever anything that demonstrates hard work and commitment, certainly that is it. I'm not surprised, nor is Barbara, about the tireless campaign you've been waging. We also know that Cindy's a tremendous asset.

To the voters and the people there in Plattsmouth, let me just say this: I've known Hal for almost 20 years now. And I've learned a lot about him. I believe he will make a difference. It is the new versus the old for the Senate. As a lawyer, as a businessman, as a four-term Congressman, he's had the experience; but now he's going to bring a breath of fresh air to that Senate. And I believe he can make a difference.

You know, dealing with a Congress completely controlled by the Democrats is not easy. It's not an easy assignment. Let me just give you a couple of examples before I let you go and let you get out to work for Hal.

Early on, I proposed tough, new Federal laws, and I believe we had—on crime. I believed that—then, as I do now—that it is time we had a little less sympathy for the criminals and a little more for the victims of crime. And incredibly, the liberal Democrats killed this legislation in a back room in the dead of the night. And that is a singular reason why we need Hal Daub in the Congress in Washington, in the Senate, in the United States Congress, to help work on these key issues, because I know where he's coming from. And the people of Nebraska should understand that we need this driving force to get control in that Senate so we'll be able to take the offense. On the tax-and-spend policies of our opponents, this liberal, Democratic Congress is tough to top.

And again, I think if we had more Republicans in the Senate we would control the agenda. We wouldn't be playing defense to the liberal agenda that's coming down the pike at me from time to time. The only tool that I've got is the veto pen. We've used it; we've used it successfully. But even where we get whipped, if I had a Hal Daub in there, we'd have a vote to sustain the President's position on these key issues.

I sometimes think that if Washington was as well-run as Lincoln, Nebraska, things would be a heck of a lot better; and so, I want to put in a pitch here for Kay Orr. I also hope you get out the vote for another dynamic candidate, Ally Milder. Barbara was out campaigning with her the other day, and both of us send her and send Kay and, of course, send Hal and Cindy our very best wishes.

This election could be won or lost depending on who gets out to the polls. Nobody could have worked harder than Hal Daub. But now the question comes: Who is going to get out to the polls? I know the Daub campaign was on the move. And I'm depending on each and every one of you to get our friends and neighbors to vote. And vote for a Senator who will work with us, not against us. Vote for one that will be good for Nebraska and, in my view, good for the values that I was elected on and that Barbara and I believe in so much. So, my appeal: Elect Hal Daub as your next Senator. Hal, go get them. And many thanks.

Mr. Daub. Mr. President, for you taking this time to focus your thoughts on Nebraska and on my Senate campaign, I'm mighty grateful. Dorothea Roberts, who's here, who's done a good job with her team of helping put this gathering together. And my wife, Cindy, is standing right beside me.

The President. Well, give her a big hug and go on out and win now. And I'm pleased you feel things are moving.

Ms. Roberts. Hello, Mr. President.

The President. Hi, Cindy.

Ms. Roberts. Mr. President, this is Dorothea. Just a minute, I'll give her to you.

Mrs. Daub. Mr. President, I bring you greetings from Plattsmouth, Nebraska, from District 2, from Cass County. We all love Hal Daub, and we love you. Thank you.

The President. Well, not at all. Good luck to all of you. Now, this is exactly the time to put on the final pressure to win on Tuesday. Good luck.

Mr. Daub. Thanks very much, Mr. President.

The President. Over and out.

Note: The President spoke by telephone at 2:05 p.m. from Houston, TX. In his remarks, he referred to Mr. Daub's wife, Cindy; Gov. Kay Orr; and Ally Milder, candidate for the House of Representatives. Mr. Daub referred to Dorothea Roberts, Republican field representative. A tape was not available for verification of the content of these remarks.

Remarks to a Reception for Congressional Candidate Genevieve Atwood in Salt Lake City, Utah
November 4, 1990

Ms. Atwood. Hello, Mr. President.

The President. Genevieve, I'm glad it's a two-way connection. I thought maybe you'd just have to listen, which would be a hardship. [*Laughter*]

Ms. Atwood. Well, no, our relationship's a two-way street, Mr. President. I'm very supportive of everything you're doing.

The President. Barbara was just thrilled to be out there in Utah, and I just want to weigh in at the last minute. She's here with me in Houston, Texas, where we're going to be voting on Tuesday. But she loved being out there with you; and she came back with glowing reports of what you're doing, of your enthusiasm, and of the groundswell of support she felt for your campaign. So, she's asked me to pass along a message, and here's what she said: "I need a new friend in Washington almost as much as Utah does. Elect Genevieve Atwood to the United States Congress."

Ms. Atwood. That's a fabulous message. We believe in that.

The President. I expect you're for that.

And the main thing is I have a wonderful feeling that the people of Utah are for that as well. But I understand that you have my friend the Governor with you there. If he is, please give Norm my very best, will you?

Ms. Atwood. He's right here. Say hi.

Governor Bangerter. I'll say it myself, Mr. President. It's delightful to hear from you, and we look forward to seeing you in Washington in February.

The President. Listen, it's nice talking to you, sir. And you know, just if you had a minute more, I want to make a couple of points on some of the issues.

I first would like to say how much I rely on both Senators Hatch and Garn; and of course, Hansen and Nielson, you know, doing a great job as well. Utah needs someone who's going to work with the delegation, not against it, for the good of State and for the good of America.

And in my view, Genevieve Atwood, with her experience as a scientist and former legislator and fourth-generation Utahn, she understands Utah's commitment to common sense and to the family values that I think are so essential in this country. And, Genevieve, I know you'll provide a strong and independent voice as Congresswoman. And believe me, in dealing with the Congress—both of whose Houses are controlled by liberal Democrats—is not the world's greatest assignment, and we get frustrated because we need more people like you there.

If you had time for just an example or two—you know, on the anticrime legislation, I proposed tough new Federal laws. And I still feel that it is about time, in our legislation, that we show a little less sympathy for the criminals and a little more for the victims of crime. And incredibly, the liberal Democrats killed this legislation in a back room in the dead of the night. And I think if we had more people like you there, Genevieve, I believe we could get done in the Congress that which the people really want done.

So, anyway, here we go. And I would only say that not only on these issues, like education and the environment—which is so precious to the people of Utah—and anticrime legislation, we're still facing that tax-and-spend mentality of the liberal Democrats. And Genevieve is a strong supporter, I'm told, of the balanced-budget amendment and that Presidential line-item veto. My view is: If Congress can't do it, give the President a shot and let me try. And I believe we could make much more progress on this deficit without any tax increases by holding the line on spending.

So, good luck on Tuesday. I would say to those there: Please get out the vote. I know things look good in this race, but don't take anything for granted. We want to sound a call that would be heard from Temple Square to the foothills of the Wasatch Mountains to the banks of the Potomac. So, go get them. And, Genevieve, we're with you. On election night, we're right there with you, both Barbara and I, sending our love and our appreciation for a wonderful woman.

Ms. Atwood. Thank you for your wonderful support. Senator Hatch is here right next to me, and a bunch of folks. Why don't we give the President a cheer. Hooray!

The President. Hey, if I had known Orrin was there, I wouldn't have said such nice things about him. Orrin, if I had known you were there, I wouldn't have said such lovely things about you. [*Laughter*]

Senator Hatch. I understand, Mr. President.

The President. Listen, thanks for everything. You have been fantastic. And my best to Jake, too. And, Governor, my respects to you, sir. And now go out and get Genevieve in there.

Ms. Atwood. All right. Thank you, Mr. President.

The President. Over and out.

Note: The President spoke by telephone at 2:12 p.m. from Houston, TX. The reception was held in Ms. Atwood's home. In his remarks, the President referred to Senators Orrin Hatch and Jake Garn, and Representatives James V. Hansen and Howard C. Nielson. A tape was not available for verification of the content of these remarks.

Remarks to a Campaign Rally for Congressional Candidate Wayne Gilchrest in Salisbury, Maryland
November 4, 1990

The President. ——After all, this is our country, and that seat of yours in the United States Congress belongs to the people of the Eastern Shore—the farmers, the fishermen, the teachers, and everyone else in that wonderful part of the State. And if something is wrong, you can do something about it. And you can elect one of your own to the Congress as someone who shares our values, our family values. And that all boils down, as far as I'm concerned, to this phrase: Elect Wayne Gilchrest!

You know, in dealing with the Congress

completely controlled—both Houses completely controlled by the liberal Democrats, I've concluded that it isn't easy. I was elected to do certain things, and we get blocked because we have too few Wayne Gilchrests in the United States Congress.

Let me give you an example: I proposed tough, new Federal laws of anticrime legislation. And I really believed that it was time that we had a little less sympathy for the criminals and a little more for the victims of crime. But incredibly, we sent up a strong anticrime package, and it got totally bogged down by the liberal Democrats trying to kill the legislation and change it right there in the dead of night. And that's a very good reason to send Wayne Gilchrest up there, because we need more Congressmen that will support strong anticrime legislation.

And then I've had to veto after veto pieces of legislation in the Congress because the Democratic Party—not the one you used to think of in the Eastern Shore way, back when once in a while you could get what they called a conservative Democrat—but the national Democratic Party that controls this Congress simply is on a continuous tax-and-spend binge. And I really believe more people like Wayne could make a big difference—I know they'd make a difference.

And so, again, I urge you to put someone who is in touch, who's in tune with the people of Salisbury and the people of the Eastern Shore there. And so, this district—

I've talked to all our political experts—this district is one of the critical districts in the country for change, the kind of change that I want to see, the kind of change that I know you want to see. So, don't let them tell you no one can make a difference. In this very district, you can make the difference, make the change that will help our country. You've got a good man there in Wayne. So, go out and work hard for him.

And God bless you all.

Mr. Gilchrest. Thank you, Mr. President, and we will. And we're looking forward to victory on Tuesday. We know that the people of Maryland are going to vote for their community, and more importantly, they're going to vote for their children.

And we know that you're busy, and we greatly appreciate this time that you have given to us. We all do.

The President. Well, not at all. And Barbara's sitting right here. We're off to go to get-out-the-vote phone bank here in Houston, Texas. And before we go, we want to send you our love and our affection. And, yes, we share your interest in these family values, and we want the best. And by golly, that's why I'm on the phone urging everybody there to vote for Wayne Gilchrest.

Over and out. And good luck to you.

Note: The President spoke by telephone at 2:20 p.m. from Houston, TX. The rally was held at Mr. Gilchrest's campaign headquarters. A tape was not available for verification of the content of these remarks.

Remarks to a Campaign Rally for Gubernatorial Candidate Arliss Sturgulewski in Anchorage, Alaska
November 4, 1990

The President. Well, hello, Anchorage. Jim, are you there?

Mr. Campbell. Yes, we can hear you. You're coming across great, Mr. President. We've got a large group here, as Arliss said, supporters that have been with us. And really, thank you for this opportunity. And also, we've just been campaigning, as Arliss

mentioned, with Senator Stevens, Senator Murkowski, Don Young this morning; and thank you for letting them get on home with us.

The President. Well, listen, first of all, let me just, please, give my very best to Ted Stevens and Frank Murkowski and Don Young. You've got a wonderful, wonderful delegation for Alaska and for the United States back there in Washington. And I'm grateful to each one of the three of them every single day. So, I first want to salute that congressional delegation, one of the greatest that we've got. And if we had more people like them in the Senate and more people like Don in the House, we would be sailing along with the agenda that Alaskans want to see fulfilled.

So, that's enough of the Washington scene, but Barbara and I are here in Houston, Texas. One day of campaigning tomorrow, and then I vote and go back to Washington. But we wanted to just send, Arliss, to send you and Jim our very best. I've known Arliss Sturgulewski for a long time, Jim Campbell, too. And they'll make a great Governor and Lieutenant Governor for the State.

You know, I would say that Alaska needs a Governor——

Mr. Campbell. Are you paying for this call? We're getting a lot of applause.

The President. Yes. [*Laughter*] Hey, listen, I'm just getting warmed up when I think of that wonderful ticket up there. But I'm glad you've got so many people there.

And let me simply say that the State needs a Governor who does not do business as usual and someone who doesn't flinch at making the tough choices and who will go in there and shake things up for all the right reasons. And of course, Arliss, that's why I so strongly support you. And I believe that everyone there, certainly—and I'm hopeful on Tuesday the rest of the State—will say the same thing: that we've got the best candidates. Far and away the best gubernatorial candidate: a 25-year record as an Alaska leader, including service on every standing State senate committee in her four terms. And this kind of rich experience in business and government will serve the State well. So, get out and vote.

Ms. Sturgulewski. Thank you, Mr. President. We look forward to working with you on ANWR [Arctic National Wildlife Refuge], on some high seas driftnet fishery issues, on some military issues. And we're really delighted at your support, look forward to working with you and our congressional delegation. And good luck on the campaign trail, and I know you wish that to us.

The President. Well, I do. But listen, I'm not finished yet, Arliss. I'm just getting warmed up here. But I wanted to mention one other issue if I could: education. I mean, Ted and Frank are working hard for our Education Excellence Act; Don Young supporting it. But I really think a lot of the answer lies at the State level. And with your experience as a schoolteacher, I believe that you can champion the cause of education in Alaska, just as I'm trying to champion the cause of education in the country.

And I need your help to help us achieve what we laid out at the Governors summit. I'm talking about the goals for national educational excellence. So, that's another reason we want to see you in there. And so, please work hard, you and Jim.

And may I just say to your supporters there, you know, I get sick and tired of all these gloomy assessments that I hear on television and read about in the papers. We have a lot to be grateful for in our country, and one of the things is, individuals can make a difference. And this cynical reporting we hear about, how everybody is gloomy and down in the dumps—I don't believe it. Alaskans have never been that way. And if you all get out and vote, you can say to yourselves on Wednesday: I made a difference. I elected Arliss and Jim, sent Don Young and Ted Stevens—Frank's already there—back to Congress, and elected Arliss and Jim at the State level. So, you can make a difference.

And please get to the polls and vote, and join Barbara and me in counting our blessings for this, the greatest country on the face of the Earth. Now go get 'em, Arliss.

Ms. Sturgulewski. We're delighted at your call. And believe me, people are energized, and they're working. And we are going to be successful on November 6th. But thanks for your call. It was wonderful.

The President. Best of luck. Over and out.

Note: The President spoke by telephone at 4:02 p.m. from Houston, TX. The rally was held at Ms. Sturgulewski's campaign headquarters. In his remarks, the President referred to Senators Ted Stevens and Frank H. Murkowski. A tape was not available for verification of the content of these remarks.

Remarks at a Republican Campaign Rally in Tyler, Texas
November 5, 1990

Thank you very, very much for that warm welcome back to Tyler and to Smith County. I am just delighted to be here. And of course, let me, at the very outset—I planned to say something special about Phil Gramm. But I want to ask everybody to look at the Gramm sign there; it says it all: Common sense, uncommon courage. What a great Senator we have up there.

In case anybody is asking "Where's George?"—I'm here in Smith County, working for a man that I believe in, that I've known for a long time, that will be a great Governor of this State: Clayton Williams.

I want to pay my respects to Bob Mosbacher, who's doing an outstanding job for his country—our country—as Secretary of Commerce. I want to thank President Ray Hawkins for permitting us to have this fantastic rally in this marvelous institution, the Tyler Junior College. And I will salute a handful of Belles right here in the front. You can't see them, but there's a bunch of marvelous people from this area that got me started in politics—1964. We took it on the chin then. We fought back, and I don't believe I'd be President without that grassroots support of these people and others like them across this State. So, thank you. And also thanks to the Apache Belles.

You know, when Claytie first contacted us about coming back to Tyler, he called our son, George, Jr., living over in Dallas. And he said that he wanted to appear with a popular but aging Texan who's risen to the top in his field. George said, "Nolan Ryan is busy. Do you want to ask my dad?" So, here we are. [*Laughter*]

And let me just say to her friends here, inasmuch as I've been the one elected to speak for the family, Barbara Bush is delighted to be with you. And I am very proud of the job she's doing as First Lady of this country. The trouble is about Barbara: She worked with our dog to write a best-selling book, and now you give the dog Alpo, and she wants to see the wine list. [*Laughter*]

But here we are on the day before this election, and I'm greatly pleased and honored to be back here in Texas, back home where Barbara and I raised our kids, in the State in which I voted in every election since 1948. And I'm proud to be here. I am a Texan, and I'm proud of it. And I know Texas quality when I see it, and that's why I want Phil Gramm and Claytie Williams elected.

And while at it, I'm pleased to support our entire Republican team: Rob Mosbacher for Lieutenant Governor; Kay Bailey Hutchinson, running for treasurer; Buster Brown for attorney general; Warren Harding for comptroller; Wes Gilbreath for land commissioner; and Rick Perry for agriculture commissioner. We have a good, quality, across-the-board team. Please go out and elect every single one of them.

You know the story about Claytie. He's a Texas original—Fort Stockton, born and bred—straight-shooter who will do what needs to be done. He believes that we can help shape the Texas of tomorrow by building on the old-fashioned values that we all have grown up with. He believes in hard work, in common sense, in strength of character. And so does Texas—the entire State.

And just another word about Phil Gramm. I watch this Senate, and I say to myself, as I fight back the liberal program: If we had more Senators like Phil Gramm, we wouldn't be talking about budget deficits, we wouldn't be talking about having to contain government spending; we could get the job done. And Phil Gramm, believe me, is a leader—the leader; I would say, for just plain common sense in the United States Senate. I want to see him win, and I want to see him win by the biggest margin we've ever elected a Senator with. So, please do your best tomorrow.

I've listened to some of the campaign rhetoric coming out of the other side, and it's sad. It is pessimistic. It is downbeat. It is tired. And it's liberal. And we are the party with a vision for the future, the party of new ideas. And if America wants to change, I think we need a Republican Congress.

And I wish we could get it now—tomorrow—and then watch what we can do.

I mentioned Phil standing out there for spending constraint. He supports a balanced-budget amendment, and so do I. And you know, the Democrat agenda up there, the Democrat agenda in the Senate and in the House, stifles growth. The Democrats wanted to raise taxes, including income taxes on the working families. I heard some campaign rhetoric yesterday down here about that. Well, let me tell you, they can call it soak the rich all day long; but what it really soaks is working Americans. They talked about a proposed surtax on the rich to raise a few billion dollars; but in the very same bill that passed by overwhelming Democratic votes, in the same bill, they socked it to the working American to the tune of $40 billion. So, don't listen to that tired, liberal, divide, class-warfare rhetoric about soaking the rich. Hold on to your wallets; they're after you, every single one of you.

You see, Phil has this unusual, kind of a nutty idea. He thinks that Americans are not taxed too little, but that Congress spends too much. And he's absolutely right about that. Maybe it's a little old-fashioned for some of the hotshot liberals out there, but this is exactly the way he feels—and it's exactly the way he votes. And I tell you this: If Congress can't restrain spending, give me what 43 Governors have: Give me that line-item veto, and let the President have a shot at trying to keep the taxes down and the spending down.

I'm glad to hear Claytie say that he's against a State income tax. I think most Texans strongly oppose that concept. I know I do. And again, if we had Claytie here in the Governor's office, I'd have somebody there that I can work with to build a better Texas.

You know, Clayton mentioned the crime proposals of his. We've got to fight crime. I can tell you that our drug czar had a good report to the Nation the other day, showing that we've turned the corner, that we're making progress in our war against drugs. But now we've got to back up those that are fighting the war with good, strong crime legislation. I believe America's fed up with crime. I hope you don't have to worry about it as much in Tyler as we do in other parts of the State and the country; but every family, wherever we are, is concerned about it. And we're fed up with it.

And we have this view—the Republicans do—that says the handcuffs don't belong on the cops or the courts, but the handcuffs belong on the criminals. And that's what we're trying to do in our anticrime legislation. Shortly after I took office, I stood out there before the Capitol and called on the Congress to pass tough, new laws to help America take back the streets. And it had strong support from Phil and had strong support from Ralph Hall, the Congressman here, had strong support from the Republicans in the House and the Senate. But in the final hours of the Congress, the Democratic liberals gutted our package to fight back against violent crime. And for my part, I believe we ought to have a little less sympathy for the criminals and a little more sympathy for the victims of crime.

And now, as I've been doing for the last few days, I want to ask you to shift gears with me, because I think that the subject of the Middle East that Claytie alluded to in his very generous opening remarks is on the minds of everybody. And I'd like to shift to a strictly nonpartisan mode and speak to those who perhaps have kids, young men and women, serving in Saudi Arabia. We are at a partisan political event, but I don't get the opportunity to crisscross the country as much as I have recently and the chance to talk directly to as many people. And so, let me just say that the former Senator, Arthur Vandenberg—some of you students might remember the Vandenberg adage which said politics ends at the water's edge. And this is a noble principle. It's one that we've gotten away from in the Vietnam era, post-Vietnam era. But when we have a couple hundred thousand kids halfway across the world, the country comes together.

And let me just tell you that I am very grateful to the Democratic leaders and the Republican leaders in both the House and the Senate, the Democratic Members and the Republican leaders in both the House and the Senate, for the strong support that they have given the President and the administration as we try to cope with this unprecedented aggression.

Let me be clear: We have no argument with the people of Iraq. We bear no hostility to the Iraqi people at all, nor do any of the over 25 countries represented on land and sea in the Gulf area. We put together a fantastic, historic coalition of nations, large and small, Arab and others, all from across the entire spectrum. They're together, and they're holding strong. But our problem is not then with the people of Iraq; our problem is with Saddam Hussein alone.

And I want to see a peaceful resolution to this crisis. Indeed, we've worked very closely, as you know, with the United Nations—rejuvenated United Nations, putting 10 resolutions into effect, resolutions that have the support of China and the Soviet Union as well as Western Europe, passing resolutions and speaking with one voice against Iraq's aggression. And I will give these sanctions—unprecedented economic sanctions—I will give these sanctions time to work. And I hope and pray that there never will be a shot fired in anger.

Let me be very, very clear: There will be no compromise on the stated objectives of the United Nations Security Council resolutions, no compromise at all, because the brutality against innocent civilians is unacceptable in terms of international law and international behavior. And the naked aggression where a big country bullies its neighbor and takes it over is against everything we believe in this country. And that aggression will not stand. So, I will do my level-best, work my heart out, hold out my hand in every way possible; but we will stop short of making one single concession because aggression that goes rewarded today will be much worse tomorrow. That's the problem, and that's why I will stand strong against the aggression of Saddam Hussein.

You know, I know I'm speaking to parents and to brothers and to sisters and to friends. But let me tell you what the Joint Chiefs tell me. They tell me that we have never had finer young men and women in uniform than we do today—every one a volunteer, fully trained, highly motivated, the best young kids in the world. And they're now halfway across the globe, and they're standing ready there in the sand and the heat of the desert sun. And we have a lot to be thankful for in this country, and Barbara and I are looking forward very much to being with them on Thanksgiving Day and bringing with them your thanks for their service to the greatest, freest country on the face of the Earth.

You know, a lot of them have filled out absentee ballots, and they're sending them in. And that brings me back now to a slightly more partisan mode. There's a lesson, though, in that—a lesson that—in the love of liberty and the precious freedom that gives America its meaning. So, tomorrow I urge all Texans—all Texans, regardless of how you're going to vote—to get out there and vote; and do not take democracy for granted.

You know, tomorrow's vote is critical, and so, my message to you all is this: You have a chance to make a difference. The cynics, these Washington pundits that we see on these tiring shows all the time—I don't know if you're like I am; maybe you enjoy those things, but I can take only so much self-flagellation. [*Laughter*] And I see all these great inside-the-beltway experts telling us everything that's wrong with the United States. And tomorrow, you can go to the polls and say what's right about it, because we've got a great candidate for Governor and we've got a great United States Senator and we have quality men and women willing to serve. Don't tell me what's wrong with this country; show us what's right about it. Get out and do your civic duty.

And thank you, and God bless you all.

Note: President Bush spoke at 11:30 a.m. in the gymnasium at Tyler Junior College. In his remarks, he referred to the Apache Belles, the college's drill team; Nolan Ryan, pitcher for the Texas Rangers baseball team; William J. Bennett, Director of National Drug Control Policy; and President Saddam Hussein of Iraq.

Remarks at a Republican Campaign Rally in Waco, Texas
November 5, 1990

The President. Hugh, thank you for that wonderful introduction, and all of you for that welcome back. And Barbara and I are very, very pleased to be here on this, the last campaigning day before we go to the polls tomorrow. And I say "we" because I have voted in every even-year election since 1948. And I don't believe we have ever had a finer young man running for the United States Congress from this district than we do in Hugh Shine. And we've never had a better statewide ticket than we've got. We have a first-class team running to win, and we need your support tomorrow—need you to get your neighbors and your friends to the polls.

I'm a little sorry we're late. Claytie and I both set off the metal detectors with our silver feet. [*Laughter*] No, I'll never forget that Democratic Convention two——

Audience members. Where's Ann? [*Laughter*]

The President. Well, I remember [Senator] Teddy Kennedy, that bastion of democracy, you know—[*laughter*]—saying, "Where's George?"

Right here, right here in Waco, supporting the best ticket we have ever had: Clayton Williams, my dear friend; my dear friend, our Congressman Hugh Shine. And of course, we've got the best United States Senator in Washington in Phil Gramm. Now, get out and get this job done.

Hey, listen, it's nice to be back here, I'll tell you. First, I want to thank the Midway High School Band. Where are they? Right over there.

A word about Phil. Who had that Phil Gramm sign right over here? I want to see that thing now. It says it best. Take a look at it: Common sense, uncommon courage. This man is a man of courage. Took his case to the people, and everybody was saying: Oh, don't do that. There's a safer way to win. Went in, regained his seat as a Republican in the House. Ran with a spectacular successful race for the Senate. And now stands to be the largest vote-getter we've ever had. Tomorrow, please remember to get out that vote.

And he's got the respect in the Senate, and he did it the old-fashioned way: He earned it, because he does his homework, and he knows a lot more about it than most Members of the United States Senate. And when I say "it," I mean how you solve the economy of this country the way we Texans want: fewer taxes and less spending. And he has been a champion of that his whole career.

And that brings me to one of our newest and brightest stars across this country, Hugh Shine—a strong, proven conservative. And he is born and bred in Texas. He's a veteran, a successful businessman—and what a wonderful family he has; Deb, we're so proud of that great family of yours—a man of conviction, a public servant with integrity, and a leader with enormous potential. You deserve this kind of man in the United States Congress. Please send Hugh up to Washington to help us on our agenda.

And as to the other star of the occasion, my friend of long standing, Clayton Williams. I am here not to oppose somebody; I am here because I am for him. I know what he can do as Governor. As we look at the plans for the future and how we fulfill our education goals, for example, I want somebody in the statehouse with whom I can continue to work—work compatibly, work on the same philosophical approach and solve the problems of Texas without a lot of further mandates from Washington, DC. And Clayton Williams is that kind of a man.

You see, there's a common theme here. Take, for example, the economy. Unlike the party that only wants to regulate and control, we're the party that wants to innovate. We want a growth agenda, and that means expanding economic opportunities for working men and women. As successful businessmen like you and Clayton Williams know how it's done, because they've done it themselves.

We've got some other good ones, businesspeople like Rob Mosbacher running for Lieutenant Governor. And I'm very proud that his dad is with us today—coming out of business himself, doing a great job as our Secretary of Commerce for the entire country.

But American men and women deserve—the working ones—deserve an economy where they can create and prosper. And that's why these three with us here want to encourage enterprise of every kind, for every Texan, from Houston to El Paso and from the Panhandle to Brownsville. And that's why in the budget negotiations, we worked so hard to create incentives to make America less dependent on foreign oil. That means jobs, and it means jobs in Texas. And I'm glad we got that done.

And we have another common theme here. We Republicans do not waver in our support of a strong national defense. For 10 years, we've fought firmly against liberal attempts to slash defense. In this recent agreement, defense took some cuts; but I can certify to the American people that, because of people like Phil Gramm in the Congress, we were able to hold the line on reasonable levels of defense spending so that I can guarantee that nobody is going to kick the United States of America around. We have a strong defense, the best in the world, and we're going to keep it that way.

You know, it is a fascinating time to be privileged to be President of the United States. Democracy has finally dawned in Eastern Europe, after a cold, dark night of 45 years. And now we bear wondrous witness to a tidal change in the currents of history. And we see America and the Soviet Union working together now to stand against aggression. And there's a reason that we're able to stand strong against aggression in the Persian Gulf: It's because we are determined that our nation's defense be nothing less than the very best. We are credible in the eyes of the entire world.

There's an old saying about defense: that when there's trouble you don't have time to go shopping. Technology doesn't happen overnight, and most defense systems take a decade or more to move from the drawing board to development and then deployment. America's strong defense is made possible by decisions made years earlier, decisions made by Republican leadership. Ask Hugh. He's a veteran, still serving with the

Reserves. And with leaders and dedicated people like that in the Congress, America will always stand strong. That is the first responsibility of a President. And I'll be delighted to be working with Hugh towards that end.

There are many, many other issues where we are on the offense. We've got a new clean air bill now. We've done something, finally, for the disabled in a progressive piece of legislation that I think is long overdue: the Americans with Disabilities Act. Some good things are happening up in Washington, but I've come to the hometown of the Texas Rangers—one of the oldest law enforcement organizations in America—to say this: We want change; Republicans want change.

And I sent tough anticrime legislation up to Capitol Hill 1 year and a half ago, and new laws to let the police and the prosecutors take violent criminals off the streets and put them away. But in the final hours of this liberal, Democrat-controlled Congress, they gutted out legislation in a back room, late at night. Well, I am not going to stop fighting for strong anticrime legislation. The liberals hate it, but America's people want it. And I need more people like Phil Gramm, and I need Hugh Shine to help me get the job done for every family in America. We believe it's high time to have a little more sympathy for the victims of crime and a little less for the criminals themselves.

And so, we need compatible government, government in Austin that's going to work with us for these national anticrime objectives, government in Austin that's going to help us on our National Drug Strategy to combat narcotics coming into every school in the United States.

And incidentally, we're making some progress on that, thank heavens. The country's finally come together behind our national drug strategy. And I can report to you, we've turned the corner. We are going to whip the battle of narcotics. We're going to win it, and we're going to then turn to the future and see what we can do to help those who have been wasted by this terrible peril of drugs.

You know, I want to just end this way. I

won't talk to you at length about Iraq, but I know everybody's interested in it. And I have a rare opportunity to talk to a lot of people in the last few days. So, I've tried to make very clear that we have a difference here in many of these domestic issues, clear differences in all of them—but when it comes to the situation in Iraq, the country is united. We're getting strong support from Democrats and Republicans alike in the Congress. The leadership on the Democratic side has been supportive. And so, I ask you now to shift to a nonpartisan basis as I mention just a couple of points.

In the first place, we are in the Gulf not alone but along with 23 countries. Some of them are Arab countries. Some of them are large countries. Some of them are small countries. But we are united in one thing: Saddam Hussein's aggression against Kuwait will not stand. And to the cynics outside who might say we have no business there, I say that unchecked and uncontrolled aggression could be world war tomorrow. And therefore, we will check this aggression. I want the solution to be peaceful. I will give the sanctions all the time that's required to see if they work. But we will not compromise on the principle that one nation cannot bully its neighbor and take it over in contravention of international law.

I think of this part of Texas as extraordinarily patriotic. I think of this part of Texas as committed to those who are serving our country. And let me tell you, every single member of the Joint Chiefs has told me that we have never had finer, more courageous young men and women serving in our Armed Forces than we do today—best trained, best motivated, best committed to the cause that is our cause.

And so, in a few weeks, Barbara and I will sit down to a Thanksgiving dinner over there. And I wouldn't dare to speak for everybody in this room; but I expect we're unanimous when I say I will take them the thanks of the very grateful people of Waco, Texas, and the surrounding areas because we owe them everything.

So, now get to the polls. We Bushes have enjoyed this. This is my first trip here for Hugh. Our son George has been here. The Silver Fox over here has been here a time or two. She's right—250 million other parents and one husband all feel the same way about it.

Listen, tomorrow is a big day. I get so tired of people saying they can't make a difference. There's a great kind of malaise in terms of the feeling about the political process. You wouldn't be here if you didn't know different. You know you can make a difference. Don't listen to those mournful pundits that come on before every election telling us how bad everything is in this, the greatest country on the face of the Earth. You can make a difference. You can do something positive. You can go out and re-elect Phil Gramm by the biggest vote ever. You can send us a Governor I can work with: Claytie Williams. And you can send a bright new star to Washington in Hugh Shine. Now go get the job done.

Thank you.

Note: President Bush spoke at 2:53 p.m. in McLennan Hall at the Waco Convention Center. In his remarks, he referred to President Saddam Hussein of Iraq. Audience members referred to Ann Richards, the Democratic gubernatorial candidate.

Statement on Signing the Departments of Veterans Affairs and Housing and Urban Development, and Independent Agencies Appropriations Act, 1991
November 5, 1990

Today I signed H.R. 5158, the "Departments of Veterans Affairs and Housing and Urban Development, and Independent Agencies Appropriations Act, 1991."

This Act meets the needs of our Nation's veterans. The Act provides $12.3 billion for

VA Medical Care, an increase of $0.9 billion over the 1990 enacted level. This increase will allow the Department to provide quality care to all eligible veterans expected to apply on a system-wide basis.

I am pleased that NASA was provided nearly a 13.5 percent increase over its fiscal year 1990 budget. While I am disappointed that the Congress would not provide the small amount of funding requested for technology development to enable future manned missions to the Moon and Mars, I am pleased that the Congress recognized the inevitability of human space exploration. NASA has the flexibility to reprogram funds to continue current in-house mission studies and synthesis activities. The human exploration of space is our destiny—we must continue to move forward.

I am greatly concerned over the significant budget reduction in the Space Station Freedom (SSF) program. SSF remains, for me, a high priority. However, I am instructing NASA to reassess its current design and try to restructure a development effort within the funding envelope recommended by the Congress. The revised program will seek to achieve a permanently manned presence, to maintain a balance among science objectives, and to preserve our commitments to our international partners and to other users.

I am equally concerned that this Act did not fund the HOPE initiative, which would enable low-income persons to take control of their lives through homeownership. We must use available Federal housing funds more effectively to provide opportunity and hope for low-income Americans. I am also disappointed that the Congress has chosen to impose new restrictions on the ability of the Secretary of Housing and Urban Development to manage his Department. It would be much better for the Congress to work cooperatively with the Administration to overcome previous HUD management problems.

I am also disappointed that the Congress failed to provide an adequate increase for the research activities of the National Science Foundation. Support for basic research, particularly individual researchers, underlies the Nation's long-term economic growth. The reductions made by the Congress are regrettable and will certainly contribute to the decline in support for individual investigators.

The Congress has an especially difficult task balancing the competing priorities funded in this diverse Act with the resources available. I appreciate their efforts. We will continue to work with the Congress to seek solutions for the deficiencies I have noted.

GEORGE BUSH

The White House,
November 5, 1990.

Note: H.R. 5158, approved November 5, was assigned Public Law No. 101–507.

Statement on Signing the Omnibus Budget Reconciliation Act of 1990
November 5, 1990

Today I am signing H.R. 5835, the "Omnibus Budget Reconciliation Act of 1990," the centerpiece of the largest deficit reduction package in history and an important measure for ensuring America's long-term economic growth. This Act is the result of long, hard work by the Administration and the Congress. No one got everything he or she wanted, but the end product is a compromise that merits enactment.

H.R. 5835, and the discretionary spending caps associated with it, will achieve nearly $500 billion—almost half a trillion dollars—in deficit reduction over the next 5 years. Over 70 percent of that deficit reduction derives from outlay reductions; less than 30 percent from revenue increases. In addition, the Act enacts significant budget process reforms to ensure that the agreement is fulfilled and that budgetary discipline is extended and strengthened.

Entitlement Reforms. The Act provides for the most comprehensive and substantial reform of mandatory "entitlement" programs ever—about $100 billion in savings from restructuring and reforms in the following major programs:

- Farm programs;
- Federal housing programs;
- Student loan programs;
- Veterans programs;
- Postal subsidies;
- Federal employee benefits; and
- Medicare.

Discretionary Program Caps. The Act establishes 5-year caps on overall discretionary spending that will result in savings of over $180 billion. To keep domestic and international spending from growing any faster than inflation, the Act creates new automatic "mini-sequesters." The Act also provides for an orderly defense reduction without threatening national security.

Energy Security. The Act provides incentives for energy conservation and for exploration and development of domestic energy resources.

Social Security. Social Security is fully protected and taken off-budget.

Enforcement and Process Reform. The Act contains the toughest enforcement system ever. The Gramm-Rudman-Hollings sequester process is extended and strengthened with caps, mini-sequesters, and a new "pay-as-you-go" system.

Credit Reform. The Act implements a new Federal accounting and budgeting system to expose and limit previously hidden (and rapidly growing) liabilities.

Tax Changes. The Act includes a tax rate cut from 33 percent to 31 percent for about 3.5 million middle and upper-middle income taxpayers and an overall decrease in taxes paid by those with incomes under $20,000. There are higher excise taxes on luxury items and limitations on itemized deductions and the personal exemption for higher income taxpayers. The total net tax changes comprise 28 percent of the deficit reduction package.

This Act creates the conditions that should allow future interest rates to be lower than they would be otherwise. Lower interest rates can benefit the entire economy. They can mean more housing starts; more Americans driving new cars; reductions in mortgage payments for homeowners; more long-term investment; greater productivity; and increased numbers of jobs.

In signing this landmark Act, I pledge the continuing best efforts of my Administration to maintain not only the letter, but the spirit of the new fiscal order for the Federal Government that is embodied in this agreement.

H.R. 5835 also contains *Child care* provisions, strongly supported by this Administration, that will enlarge the opportunities of parents to obtain the child care they desire, including care that is provided by sectarian institutions if the parents so choose. The largest portion of this new child care program will come from tax credits to people—as requested by the Administration. In addition, a Child Care and Development Block Grant program includes provisions for the issuance of child care certificates or vouchers that would enable parents to exercise their own judgment as to what type of child care best suits the particular needs of their own child.

I note my understanding of these child care provisions and sign the bill based on that understanding, as follows:

First, I understand that the definition of child care certificates in section 658P(2) ensures that States may not restrict parental choice by limiting the range of providers from whom parents may seek child care, using certificates as payment, and that such certificates shall not be considered to be grants or contracts.

Second, section 658N(a)(1)(B) specifically permits sectarian organizations that are child care providers to require that all of their employees adhere to the religious tenets and teachings of the organization and comply with rules forbidding the use of drugs or alcohol. As I understand it, the term "sectarian organization" in this provision includes religious organizations generally.

Third, as used in sections 658N(a)(2)(B) and 658N(a)(3)(B), the term "organization" means not only the particular provider but also a broader association with which that provider may be identified.

Finally, all of the provisions of the Child Care and Development Block Grant program will be interpreted in light of the requirements of the establishment and free exercise clauses of the First Amendment.

I would also note certain constitutional difficulties in other titles of the Omnibus Budget Reconciliation Act. In particular, section 4117 of the Act requires the Secretary of Health and Human Services, in certain conditions, to treat the States of Nebraska and Oklahoma as single fee schedule areas for purposes of determining the adjusted historical payment basis and the fee schedule amount for physicians' services furnished on or after January 1, 1992. Such treatment is made to depend on the Secretary's receiving written expressions of support for treatment of the State as a single fee schedule area from each member of the congressional delegation from the State and from organizations representing urban and rural physicians in the State. This provision requires the Secretary to base a substantive decision on the allocation of Federal benefits on the statements of members of congressional delegations and other persons who are not appointed by the President. Therefore, it must be understood either (1) as an attempt to vest significant authority to execute Federal law in those persons, in which case it violates the Appointments Clause, Article II, section 2; see *Buckley* v. *Valeo*, 424 U.S. 1 (1975); or (2) as an attempt to confer lawmaking power on individual members of the Congress and others, in which case it violates Article I, section 7; see *INS* v. *Chadha*, 462 U.S. 919 (1983). Accordingly, this requirement is without legal force, and I am so instructing the Secretary of Health and Human Services. I am also instructing the Attorney General and the Secretary of Health and Human Services to prepare remedial legislation to amend this section for submission to the next session of the Congress, so that the Act can be brought into compliance with the Constitution's requirements.

Further, the Constitution empowers the President to "recommend to [Congress] such Measures as he shall judge necessary and expedient." U.S. Const. Art. II, Sec. 3. Several sections of the Act raise constitutional difficulties by appearing or purporting to impose requirements that the executive branch submit legislative proposals of a predetermined kind. The executive branch has consistently treated provisions of this type as advisory rather than as mandatory, and to avoid a constitutional question will so construe the provisions at issue here.

GEORGE BUSH

The White House,
November 5, 1990.

Note: H.R. 5835, approved November 5, was assigned Public Law No. 101–508.

Statement on Signing the Treasury, Postal Service and General Government Appropriations Act, 1991
November 5, 1990

Today, I have signed into law H.R. 5241, the "Treasury, Postal Service and General Government Appropriations Act, 1991." This Act provides appropriations for a number of critical programs under the Department of the Treasury, the General Services Administration, the Office of Personnel Management, the Executive Office of the President, and several other independent agencies. Funding for these central management agencies is essential to carry out the primary financial and administrative functions of the Federal Government.

I want to take this opportunity to thank the Congress for addressing objections raised by the Administration concerning provisions that purported to forbid the implementation or enforcement of certain nondisclosure agreements required of Government employees with access to classified information. These provisions, which were first enacted in the omnibus continuing resolution for fiscal year 1988 (Public Law No. 100–202), raised profound constitutional concerns and resulted in lengthy litigation. Section 617 of H.R. 5241 accommodates the concerns of the executive branch, provided that it is not construed in a manner that interferes with my constitutional authority to protect national security information. In this connection, I note that nothing in section 617 purports to interfere with the authority of executive branch agencies to implement and enforce the prepublication review clause included in many of their nondisclosure forms.

Finally, I note that the provisions of H.R. 5241 authorizing appropriations for the Office of Management and Budget forbid the expenditure of those funds "for the purpose of reviewing any agricultural marketing orders or any activities or regulations under the provisions of the Agricultural Marketing Agreement Act of 1937 (7 U.S.C. 601 et seq.)." These restrictions raise constitutional concerns because they impair my ability as President to supervise the executive branch.

GEORGE BUSH

The White House,
November 5, 1990.

Note: H.R. 5241, approved November 5, was assigned Public Law No. 101–509.

Statement on Signing the National Defense Authorization Act for Fiscal Year 1991
November 5, 1990

Today I have signed into law H.R. 4739, the "National Defense Authorization Act for Fiscal Year 1991." This Act authorizes appropriations for Department of Defense and Department of Energy national security activities and extends and amends other programs. This Act, which reflects most of the Administration's major defense priorities, will provide for a strong national defense during fiscal year 1991.

I have signed this Act notwithstanding the reservations that I have regarding certain of its provisions. I am particularly concerned about those provisions that derogate from the President's authority under the Constitution to conduct U.S. foreign policy, including negotiations with other countries. One such provision is section 1455, which purports to require the President to begin negotiations with Japan on an agreement under which Japan would offset U.S. costs associated with the presence of our military personnel in Japan. Another is section 1702, which could be construed as requiring the Secretary of State to negotiate with foreign countries regarding restricting the export of certain goods and technology. A third is section 2802, which purports to require the President to seek to place certain questions concerning basing of the 401st Tactical Fighter Wing on the agenda of the next meeting of NATO's North Atlantic Council. Consistent with my responsibility under the Constitution for the conduct of negotiations, I will construe all these provisions to be precatory rather than mandatory.

I am concerned, as well, about certain provisions regarding the Strategic Defense Initiative. The earmarking of funds, in combination with a funding level that is $1.8 billion below the amount requested, unduly restricts the flexibility necessary for sound management and virtually guarantees that funds will be redirected away from the most promising technologies. I note also that section 221 contains criteria for conducting Strategic Defense Initiative research and development that might be construed as a constraint on the President's authority to interpret treaties. I sign this Act with the understanding that the Congress did not intend that obligation of funds for the ground-based interceptors and sensor identified in the conference report on H.R. 4739 be dependent on a determination at this time that these systems are deployable under the ABM Treaty.

Several provisions might be construed to impinge on the President's authority as Commander in Chief and as the head of the executive branch. Thus, section 1455 purports to impose a limit on the number of military personnel stationed in Japan, and section 406 purports to do the same with respect to military personnel stationed in Europe. Section 1455 permits a waiver of the limit should I determine that the national security requires it and I so notify the Congress. Section 406 permits a waiver under similar conditions, but limits the number of additional personnel that may be assigned. I shall construe these provisions consistent with my authority to deploy military personnel as necessary to fulfill my constitutional responsibilities.

A number of provisions regarding the reserve forces are of concern. Section 903 purports to require assignment of all Army Reserve operational forces to U.S. Forces Command, with no specific provisions for the Secretary of Defense to direct other assignments, including those assignments already made to unified or specified commands. Sections 1436 to 1438 establish certain standards for the allocation of aircraft to Naval Reserve, Air Force Reserve and Air National Guard units, as well as requiring assignment of the tactical airlift mission to the Air Force Reserve and Air National Guard. I shall construe these provisions consistent with my authority as Commander in Chief to deploy the Armed Forces as I see fit.

Although this Act eliminates a large number of reports to the Congress, it still imposes on the Department of Defense reporting requirements that are an unnecessary burden on its resources. In addition, certain reporting provisions raise national security concerns. Sections 1461 and 1482 purport to require prior notice to the Congress regarding initiation of, or classification changes in, special access programs. I shall construe these provisions consistent with my constitutional authority to protect sensitive national security information.

In addition, section 1409(a) refers to a classified annex that was prepared to accompany the conference report on this Act and states that the annex "shall have the force and effect of law as if enacted into law." The Congress has thus stated in the statute that the annex has not been enacted into law, but it nonetheless urges that the annex be treated as if it were law. I will certainly take into account the Congress' wishes in this regard, but will do so mindful of the fact that, according to the terms of the statute, the provisions of the annex are not law.

The Constitution empowers the President to "recommend to [Congress] such Measures as he shall judge necessary and expedient." U.S. Const. Art. II, Sec. 3. Section 1009 raises constitutional difficulties by purporting to require the submission of a report on Andean anti-drug efforts that includes specific legislative proposals. The executive branch has consistently treated provisions of this type as advisory rather than mandatory, and to avoid a constitutional question will so construe this provision.

Finally, I am concerned that several provisions of the Act that deal with the management of real property, especially in the area of rental space and specified disposals, circumvent the provisions of, or regulations related to, the Federal Property and Administrative Services Act of 1949. Generally, effective and efficient management of such real property matters is best accomplished in accordance with the Property Act.

GEORGE BUSH

The White House,
November 5, 1990.

Note: H.R. 4739, approved November 5, was assigned Public Law No. 101–510.

Statement on Signing the Department of Defense Appropriations Act, 1991
November 5, 1990

Today, I have signed H.R. 5803, the Department of Defense appropriations bill for fiscal year 1991.

This bill is generally supportive of Administration objectives and provides resources that will permit us to maintain a strong national defense.

I am concerned about requirements that could be construed to derogate from the President's authority under the Constitution to conduct United States foreign policy, including negotiations with other countries. Consistent with my responsibility under the Constitution for the conduct of negotiations, I will construe such requirements to be precatory rather than mandatory.

I note my construction of one provision of the bill. Section 8111(a) refers to a classified annex that was prepared to accompany the conference report on this bill and states that the annex "shall have the force and effect of law as if enacted into law." Congress has thus stated in the statute that the annex has not been enacted into law, but it nonetheless urges that the annex be treated as if it were law. I will certainly take into account Congress' wishes in this regard, but will do so mindful of the fact that, according to the terms of the statute, the provisions of the annex are not law.

GEORGE BUSH

The White House,
November 5, 1990.

Note: H.R. 5803, approved November 5, was assigned Public Law No. 101–511.

Statement on Signing the Department of the Interior and Related Agencies Appropriations Act, 1991
November 5, 1990

Today I signed H.R. 5769, the "Department of the Interior and Related Agencies Appropriations Act, 1991."

I am pleased that the Act includes funding for many programs important to the environment. In particular, the Act includes funds to expand our national parks, forests, and wildlife refuges, as I recommended in my budget. Many nationally significant natural and cultural resources will be protected by these appropriations. Furthermore, the Act provides funds for the commencement of my tree-planting program and the start-up of the National Tree Trust Foundation. I commend the Congress for these actions.

I have serious reservations with four provisions in this Act: those dealing with restrictions on the reorganization of the Bureau of Indian Affairs (BIA); those dealing with a permanent extension of coverage of the Federal Tort Claims Act to Indian Tribes, tribal organizations, tribal contractors, and their employees; those dealing with unconstitutional committee approval requirements; and those dealing with restrictions on preleasing, leasing, and drilling activities in the Outer Continental Shelf (OCS).

The Department of the Interior will be restricted by the Act from taking certain actions relating to a BIA reorganization. The United States has a long-standing duty to execute the Federal trust responsibility for the natural and financial resources we hold in trust for American Indian Tribes and their members. In 1789, the very first Congress assembled under the new Constitution declared, in ratifying the Northwest Ordinance of 1787, "The utmost good faith shall always be observed towards Indians." Over the years, the courts have repeatedly made it clear that Federal officials have an obligation of the highest responsibility and trust toward American Indians and their property. The courts have measured Federal performances of our Indian duties by the most exacting fiduciary standards.

I am committed to good-faith fulfillment of our obligations to Indian Tribes and their members. I look to the Secretary of the Interior as the officer responsible for fulfilling the Federal Indian trust responsibility. The Secretary is in the midst of addressing organizational changes to better fulfill that responsibility and to improve service to the Indian people generally. He is addressing some of the issues that have been the most crucial and admittedly difficult in Indian affairs. The Congress has now chosen to block this good-faith effort by the Secretary, even as he is continuing discussions with the Indian people on his improvements. I view this intervention in performance of the trustee's duties to be unfortunate and unwise.

The Act includes permanent substantive legislation with respect to the Federal Tort Claims Act that is both fiscally irresponsible and also will undermine our efforts to foster the independence and autonomy of Indian Tribes and tribal organizations.

The Act provides that Indian Tribes, tribal organizations, and Indian contractors and their employees shall be considered employees of the United States with respect to claims arising from contracts, grants, and cooperative agreements authorized by the Indian Self-Determination and Education Assistance Act and the Tribally Controlled School Grants of the Hawkins-Stafford Elementary and Secondary School Improvement Amendments of 1988. The effect of this provision would be to make the United States permanently liable for the torts of Indian Tribes, tribal organizations, and contractors. This provision is fundamentally flawed because the United States does not control and supervise the day-to-day operations of the tribes, tribal organizations, and contractors. Moreover, such control and supervision would be inappropriate and inconsistent with the relationship of the United States with the tribes.

I have supported legislation to foster the independence and autonomy of Indian Tribes and tribal organizations. Hence, supervision and control over tribes and their organizations and contractors would be wholly unacceptable. Without that supervision and control over daily activities, the United States has no opportunity to limit the risks of grave injury to persons, as well as the public fisc. The extension of governmental responsibility for private conduct under these circumstances is untenable.

Our objections to this provision are fundamental and unequivocal. We will work with the new Congress to address the underlying concerns and to repeal this provision at the first opportunity.

Several provisions of H.R. 5769 purport to condition my authority, and the authority of affected executive branch officials, to use funds otherwise appropriated by the Act on the approval of various committees of the House of Representatives and the Senate. These provisions constitute legislative veto devices of the kind declared unconstitutional in *INS* v. *Chadha*, 462 U.S. 919 (1983). Accordingly, I will treat them as having no legal force or effect in this or any other legislation in which they appear. I direct agencies confronted with these devices to consult with the Attorney General to determine whether the grant of authority in question is severable from the unconstitutional condition. See *Alaska Airlines, Inc.* v. *Brock*, 480 U.S. 678, 684–87 (1987).

Section 121 of the General Provisions applicable to the Department of the Interior, which requires the National Park Service to submit questions regarding valuation of certain mining claims to an independent panel of three arbitrators, raises constitutional concerns. Section 121(d) purports to require the National Park Service to make an offer to the claimant "to purchase said claim for the appraised value." The process of determining the amount of money which the government will offer in exchange for a claim is an exercise of significant authority, which must be undertaken by an Officer of the United States, appointed in accordance with the Appointments Clause, Article II, sec. 2, cl. 2, of the Constitution. Appraisers selected pursuant to Section 121, however, must be appointed in accordance with the procedures of the American Arbitration Association. I instruct the Secretary of the Interior to consult with the Attorney General concerning the appropriate response to Section 121 of H.R. 5769.

I also regret that the Congress continued 1-year legislative moratoria on preleasing, leasing, and drilling in certain areas of the Outer Continental Shelf. My June 26th decisions to forego such activities in many areas of the OCS made these legislative moratoria unnecessary.

Notwithstanding these reservations, I have signed the bill because its benefits—particularly the treatment of many environmental, conservation, and energy-related issues important to the Nation—outweigh my reservations.

GEORGE BUSH

The White House,
November 5, 1990.

Note: H.R. 5769, approved November 5, was assigned Public Law No. 101–512.

Statement on Signing the Foreign Operations, Export Financing, and Related Programs Appropriations Act, 1991
November 5, 1990

Today I have signed H.R. 5114, the "Foreign Operations, Export Financing, and Related Programs Appropriations Act, 1991." The Act contains many important provisions that the Administration supports. I am especially pleased that the Congress has recognized the critical importance of the issue of Egypt's military debt, and included provisions that will allow me to address this issue in a manner consistent with the national security interests of the United States. Congressional recognition of the unique Egyptian contribution in galvanizing international support against Iraqi aggression is in accord with the finest traditions of bipartisan cooperation.

I am also appreciative that the Congress has included several provisions that will increase my flexibility in conducting foreign policy. These include provisions that will afford substantial latitude in providing assistance to Eastern Europe and that will allow me to respond more quickly to new and changing developments around the world.

There are, however, a number of troublesome provisions in the Act. Of greatest concern is section 531, regarding assistance to El Salvador. Despite the important changes made to this provision in conference, I remain concerned that the structure and wording of section 531 could complicate

our efforts to achieve a satisfactory settlement in El Salvador between the democratically elected government and the Farabundo Marti National Liberation Front (FMLN).

I am concerned that the Congress has included a variety of specific provisions that could be counterproductive in carrying out our foreign relations. These provisions include conditions on assistance for Cambodia, the limiting of military assistance to Turkey below the level that I requested, and the prohibition on international military education and training for Malaysia as well as other countries.

Similarly, I must note my concern about a number of provisions that raise constitutional issues. Among these are provisions that purport to direct, or forbid, negotiations with foreign governments or entities; that require the executive branch to disclose current negotiations or present specific positions to international organizations; or that mandate representatives of certain executive branch agencies to be assigned to certain countries. In keeping with past practice, I shall treat such provisions as advisory rather than mandatory. Moreover, I retain the same concerns about section 569, prohibiting certain dealings with foreign governments, that I expressed in signing last year's appropriations Act. In the case of section 562A, which calls for the Administrator of the Agency for International Development ("AID") to conduct an on-site assessment "along the Thai-Cambodian border and within Cambodia, including Phnom Penh," I will interpret the provision so as to avoid constitutional problems. Because I have no objection to sending an AID team to certain areas along the Thai-Cambodian border, and from there that team can gather information about conditions along the border and in Cambodia itself, section 562A can be satisfied consistent with the exercise of my constitutional authority.

Despite my serious concerns about certain of its provisions, I believe that it is necessary to sign this Act in order to move forward with the job of conducting U.S. foreign policy.

GEORGE BUSH

The White House,
November 5, 1990.

Note: H.R. 5114, approved November 5, was assigned Public Law No. 101–513.

Statement on Signing the Energy and Water Development Appropriations Act, 1991
November 5, 1990

Today I signed H.R. 5019, the "Energy and Water Development Appropriations Act, 1991." I am concerned about the reduced funding provided for the Superconducting Super Collider and basic research programs. These reductions are especially unfortunate because they were used to finance large numbers of economically unjustified water projects in the Corps of Engineers and the Bureau of Reclamation.

I do recognize that the Congress kept the funding contained in this Act at a level consistent with the Budget Summit Agreement. It is my hope that one of the features of the caps in the agreement is that it will force a competition for limited funds based on merit. I will be asking the Congress in future budgets for funding based on national priorities rather than narrow interests.

In this regard, I am deeply concerned that the Congress has chosen to reduce programs in scientific research while protecting $170 million of funds earmarked by the Congress for special interest projects. Nowhere is our responsibility to apply Federal funds to our highest national priorities more crucial than in the area of scientific research. Research projects should be selected after competitive evaluation on the basis of merit and research priorities, not on the basis of parochial interest.

Sound public works projects form an important part of our Nation's infrastructure. They should be funded in a manner that minimizes total project costs and fulfills our commitments to nonfederal cost-sharing partners for orderly project development. A number of the Act's provisions and projects relating to the Army Corps of Engineers depart from this principle and concern me deeply.

—First, many of the dollars are for low-priority projects that are not in the national interest.

—Second, this Act provides Federal funding for work that in the past has been the responsibility of the local sponsor or property owner.

—Third, I am concerned that this Act initiates work that the Corps may not be able to finish due to the budget constraints agreed to by this Administration and the Congress for FY 1992 and beyond. I am, therefore, advising the Congress that continued funding of many of these projects may not be accommodated in future budgets.

It is clear that the Congress intends to continue funding construction on some elements of the Garrison Diversion project. However, as recognized by the House, the irrigation features remain a major concern. A task force under the auspices of the Secretary of the Interior has been reviewing possible alternatives. The task force recommendations reinforce Administration policy to not support Federal funding for the completion of irrigation facilities or related principal water supply works. The Administration will consider funding for other features of the project, consistent with budgetary constraints.

Sections 506 and 510 of the Act also raise serious concerns. Section 506 of the Act provides that none of the funds appropriated by H.R. 5019 or any other legislation may be used to conduct studies concerning "the possibility of changing from the currently required 'at cost' to a 'market rate' or any other noncost-based method for the pricing of hydroelectric power" by Federal power authorities. Article II, Section 3 of the Constitution grants the President authority to recommend to the Congress any legislative measures considered "necessary and expedient." Accordingly, in keeping with the well-settled obligation to construe ambiguous statutory provisions to avoid constitutional questions, I will interpret section 506 so as not to infringe on the Executive's authority to conduct studies that

might assist in the evaluation and preparation of such measures.

Section 510 of the Act prohibits the use of appropriated funds to change certain employment levels determined by the Administrators of the Federal Power Marketing Administrations. This provision must be interpreted in light of my constitutional responsibility, as head of the unitary executive branch, to supervise my subordinates. I note in this regard that section 510 does not purport to interfere with my authority, insofar as the Administrators of the Federal Power Marketing Administrations are subject to my direction and control, to direct them to establish and maintain certain employment levels. Rather, it only circumscribes the ability of other executive branch officials to alter such levels once they have been set in a manner satisfactory to me.

GEORGE BUSH

The White House,
November 5, 1990.

Note: H.R. 5019, approved November 5, was assigned Public Law No. 101–514.

Statement on Signing the Departments of Commerce, Justice, and State, the Judiciary, and Related Agencies Appropriations Act, 1991
November 5, 1990

Today I have signed into law H.R. 5021, the "Departments of Commerce, Justice, and State, the Judiciary, and Related Agencies Appropriations Act, 1991."

In signing this Act, I note that the Act creates a three-member Central European Small Enterprise Development Commission, which will formulate and contract for a 3-year management and technical assistance demonstration program in Central Europe. Because this constitutes the exercise of significant authority pursuant to the laws of the United States, the members of the Commission must be appointed in conformity with the provisions of the Appointments Clause. U.S. Const. Art. II, sec. 2, cl. 2. Thus, although the Act is silent as to the manner of appointment of these individ-

uals, it must be construed to require that the members of the Commission are to be appointed by me or my delegate. Similarly, requiring that the members of the Commission be "representatives" of private organizations would impose upon them an obligation inconsistent with the undivided duty of loyalty owed by Officers of the United States. Therefore, I am constrained to interpret the Act, as the Constitution requires, to provide for appointment of members of the Commission after due consideration of recommendations from the organizations designated in the Act.

Furthermore, as with last year's Act, I interpret the provisions on the Legal Services Corporation as not restricting the authority of future recess appointees to exercise all powers conferred upon members of the Board of the Corporation.

GEORGE BUSH

The White House,
November 5, 1990.

Note: H.R. 5021, approved November 5, was assigned Public Law No. 101–515.

Statement on Signing the Military Construction Appropriations Act, 1991
November 5, 1990

Today I signed H.R. 5313, the "Military Construction Appropriations Act, 1991."

The Military Construction Appropriations Act for fiscal year 1991 is within the funding levels of the Budget Summit Agreement. The Act provides funds for military construction, family housing, and base closure programs of the Department of Defense.

I am deeply disappointed with several provisions in the bill.

Most serious is language that would prohibit the obligation of funds to allow the United States to meet its obligations to the NATO alliance and relocate the 401st Tactical Fighter Wing to Crotone, Italy. I am especially troubled that some may perceive this as a reduction in our commitment to NATO during this period of dramatic change. Moving the 401st to this strategic location remains a crucial element of NATO defense strategy and a top priority for the United States. The Administration will continue to work with the Congress to resume our contribution and to proceed with this important effort. Meanwhile, I hope our NATO allies will continue construction of this essential base.

Appropriations for the NATO Infrastructure program are $193 million, $228 million less than the $420 million requested. This level of funding may prevent the United States from meeting its contractual obligations under treaties and agreements with our NATO allies and slow essential restoration and emergency repairs of existing overseas facilities.

Section 113 of the Act requires the Secretary of Defense to give 30 days' advance notice to certain congressional committees of any proposed military exercise involving construction costs that are over $100,000. In approving H.R. 5313, I wish to reiterate an understanding, expressed by President Reagan when he signed an Act containing a similar provision, that this section encompasses only exercises for which providing 30 days' advance notice is feasible and consistent with my constitutional authority and duty to protect the national security.

Finally, section 125 would purport to require the Department of Defense to proceed with military construction projects that may become unnecessary as we reshape the Armed Forces.

GEORGE BUSH

The White House,
November 5, 1990.

Note: H.R. 5313, approved November 5, was assigned Public Law No. 101–519.

Remarks at a Republican Campaign Rally in Houston, Texas
November 5, 1990

I think those signs say it all about our Senator: common sense, uncommon courage. That says it all about our great Senator, Phil Gramm. My heavens, we need him back there. We have an opportunity—those of us who vote here in this State have an opportunity to rack up the biggest majority for a Senator in the history of this State. So, let's get out and get that job done tomorrow.

Phil, thank you for all you do. And, Wendy—it's a moving and touching story. As long as Phil said something nice about his wife—[*laughter*]—I want to say I think we've got the best First Lady we've ever had, frankly.

And Barbara and I are both delighted to be back in Houston. I pointed out on the campaign trail today that we have voted in every even-year election since 1948 in Texas. And we're looking forward to voting on this one more than ever before——

[*At this point, audience members interrupted the President's remarks.*]

That's all right. Now, look, the guy's got it wrong. Let me help him out. No, no, look, let me just address myself to that question. He's got it wrong. What we're doing in the Persian Gulf is not anything about war for oil. What we're doing is standing up against naked aggression, and we will succeed. We will not turn back. This guy, he just has it mixed up a little bit. Don't be angry. We see these signs all over, and I will continue to try to spell out the fact that what we are standing up for is to throw Saddam Hussein out of Kuwait, to restore the leaders, and then to say naked aggression will not succeed. And that's what it's about.

And let me say to him, nobody wants war less than I do. I went through a pretty tough one. I've been there. But what I want to do is give these economic sanctions a chance to work. I want to hold our coalition—unprecedented in history—together. And I want to send a message to aggressors in the future that aggression will not pay. That's what we're doing in the Middle East. And I might add to this guy: We will simply say there can be no compromise with the U.N. resolutions. They've spelled it out, and Saddam Hussein must get out of Kuwait with no conditions. That's what the policy is about.

But I will continue to try to get that message out, loud and clear. Now, let me say this—Claytie and I were a little late getting

here. We had trouble with the magnetometers. Our silver feet got caught there as we were coming through the line. [*Laughter*] But having said that, let me add this: I've known Clayton Williams for some time. I know of his record. I know of his sincerity. I know of his integrity. And he will be a great Governor for the State of Texas. And I'm going to vote for him early tomorrow morning.

And I want to salute another who's with us today, an old friend of mine, the next Lieutenant Governor, Rob Mosbacher—and Catherine. Waged a wonderfully aggressive campaign, and we're proud of him. And that office has great power in our State, and it's about time we have a strong leader like Rob Mosbacher—[*laughter*]—Mosbacher, Moosebacher—it doesn't matter how you spell it. Rob, good luck. You've worked hard. Best of luck to you—Misbacher, Mosbacher.

And to all the others, I really believe we do have the finest, most qualified ticket that we've seen: Wes Gilbreath for land commissioner, Beau Boulter for the railroad commission, Warren Harding for State treasurer. Then we've got some that aren't up here with us, Rick Perry and Buster Brown and Kaye Bailey Hutchinson—an outstanding ticket.

And I don't know where Milo went, but I want to thank Milo Hamilton for being here. And I'm glad to see some of my friends from the Astros. And really, it's great to be back here. And it is fitting we're back here, because I remember 2 years ago, almost to the day, an occasion like this when Barbara and I were—nervous time just before our election, before I was elected President of the United States. And I looked around this room then, as I do now, and I see many people here without whose support I would not be standing here as President. And I'm grateful to each and every one of you. We've never forgotten how we got to serve this country in this way.

But this is a great city and a great comeback city and a city that knows how to live and knows how to fight back, knows how to make those dreams that we all share come true. You know, two decades ago, Houston was the first word the world heard from the Moon. And this fall, Texas is where Republicans are going to have the last word, by electing Phil Gramm, Clayton Williams, and Rob Mosbacher and the rest of our ticket.

There are enormous differences between the two tickets and certainly between our candidate for the United States Senate and our candidate for Governor of this great State. When voters understand these differences, we win. And when Texas elects leaders like Phil and Clayton and Rob Mosbacher and the others up here, America wins.

And there is something to be said about a President having a Governor with whom he can work compatibly. And it's certainly true that I need more United States Senators like Phil Gramm. And if we had them, we wouldn't be worrying about this deficit so much. We wouldn't be on a spending binge in Washington.

Phil put it best: What we need is a growth agenda, expanding economic opportunities for working men and women. Business leaders like Rob Mosbacher and Clayton Williams know how it's done. They've done it themselves. And American working men and women deserve an economy where they can create and prosper. And that's why these three here want to encourage enterprise of every kind for every Texan, from Houston to El Paso and from the Panhandle down to Brownsville. And that's why, in the budget negotiations, we worked so hard to create some incentives to make America less dependent on foreign oil. And that means sound national security policy, and those incentives will help create jobs—jobs right here in the State of Texas.

And I think we have another item, another priority, that unites us. We Republicans do not waver in our support of a strong national defense. For 10 years we've held firm against the liberal attempts to slash defense. And I am convinced that the remarkable sweep of democracy that we've seen around the world would not have happened without a credible, strong, determined, secure United States of America.

Democracy has finally dawned again in Eastern Europe. And Barbara and I are looking forward to being in Czechoslovakia not so many days from now. After a cold,

dark night of 45 years, a curtain down on the aspirations of people, the curtain is up; and there's hope, and there's opportunity, and there's optimism in Eastern Europe. And now we bear wondrous witness to a tidal change in the currents of history. We see America and the Soviet Union working together, solidly together at the United Nations, to stand against aggression. And that's a good thing; that's dramatic change. But in this last budget agreement, defense got some cuts. But I think Phil and I both can certify that we came through at substantially better levels than we thought and that we're at a level now where I can say to the American people: We are going to keep our strength; we are going to demonstrate that we are dependable allies and friends to those who stand up against tyranny around the world.

I like what Claytie said about education. Beyond a strong economy and a strong defense, we have a vision of a society where opportunity is equal to the dreams of the American people; and that means education for all, sound, with new ideas. I want a Governor who is going to help me implement the national goals that came out of the Governors' summit—the one I called at Charlottesville, Virginia, last year. I want somebody who believes as I do that we don't need more mandated programs from Washington, but that we need more of the action right here at the State level in Texas, giving parents a choice about how to educate their kids.

I sent an educational bill up there to the Congress, the Educational Excellence Act, to reward achievement, encourage accountability—fundamental education reform. And once again, if we had more like our Republican Congressmen from Texas and more in the Senate like Phil Gramm, we would pass that. Because we would then be giving more say to the parents, and we'd be recognizing the good teachers—God bless those teachers that look after our young kids every day of their lives. So, when Claytie talks about education reform, it's compatible with what Phil is working towards in the Senate and what I'm striving to do as President of the United States.

This party also knows how important it is

for America to follow her dreams, wherever they take us. And that's why last year I announced some major destinations in our space program: first, to have space station *Freedom* up before the century is out; second, for the new century, a permanent lunar base—back to the Moon, back to the future—this time, back to stay; and third, down the road, but nevertheless a goal, a manned expedition to Mars. Exploring the heavens is man's destiny, and Houston and Texas know that it is our destiny. You know it, and I know it. And I want to continue to work to keep that future alive and bright for the generations to come.

And there's one other area I want to mention, another piece of unfinished business. The men and women in this room are committed to—and I think people all across this State, no matter what walk of life they come from. I know that Clayton Williams is determined to create and protect crime-free and drug-free communities, and so am I. In Washington, Phil has taken a superb leadership role—a national leader, fighting to clamp down on crime and drugs. And he believes police and prosecutors must have the tools to get violent criminals off the streets and put them away. And, you know, I sent a tough anticrime bill to the Congress 1½ years ago—new laws to let police and prosecutors take violent criminals off the street and put them away. But in the final hours of the Congress, the Democratic liberals gutted our legislation in a back room late at night.

Well, Republicans are not going to stop fighting. We believe when we're fighting this battle that we're doing it for every community across our country. And we believe fundamentally that it's better to have a little less sympathy for the criminal and a little more for the victim of crime.

We have much to be grateful for, much to be thankful for. And 12 hours from now, the American people will vote. And tomorrow they have a chance to vote for change. I've been fascinated by the fact that many of our kids halfway around the world—the finest, most dedicated, most highly motivated troops we've ever had—are sending in absentee ballots. And sometimes I listen to that liberal cacophony saying: Oh, everything's all wrong with this country. Everything's bad—bad news, bad, bad! My view is this: We can do absolutely anything we set our sights on if we get the right kind of people in public life.

And so, what I'm here to do is say: Barbara and I are proud to be home. We're proud to be voting for Clayton Williams and Phil and Rob Mosbacher and the rest of our ticket. We don't believe that you can't make a difference. We can make a difference, and so can you if you'll get out and work tomorrow. Get your friends to the polls, and vote for these people.

Thank you, and God bless you all.

Note: The President spoke at 6:24 p.m. in the Galleria Ballroom at the Westin Galleria Hotel. In his remarks, he referred to State representatives Rick Perry and Buster Brown; Kaye Hutchinson, candidate for State treasurer; and Milo Hamilton, Houston Astros baseball announcer.

Statement on Signing the Bill Providing for the Study of Historical and Cultural Resources in Vancouver, Washington
November 5, 1990

I have today signed H.R. 5144, "An Act to provide for the study of certain historical and cultural resources located in the city of Vancouver, Washington, and for other purposes."

This legislation establishes a Vancouver Historical Study Commission to assess and make recommendations regarding the feasibility of establishing a Vancouver National Historical Reserve. This Reserve would include several properties in Vancouver that were important to the settlement of the Pacific Northwest.

Sections 4 and 5 of the Act, concerning

excess property of the Department of Defense at Vancouver Barracks, make no reference to relevant provisions of the Federal Property and Administrative Services Act of 1949, as amended. Under the provisions of the Property Act and existing Federal Property Management Regulations, the Administrator of General Services has authority to convey Federal real property, without monetary consideration, for historic purposes. Because the Congress does not appear to have intended that the Property Act would not apply, any property conveyance recommendations the Administration may make under this Act will also be in accordance with the provisions of the Property Act.

Section 6 of the Act states that any "Federal entity" conducting or supporting activities directly affecting the Vancouver historical area shall consult with the Secretary of the Interior and the Vancouver Historical Study Commission with respect to such activities. Moreover, such Federal entity is also required to "cooperate with the Secretary and the Commission in carrying out their duties under this Act and, to the maximum extent practicable, coordinate such activities with the carrying out of such duties." In order to avoid constitutional concerns, I will construe this section as not vesting the Commission, which is composed in part of officials representing State agencies, with any authority to control the activities of Federal agencies.

GEORGE BUSH

The White House,
November 5, 1990.

Note: H.R. 5144, approved November 5, was assigned Public Law No. 101–523. The statement was released by the Office of the Press Secretary on November 6.

Statement on Signing the Disadvantaged Minority Health Improvement Act of 1990
November 6, 1990

I am pleased to sign today H.R. 5702, the "Disadvantaged Minority Health Improvement Act of 1990." This legislation will improve the access of disadvantaged individuals, including minorities, to health care and health professions opportunities.

A disparity exists between the health status of disadvantaged individuals, including minorities, and the general population. My budget for FY 1991 addressed these problems by requesting $117 million for a new Minority Health Initiative. I am gratified that this Act contains the authority to implement certain key provisions of that Initiative.

Secretary Sullivan has taken an active leadership role in addressing minority health issues since being sworn in as Secretary of Health and Human Services. Because of his leadership and that of many in the Congress, this Act will improve the quality of health care services to all disadvantaged Americans. It transcends racial and ethnic differences and will be administered in a fair and nondiscriminatory way.

I support the emphasis in the Act on improving access to health care for all disadvantaged individuals, including both minority and nonminority individuals, and increasing their representation in the health professions. It is, of course, the Federal Government's responsibility to ensure that the benefits of Federal programs are offered to individuals in a manner consistent with the equal protection guarantees of the Constitution. Certain provisions of the Act concern me with respect to these guarantees. For example, subsection 4(c)(5) purports to link eligibility for school program grants to the numerical representation of races enrolled at the school. Accordingly, I am hereby instructing the Secretary of Health and Human Services to implement this and

other provisions of the Act in a nondiscriminatory and constitutional manner.

GEORGE BUSH

The White House,
November 6, 1990.

*Note: H.R. 5702, approved November 6, was
assigned Public Law No. 101–527.*

Letter to Congressional Leaders Transmitting the Report on United States Satellites and Antisatellite Weapons
November 7, 1990

Dear Mr. Speaker: (Dear Mr. President:)
In accordance with section 1008 of the
National Defense Authorization Act for
Fiscal Years 1990 and 1991 (Public Law
101–189), enclosed is a report on U.S. antisatellite weapon activities and the surviv-
ability of U.S. satellites against current and
potential antisatellite weapons deployed by
the Soviet Union.
The unclassified version of this report will

be forwarded at a later date under separate
cover.
Sincerely,

GEORGE BUSH

*Note: Identical letters were sent to Thomas
S. Foley, Speaker of the House of Represent-
atives, and Dan Quayle, President of the
Senate.*

Statement on Signing the Foreign Direct Investment and International Financial Data Improvements Act of 1990
November 7, 1990

I have today signed S. 2516, the "Foreign
Direct Investment and International Financial Data Improvements Act of 1990." This
Act requires the Secretary of Commerce to
produce an annual report on the role and
significance of foreign direct investment in
the United States. The report will provide
information with sufficient detail so that
analysis of such investment in various industry sectors and geographic areas will be improved. This improvement will be accomplished with no additional reporting requirements on businesses.
The Act allows the Bureau of Economic
Analysis, the Bureau of Labor Statistics, and
the Bureau of the Census to share identifia-
ble business establishment data in order to
achieve more meaningful information on
foreign investment. The General Accounting Office will also have limited access to
these data to perform its oversight function.

S. 2516 contains significant safeguards to
protect the confidentiality of sensitive business information and to ensure that data
provided by individual respondents will be
used exclusively for statistical and analytical
purposes. The provisions of this Act clearly
preserve the principles of exclusive statistical use and nondisclosure of confidential information. It is of paramount importance to
this Administration that these fundamental
principles of the Federal statistical system
are strictly maintained so that the accuracy
and integrity of Government data are not
threatened.

GEORGE BUSH

The White House,
November 7, 1990.

*Note: S. 2516, approved November 7, was
assigned Public Law No. 101–533.*

Presidential Determination No. 91–8—Memorandum on the Liberalization of Trade and Investment With Nicaragua
November 7, 1990

Memorandum for the Secretary of State

Subject: Presidential Determination Waiving Worker Rights Criteria with Respect to Nicaragua Pursuant to Section 212(b) of the Caribbean Basin Economic Recovery Act

By virtue of the authority vested in me by the Caribbean Basin Economic Recovery Act, as amended (19 U.S.C. 2701 *et seq.*) (hereinafter "the Act"), I hereby determine, pursuant to section 212(b) of the Act (19 U.S.C. 2702(b)), that the designation of Nicaragua as a beneficiary country under the Act will be in the national security in-

terest of the United States. Accordingly, I waive the application of paragraph (7) of section 212(b) of the Act.

You are authorized and directed to publish this determination in the *Federal Register.*

GEORGE BUSH

[*Filed with the Office of the Federal Register, 2:54 p.m., November 27, 1990*]

Note: The memorandum was released by the Office of the Press Secretary on November 8.

Letter to Congressional Leaders on the Liberalization of Trade and Investment With Nicaragua
November 7, 1990

Dear Mr. Speaker: (Dear Mr. President:)

Pursuant to section 212 of the Caribbean Basin Economic Recovery Act (CBERA), I wish to inform you of my intent to designate Nicaragua as a beneficiary of the trade-liberalizing measures provided for in this Act. Designation will entitle the products of Nicaragua, except for products excluded statutorily, to duty-free treatment. As a beneficiary, Nicaragua also may become eligible for investments using funds generated in Puerto Rico under section 936(d)(2) of the Internal Revenue Code and re-lent to eligible Caribbean Basin countries at favorable rates, and for the convention expense tax deduction under section 274(h) of the Internal Revenue Code, by entering into an exchange of information agreement with the United States on tax matters.

Designation is an important step for Nicaragua in its effort to revitalize and rebuild its weakened economy. Designation also is significant because it is further tangible evidence of the constructive cooperation between the United States and the peoples

and governments of the Caribbean Basin.

My decision to designate Nicaragua results from consultations between this Administration and the Government of Nicaragua regarding the designation criteria set forth in section 212 of the CBERA. Nicaragua has demonstrated to my satisfaction that its laws, practices, and policies are substantially in conformity with the designation criteria of the CBERA. The Government of Nicaragua has communicated on these matters by letter to Ambassador Hills, and in so doing has indicated its desire to be designated as a CBERA beneficiary (a copy of the letter is enclosed).

I intend to exercise the authority provided by the Caribbean Basin Economic Recovery Expansion Act of 1990 (CBEREA) to waive the worker rights criteria. The CBEREA amended the worker rights criteria to bring them in conformity with the worker rights criteria under the Generalized System of Preferences (GSP). Nicaragua was terminated from the GSP program in 1987 due to its worker rights practices.

Nicaragua has agreed to update its labor law. The approach of the new Nicaraguan Government is totally different from that of its predecessors, and I am confident that real change can now occur. Nevertheless, in order to ensure that Nicaragua satisfies the legal requirements of the new criteria, we would need to perform a full review, which would require several months.

Nicaragua has recently emerged from a period in which it undermined the security and stability of Central America. Nicaragua's political stability depends in large measure on its ability to make significant economic progress. However, the economic situation in Nicaragua remains precarious. Nicaragua's economic recovery hinges on stimulating the private sector, particularly in the area of foreign trade. By extending duty-free treatment to Nicaraguan imports, the United States can foster Nicaraguan political stability through enhanced economic growth. Continued political stability in Nicaragua will contribute to the stability of the region. Central America's stability and development are clearly in the national security interest of the United States.

For these reasons, I have determined, pursuant to section 212(b) of the CBERA, as amended, that it would be in the national security interest of the United States to expedite Nicaragua's CBERA beneficiary status by waiving the worker rights criteria (a copy of the determination is enclosed). On the basis of the statements and assurances in Nicaragua's letter, and taking into account information developed by the United States Embassy and through other sources, I have concluded that designation of Nicaragua as a CBERA beneficiary is appropriate at this time.

I am mindful that under section 212(e) of the CBERA, as amended, I retain the authority to suspend, withdraw, or limit the application of CBERA benefits from any designated country if a beneficiary's laws, policies, or practices are no longer in conformity with the designation criteria. The United States will keep abreast of developments in Nicaragua that are pertinent to the designation criteria—particularly with respect to worker rights.

This Administration looks forward to working closely with the Government of Nicaragua and with the private sectors of the United States and Nicaragua to ensure that the wide-ranging opportunities opened by the CBERA are fully utilized.

Sincerely,

GEORGE BUSH

Note: Identical letters were sent to Thomas S. Foley, Speaker of the House of Representatives, and Dan Quayle, President of the Senate. The letter was released by the Office of the Press Secretary on November 8. The proclamation designating Nicaragua as a CBERA beneficiary is listed in Appendix E at the end of this volume.

Statement by Press Secretary Fitzwater on the Liberalization of Trade and Investment With Nicaragua
November 8, 1990

President Bush today signed a Presidential proclamation designating Nicaragua as a beneficiary of the trade measures provided for in the Caribbean Basin Economic Recovery Act. Nicaragua's participation in the Caribbean Basin Initiative (CBI) benefits will give Nicaraguan businesses duty-free access to the U.S. market for a wide range of goods and will prompt growth in Nicaragua's export sector, which is critical for its economic recovery program.

In recognition of the disastrous economic situation which the democratically elected government of President Violeta Chamorro inherited, President Bush has determined that it is in the national interest to waive the statutory requirements that a lengthy review of worker rights in Nicaragua be conducted before CBI benefits are extended. Nevertheless, we are satisfied that the Nicaraguan Government complies with the criteria of the law and that there is labor freedom in Nicaragua. Today the Nicaraguan workers are free to organize, the press is uncensored, political activity is unrestricted, and religious activity is free from government interference. This is in strong contrast to the record of the previous government.

By promoting increased trade ties be-tween the United States and Nicaragua, President Bush's action is yet another sign of the new, friendly relationship between our two countries. The United States reiterates its strong support for the democratically elected government of Nicaragua.

Note: The proclamation is listed in Appendix E at the end of this volume.

Remarks Announcing the Resignation of William J. Bennett as Director of National Drug Control Policy and a Question-and-Answer Session With Reporters
November 8, 1990

The President. I am announcing today that Bill Bennett, America's first Director of the Office of National Drug Policy, has offered his resignation and, with much regret, I have accepted it. His decision to return to private life is obviously welcome news to his family, but there is no doubt that his energetic contributions to public life will be sorely missed.

When we took office, Bill Bennett took on one of the most important initiatives of our administration, the national drug control strategy, our blueprint, if you will, for the war on drugs. He confronted the problem head on, helping lead America's determined effort to take back the streets. And his hard work has paid off. We devoted unprecedented new resources to the fight: new money, new material, new manpower for law enforcement, for treatment, for prevention. Never before has so much effort, involving so many people, been applied to the battle against drugs.

Bill's efforts have helped spark a fundamental change in attitude, an awareness that drugs can take away your family, your job, your health, your freedom and, indeed, your very life. As we've seen on the road firsthand, he's inspired communities across the country to get involved in this battle. And I've enjoyed my many travels with him.

Both Bill and I are encouraged by recent, very promising signs that suggest the drug problem is diminishing not only in the suburbs but in the cities as well. And I know he believes, as I do, that we're on the road to victory. So, we're going to stick to our comprehensive drug strategy. We're going to renew our call for Congress to pass a true crime bill—one that's tough on criminals, not on the police. And my administration will remain on the front lines until this scourge is stopped.

On behalf of all Americans, I want to thank Bill for his leadership on this issue and express my gratitude for all that he has done to unite the Nation against the scourge of drugs. Block by block, school by school, child by child, we will take back the streets; and we will never surrender.

Bill Bennett has done a superb job for this country, and I will always be very, very grateful to him. And now I'd like to ask him to say a word or two, and then I'll be glad to take a couple of questions, and I'm sure he would as well.

Director Bennett. Mr. President, thank you very much for your words and for the confidence that you put in me in asking me to take this job. As you remember, I volunteered for the job. I had an opportunity earlier on in the Reagan administration to serve this country and the children of this country. And to have a second opportunity to do that was a rare privilege indeed. All I want to say now—and of course, I'll be happy to take questions later on about our policies and our programs—but all I want to say now, again, is thank you and talk a minute about the difference that you have made.

Your taking this issue on, your saying in that Inaugural Address that this scourge will stop, coincided with the great American change of mind about drugs. But your leadership at crucial points has made a great deal of difference. You said in your inaugural: "This scourge will stop." That was against the advice of some to take on this issue. But you took it on. Second, you remember that trip to Cartagena. And many advised you not to go, and public opinion polls were advising you not to go. But you thought it was serious and merited your being there, and you were there. About a month and a half ago, when we issued our report update on the war on drugs, you stated again that this was a top priority of yours. You have been there every time we have asked you to be there, and you have taken this issue unto yourself. The American people know that and are grateful to you for it.

The midterm elections just took place. No one has commented because, I guess, it hasn't been noticed yet. But there was hardly any sign during those elections that any Democrat sought to challenge you on the issue of drugs—because you were credible, because you have taken this task up, because everyone knows that you have taken it seriously and made an unprecedented commitment.

While we're on politics, it's my belief, Mr. President, you will conclude this term very successfully. You will be reelected as President of the United States in 1992—[laughter]—and in 1996 you will be thanked by your countrymen for a profound and great service, not least of which because in 1996, when the American people look at this issue, they will see the drug problem much improved.

Thank you very much, sir.

Persian Gulf Crisis

Q. Mr. President, Margaret Thatcher [Prime Minister of the United Kingdom] said yesterday that either Saddam Hussein [President of Iraq] get out of Kuwait soon or Britain and its allies will remove him by force. Do you agree with that, and how soon is soon?

The President. Well, let me say—I should have thrown a caveat in. I'm going to take some questions on the Middle East this afternoon, so if you'll excuse me, I'll defer them until then. But I won't take any now on that subject at all.

Q. All right. I'll try politics.

The President. Try that. [*Laughter*]

Q. Do you have a replacement?

Midterm Elections

Q. Okay. You went around the country telling Americans you had to have more Republicans in Congress to get the economy going and to cut the deficit. You didn't get any more Republicans. In fact, you lost a little ground. What does that mean for your relationship with Congress?

The President. Hey, listen, it means I didn't do as well as I'd like. I'd like to have had more; I still feel that way. I think if you want to put it in proper perspective—I think everyone is aware of the fact that the party in power normally loses in an off year. I'm told we did a little better than the norm, but that doesn't make me happy. I'd like to have more Republicans.

Q. Well, does it tie your hands now—I mean, the fact that the Democrats——

The President. No, it doesn't tie my hand. The changes were very small. I regret terribly the loss of Senator Boschwitz. He's an outstanding Republican Member of the Senate. But we lose one there. I don't want to go into a lot of political statistics, but I'm told that's far fewer than normally happens in an off year, and certainly in the House—nine, compared to some of the gloom and doom predictions is not as substantial. But look, every one that we dropped I don't like. I don't like to see us lose seats at all. I'd like to see us gain.

Administration Vacancies

Q. Mr. President, do you have a replacement for Bennett, and do you have a replacement for Elizabeth Dole [former Secretary of Labor] as a result of the election?

The President. Not yet. Not yet. And I haven't even begun to really sit down seriously with lists. Bill, out of courtesy, whispered in my ear not so long ago that he wanted to go back to private life; and maybe I've just been hoping he would think more rationally. But I understand that. I love his family, and it is right for him and his family. And somehow, I think that's going to prove to be right for me and this administration in the long run.

But, no, but we've got to start soon on that, Helen [Helen Thomas, United Press International]. I wanted to wait until after the election to keep my focus on the campaign trail and then on these big problems we're wrestling with halfway around the world. So, I'm not misleading you. Heard a lot of names floated, but we're not down to the decisionmaking point on either of these two or——

Q. Will it be a woman? And will it be someone like Lynn Martin [Republican senatorial candidate in Illinois]?

The President. Well, as I say, we're not there yet, so I can't help you. Nice try, however.

Midterm Elections

Q. Mr. President, a couple of months ago, predictions were that Republicans might actually make gains in the midterm election.

The President. Hey, listen, that's what I wanted.

Q. And then their fortune seemed to turn when you changed your mind on the possibility of new taxes and then during the drawn-out budget process. To what extent do you blame yourself, if at all, for the Republican showing in this past election?

The President. I think if the past year were significantly different than other years—in other words, if we'd have taken a bath for every off year heretofore people had gained, the party in power, I think maybe I would have had to accept a little more responsibility and blame. I'm not talking victory because I am very disappointed the way some of the races turned out. On the other hand, when you look overall, I think most people that understand American politics are saying this administration did not come out worse than predecessors. Indeed, some make the point that we came out a little better.

So, it's pretty hard to assess that. And I haven't looked at it in terms of those who

supported the budget package—whether they did worse than others. But I made very clear to the American people I was concerned with some of the provisions in the budget package. I happen to believe in the long run it's going to prove in the best interests of this country. And so, I'm not suggesting that that was popular or made me popular with everybody. But I can't really answer it until we've seen a little more analysis. You've asked a very technical question in a sense.

1992 Presidential Election

Q. Mr. President, are you running for re-election in 1992?

The President. Ann [Ann Compton, ABC News], I'm going to put you down as one of the first I'll let know when I make that decision. No decision has been made. You all go through this kind of coy dance now for a while. The minute the election is over everybody shifts gear and starts pointing at '92. It's understandable. So, therefore, I understand where you're coming from, but I can't give you an answer yet.

Q. Are you giving any consideration in not running? Is that a possibility?

The President. Not today. Not today. I'm shifting gears now and trying to shift into the role of trying to lead this country in getting things done. And we're going to have a good agenda to take to the Congress. And clearly, I want to see the country remain united in our determination to succeed halfway around the world. So, I really have not started a focus on '92.

The Economy and the Persian Gulf Crisis

Q. Mr. President, some of the polling taken in conjunction with the election, exit polls and so forth, showed an impression growing in the country that the United States is headed for war in the Middle East and very serious economic problems here at home. Would you address those fears?

The President. Well, I'm concerned about the economic situation—been very frank about that. I will be meeting with our top economic people in the next few days—a series of meetings, both inside—top economic people in the White House, and then I'll be inviting some others in to talk about it because I am concerned about a slow-down in this economy. And I'm concerned what that means to the average working-man in this country and the women that work with their kids—having to support them. I mean, it's a terrible worry that people have. And we've been enjoying rather robust growth for many years, and now we all know the economy is slower. So, I want to be sure that, to the degree a President can do something to soften the blow or to stimulate economic growth, that he tries to do it. So, we'll be having a lot of discussion about that.

And what was your part on the Gulf?

Q. About the prospects for war in the Persian Gulf?

The President. Well, I've been very clear that we want to see the sanctions be so successful we don't have to have anybody shooting over there, and I've also said we're not ruling any options out.

Civil Rights Legislation

Q. Sir, you're getting a lot of free advice on which way to go politically over the next couple of years——

The President. Yes.

Q. Mr. Viguerie and Howard Phillips [conservative Republican consultants] are telling you you've got to go right and rees-tablish your conservative credentials. Marlin [Marlin Fitzwater, Press Secretary to the President] did remind us yesterday that you are a conservative. But people like Ed Rol-lins [cochairman of the National Republican Congressional Committee] are saying you've got to be more broad-based and go after the Democrats. What do you see now? Do you have to appeal to a wider section and got to go after blacks again after the veto of the civil rights bill?

The President. One of the things I—since you raised the civil rights bill—is that I want to have a good civil rights bill. And so, we'll be sending one up early on. It will not have quotas. It will not lead to quotas. It will be fairplay in trying to eliminate dis-crimination in the workplace. And there were some politics involved in that, John [John Cochran, NBC News].

We sent a bill up there that was a very good bill, and the leaders wouldn't even permit it to be voted on because they

thought they could stick me with being anti-civil rights. I am pro-civil rights. I am pro-fairness in the workplace, against dis-crimination in the workplace. And we can fashion that kind of civil rights legislation if we can get some of the politics out of it. And maybe we can as we start a new Con-gress, because I've got a good record in that regard. I have not changed in that regard. But I don't think it is fair to recommend to the American people legislation that in my view, would inevitably result in quotas.

But now we're out of the political give-and-take on that, and I think maybe we can get something positive done.

Washington Politics

Q. Can I ask you about the reaching out in a broad-based way? And would you reach out to Ed Rollins? You willing to work with him and let him stay on?

The President. I'm not going to get into this beltway stuff. One of the things that I loved was outside—I got needled by some— let's see if I can find him or her here—a writer about saying it's nice to be outside of the beltway. It is. I didn't get one single question about the future of any individual consultant or member of whatever congres-sional or Senate committee or national com-mittee. We stayed on different subjects. So——

Q. We're here.

The President. Yes, we're here, but my mind is out there. So, I refuse to get into all of that.

Relations With Congress

Q. Mr. President, as you approach the new Congress, do you think you will be able to extend the hand of friendship the way you—the tone of the first—in your first inaugural, or do you think this will be parti-san and confrontational from the outset?

The President. Well, it takes two to— when you extend the hand somebody else has to reach out and shake it. And we've been through a highly partisan political dance here for a while. It's the great Ameri-can way. And those with whom I've worked cooperatively, needless to say, went out and tried to bash the President. And we've heard all kinds of rhetoric about how I should be doing things differently. But look, there are going to be certain things where we will continue to try to work with the Congress.

I also will be being sure I can do the best job I can in leading a united Republican Party. We have some—he mentioned a couple of critics that aren't in the Congress or anything who—there's nothing I can do to placate those who have been some of the severest critics of Ronald Reagan even. So, I'm not going to even worry about that. But I do think that it's worth trying to move the country forward. And on some areas, we're going to have to do it, and on some, I'm going to be appealing strongly for Democratic support, and in some I'm going to use the veto so as to stop a lot of bad things from happening to this country. And that veto power is there. And I am more determined than ever to use it.

I was elected to take this country in a certain direction, and the liberals in the Congress want to take it in another direction. So, our system decrees: Who wins? How are we going to move it? And they're going to shoot stuff back at me over and over again that I cannot accept. Now, will I try to avoid that? Will I say to them on a civil rights bill: "Look, I want civil rights, and I don't want quotas. You tried it your way; now let's give me a vote my way"? Absolutely. I have to do that. That's part of my responsibility. All kinds of growth incentives—when the economy is slow, you want growth incentives. So, I've got an agenda. We're going to be fashioning it. And whether they are going to be willing to cooperate, I don't know.

But it's hard when you have a majority—take capital gains. There was a majority last year in the House for it. There was a majority last year in the Senate for it. And it never could get voted on. Now, I think the American people can see that. And so, let's hope we can make progress on some of these incentives. When you have a slow economy, or worry about a slower economy, that's a good time to put incentive into the economic spectrum.

Manuel Noriega

Q. Mr. President, CNN [Cable News Network] has obtained tapes which apparently were recorded between Manuel Noriega [former Panamanian dictator charged with drug trafficking] in prison and his defense team. Although certain calls are permitted to be monitored, we understand that those with a defendant's attorneys are supposed to be privileged. Were you aware of this monitoring, or any specific order that would have authorized monitoring of privileged conversations?

The President. No, and I'm not aware of it now. I'm learning something from you. So, I'm not going to comment on it if I don't know anything about it, and I don't.

Q. Under what circumstances would you favor monitoring——

The President. I would favor abiding by the law.

Federal Budget Agreement and Taxes

Q. Mr. President, with all of your explanations on midterm perspective taken as a given, do you think you paid a political price for compromising with the Democrats and agreeing to new taxes?

The President. I don't know, because I used to get accused in this very room by question, not direct accusation, but by living and guiding myself by the polls. That was: Hey, you won't make a tough decision because of the polls. Have not heard that recently, and maybe that has something to do with how I'd answer your question. Because I don't think it was popular, what I did, with anybody. But I think it was the right thing to do, and so, I will try to make that point. You know, like the umpire, you've got to call them as you see them.

So, I have some remedial work to do, I think. I wish I could go back and give a clearer answer to whether this helped or hurt in the election, because I just don't know the answer to that. But I think in the final analysis, if it's good for the economy, long run—we're in some tough times right now—but in the long run, if it's good for the economy, then that should be good for the country. And if it's good for the country, hopefully it would be good for the views that I represent.

Q. I ask that because so many of the Governors on the Democratic side and your own side seemed to have certainly been punished where they raised taxes, and I wonder if that's a lesson you take away from this election.

The President. I think there is a lesson. I think people feel they're taxed too much. I happen to believe that, and I've said that. I haven't changed my view: that we think we ought to go out and raise people's taxes. What I think we're going to see coming down the pike at me, in terms of the offered hand, is a whole wide array of tax proposals out of the Democrats. Maybe I misread what some of their leaders said when they talked about now going back and trying to raise income tax rates. And they're going to do it over my dead veto or live veto or something like that, because it ain't going to happen, I'll guarantee you.

And so, I can identify with that. I've always felt that way. I made one compromise to try to get a budget agreement that, in my view, I felt was essential. And I got the message. I had the message long before America went to the polls to say, Hey, we don't want any more taxes; we want to do something about spending. And one of the great things about this budget agreement is that—we'll get to you in a minute—one of the great things about that is that there is some enforcement provisions in here that I am determined to live by and that I am determined to make Congress live by. And if we live by them, then we can negate the insatiable desire on the part of some in the Congress on the Democratic side to raise taxes.

But the good news on that, Wyatt [Wyatt Andrews, CBS News], is I think some of the Democrats got the message as well as Republicans. We had the message. We've understood this. And you're right, they spoke up against Governors, some Democrat, some Republican. But I don't think there's any confusion on the part of people as to how I feel about taxes. I oppose raising taxes. And we had this one compromise, and that just reinforced my view, frankly.

Q. If I may, are you saying it's one time only?

The President. I'm just saying I'm going to hold the line on taxes and fight back all these plans that are coming at me that I think will—maybe I'm getting paranoid about it when I hear them talk about let's

go out and raise taxes again—but I thought that was kind of the message coming out of the end of the budget debate. And if that's the case, we're in for a whale of a fight. And the proffered hand may miss the shake because we're not going to compromise on that.

Q. Could we go back out beyond the beltway again for a minute?

The President. Let's do it, Michel [Michel McQueen, Wall Street Journal].

Campaign Tactics

Q. A couple of years ago, the Texas Republican Party passed an "English only" amendment as part of its party platform, and you spoke out against this. You said that this was an alienating message to send to people you want to participate. This year the North Carolina Republican Party sent postcards to minority voters, Democrats, suggesting that they had given false information to elections officials, giving them false information. Is this an appropriate campaign tactic? And why have you been silent about this?

The President. Because I haven't tried to get into the campaign tactics in 50 States. On the postcard—I mean, the "English only"—I don't think it's a good thing to have. I mean, I want every kid to speak English. I've been for bilingual education all my life—continue to support it—but I think the goal of it should be that every kid in this country speak English. But I just don't think the "English only" approach is the way to do it. I think it could result in certain discrimination.

But I'm sorry, I can't help you on the details of a race for the United States Senate or a Governor's race or a congressional race. I just have not gone into that.

Q. Sir, are you saying that you don't know anything about this postcard situation?

The President. Yes, just what I've read in the papers. I've read a lot of charges and countercharges. And I've heard some people say it's bad, and I've heard others say it's not. I do recall—anytime somebody puts in what they call a voter's security program, some people raise hell about it. And that's not right, either. So, it ought to be—it depends how it's done. And I just don't know enough about what you're trying to get me into, to get into that.

Midterm Elections

Q. Mr. President, I wonder if you have any reaction to the margins of victory of Mario Cuomo [Governor of New York] and [Senator] Bill Bradley, two Democrats thought to be looking at challenging you in 2 years. [*Laughter*]

The President. I told you I'm not thinking about '92.

Q. Could you say that a little louder?

The President. I just told Michel I haven't gone into the details of all these races. I don't know. I don't know.

Director Bennett's Resignation

Q. Mr. President, may I ask you about Director Bennett? We've heard stories of threats against himself, against his family, and maybe that's why he's leaving. What do you know about that?

The President. I'd let him respond to that question, but I—maybe—Bill, why don't you——

Director Bennett. I've got one question. Come on, let me take it. [*Laughter*] So far, I've read that I am bored, restive, restless, tired, unhappy, moping about lack of media attention, sulking about not being in the Cabinet, in a snit with John Sununu [Chief of Staff to the President]—all sorts of things that I've read about—and being stampeded out of town—none of which are true.

There have been people who haven't liked me since I've been in public service. The Yale English department—they may be threatening. I don't—[*laughter*]—the National Education Association and this latest crowd. But I mean, I'm not the stampeded-out-of-town type. There's nothing there.

Q. How about personal threats to your safety?

Director Bennett. I mean, there are threats. There are always threats in this kind——

Q. ——to your safety?

Director Bennett. Yes, well they've been there since the beginning of this job, and that's always the case. I think what people are picking up on is when I went up to Alaska to talk about the recriminalization of

marijuana, which, by the way, occurred—that took place, that initiative passed. There were some anonymous threats from some potheads: that they were going to blow me up. But the notice that went out from one of the pothead societies said—[*laughter*]—said, "Come confront Bennett." But the date they put on it was 2 days after the day I was there. [*Laughter*] So, if they did leave anything dangerous, it's probably going off up there on the icecap somewhere without——

Q. Why are you leaving?

Director Bennett. I don't want to tie you up. Should we go into this?

Q. Why?

The President. No, no. I'll just take two more and then——

Director Bennett. When the President and I talked 20 months ago, we talked about things that needed to be done. I had two jobs in Government: Humanities Chairman and Secretary of Education. We decided that what we needed to do was to get a good strategy, which we've got; to get bipartisan support for it, which we've got broadly—there are still some things Democrats need to do, like the crime bill; third, that we needed to get the right amount of resources for it, which we've achieved; and fourth, begin to see some progress, some results.

We said at that time—I remember the President saying to me, "If you can get this thing started, going in the right direction, moving, I'll be very grateful." I think we got that. And so, I took the job freely, and now I leave freely.

Q. Why don't you want to see it through?

Director Bennett. Seeing it through is going to—I mean, I think if this nation stays on course, I think, we will probably beat the goals that we stated in the National Drug Control Strategy of 10 years. I think we'll be there in 5 years if the States do the things that they're supposed to do and if others do what they're supposed to do. The Federal commitment, I think, is clear—unprecedented commitment, unprecedented amount of money, resources, and so on. That's 5 years.

You know, I've had 9 years in Government. I think that's enough for now. I mean, I do want to tell my critics I am not leaving public life. And worse than that, I may not even be leaving public service forever. I may be back. One needs to be careful about this.

But I don't leave with any sense of remorse or apology. I'm proud of what we've done, and I think what we've done is a good thing and we really are making progress.

The President. With your permission, let me just take two—Jessica [Jessica Lee, USA Today] and Ellen [Ellen Warren, Knight-Ridder Newspapers]—and then leave you to the others. But before I—well, go ahead, and then I want to just conclude my part.

Taxes

Q. Mr. President, you say that your reading of the election shows that people didn't and don't want their taxes raised. Upon reflection, do you wish you had kept your campaign promise and not supported higher taxes?

The President. Do I wish I had been able to? Yes. Very much so.

Q. But sir, you told——

The President. In fact, we tried. We sent a budget up there, and it kind of died for lack of a second. It had no taxes in it. And that's a very—I wish I had a Congress who would do it just my way, because I am still convinced we can get by without having raised anybody's taxes of any kind. So, yes, I have serious regrets about that.

Q. Can you make the promise now, sir, that you will not support new taxes in the future?

The President. Can I make the promise I won't support them? Absolutely. But sometimes you run into some realities. I'm girding up my loins to go into battle to beat back the tax attempts that I think are coming because I think the American people are fed up with it. I think that was very clear. I think in my case they probably know that there had to be some compromise, at least from the way you look at does the American people support the deficit agreement or not. But I want to be on the side of no tax increases, and we're going to go right to bat again in the Congress at that. We fight that battle all the time.

Persian Gulf Crisis and Director Bennett's Resignation

Q. Mr. President, there seemed to be not very much debate about the Persian Gulf during the election, even though we have our young people there with their lives on the line. I'm wondering if you take the fact that you weren't seriously challenged by the opposition party on this matter—if you take this as support for any decision that you might make with respect to having to go to war there, without respect, say, to the House's adjournment resolution that says they should come back if you were to go to war?

The President. Jessica, I said I didn't want to take any Persian Gulf questions.

Q. It's not——

The President. Well, it is, so therefore I will reply to this, and then—this is the last one anyway. Look, we have had extensive consultations with Congress. We will continue to have extensive consultations with Congress. I think the people in the campaign, for the most part, recognized that I was trying very hard to separate support for the Persian Gulf policy from the pure head-on-head confrontation of domestic politics.

Again, I tried continually on the road to salute the Democratic leadership and Democratic Members along with Republican leadership and Republican Members for what I think has been extraordinarily solid support. And I think that support has led to good support from the American people. But we have a major foreign policy objective there. I am determined to see the objective fulfilled. I am determined to hold this coalition together. But that must be done without partisan politics intervening.

And so, that then leads me to say I will continue to consult. I know the responsibilities I have to do that. I know the importance of the support of the Congress. And I will continue to reach out to them and keep them informed and consult. And they know my views. So, I don't think that the campaign has driven any wedge between me and the leaders on Capitol Hill or of the American people on this very important problem.

Q. So, that does mean that you feel that there is widespread national support for——

The President. No question about it.

Q. ——whatever it is that you have to do, that you decide to do?

The President. Well, I like to feel the American people would support their President on whatever decision is made. And I think one way to guarantee that is to be sure that you consult, to be sure that you spell out your objectives as clearly as possible, be sure you keep their historic coalition together. And the importance of the [Secretary of State] Baker trip, for example, I think, is obvious. And so, so far, I think that the ingredients are there for full support. And I view my responsibilities as such that I must be sure that's right. I'll go the extra mile here at home and abroad to see that the common objectives as stated by the United Nations are met.

Now, I'll turn it over to Bill. And let me just say, I've read some silly speculation about Bill Bennett's leaving. And he has my total confidence. There's no internal politics that's caused him to make this decision. If he feels like it, he can tell you when he—I don't want to violate confidences—when he and I had our first and subsequent talks about this. He knows the affection that Barbara and I have for him and his family. I know the kind of sacrifice that anyone serving this country goes through not just in the controversy of the job but in terms of financial aspirations for their families that need to be educated. And so, please discount some of this understandable speculation. He has my confidence; I think I have his. And I know that he has the love and affection for his family from Barbara and me.

I think he's done an outstanding job for this country. And even his severest critics, I think, will tell you that—those that started off the most critical. We've made progress in an area that is vital to every single family in this country, and I will never get over being grateful to Bill Bennett for what he's done.

Note: The President spoke at 11:08 a.m. in the Briefing Room at the White House.

Letter Accepting the Resignation of William J. Bennett as Director of National Drug Control Policy
November 8, 1990

Dear Bill:

It is with great regret that I accept your letter of resignation as Director of National Drug Control Policy. Your strong support and steady guidance will be sorely missed.

As the first Director of National Drug Control Policy, you took on the dual task of coordinating the Federal Government's effort to fight the war on drugs while providing courageous national leadership in the battle against drug use, addiction, and drug-related crime. Your drive, determination, clarity of purpose, and deep sense of mission have helped unite the whole Nation behind this critical task.

Under your careful stewardship, our Administration published the first National Drug Control Strategy, a comprehensive blueprint for fighting drugs and drug use on every front, at every level of government, and in every city, town, and neighborhood. In the time since we presented the National Strategy to the American people, we have seen many very real and encouraging signs of progress against drugs. You have helped lay the essential groundwork for victory, and I share your fervent belief that in the months and years ahead, we will see the menace of drugs finally beaten.

Bill, both Barbara and I maintain the greatest respect and admiration for your accomplishments in public office. On behalf of all Americans, let me express our indebtedness to you for your service to the peace and health of this Nation.

Sincerely,

GEORGE BUSH

Dear Mr. President:

It is with deep respect and heartfelt gratitude that I advise you of my wish to resign as Director of the Office of National Drug Control Policy at the end of November.

When I assumed this position in March of 1989, you asked that I devote my efforts to develop a strategy to fight the terrible menace of illegal drugs. Under your leadership, and with the strong support of your Cabinet, I believe we have done that.

During the last nineteen months, we have made progress in attacking all aspects of illegal drug use in this country. While much remains to be done, I think it can be said we have witnessed a major turning point in the war on drugs. All indicators suggest that drug use—across the board—

has started to turn down. I believe that the American people have united to assure that the promise you made in your Inaugural Address will be fulfilled.

The National Drug Control Strategy that has been implemented during your Administration enjoys broad, bipartisan support. With continued effort, energy, and further refinement, this Strategy will bring this scourge under control, and provide lasting benefit to the American people. Your courageous commitment to tackle this problem is a tribute to you and your Presidency.

Thank you for the opportunity to serve.

Sincerely,

BILL
William J. Bennett

The President's News Conference on the Persian Gulf Crisis
November 8, 1990

The President. I have a brief statement, and I'd be glad to take a couple of questions and then turn to Secretary Cheney, who will take some questions. And then he will go over to the Pentagon for more of an in-depth briefing.

On August 6th, in response to the unprovoked Iraqi invasion of Kuwait, I ordered the deployment of U.S. military forces to Saudi Arabia and the Persian Gulf to deter further Iraqi aggression and to protect our interests in the region. What we've done is right, and I'm happy to say that most Members of Congress and the majority of Americans agree.

Before the invasion in August, we had succeeded in the struggle for freedom in Eastern Europe, and we'd hopefully begun a new era that offered the promise of peace. Following the invasion, I stated that if history had taught us any lesson it was that we must resist aggression or it would destroy our freedom. Just ask the people of Kuwait and the foreign nationals in hiding there and the staffs of the remaining Embassies who have experienced the horrors of

Iraq's illegal occupation, its systematic dismantling of Kuwait, and its abuse of Kuwaitis and other citizens.

The world community also must prevent an individual clearly bent on regional domination from establishing a chokehold on the world's economic lifeline. We're seeing global economic stability and growth already at risk as, each day, countries around the world pay dearly for Saddam Hussein's [President of Iraq] aggression.

From the very beginning, we and our coalition partners have shared common political goals: the immediate, complete, and unconditional withdrawal of Iraqi forces from Kuwait; restoration of Kuwait's legitimate government; protection of the lives of citizens held hostage by Iraq both in Kuwait and Iraq; and restoration of security and stability in the Persian Gulf region.

To achieve these goals, we and our allies have forged a strong diplomatic, economic, and military strategy to force Iraq to comply with these objectives. The framework of this strategy is laid out in 10 United Nations resolutions, overwhelmingly supported by the United Nations Security Council. In 3 months, the U.S. troop contribution to the multinational force in Saudi Arabia has gone from 10,000 to 230,000 as part of Operation Desert Shield. General Schwarzkopf [commander of the U.S. forces in the Persian Gulf] reports that our forces, in conjunction with other coalition forces, now have the capability to defend successfully against any further Iraqi aggression.

After consultation with King Fahd [of Saudi Arabia] and our other allies, I have today directed the Secretary of Defense to increase the size of U.S. forces committed to Desert Shield to ensure that the coalition has an adequate offensive military option should that be necessary to achieve our common goals. Toward this end, we will continue to discuss the possibility of both additional allied force contributions and appropriate United Nation actions.

Iraq's brutality, aggression, and violations of international law cannot be allowed to succeed. Secretary Baker has been consulting with our key partners in the coalition. He's met with the Amirs of Bahrain ['Isa bin Salman Al Khalifa] and Kuwait [Jabir al-Ahmad al-Jabir al-Sabah], King Fahd, President Mubarak [of Egypt], as well as the Chinese Foreign Minister [Qian Qichen], President Özal [of Turkey], [Soviet] Foreign Minister Shevardnadze, President Gorbachev. He also will be meeting with Prime Minister Thatcher [of the United Kingdom] and President Mitterrand [of France]. I've been heartened by Jim's appraisal of the strong international solidarity and determination to ensure that Iraq's aggression does not stand and is not rewarded.

But right now, Kuwait is struggling for survival. And along with many other nations, we've been called upon to help. The consequences of our not doing so would be incalculable because Iraq's aggression is not just a challenge to the security of Kuwait and other Gulf nations but to the better world that we all have hoped to build in the wake of the Cold War. And therefore, we and our allies cannot and will not shirk our responsibilities. The state of Kuwait must be restored, or no nation will be safe and the promising future we anticipate will indeed be jeopardized.

Let me conclude with a word to the young American GI's deployed in the Gulf. We are proud of each and every one of you. I know you miss your loved ones and want to know when you'll be coming home. We won't leave you there any longer than necessary. I want every single soldier out of there as soon as possible. And we're all grateful for your continued sacrifice and your commitment.

Now, with no further ado, I'd be glad to take a couple of questions. And when I leave, Dick, take some questions and then go over to the Pentagon.

Q. Mr. President, it sounds like you're going to war. You have moved from a defensive position to an offensive position, and you have not said how many more troops you are sending or, really, why.

The President. Well, I've said why right now. And I hope it's been very clear to the American people.

Q. Are there new reasons that have moved this posture?

The President. No, it's just continuing to do what we feel is necessary to complete our objectives, to fulfill our objectives, that have been clearly stated.

Q. Well, are you going to war?

The President. I would love to see a peaceful resolution to this question, and that's what I wanted.

Q. What made the change from the defense to offense?

The President. I would like to see a peaceful solution to this question. I think Saddam Hussein should fully, without condition, comply to the U.N. resolutions. And if this movement of force is what convinces him, so much the better.

Q. You said last week that the sanctions haven't had the impact that you wanted. Some members of the coalition are urging a go-slow approach. The President of Egypt says you've got to wait 2 or 3 months before you judge whether the sanctions have worked. Are you willing to wait that long?

The President. Wait for what?

Q. To see if the sanctions have worked?

The President. I think from talking to Jim Baker and recently to President Mubarak that we are in total sync with him. But I hope that the sanctions will work within a 2-month period. But I don't think we've got a difference with Egypt on this at all, Terry [Terence Hunt, Associated Press].

Q. The question is how long are you willing to give the sanctions?

The President. Well, I can't tell you how long. If I knew, I certainly wouldn't want to signal that to Saddam Hussein.

Q. Prime Minister Thatcher said yesterday that if, indeed, Saddam doesn't withdraw from Kuwait that you and the allies will use force. I haven't heard you say that before. You've talked about wanting to retain the option of war, but would you use force?

The President. Well, I don't want to say what I will or will not do. But certainly, I noted what Prime Minister Thatcher said— one of the strongest members of this coalition. And she's an eloquent spokesman for her views and speaks in a way that shows that we're all together. So, I have not ruled out the use of force at all, and I think that's evident by what we're doing here today.

Q. Sir, can I just follow that up by going back to the speech you gave at the Pentagon back in August, when you talked about oil, protecting Middle East oil reserves, and you talked about American jobs, in fact the American way of life being endangered. Yet when you went out on the campaign trail, you seemed to shy away from oil. You said demonstrators don't seem to understand that we're not going to go to war for oil. But that was one of the things you talked about. And in fact, isn't oil part of the American national interest? Isn't that a main reason we're there?

The President. It is a part of it, but it is not the main reason—or I'd say, a main reason. The main reason we're there is to set back aggression, to see that aggression is unrewarded. My argument with some of the protesters is that they seem to suggest that oil is the sole reason that we are involved in this enormous commitment. And that is simply not correct. There's a lot of other interests, and the restoration of the security and stability in the Persian Gulf region clearly relates to the world's economic interest. I'm not denying that, and I'm not backing away from the fact that all the Western world has real interest in that. But my argument with those people is that they are missing the point. The point is: It is the aggression against Kuwait that has caused this coalition to come together as it has.

Q. Do you feel that you are free to take offensive action without any kind of U.N. resolution authorizing it?

The President. Yes, we have authority. But we've been great believers in going to the United Nations. I think one of the major successes has been the ability to have world opinion totally on our side because of U.N. action. The peacekeeping function of the United Nations has indeed been rejuvenated by the actions of the Security Council.

Way in the back, because I've been accused by a distinguished senior reporter of not getting into the back of the room, so I'd like to rectify that.

Q. Mr. President, do you yet have the support you need in order to secure an additional resolution from the U.N. Security Council to explicitly authorize the use of force? Do you now have sufficient support on the Security Council to get that?

The President. I would say that the Baker mission is—what it is about is consultation. That subject will be discussed in some ways, I'm sure, but that's not why he's there. We're talking about a wide array of issues, and so I'd say we have not tried to specifically poll the other 14 members of the Security Council along those lines. So, I can't answer whether we would or not.

Q. If I may follow: Has any country told you they would block such a resolution?

The President. Some may have said such a thing, but it's not been brought to my attention at all. And again, I think I'd know if that were the case. But I don't think so.

Q. Mr. President, it would seem that the situation at the U.S. Embassy in Kuwait is crucial to the future of the overall situation in the Gulf. What is the latest there? What is the situation with their food and water supplies? And do you have any plan in the works to resupply them?

The President. I think it's unconscionable to try to starve people out and to isolate them from food and supplies of all kinds, and that's exactly what's going on. In terms of how long they can survive, I'm not sure I could give you a specific answer, but I believe the answer would be a few weeks, something of that nature.

Q. Are there plans to resupply them when they run out or——

The President. Well, if there were, given the hostile environment in which these people are living, it would be unproductive to discuss it.

Q. Mr. President, what has happened in the last 2 weeks that has led you to put now an offensive force into Saudi Arabia?

The President. Well, we have not only offensive but defensive forces there already. And what leads me to do this is just because I believe, upon the advice of our able Secretary of Defense and others, that this is in the best security interests of our people that are there and of the coalition. I think it is just a guarantee of the safety of all, and I think it sends a very strong signal—another strong signal—to Saddam Hussein that we are very, very serious about seeing the United Nations resolutions complied to in their entirety, without any kind of watering down.

Q. Would you say that we're in a critical phase now between a peaceful solution and a possible armed conflict?

The President. I wouldn't phrase it that way.

Q. Mr. President, the longer that you wait and the longer that no action is taken in Kuwait, the less and less there seems to be of Kuwait. What's the point of waiting if there's not going to be anything left of that country when you finally decide to go in?

The President. Well, I've told you that I would like to feel that Saddam Hussein would come to his senses and comply under economic pressure with the sanctions that have been taken in the United Nations and with the objectives. I would like to think the economic sanctions would compel him to do that which he has been unwilling to do. Regrettably, he keeps reiterating his view that this is not Kuwait but Province 19, and that is unacceptable to the United States and to our partners. So, I think we're giving these sanctions time to work. We're giving world opinion time to mobilize and impress on him that we're all serious. But now we're moving up our forces for the reasons I've given you.

Q. But there might not be much left of Kuwait.

The President. Well, that worries me. It worries me very much, as do the lives of those who have been forced into hiding by his brutality and his violation of international law. Of course, it concerns me deeply. And I've spoken about that, the dismantling of Kuwait and the systematic brutality that is exercised against the citizens of Kuwait. And as each day goes by it's worse. So, I take your point that it's—I guess it's your point—that it's a very bad situation. But I just keep reiterating my determination to see our objectives fulfilled here.

Q. Sir, on your consultation that your Secretary of State's doing now in Moscow, could you just spell out for us what your understanding is as of today with Mikhail Gorbachev on the use of force?

The President. Well, I talked to Jim Baker—it's a very timely question because I talked to him, just before coming in here, from Moscow; and he had a long series of consultations and discussions there with the Foreign Minister and with Mr. Gorbachev. I am convinced, from what the Secretary has told me, that we are on the same wavelength in terms of the objectives that I spelled out here. But I can't go in with you into what the Soviet position will be on the use of force. I don't think they've been asked to send forces. Is that—maybe I missed the question.

Q. Mr. Shevardnadze on the record today said that they, too, would not rule out the use of force, while they still wanted a peaceful solution. Does that at least help you send the kind of signal to Saddam Hussein that you're also trying to send here?

The President. I think it is very helpful. But I think the signal of solidarity between the United States and the Soviet Union and the rest of the Security Council has already gone out. But, no, I think that it is very helpful to have a position like that stated and restated, because that's the way the whole world feels. And it is good to have this solid front between ourselves and the Soviet Union. And I think Jim felt that he had a constructive visit with the Chinese Foreign Minister. And he's looking forward to his meetings with President Mitterrand and Prime Minister Thatcher in the next couple of days. But his trip has been extraordinarily helpful in sending that signal of solidarity and determination on the part of those that are involved here, strong determination.

I'm going to take a couple more, and then let Dick take some questions.

Q. I understand that we're going to be getting that briefing and General Powell [Chairman of the Joint Chiefs of Staff] will speak later, but can you please give us some sense of the numbers and types of reinforcements that you're sending to the Gulf? And do you believe that this will be the final deployment? We keep seeing the numbers ratcheting up and hearing that this should be sufficient to do the job.

The President. Let me simply say we're talking about substantial numbers. I will defer, with your permission, of course, to the Secretary of Defense and the Chairman of the Joint Chiefs, who will be able to help more than I will on the details of this move. But I can't say whether—after this is completed—whether there will be anything else done or not. I mean, I am still hopeful that Saddam Hussein will get the message that he is not going to prevail and that he has to get out of Kuwait without condition, and that the rulers have to come back and that the stability of the Gulf must be guaranteed. So, I would simply leave it there and, if you would, let the defense experts take the rest of it.

Q. As you have consulted—if I may follow up—on this deployment and, in fact, on the military situation overall with the other countries involved in the multinational forces, there have been complaints, observations out of Israel that, were there to be offensive action, there needs to be coordination or some sort of chain of command involving the Israelis, too, where they may end up being involved. To what extent are you communicating with the Israelis, and to what extent do you envision any role or possible role for the Israelis should this come to war?

The President. I think the whole world knows that the United States has a very special relationship with Israel—a strong relationship. I think we are in close touch with the key players there in terms of our objectives, and I think they have conducted themselves regarding all of this very well, indeed. But I am not going to discuss any more details than that. But I feel that we're on a good wavelength there. We had some differences, obviously.

One and one, and then I've got to go.

Q. Mr. President, to follow up on Wyatt's [Wyatt Andrews, CBS News] question: After Foreign Minister Shevardnadze made his comments today, President Gorbachev seemed to say that it was too early to talk about the use of force. Are the Soviets sending us mixed signals——

The President. No——

Q.——or is this just an indication that—like President Mubarak made earlier in the week—that some of our allies want more time to try to find a diplomatic solution before use of force?

The President. I don't get the feeling we're getting any mixed signals at all from the Soviets, particularly after I've talked to Jim Baker. I know there was some feeling there were mixed signals because of Mr. Primakov's [Soviet Presidential Council member] mission, but upon the completion of that, I think people recognize that we are still very much in agreement with the Soviet on matters as it relates to the Gulf. It's good, Ann [Ann Devroy, Washington Post], and it's strong. And I just can't worry about that point at all, after talking to Jim Baker.

Q. Does Jim Baker have an explanation for the difference between Mr. Shevardnadze's remarks and Mr. Gorbachev's remarks today?

The President. No. He made the point that we were together with them, and that was not discussed—any differences.

Last one, on the aisle.

Q. Mr. President, I have a very important question to ask you.

The President. Only if he'll yield. You know, in the Congress, they say, "I yield to the distinguished lady from Texas." But if he don't want to yield, I'm sorry; I've recognized the gentleman.

Q. Some members of your administration——

Q. I don't expect him to yield, but I would expect you to. [*Laughter*]

The President. Sarah [Sarah McClendon, McClendon News], I've disappointed you so much.

Please go ahead.

Q. Some members of your administration are convinced that Saddam Hussein will not move until the 11th hour, or 11:59, when he is totally convinced that you are about to use military force. Why is he not convinced now, do you think? How do you expect that you will be able to get to that 11:59 minute?

The President. Well, I'm not sure I accept the 11:59 analogy. But if there has ever been any doubt in his mind about the seriousness of the West and of the other Arab countries and of the coalition—put it that way—I think that those doubts are rapidly being dispelled. You see, I do believe that when he moved into Kuwait I think he felt he was going to have just an easy time of it and that the world would not rise up in arms against the aggression. I think he miscalculated there. I believe he thought he could just take over Kuwait and then there would be a lot of talk and discussion and he would be able to turn Kuwait, a sovereign nation, a member of the Arab League, a member of the United Nations, into Province 19.

And the United States, along with other countries, said no, we're not going to permit this aggression to stand, because an unchecked aggression today could lead to some horrible world conflagration tomorrow. And so, I think there's where the miscalculation originally was. I find it hard to believe that today, November 8th, he does not understand that he's up against a determined, unprecedented alliance.

And so, I hope that he is rethinking his position of unyielding opposition to the will of the rest of the world. And I would think that when he surveys the force that's there, the force that's going, what other countries are doing in this regard, he will recognize that he is up against just a foe that he can't possibly manage militarily. Margaret Thatcher touched on that yesterday, and I thought she did it very well, indeed. And so, if nothing else happens, I'm convinced that this move will show him how serious we are as a significant partner in this coalition. I think it's a good thing, and it will have strong support from others around the world. Let's hope he comes to his senses and does tomorrow that which he should have done weeks ago, because this aggression simply will not stand.

Now, Dick, it's all yours.

Note: The President's 65th news conference began at 4:04 p.m. in the Briefing Room at the White House.

Statement on Signing the Nutrition Labeling and Education Act of 1990
November 8, 1990

Today I am signing H.R. 3562, the "Nutrition Labeling and Education Act of 1990." This legislation amends the Federal Food, Drug, and Cosmetic Act to require nutrition labeling on certain foods and to regulate health claims about nutrients in foods.

This Act makes two significant changes in current law. First, it requires food manufacturers to include more nutrition information on their labels to assist consumers in selecting a healthful diet. Second, H.R. 3562 would prohibit food manufacturers from making health claims on their labels unless the claims are permitted by the Department of Health and Human Services.

I note that one provision of the Act requires the Secretary of Health and Human Services to contract for a study of the effectiveness of the regulations implementing certain provisions of the Federal Food, Drug, and Cosmetic Act and to undertake regulatory action using the results of this study. As the Constitution requires, I understand this provision to reserve to the Secretary of Health and Human Services the authority to formulate the regulatory proposals required by this legislation, taking into consideration the recommendations of the contractor's study.

GEORGE BUSH

The White House,
November 8, 1990.

Note: H.R. 3562, approved November 8, was assigned Public Law No. 101–535. The statement was released by the Office of the Press Secretary on November 9.

Statement on Signing the Bill Amending the Employee Retirement Income Security Act of 1974
November 8, 1990

Today I am signing H.R. 5872, a bill "To amend title I of the Employee Retirement Income Security Act of 1974 to require qualifying employer securities to include interest in publicly traded partnerships."

In approving this legislation, I wish to make clear that the scope of the bill is limited. It is my understanding that the bill will change provisions of the Employee Retirement Income Security Act with respect to the treatment of investments in publicly traded partnerships under certain provisions governing fiduciary duties and prohibited transactions. H.R. 5872 will not change existing tax rules that prohibit publicly traded partnerships from maintaining certain forms of tax-qualified plans such as employee stock ownership plans.

GEORGE BUSH

The White House,
November 8, 1990.

Note: H.R. 5872, approved November 8, was assigned Public Law No. 101–540. The statement was released by the Office of the Press Secretary on November 9.

Statement on Signing the Bill Extending Nondiscriminatory Tariff Treatment to Products of Czechoslovakia
November 8, 1990

As I prepare for my visit to Prague on November 17 and 18, I am particularly pleased to sign H.J. Res. 649 that approves the extension of nondiscriminatory tariff treatment to products of the Czech and Slovak Federal Republic. I thank the Congress for its close cooperation and prompt approval of this measure that will mark an important milestone not only in U.S.-Czechoslovak relations, but also in Czechoslovakia's reintegration into the global economy and the community of free nations.

Once most-favored-nation (MFN) tariff treatment is implemented, Czechoslovakia will become the first Eastern European nation to receive such treatment for its exports to the United States since the revolutions of 1989. With the assistance and endorsement of the Congress, we already have launched efforts that should result in the eventual extension of similar treatment to products of the Soviet Union and Bulgaria.

The enactment of H.J. Res. 649 represents a significant step on our part to bring into force the U.S.-Czechoslovakia Trade Agreement signed by our two governments last April. Upon formal approval of the Agreement by the Federal Assembly and an exchange of diplomatic notes between our governments confirming mutual approval, the Agreement will extend MFN tariff treatment to Czechoslovak exports to the United States and U.S. exports to Czechoslovakia. These sharply lower tariffs will provide the impetus for greatly expanded trade between the United States and Czechoslovakia and the first step toward a normalization of our bilateral trade relations.

In addition to extending MFN tariff treatment, the Trade Agreement contains important guarantees for American businesses engaging in trade with Czechoslovakia, including the right to nondiscrimination in renting office space, in paying for local goods, and in establishing bank accounts. Any hard currency earnings from trade may be repatriated immediately. Through this Agreement, the Czechoslovak Government has also committed to upgrade significantly its protection of intellectual property rights, bringing its intellectual property regime to a level on a par with that of other industrialized nations.

The Czechoslovak Government already has made tremendous strides in its movement toward economic reform and trade liberalization. The implementation of this Agreement and the establishment of U.S.-Czechoslovak trade relations on a basis of nondiscrimination will serve to solidify these reforms and ensure Czechoslovakia's role as an important partner in the global trading system.

GEORGE BUSH

The White House,
November 8, 1990.

Note: H.J. Res. 649, approved November 8, was assigned Public Law No. 101–541. The statement was released by the Office of the Press Secretary on November 9.

Memorandum of Disapproval for the Orphan Drug Amendments of 1990
November 8, 1990

I am withholding my approval of H.R. 4638, the "Orphan Drug Amendments of 1990." This legislation would make substantive changes to the orphan drug provisions of the Federal Food, Drug, and Cosmetic Act and the Orphan Drug Act.

Enacted in 1983, the Orphan Drug Act created economic incentives for drug companies to develop drugs for rare diseases and conditions—so-called "orphan drugs." Typically, these drugs would not be profitable to develop because of their small patient populations.

By any measure, the Orphan Drug Act has been a tremendous success. A total of 49 new drugs for rare diseases have been approved under this program, and 370 others are in the development stage. These drugs have provided lifesaving treatments for such terrible diseases as enzyme deficiency, which affects adversely the immune system of about 40 children nationwide. Until the orphan drug was developed to treat these children, they had to spend their entire lives in the protection of an isolation bubble. One of the first orphan drugs is another example of a triumph. The most difficult form of leprosy affects only 4,000 people. A drug known for over 14 years to be effective in treating this condition was not being marketed by any drug company, because it was considered unprofitable—until the Orphan Drug Act provided the marketing incentive. In a similar manner, orphan drugs provide treatment for terrible diseases for which there is usually no alternative therapy.

I have serious concerns about the effect that H.R. 4638 would have upon the incentive of drug companies to develop orphan drugs. I believe we must not endanger the success of this program, which is due in large measure to the existence of the "market exclusivity" provision in the Orphan Drug Act that allows companies to have exclusive marketing rights to an orphan drug for 7 years. Weakening the current 7-year exclusivity provision would certainly discourage development of desperately needed new orphan drugs.

Under current law, firms may apply to develop the same orphan drug, but only the first firm to have its drug approved receives market exclusivity. The certainty of this 7-year period is the basis of the economic incentive to attract drug firms to invest in orphan drugs.

The bill would make two major changes to the market exclusivity provisions of the Orphan Drug Act. First, the bill provides for "shared exclusivity." Firms that can demonstrate that they have developed the orphan drug simultaneously would be allowed to share the market with the firm initially awarded the market exclusivity. Second, the bill requires the Food and Drug Administration to withdraw the marketing exclusivity as soon as the patient population exceeds a 200,000 patient limit. Both of these changes have the effect of weakening the marketing incentives provided by the Act. Under this bill, the length of the market exclusivity period will depend on how quickly the patient population grows and whether other firms file claims for simultaneous development.

In addition, as currently constructed, the 200,000 patient population limit would be applied to orphan drugs approved prior to the enactment of the bill as well as to those approved in the future. This retroactive rule change would send a troublesome signal to all those who might wish to develop orphan drugs that the Federal Government may change unilaterally the rules for firms that made investment decisions based on the expectation of 7 years of market exclusivity.

I am aware that this bill was passed after a number of compromises among Members of Congress. I am extremely concerned, however, that individuals with rare diseases may suffer because of changes that this bill would make in the incentives to develop new drug treatments. Accordingly, I am withholding my approval of H.R. 4638.

GEORGE BUSH

The White House,
November 8, 1990.

Note: The President's last day for action on this bill was November 8. The memorandum was released by the Office of the Press Secretary on November 9.

Final Sequester Order
November 9, 1990

By the authority vested in me as President by the statutes of the United States of America, including section 254 of the Balanced Budget and Emergency Deficit Control Act of 1985 (Public Law 99–177), as amended by the Balanced Budget and Emergency Deficit Control Reaffirmation Act of 1987 (Public Law 100–119) and Title XIII of the Omnibus Reconciliation Act of 1990 (Public Law 101–508) (hereafter referred to as "the Act"), I hereby order that the following actions be taken immediately to implement the sequestrations and reductions determined by the Director of the Office of Management and Budget as set forth in his report dated November 9, 1990, under sections 251 and 254 of the Act:

(1) Budgetary resources for each non-exempt account within the international category of discretionary spending shall be reduced as specified by the Director of the Office of Management and Budget in his report of November 9, 1990.

(2) Pursuant to sections 250(c)(6) and 251, budgetary resources subject to sequestration shall be new budget authority; new loan guarantee commitments or limitations; new direct loan obligations, commitments, or limitations; and obligation limitations.

(3) For accounts making commitments for guaranteed loans as authorized by substantive law, the head of each Department or agency is directed to reduce the level of such commitments or obligations to the extent necessary to conform to the limitations established by the Act and specified

by the Director of the Office of Management and Budget in his report of November 9, 1990.

All sequestrations shall be made in strict accordance with the specifications of the November 9th report of the Director of the Office of Management and Budget and the requirements of sections 251 and 254.

GEORGE BUSH

The White House,
November 9, 1990.

Appointment of Remedios Diaz-Oliver as a Member of the Advisory Committee for Trade Policy and Negotiations
November 9, 1990

The President today announced his intention to appoint Remedios Diaz-Oliver, of Florida, to be a member of the Advisory Committee for Trade Policy and Negotiations for a term of 2 years. She would succeed John R. Faust, Jr.

Since 1977 Ms. Diaz-Oliver has served as president and chief executive officer of American International Container, Inc., in Miami, FL. Prior to this she was vice president and sales manager of Richford Industries, Inc., of Miami, FL, 1961–1976. In addition, she has served as a director and consultant for New World School of Languages in Miami, 1964–1966.

Ms. Diaz-Oliver graduated from Havana Business University and Havana College. She is married to Fausto Diaz-Oliver, has two children, and resides in Miami, FL.

Notice of the Continuation of the National Emergency With Respect to Iran
November 9, 1990

On November 14, 1979, by Executive Order No. 12170, the President declared a national emergency to deal with the threat to the national security, foreign policy, and economy of the United States constituted by the situation in Iran. Notices of the continuation of this national emergency have been transmitted annually by the President to the Congress and the *Federal Register*, most recently on October 30, 1989. Because our relations with Iran have not yet returned to normal, and the process of implementing the January 19, 1981, agreements with Iran is still underway, the national emergency declared on November 14, 1979, must continue in effect beyond November 14, 1990. Therefore, in accordance with section 202(d) of the National Emergencies Act (50 U.S.C. 1622(d)), I am continuing the national emergency with respect to Iran. This notice shall be published in the *Federal Register* and transmitted to the Congress.

GEORGE BUSH

The White House,
November 9, 1990.

[*Filed with the Office of the Federal Register, 5:12 p.m., November 9, 1990*]

Note: The notice was released by the Office of the Press Secretary on November 13.

Letter to Congressional Leaders on the Continuation of the National Emergency With Respect to Iran
November 9, 1990

Dear Mr. Speaker: *(Dear Mr. President:)*

Section 202(d) of the National Emergencies Act (50 U.S.C. 1622(d)) provides for the automatic termination of a national emergency unless, prior to the anniversary date of its declaration, the President publishes in the *Federal Register* and transmits to the Congress a notice stating that the emergency is to continue in effect beyond the anniversary date. In accordance with this provision, I have sent the enclosed notice, stating that the Iran emergency is to continue in effect beyond November 14, 1990, to the *Federal Register* for publication. Similar notices have been sent annually to the Congress and the *Federal Register* since November 12, 1980, most recently on October 30, 1989.

The crisis between the United States and Iran that began in 1979 has not been fully resolved. While the international tribunal established to adjudicate claims of U.S. nationals against Iran and of Iranian nationals against the United States continues to function, normalization of commercial and diplomatic relations between the United States and Iran has not been achieved. In these circumstances, I have determined that it is necessary to maintain in force the broad authorities that may be needed in the process of implementing the January 1981 agreements with Iran and in the eventual normalization of relations with that country.

Sincerely,

GEORGE BUSH

Note: Identical letters were sent to Thomas S. Foley, Speaker of the House of Representatives, and Dan Quayle, President of the Senate. The letter was released by the Office of the Press Secretary on November 13.

Remarks at the Presentation Ceremony for the National Medals of Science and Technology
November 13, 1990

Welcome, everybody. Thank you all. Please be seated. And delighted to see you here. Pleased to see Secretary Mosbacher, our Secretary of Commerce; Secretary Watkins, Secretary of Energy; and of course, Dr. Bromley; Admiral Truly, right here in front, of NASA. Mike—Governor Castle, good to see you, sir. And we especially want to greet our honored guests, this extraordinary gathering of scientific and technological genius. Welcome to the White House, and welcome to the presentation of the 1990 National Medals of Science and the National Medals of Technology.

The timing of these awards is fortuitous. A year ago this week, Barbara and I awarded medals to some of the artistic giants of our time: Alfred Eisenstaedt and Dizzy Gillespie and John Updike, among others. And with all that assembled talent, guess what led the evening news: the Rose Garden presentation of the national turkey. [*Laughter*] So, you're in luck. [*Laughter*] This year the turkey doesn't get here until Thursday. [*Laughter*]

And this gathering marks a proud moment for me, just as it was when this year's Nobel Prizes were announced and it turned out that eight of the nine winners in science and economics were born in the United States of America. It is, indeed, a tribute to America's frontier spirit and to our nation's steadfast resolve and sense of the future. For when it comes to leadership in science and technology, best in America means best in the world.

America's tradition of excellence has long been nurtured by a tradition of free inquiry aimed at the simple goal of better understanding ourselves and the world. In the 1945 report that led to the founding of the NSF, the National Science Foundation, Vannevar Bush—no relation—wrote that "As long as scientists are free to pursue the truth wherever it may lead, there will be a flow of new scientific knowledge to those who can apply it to practical problems."

And so it is today. More and more, nearly every product, from electronics to agriculture, incorporates the latest in technology. And more and more, our nation depends on basic scientific research to spur economic growth, longer and healthier lives, a more secure world and, indeed, a safer environment.

Today our government must help carry that research forward and contribute to the development of generic technologies that build on basic discoveries. If America is to maintain and strengthen our competitive position, we must continue not only to create new technologies but learn to more effectively translate those technologies into commercial products. In this way, we can help leverage the R&D of the private sector, helping whole industries advance in an increasingly competitive global market.

The budget highlights our administration's commitment to science and technology. We won double-digit increases for both NASA and the NSF and expanded funds to investigate global climate change. We remain committed to doing even more, doubling the NSF budget over 5 years and extending the tax credit for R&E, research and experimentation. And we're going to keep raising America's sights. Space station *Freedom* will give us a permanent presence in Earth orbit, and the Space Exploration Initiative will take us to the Moon and Mars and beyond—back to space, back to the future, and this time back to stay.

Thirty years from now, when the Nobel Prizes are announced, I want America to be well represented. And 30 years from now, when the Medals of Science and of Technology are bestowed, I want to see America graced by a group as accomplished as that here today. Many of today's honorees serve as prime examples of how we can effective-ly translate basic science into commercial technology. I think of Millie Dresselhaus, arguably the most important and prominent woman physicist and engineer of her generation, whose hard work helped to revolutionize semiconductors, or Allan Cormack, whose pioneering efforts earned him a Nobel Prize and made CAT scan a household word, and scholars as diverse as Boston's Baruj Benacerraf or Seattle's Donnall Thomas, another Nobel laureate, whose contributions to immunology may lead to new answers in our battle against cancer and AIDS. Scientists like you have, indeed, helped America to understand that AIDS is a disease, not a disgrace. And scientists like you who have helped America to appreciate our responsibility to those who are living with HIV and AIDS. And they deserve our compassion, they deserve our care, and they deserve more than a chance: They deserve a cure.

Another legacy of these prestigious medals and the work they honor must be the cultivation of excellence in science and math in classrooms across America. The National Science Scholars program we proposed soon after taking office has now been enacted and will encourage budding scholars of today to become the scientists of tomorrow. Guiding our efforts is an ambitious but critical goal for this decade: By the year 2000, U.S. students will be first in the world in science and math.

This week is Education Week, and its theme is "Educating Everyone Takes Everyone," a fitting motto for the challenges that lie ahead. If we are truly to remain a world leader in science and technology, then we must achieve a renaissance of quality in our schools and we must tap the talent, the energy, and the commitment of all our families, businesses, and universities.

The people we honor today are American trailblazers, real-life pioneers who pressed the very limits of their fields. You have distinguished not only yourselves but also your nation. And that's why America continues to need and want and appreciate your creativity, your genius, and your diversity.

Thank you. Congratulations to all. And God bless the United States. Thank you for coming.

Note: The President spoke at 2:01 p.m. in the East Room at the White House. In his remarks, he referred to D. Allan Bromley, Director of the Office of Science and Technology Policy; Richard H. Truly, Administrator of the National Aeronautics and Space Administration; and Gov. Michael Castle of Delaware.

Remarks Following Discussions With Giulio Andreotti, Prime Minister of Italy and President of the European Council
November 13, 1990

The President. I was delighted to have the opportunity for these extended discussions with my friend Giulio Andreotti. This is my first official meeting with the leader of the European Community in his capacity as President of the EC Council. And as such, it fulfills an agreement that I made with Prime Minister Haughey during the Irish EC Presidency.

I look forward to regular working sessions with future EC Presidency representatives and consider this the beginning of a valuable new tradition. I, of course, also wanted to extend a warm welcome to the EC Commission President, an old friend, Jacques Delors, and of course, the Foreign Minister of Italy, Foreign Minister De Michelis, who have made valuable contributions in these discussions that we had there in the Cabinet Room.

We discussed at length our goals for the Uruguay round and our strong conviction that we must succeed in substantial trade liberalization and strengthening the multilateral world trading system. And I, for my part, and Prime Minister Andreotti and President Delors, on behalf of the Community and its member states, have pledged to make every effort to ensure that the round concludes successfully in the coming weeks. Indeed, there will be follow-on meetings tomorrow with President Delors.

We also continued our discussions on the crisis in the Gulf. We've worked closely with our EC colleagues on all aspects of the Gulf situation since the invasion of Kuwait, and we've cooperated to pass and maintain effective U.N. Security Council sanctions. Our continuing consultations are providing vital assistance to the frontline states. And I want to salute Prime Minister Andreotti for his strong leadership and for the Community's firm resolve in the international effort in the Gulf.

Through our consultations today and in the future, we are strengthening the transatlantic partnership, a partnership which will continue to unite the United States and Europe in advancing our shared values of political and economic freedom.

Mr. Prime Minister, thank you for coming, sir, and have a safe trip home.

The Prime Minister. I thank you, Mr. President, for the welcome you gave to me and to President Delors and Minister De Michelis.

The close relationship between the United States of America and the European Community constitutes a point, and has constituted a point, of great strength for the maintenance of stability and peace in the world.

What occurred in Kuwait is rightly deemed to be untolerable. If it were allowed to occupy and to annex a country without any opposition, then this would mean the end of the juridical order system which exists in the world. The effort being carried out by the United Nations with the contribution of all of us is aimed at obtaining three results: first, the liberation of Kuwait and the return of the legality in the country; second, the freeing of the hostages; and third, the establishment of a system of security in all the countries in the Middle East capable of assuring a reciprocal peace in that area and a reciprocal respect amongst their peoples.

As President Bush has said in his speech in front of the United Nations on the 1st of October, there can be no simultaneity to solve all the problems in the area, but there exists a connection amongst them and a strong commitment to bring back peace and security in the Middle East. And all our efforts must be aimed at achieving these goals in a peaceful way.

Lastly, I want to say that we have worked out the wording of the declaration of the relationship between the EC and the United States of America. I know that there has been only one word in brackets, and I hope this will be very soon solved so that in Paris next week we can have the issuance of this declaration.

And lastly, as President Bush has said, during the meeting, we have devoted a great part of it to discuss at length the problems connected with the Uruguay round, and with great clarity and also with the will to reach a positive conclusion. And we believe truly that should this agreement not be achieved, then it would bring about serious damages, in particular to the less developed countries.

I will have the pleasure of meeting next week in Paris President Bush, and I would like just to emphasize how important it is, this formula of cooperation for security in Europe. Also, before 1975, relations between Europe and the American continent were very good. But as of 1975, United States of America and Canada are Europe. And it is not a fantasy to say that it was in that very moment that the new history for United States, for Canada, and for Europe, and for the whole world had started. And we must have this policy of cooperation and security guide always our steps in the future in our decisions.

Thank you, President Bush, also for having me, for this welcome, and having bid me a good return, because now I will not suffer today of jet lag since I'm leaving tonight. [*Laughter*]

The President. So pleased you were here, sir. Thank you.

Note: The President spoke at 5:49 p.m. at the South Portico of the White House. The Prime Minister spoke in Italian, and his remarks were translated by an interpreter.

Statement by Press Secretary Fitzwater on President Bush's Meeting With Giulio Andreotti, Prime Minister of Italy and President of the European Council
November 13, 1990

Italian Prime Minister Giulio Andreotti, in his capacity as President of the European Community, met with President Bush today from 4:00 to 5:30 p.m. The two leaders met privately for approximately 30 minutes on bilateral issues. Prime Minister Andreotti was joined by EC Commission President Jacques Delors and by Italian Foreign Minister De Michelis in the plenary session. Secretaries Baker and Brady and national security adviser Scowcroft attended on the U.S. side.

President Bush had fruitful discussions with the Prime Minister on a wide range of issues of mutual interest to the United States and the EC. He particularly praised the Community's firm resolve in the international effort to contain Iraqi aggression in the Gulf region and singled out Prime Minister Andreotti's leadership in this regard.

President Bush also discussed with the Prime Minister and with Commission President Delors the importance of achieving success in the Uruguay round trade negotiations, in the interest of strengthening and further liberalizing the international trading system. It was agreed that renewed efforts at top political levels would be made so as to achieve the common ground on the issue of agricultural subsidies which is needed to move beyond the present impasse in the GATT negotiations.

There was also discussion of the close partnership that both the United States and the EC seek on the whole range of issues of mutual interest. In this connection, a U.S.–EC Declaration of Principles is currently in the final stages of preparation. The declaration would further institutionalize the already extensive U.S.–EC consultations that exist on most issues of common interest.

Note: The statement referred to Secretary of State James A. Baker III and Secretary of the Treasury Nicholas F. Brady.

Remarks at a Dinner for the Senate Republican Leadership
November 13, 1990

Bob, thank you very much for those kind words, and let me just say how pleased Barbara and I are to be here. You all did a smart thing today in returning a true Republican leader to office: Bob Dole. In fact, Millie has already sent her congratulations to Leader. [*Laughter*]

I really wanted to be here for a lot of reasons, but one of them is because Bob has led our policy with style and wit, and with precision, with integrity. I've come to count on him every single day. And he's been a great Republican leader, as great as any in the past. And I say that—we had another great one sitting here tonight: Howard Baker. And I also think of Joy's dad, Everett Dirksen—great, great leaders. But I think we would all agree that Bob Dole is doing an exceptional and an outstanding job. And again, I count my blessings that he's leader in the United States Senate for our party.

While I'm at it, I want to congratulate the new head of the Red Cross, someone I will miss at our Cabinet meetings. And I'm very sorry she couldn't be with us. She's up still laboring under the Labor portfolio up there in New York at a big meeting of the AFL–CIO, I believe it is. But anyway, let me just say to you, my friends in the Senate, what I've tried to tell outside world when Elizabeth [Dole] and I walked into the press room: She has done an outstanding job for this country. And it's right and proper now that she go on to this new challenge. But what a superb Secretary of Labor she's been. Bob, tell her we miss her here tonight.

And of course, then, on the rest our leadership: Al Simpson, back from a landslide, proving that adage that you can fool some of the people all of the time. [*Laughter*] But nevertheless, I congratulate him. And a

congratulations to the newly elected conference chairman, Thad Cochran; and the secretary, Senator Bob Kasten; to Phil Gramm, a fellow Texan, senatorial campaign committee chairman; Don Nichols, now the new policy committee chairman. And I look forward to working closely with every single one of you. And I would say to those who didn't make it: You didn't lose at all. And I detected at least a wonderful spirit of comradery upstairs. And the party here in the Senate is together and strong, and we've got great new leadership.

Let me also acknowledge the four Senators among us who have left their mark on our party and our nation. Senator Bill Armstrong has been a superb chairman of the policy committee, and now he returns to Colorado. What a great Senator he's been.

And I didn't see Gordon Humphrey, but if he's here, let me say that he's done an outstanding job. And now he's taken his case back at the grassroots level in the State of New Hampshire. And I admire him, and I respect him for that. And when I arrived in Washington as—you won't believe this—a skinny freshman in the House of Representatives, one of the first friends that I found was a colleague by the name of Jim McClure. We were elected in November in 1966, and since then I've seen him leave the House and become a truly great Senator from Idaho. And over the years, I can just say that Barbara and I have treasured our friendship with Jim and Louise. And I wish him all the very best, if he's out there—I think he is somewhere.

And then, of course, Bob so appropriately saluted the other leaving a legacy of leadership here: Rudy Boschwitz. Rudy was on the national committee when I was chairman of the Republican committee, and we've been friends ever since. And I'll tell you, if there was ever a hurt—a personal hurt—coming out of this election, it was the Minnesota Senate race. But I have this wonderful, warm feeling that we haven't heard the last from Rudy Boschwitz. And I'll tell you, we love him, and we thank him for what he did.

And then, of course, I just want to add my hearty congratulations to Hank Brown, to Larry Craig, and to Bob Smith, and to say that I look forward to working with all of you. You've won a great victory for our party, and I think we're going to win a lot of victories for our country. And so, once again, to the three newly elected Members of this Senate, congratulations and best of luck to each and every one of you.

And now let me just conclude by saying that we gather here 1 week—it seems like eons ago to me—but 1 week after the American people turned to the polls and returned to Washington a government divided. It's a government that's divided by party; it's a government that's divided by purpose and vision. But our purpose as a party and my purpose remains undivided and clear. And we are as committed as ever to private sector, progrowth solutions, expanding our economy, not arguing over how the economic pie should be divided. We are as committed as ever to opportunity, not the failed policies that we fought here in the last Congress on the taxing and spending of the liberals. And we will, as a Republican President and Republican Senators, fight the opposition and fight the special interests for the sake of the national interest.

You know the world is changing, and those changes are going to produce exciting new challenges. Working together, we can prepare this great country to meet those challenges and lead the world into the 21st century. In my view, a lot of the action is going to be at the State level. And this brings me to one who left the Senate to move to the State level, and the biggest State in the United States. And I'm talking, of course, about Pete Wilson and his superb win out there in California.

As I look at our national agenda, it seems to me we've got to keep in mind that the government closest to the people does govern best. And, Pete, I look forward to working with you. I know all the Senate does in working with you and the other Republican Governors and other Governors to make this country just a little better.

You know, in the year ahead, perhaps we should draw some inspiration from a great American of the last century. I want to read you some words: "Make no little plans. They have no magic to stir men's blood and probably in themselves will not be realized. Make big plans. Aim high in hope and work, remembering that a noble idea once recorded will never die, but long after we are gone will be a living thing."

The man who wrote those words was Daniel Burnham, the architect who conceived and built this great Union Station. And as we had a chance earlier to look around at the ceilings and the gilded geometry that sprang from one man's imagination, let's remember to make big plans, to aim high in hope and work.

These are not particularly easy times. As we look—Bob referred to the situation in the Gulf. It is my view that the United States will not and must not fail in its objectives. And the objectives are clearly outlined in the 10 resolutions of the United Nations Security Council. And it isn't a question simply of the economic interests of the world—and they are enormous, as you see the Third World driven to its knees already by the results of Saddam Hussein's aggression against Kuwait. It isn't simply the economic matters—and they are enormous because we have enormous economic stakes in what happens in that part of the world. And I can think of nothing worse than to see an aggression rewarded and then tomorrow to have the economic noose tightened even further. We're already feeling the pinches in this country of what he's done.

But there's another and a more fundamental principle involved, and that is that one big nation not take over another, one big nation cannot bully and beat into submission another. And it is my view that the United States alone can lead and stand on principle to be sure that we don't set a dangerous precedent for tomorrow.

And so, I stand here to tell you that I am

grateful for your support. And I am more determined than I've ever been that we hold this magnificent historic coalition together and that we not fall short of our objectives which have been clearly stated. The United States will not and must not fail. And to achieve that end, I need your support. And I'm grateful for that which you have already given to me and, thus, to our country. But these are serious times, and I expect I would be falling short of what's in my heart if I didn't tell you I am grateful to each and every one of you who

have been able to support us in these very difficult times.

Thank you, and God bless you all. And, Bob, thank you for your magnificent leadership once again.

Note: The President spoke at 7:54 p.m. in the East Hall at Union Station. In his remarks, he referred to Howard Baker's wife, Joy; Jim McClure's wife, Louise; and President Saddam Hussein of Iraq. He also referred to the First Family's dog, Millie, and Senator Dole's dog, Leader.

Letter to Congressional Leaders on the Extension of Active Duty of the Selected Reserve of the Armed Forces
November 13, 1990

Dear Mr. Speaker: (Dear Mr. President:)

I have today, pursuant to section 673b(i) of title 10, United States Code, authorized the Secretary of Defense, and the Secretary of Transportation with respect to the Coast Guard when it is not operating as a service within the Department of the Navy, to extend for an additional 90 days the period of active duty of units and individual members not assigned to units organized to serve as units of the Selected Reserve ordered to active duty pursuant to section 673b(a) of title 10, United States Code and Executive Order No. 12727 of August 22, 1990. The continued need for units and members of the Selected Reserve to augment the active Armed Forces of the

United States for the effective support and conduct of operational missions in and around the Arabian Peninsula necessitates this action.

A copy of the Executive order implementing this action is attached.

Sincerely,

GEORGE BUSH

Note: Identical letters were sent to Thomas S. Foley, Speaker of the House of Representatives, and Dan Quayle, President of the Senate. The letter was released by the Office of the Press Secretary on November 14. The Executive order is listed in Appendix E at the end of this volume.

Remarks at the Presentation Ceremony for the President's Environmental Youth Awards
November 14, 1990

Well, this is a big day at the White House. I'm glad to see you all here. And I heard those kind comments by our outstanding head of EPA, Bill Reilly. And let me just say to all of you environmentalists, we are very blessed in this country to have a man like Bill Reilly taking on this extraordinarily

complicated task and doing such a great job. I want to welcome Mike Deland, head of our Council [on Environmental Quality] here, who's also doing a superb job on the environment; Ted Sanders, from the Education Department, our Under Secretary; and Frank Bracken, the Under Secretary of the

Department of the Interior—both so interested in this work—and of course, our hardworking EPA youth coordinators and our regional administrators. And especially, I'm pleased to come over to welcome the young champions for the environment, all of you.

And all of you know that protecting the environment is not a spectator sport; we all have to be a part of the solution. And that's why the past year has been so encouraging. So many people, in so many ways, are getting involved—even the Simpsons.

You know, Bart Simpson dropped me a line the other day when I told him you were coming—true story—and he wrote me saying: "When I mess up my bedroom, my mom comes in and yells, but eventually she cleans it up and everything's cool. But when we mess up the environment, we're the ones who are going to be yelling, and it definitely won't be cool." Well, this is one of those rare moments when Bart makes sense. [*Laughter*] Wise beyond his years, just as all of you are wise beyond yours.

Just yesterday, here at the White House, I had the honor, the pleasure of awarding the Medal of Science and the Medal of Technology to some distinguished American scientists, engineers, and mathematicians. But the awards that we're making today are no less significant. In fact, when I heard about the projects for this year's awards, I was struck by the sophistication of these projects. Some have grown to national, even international stature. Others have changed the way whole communities operate. But all have made permanent improvements to our natural environment.

Today, in the middle of American Education Week, it's a pleasure to recognize the efforts of students who represent citizenship at its most responsible and the adult sponsors who worked so hard with them. Together, they've proved something too many tend to forget, and that is that in this country it's the individual that counts. It's the individual who makes a difference.

I think of one young man, in particular, who won this award last year for launching a recycling program. He stood on this stage and asked me if the White House did any recycling. You talk about pressure. [*Laughter*] This guy came in here—it's not often that lobbyists come disguised as high school

kids. [*Laughter*] Well, I told him that I didn't think we had a recycling program, but that we'd sure be working on it. And you know, if anyone can teach old dogs new tricks, kids can. And so, now I can say to this year's award winners: We learned something from people like you, and now we've a recycling program in the White House.

And if it's true, as some say, that we're all borrowing the Earth from future generations, it's also true that the Earth will be preserved by millions of small decisions made every day by every one of us. And they're the kind of small decisions that make a world of difference, whether it's recycling aluminum cans, conserving water, turning off a lightbulb, even just keeping the refrigerator door closed.

Like that scene in the "Teenage Mutant—bear with me—Ninja Turtles." [*Laughter*] They're standing in front of the refrigerator, deciding what to have for dinner. And one of them is standing there with the door open. So, another one says, "Think with the door closed, then get what you want." "Okay," the first one says, "I'm thinking. Tonight we'll have broccoli." [*Laughter*] And fortunately, he pulls out a pizza. So, there's a happy ending to this story. [*Laughter*]

And if more of us think with the door closed and our minds open, we can all bring environmental ignorance to a happy ending. Because, to quote one of those Mutant Turtle characters, "There are no passengers on Spaceship Earth, only crew."

So, with those words of wisdom, let me go on now to the highlight of the day, and that is to the awards for the distinguished crew that is with us today. And let me say, in advance, congratulations to each and every one of you.

[*At this point, the awards were presented.*]

Well done, everybody. What a great day. What an inspiring day here at the White House. Thank you all very, very much.

Note: The President spoke at 10:28 a.m. in Room 450 of the Old Executive Office Building. Bart Simpson was a character in the television show "The Simpsons."

Letter to Congressional Leaders Transmitting a Report on the Potential Effects of Space Nuclear Reactors on Gamma-Ray Astronomy Missions
November 14, 1990

Dear Mr. Speaker: (Dear Mr. President:)
I herewith forward a Report on the Potential Effects of Space Nuclear Reactors on Gamma-Ray Astronomy Missions pursuant to section 1012 of the National Defense Authorization Act for Fiscal Years 1990 and 1991 (Public Law 101–189).
Sincerely,

GEORGE BUSH

Note: Identical letters were sent to Thomas S. Foley, Speaker of the House of Representatives, and Dan Quayle, President of the Senate.

Remarks at the Thanksgiving Turkey Presentation Ceremony
November 14, 1990

Is that the bird? Hey, Sam! I know you've been waiting out here and getting cold, but I want to welcome all you kids and all you older kids to the Rose Garden, especially Tom over there. After everything that's been going on in Washington these past few months, it's great to finally be sharing a stage with someone I can call a turkey and get away with it. [*Laughter*] So, I welcome him. I want to assure those of you who fear that a terrible fate awaits Tom Turkey that we've decided to spare him. He will not be subjected to questions from the Washington press corps after this ceremony. [*Laughter*]

Tom, since you come from North Carolina, and out of respect for the Governor of that State, my friend Jim Martin, I'm going to give you a Presidential pardon, and you can spend the rest of your life at a nearby children's farm. So, he'll be all right at Thanksgiving. Other turkeys may not; this one's going to be okay.

I'm glad to see the kids from the Key Elementary School and the New Hampshire Estates Elementary School. Here's a story you can take back to your teachers. Ben Franklin was upset that the bald eagle was named our national symbol because he wanted it to be the turkey. He said: "The turkey is a much more respectable bird,

and a true original native of America." I'm sure that's a sentiment that Wyatt Upchurch and Stuart Proctor here and the National Turkey Federation would strongly applaud.

You know, Thanksgiving is really special to me because it's a truly American holiday, one that sums up the good, generous heart of this country. And it reminds us of our real American values, the ones we just can't afford to forget: values like deep gratitude for the rich blessings of this great land, unselfish generosity towards those in need, and commitment to the primary importance of family.

With those values in mind, inside there in the Oval Office, I just signed the 1990 Thanksgiving Day Proclamation, continuing a Presidential tradition that was begun by our first President, George Washington. I was pleased to have five religious leaders from different denominations on hand for the signing. And continuing an even longer tradition that dates back to the Pilgrims, we can draw our inspiration from these early Americans. They suffered and lost so much and yet gave a day of genuine rejoicing for the little bit that they did have. How much more gratitude we, who have so much, owe today to our God, our fellow citizens, our country, and our brave service men and women so far from home this holiday.

Barbara and I will be with them, incidentally, Thanksgiving Day—with some of them over in Saudi Arabia. And I know I'll express what's in the heart of every American when I shake their hands—young men and young women—and say: Thank you. Thank you for standing for freedom, for our security, and for peace in our world.

And perhaps their sacrifice will make those of us at home this Thanksgiving Day reflect even more deeply. So that when we give thanks for our food, we will think of those that are ravaged by hunger; when we give thanks for our health, we will think of those imprisoned by pain or illness or despair; when we give thanks for our freedom, we will also think of those who live in darkness or tyranny; when we give thanks for our future, we will think of those who don't know hope. And we will realize that

we have two obligations above all others. First: We must not take for granted the blessings of our lives. And second: For our lives to have true meaning, we must share with others. For this holiday reminds us that it's inner riches, not external wealth, by which we are measured. After all, Thanksgiving is not a time of the year, but it really is an attitude of the heart.

Thanks for coming. God bless everyone here, your families, all those being held hostage, and our service men and women here and abroad. And to all you kids, Happy Thanksgiving. I'm glad you came to the White House. Thanks a lot.

Note: The President spoke at 1:42 p.m. in the Rose Garden at the White House. In his remarks, he referred to Wyatt Upchurch and Stuart Proctor, president and executive vice president of the National Turkey Federation. The proclamation is listed in Appendix E at the end of this volume.

Letter to Congressional Leaders on National Emergency Construction Authority
November 14, 1990

Dear Mr. Speaker: (Dear Mr. President:)
Enclosed is an Executive order entitled "National Emergency Construction Authority." I signed the order today to make available to the Department of Defense the emergency construction authority contained at section 2808 of title 10, United States Code. This authority will enable the Secretary of Defense to undertake military construction projects that he deems necessary to respond to the threat caused by the Iraqi invasion of Kuwait.

Without this authority, all military construction in support of Operation Desert Shield or any other operation responding to the Iraqi invasion of Kuwait would have to be included in a military construction authorization act and an appropriations act. Operational requirements do not permit such an extended process for construction of much-needed facilities. This Executive

order will permit the Secretary of Defense and the Secretaries of the military departments, if the Secretary of Defense determines a delegation of his authority to be appropriate, to prioritize the construction needs of the military departments and to construct facilities not otherwise authorized by law.

Sincerely,

GEORGE BUSH

Note: Identical letters were sent to Thomas S. Foley, Speaker of the House of Representatives, and Dan Quayle, President of the Senate. The letter was released by the Office of the Press Secretary on November 15. An original was not available for verification of the content of this letter. The Executive order is listed in Appendix E at the end of this volume.

Appointment of Ann Windham Wallace as Director of the Office of Consumer Affairs
November 15, 1990

The President today announced his intention to appoint Ann Windham Wallace, of Texas, as Director of the Office of Consumer Affairs at the Department of Health and Human Services. She would succeed Bonnie Guiton.

Since 1987 Ms. Wallace has served as director of the Governor's office of community leadership and volunteer services and director of the Governor's commission for women in Austin, TX. Prior to this, she has participated in many civic and political activities in Austin, TX, including cochairman of Family Community Leadership, community adviser for the Austin Junior League, member of the Task Forces on Displaced Homemakers and Childsave, and adviser for the Governor's committee for disabled persons, 1987.

Ms. Wallace attended the University of Texas at Austin. She was born March 1, 1926, in Okmulgee, OK. Ms. Wallace resides in Austin, TX.

Remarks on Signing the Bill Amending the Clean Air Act
November 15, 1990

Thank you all very much. Thank you so much for being here. I would first like to welcome the Ambassador from Canada, our friend, Derek Burney, who represents, I think, by being here, his countrymen's concern for our common environment.

It is a pleasure to have several of our Cabinet here today: of course, Secretary Lujan here, Interior; and Jim Watkins; as well as Bill Reilly, the Administrator of EPA. Susan Engeleiter is here. Also, Madeleine, I want to welcome you—Governor Kunin, the Governor of Vermont, is with us today who has a big stake in all of this, and welcome.

I also want to welcome the leaders from the Senate side: the majority leader, Senator Mitchell, who has always had a keen interest in this, and of course, Bob Dole, Republican leader—both with us today. And of course, if I get singling out all the Members who are here of Congress, I'll be here all day. And I'm just glad you all are here. The Speaker and others, unfortunately, couldn't be here—majority and minority leader. But we have many of the committee leaders that worked the hardest here. I'll get in trouble, but I see John Dingell, and I want to thank him and so many others.

Please let's stop there. Let me just welcome the Members of Congress who have done so much on all of this.

Thanksgiving is still a week away, but I believe this really is a true red-letter day for all Americans. Today we add a long-awaited and long-needed chapter in our environmental history, and we begin a new era for clean air.

This last weekend, I spent some pleasant hours up at Camp David. Saturday and Sunday really were fantastic—clear and crisp and beautiful, bright sunshine and those magnificent fall colors. And it was great to get out in the woods. But no American should have to drive out of town to breath clean air. Every city in America should have clean air. And with this legislation, I firmly believe we will.

I first made a commitment to comprehensive clean air legislation when I was running for this job, and soon after coming into office, we developed a comprehensive clean air proposal. I think we did have consultation in the best spirit with the Democratic leadership and with the Republican leadership in the Congress, with environmentalists and with representatives of industry, because I believed, and I think we all felt, that it was time for a new approach. It was time to break the logjam that hindered progress on clean air for 13 years. And so, I told our best minds, assembled that morning a year and a half ago, every American expects and deserves to breathe clean air. And as President, it is my mission to guarantee it for this generation and for the generations to come.

Well, as we used to say in the Navy: Mission defined, mission accomplished. Today I am very proud on behalf of everyone here to sign this clean air bill—Clean Air Act of 1990.

This landmark legislation will reduce air pollution each year by 56 billion pounds—that's 224 pounds for every man, woman, and child in America. It will go after the three main types of air pollution: acid rain, smog, and toxic air pollutants. This bill will cut emissions that cause acid rain in half and permanently cap them at these new levels. It will reduce pollutants that cause smog in our cities by 40 percent, so that by the year 2000, over 100 major American cities with poor air quality will have safer, healthier air. And it will cut dangerous air toxics emissions by over 75 percent, using new technologies. And by the next decade, its alternative fuel provisions will help reduce our dependence on foreign oil. This bill means cleaner cars, cleaner power plants, cleaner factories, and cleaner fuels; and it means a cleaner America. Virtually every person in every city and every town will enjoy its benefits.

This legislation isn't just the centerpiece of our environmental agenda. It is simply the most significant air pollution legislation in our nation's history, and it restores America's place as the global leader in environmental protection.

Nineteen ninety is now a milestone year for the environment. I also hope that it will be remembered as an important year for environmental cooperation. There were several members of my administration who saw to it, through thick and thin, that this bill got to my desk: Bill Reilly, the EPA Administrator; Jim Watkins, the Secretary of Energy. From my own staff, our Chief of Staff worked tirelessly—John Sununu. Roger Porter did an outstanding job, working day in and day out with the Members of Con-

gress. Boyden Gray—the same thing. Bob Grady and so many others. And they did a great job on this.

And I also want to thank once again the Senators and Members of Congress from both sides of the aisle. Many of you are with us today, and as I mentioned earlier, others couldn't be with us today. But it isn't because of lack of interest. Congress is out; many are scattered to the winds. But the list is too long to single out everybody from the Hill that worked on this. But again, I just want to thank you that are here today and the others who couldn't be with us for your commitment and dedication—as well as the Governors, the Governors and the experts from local governments who were also instrumental in building true bipartisan support for this legislation.

We met with business leaders who saw stewardship to the environment as a key to long-term economic growth. And we met with academics and innovative problem-solvers from every side who have helped build the foundation for this approach.

I want to commend the environmental groups that we've met with, like the Environmental Defense Fund, under the leadership of Fred Krupp, for bringing creativity to the table to end what could have been a hopeless stalemate.

We all had tough choices to make. Some said we went too far; others said we didn't go far enough. But despite our differences, we all agreed on the goal: clean air for all Americans. We agreed on the means: a new Clean Air Act.

And we all agreed it was time to take a new approach. This bill is both ambitious in its goals and innovative in its methods. For the first time, we've moved away from the redtape bureaucratic approach of the past. The old tradition of command and control regulation is not the answer. By relying on the marketplace, we can achieve the ambitious environmental goals we have as a country in the most efficient and cost-effective way possible. We'll have to take advantage of the innovation, energy, and ingenuity of every American, drawing local communities and the private sector into the cause. It's time for a new kind of environmentalism, driven by the knowledge that a sound ecology and a strong economy can coexist.

The approach in this bill balances economic growth and environmental protection. The approach is comprehensive, cost-effective; and most of all, it will work. The first major pollution reductions are where we need them most. It offers incentives, choice, and flexibility for industry to find the best solutions, all in the context of continued economic growth. The bill is balanced: It will stimulate the use of natural gas from the wells of Texas and Louisiana; and fuels made from the farms of Iowa, Illinois, the great Midwest; and cleaner, low-sulfur coal from the hills of West Virginia to the Rocky Mountain States. This bill can make America the global leader in developing a new generation of environmental technologies to which the world is now turning.

But it does more. The legislation sets reasonable deadlines for those who must comply; but once deadlines go by, once they pass, the penalties are severe. American heritage is precious. We will not turn our backs or look the other way. That means polluters must pay. And so, there is a new breeze blowing, a new current of concern for the environment. Today marks a great victory for the environment, a day when we have strengthened our clean air statutes, already the world's toughest. This legislation is not only in America's interest; like so many of the environmental issues that we are working on, this bill is in the interest of people all over the world.

And the new environmental ethos is growing. We see it in community efforts and in school involvement across America, and we're seeing it in the innovative response of private industry—in alternative fuel service stations, electric vehicles. These companies understand we must pioneer new technology, find new solutions, envision new horizons if we're to build a bright future and a better America for our children.

There's an old saying: "We don't inherit the Earth from our parents. We borrow it from our children." We have succeeded today because of a common sense of global stewardship, a sense that it is the Earth that endures and that all of us are simply holding a sacred trust left for future generations. For the sake of future generations, I again thank each and every one of you for your commitment to our precious environment. I am now honored to sign this clean air bill into law.

Thank you all who have worked so hard for this day to become possible. Thank you, and God bless all of you.

[At this point, the President signed the bill.]

Maybe we could have the symbolism—I don't think there's any protocol, but if I could just invite the front row here to come up with Members of Congress, we'd at least show that this is an across-the-board—*[applause]*——

Please, go in peace. This symbolism—we've omitted some real fine movers and shakers there, but again, my thanks to all of you. Thank you all for being with us.

Note: The President spoke at 2:32 p.m. in the East Room at the White House. In his remarks, he referred to Susan S. Engeleiter, Administrator of the Small Business Administration; Representative John D. Dingell; Roger B. Porter, Assistant to the President for Economic and Domestic Policy; C. Boyden Gray, Counsel to the President; and Robert Grady, Associate Director for Natural Resources, Energy and Science at the Office of Management and Budget. S. 1630, approved November 15, was assigned Public Law No. 101–549.

Statement on Signing the Bill Amending the Clean Air Act
November 15, 1990

Today I am signing S. 1630, a bill to amend the Clean Air Act. I take great pleasure in signing S. 1630 as a demonstration to the American people of my determination that each and every American shall breathe clean air.

In July of 1989, I sent to the Congress a proposal to amend the Clean Air Act of 1970. My proposal was designed to improve our ability to control urban smog and reduce automobile and air toxic emissions, and to provide the enforcement authority necessary to make the law work. It also proposed new initiatives to cut acid rain in half and to promote cleaner automotive fuels.

As a result of that proposal, the 13-year legislative logjam has now been broken. S. 1630 contains all of the essential features of my original proposal and will lead to the achievement of the goals I originally set out. The bill I am signing today will permanently reduce sulfur dioxide emissions by 10 million tons below 1980 levels. It will cut NO_x emissions by two million tons from projected year 2000 levels and reduce air toxic emissions by over 75 percent.

The bill will allow the Nation finally to meet air quality standards in every city; and, in total, almost 30 million tons per year of dangerous chemicals and noxious pollutants will be prevented from fouling the air.

The result of this new Clean Air Act will be that cancer risk, respiratory disease, heart ailments, and reproductive disorders will be reduced; damage to lakes, streams, parks, crops, and forests will greatly be lessened; and visibility will be notably improved. As an added benefit, energy security will on balance be enhanced as utilities and automobiles switch to cleaner burning alternative fuels.

The innovative use of market incentives in the bill represents the turning of a new page in our approach to environmental problems in this country. The acid rain allowance trading program will be the first large-scale regulatory use of market incentives and is already being seen as a model for regulatory reform efforts here and abroad. The acid rain program is based on some simple concepts—that we should set tough standards, allow freedom of choice in how to meet them, and let the power of markets help us allocate the costs most efficiently.

By employing a system that generates the most environmental protection for every dollar spent, the trading system lays the groundwork for a new era of smarter government regulation; one that is more compatible with economic growth than using only the command and control approaches of the past. Other provisions to increase flexibility include increased opportunities for emissions trading and performance standards for fuel refiners to encourage alternative fuel reformulations. In all, these path-breaking features allow us to implement the legislation in a way that achieves my environmental goals at an acceptable cost. The result will be the dawning of a new era in regulatory policy, one that relies on the market to reconcile the environment and the economy.

To address the serious concerns raised by the cost of this legislation, I am directing Bill Reilly, Administrator of the Environmental Protection Agency, to implement this bill in the most cost-effective manner possible. This means ensuring that plants can continue to use emission trading and netting to the maximum extent allowed by law; that the Administration's proposed policy on WEPCO is implemented to the extent allowed by law as quickly as possible; and that the permit program is phased in over time in an orderly, nondisruptive manner. This Administration will also pursue the use of more realistic assumptions when estimating risk. These implementation strategies will help keep unnecessary costs and job losses down, while ensuring the achievement of the environmental goals of this bill in the most efficient manner possible.

Unfortunately, I must note several provisions of the bill that raise serious constitutional concerns. I strongly object to the bill's restrictions on removal or review of the Chemical Safety Investigation Board. Although the Board's principal functions are investigatory and advisory, it has also been given regulatory and enforcement authorities clearly assigned by the Constitution to the executive branch. As such, the provisions purporting to limit my authority to remove Board members and provide them with policy guidance raise serious constitutional questions. Accordingly, although I believe that these provisions are severable, I am directing the Administrator of the Environmental Protection Agency to submit curative legislation in the next session of Congress insuring that the Board's activities are consistent with the Constitution. This legislation will also address the serious constitutional concerns created by those provisions relating to the Board that invade the deliberative processes of the executive branch. Similarly, because the Urban Air Toxics Research Center created by the bill exercises executive grant-making authorities, the provision of the bill vesting appointment of part of its Board in Members of Congress violates this principle. This defect must also be rectified by curative legislation.

In addition, there are certain aspects of the bill's enforcement provisions that raise constitutional questions. I note that in providing for citizen suits for civil penalties, the Congress has codified the Supreme Court's interpretation of such provisions in the *Gwaltney* case. As the Constitution requires, litigants must show, at a minimum, intermittent, rather than purely past, violations of the statute in order to bring suit. This requirement respects the constitutional limitations on the judicial power and avoids an intrusion into the law-enforcement responsibilities of the executive branch. I should also note my interpretation of the provision permitting courts to order that civil penalties be used in beneficial mitigation projects consistent with the Act and enhancing public health or the environment. Because the Congress may not impose on courts responsibilities inconsist-

ent with their judicial function, I do not interpret this provision as imposing administrative responsibilities on the courts.

Even before the signing of this bill, the American public has begun to respond to the environmental leadership it embodies. In response to the direction we have signalled in this legislation:

—Cleaner reformulated gasolines are being produced by our leading refiners and are eagerly being sought out by consumers.

—Cleaner natural-gas-fueled trucks, electric vehicles, and flexible-fueled vehicles are or will soon be manufactured by domestic auto producers.

—Commitments have been made by the chief executives of leading chemical industries to reduce voluntarily their air toxic emissions by as much as 90 percent.

The speed with which companies and the public are voluntarily getting a head start is testimony to the need and timeliness of the measures I proposed and the Congress has now passed.

Passage of this bill is an indication that the Congress shares my commitment to a strong Clean Air Act, to a clean environment, and to the achievement of the goals I originally set forth.

GEORGE BUSH

The White House,
November 15, 1990.

Note: S. 1630, approved November 15, was assigned Public Law No. 101–549.

Nomination of Susannah Simpson Kent To Be Director of the Institute of Museum Services
November 15, 1990

The President today announced his intention to nominate Susannah Simpson Kent, of Pennsylvania, to be Director of the Institute of Museum Services, National Foundation on the Arts and the Humanities. She would succeed Daphne Wood Murray.

Mrs. Kent has been involved with muse-

ums throughout her life. Her managerial, volunteer, and research experience includes work with history, natural history, and art museums, and also with nature centers and other environmental conservation organizations.

Mrs. Kent graduated from Smith College

in 1957 with a B.A. in English. She pursued the study of economics at New York University before receiving her master of arts degree in American history from Yale University, where she also engaged in East Asian studies. Mrs. Kent is currently a master's degree candidate in museum studies at the George Washington University in Washington, DC. She is married, has two children, and resides in Washington, DC.

Statement on Signing the Chief Financial Officers Act of 1990
November 15, 1990

Today I have signed H.R. 5687, the "Chief Financial Officers Act of 1990." The Act provides new tools to improve the management of the Federal Government. It establishes Chief Financial Officers in 23 major executive agencies as well as a new Deputy Director for Management and a Controller in the Office of Management and Budget. The establishment of a Deputy Director for Management in OMB will strengthen and institutionalize the "M" in OMB.

Improving the Government's stewardship over public funds is critically important. The Act will help us to strengthen the systems that provide the President, the Congress, and the American people with the information necessary to make informed decisions on how public funds are spent. It will also help ensure that these data are timely and reflect more accurately the true costs of running the Federal Government.

The Act reinforces my Administration's efforts to establish Federal accounting standards, integrate and modernize the Government's financial systems, and produce audited financial statements. The operations and financial condition of Government must be accurately and publicly reported. I am pleased to note that the Act's priorities for management improvements coincide with those of my Administration. We look forward to working with the Congress on implementing the Act.

I also want to thank Congressmen Conyers and Horton and Senators Glenn and Roth for working with us in developing H.R. 5687.

GEORGE BUSH

The White House,
November 15, 1990.

Note: H.R. 5687, approved November 15, was assigned Public Law No. 101–576. The statement was released by the Office of the Press Secretary on November 16. An original was not available for verification of the content of this statement.

Statement on Signing the Bill Ensuring the Applicability of Patent Law to Activities in Outer Space
November 15, 1990

Today I am signing S. 459, legislation that will ensure the applicability of U.S. patent laws to our activities in outer space. This important and necessary legislation will remedy the current uncertainty in patent law as to the jurisdiction that applies to activities in outer space. This uncertainty arises primarily because the existing patent laws of most countries generally have no extraterritorial effect.

S. 459 will specifically ensure that U.S. patent laws apply to inventions made, used, or sold in space on vehicles under the jurisdiction or control of the United States. The Act is consistent with the purpose of our patent laws—to promote the progress of science and useful arts. With the enactment of this legislation, U.S. commercial entities will know that their activities in space will receive the same patent protection that they would receive if conducted on Earth. The certainty that inventions that advance space technology will be recognized under our patent laws will further encourage the private sector to undertake commercial space ventures, which is one of the important objectives of our National Space Policy.

This legislation is also important because it represents the final step required in implementation of the Intergovernmental Agreement on Space Station Cooperation between the United States and our international partners—Canada, Japan, and the Eu-

ropean Space Agency. The Act provides the flexibility required to carry out commitments regarding the applicability of U.S. patent laws under the Agreement for the development, operation, and utilization of Space Station *Freedom.*

GEORGE BUSH

The White House,
November 15, 1990.

Note: S. 459, approved November 15, was assigned Public Law No. 101–580. The statement was released by the Office of the Press Secretary on November 16. An original was not available for verification of the content of this statement.

Statement on Signing the Excellence in Mathematics, Science and Engineering Education Act of 1990
November 16, 1990

Today I am signing H.R. 996, the "Excellence in Mathematics, Science and Engineering Education Act of 1990." This Act is intended to encourage students to pursue fields of study in which Americans must excel if the United States is to maintain and advance its competitive position in the markets of the world. Excellence in these areas is crucial to developing both the professionals—scientists and engineers—and a work force that this country needs.

Mathematics and science education are an important priority for this Administration and the Nation. In September 1989, the Nation's Governors and I held the Education Summit, which led to the identification of six National Education Goals, two of which directly address science and mathematics achievement.

In developing the FY 1991 budget immediately following the Education Summit, the Administration took important steps to strengthen programs of Federal agencies and to increase funding for science and mathematics education. We intend to further develop that initiative through the work of a new interagency committee that is developing a strategic plan and priorities

for the Administration's program in science and mathematics education.

I am pleased that the Congress has included in H.R. 996 a version of the National Science Scholars program that I proposed in April 1989. This program will award scholarships to high school students who have excelled in science and mathematics to encourage them to continue their education in these subjects at the undergraduate level. This new program will provide an important vehicle for demonstrating the Nation's commitment to excellence in science, mathematics, and engineering achievement and to the recognition of excellent young people who are pursuing higher education and careers in those fields.

I note that, under this legislation, State nominating committees will nominate students for the National Science Scholars program. Members of Congress will nominate students for scholarships under the National Academy of Science, Space, and Technology program authorized by H.R. 996. Determining eligibility for Federal funds is a significant governmental duty that, under the Appointments Clause of the Constitution, may be performed only by officers of the

United States.

The Act requires that the nominating committees for the National Science Scholars program present to the President the names of four candidates, at least half of whom must be female, from each congressional district. The Act also requires the President to select two scholarship recipients, at least one of whom must be female, from each congressional district. This rigid selection quota based on sex is inconsistent with the Constitution. While I am pleased that the Congress answered my request for a National Science Scholars program, I will ask the Attorney General and the Secretary of Education to prepare legislation that will bring this Act into compliance with the Constitution.

H.R. 996 makes recipients of science scholarships who are convicted of felonies, or certain crimes involving controlled substances, ineligible for further scholarships authorized under the Act. These individuals would also be required to repay, with interest, any scholarships received. I interpret the phrase "[e]xcept as provided . . . by . . . section 5301 of the Anti-Drug Abuse Act of 1988" to mean that H.R. 996 in no way limits or eliminates the penalties imposed under section 5301. Thus, a person who is convicted of a Federal drug felony could, in addition to forfeiting future awards and repaying past awards, still be denied other Federal benefits pursuant to section 5301.

Section 721 of H.R. 996 is an objectionable provision that would extend until January 1, 1991, the comment period on a regulation proposed by the Secretary of Education to address an abuse of the student loan programs. The Department and its Inspector General have clearly documented the abuse. By extending the comment period, section 721 will unnecessarily impede the Secretary's ability to counter this abuse in a timely manner. Nevertheless, I expect the Department of Education to develop a sound final regulation—based on comments received during the extended comment period—to be effective for the 1991-1992 school year.

For the United States to attain the National Education Goals, particularly those in science and mathematics achievement, the Administration, the Congress, the States, local schools, and parents will all have to work together. H.R. 996 is one indication of this broad concern and cooperation. There is a continuing challenge, however, for all of us to work together in developing a truly national effort to make American students first in the world in science and mathematics achievement. I hope that all Americans will join me in this effort.

GEORGE BUSH

The White House,
November 16, 1990.

Note: H.R. 996, approved November 16, was assigned Public Law No. 101–589.

Remarks on Signing Environmental Protection, Research, and Education Bills
November 16, 1990

First, a warm welcome to the Members of Congress who are with us today. And I am delighted to see Secretary Lujan and our Administrator, Bill Reilly, with us; Mike Deland of the Council; John Knauss, the head of NOAA; and other distinguished guests. I want to just say, What a beautiful day, and a warm welcome to the White House.

We're here beside Lady Bird Johnson's tree, a willow oak planted in 1964. And Lady Bird once said she wants to be remembered as one who planted trees. And when I look out at the oak from the Oval Office window right here, at this magnificent oak on a beautiful fall day such as this, I understand Lady Bird and her advice to "know and enjoy the world around you."

Yesterday I signed into law the Clean Air Act of 1990, the centerpiece of our commitment to preserve and protect our environment. It makes our air pollution laws, already the world's toughest, even tougher. This year's clean air act is the most significant air pollution legislation in American history, and it restores America's place as the global leader in environmental protection.

Our agenda for the environment is broad and ambitious, one that encompasses not just the air we breathe but also verdant forests and grassy meadows, majestic rivers and lakes, and pristine coastal shorelines. Clearly, all of us must work together to preserve America's natural beauty.

Several bills that I am signing this morning will protect some of the most precious expanses of America, from the sands of the Mojave Desert to the undersea landscapes of the Purple Isles of the Florida Keys to the broad waters of the Great Lakes and Lake Champlain. One of the bills creates the National Forest Foundation, establishes two new wildlife refuges, and strengthens marine research programs and environmental law enforcement.

And we've not neglected our global responsibilities. Today I will sign legislation enhancing the preservation of Antarctica's vast and unique ecosystem, and I will sign legislation confirming our commitment to build a sound research base regarding global climate change.

And finally, there is environmental awareness, giving teachers the tools to teach our kids about the importance of conservation through the National Environmental Education Act.

Early in this century, the original environmental President, Theodore Roosevelt, said that children should be taught to read and enjoy what he called the wonder book of nature because he believed that our environment belongs not only to today's generation but to the next generation as well.

You're never too young or too old to learn about the wonders of nature. Those of us long in the tooth never tire of that sense of splendor one feels in the outdoors, and we love to see the wide eyes of a child at the moment they first see a cascading waterfall or a bottomless canyon or even a real, live, dangerous animal, like the turkey we had here yesterday. [*Laughter*]

These bills I'm about to sign are about what the future will hold for our kids. And that is why our environmental agenda is forward-looking—to the next generation and the generations that will follow. And so, it is with them in mind, those who will inherit this stewardship, that I am delighted to sign these eight bills into law.

And I would like to ask the seven Members of Congress who are with us if you all would come up here, and I'd ask that the Secretaries come over here behind me. And you guys come here, and we'll just get this over with. And thank you all for coming to the White House on this very special and spectacularly beautiful day.

Note: The President spoke at 10:18 a.m. on the South Lawn of the White House. In his remarks, he referred to Secretary of the Interior Manuel Lujan, Jr.; William K. Reilly, Administrator of the Environmental Protection Agency; Michael R. Deland, Chairman of the Council on Environmental Quality; and John A. Knauss, Under Secretary of Commerce for Oceans and Atmosphere and Administrator of the National Oceanic Atmospheric Administration.

Statement on Signing the Antarctic Protection Act of 1990
November 16, 1990

I have today signed H.R. 3977, the "Antarctic Protection Act of 1990." The Antarctic continent is a vast, unspoiled land whose associated and dependent ecosystems provide habitat for many unique species of wildlife and a natural laboratory from which to monitor critical aspects of stratospheric ozone depletion and global climate change. There is a need to better protect Antarctica's fragile environment by concluding a new environmental protection agreement to supplement the existing protections provided by the Antarctic Treaty of 1959 and related international agreements.

Any new agreement must reinforce the essential elements of U.S. Antarctic policy:

- maintenance of Antarctica as a zone of peace;
- comprehensive protection of the unique Antarctic environment;
- preservation of the unparalleled opportunities Antarctica offers for environmentally sound scientific research essential to understanding the dynamics of the planet's natural systems; and
- maintenance of the Antarctic Treaty and Antarctic Treaty systems as the framework for pursuing these goals.

Overall, H.R. 3977 is in accord with that policy. I am signing the legislation because it was amended in a manner that can be considered consistent with my Administration's position on Antarctic issues. This posi-

tion includes advocacy of a strong environmental protection agreement to supplement the Antarctic Treaty.

In signing the bill, I wish to make clear that the provision regarding the submission of international agreements to the Senate and the provision stating that the Secretary of State should enter into certain international negotiations are purely hortatory and do not limit the President's constitutional authority for the conduct of foreign affairs. I also note that I will construe the parts of the bill applicable to the activities of Federal agencies in light of the constitutional principle that commits the resolution of disputes between components of the executive branch to me rather than to the courts.

GEORGE BUSH

The White House,
November 16, 1990.

Note: H.R. 3977, approved November 16, was assigned Public Law No. 101–594. An original was not available for verification of the content of this statement.

Statement on Signing the Great Lakes Critical Programs Act of 1990
November 16, 1990

Today I am pleased to sign H.R. 4323, the "Great Lakes Critical Programs Act of 1990," which amends the Federal Water Pollution Control Act with respect to water quality in the Great Lakes. Although the United States and Canada, working together, have made much progress in cleaning up the Great Lakes, much work remains to be done. This Act will provide a substantial boost to our efforts by providing additional tools to make progress on much needed planning and cleanup activities.

Passage of this bill is an indication that the Congress shares my commitment to protecting the environment and my desire to clean up and maintain these bodies of water that are important recreationally and historically to the people of the United States and Canada.

In addition to its provisions concerning the Great Lakes, the Act would establish two "management conferences" responsible for managing Lake Champlain and Onondaga Lake in New York. The provision establishing the management conference for Onondaga Lake is repeated in S. 2740, which also passed in the final days of the Congress. Unfortunately, as structured by these provisions, these management conferences present serious constitutional concerns under the Appointments Clause of the Constitution.

H.R. 4323 designates State governors, State legislators, and other State and local officials to serve on each management conference. The Act then vests significant governmental authority in these State and local government officials by giving the management conferences and State governors substantial control over the making of Federal grants and the implementation of the management programs for Lake Champlain and Onondaga Lake. Because such power may be exercised only by officers appointed consistent with the Appointments Clause, and not by State governors or other State or local officials, the management conferences created by the Act are inconsistent with this constitutional requirement. Accordingly, although I am signing H.R. 4323 today, I

will request the Secretary of Defense, the Administrator of the Environmental Protection Agency, and the Attorney General to submit legislation to correct this constitutional problem.

GEORGE BUSH

The White House,
November 16, 1990.

Note: H.R. 4323, approved November 16, was assigned Public Law No. 101–596.

Statement on Signing the Fort Hall Indian Water Rights Act of 1990
November 16, 1990

Today I have signed H.R. 5308 the "Fort Hall Indian Water Rights Act of 1990." The agreement implemented by this Act is the end product of 5 years of intense, good-faith negotiation among the parties with competing claims to the waters of the Upper Snake River Basin in Idaho. These parties include the Shoshone and Bannock Indian Tribes, non-Indian water users, the State of Idaho, and the Departments of Justice and the Interior on behalf of the United States and as trustee of the Tribes' water rights. I applaud the spirit of compromise that allowed the parties to resolve their differences without the need to resort to the costly and often divisive litigation by which many other western water disputes are decided.

H.R. 5308 is acceptable to the Administration for several reasons. First, it contains a very favorable quantification of the Shoshone and Bannock Tribes' water rights and also provides certain storage and marketing rights that further enhance the value of those rights. Second, it fully protects the interests of the United States and other potentially affected tribes. Third, it settles with finality virtually all disputes and litigation over the water at issue, allowing all parties—State, local, and tribal—to proceed confidently in the use and development of their water rights. Finally, it does all of this with a relatively modest Federal contribution, in accordance with the Administration's criteria and procedures for Indian

water rights claim settlements, and without the necessity for Federal construction of significant new storage or irrigation facilities.

Unfortunately, very late in the legislative process and without a request for Administration comment, the Congress included an objectionable provision in the implementing legislation. Section 8(c) could be interpreted to allow the Tribes to collect from the Claims and Judgment Fund monies that the Act authorizes to be appropriated and paid to the Tribe, should such monies not be appropriated by the Congress within specified periods. So interpreted, this provision would constitute a circumvention of the normal appropriations process and an unwarranted use of the Claims and Judgment Fund.

Owing to the many otherwise redeeming aspects of H.R. 5308, and the unique circumstances surrounding the addition of the objectionable provision to Section 8(c), I have signed H.R. 5308. I am quite concerned, however, that the objectionable provision might become a precedent for the inclusion of similar provisions in future legislation, which would not be acceptable to the Administration. Accordingly, I have directed the Secretary of the Interior, the Attorney General, and others to communicate in the future a firm policy against the inclusion of such provisions in future legislation, the violation of which will lead to Executive disapproval.

GEORGE BUSH

The White House,
November 16, 1990.

Note: H.R. 5308, approved November 16, was assigned Public Law No. 101–602.

Statement on Signing the Aviation Security Improvement Act of 1990
November 16, 1990

I am pleased to sign H.R. 5732, the "Aviation Security Improvement Act of 1990," and to reaffirm our Nation's determination to bolster international aviation security in the face of threats by terrorists.

This Act implements recommendations of the President's Commission on Aviation Security and Terrorism, which I appointed last year in the aftermath of the tragic bombing of Pan American Flight 103 over Lockerbie, Scotland. My Administration already has put many of the recommendations into effect and taken other steps to improve aviation security. This Act is a continuation of the process. The relatives and friends of the Pan Am victims deserve great credit for their persistence in helping to improve aviation security. Credit also is due to members of the Commission and the Congress who worked together with us to improve the bill. H.R. 5732 is a living memorial to those whose lives were so cruelly cut short by the terrorists responsible for bombing Pan Am 103.

I do have reservations about certain provisions of this Act. I am particularly concerned with those provisions that purport to restrict the President's authority under the Constitution to conduct our foreign policy, including the authority to conduct negotiations on behalf of the United States. For example, the Act includes requirements that the Secretary of State conduct negotiations on aviation security issues, including the control of terrorism.

While, as a policy matter, I will always endeavor to consult with the Congress on such foreign policy issues, I am obligated to defend the constitutional authority of the Presidency. Accordingly, I direct executive branch officials affected by H.R. 5732 to interpret its provisions so as not to conflict with my constitutional authority in the field of foreign affairs.

In signing this legislation, I am doing more than signing a bill into law. This Act reflects the workings of the American democracy, an effort by private citizens, the Congress, and the executive branch to join in the common cause against international terrorism. H.R. 5732 is an expression of our national unity and determination to continue our fight against international terrorists and to help prevent another tragedy like Pan Am 103.

GEORGE BUSH

The White House,
November 16, 1990.

Note: H.R. 5732, approved November 16, was assigned Public Law No. 101–604.

Statement on Signing the Bill Designating Florida Keys Coastal Waters as a National Marine Sanctuary
November 16, 1990

On Earth Day of this year, I stated that "the Florida coral reefs are one of the most diverse ecosystems in the world and a unique national treasure. Protecting the reefs from damage, both from vessel groundings and pollution, is imperative." Today I take great pleasure in signing H.R. 5909—a bill that designates 2,600 square nautical miles of coastal waters off the Florida Keys as our Nation's ninth national marine sanctuary. The new Florida Keys National Marine Sanctuary covers the entire Florida reef tract, as well as part of one of America's favorite fishing areas, the Florida Bay "backcountry."

National marine sanctuaries should only be designated after adherence to the comprehensive evaluation and designation procedures set forth in the Marine Protection, Research, and Sanctuaries Act (the "Act") of 1972. Department of Commerce studies supporting designation of a Florida Keys National Marine Sanctuary, however, justify bypassing part of the usual process in this instance.

My approval of the legislation demonstrates this Nation's resolve to preserve ecologically unique ocean areas. Next year, through the process set forth in the Act, we intend to designate several other national marine sanctuaries including the Flower Garden Banks in the Gulf of Mexico; Monterey Bay, California; and the Olympic Coast off the State of Washington.

I am pleased that the bill makes the Department of Commerce's National Oceanic and Atmospheric Administration (NOAA) responsible for developing and implementing the management plan for the Sanctuary. NOAA has managed our other national marine sanctuaries well and, in cooperation with the Florida Department of Natural Resources, has had great success in managing the existing Key Largo and Looe Key National Marine Sanctuaries off Florida. Those two Sanctuaries eventually will become part of the new Sanctuary.

Designation of the Florida Keys National Marine Sanctuary will complement and augment existing Federal Government, Florida State and local government, and private sector efforts to protect the marine resources of the Florida Keys. It is an accomplishment of which we can all be proud.

GEORGE BUSH

The White House,
November 16, 1990.

Note: H.R. 5909, approved November 16, was assigned Public Law No. 101–605. An original was not available for verification of the content of this statement.

Statement on Signing the Consumer Product Safety Improvement Act of 1990
November 16, 1990

Today I am pleased to sign S. 605, the "Consumer Product Safety Improvement Act of 1990." This legislation authorizes appropriations through FY 1992 for the Consumer Product Safety Commission (CPSC) and makes certain other changes to existing consumer protection laws.

The Act reduces the number of commissioners required for a quorum from three to two when only three members are serving on the Commission. This ensures the agency's ability to carry out its statutory mandate. In addition, the Act improves the agency's regulatory process and increases

civil penalties for manufacturers violating consumer protection laws. These changes will help the agency to carry out its mandate of protecting the public against unreasonable risks of injury associated with consumer products.

I remain concerned about certain new information reporting requirements contained in section 37 of the Act. Requiring manufacturers, distributors, or retailers to report to the CPSC when a civil action results in a final settlement, as provided in section 37, compromises the validity of the information. That a civil action was settled out of court is not an indication of whether the product caused the harm.

I note that one provision of this Act warrants careful construction to avoid constitutional difficulties. Section 118 permits State Attorneys General alleging violations of certain provisions of the Consumer Product Safety Act to bring actions to seek injunctive relief. Consistent with the Constitution, I understand this provision to permit States to seek relief only when they otherwise possess standing under Article III.

GEORGE BUSH

The White House,
November 16, 1990.

Note: S. 605, approved November 16, was assigned Public Law No. 101–608.

Statement on Signing the Bill Amending the Arctic Research and Policy Act of 1984
November 16, 1990

I am today signing S. 677, an Act that amends the Arctic Research and Policy Act of 1984. These amendments are intended to facilitate the work of the Arctic Research Commission and the Interagency Arctic Research Policy Committee in developing and implementing a research policy to guide scientific efforts in the Arctic.

Two provisions of the Act warrant careful construction to avoid constitutional difficulties. Section 3(b) requires that the Arctic Research Commission report concurrently to the President and the Congress on its activities during the preceding fiscal year. I construe this section to permit the President to review the Commission's report before it is submitted to the Congress. Section 6 of the Act requires the Interagency Arctic Research Policy Committee to submit to the Congress a report that details, among other things, its responses to the recommendations of the Commission. I do not construe this language to detract from my authority to protect the confidentiality of communications within the executive branch.

GEORGE BUSH

The White House,
November 16, 1990.

Note: S. 677, approved November 16, was assigned Public Law No. 101–609.

Statement on Signing the National and Community Service Act of 1990
November 16, 1990

Today I am signing S. 1430, the "National and Community Service Act of 1990." There can be no nobler goal than to strengthen the American ethic of community service and to help translate this ethic into meaningful action. S. 1430 will make an important contribution to achieving this goal.

I am particularly pleased that S. 1430 includes provisions for the initial funding of a private, nonprofit foundation that will promote the ethic of community service, disseminate information about successful local activities to other communities across the Nation, and stimulate the development of new leaders and their community service initiatives. Government cannot rebuild a family or reclaim a sense of neighborhood, and no bureaucratic program will ever solve the pressing human problems that can be addressed by a vast galaxy of people working voluntarily in their own backyards. The Points of Light Foundation will help that galaxy to grow and flourish in the years ahead.

S. 1430 also includes a number of new programs that use more traditional techniques of fostering community service, including Federal grants and demonstration projects. An important role can be played by programs of this kind, and I am committed to ensuring that these new initiatives are administered in an effective fashion. I note that participants in some of the new programs will be paid by the Government to engage in community service. Although the use of financial incentives may be appropriate in some circumstances, I have reservations about the wisdom of employing "paid volunteers" to the extent contemplated by S. 1430.

I must also note that there are constitutional defects in two provisions of S. 1430. Section 190 creates a Commission on National and Community Service to administer several of the programs established by the Act. The Commission in turn is to be administered by a Board of Directors composed of 21 members appointed by the President and confirmed by the Senate. Section 190(b), however, purports to limit the President's choice of nominees to the Board. Under section 190(b), the Board must be "balanced according to the race, ethnicity[,] age and gender of its members"; must include no more than 11 members of the same political party; must include seven members nominated by the Speaker of the House of Representatives; and must include seven members nominated by the Majority Leader of the Senate.

Under the Appointments Clause of the Constitution, article II, section 2, clause 2, congressional participation in such appointments may be exercised only through the Senate's advice and consent with respect to Presidential nominees. Accordingly, the restrictions in section 190(b) on my choice of nominees to the Board of Directors are without legal force or effect. I direct the Attorney General to prepare remedial legislation for submission to the Congress during its next session, so that the Act can be brought into compliance with the Constitution's requirements.

In addition, section 602(b) of S. 1430 purports to condition my authority to transfer certain funds from one account to another on the subsequent approval of congressional committees. This attempt to condition my authority constitutes a legislative veto device of the kind declared unconstitutional in *INS* v. *Chadha*, 462 U.S. 919 (1983), and I will treat it as having no legal force or effect.

GEORGE BUSH

The White House,
November 16, 1990.

Note: S. 1430, approved November 16, was assigned Public Law No. 101–610.

Statement on Signing the National Earthquake Hazards Reduction Program Reauthorization Act
November 16, 1990

I have today signed S. 2789, the "National Earthquake Hazards Reduction Program Reauthorization Act." This Act authorizes appropriations for earthquake prevention and preparedness programs carried out by the Federal Government. It also modifies these programs in various respects.

In signing this Act I note that I will construe one section to avoid constitutional issues. Section 7 of the bill requires the National Earthquake Hazards Reduction Program Advisory Committee, whose members are to be appointed by the Federal Emergency Management Agency (FEMA), to provide policy recommendations to FEMA and other Executive branch entities concerned with earthquake disasters. Section 7 further requires the Advisory Committee to "submit a written report directly to Congress, without review by the Office of Management and Budget or any other agency, . . . which shall describe any recommendations" that the Advisory Committee has made. I shall interpret these provisions in light of my constitutional responsibility, as head of the unitary Executive branch, to supervise my subordinates as I deem appropriate.

GEORGE BUSH

The White House,
November 16, 1990.

Note: S. 2789, approved November 16, was assigned Public Law No. 101–614.

Statement on Signing the National Environmental Education Act
November 16, 1990

I am today signing S. 3176, the "National Environmental Education Act." This Act establishes an Office of Environmental Education within the Environmental Protection Agency to support and coordinate various educational, training, and awards programs.

While our environmental laws and regulatory programs are achieving their ends, this is no longer a sufficient approach given the magnitude and nature of the environmental problems we face. We must also encourage voluntary changes in individual habits. On September 19, 1989, in Spokane I spoke of the importance of the environmental ethic: "Through millions of individual decisions—simple, everyday, personal choices—we are determining the fate of the Earth. So the conclusion is also simple: We're all responsible, and it's surprisingly easy to move from being part of the problem to being part of the solution."

Environmental education heightens public sensitivity to the consequences of individual and collective actions, while also preparing future environmental management professionals. Hence, this legislation helps empower people to do the right for the environment through education and fostering awareness.

While I enthusiastically support the goals of this legislation, I must note my reservations about two provisions of the bill that raise constitutional questions. First, Section 10 of the bill establishes an Environmental Education and Training Foundation. The bill provides that the Foundation shall be a nonprofit, charitable corporation; that it shall not be an agency or establishment of the United States; and that appointment to the Foundation's board of directors shall not constitute employment by, or the holding of an office of, the United States. These statements are contradicted by the facts that the Foundation is established by the Congress; funded by the Congress; endowed with the sole purpose of furthering the activities and services of a Federal agency, the Environmental Protection Agency; and by the fact that the Foundation's Directors are appointed by the Administrator of the EPA.

Entities that are neither clearly governmental nor clearly private should not be created. The establishment of such entities is unwise. It undermines the separation of powers principles of our Constitution, blurring the distinction between public and private entities in a way that may diminish the political accountability of government. Accordingly, I instruct the Attorney General and the Administrator of the Environmental Protection Agency to prepare legislation for submission to the next Congress that will cure the serious defects in this legislation.

I also note that Section 9(b)(1) of the bill purports to require that the Administrator of EPA receive advice concerning the execution of his functions under this bill exclusively from a specified advisory council. This requirement unconstitutionally limits the range of advice that one of my subordinates may receive in the execution of his duties. I instruct the Attorney General and the Administrator to prepare legislation that will cure this problem as well.

GEORGE BUSH

The White House,
November 16, 1990.

Note: S. 3176, approved November 16, was assigned Public Law No. 101–619. An original was not available for verification of the content of this statement.

Memorandum of Disapproval for the Private Relief Bill Providing Benefits to Joan R. Daronco
November 16, 1990

In the closing days of the 101st Congress, two bills were passed providing for somewhat different benefits for the surviving spouses of assassinated Federal judges. These survivors have suffered profound and tragic losses, and they have our deepest sympathies. I am pleased that the Congress has passed legislation allowing these individuals to receive additional benefits.

One bill—H.R. 5316, the "Judicial Improvements Act of 1990"—has not yet been presented to me for approval. Upon its presentation to me, I plan to approve H.R. 5316, which contains provisions that would increase the benefits, subject to certain limits, for surviving spouses of all assassinated Federal judges on an equitable basis.

My approval of H.R. 5316 makes the approval of another bill—H.R. 3134—unnecessary. Therefore, I am withholding my approval of H.R. 3134, a bill which would have provided somewhat different benefits for Mrs. Joan R. Daronco. This action, in conjunction with my planned approval of H.R. 5316, will ensure that Mrs. Daronco and all such surviving spouses receive their benefits in an equitable manner.

GEORGE BUSH

The White House,
November 16, 1990.

Note: The President's last day for action on this bill was November 17. An original was not available for verification of the content of this memorandum.

Memorandum of Disapproval for the Indian Preference Act of 1990
November 16, 1990

I am withholding my approval of S. 321, the "Indian Preference Act of 1990." S. 321 would establish, among other things, a program to provide preferences to qualifying Indian enterprises in the award of Federal grants or contracts using funds appropriated for the benefit of Indians. The bill would impose new, expensive, and often duplicative program responsibilities on the Secretary of the Interior that would be difficult to implement. It would also likely result in Federal agencies assuming new, unfunded liabilities related to Indian preference enterprises.

My Administration strongly supports the goals of S. 321 and is committed to helping alleviate the widespread unemployment and underemployment on Indian reservations. Moreover, the Administration supports efforts to prevent companies from misusing Federal Indian preference programs. Accordingly, amendments are needed to the "Buy Indian Act" to increase Indian economic self-sufficiency and employment opportunities and to prevent utilization of preference provisions by nonqualifying companies. However, S. 321 is seriously flawed and would create more problems than it would solve.

I am withholding my approval of S. 321

to allow further review of the issues in the 102nd Congress. Many of the issues raised by S. 321 are complex and deserve a full airing in both Houses of Congress. The House passed S. 321 in the final days of the 101st Congress without sufficient consideration of these complex issues.

In the interim, I am directing the Secretary of the Interior to take the necessary steps to address the contracting problems identified in the November 1989 report of the Special Committee on Investigations of the Senate Select Committee on Indian Affairs.

In particular, I am directing the Secretary

to issue guidelines that set forth specific procedures to govern Bureau of Indian Affairs field contracting officers in conducting pre-award reviews of grants and contracts. I am also directing the Secretary to develop and submit proposed regulations to implement the "Buy Indian Act" for Executive review within 90 days.

GEORGE BUSH

The White House,
November 16, 1990.

Note: The President's last day for action on this bill was November 21.

Letter to Congressional Leaders on the Deployment of Additional United States Armed Forces to the Persian Gulf
November 16, 1990

Dear Mr. Speaker: (Dear Mr. President:)

There have been a number of important developments in the Persian Gulf region since my letter of August 9, 1990, informing you of the deployment of U.S. Armed Forces in response to Iraq's invasion of Kuwait. In the spirit of consultation and cooperation between our two branches of Government and in the firm belief that working together as we have we can best protect and advance the Nation's interests, I wanted to update you on these developments.

As you are aware, the United States and Allied and other friendly governments have introduced elements of their Armed Forces into the region in response to Iraq's unprovoked and unlawful aggression and at the request of regional governments. In view of Iraq's continued occupation of Kuwait, defiance of 10 U.N. Security Council resolutions demanding unconditional withdrawal, and sustained threat to other friendly countries in the region, I determined that the U.S. deployments begun in August should continue. Accordingly, on November 8, after consultations with our Allies and coalition partners, I announced the continued deployment of U.S. Armed Forces to the Persian Gulf region. These Forces include a

heavy U.S. Army Corps and a Marine expeditionary force with an additional brigade. In addition, three aircraft carriers, a battleship, appropriate escort ships, a naval amphibious landing group, and a squadron of maritime prepositioning ships will join other naval units in the area.

I want to emphasize that this deployment is in line with the steady buildup of U.S. Armed Forces in the region over the last 3 months and is a continuation of the deployment described in my letter of August 9. I also want to emphasize that the mission of our Armed Forces has not changed. Our Forces are in the Gulf region in the exercise of our inherent right of individual and collective self-defense against Iraq's aggression and consistent with U.N. Security Council resolutions related to Iraq's ongoing occupation of Kuwait. The United States and other nations continue to seek a peaceful resolution of the crisis. We and our coalition partners share the common goals of achieving the immediate, complete, and unconditional withdrawal of Iraqi forces from Kuwait, the restoration of Kuwait's legitimate government, the protection of the lives of citizens held hostage by Iraq both in Kuwait and Iraq, and the restoration of security and stability in the region. The deployment will ensure that the coalition has an adequate offensive military option should that be necessary to achieve our common goals.

In my August 9 letter, I indicated that I did not believe that involvement in hostilities was imminent. Indeed, it was my belief that the deployment would facilitate a peaceful resolution of the crisis. I also stated that our Armed Forces would remain in the Persian Gulf region so long as required to contribute to the security of the region and desired by host governments. My view on these matters has not changed.

I appreciate the views you and other members of the congressional leadership have expressed throughout the past 3 months during our consultations. I look forward to continued consultation and cooperation with the Congress in pursuit of peace, stability, and security in the Gulf region.

Sincerely,

GEORGE BUSH

Note: Identical letters were sent to Thomas S. Foley, Speaker of the House of Representatives, and Robert C. Byrd, President pro tempore of the Senate.

Letter to Congressional Leaders Reporting on the Declaration of a National Emergency Concerning Chemical and Biological Weapons Proliferation
November 16, 1990

Dear Mr. Speaker: (Dear Mr. President:)

Pursuant to section 204(b) of the International Emergency Economic Powers Act, 50 U.S.C. section 1703(b), and section 201 of the National Emergencies Act, 50 U.S.C. section 1621, I hereby report that I have exercised my statutory authority to declare a national emergency and to issue an Executive order that:

—directs the Secretary of State and the Secretary of Commerce to use their existing legal authorities to control exports that they determine would assist foreign countries in acquiring the capability to produce, stockpile, deliver, or use chemical or biological weapons;

—directs the Secretary of Commerce to prohibit exports that would assist foreign countries in chemical and biological weapons programs;

—directs the Secretary of State to pursue early negotiations to adopt comparable effective controls on goods and technology that could assist countries in chemical and biological weapons programs;

—directs the Secretary of State to ensure that the early achievement of a global convention banning chemical weapons, with adequate verification provisions, shall be a top priority of U.S. foreign policy;

—directs the imposition of procurement and import sanctions on foreign persons who knowingly and materially contribute to the efforts of foreign countries that use chemical and biological weapons in violation of international law or make substantial preparations to do so;

—directs the imposition of sanctions against foreign countries that use chemical or biological weapons in violation of international law, and authorizes the imposition of sanctions against countries that are making substantial preparations to use such weapons or that have developed, produced, or stockpiled such weapons in violation of international law.

The Secretary of State, the Secretary of the Treasury, and the Secretary of Commerce are authorized to issue regulations implementing these requirements. I am enclosing a copy of the Executive order that I have issued exercising these authorities.

I have authorized these actions in view of the danger posed to the national security and foreign policy of the United States by the continuing proliferation of chemical and biological weapons, and the need for stronger unilateral and multilateral controls. This is especially true at this time due to events in the Persian Gulf, and the threats that have been made regarding the use of chemical weapons. We are calling upon other countries to work together to strengthen our efforts and to develop multilateral controls that will effectively address this global threat.

Sincerely,

GEORGE BUSH

Note: Identical letters were sent to Thomas S. Foley, Speaker of the House of Representatives, and Dan Quayle, President of the Senate. The Executive order is listed in Appendix E at the end of this volume.

Memorandum of Disapproval for the Omnibus Export Amendments Act of 1990
November 16, 1990

I am withholding my approval of H.R. 4653, the "Omnibus Export Amendments Act of 1990." Although this legislation contains constructive provisions, it would severely constrain Presidential authority in carrying out foreign policy.

I agree with the principal goals of this bill, which include improved export controls for, and sanctions against the use of, chemical and biological weapons; sanctions on Iraq; missile technology sanctions; and reauthorization of the Export Administration Act. Indeed, I have recently signed into law provisions on missile technology sanctions and sanctions against Iraq comparable to those contained in this bill. H.R. 4653, however, contains elements that I believe would undermine these objectives and our ability to act quickly, decisively, and multilaterally at a time when we must be able to do so. These provisions unduly interfere with the President's constitutional responsibilities for carrying out foreign policy. Rather than signing the bill, I am directing action under existing authorities to accomplish the bill's principal goals.

I am pleased that the Congress endorses my goal of stemming the dangerous proliferation of chemical and biological weapons. The Administration has worked closely with the Congress to design appropriate and effective legislation to improve our ability to impose sanctions on the nations that use such weapons and any companies that contribute to their spread. Indeed, the Admin-

istration supported the House version of the sanctions provision. Throughout discussions with the Congress, my Administration insisted that any such legislation should not harm cooperation with our partners and should respect the President's constitutional responsibilities. Unfortunately, as reported from conference, H.R. 4653 does not safeguard those responsibilities, nor does it meet our broader foreign policy goals.

The major flaw in H.R. 4653 is not the requirement of sanctions, but the rigid way in which they are imposed. The mandatory imposition of unilateral sanctions as provided in this bill would harm U.S. economic interests and provoke friendly countries who are essential to our efforts to resist Iraqi aggression. If there is one lesson we have all learned in Operation Desert Shield, it is that multilateral support enhances the effectiveness of sanctions.

Because of my deep concern about the serious threat posed by chemical and biological weapons, I have signed an Executive order directing the imposition of the sanctions contained in this bill and implementing new chemical and biological weapon export controls. This Executive order goes beyond H.R. 4653 in some respects. It sets forth a clear set of stringent sanctions, while encouraging negotiations with our friends and allies. It imposes an economic penalty on companies that contribute to the spread of these weapons and on countries that actually use such weapons or are making preparations to do so. At the same time, it allows the President necessary flexibility in implementing these sanctions and penalties. Furthermore, the Executive order reaffirms my determination to achieve early conclusion of a verifiable global convention to prevent the production and use of chemical weapons.

The Executive order also directs the establishment of enhanced proliferation controls, carefully targeted on exports, projects, and countries of concern. On this issue, as with other important export control matters, my goal is to pursue effective, multilateral export controls that send the clear message that the United States will not tolerate violations of international law.

I am also concerned that other features of H.R. 4653 would hamper our efforts to improve the effectiveness of export controls. In the rapidly changing situation in Eastern Europe, and in bilateral relationships with the Soviet Union, we have demonstrated the ability to adjust, in cooperation with our allies, export controls on high technology to reflect the new strategic relationships. Last May I asked our allies to liberalize dramatically our multilateral export controls. Negotiations designed to liberalize trade to encourage democratic institutions and open market economies will continue. Our multilateral export controls have contributed significantly to the positive changes brought about in West-East relations. The micromanagement of export controls mandated by H.R. 4653 can only damage these ongoing efforts.

In other areas, H.R. 4653 would be harmful to closely linked U.S. economic and foreign policy interests. For example, under section 128 of the bill there would be extraterritorial application of U.S. law that could force foreign subsidiaries of U.S. firms to choose between violating U.S. or host country laws.

Other sections of H.R. 4653 contain useful provisions that will be implemented as soon as possible. However, additional legal authority is not required to make our export control system reflect the economic and national security realities of today's world. In response to recent world events, I am directing Executive departments and agencies to implement the following changes:

—By June 1, 1991, the United States will eliminate all dual-use export licenses under section 5 of the Export Administration Act to members of the export control group known as CoCom, consistent with multilateral arrangements. In addition, all re-export licenses under section 5 to and from CoCom will be eliminated, consistent with multilateral arrangements.

—By June 1, 1991, the United States will remove from the U.S. munitions list all items contained on the CoCom dual-use list unless significant U.S. national security interests would be jeopardized.

—By January 1, 1991, U.S. review of export licenses subject to CoCom Favorable Consideration and National Discretion procedures will be reduced to 30 and 15 days, respectively.

—By January 1, 1991, new interagency procedures will be instituted to make dual-use export license decisions more predictable and timely.

—By January 1, 1991, the Secretary of State will initiate negotiations to ensure that supercomputer export controls are multilateral in nature and not undermined by the policies of other supplier countries. By June 1, 1991, in consultation with industry, we will devise and publish a method to index supercomputer license conditions to reflect rapid advances in the industry and changes in strategic concerns.

—By January 1, 1991, we will significantly increase the threshold for Distribution Licenses to free world destinations and ensure that at least annually these thresholds are adjusted to reflect changes in technology and are consistent with international relationships, including changing requirements to stem the proliferation of missile technology and nuclear, chemical and biological weapons.

In summary, H.R. 4653 contains serious and unacceptable flaws that would hamper our efforts to prevent the proliferation of weapons of mass destruction and to ease restrictions on the legitimate sale of dual-use goods to acceptable users. Rather than sign this bill, I have chosen to take a series of steps under existing authorities to ensure that mutually shared objectives are met in a timely and effective manner. I will work with the Congress, upon its return, to enact an appropriate extension of the Export Administration Act.

GEORGE BUSH

The White House,
November 16, 1990.

Note: The President's last day for action on this bill was November 17. The Executive order on chemical and biological weapons proliferation is listed in Appendix E at the end of this volume.

Memorandum on the Egyptian Military Debt
November 16, 1990

Memorandum for the Secretary of the Treasury and the Secretary of Defense

Subject: Delegation of Authority Regarding Egyptian Military Debt

By virtue of the authority vested in me by the Constitution and laws of the United States of America, including section 592 of the Foreign Operations, Export Financing, and Related Programs Appropriations Act, 1991 (Public Law 101–513) (the "Act"), and section 301 of title 3 of the United States Code, I hereby:

(1) delegate to the Secretary of the Treasury the functions vested in me by section

592(c)(1) of the Act; and

(2) delegate to the Secretary of Defense the functions vested in me by section 592(c)(2) of the Act, except that those under subparagraph (C) thereof shall be subject to the concurrence of the Secretary of the Treasury.

The Secretary of the Treasury is authorized and directed to publish this memorandum in the *Federal Register.*

GEORGE BUSH

[*Filed with the Office of the Federal Register, 4:22 p.m., November 28, 1990*]

Appointment of Jeannette Louise Naylor as Deputy Assistant to the President and Deputy Director of Presidential Personnel
November 16, 1990

The President today announced his intention to appoint Jeannette Louise Naylor as Deputy Assistant to the President and Deputy Director of Presidential Personnel. She would succeed Roscoe B. Starek III.

Currently Miss Naylor is Special Assistant to the President and Associate Director of Presidential Personnel. From January 1988 to December 1988, Miss Naylor was senior project manager with International Skye Associates, Inc., a Washington, DC, consulting firm. From 1983 to 1987, Miss Naylor was development officer for the National Endowment for the Arts, where she was

responsible for fostering partnership efforts with the private sector in support of the arts. She also served as liaison to the President's Committee on the Arts and the Humanities. Miss Naylor served as eagle representative for the Republican National Committee from 1981 to 1983. Prior to moving to Washington, Miss Naylor was finance director of the Republican Party of Texas from 1979 to 1981 and assistant finance director for the Jim Baker for attorney general campaign in 1978.

Miss Naylor received her bachelor's degree in psychology and sociology from

Trinity University in San Antonio, TX, in 1978. She resides in Arlington, VA, and is involved in numerous charitable organizations in the Washington area.

Nomination of Alixe Reed Glen To Be an Assistant Secretary of Health and Human Services
November 16, 1990

The President today announced his intention to nominate Alixe Reed Glen to be Assistant Secretary of Health and Human Services (Public Affairs). She would succeed Kay Cole James.

Since January 1989 Ms. Glen has served as Special Assistant to the President and Deputy Press Secretary at the White House. Prior to this, she has served as deputy press secretary for the George Bush for President campaign, 1987–1989; press officer at the

Peace Corps, 1986–1987; and associate producer, "Crossfire" at Cable News Network, 1985–1986. In addition, Ms. Glen served as Assistant Press Secretary in the Office of the Vice President at the White House, 1981–1985.

Ms. Glen graduated from Hollins College (B.A., 1979). She was born August 24, 1957, in Greenwich, CT. Ms. Glen is married and resides in Washington, DC.

Statement by Press Secretary Fitzwater on the President's Meetings With National Leaders in Prague, Czechoslovakia
November 17, 1990

President Bush and President Havel met at 10 o'clock this morning at Hradcany Castle in the first meeting of the visit. President Havel welcomed President Bush on this historic occasion, the first-year anniversary of the revolution. The two leaders discussed the economic development of Czechoslovakia, including the need to get U.S. investment. President Bush said the United States is concerned about the international oil situation. President Bush said there is a disruption in supply, but it is the speculation about the Persian Gulf that has driven up prices. President Havel said their economy depends on an uninterrupted flow of oil from the Soviet Union, and that has been a problem in the current situation.

The two leaders discussed the CSCE and the prospects for locating a new Secretariat in Prague. Both leaders stressed the interest in seeing a successful CSCE meeting, particularly on issues of arms control and human rights.

Federal Leaders

President Bush met at approximately 10:40 with Federal leaders to discuss economic conditions. The President said the talks with the IMF and World Bank are progressing well. They also discussed oil supplies and their impact on this country. They emphasized the important role of private investment in improving the economy of Czechoslovakia.

Czech Leaders

President Bush met with Czech leaders at approximately 11 a.m. They emphasized that they wanted to help themselves economically as much as they can. One of the leaders quoted Mark Twain by saying "a helping hand is usually found at the end of your arm." President Bush spoke of the strength of the U.S. system in which 50 States have strong views, but cooperate comfortably with the Federal Government. President Bush also spoke of the need for stability in Czechoslovakia as they deal with private investors from the United States. President Bush also raised the matter of the environment, saying that pollution is a high cost that we must be concerned about.

Slovak Leaders

President Bush met at approximately 11:30 with Slovak leaders. He wished them success and emphasized the need for stability. The Slovak leaders commented on the United States as a melting pot that has accepted nationalities from all over the world. They pointed out they are working hard to get private investment and asked if more of their people could come to the United States for training in various production skills.

President Bush said "our vision is a Europe whole and free." President Bush remarked on the warm welcome of the crowds that lined the streets on the way into Prague from the airport.

Dubček

At approximately 12:15 President Bush called on Alexander Dubček, President of the Federal Assembly, and greeted him warmly, acknowledging his historic role in the move towards freedom in Czechoslovakia. President Dubček recalled his visit to the United States and said that President Bush's visit constitutes a most prominent day for U.S.-Czechoslovak relations. President Bush and President Dubček discussed the role of the Federal Assembly and its important role in the building of democracy. President Bush concluded the meeting by signing a large, brown leather guest book, giving the signing pen to President Dubček. President Bush signed: "With great happiness and warm best wishes, George Bush, November 17, 1990."

Note: In the morning, President Bush arrived at Ruzyne Airport, where he was accorded a formal welcome with full military honors.

Remarks to the Federal Assembly in Prague, Czechoslovakia
November 17, 1990

President Havel, thank you, sir, for greeting us with such warmth today. And to Chairman Dubček, thank you, sir, for that really warm and generous introduction. May I salute the Prime Ministers of the Czech and Slovak Republics; the Members of the Assembly; and most of all, the people of Czechoslovakia. It is an honor for me, the first American President ever to visit your country, to bring you the greetings of the American people on this, the first anniversary of Czechoslovakia's return to freedom.

One year ago today, in the streets and squares of this city, the people of Prague gathered, first by twos and threes, and then by thousands—in the night air, an autumn chill; in their minds, memories of a spring 20 years past. The Velvet Revolution had begun.

That revolution succeeded without a single shot. Your weapons proved far superior to any in the state's arsenal. In the face of force, you deployed the power of principle. Against a wall of lies, you advanced the truth. Out of a thousand acts of courage, Czech and Slovak, emerged a single voice. Its message: The time had come to bring freedom home to Czechoslovakia.

Your revolution was also a renewal: a renewal of the deeply held principles that bind my country, the United States of America, to yours; principles enshrined in your Declaration of Independence, issued in the United States in 1918 by Tomáš Masaryk, your first President, and Milan Stafanik, proud Slovak patriot; principles inspired by the ringing words of our own Thomas Jefferson more than two centuries ago.

In my homeland, those principles were put into practice when we adopted our Constitution and its Bill of Rights. And last night, I carried copies of those documents as we flew from Washington to Prague, copies that I guess were passed out to you as you came in today. And during this historic time, as you consider the adoption of your own federal system and bill of rights, I offer them to you in friendship, for the common principles and common bonds our peoples have long shared.

Generations of Americans, Czechs, and Slovaks sustained these common bonds. In the battle to defeat Nazi tyranny, America stood with the courageous Czech and Slovak partisans fighting for freedom. Through the long dark decades after 1948, we, like you, refused to accept Europe's division. Through Radio Free Europe and the Voice of America, we held aloft the ideal of truth, and we spoke a common language of hope.

At long last, the grip of the dictators weakened; Czechoslovakia seized its chance to rise up, to reclaim your rights as a free people and as a sovereign nation.

Today, as fellow citizens of free governments, we share the fruits of our common resolve. Europe, East and West, stands at the threshold of a new era: an era of peace, prosperity, and security unparalleled in the long history of this continent. Today Europe's long division is ending. Today, once more, Czechoslovakia is free.

Czechoslovakia's revolution is over, but its renaissance has just begun. Your work and ours is far from complete. Your nation, like your neighbors to the north and south, faces the unprecedented task of building a stable, democratic rule and a prosperous market economy on the ruins of totalitarianism. I am here today to say that we will not fail you in this decisive moment. America will stand with you to that end.

America stands ready to help Czechoslovakia realize the progress and prosperity now within reach. Today our two countries will conclude agreements giving Czechoslovakia the fullest access to American markets, American investment, and American technology. To help unleash the creativity and drive of the Czechs and Slovak people, I will urge our Congress to authorize a $60-million Czechoslovak-American Enterprise Fund. In addition, to help build your private sector, the United States will extend

prompt economic assistance from the $370 million now committed to central and eastern Europe for the coming year.

We also welcome the active involvement of the American private sector. I am pleased to see that yesterday your government entered into a promising, multimillion-dollar joint venture with Bell Atlantic and U.S. West to modernize your country's communications network. I am sure this will be the first of many large-scale investments in the future of a free Czechoslovakia.

In response to this region's severe energy problems, we expect the IMF—at our initiative—to lend up to $5 billion in 1991 to central and eastern Europe, and the World Bank will commit an additional $9 billion over the next 3 years.

In addition to these economic initiatives, we seek to renew the free and open exchange denied our peoples for so many years. I am pleased to announce the reopening of the American consulate in Bratislava in the Republic of Slovakia and, just yesterday, the selection of a site for our new cultural center in Prague. Our newly established International Media Fund promises to contribute expertise and encouragement to your nation's free and independent media. And I am gratified that your government and my country's Institute for East-West Security Studies will soon open a European Studies Center in Stirin, an important partnership of the intellect between European and American scholars.

And let me say once again: Prague should be the home to the permanent Secretariat of the Conference on Security and Cooperation in Europe. In Paris, I am confident that I will find unanimous support for this initiative. It is right that this city, once on the fault line of cold war and conflict, now at the heart of the new and united Europe, play a central role as the CSCE seeks to expand the frontiers of freedom in Europe.

At the Paris summit of the CSCE, the nations of North America and Europe will sign historic documents: a treaty to provide deep reductions in conventional armed forces in Europe, a CSCE summit declaration charting the future role of CSCE in ending Europe's division. The Atlantic alliance, the foundation of European stability, has pledged itself to the same goal.

Working together, we can fulfill the promise of a Europe that reaches its democratic destiny, a Europe that is truly whole and free. But this continent's reconciliation is only part of the larger vision for our world, a vision which I ask you to share.

Let me draw on the life and writings of the gentleman that is sitting over my right shoulder, President Havel—let me draw on those just to make my point. Several years ago, Mr. Havel wrote about the Western visitors who came to see your so-called dissidents, asking how they could help your cause. He wondered about that question, wondered why visitors from the West couldn't see that your cause was their cause, too. Mr. Havel wrote, and I quote: "Are not my dim prospects or my hopes his dim prospects and hopes as well? Is not the destruction of humans in Prague a destruction of all humans? Is not indifference to what is happening here a preparation for the same kind of misery elsewhere?"

Dissident Havel—now President Havel—spoke then of a shared destiny, spoke out of a sure sense that the fate of all mankind is linked. Czechs and Slovaks understand this vision and the challenge. For half a century, your struggle for freedom was cut short not by one but by two of the cruelest tyrannies history has ever known. You know what it means to live under regimes whose vision of world order holds no place for freedom. As heirs of Jan Hus, whose statue stands just a few blocks from us, as countrymen of Comenius, the son of Moravia, whose name graces your great University of Bratislava, you have always looked to the far horizon to take your bearings from principles that are universal. As small nations, whose very existence demands constant vigilance, you have always understood that your future depends not only on your own heroic actions here but on the broader principles that govern the greater world in which you live. We must recognize that no people, no continent, can stand alone, secure unto itself. Our fates, our futures are intertwined.

That, you see, is why Europe's celebration of freedom brings with it a new responsibility. Now that democracy has proven its power, Europe has both the op-portunity and the challenge to join us in leadership, to work with us in common cause towards this new commonwealth of freedom.

This commonwealth rests on shared principles, upon four cornerstones that constitute our common values: an unshakable belief in the dignity and rights of man and the conviction that just government derives its power from the people, the belief that men and women everywhere must be free to enjoy the fruits of their labor and that the rule of law must govern the conduct of nations.

The United States welcomes the new democracies of central and eastern Europe fully into the commonwealth of freedom, a moral community united in its dedication to free ideals. We wish to encourage the Soviet Union to go forward with their reforms, as difficult as the course may seem. They will find our community ready to welcome them and to help them as they, too, commit themselves to this commonwealth of freedom.

Every new nation that embraces these common values, every new nation that joins the ranks of this commonwealth of freedom, advances us one step closer to a new world order, a world in which the use of force gives way to a shared respect for the rule of law. This new world will be incomplete without a vision that extends beyond the boundaries of Europe alone. Now that unity is within reach in Europe is no time for our vision of change to stop at the edge of this continent.

The principles guiding our two nations, the principles at work in our two revolutions, are not Czech or Slovak or American alone. These principles are universal, rooted in the love of liberty and the rights of man.

Now, after four decades of conflict and cold war, we are entering an era of great promise; and yet our freedom, the freedom of people everywhere, remains under threat from regimes for whom the rights of man and rule of law mean nothing. And that is why our response to the challenge in the Persian Gulf is critical. The current crisis there is a warning to America as well as to Europe that we cannot turn inward, somehow isolate ourselves from global challenges. Iraq's brutal aggression against Kuwait is a rude reminder that none of us can remain secure when aggression remains unchecked.

I have this feeling in my heart that no peoples understand better what is at stake in the Gulf than Czechs and Slovaks. You know from your own bitter experience that the world cannot turn a blind eye to aggression. You know the futility and vain hope that aggressors can be appeased. You know the tragic consequences when nations confronted with aggression choose to tell themselves it is no concern of theirs, just a "quarrel in a faraway country between a people of whom we know nothing."

We Americans, too, have learned. We know the costs, to ourselves and to the whole of Europe, of our isolationism after the First World War. We know that America must resist the temptation to consider our work complete. We must remain committed to the cause of freedom in the world.

And more and more, the Soviet Union is demonstrating its commitment to act as a constructive force for international stability. More and more, the United Nations is functioning as its creators intended it: free from the ideological confrontation that frustrated collective action, rendered impotent the peacekeeping function of that body.

From this first crisis of the post-cold-war era comes an historic opportunity: the opportunity to draw upon the great and growing strength of the commonwealth of freedom and forge for all nations a new world order far more stable and secure than any we have known.

Today I am very proud to join Czechoslovakia as it celebrates a year in freedom. I salute you for your courage and your vision, for all that you have endured, and for all you are destined to achieve. And I challenge you, as you take your rightful place in the center of Europe, to look beyond the confines of this continent to join with your neighbors in Europe and in North America to build a true commonwealth of freedom so that the peace and prosperity you seek—the peace and prosperity we shall share—will be the peace and prosperity of all mankind.

Once again, thank you for this warm welcome, and may God bless the people of Czechoslovakia.

Note: The President spoke at 12:36 p.m. in the Federal Assembly Hall. In his remarks, he referred to Alexander Dubček, Chairman of the Federal Assembly.

Question-and-Answer Session With Reporters Following Discussions With President Václav Havel in Prague, Czechoslovakia
November 17, 1990

President Havel. Dear friends, let me welcome you to this brief meeting with our honored guest, President Bush, and myself. We are ready to answer your questions. But before doing so, perhaps I should briefly explain what President Bush and I have been discussing.

We have touched up on a number of different matters, but we focused primarily on the following subjects. We have presented our information on the present situation in Czechoslovakia, and possibilities of a possible assistance or cooperation on the part of the United States have been discussed. Secondly, we have dwelled upon the future of Europe in the light of the forthcoming CSCE summit in Paris and upon the future of the Helsinki process. And on that score, we have found that our views there are very close to each other, if not even identical. And sadly, we have talked at some length about the situation in the Persian Gulf.

You can ask us questions that shall be answered alternately by President Bush and myself, with me being the one to answer the first question.

U.S. Assistance for Czechoslovakia

Q. President Havel, are you satisfied with the assistance you're getting? You seem to not be saying that your views are identical on that subject with the President.

President Havel. President Bush shows a lot of understanding for our problems, and he has already pledged certain forms of assistance in the statement he delivered in the Federal Assembly, which you have suddenly had.

Q. President Bush, even though you did outline some assistance today in your speech, proportionately it's fairly miniscule compared to what Czechoslovakia needs. Are you prepared to consider further direct U.S. assistance?

President Bush. Well, I think we've spelled out what we can do in terms of direct assistance right now. The thing that is of most import to Czechoslovakia is increased support from the IMF and the World Bank. And I made clear to President Havel that we will be very supportive in that connection.

In addition, the thing that would be of most benefit to Czechoslovakia and to the United States would be increased investment and increased private-sector help. And that we've discussed; and then that, I think we both agree, would be the best answer—certainly long-range answer—for the vitality and growth of Czechoslovakia.

President Havel. I think we should give an opportunity, also, to the Czechoslovak media.

Q. Mr. President Bush, have you spoken to Mr. Havel about American assistance in the science and technology fields and especially in education of the people? Would you be more concrete?

President Bush. We didn't discuss S&T as much. We did talk about educational exchanges, but we did not dwell on the science and technology. Certainly, I would say we would be ready to cooperate in every way in that field, however.

Soviet Union and Eastern Europe

Q. President Havel, can I ask you about the situation in the Soviet Union, as you watch it—the tensions that we see that Mr. Gorbachev is facing? What concerns do you have about the breakup of the Soviet Union

and how that would affect Central European countries?

President Havel. The fact that the Soviet Union is currently undergoing the most sweeping, the most far-reaching changes in its entire history is more than evident, but it is not yet clear what the future arrangement of the Soviet Union will be. But it is our firm belief that the changes may be accomplished in a rapid and peaceful way without any bloodshed and that they may give the individual Republics and the peoples of the Soviet Union the measure of autonomy which they desire.

Q. President Bush, what's your opinion on the plan of economic help to U.S.S.R. through Eastern Europe which was proposed by Minister Dienstbier [Foreign Minister of Czechoslovakia] in his speech at Harvard University earlier this year? And was this topic on the program of your talks in Czechoslovakia?

President Bush. I'm sorry, I didn't hear the first part.

We didn't discuss that in great detail, but I am convinced that the United States—and I tried to say this in our speech to the joint session—has an enormous stake. We do not want to see Czechoslovakia, Poland, and Hungary off in some kind of no man's land. And thus, we did discuss future security arrangements. It is my view—and I would let the Czechoslovakian Government speak for itself—that some more active role in the CSCE process will contribute to the stability of Europe and fully include Czechoslovakia in the decisions that lie ahead for Europe.

Persian Gulf Crisis

Q. President Bush, in your speech in Parliament, you said we Czechoslovaks understand better than any other nation the Kuwaiti situation. Suppose that something similar happens in our part of the world. What attitude U.S. would adopt since we have no oil here?

President Bush. I'm glad you raised that, because one thing that is very clear to me is that what Saddam Hussein has done in taking over Kuwait is devastating to the economies of eastern Europe, say nothing of the economies of the West and every other part of the world. This naked aggression against Kuwait has clearly had an adverse effect on the economies of every single country because of the disproportionate amount of the GNP that is assigned to energy. And so, I am very clear that it is not simply the United States and other countries in the West that are getting hurt by Saddam Hussein's aggression and what that means in terms of higher oil prices but every country as well. Clearly, this is true in Eastern Europe.

Your question, other than that, is too hypothetical for me to say what we might do under some hypothetical situation. But I can guarantee you, we are going to continue to stand against this aggression and do our level-best to see that the United Nations resolutions are fully implemented—hopefully, in a peaceful manner. But Saddam Hussein has got to withdraw from Kuwait without condition, and the legitimate leaders have to be restored, and the hostages—and Czechoslovakia has some, and so does the United States—must be freed. This inhumane treatment of hostages is unacceptable. And then there must be a stable order in the Gulf.

So, these objectives will be fulfilled. And my little few hours I've had here on this visit convinced me that it's everybody that's being hurt by this aggression.

Q. President Havel, do you agree with President Bush's views on the Gulf, and do you believe the United States is acting responsibly in the Gulf?

President Havel. Czechoslovakia has made it very clear on a number of occasions that it is necessary to resist evil, that it is necessary to resist aggression, because our own history has taught us ample lessons about the consequences of appeasement.

Dear friends, unless you want the winds to carry us away, you have to accept the situation that there is room for one more question only. [*Laughter*]

Q. President Havel, do you fear that the Gulf situation is taking too much money away from the kind of problems that it could solve in Eastern Europe?

President Bush. ——talking about oil prices?

President Havel. It is my opinion that all the resources that are expended on resisting aggression anywhere in the world finally turned to the good of all humankind.

President Bush. Thank you very much. You heard our host.

President Havel. Thank you all for your attention.

Q. President Bush, there is some feeling that you are too much in a hurry. What do you think of a moratorium that's being called for, in terms of hostilities in the Gulf, by Mubarak and other leaders?

President Bush. Mr. Mubarak and I see eye to eye on this situation in the Gulf.

Note: President Havel spoke at 2:48 p.m. in the Music Room at Hradcany Castle, his residence and the seat of the national government. He spoke in Czech, and his remarks were translated by an interpreter. In his remarks, President Bush referred to President Saddam Hussein of Iraq and President Mohammed Hosni Mubarak of Egypt. Following the question-and-answer session, President Bush met with Cardinal Tomasek at the Archbishop's Palace.

Remarks in Prague, Czechoslovakia, at a Ceremony Commemorating the End of Communist Rule
November 17, 1990

Thank you, Mr. President, and thank you, my Czech and Slovak friends. It is a tremendous honor to me to be the first sitting American President to visit this proud and beautiful country and to be able to join you on the first anniversary of the extraordinary Velvet Revolution. What a powerfully moving sight it is.

There are no leaves on the trees, and yet it is Prague Spring. There are no flowers in bloom, and yet it is Prague Spring. The calendar says November 17th, and yet it is Prague Spring.

Your Declaration of Independence proclaims: "The forces of darkness have served the victory of light. The longed-for age of humanity is dawning." Today the freedom-loving people of the world can bear witness that this age of humanity has now finally and truly dawned on this splendid nation.

Seven decades ago, an unprecedented partnership began between two Presidents: the philosopher, Tomáš Masaryk, and the idealistic scholar, Woodrow Wilson. It was a partnership as well among Czechs and Slovaks to join together in federation. And, yes, it was a long, hard road from their work on your Declaration of Independence to this magnificent celebration today. I am proud to walk these last steps with you as one shared journey ends and another begins.

Our countries share a history. We share a vision. And we share a friendship, a friendship Masaryk described to Czech-American soldiers 70 years ago. He said: "Do not forget that the same ideals, the same principles ever unite us. Do not forget us as we shall never forget you." That is why I'm here today. We have not forgotten.

The world will never forget what happened here in this square where the history of freedom was written—the days of anguish, the days of hope. So many times, you came here bearing candles against the dark night, answering the call of Comenius to follow "the way of light." These brave flames came to symbolize your fiercely burning national pride.

A year ago, the world saw you face down totalitarianism. We saw the peaceful crowds swell day by day in numbers and in resolve. We saw the few candles grow into a blaze. We saw this square become a beacon of hope for an entire nation as it gave birth to your new era of freedom.

This victory owes its heart to two great heroes. Alexander Dubček—22 years ago, he led this nation in its first sweet taste of liberty. His are the will and compassion that are the living Czechoslovakia. And then President Havel, a man of wisdom, a man of tremendous moral courage. In the dark years, on one side stood the state; on the other side, Havel. On one side, tyranny; on the other, this man of vision and truth. Among the first was Havel, and now there are millions.

Today a Europe whole and free is within our reach. We've seen a new world of freedom born amid shouts of joy; born full of hope, barreling with confidence toward a new century; a new world born of a revolution that linked this square with others— Gdansk, Budapest, Berlin—a revolution that joined together people fueled by courage and by humanity's essential quest for freedom.

For four decades, our two nations waited across the divide between East and West, two peoples united in spirit, in vision, and yet separated by conflict. Today the United States and Czechoslovakia stand together, united once more in our devotion to the democratic ideal.

Now, with the division of Europe ending and democracy ascending in the East, the challenge is to move forward. In Czechoslovakia: from revolution to renaissance, across this continent toward a new Europe in which each nation and every culture can flourish and breathe free. On both sides of the Atlantic: toward a commonwealth based on our shared principles and our hopes for the whole world, a commonwealth inspired by the words of your great Comenius written three centuries ago: "Let us have but one end in view: the welfare of humanity."

A thousand miles to the south, this new commonwealth of freedom now faces a terrible test. Czechoslovakia was one of the first nations to condemn the outrage in the Persian Gulf, one of the first to measure the magnitude of the wrong committed in the name of territorial ambition. It is no coincidence that appeasement's lonely victim half a century ago should be among the first to understand that there is right and there is wrong, there is good and there is evil, and there are sacrifices worth making.

There is no question about what binds our nations, and so many others, in common cause. There is no question that ours is a just cause and that good will prevail. The darkness in the desert sky cannot stand against the way of light. I salute your courageous President when he joins us in saying that Saddam Hussein's aggression must not be rewarded.

Earlier today I told your Parliament, we know this is a difficult time for you, but also a time of extraordinary optimism. As you undertake political and economic reform, know one thing: America will not fail you in this decisive moment. America will stand with you. We will continue along the road mapped out by our Presidents more than 70 years ago, a road whose goal was described by Woodrow Wilson: "to bring peace and safety to all nations and make the world itself at last free."

For the past 70 years, your Declaration of Independence has been preserved and cherished in our Library of Congress. I say, it is time for Masaryk's words to come home. And as humanity and liberty return to Czechoslovakia, so, too, will this treasured document.

On behalf of the people of the United States, I am proud to be able to tell the people of Czechoslovakia: 1989 was the year that freedom came home to Czechoslovakia; 1990 will be the year your Declaration of Independence came home to the golden city of Prague. May it be for future generations a reminder of the ties that bind our nations and the principles that bind all humanity.

In 1776, when our Declaration of Independence was first read in public, a bell tolled to proclaim the defiant thrill of that moment. That bell—we call it, at home, the Liberty Bell—has for 200 years symbolized our nation's deepest dedication to freedom—dedication like your own. Inscribed on this bell are the words: "Proclaim liberty throughout all the land." We want to help you proclaim your new liberty throughout all this proud and beautiful land, and so today we give to you our last replica of the Liberty Bell. You know, one of our patriotic songs proclaims, "Sweet land of liberty—from every mountainside, let freedom ring."

And so, when bells ring in Wenceslas Square or in Bratislava or anywhere in this glorious country, think of this bell and know that all bells are tolling for your precious liberty, now and forever. And so, now I am proud to ring this bell three times. Once for your courage, once for your freedom, and once for your children.

[At this point, the President rang the bell.]

May God bless Czechoslovakia. Thank you all very much.

Note: The President spoke at 4:13 p.m. in Wenceslas Square. Prior to his remarks, he participated in a wreath-laying ceremony at the St. Wenceslas Memorial. In his remarks, he referred to President Saddam Hussein of Iraq. A tape was not available for verification of the content of these remarks.

Statement by Press Secretary Fitzwater on the Czechoslovakia-United States Trade Agreement
November 17, 1990

The United States and Czechoslovakia today exchanged diplomatic notes bringing into force the trade agreement signed by the two Governments last April. The agreement extends most-favored-nation (MFN) tariff treatment to Czechoslovak exports to the United States and U.S. exports to Czechoslovakia. President Bush expressed his hope that the mutual extension of MFN tariff treatment will "provide the impetus for greatly expanded trade between our two countries and the first step toward a normalization of our bilateral trade relations." The exchange follows approval of the agreement on November 16, 1990, by the Czechoslovak Federal Assembly. The U.S. Congress approved the extension of MFN on October 23.

The agreement, along with its side letters on trade and financial matters, intellectual property, and tourism, contains important guarantees for American businesses, including the right to nondiscrimination in renting office space, paying for local goods, and establishing bank accounts. Through this agreement, the Czechoslovak Government has also committed to upgrade substantially its protection of intellectual property rights, bringing its intellectual property regime to a level on a par with that of other industrialized nations.

The implementation of this agreement coincides with the next phase of Czechoslovakia's concerted efforts at market reform and trade liberalization. The Government of Czechoslovakia has announced plans to activate a number of important reform measures in January 1991, including price liberalization through the delinking of retail and wholesale prices, internal currency convertibility, and the privatization of large state enterprises through the establishment of joint ventures with foreign entities.

President Bush praised Czechoslovakia's reform efforts as "impressive initiatives, heralding a new age in Czechoslovakia's relations with the international trading system." The President also expressed his hope that Czechoslovakia's reforms would continue to move the country towards full trade liberalization.

Combined with the current and planned reforms in Czechoslovakia, the extension of MFN should result in the threefold increase in bilateral trade over the next few years, setting the stage for a strong trade relationship between our two countries.

Radio Address to the People of Czechoslovakia
November 17, 1990

Indeed, it is an honor for me to be here on the first anniversary of your Velvet Revolution. And I'm doubly honored to be the first American President ever to visit Czechoslovakia. And President Havel, I thank you for inviting me to visit your country. Barbara and I are delighted to be here, and I'm flattered that you invited me to join you in this weekly radio talk.

I spent a marvelous and moving day here in Prague. I met the new leaders of Czechoslovakia, both Federal and Republic. And I spoke before your Federal Assembly, that hall that has now sprung to life in building your new democracy. And on Wenceslas Square, I joined you in celebrating the first anniversary of your Velvet Revolution. And it's really been among the most thrilling days of my life.

The ties between our two countries are unique, going way back to the creation of the Czechoslovak state. And Americans feel a special attachment to your Czech and Slovak federation.

Our peoples were cut off from each other for most of the Communist period, and we've now begun making up for what we missed through those two generations. And I regret that I was unable to visit Slovakia during this brief visit, so let me extend a special word or greeting to the people of Slovakia and say how delighted I am that the United States will soon reopen its consulate there in Bratislava.

And let me say to all the citizens of the Czech and Slovak Federal Republic: We rejoice with you in your liberty, and we pledge that we will not fail you in this decisive moment of your history.

President Havel, once again, sir, my thanks to you for allowing me to join you on the airwaves of free Czechoslovakia. God bless you all.

Note: The address was recorded at 6:40 p.m. on November 17 at Hradcany Castle in Prague, Czechoslovakia, and was broadcast as a part of President Havel's weekly radio program at 2 p.m. on November 18. Following the recording session, President Bush attended a reception at the castle hosted by President Havel. Later, President Bush went to the U.S. Ambassador's residence, where he stayed overnight.

Exchange With Reporters Aboard Air Force One
November 18, 1990

Chancellor Helmut Kohl of Germany

The President. ——here's why. I want to save it all for Germany or France or Saudi Arabia.

Q. Why?

The President. Why? That's what I asked——

Q. You called Kohl this morning? What was that about?

The President. Called him?

Q. In the last few days?

The President. No.

Q. Yesterday?

The President. No.

Q. What about GATT? Yesterday I was asking Marlin about GATT and about whether or not you were going to bring that up today.

Mr. Fitzwater. I think it's been a couple weeks since you called Chancellor Kohl.

The President. Yes. I haven't talked to him today. Mark that: Did not call Kohl.

Soviet Union/Persian Gulf Crisis

Q. What do you think about the changes in the Soviet Union?

The President. Very interesting. I'll have a chance to talk to Mr. Gorbachev about all of that.

But this visit was very moving and very emotional and very good. And I thought what Havel said yesterday should be well noted around the world, not just on his aspirations for his own country but what he said as it related to aggression in the Middle East, because this country has learned what it means to be taken over. And all during dinner and afterward, talking to the people, the patriots there, why, it just redoubles my conviction that aggression can't stand. And I think he answered that question very directly to one of you all yesterday which was very, very forceful.

Q. Everybody thinks you're going to war——

The President. The United Nations——

Q. ——in late January.

The President. ——resolutions will prevail. I'm convinced of it.

Q. So what about Bennett [former Director of National Drug Control Policy]——

The President. And I was very pleased with the support yesterday that I saw in that—I think it was your poll, wasn't it? ABC? Its strong support for what we're doing—very strong. You can write the story one way; but when you analyze the results of the poll, why, it was very, very positive. I think some were frustrated we haven't moved sooner, and some are frustrated we may be moving too fast. But if we add it all up, there is strong support for what the United States is doing at home, and I think there's strong support for what we're doing around the world. I'm sure of it in Czechoslovakia. I can guarantee you that.

Q. Do you consider that a green light?

The President. I consider it a solid front.

Q. A what?

The President. A solid front. Because I think this: What we learn here today is just one more affirmation that the United Nations is correct in its resolutions.

Q. Are you planning a TV speech when you get back to the States?

The President. Haven't planned it, but there may well be one.

Q. How close are you to getting enough votes in the U.N. to go for a——

The President. We're not discussing that now. We're just doing a little consultation.

William J. Bennett

Q. Did you really pick Bennett to head the——

The President. We're not discussing that now.

Q. ——Republican National Committee?

The President. I don't know—a lot happens when I leave. We've got to wait and do a little—[*laughter*]——

Q. This happened without your knowledge?

The President. Yes. Isn't that amazing?

Q. Shocking.

Arms Reduction Agreements and the Conference on Security and Cooperation in Europe

Q. Are you intending for the Gulf to make everybody forget about CSCE?

Q. Don't you think that's the effect of what you're doing on this——

The President. I don't know. I hope you write the importance of this arms control agreement. I will say it's important. It seems to have been overshadowed by what's happening in the Gulf, but it is a significant milestone.

Q. How about START [strategic arms reduction talks]?

The President. And you've got to put CSCE in a broad context. I mean, when I was talking to the Czechs yesterday about not having them and the other Eastern European countries in some no man's land, that leads one to the importance of CSCE for the ongoing consideration of European interest with them as a part of it. So, that's——

Q. What about START?

Q. How about the expansion of NATO?

The President. They are observers in NATO, but I think for the broader participation, the CSCE will have some applications.

Q. How closely are you tracking how much material the Russians are moving east of the Urals?

The President. I can't answer that. I've not been briefed on how much they're moving east of the Urals.

Q. So, it doesn't concern you?

The President. I have not followed recently. I'm sure that if it were a real concern, I'd know about it.

Q. Are you going to go to Moscow to sign the START agreement in January?

The President. When the START agreement is ready to sign, I'll go to Moscow and sign it.

Q. When do you think it will be ready?

The President. I can't help you with that, but maybe I'll be able to help you with that question after I see Mr. Gorbachev.

Agricultural Subsidies

Q. How much of your discussions with Kohl are going to relate to the Gulf as compared to CSCE, and what's the agenda look like?

The President. I don't know. Of course, there's also the trade area with Kohl that we've got to talk about. So, I don't know how it will break out. But I have such a warm, pleasant relationship with him that I've always been able to talk very frankly, and I don't feel inhibited or restricted by any talking points or allocation of his time on a subject.

Q. Is he the main stumbling block on the subsidy——

The President. No.

Q. You think you'll get better results out of him after his elections? Is that why you're going to Brussels on GATT?

The President. I don't know. I think that he basically is with us in terms of freer trade. I mean, there's no question in my mind about that. But whether the election is an inhibiting factor, I'd have to make that determination after I've talked to him.

Q. You still plan to go to Brussels, though?

The President. When?

Q. I'm sorry, we still will attend the Brussels GATT meeting; we're not going to pull out on that?

The President. Well, let's wait until we finish the discussions over here and then see what we get.

Visit With U.S. Troops in Saudi Arabia

Q. Why did you ask the Members of Congress along for the Saudi Arabia stop?

The President. Well, I just think it's a good thing to have the leadership with you on a trip of this nature. They're very emotionally involved. And I think it's most appropriate that they come. And they all seemed to accept with alacrity, so I guess they have no reservations at all.

Q. Why not some of the critics which you wouldn't include among the leaders that you've invited? They've been the most support, I think. [Senator] Moynihan or——

The President. Well, I deal with the leadership. I can't deal with every Member of Congress. You've got 435 in the House, remember, Ann [Ann Compton, ABC News], and you've got 100 in the Senate. So, plenty of Congressmen go over there on their own, but the President should invite the leaders.

Q. Is there some reason why [Representative] Gephardt is not on the list for Saudi Arabia?

The President. Well, only the fact that we have two from the House and two from the Senate. But it would have been the most appropriate if—in fact, there was some discussion that if the Speaker couldn't go, then clearly Gephardt would have been——

Thank you all. See, I've exhausted your questions.

Q. Will we get another shot at you this afternoon?

The President. I doubt that.

Q. No?

The President. We don't want overexpo-

sure. You know, once—I think it was Helen [Helen Thomas, United Press International] who said we're having too many——

Q. Never. I never said that in my life.

The President. You sure?

Note: The exchange occurred while the President was en route from Prague, Czechoslovakia, to Ludwigshafen, Germany. Marlin Fitzwater was Press Secretary to the President. Earlier in the morning, the President met with members of the U.S. Embassy community and participated in a departure ceremony with national leaders at Ruzyne Airport. A tape was not available for verification of the content of this exchange.

Remarks to the Residents of Speyer, Germany
November 18, 1990

Thank you, Chancellor Kohl. And I'm delighted to be back in the Rhine country, in the beautiful village of Speyer, to be with your great Chancellor and, most of all, to be the first American President to visit the new Germany. It is also a sign of the times that just a week ago the Soviet President, Mikhail Gorbachev, walked your streets, saw your majestic cathedral, and joined with you in the celebration of German unity.

When we were here last year, Germans still lived in two societies: one free and one oppressed; one alive, the other frozen in tyranny; two very different governments, but one people, one Germany.

In May of 1989, I talked to the citizens of Mainz; and on that day, we spoke not only of our mutual defense but of our shared values, not just of the matters of the mind but of the deeper aspirations of the heart. And we heard the call for a common European home, but insisted on another home: one in which all within would be free to move from room to room, free to enjoy their right of self-determination.

I will never forget November 1989, when word came from Berlin: The wall has been breached. And soon the world was trans-

fixed by startling images, scenes of celebration and triumph as thousands of Germans joined hands across a mass of concrete that had divided your nation for far too long. That was an exciting moment, and I'm delighted today to celebrate that moment in the home area of the first Chancellor of this new Germany, Chancellor Helmut Kohl, the man who united Germany.

I'm also here because the unification of Germany is not just cause for celebration by one people; it's a cause for celebration for all who love freedom. And let me just tell you: No people on Earth are more thrilled by your achievement than your friends in America.

I see the rains are coming. [*Laughter*] So, I will conclude, mercifully, by saying thank you to all the citizens of this marvelous part of Germany. Thank you for this warm welcome for Barbara and me and, I say symbolically, for the United States of America. And thank you, Chancellor, for your words about standing together in the face of tyranny, standing together to see that aggression will not pay in this world. God bless the people of a united Germany. Thank you. God bless each and every one of you. Thank you for this warm hospitality. Good luck.

Note: The President spoke at 12:50 p.m. in the town square. Prior to his remarks, he *attended an organ recital at Speyer Cathedral. A tape was not available for verification of the content of these remarks.*

Remarks and a Question-and-Answer Session With Reporters Following a Luncheon With Chancellor Helmut Kohl in Ludwigshafen, Germany
November 18, 1990

The President. Another marvelous meal, I'll tell you that.

The Chancellor. Mr. President, Mrs. Bush, ladies and gentlemen, allow me to thank you once again very warmly for having met with me here in my home region. The weather doesn't correspond at all to the kind of mood we're in and to the overall feeling, but unfortunately, November in Germany means rain.

But the relationship between the Federal Republic of Germany and the United States of America is an excellent one; and this is due, first and foremost, to the personal involvement of President Bush. I've already said this in my short statement in front of Speyer Cathedral.

The 3d of October, 1990, the day of German unity, would not have been possible, would, indeed, have been inconceivable, without the help and support which we received from the Americans throughout the century; and we'll never forget this. Right now, over the next few years, over the next few decades, indeed, we, the united Germany, want to do our utmost in order to foster and deepen this relationship, particularly among young people. We want to promote the exchange of students, of high school students, and scientists, scholars, and this in the closest possible way. And obviously, Mr. President, I would be most pleased to see as many American companies as possible investing in the new states, the new Federal lander, which was formerly the German Democratic Republic, GDR.

I know that the President of the United States is a very busy man indeed. But if perhaps in one of your next speeches in front of the chamber of industry and commerce in the U.S. you were in a position to introduce a few remarks about the possibilities of investment in the eastern part of Germany, in what was formerly the GDR, I think that would be a very good and very beneficial thing.

Today we talked about a number of issues where we think we can help each other. We exchanged views, and we expressed agreement on the fact that we hope that the next GATT round, the Uruguay round, may be a successful one. We're going to work on that one also over the next few weeks. And we talked about the challenge to the international community in the Middle East, in Kuwait, and in Iraq.

We were in agreement here that it is very important, indeed, that the international community stand together here, stand fast in the coalition. And this on the basis of the U.N. resolutions, in the sense that we want to see respect for international law restored. And we were in agreement that it is of utmost importance to see a release of all hostages of all nationalities as soon as possible. And that this, indeed, was one of the most important prerequisites for any further talks.

We also said that it was our wish that negotiations would lead to a peaceful outcome of the situation there, but that these negotiations can only be successful if both sides want their success and if the consequences of this assault are removed.

Again, Mr. President, thank you very much for coming here. Thank you, Barbara, and with all my heart, let me wish you all the best and the best of success in your very difficult office. And may God bless you.

The President. Thank you, sir, and may we thank you and Mrs. Kohl for your hospitality. There's something very special about conducting the kind of discussions we had within the home of two friends, in a warm ambience, and in a setting that lends itself to frank and open discussions and agreement as the Chancellor's outlined. And again, we're very grateful to you for this extraordinary hospitality. Thank you all very much.

Persian Gulf Crisis

Q. Mr. President, in your prepared speech today, you said that a united Germany must take responsibility for leadership in the world. What would you like to see Germany do in the Persian Gulf crisis?

The President. I think exactly what the Chancellor says: keep the coalition together. In my view, they are fulfilling their roles. When I was talking about their leadership, clearly anybody that takes a look at the map and understands the realities of the world knows that this united Germany is, and will be, a tremendous force for peace and certainly for economic good in the world. So, I think we're together with Germany, both in the Gulf—I made no special

request of Chancellor Kohl at all. But I agree with him that this coalition is holding and should continue to hold, and thus, the best way to get a peaceful solution: send a solid signal to Saddam Hussein [President of Iraq] that his aggression will not be rewarded.

Q. Do you think you see eye to eye on the possibility of——

The President. I've read what he's said, and I think we're in very close accord here. We're not ruling out any options; we're not ruling any options in. I want to see a peaceful resolution to this question.

Q. The Chancellor, in a radio address today, warned of the consequences of military action in the Persian Gulf. Did he deliver a similar warning to you?

The President. He made very clear he'd like to see a peaceful resolution to this question, and so would I.

Note: The President spoke at 3:30 p.m. outside Chancellor Kohl's residence. Later in the afternoon, the President traveled to Paris, France. In the evening, he attended a dinner at the Palais de l'Elysée hosted by President François Mitterrand of France. Following the dinner, President Bush went to the home of the U.S. Ambassador, his residence during his stay in Paris. A tape was not available for verification of the content of these remarks.

Remarks and an Exchange With Reporters Following Discussions With Prime Minister Margaret Thatcher of the United Kingdom in Paris, France
November 19, 1990

The President. We've had a very delightful breakfast, and I want to thank the Prime Minister for coming over. Not surprisingly, we see eye to eye on matters in the Gulf. And we had an opportunity to discuss trade, the importance of getting on to a successful conclusion of the GATT round. And thank you, Prime Minister, for coming at this early hour. But once again, I've learned a lot, and I feel very comfortable that the U.K. and the United States are looking at these major problems through the same

prism.

The Prime Minister. It's been a very good breakfast meeting. We see so similarly on most things. We have the same firmness on the Gulf, the same horror that hostages are kept at all—they should be released immediately—the same firmness that if Saddam Hussein [President of Iraq] does not withdraw from Kuwait, the military option would have to be used.

We also come together on a day when—if the United States and the United Kingdom and Europe had not stayed absolutely firm in defense, we should never be in a position to sign the agreement that will be signed today. That, I think, is a very, very good message to the world to stay firm in defense, because you never know what uncertainties may arise.

On other things, you know we and the United States believe firmly in free trade. That is what gets a prosperous world. And we're deeply concerned about the GATT round. And as you know, I have done my level-best to see that Europe puts forward reasonable proposals—indeed, put forward any proposals. We're not through the difficulties yet, and it's important that the Uruguay round does succeed.

Persian Gulf Crisis

Q. Mrs. Thatcher, do you think there's going to be a war, a shooting war, in the Gulf? You have a lot of experience with the Middle East and certainly Britain's ties with Iraq. What do you think?

The Prime Minister. There will be one fair way to avoid that, and that would be for Saddam Hussein to withdraw quickly, totally.

Q. Does that answer the question?

The Prime Minister. Yes, it does.

Q. Do you think it——

The Prime Minister. If he does not, then he has to be removed by force. This is evil. The things that are going on in Kuwait are terrifying. They are brutal. And most people understand that evil has to be stopped. Either he withdraws or the military option has to be used.

Q. Mr. President, I know that you think this latest hostage offer from Saddam Hussein is a cynical manipulation of hostage families——

The President. Yes, I do.

Q. ——but could it serve in any way as a possible precursor for some kind of negotiation to get him out of Kuwait?

The President. I can't read his mind, but when you have done something as outrageously illegal as grabbing somebody's innocent civilians and holding them hostage—kidnaping them, if you will—there should be no reward for that. And he ought to have released them long ago. And he ought to release them now. And this cynicism of

starting to release them on Christmas Day will be seen by the world as a total ploy. And so, if you mean does it offer me hope that he's getting flexible, I don't think so. I think it's a cynical ploy to rally public opinion. And it is so brutal to parcel out human life in that way that I think it will backfire in terms of what he expected from it.

Q. Mr. President, en route here, President Gorbachev in Italy said he was convinced a peaceful way would be found out of this crisis. And he spoke of new ideas; the implication seeming to be new initiatives in the diplomatic front. Do you to any degree share that optimism? I know you've said you're hopeful that a peaceful way can be found, but do you share the optimism that Mr. Gorbachev appears to be expressing? And do you know anything about new ideas?

The President. I'll talk to him, but I have not seen anything to make me believe there is a new approach that fulfills the obligations entailed under the United Nations resolutions. Because there can be no compromise. You cannot reward aggression. But I will be seeing him, and Mr. Gorbachev has been very solid in support of the United Nations. So I'm anxious to know if there's something new that he's thinking of, but I can't think what it is.

Q. Could you address that question?

The Prime Minister. Saddam Hussein should obey the United Nations resolutions and withdraw immediately. What we've got now is not peace. There's no peace in Kuwait; there's evil. There is daily brutality. There is cruelty. They're shooting people because they have attempted to hide and protect foreigners in Kuwait. That is not peace. It is the worst brutality and evil. Unless he leaves, he will have to be made to leave by force. I think you just have to get the fundamentals straight. He plays with human beings as if they were pawns. Unless you stop this man, there will be no peace in the world, let alone in the Middle East.

Can I just say, the mere heads of government have to get to the conference before heads of state. [*Laughter*] So can I just——

British Conservative Party Leadership Election

Q. One British question. Are you going to survive——

Q. Are you going to survive tomorrow? Are you going to survive the political challenge?

The Prime Minister. I most earnestly believe so.

The President. Thank you all very much.

Conventional Arms Reduction in Europe

Q. I'd like another conference question, Mr. President.

The President. A what?

Q. A conference question.

Q. Can we ask you about——

The President. I'm going to take one more question, and then I'm leaving.

Q. I'd like to know if you see any irony in coming together to sign this treaty that reduces conventional arms and celebrates peace in Europe while you push this tough hard line against Saddam Hussein.

The President. I don't see any irony in it whatsoever. What I see is the fact that we're able to enter into a CFE [conventional armed forces in Europe] agreement with full cooperation and support of the Soviet Union who, heretofore, has been an enormous adversary of the West. And now this reduces to practically nil the tensions that have existed. It is the farthest reaching arms control agreement in history; and it signals the new world order that is emerging, and to some degree has emerged, and that is the best hope for rolling back the brutality and the aggression of Saddam Hussein, who has nothing to do with the CFE agreement.

So what it does is show a solidification of forces that in recent history have been on opposite sides of some of these questions. So if there's any message coming out of CFE for Saddam Hussein, it ought to be: Look what you're up against here. Here are people that since World War II have tension and, at times, conflict; and now they're together as they take a gigantic step forward in arms control. And they're together as they stand in the United Nations against your brutal, naked aggression. So, if there's any connection, that's the message that I'd like to see come out of all of this.

Persian Gulf Crisis

Q. What about the timing—doing this on the eve of the conference—is he trying to spoil or send a message——

The President. I don't know that it has anything to do with the CSCE conference, but if it is, it's to try to glom up a little support for his brutality. And I think—you heard Prime Minister Thatcher—I feel the same way. I'm sure President Mitterrand [of France] will feel the same way. So, if his move is timed to get support for him in CSCE, I think it will fail. I can't imagine anybody that has citizens held hostage by his brutality there succumbing to this siren's call of a 3-month release starting in a month and a half from now. It is so brutal and so cruel that it becomes obvious.

Q. Well, sir, do you think he's trying to buy time with this?

The President. Probably trying to buy anything—public support, time—anything. But the longer he focuses on holding innocents against their will, the more he points to his own brutality, and that's exactly what's happened here. And there is no room for compromise on what he's doing.

Q. Would you say the same thing Mrs. Thatcher just said: that if he doesn't get out, he must be forced out of Kuwait?

The President. I've already given my position. We're not ruling out any options at all.

Q. But she didn't say that. She said you must——

The President. I told you how I'd say it.

Q. Mr. President, a lot of people——

The President. We won't press ourselves——

British Conservative Party Leadership Election

Q. Did you wish Mrs. Thatcher luck?

The President. Did I what?

Q. Did you wish the Prime Minister luck?

The President. I stay out of all of this, but we have a superb relationship with Mrs. Thatcher. It is, indeed, a special relationship. And far be it from me to figure out the internal politics of a party in the United Kingdom, just as I would not like to ask her to figure out the similar problems that might exist in the Democratic Party or the Republican Party in the United States.

Q. But the special relationship would continue, would it not?

The President. The special relationship is good and strong. And I'm not going to say anything that would look like I'm trying to intervene into the proceedings over there.

Persian Gulf Crisis

Q. Mr. President, are you at all concerned that the perception seems to be that other leaders are trying to restrain you and Mrs. Thatcher? You're the only ones——

The President. No, I don't get that at all. I didn't pick that up at all. I had dinner with President Mitterrand last night. That's nonexistent.

Q. A lot of people think your buildup——

Q. What was Chancellor Kohl [of Germany] up to yesterday with his remarks about negotiating and finding a way to help Saddam Hussein ease his way out of the situation? That sounds like concessions.

The President. Listen, he can ease out fine. There will be no concession. And I agree with Chancellor Kohl that it would be nice to have a peaceful resolution to this question. That's what we've been trying to do. We're ratcheting up pressure on this man, and I hope as soon as he understands that he cannot prevail that he will do that which he did in Iran: 180 degrees and head north. That's what he ought to do.

Q. Can I ask you: Are you under pressure from these allies to reach a negotiated settlement?

The President. No, I'm under pressure from my own—what I believe in my heart: that I'd like to see a peaceful solution to this question. Most of the forces are American kids over there. And anybody feels a certain responsibility for them. I also feel a responsibility to see that this aggression does not go rewarded. So, no, I'm not under any pressure from them.

Q. A lot of people think that sending 400,000 troops—that you will feel inevitably that you have to use them.

The President. There won't have to be a shot fired in anger if he does what he's supposed to do, which is to comply fully, without condition, to the United Nations resolutions. That's the way to get the peaceful solution to this question, and that is the only way to get a peaceful solution because

it's not going to go on forever. It simply cannot go on forever and won't go on forever.

Q. Do you think he's softening?

Q. Chancellor Kohl seemed to indicate that, really, we ought to really push hard on negotiations. You don't really talk about negotiations very much.

The President. I've seen the different negotiation efforts. I've seen people try for a so-called Arab solution. And they all fall short. The reason they fall short is that, in the final analysis, Saddam Hussein tells every single person that tries to be in a negotiating role, Kuwait is a province of Iraq. That is unacceptable. That's unacceptable to the United Nations. Clearly, it is unacceptable to the United States. And that's why it fails.

You can't negotiate with a terrorist. If a person kidnaps another, should the kidnapper be given face? Should that person be given some way out so he can have a little face when he gets back into the world? The answer is no, you do not compromise with that. And therein lies the problem. And Chancellor Kohl knows that very well indeed. But do I share his aspirations for a peaceful resolution to this question? Absolutely.

Q. Mr. President, isn't that exactly why, though, it appears to undercut your effort: for you to be talking pressure, him to be talking negotiation?

The President. I talked to Chancellor Kohl for 2 hours, and as I told you yesterday, I feel totally on the same wavelength with him.

Q. Why do you suppose he gives that radio interview then and talks about negotiated settlement and you've just outlined the case why it won't work?

The President. We've talked about whether there's any way to get a negotiated settlement. But he has no—I don't think—you can ask him—he'll be around—what he means by negotiated settlement. But he does not mean compromise on these U.N. resolutions, I can guarantee you. And if somebody can find a way to talk sense to Saddam Hussein and make him do in Kuwait that which he did in Iran—turn tail 180 degrees and head east, as it was in

Iran—and do the same thing in Kuwait, so be it. He did it in Iran because he didn't want to face two fronts, I think.

But that is a reason that—some will tell you—makes it very difficult for him to do what he ought to do: get out of Kuwait. But that doesn't make the rationale, the moral underpinning, any less compelling. That rationale is there. You do not brutalize a neighbor. You do not kill and torture. You do not hold innocent civilians. You do not beleaguer an embassy and try to starve its people out in direct contravention of U.N. resolutions. And that's exactly what he's doing. And every day that goes by, it just strengthens my resolve.

Aid to the Soviet Union

Q. Mr. President, on your meeting tonight with Mr. Gorbachev, are you inclined to go along with providing some humanitarian aid to the Soviet Union?

The President. We would always be open-minded on humanitarian aid if there's a real need there. We have certain inhibitions under United States law; but if there are food shortages, for example, and the United States was in a position to help, clearly we'd want to try. And that's the right and humane thing to do as a country moves towards us and relations are greatly improved. And I would want to try to help.

But they know that we have some legal constraints under our own system of law there that prohibits our doing certain things in that regard.

Q. Do you worry about him during this bleak winter coming up?

The President. I worry about the Soviet people during the bleak winter coming up if, indeed, it proves to be as severe as some of the reports indicate. And these people are—as we travel extensively inside the Soviet Union, we Americans—and many are there now in very different numbers and in different ways than in previous times—I think there's a recognition that we want to try to help with the evolution of market systems and the change that's taking place. And you also want to help new friends if they're in jeopardy. So, I want to seek for ways to try to help, but we've got certain provisions in our laws that put constraints on me.

U.S. Embassy in Kuwait

Q. How's the food holding up in the Embassy in Kuwait?

The President. Still tuna fish. Still tuna fish.

Thank you all very much.

Note: The President spoke at 9:02 a.m. at the U.S. Ambassador's residence.

Treaty on Conventional Armed Forces in Europe
November 19, 1990

DECLARATION OF THE STATES PARTIES TO THE TREATY ON CONVENTIONAL ARMED FORCES IN EUROPE WITH RESPECT TO PERSONNEL STRENGTH

In connection with the signature of the Treaty on Conventional Armed Forces in Europe of November 19, 1990, and with a view to the follow-on negotiations referred to in Article XVIII of that Treaty, the States Parties to that Treaty declare that, for the period of these negotiations, they will not increase the total peacetime authorized personnel strength of their conventional armed forces pursuant to the Mandate in

the area of application.

DECLARATION OF THE STATES PARTIES TO THE TREATY ON CONVENTIONAL ARMED FORCES IN EUROPE WITH RESPECT TO LAND-BASED NAVAL AIRCRAFT

To promote the implementation of the Treaty on Conventional Armed Forces in Europe, the States Parties to the Treaty undertake the following political commitments outside the framework of the Treaty.

1. No one State will have in the area of

application of the treaty more than 400 permanently land-based combat naval aircraft. It is understood that this commitment applies to combat aircraft armed and equipped to engage surface or air targets and excludes types designed as maritime patrol aircraft.

2. The aggregate number of such permanently land-based combat naval aircraft held by either of the two groups of States defined under the terms of the Treaty will not exceed 430.

3. No one State will hold in its naval forces within the area of application any permanently land-based attack helicopters.

4. The limitations provided for in this Declaration will apply beginning 40 months after entry into force of the Treaty on Conventional Armed Forces in Europe.

5. This Declaration will become effective as of entry into force of the Treaty on Conventional Armed Forces in Europe.

WHITE HOUSE FACT SHEET

Today the 22 members of NATO and the Warsaw Pact signed a landmark agreement limiting conventional armed forces in Europe (CFE). The CFE treaty will establish parity in major conventional armaments between East and West in Europe from the Atlantic to the Urals. The treaty will limit the size of Soviet forces to about one third of the total armaments permitted to all the countries in Europe. The treaty includes an unprecedented monitoring regime, including detailed information exchange, on-site inspection, challenge inspection, and monitoring of destruction.

East-West Limits

The treaty sets equal ceilings from the Atlantic to the Urals on key armaments essential for conducting surprise attack and initiating large-scale offensive operations. Neither side may have more than:

20,000 tanks
20,000 artillery pieces
30,000 armored combat vehicles (ACV's)
6,800 combat aircraft
2,000 attack helicopters.

To further limit the readiness of armed forces, the treaty sets equal ceilings on equipment that may be with active units. Other ground equipment must be in designated permanent storage sites. The limits for equipment each side may have in active units are:

16,500 tanks
17,000 artillery pieces
27,300 armored combat vehicles (ACV's).

In connection with the CFE treaty, the six members of the Warsaw Pact signed a treaty in Budapest on November 3, 1990, which divides the Warsaw Pact allocation by country. The members of NATO have consulted through NATO mechanisms and have agreed on national entitlements. These national entitlements may be adjusted.

Country Ceilings

The treaty limits the proportion of armaments that can be held by any one country in Europe to about one third of the total for all countries in Europe—the "sufficiency" rule. This provision constrains the size of Soviet forces more than any other in the treaty. These limits are:

13,300 tanks
13,700 artillery pieces
20,000 armored combat vehicles (ACV's)
5,150 combat aircraft
1,500 attack helicopters.

Regional Arrangements

In addition to limits on the number of armaments in each category on each side, the treaty also includes regional limits to prevent destabilizing force concentrations of ground equipment.

Destruction

Equipment reduced to meet the ceilings must be destroyed or, in a limited number of cases, have its military capability destroyed, allowing the chassis to be used for nonmilitary purposes. After the treaty enters into force, there will be a 4-month baseline inspection period. After the 4-month baseline period, 25 percent of the destruction must be complete by the end of 1 year, 60 percent by the end of 2 years, and all destruction required by the treaty must be complete by the end of 3 years. Parties have 5 years to convert limited amounts of equipment.

Large amounts of equipment will be destroyed to meet the obligations of the CFE treaty. The Soviet Union alone will be obliged to destroy thousands of weapons, much more equipment than will be reduced by all the NATO countries combined. NATO will meet its destruction obligations by destroying its oldest equipment. In a process called "cascading," NATO members with newer equipment, including the U.S., have agreed to transfer some of this equipment to allies with older equipment. Cascading will not reduce NATO's destruction obligation. Under the cascading system, no U.S. equipment must be destroyed to meet CFE ceilings. Some 2,000 pieces of U.S. equipment will be transferred to our NATO allies.

Verification

The treaty includes unprecedented provisions for detailed information exchanges, on-site inspections, challenge inspections, and on-site monitoring of destruction. At the initiative of the U.S., NATO has established a system to cooperate in monitoring the treaty. Parties have an unlimited right to monitor the process of destruction.

The CFE treaty is of unlimited duration and will enter into force 10 days after all parties have ratified the agreement.

Note: In the morning, the Treaty on Conventional Armed Forces in Europe was signed in a ceremony in the Salle des Fêtes at the Palais de l'Elysée. The declarations and fact sheet were made available by the Office of the Press Secretary as three separate documents, but the declarations were not issued as White House press releases.

Remarks to the Conference on Security and Cooperation in Europe in Paris, France
November 19, 1990

Mr. Chairman, this is a glorious day for Europe. This morning I signed for my country an arms control agreement which ends the military confrontation that has cursed this continent for decades. This afternoon we welcome a summit document, a Charter of Paris, which expresses the common aspirations of our society. It is right that we gather here in this magnificent city, a city of civilization, to declare our hopes for the future and to mark a grand turn in the course of history.

Today we do justice to the original framers of the Helsinki Final Act. The goals they set have proven their worth, thanks to the courage of so many who dared not merely to hope but to act. We salute men of courage—Havel and Mazowiecki and Antall, here with us today, and all the other activists—who took Helsinki's goals as solemn commitments and who suffered so that these commitments would be honored. And we salute all those individuals and private groups in the West who showed that the

protection of human rights is not just the business of governments; it's everyone's business—nongovernmental organizations, the press, religious leaders, and ordinary citizens.

Their dreams are being realized before our eyes. The new democracies of central and eastern Europe have ended decades of repression to rediscover their birthright of freedom. In the Soviet Union, the seeds of democracy and human rights have found new soil. And at long last, the cruel division of Germany has come to an end. A continent frozen in hostility for so long has become a continent of revolutionary change. To assure that this change occurs in a secure framework, we've completed a conventional arms control treaty that transforms the military map of this continent. We are adopting confidence in security-building measures that will contribute to lasting peace through openness. This morning, 22 of us signed a solemn undertaking on the nonuse of force.

But today, as old political divisions disappear, other sources of tension—some ancient, some new—are emerging. National disputes persist. Abuses of minority and human rights continue. Where millions had once been denied the freedom to move, now millions feel compelled to move to escape economic or political hardship.

We are witnessing in several countries the ugly resurgence of anti-Semitism and other ethnic, racial, and religious intolerance. Bigotry and hatred have no place in civilized nations. Minorities enrich our societies. Protection of their rights is a prerequisite for stability.

Europe is entering unknown waters. The CSCE is ideally suited to help its member states navigate. We have articulated fine standards for national behavior; and now it is our task to bring CSCE down to Earth, making it part of everyday politics, building and drawing on its strength to address the new challenges. My government put forward some ideas for the future development of the CSCE earlier this year, and I hope that they contributed to the initiatives that the members of the North Atlantic alliance announced at our London summit in July. And I am pleased to see that so many of the ideas discussed there have emerged in a summit declaration that we will sign this week.

Let me highlight how we think some of these initiatives and others will help the CSCE put its principles into practice. The declaration we will sign establishes an agenda to guide our work until we meet again in Helsinki. This is important work on issues vital to all of us. The peaceful settlement of disputes, the role of minorities in our societies, the construction of democratic institutions and, most fundamental of all, enhancement of human rights.

We've also agreed that we must deepen the security of our community by extending our talks on conventional forces, expanding the benefits of confidence-building measures, and successfully concluding an agreement on "open skies."

Finally, we recognize that, as Europe mends its wounds, so CSCE can mature. We've established a framework for regular political consultations and institutions to re-inforce that framework. The Secretariat, the Office of Free Elections, and the Center for the Prevention of Conflict—let's face it, they are modest, but significant steps towards the new order we all seek. We welcome, too, the call for a new parliamentary dimension in CSCE which can give another voice to the democratic values that we all share.

Two days ago in Prague, I called on Europe and America to work in common cause toward a new commonwealth for freedom based on these shared principles: a belief in the fundamental dignity and rights of the individuals, a belief that governments can be empowered only by the people and must answer to them, a belief that individuals should be able to enjoy the fruits of their labor, and a belief that governments and nations must live by a rule of law as a prerequisite for human progress. These are the principles that guide our nations and the CSCE. And yet to secure them in our two continents, they must be secure in the world as a whole.

As we consecrate those principles here today, those same principles are grossly violated in the Persian Gulf. I'd like to quote a sentence from the joint statement issued by President Gorbachev and myself in September at Helsinki. And here's the quote: "Nothing short of complete implementation of the United Nations Security Council resolutions is acceptable."

Well, can there be room for any other view here, in a continent that has suffered so much from aggression and its companion, appeasement? The principles that have given life to CSCE, that have guided our success in Europe have no geographic limits. Our success here can be neither profound nor enduring if the rule of law is shamelessly disregarded elsewhere.

As we entered the cold war in the spring of 1947, the American Secretary of State, George Marshall—he made an important point which I'd like to quote: "Problems which bear directly on the future of our civilization cannot be disposed of by general talk or vague formulae. They require concrete solutions for definite and extremely complicated questions—questions that have to do with boundaries, with power to prevent military aggression, with people who have bitter memories with the production and control of things which are essential to the lives of millions of people."

We in the CSCE have come far in the last few months in finding those concrete solutions, and now we should build on this success here, and we should stand on it squarely everywhere.

Thank you all very much.

Note: The President spoke at 4:10 p.m. at the Kleber Center. In his remarks, he referred to Chancellor Helmut Kohl of Germany, Conference Chairman of the day; President Václav Havel of Czechoslovakia; Prime Minister Tadeusz Mazowiecki of Poland; and Prime Minister Jozsef Antall of Hungary.

Text of the Joint Declaration of Twenty-Two States
November 19, 1990

The Heads of State or Government of Belgium, Bulgaria, Canada, the Czech and Slovak Federal Republic, Denmark, France, Germany, Greece, Hungary, Iceland, Italy, Luxembourg, the Netherlands, Norway, Poland, Portugal, Romania, Spain, Turkey, the Union of Soviet Socialist Republics, the United Kingdom and the United States of America

—greatly welcoming the historic changes in Europe,
—gratified by the growing implementation throughout Europe of a common commitment to pluralist democracy, the rule of law and human rights, which are essential to lasting security on the continent,
—affirming the end of the era of division and confrontation which has lasted for more than four decades, the improvement in relations among their countries and the contribution this makes to the security of all,
—confident that the signature of the Treaty on Conventional Armed Forces in Europe represents a major contribution to the common objective of increased security and stability in Europe, and
—convinced that these developments must form part of a continuing process of co-operation in building the structures of a more united continent,

Issue the following Declaration:

1. The signatories solemnly declare that, in the new era of European relations which is beginning, they are no longer adversaries, will build new partnerships and extend to each other the hand of friendship.

2. They recall their obligations under the Charter of the United Nations and reaffirm all of their commitments under the Helsinki Final Act. They stress that all of the ten Helsinki Principles are of primary significance and that, accordingly, they will be equally and unreservedly applied, each of them being interpreted taking into account the others. In that context, they affirm their obligation and commitment to refrain from the threat or use of force against the territorial integrity or the political independence of any State, from seeking to change existing borders by threat or use of force, and from acting in any other manner inconsistent with the principles and purposes of those documents. None of their weapons will ever be used except in self-defense or otherwise in accordance with the Charter of the United Nations.

3. They recognize that security is indivisible and that the security of each of their countries is inextricably linked to the security of all the States participating in the Conference on Security and Co-operation in Europe.

4. They undertake to maintain only such military capabilities as are necessary to prevent war and provide for effective defense. They will bear in mind the relationship between military capabilities and doctrines.

5. They reaffirm that every State has the right to be or not to be a party to a treaty

of alliance.

6. They note with approval the intensification of political and military contacts among them to promote mutual understanding and confidence. They welcome in this context the positive responses made to recent proposals for new regular diplomatic liaison.

7. They declare their determination to contribute actively to conventional, nuclear and chemical arms control and disarmament agreements which enhance security and stability for all. In particular, they call for the early entry into force of the Treaty on Conventional Armed Forces in Europe and commit themselves to continue the process of strengthening peace in Europe through conventional arms control within the framework of the CSCE. They welcome the prospect of new negotiations between the United States and the Soviet Union on the reduction of their short-range nuclear forces.

8. They welcome the contribution that confidence- and security-building measures have made to lessening tensions and fully support the further development of such measures. They reaffirm the importance of the "Open Skies" initiative and their determination to bring the negotiations to a successful conclusion as soon as possible.

9. They pledge to work together with the other CSCE participating States to strengthen the CSCE process so that it can make an even greater contribution to security and stability in Europe. They recognize in particular the need to enhance political consultations among CSCE participants and to develop other CSCE mechanisms. They are convinced that the Treaty on Conventional Armed Forces in Europe and agreement on a substantial new set of CSBMs, together with new patterns of co-operation in the framework of the CSCE, will lead to increased security and thus to enduring peace and stability in Europe.

10. They believe that the preceding points reflect the deep longing of their peoples for close co-operation and mutual understanding and declare that they will work steadily for the further development of their relations in accordance with the present Declaration as well as with the principles set forth in the Helsinki Final Act.

The original of this Declaration of which the English, French, German, Italian, Russian and Spanish texts are equally authentic will be transmitted to the Government of France which will retain it in its archives. The Government of France is requested to transmit the text of the Declaration to the Secretary-General of the United Nations, with a view to its circulation to all the members of the organization as an official document of the United Nations, indicating that it is not eligible for registration under Article 102 of the Charter of the United Nations. Each of the signatory States will receive from the Government of France a true copy of this Declaration.

In witness whereof the undersigned High Representatives have subscribed their signatures below.

Note: The declaration was made available by the Office of the Press Secretary, but was not issued as a White House press release.

Exchange With Reporters Prior to a Meeting With President Mikhail Gorbachev of the Soviet Union in Paris, France
November 19, 1990

Persian Gulf Crisis

Q. Mr. Gorbachev.

President Gorbachev. Maybe we'll have something to say to you after our talk.

Q. Well, Saddam Hussein is building up his troops—200,000 more troops in Kuwait. What do you think that means? And what new ideas have you brought to the President?

President Gorbachev. You're very knowledgeable.

Q. Thank you. [*Laughter*]

President Bush. That is the new idea. [*Laughter*]

President Gorbachev. I'll say just a couple of words because it's easier for me than for the President because I think he suffers from jet lag a little more. So, I think we'll complete our understanding on a number of topics, and central to our discussion probably will be the Persian Gulf crisis. I think you must know that we're not going to change our position. We certainly will seek to resolve that situation, and we must be firm in our position in that.

Q. What is your position?

President Gorbachev. You don't know our position?

Q. Is it force or patience? President Gorbachev, is it force or patience?

President Gorbachev. Well, I think we all need patience, but that does not mean that we are going to relax, we are going to retreat. No, we are going to demand in a very resolute way. And the fact that we are working together, not only the Soviet Union and the United States but the United Nations and the whole are acting together, allows me to expect that in this very difficult crisis, resolutions will be found. And we will not waste time.

President Bush. We've got one more wave.

Q. Will there be a press conference afterwards?

President Bush. Not me. I had one this morning.

Q. President Bush, are you satisfied with what President Gorbachev——

President Bush. I'm looking forward to these consultations, and I'm very pleased with the way the Soviet Union and the United States have worked together at the United Nations. We'll continue to—to be very open lines of communication, and I have no reason to be anything other than very satisfied.

Thank you all very much.

Soviet Union-U.S. Relations

[*At this point, a reporter asked a question in Russian, and a translation was not provided.*]

President Gorbachev. By the way, I tried to speak to that in my speech, and I showed that without the kind of U.S.-Soviet relationship as exists now nothing positive would have happened in Europe and in the world. That has not diminished the role of the—but that's the reality.

President Bush. And inasmuch as you mentioned my name, I totally agree with that. And what's been lost today because events in other parts of the world is the significance of this meeting here in Paris, and it was historic. And President Gorbachev is correct. The fact that the Soviet Union and the United States could work together not only to achieve an arms control agreement but to start looking into the future with harmony and in cooperation is very, very promising for the new world order, for a Europe whole and free, and for peace in the world. So, somehow that's been lost today, given the understandable concerns about the Persian Gulf. But I'm glad you asked it because it is a highly significant point.

And thank you all very much.

U.S. Role in European Affairs

[*At this point, a reporter asked a question in Russian, and a translation was not provided.*]

President Gorbachev. At this meeting, I don't think that the United States is, so to say, passing the ruling to others. The United States here is a participant who will continue to participate in all European matters; and that's, I think, the only way that is possible, that is conceivable, in European—and he has an understanding——

President Bush. There's only one problem in all of this. That is you get a little jet lag when you have to come from Washington, DC. It's easier for you. [*Laughter*]

Thank you all very much.

Note: The exchange took place in the afternoon at the U.S. Ambassador's residence. Saddam Hussein was President of Iraq. A tape was not available for verification of the content of this exchange.

Statement by Press Secretary Fitzwater on President Bush's Meetings With President Turgut Özal of Turkey and Prime Minister Tadeusz Mazowiecki of Poland
November 20, 1990

Özal

President Bush held a wide-ranging discussion for approximately 1 hour with President Özal of Turkey this afternoon, with particular attention to the Persian Gulf. Their discussion was characterized by the same close cooperation that we have enjoyed with Turkey. President Bush noted that Turkey is showing real leadership in the international response to Iraq's aggression against Kuwait and that the United States is committed to helping Turkey to deal with the effects of that situation on Turkey.

President Bush accepted President Özal's previous invitation to pay a state visit to Turkey in the first part of 1991. President Bush's visit will symbolize the particularly close ties between the United States and Turkey and is intended to contribute to a continuation of the excellent relations between the two countries. President Bush and President Özal agreed to confirm a date for the meeting soon. The last Ameri-can President to visit Turkey was President Eisenhower in 1959.

Mazowiecki

President Bush met for approximately 20 minutes with Polish Prime Minister Mazowiecki. They discussed the Polish debt situation, and President Bush stated the U.S. concerns and understanding of this matter and noted that the United States will be addressing it seriously. Prime Minister Mazowiecki reemphasized Polish support of the United Nations Gulf policy and stated that Poland will shortly be sending a hospital ship and a rescue ship to the area. President Bush expressed his gratitude for the Polish effort in support of the international community's stand against the Iraqi aggression in Kuwait. President Bush reiterated the need for the international community to continue in its firm resolve against the Iraqi aggression so that Saddam Hussein [President of Iraq] fully recognizes he has no choice but to comply with the United Nations resolutions.

Exchange With Reporters Prior to a Meeting With Prime Minister Constantine Mitsotakis of Greece in Paris, France
November 21, 1990

Persian Gulf Crisis

Q. Mr. President, did you have a breakthrough with President Gorbachev on the Persian Gulf in terms of a resolution you're seeking? Do you think there's been a little give there?

The President. Helen [Helen Thomas, United Press International], I've said all along—and please go back and look at it—that we're on the same wavelength with the Soviet Union. And I still feel that way—same wavelength in regard to the United Nations. So, I won't go beyond that. But I feel I've been consistent here, and I feel the Soviets have been consistent.

Q. Well, there seems to be a little more optimism since yesterday, since Baker's talks.

The President. Well, I've been optimistic all along. We're on the same wavelength; that's the only point I'm trying to make. I think that we're in good synchronization with them and with many other countries as we face the problems of the Gulf. And I might say that the Greeks have been totally on board and understanding about our collective objectives in the Gulf, and I'm very grateful to them.

President's Visit to Greece

Q. You're going there in January?

The President. I hope to be going to Greece early in the year, yes. I don't know that I'm getting ahead of the groove, but I'll tell you that I want very much to do that. And I don't know the exact date, but I know you asked me, and I'm looking forward to my first visit there as President. I've been there several other times, of course.

Persian Gulf Crisis

Q. Are you setting a deadline, sir, for the Iraqis to get out of Kuwait?

The President. We'll just watch the way all of this develops. Everybody is convinced they must get out of Kuwait with no concessions, and that's what's emerging here. Some people have been writing the story one way, and some writing it another. All that I understand. But please understand we are on the same wavelength with the Soviet Union and almost all the others on the Security Council, and certainly with countries like Greece and others around the world who may not be on the Security Council. But know what it means when aggression comes along, and know that we have to reverse this aggression that is brutalizing the people of Kuwait, the hostages in Iraq. And indeed, I haven't lessened my concerns about the United States Embassy in Kuwait.

I'm not sure the American people have focused on the fact that Saddam Hussein continues to violate the United Nations resolution and continues to try to starve out our Embassy in Kuwait. But all of these points—whether it's hostages in Iraq, whether it's an Embassy in Kuwait, whether it's the aggression itself—it seems that on all of those points we have agreement with most of the people—if not all—that I've talked to here at the CSCE. So, I leave Paris feeling that we are still together as countries that want to see this aggression reversed and want to see this man unilaterally, without condition get out of Kuwait.

People are beginning to see the cynicism, his brutality, the way he plays around with the lives of the hostages. It is brutal. It is cruel. And I didn't see one single country here that had anything other than condemnation of that kind of behavior. And I talked to almost everybody that sat around that table.

Q. Again, sir, though, is there a deadline——

The President. Listen, I've got a lot of business to do with my good friend.

Note: The exchange began at 8 a.m. in the Drawing Room at the U.S. Embassy. In his remarks, the President referred to talks between Secretary of State James A. Baker III and Soviet Foreign Minister Eduard Shevardnadze. Saddam Hussein was President of Iraq. A tape was not available for verification of the content of these remarks.

Remarks and a Question-and-Answer Session With Reporters in Paris, France
November 21, 1990

The President. We're going to have a statement on what transpired here in the CSCE talks. And really, the first sentence, although written in the past tense, says it all: that in signing the Charter of Paris this morning, we have closed a chapter of history. I'm about to sign this, and we are closing a chapter in history. The cold war is

over, and now we move on to working with the various countries in the CSCE and others for a peaceful and stable Europe.

And so, I've been very pleased with that part of the agenda. I commend those who worked hard on the CFE [conventional armed forces in Europe] treaty. It's been lost because of understandable interest in the Gulf, but it was the most significant arms control treaty perhaps in history.

And we've had a lot of active bilateral talks. Secretary Baker, who is with us, has had extensive consultations. And the mood with the CSCE partners I think is very positive.

And then I would comment on the Gulf—as I did in there—that we're together. One thing to note is that the countries of Eastern Europe, against whom force and aggression was used in the past, are as solid, if not more solid, than anybody in terms of support for what the United States and others are trying to do in the Gulf. It is very moving when you hear a Václav Havel or the Polish delegation talking about the need to have the United Nations resolutions against Iraq complied with in their entirety. No compromise! The Greek Prime Minister just left—solid as a rock, strongly in support. And of course, you know how the Turks feel.

And so, this was very encouraging to me that the world is still strongly together. And member after member came up to me and said: Thank God for the United States leadership in standing up against this aggression. And it just happened all the time.

So, that subject was in every corridor, in every bilateral discussion, on everybody's mind. And yet things are holding together very well indeed. I can understand when Saddam Hussein takes a propaganda move everybody starts writing, well, the coalition is coming apart, or he may divide the support. It's not happening. The coalition is together. The support is not getting divided. And people are seeing more clearly that Saddam Hussein's aggression cannot pay off and that whatever steps are necessary to support fully, without compromise, the United Nations resolutions must be taken. And so, I'm encouraged, very encouraged, about this holding together of a coalition that's in the sands and on the seas of the Gulf and in terms of the support from countries across the board that may not be there in physical presence.

Persian Gulf Crisis

Q. Are you seeking a resolution from the U.N. to authorize the use of military force if needed? And I'd like to follow it up.

The President. Go ahead. Or do you want me—do you want an answer first?

Q. Okay. We've gotten a lot of statements that really take an English interpreter to find out what you and the Soviets are really saying.

The President. Exactly. And I can understand your frustration about that, but when you're dealing with the technicalities of diplomacy and each is trying to understand where the other heartbeat is—I can only tell you that we are together with the Soviet Union. The process is going forward properly. There have not been the diversions that I have read about. The reception with Mr. Gorbachev, the reception we had here, and the dinner and the meeting I had were—the last word I would use to describe them was "chilly." And I read that in several places in the American headlines. It wasn't chilly.

Gorbachev told me last night that in his view it was the best meeting we've had. And I've felt that way from the very beginning. And it was frank and open and, I think, in broad agreement. And so, I want to lay that one to rest because it really was relaxing. Anybody that was at the dinner can tell you that there's never been a more relaxed occasion. And that stemmed from the fact that Jim Baker and Shevardnadze had hammered out a lot of the difficulties, and Gorbachev and I saw eye to eye on these issues.

Now in terms of timing and what we might do at the United Nations, sometimes we can't be quite as forthcoming as you would understandably like, but more important than trying for me to get some headline is to have the process go forward properly. And that's exactly what is happening. It's extensive consultation. But let me just sum it up, Helen [Helen Thomas, United Press International]. I leave Paris in a few hours feeling not only are we together with the Soviet Union but that we are together with most of the members of the Security Council, and certainly together with the CSCE members.

Q. Well, on the first part of the question: Are you seeking a resolution—what stage are you in?

The President. I'm just working carefully

with the process, and I'm not directly responding to your question because more important than the headline that would come from the question is that we get the results we want. And I would just leave it there and please ask your understanding that when you're trying to hold a coalition together and trying to take collective action it requires some behind-the-scenes discussions and negotiation. But I can sum it up for you to say that—well, put it this way: What came out of the Baker-Shevardnadze meeting really says it all. And I'd leave it right there. But that I would characterize as saying, things are on track. But I can't go into every behind-the-scene detail. I certainly understand your wanting to know about them, but there are some things—to get them done you have to have all the diplomacy done behind the scenes.

Yes, Brit [Brit Hume, ABC News]?

Q. Mr. President, are you not concerned that this phased release of hostages which Saddam Hussein has announced he will do would interfere with any effort you might undertake to have sterner measures against him during the very time when a series of hostage releases is underway, particularly in the eyes of other leaders and European leaders?

The President. No, because I believe that that cynical dealing of human life, parceling out lives from Christmas to March, has backfired on Saddam Hussein. I think people have seen it as a cynical, cruel ploy. And every person I talked to at the CSCE meeting summarized it that way. So, I don't see it working the way he wants. And the way he wants is to divide the coalition, hand over human life here or there to some visitor and try to undermine not just what the United States is doing but what the whole coalition is doing.

So, I don't see it with any downside. When it first came out I wondered a little bit. I saw it as a cynical ploy, and I wasn't quite sure how others would see it. But I'm telling you I talked to a lot of people yesterday, and I don't know whether Jim got the same reaction, but it was universally condemnatory. And they said this is just another cynical ploy by an embattled dictator who's trying to drive wedges between us and the rest of the world, and it will not

succeed. And it hasn't altered my view of what I might or might not do in one single way.

Q. Mr. President, it's been widely reported that there is some sort of a deadline that you're trying to reach an agreement on for Iraq to get out of Kuwait. Is that correct?

The President. Well, the deadline should have been the day the U.N. passed its first resolution or, in my view, the day he first went in. But I have no specific deadline in mind. But we are just going to keep ratcheting up that pressure until the man does what he should have done long ago. And so, I can't help you on a specific deadline at this point.

Q. Mr. President, you spoke with some passion in there about the condition of the people at the Embassy in Kuwait. What is the condition of the people at the Embassy in Kuwait, and what might you be able to do about it?

The President. Well, the condition is that they are still in a beleaguered state. Americans are in there, in an embassy that is supposed to be sacrosanct. And it is being violated. The people are being—the attempt by Saddam Hussein to starve them out in face of a United Nations resolution that calls for replenishment is getting nothing but hatred, more hatred for Saddam Hussein, around the world, because other people see our Embassy in this beleaguered state and say: Well, what will happen to my Embassy tomorrow?

There's a precedent here that transcends the Gulf. And so in terms of how people look at the problem, there's a universal condemnation of what he is doing. In terms of how long the people can last, I don't know the answer to that. I know at first, the first reports we got were sometime in November, but then they discovered a little new water supply that apparently can be purified. So I can't give you a specific time, but I think the time has slipped into December some, hasn't it, Jim? But leave it in a very general way, but I know it's not within the next few days that they have to pull down the flag.

Q. Is he going to succeed in starving them out?

The President. The answer is: Not if I can

do anything about it.

Q. What can you do about it?

The President. Well, I guess the last thing that would be productive would be to say what I might do about it.

Q. Mr. President, you referred to the meeting with Secretary Baker and Shevardnadze. What exactly did they agree to?

The President. Well, I'll let the Secretary talk to that after I finish, which I'm about to do, but let him talk about it. But I think what you're seeing is the relationship in its real light, after the Baker-Shevardnadze story, because what I thought came out wrong yesterday was great divisions between Gorbachev and me on how we're looking at the next steps to get Saddam Hussein to turn around this aggression. And I think the major thing that came out of the Baker-Shevardnadze meeting was kind of: Look, we are together; we are working together. And if we have differences—and I would think if we did they would be extraordinarily minor—that they can be resolved.

But we are on the same wavelength. We are together. And that's what I saw coming out of Jim's meeting. Just as it was the result of the Gorbachev-Bush meeting.

Q. Do you think there's a chance that U.N. action could be taken this month?

The President. Well, I would just say stay tuned, because we're doing an awful lot of diplomatic work behind the scenes; other countries are doing diplomatic work behind the scenes. And I'd say certainly there's a chance, but I can't give you dates or time or what the resolution would contain because more important to me than to get a splash peak of interest is to see that it works out properly.

This is the last one, and then I really do have to head on over to the——

Q. Thank you, Mr. President. A couple of questions about the next stop in Saudi Arabia? First of all, what do you hope to accomplish there in your meetings and in your visits with the troops? And secondly, we've had a lot of questions from people back home about concerns for your safety while you're over there. What can you say to that?

The President. Let me answer the second part first. I have never felt more secure in going anyplace than I do in going to see our troops over there. There's a lot of young men and women there who I think are looking forward to the visit, and I think my own personal safety and Barbara's is just guaranteed. It really doesn't enter my mind at all. And so, it is not a risky mission, in my view, not in the least. And I'd tell you if I felt any tremors, and I don't.

I remember when we went down to Cartagena, people were saying: Well, this was rather dangerous. Well, even there I felt secure. I think that was vindicated by the result. So, let me just assure people who are concerned that there is no risk, and I feel very, very comfortable about that.

And then, why? It's Thanksgiving, and gosh, we have a lot to be thankful for at this time of year—this particular year, too. And so, I will be trying as best I can, right from the heart, to express my thanks to the young men and women that are serving over there. It is a time for prayer; it is a time when we all thank God for our blessings. And I will try through this visit, perhaps only symbolically, to tell every single man and woman over there that we thank them and we thank God for the blessings that we have and that we are going to prevail. They're not there on a mission impossible.

The very fact that they are there in these numbers offers the best chance for a peaceful resolution to this crisis. And I'll be telling them that, and I'll be saying: Thank you. Thank you from this grateful heart. And I know I speak for all the American people on this one. I don't care where they're coming from on resolutions or whether the President is moving too slow or whether he's moving too fast. If I do nothing else, I will convey to them the heartfelt thanks of the American people at this very special time of year for Americans.

Thank you all so much.

Prime Minister Margaret Thatcher of the United Kingdom

Q. Mr. President, a non-Gulf question.

The President. There is no such thing as non-Gulf.

Q. Did you speak to Mrs. Thatcher last night?

The President. I did.

Q. What did you say to her?

The President. Well, I said, how's it going? [*Laughter*]

Q. And what did she say to you?

The President. That's a different matter. [*Laughter*] No, she seemed very determined. Nobody ever said she was anything other than that.

Q. And she didn't seem down?

The President. No. I'll tell you, to show up there in the wake of a traumatic election process, during a traumatic election process of this nature, I thought in itself showed her fiber and her steel. And she couldn't have been more pleasant. Barbara had more chance to talk to her than I did. There was a lot of standing around there, and we—said they walked in together. But I think we both felt that she was determined. And I respect her. A lot of people might have said it's been too traumatic a day and gone to the hotel, but not Margaret Thatcher.

Thank you.

Note: The President spoke in the morning at the U.S. Ambassador's residence. In his remarks, he referred to President Václav Havel of Czechoslovakia, Prime Minister Constantine Mitsotakis of Greece, President Saddam Hussein of Iraq, and Soviet Foreign Minister Eduard Shevardnadze.

Text of the Charter of Paris for a New Europe
November 21, 1990

A New Era of Democracy, Peace and Unity

We, the Heads of State or Government of the States participating in the Conference on Security and Co-operation in Europe, have assembled in Paris at a time of profound change and historic expectations. The era of confrontation and division of Europe has ended. We declare that henceforth our relations will be founded on respect and co-operation.

Europe is liberating itself from the legacy of the past. The courage of men and women, the strength of the will of the peoples and the power of the ideas of the Helsinki Final Act have opened a new era of democracy, peace and unity in Europe.

Ours is a time for fulfilling the hopes and expectations our peoples have cherished for decades: steadfast commitment to democracy based on human rights and fundamental freedoms; prosperity through economic liberty and social justice; and equal security for all our countries.

The Ten Principles of the Final Act will guide us towards this ambitious future, just as they have lighted our way towards better relations for the past fifteen years. Full implementation of all CSCE commitments must form the basis for the initiatives we are now taking to enable our nations to live in accordance with their aspirations.

Human Rights, Democracy and Rule of Law

We undertake to build, consolidate and strengthen democracy as the only system of government of our nations. In this endeavour, we will abide by the following:

Human rights and fundamental freedoms are the birthright of all human beings, are inalienable and are guaranteed by law. Their protection and promotion is the first responsibility of government. Respect for them is an essential safeguard against an over-mighty State. Their observance and full exercise are the foundation of freedom, justice and peace.

Democratic government is based on the will of the people, expressed regularly through free and fair elections. Democracy has as its foundation respect for the human person and the rule of law. Democracy is the best safeguard of freedom of expression, tolerance of all groups of society, and equality of opportunity for each person.

Democracy, with its representative and pluralist character, entails accountability to the electorate, the obligation of public authorities to comply with the law and justice administered impartially. No one will be above the law.

We affirm that, without discrimination,

every individual has the right to:

freedom of thought, conscience and religion or belief,
freedom of expression,
freedom of association and peaceful assembly,
freedom of movement;

no one will be:

subject to arbitrary arrest or detention,
subject to torture or other cruel, inhuman or degrading treatment or punishment;

everyone also has the right:

to know and act upon his rights,
to participate in free and fair elections,
to fair and public trial if charged with an offence,
to own property alone or in association and to exercise individual enterprise,
to enjoy his economic, social and cultural rights.

We affirm that the ethnic, cultural, linguistic and religious identity of national minorities will be protected and that persons belonging to national minorities have the right freely to express, preserve and develop that identity without any discrimination and in full equality before the law.

We will ensure that everyone will enjoy recourse to effective remedies, national or international, against any violation of his rights.

Full respect for these precepts is the bedrock on which we will seek to construct the new Europe.

Our States will co-operate and support each other with the aim of making democratic gains irreversible.

Economic Liberty and Responsibility

Economic liberty, social justice and environmental responsibility are indispensable for prosperity.

The free will of the individual, exercised in democracy and protected by the rule of law, forms the necessary basis for successful economic and social development. We will promote economic activity which respects and upholds human dignity.

Freedom and political pluralism are necessary elements in our common objective of developing market economies towards sustainable economic growth, prosperity, social justice, expanding employment and efficient use of economic resources. The success of the transition to market economy by countries making efforts to this effect is important and in the interest of us all. It will enable us to share a higher level of prosperity which is our common objective. We will co-operate to this end.

Preservation of the environment is a shared responsibility of all our nations. While supporting national and regional efforts in this field, we must also look to the pressing need for joint action on a wider scale.

Friendly Relations among Participating States

Now that a new era is dawning in Europe, we are determined to expand and strengthen friendly relations and co-operation among the States of Europe, the United States of America and Canada, and to promote friendship among our peoples.

To uphold and promote democracy, peace and unity in Europe, we solemnly pledge our full commitment to the Ten Principles of the Helsinki Final Act. We affirm the continuing validity of the Ten Principles and our determination to put them into practice. All the Principles apply equally and unreservedly, each of them being interpreted taking into account the others. They form the basis for our relations.

In accordance with our obligations under the Charter of the United Nations and commitments under the Helsinki Final Act, we renew our pledge to refrain from the threat or use of force against the territorial integrity or political independence of any State, or from acting in any other manner inconsistent with the principles or purposes of those documents. We recall that non-compliance with obligations under the Charter of the United Nations constitutes a violation of international law.

We reaffirm our commitment to settle disputes by peaceful means. We decide to develop mechanisms for the prevention and resolution of conflicts among the participating States.

With the ending of the division of Europe, we will strive for a new quality in our security relations while fully respecting each other's freedom of choice in that respect. Security is indivisible and the security of every participating State is inseparably linked to that of all the others. We therefore pledge to co-operate in strengthening confidence and security among us and in promoting arms control and disarmament.

We welcome the Joint Declaration of Twenty-Two States on the improvement of their relations.

Our relations will rest on our common adherence to democratic values and to human rights and fundamental freedoms. We are convinced that in order to strengthen peace and security among our States, the advancement of democracy, and respect for and effective exercise of human rights, are indispensable. We reaffirm the equal rights of peoples and their right to self-determination in conformity with the Charter of the United Nations and with the relevant norms of international law, including those relating to territorial integrity of States.

We are determined to enhance political consultation and to widen co-operation to solve economic, social, environmental, cultural and humanitarian problems. This common resolve and our growing interdependence will help to overcome the mistrust of decades, to increase stability and to build a united Europe.

We want Europe to be a source of peace, open to dialogue and to co-operation with other countries, welcoming exchanges and involved in the search for common responses to the challenges of the future.

Security

Friendly relations among us will benefit from the consolidation of democracy and improved security.

We welcome the signature of the Treaty on Conventional Armed Forces in Europe by twenty-two participating States, which will lead to lower levels of armed forces. We endorse the adoption of a substantial new set of Confidence- and Security-building Measures which will lead to increased transparency and confidence among all participating States. These are important steps towards enhanced stability and security in Europe.

The unprecedented reduction in armed forces resulting from the Treaty on Conventional Armed Forces in Europe, together with new approaches to security and co-operation within the CSCE process, will lead to a new perception of security in Europe and a new dimension in our relations. In this context we fully recognize the freedom of States to choose their own security arrangements.

Unity

Europe whole and free is calling for a new beginning. We invite our peoples to join in this great endeavour.

We note with great satisfaction the Treaty on the Final Settlement with respect to Germany signed in Moscow on 12 September 1990 and sincerely welcome the fact that the German people have united to become one State in accordance with the principles of the Final Act of the Conference on Security and Co-operation in Europe and in full accord with their neighbours. The establishment of the national unity of Germany is an important contribution to a just and lasting order of peace for a united, democratic Europe aware of its responsibility for stability, peace and co-operation.

The participation of both North American and European States is a fundamental characteristic of the CSCE; it underlies its past achievements and is essential to the future of the CSCE process. An abiding adherence to shared values and our common heritage are the ties which bind us together. With all the rich diversity of our nations, we are united in our commitment to expand our co-operation in all fields. The challenges confronting us can only be met by common action, co-operation and solidarity.

The CSCE and the World

The destiny of our nations is linked to that of all other nations. We support fully the United Nations and the enhancement of its role in promoting international peace, security and justice. We reaffirm our commitment to the principles and purposes of the United Nations as enshrined in the Charter and condemn all violations of these principles. We recognize with satisfaction the growing role of the United Nations in world affairs and its increasing effectiveness, fostered by the improvement in relations among our States.

Aware of the dire needs of a great part of the world, we commit ourselves to solidarity with all other countries. Therefore, we issue a call from Paris today to all the nations of the world. We stand ready to join with any and all States in common efforts to protect and advance the community of fundamental human values.

GUIDELINES FOR THE FUTURE

Proceeding from our firm commitment to the full implementation of all CSCE principles and provisions, we now resolve to give a new impetus to a balanced and comprehensive development of our co-operation in order to address the needs and aspirations of our peoples.

Human Dimension

We declare our respect for human rights and fundamental freedoms to be irrevocable. We will fully implement and build upon the provisions relating to the human dimension of the CSCE.

Proceeding from the Document of the Copenhagen Meeting of the Conference on the Human Dimension, we will co-operate to strengthen democratic institutions and to promote the application of the rule of law. To that end, we decide to convene a seminar of experts in Oslo from 4 to 15 November 1991.

Determined to foster the rich contribution of national minorities to the life of our societies, we undertake further to improve their situation. We reaffirm our deep conviction that friendly relations among our peoples, as well as peace, justice, stability and democracy, require that the ethnic, cultural, linguistic and religious identity of national minorities be protected and conditions for the promotion of that identity be created. We declare that questions related to national minorities can only be satisfactorily resolved in a democratic political framework. We further acknowledge that the rights of persons belonging to national minorities must be fully respected as part of universal human rights. Being aware of the urgent need for increased co-operation on, as well as better protection of, national minorities, we decide to convene a meeting of experts on national minorities to be held in Geneva from 1 to 19 July 1991.

We express our determination to combat all forms of racial and ethnic hatred, anti-semitism, xenophobia and discrimination against anyone as well as persecution on religious and ideological grounds.

In accordance with our CSCE commitments, we stress that free movement and contacts among our citizens as well as the free flow of information and ideas are crucial for the maintenance and development of free societies and flourishing cultures. We welcome increased tourism and visits among our countries.

The human dimension mechanism has proved its usefulness, and we are consequently determined to expand it to include new procedures involving, *inter alia*, the services of experts or a roster of eminent persons experienced in human rights issues which could be raised under the mechanism. We shall provide, in the context of the mechanism, for individuals to be involved in the protection of their rights. Therefore, we undertake to develop further our commitments in this respect, in particular at the Moscow Meeting of the Conference on the Human Dimension, without prejudice to obligations under existing international instruments to which our States may be parties.

We recognize the important contribution of the Council of Europe to the promotion of human rights and the principles of democracy and the rule of law as well as to the development of cultural co-operation. We welcome moves by several participating States to join the Council of Europe and adhere to its European Convention on Human Rights. We welcome as well the readiness of the Council of Europe to make its experience available to the CSCE.

Security

The changing political and military environment in Europe opens new possibilities for common efforts in the field of military security. We will build on the important achievements attained in the Treaty on Conventional Armed Forces in Europe and in the Negotiations on Confidence- and Security-building Measures. We undertake to continue the CSBM negotiations under the same mandate, and to seek to conclude them no later than the Follow-up Meeting of the CSCE to be held in Helsinki in 1992. We also welcome the decision of the participating States concerned to continue the CFE negotiation under the same mandate and to seek to conclude it no later than the Helsinki Follow-up Meeting. Following a period for national preparations, we look forward to a more structured co-operation among all participating States on security matters, and to discussions and consultations among the thirty-four participating States aimed at establishing by 1992, from the conclusion of the Helsinki Follow-up Meeting, new negotiations on disarmament and confidence and security building open to all participating States.

We call for the earliest possible conclusion of the Convention on an effectively verifiable, global and comprehensive ban on chemical weapons, and we intend to be original signatories to it.

We reaffirm the importance of the Open Skies initiative and call for the successful conclusion of the negotiations as soon as possible.

Although the threat of conflict in Europe has diminished, other dangers threaten the stability of our societies. We are determined to co-operate in defending democratic institutions against activities which violate the independence, sovereign equality or territorial integrity of the participating States. These include illegal activities involving outside pressure, coercion and subversion.

We unreservedly condemn, as criminal, all acts, methods and practices of terrorism and express our determination to work for its eradication both bilaterally and through multilateral co-operation. We will also join together in combating illicit trafficking in drugs.

Being aware that an essential complement to the duty of States to refrain from the threat or use of force is the peaceful settlement of disputes, both being essential factors for the maintenance and consolida-

tion of international peace and security, we will not only seek effective ways of preventing, through political means, conflicts which may yet emerge, but also define, in conformity with international law, appropriate mechanisms for the peaceful resolution of any disputes which may arise. Accordingly, we undertake to seek new forms of co-operation in this area, in particular a range of methods for the peaceful settlement of disputes, including mandatory third-party involvement. We stress that full use should be made in this context of the opportunity of the Meeting on the Peaceful Settlement of Disputes which will be convened in Valletta at the beginning of 1991. The Council of Ministers for Foreign Affairs will take into account the Report of the Valletta Meeting.

Economic Co-operation

We stress that economic co-operation based on market economy constitutes an essential element of our relations and will be instrumental in the construction of a prosperous and united Europe. Democratic institutions and economic liberty foster economic and social progress, as recognized in the Document of the Bonn Conference on Economic Co-operation, the results of which we strongly support.

We underline that co-operation in the economic field, science and technology is now an important pillar of the CSCE. The participating States should periodically review progress and give new impulses in these fields.

We are convinced that our overall economic co-operation should be expanded, free enterprise encouraged and trade increased and diversified according to GATT rules. We will promote social justice and progress and further the welfare of our peoples. We recognize in this context the importance of effective policies to address the problem of unemployment.

We reaffirm the need to continue to support democratic countries in transition towards the establishment of market economy and the creation of the basis for self-sustained economic and social growth, as already undertaken by the Group of twenty-four countries. We further underline the necessity of their increased integration, involving the acceptance of disciplines as well as benefits, into the international economic and financial system.

We consider that increased emphasis on economic co-operation within the CSCE process should take into account the interests of developing participating States.

We recall the link between respect for and promotion of human rights and fundamental freedoms and scientific progress. Co-operation in the field of science and technology will play an essential role in economic and social development. Therefore, it must evolve towards a greater sharing of appropriate scientific and technological information and knowledge with a view to overcoming the technological gap which exists among the participating States. We further encourage the participating States to work together in order to develop human potential and the spirit of free enterprise.

We are determined to give the necessary impetus to co-operation among our States in the fields of energy, transport and tourism for economic and social development. We welcome, in particular, practical steps to create optimal conditions for the economic and rational development of energy resources, with due regard for environmental considerations.

We recognize the important role of the European Community in the political and economic development of Europe. International economic organizations such as the United Nations Economic Commission for Europe (ECE), the Bretton Woods Institutions, the Organisation for Economic Co-operation and Development (OECD), the European Free Trade Association (EFTA) and the International Chamber of Commerce (ICC) also have a significant task in promoting economic co-operation, which will be further enhanced by the establishment of the European Bank for Reconstruction and Development (EBRD). In order to pursue our objectives, we stress the necessity for effective co-ordination of the activities of these organizations and emphasize the need to find methods for all our States to take part in these activities.

Environment

We recognize the urgent need to tackle the problems of the environment and the importance of individual and co-operative efforts in this area. We pledge to intensify our endeavours to protect and improve our environment in order to restore and maintain a sound ecological balance in air, water and soil. Therefore, we are determined to make full use of the CSCE as a framework for the formulation of common environmental commitments and objectives, and thus to pursue the work reflected in the Report of the Sofia Meeting on the Protection of the Environment.

We emphasize the significant role of a well-informed society in enabling the public and individuals to take initiatives to improve the environment. To this end, we commit ourselves to promoting public awareness and education on the environment as well as the public reporting of the environmental impact of policies, projects and programmes.

We attach priority to the introduction of clean and low-waste technology, being aware of the need to support countries which do not yet have their own means for appropriate measures.

We underline that environmental policies should be supported by appropriate legislative measures and administrative structures to ensure their effective implementation.

We stress the need for new measures providing for the systematic evaluation of compliance with the existing commitments and, moreover, for the development of more ambitious commitments with regard to notification and exchange of information about the state of the environment and potential environmental hazards. We also welcome the creation of the European Environment Agency (EEA).

We welcome the operational activities, problem-oriented studies and policy reviews in various existing international organizations engaged in the protection of the environment, such as the United Nations Environment Programme (UNEP), the United Nations Economic Commission for Europe (ECE) and the Organisation for Economic Co-operation and Development (OECD). We emphasize the need for strengthening their co-operation and for their efficient co-ordination.

Culture

We recognize the essential contribution of our common European culture and our shared values in overcoming the division of the continent. Therefore, we underline our attachment to creative freedom and to the protection and promotion of our cultural and spiritual heritage, in all its richness and diversity.

In view of the recent changes in Europe, we stress the increased importance of the Cracow Symposium and we look forward to its consideration of guidelines for intensified co-operation in the field of culture. We invite the Council of Europe to contribute to this Symposium.

In order to promote greater familiarity amongst our peoples, we favour the establishment of cultural centres in cities of other participating States as well as increased co-operation in the audio-visual field and wider exchange in music, theatre, literature and the arts.

We resolve to make special efforts in our national policies to promote better understanding, in particular among young people, through cultural exchanges, co-operation in all fields of education and, more specifically, through teaching and training in the languages of other participating States. We intend to consider first results of this action at the Helsinki Follow-up Meeting in 1992.

Migrant Workers

We recognize that the issues of migrant workers and their families legally residing in host countries have economic, cultural and social aspects as well as their human dimension. We reaffirm that the protection and promotion of their rights, as well as the implementation of relevant international obligations, is our common concern.

Mediterranean

We consider that the fundamental political changes that have occurred in Europe have a positive relevance to the Mediterranean region. Thus, we will continue efforts to strengthen security and co-operation in the Mediterranean as an important factor for stability in Europe. We welcome the Report of the Palma de Mallorca Meeting on the Mediterranean, the results of which we all support.

We are concerned with the continuing tensions in the region, and renew our determination to intensify efforts towards finding just, viable and lasting solutions, through peaceful means, to outstanding crucial problems, based on respect for the principles of the Final Act.

We wish to promote favourable conditions for a harmonious development and diversification of relations with the non-participating Mediterranean States. Enhanced co-operation with these States will be pursued with the aim of promoting economic and social development and thereby enhancing stability in the region. To this end, we will strive together with these countries towards a substantial narrowing of the prosperity gap between Europe and its Mediterranean neighbours.

Non-governmental Organizations

We recall the major role that non-governmental organizations, religious and other groups and individuals have played in the achievement of the objectives of the CSCE and will further facilitate their activities for the implementation of the CSC commitments by the participating States. These organizations, groups and individuals must be involved in an appropriate way in the activities and new structures of the CSCE in order to fulfill their important tasks.

NEW STRUCTURES AND INSTITUTIONS OF THE CSCE PROCESS

Our common efforts to consolidate respect for human rights, democracy and the rule of law, to strengthen peace and to promote unity in Europe require a new quality of political dialogue and co-operation and thus development of the structures of the CSCE.

The intensification of our consultations at all levels is of prime importance in shaping our future relations. To this end, we decide on the following:

We, the Heads of State or Government, shall meet next time in Helsinki on the occasion of the CSCE Follow-up Meeting 1992. Thereafter, we will meet on the occasion of subsequent follow-up meetings.

Our Ministers for Foreign Affairs will

meet, as a Council, regularly and at least once a year. These meetings will provide the central forum for political consultations within the CSCE process. The Council will consider issues relevant to the Conference on Security and Co-operation in Europe and take appropriate decisions.

The first meeting of the Council will take place in Berlin.

A Committee of Senior Officials will prepare the meetings of the Council and carry out its decisions. The Committee will review current issues and may take appropriate decisions, including in the form of recommendations to the Council.

Additional meetings of the representatives of the participating States may be agreed upon to discuss questions of urgent concern.

The Council will examine the development of provisions for convening meetings of the Committee of Senior Officials in emergency situations.

Meetings of other Ministers may also be agreed by the participating States.

In order to provide administrative support for these consultations we establish a Secretariat in Prague.

Follow-up meetings of the participating States will be held, as a rule, every two years to allow the participating States to take stock of developments, review the implementation of their commitments and consider further steps in the CSCE process.

We decide to create a Conflict Prevention Centre in Vienna to assist the Council in reducing the risk of conflict.

We decide to establish an Office for Free Elections in Warsaw to facilitate contacts and the exchange of information on elections within participating States.

Recognizing the important role parliamentarians can play in the CSCE process, we call for greater parliamentary involvement in the CSCE, in particular through the creation of a CSCE parliamentary assembly, involving members of parliaments from all participating States. To this end, we urge that contacts be pursued at parliamentary level to discuss the field of activities, working methods and rules of procedure of such a CSCE parliamentary structure, drawing on existing experience and work already undertaken in this field.

We ask our Ministers for Foreign Affairs to review this matter on the occasion of their first meeting as a Council.

Procedural and organizational modalities relating to certain provisions contained in the Charter of Paris for a New Europe are set out in the Supplementary Document which is adopted together with the Charter of Paris.

We entrust to the Council the further steps which may be required to ensure the implementation of decisions contained in the present document, as well as in the Supplementary Document, and to consider further efforts for the strengthening of security and co-operation in Europe. The Council may adopt any amendment to the supplementary document which it may deem appropriate.

The original of the Charter of Paris for a New Europe, drawn up in English, French, German, Italian, Russian and Spanish, will be transmitted to the Government of the French Republic, which will retain it in its archives. Each of the participating States will receive from the Government of the French Republic a true copy of the Charter of Paris.

The text of the Charter of Paris will be published in each participating State, which will disseminate it and make it known as widely as possible.

The Government of the French Republic is requested to transmit to the Secretary-General of the United Nations the text of the Charter of Paris for a New Europe which is not eligible for registration under Article 102 of the Charter of the United Nations, with a view to its circulation to all the members of the Organization as an official document of the United Nations.

The Government of the French Republic is also requested to transmit the text of the Charter of Paris to all the other international organizations mentioned in the text.

Wherefore, we, the undersigned High Representatives of the participating States, mindful of the high political significance we attach to the results of the Summit Meeting, and declaring our determination to act in accordance with the provisions we have adopted, have subscribed our signatures below:

[*Signatures of the representatives of sub-*

scribing nations were attached at this point.]

Note: The charter was made available by the Office of the Press Secretary, but was not issued as a White House press release.

Thanksgiving Day Message to American Troops
November 21, 1990

As we gather together for Thanksgiving this year, America has much to be truly grateful for. To those of you who are spending this holiday away from your loved ones to defend our nation's security and that of our allies, I am deeply grateful. To those of you on duty in the Persian Gulf, I say a special thank you.

Recent events prove the world is still a dangerous and unstable place. Along with the triumph of freedom around the world comes new challenges, especially in the Middle East. Once again, you, the men and women of our Armed Forces, have responded to the call of duty to protect freedom and stand firm against aggression. And once again, you have the full support of the American people and the thanks of this President.

You know, Barbara and I have spent a lot of Thanksgivings with a family we're proud of. Well, this year is no different, as we spend Thanksgiving in the Persian Gulf. And as Americans celebrate this special day back home, know that you are in their hearts. America is proud of you and the job you're doing. Almost 2 years ago, I began my Inaugural Address with a prayer, seeking God's wisdom and guidance in all that

we face. Earlier this month, with American troops facing down aggression overseas, I asked the Nation to join me in prayer, a prayer for the brave service men and women in whom we entrust the future of this country—as well as for those Americans held hostage. Now, this Thanksgiving, I hope that all Americans of all faiths and walks of life will bow their heads in appreciation for God's power to protect us and His wisdom to guide us.

As members of our Armed Forces worldwide, your strength and readiness allow the flames of freedom and democracy to glow brightly. You represent America's best—the world's best hope for the future. No matter where you are, I hope you're safe and well. The entire Bush family wishes you and your family a happy Thanksgiving. May God bless you and bring you home safely and soon.

Note: This message was recorded on October 18 in the Oval Office at the White House. It was broadcast on the Armed Forces Radio Network to American troops worldwide on Thanksgiving Day. A tape was not available for verification of the content of this message.

Remarks and a Question-and-Answer Session With Reporters in Jeddah, Saudi Arabia, Following Discussions With Amir Jabir al-Ahmad al-Jabir Al Sabah of Kuwait
November 21, 1990

The President. May I say that I just had a very useful meeting with His Highness, the Amir, and I reiterated the total commitment of the United States to the objectives that are enshrined in 10 United Nations Security Council resolutions. And as you all know, these objectives include Iraq's immediate and unconditional withdrawal from Kuwait, the restoration of Kuwait's legitimate government, the release of all individuals held against their will from whatever country they come, and it also includes the eventual stability and security of the Gulf.

We agreed on the desirability that these objectives be realized peacefully. At the same time, we also agreed that all options remained open and that steps needed to be taken right now in order to make these options credible and effective.

His Highness the Amir told me of the atrocities and acts of destruction that are being committed daily against the Kuwaiti people by the forces of Saddam Hussein. It is a moving and touching and horrible story. And I come away from this conversation more committed than ever to seeing this cruel occupation come to an end and those responsible for this violence called to account.

Let me just close by saying that this is my second meeting with His Highness the Amir since the tragic events of August 2d. And as I told him, I both hope and expect that our next meeting will take place in liberated Kuwait.

The Amir. Mr. President, it is with great pleasure that I meet with you once again, this time on the land of the Kingdom of Saudi Arabia, a land that is very dear to us and friendly to us all. Although this meeting takes place under tragic circumstances for my country and my people, we nevertheless find some solace in the honorable stance taken by the world community and respect of our cause, on the side of justice and righteousness in an unprecedented matter as to make it an historical turning point in international relations.

In this context, I feel duty-bound to single out the decisive role of the United States—people and administration—in standing up in the face of aggression. The American resolve did not come as a surprise, for your people are the descendants of the Pilgrim fathers who, centuries ago, preferred risking their lives in search of freedom in a far and unknown world rather than accepting to live under oppression and injustice, thereby setting a tradition of standing up for justice and opposing aggression.

Their hopes were realized, and they built a free world that rejects despotism and oppression. And so, it became a refuge for all freedom-lovers. Today, the descendants of the Pilgrim fathers reversed their historic crossing in aid of freedom yet once again, again to dissipate the dark shadows cast by another dictator on the land of the free, true to their tradition and true to the tradition of their ancestors to which they have always adhered.

Mr. President, it is with affliction in our hearts that every day passes, knowing how much suffering our people and peoples of other nationalities are being subjected to in an ever-increasing manner, and the darkness that has befallen their homeland, making them vulnerable to unprecedented inhuman treatment, depriving them even from food and medicine.

The people of Kuwait inside their country, unarmed and outnumbered, are unanimously engaged in a passive resistance against the invaders with a rare bravery against all odds and under the most adverse circumstances. So much that the aggressors has lost his senses and indulged in its fury of frustration in the practice of oppression and brutality in an ever-increasing manner.

No doubt, Mr. President, your Ambassador [Nathaniel W. Howell] and what have remained of Western diplomats that have managed so bravely to continue living in

Kuwait, sharing the suffering of the Kuwaiti people, will testify to this fact. And there is not the slightest talk that the flagrant aggressor would give up his intransigence and his determination to defy the collective will of the world community or his indulgence in the exercise of cheap tricks and playing with the sentiments of people with the issue of hostages, whom he should not have detained in the first place. And his attempt to connect and justify his aggression with that of Arabs, as he is comparing an evil with more evil, thereby exposing his people and his nation to serious dangers, the extent of which cannot be predicted.

Nevertheless, we are sure of the inevitability of the triumph of right over wrong, and in that we place our hope. For our faith is strong, and our confidence in the firm support of our brothers and our friends is limitless.

Last but not least, I present my sincere felicitation to you and, through you, to the American people and their sons who have come to the Gulf to deter the aggressor, on the occasion of Thanksgiving Day, the anniversary of those brave men who had refused to succumb to oppression.

Thank you, Mr. President.

Persian Gulf Crisis

Q. Mr. President, what do you mean by that steps should be taken right now?

The President. What did I mean by them? I think he ought to step out of Kuwait immediately and release all the hostages.

Q. Sir, are you suggesting you should take some action?

The President. We are taking action. We are moving considerable force here. And I hope that will get the message to Saddam Hussein how serious not only the United States is but other countries are because others are moving forces, too. And besides that, his most recent cruel ploy of talking about kind of dribbling out hostages, some of which he'd start releasing on Christmas Day and then spread that over 2 months— that ploy has backfired on him. Everybody I talked to in Paris felt that it was a cruel gambit, a cruel ploy. And the Amir has said he shouldn't have held these hostages in the first place, and that is correct.

Q. President Gorbachev today called for a Security Council meeting.

The President. Well, good.

Q. What do you think of that? And is that of your making?

The President. I think this is just fine.

Q. What do you expect to come of it?

The President. Well, we'll discuss that when we get to the Security Council. But I think there's been general understanding that the United States has been in favor of such a step. And I would expect there would be yet another resolution strongly against Saddam Hussein. But we'll wait to see what that resolution does.

Q. ——new atrocities tonight from the Amir, atrocities that you haven't heard about before——

The President. He showed me some pictures that are so cruel and so brutal, the treatment of Kuwaitis so cruel and so brutal that it just turns your stomach. And so, we talked about some. But there will be a chance for the world to have a little window on this because this matter is going to be aired in the United Nations next week. And justice demands that the world listen and understand exactly the kind of brutality that Saddam Hussein has wrought upon innocent kids and families in Kuwait. And what he's doing to hostages in Kuwait today is appalling.

One thing I learned is that he's announced the death penalty for those who harbor innocent civilians. If you hide innocent civilians and you're caught by his brutes, you get the death penalty. And that is pretty brutal, and it's just one more piece of evidence that this brutality must not be rewarded.

Q. Mr. President, you're going on to Geneva to meet with President Assad. Can you tell us what you expect to undertake with him and why are you meeting with President Assad when the United——

The President. He is a coalition partner. He's in the process of moving substantial force here. We've worked to help others build a big, strong coalition. And I will be talking to him about our common objectives in the Gulf, and they are common objectives because I understand that the Syrians want to see Saddam Hussein out of Kuwait just as much as we do.

Q. Do you have any problems sitting down with President Assad given the problems with terrorism that the two countries have?

The President. I have no problem sitting down with him for this common objective. And it's important that this coalition stay together. It's important that everybody that's a part of it feel a part of it. And I'm going to be discussing that with him.

Q. Mr. President, considering the atrocities, how can you wait any longer? It's been 3 months.

The President. Well, I've indicated we were moving substantial force. Others are moving forces. And we are still hoping that the man will come to his senses and do that which he should have done in August, and that is to get out of Kuwait without condition. And I can't tell you or Saddam Hussein how long is long enough. In my view, 1 day was long enough. But how long this coalition will wait before other options are exercised? I'm sorry, I can't help you with that.

Q. Could you give us some idea of the U.N. resolution you're after, Mr. President?

The President. No, I'll let that evolve. We're still in consultation, Secretary Baker having consulted widely. I've had a chance to discuss that with the Kuwaitis here this evening, and there will be more consultation before that resolution gets into final form. But I can view this as very positive. I had not heard Mr. Gorbachev's comments, but I know what he and I have talked about, and I know what Secretary Baker and Mr. Shevardnadze have talked about, and it is all positive.

And for those who interpreted my meeting with Mr. Gorbachev as chilly, they just simply misinterpreted. It was the best meeting I've ever had with the man, and we've had very, very good ones in the past. So, I'm glad this thing is evolving and we now see the differences that some over there in Paris thought might exist between the Soviets on the way we're looking at this question. They are determined to see Saddam Hussein comply with the United Nations resolutions and get out of Kuwait without condition. I'm absolutely certain of it.

I've got time for just one or two more.

Q. Despite the tough talk by the United States and other countries, Saddam Hussein is not budging, and he's increasing the pressure in Kuwait. What's your comment, sir?

The President. The pressure is increasing on Saddam Hussein. And if he doesn't understand it now, he will soon. But I think he's beginning to understand it. Most reports we get indicate that the sanctions are having some effect; I can't tell you how much. Unless he's blind, he sees a strong coalition armed force still mobilizing against him, and I would think that he's beginning to get the message.

Now, in terms of his cruelty and his brutality, yes, it does continue. It continues in Kuwait. It continues in the holding of these hostages. So, we're not happy and we're not relaxed about his fully understanding that he must unconditionally get out of Kuwait, but we're going to keep on getting that message out there. And it's a solid message.

I'll tell you, I don't know if you were in Paris, but it was a solid front against the man from all the countries represented. And one thing I found that was very interesting: that those countries in Eastern Europe that have suffered in the past from aggression are very, very strong in support of what we all are doing as it relates to the Gulf.

Q. Mr. President, have you discussed with the Amir of Kuwait a timetable for war?

The President. We've discussed a lot of things and we did not put any time—dates on that category of discussion, no.

Q. Are you suggesting now you're going to the United Nations, or your lieutenants will, to present these pictures to the U.N. in some fashion?

The President. Well, there are going to be—Jim can help you. There's already a scheduled session.

Secretary Baker. Monday and Tuesday in the Security Council there will be some hearings with respect to the atrocities that have been committed. The government of Kuwait has asked for these hearings.

Q. Sir, is this a preamble for the force resolution you've been seeking?

The President. It's just more information getting out because I think there's a lot of people around the world and all of the U.N.

countries that don't really appreciate yet the brutality of Saddam Hussein. Most see it, and the world is obviously united against it. But I don't think they have the full impact yet, and perhaps these hearings will drive home to the man on the street in these various countries the brutality of Saddam Hussein.

Q. Do you feel the pressure of the November 30 deadline when we have to give up the chairmanship of the U.N. Security Council?

The President. No, I don't feel great pressure on it, but I feel that we should act and take action before November 30th. I think we should take action right away in the United Nations for more resolutions. Stay tuned.

Q. Mr. President, there's been much talk about a window of opportunity and that's why Saddam Hussein set this March 25th last date for the recent release of hostages. Is the window of opportunity really nonexistent? They talked about the desert storms and the desert heat and Ramadan and all that. In your own mind, is there such a thing as a window of opportunity?

The President. Well, I think that the window of opportunity for Saddam Hussein is right now. I think he should withdraw unconditionally from Kuwait right now and stop the brutality against the innocent women and children and men of Kuwait and innocent hostages from other countries. So, I think your question, John, gets to the question of how long can we permit the sanctions to be the sole action-forcing event. And I just can't help you with how long.

Q. Will you be satisfied, Mr. President, if the U.N. gives you something less than a resolution authorizing force?

The President. Nice try, Terry [Terence Hunt, Associated Press]. We're not going to discuss the content of the U.N. resolution until we're ready to table it and until extensive consultations have been concluded. And they are continuing. They will be continuing right up through the next few days. So, I just leave it right there.

Thank you all very much.

Note: The President spoke at 9:27 p.m. at the Al-Hamra Guest Palace. Prior to their remarks, he and the Amir participated in a bilateral meeting with U.S. and Kuwaiti officials. In his remarks, President Bush referred to President Saddam Hussein of Iraq and Soviet Foreign Minister Eduard Shevardnadze.

Statement on Signing the Bill Modifying the Boundaries of the Alaska Maritime National Wildlife Refuge
November 21, 1990

Today I am signing H.R. 5264, an Act "To authorize modification of the boundaries of the Alaska Maritime National Wildlife Refuge." Under this Act, the United States will acquire, through a land exchange with an Alaska Native Corporation, an environmentally significant tract of wetlands for the Refuge. These wetlands are an important wintering habitat for several species of ducks, and I agree that a land exchange of the kind contemplated in H.R. 5264 offers an appropriate method for carrying out this effort at environmental preservation.

Unfortunately, H.R. 5264 contains important constitutional defects. Under the Act, the amount of Federal land to be exchanged for the wetlands in question must be determined by "independent" appraisers, who would not be subject to supervision by the President. This is contrary to Article II of the Constitution. In addition, one or more of the appraisers would be chosen in a manner inconsistent with the Appointments Clause of the Constitution, Art. II, sec. 2, cl. 2.

I have no doubt that these constitutional defects were the result of inadvertence. Because the Act does not provide a mechanism for carrying out the land exchange in a manner consistent with the Constitution, however, it cannot be fully implemented until its constitutional deficiencies are rectified. Accordingly, the appraiser appointed by the Secretary of the Interior pursuant to section 3(a) of the Act will be instructed by the Secretary not to complete his appraisal until the Secretary is informed by the Department of Justice that adequate technical corrections legislation has been enacted.

GEORGE BUSH

The White House,
November 21, 1990.

Note: H.R. 5264, approved November 21, was assigned Public Law No. 101–622.

Statement on Signing the International Narcotics Control Act, 1990
November 21, 1990

Today I have signed H.R. 5567, the "International Narcotics Control Act, 1990." I am pleased that the Act contains certain provisions that will assist the Administration in implementing our international narcotics control strategy.

I have, however, a number of serious reservations about the Act. In general, I am concerned that many provisions of the Act would unreasonably undercut the flexibility needed by the Administration to implement effectively our international counternarcotics program. Despite the fact that the Administration has consistently kept the relevant congressional committees fully informed of its efforts to implement an international counternarcotics strategy, the Act includes cumbersome reporting, determination, and notification requirements that could impair the effectiveness of the program.

Many of these provisions, however, need not impair implementation of our counternarcotics strategy because, as a matter of law, they may not apply to funds appropriated in the recently enacted Foreign Operations, Export Financing, and Related Programs Appropriations Act (P.L. 101–513). This is because many of the restrictions of H.R. 5567 expressly apply only to funds authorized to be appropriated by H.R. 5567, and funds appropriated by P.L. 101–513 were not expressly made available under the authorization contained in H.R. 5567. Accordingly, I sign H.R. 5567 into law with the understanding that it may not subject our counternarcotics program to the most burdensome constraints of H.R. 5567. Nevertheless, recognizing the concerns that the provisions of H.R. 5567 reflect, we will work with the Congress to help ensure that congressional concerns are carefully considered in the implementation of our programs.

The Administration is committed to conditioning Andean counternarcotics assistance on effective counternarcotics performance, the implementation of sound economic policies, and respect for human rights. I note that section 4 requires that I make certain determinations on additional conditionality as a prerequisite to furnishing assistance authorized to be appropriated by sections 2(a) and 3(a) of the Act, or provided pursuant to section 517 of the Foreign Assistance Act of 1961, as amended. I do not believe that the Congress intended this provision to require a termination of vital antinarcotics assistance, and, to the degree appropriate, will interpret the section 4 requirements in a manner consistent with the shared concerns of the Congress and myself regarding the effective implementation of the Andean initiative. For instance, I appreciate the concern expressed in the Act regarding the control of the governments of these countries over police and military operations related to counternarcotics and counterinsurgency activities. I understand, however, that this legislation would not preclude my ability to make the necessary determinations if the amount and nature of government control is sufficient to ensure that assistance is effective. I am signing the Act on the basis of this understanding.

I have certain additional concerns. First,

while the Administration is already working toward the goal of increasing host country capability to conduct air operations, the arbitrary deadline contained in section 13 could endanger the lives and property of U.S. and foreign citizens. Second, I regret that the Congress has not provided a satisfactory provision regarding title to aircraft, and I hope to work with the new Congress to resolve this important problem.

Finally, I do not believe as a matter of principle that development and economic assistance should be necessarily conditioned on the same standards as military assistance, since its nature and purpose is considerably different. Subjecting these countries to a degree of scrutiny unmatched in other assistance programs risks alienating the very countries that we are seeking to engage in our narcotics control efforts.

GEORGE BUSH

The White House,
November 21, 1990.

Note: H.R. 5567, approved November 21, was assigned Public Law No. 101–623.

Remarks to the Military Airlift Command in Dhahran, Saudi Arabia
November 22, 1990

Thank you all. Thank you for that warm welcome. I'm just delighted to be here, and so is Barbara. And I don't normally speak for the joint leadership of the United States Congress, but it is most fitting that on this Thanksgiving Day we have with me here the Speaker of the House, Tom Foley; Bob Michel, the minority leader in our House; Senator Mitchell, the leader in the United States Senate; and Bob Dole, the minority leader in the Senate. I'm just delighted they're out here with us.

And, of course, I salute not only Colonel McBroom but also General Schwarzkopf. And, Norm, we have a little present for you. It comes from the families and friends of our troops around the world, and it's just exactly your size. [*Laughter*] This thing will fit you. [*Laughter*]

Well, Barbara and I are very proud to be sharing this Thanksgiving with the men and women of our allied forces. And later we're going to visit your partners in the Army, the Navy, Coast Guard, Marines—together, the finest Armed Forces in the entire world. And we are here because we believe in freedom: our freedom and the freedom of others. And we're here because we believe in principle. And we're here because we believe in you.

And I'm very impressed with the Air Force—people like Airman First Class Wade West. He was home on leave to get married when this got started. On August 7th he was called up. Within an hour he had the ceremony performed—his wedding ceremony—and left for the Middle East. You talk about a guy who gets things done. [*Laughter*] Fantastic.

Over the past 4 months, you have launched what history will judge as one of the most important deployments of allied military power since 1945. And I'm here today to personally thank you—the Saudi, Kuwaiti, British, and American air men and women here today, and the forces from 23 other nations—here to see that an unprecedented series of U.N. resolutions is honored.

Thanksgiving is indeed the oldest, some say the most American of holidays, dating back to our very origins as a people. It's a day apart from all others—a day of peace, a day of thanks, a day to remember what we stand for and, this Thanksgiving, why we're here. It isn't all that complicated. Earlier this week I set out the key reasons why we're here, making a stand in defense of peace and freedom. And we're here to protect freedom, here to protect the future, and here to protect innocent lives.

First, freedom: Protecting freedom means standing up to aggression. The brutality inflicted on the people of Kuwait and on innocent citizens of every country must not be rewarded. Kuwait is small, but one conquered nation is one too many. And remember, remember, the invasion of Kuwait was without provocation. The invasion of Kuwait was without excuse. And the invasion of Kuwait simply will not stand.

Second: Protecting our future means protecting our national security and the stability and security of the Gulf area that is so vital to all nations. Today the worldwide march of freedom is threatened by a man hell-bent on gaining a choke-hold on the world's economic lifeline. And that's why Iraq's aggression is not just a challenge to the security of our friends in the Gulf but to the new partnership of nations we're all hoping to build. Energy security is national security for us and for every country.

And third: We're here to protect innocent lives, including American lives. Every diplomat and every citizen of every country held hostage must be freed.

Three simple reasons—protecting freedom, protecting our future, protecting innocent lives—any one is reason enough why Iraq's unprincipled, unprovoked aggression must not go unchallenged. Together, as 10 United Nations Security Council resolutions made clear, they are a compelling case for your mission.

What we're confronting is a classic bully who thinks he can get away with kicking sand in the face of the world. And so far, we have acted with restraint, as is our way. But Saddam is making the mistake of his life if he confuses an abundance of restraint and patience with a lack of resolve. And every day that passes brings Saddam Hussein one step closer to realizing his goal of a nuclear weapons arsenal. And that's another reason, frankly, why, more and more, our mission is marked by a real sense of urgency.

Our objectives in the Gulf have never varied. We want a free and restored Kuwait, protect American citizens, safeguard the security and stability of the region. To force Iraq to comply, we and our allies have forged a strong, diplomatic, economic and, yes, military strategy. No President, none at all, is quick to order American troops abroad. But there are times when all nations that value freedom must confront aggression.

Sometimes it's a question of some pain—some pain now to avoid even worse pain later. In World War II, the world paid dearly for appeasing an aggressor who could have been stopped early on. We're not going to make that mistake again. We will not appease this aggressor.

The world is still a dangerous place, and those in uniform will always bear the heaviest burden. And we want every single American home. And this we promise: No American will be kept in the Gulf a single day longer than necessary. But we won't pull punches. We're not here on some exercise. This is a real world situation, and we're not walking away until our mission is done, until the invader is out of Kuwait.

There is no way Americans can forget the contribution you are making to world peace and to our country. Year after year on this very special day, special to every American, no doubt each of you has given thanks to your country. This year your country gives thanks to you. We think of you with pride in our hearts and a prayer on our lips.

May God bless you and watch over you. To those with whom we stand shoulder to shoulder, our friends from other lands, may God bless each and every one of you. And may God bless the United States of America. Thank you very much. Thank you. Good to see all of you. Thank you.

Note: The President spoke at 11:05 a.m. at the Military Airlift Command ramp at Dhahran International Airport. In his remarks, he referred to Col. John McBroom, commander of the 1st Tactical Fighter Wing; Gen. H. Norman Schwarzkopf, commander of U.S. forces in the Persian Gulf; and President Saddam Hussein of Iraq.

Remarks to United States Army Troops Near Dhahran, Saudi Arabia
November 22, 1990

Hey, listen, thanks for that warm desert welcome, and I mean warm. Let me first introduce you to the leaders of the United States Congress. This is Speaker Tom Foley, the Speaker of the House. Next to him, Senator George Mitchell, the leader of the United States Senate. Senator Bob Dole, minority leader. And Congressman Bob Michel of Illinois, the minority leader. And to you, Ted—Colonel Reid—thank you, sir. And let me give a special salute, if I might, to the host unit for our visit, the 2d Battalion of the 18th Infantry Regiment.

I can't do much about this warm weather, but I hope you're getting enough MRE's. [*Laughter*] I'm told that's a military term meaning "I'd rather have a Bud Light." [*Laughter*] Now, look, look, we know that the days can get pretty long out here, and you'll be glad to know that if it goes on too long we have a secret weapon in reserve. If push comes to shove, we're going to get Roseanne Barr to go to Iraq and sing the national anthem. Baghdad Betty, eat your heart out. [*Laughter*]

Barbara and I are very, very pleased to be here today, joined by the bipartisan leadership of the Congress on this mission of peace, this mission of pride. And we're honored to be here to tell you that on this special Thanksgiving Day, Americans will thank God for many things, but first they will thank God for each one of you.

The 18th Airborne, with the strength of the 197th Infantry Brigade and the 24th Infantry Division—[*applause*]—okay, you're entitled to 2 seconds—[*laughter*]—and so many other brave Americans, has spearheaded what history will judge as one of the most important deployments of military power in the last half century. You've done it for principle, you've done it for freedom, and you've done it to make America proud. And so, I've come out here today personally to thank you, the men and women who endured much and sacrificed more to stand tall against aggression.

I hope you'll excuse a personal reference, but seeing you all here brings back a personal memory of another Thanksgiving—another group of young Americans far from home—and for me it was November 23, 1944. And I was 20 years old and 6 days away from my last mission as a carrier pilot. And our ship, the *San Jacinto,* laid off the coast of the Philippines. And while we celebrated without family that year, like you, we all came together as friends and as part of something bigger than ourselves to thank God for our blessings. And we joined together then, as you are now, as a part of a proud force for freedom.

You know, back then, the 24th was there in the northern Philippines, as I was flying raids in the south on Manila Bay; and 10,000 miles away in another theater where the stakes were just as high—one well-known to some standing right with me—the predecessor of today's 197th were on the front lines of the fight for Europe. And they don't call you "forever forward" for nothing. And now, almost 50 years later, there are still proud troops like you, commanders like you, Americans like you ready to stand in defense of peace and freedom. And the whole world—and believe me—I'm just here from Paris where I met with all the CSCE countries of Europe—the whole world thanks you.

Today we face a similar mission, but in a world far different than the one we faced in 1944. Today we have a vision of a new partnership of nations united by principle and seeking a lasting peace for this generation and generations to come. And that is why we are here in this land so far from husbands and wives and parents and children on this day, this special day for Americans, this Thanksgiving Day. And that's why we sacrificed, so that those kids and all children can grow up in a new world, a safer and a better world.

And simply put, we are here to guarantee that freedom is protected and that Iraq's aggression will not be rewarded. We must send a signal to any would-be Saddam Husseins that the world will not tolerate tyrants who violate every standard of civilized behavior—invading, bullying, and swallowing whole a peaceful neighbor. We will not tolerate the raping and the brutalizing and the kidnaping and the killing of innocent civilians. And we will not tolerate those who try to starve out foreign embassies, breaking a diplomatic code of conduct that has been in place for centuries.

You see, we must also ensure our future. Clearly, our national security's at stake here in the Gulf, not just from the threat of force but from the potential economic blackmail of a Gulf dominated by a power-hungry Iraq. Even now, without an actual shortage of oil, Saddam's aggression is directly responsible for skyrocketing oil prices, causing serious problems at home and throughout the entire world, especially for smaller countries who are hurt the most.

You know, in Eastern Europe, the economic shock wave of the Gulf threatens to disrupt the already difficult process of creating both new and democratic governments and free market economies. And while Saddam loudly professes his desire to help the most impoverished nations of the region—the have-nots, he calls them—his aggression is taking a terrible toll on the already hard lives of millions. And we can't hope to achieve our vision of a new world order, the safer and better world for all our kids, if the economic destiny of the world can be threatened by a vicious dictator. The world cannot, must not and, in my view, will not let this aggression stand.

And finally—and I know you don't forget it, and I hope no American forgets it on this special day when we give our thanks to our God—finally, innocent lives are at stake here. The cynical manipulation of civilians, be it as bargaining chips or as pawns to deter attack, is an affront to acceptable behavior. And nothing is more cynical than Iraq's announcement earlier this week that the hostages would be freed in batches like chattel, beginning Christmas Day. There is no reason to wait for Christmas. I say to him today: Free the hostages—all the hostages—and free them today, or you're going to pay the price.

And it is also time that Saddam conformed to the unanimous demand of the United Nations. And remember, we're not in this alone—all the countries in the United Nations standing up. It is the United Nations against Saddam Hussein. It is not Iraq against the United States. It's also time, then, that he conformed to the unanimous demand of the United Nations that our Embassy be resupplied and that our diplomats treated with the respect they deserve under international law. The outrageous treatment of the United States Embassy in Kuwait must stop.

So, to sum it up, the United States is joined in the Gulf with other members of the United Nations for these three simple reasons: First, to ensure that freedom will be protected and aggression will not be rewarded; second, to protect our future by ensuring our national security; and finally, to protect innocent lives.

Any one is reason enough why Iraq's unprincipled, unprovoked aggression must not go unchallenged. And together, as 10 United Nations Security Council resolutions make clear, they are a compelling argument for your important mission. All of us know only too well the inevitable outcome of appeasement. The kind of aggression we see in Kuwait today is not just a threat to regional peace but a promise of wider conflict tomorrow.

And we understand that we can sacrifice now, or we can pay an even stiffer price later as Saddam moves to multiply his weapons of mass destruction: chemical, biological and, most ominous, nuclear. And we all know that Saddam Hussein has never possessed a weapon that he hasn't used. And we will not allow the hope for a more peaceful world to rest in the hands of this brutal dictator.

Our goals in the Gulf have never changed. We have no quarrel at all—and I'll repeat it here—we have no quarrel with the Iraqi people. It is with the outrageous aggression of Saddam Hussein. We want the immediate, complete, and unconditional withdrawal of all Iraqi forces from Kuwait. We want the reestablishment of Kuwait's legitimate government. We want the protection of lives of American citizens and the restoration of the security and stability of the Gulf.

No President, believe me, no President is quick to order American troops abroad. But there are times when all nations that value their own freedom and hope for a new world of freedom must confront aggression. You know, you guys know it, all of you men and women out here in the sands know it, and we still live in dangerous times. And those in uniform, I guess, will always continue to bear the heaviest burden. We want every single American soldier home.

And this we promise: No American will be kept in the Gulf a single day longer than necessary. But we won't pull punches. We are not here on some exercise. This is a real world situation. And we're not walking away until our mission is done.

I think Americans understand the contribution that you are making to world peace and to our own country. And on this very special Thanksgiving Day, when every American thanks God for our blessings, we think of you. Barbara and I will always remember this time out here that we've shared with you all today. And so, we want you to know that you have our love and our prayers, and we're proud of each and every one of you.

May God bless you and watch over you. And may God bless the greatest country on the face of the Earth, the United States of America. Thank you. God bless you all.

Note: The President spoke at 12:30 p.m. at an Army tactical site in the desert. In his remarks, he referred to Col. Ted Reid, commander of the 197th Infantry Brigade, and President Saddam Hussein of Iraq. Following his remarks, the President and Mrs. Bush had Thanksgiving dinner with the troops.

Remarks During a Thanksgiving Day Service on Board the U.S.S. *Nassau* in the Persian Gulf
November 22, 1990

Thank you, Chaplain Bebee. And let me thank Captain Dow. Let me, on behalf of Barbara and myself and the four congressional leaders that are with us—the Speaker of the House of Representatives, Tom Foley; the leader of the United States Senate, George Mitchell; the minority leader of the House, Bob Michel; and the minority leader of the Senate, Bob Dole—express to all of you our joy at being here and our great respect for what all aboard *Nassau* and all that are out here from other units, including our CINC, General Schwarzkopf, are doing. It's a joy to be with you. And I want to thank once again Captain Dow and the ship's company for, I know, an unusual amount of arrangements that go with one of these visits. But we promise to leave on time. [*Laughter*]

Barbara and I treasure this distinctly American sense of sharing with the families and friends in the faith of our fathers. For many of us, this is a time of contemplation about things greater than ourselves, an opportunity to seek perspective. I notice that Chaplain Bebee called his sermon a meditation. And I'm reminded of the story of the kid that went to church with his grandfather. And he said to the grandfather, "Grandfather, what are all the flags there along the side of the church?" The grandfather said, "Well, that's for those who died in service." The kid said, "Oh, really? The 9 o'clock or the 11 o'clock service?" And I noticed how brief your chaplain was, and I will try to be the same.

I notice that both Chaplain Dallmann and Chaplain Bebee referred to the Pilgrim fathers. In the early days, Americans gave thanks for the Lord's many blessings. And those, as was pointed out to us here today in the meditation, were indeed hard times—times of privation, lonely times in foreign surroundings, dangerous times, fearful, perilous. What is so remarkable about the first Thanksgiving is that those hearty souls were giving thanks in an age of extreme adversity, recognizing the Lord's bounty during extraordinary hardship, understanding that his bounty is not in things material but more importantly in things spiritual.

I reminded some at an Army base a while ago that this reminds me a bit of a Thanksgiving that I spend 46 years ago on a carrier, U.S.S. *San Jacinto* CVL30, off the coast of the Philippines during World War II. I found then that the Lord does provide many blessings to men and women who face adversity in the name of a noble purpose. They are the blessings of faith and friendship, strength and determination, courage and camaraderie and dedication to duty. And I found that the Lord allows the human spirit the inner resolve to find optimism and hope amidst the most challenging and difficult times. He instills confidence when despair tries to defeat us and inspires teamwork when the individual feels overwhelmed by the events of day to day.

Thanksgiving reminds us of America's most cherished values. Freedom was, indeed, as we've heard from our chaplain, the watchword for the *Mayflower*'s journey. Freedom united the Pilgrims in a common purpose. Freedom was the idea that inspired the first Thanksgiving of the colony there at Plymouth Bay.

The grand experiment called America is but a recent manifestation of humanity's timeless yearning to be free. Only in freedom can we achieve humanity's greatest hope: peace. From the wisdom of Solomon to the wonder of the Sermon on the Mount, from the prophecies of Isaiah to the teachings of Islam, the holy books that are our common heritage speak often of the many blessings bestowed upon mankind, often of the love of liberty, often of the cause of peace. And so, I would like to close these remarks with a prayer.

Lord, bless us and keep us. Show us your way, the way of liberty and love. Soften the hearts of those who would do us harm. Strengthen the hearts of those who protect and defend us. Sustain the hearts of those at home who pray for our safe return. We rely upon your guidance and trust in your judgment, for we are one nation under God. Amidst this threat of war, help us find the will to search for peace. As was said upon the Mount: "Blessed are the peacemakers, for they shall be called the children of God." Amen.

Thank you all very much for inviting these four congressional leaders, for inviting Barbara and me to share this very special day with the sailors, the marines, the coastguardsmen all out here aboard the U.S.S. *Nassau* today on this spectacularly beautiful day halfway around the world from the home that we love.

I cannot overstate to you the outpouring of support from your friends and families. General Schwarzkopf was telling me of the mail system here: You get a lot of mail that doesn't even have a name on it, and they spread it all around. I hope some of you have received it. And it does express the support that the American people have for you on this important mission.

So, God bless you all on this very special day. And God bless the United States of America. Thank you.

Note: The President spoke at 2:23 p.m. on the flight deck. In his remarks, he referred to Capt. Jack Dow, commanding officer of the U.S.S. "Nassau," and Gen. H. Norman Schwarzkopf, commander of U.S. forces in the Persian Gulf.

Remarks to Allied Armed Forces Near Dhahran, Saudi Arabia
November 22, 1990

With us today, we have four very special guests out here. The leaders, if you will, the top leadership of the United States Congress: the Speaker of the House, Tom Foley; the leader of the Senate, George Mitchell, next to him, Senator Mitchell; Congressman Bob Michel, the Republican leader, minority leader in the House; and Senator Bob Dole [Senate minority leader].

Let me just say how pleased that Barbara

and I are to be here. And I want to thank all of you for this welcome, this warm welcome. I want to thank General Myatt for greeting us—Mike Myatt—and all of his people. I want to thank General Boomer. I want to thank Brigadier General Cordingly of the famed Desert Rats who are with us here.

I guess like all of you, Barbara and I always try to spend our Thanksgiving with our own family. I know that's true of these leaders in the Congress. But after spending the morning visiting with the men and women of our Army, Air Force, Navy, and Coast Guard, and now with the First Marine Division here today, there could hardly be a prouder moment than sharing Thanksgiving with this family, this American family out here.

This is quite a crowd. I can't help but think of the warning one soldier gave comedian Steve Martin last month—true story. He said, "You'd better be funny. We've got bullets." [*Laughter*] Well, look at it this way: You guys better be nice to me. I've got Norm Schwarzkopf with me. [*Laughter*] And I've got Al Gray back there, so— [*laughter*].

But I do first want to give a very special welcome to our staunch friends and allies, to General Cordingly and the famed Desert Rats. You, too, are a long way from home this day and your families. And I hope you will forgive me if I focus on the fact that this, at home for Americans, is our very special Thanksgiving Day.

As we gather it is dawn in America at— lost track—10 minutes of eight on the East Coast and about 10 minutes to six out on the West and the beginning of our day of thanksgiving and remembrance. You know, as you drive by the farms and the cities in the early morning light, the windows all look the same. But inside each house and apartment there are people with stories to tell, families bound together in hope and love. And believe me on this one, in all of those homes, in all of those families, you right here out in this desert are very much on the minds of the American people in all of those families.

You know, Thanksgiving is the oldest, some might say the most American of holidays, dating back to our very origins as a people. And it's a day, I think we would all agree, separate and apart from others. It's a day of peace; it's a day of thanks; a day to remember what we stand for and what it means to be an American and why our forebears sacrificed so much to cross ocean and build a great land. And on this day, with all that America has to be thankful for, it is fair for Americans to say, why are we here?

It's not all that complicated. There are three key reasons why we're here with our U.N. allies making a stand in defense of peace and freedom. We're here to protect freedom. We're here to protect our future. And we're here to protect innocent life.

And number one, protecting freedom means standing up to aggression. You know, the brutality inflicted on the people of Kuwait and on innocent citizens of every country must not be rewarded. Because a bully unchecked today is a bully unleashed for tomorrow.

Last August 2d, this brutal dictator set out to wipe another country from the face of the Earth. And Kuwait, a little, tiny country, awoke to the flashing guns of cold-blooded troops, to fire and ice of Saddam Hussein's invasion. Now Kuwait is struggling for survival, an entire nation ransacked, looted, held hostage. Maybe you can strike a name from the maps, but you can't strike a country from the hearts of its people. The invasion of Kuwait was without provocation, the looting of Kuwait is without excuse, and the occupation of Kuwait will not stand.

And number two, our mission is about protecting national security, which is to say protecting our future. Because energy security is national security for us and, indeed, for every country.

Last year on a snowy Thanksgiving eve up there at Camp David, I spoke to the American people about the newly fallen Berlin Wall. The piece of the wall that sits on my desk is a reminder of our steadfast role in the worldwide explosion of freedom. But now the march of freedom must not be threatened by the man whose invasion of Kuwait is causing great economic hardship in the countries which can afford it the least.

We just saw it in Czechoslovakia. Barbara

and I are just back from Czechoslovakia, where the progress of their peaceful revolution has already been damaged by the shock waves from Iraq's aggression. President Havel told me that Saddam's aggression is having a severe effect on his struggling economy. And every day that goes by increases the damage. But when he was asked if our action in the Gulf was taking too much money away from the problems of Eastern Europe, he answered plainly. He said, "All the resources that are expended on resisting aggression anywhere in the world are finally turned to the good of all humankind." This from that playwright that was jailed not so many months ago by aggression itself. Listen to the words of this man who stands for freedom.

Václav Havel is right. Iraq's aggression is not just a challenge to the security of Kuwait and the other Gulf neighbors but to the better world we all hope to build in the wake of the cold war. We're not talking simply about the price of gas; we are talking about the price of liberty.

Number three, we're here because innocent lives are at stake. We've all heard of atrocities in Kuwait that would make the strongest among us weep. It turns your stomach when you listen to the tales of those that have escaped the brutality of Saddam, the invader. Mass hangings. Babies pulled from incubators and scattered like firewood across the floor. Kids shot for failing to display the photos of Saddam Hussein. And he has unleashed a horror on the people of Kuwait.

Our diplomats and our citizens held hostage must be freed. And it's time to stop toying with the American hostages. And it's time for Saddam to stop trying to starve out our little beleaguered Embassy in Kuwait City. And the same, General Cordingly, is true of the British Embassy that is courageously holding on—the two of us side by side in Kuwait as we're shoulder to shoulder in the sands of Saudi Arabia. And it's time to put an end to this cruel hostage bazaar, bartering in human beings like the days of the slave trade. Because if we let Iraq get away with this abuse now, Americans will pay a price in future hostage-taking for decades to come, and so will other nations.

Three simple reasons: protecting freedom, protecting our future, protecting innocent lives. And any one is reason enough why Iraq's unprincipled, unprovoked aggression must not go unchallenged. Together they make a compelling case for you to be away from your families on this special Thanksgiving Day. They make a compelling case for your mission.

No President is quick to order American troops abroad. But there are times when any nation that values its own freedom must confront aggression. Czechoslovakia—they know firsthand about the folly of appeasement. They know about the tyranny of dictatorial conquest. And in the World War that followed, the world paid dearly for appeasing an aggressor who should and could have been stopped. We're not going to make that mistake again. We will not appease this aggressor.

As in World War II—the threat to American lives from a seemingly distant enemy must be measured against the nature of the aggression itself: a dictator who has gassed his own people—innocent women and children—unleashing chemical weapons of mass destruction, weapons that were considered unthinkable in the civilized world for over 70 years.

And let me say this: Those who would measure the timetable for Saddam's atomic program in years may be seriously underestimating the reality of that situation and the gravity of the threat. Every day that passes brings Saddam one step closer to realizing his goal of a nuclear weapons arsenal. And that's why more and more, your mission is marked by a real sense of urgency. You know, no one knows precisely when this dictator may acquire atomic weapons, or exactly who they may be aimed at down the road. But we do know this for sure: He has never possessed a weapon that he didn't use. What we're confronting is a classic bully who thinks he can get away with kicking sand in the face of the world.

So far, I've tried to act with restraint and patience. I think that's the American way. But Saddam is making the mistake of his life if he confuses an abundance of restraint—confuses that with a lack of resolve.

Over the past 4 months, you have launched what history will judge as one of the most important deployments of allied military power since 1945. And I have come here today to personally thank you. The world is watching. Our objectives in the Gulf have never varied. We want to free and restore Kuwait's government, protect American citizens abroad, safeguard the security and stability of the region. The united world has spelled out these objectives in 10 United Nations Security Council resolutions. To force Iraq to comply, we and our allies have forged a strong diplomatic, economic, and military strategy. But the Iraqi dictator still hasn't gotten the message.

Maybe he's confused by his own propaganda, this ridiculous radio broadcast that I understand the marines have labeled "Baghdad Betty." [*Laughter*] Well, she plays all the oldies, so one guy suggested we send Iraq a tape of M.C. Hammer and a note that says: This is how we entertain ourselves. Just imagine how we fight.

We have been patient. We've gone to the United Nations time and time again. I'm prepared to go another time. We still hope for a peaceful settlement, but the world is a dangerous place. And we must make all of these options credible. Those in uniform, it seems to me, will always bear the heaviest burden. We understand something of what you endure—the waiting, the uncertainty, the demands of family and military life. And we want every single troop home. We want every Brit to be able to go home as soon as possible. We want every single American home. And this I promise: No American will be kept in the Gulf a single day longer than necessary. But we won't pull punches; we are not here on some exercise. This is a real-world situation. And we're not walking away until our mission is done, until the invader is out of Kuwait. And that may well be where you come in.

As we meet, it is dawn in America. It is Thanksgiving Day. The church bells ring an hour of prayer, a day of rest, a nation at peace. And especially today, Americans understand the contribution that you all are making to world peace and to our country. Year after year on this special day, no doubt

each of you has given thanks for your country. This year, your country gives thanks for you. Thanksgiving is a day of prayer, a day when we thank God for our many, many blessings. And I have done that today. This has been an unforgettable visit, an unforgettable visit.

And I leave—as I know our Congressmen do, and I know Barbara does—with pride in our heart, a prayer on our lips. God bless you all. God bless our faithful allies, the United Kingdom. God bless the Marines, and may God bless the greatest, freest country on the face of the Earth, the United States of America. Thank you and bless you all. Good luck to all of you guys.

Now, wait a minute, we've got a challenge to offer here. I brought you a present because I thought maybe you could find a place to use these things. No, and it's not a flyswatter. All right, I want to get the general to organize a little tournament around here. And I'll bet you—and I invite the winners—this team—you need two on a team here—invite the winners to the White House as soon as you get through your workout here. And my son and I will be prepared at any time, at your convenience, to take on the winners on the White House horseshoe pit. It's a challenge; it's a firm invitation. I want the two best men you've got, possibly women—we had a woman champion in the White House this year—come and get it. I think we can whip you. Good luck.

Note: The President spoke at 3:50 p.m. to troops gathered at a Marine tactical site in the desert. In his remarks, he referred to Brig. Gen. J.M. Myatt, commanding general, 1st Marine Division; Lt. Gen. Walt Boomer, commanding general, I Marine Expeditionary Force; Brig. Gen. Patrick Cordingly, commander of the British 7th Armoured Battalion; Gen. H. Norman Schwarzkopf, commander of U.S. forces in the Persian Gulf; Gen. A.M. Gray, Jr., Commandant of the Marine Corps; and President Saddam Hussein of Iraq. Following his remarks, the President and Mrs. Bush had Thanksgiving dinner with the troops.

Exchange With Reporters Near Dhahran, Saudi Arabia
November 22, 1990

U.S. Armed Forces

Q. ——the other force was here, and something like four to one?

The President. Well, we're by far the largest country. Also, when you're the leader in the world for peace and for freedom, you bear a disproportionate responsibility. We're prepared to do that. I'm pleased that 23 countries are involved. I'm pleased that other forces are moving in. I saw the famed Desert Rats here today—I'm very proud, once again, we're shoulder to shoulder with the Brits, for example. We have Arab forces here. But we're the United States of America; we have a disproportionate responsibility to lead and to stand for something. And that's what we're doing.

Prime Minister Thatcher of the United Kingdom

Q. Speaking of the Brits, what is your reaction to Margaret Thatcher's decision to resign?

The President. Well, of course you know of my high regard for Prime Minister Thatcher. We will obviously work with the next Prime Minister, and I expect that, knowing the fiber there, that they'll stay right on course with us. But on a very personal sense, I would send my best to her at this difficult time. She's been a staunch friend and ally. She's a woman of principle; she's stood for what she believes. You always know where she was and what she believed. I think everybody in America would agree that Margaret Thatcher has been an outstanding ally for the United States. I'm certain that this will continue with the United Kingdom.

But on a personal basis, I'll miss her because I value her counsel, I value her long experience—the wisdom that comes from her long experience. She has been an outstanding Prime Minister for the United Kingdom and an outstanding friend to the United States.

President's Visit With the Troops

Q. Mr. President, on today, what did you learn by walking in the same footsteps of the soldiers you've sent here?

The President. I learned a lot about the kids just from looking them in the eye. And I learned once again something I already knew: how lucky we are to have this all-volunteer force as strong, as well-trained, and as highly motivated as they are. And I learned they are just like my own kids. Probably wish they were home Thanksgiving Day in the United States. And I learned that they're willing to be apart from their own loved ones because they feel it is their duty and their obligation. And they're strong and they're tough, and I've been very moved by today, I'll tell you.

Q. Had you been concerned about the morale, sir, given the fact that it's over 4 months now and they've had nothing to fight?

The President. Well, I think the waiting is a difficult part of this. But I think they, like their President, would prefer a peaceful solution. But like their President, I sense a certain resolve on their part that if they have to do something they're prepared to do it. And they want to do it and do it fast. And they want to do it and get it over. I can understand that. I was in their shape 40-some years ago to this very day—46. So, I've been very moved and motivated myself by this.

And I'll go the extra mile for peace. We've been doing it. We've been showing patience and restraint. But I also know that this Saddam Hussein is cruel and he's brutal, and he's violating the rights of individuals. And I don't believe there's a marine out here, or an Army person or a Navy person or an Air Force man or woman, or a British Rat or our Arab allies that are not as upset as I am about the way innocent civilians are being treated. And I'll damn sure tell you: I'm upset about it. We'll try the peaceful route. We're trying it. But there will be no compromise with this kind of aggression. We're not going to compromise.

1675

Iraqi Nuclear Capability

Q. Sir, you've talked increasingly today about a nuclear—Saddam's nuclear capability—

The President. Yes, I'm concerned about it.

Q. What's behind that?

The President. There's nothing behind it. It's just the fact that I think the longer it goes on, why, I'm concerned about it. That's what's behind it.

Q. Do you have new information, more so than you thought before?

The President. I would just stay with what I've said here today. When I said, remember, that he's used every weapon that he's had, I'm thinking primarily of the brutality of those chemical weapons that he did use on his own people. And I hope the American people understand this more clearly now. But I darn sure get the feeling that

the people out here understand it.

President's Visit With the Troops

Q. Was this an emotional day for you, sir?

The President. It was a very emotional day for me. And I think we are very fortunate to have this kind of dedicated young men and young women in the sands of Saudi Arabia today. It's only the United States that can lead like this—it's only the United States of America. We have others with us, but these are the ones that are doing the heavy lifting. And God bless them all.

Note: The exchange took place at a Marine tactical site in the desert. In his remarks, President Bush referred to President Saddam Hussein of Iraq. A tape was not available for verification of the content of this exchange.

Remarks and a Question-and-Answer Session With Reporters Following Discussions With President Mohammed Hosni Mubarak in Cairo, Egypt
November 23, 1990

President Mubarak. We welcome President Bush in Egypt as an outstanding leader of a great nation. We welcome him as a true friend, as a man of principles and determination, a statesman endowed with vision and compassion. We value the contribution he has made to strengthen Egyptian-American friendship, bringing it to a higher level of cooperation based on principles and mutual respect.

We are proud of this partnership which has helped us to advance the cause of peace and the fraternity among all nations, to stand for eradication of injustice and the elimination of war and violence, and to contribute to the construction of a new world order—a world in which all nations, big or small, have a right to live in peace and dignity.

In our talks today we pursued our discussion of several issues of common concern. We came out of these talks with a better understanding of how to deal with the chal-

lenge of our time. In the difficult weeks ahead we will leave no stone unturned in our search for a peaceful solution to the Gulf crisis. But let no one be in doubt that the status quo of occupation and repression is totally unacceptable to us and in the entire world. It is a threat to peace and security everywhere and a grave violation of the rule of law. It undermines the very foundation of our modern civilization. Hence, the Iraqi invasion must be reversed and Kuwait must be liberated. No tactics will divert us from our objective. No act of defiance will weaken our resolve or shake our determination. To both of us it's a matter of principle and moral commitment. If we fail to meet that challenge, the consequences will be grave for all nations. We cannot compromise on principle and moral values. Nor can we bargain on the fundamental right of peoples to live in freedom and dignity.

As you work together with the family of nations in order to bring the tragedy of the Gulf to an end, we shall address other problems with the same zeal and commitment. In the right context, the plight of the Palestinian people must be brought under focus. Their inherent right to self-determination should be exercised. The holy shrines of Jerusalem must be respected and protected.

Mr. President, you came to us in peace, and we greet you in peace. We stand here together at a crucial moment in the history of our region and the whole world. That moment has its great risks, but it equally holds great promises and offers tremendous opportunities. We stand united in order to realize these promises for the good of all peoples of the Middle East and the whole world. We shall continue—we shall continue to build on what we achieved today for the benefit of our nations and that of humanity.

Thank you.

President Bush. Thank you, Mr. President. And let me just add that I had a very useful set of talks with my close and trusted friend of longstanding, President Hosni Mubarak. Let me just say at the outset how pleased Barbara and I are to be back here in Cairo and how pleased I am to have had such a long, productive meeting.

We reviewed the situation in the Gulf. And we agreed that while a peaceful solution brought about by sanctions is clearly preferable, steps must be taken now by all members of the international coalition so as to ensure that credible alternatives are available before much more time passes. There is complete identity of views between us on the need for Saddam Hussein [President of Iraq] to withdraw right away and withdraw without condition. So-called partial solutions are out of the question.

We also discussed the challenges to regional security that will continue to exist even should Saddam withdraw. Clearly, safeguards are required to ensure that such aggression does not recur and that Saddam does not turn to weapons of mass destruction to further his goals.

Let me just end these brief introductory remarks by reiterating our common commitment to continue working closely together to ensure that we succeed. The U.S.-Egyptian relationship is extremely close and is a true force for peace in the region. And I believe that much of the credit belongs to President Mubarak's leadership. I'm thus extremely happy to be here and to have had this opportunity to exchange views and to benefit once again from his counsel and insight.

Thank you, sir, for your hospitality.

Persian Gulf Crisis

Q. President Mubarak—I have a question for both Presidents, please. You both used very strong language in recent days talking about removing Iraq from Kuwait and calling for the need for unity, and yet there are divisions on both sides. The Arab world is not united. Even yesterday Yemen suggested an Arab solution was needed. And, Mr. President, in Congress there's a lot of support for your present policy, but there seems to be a lot of skepticism over moving one step further. How have you both reached accommodation with—you, sir, with Congress and you, sir, with other Arab nations—in getting the unity that you're looking for?

President Mubarak. Your question is not a difficult question to answer, but I would like to tell you, in Yemen they said they are not going to vote for using force. They are looking for an Arab solution. Any kind of solution, whether it is an Arab solution, French solution, British, American, Moslem, Christian solution, it depends on two points: complete withdrawal without any precondition; then, the return of legitimate government to Kuwait.

If they are asking for no use of force, all of us don't want to use force. All of us want a peaceful solution, a complete withdrawal and the return back of the legitimate government of Kuwait to Kuwait. So, if anybody could solve this problem or could reach these goals peacefully, all of us will be very pleased, and we'll clap hands for them. So, there is no other solution except withdrawal and legitimate government to return back without any precondition.

President Bush. And I would simply add to that, the way to have Congress on board is to continue to explain what our principles are, to continue to explain that we must be successful, to demonstrate to the American people and to the people of the world that what President Mubarak has said is true: We all want a peaceful solution. We have been extraordinarily patient. The United Nations has passed 10 resolutions. And I will simply go home and talk—continue the consultations, that most Congressmen believe have been extensive—to make clear that they understand how we must remain determined and we must keep all options open.

And you mentioned Yemen. Yemen has supported some resolutions in the United Nations, and they have not supported others. We are not suggesting that every country in every part of the world feels as strongly about this as we do. But I can assure you, coming out of Paris, that the world still has violent disapproval of what Saddam Hussein has done. And I believe they will be supportive of any action that this superb coalition takes.

Q. President Mubarak, you have made clear that you, as President Bush and others, would much prefer a peaceful solution. If, however, that is impossible and if you have to resort to war to solve the current crisis, it is not clear from press accounts what the role of the Egyptian army would be. Would it be an army that would come in afterwards to help peacefully occupy Kuwait, or would it be in the forefront of the forces trying to retake Kuwait?

President Mubarak. Look, we have discussed all these points from the beginning with the President and the other friends. We send the forces there, and all of us know what will be the mission of the force. And I'm not in a position to tell you the details—where the forces are going to stay or going to move—but we have our plan coordinated with all the forces there. Whenever the use of force is needed and this option is going to be implemented, we have to act there.

Q. ——the word "patience" seems to have been forgotten in coalition lexicon in recent days. Why the urgency? I know you explained the potentiality of nuclear power and so forth. Is it Ramadan? Are you just running out—I mean, what is forcing you to move so fast—which is obviously the military option because President Mubarak

sounded so pessimistic today?

President Bush. We haven't given up on the peaceful solution at all. We have been patient. I thought just before I spoke here that I used the word patience. If not, I'm glad you reminded me. We have been very, very patient. This man should have gotten out of Kuwait with no concession, no condition, long ago. We've gone to the United Nations for 10 different resolutions, and indeed there will be another resolution. We have shown patience. We have explored all diplomatic options. We have had many people making inquiries of peace on behalf of Arabs and on behalf of others to this man. And I'm simply saying we're going to hold this coalition together, we're going to keep all options open, and we're going to see what happens.

But there's no timeframe, nothing—no holiday, as you mentioned—that's driving any decisions that I'll make, I can guarantee you that. President Mubarak can speak for himself. But we're getting tired of the status quo, and so is the rest of the world. And I think you'll see that in the discussions that are going to be held in the United Nations. I think the world will see the horror of what has been wrought on Kuwait by Saddam Hussein when the Kuwaitis are permitted to present the tales of brutality that just abound there in Kuwait. It's been awful what's happened. And I'm not sure the world fully understands that, so we do need a little more time to present that.

Q. Well, he has been stopped from any further aggression against——

President Bush. That's not the point, Helen [Helen Thomas, United Press International]. The point is he is still in Kuwait. And as long as he is there, this coalition will hold together, and we will not rest until he is out of there. And that is the point. And all options remain open. And I am convinced after my visit yesterday, all options are credible.

Q. I have a question——

President Bush. For me or for the President? Who is it for?

Q. For President Bush—for you, sir.

President Bush. Yes, ma'am.

Q. Can we draw some lessons from the CSCE conference and—applying similar mechanisms in the Middle East? Have you discussed such futuristic plans with President Mubarak and King Fahd [of Saudi Arabia]—this is number one. Number two, what is your reaction to Mr. Shamir's [Prime Minister of Israel] statements concerning the occupied territories and the settling of Jews?

President Bush. First, on the CSCE. This isn't directly responsive to your question, but I'll say this to our friends here in Cairo—and I did not mention this to my friend President Mubarak: Those countries, the newest members around the CSCE corridors, the Eastern European countries, were perhaps the strongest in their conviction that Saddam Hussein's aggression not be rewarded.

Václav Havel [President of Czechoslovakia] was eloquent—indeed, he spoke at a press conference on it—[Prime Minister] Antall of Hungary, and [Prime Minister] Mazowiecki of Poland. And the reason is because they had been aggressed against by a different Soviet Union in the past. They know what it is to be oppressed and to have aggression succeed. So, this was one of the reasons, I think, there was strong support for what we are doing in terms of a future world order.

You heard President Mubarak refer to that. This, the integration of Arab countries into a CSCE process, wasn't discussed but implicit in our optimistic assessment that once Iraq is out of the way—once the Iraq-Kuwait struggle is out of the way—we can have a new world order. And that new world order certainly offers a much better chance for peace for the Middle East.

In terms of the Palestine question and in terms of what Mr. Shamir has said, I've learned something: not to comment until I actually see the quote. But the United States remains determined to be helpful, to be a catalyst in bringing peace to the West Bank question. And we are supportive—we have always been—of Security Council Resolution 242. We tried very hard before this aggression by Iraq—which is unrelated in my view—but we tried very hard to be a catalyst for peace talks to get going. And let me just say here we are still determined to play a very useful role in a peaceful resolution of this question.

And it is not something that we have forgotten. What I am equally determined to do is keep these two questions separate. There should not be any linkage. Saddam Hussein should not be able to hide behind the difficulty in one area so he can continue his aggression and brutality and torture in another.

And so, there has been a separation, but let me reassure you, the United States remains extraordinarily interested and hope we can be helpful in a lasting solution—peaceful solution—to the whole question of the entire Middle East.

Q. President Mubarak, could I ask you, please, about the role of President Assad of Syria? We understand that you were instrumental in urging Mr. Bush to meet with President Assad. I'd like to know why, sir. And I'd also like to ask President Bush why it is that not all that long ago it was Saddam Hussein that the U.S. was dealing with in the Middle East and Assad who was on the outs, and now things have reversed themselves.

President Bush. Well, you want me to go first? I'd ask you to repeat the question, because I didn't hear the first part of it. But if the question is why our outrage against Saddam Hussein today, when we had tried to improve relations—he hadn't invaded Kuwait. He hadn't raped, pillaged, and plundered the people in Kuwait and the city of Kuwait itself. He hadn't violated this fundamental norm of international behavior. And indeed, other countries have tried to improve relations with him. And ours was one of them. I've said to you before, given what he's done now, maybe that is something we shouldn't have undertaken.

Now, what was your——

Q. Well, the question was really the role reversal and the fact that Mr. Assad is the one who has been on the list of those responsible——

President Bush. Mr. Assad is lined up with us with a commitment to force. Having seen those American kids in the desert yesterday, I will work with those that have stood forward and said, We are not going to permit Saddam Hussein's aggression to succeed. That doesn't mean we have no differences with Syria; we've got big differences on certain categories, and I'll be glad to discuss them with President Hafiz Assad when I meet with him.

But they are on the front line, or will be, standing up against this aggression. Out of this, I would only say I will work with those countries whose very presence enhances our chance of success in reversing this aggression. As long as I have one American troop—one man, one woman left there in the armed forces in this Gulf, I will continue to work closely with all those who stand up against this aggression. Then I reserve the right bilaterally to point out any differences I have with a country, just as that country will probably, frankly, point out the differences they have with me.

President Mubarak. I think the President has answered the question completely. I would like to add one more point: that Syria is considered in this area one of the key countries and a good supporter to the goals which we are supporting. So, we shouldn't neglect her.

Q. Could I follow that up, sir?

Q. Mr. President——

President Bush. I've got three at once, I can't hear. I'm confused. There's three questions——

Q. President Mubarak, could I follow that up by simply asking you, sir, why you recommended the meeting? It seems that, based on what President Bush said the other day, that the concern was that President Assad was feeling left out, that it wasn't profitable for President Bush to meet with him, and you wanted to change that. You wanted to bring Assad in, out of the closet, so to speak.

President Mubarak. I said that President Assad is a key leader in this area. Secondly, President Assad is against the occupation of Kuwait. Third, President Assad has his forces now beside our forces and beside other Arab forces in Saudi Arabia for the purpose of liberating Kuwait. So, we shouldn't neglect him. He is a very important partner there.

Q. Was he feeling left out, sir? Was he feeling left out because President Bush wasn't meeting him?

President Mubarak. I think President Bush could answer you this question. But he is participating in the whole thing now in Saudi Arabia.

President Bush. I don't know whether he's feeling left out or not, but as I say, he is an important coalition partner, and I think it is appropriate that we discuss many questions that relate to the brutal aggression by Saddam Hussein against Kuwait. We do have a common goal here, a common purpose here. And so, I'm looking forward to it.

I can't tell you—I had no signals on a personal level that he was feeling left out, but I think the people that I've talked to on this trip, including President Mubarak and including those I talked to in Saudi Arabia and elsewhere, feel that it is good—and talked to some in Europe about this behind the scenes—feel that it is good this meeting is taking place. Because there's a lot of countries—different views on a lot of different questions—that are together on this one question, the reversal of the aggression. And I think there was some feeling in all these places that it was important to include him in. They did not say whether he was feeling left—yes, sir.

Q. Concerning Mr. Baker's [Secretary of State] visit to Yemen and the statement that followed, Mr. Bush, how far away are you now from achieving a U.N. resolution on the use of force? And if you fail to get one, is the United States willing to go with its allies in Saudi Arabia and in the Gulf, to go to war without U.N. backing?

President Bush. Well, I was asked that question earlier on, and I do feel we have the authority to do what we have to do. But we have tried very hard to work within the U.N. confines, within the Security Council. And I am confident that we will be successful in the Security Council.

The world is getting tired of this. And the Security Council is tired of the fact that resolutions have been passed calling for immediate withdrawal, and they haven't been implemented; calling for recognition of the safety and the right to resupply an embassy, and that has not been complied with. And I can tell you, sir, I am getting increasingly frustrated about the treatment of the U.S. Embassy and the treatment of innocent hostages.

So, I saw the report from our Secretary of

State. We would like to get Yemen on board, and we'll keep working on that. I think it's in the best interest of Yemen to stand up against aggression in whatever way is required. But the fact that one country, which has approved some resolutions and has not approved others, might have reservations about this one—that's the way it is. But we're going to keep working on it, and I think we're very, very close now.

Q. President Bush, you are seeking a U.N. mandate to force Iraq out of Kuwait. Would you prefer it setting a time limit, or rather not? And, with your permission, how would our mutual cooperation be more defined to cope with Egypt's political and economic responsibilities in our region? Thank you.

President Bush. Well, I think on the U.N. debate, we'll be discussing not only the need to consider further action but perhaps a timeframe. I'm not clear on that, and as I say, I want to work within the United Nations Security Council. In terms of Egypt, that's a bilateral question. And I think we have good bilateral relations.

I'm very pleased that the debt forgiveness program is of benefit to the man on the street in Egypt. I know—I don't want to put words in his mouth, but President Mubarak expressed to me, asked me to express to the American people, his thanks for this. And this is a highly significant move that gives a certain flexibility to Egypt.

But, look, let me just say we will continue to explore every way to work cooperatively with Egypt, whether it's in the private sector, whether it's through the various programs that we have in effect. Because we have this international problem that draws us together now in the Gulf, the Gulf crisis, but we also have a longstanding relationship of working together on the bilateral problems. And I think that that recent action by the Congress—and actively supported by the President, indeed, requested by the President—on debt forgiveness is just one more manifestation of that.

Q. What is after Kuwait? What is after Kuwait, whether it is solved peacefully or by force, what is after Kuwait?

President Bush. Are you asking President Mubarak or me?

Q. President Mubarak.

President Bush. That's great. [*Laughter*]

President Mubarak. Of course, you know, after Kuwait, after solving the problem of Kuwait or exactly after liberating Kuwait, either withdrawal or using any other options, there should be some kind of measures to keep this area stable and to avoid any more tension and any more war.

Q. And the borders? Something about the borders?

President Mubarak. Remarking the borders, if it is needed for Arab forces to stay there, this will start from the people of the Gulf themselves. Let them study it; let they propose what they need; let we find out what kind of decision could we reach.

Q. Mr. President, I'd like to ask about Israel. You're probably aware that many have reacted in Israel with a sense of insult that could you go meet Assad and not stop in Israel. I wonder if—given what you said today about the separation, I believe you put it, with policy there—that you in any way intended that message?

President Bush. No, certainly not. I think the Prime Minister of Israel's comments show a certain understanding about what I'm trying to do. We will continue to have meetings with Israel. So, I haven't picked up anything like that at all. I've seen some press reports that express a difference. But, look, I'm focusing now on these meetings, on this trip, on this Gulf coalition. Syria is a part of it. Nobody should read more into it or less into it than that they are an important part of this coalition. So, I think that's manageable. I'm hoping to see Prime Minister Shamir when he comes to the United States, and indeed, we're in very close contact all up and down our bureaucratic level. So, I'm glad you asked it because I hope there's no misunderstanding. If there is, I'd like to lay it to rest.

This relates to the reversal of aggression, and I happen to feel that not only is that in the interest of the United States, I think it's in the interest of all countries, and that would include every country in the Middle East, which obviously includes the State of Israel. It is in their interest that we prevail, and it is in the interest of Syria, and it is in the interest of Egypt, and it is in the interest of the United States that we prevail against Saddam Hussein. That's what this is about. And we are going to prevail, and I never felt more sure of that than I do today.

Q. If I may follow. The question, as I'm sure you know with your expertise in foreign affairs, is that you can do much of what you want to do diplomatically with a phone call, without a meeting that rewards terrorism.

President Bush. That what?

Q. If you wanted to meet, or if you wanted to speak to President Assad about the Gulf situation, you could do that, as you often do, with a telephone call. But the allegation is that if you meet him personally——

President Bush. I've already had a telephone call with him. Now we're going to have a meeting. That should no way indicate that there are no differences between the United States and Syria on a wide array of questions. There are; everybody knows that. But we are together on this question, and now I want to be sure that we are solidly together in every way. And that is in the interest of every country.

President Mubarak. Could I add some words?

President Bush. Yes, please.

President Mubarak. I think no problem—it's not a big problem just to—that President Bush could meet with President Assad. As far as their meeting for peace questions, we should encourage that. The whole world needs peace. Whenever there is peace, there is stability. And a telephone call—there is great difference between solving the problem, some problems, with telephone calls and sitting with each other and have direct talks. This may be, in some issues, very effective. Thank you.

President Bush. This, I'm told by our leader over here on the right, not on the left this time, is the last question.

New World Order

Q. You said, President Bush, that a new world order would emerge once the Gulf crisis has been solved. How do you envisage this new world order?

President Bush. Well, I envisage it, one, where the whole—once we're—let me start over. Once we set back this aggression, and once it is clear that the security and the

stability of the Gulf are enhanced by whatever arrangements are set into place—once that this invading dictator gets out of Kuwait—then I think that it's clear we're going to have an opportunity, given the diversity of this coalition, to work more closely together. And part of that—I want to see a solution to the question of the West Bank, for example. But I think if we work cooperatively as are—with our common sights set—this aggressor will not succeed—it opens up all kinds of possibilities for a new world order.

We're already seeing that world order means world. And we're beginning to see that with what happened out of the—well, just as a result of the actions that led up to this successful CSCE meeting. I'm going down to South America, and the evolving democracies there are strengthening their economies, and we've got a program that I think will be very helpful there.

But as it relates to the Middle East, I think we've got all kinds of potentials for peace, given the fact that we've come together almost unanimously, standing up against this brutal dictator. And out of that and out of the contexts that go with that, I hope we can be catalytic in solving other problems, and I think that will lead to a new world order that has much better chance for peace for our children and our grandchildren.

So, that is the optimistic part of all of this. Right now we're facing a brutal dictator, and we've got to do something about it—a man that's holding hostages and all of this. It's just unconscionable what the man is doing. But as we unite and as we prove to be successful—and we will be successful—I think we can then see all around this concept that aggression will not pay, that we have a better shot for world peace. And I will work my hardest to be sure that the United States plays an active role in that, whether it be in the Middle East or whether it be in the rest of the world.

That is the exciting part. The more troubling aspect is how do we get this brutal dictator out of Kuwait now? And that one we've been talking about.

President Mubarak. Thank you.

President Bush. Thank you all.

Note: President Mubarak spoke at 12:35 p.m. in the main hall of Itihahdia Palace. Prior to their remarks, the two Presidents *met privately and with U.S. and Egyptian officials at Qubba Palace.*

Exchange With Reporters in Geneva, Switzerland, Prior to a Meeting With President Hafiz al-Assad of Syria
November 23, 1990

Media Relations

Q. What do you think about Israel's disappointment, Mr. President?

Q. Gentlemen, if Saddam Hussein [President of Iraq] does not cooperate and withdraw, is war inevitable?

President Bush. I explained to the President that I do not take questions at what is billed as a photo opportunity. Of course, I also said that he's free to take questions if he wants. But I hope all will excuse me, but that's—understand the groundrules.

Q. President Assad, will you commit your troops to an offensive action?

President Assad. Do you expect in such a big press conference that we speak about offensive or defensive action? [*Laughter*]

Q. Yes.

Q. Yes.

Q. Do you think we'll have another opportunity?

President Assad. Always politicians and statesmen would like to speak to pressmen so that they do not arouse their anger. But they like to give statements in the right times, in the suitable times. Who knows, there may come some good times to give you some statements.

Q. Inshallah [God willing]. [*Laughter*]

President Bush. That's Helen Thomas, United Press. Thank you all very much. We've got a lot of business to do.

President Assad. Do not forget what has been said. Do not carry home——

President Bush. Thank you all very much. It was wonderful. Thank you. [*Laughter*]

President Assad. These words will not appear in pictures. [*Laughter*]

President Bush. They may appear on one of these things, though. They pick up everything we say. [*Laughter*]

Q. But what about Europe? Excuse me, we are in Europe.

President Bush. I am pleased to be in Europe.

Note: The exchange took place at 7 p.m. in the Holiday Inn Crowne Plaza Hotel. Following the meeting, the President and Mrs. Bush traveled to Camp David, MD. A tape was not available for verification of the content of this exchange.

Statement by Press Secretary Fitzwater on President Bush's Meeting With President Hafiz al-Assad of Syria
November 23, 1990

President Bush and President Assad met for approximately 3 hours in Geneva. They had a discussion that can be accurately characterized as full and frank and that covered in depth a broad range of bilateral and regional concerns.

On the situation in the Gulf, the two Presidents agreed that Iraq's occupation of Kuwait is unacceptable, as are any partial solutions. They expressed their preference for a peaceful solution of the crisis in conformity with Arab League and U.N. resolutions. They also agreed that Iraq should receive no reward for its aggression and that

Kuwait's territory and legitimate government must be restored fully.

On Lebanon, the two Presidents noted areas of progress and emphasized the necessity for the implementation of the Taif accords.

President Bush and President Assad also discussed the Middle East peace process and the importance of moving ahead consistent with United Nations Resolutions 242 and 338.

President Bush urged Syria to do everything in its power to help bring about the release of all hostages being held in Lebanon. The two leaders also discussed human rights issues.

Last, the two Presidents had an extended conversation on the question of terrorism, agreeing to continue the U.S.-Syrian dialog with the goal of achieving positive results.

Remarks at the Arrival Ceremony in Monterrey, Mexico
November 26, 1990

To President Salinas and Mrs. Salinas, to Governor and Mrs. Trevino, Mayor Rizzo, Mrs. Rizzo, friends and neighbors, and all the wonderful people of Monterrey, thank you for that welcome. Barbara and I are honored by all you've done, for all of the work that has gone into preparations for our visit. *Muchas gracias* [Thank you very much].

It is an honor to stand with you, before this magnificent palace, at such a promising moment in our shared history. For I believe that our two peoples are now on the eve of an era more cooperative and more prosperous than ever we have known before.

In this plaza, I can stand before Mexico's greatest heroes: Hidalgo and Morelos, who set this great nation on the road to independence; Juárez and Escobedo, who defined and defended the principles of justice and freedom that guide Mexico even to this day; and above all, the Mexican people themselves—all of you here tonight—who are the lifeblood of this great city and of this great nation.

So, I've come to Mexico tonight with a message of respect, of admiration, and hope for a brighter future shared by our two countries. And I am very pleased to be working closely with your dynamic and creative President, Carlos Salinas. He is the architect of a breathtaking economic transformation, and he is a great world leader. In his inaugural address, he expressed his "certainty that Mexico—because of its history, dimensions, and the quality of its people—deserves to hold a stronger position among the nations of the world." President Salinas, I agree. And because of your Presidency, Mexico does hold a stronger position among the nations of the world.

In our consultations, President Salinas and I are discussing how we can achieve a brighter and more prosperous future for both of our nations. I believe that U.S.-Mexican relations have never been better. And let me tell you, as President of the United States, this relationship is of vital importance to my country. We will never neglect it. We are neighbors, and we are friends.

We want to work together toward the free and open trade so vital to creating jobs and enterprise in your economy and our own. We want to look for new progress against the scourge of drugs, so threatening to our youth. We have a precious environment to protect and future generations to educate.

And there are challenges, too, in the world beyond our borders. Reconstruction in Central America, the restoration of stability in the Persian Gulf region, the successful conclusion of world trade talks—these are all issues that President Salinas and I are discussing together.

We are joined by our faith in freedom. And in the words of a great son of Mexico, Octavio Paz, liberty "is a movement of consciousness that leads us, at certain moments, to utter one or two words: Yes, or no." And together, let us say yes to liberty. And let us commence a new era for both our nations where what stretches between us is not a barrier but a bridge.

And so, with candor and mutual respect as our guides, let us cross over into a new era of shared progress and prosperity—for a stronger Mexico and a stronger United States and a better world.

Thank you for this warm reception. God bless the people of Monterrey. God bless the people of Mexico. And God bless the whole world in peace. And viva Mexico! Thank you.

Note: President Bush spoke at 6:15 p.m. at Heroes Plaza. A tape was not available for verification of the content of these remarks.

Statement by Press Secretary Fitzwater on President Bush's Discussions With President Carlos Salinas de Gortari in Agualeguas, Mexico
November 26, 1990

President Bush and President Salinas had lunch at the Salinas family home in Agualeguas and discussed a number of bilateral and regional issues. President Bush enjoyed the family home environment and the stay in this picturesque Mexican town. It was another opportunity, in an informal environment, for the two leaders to discuss the warm relationship between the United States and Mexico.

Much of their discussion focused on the free-trade agreement and the status of talks that have been held so far. Both Presidents are interested in pursuing the agreement as fast as possible and attach high priority to its successful conclusion.

President Bush and President Salinas also discussed increased cooperation in the war against drug trafficking, and they empha-

sized a commitment to do everything possible to end border violence.

The leaders discussed the situation in El Salvador, agreeing to press for a cease-fire and a negotiated settlement to the situation.

These issues and others will be discussed in greater detail at tomorrow morning's business session and the plenary meeting involving Cabinet officers in both countries. President Bush believes the first day has been enormously successful and appreciates the generous hospitality of President Salinas and the Mexican people. Both the President and Mrs. Bush were overwhelmed by the warmth and enthusiasm of the crowds that greeted them in Monterrey and the numbers of citizens who followed their motorcade into the city. It was a very heartwarming welcome to be received in such an enthusiastic manner.

Remarks to Community Members in Monterrey, Mexico
November 27, 1990

President and Cecilia Salinas, Secretary Solana, Ambassadors Petricioli and Negroponte, members of both Cabinets, we are delighted to be here. And at the outset of these remarks, may I thank everyone responsible for providing us with this magnificent forum in this magnificent theater and to thank the guests who are here—Presi-

dent Salinas telling me that they come from all across the country. We are honored, and I am very proud to be here.

Mr. President, Barbara and I are touched and deeply impressed by the wonderful reception that we've been given by the people of your home State, from Charreada in Agualeguas to the bustling crowds of Monterrey. For our part, it's great to see Saddleback Mountain and to be with the civic leaders of this truly magnificent city, this truly great country. And it's also a pleasure to again spend time with your President. From the chambers of the United Nations to the halls of the Kremlin to the palaces of Paris and Prague, the world recognizes that Mexico has one of the most dynamic and creative leaders of our generation, your President, President Salinas. When I say "our generation," I've got to be a little careful about this young President. [*Laughter*]

Little surprise, then, that one of my first acts as President-elect was to meet with your President in Barbara and my hometown of Houston, Texas. Yesterday President Salinas returned the favor by sharing with us the beauty of his hometown. And it was there in Agualeguas that I saw many similarities of our backgrounds. Both of us are the sons of Senators. Both of us were raised to believe in public service. And both of us know that what is true for two people is true for two nations: Friendship makes us stronger.

I know that my country is also stronger because of Mexico's contribution to our cultural heritage—a rich bequest of architecture, language, and culture. And in a more personal way, it's a heritage bestowed on the Bush family. Our son Jeb has lived in your country. His wife Columba was born in your country, grew up in León and Guanajuato. And their union has given Barbara and me three beloved grandchildren. So, when I speak of Americans and Mexicans, I can only say: *Somos una familia*—we are one family.

Of course, we're still distinct societies with very different identities, as we should be. But we've, at long last, discarded hollow fears and wornout cliches. And as the world watches, we're working together in a spirit of mutual respect.

The world is also watching because President Salinas is leading Mexico through an era of exciting, unprecedented reform. Like the Aztec eagle, Mexico is rising again as a 21st-century giant, greater than ever. The Mexican renaissance has begun.

Right from the start, President Salinas, his

fellow leaders, and the Mexican people have shown unflagging courage, even in the midst of a grave financial crisis, high inflation, and a devastating hurricane. Such courage does not go unrewarded, and that's why Mexico is growing stronger by the day.

The world celebrates the impressive success Mexico has achieved in opening its economy so quickly, in restructuring its debt more creatively, and in reforming its national economy more wisely. These are bold moves, but we live in a time that demands bold action.

The world has not seen such rapid change since the last meeting in Monterrey between a U.S. President and a Mexican President. In 1943, when President Franklin Delano Roosevelt came here to consult with President Ávila Camacho, we were allies in a life-or-death struggle against tyranny. That war ended in 1945. Another struggle, a cold war, came to a peaceful end in 1990. Yet even as the challenges change, the nature of our relationship as colleagues, neighbors, and friends endures and grows. This is what we mean by the spirit of Houston and Monterrey.

And it is in this spirit of friendship that we can work together to confront new challenges: to advance democracy and human rights, to provide for the economic prosperity and well-being of our citizens, to struggle together to protect our youth from drugs, and to protect our common environment from pollution.

As we meet, we are poised to conclude negotiations on international trade that will bring greater opportunity to our peoples. We must press now for the successful conclusion of the world trade talks known as the Uruguay round of GATT. The critical moment is at hand; we must not let the Uruguay round fail. As two of the world's largest economies, we must insist that all our trading partners act in a spirit of fairness and openness. We know all too well that trade-distorting subsidies and artificial barriers create winners and losers before the game even begins. We must insist that trade with the nations of Europe, Asia, and elsewhere at the very least be conducted on a level playing field.

Certainly, we've seen what trade liberalization can do just between two countries. Since Mexico entered GATT and lowered its tariffs, our two-way trade has boomed, from $34.8 billion in 1987 to over $50 billion in 1989; and figures are still climbing in 1990.

The maquiladora industry alone boasts of more than 1,700 plants, all generating foreign exchange for Mexico. The reason? Go to the leading automotive or electronics plants here in northern Mexico, and you'll find standards that are not excelled anywhere in the world. The world is demanding quality, and the U.S. and Mexican workers can provide it.

But the size and sophistication of U.S.-Mexico trade today only hints at our potential. We can create and share unprecedented prosperity and jobs. That is why we both want to conclude a bilateral free-trade agreement.

This agreement will not only allow us to expand markets, it will allow us to expand opportunity. Together, we can allow two economies to work in complementary ways. Together, we can produce goods and services that are world-class competitive. Free trade is good for the United States and good for Mexico—good for American workers and good for the workers of Mexico. I really look forward to the day when we will meet to sign our names to a free-trade agreement that will write a new page in North American history.

But while we endorse expanded trade, we reject the idea of a world divided into two isolated trading blocs. The United States and Mexico must set an example for all nations. In my Enterprise for the Americas Initiative, I sketched out a vision of a hemisphere open to the free movement of goods, services, and ideas, from Anchorage to Montevideo. This is a vision that President Salinas shares, for he knows that Mexico is a critical link in this chain of progress.

Your great poet and Nobel laureate Octavio Paz wrote that "Mexico has been, and is, a boundary between peoples and civilizations. Boundaries, however, are not only disjunctive obstacles, they are also bridges." So, let our work together build ever more bridges to join North and South.

But of course, our bilateral cooperation extends far beyond commerce. Our peoples live in peace and freedom; but halfway around the world, a brutal, unprovoked aggression shattered the peaceful desert sky. Once again, Mexico and the United States stand united in rejecting aggression, this time, that of the dictator of Iraq. Mexico is opposing this aggression with a strong and respected voice in the United Nations and by increasing its contribution to the world oil market. And so, I am here today to thank Mexico and thank your President and to salute the Mexican people for your world leadership.

What could not be done in the past can be done today. The world of global conflict is giving way to a new world order of global cooperation.

Next week, when I visit your sister republics in South America, I'll discuss the historic nuclear nonproliferation treaty pioneered by Mexico in 1967. This treaty has played an important role in keeping this hemisphere free of the dangerous competition of nuclear weapons that threatens so many other regions of the world.

But there's another threat to the peace, one that's more subtle, one that knows no nationality and respects no borders. I'm talking about drugs and the violence they bring, that President Salinas so eloquently spoke about a minute ago. Both President Salinas and I have committed our governments to a decisive victory over drug trafficking.

Like all conflicts, the drug war claims casualties. Each time a hero falls, it doesn't matter if he loses his life on my side or your side of the border. Let no one doubt our resolve. We will not be divided against each other, dissuaded from seeking justice, or frightened into submission. We must not flag or fail. We must and we will win together this war on drugs.

I think we've always known it, but we know now that what affects one of us affects both of us. This is no less true when it comes to our common environment—critical to the future of both our nations. A few weeks ago, I signed the first comprehensive clean air legislation in 13 years, new legislation that will benefit not just my country but the whole world. We're also working with you to improve air quality in our large cities and reduce pollution along our common border. If I may paraphrase your President, the children of Los Angeles and Mexico City deserve blue skies by day and stars to wish upon by night. That bright and hopeful future must be our mission because our children and their children deserve nothing less.

Your President and I also understand that our two nations have much to share in a greater marketplace: the marketplace of ideas. That's why we've created the U.S.-Mexico Commission for Educational and Cultural Cooperation, a new way to promote a dialog among our scholars and our artists and our educators. And when our brightest men and women confer, I believe that one of the things they will tell us is this: We're facing a new century, so let us begin this new century not simply as neighbors but as friends. Let us begin this new century not as mere partners in trade but

as partners in leadership.

Standing alone, we're still the nations that produced giants of leadership like Washington and Hidalgo, giants of freedom like Lincoln and Juárez, and giants of the spirit like Carl Sandburg and Octavio Paz. But as great as our two nations are when we stand together, we are never taller than when we stand for principle.

Once again, thank you for this extraordinarily gracious hospitality. May God bless you all and the peoples of the United States and Mexico. Thank you very, very much.

Note: President Bush spoke at 11:15 a.m. at the Teatro de la Ciudad. In his remarks, he referred to President Carlos Salinas de Gortari's wife, Cecilia; Secretary of Foreign Relations Fernando Solana Morales of Mexico; Gustavo Petricioli, Mexico's Ambassador to the United States; John D. Negroponte, U.S. Ambassador to Mexico; and President Saddam Hussein of Iraq.

Remarks at a Meeting With Mexican and American Business Leaders in Monterrey, Mexico
November 27, 1990

Thank you, my friends. Thank you, Mr. Minister, Jaime Serra, for that kind introduction, and to all of you for that warm reception. Mr. Sada, I enjoyed your remarks, sir, and thank you for your comments about Texas. I expect Bob Mosbacher would respond also in this way, or our Secretary of State Jim Baker, and quite a few others in our administration.

But I am just delighted to be here. And really, in Monterrey I have felt the warmth of the friendship that has grown between our countries. I like to feel it's always been there. But I can tell you at the outset of these brief remarks, I don't ever remember a time when Mexican and U.S. relations were better. They are superb, and I'm going to keep working my heart out to make them even better still.

I want to salute the business people from Mexico and again express my appreciation to the business leaders from the United

States that are with us today. We had a very important breakfast. This meeting, I'm told, has gotten into a lot of technical questions; and if we do have time for questions afterward and you ask me about flower duties or something of that nature, I will pass the question off to our able Ambassador Carla Hills or our able Secretary Bob Mosbacher.

But you know, preparing for this trip, I noted that 47 years ago, 1943, the last American President to visit Monterrey, Franklin D. Roosevelt, told of his hopes that one day every Mexican and American President would feel at "liberty to visit each other just as neighbors visit each other"—and he went on—"just as neighbors talk things over and get to know one another." Today that ideal of a special relationship between the United States and Mexico is no longer a dream; it is real. It's as real as the spirit and drive, the compassion and the courage of this great President of yours,

President Salinas, and of the Mexican people themselves.

Bernal Díaz, a great 16th century writer, once wrote of Mexico that "never in the world would there be discovered other lands such as these." The Mexico of 1990 lives up to that early vision. Yours is a land of beauty, the boundless energy of a creative people. It's a land of optimism and a land of infinite opportunity. You're a nation proud of yesterday and hopeful for the future, and it's a future that the United States wants to participate in. We want to share in that future.

It's easy to see why Mexico is so strong and why the relationship between our two nations has never been better, never been more important. Today more people than ever before are establishing between us stronger social, cultural, and economic ties.

Today our governments are working closely to win this war on drugs, a war that takes a terrible toll on the lifeblood of both Mexico and the United States. Our law enforcement officials have been meeting regularly with their counterparts in Mexico and working very closely together. Their efforts are beginning to pay off, as we see more illegal drugs seized than ever before.

We also see more and more universities on both sides of the border developing exchange programs as we work to encourage intellectual achievement and better understanding between our peoples. And we're working together on a host of common endeavors to protect our environment.

But it is difficult to imagine any theme more vital than the one that I'm told you have been discussing here this morning: how the private sector can create and expand the economic resources that sustain our relationship as a whole. I can tell you that I am convinced that the most important step that we can take together as two nations and as two peoples with drive and determination is the conclusion of this free-trade agreement between the United States and Mexico.

You know that agreement is important because free trade means more jobs and productivity for both Mexicans and Americans. You understand the economic importance of the United States; and America, too, realizes the importance of Mexico. Consider that Mexico is now America's third largest trading partner—$52 billion in trade in 1989—and this year's number I understand will be even higher. Since every billion dollars of exports creates roughly 25,000 jobs, more cooperation means more prosperity for more people.

I know there's no blueprint, no one-size-fits-all approach, to progress and reform. Each nation must decide how best to achieve economic growth. But it was President Salinas who said in his recent State of the Union Address: "Mexico doesn't want to be a third world nation. It wants to be a first world nation." He understands that prosperity in this hemisphere depends on trade, not aid. Already, your automotive, electronic, tourism, and other industries have shown world-class productive capability. And when you grow, we grow. A Mexico that wants to get out and compete has selling power, but it also has buying power. And that's a good Mexico—good for America.

Negotiating this free-trade agreement is not going to be easy. You're going to hear criticism—we all will—just as we did when we negotiated our free-trade agreement with our neighbors to the north, with Canada. But we should remember what trade liberalization can and already has done. In 1988, Mexico entered the GATT, and our bilateral trade with Mexico soared to over $50 billion—up $17 billion from the year before the GATT entry.

Virtually everyone favors free trade and fair trade, but not everyone has the vision to make it a reality. I believe that we do; I believe that Mexico and the United States do. And I ask you not only to help make it happen but to make it succeed. Both our peoples can then look to a future of peace and prosperity—a proud future for two nations sharing not just common borders, not just common ideals, but a friendship that will last for generations.

I can't tell you what a joy it was yesterday to be in President Salinas' home with our family and his family. It was more than symbolic because of the hospitality—was just exceptional. But I think it sent a signal—I hope it did send a signal—that we are true friends, North and South, Mexico and the United States of America. We have so much in common.

I want to thank you all for your kindness. I want to thank you for participating in this important forum. I want to thank you on my wife's behalf for this exceptional hospitality on this truly wonderful visit. And I want to express my thanks once again to President Salinas, to Minister Jaime Serra. And God bless the great nation of Mexico. Thank you all very, very much.

[At this point, an audience member asked a question in Spanish, and a translation was not provided.]

The President. In the first place, I don't think that protectionism in our country is very strong. As the gigantic United States economy slows down—it may slow down even more—it concerns me that some in our country and some in our Congress might turn inward to what you properly label as a protectionist mode. I don't think it is a major problem. And the reason I don't is because, in part, of our relatively slow, gigantic economy—some will tell you parts of our country are in recession; others are saying it's just very, very close to very fractional growth. But nevertheless, in spite of these differences, our exports are very, very strong.

And I think most Americans realize that if we are going to export we better not be protectionists. You can't have it both ways. We shouldn't want to have it both ways. So, I don't think, as we go forward on a free-trade agreement, that it's going to get caught up in the evil vise of U.S. protectionism.

I think one thing that would be extraordinarily helpful in that regard is a successful conclusion of the GATT round, the Uruguay round, because I think that would send a very strong signal.

And if we are successful, we're going to have—Ambassador Hills, Secretary Mosbacher, and myself as President—we're going to have some problems with certain elements, certain groups, in the United States Congress. But I am convinced that a successful negotiation in conclusion of the Uruguay round will be approved strongly by the Congress, and I think it would be extraordinarily helpful in setting back any enthusiasm for protection that might exist in our country.

Recently, I had to veto a piece of legislation which I'm sure you're familiar with regarding textiles. Now, that was a manifestation of protectionism—lingering protectionism, you might say. But the veto was sustained. It was just before an election. The popular vote was the other way, opposite my position, and I understood this. But the veto was sustained. And this President will continue to veto protectionist legislation. I may not get majorities in the Congress, but I think I will have enough support in the Congress to see that we don't throw up any legal impediments to the work that's going forward on the Mexican-U.S. free-trade agreement.

So, I'm glad you raised it. It is a concern. It is not an overwhelming concern. I think it's something that can be managed. And I feel, from talking to a lot of Members of Congress and to some of our own people about this, that there is genuine enthusiasm for this project that would override any vestiges of protectionism.

Note: The President spoke at 11:59 a.m. in the ballroom at the Casino Monterrey. In his opening remarks, he referred to Secretary of Commerce Jaime José Serra Puche of Mexico; Bernardo Garza Sada, prominent Mexican businessman; Secretary of Commerce Robert A. Mosbacher; and U.S. Trade Representative Carla A. Hills.

Toast at the State Luncheon Hosted by President Carlos Salinas de Gortari in Monterrey, Mexico
November 27, 1990

President Salinas, if I may, I want to thank you for your hospitality and friendship, and your counsel and your commitment to a stronger relationship between our two countries.

For both President Salinas and I, home is no more than 200 miles from our common border. He referred to this. We both grew up in families with a heritage of public service, and we were inaugurated at the same time in history. When we first met in Houston in 1988, neither of us had yet assumed office, but both were fully aware of the challenges facing us in the relationships between our nations.

No country is more important to the United States than Mexico is. The United States bears the imprint of your culture. Your nation is our third largest trading partner. Twelve million Americans—twelve million—call Mexico their cultural homeland. We've faced many challenges together, whether it's the conflict of Central America or the drug lords in the Andes.

In our Houston meeting and in our many meetings since then, you've always brought Mexico's perspective into positive focus, pointing the way to the kind of communication and cooperation that has benefited us both so much. And now we're on the verge of negotiating an historic free-trade agreement, the symbol of how far our two countries have come in learning to understand, respect, and work with one another. This agreement will unleash powerful energies in both economies. Countless new ventures will emerge. More jobs, higher standards of living, and greater productivity will make us both more competitive in the global arena.

As you said in your State of the Union Message, "We want to harness the new winds of change that are blowing beyond our borders." And without ignoring risks, you celebrated new freedoms, and you saw fresh hope.

Mr. President, as I leave Monterrey, my views are reinforced. I share your views enthusiastically. We're not on an easy path, but I firmly believe we are on the right one. And I sincerely hope that our two nations share the same path of freedom and opportunity for years to come.

And so, in the spirit of Houston and Monterrey, I raise my glass to a great leader and a great nation, a man who has raised Mexican-U.S. relations to a new level, to President Carlos Salinas de Gortari and to Mexico.

God bless you all, and thank you for a wonderful visit.

Note: The President spoke at 1:08 p.m. in the courtyard of the Governor's Palace. Following the luncheon, he participated in a departure ceremony at General Mariano Escobedo International Airport and returned to Washington, DC. A tape was not available for verification of the content of these remarks.

Mexico-United States Joint Statement
November 27, 1990

JOINT PRESS STATEMENT AT THE CONCLUSION OF PRESIDENT BUSH'S STATE VISIT TO MEXICO HELD IN MONTERREY ON NOVEMBER 27, 1990.

At the invitation of President Carlos Salinas de Gortari, President George Bush of the United States of America paid a state visit to Mexico, November 26–27, 1990. During this visit the two Presidents exchanged views on an extensive agenda of common interest.

Both Presidents, reflecting the climate of friendship and cordiality of relations between the two countries and the intention reaffirmed by both heads of state in previous meetings for this climate to materialize in concrete results to enhance the symbols of good neighborliness, held a friendly and cordial dialogue on the most important issues on the bilateral agenda as well as on regional and global matters.

Presidents Bush and Salinas de Gortari underscored that the best means to strengthen bilateral relations in the future is through dialogue with mutual respect for each other's sovereignty. They stressed their conviction that bilateral relations should be evaluated as a whole, without allowing any single issue, regardless of its complexity, to detract from the need for maintaining such a dialogue, in order to ensure that relations remain at their present optimum level.

The diversity and complexity of Mexico-United States affairs should be viewed as a challenge and as an opportunity that encourage nations to pay unceasing attention to this relationship and to take effective measures to solve problems still pending.

In reviewing recent achievements, the Presidents noted the progress achieved in areas such as trade, financial cooperation, border issues, the fight against international drug traffic and abuse, cooperation for environmental protection, and strengthening of cultural and educational exchange, and tourism. The Presidents also stated that such achievements are largely due to the excellent cooperation between the Governments within the framework of the binational commission, through which a substantial number of Cabinet members of both countries and leaders of U.S. agencies and Mexican decentralized organizations can meet to hold a dialogue at least once a year.

Free Trade Agreement

In the area of the rapidly expanding trade and investment, the Presidents reaffirmed their commitment in regard to the need to promote trade liberalization and to continue consultations towards a free trade agreement between Mexico and the United States, contemplating the way in which Canada might consider joining such negoti-

ations.

Enterprise for the Americas and Uruguay Round

The Presidents also focused on the current status of consultations with Latin American countries about the Enterprise for the Americas, and reaffirmed their commitment to a successful conclusion of the Uruguay round.

Border Issues

The Presidents' discussion included a general examination of issues concerning their common border, noting that it is one of the most heavily utilized in the world.

Both governments, having agreed to facilitate the rapid passage through ports of entry, and conscious of the vital importance for border communities of both nationalities of prompt attention in the ports of entry of the two countries, and affirming their interest in achieving improved facilitation of services, including operating hours, expressed their satisfaction with the establishment of new border ports, and with the progress in the construction of the Zaragoza-Ysleta, Colombia-Dolores and Lucio Blanco-Los Indios bridges, as well as the authorization for nine new ports of entry.

The Presidents shared their concern about the cases of violence on both sides of the border. They strongly condemned such acts of violence and instructed their respective authorities to propose, through the subgroup on consular affairs and protection of the binational commission and other timely high-level meetings, joint recommendations calling for new specific mechanisms with the objectives of arriving at a satisfactory solution of pending cases and creating awareness in order to prevent the repetition of such incidents in the future.

Tuna Exports

President Salinas informed President Bush of his concern about the impact of the tuna embargo on Mexico. President Bush noted the recent judicial action in support of the administration's position that the embargo be stayed, and pledged to work cooperatively with Mexico bilaterally and other nations to seek alternative solutions to this problem, including a multilateral convention.

On the same subject, President Salinas ratified his Government's intention of taking part in multilateral agreements—based on equity and appropriate scientific evidence—for the conservation of marine species, including tuna and marine mammals.

The War Against Drug Trafficking and Drug Abuse

In reference to the fight against international drug trafficking, Presidents Salinas and Bush reaffirmed their conviction that only through efficient international cooperation, based on strict respect for each country's sovereignty, can drug trafficking be fought, and at the same time the demand for drugs reduced.

The Presidents underscored that in this war it is the exclusive responsibility of each country to reinforce in its respective jurisdiction applicable national laws.

The Presidents also reaffirmed once more their recognition of the courage shown by officials waging the war on drug trafficking in each country.

The Governments of Mexico and the United States further reaffirmed their intention of continuing the expeditious consultations concerning the exchange of the instruments of ratification of the mutual legal assistance agreement. President Salinas de Gortari pointed out that the Mexican Senate would have to be informed of the results of such consultations in accordance with the Mexican Constitution.

Environmental Cooperation

The Presidents emphasized the need for ongoing cooperation in the area of environmental protection.

Both Presidents instructed the authorities responsible for environmental affairs of their countries to prepare a comprehensive plan designed to periodically examine ways and means to reinforce border cooperation in this regard, based on the 1983 bilateral agreement. Such a mechanism should seek ways to improve coordination and cooperation, with a view to solving the problems of air, soil, and water quality and of hazardous wastes. State and municipal authorities of both governments and private organizations

in both countries should participate in such tasks as appropriate.

Educational Cooperation

The Presidents expressed their satisfaction with the signing of an agreement to create the United States-Mexico Commission for Educational and Cultural Exchange for Scholarships, stressing the significant participation of the private sector in the Executive Board of said Commission.

Financial Cooperation

The Presidents examined the measures adopted against money laundering, as well as those designed to avoid double taxation and agreed to pursue negotiations on issues in this area.

Tourism

The Presidents agreed on the need to facilitate tourist exchange and transportation even further. To that end they agreed to support mechanisms such as the signing of a memorandum of understanding for charter buses to bring tourists into Mexico and to encourage and promote investments in this area.

World Affairs

In the area of regional and global matters, the two Presidents held an extensive exchange of views and information. President Salinas de Gortari informed President Bush of Mexico's intention to cooperate in the search for a negotiated solution to the conflict in El Salvador, in support of the measures taken by the Secretary General of the UN based on resolutions of the Security Council.

In turn, President Bush provided a detailed explanation and assessment of the Persian Gulf situation from the U.S. perspective after his recent visit to that area. The two Presidents once again expressed the desire for a peaceful resolution to the situation in accord with UN resolutions, and exhorted the Government of Iraq to effect an immediate unconditional withdrawal from Kuwait and to release at once all hostages that still remain in that country. Both Presidents expressed their satisfaction with the prevailing spirit of a frank and positive dialogue, both between themselves and their administrations, reflecting the unswerving will to sustain and strengthen the friendly relations between Mexico and the United States.

Note: The joint statement was made available by the Office of the Press Secretary, but was not issued as a White House press release.

Remarks on Signing the Food, Agriculture, Conservation, and Trade Act of 1990
November 28, 1990

Thank you very much. Thank you all. Well, thank you all very much. Delighted to have you here at the White House. Let me first thank Secretary Yeutter for all his hard work, and then the front row of heavy hitters here from the United States Congress: Chairman Leahy and, of course, the minority leader, Senator Dole; Senator Cochran; Senator Lugar; Senator Bond—all extremely interested, all terribly important to this legislation. I understand, Clayt, that there's quite a few people from the Department here, and I want to take this opportunity to thank them.

You know, there's no question here or anyplace else how crucial a strong agricultural sector is to the future of this country. From the fields to the supermarkets, agriculture creates 1 of every 7 jobs in this country; 8 out of 10 of them off the farm, spreading the seeds of economic growth across the entire country.

America grew to greatness on the strength of own agriculture. For that, I know that all of us will always be proud and thankful to America's farmers. Our farmers are the best. Period! They outproduce every other nation in the world by far, and even outproduce some continents. They're world champion providers.

We're in the Uruguay round negotiations, making every effort to achieve substantial agricultural reform, which will include major reductions in trade-distorting barriers. We want to bring home a fair deal for American farmers, and I can assure you there will not be a signature on one that is not fair.

Here at home, the legislation I'm about to sign will help our farmers continue to be leaders in global agricultural trade. We've been working closely with the leadership in the Congress to get a farm bill that keeps our farmers competitive and keeps our rural areas environmentally sound. And I believe, after talking to some of the Members here, that this bill meets that standard. It's a market-oriented bill that lets farmers make more of their own production decisions based on the market rather than on government support prices. It also encourages the research that is so crucial to helping our farmers maintain their global lead in agriculture.

The 1985 farm bill was a success. Farm income has been at record-high levels for the last 3 years. This bill, and the reconciliation bill that accompanied it, continue and expand the market orientation of that law. Farmers will have greater flexibility to enhance their income by having the choice to make their own production decisions in response to market signals. Moreover, for every percentage point that is shaved from interest rates and inflation due to deficit reduction, farm income benefits by over a billion dollars.

Because farmers have always been important stewards of the Earth, this farm bill will help farmers protect water quality and wildlife habitat. And its greater flexibility will boost crop rotation, in turn helping to control weeds and pests and erosion. There's more in this legislation to protect our environment. In fact, this is the most environmentally progressive farm bill ever signed. It creates a wetlands reserve; improves the Conservation Reserve Program; and encourages urban forestry initiatives, including funding for a program that's near and dear to my heart, the America the

Beautiful Initiative. That moves us toward our goal of planting a billion trees across America.

For the sake of low-income Americans, I'm particularly pleased with the 5-year continuation of the Food Stamp Program, the foundation for food assistance for Americans in need. Congress and this administration worked closely together to develop a program that is easier for recipients to use and reauthorizes the Commodity Supplemental Food Program and the Emergency Food Assistance Program.

So, to the Members of Congress who worked so hard to get this bill passed—to Senator Leahy and Dick Lugar of the Senate Agricultural Committee; then in the House side to Congressmen Kika de la Garza, the chairman, and Ed Madigan, who couldn't be with us today; and to all involved here—and I'll single out again our minority leader in the Senate, Bob Dole—well done.

And to you, Clayt, and the dedicated people at the Department who worked so tirelessly with Congress to get this farm bill written and passed: You've given this ad-

ministration a farm bill of which I think we can all be very proud.

And to all of you here today from the State ASCS [Agricultural Stabilization and Conservation Service] offices, who will be working so hard to implement this bill in the coming years, thank you for taking on this crucial task. You're helping assure a bright future for farming in America.

And now, with no further ado, I'd like to ask these five Members of Congress and the United States Senate to come up as we sign this legislation.

[At this point, the President signed the legislation.]

Listen, thank you all very much for coming, and he who lifts it can have it. *[Laughter]*

Note: The President spoke at 11:07 a.m. in Room 450 of the Old Executive Office Building. In his remarks, he referred to Secretary of Agriculture Clayton K. Yeutter. The President's closing comments referred to the large size of the bill. S. 2830, approved November 28, was assigned Public Law No. 101–624.

Statement on Signing the Food, Agriculture, Conservation, and Trade Act of 1990
November 28, 1990

I am pleased to sign S. 2830, the "Food, Agriculture, Conservation, and Trade Act of 1990." This Act represents the culmination of many long months of effort by the Congress and the Administration. The effort has been worthwhile, for this farm bill addresses several goals, shared by my Administration and the Congress: keeping American farmers competitive in world markets, assisting farmers in their efforts to protect our environment, and stabilizing the farm economy and our food supply. I also applaud the reauthorization of the nutrition assistance programs vital to the good health of our low-income Americans.

I am most pleased with those aspects of the 1990 farm bill that continue the

market-oriented shift begun in the 1985 legislation. Increased planting flexibility, farmers' control over their own production decisions, and greater reliance on signals from the market rather than on Government support programs are key to this market-oriented shift. Increased flexibility in planting choices contained in the 1990 farm bill will allow farmers to break out of the traditional farm program straitjacket, which bound them to produce the same crop year after year, regardless of market opportunities.

In the Uruguay Round, we are committed to reducing market barriers and export subsidies that deny our farmers competitive access to market opportunities around the world.

Agriculture will greatly benefit from the reduction of the Federal deficit because interest rates and inflation will be less. For every percentage point that interest rates fall, farm income is estimated to increase by three-quarters of a billion dollars annually. For every percentage point shaved off inflation in the cost of production, farm income is estimated to grow by one-half billion dollars annually. American farmers have always made the most of such opportunities.

From a budget perspective, the reductions in spending in this bill and in the related provisions of the Omnibus Budget Reconciliation Act of 1990—a total of around $13 billion over the next 5 years—will assist in the effort to reduce the deficit and reduce interest rates and inflation.

Planting flexibility available through the 1990 bill provides a further important step in harmonizing the protection and enhancement of the environment with commodity support programs. Farmers have always been recognized as stewards of the land, and now I call upon them to continue their leadership. Many provisions of this farm bill will help farmers protect water quality and wildlife habitat. Greater planting flexibility will boost the use of crop rotation, which will in turn enhance soil fertility and aid in the control of weeds, pests, and soil degradation. The Congress reaffirmed its commitment, which I share, to the preservation of wetlands in establishing goals for enrolling land in a Wetland Reserve Program.

The forestry provisions of the farm bill provide the authorization for my America the Beautiful Initiative. Although appropriations to date may not be sufficient to ensure that my goal of planting one billion trees annually is fully met, strides in that direction are incorporated in the legislation. I will continue to work with the Congress to see that our mutual concerns for our Nation's forest resources are fully met.

I am particularly pleased with the 5-year continuation of the food stamp programs, the foundation for food assistance for low-income Americans, and the reauthorization of the Commodity Supplemental Food Program, the Emergency Food Assistance Programs, and the Food Distribution Program on Indian Reservations. The Congress, the

Administration, and the States worked together to enhance food stamp program integrity to ensure that benefits are used as intended. Coupled with last year's reauthorization of the Child Nutrition Program, and the Special Supplemental Food Program for Woman, Infants, and Children, the Nation's food assistance programs are now in place for years to come, ensuring that the bounty of American agriculture is shared with all Americans. However, I am concerned that the bill forgives the States' obligations to repay the Federal Government for past errors in payments. Given the demands on Federal resources, everything possible must be done to require their efficient and fair use.

I am also pleased that this farm bill reforms and streamlines the administration of our overseas food aid programs and continues our export programs that keep American products competitive in world markets. Of particular importance to me are provisions that would implement parts of my Enterprise for the Americas Initiative aimed at helping Latin American and Caribbean countries and grant authority to reduce needy countries' debt repayment obligations under the Food for Peace Program.

I am also pleased that the Congress has endorsed the Administration's initiative for growth in the size of the competitive research grant program for agriculture. Only by ensuring that the best minds produce the best science can we build a secure foundation for future technological advances in farming. However, while the Federal Government has a critical and unique role to play in supporting such basic science. I do not see a corresponding need to subsidize private sector activities in product development. Consequently, while I strongly favor the idea of commercializing emerging innovative technologies, I do not support the establishment of the Alternative Agricultural Research and Commercialization Board to provide federally subsidized grants and loans to the private sector for this program.

Some aspects of the rural development title will help to improve the economic vitality of rural America. In particular, formation of a new Rural Development Administration presents an opportunity to improve coordination of important community and business programs. However, many other rural development provisions could greatly increase Federal costs without necessarily improving the welfare of rural America. In particular, the provisions regarding rural telephone loans represent unwarranted increases in Federal subsidies and risk. Telephone borrowers, many of whom are large and profitable holding companies, can now use Federal loans to build office buildings, can determine their own loan terms, and can have their required debt service margin reduced. These changes reduce the Administration's ability to manage properly telephone loan risk, and in effect turn control of the program over to the borrowers.

I also note that in enacting amendments to the law governing the Rural Telephone Bank Board, the Congress provided that the members of the Board would exercise management authority "within the limitations prescribed by law." Consistent with my obligation to construe statutory provisions to avoid raising constitutional questions, I construe this savings provision to embody the recognition that those Board members not appointed in conformity with the Constitution cannot exercise the authority vested by the Constitution in officers of the United States.

I further note that a number of other provisions of the bill could be construed to vest governmental authority in private parties. These provisions appear to raise constitutional concerns, and I am accordingly directing the Secretary of Agriculture to consult the Attorney General to consider whether curative legislation or other action is needed to ensure that these authorities are exercised as the Constitution requires.

In spite of these drawbacks, on balance I have before me a farm bill that will enhance the competitiveness of our farmers and the health of our citizens. My gratitude goes to those who have worked so tirelessly to produce this legislation: concerned citizens, Members of Congress, and my own Administration. I look forward to continued prosperity in the agricultural economy and good health and nutrition for our citizens.

This is not a perfect farm bill either from my perspective or from that of many Members of Congress. But the vision of all who worked on this legislation is the same: prosperity for our agricultural sector and the nutritional well-being of our people. The bill before me is faithful to our shared vision.

GEORGE BUSH

The White House,
Nov. 28, 1990.

Note: S. 2830, approved November 28, was assigned Public Law No. 101–624.

Remarks on Signing the Cranston-Gonzalez National Affordable Housing Act
November 28, 1990

Well, thank you all very much for being here today. And of course, it's great to be with our enthusiastic and effective Secretary of HUD, Jack Kemp, who deserves great credit for what we're about to do here. And of course, I want to salute the Members of Congress—they've been so helpful and instrumental in this—who are with us today. I see Kit Bond, and Al D'Amato was to be—they're sitting there. And I want to thank, particularly, the chairmen of the Banking Committee, Senator Riegle and Congressman Henry B. Gonzalez, for their work on this. I'm told that their counterparts, Jake Garn and Chalmers Wylie, are not with us today, the ranking Republicans on the committee; but I also want to thank them for their remarkable efforts.

I understand that some mayors are in town. Quite a few mayors and other local elected officials are with us, and I want to welcome them to the White House. I'm told that Kimi Gray is here, over here. And,

Kimi, you're kind of a symbol of hope for the aspirations of a lot of people, and I'm just delighted you're here with us today.

Now, let me start with a story, a bit of history—1862, the middle of the Civil War. And on May 20th of that year, Abraham Lincoln sat down with pen in hand and signed into law the Homestead Act of 1862. And that bill gave 160 acres to any family who wanted to make a go of it in the wilderness and reach for the American dream.

It is one of the most successful endeavors in American history, causing the great land rush to the Wild West and forming the vision for a new homesteading program in urban America today. Because Abraham Lincoln's Homestead Act empowered people, it freed people from the burden of poverty. It freed them to control their own destinies, to create their own opportunities, and to live the vision of the American dream. Likewise today, creating the opportunity for low-income Americans to become property owners is a key to fighting poverty and offering real hope to thousands.

I've said before that a cornerstone of our effort to reduce the heavy hand of government is this idea of empowering people, not bureaucracies, and giving people—working people, poor people, everyone—control over their own lives and access to property and jobs so that all Americans can have a life of dignity, responsibility, and economic opportunity. Secretary Kemp has long been a champion of this idea, and that's why I have appointed him as Chairman of the Domestic Policy Council's Economic Empowerment Task Force.

The status quo of centralized bureaucracy is not working for the people—the ones who need affordable housing; the ones who want to choose the best schools for their kids or child care for their younger children; the ones who want to pull themselves out of dependency and into a life of self-sufficiency in a safe, clean, and drug-free community. It's the people who have the best answers for themselves and their families, not the Government.

And that's exactly what the National Affordable Housing Act that I'm about to sign here does in several ways: It puts power in the hands of people. First, it authorizes a major administration initiative: Homeownership and Opportunity for People Everywhere, the HOPE Initiative. HOPE will provide new opportunities for low-income families to buy their own homes—urban homesteaders, if you will—and helps the residents of public housing to buy their own units. Tenant management, control and, ultimately, ownership of public housing is an idea whose time has come. And let me just tell you why.

When the people who live in public housing are in charge, the results are remarkable: more people pay their rent, maintenance improves, operating costs decline, and crime rates plummet. Employment goes up, more kids stay in school, and neighborhoods spring back to life. And the reason? Because each resident simply now has a stake in society—an equity stake—a chance to make a go of it, to live the American dream for themselves.

We want public housing to become a springboard for independence, not a bottomless pit for dependency. HUD used to be asked to give awards for public housing residents who stayed in public housing the longest, and we stopped doing that. Jack made a significant change there. And now—and even more so with this bill—we're offering incentives to public housing tenants who move out and move up into the productive economic mainstream. These are the people who will help us meet our goal of 1 million new homeowners by 1992.

But there's more. This bill contains Home Investment Partnerships, a new block grant to provide incentives to States, localities, and nonprofit organizations to provide people who currently rent with vouchers, tenant-based assistance, and rehabilitation of existing housing, because affordable housing is in everybody's interest. And in addition to housing assistance for migrant farm workers, the elderly, and the disabled, this legislation also creates the Shelter Plus Care Program to assist homeless persons who are mentally ill, who have a drug abuse problem or other problems, to give them the support they need to keep them from returning to a desolate life on the streets.

Finally, it reforms certain programs in the FHA, in the Federal Housing Administration, to make them more financially sound. The National Affordable Housing Act gives people the best kind of government assistance: It provides opportunity, and it encourages responsibility without the shackles of dependency. And that is really the American dream, for no matter where people live or how much money they have, all people yearn to control their own lives. Abraham Lincoln knew this, and his vision lives on today as the foundation for our efforts to empower all Americans.

And so, it is with that in mind—the undying ideal of hope and opportunity for all—that I am pleased to sign this bill into law.

And once again, I want to thank each and every Member of Congress who has worked hard on this legislation, particularly the two

chairmen that are with us today. And of course, again, my respects for his leadership to Jack Kemp, the Secretary of HUD. Thank you all for joining us today.

And now, if I can lift it up, I'll sign it. [*Laughter*]

Note: The President spoke at 2:05 p.m. in the East Room at the White House. In his remarks, he referred to Senators Christopher S. Bond and Alfonse M. D'Amato, and Kimi O. Gray, chairperson of the National Association of Resident Management Corps. and chairperson of the Kenilworth-Parkside Resident Management Corp. S. 566, approved November 28, was assigned Public Law No. 101–625.

Statement on Signing the Cranston-Gonzalez National Affordable Housing Act
November 28, 1990

It is with great pleasure that I today sign S. 566, the "Cranston-Gonzalez National Affordable Housing Act." In addition to extending and reforming existing housing programs, this Act creates and expands innovative new programs proposed by this Administration. These new programs will advance opportunities for homeownership and economic self-sufficiency in our Nation's most distressed communities. This Act is an exciting bipartisan initiative to break down the walls separating low-income people from the American dream of opportunity and homeownership.

I want to note the contributions of several people to the enactment of this landmark legislation, starting with Secretary of Housing and Urban Development Jack Kemp. Secretary Kemp has brought a unique vision to his job and a commitment to empowerment as a tool to encourage individual dignity and initiative and reward productive work effort.

Many Members of Congress also made significant contributions to the bipartisan effort to produce a housing bill. A few deserve special recognition. Senators Alan

Cranston and Al D'Amato have devoted the last several years to the passage of a comprehensive housing bill, and we would not be here today without their efforts. Likewise, I want to recognize the efforts of Congressmen Henry Gonzalez and Chalmers Wylie, whose spirit of cooperation throughout the legislative process helped bring us to this point.

S. 566 contains the Homeownership and Opportunity for People Everywhere—HOPE—initiatives that my Administration submitted to the Congress earlier this year. HOPE represents a dramatic and fundamental restructuring of housing policy. It recognizes that the poor and low-income tenants—not public housing authorities and developers—are our clients. HOPE will do what traditional programs have not done: empower low-income families to achieve self-sufficiency and to have a stake in their communities by promoting resident management as well as other forms of homeownership.

The cornerstone of HOPE is a program to provide grants to enable low-income families and tenants to become homeowners.

HOPE homeownership grants can be used for planning activities, including the development of resident management corporations. They can also be used for rehabilitation and post-sale subsidies to help ensure the success of homeownership. HOPE grants are eligible to be used in public housing and vacant, foreclosed, and distressed single-family and multifamily properties.

The legislation also includes my Administration's Operation Bootstrap—or Family Self-Sufficiency—proposal. In the past, public housing was seen as a long-term residence for low-income people. My Administration believes that Federal housing subsidies should serve as transitional tools to help low-income families achieve self-sufficiency, move up and into the private housing market, and join the economic mainstream. The Family Self-Sufficiency Program will ensure that all new housing voucher and certificate assistance is coordinated with employment counseling, job training, child care, transportation, and other services to encourage upward mobility.

S. 566 also authorizes our HOPE for Elderly Independence proposal to combine vouchers and certificates with supportive services to assist the frail elderly. In addition, it authorizes Shelter Plus Care, which couples housing assistance and other services to homeless persons with disabilities and their families.

This Act also reflects the efforts of the Administration and the Congress to enact needed reforms to the Federal Housing Administration's (FHA) single-family mortgage insurance program. These reforms will ensure that FHA is actuarially safe and financially sound. The Act's provisions meet the four principal objectives of my Administration's original FHA reform proposals: the achievement of adequate minimum capital standards by the earliest possible date; insurance premiums that reflect the risk of default; minimum equity contributions by borrowers to protect them and the insurance fund from default risk; and maintaining the emphasis of FHA on low- and moderate-income homebuyers. With these reforms, we will be ensuring the availability of FHA for future generations of families seeking to achieve homeownership.

I am pleased that this Act contains a solution to the preservation and prepayment question that reflects the Administration's basic principles. These include protecting project residents from becoming homeless as a result of a mortgage prepayment; emphasizing alternative prepayment strategies that provide opportunities for homeownership; and honoring the contracts between project owners and the Federal Government.

One important preservation strategy is to provide project owners with economic incentives to maintain their properties for low-income use. I am concerned, however, that the incentives in S. 566 are more generous than are necessary, providing excessive benefits over the long term that will be paid by all taxpayers. Nonetheless, I recognize that this preservation proposal is a compromise and that it represents a good-faith effort by the Congress to meet the Administration's concern that limited Federal funds be provided to those who need assistance.

This legislation provides a new block grant, HOME Investment Partnerships, to promote partnerships among the Federal Government, States, localities, nonprofit organizations, and private industry. These partnerships will seek to utilize effectively all available resources and a wide variety of approaches to meet housing needs.

My Administration has been concerned that the HOME program not become a vehicle for the production of new, federally subsidized rental housing at the expense of other, more efficient and better targeted subsidies, such as rental assistance to poor tenants.

I believe this legislation addresses our concerns, because it provides for a wide variety of uses for HOME funds, including tenant-based assistance. It also imposes higher State and local matching requirements for new construction than for tenant-based assistance or minor rehabilitation. In addition, it requires that 90 percent of HOME funds be targeted to families with incomes at 60 percent or below the area median income.

Unfortunately, this Act also sets aside up

to 15 percent of total HOME funds in FY 1992 to be used solely for a rental housing production program. I do not believe that the earmarking of funds for new construction is consistent with the goal of providing States and localities with maximum flexibility to meet their specific affordable housing needs.

I am further concerned that this legislation, in several instances, would relax long-standing provisions of current law that provide a preference for housing assistance for those families who are most in need. Although the Federal Government currently serves about 4.3 million low-income families, there are about 4 million additional families, most of them very low income, whose housing needs have not been met. We should not divert assistance from those who need it most.

Several additional provisions warrant careful construction to avoid constitutional concerns. For example, section 302(b)(7) of the Act calls on the President to appoint one member of the Board of Directors of the National Homeownership Trust to represent consumer interests. In light of the President's power under article II, section 2 of the Constitution, I sign this bill with the understanding that the individual appointed by the President to serve on the Board represents the United States as an officer of the United States. The requirement that this individual represent consumer interests does not constrain the President's constitutional authority to appoint officers of the United States, subject only to the advice and consent of the Senate.

Section 943(e)(3)(A) provides that the National Commission on Manufactured Housing "may secure directly from any department or agency of the United States such data and information as the Commission may require." I sign the bill with the understanding that this provision does not limit the constitutional ability of the President to withhold information, the disclosure of which might significantly impair the conduct of foreign relations, the national security, or the deliberative processes of the executive branch or the performance of its constitutional duties.

Finally, it is the Federal Government's responsibility to ensure that the benefits of Federal programs are offered to individuals in a way consistent with the equal protection guarantee of the Constitution. In that regard, I am concerned about section 958(a) of the Act, which provides a preference to native Hawaiians for housing assistance programs for housing located in the Hawaiian homelands; section 958(d)(1), which defines "native Hawaiian" in a race-based fashion; and section 911, which would exempt this preference from the provisions of the Housing and Community Development Act of 1974 relating to nondiscrimination on the basis of race. This race-based classification cannot be derived from the constitutional authority granted to the Congress and the executive branch to benefit native Americans as members of tribes. I direct the Attorney General and the Secretary of Housing and Urban Development to prepare remedial legislation for submission to Congress during its next session, so that this Act, and similar provisions in other Acts, can be brought into compliance with the Constitution's requirements.

I am pleased that, in crafting this legislation, the Congress also has modified a number of the rural housing programs administered by the Department of Agriculture's Farmers Home Administration. As a result, these programs will be more responsive to the needs of low-income residents of small towns and rural areas. A significant change is a new program of guaranteed loans for homeownership by low- and moderate-income residents in rural areas. This housing reform will provide assistance to these individuals and families more effectively and efficiently.

In conclusion, this legislation represents true bipartisanship, considerable give-and-take, and good-faith negotiation between the Congress and the Administration. It reforms and reauthorizes existing programs to provide for community development, to operate and modernize public housing, and to assist in meeting the needs of low-income families, the elderly, and the handicapped. In addition, through HOPE, it provides the potential for the redirection of housing policy back toward the poor.

The signing of the "Cranston-Gonzalez National Affordable Housing Act" presents us with an opportunity to renew our commitment to the goals we all share: decent, safe, and affordable housing for all Americans.

GEORGE BUSH

The White House,
November 28, 1990.

Note: S. 566, approved November 28, was assigned Public Law No. 101–625.

Statement on Signing the Fishery Conservation Amendments of 1990
November 28, 1990

I am today signing H.R. 2061, the "Fishery Conservation Amendments of 1990," notwithstanding reservations I have concerning some of its provisions.

H.R. 2061 authorizes appropriations for and amends the Magnuson Fishery Conservation and Management Act, which provides the primary authority for the conservation and management of fishery resources within the 200-mile Exclusive Economic Zone (EEZ) off our coasts. Many of the amendments made by H.R. 2061 will enable us to better conserve and manage our precious fishery resources.

However, numerous provisions of the Act could be construed to encroach upon the President's authority under the Constitution to conduct foreign relations, including the unfettered conduct of negotiations with foreign nations. Further, one provision directs that fishery management plans prepared or approved by the Secretary of Commerce contain "regulations implementing recommendations by international organizations in which the United States participates." If this provision were construed to require the Secretary to implement the recommendations of international organizations in which the United States participates, it would unconstitutionally subject the executive branch to the control of international bodies that are not politically accountable to the American people. Finally, two provisions purport to direct the Secretary to make legislative recommendations to the Congress. Under Article II, Section 3 of the Constitution, the President possesses the exclusive authority to determine which legislative measures he and his subordinates will recommend.

To avoid constitutional questions that might otherwise arise, I will construe all these provisions to be advisory, not mandatory.

I am concerned that several of the Act's provisions regarding highly migratory species not be construed to create a gap in the authority of the United States to manage those species. Current law defines "highly migratory species" to mean only species of tuna and excludes such species from the exclusive fishery management authority asserted by the United States in our EEZ. H.R. 2061 would eliminate this exclusion effective January 1, 1992. Thus, effective as of that date, the United States will assert management authority over tuna in its EEZ. As a matter of international law, effective immediately the United States will recognize similar assertions by coastal nations regarding their exclusive economic zones.

The Act also expands the definition of "highly migratory species" to include marlin, ocean sharks, sailfishes, and swordfish—non-tuna species for which management authority is presently asserted and exercised. Consequently, H.R. 2061 could be interpreted to expand the exclusion and thus withdraw the authority to manage these species until the exclusion is eliminated in 1992. It is my understanding that the Congress intended the management of these species to continue.

Accordingly, for purposes of the tuna exclusion that remains in effect until 1992, I will not construe the revised definition to take effect. For all other purposes, the revised definition takes effect immediately.

Thus, the authority of the United States to manage the species added to the definition will continue, and the responsibility for managing those species will transfer immediately from specified fishery management councils to the Secretary.

Finally, the Act contains a provision that departs from procedures currently governing challenges to regulatory action taken under the Magnuson Fishery Conservation and Management Act. The provision severely threatens the ability of the Attorney General to provide reasoned and responsible representation to the Secretary of Commerce in response to administrative challenges to the Secretary's rule-making authority under the Act. It also imposes unnecessarily burdensome filing requirements on the Secretary. The Attorney General and the Secretary will propose corrective legislation next year to cure these procedural difficulties.

GEORGE BUSH

The White House,
November 28, 1990.

Note: H.R. 2061, approved November 28, was assigned Public Law No. 101–627.

Statement on Signing the Bill Authorizing the Conveyance of Land by the Rumsey Indian Rancheria
November 28, 1990

Today I have signed H.R. 3703, an Act "To authorize the Rumsey Indian Rancheria to convey a certain parcel of land." H.R. 3703 contains numerous provisions that will promote the economic and social welfare of native Americans. Those provisions that provide for the prevention, identification, treatment, and investigation of child abuse and neglect on Indian reservations are meritorious. I must, however, take note of two issues that raise serious concerns.

First, sections 405, 504, and 507 purport to require the Secretary of the Interior and the Secretary of Health and Human Services to submit various reports to the Congress containing legislative recommendations. The Constitution grants to the President the power to recommend to the Congress such measures as he judges necessary and expedient. Accordingly, I shall treat the provisions on legislative recommendations as advisory rather than mandatory.

Second, section 316 authorizes the Secretary of the Interior to enter into cooperative agreements with Indian tribes for certain purposes and provides that the Indian tribes and their contractors will be immune from liability. Furthermore, section 316 makes the United States liable in their stead for tortious acts committed under those contracts. This provision will make the U.S. Government a veritable insurer for tribal activities under circumstances in which the United States otherwise would not be liable.

I do not believe that the United States should indemnify Indian tribes and their contractors or assume the enormous liability that this provision could generate. This provision, like the one in Public Law 101–512, the "Department of the Interior and Related Agencies Appropriations Act, 1991," violates the existing means for determining whether public funds will be put at risk for the acts of specific individuals. We will seek repeal of this and any other such provision in the next Congress. I hereby instruct the Attorney General and the Secretary of the Interior to prepare for submission to the Congress legislation that will repeal this section.

GEORGE BUSH

The White House,
November 28, 1990.

Note: H.R. 3703, approved November 28, was assigned Public Law No. 101–630.

Statement on Signing the Water Resources Development Act of 1990
November 28, 1990

Today I am signing S. 2740, the "Water Resources Development Act of 1990," which authorizes water resources projects and programs in support of the Department of the Army Civil Works mission.

In signing this bill, I endorse the biennial cycle of water sources development legislation for the Army Civil Works program implemented by the Army Corps of Engineers. In addition to authorizing worthwhile water resources projects, the legislation includes a number of provisions that protect and restore this Nation's environment, which I wholeheartedly support. S. 2740 also preserves the fundamental cost-sharing and policy reforms of the Water Resources Development Act of 1986. I believe, on balance, that it reflects acceptable compromises between the executive and the legislative branches on a variety of issues of common interest.

However, I am concerned that S. 2740 contains a number of troubling special-interest provisions. For example, it contains a provision to require the Army to finance a replacement highway bridge where no legal obligation or Federal interest exists for such a replacement, and a provision for the exchange of leasehold interests for excess Federal property when such an exchange is inappropriate. Provisions such as these set undesirable precedents for the Federal Government.

In addition, a number of provisions in the Act require the Government to undertake projects and studies that traditionally have been pursued by nonfederal interests, such as constructing recreation facilities associat-

ed with a project, which are not a required or an integral part of the project. I believe, however, that the potential negative impacts of such provisions on Federal water resources policies and on the availability of Federal funds can be minimized through intensive management and through the annual budget process.

Finally, the Act contains a constitutional problem. Section 411 establishes a management conference responsible for managing Onondaga Lake in New York. The same provision also appears in H.R. 4323, legislation I approved earlier this month. The power both Acts give to State Governors and to State and local officials who serve on the management conference may only be exercised by officials who are selected pursuant to the Appointments Clause of the Constitution. Because the Act is inconsistent with this requirement, I am directing the Secretary of Defense, the Administrator of the Environmental Protection Agency, and the Attorney General to submit legislation to correct this constitutional problem.

Because I believe in a strong water resources program, and despite my concerns about a number of inappropriate provisions, I have approved this bill.

GEORGE BUSH

The White House,
November 28, 1990.

Note: S. 2740, approved November 28, was assigned Public Law No. 101–640. The statement was released by the Office of the Press Secretary on November 29.

Statement on Signing the Independent Safety Board Act Amendments of 1990
November 28, 1990

Today I am signing S. 3012, the "Independent Safety Board Act Amendments of

1990." This Act will enable the National Transportation Safety Board (NTSB) to continue in its role as the world's leading transportation investigative agency. Through the Board's efforts, everything from air transportation to pipelines will continue to be subjected to the Board's careful scrutiny and thoughtful recommendations.

My endorsement of this Act is based on my understanding that the amendment contained in section 3, which grants "sole authority" over certain testing to this agency, is intended, as the Senate report notes, to address NTSB's "difficulty with respect to *courts* interfering in the investigatory process with respect to testing. . . ." Accordingly, the amendment does not purport to limit the constitutional authority of the President.

I am also concerned that the provisions in S. 3012 dealing with the disclosure of airline cockpit voice recorder transcripts and recordings be interpreted in a manner that is fair to all parties. It is important to protect these materials from sensationalism and unwarranted disclosure, but it is also important that courts provide prompt and complete disclosure to litigants with an interest in judicial proceedings involving aircraft accidents. Every effort should be made to construe the provisions in S. 3012 in a way that preserves an appropriate balance between these goals.

GEORGE BUSH

The White House,
November 28, 1990.

Note: S. 3012, approved November 28, was assigned Public Law No. 101–641. The statement was released by the Office of the Press Secretary on November 29.

Letter to Congressional Leaders Reporting on the National Emergency With Respect to Iran
November 29, 1990

Dear Mr. Speaker: (*Dear Mr. President:*)

I hereby report to the Congress on developments since the last report of May 14, 1990, concerning the national emergency with respect to Iran that was declared in Executive Order No. 12170 of November 14, 1979, and matters relating to Executive Order No. 12613 of October 29, 1987. This report is submitted pursuant to Section 204(c) of the International Emergency Economic Powers Act, 50 U.S.C. 1703(c), and Section 505(c) of the International Security and Development Cooperation Act of 1985, 22 U.S.C. 2349aa–9. This report covers events through September 30, 1990, including those that occurred since the last report under Executive Order No. 12170 dated May 14, 1990. That report covered events through March 31, 1990.

1. Since the last report, there have been no amendments to the Iranian Transactions Regulations, 31 C.F.R. Part 560 (the "ITRs"), administered by the Office of Foreign Assets Control ("FAC"). The Iranian Assets Control Regulations, 31 C.F.R. Part 535 (the "IACRs"), were amended on October 5, 1990, 55 FR 40830, to implement the Settlement Agreement in Claims of less than $250,000.00, Case No. 86 and Case No. B38, dated May 13, 1990, in which the Governments of the United States and Iran settled certain U.S. private claims of less than $250,000.00, and all outstanding and potential U.S. government claims arising in relation to case number 86 or B38.

The major focus of licensing activity under the ITRs remains the importation of certain non-fungible Iranian-origin goods, principally carpets, which were located outside Iran before the embargo was imposed, and where no payment or benefit accrued to Iran after the effective date of the embargo. Since March 31, 1990, FAC has made 87 licensing determinations under the ITRs.

During the reporting period, the Customs Service has effected numerous seizures of Iranian-origin merchandise, primarily carpets, caviar, pistachios, jewelry, and gold and sterling silver artifacts, for violations of the ITRs. FAC and Customs Service investigations of these violations have resulted in forfeiture actions and impositions of civil monetary penalties amounting to $141,413.00. Numerous additional forfeiture and civil penalties actions are under review.

The *United States* v. *Hamed Mohseni,* a case brought in the Eastern District of Wisconsin, the defendant was indicted on June 12, 1990, for willful falsification of documents in an attempt to illegally enter Iranian carpets into U.S. trade by misdescribing their origin as Pakistani. Mohseni pled guilty to this charge on August 12, 1990. On October 22, 1990, Mohseni was sentenced to 2 years' probation, 1 month's incarceration, and a criminal fine of $1,050.00. Additionally, the Court ordered the forfeiture of four Iranian carpets having a wholesale value of $40,000.00.

In a related case in the Eastern District of Wisconsin, *United States* v. *Geoffrey A. Orley,* the defendant, an attorney and licensed securities broker, entered into a plea agreement on May 23, 1990, admitting to filing false documents to further an Iranian carpet smuggling scheme. Orley was convicted on September 17, 1990. A sentencing date has not been set. As part of their plea agreements, Geoffrey Orley and Hamed Mohseni have agreed to cooperate with the U.S. Government and to testify in pending criminal proceedings against two additional defendants. Multi-count indictments are anticipated in the latter cases.

2. The Iran-United States Claims Tribunal (the "Tribunal"), established at The Hague pursuant to the Algiers Accords, continues to make progress in arbitrating the claims before it. Since the last report, the Tribunal has rendered 13 awards, for a total of 489 awards. Of that total, 344 have been awards in favor of American claimants: 213 of these were awards on agreed terms, authorizing and approving payment of settlements negotiated by the parties, and 131 were decisions adjudicated on the merits. The Tribunal has dismissed a total of 32 other claims on the merits and 70 for jurisdictional reasons. Of the 43 remaining awards, two were withdrawn and 41 were in favor of Iranian claimants. As of September 30, 1990,

awards to successful American claimants from the Security Account held by the NV Settlement Bank stood at $2,004,184,294.21.

As of September 30, 1990, the Security Account has fallen below the required balance of $500 million 34 times. Iran has replenished the account 34 times, as required by the Algiers Accords, by transferring funds from the separate account held by the NV Settlement Bank in which interest on the Security Account is deposited. Iran has also replenished the account twice when it was not required by the Accords, for a total of 36 replenishments. Additionally, the account was replenished on September 21 in the amount of $200 million pursuant to a settlement agreement with the United States Government. A further replenishment of $228,804.05 on September 24 was related to the transfer of the unutilized balance of a letter of credit. As of September 30, 1990, the total amount in the Security Account was $271,986,604.21, and the total amount in the interest account was $5,247,131.38. The aggregate amount that has been transferred from the interest account to the Security Account is $832,872,986.47.

3. The Tribunal continues to make progress in the arbitration of claims of U.S. nationals for $250,000.00 or more. Over 80 percent of the nonbank claims have now been disposed of through adjudication, settlement, or voluntary withdrawal, leaving 133 such claims on the docket. The largest of the large claims, the progress of which has been slowed by their complexity, are finally being decided, sometimes with sizable damage awards to the U.S. claimant. In the largest settlement to date, Amoco settled its two pending cases against the National Iranian Oil Co. for a payment of $600 million. Since the last report, 12 large claims have been decided.

4. On May 13, 1990, the United States and Iran signed an agreement settling the claims of U.S. nationals against Iran of less than $250,000.00 and certain U.S. claims against Iran for outstanding loans made by the Agency for International Development. On June 22, 1990, the Iran-U.S. Claims Tribunal issued Award No. 483 recording and giving effect to the settlement agreement.

This award terminated the small claims pending before the Tribunal. Under the IACRs, the award constitutes the Tribunal's final disposition of small claims. The award provided for the payment of $105 million to the United States out of the Security Account. Of that amount, $50 million will be available for the settlement of the small claims through a program established at the Foreign Claims Settlement Commission at the Department of Justice. On June 28, 1990, the Department of State formally transferred the small claims program to the Foreign Claims Settlement Commission, as envisioned by the settlement agreement and the Iran Claims Settlement Act.

Originally, 2,795 small claims were filed with the Tribunal. The small claims settlement agreement covers 2,361 claims that were pending at the Tribunal on the date of the signing of the agreement, 10 claims that were dismissed by the Tribunal for lack of jurisdiction, 326 claims that were filed with the Tribunal but subsequently voluntarily withdrawn, and 415 claims that were submitted to the State Department but not timely filed with the Tribunal. All other claims filed with the Tribunal but not covered by the agreement had already been resolved through awards or settlements between the parties.

5. In coordination with concerned Government agencies, the Department of State continues to present United States Government claims against Iran, as well as responses by the United States Government to claims brought against it by Iran. Since the last report, the Department has filed pleadings in eight government-to-government claims. Two such claims have been settled. Regarding Case No. B/1, in return for Iran's agreement not to seek return of the full balance of its Foreign Military Sales Trust Fund from the United States in advance of adjudication of its claims on the merits, the United States transferred $200 million from the Trust Fund to the Security Account, where it will be available for payment of Tribunal awards to successful U.S. claimants.

6. Since the last report, eight bank syndicates have completed negotiations with Bank Markazi Jomhouri Islami Iran ("Bank Markazi," Iran's central bank) and have been paid a total of $4,393,148.93 for interest accruing for the period January 1–18, 1981 ("January Interest"). These payments were made from Dollar Account No. 1 at the Federal Reserve Bank of New York ("FRBNY"). In addition, under the April 13, 1988, agreement between the FRBNY and Bank Markazi, the FRBNY returned $4,693,421.29 of Iranian funds to Bank Markazi.

7. The situation reviewed above continues to implicate important diplomatic, financial, and legal interests of the United States and its nationals and presents an unusual challenge to the national security and foreign policy of the United States. The Iranian Assets Control Regulations, issued pursuant to Executive Order No. 12170, continue to play an important role in structuring our relationship with Iran and in enabling the United States to implement properly the Algiers Accords. Similarly, the Iranian Transactions Regulations, issued pursuant to Executive Order No. 12613, continue to advance important objectives in combatting international terrorism. I shall continue to exercise the powers at my disposal to deal with these problems and will continue to report periodically to the Congress on significant developments.

Sincerely,

GEORGE BUSH

Note: Identical letters were sent to Thomas S. Foley, Speaker of the House of Representatives, and Dan Quayle, President of the Senate.

Letter to Congressional Leaders Reporting on the Cyprus Conflict
November 29, 1990

Dear Mr. Speaker: (Dear Mr. Chairman:)

In accordance with Public Law 95–384 (92 Stat. 739; 22 USC 2373(c)), I am submitting to you this bimonthly report on progress toward a negotiated settlement of the Cyprus question.

This report covers the period from August through early October 1990, a time in which both U.N. and U.S. efforts concentrated on trying to get the Cyprus intercommunal talks restarted.

In early August, the Secretary General sent his Special Representative on Cyprus, Ambassador Oscar Camilion, and Mr. Gustave Feissel of the Secretary General's New York staff to Ankara and Athens. In both capitals the two U.N. officials discussed the continuing stalemate in the negotiations and asked for Turkish and Greek Government support in furthering the Secretary General's "plan of action," which he outlined in his report to the U.N. Security Council on July 12.

Both the Turkish and Greek Governments conveyed their willingness to cooperate with the U.N., and on September 11 the UNSYG's spokesman released the following statement in New York in describing the status of the Cyprus negotiations:

"In recent days, I have been asked about the intentions of the Secretary General with regard to his mission of good offices in Cyprus and the questions that have been raised about the application of Cyprus to the EC.

"The Security Council has called on the leaders of the two communities in Cyprus to pursue their efforts to reach freely a mutually acceptable solution and to cooperate, on an equal footing, with the Secretary General. To achieve this goal, the members of the Council have endorsed the plan of action proposed by the Secretary General in his report of 12 July.

"In resolution 649 (1990), the Council has made it clear that the solution being sought has to be a bi-communal and bi-zonal federation that will ensure the sovereignty, independence, territorial integrity and non-alignment of Cyprus and will exclude union in part or in whole with any other country or any form of partition or secession.

"The overall agreement to be negotiated by the two leaders must cover all the issues that make up the Cyprus question. It is envisaged that matters related to the membership of Cyprus in the EC will be discussed in this connection.

"The Secretary General is concerned by the continued deterioration of the situation in Cyprus due to developments in past months and the lack of progress in the negotiating process. This trend must be reversed. He therefore hopes that it will be possible to implement his plan of action without delay."

Six days later, on September 17, 1990, the Council of the European Community, meeting in Brussels, considered the Government of Cyprus' July 4 application for membership in the European Community and decided to refer the application to the Commission of the European Community for study.

On September 25, during Turkish President Ozal's meeting with me, we discussed ways of supporting the U.N. Secretary General in his attempts to promote reconciliation on the island. Secretary of State Baker also had several such conversations with Greek Foreign Minister Samaras in the same period. On September 25, Under Secretary of State Kimmitt met with Cypriot President Vassiliou in New York to stress continuing U.S. support for U.N.-sponsored efforts in Cyprus. President Vassiliou, in turn, recalled his speech earlier that day before the UNGA in which he insisted that "a just and viable solution to the Cyprus problem necessitates that negotiations are entered into in good faith and are result-oriented. We have, time and time again, displayed our commitment as well as our good will during the course of negotiations. We have presented proposals to the Turkish Cypriot side going far beyond the protection of cultural, religious and linguistic identity, aiming at creating a federation consisting of two regions, one to be administered by the Turkish Cypriot community and the other by the Greek Cypriot."

President Vassiliou returned to Cyprus several days later and, in a speech before a special session of his House of Representatives marking the island's 30th anniversary of its independence, he included the following notable passage:

"Naturally foremost in our hearts and our minds is the national problem which is directly connected with our survival and on whose solution much else depends. We carry 30 years of experience as well as many wounds from which all of us, Greek Cypriots and Turkish Cypriots should learn. Mistakes and omissions were made by both sides in the past. However, history and our present situation have convinced us that all these, as well as foreign interventions, do not serve the interest of any Cypriot. Our destiny was and remains common. Consequently, with goodwill, tolerance, mutual respect for our differences and views, we can find a solution acceptable to all. We can and we must pinpoint the points which unite us and serve us all and build on them. The future cannot be secured with separatist trends and sterile confrontation. Through contact and the exchange of views on all levels, a climate of mutual trust and understanding can be created, which will eliminate the mistrust created and maintained by isolation. That is why we work for rapprochement."

In late September, the U.N. Secretary General and his advisers reached agreement on how their "plan of action" would be implemented. Ambassador Camilion and Mr. Feissel returned to Cyprus in mid-October to begin a series of separate meetings with the leaders of the Turkish Cypriot and Greek Cypriot communities to see if work could be restarted on a draft outline for a Cyprus settlement. My special Cyprus Coordinator, Nelson Ledsky, met with these U.N. negotiators and with representatives of the interested parties in New York and travelled to the eastern Mediterranean in late October, to reemphasize U.S. support for the U.N. negotiating effort. The UNSYG has sent a further report to the U.N. Security Council detailing the status of the negotiations through October 31.

Sincerely,

GEORGE BUSH

Note: Identical letters were sent to Thomas S. Foley, Speaker of the House of Representatives, and Claiborne Pell, chairman of the Senate Foreign Relations Committee.

Statement by Press Secretary Fitzwater on Argentine and Brazilian Compliance With Nuclear Safeguards and Nonproliferation Regimes
November 29, 1990

The United States applauds the November 28 announcement by Argentina and Brazil to work with the International Atomic Energy Agency (IAEA) to apply safeguards to all nuclear facilities and activities in their countries and to bring into force the Treaty of Tlatelolco, which establishes a nuclear weapon-free zone in Latin America. The prospects for a Latin America forever free from the dangers of nuclear weapons have brightened.

President Menem and President Collor have acted boldly to enhance regional and world stability in pledging to use nuclear energy only for peaceful purposes. We anticipate that yesterday's announcement of mutual inspections and negotiations with the IAEA will lead to the early implementation of a full-scope IAEA safeguards agreement. This will facilitate peaceful nuclear cooperation with Brazil and Argentina while broadening their access to other advanced technologies.

We also welcome and commend the commitment by the Governments of Argentina and Brazil to bring the Treaty of Tlatelolco into force. We urge them to do so swiftly. We also urge those countries in Latin

America which have not done so to bring the treaty into force as Argentina and Brazil are pledging to do and to support the international community's nonproliferation regime. President Bush will visit the region next week and looks forward to discussing these issues in greater detail with Presidents Menem and Collor.

Statement on Signing the Stewart B. McKinney Homeless Assistance Amendments Act of 1990
November 29, 1990

It is with great pleasure that I have today signed H.R. 3789, the Stewart B. McKinney Homeless Assistance Amendments Act of 1990. Congress first enacted the Stewart B. McKinney Homeless Assistance Act in 1987, and the act signed today will reauthorize a broad array of programs to assist the homeless, amend current programs, and authorize certain new programs to address the continuing needs of homeless, especially the mentally ill and substance abusers.

Since 1987 the McKinney Act has provided over $2 billion for programs to assist the homeless. H.R. 3789 will authorize the new *Shelter Plus Care Program*, an administration proposal, which will help link rental housing assistance to other supportive services for the homeless.

Under the provisions of H.R. 3789, the Department of Health and Human Services is authorized to establish a Family Support Centers demonstration program that will provide a number of health and related services for low-income individuals who were previously homeless or are at risk of becoming homeless. The act also authorizes additional grants to the States that would be focused on those who are currently homeless and suffer from both substance abuse and mental illness.

H.R. 3789 recognizes that the homeless often have needs that go beyond housing assistance. By providing health services, substance abuse services, and counseling in addition to housing assistance, this act enhances the administration's ability to address the needs of the homeless in all their complexity.

Note: H.R. 3789, approved November 29, was assigned Public Law No. 101–645.

Statement on Signing the Bill on Wetland and Coastal Inland Waters Protection and Restoration Programs
November 29, 1990

Today I am signing H.R. 5390, "An Act to prevent and control infestation of the coastal inland waters of the United States by the zebra mussel and other nonindigenous aquatic nuisance species, to reauthorize the National Sea Grant College Program, and for other purposes." This Act is designed to minimize, monitor, and control nonindigenous species that become established in the United States, particularly the zebra mussel; establish wetlands protection and restoration programs in Louisiana and nationally; and promote fish and wildlife conservation in the Great Lakes.

Title III of this Act designates a State official not subject to executive control as a member of the Louisiana Coastal Wetlands Conservation and Restoration Task Force. This official would be the only member of the Task Force whose appointment would not conform to the Appointments Clause of the Constitution.

The Task Force will set priorities for wetlands restoration and formulate Federal conservation and restoration plans. Certain of its duties, which ultimately determine funding levels for particular restoration projects, are an exercise of significant authority that must be undertaken by an officer of the United States, appointed in accordance with the Appointments Clause, Article II, sec. 2, cl. 2, of the Constitution.

In order to constitutionally enforce this program, I instruct the Task Force to promulgate its priorities list under section 303(a)(2) "by a majority vote of those Task Force members who are present and voting," and to consider the State official to be a nonvoting member of the Task Force for this purpose. Moreover, the Secretary of the Army should construe "lead Task Force member" to include only those members appointed in conformity with the Appointments Clause.

GEORGE BUSH

The White House,
November 29, 1990.

Note: H.R. 5390, approved November 29, was assigned Public Law No. 101–646.

Remarks to the Association of Bank Holding Companies
November 29, 1990

Well, thank you all very much. And it is a pleasure to do what's known in Washington as a cameo appearance, a drop-by. But I'm delighted to be here—these very busy and very interesting times. I first want to thank Gene Miller and, of course, my friend—I don't want to put him in an age category, but my classmate—Lud Ashley, an old friend, and, of course, the leading lights of the banking industry here today.

Back in February of 1989, the members of your organization came out early for our S&L program, the reform bill. Your strong support helped us take a critical first step toward restoring the integrity of our S&L system, and we are very grateful for that. And since then, Nick Brady, who is known to, I guess, everybody here, has been conducting a thorough review of the key issues and the concerns of the American banking system.

What he's found is the need for significant structural reform, reforms that keep pace with the revolutionary changes in financial services that have marked the past two decades. And today in the age of the ATM and the 800 number, and in the face of intense competition from nonbanks to meet the consumer's credit needs, we must rethink and reexamine our existing regulations and the need for change.

The regulatory system that served us very well, indeed, from its inception in the thirties, is today, in my view, increasingly outmoded, is likely to prevent banks from staying competitive as it is to allow them to serve customers and sustain confidence in the system. The result can be counterproductive: Denying banks the opportunity to enter new markets actually encourages risky ventures that fall within the old rules and regulations.

In January, the Treasury Department will make its recommendations on comprehensive banking reforms, including provisions on deposit insurance. The legislation that we will propose will make a significant contribution to the long-term health of the banking system. And once again, I will be in close touch with Lud and Gene and all of you here today to help secure a speedy passage of this reform package in the 102d Congress. What's at stake is not just the confidence of the American people in the banking system but the profitability and the competitiveness of a key American industry, because our banking system can never be truly safe if it's not also economically sound.

Lud tells me the theme of the conference is managing risk. And I don't need to tell you how the events of the past few months

1711

have clouded over the crystal ball out there for everybody. For the people in this room who face the challenge of mapping corporate strategies in an environment that at best is uncertain, the task you face is extraordinarily complex.

I know that—I see Jim Leach back here, another old friend of mine, and I know that he's been up here preaching some wisdom. I'm not sure exactly what he says, but listen carefully to him. [*Laughter*] He's one of the sanest and greatest Members of the Congress, I can tell you that. I also understand that Richard Breeden was here—I don't know if he's here now—but the head of the SEC [Securities and Exchange Commission] was here—good man. They've spoken about—in more detail than I'm capable—spoke to you about the challenges that confront you. And they are serious. No question about it.

Interest rates, frankly, are higher than any of us would like them to be. I am very hopeful—and I'm not one who is a Fed basher or anything of that nature—but I'm hopeful that the deficit agreement that was not the world's most popular piece of legislation—budget deficit agreement will lead eventually to lower rates. And of course, we've seen some come down. I happen to think that's very good for the economy. I know your concerns about a credit crunch, and we've been having a series of very interesting meetings with private sector people at the White House, which has helped me understand better the credit crunch.

I mentioned earlier the concept that some of you all have in this industry of overregulation or excessive zeal in the regulatory business, and I think we're now more attuned to that problem than heretofore. And so, what I hope is, is when we get the new Congress here we can take more of a leadership role out of the White House in not only helping to strengthen the business that you all are in but to sometimes relieve a little pressure from the overzealous nature of some of the regulations.

So, we are in a period that concerns me of a sluggish economy. I suspect that each one of you here has economists that you believe in. And some are saying recession, and some are saying slowdown, and some

saying downturn. But one positive thing is that most, if not all, people are suggesting that whatever it is, it won't be long lasting. And I think that is very important to the overall good of the American people. I am confident that it will run its course. I think it will be relatively slow, based on the expert opinions to which I have access. I am certain that the institutions that are represented here and all of you business leaders in this room will play a leading role in reviving the economy and returning to the path of expansion and opportunity and growth.

So, I might add just a comment or two about the effects of what's happening halfway around the world on our own economy and on the economies of other countries. One of the most fascinating visits that I had on this recent trip to Europe—a trip that preceded another good trip, incidentally, for those of you who are interested in matters south of our border, a trip to Mexico—but one of the things that was really fascinating to me about the trip to Europe were the talks I had with the eastern European leaders.

I started my trip by going to see [President] Václav Havel in Czechoslovakia. Here's a country whose economy is being devastated by what Saddam Hussein is doing in the Persian Gulf. I think he used a figure of $1.5 billion for 1 year estimated strain on that fragile economy. Comes at a very bad time for him. We had a little press conference outside of what they call the Castle there, which is his headquarters, in that marvelous center of Prague, and he was asked a question. And I think some who were inquiring thought that maybe there would be a wedge driven between the steadfast position of the United States, as we approach the dictator Saddam Hussein, and Czechoslovakia. But to the surprise of some, but not to me, since I had talked to him about it, in spite of the economic hardship to Czechoslovakia, he was about as strong as you could possibly be in standing up against the rape, the pillage, and the plunder, and the aggression against Kuwait. That was true also of the Polish and Hungarian leaders with whom I met a few days later in Paris at the CSCE meeting.

And so, on this subject of the Gulf, it is clear to me that those who can afford it the least are those who are getting hurt the worst by the speculation that's resulted in these higher oil prices. Some of you may have heard Alan Greenspan [Chairman of the Board of Governors, Federal Reserve System] in his rather eloquent testimony talking a day or two ago about the effect that the oil increases are having on the United States economy and what that means, trying to assess the slowdown or the recession or whatever one would call exactly what we're in now.

And it's very clear that they are having a very bad effect on our economy. But one of the reasons that the world is holding together as well as it is, is that the smallest countries—and many of them, Moslem countries—feel just as strongly as we do, and others, that the aggression must be returned not simply on the moral basis, which certainly is a profound reason to see the aggression turned around, but on the economic basis as well. Their economies are being hurt. It's not just eastern Europe. Take a look at Senegal. Some of you all do business all through Africa, and take a look at some of the countries that really are in tough shape there, and then see what the result of Saddam Hussein's aggression is doing to them. And then add to it what's happened in the United States. And that whole economic side of this equation comes much more clearly into focus.

I'm hopeful that this afternoon the United Nations will pass—I believe it's its 13th resolution, maybe it's its 11th. But as one who served at the United Nations with sometimes frustration because of the failure of the so-called peacekeeping function of the U.N., I think one of the exciting and positive things to be coming out of all this strife and problems halfway around the world is the rejuvenation of the United Nations peacekeeping function.

It is not insignificant that it's not the United States alone but the United States backed—or in conjunction with the rest of the Security Council—indeed, with most of the members of the United Nations itself strongly supporting what we are about in trying to reverse the aggression over there. So, my point is, there's a moral underpin-

ning to what we're doing. To me, it is very, very clear, and I don't intend to waver one single bit.

But there's also an economic side to this equation, and economic effects are devastating those who can afford it the least. So, we're embarked on a very interesting path here, and I hope that the resolution—that it will be peaceful. That is certainly what everybody aspires to, certainly the President, who is also the Commander in Chief of the Armed Forces. But I think the main thing that I hope will come out of today's session of the United Nations is that we send perhaps the clearest signal of all to Saddam Hussein that the world is deadly serious about reversing this aggression and about lifting this economic oppression that he has wrought on many, many countries that can ill afford it.

So, we'll see where we go. I hope my optimism I feel at this point is not misplaced. If it is, we just go right back to the drawing board, because I know that we have to prevail. And I expect all of you who do business abroad, as most of you do, understand exactly what I'm talking about when I talk about the horrible economic effects that this man's aggression is having on all the economies of the world.

Listen, it is a great pleasure to be here. I salute you and your work. I'm delighted to be with you, and I would welcome from the private sector any input on how the Government, by either getting out of the way or by in one way or another doing our business better, can strengthen and encourage the banking system of this country. It is vital. And we've taken it for granted for years and years as a sign of the greatest stability—one of the great stable points of our country. And I'm confident that if we conduct ourselves right and if you do your business right, that principle will be out there for all to see in the days ahead.

Thank you, and good luck to you in your work. And thank you for letting me come by for this cameo appearance. Thanks a lot.

Note: The President spoke at 1:26 p.m. in the ballroom of the Willard Hotel. In his remarks, he referred to Eugene Miller, chairman and chief executive officer of Co-

merica Corp, Inc.; Thomas Ludlow Ashley, president of the Association of Bank Holding Companies; Secretary of the Treasury

Nicholas F. Brady; and President Saddam Hussein of Iraq.

Remarks at a Reception for Participants in Students Taking Action and Responsibility in Service
November 29, 1990

Looking out on these shining faces today, Barbara and I remember a summer day on the South Lawn more than a year ago when I challenged—called upon—every young person in America to make service to those in need a central and enduring part of their lives. And we are just delighted to be here to celebrate one significant result of that day, a new, exciting educational initiative called StarServe.

I want to first express my thanks to an old friend, several old friends, and I'm talking, of course, about Mike Love and the Beach Boys. Mike said that he was motivated to go out and help young people respond to this call. And he did, and he's done it, and he's given of himself, and so have his wonderful colleagues. And we are very grateful to them. I want to thank the Kraft General Foods Foundation for its underpinning, its financial support; and, of course, the United Way for its expertise.

Thanks to all the young people gathered here and, of course, to the stars who support StarServe and given of themselves as well. You and other stars who have already agreed to participate in this effort show that real stars—real stars—use their influence to encourage those who admire them to do likewise. As we speak, the materials of StarServe are being sent to more than 100,000 educators of students in grades 4 through 12 throughout the country.

And of course, StarServe isn't creating youth community service; many young people are already undertaking meaningful projects all around the country. There's no better example of this than Diane Wurst's third grade class in Polk, Nebraska, who, as we've heard, was our 48th daily Point of Light. Each school day for the last 7 years, each one—you heard from one of them—

but each one of these third graders has telephoned these homebound seniors, offering words of comfort and cheer. You've heard from her and then got another little window by Trent there—visiting their elderly friends on weekends and holidays, assuring those who are alone that someone cares.

While there are other outstanding examples of youth service, I want every young American, from 5 to 25, to be a Point of Light in his or her community. Whether it's lonely senior citizens, a troubled classmate or acquaintance, someone who's burdened by drug abuse, illiteracy, homelessness or hunger, there's a need right next door, down the hall, or in your own backyard that you can meet.

StarServe is one of the first independent initiatives of the Points of Light Foundation, the new, nonprofit, nonpartisan foundation on which I'm pleased to serve as honorary chairman. By making service creative and educational for young Americans, StarServe will help the foundation achieve its goal of engaging all Americans in service. Barbara and I believe that if, at an early age, you learn to serve those in need, it will become the way you live your whole life, bringing a sense of meaning and adventure that simply can't be matched.

StarServe shows that businesses can, indeed, help young people make their service ideas a reality, that nonprofits can provide invaluable counsel to those who are new to community service, and that the worlds of entertainment and media can use their influence to make service a pervasive part of the popular culture. I especially like the name of this project, StarServe, Students Taking Action and Responsibility in Service. Every young person wants to be a star.

Well, every young person has a gift to give to someone in need, and America needs your gifts now as never before. And so to all young Americans I say, answer the call to serve your community and be a star. Thank you all very, very much.

Note: The President spoke at 2:19 p.m. in the East Room at the White House. In his remarks, he referred to the Beach Boys, a popular music group, and their vocalist, Mike Love; and Trent Stevens, a third-grade student at Polk Public School in Polk, NE.

Statement on Signing the Crime Control Act of 1990
November 29, 1990

Today I sign into law S. 3266, the "Crime Control Act of 1990." The Act contains important steps forward in several areas, particularly Federal debt collection and prosecution of financial institutions fraud. It also provides further protection for children from child abuse and child pornography. However, I must note my deep disappointment over many provisions noticeably absent from the legislation.

Over a year and a half ago, with the support of State and local police and prosecutors, I submitted to the Congress a comprehensive legislative package to assist law enforcement efforts in keeping violent criminals off our Nation's streets. That legislation contained a death penalty for the most heinous Federal crimes, including mail bombing and terrorist murder; comprehensive reform of *habeas corpus* proceedings that continue to nullify State death penalty laws through repetitive hearings and endless delays; reform of the exclusionary rule to allow juries to consider all evidence gathered by law enforcement officers acting in good faith; and enhanced penalties for the criminal use of firearms.

Despite the fact that each of these proposals passed one or both Houses of Congress, *none* is included in the legislation I am signing today. At the eleventh hour, these reforms were stripped from the crime bill by the conference committee.

I am also disturbed by provisions in S. 3266 that unnecessarily constrain the discretion of State and local governments. Examples are found in Title VIII's "rural drug enforcement" program; in Title XV's "drug-free school zones" program; and in Title

XVIII's program for "correctional options incentives." Most egregiously, section 1702 inappropriately overrides legitimate State firearms laws with a new and unnecessary Federal law. The policies reflected in these provisions could legitimately be adopted by the States, but they should not be imposed on the States by the Congress.

Habeas corpus litigation is another area in which congressional policies may impede effective State law enforcement. In Public Law 101–515, the Congress appropriated substantial funds for "Death Penalty Resource Centers." Because S. 3266 does not include the reform of the *habeas corpus* system that I proposed, these Federal funds will inevitably be used in part to foster repetitive attacks on State court judgments and to delay unjustly the implementation of State sentences.

While this is not the crime bill I asked the Congress to pass, I am pleased with the tools S. 3266 provides for fighting financial institutions fraud. S. 3266 establishes within the Department of Justice an Office of Special Counsel for Financial Institutions Fraud, a Financial Institutions Fraud Unit, Financial Institutions Fraud Task Forces, and a Senior Interagency Group. In addition, the bill enhances the ability of the Federal banking agencies and the Department of Justice to seize the assets of wrongdoers and makes it more difficult for those wrongdoers to use bankruptcy to avoid civil or criminal penalties.

Furthermore, this Act improves significantly the ability of the Department of Justice to collect millions of dollars owed to the Federal Government. For the first time, the Congress has provided United States attorneys with uniform civil procedures for the collection of debts owed to the American taxpayers.

Americans have the right to be free from fear in their homes, in their streets, and in their neighborhoods. I call on the Congress to implement the remainder of the comprehensive crime package, which fell short of becoming law this session. The American people deserve tough, new laws to help us prevail in the fight against drugs and crime.

GEORGE BUSH

The White House,
November 29, 1990.

Note: S. 3266, approved November 29, was assigned Public Law No. 101–647.

Statement on Signing the Negotiated Rulemaking Act of 1990
November 29, 1990

Today I am signing S. 303, the "Negotiated Rulemaking Act of 1990." This Act will encourage Federal agencies to use negotiation in the regulatory process, to the extent that it may be appropriate, as a means of avoiding costly and time-consuming litigation.

In approving this bill, I must emphasize that Federal officials will retain their full statutory and constitutional responsibility to make all administrative determinations on regulatory matters. Under the Appointments Clause of the Constitution, Article II, Sec. 2, Cl. 2, governmental authority may be exercised only by officers of the United States.

The Act does not require an agency to adopt, or even to publish as a proposed rule, a consensus reached by a negotiated rulemaking advisory committee. Nor does the Act supplant either the role of the public in commenting on a proposed rule in accordance with the Administrative Procedure Act, or the responsibility of Government officials to consider such comments and to decide on and draft the text of a final rule. In this regard, I note that a negotiated rulemaking advisory committee has completed its function after it has recommended a proposed rule to the rulemaking agency.

I must also emphasize that S. 303 does not derogate in any way from existing agency authority to utilize or experiment with any lawful form of rulemaking, including negotiated rulemaking.

GEORGE BUSH

The White House,
November 29, 1990.

Note: S. 303, approved November 29, was assigned Public Law No. 101–648.

Remarks on Signing the Immigration Act of 1990
November 29, 1990

Thank you very much for coming, everybody. And first, may I salute the Attorney General and Secretary Ed Derwinski, and also, welcome the distinguished Members of Congress who are with us today: Senator Kennedy and Senator Thurmond, Senator Simpson, Senator Simon. Ham Fish was to be here; Congressmen Morrison and Lamar Smith are with us. I don't know whether Ham wedged into the back or not. But in any event, welcome to all of you.

Today I am pleased to sign S. 358, the Immigration Act of 1990. It is the most comprehensive reform of our immigration laws in 66 years. Nearly all Americans have ancestors who braved the oceans—liberty-loving risk takers in search of an ideal—the largest voluntary migrations in recorded history. Across the Pacific, across the Atlantic, they came from every point on the compass—many passing beneath the Statue of Liberty—with fear and vision, with sorrow and adventure, fleeing tyranny or terror, seeking haven, and all seeking hope.

And now we stand again before an open door—a door into tomorrow. Immigration reform began in 1986 with an effort to close the back door on illegal immigration. And now as we open the front door to increased legal immigration, this bill provides long-needed enforcement authority. It also credits the special role of immigrants to America, and it will promote a more competitive economy, respect for the family unit, and swift punishment for drugs and crime.

Immigration is not just a link to America's past; it's also a bridge to America's future. This bill provides for vital increases for entry on the basis of skills, infusing the ranks of our scientists and engineers and educators with new blood and new ideas. And it also boosts our war on drugs and crime, allowing us to send back alien offenders who threaten our streets and who

make up nearly a fourth of our Federal prison populations. It'll help secure our borders, the front lines of the drug war. It also revises the exclusion grounds for the first time since enactment in 1952, putting an end to the kind of political litmus tests that might have excluded even some of the heroes of the Eastern European Revolution of 1989.

This bill is good for families, good for business, good for crime fighting, and good for America. We welcome both it and the generations of future Americans who it will bring in to strengthen our great country.

And now I am honored and pleased to sign into law the Immigration Act of 1990. And I'd like to ask the Members of Congress—if you all would come up—if we do this. Ed, if you'll get on one side and Dick on the other.

[*At this point, the President signed the bill.*]

There we go. Well done. Thank you.

Note: The President spoke at 2:28 p.m. in the Roosevelt Room at the White House. In his remarks, he referred to Attorney General Dick Thornburgh; Secretary of Veterans Affairs Edward J. Derwinski; and Representative Hamilton Fish, Jr. S. 358, approved November 29, was assigned Public Law No. 101–649.

Statement on Signing the Immigration Act of 1990
November 29, 1990

Today I am pleased to sign S. 358, the "Immigration Act of 1990"—the most comprehensive reform of our immigration laws in 66 years. This Act recognizes the fundamental importance and historic contributions of immigrants to our country. S. 358 accomplishes what this Administration sought from the outset of the immigration reform process: a complementary blending of our tradition of family reunification with increased immigration of skilled individuals to meet our economic needs.

The legislation meets several objectives of this Administration's domestic policy agenda—cultivation of a more competitive

economy, support for the family as the essential unit of society, and swift and effective punishment for drug-related and other violent crime.

S. 358 provides for a significant increase in the overall number of immigrants permitted to enter the United States each year. The Act maintains our Nation's historic commitment to family reunification by increasing the number of immigrant visas allocated on the basis of family ties.

At the same time, S. 358 dramatically increases the number of immigrants who may be admitted to the United States because of the skills they have and the needs of our economy. This legislation will encourage the immigration of exceptionally talented people, such as scientists, engineers, and educators. Other provisions of S. 358 will promote the initiation of new business in rural areas and the investment of foreign capital in our economy.

I am also pleased to note that this Act facilitates immigration not just in numerical terms, but also in terms of basic entry rights of those beyond our borders. S. 358 revises the politically related "exclusion grounds" for the first time since their enactment in 1952. These revised grounds lift unnecessary restrictions on those who may enter the United States. At the same time, they retain important administrative checks in the interest of national security as well as the health and welfare of U.S. citizens.

Immigration reform began in 1986 with an effort to close the "back door" on illegal immigration through enactment of the 1986 Immigration Reform and Control Act (IRCA). Now, as we open the "front door" to increased legal immigration, I am pleased that this Act also provides needed enforcement authority.

S. 358 meets several objectives of my Administration's war on drugs and violent crime. Specifically, it provides for the expeditious deportation of aliens who, by their violent criminal acts, forfeit their right to remain in this country. These offenders, comprising nearly a quarter of our Federal prison population, jeopardize the safety and well-being of every American resident. In addition, S. 358 improves this Administration's ability to secure the U.S. border—the front lines of the war on drugs—by clarifying the authority of Immigration and Naturalization Service enforcement officers to make arrests and carry firearms.

S. 358 also improves the antidiscrimination provisions of the IRCA. These amendments will help deter discrimination that might be related to the implementation of "employer sanctions" under the 1986 law. In this regard, S. 358 helps to remedy unfortunate side effects of this important deterrent to illegal immigration.

In signing this legislation, I am concerned with the provision of S. 358 that creates a new form of relief known as "temporary protected status." The power to grant temporary protected status would be, except as specifically provided, the "exclusive authority" by which the Attorney General could allow otherwise deportable aliens to remain here temporarily because of their nationality or their region of origin. I do not interpret this provision as detracting from any authority of the executive branch to exercise prosecutorial discretion in suitable immigration cases. Any attempt to do so would raise serious constitutional questions.

GEORGE BUSH

The White House,
November 29, 1990.

Note: S. 358, approved November 29, was assigned Public Law No. 101–649.

Statement on the United Nations Security Council Resolution Authorizing the Use of Force Against Iraq
November 29, 1990

The United Nations Security Council vote underscores the unity and determination of the international community to end Iraq's illegal occupation of Kuwait. We are pleased to note the common stance and determination of the world in this endeavor. The United States will continue working with all countries for the express purpose of having the United Nations Security Council resolution fully implemented. We continue to favor a peaceful settlement of this crisis; at the same time, and as the Security Council vote demonstrates, there is growing resolve that Saddam's occupation of Kuwait not be allowed to stand and that all necessary means be employed to ensure this is the case.

Note: Saddam Hussein was President of Iraq.

The President's News Conference
November 30, 1990

The President. I have a statement, an opening statement, that is a little longer than normal; and I'd ask your indulgence. And then I will be glad to respond to questions.

We're in the Gulf because the world must not and cannot reward aggression. And we're there because our vital interests are at stake. And we're in the Gulf because of the brutality of Saddam Hussein. We're dealing with a dangerous dictator all too willing to use force who has weapons of mass destruction and is seeking new ones and who desires to control one of the world's key resources—all at a time in history when the rules of the post-cold-war world are being written.

Our objectives remain what they were since the outset. We seek Iraq's immediate and unconditional withdrawal from Kuwait. We seek the restoration of Kuwait's legitimate government. We seek the release of all hostages and the free functioning of all embassies. And we seek the stability and security of this critical region of the world.

We are not alone in these goals and objectives. The United Nations, invigorated with a new sense of purpose, is in full agreement. The United Nations Security Council has endorsed 12 resolutions to condemn Iraq's unprovoked invasion and occupation of Kuwait, implement tough economic sanctions to stop all trade in and out of Iraq, and authorize the use of force to compel Saddam to comply.

Saddam Hussein has tried every way he knows how to make this a fight between Iraq and the United States, and clearly, he has failed. Forces of 26 other nations are standing shoulder to shoulder with our troops in the Gulf. The fact is that it is not the United States against Iraq; it is Iraq against the world. And there's never been a clearer demonstration of a world united against appeasement and aggression.

Yesterday's United Nations Security Council resolution was historic. Once again, the Security Council has enhanced the legitimate peacekeeping function of the United Nations. Until yesterday, Saddam may not have understood what he's up against in terms of world opinion, and I'm hopeful that now he will realize that he must leave Kuwait immediately.

I'm continually asked how effective are the U.N. sanctions that was put into effect on August 6th. I don't know the answer to that question. Clearly, the sanctions are having some effect, but I can't tell you that the sanctions alone will get the job done. And thus, I welcome yesterday's United Nations action.

The fledgling democracies in Eastern Europe are being severely damaged by the economic effects of Saddam's actions. The developing countries of Africa and in our hemisphere are being victimized by this dictator's rape of his neighbor Kuwait. Those who feel that there is no down side to waiting months and months must consider the devastating damage being done every day to the fragile economies of those countries that can afford it the least.

As Chairman Alan Greenspan [Board of Governors, Federal Reserve System] testified just the other day, the increase in oil prices resulting directly from Saddam's invasion is hurting our country, too. Our economy, as I said the other day, is at best in a serious slowdown, and if uncertainty remains in the energy markets, the slowdown will get worse.

I've spelled out once again our reasons for sending troops to the Gulf. Let me tell you the things that concern me most. First, I put the immorality of the invasion of Kuwait itself. No nation should rape, pillage, and brutalize its neighbor. No nation should be able to wipe a member state of the United Nations and the Arab League off the face of the Earth.

I'm deeply concerned about all the hostages—innocent people held against their will in direct contravention of international law. Then there's this cynical and brutal policy of forcing people to beg for their release, parceling out human lives to families and traveling emissaries like so much chattel.

I'm deeply concerned about our own Embassy in Kuwait. The flag is still flying there. A handful of beleaguered Americans remain inside the Embassy unable to come and go. This treatment of our Embassy violates every civilized principle of diplomacy. It demeans our people; it demeans our country. And I am determined that this Embassy, as called for under Security Council Resolution 674, be fully replenished and our people free to come home. What kind of precedent will these actions set for the future if Saddam's violation of international law goes unchallenged?

I'm also deeply concerned about the future of Kuwait itself. The tales of rape and assassination, of cold-blooded murder and rampant looting are almost beyond belief. The whole civilized world must unite and say: This kind of treatment of people must end. And those who violate the Kuwait people must be brought to justice.

I'm deeply concerned about Saddam's efforts to acquire nuclear weapons. Imagine his ability to blackmail his neighbors should he possess a nuclear device. We've seen him use chemical weapons on his own people. We've seen him take his own country, one that should be wealthy and prosperous, and turn it into a poor country all because of insatiable appetite for military equipment and conquest.

I've been asked why I ordered more troops to the Gulf. I remain hopeful that we can achieve a peaceful solution to this crisis. But if force is required, we and the other 26 countries who have troops in the area will have enough power to get the job done.

In our country, I know that there are fears about another Vietnam. Let me assure you, should military action be required, this will not be another Vietnam. This will not be a protracted, drawn-out war. The forces arrayed are different. The opposition is different. The resupply of Saddam's military would be very different. The countries united against him in the United Nations are different. The topography of Kuwait is different. And the motivation of our all-volunteer force is superb.

I want peace. I want peace, not war. But if there must be war, we will not permit our troops to have their hands tied behind their backs. And I pledge to you: There will not be any murky ending. If one American soldier has to go into battle, that soldier will have enough force behind him to win and then get out as soon as possible, as soon as the U.N. objectives have been achieved. I will never—ever—agree to a halfway effort.

Let me repeat: We have no argument with the people of Iraq; indeed, we have only friendship for the people there. Further, I repeat that we have no desire to keep one single American soldier in the Gulf a single day longer than is necessary to achieve the objectives set out above.

No one wants to see a peaceful solution to this crisis more than I do. And at the same time, no one is more determined than I am to see Saddam's aggression reversed.

Lastly, people now caution patience. The United States and the entire world have been patient. I will continue to be patient. But yesterday's U.N. resolution, the 13th by the Security Council, properly says to Saddam Hussein: Time is running out. You must leave Kuwait. And we've given you time to do just exactly that.

Many people have talked directly to Saddam Hussein and to his Foreign Minister Tariq 'Aziz. All have been frustrated by Iraq's ironclad insistence that it will not leave Kuwait. However, to go the extra mile for peace, I will issue an invitation to Foreign Minister Tariq 'Aziz to come to Washington at a mutually convenient time during the latter part of the week of December 10th to meet with me. I'll invite Ambassadors of several of our coalition partners in the Gulf to join me at that meeting. In addition, I'm asking Secretary Jim Baker to go to Baghdad to see Saddam Hussein. And I will suggest to Iraq's President that he receive the Secretary of State at a mutually convenient time between December 15th and January 15th of next year.

Within the mandate of the United Nations resolutions, I will be prepared, and so will Secretary Baker, to discuss all aspects of the Gulf crisis. However, to be very clear about these efforts to exhaust all means for achieving a political and diplomatic solution, I am not suggesting discussions that will result in anything less than Iraq's complete withdrawal from Kuwait, restoration of Kuwait's legitimate government, and freedom for all hostages.

Thank you very much. And I will be glad to respond to a few questions.

Persian Gulf Crisis

Q. Mr. President, now that you have a clear-cut U.N. resolution on use of force, doesn't that force you into a position if these talks between the Secretary of State break down—doesn't this force you into the position of having to use force on January 15th if Saddam Hussein hasn't left? And if not, won't we be perceived as the one who blinked first?

The President. No, the date was not a date at which point force had to be used.

Q. If I could just follow up with another question. Are you going to ask Congress for approval of this resolution—would you like to see Congress pass the same kind of resolution that the U.N. passed?

The President. I'd love to see Congress pass a resolution enthusiastically endorsing what the United Nations has done, yes. But we're in consultation on that, and I have no plans to call a special session. I'm not opposed to it, but we're involved in consultations right now. I have talked to several Members of Congress. I've talked to leaders in the House. I've talked to several on the Republican side and Democratic side in the Senate. And I want to be sure that these consultations are complete.

Some feel a lame-duck session is not good, that the new Members should have a right to have a say. Others feel that we ought to move right now. The Congress, as you know, in their adjournment resolution, had a provision in there that they could come back and take this up. They are a coequal branch of government; they can do that if they want to. But we will continue our consultations. They'll follow, incidentally, today, this with a meeting with the leader-

ship. So, I'll get a little better feel for that as we go along.

Q. Mr. President, you say you're confident that American troops will prevail against Saddam if they're called upon?

The President. Oh, absolutely.

Q. But at what price? How many Americans?

The President. Oh, I can't give you any figures, of course. But I can say that the movement of this additional force safeguards the lives of every American and every one of our allies in the Gulf.

Yes, Brit [Brit Hume, ABC News]?

Q. Mr. President, in recent days, senior members of the administration have emphatically rejected the idea of any special emissaries or diplomatic envoys to or from Iraq to discuss this on your part. What changed your mind, sir?

The President. The United Nations resolution, I think, has a good chance of making Saddam Hussein understand what it is he's up against. I have not felt that he got the message. I hope this will do it. But I am convinced that these two direct meetings that I've discussed here will guarantee to all the people of the world, certainly to the American people, that Saddam Hussein not misunderstand, not misinterpret. I keep hearing: Well, people won't give him the news. Unlike the President of the United States, who gets good news and bad news very faithfully, I am told that Saddam Hussein's troops don't bring him the bad news; and I'm told that he is somewhat isolated. And I think this U.N. resolution will help de-isolate him, and I think the two proposals that I have made here will help. So, it's just going the extra step, Brit, that's what it is. And it's a decision that I personally made.

Q. You indicate that this date is not actually a deadline for the use of force, merely a date after which force would be permissible. How do you avoid the impression, should that date come and go without military action, that the U.S.-led coalition has, in fact, blinked?

The President. Well, we've got to look at events at the time, but I don't think there will ever be a perception that the United States is going to blink in this situation.

That's why I had some of the words in this statement that I had.

Q. Mr. President, you've just spoken about the weapons of mass destruction—nuclear weapons—and also that one of your goals is to try to reach stability in the region. Can you reach stability in the region with Saddam Hussein in power?

The President. I think most countries, members of the United Nations, feel that there have to be some safeguards put into effect in terms of guaranteeing the security and stability of the Gulf. And so, I would think that the status quo ante will not be enough. And I think there are sanctions in place now, and I think it would be very proper to discuss what those safeguards should be after there has been a total compliance with the United Nations resolutions.

Q. Sir, could I just follow up. I just notice that originally when you outlined your goals you included stability in the region. You seem to summarize them when you talk about these talks with Saddam Hussein. But you only mentioned the first three; you didn't mention stability in the region.

The President. Well, was I talking about the U.N. resolution? Which security and stability I don't think was a part of the U.N. resolution. It is certainly part of the world's objective, however. I think that may be the technical difference. But, look, it is critical, and it is very, very important.

Q. Mr. President, I want to ask if your comments about the Kuwaiti Embassy—whether it's fair to conclude, based on those, that you will neither close the Embassy nor permit those Americans to be starved out?

The President. I will not say exactly what I will do or exactly what I won't do. There is a very interesting report that we got in this morning saying that some Iraqis showed up at the Kuwaiti Embassy, our Embassy in Kuwait, and delivered fruit, vegetables, and a case of Iraqi cigarettes to Embassy Kuwait. And apparently, there's going to be another delivery tomorrow, including soda pop. And they asked what medical supplies were required.

Q. No mail?

The President. It doesn't say that. The Embassy will apparently provide a list tomorrow. And the electricity is still cut off.

So, this is kind of an interesting little development. But somebody said to me: Well, hey, what about if there's some provocation—they asked me in the leadership meeting. I said, consider me provoked when it comes to the United States Embassy. Consider me provoked when I see Americans without proper food and medical equipment.

Q. May I follow? Do you take it from that communique that you've received there that the Iraqis have the message and want to eliminate that as a potential tripwire?

The President. I don't know. It's too—the best question, right on target, one that we were discussing inside. Let's try to be optimistic and say this could be a positive sign, but it's so far short of compliance with international law that I can't be rejoicing. But it is a very interesting development.

Q. You've been getting some pretty negative comments up on the Hill from these hearings being held this week. Now, this morning, you said this would not be a long, protracted Vietnam-type war. However, General Odom, the former head of the NSA [National Security Agency], testified just this morning before the Senate Armed Services that, in fact, we'd have to be there for decades. Now, presumably, he means even after military combat we'd have to have people in place there, at least part of a peacekeeping force. Do you see our commitment there to extend that far?

The President. No, I don't.

Q. May I ask you something else? Al Gore yesterday takes issue with your comments and the comments of some of your aides, such as Brent Scowcroft [Assistant to the President for National Security Affairs], about Saddam being able to churn out a nuclear weapon within a matter of months. Gore, who has had some private briefings, apparently, has from some of you people, indicates that your administration statements are misleading.

The President. I disagree with the Senator. And if he wants to gamble on the future about the construction of atomic weapons by Saddam Hussein, I don't. I know what the intelligence says—every bit of it. I can't share it, obviously, because we don't comment on intelligence matters. But

I am concerned—from the very first time I spoke on this subject—I think in August, I mentioned weapons of mass destruction, I believe—certainly early on—and I am concerned about it. And if Senator Gore has a difference of opinion and is not concerned about it, we just have an honest difference there. I am concerned about Saddam Hussein's attempt to accelerate the construction or possession of a nuclear weapon. And I might as well share that as honestly as I can.

Q. Sir, are you saying that he could develop a warhead next year?

The President. I'm not giving you a timeframe. But you've seen the estimates, some of which I guess are accurate, in the papers. And there's a lot of scientists that come down on different sides. Senator Gore, I'm sure, is an intelligence fellow, and he—but I don't think he has access to absolutely all; maybe he does. But I am not going to err on the side of underestimation when it comes to this question.

Q. Mr. President, your announcement about Tariq 'Aziz and Secretary Baker—have you had any signals, any indications from the Iraqis, that they would welcome this, that they are indeed looking for this kind of communication?

The President. No. The only thing I've heard is that they want to talk. Here's an opportunity. But no, I've not had any diplomatic signals or signals of other kinds.

Q. And of those 26 nations that you list in the area, how many of those are equally committed to offensive action rather than just defensive action?

The President. I can't give you the answer to that because I don't really know. But I expect that there is enthusiasm in all quarters of those countries for the U.N. action that was taken yesterday.

Q. Well, with all respect, shouldn't you know how many would follow your troops into battle?

The President. I know that what I said is true about if we have to go into battle. I'm satisfied I know enough about that. I went over in detail, as you well imagine a President should because I have the responsibility as Commander in Chief, what might happen if we have to use force.

I repeat: I hope we'll never have to have one single shot fired in anger.

Q. Iraq has been constantly calling for dialog. Aren't you concerned that those two missions, Tariq 'Aziz and James Baker, will lead Saddam Hussein to claim that the U.S. is showing a sign of weakness?

The President. Because Baker goes to Baghdad?

Q. Aren't you concerned that that will be the position of Saddam Hussein?

The President. No, I'm not. I'm concerned some might say that is an ultimatum in which—all it is, is an effort to be sure that he understands the commitment of the United States; that he understands that anything that is done must be done inside the confines of the United Nations resolutions that have been passed; that there will be no contingency, there can be no face-saving—that's not what this is about. This is to be sure that he understands how strongly the President of the United States feels about implementing to a tee, without concession, the United Nations position. Some have told me that he's not getting the message of how determined we are. I can't think of any better way to do it at this juncture, in the wake of the U.N. resolution, than this face-to-face meeting. I'm not sure he'll agree to it.

Q. Today's press conference seems to amount to again more talk of preparations for war. Can you describe what you think your responsibilities are in terms of Congress as we head into this period, since they seem to think that and agree that you're consulting, talking, but you seem reluctant to go and get a resolution that mimics the U.N. resolution. What do you think your responsibilities are to Congress and to the people that elected them?

The President. Full consultation. Get them in on the——

Q. Any more than telling them before you do something?

The President. I'm leveling with them on where I think matters are right now. You've put your interpretation on my remarks. There were plenty of comments in there about hoping that we will have a peaceful resolution, that the best answer to get a peaceful resolution is to have Saddam Hussein know how determined everybody is.

You see, I think yesterday's U.N. resolution was a step towards peace, not a step towards war, because I believe that when Saddam Hussein finally gets the message and understands what he's up against in terms of world opinion and other things that he will do that in Kuwait which he did in Iran.

Trade With the Soviet Union and U.S. Aid

Q. Thank you, Mr. President. The Soviet Union did, indeed, vote on our side as far as the resolution allowing force if it's necessary. Are we going to offer the Soviet Union any compromise on export credits? As you know, there's some concern that they think there is a de facto grain embargo going on because we won't offer export credits in their very needy time.

The President. The matters are totally separate and unrelated. But I am concerned about this. And I've talked with Mr. Gorbachev of a willingness to entertain proposals for food, particularly if the reports prove to be accurate in terms of the severe winter and the hardship that this will inflict on the Soviet people.

I have asked our own top people here to come up with recommendations for me, next week, as what to do about Jackson-Vanik. It has been my position that the Soviets should pass the necessary emigration legislation. That has not taken place. But some are saying that I now have a clearer waiver authority than I thought. And I do not want to work hardship on any sector of the American economy. I'm one of those strongest proponents against a grain embargo, and yet I'm told that some in middle America think that our position is really almost resulting in a grain embargo. And I want to dispel any notion that I am for the grain embargo.

The Soviets are concerned about many aspects of this legislation. So, I'm facing a decision as to what to do. Should we try to waive Vanik, and should we then extend credits under the CCC [Commodity Credit Corporation]? There are other agricultural programs that I think we can go forward with immediately without waiver of Jackson-Vanik. But it's an evolving question here. And I don't know exactly what I am going to do, because we're caught between

some strong and understandable economic interests at home and, on the other hand, a position of wanting to stand for free and fair emigration.

One thing that is important to note, however, is that the exodus of Soviet Jews from the Soviet Union is high. And I'd like to take some credit for our administration in this, because we've been steadfast in encouraging the exodus of Soviet Jews. And so, that will weigh on my consideration when I get down to have to make this final decision about the waiver of Jackson-Vanik.

Emigration of Soviet Jews to the United States

Q. On that, would you consider another increase of the quota that—the number of people that could emigrate to the United States? Would we increase the amount that we'd accept?

The President. We're reviewing the whole policy at this juncture.

Persian Gulf Crisis

Q. Mr. President, Arab experts suggest that Saddam Hussein has hinted in his remarks that he would like to have some sort of deal, but he wouldn't necessarily hold to his demands. Now you're saying you're willing to meet with him. Are you willing to offer him anything in these meetings in return for a pullout, such as a conference on the Middle East?

The President. No. Those two items are totally separate. We've made that very, very clear. And what I have said is that these discussions will be done within the U.N. mandate. I'm not all that hopeful that we'll get big results out of all of this. It's going the extra mile. It's taking the extra step. But I can't tell you that I think we're going to have great success on all of this because our partnership in the world is together on the fact that we cannot stop short of total fulfillment, without condition, of the United Nations resolutions.

Q. What then is the point of the meeting? Are you just delivering ultimatums?

The President. No, this isn't an ultimatum at all. And I hope what it does is demonstrate that we are prepared to go face to face and tell him how committed we are to the United Nations resolutions. I've told you I don't think he has felt this commitment. As I said earlier, he may feel it a little more strongly now that we did what many skeptics thought couldn't happen—that the United Nations Security Council did, and that is come together and pass this very important resolution.

So, one thing is he has got to understand what the alternatives are to complying with the United Nations resolutions. And the best way to get that across is one on one—Baker looking him right in the eye. I've been told that he doesn't necessarily believe that I am totally committed to what I've been saying. And here's a good opportunity to have him understand that face to face.

So, we want to make the case to him directly for complying with the United Nations resolutions, make the case to him from a Secretary of State who's incessantly worked to get this resolution through—the strength of the commitment of the international community—and then try to persuade him to reconsider his position and to take the steps necessary for a peaceful resolution of the crisis. But it isn't a trip of concession. When you've done what he's done, I don't see that there's room for concession, there's room for giving something to save face. That's not the way you treat with aggression. And we're not going to treat with it any differently than I've outlined here.

Yes, and then Maureen [Maureen Santini, New York Daily News]. I told Maureen I'd—you two, and then I'll go peacefully.

Q. With high oil prices hurting the world——

The President. ——you're whipsawed today; it's terrible. The statement was so long at the beginning. I apologize for that.

Q. You don't have to give to everybody up front.

The President. Well, Helen—I mean, Sarah [Sarah McClendon, McClendon News]. Thank you, Sarah. I didn't see your hand up.

Q. It sure has been up for an hour. [*Laughter*]

The President. Even before I got here? [*Laughter*] Sarah, you get the last question. We did this before, and I got in real trouble.

Go ahead—two.

Q. Mr. President, you mentioned the damage that high oil prices are doing to the world economy. Should Saudi Arabia and other producers share more of their windfall?

The President. I think they're doing a pretty good job in underwriting the costs to various countries and helping third party countries that have been hurt by all of this. But I think everybody should go the extra mile to help others. And I was pleased when I was talking in Mexico, for example, with President Salinas, that he is selling oil—to try to help the burden by selling oil at bargain prices off this inflated world price. So, I think everybody should try to help. And I think the Saudis have made a lot of commitments to countries in trying to help out. I hope they will continue to do that, and I'm confident they will.

Q. If I could follow, sir: Should Saudi Arabia have a military draft?

The President. That's for the Saudi Arabians to decide. I don't think the United States needs one, incidentally.

Q. Mr. President, if you ultimately feel that you have to ask Americans to support the use of force, what that, of course, means is that you have to ask some parents to give up the lives of their children.

The President. I know it.

Q. What I was wondering was: We all know how important your children are to you. Do you feel that this issue is important enough to you that you could conceive of giving up one of their lives for it?

The President. You know, Maureen, you put your finger on a very difficult question. People say to me, How many lives? How many lives can you expend? Each one is precious. I don't want to reminisce, but I've been there. I know what it's like to have fallen comrades and see young kids die in battle. It's only the President that should be asked to make the decision: Is it worth it? How many lives is it worth? Is it worth it to commit one life, put one life in harm's way to achieve these objectives? And that's why I want to get a peaceful resolution to this question.

You ought to read my mail. It is so heart-moving. Supportive, and yet: Please bring my kid home. Please bring my husband home. It's a tough question. But a President has to make the right decision. These are worldwide principles of moral importance. I will do my level-best to bring those kids home without one single shot fired in anger. And if a shot is fired in anger, I want to guarantee each person that their kid, whose life is in harm's way, will have the maximum support, will have the best chance to come home alive, and will be backed up to the hilt.

Because of that question that weighs on my mind, I added that language this morning about how this will not be a Vietnam. They can criticize me for moving force. And if we've got one kid that's apt to be in harm's way, I want him backed up to the hilt by American firepower, and others as well. That's why I'm working as hard as I am not only to hold this coalition together but to strengthen it. The best way to safeguard the lives of Americans is for Saddam Hussein to do that what he should have done long ago. And if force has to be used, the best way to safeguard lives is to see that you've got the best and you're willing to use it. That's my posture.

Q. Sir, why do you seem to be avoiding the people's representatives having an opportunity to talk on this and to express their opinion? You know Congress, and yet you're avoiding it. You know that the Constitution gives the power not only to declare war, but to provide the money and to say other things about what shall be done with troops. That's the Constitution. Yet you seem to be avoiding that. The experts on Capitol Hill say that what you have done by prenotification, calling two or three Members and saying we're on the way— you've already made the decision. You're notifying them; that's prenotification. That's not consulting with Congress. They say you should sit down and have a back-and-forth with them.

The President. Yes.

Q. And I want to remind you that when Foley speaks as Speaker of the House, he may be Speaker of the House, but he sure as hell doesn't represent Florida and Texas.

The President. Sarah, therein, you've properly brought up the dilemma I face.

There are 435 Members of the United States Congress, there are 100——

Q. But——

The President. May I finish, please? There are 100 Members of the United States Senate. Each one has a view as to what I ought not to do, and that's fine. They have the power under the resolution of adjournment to come back 20 seconds from now and to take a voice, to stand, to take a common position. If they want to come back here and endorse what the President of the United States has done and what the United Nations Security Council has done, come on, we're ready. I'd like to see it happen. But what I don't want to do is have it come back and end up where you have 435 voices in one House and 100 on the other saying what not to do and saying— kind of a hand-wringing operation that would send bad signals. I welcome these hearings. We're having hearings. We're consulting. I've told you I'm consulting. I'll be honest with you: I cannot consult with 535 strong-willed individuals. I can't do it, nor does my responsibility under the Constitution compel me to do that. And I think everyone would agree that we have had more consultations than previous administrations.

Q. Sir, we have a majority rule in this country, and you seem to be afraid of it.

The President. No, I'm not afraid of it at all. We have a tripartite form of government. And I know my strengths, and I know the limitations on the Presidency. This is an interesting debate, Sarah. [*Laughter*] And I know my limitations. And I know what I can do, and I know what previous Presidents have done. And I am still determined to consult the extra mile. You want to continue to debate?

Q. You and Jim Baker give the other countries a chance to talk, and you give the United Nations a chance to talk, but you won't give the United States people a chance to debate with you.

The President. Well now, that's an absurd comment, Sarah, from a bright person like you. That is absolutely absurd. They're holding hearings. They're talking. They have the power under the adjournment resolution to reconvene this minute. Some in the

House want to come back now; some want to talk about it later on. Some in the Senate want to come right back now and immediately endorse what the President has done and what the Security Council resolution is—and I'm for that—but some don't. And so, consultation is going on. Please do not assign to me improper motives. They're talking right now. They're having endless hearings by endless experts up there, each one with a slightly different view. And

that's the American way. And that's fine. And I know what the responsibilities of the President are, and I am fulfilling those responsibilities.

Note: The President's 66th news conference began at approximately 11 a.m. in the Briefing Room at the White House. In his opening remarks, he referred to President Saddam Hussein of Iraq.

Exchange With Reporters Prior to a Meeting With Foreign Minister Qian Qichen of China
November 30, 1990

Q. Mr. President, has China atoned for Tiananmen Square?

The President. Have they what?

Q. Have they atoned for Tiananmen Square?

The President. Well, I think the Chinese Government knows that we have some differences on this whole broad question of human rights, but we have many things in common. And one good thing is, we have a very frank relationship with this Foreign Minister and an ability to discuss things openly. He's got some problems with some things, perhaps, we've done, and in this area there are some differences. But that's one of the purposes of this kind of meeting—is to reduce these differences and to go forward.

We've worked closely on the broad concept of stopping aggression. And of course, that is something that we have in common with this very important country, China. So, I'm looking forward to full discussions with this Foreign Minister.

Q. Are you thinking of eliminating sanctions?

The President. We're going to discuss a wide array of questions, and I think it will

go very well. And, as I say, both sides are trying to strengthen and build on this relationship that both recognize as important. And I will have every opportunity to express to the Foreign Minister, and I expect he will report that back very accurately to the leaders in Beijing, how strongly I feel on some of these questions. And he'll have every opportunity today to present China's views on these important questions.

I'm always inclined to emphasize the positive. And there are many positive and very important aspects to this relationship— very important. And not the least of which is that China and the United States have made common ground in terms of standing up against aggression. And that is important to every American; it is important, I think, to the Chinese side as well.

Mr. Fitzwater. Lights. Thank you.

The President. Thank you, guys. It's been a great pleasure. [*Laughter*]

How many brave souls are going to South America? All right. Rest up.

Note: The exchange began at 1:30 p.m. in the Oval Office at the White House. Marlin Fitzwater was Press Secretary to the President.

Remarks Announcing the Nomination of Bob Martinez To Be Director of National Drug Control Policy
November 30, 1990

The President. During the past couple of years, we've devoted unprecedented resources to the war on drugs. Bill Bennett—I mentioned this just the other day—has been an outstanding leader of that fight. I'm pleased that in stepping down as Director of the Office of National Drug Control Policy, he is now willing to take on the challenge of chairing the Republican National Committee. I have recommended Bill Bennett to the members of the RNC to serve in the post of chairman, and I've also recommended that Lee Atwater serve as general chairman of the Republican Party.

Bill is a man of proven leadership, intellect, and commitment whose drive and determination will be a tremendous asset to the Republican Party organizations and operations, and I am grateful that he has accepted this important task. And I might add that I am delighted that Lee Atwater will continue to provide valued counsel as general chairman of the party. He has been, as you all know, a close adviser and political strategist—chief political strategist—and a good friend. I certainly wish him Godspeed in his fight and in his recovery.

Today, I'm also pleased to announce the appointment of a superbly qualified individual, Governor Bob Martinez, to succeed Bill Bennett as our nation's new Drug Policy Director—a battlefield promotion, if you will, for a leader who has earned his stripes on the front lines of the drug war. Governor Martinez can and will hit the ground running. He needs no primer. As the National Governors' Association's lead Governor on substance abuse and drug trafficking, he has been contributing to our national drug control strategy for over 2 years.

As Governor, Bob Martinez has introduced some of our most innovative and effective new tools against drugs. He was the first to name a State drug czar and one of the first to bring the National Guard into the fight. He stiffened the Florida Code and then added the prison space to enforce it. He's enacted new laws that take career criminals off the streets; launched a successful boot camp program; moved to revoke drivers licenses for drug users; supported, always, effective drug treatment; and established drug-free school zones.

As a Governor who signed more than 130 death warrants, he understands tough choices and the need for penalties as tough as the criminals that we face.

As a former Governor and mayor, Bob will be especially effective in joining hands with State and local leaders. As a teacher who has spent 7 years in the classroom, he knows the longterm key to winning this effort is to stop drug use before it starts. As a businessman, he knows the challenges we face in making the workplace drug-free. And as a Spanish-speaking leader who has probed the problem firsthand in Bolivia and Colombia, he's in a unique position to work with our Latin American allies.

Bob Martinez is the grandson of Spanish immigrants, the son of a waiter, a man who worked his way through school. My predecessor called him "the embodiment of the American dream." He's now about to take on his toughest challenge yet—with all respect to your present employment—the scourge that is today the American nightmare.

Governor, we congratulate you. We wish you luck. I want to thank you for taking on this important task. You know you've got big shoes to fill, and we're going to stand with you in this important fight. America, as Bill has so eloquently stated—Bill Bennett—is making progress against drugs. Thanks to the leadership of people like Bill Bennett, we're going to continue to do so. We're all pleased that Bill's very able chief of staff, John Walters, will carry on the fight until Governor Martinez assumes the helm. There are many battles ahead. And we're going to renew our call to Congress to pass a true crime bill—one that's tough on criminals, not on the police—and we'll remain on the front lines. We will take back the streets.

Bob—Governor Martinez—I look forward to working with you as closely as I have with Bill Bennett.

Bill, I look forward to working with you in an entirely different assignment. We'll have many, many contacts, I can assure you.

But thank you all very much, and now I will turn this over to Governor Martinez with my warm best wishes. Thanks for taking this on. Thank you all.

Reporter. Mr. President, can I ask you a question about your phone calls to the leaders of the Middle East today—what the response was?

The President. Doing very well. But let's turn it over—they've all been very, very positive.

Note: The President spoke at 2:30 p.m. in the Briefing Room at the White House.

Statement by Press Secretary Fitzwater on President Bush's Telephone Conversations With Foreign Leaders
November 30, 1990

President Bush called a number of foreign leaders this afternoon to discuss his proposal that Iraqi Foreign Minister Tariq 'Aziz meet with U.S. and other representatives in December, and that Secretary of State Baker travel to Baghdad to meet with [President] Saddam Hussein. All the leaders received President Bush's initiative enthusiastically and reiterated their desires for achieving the complete and unconditional withdrawal of Iraq from Kuwait, the restoration of the legitimate government of Kuwait, and the release of all hostages. President Bush spoke with Presidents Mubarak [of Egypt] and Özal [of Turkey], King Fahd [of Saudi Arabia], Prime Minister Major [of the United Kingdom], and the Amir of Kuwait.

Memorandum of Disapproval for the Intelligence Authorization Act, Fiscal Year 1991
November 30, 1990

I have withheld my signature from S. 2834, the proposed "Intelligence Authorization Act, Fiscal Year 1991," thereby preventing it from becoming law. I am compelled to take this action due to the bill's treatment of one highly sensitive and important issue that directly affects the Nation's security, although there also are several objectionable elements of the bill that trouble me.

I cannot accept the broad language that was added in Conference to the definition of covert action. Section 602 of the bill defines "covert action" to include any "request" by the United States to a foreign government or a private citizen to conduct a covert action on behalf of the United States. This provision purports to regulate diplomacy by the President and other members of the executive branch by forbidding the expression of certain views to foreign governments and private citizens absent compliance with specified procedures; this could require, in most instances, prior reporting to the Congress of the intent to express those views.

I am particularly concerned that the vagueness of this provision could seriously impair the effective conduct of our Nation's foreign relations. It is unclear exactly what sort of discussions with foreign governments would constitute reportable "requests" under this provision, and the very possibility of a broad construction of this term could have a chilling effect on the ability of our diplomats to conduct highly sensitive discussions concerning projects that are vital to our national security. Furthermore, the mere existence of this provision could deter foreign governments from discussing certain topics with the United States at all. Such a provision could result in frequent and divisive disputes on whether an activity is covered by the definition and whether individuals in the executive branch have complied with a statutory requirement.

My objections to this provision should not be misinterpreted to mean that executive branch officials can somehow conduct activities otherwise prohibited by law or Executive order. Quite the contrary. It remains Administration policy that our intelligence services will not ask third parties to carry out activities that they are themselves forbidden to undertake under Executive Order No. 12333 on U.S. intelligence activities. I have also directed that the notice to the Congress of covert actions indicate whether a foreign government will participate significantly.

Beyond this issue, I am also concerned by the treatment in the Joint Explanatory Statement accompanying the Conference Report of notification to the Congress of covert actions. I reached an accommodation with the Intelligence Committees on the issue of notifying the Congress of covert actions "in a timely fashion," as required by current law, and have provided letters to the Intelligence Committees outlining how I intend to provide such notice. I was consequently dismayed by the fact that language was inserted in the Joint Explanatory Statement accompanying the Conference Report that could be construed to undercut the agreement reached with the Committees. This language asserts that prior notice may be withheld only in "exigent circumstances" and that notice "in a timely fash-

ion" should now be interpreted to mean "within a few days" without exception. Such an interpretation would unconstitutionally infringe on the authority of the President and impair any Administration's effective implementation of covert action programs. I deeply regret this action.

Additionally, I am concerned that there are several legislatively directed policy determinations restricting programs of vital importance to the United States that I do not believe are helpful to U.S. foreign policy. This bill, like its predecessor last year, also contains language that purports to condition specified actions on the President's obtaining the prior approval of committees of the Congress. This language is clearly unconstitutional under the Presentment clause of the Constitution and the Supreme Court's decision in *INS* v. *Chadha,* 462 U.S. 919 (1983). I again urge the Congress to cease including such unconstitutional provisions in bills presented to me for signature.

This Administration has had a good relationship with the Intelligence Committees. I am willing to work with the Congress to address the primary issue that has prompted my veto as well as other difficulties with the bill. I will also continue to work with the Congress to ensure there is no change in our shared understanding of what constitutes a covert action, particularly with respect to the historic missions of the armed forces. I am confident that these issues can be resolved quickly in the next Congress through mutual trust and a good-faith effort on the part of the Administration and the Congress.

GEORGE BUSH

The White House,
November 30, 1990.

Note: The President's last day for action on this bill was November 30.

Statement on Signing the Judicial Improvements Act of 1990
December 1, 1990

I am very pleased to sign H.R. 5316, the "Judicial Improvements Act of 1990." Most important, Title II of this Act provides for 85 new Federal judgeships. These additional judicial resources will provide needed assistance in our fight against crime and drugs by enhancing our courts' ability to provide swift and fair justice. They will also increase civil litigants' access to prompt judicial resolution of their cases. H.R. 5316 also contains other useful provisions. Title I makes valuable suggestions for improving the management of the civil justice system; and Title III establishes a new retirement system for Claims Court judges and assures adequate retirement benefits for the spouses of assas-sinated Federal judges. I am very grateful to Members of both Houses and both political parties, particularly Senators Biden and Thurmond and Congressmen Brooks and Fish, as well as to the Judicial Conference and the Administrative Office of the U.S. Courts, for the effort they invested in devising this important piece of legislation.

GEORGE BUSH

The White House,
December 1, 1990.

Note: H.R. 5316, approved December 1, was assigned Public Law No. 101–650.

Written Responses to Questions Submitted by the South American Press
November 30, 1990

Chile-U.S. Relations

Q. In the relations between the United States and Chile, what are the main items that you would like to see resolved and in what manner?

The President. More than anything else, I would like to convey to the Chilean people my most heartfelt congratulations and support for their transition to civilian democracy. It is a transition which was fraught with difficulties and challenges, but the people of Chile have carried it off with great courage, intelligence, and dignity. Those of us who hoped and worked for this objective feel that the democratic ideal throughout the world has been enhanced by Chile's example. Equally important, Chile has managed to bring about its democratic transition without undermining the economic progress that it has made in recent years.

It is important to keep this larger context in mind as we look at specific items on our bilateral agenda. It is no secret that our agenda during the first months of President Aylwin's term has been dominated by issues left over from the past, principally by the questions of restoration of GSP to Chile and a framework for settlement of the issues generated by the Letelier case.

Many Chileans have felt frustration or even irritation about the slowness with which these questions have been resolved. All I can say is that in democracies, things don't move as fast as they do under other systems; that is the price we pay for consultation and deliberation. The reassuring thing is that decisions do get made, however. I am happy that we have been able to begin the process of restoring GSP to Chile and that the Chilean Congress has passed the "Cumplido" law transferring jurisdiction over the Letelier case from military to civilian courts. This will make it possible to eliminate restrictions on defense cooperation, something we want to do.

Enterprise for the Americas and Trade Negotiations

Q. How do you plan to implement the Enterprise for the Americas Initiative, especially concerning trade, since you have a mainly Democratic Congress with protectionist attitudes and no trade agreement has been reached in Uruguay round GATT talks? How will you address both issues? How do you expect Latin America to believe in a free market economy if measures are taken in the U.S. Congress to protect your economy?

The President. The short answer to your question is that we have to work hard to get the results we want and believe are right, which will provide economic growth for both the United States and our hemispheric partners. We need our Congress to approve legislation for certain parts of the Enterprise for the Americas. This includes legislation for the restructuring of official debt and for the investment fund we would like to see in the Inter-American Development Bank. Fortunately, the reaction in the Congress to the Enterprise initiative has been very positive, which pleases me enormously. We have already succeeded in getting one piece of the Enterprise legislation passed through our Congress, regarding P.L. 480 debt, despite our budget problems and the crunch of legislation that we always face at the end of a legislative term. We are taking steps to implement this legislation, and we are prepared to enter into negotiations with countries eligible under the legislation to reduce their P.L. 480 debt.

You have my commitment that I will be back to the Congress when it reconvenes in January 1991, seeking passage of the other portions of the Enterprise legislation. I feel confident that a bipartisan spirit will prevail, because I am convinced that the vast majority of the Members of Congress recognize the mutual benefits such an agreement could bring and support good relations between the United States and our partners in this hemisphere. This is not to say that protectionist pressures do not exist. They do in our Congress, as they do in all legislatures of democratic countries. I have used my veto power (for example, with the textile bill earlier this year) to prevent protectionist pressures at home from hurting our economy or damaging important foreign policy interests.

The other point you touched on is the Uruguay round. I want you to know that I am making every effort to ensure that these talks produce an outcome that results in expanding world trade substantially. Our position is clear: We all need a successful conclusion to the Uruguay round, one that opens markets worldwide. I am glad that other countries in this hemisphere share this view and have worked hard to bring it about. We look forward to working closely with Chile and other trading nations to achieve good market-opening agreements and substantial agricultural reforms.

Brazil-U.S. Relations

Q. Mr. President, many Brazilians think that the prospect of better relations between Brazil and the United States that emerged from your personal contacts with President Collor earlier this year are fading under the difficulties of new trade frictions and the old debt problem. I would like to ask you two questions in this regard: Your government has recently joined the other G–7 members in demanding that Brazil "resolve its debt arrears problem with the commercial banks" before any further long-term financial agreements can be negotiated. The Brazilian Government argues that this approach is not acceptable because it would compromise the market-oriented economic stabilization program that you have endorsed. The issue is likely to be central to your talks in Brasilia. How will you deal with it?

The President. You've posed a very complex question, and I will try to do it justice. In the first place, I would like to tell you that I have the highest respect for President Collor and what he is trying to do to reform and modernize the economy of Brazil. To bring about such dramatic change in a huge country like Brazil, which has more than 150 million people, deserves respect and admiration.

Our relations with Brazil are based on the solid appreciation that we share a common commitment to democratic civilian rule and economic prosperity for our citizens. With such large, competitive, and varied economies as those of the United States and Brazil, there will always be some trade frictions. What most of you may not realize is the progress we have made in addressing these trade issues. As other problems crop up, they will need to be worked on. As long as I am President, the United States will seek to address these problems in a spirit of creative problem-solving.

With regard to your question about Brazil's debt, the United States is eager to see a long-term solution that is consistent with the international debt strategy and will give Brazil the opportunity to grow and trade its way to economic health. This is a process of negotiation and has to be seen as such. While I will want to discuss this issue with President Collor, I do not see it as central to my discussions in Brazil. This is one of many issues we will want to discuss, with the goal of understanding each other's position well and looking for ways to advance common objectives.

U.S. Trade With South America

Q. The United States has proposed a framework trade agreement to Brazil and three other South American nations but has rejected a Brazilian proposal to discuss such an important issue as the access to advanced U.S. technology in the context of the agreement. Why? Is it a commercial problem or a security related problem?

The President. First of all, I must point out that the inspiration for doing a five-country framework agreement came from Brazil, Argentina, Uruguay, and Paraguay. Much as I might like to claim credit for this innovative suggestion, I cannot; it came from South America. We were pleased to move forward on this suggestion because it clearly advances the goals of regional and hemispheric economic integration that are at the heart of the Enterprise for the Americas proposal.

Second, I think you may be reading more into our position than there really is. The framework agreements we have negotiated with other countries are directed at trade and investment. There is plenty that we can do and need to do in these areas. While we are indeed willing to talk about trade-related technology questions, we were concerned that if we tried to do too much, we would end up with a structure that was too difficult to manage. There's a saying in English which says, "Don't bite off more than you can chew." I understand there is a similar phrase in Spanish which says, "*El que mucho abarca, poco aprieta.*" We want the framework agreements to work on difficult issues, but not to have them solve *all* the issues.

Latin America-U.S. Relations

Q. Mr. President, in Latin America there are numerous questions about the motives and objectives that led you to launch the Enterprise for the Americas Initiative. Would you explain your view of Latin America today, the motives that brought you to propose the initiative and, if you could be more specific, in what fields and during what time period do you expect the most important aspects of the initiative to be achieved?

The President. With regard to this hemisphere, the first year of my administration was devoted largely to two subjects: restoration of democracy in Central America and the war on drugs. With the triumph of democracy in Nicaragua, the end of dictatorship in Panama, and with the drug strategy launched, I became convinced that the United States needed to take a longer range look at relations in this hemisphere. In part, I was also reacting to concerns expressed to me by the region's leaders, who told me they worried that the amazing events in Central and Eastern Europe would cause us to forget this hemisphere and devote all our resources to Europe.

I gave these Latin American and Caribbean leaders my commitment that the United States would remain engaged in this hemisphere. As I told several leaders, the Americas are our common homeland, and we cannot forget this. For this reason, I asked my top economic and policy advisers to examine our policy in the region and give me ideas on innovative approaches the United States could take to complement economic reforms being implemented by Latin American and Caribbean governments.

The result of this review was the June 27 Enterprise for the Americas Initiative. My goal was to propose a mix of long-term and short-term objectives, covering the areas of trade, investment, debt, and the environment. In trade, I set out a challenge: that we act together to create a free trade area for the entire hemisphere. To get there, we are already working on a free trade agreement with Mexico, and we have signed bilateral framework agreements with Bolivia, Colombia, Ecuador, Chile, Honduras, and Costa Rica. In response to a suggestion from Brazil, Uruguay, Paraguay, and Argentina, we have agreed to negotiate a multicountry framework agreement.

In the investment area, we suggested creation of new Inter-American Development Bank programs and an additional multilateral investment fund and to improve the hemisphere's investment potential. We are seeking congressional approval of funding to contribute to multilateral. On debt, we have secured passage through the U.S. Congress of the first element of our package for reducing official debt. As you know, one of the features of this proposal is to use interest paid on the remaining debt stock to fund environmental projects. As soon as the U.S. Congress reconvenes in January, we will be working for passage of the rest of the legislative package.

As we look to the future, however, we should not be doing so in terms of unrealistic deadlines saying that "on such-and-such a date, all of the region's problems will be solved." What we are offering is a commitment to work actively and creatively with this hemisphere, to consult frequently, and to seek solutions which lead to greater prosperity and well-being for all, in what we hope will be the world's first "hemisphere of democracy."

Uruguay-U.S. Relations

Q. Uruguay is a tiny country that, despite its important democratic tradition, [seems] many times to have been ignored by the United States. This Presidential visit, for example, is the first one in 30 years. What brought Latin America to your attention, created an interest in visiting Uruguay, and what benefits might Uruguay gain from this new relationship with the U.S.?

The President. It has been too long since a President of the United States visited Uruguay. President Eisenhower visited Montevideo in 1960, and President Lyndon Johnson made a brief trip to Punta del Este in 1967, I believe.

Uruguay may be a small country, but it is one which has throughout its history played a creative and innovative role in world affairs. It is also a nation of immigrants, a fact that serves as a point of linkage with the United States. For example, I recently accepted the credentials of your Ambassador to the United States, Eduardo MacGillycuddy. Ambassador MacGillycuddy is a distant cousin of a United States Senator from Florida, Connie Mack. Ambassador MacGillycuddy's grandfather was a brother of the Philadelphia Phillies baseball legend by the same name.

Let me offer another example. As I mentioned above, we are in the midst of trying to complete the most ambitious trade expansion program in decades. If this effort succeeds, it could expand world trade by $500 billion. It is no accident that this round of world trade talks is called the Uruguay round, after the country which served as sponsor for its launching.

I can point to other things as well. President Lacalle was the first President of this region to telephone me after I announced the Enterprise for the Americas Initiative on June 27. His support has been a strong stimulus to me to make this proposal work. To make it work, we will need the help of institutions such as the Inter-American Development Bank, which is headed by another Uruguayan, Enrique Iglesias.

For all these reasons, I am eager to visit Uruguay, to consult with President Lacalle, and speak to the Uruguayan Congress. I would not speak only in terms of benefits to Uruguay from the visit. We are looking for answers that will benefit the whole hemisphere, such as the ones we can derive from a successful Uruguay round and a free trade area stretching from Alaska to Tierra del Fuego.

Argentine Economy

Q. Argentina is working on the economic integration with Brazil and other countries in the Southern Cone and, at the same time, has started a process of deep restructuring of its economy and its institutional frame. What is your impression of the fact that privatization of two big state corporations (an airline and a telephone company) has been achieved with the participation of American capital, but not of American management or technology?

The President. I think the most important part of your question relates to what is going on in Argentina today. Difficult, sometimes painful, economic choices are being made by President Menem. These choices involve the transformation of very large sectors of the Argentine economy. Like many other leaders of this hemisphere, President Menem is making the difficult choices and implementing economic reform policies to make Argentina more competitive and guarantee the country's long-term economic health.

Privatization has played a part in this economic restructuring. As your question noted, instead of continuing to have the economy dominated by an inefficient state apparatus, which has stifled initiative and blocked economic growth, the Government of Argentina has adopted policies aimed at privatizing businesses such as the airline and the telephone company. This has reduced Argentina's debt burden and brought back to these companies the incentive to compete for investment and for clients. Quite frankly, I believe that good airlines can and should depend on their passengers for their revenues and not depend on the taxpayers.

As for the participation of United States investors—whether this be in the form of capital, of technology, or of management—as long as there is a level playing field, and by that I mean that the rules are the same for all investors, I think that rational economic choices will be made. That's what freedom to compete is all about, whether it is in Argentina or Alaska.

U.S. Trade Policies

Q. At the final stage of the Uruguay round of GATT, the U.S. is standing again against subsidies and all kinds of protectionist trade barriers for agricultural products. Nevertheless, the Government is subsidizing some grain exports, with potential harm for Argentina and other countries in the hemisphere, and is keeping some tariffs that make difficult the entrance of products like, for example, Argentine leathers. Is it possible that the administration could modify these policies in favor of a more consistent attitude with respect to all forms of protectionism?

The President. I know that the Commerce Department's decision to impose countervailing duties on Argentine leather was unpopular with the leather industry in Argentina. But here are some economic facts: By forbidding the export of hides from Argentina, prices for these hides in Argentina are driven down because they can only be sold in the domestic market. This means that leather exported from Argentine commerce to other markets, such as the United States, is priced artificially low.

Argentina's competitors in the U.S. thought this was unfair and complained to our authorities. Following a very detailed and open process in accordance with our law, in which the Argentine industry was represented by experienced counsel, the Commerce Department agreed that a subsidy was being provided by virtue of the Argentine Government's policy prohibiting the export of hides. This is not an issue where the President of the United States can intervene to tip the scales one way or another. The solution is for Argentina to allow exports of hides, so that its leather will be priced according to the forces of the international market.

I should note that this has been a long-standing sore point in our bilateral relationship. Several years ago, we had negotiated a solution under the section 301 provision, but because the agreement was not fulfilled by Argentina, U.S. industry felt it had no recourse but to seek relief under U.S. trade laws.

With regard to wheat, I assume you are referring to the Export Enhancement Program. This program was designed to keep U.S. wheat competitively priced with the wheat being sold by other producers, primarily the European Community. We hope that a successful outcome of the agricultural talks in the Uruguay round will make this and other export subsidy programs superfluous.

Petroleum

Q. Venezuela has increased its oil production by half a million barrels daily to help in the Gulf crisis and is opening its doors again to U.S. private investment in the oil sector. Recently, President Carlos Andrés Pérez stated that his country deplored the speculation which was driving oil prices up and hurting the American consumer. He said it was not in Venezuela's interest, either, to be subject to ups and downs in prices and appealed for a meeting between the major oil producing nations and the leading consumer countries to work out some kind of stabilization program for international oil prices. The U.S. has not reacted to this proposal, made first 2 months ago.

Although your country supports a market economy, it has joined in stabilization agreements in the past for various products. Would you consider this for oil, especially now that the market has been disrupted by the Gulf crisis, and the future well-being of the Gulf nations as well as other producers such as Venezuela, not to mention various of your own States, which produce oil and are dependent upon a steady and reasonable oil income?

The President. You have posed a detailed question which requires a detailed reply. In the first place, I must pay tribute to the extremely positive role that Venezuela, and particularly President Carlos Andrés Pérez, has played in the months since Iraq invaded Kuwait. He worked hard with Saudi Arabia to ensure that members of the Organization of Petroleum Exporting Countries (OPEC) increased supplies to cover the shortfall caused by the loss of Kuwaiti oil and the embargo on Iraqi exports. Venezuela and CAP have been a force for stability in oil supplies.

We have also welcomed President Pérez' efforts to prevent wild swings in world oil prices. As he has correctly pointed out, these are bad for producers, and they are bad for consumers. A recession in the industrialized world will not help OPEC members such as Venezuela, and far-sighted leaders such as President Pérez have been among the first to realize this.

I know that Venezuela has suggested convening a meeting between oil producing countries and oil consumers. Our reaction has been rather guarded. If there were an absence of communication between producing countries and consuming countries,

bringing the two sides together might be worth studying. In the case of the oil market, however, producers and consumers are talking to each other all the time, sharing statistics and projections regarding both supply and demand, and doing so in a number of different contexts. These bilateral and other channels are in my opinion working sufficiently well that we do not have to create another formal medium of communication.

As for your suggestion for joint action by producers and consumers to stabilize the price, I do not believe this is an idea which is workable. Even if producers and consumers could agree on what a stable price should be, and I think this in itself would prove impossible, I have a more fundamental objection. I believe that in general market mechanisms are more efficient and effective, and this includes the market for oil.

One final point. I agree with President Pérez that we need to increase the production of oil from areas of the world such as Latin America and the Caribbean in order to diversify world supplies. I believe that private investment funds are available for this effort and will go to countries which have hospitable investment climates. There is more that we can do in this area, and I look forward to discussing this issue with President Pérez and his advisers when I am in Caracas.

Persian Gulf Crisis

Q. Reliable opinion polls in Latin America reveal that people condemn Saddam Hussein [President of Iraq] but are against the U.S. going to war and favor a diplomatic resolution of the conflict. Will you reject any political settlement in the Gulf?

The President. As you know, I just returned from a visit to Saudi Arabia, during which I visited with U.S. forces. So, let me try to answer your question in the following way. On August 2, 1990, Saddam Hussein attacked the tiny nation of Kuwait, occupied it with extreme violence, and then announced that Kuwait had ceased to exist— that it had been incorporated into Iraq. Since August 2, there have been a flood of reliable reports that Iraqi occupation troops have been engaged in a systematic looting of Kuwait, dismantling buildings, seizing assets, and driving private cars back with them to Iraq.

The response by the international community has been based on two premises: first, that Iraq has committed naked and unprovoked aggression against Kuwait, and second, that Kuwait's status as a sovereign state must be restored. The only way that Kuwait's sovereignty can be restored is for the occupying Iraqi troops to leave Kuwait.

This position has been embodied in numerous resolutions of the United Nations Security Council. The community of Latin American and Caribbean States spoke out strongly in condemnation of the invasion of Kuwait and in support of the sanctions that the United Nations imposed. Argentina has sent a force of two ships to the Gulf to cooperate with the multinational force, an action which we applaud.

The United States is not eager to see armed conflict in the Gulf. As President, I ordered American forces to the area to block Iraqi aggression and to support the demands of the international community for restoration of Kuwait's sovereignty. We

have not rushed to use force, preferring to give the international sanctions a chance to work and to let the Iraqi leadership see clearly that they have the whole world arrayed against them.

However, for the international community's sanctions to be credible, they must be backed up with the possibility of coercion. Those who rule by force frequently understand only the language of force. The United States, acting in concert with countless other countries, has taken actions to ensure that Saddam Hussein understands that the international community can indeed use coercion against him if he remains unwilling to understand the voice of reason and diplomacy. Force is not our preferred option, but it is a real option. Our preference is for Saddam Hussein to order his troops out of Kuwait, and thereby make possible the restoration of full Kuwaiti sovereignty.

Note: The questions were submitted by El Mercurio of Chile, Estado de São Paulo of Brazil, El Pais of Uruguay, La Nación of Argentina, and El Nacional of Venezuela. The Office of the Press Secretary issued the press release on December 3.

Remarks to a Joint Session of the Congress in Brasilia, Brazil
December 3, 1990

Mr. President of the National Congress and Mr. President of the Chamber of Deputies; and to our two most articulate speakers, Senator Tito and Deputy Fiuza; and Mr. Acting President of the Supreme Court; esteemed Papal Nuncio and members of the diplomatic corps; Mr. Archbishop; Honorable Ministers of State and Governors of the Federal District; and honorable Deputies and Senators: It is a privilege, it is an honor to join you in this great hall of democracy.

My thoughts today could have no better forum than this National Congress; my words, no better audience than the people of Brazil. We meet at an extraordinary moment in our shared history, a time of

serious challenges and important choices that calls for mutual respect, candor, and collective will. I've met with many Latin and Caribbean leaders. And beyond any single issue that we've discussed, all of us have been galvanized by a new era of hope and opportunity throughout the Americas, especially here in Brazil.

By pioneering bold new economic reforms and consolidating its democracy, Brazil today is poised to enter the 21st century as a leader among nations. That is a tribute to a leader whose friendship and vision I value and respect, a man who represents a new generation of democratic leadership now sweeping across Latin America, your dynamic new President, Fernando Collor de Mello. President Collor has spoken eloquently of Brazil's rightful place at the table of the First World, and I agree. I believe it is time, in fact, to end the false distinctions between the First World and Third World that have too long limited political and economic relations in the Americas. Let us instead speak of the New World.

This hemisphere has always found strength in diversity. After all, here I stand, addressing Portuguese speakers in English, because of an Italian sailing on behalf of Spain five centuries ago. What we hold in common transcends borders and translates into any language. The nations of the Americas all struggled and gained independence from the old ways of the Old World, ended the injustice of slavery and colonialism, and built republics of promise and renewal around the dignity and the power of the individual and the rule of law.

Now, as we approach the 500th anniversary of Columbus' discovery of Americas and the arrival of Cabral's Portuguese fleet in Brazil, this is our moment to chart the course for the New World, a course of freedom, a course of democracy, a course of prosperity. We've all witnessed in wonder the dawn of democracy in Eastern Europe. But in the Americas, we, too, have seen extraordinary political and economic change that is transforming the face of this hemisphere—nowhere more so than right here, no more so than in the great nation of Brazil. The changes you are carrying out in your economy—reducing the size of the state, privatizing enterprises, combating inflation, and liberalizing trade—are the keys to growth and prosperity in a global economy of the 21st century, whose outlines we already see today. I am here to tell you that you are not only on the right path but the United States wants you to succeed and supports your efforts every step of the way. I believe that we've just begun to press forward toward the real promise of the Americas.

Territories may end at borders, but mankind's capacity for progress knows no bounds. Continents may end at the water's edge, but human potential knows only those limits set by human imagination. The Americas' role in the world is not defined by geography; it is defined by its people and its ideals. I truly believe that we are approaching a new dawn in the New World.

Our thinking must be bold; our will, resolute. Our challenge now is to hew out of a wilderness of competing interests a new kind of opportunity in the Americas. To fulfill the New World's destiny, all of the Americas and the Caribbean must embark on a venture for the coming century: to create the first fully democratic hemisphere in the history of mankind, the first hemisphere devoted to the democratic ideal—to unleash the power of free people, free elections, and free markets.

Two weeks ago in Czechoslovakia, I spoke to a people that had paid dearly for its freedom. I talked about a new commonwealth of freedom based on four key principles. This hemisphere already shares these convictions: an unshakable belief in the dignity and rights of man, the conviction that just government derives its power from the people, the belief that men and women everywhere must be free to enjoy the fruits of their labor, and four, that the rule of law must govern the conduct of nations. Every nation that joins this commonwealth of freedom advances us one step closer to a new world order. We must persist until this victory for freedom and democracy is won completely.

It is also within our power to make this hemisphere the largest free-trading partnership of sovereign nations in the world. From the northernmost reaches of Canada to the tip of Cape Horn, we see a future where growing opportunity, the power of technology, and the benefits of prosperity are developed and shared by all. Change will not come easily. Economies now dependent on protection and state regulation must open to competition. The transition, for the time being, will be painful. Many in the Americas will have to make serious adjustments to compete with Southeast Asia and to take advantage of the European market after 1992. But we are confident that solutions will be found—by Brazilians, by Chileans, by Venezuelans—by all of the Americas.

And the results—growing economies and sound currencies—will bring unprecedented prosperity and growth for all our citizens to share. That was the vision of the Enterprise for the Americas Initiative that we announced last June. And Deputy Fiuza, I listened very carefully to your strong speech in this regard, and I thank you for those frank and forceful comments. The initiative calls for a major hemispheric effort to unify the New World in the three key areas of trade, investment, and debt.

In trade, our first priority should be to promote long-term growth. And the most effective first step is the successful conclusion of the Uruguay round, now in its final stages in Brussels. An end to export subsidies on agricultural goods and new openings for developing-country exports mean new market opportunities and a higher standard of living for the farmer in Para, the textile worker in Santa Catarina, and the engineer in São Paulo.

But the Uruguay round and bilateral trade agreements are only first steps. The Southern Cone Common Market, now developing under the leadership of your President and his colleagues in neighboring countries, is another major step toward the world's first hemispheric free trade zone.

To promote new investment in the Americas, the dead hand of state control must be lifted. We must allow entrepreneurs the flexibility to adapt, create, and produce. So, as we chart a course for the future of the New World, let us hold firmly in our minds an unshakable conviction in the importance and benefit of free enterprise. Let us work together so that any man or woman who wants to launch a new enterprise views the state as an ally, not as an obstacle, and all who pursue the fruits of the free market see other nations not as threats to sovereignty but as partners in trade and mutual prosperity.

Individuals cannot succeed if government is burdened by debt. So, the third leg of our Enterprise for the Americas Initiative is a comprehensive commitment to work with Brazil and others in Latin America to restructure U.S. official debt. Our new approach to official debt will complement commercial debt restructuring through the Brady plan. I understand the importance to Brazil and, indeed, to the international financial community of reaching a new and

effective agreement on commercial debt. I believe, through your program of economic reform, you have taken the first crucial step toward that goal. Global capital flows will be vital to your development, and we are ready to assist wherever possible.

We've submitted a request to our Congress for the authority to implement our proposals. But we know that real solutions must involve all of us in the Americas. That's why we envision a permanent partnership between all the nations of the Americas to confront challenges that know no borders. We envision a hemisphere where a collaborative commitment is shared to protect our environmental legacy. There can be no sustained economic growth without respect for the environment. That's why the Enterprise for the Americas Initiative joins environmental protection with bilateral debt relief not as a challenge to national sovereignty—not as a challenge to the sovereignty, in this case, of Brazil—but as an affirmation of shared international interests. Senator Tito—and I do appreciate, sir, your using this podium for a frank exchange here—talked about partners in growth—I believe you said, sir—partners in growth rather than shareholders of misery. That is what you want, and that is what we want.

I encourage Brazil and other creditor nations to convert debt into funds for the environment. The entire world stands in awe of Brazil's unique endowment of wildlife, trees, and plants in the Amazon and the Atlantic rain forests. No nation on Earth—none—is as rich in flora and fauna, with all of their potential to provide future medicines and foods and crops and fibers. Your hosting of the United Nations Conference on Environment and Development in 1992 places Brazil in a position of true global leadership. We hope that conference will mark the culmination of a number of initiatives to protect and wisely utilize the world's resources.

We also are challenged to make ours a hemisphere where sovereign nations are joined in collective determination to eradicate the disease of drugs. On this one, the time for blame is long over. We in the United States recognize that we must do more to reduce what seems to you as insatiable demand. And you understand that the spreading tentacles of the drug trade threaten any democratic society. President Collor has taken a strong position against drugs for the sake of youth in Brazil. I know full well it is a demand problem as well as a supply problem for my country, and I pledge the full efforts of my government to continue to dampen demand. There is only one answer to the drug problem in this hemisphere, and that is to defeat these narco-traffickers who prey on our children, once and for all.

And finally, in this era of great challenges around the world, we want the Western Hemisphere to be a model to the world for security, stability, and peace. Together, let us ensure that this hemisphere stands united to prevent the spread of nuclear weapons or new, more dangerous ballistic missiles anywhere in the world. We hope that all countries in this hemisphere will follow Brazil's and Argentina's recent decision to bring the nonproliferation treaty, Tlatelolco, into force. I want to applaud, as many other nations have done, the recent announcement by Brazil and Argentina that together they will ensure that no nuclear program in their countries is used for anything but peaceful purposes. We applaud your decision to move forward on full-scope nuclear safeguards.

But your leadership today goes beyond this hemisphere. Just as Brazil made valiant contributions to the cause of freedom in World War II, you were among the very first to implement the sanctions against Iraq. I realize the sacrifices that Saddam's brutality has caused this nation and its people, has caused many nations around the world. In this country, I was told this morning, the impact—$5 billion in higher oil prices alone for 1 year—$5 billion to your economy, struggling to move forward, because of the brutality and the aggression of Saddam Hussein. In Czechoslovakia, a country that knows about aggression, Václav Havel told me, $1.5 billion just because of the aggression of Saddam Hussein. I salute your leadership in the world's community and united stand against Iraq's aggression and in defense of the rule of law.

Our nations long ago achieved independence from the Old World. And so, now let us work toward a new declaration of interdependence among the American nations of the New World. If, as Jose Bonifacio once said, "Brazilians are enthusiasts of a beautiful ideal," let us not limit the New World's potential with old thinking. After the half millennium we've had in this hemisphere to form our nations and find our way, let the nations of the Americas now fulfill their common potential.

Standing on this central plateau, soon to be the seat of great decisions, President Kubitschek said this: "I look once again at the future of my country and see this dawn with unyielding faith and unlimited confidence in its great destiny."

My friends, our neighbors, let the new dawn come to Brazil and to the New World, and let us fulfill the promise of these great lands.

Thank you very much. And may God bless the people of Brazil. Thank you very, very much.

Note: President Bush spoke at 11:28 a.m. in the House Chamber of the Brazilian Congress Building. In his remarks, he referred to Nelson Carneiro, President of the Senate; Antonio Paes de Andrade, President of the Chamber of Deputies; Senator Ronan Tito, leader of the Brazilian Democratic Movement Party; Ricardo Fiuza, Member of the Chamber of Deputies; Minister Aldir Guimarães, Acting President of the Supreme Court; Dom Carlo Furno, the Papal Nuncio; Dom Jose Freire Falcão, Archbishop of Brasilia; President Saddam Hussein of Iraq; and President Václav Havel of Czechoslovakia.

Remarks at a Luncheon for the Business Community in Brasilia, Brazil
December 3, 1990

Thank you, Ambassador, for your introduction and for your hospitality, you and Peggy. I seldom speak on behalf of a group of Brazilian businessmen, but thanks for the hospitality at this luncheon, too. We're delighted to be here. Let me salute the Minister of Justice, Your Excellency; and the Minister of the Economy, who is with us; the Minister of Agriculture, who is with us. I just want to say thank you to all the guests, some who've come from a long, long way. I want to salute the Minister of the Infrastructure, who is here, and each and every one of you.

I'm delighted to be here today, as was Secretary Mosbacher last spring, with some of this nation's most distinguished business leaders to discuss very briefly our dynamic bilateral relationship and our relationship with the rest of the major trading nations of the world. I'm delighted that Secretary Brady, our Secretary of the Treasury, is with us here today.

The success of this economy—he and I agree on this—the success of your economy, the world's eighth largest, is truly vital to the well-being of all nations in the Americas. In talking with your President—your able President—my friend, this morning, President Collor, I was impressed with his vision of a *"Brazil Novo."* He is determined that this great country will grow and prosper throughout the nineties. And he believes that with a market economy Brazil will take its rightful place at the first table of nations. And I wholeheartedly share that view.

This morning, I was deeply honored to be able to speak before a joint session of your Congress, and I spoke there of the daunting task that awaits us: the construction of a new economic relationship for the whole Western Hemisphere. Our shared future is borne of the triumph of democracy in this hemisphere and is directed towards the next necessary steps: raising the standard of living and expanding the economic opportunity of all the people in Latin America. I

call this initiative the Enterprise for the Americas, a vision of a community of the Americas, free of barriers to trade and investment and free of the burden of debt.

The United States is Brazil's largest investor and trading partner. And we are excited at the prospect of a growing market economy in Brazil. And we recognize that it is the private sector that is the locomotive for economic growth. As business leaders and entrepreneurs, your role in building a more open market in Brazil has been and will be a key part of our growing trade relationship.

This week in Brussels, trade ministers are meeting over there for the final negotiation of the Uruguay round. The U.S. and Brazil agree on the need to phase out agricultural subsidies. Taken with our progress on the other ambitious topics of the negotiation, a success at the GATT in Brussels will represent new market opportunities and more profits for Brazilians. We just have to be successful in this GATT round.

You, more than most, know that the dead hand of state control has got to be lifted to unleash the creativity of entrepreneurs and business leaders such as those represented here today, yourselves, and to give your businesses the flexibility to adapt to changing markets. The U.S. has already invested almost $15 billion in this country, and Brazilians know what foreign investment can help produce: meaningful jobs for your workers and expanded goods and services for your customers.

The first steps to implement the Enterprise for Americas Initiative are already underway. The nations of Brazil, Argentina, Uruguay, Paraguay, and the United States are drafting now a framework agreement to make its principles a reality. I urge each and every one of you to stand with us in support of this enterprise, to stand with us on the side of the future, and on the side of order and progress—as the flag of Brazil reads—and the changes to come.

In the short run, economic change will be

difficult and painful for many. But the long-term results—a growing economy and a sound currency—will lead to new opportunities and a better quality of life for all the people of Brazil and, indeed, for the rest of the hemisphere. That is what your President meant with his vision of economic growth for the "*Brazil Novo.*"

In the 19th century, Brazilians declared their independence from the Old World and founded their republic. And now, as we approach a new century, we embark on what I see as a voyage of rediscovery. Brazilians have joined the move toward greater prosperity and freedom for the people of this hemisphere, toward a new dawn for the New World.

Well, I just want to say thank you, then, to all of you for participating in this. We need your help to make all of these dreams come true. And I want to thank you for the warm welcome in this receiving line. You do make me feel welcome here in Brazil, and I am delighted to be back. And God bless you all and your wonderful nation of Brazil. Thank you all very much for coming.

Note: The President spoke at 1:48 p.m. at the U.S. Ambassador's residence. In his remarks, he referred to U.S. Ambassador Richard Melton and his wife, Peggy; Minister of Justice Bernardo Cabral; Minister of Economy Zelia Cardoso de Mello; Minister of Agriculture Antonio Cabreira Filho; Minister of Infrastructure Ozires Silva; and U.S. Secretary of Commerce Robert A. Mosbacher.

Toast at a State Dinner in Brasilia, Brazil
December 3, 1990

President Collor and Mr. Vice President, Mr. President of the Senate, Mr. Archbishop, Mr. President of the Chamber of Deputies, and Mr. Acting President of the Supreme Court, Minister of Foreign Relations, and Ministers of State, members of the Cabinet, Ambassador and Mrs. Melton, and all you distinguished guests: I am deeply grateful to all of you here and to the people of Brazil for your gracious hospitality.

I fouled this up at lunch, so I want to be sure if we're going to—are you going to translate it all, or just one part? Okay.

In fact, it won't be easy to leave here. I'm told that one American Ambassador stayed in your country for 21 years—obviously, a very smart man. I'm here for 24 hours.

But it was a great honor for me to address your Congress this morning. And it was a memorable moment; but more than that, it was, it seemed to me, an affirmation of the proud heritage we share and a reminder that we have much reason for hope in the future.

And again tonight I want to thank the leaders of Congress. And I also want to ad lib here, because I understand I was invited today to go to the Supreme Court. We have great respect in the United States for an independent judiciary. And I am very grateful to the Justices, some of whom are here tonight, that invited me to the Court. And I am only sorry that I did not have the opportunity to take you up on your invitation. But this occasion tonight gives me a chance to salute you, the members of the Court, for whom we have so much respect.

Our two nations have a great deal in common. We put our faith in similar forms of representative government, and we've had Ambassadors in each other's capitals since the earliest years of this century. Our relations have been long; our devotion to freedom, constant; our commitment to peace, enduring. And now I'm convinced that the time has come to move our relations toward a new and higher plane, to eliminate the false schism between what we once called the First and Third Worlds. As President Collor speaks of a *Brazil Novo*, we should also speak of a new world, defined by its ideals of freedom, democracy, and prosperity shared by all.

All of us in the Americas share a common

economic and political vision: an unshakable belief that extraordinary achievements are possible when the imagination and industry of the individual is unleashed. I believe we've just begun to tap the true potentials of the Americas, and it is within our power to bring a new dawn to the New World.

Our Enterprise for the Americas Initiative is a major step forward, helping us explore the many new areas of our common destiny in a spirit of optimism and hope for all peoples of the hemisphere.

Mr. President, you, sir, have courageously resolved to make profound changes in your economy; and I believe that those changes will reap handsome benefits for the people of Brazil, for all the people of Brazil.

We have a common interest in expanding trade and protecting it from the damage that perceived inequities would inflict on our economic partnership. No country would gain if our common policy of an open and fair international trading system isn't fulfilled.

We share common environmental concerns, knowing that the destruction of irreplaceable resources, wherever they're found, compromises mankind's well-being

everywhere. I'm confident that we will continue to find shared solutions to global environmental challenges.

Together, our opportunities are boundless, and so let us forge a closer and more vital partnership to ensure lasting prosperity for all our people.

And now I would like to ask you to join me in raising a glass to the health and happiness of the people of Brazil; to our friend and admired President of Brazil, Fernando Collor; and to the friendship between our two great nations. And thank you for an unforgettable visit. Thank you all.

Note: The President spoke at 9:58 p.m. at the Foreign Ministry Building. In his remarks, he referred to Vice President Itamar Franco; Nelson Carneiro, President of the Senate; Dom Jose Freire Falcão, Archbishop of Brasilia; Antonio Paes de Andrade, President of the Chamber of Deputies; Minister Aldir Guimarães, Acting President of the Supreme Court; José Francisco Rezek, Minister of Foreign Affairs; and U.S. Ambassador Richard Melton and his wife, Peggy. Following the dinner, the President went to the U.S. Ambassador's residence, where he stayed overnight.

Question-and-Answer Session With Reporters in Montevideo, Uruguay
December 4, 1990

President Lacalle. I'd like to welcome you all to this press availability. I know the important figure here is President Bush and not me, but I would also be prepared to answer any questions in my broken English, which is, of course, our common language here. I'd appreciate it if you'd identify yourselves, and I would give the floor to President Bush.

President Bush. Just a brief opening statement, with your permission, sir—first, to say how pleased I am to be here with my friend President Lacalle. This President and his proud country are leaders on the crucial issues that face this hemisphere and the world today.

Uruguay was one of the leaders in return to democracy in Latin America. And the global trade talks that are now underway in Brussels began right here in this nation. An essential ingredient for a successful conclusion of the GATT round is agriculture, and this President has taken a world leadership position on seeing that agriculture is included and satisfactorily addressed.

In spite of the economic hardship inflicted on this country, President Lacalle and Uruguay have taken a leadership role in strongly supporting United Nations sanctions against Iraq, and I salute him for this. This isn't easy. This requires a certain degree of sacrifice for the people here, but they've been steadfast in standing up to this aggression.

And this President was the first one to telephone me after I announced my Enterprise for the Americas Initiative. And we've been talking how to fully implement that.

I'm sorry I won't be going to Paraguay on this trip; but by the time the trip is over, it will have been to here, Uruguay, and to Brazil and to Argentina. And there we will be talking about the negotiations on a far-reaching regional framework agreement on trade and investment, which is the first crucial step toward our common goal of a hemisphere in which trade is free for all.

Once again, my thanks to you, sir.

President Lacalle. Thank you, sir.

Persian Gulf Crisis

Q. Mr. President, Terry Hunt, of the Associated Press. I'd like to ask you: Last week General Jones and Admiral Crowe, both former Chairmen of the Joint Chiefs, said that they thought that you ought to give sanctions against Iraq a year to 18 months to work before you resort to military action. Do you think that's unreasonable?

President Bush. I don't agree with them.

Q. How long do you think that you should give sanctions?

President Bush. I can't say how long, but I don't agree with them.

Q. To follow that up, please: Secretary Cheney said yesterday up on the Hill that it is his personal view that sanctions just won't work, that they can't work—that after a passage of time, the embargo will begin to slip, that Saddam Hussein [President of Iraq] is just too brutal and the Iraqi people are either too self-sufficient or too resilient to be bowed by that kind of economic pressure. Do you share that view, which is, in essence, saying that this stage and time only the threat of imminent war has the potential for making Saddam Hussein bow?

President Bush. I am convinced that Saddam Hussein, up until now at least, has not gotten the message. And the United Nations resolution speaks for itself. To me, it was loud and clear. But I don't think Saddam Hussein yet understands that. And therefore, the best hope for peace is for him to understand that all means—all means—necessary to fulfill these resolutions

will be used against him. And I hope he gets the message.

Q. But are we at the point where we can say that it's no longer realistic to expect that the sanctions are going to bring him around to that point of view?

President Bush. Well, as you know, I've not been one who has been convinced that sanctions alone would bring him to his senses, but they're having some effect. But I—put it this way, I thought Secretary Cheney did a superb job in his testimony. In fact, I thought it was so good that I sent him a message yesterday, and also one to Colin Powell [Chairman of the Joint Chiefs of Staff].

Marxism

Q. I would like to ask you, now that Marxist systems all over the world are falling apart, in eastern Europe, et cetera, what do you find to be the meaning of the fact that there is a Marxist mayor recently elected here in Montevideo?

President Bush. I don't know much about the Marxist mayor. But this is a democratic country; people can run for office. We elected a Socialist to the Congress of the United States—the State of Vermont did the other day. So, I have no hangups. And I'll look him in the eye and thank him for what I understand will be his hospitality to me, but just so he doesn't ask me to endorse his Marxist views, because I think marxism is declining around the world. But I don't know what his view is.

You know, when I was in Italy, the head of the Congress there was a Marxist woman. I had no difficulty going over and speaking civilly to her, and she was very civil to me. So, I found that there's all different degrees of that, of marxism, just as there are of socialism and just as there are of, I guess, adherence to democracy. So, I have no hangups at all. If the guy wants to welcome me to the city—I already feel welcome, and I'd like to be rewelcomed.

Persian Gulf Crisis

Q. President Lacalle, please excuse one further question to President Bush on the Gulf, which I know is not the main subject of your discussions here today.

Mr. President, there are newspaper reports today indicating that the five permanent members of the U.N. Security Council agreed last night that when Secretary Baker meets with Saddam . . . Kuwait a firm commitment that there will be no attack on him and his regime. Is that correct, sir, and can you elaborate?

President Bush. No. Do you mean when the five permanent members were in New York?

Q. Well, please don't hold me to the absolute details, sir, of what may have been the form of such an agreement. But may I phrase the question by asking you if there is such a plan, and do you and Secretary Baker plan to offer such a promise in the meetings that are coming up?

President Bush. Brit [Brit Hume, ABC News], I'm not in a negotiating mood or anything of that nature when I meet with Foreign Minister of Iraq 'Aziz. And I think what I want to do is make very clear to him that the best way to preserve the peace is to go forward and fully implement the U.N. resolutions. But I don't know of any meeting of that nature of the five permanent members—at the Foreign Minister level or any level—to discuss that.

Q. Excuse me, sir, but such an offer, if it could be called that, would not be inconsistent with the positions you've taken. And I'm just wondering if that is indeed something you feel that you would be in a position to say at that time.

President Bush. Well, let's wait and see how these talks go. And I know what I've told you I'm going to say. And what else I'd say—well, I'll take some time to figure that all out, but don't want to get the message softened down. The message is: Get out of Kuwait in full compliance with all United Nations resolutions. Now, I saw something that Jim Baker said to that effect the other day, and I did not have any problem with that at all.

But I don't—Brit, I think you're on a wrong track. I don't think there was any meeting of the minds, but maybe something happened up there I'm not aware of.

Uruguayan Debt and Regional Alliances

Q. I represent Channel 10, Mr. President, and I would like to ask you how you see the regional alliances such as the MerCoSur, which is being worked on, in terms of economic development. As President Lacalle said, our wanting not help but growth—how does all of this fit in with the treatment of Uruguay's foreign debt?

President Bush. Well, in the first place, Uruguay is taking a very forward and, I think, proper position on the debt situation. It isn't easy, but I am convinced that this forward-looking position will add to further investment in Uruguay and further confidence in international financial markets in Uruguay, which is bound to benefit the people of Uruguay.

And lastly, regional alignments don't trouble us at all because we're all moving in this hemisphere toward a much more open trading system. And that, too, will benefit the peoples of all the countries, I believe.

Persian Gulf Crisis

Q. Again, for Mr. Bush—I am sorry—but again, on the Persian Gulf. Is it possible that in U.S. talks with Iraqi officials that the U.S. could make it clear with Iraq that the U.S. values the resolution of the Palestinian issue, but also make it clear that the Persian Gulf and the Palestinian issue are totally separate? Can you do that—both?

President Bush. I will not be endeavoring to do that. I think people around the world know of our interest in seeing a peaceful and permanent solution to the question in the West Bank and the Palestinian question, but there will be no linkage. There will be no linkage whatsoever. The whole world knows that Saddam Hussein has been trying for linkage, and in the talks we have there will be no linkage.

Q. Will you mention the subject at all in the talks?

Enterprise for the Americas Initiative

Q. I am from the newspaper La Republica. The Alliance for Progress was something from which we awaited solutions to get out of our situation of underdevelopment. In what way is the Enterprise for the Americas Initiative going to make it possible for us to grow, to promote the entry into our countries of risk capital, and to promote the entry into the large markets of the United States and Canada of our goods and merchandise?

President Bush. In the first place, we foresee a whole hemisphere of much more open trade—free trade, if you will—down the line. But secondly, you're dealing in a hemisphere that has already moved since the Alliance for Progress down the path of democracy toward free markets, toward privatization. I don't want this Enterprise Initiative to be just more rhetoric; we want action. This President wants action. But the climate for this kind of action is so much better today that I think we will be successful to go along the course we've been discussing here. We're different times, different times.

Agricultural Trade Policy

Q. On GATT, is there any room for compromise, President Bush, in your position on reducing farm subsidies? Would you settle for something less than a sweeping 75-percent to 90-percent reduction to get agreement in Brussels?

President Bush. First, we're all in this together—Uruguay and the United States. All countries in this hemisphere want to have agriculture—I believe all countries—want to have agriculture as a significant part of this GATT round, for it to be successful.

But to get to your question, Gene [Gene Gibbons, Reuters], we are not locked on a specific figure; we are locked on the fact that there has to be inclusion of all categories. And I think therein lies the difficulty that's taken place in Brussels as of very, very recently.

Q. May I follow up, President Lacalle, to ask if you share President Bush's position that no agreement is better than a bad agreement on GATT?

President Lacalle. Well, we are in the same boat, as we say here, in this GATT negotiation. Of course, every negotiation has its turning point. Now we are saying, and saying loud, that it's a package that every issue must be inside it. This has hurt millions of people. This agriculture policy has hurt millions of people two ways: through subsidies that go into our own markets and compete against the products of the agricultural countries and, at the same time, through protectionist barriers that

don't open the markets of certain very wealthy parts of the world to we, the farmers of the world.

But at the same time, we have the other issues. So, we are taking a pragmatic view towards the negotiation. We are saying agriculture must be inside. I'm not telling you what kind of percentage I'm prepared to accept, but it must be in the package, and it cannot be the percentage that has been officially offered up to now.

U.S. Forces in Panama

Q. President Bush, when you arrived here you said we were entering a new era in our relations. On the one hand, you're talking about a deepening of relations, and on the other, you continue having your troops in Panama. Don't you see something contradictory to that?

President Bush. You want a yes or no answer? No. I don't see anything contradictory. These are not occupying forces. These are not aggression forces. These are not forces that have raped, pillaged, and plundered the people of Kuwait. And I don't see a similarity at all.

Persian Gulf Crisis

Q. I'm Charles Bierbauer of CNN [Cable News Network]. A question for each of you, if I may. Let me start with President Bush. You've repeatedly made reference to the economic cost of the Persian Gulf to countries such as Uruguay, Brazil, Czechoslovakia. Some in your administration say that those costs are unwarranted given the current oil availability. Are you doing anything at all, or should you, to reduce the oil prices and to reduce the burden on these countries?

President Bush. The economic burden on these small countries and on the United States are heavy. You heard Chairman Greenspan [Board of Governors, Federal Reserve System] testify the other day. And all I can do is try to make clear as best I can as President that there is not an oil shortage today. And hopefully, some of those speculators will listen to that and look at the facts and see that that is true. In the meantime, countries are being devastated by the price that is driven through speculation or driven through fear.

And lastly, I can make clear that this is not going to go on forever. I think some worry very much about that. And it is not going to go on forever.

World Power Alignment

Q. President Lacalle, I wanted to ask you a related question. In June, at the OAS [Organization of American States] meeting, you voiced concern about the weight the superpowers exerted upon the other Latin American nations—the inequity of that historically. Do you feel in this instance of the Persian Gulf and in general that you are still feeling the exerted weight of the superpower of the United States upon your country?

President Lacalle. I think that in the quality of international relationship, the world has changed. Of course, small countries prefer a multipolar world than a bipolar world. And I think we are in the midst of a big change. We haven't realized what the year '90 brought as a change of the political equation the world over. Of course, these historical facts are seen afterwards, and we rationalize them afterwards. But I think a whole new time of much more equal relationship between the countries, big and small, is dawning. And the interdependence of the economic problems makes everybody feel that we are in the same boat once again, the same example. So, I think that, of course, the power, the presence of important countries and big powers like the States are felt much more than other countries. But we are in an era of mutual respect and consultation that will, I think, substitute the world we knew last year.

Technology Gap

Q. President Bush, your Enterprise for the Americas Initiative—in putting forward the idea of a free market, does it take into account the gap between underdeveloped countries and the impossibility that the underdeveloped countries have to compete technologically from the point of view of know-how? Does the Enterprise have any plan in it to do something about technological or technical conversion to allow the underdeveloped countries to compete with the large ones?

President Bush. Mainly through technolo-

gy transfer. And, yes, the United States is moving vigorously forward with countries in terms of technology transfer. I'm not sure that's directly responsive.

Q. In view of the fact that the underdeveloped countries find it impossible to acquire this know-how.

President Bush. Well, it's not impossible. And the answer is: Move briskly to privatization, to free markets, to market economies, and keep going down that path. And that will attract investment, and that investment will close the technological gap. So, I'd say that is the answer to countries that are moving forward now into this period of change.

Leftist Governments in South America

Q. When Allende was President of Chile, as a Socialist government, Chile was considered to be a security risk to the United States. If Uruguay were to bring to power a coalition of the left—Socialist Communists, et cetera—if that kind of coalition came to government, would it be considered to be a risk to the security of the United States? And secondly, the Enterprise for the Americas regime—would it apply to a country which would elect a Socialist government?

President Bush. The success of the Enterprise for Americas depends a lot on moving down this market-economy route. Most Socialists governments or Communist governments want the goods and services produced to be owned by the state. That is a formula for disaster. That is a failed formula. So, the question is very hypothetical, but it seems unlikely to me that the country would move in that direction these days, when you see the whole world moving away from the failed ideology of communism.

[*At this point President Lacalle knocked over a glass.*]

President Lacalle. It's a gimmick. [*Laughter*]

Argentine Military Rebellion

Q. Yesterday, we were witnesses to what happened in Argentina. Do you think that democracies are stable in this part of the continent?

President Bush. Yes, I do. And I think that the incidents yesterday, as I read it, were aimed not at the government, but it was a military-versus-military controversy. And so, I am very pleased to be going to Argentina, and I salute President Menem there for what he has done and is trying to do in moving Argentina further down democracy's path and doing something in the economic system along the lines that we've been talking about here today.

Meeting With President Lacalle

Q. What bilateral issues were dealt with in your meeting with President Lacalle, President Bush?

President Bush. Mainly, sir, on trade and investment. We're talking about science and technology. Indeed, as a result of our preliminary meeting, President Lacalle has very generously invited my Science Advisor, Dr. Bromley, to spend an hour with him today on that subject. And so, these were the main subjects, but there were one or two others I think we touched on. But those were the main subjects—trade, investment, economics dominated the meeting on a bilateral basis, sir.

The technology also touched on the environment questions. Even though those are global, there are some interests of bilateral concern there.

President Lacalle. Thank you, everybody. Welcome, once again to Montevideo.

Note: President Lacalle spoke at 2:45 p.m. in the Salón de Actos at the Edificio Libertad. A reporter referred to the Mercado Comun del Sur (MerCoSur) negotiations to create a Southern Cone common market, composed of Brazil, Argentina, Uruguay, and Paraguay. Ellipses in these remarks indicate that material was missing on the press release. A tape was not available for verification of the content of the question-and-answer session.

Remarks to a Joint Session of the Congress in Montevideo, Uruguay
December 4, 1990

Mr. Vice President, distinguished Members of Congress, ladies and gentlemen, and citizens of Uruguay:

First off, all of us have been deeply touched by your warm welcome. From the minute I've gotten here, I've felt at home. And indeed, Montevideo is graced by images that were once familiar features in our own nation's frontier tradition: the dramatic statues of Belloni and Zorrilla depicting covered wagons, a stagecoach, the gaucho himself. For a moment, I thought I was back home in Texas.

The peoples of our two countries have long been linked by bonds of tradition and belief. Both emphasize equality. Both place their trust in the individual. Both are deeply rooted to the land. Indeed, Uruguay is blessed with some of the best farmland in the world, and flying over it this morning, it reminded me of the fertile heartland of the United States. But the truth is, there is no place quite like Uruguay, this heart-shaped country that's not only at the heart of the Southern Cone but at the heart of South America's exciting new movement towards free markets and free ideas.

Uruguay appears small on the map, but looms large in real life—large in land, large in character, large in heritage, and large in dreams. More than a century ago, W.H. Hudson crossed Uruguay's rolling grasslands and purple banks and brought them vividly to life in his epic saga "The Purple Land." The Uruguay he saw was a trackless prairie of vast spaces and limitless horizons. Today the horizons of Uruguay once again open up to a future without limit. Just look around. Behind me, José Artigas, father of a modern nation. And before me, the Uruguayan Congress, a new generation of pioneers seeking not to tame a land but to build a nation.

Our visit comes at a time when the Western Hemisphere looks out upon a new era, an era not for the First World or the Third

World but an era that marks a new dawn for the New World. Together, we're embarked on a journey spurred by profound worldwide changes: political renewal, economic restructuring, social realignment. And together we're leading the way.

We have a unique chance to realize the dreams and ambitions of the people who came to the Americas, north and south, seeking a better life for themselves and for those who followed. Like the United States, Uruguay is a nation of immigrants, and the history of our Republics is told in the history of our families.

One such family was the MacGillycuddys of Ireland, who left the shores of Europe in the last century. One went north, and one went south. Both worked hard, prayed to the same God, learned the language of their adopted countries. And today their grandchildren are the children of the Americas: Eduardo MacGillycuddy, Uruguay's Ambassador to Washington, and Cornelius MacGillycuddy, better known in my country as United States Senator Connie Mack—common dreams, common bonds, common families.

This is my first trip to Uruguay, and yet I feel I know your President, President Lacalle, well. We met in Washington last February, and again in October in New York. Not only does your President have a vision for his country, but he has the rare talent of being able to act on his vision for the benefit of the people.

Last June I announced the Enterprise for the Americas Initiative, an ambitious new plan to increase trade, investment, and growth throughout the hemisphere. It is a major step in our shared dream for the world's first completely democratic hemisphere. And President Lacalle was the first, the very first leader, to call me to discuss how we could work together to realize its objectives.

The world is changing faster than anyone believed possible. Fundamental changes are sweeping Uruguay and Latin America. From Tierra del Fuego to the Texas border, old ways of doing business are being reexamined, and new ideas are on the march. The democratic form of government has come to be recognized as the heart of political legitimacy. The democratic ideal has not triumphed everywhere and, to be sure, not all men live today in total freedom or in democracy; but we've reached the point where all are demanding to live in freedom as their God-given right.

The Western Hemisphere can take pride in having launched this worldwide transformation from dictatorship to democracy. And nowhere has the process been more impressive than right here, where your people have demonstrated the courage, cooperation, and self-sacrifice necessary to win success. The transition was difficult, but the potential rewards are great. The conversion of the hemisphere to representative government and to rational economic management opens up the possibility of unprecedented mutual respect and common purpose across the Americas.

Here in Uruguay, President Lacalle has set forth a bold program to restructure the economy, changes which will improve Uruguay's overall strength and prosperity. In time, the economy will produce more goods and services, provide more jobs for all and, in short, improve Uruguay's very quality of life.

But look, fundamental changes often involve costs. There are no easy solutions, no quick fixes. But you are not alone. Our Enterprise for the Americas Initiative is aimed at extending a helping hand to our neighbors in South America on trade, investment, and debt reduction.

I know some in Latin America fear we've become preoccupied with the dramatic developments in the Old World. Let me assure you today that we have not. The Enterprise for the Americas Initiative represents a fundamental shift in our relationship with Latin America. It recognizes a simple truth, a truth President Lacalle recognized last June at the Organization of American States, a truth that has now been heard and embraced throughout the Americas. "Prosperity in our hemisphere," he said, "depends on trade, not aid."

In order to promote trade, we are working toward a framework agreement with Uruguay, Brazil, Argentina, and Paraguay that commits us to explore practical ways to reduce trade and investment barriers. A strong multilateral trading system is the cornerstone of a healthy, expanding world economy, benefiting both developing and developed nations alike. That's why I have made the successful conclusion of the Uruguay round of the GATT a top trade priority, and that's why it has such a prominent place in my Enterprise for the Americas Initiative. It presents us an extraordinary opportunity for unparalleled economic growth for all nations, well into the 21st century.

In the final talks at the GATT this week, we stand firmly with you and other Latin nations in insisting that countries sharply reduce the agricultural subsidies that distort world trade. The land has historically been at the heart of both our economies; and from Montevideo to Montana, our farmers and our ranchers enjoyed shared traditions, shared interests, and shared concerns.

As our trade ministers meet in Brussels this week, I want to speak to them from the place where the round began. It began with a commitment to expansion of world trade, so let us finish the round in the same spirit, translating good intentions into firm commitments that will benefit us all by substantially expanding world trade. As the traveler in "The Purple Land" says: "We lose half our opportunities in life through too much caution." The new dawn is breaking. The stakes are high. Let's successfully conclude the GATT round—and that means opening up Europe's market to this hemisphere's agricultural products.

The Enterprise for the Americas Initiative also acknowledges that improved trade must be bolstered by assistance with investment and with debt. To promote investment, we've been working with the Inter-American Development Bank to create a sectoral loan program. The IDB's response has been outstanding. That's no surprise; it's led by an Uruguayan, Enrique Iglesias. We will also help countries committed to economic and investment reform to shake loose the burden of debt.

First, I want to congratulate President Lacalle on his successful negotiation of a debt agreement with the commercial banks under the Brady plan. That is a vote of confidence in Uruguay's economic policies by the international financial community. And we've also asked our Congress to approve a new package to reduce Uruguay's official debt. This will allow us to convert other payments to investment in industry and to swap debt for nature to protect your natural beauty. Environmental destruction knows no borders. And it is our responsibility to leave future generations not only a more prosperous world but a cleaner and a safer world.

A safer world also means a world free from the scourge of this hemisphere, the scourge called cocaine. And for the sake of our kids, every country must do its part to stop the explosive cycle of drugs, dependency, and dollars. And let me assure you, we are doing our level-best to reduce demand in the United States for these outrageous illegal narcotics.

And finally, a safer world also means a world safe for freedom, a world governed by the rule of law. And just a few minutes ago, I was privileged to meet with your Supreme Court. A free, honest, and impartial judicial system is fundamental to the freedom of a democracy, just as the rule of law is fundamental to the freedom of the world.

What the world faces in the Persian Gulf, believe me, is fundamental. We will not—we must not—reward a nation that would wipe another country off the face of the Earth. We will not reward a nation that has literally—and the tales are agonizing—has literally raped and terrorized its smaller neighbor. We will not reward a nation that kidnaps people and holds them hostage, staking them out as human shields, a nation that violates the sanctity of foreign embassies. And we will not reward a nation whose unprovoked aggression is driving economies all around the world into ever-greater financial distress.

I want to just say a special word in tribute to your President and to your proud democracy. Uruguay has shown great courage and commitment in support for United Nations sanctions against Iraqi aggression. Some may not realize this, but Uruguay paid a double price, a double price for upholding these sanctions: first, in higher oil prices, but also in substantial markets lost, for now, for your products. And yet you never flinched; your country never flinched. You never wavered in support of these U.N. sanctions.

You know, some seek to portray the crisis in the Gulf as a conflict between Iraq and the United States. In truth, as your example clearly demonstrates, it is a conflict between a united world community and an isolated, brutal dictator; the rule of law against Saddam Hussein's brutal aggression. And that's why I'm convinced, totally convinced, that the world community will prevail in the end.

The U.N. sanctions in their entirety will be upheld, and aggression will not be rewarded. That—and it will come—that will be a great victory for peace and global security. And I want to take this occasion, once again, to salute you, to salute your nation for your leadership in this struggle.

You know, in Czechoslovakia, President Havel told me the cost to his country was $1.5 billion. In Brazil yesterday, President Collor told me $5 billion is his estimated annual cost. And here in Uruguay, President Lacalle said the impact is substantial. All because of Iraq's determination to violate the sanctity and the sovereignty of little Kuwait.

No one in your great country needs to be told about sovereignty. In 1811 Artigas and his gauchos led an exodus of free Uruguayans who refused to submit to the control of foreign despots. His demand was simple: complete autonomy for Uruguay. His dream was not realized overnight, but today many believe that had it not been for Artigas' brave stand Uruguay would surely been absorbed into another nation.

Exactly 30 years ago, President Eisenhower spoke to the people of Uruguay from this very podium. Our message hasn't changed. He said: "The United States does not covet a single acre of land that belongs to another. We don't wish to control or dictate to another government." And he went on, "We believe that the people of every nation are endowed with the right of free choice and that the most sacred obligation of the world community is to guarantee such choice to all."

A generation later, Juan Lavalleja and the 33 Immortals completed Uruguay's transition to sovereign freedom. Today their legacy has fallen to you—an inheritance from Uruguay and for all of the Americas. Today the new 33 Immortals are the very nations of this continent, the OAS nations, now barreling in confidence towards the new century. All of us have a stake in working together. Our goal is to work with Latin America to build a hemisphere where trade and investment are unfettered, private enterprise can flourish, and individual rights are respected.

I see a hemisphere with strong democratic institutions and leaders and ever-expanding economic opportunity for all members of society, a society free of drugs and crime, a cleaner environment, and a new era of cooperation between Latin America and the United States.

Yours is a colorful land of spectacular beauty, from the lush green expanses outside Salto to the purple banks of the Yi River to the white beaches of Punta del Este. And as a new dawn breaks over the New World, Uruguay and all the hemisphere will continue on our voyage of discovery guided by the true colors of the Americas—the colors of free ideas, free markets, and free trade. And as you travel, we will be watching with great hopes, and we will be standing with you. God speed you on this journey, and God bless the wonderful people of this country.

Thank you very, very much.

Note: President Bush spoke at 4:37 p.m. in the Salón de Actos at the Edificio Libertad. In his remarks, he referred to Vice President Gonzalo Aguirre of Uruguay and President Saddam Hussein of Iraq.

Question-and-Answer Session With Reporters in Buenos Aires, Argentina
December 5, 1990

President Menem. Ladies and gentlemen, it's a great moment of pride on the part of the President of Argentina to share this press conference with the President of the United States, and my good friend, George Bush. It has been 30 years since a President from the country to the north has come here on a visit, and never has there ever been a circumstance like this. This is the first time that we have ever heard a proposal of the magnitude of the President's Initiative for the Americas. So, in this fiesta of good neighborliness, the President is visiting Latin America.

Things are now very good, and they will get better after this visit which he is making to Brazil, to Uruguay, to Venezuela, and to our Argentina.

Mr. President, thank you so very much for your visit and for your friendship. And I hope that the few hours that you spend here will serve to rest your mind and to prepare you to continue the great work you are doing from the country which is the most powerful in the world to preserve peace in the world.

President Bush. Thank you very much, Mr. President. And let me just make a couple of brief comments before we go to the questions.

Today my esteemed friend the President of Argentina and I talked about the consolidation of democracy, and we talked about the movement toward free and open economies. It is important to point out that under the leadership of President Menem, Argentina has been a leader in all of this—all of this.

Argentina helped lead the way in restoring democracy. And President Menem and the Argentine people proved again this week that they will not permit any group to return Argentina to the days of violence and dictatorship, in a superb show of strength and commitment.

And in these days of free economies, President Menem has taken the lead in privatization and in many other areas.

And lastly, I'm very grateful for Argentine's leadership and support for the world's common purpose in the Persian Gulf. And so, I'm here to salute the President, Argentine's leadership, and move toward solidifying democracy and improving the lot of its people through strengthening their economy. And I'm here with a feeling of great respect for the Argentine people and for the distinguished President, Carlos Menem, my friend.

President Menem. Thank you very much.

President Bush. Now, how are we going to proceed here? Who's in charge of questions? Oh, right over here. Excuse me.

Argentina-U.S. Relations

Q. Taking up the words of President Menem, I would like to ask you, Mr. President, what is the vision of the United States of Argentina? And how does the United States intend to implement its initiative to come to the help of Argentina in these major efforts that it is making?

President Bush. Well, the vision is of a democratic Argentina whose economy is one of the world's leading and most productive economies. That's the vision.

And because your President has taken the lead in matters such as privatization, I am confident that not only will our bilateral relation continue to improve but also it enables us to work very closely with the four countries that have joined together—Paraguay, Argentina, Brazil, and Uruguay—joined together in the Southern Cone to open up markets.

And thirdly, I see Argentina and the United States working closely in multilateral forums. And we've been staunchly together, for example, in trying to have a successful conclusion of the Uruguay round.

And lastly, because of the steps President Menem has courageously taken, I think that will lead to a happy ending, happy solution, to the overall foreign debt problem that Argentina faces. The private banks, seeing these moves towards privatization and open markets, will be much more inclined to work bilaterally with President Menem and Argentine to bring debt relief, needed debt relief, to the Argentinean economy.

Agricultural Trade Negotiations

Q. Norman Sandler, UPI [United Press International]. Mr. President, speaking of the GATT round, Carla Hills today was pessimistic about the outcome, and Clayton Yeutter said the United States may be prepared to propose retaliatory subsidies if it ends in failure. Is that kind of threat, given the impact it would have on Argentina and other Latin American countries, really consistent with the kind of theme of free trade you're trying to promote on this trip?

President Bush. I have not seen these comments. I have full confidence in Carla Hills and Secretary Yeutter. I believe that the United States and Argentina are totally in accord in our approach to the agriculture being included in the GATT round. There cannot be a successful conclusion to the GATT round without agriculture being included. And so, I expect that's what Carla and Clayton Yeutter are saying over there. But if that round fails, we will work bilaterally with the Argentine to see that their trade with us is not set back. But both of us want to see it internationalized through a successful conclusion of the GATT round.

Q. Can I just clarify by asking whether you're saying that any retaliatory subsidies would be targeted at, say, Europe; and in Latin America would be spared?

President Bush. Too hypothetical. We are still working to get a successful conclusion of this round. I'm not in the business of talking retaliation while people are still meeting and discussing this—trying to get this round worked out satisfactorily.

Argentine Economy

Q. Given the past failures of attempt at international orders to govern Latin American economy, what practical methods would you think of using with your new initiative to bring practical implementation to the steps you have proposed?

President Bush. Well, I think the practical considerations are already being manifested. I think we can reduce some of the government obligations, for example, and I

think we're in the process of doing just exactly that. That's a very important one to start with. I think we can try to be helpful with the private banks, although President Menem knows that this is a decision between the banks and the Argentine Government.

But the benefits that accrue to the Argentine are not benefits laid upon their head by the United States; they are benefits that accrue from the fundamental reforms that this President has put into effect and is continuing to put into effect. I would cite only one: the benefits to the people that have accrued from the privatization that he courageously undertook. So, it isn't that we're bestowing benefits; this is a relationship of mutual respect where we're working towards the same economic objectives.

Persian Gulf Crisis

Q. Mr. President, are there startings of a deal with the Persian Gulf? There are rumors that Saddam Hussein is willing to withdraw from Kuwait and let the Amir return if he is given control of the oilfield on the border and perhaps given access to the Gulf. Do you know anything about this?

President Bush. No. The answer to your question is no, thank you very much.

Q. Terry Hunt, AP [Associated Press]. Do you view these talks with Mr. 'Aziz [Foreign Minister of Iraq] and between [Secretary of State] Baker and Saddam as negotiations in which there will be some give-and-take?

President Bush. I view these talks as confined by—or put it this way, mandated by the United Nations Security Council resolutions, period. That means no concession of territory. That means freedom of innocent people that are held against their will. That means respect for embassies, I might add. And that means the eventual security and stability in the Gulf, although that's not specified in the resolution.

But I don't view these talks as having anything to do about concessions that stop short of full implementation of the U.N. Security Council resolutions. And I felt strongly about that when I met with President Menem, and I feel more strongly about it now because he agrees totally with that.

And he is a participant and a leader of an important country that is allied with us in this worldwide effort.

Argentine Economy

Q. Mr. President, you've just referred to the efforts that the Argentine Government is making in the economic field. I'd like to ask you what possibilities there are that your government will encourage North American capital to invest in our country under present circumstances?

President Bush. That is a strong part of this whole working together for economic recovery and revitalization. We have an organization in the United States called OPIC which guarantees foreign investment. They are very interested in bringing more investors to the Argentine.

We have other government agencies that are interested in furthering investment. The Ex-Im Bank would be one of them. To the degree we can encourage multilateral lending agencies to support the new Argentine with its new approach to privatization and free markets, we would be willing to do this.

So, there will be many bilateral ways in which we can further the economic growth that President Menem envisions and growth that I'm confident will inure to the benefit of all the people in Argentina.

Persian Gulf Crisis

Q. Mr. President, we are being—Messrs. President—it is for both of you actually, but first for President Bush—we are hearing from an official in Baghdad, an official who has said that Iraq would not leave Kuwait, that in these upcoming discussions all issues are on the table—everything, in this official's words. You said yesterday that you didn't detect that Saddam Hussein has yet gotten the message. Are you getting any indication that there is, indeed, some softening of the Iraqi position? Are you prepared to have all issues on the table? Do you feel this is helpful?

President Bush. I'm not optimistic. I see no evidence that Saddam Hussein is ready to comply fully without condition with the U.N. resolutions.

Q. What then, sir, if I may follow, are your expectations for these discussions you are to have, and what do you make of comments like those that we are picking up?

President Bush. Who's your source? Who's saying it? Can you help me? And then I can answer the question better.

Q. I wish I could, sir, but my understanding is that it is a senior Iraqi official.

President Bush. Oh, in the Government. May I start by saying the reason I ask what the source is, is we hear so many rumors about deals. And yet every time an Iraqi official on the record speaks, it is that they will not withdraw from Kuwait. In my view—and I think it's the view of the entire world; I know it's the view of my esteemed friend here—is that they must withdraw without condition. When naked aggression takes place, it's not a question of finding face for the aggressor. When a country is literally raped and pillaged, let the world go out and try to find some reason to save face for he who has raped and pillaged that country?

So, I hope there proves to be some reason for withdrawal without condition. But in answer to your question, no, I have no feeling whatsoever that Saddam Hussein is willing to do now that which he should have done 5 months ago—4 months ago.

President Menem. We have said before that we wholeheartedly condemn what Iraq has done, to invade and occupy a territory which does not belong to it. We are the only country in Latin America which has sent ships to help enforce the embargo against Iraq. I share everything that has been said here by the President of the United States. An aggressor cannot condition his withdrawal on the satisfaction of his conditions. The only way is for Iraq to withdraw without any preconditions.

Q. We have seen, Mr. President, that the American journalists are deeply concerned with things that happen in your country. So are we concerned with things that happen in our country. We sent——

President Bush. I missed who you're with. I missed your identity.

Q. Mendoza from Channel 7. We sent two vessels; we back you up. What does the United States do for Argentina? We sent two vessels to the Gulf. You have tried to explain to a Latin American President your position towards the Gulf. What has the United States done for Argentina? And to say to the President, is that all right for you?

President Bush. May I answer your question?

Q. Yes.

President Bush. I don't believe Argentina is sending frigates to the Gulf to help the United States. I think they're sending frigates to the Gulf because they believe, as we do, that we must stand up against this brutal aggression.

Q. So, the United States does not feel, Mr. President, personally helped or backed up by Argentina? You think this is democracy all over the world?

President Bush. I think we're in this as the whole world. You've seen that manifested at the United Nations, and you see it manifested in the diversity and number of the force deployed against Saddam Hussein. People aren't doing this for the United States; they're doing it for world order and international law and because they feel as strongly as I do—your President feels as strongly as I do—about brutal aggression of this sort. He's not trying to do us a favor; he's doing what is right, what the United Nations agrees. We both agree that the peacekeeping function of the United Nations has been revitalized and have a real

chance now to be more meaningful in the future.

President Menem. Argentina complied in sending those ships with U.N. resolutions adopted by the Security Council. We did it for the sake of peace and out of solidarity with the country victim of aggression. And this is an attitude we intend to maintain.

We have a friendship with the United States which is really unprecedented. But it was not in that framework that we acted. We do not seek any retribution or any reward. That would be undignified. And if there is anything that the Argentines are known for, it is their sense of dignity. We don't want any help or aid. We want to work with the United States and other countries to preserve peace, which is tantamount to saying to preserve life. We do not seek any counterpart or anything in return. And in fact, were it offered, we would not accept it.

The United States President would be glad to stay here with you all afternoon. So would I. But the Congress is waiting for him, so please respect his schedule.

Thank you.

Note: The session began at 3 p.m. in the Sala de Conferencia at Casa de Rosata. President Menem spoke in Spanish, and his remarks were translated by an interpreter.

Remarks to a Joint Session of the Congress in Buenos Aires, Argentina
December 5, 1990

Thank you, Mr. President of the Senate, Eduardo Duhalde. Thank you for those wonderful remarks. To the President pro tem of the Senate, Senator Menem; and the President of the Chamber of Deputies, Dr. Pierri; distinguished members of the Supreme Court; distinguished members of the military; distinguished legislators and government officials; and ladies and gentlemen: I am honored to be with you in this very beautiful Hall of Democracy, with so many Members of your Congress. And I am privileged to be with you at this special time in

history—both your own history and the history we share as members of the same hemisphere—for we live in an era of dramatic change.

Some may have thought that the events of Monday would make me change my plans. To the contrary, they strengthened my resolve to come to Argentina, to stand shoulder to shoulder with President Menem and the Argentine people, who love democracy and refuse to see it subverted.

The message today from Argentina is clear: Democracy is here to stay. Too many brave people sacrificed and died to bring democracy back to Latin America. Let those who would attack constitutional democracy understand: In Latin America the day of the dictator is over. Violent assaults upon the rule of law represent the old way of thinking, the old way of acting this history has left behind. It is time to think anew.

No longer should we think in terms of the Old World, where our roots lie, or of the First World or the Third World. No, we must move beyond the labels that once separated us to grasp the common future that unites us. Argentina, the United States, and the other nations in this continent share the promise of a new dawn in a new world.

So, I have come to Argentina to speak about change—you heard it first from the Vice President—the kind of positive, hopeful change symbolized by the Sun of the Spirit of May in your dramatic seal.

There's an old saying that when North Americans meet Argentines, they look into a mirror. I've felt that. Much here seems familiar: the cattle, the seas of grass, the love of liberty, the shared belief in the dignity of the individual, our common European roots and shared colonial past, the warm energy and the spirit of the people, even our interest in sport—we look forward to welcoming your team to the United States in 1994 for our first hosting of the World Cup, for example. But above all, above all, we share a devotion and a commitment to our respective nations that would have pleased General San Martín, who wrote: "Love for one's native land fuels noble souls."

All of this is part of the unique bond between our countries, but it's also recent history that unites us. Your return of democracy has brought our peoples closer than ever before. Your sacrifice during past decades caused us deep anguish and concern. But your people did not lose faith in the democratic ideal, and the United States did not lose faith in you.

As we prepare, with optimism and anticipation, for the challenges facing this hemisphere and the rest of the world, some things are clear. We all know that we want to live in a new world that is a model of security and stability. This means regional arms control—as well as nuclear, missile,

and chemical nonproliferation—and the collective determination to face down aggression.

As I said the day before yesterday in Brasilia, the United States applauds the decision announced November 28th by the leaders of Argentina and Brazil to move forward on nuclear safeguards and to bring the Treaty of Tlatelolco into force. We hope you will move quickly to realize both of these commitments, as they have a direct, measurable impact on regional and world security. Such action will also allow the United States and other countries to expand significantly the range of our nuclear and other technical cooperation. We are eager and we are ready to do so.

In the current crisis halfway around the world in the Gulf, you have also shown strength and vision by helping to lead international efforts to stop Saddam's brutal aggression. Your contribution to the multinational force in the Gulf is a statement of your commitment to peace and a commitment to the rule of law and a clear sign that you are assuming your rightful place as a leader among freedom-loving nations.

Argentina and President Menem have not limited their efforts to promoting international security. Here in this great country, you have embarked on another courageous action: the restoration of your economic dynamism. Your President, Carlos Menem, has defined the challenge that we face to day. He said: "To take advantage of democratic experiences, to propel economic growth and progress, is the principal crossroads and challenge for our peoples and governments."

It is a difficult challenge, as I believe few Presidents have ever taken office under more testing circumstances than did President Menem. And yet he and his colleagues in this Congress did not shrink from the task at hand. Instead, you've set into motion a forward-looking structural, economic, and social transformation of this great country.

We know of the painful short-term sacrifices that you are being called upon to make, in what your own President has called surgery without anesthesia. For this tremendous undertaking to succeed, it will not take miracles; it will take work. But know that the United States is prepared to work with you every step of the way.

Just yesterday we signed two new agreements, a mutual legal assistance treaty and a mutual customs cooperation agreement. And last June, to help this movement in your nation and the others of this continent, we proposed the Enterprise for the Americas Initiative, which calls for a major hemispheric effort to expand trade and investment and to reduce debt; to unleash energy; to encourage initiative; and to let the incentive of reward inspire people to better themselves, their families, and their futures. We are absolutely committed to this initiative as a major priority. It will give impetus to the essential economic restructuring which you already have underway, and it will sustain and deepen this process in tangible ways.

The initiative is our hemisphere's new declaration of interdependence. For economic revolution is the equal of political revolution, and economic cooperation must be embraced not as a threat to privilege for a few but as the key to prosperity for all. We know that prosperity in our hemisphere depends on trade, not aid. And it is within our power to make our region the largest trading center of sovereign nations in the world. Already, the Southern Cone common market is moving us closer to our ultimate objective: a free-trade system that links all of the Americas. We support you in this and look forward to completing a framework agreement on trade and investment between the United States and the Southern Cone.

But to promote long-term growth, we need the successful conclusion of the Uruguay round. The negotiators must succeed in their efforts to reduce or eliminate tariffs, subsidies, and other barriers to agricultural products. This will mean new market opportunities for the farmer in Buenos Aires Province, the agricultural workers in Jujuy, and the engineer in Rosario.

No act could be more significant for your nation than the move toward a market-oriented economy, a move crucial to attracting foreign investment. You see, it lays the groundwork for your future, building a road that leads to a modern, growing Argentina. A free-enterprise economy will encourage

capital investment, greater individual initiative, and real prosperity for this and future generations. With the help of the Inter-American Development Bank, we want to encourage the reform and the opening of investment regimes. The spirit of enterprise will unleash your great potential and assure this nation of its position as one of the most vigorous nations in the world.

The reforms that you are carrying out in your economy, including your bold program of privatization, are not only the key to economic growth and expanded opportunity; they are also the first crucial steps under the Brady plan to achieve debt reduction with your commercial creditors. I understand the burden of debt that weighs on Argentina, but I believe that today—like Mexico, Venezuela, Uruguay, and Costa Rica—Argentina is on the right road to reduce that burden under the Brady plan.

The way we deal with our common economic realities can be a stepping-stone to a permanent partnership among all the nations of the Americas. I believe we are on the brink of something unprecedented in world history—the first wholly democratic hemisphere. Think of it: the first hemisphere devoted to freedom—to free speech, to free elections, free enterprise, free trade, free markets.

And that's why I've come to your country: to celebrate what we share, to recommit the United States of America to the movement toward democracy and prosperity all throughout the Americas, to stress the vital importance of mutual cooperation and understanding among traditional friends. For we read in Martin Fierro: "brothers should stand by each other, because this is the first law." And he goes on: "keep a true bond between you at each and every time."

You know, Argentina is a great nation with enormous resources, but none more impressive than the Argentinean people themselves. When this century began, Argentina was among the most prosperous and productive nations in the entire world. And I am totally confident that Argentina will be such an economic leader again and continue to lead this hemisphere.

Together, yet from our own beloved lands, we will watch freedom, democracy, and prosperity grow. We will watch it from the vantage point of two countries strong in liberty and expanding in economy. And we can look forward together with shared optimism to the 21st century, to the brilliant new dawn of a splendid new world.

Thank you all very much for this warm welcome. I am delighted to have been your guest here today. Thank you.

Note: The President spoke at 4:45 p.m. in the Congressional Chamber at the Palacio del Congreso. In his remarks, he referred to Eduardo Duhalde, President of the Senate and Vice President of Argentina, and President Saddam Hussein of Iraq.

Toast at a State Dinner in Buenos Aires, Argentina
December 5, 1990

Mr. President, my friend Carlos Menem, thank you for those very kind words. And it has been a very great honor for Dorothy, our daughter, and me and for the rest of us on the American side to be received in this magnificent setting, to be received so warmly by your people, and to be received so warmly by your very special President, Carlos Menem. We are simply delighted to be here in this beautiful country that has rejoined the ranks of the world's great democracies, a democracy built on what your national anthem refers to as the "sacred cry" of freedom.

I liked what your President said about a nation together for the final takeoff. And Carlos—or Mr. President—[*laughter*]—I have the feeling that you have involved the people and that the people are proud in their support. And this week, by your firm action, supported by the people, you proved again that no one will take away the freedom of the Argentinean people.

You've helped reestablish this wonderful democratic tradition, and I salute your bold reform of the economy. You're rising to the challenges laid out in the Enterprise for the Americas Initiative for all nations in the hemisphere to join together to boost trade, investment, and growth.

Today President Menem and I talked at length about these issues and how best to bring economic recovery to this hemisphere. We recalled progress already made. And I spoke at some length about these ideas, which are of immense importance to our nations, during my speech at your Congress earlier today. And tonight President Menem has given an eloquent response, and I thank him.

But even though we've been here just a short time, this visit has again reminded me of the likenesses that unite our peoples. Think of our nations' beauty. One of America's patriotic songs—"purple mountains' majesty" and "amber waves of grain"—that would define Argentina, as would the words of Jose [Jorge] Luis Borges, describing this city's "silent magic that captures newcomers almost totally." Think of the splendor of the Andes, the jungles of Misiones, or the valleys of Patagonia; and they match the sweep of the continent that is America. And think, also, of other likenesses. We both were founded on equality and liberty. Each of us reveres the individual: you, the gaucho; we, the cowboy. We both honor values like work, family, belief in country, belief in God.

These likenesses have helped Argentina create a world where, as President Menem said last year, "More and more, every day, we all depend upon one another." And I agree. And I want to thank you, Mr. President, and your people for standing as allies in the Persian Gulf against Saddam Hussein's naked aggression. Together, we will do what is right, and we will do what is good—and we will prevail.

In that spirit and with real gratitude in my heart, I ask our guests to stand and raise their glasses: To the nation of Argentina; to friendship between us that has never been more strong; and to the health of my friend and distinguished colleague, Carlos Menem, the President of Argentina.

Note: President Bush spoke at 10:06 p.m. at the Sociedad Rural Restaurante. In his remarks, he referred to his daughter, Dorothy LeBlond, and President Saddam Hussein of Iraq. Following the dinner, President Bush went to the U.S. Ambassador's residence, where he stayed overnight. A tape was not available for verification of the content of these remarks.

Remarks at the Arrival Ceremony in Santiago, Chile
December 6, 1990

President Aylwin and members of the Chilean Government, I am deeply honored to bring to all the people of Chile the greetings of the American people.

These past few days, from Brasilia to Montevideo to Buenos Aires, I have witnessed firsthand the irresistible power of the democratic ideal. Around the world, across the Americas, a democratic renaissance is underway. Along with the return to free government is a parallel movement toward free markets. Here in our hemisphere, democracy's made great gains. At long last we're moving closer to the common destiny that once moved Chile's great champion of freedom, Bernardo O'Higgins, to write: "The Americas are giving great hope to philosophers and patriots alike."

Chile's peaceful return to the ranks of the world's democracies is cause for pride and celebration. And Chile's record of economic accomplishment is a lesson for Latin America in the power of the free market. Nowhere among the nations of this continent has the pace of free-market reform gone farther, faster than right here in Chile.

In just a few minutes from now, President Aylwin and I will proceed to his home to hold private discussions to continue the open and honest dialog that we began 2 months ago at the White House. And just a few hours from now, I will have the honor to address the Chilean National Congress, gathering in special session at the port of Valparaiso. And tomorrow I meet with leading members of the Chilean business community.

As you say here, brick by brick, houses are built; and so, too, are the foundations of lasting friendship built by each additional contact between the people of our two nations. America and Chile do share a bright destiny based on common ideals. Let me say to President Aylwin and to the people of Chile, it is in the spirit of those shared ideals that I come to Chile today.

Thank you for this warm welcome, and may God bless the people of Chile.

Note: The President spoke at 11:45 a.m. on the tarmac at Arturo Merino Benitez Airport.

Question-and-Answer Session With Reporters in Santiago, Chile
December 6, 1990

Chilean Political Transition

Q. President Bush, we would like to know your opinion of the political transition of Chile and on the behavior of the Armed Forces of Chile during this period of transition. We would like your comments.

President Bush. Well, it seems to me that there is great enthusiasm in the United States for this transition, for this solidification of Chile's democracy. And I'm not an expert on how the army and the civilian-controlled government is interacting, but from the United States standpoint, Chile is projecting a commitment to democracy and a country that is controlled by a popularly elected President. And that's the signal that is going out all around the world and is being so well received in the United States and in other countries as well.

Mr. Hunt of the AP [Associated Press].

Persian Gulf Crisis

Q. Mr. President, do you view this promise by Saddam Hussein [President of Iraq] to release the hostages as credible, and will it affect the U.S. war footing in the Persian Gulf?

President Bush. I hope it is credible.

Do you want to get translation of the question first? The question was——

Q. Do you view the promise by Saddam Hussein to release the hostages as credible, and will it affect the U.S. war footing in the Gulf?

President Bush. One, I hope it is credible. Two, no single hostage should have been taken in the first place. And I hope that it shows that the strategy is working and that Saddam understands that his hostage policy has incurred the condemnation of the whole world. And we've got to continue to keep the pressure on. And this would be welcomed, if true, but it will not change my thinking on his need to comply 100 percent, without condition, to the U.N. resolutions.

Chile-U.S. Trade

Q. Mr. President, when you came down at the airport, you really gave good impression on the economic policy and how efficient is market economy. However, many products of Chile still have many problems entering into the American markets. How long will the Chileans have to wait until they have real free trade with the United States?

President Bush. In the first place, the best thing to reduce barriers is to have a successful conclusion of the GATT round, which now appears to be in trouble because the agriculture question has not been accepted by several key players in this negotiation.

Secondly, we had good discussions with the President of Chile and his top officials here at lunch on how we can move forward on a trade agreement between the United States and Chile that also would be helpful in reducing barriers to bilateral trade.

Persian Gulf Crisis

Q. Mr. President, thank you. I wonder if you'd take the context of what's going on since you got the U.N. resolution authorizing the use of force. You know, you made the announcement last week that they were resupplying or helping to resupply the U.S. Embassy, now the announcement on the hostages. My question, Mr. President, is whether you believe Saddam is serious about diffusing the tensions, or is he playing chess?

President Bush. Well, first, I don't consider a couple of cases of Pepsi Cola a serious release on our beleaguered Embassy in Kuwait. I hope, though, in response to the broader aspects of your question, that Saddam Hussein is getting the message, the message so clearly stated in the last U.N. resolution. And the release of all hostages would be a very good thing, but the problem is the aggression against Kuwait. And the man must leave Kuwait without reservation, without condition. And the whole world is united in this. And I will not speak for Chile, but I believe the Chileans agree with that.

Chile-U.S. Trade

Q. President Aylwin, with the United States is the case of the poisoned grapes. During the lunch with President Bush, did you advance something of that matter? Is he going to have some conversation or ask for a position for the damage done and the losses of Chilean exporters?

President Aylwin. During the luncheon that we had and up to now, we have spoken about many topics related to the world situation and the relationship between Chile and the United States. As President Bush has said, we have progress in the idea of a bilateral treaty of free trade between our two countries.

I have pointed out to the President our satisfaction for the progress: the position of the United States concerning the topics as to what is concerning the insurance investment, the General Preference System, and the Kennedy amendment. The topic you're talking about is going to be the subject of some of our conversations in the meeting that we will have this afternoon, President Bush and myself.

President Bush. Let me say I will be prepared to fully discuss that and to assure the people of Chile that there is no discrimination that was intended or that is intended, and that I'm glad our country is moving briskly forward on these bilateral trade matters.

Mr. Cochran, NBC.

Middle East Peace Conference and the Persian Gulf Crisis

Q. Mr. President, there were reports this morning out of New York, apparently, linking American diplomats to a suggestion that the U.S. might go along with a U.N. resolution backing a Mideast peace conference. This was linked with Saddam's latest statement about the hostages. Since then we understand that Secretary Baker has denied any change in the U.S. position. Certainly, you have said there should never be any linkage, and you're aware that Saddam is trying to link them. However, having said that there is no linkage, can you offer any hope that the United States might take a favorable position toward a Mideast peace conference?

President Bush. The question is the aggression against Kuwait. There will be, and is, no linkage to the West Bank question. And to help clarify, I would refer people to Secretary Baker's statement today, to my comments at a press conference in Helsinki with Mr. Gorbachev, and to what I said at the United Nations in my speech. I hope that will make clear there is no linkage. The United States, of course, remains interested in a solution to that other question; but there is no linkage with what has to happen in Kuwait or what will happen in Kuwait.

Tough way to make a living. [*Laughter*]

Assassination of Former Chilean Ambassador Orlando Letelier

Q. One of the main people accused of the Letelier crime, General Manuel Contreras, one of the first persons accused of participating in the crime of the death of Letelier—he said that the people responsible for that crime had to be searched for in the United States. What is your opinion about this particular point?

President Bush. I'm afraid I don't know the details of what he was referring to, so I just can't help you. I think the President has moved to try to get that contentious matter cleared up, but I just am sorry, I don't know the details of that enough to know to whom he's referring.

Jim, excuse me, did you finish? Sorry, I thought you—too bad. [*Laughter*]

Q. To bring Mr. Contreras before the civil courts, will that satisfy the United States?

President Bush. I know what you're talking about, but I just can't respond on that specific point because I honestly don't know the answer to that question.

Persian Gulf Crisis

Q. Mr. President, in making his announcement today, Saddam Hussein said he was moved to release these hostages by what he called positive diplomatic changes. Are there any secret negotiations, backdoor negotiations, going on now between the Iraqis and the U.S.? And when you sit down with Foreign Minister 'Aziz, will you be laying down the law, or will you be offering further incentives to encourage Iraq to leave Kuwait?

President Bush. One, there are no secret negotiations, direct or indirect, with Iraq over this question—none. And there will be none—secret negotiations of that nature. Secondly, I am not looking for incentive or further incentive. What I want to do is be sure, by going this last, extra step for peace, that the Iraqis know from me, and 'Aziz knows from me, and Saddam Hussein knows directly from the Secretary of State, what is at stake in this matter and how supportive the United States is of the consolidated U.N. position. And that's what it's about.

And I said that before, and I'll keep repeating it because I don't want any people to think there are secret negotiations going on or that I, on behalf of this worldwide coalition, will even consider making a concession, if you will, or you can call it incentive—incentive, if you will. That is not what these meeting are about.

Chile-U.S. Trade

Q. President Bush, although President Aylwin has said that you're going to talk about the grapes in private conversations, I would like to know what action would your government be able to take regarding this problem that was originated and that has had a negative effect on Chilean exports? And several studies have proved that they were poisoned in the United States.

President Bush. Well, I will discuss this very sensitive question. I can't tell you what steps my country, if any, will take, I do ask you to understand that the question of poison foods and poison medicines is viewed with great seriousness in the United States.

And I think back to an incident involving no international trade, but an incident involving Tylenol, where the company had— one capsule of Tylenol had been poisoned, and that company went to great ends to remove that Tylenol and to change their packaging and to correct this scare. And I cite that so people in Chile will know that it isn't the Chilean grape that was singled out. This is the way, in the United States, we approach matters that can adversely affect the health of our people.

To show that persistence pays off, I'll recognize this gentleman over here, even though he's not with the North American press.

Enterprise for the Americas Initiative

Q. Mr. President, the Initiative for the Americas has been considered as a positive and in an optimistic way by most of the governments of Latin America and the Caribbean. However, there are also strong criticisms concerning the bureaucratic contradictions between your discourse and that of the American Congress, which has meant that there seems to be no real will on behalf of the key agencies of the United States in order to progress in a more speedy way towards integration in our continent.

President Bush. I think that there is a determination to move forward. Some of these procedures take a long time. And, yes, Congress in our system must be brought along as a full partner. And secondly, this initiative is not going to be an empty

slogan; I am determined to follow up on this. And I think the countries with whom I have talked feel that the process is moving forward properly. I wish it could be much faster. But let me gun down, let me shoot down in flames, this concept that some bureaucracy in our government will block this initiative. It will not. This initiative will be successful.

Middle East Peace Conference and the Persian Gulf Crisis

Q. Mr. President, I'd like to come back to John's question about a Middle East peace conference. You've so strongly and your aides have so vehemently denied any intention to move to a Palestinian conference of any sort. Is that because you are simply concerned that Saddam Hussein would say, see, I have extracted something from President Bush? Or, if not, just what conditions remain to be met for you to agree to a Mideast peace conference?

President Bush. From the very beginning Saddam Hussein has tried to justify his illegal aggression against Kuwait based on an overall Middle East problem that involves the West Bank and the Palestine question. And we are not going to get diverted from the full implementation of the United Nations resolutions in order to give him some face-saving way out of something he shouldn't have gotten into in the first place.

As you know, Jim Baker has been very active up until quite recently in trying to move that whole peace process forward. We continue to be very interested in moving the peace process forward. But it will not be linked in any way with Saddam Hussein's aggression. I don't care about face; he doesn't need any face. He needs to get out of Kuwait without trying to complicate this matter by talking about some Middle East peace settlement or peace conference. It is clear what his ploy is, and that ploy is not going to be successful.

Assassination of Former Chilean Ambassador Orlando Letelier

Q. My question is for both Presidents. I would like to know how far the United States intends to cooperate in the solution of the Letelier case. Mr. Bush, what do you think—that this case would go to the civil justice in any case?

President Bush. That question has a familiar ring.

Q. It's different.

President Bush. Oh, it is? Well, help me, because I don't understand the technical differences here.

Q. How far is the United States willing to go in order to——

President Bush. Get to the bottom of the matter?

Q. Yes.

President Bush. As far as we can. We want to cooperate fully.

President Aylwin. On our side, we think that the fact that a civilian court—an administer of the court, a special prosecutor that would be appointed at the petition of the Government by the Supreme Court, will lead to a full clarification of the responsibilities involved in that case. According to the purpose of the Government that in all matters concerned with human rights, there should be a full clarification of truth and justice be made.

We regret that we are just in time—President Bush has to travel to Valparaiso to meet with Congress. He's got to be there in 1 more hour.

President Bush. Thank you, President.

Persian Gulf Crisis

Q. ——pass a resolution. There is a report that the Perm Five have basically agreed on an alternative that essentially reiterates the U.S. position.

President Bush. Well, let's watch that unfold. That whole question has been on the table for some time.

Q. But you were so adamant in your refusal to grant Saddam even the appearance of linkage there.

President Bush. There will be no appearance of linkage. There will be no linkage.

Q. But you still——

President Bush. ——very, very clear. And that is the point I want to make. And the United States position on the other question is well-known, very well-known. There has been no change in it. But the concept of linking this in to help him save face or to compel him or encourage him to do that which he should have done in August, to correct that which he did in August, is simply unacceptable not just to the United States but to all the members of this coalition. And I will keep driving that point home. There can be no confusion about it. There can be no misunderstanding about it. There is no give on the United States side on that question. And there will be no give.

And I'm pleased that he—with the hostage question and the Pepsi Cola to the Embassy, there seems to be a little movement here and a little move there. But my mission is to have him understand that we are very, very serious about full implementation of the United Nations Security Council resolutions in full, without condition. And I'm going to keep making the point because every day I get asked questions about some new rumor. And you have to ask them, and I have to gun them down because there is no behind-the-scene negotiation. And it looks like we're getting on track, although I can't confirm it, with when 'Aziz might be coming; but it will not be with some secret agenda going on in one room and something for public consumption in another. It will not be that kind of a——

President Bush's Trip to Moscow

Q. Why did you cancel the Moscow trip, Mr. President? Mr. President, the Moscow trip—Moscow is off now in January, is that right?

President Bush. Not totally.

Q. Is it off?

President Bush. Not as far as I'm concerned.

Note: The question-and-answer session began at 1:55 p.m. at President Patricio Aylwin Azocar's residence. President Aylwin spoke in Spanish, and his remarks were translated by an interpreter.

Remarks to a Joint Session of the Congress in Valparaiso, Chile
December 6, 1990

Well, first, may I salute the President of the Senate, President Valdes. And far be it from me to lecture to his colleagues in these distinguished bodies. But I first knew him years ago when he served the United Nations with such distinction. And I would simply say to everybody here, I think we can all understand why, with that service behind him, he has what I would say is a very forward-looking, global view. And I respect his views. And thank you very much, Mr. President, not only for your remarks but for your welcome.

I want to salute the President of the Chamber of Deputies, Jose Viera Gallo; Members of the national Congress; and all the people of Chile. And really, it is for me, having come out of our Congress in the United States, a great privilege to address you today and to bring you on behalf of the American people our heartfelt congratulations on Chile's return to democratic rule.

Here amid the hills of Valparaiso, here in the halls of this beautiful assembly, stands proof that Chile has returned to the democratic path—proof that in Chile, once more, the people shall govern. It is my hope that this visit will renew and strengthen the ties between our two nations that trace back to the first days of Chilean independence, to your first Congress, convened on the 4th of July, 1811; to the guiding principles we share, the community of ideas that link your new nation to our own nation nearly 180 years ago. At the center of that community of ideas stand the shining principles that unite us today: individual liberty and democracy.

In the past year, the world has focused on the dramatic events that brought freedom and democracy to Eastern Europe and an end to an era of cold war and conflict that your President just talked about. But the principles at the root of those revolutions across the Atlantic are the very same that give life to our own democratic destiny. And in spite of the remarkable events unfolding in Europe, we should not lose sight of the fact that the triumph of the democratic ideal promises to make the Americas the first fully free hemisphere in all of history.

Chileans can take great pride in the role they have played in Latin America's democratic renaissance. Since the plebiscite of October 1988, Chile has undergone a political transformation every bit as far-reaching as the revolutions that changed the face of Eastern Europe. When others, frustrated by the long years under autocratic rule, might have engaged in recrimination, you, Chile, chose reconciliation. When others might have consumed themselves with settling scores, Chile chose to draw a positive lesson from the agony and the pain of the past.

Every year under autocratic rule served only to deepen your devotion to freedom and tolerance and respect for human rights, to strengthen Chile's collective resolve to make this return to democracy permanent and to make it irreversible. Chile's peaceful return to the way of democracy owes much to the leadership of a man of vision, a man of great moral courage, President Patricio Aylwin. But as President Aylwin understands, as everyone in this chamber knows, democracy's ultimate success rests not on the shoulders of one man alone but on the collective commitment of every Chilean— every citizen in every region, from every station in society—to put allegiance to democracy above any differences that divide you.

Chile has also been a part of a greater collective commitment through your steadfast participation in the international coalition now facing down aggression in the Persian Gulf. Chile, at considerable expense to your own economy, is upholding the sanctions against Iraq, despite the costs, because of the far greater cost to world stability should brutal aggression go unchecked. You understand, through hard experience, the fundamental importance of the rule of law.

As a friend of Chile, as the representative of a fellow democracy, I have deep respect for all that this nation has done to move forward, in peace, to this new day of freedom.

What is happening here in Chile is part, you see, of a larger movement that is sweeping this continent. Centuries ago, the Americas represented to the explorers of Europe the New World, an uncharted territory of promise and possibility. In the dawn of Chile's own independence, Bernardo O'Higgins, the Chilean patriot and patron of liberty for all of Latin America, spoke of Americas' shared destiny when he wrote: "The day of liberty has arrived for the Americas. From the Mississippi to Cape Horn, an area comprising almost half the world, we now proclaim the independence of the New World."

At long last, the new world O'Higgins wrote about is dawning across the Americas, a new dawn of democracy in which all men and women are free to live, work, and to worship as they please. My travels these past few days have made me more certain than ever that the Americas share a common democratic destiny and that Latin America's future lies with free government and free markets.

Chile, now returned to the democratic path, has long recognized the merits of a free-market economy. From the day Diego de Almagro first set foot on what is now Chilean soil, your lifeblood and link to the world has been trade. What has been true for Chile throughout its long history is today increasingly true for all nations.

Chile has moved farther, faster, than any other nation in South America toward real free-market reform. And the payoff is evident to all: 7 straight years of economic growth; in exports alone, a 15- to 20-percent increase in value in each of the past 5 years.

This explosive growth has secured for Chile a growing impact on the world economy. Today the farmer in San Fernando labors not just to feed his family, or even his village, but to deliver products to the dinner tables of Japan, Europe, and the United States. From the miner in Calama, the world obtains the raw materials it puts to use in everything from new homes to skyscrapers to space shuttles.

Chile's success—your success—is the product of wise policy, a comprehensive plan to transform this nation's economy into an engine for growth. Chile has worked to create an open and inviting investment climate for foreign capital. Since 1985 about $2.5 billion in new investment has flowed into Chile. Capital flight, which has sapped the economic strength of so many Latin nations, has now reversed itself, turned around, with returning funds spurring new investment here at home. And Chile has pioneered some of the world's most creative debt-reduction programs—these debt-for-equity swaps, exchanges that have transformed debt from a deadweight on development into new opportunities for growth.

Chile is a land of tremendous natural resources, near limitless potential: the mineral wealth of the arid Atacama; the black earth of the Central Valley; the safe haven here at Valparaiso, for centuries Chile's main port of entry and access point to the world beyond. But all of these abundant resources pale in comparison to this nation's most significant asset: the vast human potential of the people of Chile. Give to the people of Chile the opportunity to better themselves—to provide for their families, their children—and Chile will build its future. And let the people reap the rewards of their own hard work, and incentive will spur enterprise. The future of Chile is the sum total of every individual's hopes and dreams. Unleash these energies and uncover a reservoir of riches. Tap this source and transform a nation.

What has worked here in Chile can work across this continent. Last June, as your President mentioned, I introduced an initiative that I call Enterprise for the Americas—a comprehensive plan to reduce the crippling burden of debt and increase trade and investment across the Americas, for North or South, for Central. The Enterprise for the Americas Initiative challenges all countries in Latin America, and the Caribbean area, too, to commit themselves to the free-market policies that will help them attract the new capital central to achieving strong economic growth. To this end, Enterprise for the Americas seeks to promote open-investment policies through a new lending program in the Inter-American Development Bank, as well as the creation of a multilateral fund to support investment reform.

We recognize that the burden of external debt weighs heavily on efforts to breathe new life into Latin America and Caribbean economies. For that reason, the United States will help countries committed to free-market reform shake loose this burden of debt. Chile's strong economic performance makes it a prime candidate for the debt-reduction measures proposed as part of the Enterprise for the Americas Initiative.

And finally, our initiative recognizes the critical importance of our environment and the need to design debt-reduction measures that encourage environmental protection and conservation.

Enterprise for the Americas has generated great hope in the future of free markets across the continent. Already, during President Aylwin's recent visit to Washington, our two countries have signed a bilateral trade and investment framework under this initiative. And I look to Chile to continue to lead the way; to remain at the forefront of the free-market movement that's now beginning to take hold all across Latin America; to work together toward the ultimate aim of the Enterprise for the Americas, which is the creation of a hemispheric trade zone—that is free, a free-trade zone—from the Arctic regions in the north down to the southernmost tip of Cape Horn.

I want to see our two nations work together to bring down barriers to free and fair trade, not just here in the Americas but around the world. The great economic lesson of the past half-century is that protectionism stifles progress and that free markets breed prosperity.

And that's why the successful completion of this current Uruguay round negotiations remains my highest trade priority. In the Uruguay talks, both our nations have sought a deep reduction and, ultimately, the complete elimination of counterproductive agricultural subsidies. And together with Chile and other neighbors in the hemisphere, we here in the Americas constitute a potent force for free trade. So, let me say to all of you today: The United States stands ready to forge this new partnership in prosperity.

Some scholars say the word "Chile" means the ends of the Earth. Today what Chile means to the world is far different. Your nation is at the very center of the democratic revival transforming our entire continent, bringing us closer each passing day to the new world we seek. Because what matters in this new world is not the vast distances that separate us but the vital ideals that bring us together.

So, let today mark the beginning of a new partnership between our peoples. And let us all, across the Americas, work together toward a new world, toward that new dawn of democracy in which every nation is the home of liberty, democracy, and progress.

Once again, thank you from a very grateful heart for this welcome here in Chile. And may God bless the people of your great country. Thank you all very, very much.

Note: The President spoke at 4:25 p.m. in the Salón de Honor at the National Congress Building.

Toast at a State Dinner in Santiago, Chile
December 6, 1990

President Aylwin, thank you for your hospitality and for your generosity during my visit to your beautiful country. We first met earlier this year at the White House, and I hope we will have many more opportunities to exchange views and to work together.

In accepting Ambassador Silva's credentials as Chile's representative in the United States, I said: "We are happy for Chile and optimistic about its future. Your country's deep democratic tradition, its strong economy, and the richly deserved reputation of the Chilean people for dynamism and creativity reinforce our confidence." I shouldn't have been so restrained. Now that I've had the opportunity to visit Chile, I am even more convinced that Chile's future is bright. You deserve your reputation as an economic model for other countries in the region and in the world. Your economic growth is the pride of Latin America, and your commitment to market-based solutions inspires the hemisphere.

It is a pleasure to hear freedom spoken of as the recognized right of all people not only to elect their own government but to control their own destiny and follow their dreams. And it's a pleasure to listen to the language of optimism: to hear trade barriers spoken of as obstacles to eliminate and openness as the path to prosperity. Today I've heard economic growth and development discussed not as ends in themselves but as the means to raise the standard of living and to broaden opportunity for all Chile's citizens, as the means to a better life for her people.

Earlier this year, Mr. President, you observed, "Chileans, with a tradition of democratic institutions, of respect for human rights, of the rule of law, have chosen to remake their society based on those values which honored their country in the past. At the same time," you went on, "we want to seek progress and economic development based on an open and competitive system in which all creative initiatives find space for expression."

And so, it is with a noble spirit and honorable values that the Chilean people are remaking their society, a society founded on democracy and economic liberty. To achieve this, the people of Chile have freely chosen leaders of vision and courage. And you, President Aylwin, are an outstanding example. Earlier today, when I met your children and your grandchildren, I got a glimpse of the values underlying your leadership: family and faith in God and faith in the future.

To the bright future of this nation; to the freedom-loving people of Chile; to all the government officials who came to greet me at the airport; and to you, Mr. President, I raise my glass in a toast: May the renewed friendship between our two great nations remain as strong and healthy as the optimism that characterizes our two peoples.

Thank you, and may God bless your great country.

Note: The President spoke at 9:40 p.m. in the Patio de Los Naranjos at La Moneda Palace. Following the dinner, he went to the U.S. Ambassador's residence, where he stayed overnight. A tape was not available for verification of the content of these remarks.

Remarks at the American Chamber of Commerce Breakfast in Santiago, Chile
December 7, 1990

That applause did sound heartfelt. I'm reminded of when General Gray went over to see the Marines in Saudi Arabia the other day. He was talking to them, and he looked at them, and he said, "You have good morale. Remember that." [*Laughter*] Thank you for your heartfelt applause. Hey, look, I am simply delighted to be here; and I want to salute all the members of AmCham because what you're doing is very, very important as North America, the United States, and Chile go forward together towards the very next century. We've got a wonderfully promising setup between our countries now, but it's going to be most successful if your work is successful. So, I salute you. When our Ambassador said I might come over here, I accepted with alacrity.

It is an honor for me to be here and to be the first American President, as Ed pointed out, to visit Chile in 30 years. Ed referred to our entourage. That is a polite way of saying invasion squad—[*laughter*]—because when a President goes, an awful lot of people go with me. And I don't want to hurt any feelings, but there is one with me today who interacts very closely on everything that has to do with the business of AmCham. I would simply like him to stand up in case he has not been introduced. That's our Secretary of the Treasury, Nick Brady. Nick.

As many of you on the U.S. side of AmCham know, he comes out of a distinguished private-sector business background. I think that is very, very important to have in my Cabinet and amongst my very, very top advisers. So, I want to say both he and I are delighted to be here, and the rest of us—Secretary Eagleburger is with us and Bob Gates and many others, all of whom are making a significant contribution to this trip. Let me just put it this way: I think we've got a damn good Ambassador in Chile, Ambassador Gillespie, and I think you've got an outstanding Ambassador in Washington, DC, and that's good. That's going to help this relationship be even better.

Mr. Minister, I salute you, sir, and thank you—I see the Finance Minister. I think this bodes well to have this high-level attention on the part of the Chile Government and on the part of the U.S. Government to the work of this chamber. So, I welcome all of you, and I'm very glad to be here.

You know, on that Eisenhower visit three decades ago, he said this to your country's Congress: The friendship between two nations is based on "shared philosophy—faith in God, respect for the spiritual dignity of man, and the conviction that government must be the servant of the people." Today our two nations are united as never before by those beliefs that Dwight Eisenhower spoke of so eloquently. But we're also united in another way: through our commitment to bring democracy and prosperity to all the people of this hemisphere.

As business leaders, it seems to me you have an especially crucial role to play——

[*At this point, a spotlight fell, creating a loud noise which interrupted the President's remarks.*]

Bombs bursting in air—they sang about it; here it is. [*Laughter*] And incidentally, thank you for that wonderful rendition of both Chile's national anthem and the anthem of the United States of America. Thank you, sir, very, very much—all of you.

But as I was saying, you business leaders do have an especially crucial role to play: to ensure that Chile continues down this clear path to prosperity. Already, as Ed said, you have helped the United States become Chile's largest trading partner. We want to expand that trade. I made that very clear to your able President yesterday. We want to expand it further, and we will, but only if both economies—and I realize this is a two-way street—if both economies continue to remain open: open to ideas, open to reform, and especially open to free-market creativity.

That requires continued support for Chile's embrace of democracy. As your President told the Council of the Americas: "Chile is showing that an expanding, stable, and equitable economy is compatible with an open and democratic political system."

But you in AmCham have done more than consolidate democracy. You've also shown the spirit of voluntarism that is so essential, so crucial, to the success of free-market societies, especially through the important Telethon for Children, for example, that begins today. You understand that freedom bears special responsibilities, and I salute you for that.

President Aylwin knows that the tide toward freedom, once begun, is irresistible. In that spirit, we can take great pride in recently concluding a trade and investment framework agreement between our two countries. America's confidence in Chilean business is a major reason for this accomplishment. And yet even better times, I believe, lie ahead.

Last June, as I'm sure you're familiar, I proposed the Enterprise for the Americas Initiative to begin a new economic partnership in this hemisphere to help bring prosperity to Chile and its neighbors through free trade, official debt reduction, and foreign investment. It is designed to build on market-oriented economic reforms pioneered by Chile and now sweeping across all of Latin America. Through the Enterprise for the Americas, we can and we must create free and open trade throughout the hemisphere. And let me be clear: I know this is a two-way street. I know that we have much to do in the United States, as the countries south of our border have much left to do.

Progress on free trade can help to actively stem the siren song of protectionism, but free trade is just one way to reach this new world we envision. A second is this official debt reduction. The Enterprise for the Americas Initiative includes proposals to address debt reduction in Latin America. Our Congress has authorized the reduction of food assistance debt, and I will do all that I can to see that our Congress approves the reduction of other U.S. bilateral debt next year. I am pleased that Chile has been a pioneer of similar creative programs to reduce commercial debt.

Reducing the crippling burden of debt is also crucial to achieving the final part of Enterprise for the Americas, and that is increased investment. You know, since 1985 about $2.5 billion U.S. investment dollars have flowed into Chile. And from 1990 to '95, a projected $13.2 billion will aid Chile's development.

But we want to spur even more investment. The Inter-American Development Bank is moving forward on a new lending program to help countries improve their ability to attract more investment. In addition, OPIC, the Overseas Private Investment Corporation, has begun to encourage investment in Chile. And because Chile is already a pioneer, OPIC members will visit here early next year, bringing a group of private investors to discuss investment and joint-venture opportunities.

What's more, your companies have become an example of reform. Chile, indeed Latin America as a whole, is already proving that market forces work and that market forces are the way to prosperity.

Less than a decade from now, we will enter the 21st century. Already, we see the outline of that century. It will be a world in which those nations which modernize and compete will prosper, a world in which investment and trade will create opportunity and growth. So, my message today is: Let's join together to work towards this new world of progress. And it's a new world of hope, I might add, for all the peoples of the Americas.

I would say this to, well, both the Americans and the Chileans in this office. I know that it must appear to you at times that—because of the fascinating changes taking place inside the Soviet Union and, indeed, taking place in Eastern Europe—that there is a propensity on our part, the part of this administration and previous administrations, perhaps, to neglect South America. I want to assure you that that is not the heartbeat of our administration or, indeed, of our country. There will be no neglect.

We don't need slogans; I want the Enterprise for the Americas to be something more than three words. I want it to be successful. I can promise you today, the business men from the U.S. side, the business men and women from the Chilean side, that we will work to make this successful. We will work to make these seeds bear fruit. We are not going to neglect Central or South America. This is our hemisphere, and we want it to be successful.

May I, in conclusion, express my appreciation to our hosts here today—U.S., Chilean—that join together in this chamber. May I say to the official representatives of the administration in Chile, I just couldn't be more appreciative for the warmth of your hospitality here in Santiago and there in Valparaiso. I leave Chile stimulated by what I see, warmed by the embrace of the people on the streets, and grateful to each and every one of you for your part in strengthening relations between our two countries.

God bless you all, and thank you very much.

Note: The President spoke at 8:25 a.m. in the Salón de Directorio at the Holiday Inn Crowne Plaza Hotel. In his opening remarks, he referred to Gen. A.M. Gray, Jr., Commandant of the Marine Corps; Edward Tillman, president of the American Chamber of Commerce; Lawrence S. Eagleburger, Deputy Secretary of State; Robert M. Gates, Assistant to the President and Deputy for National Security Affairs; Charles A. Gillespie, U.S. Ambassador to Chile; Patricio Silva, Chilean Ambassador to the United States; and Alejandro Foxley Riesco, Minister of Finance. A tape was not available for verification of the content of these remarks.

Statement on the Uruguay Round Multilateral Trade Negotiations
December 7, 1990

The United States went to Brussels prepared to conclude ambitious market-opening agreements in all areas of the Uruguay round.

Unfortunately, the Brussels meeting has ended without result due to the inability of nations with substantial economic strength—the European Community (EC), Japan, and Korea—to negotiate fundamental agricultural reform. This is all the more disappointing given the very constructive attitude taken by many developing countries, particularly many of our friends in Latin America.

The United States remains committed to maintaining and strengthening the multilateral trading system and to a timely and successful conclusion of the round. We will do all we can to bring this about while continuing to insist upon agreements that genuinely liberalize trade. Accordingly, it is our hope that participants, especially the EC, will take this opportunity to reflect upon their position on agriculture and develop the political will to negotiate real market-opening agreements while there is still time to do so.

Toast at a State Dinner in Caracas, Venezuela
December 7, 1990

Mr. President, thank you for those very kind words and a very important speech. It is wonderful to be back in this great nation and this lovely city of Caracas. I well remember my last visit to Venezuela, a much more somber occasion. I was in your country as Vice President in December of 1981 to pay my respects to a great founding father and defender of Venezuelan democracy, Rómulo Betancourt.

Now, 9 years later, there is cause to rejoice, for the vision of Betancourt and Carlos Andrés Pérez is being realized in the Americas. Just look at what's happened in one decade: Democracy has been restored in Argentina, Peru, Ecuador, Bolivia, Brazil, Uruguay, El Salvador, Nicaragua, Guatemala, Honduras, Chile, and Paraguay, leaving Cuba as the lonely totalitarian holdout in our hemisphere. So, we are close, very close, to a democratic hemisphere, from Alaska to Argentina. And I am here today to declare that this era of peaceful change came about, in no small part, because of the unwavering leadership and example of a democratic Venezuela.

Like President Betancourt, you, Mr. President, have been a creative democratic leader. Like Simón Bolívar, you have carried on a legacy as a standard-bearer of liberty. Mr. President—CAP, to me and many other leaders in this hemisphere—[laughter]—those who love freedom in the Americas know that you and Venezuela are always on their side. And it's because of your leadership that we're seeing, once again, that freedom at the ballot box inevitably leads to freedom in the marketplace, that free political systems and free enterprise go hand in hand—just one more reason why Venezuela's future is as limitless as your people's industry and imagination.

I know that the economic reform program that you launched upon taking office has been, at times, difficult. But you've stayed true to principle, and you stayed true to Venezuela's future—a future of prosperity and democracy.

The good relations that exist between my government and yours are especially welcome because my family, the Bush family, has had a close connection to Venezuela. Our son Jeb lived and worked here in Caracas not so many years ago. And I certainly know firsthand how important Venezuela's leadership is to my country and how a prosperous and democratic Venezuela is essential to our hemispheric community. And that is why I especially look forward to cooperating closely with Venezuela in carrying out our Enterprise for the Americas Initiative.

It is my hope that the day will be brought closer when, as Simón Bolívar wrote in 1818, all of the New World can assume a place "with a description of majesty and grandeur unprecedented in the Old World."

And so, with a heart full of gratitude and thanks, let me close with a toast to President Pérez and the Venezuelan people. I believe it will be recognized and appreciated here: *"Manos a la obra!"* [Let's get on with it!]

Note: The President spoke at 9:35 p.m. in the garden at La Casona. Following the dinner, he went to the U.S. Ambassador's residence, where he stayed overnight. A tape was not available for verification of the content of these remarks.

White House Fact Sheet on the Venezuela-United States Science and Technical Cooperation Agreement
December 8, 1990

On Thursday, December 6, 1990, the Government of the United States of America and the Government of Venezuela agreed to enter into a 5-year agreement on cooperation in science and technology. This agreement renews the United States-Venezuela agreement for scientific and technical cooperation which expired in July 1988. It will serve as an important instrument to revitalize scientific and technical cooperation between the two countries.

The agreement was signed at the Ministry of Foreign Affairs by Dr. D. Allan Bromley, Assistant to the President for Science and Technology and Director of the White House Office of Science and Technology Policy, for the United States and by Minister Dulce Arnao de Uzcátegui for the Government of Venezuela.

The principal objective of the agreement is to provide additional opportunities to exchange ideas, information, skills, and techniques and to collaborate on problems of mutual interest. Cooperation may include exchanges of scientific and technical information, exchanges of scientists and technical experts, the convening of joint seminars and meetings, and the conduct of joint research projects in the basic and applied sciences.

The agreement will serve as an important catalyst to improve and enhance scientific technical cooperation between the two countries, particularly in areas such as environment and global change—including biodiversity, forestry management, and mining pollution in the Venezuelan Amazon—geosciences, and materials and standards research.

The agreement contains two annexes covering intellectual property and security obligations. The intellectual property annex ensures adequate and effective protection of intellectual property and equitable allocation of intellectual property rights arising from cooperative S&T activities. Certain areas of cooperation (drinks and food products for humans or animals, medicines of all kinds, pharmaceutical and chemical preparations, reactions, and compounds) are excluded from cooperation because the Venezuelan patent law does not provide adequate protection in these areas.

The security obligations annexes provide protection for any classified material that might inadvertently result from S&T cooperation and protection for any national security export-controlled equipment or technology involved in the cooperation.

Considering our common interest in promoting scientific research and technological development and recognizing the benefits which will be derived as a result of enhanced close cooperation, the United States and Venezuela look forward to implementation of the agreement.

Question-and-Answer Session With Reporters in Caracas, Venezuela
December 8, 1990

President Pérez. Gentlemen of the press, your friends, welcome. It is with great pleasure that I see myself here accompanying President Bush at his press conference. [*Laughter*] So, please go and ask him the questions and leave me alone. [*Laughter*]

President Bush. May I have a brief statement, with your permission?

President Pérez. Yes.

President Bush. Well, let me just say that it is fitting that I end this trip here in Caracas with my good, esteemed friend President Carlos Andrés Pérez. And the talks we've had have been warm, informative, and extraordinarily positive, as they always are when we meet.

Venezuela, under this President, is a leader in the great movements that we're seeing all through Latin America: consolidation of democracy; the movement to strip away barriers to economic growth, liberate free enterprise; and the movement to break down trade barriers throughout the Americas; and above all, the movement toward a new hemispheric partnership.

Just look at three points on the Venezuelan success story. They've gone from negative economic growth to real growth, they've cut the debt burden substantially, and they're attracting new investment—all goals of this new Enterprise for the Americas. And they're out front in these regards.

So, with respect, my friend, I salute you for these and many other achievements. Thank you for your hospitality.

[*At this point, a reporter asked a question in Spanish, and a translation was not provided.*]

Persian Gulf Crisis

President Bush. First, I agree with the hypothesis that Venezuela is a very dependable friend in this regard, in this question of oil. Venezuela stepped up early on with an offer to increase production and thus stabilize the world price. And we sign no agreements here today, but we did share the view that now, and in the future—after the Iraq matter is solved, the question of Kuwait is solved—we must do better planning to forestall any future disruptions to the entire world.

And the President pointed out to me that the most fragile economies in Central and South America are those being hurt the worst by Saddam Hussein's [President of Iraq] brutality against Kuwait.

Norm [Norman Sandler, United Press International]?

Q. Mr. President, your spokesman said last night that the threat of war in the Persian Gulf remains as strong as ever, despite what you described yesterday as movement—a little here, a little there. What I'd like to ask you is: Isn't the rationale for war, though, and perhaps even, indeed, the risk for war, diminished at this point by the prospective release of the hostages? And in fact, thanks to Venezuela and other countries, Saddam Hussein is now successfully isolated from a world that no longer needs his oil?

President Bush. I want a peaceful solution. I don't feel we are closer to a peaceful solution, and the reason I don't is because Saddam Hussein continues insisting that Kuwait is a province of Iraq and that he will not get out of Kuwait. And that is the fundamental point around which the whole world is united against him.

I'm glad the hostages are coming home. They never should have been taken in the first place. When you kidnap somebody, you should not expect a reward when you let the person go.

Q. Mr. President, doesn't it make it more difficult to convince other countries to still stand up against Saddam and perhaps go to war against him when two main concerns are no longer valid—the lives of foreign nationals in those two countries and the adequacy of oil supplies?

President Bush. No, it makes it no more difficult at all.

[*At this point, a reporter asked a question in Spanish, and a translation was not provided.*]

U.S. Forces in Panama

President Bush. As you know, there are certain treaty rights that apply to this situation. There are certain treaty rights there. We want to see Panama's democracy be successful, and we would like to see them perfect their own police-keeping function so that they don't need any outside assistance to guarantee against uprisings.

Q. How much longer do you think you will be there?

President Bush. We were discussing this today in terms of how long it will take Panama to perfect its democracy, and I can't give you an estimate.

Where's Terry [Terence Hunt, Associated Press]? He's supposed to have the next one.

Persian Gulf Crisis

Q. Mr. President, why are you giving Saddam Hussein the satisfaction of withdrawing American diplomats from Kuwait as he demanded? Is that a payback for the release of the hostages?

President Bush. It is no payback. And the feeling is that when every single American is out of Kuwait we will clear the decks, and the Embassy will have ceased to be fulfilling any day-to-day functions. But there is no payback; there is no change in my determination to get Saddam Hussein out of Kuwait in compliance with the United Nations resolutions.

Q. Britain is keeping its diplomats there. Don't you think that giving up our presence there is a reward to Saddam?

President Bush. I have great respect for whatever Britain decides to do. I'm not sure I know exactly what their plan is once their people are released. I think you can make the case that this facilitates the tough decisions that might lie ahead.

[*At this point, a reporter asked a question in Spanish, and a translation was not provided.*]

Free and Fair Trade

President Bush. One of the reasons to have a successful GATT round is to eliminate barriers that the United States has, barriers that Venezuela has to certain kinds of services and goods from the United States. So, we want to see the GATT round, which has now fallen on hard times—and I hope temporarily—be successful. And if that can't get the job done, then we move forward trying to reduce barriers bilaterally. We have barriers; Venezuela has barriers. But our objectives are the same—free and fair trade—and they haven't changed.

Gene Gibbons [Reuters]?

Persian Gulf Crisis

Q. Mr. President, you just said that removing American diplomatic personnel from Kuwait facilitated tough decisions that might be ahead. What did you mean by that?

President Bush. I just mean that when you don't have Americans there and if force is required—that's just one less worry I've got. I have said from the very beginning that this cruel policy of taking hostages and holding them in hopes that that will change the policy of this alliance is fruitless. But I am very glad that these people are coming out.

Q. I wonder, sir, if I could ask the question of Mr. Pérez, if he supports use of force in the Gulf and if he expects it to be necessary, given the release of the hostages?

President Pérez. Venezuela has stated categorically its support to the decisions made by the United Nations organization. And we have congratulated President Bush for the prudent decision he has made after the latest United Nations decision to invite the Foreign Minister of Iraq [Tariq 'Aziz] to Washington and to send Secretary of State Baker to Iraq. And I would like to add that we small countries, such as Venezuela, cannot truly accept that for anybody to be able to delete by force the boundaries of an existing nation. We are therefore automatically in favor of the restoration of freedom and sovereignty to Kuwait.

President Bush. Mr. Bierbauer [Charles Bierbauer, Cable News Network] is on my list here. We've got a list. We've got a new system here.

[*At this point, a reporter asked a question in Spanish, and a translation was not provided.*]

Cuba

President Bush. Eastern Europe returned democracy to itself, and someday the Cuban people will return democracy to themselves.

Charles, last one.

Persian Gulf Crisis

Q. Mr. President, an oil question. You've talked repeatedly about how small countries are suffering. President Pérez has mentioned that as well. And yet you seem to be relying upon the market system to set the price. Isn't this a situation where either of your countries, sirs, could do more to keep these smaller and underdeveloped countries from suffering as much as they have? I don't see any evidence of it.

President Bush. The best thing the United States can do is help get to the cause and do something about that, and that means to get Saddam Hussein without condition out of Kuwait.

In the meantime, I will do my level-best to point out to the world that there is no current shortage and that what we're seeing is paper barrels of oil traded in the futures market. And they go up, and they go down with every little rumor that is printed. And so, I think the best thing to do is to continue to educate the whole world on the facts, and that is that there is not a shortage today. And I would salute Venezuela for what they've done in trying to help,

through their own production, some of these countries that are hurt the most. And certainly we are trying through various programs to try to be of assistance wherever we can.

Q. I'm wondering if I could get President Pérez's response to this and whether—is there some way to divert these windfall oil profits to those countries who are suffering?

President Pérez. Venezuela and Mexico are doing it already. We are assisting the countries of Central America and the countries of the Caribbean. And we are also, at this time of crisis, trying to help them to finance their oil imports. Now, unfortunately, we cannot do the same with all of our Latin American clients simply because we, too, have our own difficulties. And besides, the surplus money we are getting now for the oil we sell is not going to be spent; we are going to deposit it into a macroeconomic stabilization fund so as to be able to take care of the difficulties in oil prices we know will appear in the future.

Now, I did take this opportunity to emphasize to President Bush the fact that what we should do is seek an agreement between producer and consumer countries so as to make the world understand that the price of oil is not based on true shortage of oil—this does not exist—but simply on the speculation.

President Bush. Thank you for your cooperation and understanding. Thanks.

Note: The question-and-answer session began at 11:55 a.m. in the Inner Courtyard at the Miraflores Palace. A tape was not available for verification of the content of this session.

Remarks at a Luncheon Hosted by the Venezuelan-American Chambers of Commerce in Caracas, Venezuela
December 8, 1990

President Pérez, you do us honor, sir, by being here today. And may I take this opportunity before my remarks to thank you for the exceptional and wonderful and extraordinary hospitality that you have given

to me and to Dorothy and to all of the rest of the people traveling with me. I'll never forget it, and thank you, sir.

To John Werner, the President of VenAmCham, thank you, sir, for your hospitality and giving us this forum. And of course, thank you for that very special scholarship fund that has been set up in our names. It will mean a great deal to Barbara Bush, I can assure you. Her commitment to education, I think, is well-known. But in any event, this is such a generous and wonderful thing you've done.

To Secretary Brady and our Ambassadors and Dr. Morales Bello and Dr. Figueredo, the members of the Court, the chamber leadership, and all out here, thank you.

You know, in the last week, I've looked out my window of Air Force One and seen the jungles of Brazil, the snowy peaks of the Andes, the tropical beauty of the Orinoco Basin; but I have to say, among the great sights of all the Americas is your lovely city. As you know—if you'll excuse me, a personal note; John and I were talking about this—our son Jeb came here and opened an office here several years ago for a Texas bank. And he was a member of this distinguished Chamber of Commerce. He and our daughter-in-law Columba loved living here. I have been here several times, starting, I think it was, 30 years ago. So, it's a delight to return to this great capital, so well-known to the Bush family, so well-known and so highly respected all across my country.

This marks my last stop on the South American Continent on this trip, and so, I thought it only appropriate to speak today not just of the relations of our two countries but of our shared concern for the future of our hemisphere. After all, Venezuela has always been a South American leader—and so, I might add, has this President of yours.

President Carlos Andrés Pérez is justly proud of his past successes. But again, CAP wants to do more than strengthen the democratic traditions of one country. He's a tireless promoter of universal liberty, and that's why he is respected and admired throughout the world.

Our working relationship as heads of state is strong; our friendship a bridge between our nations. But something even more profound is at work here. The United States and Latin America are developing a new understanding of each other. We are, at long last, working together in a spirit of mutual respect, for the greater good of the Americas.

This is only natural. Like your country, the United States won its liberty from European princes and powers. From the vision of Bolívar to that of George Washington, our nations were born for the sake of freedom.

As we near the 500th anniversary of Christopher Columbus' epic voyage, we are making a discovery of our own, of a new relationship between North and South. As I've said during this journey, we should not speak of a First World or a Third World but of our New World.

No nation has been a stronger voice for freedom than Venezuela. It was, after all, here in Caracas that many of today's democratic leaders from across the continent found safe harbor. When Caracas looks south, you behold a continent in which all leaders have, for the first time, been chosen by their people and have faith in their people.

This trip has reinforced what I have long believed: Latin America today is a profile in courage because the people of this continent—shopkeepers and students, political leaders and trade unionists—have struggled, sacrificed, and died to restore the rule of law and to defend democracy. Cities once under martial law, peoples once living in fear are now reborn in hope.

Look at the recent flareup in Argentina. A handful of army officers tried to settle a dispute with superior officers by force. And President Menem moved quickly, and the people never wavered in support of their elected government. The vast majority of the Armed Forces defended their Constitution and obeyed their civilian Commander in Chief.

Latin America today is also a profile in courage because the leaders and people of this hemisphere have thrown off the shackles of an outmoded set of ideas about how to promote economic growth. They've embarked instead on a bold new course.

Two decades ago, Latin America followed an economic model based on the flawed idea that the people of this continent could not compete in a modern marketplace and that the state had to shelter local industries and protect them behind high tariff walls and protectionist barriers, and that an increasingly intrusive state, rather than a liberated people, was the formula for economic growth.

Those policies were promoted as the path to development, particularly for the poor. You and I know, regrettably, that the opposite was true. For the closed economic systems that were created smothered growth and thwarted upward mobility for ordinary people. They instead created a rigged system based on privilege in which only a handful could prosper through their connections with the state.

Today, throughout this hemisphere, a new generation of bold democratic leaders has confronted that sterile status quo, and they have breathed new life into Latin America. I've met with five of these leaders: Carlos Menem, Fernando Collor, Luis Alberto Lacalle, and Patricio Aylwin and, of course, here in your country, Carlos Andrés Pérez. You're the bold pioneers of a new path to development in this continent: stripping away state controls, selling off inefficient state-owned enterprises, realigning overvalued exchange rates, and bringing down tariff walls. These leaders understand that the road to growth, jobs, and rising income is through new investment, expanded trade, and unleashing the energy of entrepreneurs.

I want to work in partnership with this new breed of leadership. And that is why I have proposed our Enterprise for the Americas Initiative: to open doors to the free movement of goods and ideas between our countries; to work for a sound financial footing, reduce debt burdens, and increase trade, investment, and opportunity for all Americans. And so, the Enterprise for the Americas seeks to promote open investment policies through new lending in the Inter-American Development Bank, as well as the creation of a multilateral fund to support investment reform.

Venezuela has already embarked on the difficult path of economic reform. Your President recognizes these steps have created hardship for many Venezuelans. President Pérez correctly believes that in the long run all Venezuelans will benefit and prosper from reform.

Trade ties between our nations also continue to broaden and to strengthen. And that doesn't mean only oil but an impressive array of new products that are helping to create jobs. And more, much more, lies ahead. Under the Enterprise for the Americas Initiative, we are negotiating a framework agreement on trade and investment to resolve specific problems and to identify new areas of cooperation. This is a first step toward free and open trade throughout the Americas.

Trade and investment are only two pillars of our Enterprise for the Americas Initiative. We recognize that the burden of external debt weighs heavily on efforts to breathe new life into Latin America and Caribbean economies. And for that reason—as the third pillar in this comprehensive approach—the United States will help countries committed to free-market reform shake loose this burden of debt.

You can be proud that, under President Carlos Andrés Pérez's leadership, Venezuela—in the lead—has reached a debt-reduction agreement with the commercial banks under the Brady plan. This agreement is a vote of confidence by the international financial community in Venezuela's economic policies.

Our Enterprise for the Americas Initiative is more than a slogan; it is more than just another program. It is a challenge to commit ourselves to free markets and to the free flow of capital, central to achieving economic growth and lasting prosperity. And that's why I've come to Latin America this week, to extend my hand in an offer of a new partnership, based on mutual respect and mutual responsibility. Ours is more than an economic partnership; it is a moral partnership.

Your President and I stand together on serious challenges facing all civilized nations—challenges that ask us to choose, literally, between right and wrong, between good and evil. Our country is the world's largest buyer of cocaine, and so we're fighting hard at home to reduce demand. We're doing it through increased education and treatment efforts that are already showing positive results. Your neighbors are the world's largest suppliers. Little surprise, then, that as much as 80 tons of cocaine a year move through Venezuela. Carlos Andrés Pérez and I agree, there can be no compromise with this obscene traffic in human addiction and human lives. We are committed to nothing less than decisive victory over the drug lords. Just a few weeks ago, we signed a bilateral money laundering agreement to help sever the flow of cash from the back streets to the banks. President Pérez and I are standing firm, and we will win this war on drugs.

On another important moral question, Venezuela has already shown magnificent leadership by working with the world community to counter the aggression of Saddam Hussein. You acted resolutely and responsibly in denouncing Iraq's conquest of Kuwait in the United Nations; and as a reliable supplier of oil, you have demonstrated determination at a time when the dictator of Iraq threatens the world's economy through economic blackmail. And I applaud your leadership.

Among the many shared challenges I've addressed today, there is one vision: In the Americas, we are many nations with a single destiny. We see a new dawn, where ordinary men and women decide who shall govern and where economic freedoms are not threats to privilege but keys to prosperity.

And that's what our Enterprise for the Americas is all about, and that is what the new partnership we seek is all about. It's a partnership with Latin America to strengthen democratic institutions and defend the rule of law; a partnership to move forward together to safeguard our environmental heritage, to protect the children of the Americas from the scourge of drugs, to prevent the spread of deadly chemical or nuclear weapons of war; a partnership to bring down debt, promote investment, and expand free trade so that all the citizens of the Americas can enjoy rising incomes and expanding opportunities. If we seize this opportunity, the partnership between the United States and Latin America can become a model for all nations into the 21st century.

Some may dismiss this vision as a dream. I am confident that it is already becoming a reality. You see, I believe the day will soon come when every man and woman in the Americas is a citizen of the world's first completely democratic hemisphere, a hemisphere in which human rights are respected—the strong are just; the weak, secure; and the rule of law prevails. And I believe the day will soon come when Latin America and the United States unite together in the world's first hemisphere in which trade is free, technology shared, and the benefits of prosperity are open to all. This week in South America—ending with this inspiring visit to Venezuela—leaves me more dedicated than ever to work with you to make that dream come true.

Thank you for this warm welcome, and may God bless you all in your important work. Thank you very much.

Note: President Bush spoke at 1:43 p.m. in the Grand Salón at the Caracas Hilton Hotel. In his remarks, he referred to his daughter, Dorothy LeBlond; Michael Skol, U.S. Ambassador to Venezuela; Simon Alberto Consalvi, Venezuelan Ambassador to the United States; David Morales Bello, President of the Venezuelan Congress; Foreign Minister Reinaldo Figueredo Planchart of Venezuela; President Carlos Saúl Menem of Argentina; President Fernando Collor de Mello of Brazil; President Luis Alberto Lacalle of Uruguay; and President Patricio Aylwin Azocar of Chile. A tape was not available for verification of the content of these remarks.

Statement on the Ratification of Soviet Union-United States Nuclear Testing Limitation Agreements
December 8, 1990

I have today signed the instruments of ratification of the Treaties Between the United States of America and the Union of Soviet Socialist Republics on the Limitation of Underground Nuclear Weapon Tests and on Underground Nuclear Explosions for Peaceful Purposes, and their respective Protocols. I was gratified that the United States Senate gave its advice and consent to ratification of these Treaties.

During consideration of the Treaties, statements were made by several Senators on the law of treaty interpretation. I believe that the views on this issue contained in President Reagan's message to the Senate of June 10, 1988, reflect the proper roles of the President and the Senate in this area.

In any event, I do not believe that any difference of views on this issue will have any practical effect on the implementation of the Treaties. Any question of interpreta-

tion that may arise undoubtedly will be handled in a spirit of mutual accommodation and respect. In this spirit, I look forward to the exchange of instruments of ratification and the entry into force of the Treaties and express my hope that it will lead to even more important advances in arms control and the preservation of world peace and security.

GEORGE BUSH

The White House,
December 8, 1990.

Note: This statement was released by the Office of the Press Secretary on December 10.

Remarks on Signing the Human Rights Day, Bill of Rights Day, and Human Rights Week Proclamation
December 10, 1990

Welcome to all of you. First, let me salute the former Chief Justice Warren Burger and thank him for all he's done commemorating our Constitution and Bill of Rights over the last few years—and still actively engaged. I want to salute Bruce Gelb, who I understand is here, Director of USIA; Ambassador Schifter; VOA Director Carlson; Ambassador Jewel LaFontant-Mankarious; and the members of the diplomatic corps that are with us today.

It's an honor to mark this important occasion with so many of the men and women who make it their calling to advance the cause of freedom and human rights around the world. It's a special pleasure to meet with you as we look back on a year in which the cause of freedom has made such gains; a year in which the collapse of the Communist idea and end of four long decades of cold war and conflict enabled the world to look with new hope toward an era of peace, an era of freedom.

With freedom's advance come new challenges. This is especially true in Europe, the continent that for so long stood at the heart

of the East-West conflict. There the Revolution of '89 has given way to the renaissance of 1990, to the difficult business of democracy-building. The hard work of consolidating these great gains has just begun. America can take pride in the role that we've played in this revolution, but not make the mistake of thinking that our work is now over.

Today, as so many of the newly emerging democracies struggle to put in place the foundation stones of freedom, the American example can light the way forward. Former Chief Justice Burger, as I mentioned, is a special guest, in a sense, to mark with us the fact that the new year we soon begin, 1991, is the 200th anniversary of the American Bill of Rights. Last month when I addressed the Federal Assembly in Czechoslovakia, a country which is now engaged in establishing the institutions of free government, I brought with me copies for every Member of our Constitution and our Bill of Rights, in the spirit of friendship, as a symbol of the common principles that bind all free people.

The authors of our Constitution and our Bill of Rights did their work not simply for one nation or one era but for the ages. Our assistance, not just material but moral and intellectual, can help our friends in Eastern Europe build a democracy that endures. As we work to further the cause of human rights, we must remember: The only alternative to the tyranny of men is the rule of law.

This advance in human rights is not confined to one continent alone. I have just got back 2 days ago from a trip to South America. I visited five countries, each one now back on the democratic path. One of them, Argentina, turned back an antidemocratic challenge just 2 days before I got there. When we arrived in Buenos Aires, you could see and feel the depth of Argentina's dedication to democracy and its ideals. As I said there: The day of the dictator is over; the war of ideas has been won by democracy.

Human rights and respect for all it entails—freedom of religion, freedom of speech, and other individual liberties, including property rights, free elections, multiparty systems—these fundamental rights are gaining ground the whole world over, in Latin America and in Asia, where free-market principles now power some of the world's fastest growing economies. I want to see our hemisphere—this hemisphere—be the first totally democratic hemisphere.

There is one outstanding example where it is not totally free and where human rights are not respected, and that's Cuba. And I hope someday soon that that will join the family of democratic nations here.

Across the continent of Africa, too often neglected during the years of East-West conflict, the issue of human rights is now of key importance. These new challenges and the great gains we've all witnessed cannot obscure the fact that this day and every day millions of men, women, children around the world continue to be denied the freedom to live, work, and worship as they wish. So, here too, then, is work to be done.

This nation and its people cannot be true to what is best in us if we fail to speak out for those whose voices are silent. In a world where human rights are routinely denied in too many lands, nowhere is that situation more tragic and more urgent today than in Kuwait. You know, we must speak out and stand up for the Kuwaiti people, a people whose very nation is now in the grasp of a tyrant unmoved by human decency. The reports, these eyewitness accounts that I've heard from Kuwaiti citizens, are a catalog of human misery: looting, torture, rape, summary execution—acts of unspeakable cruelty. What has happened to Kuwait is more than an invasion; it is a systematic assault on the soul of a nation. As long as such assaults occur, as long as inhumane regimes deny basic human rights, our work is not done.

And so, today I sign these documents. Words on paper—just as our own Constitution, our own Bill of Rights, our own Declaration of Independence are nothing more than words—and yet nothing less than the sum of human hope. As I sign these, I call on every American to see that the ideals enshrined in these words shine forth in our deeds as the very essence of all that America stands for.

Once again, thank each and every one of you for coming. May God bless all of you for your work in the cause of freedom.

And now I will sign the proclamation designating December 15th the Bill of Rights Day, and marking today, December 10th, as Human Rights Day.

Mr. Chief Justice, will you join me, please, here, sir?

Note: The President spoke at 1:31 p.m. in Room 450 of the Old Executive Office Building. In his remarks, he referred to Richard W. Carlson, U.S. Information Agency Associate Director for the Voice of America, and Jewel LaFontant-Mankarious, Assistant Secretary of State for Refugee Affairs. A tape was not available for verification of the content of these remarks. The proclamation is listed in Appendix E at the end of this volume.

Statement by Press Secretary Fitzwater on President Bush's Meeting With President Vytautus Landsbergis of Lithuania
December 10, 1990

President Bush met for one-half hour today in the Oval Office with Lithuanian President Vytautus Landsbergis and an accompanying delegation of officials from Lithuania. Landsbergis, who requested the meeting, is on a private visit to the United States. President Bush noted the value of personal contacts with the Baltic leaders, who have shown discipline and foresight in their commitment to a nonviolent solution to their problems with the Soviet Government.

President Bush reaffirmed United States policy pertaining to the Baltic States. He told President Landsbergis the United States supports the right of Lithuania and other Baltic States to self-determination.

President Bush added that the United States has never recognized the forcible incorporation of the Baltic States into the U.S.S.R. and assured President Landsbergis that this policy would not change. President Bush indicated that he and other senior administration officials had made this point directly on more than one occasion to senior Soviet officials.

President Bush stressed that the United States wanted a peaceful solution to the problem between the Baltic States and the U.S.S.R. and hoped the Soviet Government would work constructively with Baltic leaders without resorting to threats, intimidation, or the use of force.

Message on the Observance of Hanukkah
December 11, 1990

I am delighted to send greetings to Jews in this country and around the world as you celebrate the festival of Hanukkah.

The Jewish religion is rich with tradition, and this special holiday is one of both teaching and joy. It commemorates the faith and the perseverance of Judah Maccabee and his followers, who were able to defeat their oppressors and rededicate the Temple in Jerusalem. According to tradition, even though the Maccabees could find enough purified oil in the Temple to keep the sacred menorah burning for only one night of celebration, the oil lasted for eight days and eight nights.

This story of abiding trust in the mercy and justice of the Almighty continues to be a source of inspiration to Jews around the world. The miracle of the Lights illustrates that the power of the Lord can overcome what seem to be impossible obstacles and that working together to achieve common objectives can make the world a brighter place for all.

Barbara and the entire Bush family join with me in sending our best wishes for a memorable Hanukkah.

GEORGE BUSH

Remarks at a White House Conference on Drunk and Drugged Driving Awareness
December 11, 1990

Thank you all very much. Chevy Chase has arrived. [*Laughter*] Let me first salute

Jerry Curry, our Administrator, and Sam Skinner, the Secretary—both of whom are doing an outstanding job. When I heard that this group was going to gather here, I just wanted to come by and encourage you to do even more and personally thank you for the tremendous job that you're doing to raise the awareness of drunk driving.

I firmly believe that drunk driving is a national crisis. Sam has driven this into my head day in and day out with his commitment to the cause. He and I have agreed that fighting this crisis is one of the key goals of our administration. Along with all the work that he and Mr. Curry have done at Transportation, I want to commend all the community groups, the different Points of Light we probably don't even know about, in a collective sense, all the groups— certainly, those represented here that are engaged in this battle.

Mickey Sadoff, my heavens, what she's done—head of the Mothers Against Drunk Driving—we salute you, and I promise to stick my ribbon on one of the cars, if I can catch it out there. So, I hope you'll see it. But the activities of that group, along with those of so many others, including leaders in business, industry, and all across—everywhere—labor—have helped dramatically alter the public perception of drinking and driving.

Progress has been made. I had a little session with Mickey in the hall. Nobody is relaxed about it. Everybody's still determined to do more. But progress has been made. The proportion of alcohol-related traffic deaths is down, as is the number of total drunk-driving fatalities.

Two other highlights of this year: a first-ever U.S. traffic safety summit this April in Chicago sponsored by Secretary Skinner, which generated new ideas for curbing drunk drivers, and approval by the U.S. Supreme Court for sobriety checkpoints, a major goal of the Department of Transportation.

This holiday season reminds us that this is a time for Americans to remember that drinking and driving is a deadly combination. That's why I was glad to see this joint effort between the Advertising Council and the Department of Transportation, which has begun to show up in print and on the television as well. This campaign has touched millions of Americans with its simple message of individual responsibility.

Speaking of responsibility, I'm on my way down the hall right now, right down from here, to our little studio to cut some public service announcements, encouraging designated drivers, just one of your many ideas that are making a difference.

So, thank you all; God bless you in your work, and I hope each and every one of you have a very Merry Christmas. Thank you so much.

Note: The President spoke at 2:07 p.m. in Room 450 of the Old Executive Office Building. In his remarks, he referred to Jerry R. Curry, Administrator of the National Highway Traffic Safety Administration. A tape was not available for verification of the content of these remarks.

Nomination of Donald A. Henderson To Be an Associate Director of the Office of Science and Technology Policy
December 11, 1990

The President today announced his intention to nominate Donald A. Henderson, of Maryland, to be an Associate Director of the Office of Science and Technology Policy for Life Sciences. He would succeed James B. Wyngaarden.

Since 1977, Dr. Henderson has served as dean and professor of epidemiology and international health at the Johns Hopkins School of Hygiene and Public Health in Baltimore, MD. Prior to this he served as chief medical officer for smallpox eradication program of the World Health Organization in Geneva, Switzerland, 1966–1977. In addition, Dr. Henderson served with the Communicable Diseases Center at the Department of Health, Education, and Welfare in several capacities: chief of the smallpox eradication program, 1965–1966; chief of the surveillance section in the epidemiology branch, 1961–1965; assistant chief of epidemiology branch and chief of the Epidemic Intelligence Service, 1960–1961; chief of the Epidemic Intelligence Service and assistant to the chief in the epidemiology branch, 1956–1957; and assistant chief of the Epidemic Intelligence Service, 1955–1956. Dr. Henderson served at the Mary Imogene Bassett Hospital in Cooperstown, NY, as a resident in medicine, 1954–1955, and an intern in medicine, 1954–1955. In 1986 Dr. Henderson was awarded the National Medal of Science.

Dr. Henderson graduated from Oberlin College (A.B., 1950), University of Rochester School of Medicine (M.D., 1954), and Johns Hopkins University School of Hygiene and Public Health (M.P.H., 1960). He was born September 7, 1928, in Cleveland, OH. Dr. Henderson served as a commissioned officer for the U.S. Public Health Service, 1955–1977. Dr. Henderson is married, has three children, and resides in Baltimore, MD.

Remarks on the Observance of Hanukkah
December 12, 1990

Thank you, rabbis, for those lovely words and for the gift of this lovely menorah. It's wonderful to see the students—the Gesher Jewish Day School. I'm so glad you could join us all here today to sing. You haven't sung yet, have you? [*Laughter*] Oh, good, because I didn't want to miss that.

Let me say that Barbara and I and Marilyn and Dan Quayle want to just welcome everybody here to the White House for the second year of these Hanukkah celebrations. It's a holiday of hope, for it shows us the glory of God in our own lives and the power of miracles in the world. Last year at this ceremony, we spoke of our efforts to help Vladimir Raiz and other brave refuseniks—help them leave the Soviet Union. By Passover, Vladimir was a free man. But the story really doesn't stop there. In addition to Zev Raiz, more than 150,000 Soviet Jews emigrated this year to new homes, new lives of liberty and dignity.

In fact, I am told that one kid, one child with us today from the Gesher Jewish Day School, Lidia Shestopalova—where's Lidia? Here she is, right there. Now, Lidia, if that's—oh, I'm so glad you're here. But she recently arrived from the Soviet Union. And so, we welcome you to this country, and we continue to pray for all those who are seeking freedom. Thank you, Lidia.

Now, sit down and be relaxed here. We're so glad you're here. And you're so beautiful.

The ancient story of the first Hanukkah is one of victory over persecution, aggression, and intolerance. But the struggle has continued for your people through the centuries. In fact, the first wave of Jewish immigrants came to this country as early as 1654 to live a life free from intolerance and persecution.

Two hundred years ago, George Washington wrote a letter to a Jewish congregation in Newport, Rhode Island, in which he said the United States Government would give "to bigotry no sanction, to persecution no assistance." In this new country, Washington said, "Everyone shall sit in safety under his own vine and fig tree and there shall be none to make him afraid." These words embody the American ideal of freedom of worship, an ideal that we reaffirm here today and that we pass on to the generations that follow us.

I understand that these kids—I guess you're next—are going to sing for us. I'm looking forward to it. I know Barbara is, and I know Marilyn and I know Dan are as well. I was pretty good last year at this game, dreidel. Some said it was beginner's luck, but I'm ready for that. Also, I'm relying heavily on my partner here to prevail.

[*Laughter*] He's a pro in this. So, why don't we just have a few songs, and then we'll have a little match here.

But the main thing is, thank you for coming. Thank you for coming here to the White House at this very special time of year. And thank you, rabbis, for your inspirational words, your prayers, and being with us here today, too. And Happy Hanukkah to everyone. Now, let the show begin.

Note: The President spoke at 11:45 a.m. in Room 450 of the Old Executive Office Building. A tape was not available for verification of the content of these remarks.

Remarks at the Jobs for America's Graduates Awards Ceremony
December 12, 1990

Thank you, Governor McKernan, for those very kind words. And let me also thank you, given all you have on your plate, for your responsibilities and services—chairman. I also want to single out just a few here. I noticed you commented on the former Governor, now Senator, Chuck Robb's participation—chairman now, to those who don't know this, of the executive committee of Jobs for America's Graduates; Ken Smith, who—for the president; Julie Nixon Eisenhower, who's done an awful lot to make this day possible through her commitment.

And, of course, I want to salute the others that are with us: Governor Wilder of Virginia, and Governor Castle is here from Delaware, Governor Stephens of Montana. And then Kit Bond, a former Governor, I understand is with us, and there he is over here. And then especially to salute Pete Du Pont, the former Governor of Delaware, who really presided over the genesis and really with a stimulating word and thought behind all of this. And I'm delighted to be with all of you distinguished people who have made such a contribution.

Also, I saw earlier Bill Brock, a former Senator, and I know of his interest in all of this, too. And I want to congratulate those Governors not here; it all adds up to a total of 19 Governors being honored here today. And then again, I see a lot of those in town who do the heavy lifting when it comes to supporting all these worthy causes. And I want to thank each and every one of you and your foundations and your companies for seeing the light and getting out front on this important one.

My own interest, as Jock says, dates back to the very beginning—not really the beginning because Pete gets the credit for that—but back to my time on the board of directors, when the JAG—Jobs for America's Graduates—was nothing more than this idea with plenty of promise. And that's why it is with special pride that I meet with all of you, the ones, literally, who have taken the idea and put it into action with, I think, spectacular results.

One of my great pleasures as President is to shine the spotlight on the success stories. Barbara calls it being a cheerleader. Well, she's darn good at it, too, I might add. But I think we are advantaged in having this special forum from which we can point out to the country the great successes that are taking place. And certainly today, JAG— Jobs for America's Graduates—deserves to be center stage. This organization has enjoyed lasting support from State officials, Governors, and from the business community. And it's all for one simple reason: It works; JAG works.

Take a look at the statistics: 92 percent of the young people in this program were able to complete their high school diploma or their GED last year—92 percent. And it doesn't stop there. That's what Pete impressed on me and Jock has reimpressed on me. The program assists these new graduates during that critical school-to-work transition. Eighty-three percent of the young people participating made a successful transition into the working world, the armed services, or on to their next level of education. And JAG accomplished all this at half the average cost of other youth employment programs.

You've been especially effective, I'd say, in the inner cities. Kids from low-income households, whose plans for the future don't include college and may not even include finishing high school—JAG takes aim at these at-risk kids; the ones who, without the right help, without the right encouragement, might find themselves out of school, on their own, no hope, no prospects, without a future, if you will. JAG catches these kids before they drop through the cracks—20,000 last year alone.

And since I know a little about this organization, I know that you're not resting on your laurels. I'm especially pleased that, with what Jock said here, that JAG has joined this nationwide Points of Light movement with today's announcement that each participant will be expected to engage in community service activities. JAG's been especially effective—I said the urban area—also in the urban schools. And I urge you to extend this inner-city outreach, expand this proven program to as many cities and schools as possible. It's my hope that, before long, there will be a Jobs for America's Graduates program in every State in this country because as great as it is to see these award winners here today—and I met with them upstairs—there's a place in this room for all 50 Governors to be here. And it's no surprise to me that this success is taking place then at the State and local level.

Last fall, as the Governors and I forged our historic partnership at the education summit, we recognized that excellence in education required an effort that was not Federal but national, one that brought all levels of government together in common cause to improve America's schools. We've got to follow through on those goals.

I might say parenthetically just a word about a very new development. This morning, Secretary Cavazos, the Secretary of Education, my dear friend, resigned as Secretary. And I think of the contribution he made to establishing these national schools. And I think the country will always be very, very grateful to him for his service to country.

Since then, since that get-together, we've made real progress. A set of six national goals are now in place, as is this target date still in place for the year 2000. Efforts to expand flexibility and also accountability in education are underway. These efforts are underway. And at that summit, as Jock well knows—Governor McKernan—the Governors also committed to undertake a major State-by-State effort to restructure the education system.

And I want to turn now to this challenge, the need for a reform effort that results in nothing less than the restructuring of American education. The people in this room are critical to this reform effort: corporate leaders, who know education is the key to competitiveness; Governors, from Maine to California, along with top education officials from each State; teachers and principals, whose daily dedication and commitment will mold tomorrow's citizens; and finally, students, young people, for whom the word education means hope and happiness, opportunity, and achievement.

Let me explain to all of you about what I mean, just briefly, about restructuring our schools. I'll limit myself to the broad principles, because the last thing we need if we want real restructuring is a set of prescriptions, a bureaucratic blueprint from on-high Washington, mandating the States.

One of the keys to this approach is empowering people, not the bureaucracies. And central to empowerment is this concept of choice—empowering parents to decide which school is best for their children. Choice, you see, is the catalyst for change, the fundamental reform that drives forward all the others.

Let me lay out five principles that should guide our efforts to restructure our schools, principles that empower parents, expand choice, and encourage excellence in education: high expectations, decentralized authority, schools that are responsive, market-oriented, and performance-tested.

Take the first: high expectations. We've got to raise our sights, for our students, for our schools. We've seen the statistics. American kids already rank too low compared to our chief industrial competitors. America can't settle for a C average if we really mean to compete and get ahead. America's schools must, and will, aspire to world-class standards.

Secondly, we've got to decentralize authority. It wouldn't be fair to raise expectations, to ask more of our schools and our students, if we tie the hands of the teachers and the principals, particularly those who make the difference. After all, the secret to our schools' success isn't the size of the bureaucracy. We succeed or fail one student at a time. And the secret is the principal who commands respect and cares deeply about each and every kid who walks into that school, and that special teacher who starts with the same tests and books and blackboard and then makes learning come alive. For years, we've stifled our schools with requirements and redtape. Let's give our schools something teachers and principals don't have enough of: authority. And then let's hold them accountable for the results.

Third, we need responsive schools, customer-driven if you will, schools that involve and engage students and their parents—the real experts on what's best for their kids. That's central to the concept of choice. Everywhere choice has been tried, choice has worked, in large part because it has brought parents into the process, into that whole process of shaping their kids education. We need schools that are open to the input from the business community, real-world institutions that can work with our schools to educate the kind of employees they'll need tomorrow. If we want schools that work we've got to realize that there isn't any centralized monopoly on wisdom.

Fourth, restructuring means making our schools more market-oriented. We know what competition means in the business world. It's time we recognize that competition can spur excellence in our schools. Let them open their doors to experts from outside the teaching profession who are willing to share their wisdom in the schools. We've got to expand what they call alternative certification and tap the wealth of teaching in our society. There's a lot of talent out there that's precluded by mindless regulation from participating in our schools as teachers. Tap the wealth of that teaching talent that's been kept out of the classroom

simply because they lack a teaching certificate.

Fifth and finally, we need to make sure the yardstick we use to measure our achievement is performance-based. All the necessary attention to rules and regulations and procedures, all the measures of dollars spent, all the hardware and software, statistics and studies cannot be allowed to obscure the one measure that matters. And what matters is what works: results—what kind of kid walks out of that classroom and into society, what our kids know, whether we've taught them how to learn. And one thing more while the subject is performance: We hold students accountable for their own failure. Well, let's do the same, then, for our schools.

These five principles—high expectations, decentralized authority, schools that are responsive, market-oriented, and performance-based—these five can guide our efforts as we restructure American education to meet the ambitious goals that have been set for our nation's students and for our schools, first set by the Governors of the 50 States, as we lead America forward to what I hope will be an education renaissance, a system that can compete with any in the world. We've got to redouble our efforts to achieve these goals. This restructuring must take place. I don't have to tell the corporate leaders in this room that America can't expect to remain a first-class economy if we settle for second-rate schools. And let me assure you, there is a role in this restructuring for everybody here, for your energy, for your ideas, for your commitment to educational excellence.

Before I close, let me just thank once again the companies and the foundations and the individuals whose contributions help keep Jobs for America's Graduates going strong. The help you provide to each young person literally lasts a lifetime. And to those students here with us today, let me recognize your accomplishments, but let me ask something else as well. Just as you've been helped along the way, make it your mission to reach out your hand to all the other kids like you who have everything they need to succeed except encouragement.

So, once again, I really wanted to come over here, Jock, to thank you, to thank the other Governors and Senators that are with us here today, thank you for all you're doing to help the kids of this country. May you all have a wonderfully merry Christmas. And may God bless the United States. Thank you very, very much.

Note: The President spoke at 12:35 p.m. in the ballroom at the National Press Club. In *his remarks, he referred to the following officials of Jobs for America's Graduates: Gov. John R. McKernan of Maine, chairman of the board of directors; Julie Nixon Eisenhower, chairman of the resource development committee; and Senator Christopher S. Bond, former Governor of Missouri, member of the board of directors. A tape was not available for verification of the content of these remarks.*

Remarks on the Waiver of the Jackson-Vanik Amendment and on Economic Assistance to the Soviet Union
December 12, 1990

The President. Mr. Minister, welcome. I have a brief statement, and then I will turn the conference here—press conference—over to Minister Shevardnadze and Secretary of State Baker to respond to questions. But I have just had an opportunity to discuss with Foreign Minister Shevardnadze a number of issues of U.S.-Soviet relations, including our cooperation in the Gulf. And I'm pleased with the great progress that we made on START and hopeful that we will be ready to sign a treaty at a summit in Moscow on February 11 through 13th.

We also talked at length about the situation in the Soviet Union and the response of the United States to the economic problems there. I asked Minister Shevardnadze to convey to President Gorbachev my desire to respond both to the short-term needs of the Soviet Union and to contribute to fundamental economic reform—long supported *perestroika*, and continue to.

We discussed frankly the relationship of economic change in the Soviet Union to the critical task of democratization. And I reiterated our strong desire to see both political and economic reform continue because they are inextricably linked. I outlined specific and important steps that we're willing to take in support of reform. And after consulting closely with Secretary Yeutter as well as Secretaries Brady and Baker, I told Minister Shevardnadze that I am prepared to respond to a Soviet request for credit

guarantees for purchase of agricultural commodities through a waiver of the Jackson-Vanik amendment.

While I've taken this step I still look forward to a passage of the Soviet emigration law codifying the generally excellent practices of the past year. And this then will permit us to make further progress toward the normalization of the U.S.-Soviet economic relationship.

In addition, we have proposed to the Soviets a special technical assistance project to help in assessing their food distribution problem and to support market reforms. I will also authorize a joint public-private medical assistance effort to help the Soviet Union cope with immediate shortages of pharmaceuticals and basic medical supplies.

In the longer term, only steps that the Soviet Union itself takes can assure the economic health there. Thus, to promote fundamental economic reform I will propose that the World Bank and the IMF work out with the Soviet Union a special association to give the U.S.S.R. access to the considerable financial and economic expertise of those institutions. I have asked Secretary of the Treasury Nick Brady, as U.S. Governor of both institutions, to pursue this proposal with them and also with our other allies, who I'm sure will be in accord.

As I have said before, I want *perestroika* to succeed. The Soviet Union is facing tough times, difficult times. But I believe that this is a good reason to act now in order to help the Soviet Union stay the course of democratization and to undertake market reforms. The United States has an interest in the Soviet Union—able to play a role as a full and prosperous member of the international community of states. And I am hopeful that these initiatives will further that goal.

Mr. Minister, we're delighted you're here, and now I'll turn this over to you and Jim Baker.

Note: The President spoke at 4:06 p.m. in the Rose Garden at the White House. A tape was not available for verification of the content of these remarks.

White House Fact Sheet on the Waiver of the Jackson-Vanik Amendment
December 12, 1990

The President has decided to waive for the Soviet Union application of the freedom of emigration provisions contained in the Jackson-Vanik amendment (section 402) to the 1974 Trade Act. The Jackson-Vanik amendment effectively bars access to official credit and credit guarantee programs to countries which restrict emigration. The President made this decision:

- based on the liberalization of Soviet emigration policy in recent years by which an estimated 360,000 people will emigrate in 1990;
- after receiving assurances that this policy will continue, and
- to make food available to the Soviet Union in the form of up to $1 billion in Commodity Credit Corporation (CCC) credit guarantees for the purchase of U.S. agricultural products.

The President's waiver will be valid until at least July 1991, at which time he will need to determine whether to extend the waiver.

While the President has taken this action on Jackson-Vanik, he does not plan at this time to send the U.S.-Soviet trade agreement, signed during the Washington summit in June 1990, to the Congress. Only when the trade agreement is approved by Congress and takes effect could the Soviet Union receive most-favored-nation trading status.

The immediate effect of the President's action is to make the Soviet Union eligible for export credit guarantees under the CCC General Sales Manager program for the purchase of American agricultural products. This form of food assistance responds to Soviet requests for credit guarantees and will help the Soviet authorities address current food shortages. The waiver will also restore Soviet eligibility for Export-Import Bank credits and credit guarantees. However, the Stevenson amendment to the Ex-Im Bank Act and the Byrd Amendment to the 1974 Trade Act limit credits and guarantees to $300 million, with a subceiling of $40 million and other restrictions on Ex-Im Bank credits or guarantees in support of the fossil fuel industry.

In accordance with the requirements of Jackson-Vanik, before formally executing a waiver the President will report to Congress his determination that a waiver will substantially promote its freedom of emigration objectives in the Soviet Union. This report will also state that he has received the required assurances on Soviet emigration practices.

White House Fact Sheet on the Medical Assistance Program for the Soviet Union
December 12, 1990

The President has decided to establish a mixed public-private medical assistance effort to help the Soviet Union deal with acute, immediate shortages of pharmaceutical and basic medical supplies. The effort would rely on private voluntary organizations, with U.S. Government support, to provide and distribute medicines and medical supplies within the Soviet Union. At least initially, these medicines and supplies would be donated by U.S. firms.

A U.S. task force, with representatives from the U.S. Government and private voluntary organizations, will be set up to coordinate and facilitate the overall relief effort.

- The Agency for International Development (AID) will contact private voluntary organizations and pharmaceutical firms to solicit donations. AID will provide financial assistance to participating private voluntary organizations.

- U.S. private voluntary organizations will organize, deliver, and distribute privately donated medical and pharmaceutical supplies in the Soviet Union.
- The U.S. Embassy in Moscow, working with Soviet authorities in the central government and at the republic and city level, and with U.S. private voluntary organizations already in the Soviet Union, will work to identify specific needs and medical assistance priorities.

The magnitude of the program and the specific materials to be provided will depend on both this detailed assessment of needs and the extent of private interest in this effort.

Ideally, U.S. assistance will be targeted at specific groups in the population needing medical supplies (e.g., disposable syringes for infants, insulin for diabetics, drugs for those with leukemia, etc.).

White House Fact Sheet on Technical Assistance in Food Distribution and Marketing for the Soviet Union
December 12, 1990

The United States is prepared to send to the Soviet Union this month a team of private and public sector experts in the field of food distribution and marketing. The team's mission will be to assess the problems of food distribution, and provide technical assistance to central, republic, and local authorities in the Soviet Union.

The team will identify ways to strengthen and support market forces in the Soviet Union's food marketing system, consider alternatives to assist vulnerable populations, and recommend measures to improve the availability of food to the Soviet people.

The team will include experts from the U.S. private sector, universities, private voluntary organizations, and the U.S. Government. Team members will work closely with Soviet Government officials, as well as officials of the republic governments.

Excerpt of a White House Fact Sheet on the Soviet Union and International Financial Institutions
December 12, 1990

The President has proposed a special association of the Soviet Union with the International Monetary Fund (IMF) and the World Bank that will give Moscow access to the economic and financial expertise in those institutions. He has asked Secretary of the Treasury Brady, as U.S. Governor of the IMF and World Bank, to pursue this proposal with the institutions and other countries and to develop with them the necessary new arrangements.

We believe it is best for the Soviet Union to establish such a relationship with these institutions before addressing the issue of full membership.

Remarks at the Presentation Ceremony for the Malcolm Baldrige National Quality Awards
December 13, 1990

May I, too, salute the Deputy Secretary, Mr. Murrin—and of course, the Secretaries from the other Cabinet Departments that are here. I'm delighted to see all of you. I want to single out our Science Advisor that was to be here, Allan Bromley—I'm not sure he is—but in any event, very much interested in this whole field of competitiveness. Dick Truly of NASA—a keen stake in seeing the quality of all performed. I want to salute the Cadillac general manager, John Grettenberger; John Akers, who is the president and CEO of IBM, chairman of the board; the president and chairman of the board of Federal Express, who's with us, Fred Smith—we'll be seeing these all in a bit; and John Wallace, from Houston, who is the CEO of the Wallace Company.

And then I also want to salute the Members of Congress who are good enough to be with us today, members of the Baldrige family. How I love Mac Baldrige. Welcome home! And congratulations especially to these winners. And I'm proud to see some who were honored last year.

I want to single out Bob Mosbacher here, who is doing a splendid job as our Secretary of Commerce—a quality job, I might say. Quality is it. Quality for our administration. And we're here today to present these four awards, as I say, named for another man of quality, and that again is former Secretary Mac Baldrige. What a great guy.

He was—you know, some forget this, but Mac, prior to becoming Secretary of Commerce, was a true leader in business. And when it came business, he really did understand that quality cannot be assured with some slogan or an ad campaign. And he knew that it begins with winning and keeping business. And it begins with understanding that only customers can define quality. And in short, it begins and ends with the unsentimental judgment of the marketplace.

Once quality separated winning firms from sluggish ones. That time has long since passed. And with the fierce competition of the international market, quality means survival, and nothing less.

The renewed commitment by America to quality can be seen in the explosion of applications to receive the Baldrige Award. In just a few years, the National Quality Award has literally become the standard of business excellence. And the renewed spirit of excellence in business, of making quality an integral part of America's corporate strategy, has truly, I believe, made us more competitive in the international arena. Exports have already increased nearly 8 percent from year-ago levels, and the figure keep on rising.

To compete and win in the international arena, United States companies are simply going to have to offer product and services that are world-class. And that's the purpose behind this award. And it's a national purpose.

So, we're here today not only to honor these four deserving firms but to promote an awareness of quality in American business and to share successful management strategies—strategies that can, indeed, sharpen America's lead in the world marketplace. Each of these companies offers unique lessons. But these four companies also found success in a few basic principles. They learned that quality control cannot be imposed from top to bottom. They understand that quality management must cut through organization charts, across departments and offices. A quality culture does not depend on titles and job descriptions. And finally, these winning companies also realize that they are only as strong as the intelligence, judgment, and character of their employees.

This year, the Malcolm Baldrige National Quality Award is going to all three award categories: manufacturing, small business and, for the first time, service. The winners with us today were selected from a population of American organizations that requested more than 180,000 application guidelines this year. And what I said of last year's honorees applies today: Most companies catch hell from the competition. But these companies are in the lead because no competitor gave them a tougher time than they gave themselves.

Three of our winners are household names. Let me start with IBM at Rochester, a company that proves that quality coupled with employee training and education is simply good business. In fact, IBM Rochester spends five times—five times—the national average on education and training—and just one reason why IBM Rochester is globally competitive.

And the next recipient is another household name, the first automotive company to earn this award: Cadillac. And when many companies speak of quality changes, they speak of improvement in management. This company speaks of a "culture change," a clear recognition that Cadillac knows that quality begins with the morale and idea of its people. Cadillac executives, plant managers, or union representatives—all have worked together to help win this award. Quality councils are at work at each of the company's seven major facilities, supported by hundreds of company teams. And Cadillac shows that labor-management cooperations indeed yields quality results.

The next recipient is Federal Express, the first large service company to earn this award. This is a critical recognition because so much of our work force and our national wealth comes from the service sector. And Federal Express is simply nothing less than a model for all other service corporations. From ground zero in 1973, Federal Express has shot up to one of the world's largest transportation companies, with more than 90,000 employees making 1.5 million shipments a day. As with IBM Rochester and Cadillac, the secret of success for Federal Express is its training and reliance on its employees. With a no-layoff philosophy and extensive training, Federal Express attracts top-notch, motivated people. In fact, during the last 5 years, nearly 100 percent of Federal Express employees surveyed responded that they were proud to be a part of their company. And that's why Federal Express delivers. And all American workers should feel they are as much a part of their companies.

And that brings me then to the Wallace Company of Houston, Texas, the first small service business to be recognized. This family-owned firm extends its family approach to all of Wallace's 280 skilled and well-trained employees, people who think of themselves as "associates."

The Wallace Company prove that quality is not just for the Fortune 500. This small distributor of industrial goods not only survived the recent rough economic times in Houston, it proved that even in tough times you can still commit to long-term improvements in quality.

In business, success is its own reward. But the men and women of these four firms have given all Americans a standard of excellence—a standard to emulate, a standard to surpass. And they have proven that quality management is not just a strategy. It must be a new style of working, even a new style of thinking. A dedication to quality and excellence is more than good business. It's a way of life, giving something back to society, offering your best to others.

And so, for all of that, you have my admiration—my heartiest congratulations to every single American worker that you represent. And may I say to all of you, thank you and Merry Christmas. And I'm very proud to be here to participate in this ceremony. Thank you all.

Note: The President spoke at 11:23 a.m. in the Grand Hall at the Department of Commerce. In his remarks, he referred to Deputy Secretary of Commerce Thomas J. Murrin and Richard H. Truly, Administrator of the National Aeronautics and Space Administration.

Remarks at a Briefing on the Points of Light Foundation
December 13, 1990

Thank you very, very much. A warm welcome to the White House. Merry Christmas! Happy holidays! We're beginning to get the spirit around here. And may I salute the Attorney General and thank him for his leadership and for his keen interest in the subject that you've been discussing, that I'm about to discuss. Because I am really delighted to be here to help introduce the Points of Light Foundation to this impressive group of nonprofit organizations and State leaders and to announce three initiatives designed to reduce barriers hindering voluntary service efforts.

Since our founding, America has been distinguished among nations for the extraordinary degree to which our people have voluntarily banded together to help those among us in need. And today we're faced with perhaps more pressing needs than at any time in our history—needs that many of your organizations, the organizations represented here today, strive to meet year in and year out.

The needs of our nation are so great that the Points of Light Foundation seeks to make direct and consequential service aimed at serious social problems central to the life and work of every American. To achieve this goal, most institutions will need to adopt a new way of thinking. They must come to see solving these social problems as not just the responsibility of government and nonprofit organizations. Institutions will have to refine their missions to include the engagement of all of their members in community problem-solving.

Of course, service to others is and has been the mission of much of the nonprofit community. But your challenge is to find a way to engage all of your members in service. To help engage all of your members in service, the foundation is urging every institution to appoint Points of Light representatives. And to ensure that every community has multiple places to which individuals and institutions can turn for counsel about how to serve others and where to obtain service, the foundation is calling on a wide variety of institution to become what we call Points of Light centers.

As part of my commitment to advance the Points of Light movement, I'm determined to help remove barriers to service. Now, no obstacle—no obstacle is more chilling than the fear of personal liability and the high cost of insurance to protect against liability. Often programs are curtailed or those contemplated are not undertaken because of the fear of personal liability—outrageous claims, often, about personal liability. And I'm aware of the genuine interest that volunteer leaders in this room have expressed in limiting exposure to the risk of liability and the high cost of insurance.

And therefore, today I am announcing three new initiatives that will bring about much-needed change. First, I call on the nonprofit community to support a private, nongovernmentally controlled national volunteer risk management center, a central place to which volunteer organizations can turn for advice and for assistance. A task force has been formed to report on June 1st on the progress being made toward achieving this objective.

A second major initiative is the promulgation of a model State statute to protect volunteers who work with 501(c) nonprofit organizations and volunteers who work with local and State governments. This statute encourages volunteers to contribute their services for the good of their communities. And at the same time, it provides a reasonable basis for the recovery of damages which may arise from volunteer activity.

We have several distinguished State legislators with us today who are eager to support the effort of volunteers. And I call on you and other State legislators here across America to pass this legislation during the next session.

In addition to these two important initiatives, I will send to the Congress amendments to the Federal Risk Retention Act that will make it easier for organizations to form purchasing groups to obtain liability insurance at affordable rates.

With these three initiatives I am confi-dent that voluntary community service can be encouraged, increased, and strengthened. I've often said that from now on in America any definition of a successful life must include serving others. By working together, we can—I really believe that we can achieve our goal of making community service central to the life and work of every individual and institution, and in the process redefine the meaning of success in America.

I really popped in here to thank you for coming by today, to thank you and your organizations for what you're doing, to encourage the State legislators to take that extra step to guarantee to do their part, as I will try to do mine, to free up the volunteer from needless fear on a personal liability account. And we've got to do it. We've got to be successful. And I'm confident we will.

Thank you all. And I hope you have a wonderful Christmas. Thank you very, very much.

Note: The President spoke at 11:55 p.m. in Room 450 of the Old Executive Office Building. In his remarks, he referred to Attorney General Dick Thornburgh.

Exchange With Reporters Prior to a Meeting With Hostages Released by Iraq
December 13, 1990

The President. But what this man put the world through—I just can't express it. And I think you all have expressed it, coming home, with a clarity that has brought this home to the American people. I'm very anxious to hear from each of you, how you read it, and what you think is happening there.

Q. Should you give something in return for their freedom, Mr. President?

The President. Did I what?

Q. Should you give something in return for their freedom?

The President. Hell, no! Not one thing! You don't reward a kidnaper. You don't reward somebody that has done something that he shouldn't have done in the first place. And that's a fundamental, international——

Q. Do you think Saddam——

The President. I'm not going to take any-more questions, because I want to get into this briefing. But the answer to your question, if you have any doubt about it, is no. [*Laughter*]

Q. Has he defused the tension? Do you think he'll successfully be able to defuse the tension?

The President. What tension?

Q. The tension of the situation.

The President. One way or another we will.

Note: The exchange began at 3:25 p.m. in

the Cabinet Room at the White House. In his remarks, President Bush referred to President Saddam Hussein of Iraq. President Bush met with former hostages Robert *Hanby, Glenn Coleman, Ralph Montgomery, Ernest Alexander, John Cole, Antonio Mireles, and Billy Rosebush, and their families.*

Remarks on Lighting the National Christmas Tree
December 13, 1990

Joe, thank you very much. Thank you, Joe Riley. And thank you, Jane Powell and Willard Scott and Ricky Van Shelton and Ruth Brown and the Army Band, the magnificent University of Wyoming Chorale and our members of the clergy, the California Raisins and, of course, Santa Claus. And may I give a special welcome to the American hostages, just home from Kuwait and Iraq, who are with us here tonight. And my thanks to Secretary Lujan and the Department of the Interior, and a special thanks to the National Coal Association for this year's holiday gift: the 57 beautiful State and territorial trees lining our Pathway of Peace. It's a wonderful 1990's tale of careful stewardship and rebirth, for these trees were grown on mined land that has been reclaimed.

This Christmas tree lighting is always a very special moment. People talk of the magic of the season. Well, what is more magical than the way light dispels the darkness? And I've read that white light is actually made up of all the colors of the rainbow. So, that's what we see in the glow of this tree—red and blue and yellow bulbs mixing together to become something new—one light that represents both unity and diversity. And that's how I like to look at America: All of us, all different, all working together, giving the best of ourselves to make this country the strong, beautiful land that it is.

You know, there are so many emotions that we share tonight. We feel joy thinking of how freedom has at last illuminated the dark corners of Eastern Europe—and democracy coming to most of our own hemisphere. We feel pride thinking of our young men and women standing strong in the harsh, distant deserts and on the waters of the Persian Gulf—and for their courage is the true eternal flame which will never be extinguished. And we think of their parents and their loved ones here at home who miss them very much. And we join them all in praying for their safe return of their soldier or their airman or their marine or their sailor. And let us also add a prayer for those Americans—for many years, but still held hostage against their will in the Middle East.

And here tonight we also feel determination that the bright warmth of this holiday season will stay with us all year and that we will be guided by our inner North Star, making family unity and community service and national pride the center of our lives. We're determined that our nation will become a constellation of hope made up of thousands of separate Points of Light, people helping those in need across our land. People like the more than 100 representatives of daily Points of Light here tonight—individuals like W.W. Johnson, and volunteers for groups like the Higher Achievement Program and the D.C. Central Kitchen and Mary's House. And following the lead of these Points of Light, let all of us echo that beautiful carol "O Little Town of Bethlehem," and like that long-ago Star, let us shine in all "dark streets" and to all people in the "deep and dreamless sleep" of loneliness and despair.

For nearly 70 years Presidents have taken part in this tradition: flipping a switch to send thousands of lights sparkling into the chill night sky. As we gather here, we're doing what generations before us have done: watching our national Christmas tree become a brilliant symbol of hope, of peace, and of compassion for all the world. And so, let us pledge together that we will keep forever bright this shining legacy we celebrate here tonight. God bless the United States of America, and happy holidays to everybody. Merry Christmas! And now I will light the tree.

Note: The President spoke at 5:50 p.m. on the Ellipse during the annual Christmas Pageant of Peace. In his remarks, he referred to Joe Riley, president of the Christmas Pageant of Peace; actress Jane Powell; and entertainers Ricky Van Shelton, Ruth Brown, and the California Raisins. Television weatherman Willard Scott was dressed as Santa Claus.

Statement by Press Secretary Fitzwater on the President's Export Control Initiatives
December 13, 1990

The President has approved a series of export control initiatives that reflect changing strategic concerns of the United States. These include a package of procedural reforms to streamline and clarify export license processing, while enhancing our export controls to stem the spread of missile technology and nuclear, chemical, and biological weapons. The President also decided a number of pending high-performance computer export license applications to Brazil, India, and the People's Republic of China that had raised a number of national security concerns.

Export Licensing Procedures

In his recent announcement of disapproval of the Omnibus Export Amendments Act of 1990, President Bush directed U.S. agencies to institute, by January 1, 1991, new procedures to make dual-use export licensing decisions faster and more predictable, while fully accounting for proliferation and other national security concerns. Details of the new procedures are provided in a separate fact sheet.

The President determined that "American exporters are entitled to prompt review of export license applications submitted to the United States Government," and that there is a "presumption of approval of such applications based on our commitment to an open international trading system and the need to ensure American competitiveness." At the same time, he emphasized that none of these changes "signal a lessening of our determination to weigh cautiously license applications raising potential nonproliferation or broader national security concerns."

Approval of Computer Exports

In addition to these procedural reforms, the President made decisions on a number of long-pending high-performance computer export licenses for Brazil, India, and the People's Republic of China. These exports presented complicated and far-reaching policy issues. The President approved several of the license applications, but because of the potential strategic applications of such computers, he also required the imposition of stringent safeguards to ensure that the computers will be used exclusively for peaceful civilian purposes. The companies affected by these decisions will be notified by the Commerce Department of the actions taken on the licenses.

Enhanced Proliferation Control Initiative

Following on the President's call in his speech before the U.N. General Assembly to "redouble our efforts to stem the spread" of missile technology as well as nuclear, chemical, and biological weapons, an "Enhanced Proliferation Control Initiative" has been adopted. The package, more fully described in an attached fact sheet, includes the following elements:

—Worldwide export controls on 50 chemicals that can be used to manufacture chemical weapons.

—Export licenses for proposed exports that may be related to the develop-

ment of missiles or chemical and biological weapons. (Such licenses are already required for items that may be used for nuclear weapons.)
—Civil and criminal penalties against U.S. citizens who knowingly participate in activities that promote the spread of missile technology and chemical weapons. (Similar penalties already apply in the areas of nuclear and biological weapons.)

The package, which is scheduled for implementation by February 16, will implement portions of Executive Order No. 12735, issued by the President on November 16, 1990, as part of his efforts to combat the spread of chemical and biological weapons.

Note: The Executive order is listed in Appendix E at the end of this volume.

Remarks on the Nomination of the Secretary of Labor and the Persian Gulf Crisis and a Question-and-Answer Session With Reporters
December 14, 1990

The President. I have two brief statements that I'd like to make this afternoon.

First, I have today asked a distinguished public servant and a cherished friend to become Secretary of the Department of Labor. Lynn Martin, a former Congresswoman from Illinois, has agreed to assume the direction of this very important Cabinet office. She and I have known each other for many years. She was an outstanding Member of Congress and an unofficial adviser to me. She has shared with me her wisdom on any number of legislative issues. And I am delighted to have her working at my side on labor matters as we enter the decade of the nineties.

She's a mother who knows the need for child care. She's a professional who understands the business-labor relationship. And as a Congresswoman, she's spent years dealing with the concerns and aspirations of the working Americans from every walk of life. And I know that she will serve with great distinction in our Cabinet.

Lynn was in Illinois this afternoon when I called her, and she will be in Washington on Monday. And I look forward to meeting her here in the White House to talk about her direction of the Department of Labor.

And now I'd like to take up another subject, a second one. On November 30th, in offering direct meetings between the United States and Iraq, I offered to go the extra mile for a peaceful solution to the Gulf question. And I wanted to make clear to Saddam Hussein the absolute determination of the coalition that he comply fully with the Security Council resolutions. Iraqi aggression cannot be rewarded.

And so, I have asked the Secretary of State to be available to go to Baghdad anytime, up to and including January 3d, which is over 5 months after the invasion of Kuwait and only 12 days before the United Nations deadline for withdrawal. That deadline is real.

To show flexibility, I have offered any one of 15 dates for Secretary Baker to go to Baghdad, and the Iraqis have offered only one date. In offering to go the extra mile for peace, however, I did not offer to be a party to Saddam Hussein's manipulation.

Saddam Hussein is not too busy to see on short notice Kurt Waldheim, Willy Brandt, Muhammad Ali, Ted Heath, John Connally, Ramsey Clark, and many, many others on very short notice. It simply is not credible that he cannot, over a 2-week period, make a couple of hours available for the Secretary of State on an issue of this importance—unless, of course, he is seeking to circumvent the United Nations deadline.

Look, I want a peaceful solution to this crisis. But I will not be a party to circumventing or diluting the United Nations deadline which I think offers the very best chance for a peaceful solution. So, I wanted to get out my feeling about these proposed meetings.

Persian Gulf Crisis

Q. What's wrong with the January 12th date that he set? Why would that dilute it unless you're afraid that he might come up with some offer or something?

The President. In the first place, the United Nations resolutions that pertain say that he has to be out of Kuwait. I wish now that I had been a little more explicit in my first announcement of what I mean by mutually convenient dates. But I was not then, and am not now, prepared to have this man manipulate the purpose of the Secretary of State's visit. So, we've made an offer of many, many dates. But remember, the United Nations resolution calls for total withdrawal by this date.

Q. Does your statement today indicate that you would not accept January 5th or 7th or 9th?

The President. Yes, we've offered 15 days, and he ought to get moving and do something reasonable, if he really wants to move for peace.

Q. Mr. President, is there a date at which you would withdraw the offer to meet? The Senators this morning say you're willing to forgo talks now.

The President. We're not going to do them on terms that would appear to the world to be an effort to circumvent the United Nations resolution. I mean, he's got a massive force there, and that force has to be out on the 15th day of January under the United Nations resolutions. So, we'll see, we'll see how it goes.

I would say that we've given so many alternatives here that he ought to accept one of these if he's serious. Now, if it's simply that he's trying to manipulate, that is what I will have no part of.

Q. Are you telling him there is——

The President. I'll be right there, Helen. [Helen Thomas, United Press International]. We've just got to take what they call a follow-on here.

Q. Is there a deadline for him to accept your offer?

The President. No, we're not putting deadlines on it. The 'Aziz meeting is on

hold, I guess. But I say "I guess" because we've made clear to them that it's kind of a home-and-home arrangement here.

Q. You said the deadline is real. Does that mean you think you have carte blanche to start a war after January 15th, or on January 15th?

The President. I'm saying that the United Nations resolution is very clear as it regards January 15th. And I will continue now to work for a peaceful solution.

Q. You do think you can go to war after that, is that right?

The President. What do you mean, "can go to war"?

Q. You can start a war.

The President. I think that the United Nations resolutions should be fully implemented.

Q. Mr. President, when Congress comes back in January, will you ask Congress for specific authority to take offensive action?

The President. We're talking about that, and I'm very pleased with the support we've had in Congress. And I'm very pleased with the level of support from the American people. You see, as these hostages have come home, I think the people have understood—the American people—much more clearly what's at stake. As they've seen the testimony about the brutality to the Kuwaiti people that was so compelling at the United Nations, I think people have said: Wait a minute, this policy deserves support. So, I'm pleased with the support. I think that's being manifested in more support by the Congress.

But I will be talking to the leaders, continuing to consult. What I told the leaders in the Cabinet Room a few weeks ago: If you want to come in here and strongly endorse what I'm doing or endorse the United Nations resolution, I welcome that because I think it would send a very strong, clear signal to the world.

Q. Sir, why are you afraid to go before Congress and consult with them and get their advice and get their approval?

The President. Hey, listen, Sarah [Sarah McClendon, McClendon News], I was consulting with them as recently as this morning—five Members of Congress. And we will continue to consult with them.

Q. That's not 535.

The President. We're doing it all the time. I'm on the phone almost every day to them. We've had leadership meeting after leadership meeting. Oh, listen, I explained this to you in the press room a while back, this same question. Come on.

Q. Yes, sir. You should see my mail.

The President. You ought to see mine.

Q. My mail is against war.

Q. Are you saying that if Saddam Hussein won't meet by January 3d, there simply will be no meeting?

The President. I'm saying that we've given him 15 dates, and he ought to take one of them. I don't like to draw deadlines in the sand here. But there would have to be some compelling reason for me to change it because I don't want to move this up against the United Nations deadline. If you'll read the U.N. resolutions, you'll see that he should be totally out, totally out of Kuwait by January 15th. That's a massive undertaking.

Q. Mr. President, if I may follow up. You're saying maybe January 4th or 5th, but——

The President. I'm not saying that; you're saying that. I've put it as clearly as I can. I hope there's no obfuscation.

Q. Mr. President, what is your thinking today about Saddam Hussein's nuclear and chemical capability? Will international safeguards be enough to control it, or——

The President. I am very much concerned about it. I think that Congress and the American people are getting increasingly concerned about his—it's not just nuclear, which concerns me, but it's other unconventional war capabilities. I'm talking about, for example in this context, chemical weapons that he has used on his own people already. So, yes, I am very concerned about it. And any arrangement that is going to keep the rest of the world happy will have to address itself to this unconventional war capability of Saddam Hussein. Anybody that will take the reckless action he has taken militarily against a neighbor, must be contained in this era when we're all concerned about nuclear proliferation.

So I'm glad you brought it up, because this morning I met with a group of people who were supportive of our policy. And they are emphasizing to me as they go across the country the concern by the American people, on the part of the American people, about his possession of these unconventional weapons and his desire to acquire nuclear weapons. And I told, I believe it was, a press conference with most of you present—I said if I got to err on the side how long—I've addressed myself to the question, how long will it take for him to get weapons—I will err on the cautious side, on the conservative side. And I am concerned that he could acquire weapons in a very short period of time—a weapon in a very short period of time. And that is a factor that is serious as I contemplate how he is compelled to live up to the United Nations resolution.

Minority Scholarships

Q. Mr. President, do you support the Department of Education regulations barring race-based scholarships, or do you plan to rescind them?

The President. We're looking at it right now. The man that had something do with them—I was looking at his background today—is an extraordinarily sensitive, very intelligent person. So, I've asked our staff here to give me a quick readout on that so we can make a determination. But I don't think in this case anybody would accuse the person that promulgated those resolutions of doing it on a racist basis. That's one thing I'm very pleased about.

I've got time for one more, and then I really do have to go.

Persian Gulf Crisis

Q. Mr. President, right now the issue of chemical possession of weapons and nuclear weapons is not part of a United Nations resolution. Will you go back to the U.N. and get that made part of one of the requirements for Saddam Hussein? And will you move on that unilaterally?

The President. I don't think it's unilateral because I think all our coalition partners share my concerns about his possession of unconventional weapons and his attempt to get more. But I don't have plans at this moment to take this to the United Nations. But believe me, it is very much in my thinking as I contemplate what action to take to enforce the United Nations resolutions.

Thank you all, and have a great weekend.

Secretary of Education Nomination

Q. Mr. President, have you got an Education Secretary?

The President. Getting close.

Thank you, Marlin. Well done. Thank you for your assistance, fellows.

Note: President Bush spoke at 2:30 p.m. on the South Lawn of the White House, prior to leaving for Camp David, MD. In his remarks, he referred to President Saddam Hussein and Foreign Minister Tariq 'Aziz of Iraq and Marlin Fitzwater, Press Secretary to the President.

Remarks on Cabinet Nominations and a Question-and-Answer Session With Reporters
December 17, 1990

The President. I have a brief statement, and then I will ask the two with me to make comment, and then I'll be glad to take maybe two questions and turn the meeting over to both of these.

On Friday, I announced that Congresswoman Lynn Martin of Illinois had agreed to take on the job of Secretary of Labor, and I've been visiting with her again about that just now in the Oval Office. And it is very clear to me that she's going to bring extraordinary insight, a lot of talent to this very important Cabinet Department. Working Americans have a friend in Lynn Martin, and she understands the challenges facing our work force. She knows that it's going to take this nation, to remain competitive as we head into the 21st century, a strong, competitive work force. She also knows that only a quality work force will produce quality goods and services, and that means workers that are motivated, highly trained and, most of all, educated.

Education is indeed the centerpiece of the democratic ideal. And the historic meeting that I held in 1989 with the Nation's Governors in Charlottesville set this nation firmly on a course toward education reform. And so, it is especially significant today that I am able to announce that former Governor of Tennessee Lamar Alexander is my nominee to assume the helm at the Department of Education.

Lamar, if you will remember, was at the forefront of the movement to restructure our nation's schools. When he was chairman of the National Governors' Association, he was instrumental in bringing education reform to the very top of the agenda. No Governor in the country is so clearly identified with the imperative to improve education in America. And as I said in Charlottesville, education is our most enduring legacy, vital to everything we are and can become. And much of what went on in Charlottesville was started a couple of years earlier by Lamar Alexander.

You know, Lamar, that working with your former colleagues, we have agreed on six very ambitious national goals for American education. And our mission is clear, and I look forward to your leadership to help us achieve these goals by the year 2000. I am delighted and grateful to both of you for undertaking these two very important assignments.

Lynn, do you want to say a word?

Representative Martin. Thank you, Mr. President. American men and women are the finest in the world. They know we're not just facing a changing decade but a century to come. I look forward to making sure that the future for the American worker is even brighter; that with common sense and compassion and the competence that is part of the Bush administration, that we will make sure the 1990's are a time to be remembered as a pinnacle for chance and opportunity for the men and women who compose the working force for America.

And I look forward to working with Lamar Alexander. His education and that change are part of what the future holds. If I do my job it means that somewhere, sometime, someone's life will be better, someone will have a better chance. And that's really what government is supposed to be about.

And for a moment, perhaps because it's the Christmas season and a holiday season for everyone, I'd like to give a special thanks not just, of course, to the President but to his White House staff, who's been incredibly cooperative, and to two Democratic Senators from my home State of Illinois, who have gone well beyond what they've ever had to say or do to be extraordinarily gracious. And perhaps that says what's really right about our political system—that when it comes time to make sure that a future is better, that working together we can make it happen. Thank you very much.

The President. Lamar?

Governor Alexander. Mr. President, and Lynn. Mr. President, I remember the first thing you did during your inauguration week, because I was sitting right over here: you met with teachers. And I remember you said to them a little story about Sam Houston, that he wrote once that the most important contribution he ever made in life was the year he spent teaching in Maryville, Tennessee. My home is Maryville, Tennessee, and my parents were teachers. When I was a Governor I discovered that our State's major need was better schools, colleges, and universities. For the last 3 years, I've had the privilege of being president of a very good State university.

So, Mr. President, you've asked me to do something that I know you value and I've learned to value very, very much. The best example I can give of that is the big new Saturn plant in Tennessee. Families have moved there from all over America to learn how to try to build an American car that can compete with Japanese and European cars. And the UAW foreman there tells me that after they found out what it takes to do that, that they asked two questions. The second question is: Where can I get good schools for our children? And the first question is: Where can I go back to school?

If we're going to have the kind of America that we want to have—if we're going to understand our democracy, going to be competitive, if we're going to keep our good jobs—we're going to have to answer those questions: Where can we find better schools for our children and—something we often miss that Lynn brought up—where can working men and women in America go back to school themselves, so we can retrain today's work force?

I think we're fortunate to have a President who, in the midst of trying to stay one step ahead of this busy, dangerous world, is willing to try to be an education President. I think my job is to understand his goals, develop a plan, and to help him do that. And I appreciate and am grateful for the chance to do that.

Q. Mr. President?

The President. Thank you very much. May I introduce to you Mrs. Alexander, who's with us, came up from Tennessee today also. Some of you may remember her from the Governor's days. But we're just delighted you're with us.

Yes, Helen [Helen Thomas, United Press International]?

Persian Gulf Crisis

Q. Mr. President, the Iraqis are saying that only they have the right to call the shots on dates for talks. And Secretary Baker seems more hopeful. What's your stand today?

The President. Mine has not changed since yesterday. And I spelled out my position as clearly as I possibly can. So, I hope these talks will take place. But I saw the statements out of Iraq. Those statements concern me far less than the statements I see that there is no flexibility on Saddam Hussein's part about what he calls Province 19, which flies directly in the face of the United Nations action. That's the substance of all this, and that's what concerns me.

Q. Do you think we're closer to hostilities?

The President. I hope not. I certainly hope not.

Yes, Terry [Terence Hunt, Associated Press], and then Jim [James A. Miklaszewski, NBC News]. Then I'm going.

Q. Is there any flexibility in your insistence on that January 3d deadline for getting talks going, or if it doesn't happen by then are you just going to throw in the towel and wait until the 15th?

The President. Let me say, Terry, I think people understand that when you give a person 15 dates, a man who's been meeting on 20 minutes' notice with a wide group of leaders from all over the world and characters from all over the world, that we've been very flexible on this. And so, I just would leave it calmly where it sits right now, without speculating on what I might or might not do. The U.N. resolutions are clear. He must be out of Kuwait—that means entirely—by January 15th. It's very clear to the world that that's what the objective is. So, if you try to keep—for reasons of his own—moving down towards that deadline, it just seems obvious to the world what he's doing.

Q. Actually, you sound a little more flexible today than you did on Friday. You said you don't care to speculate——

The President. I'm just in a calmer mood today. [*Laughter*] Calm.

Q. Why?

The President. Monday morning, Monday morning. Monday morning. Got a big day out there, and I just didn't want to get too fired up here this early in the morning. [*Laughter*]

Q. Well, what difference, Mr. President— if it could mean averting armed conflict— what difference does 9 days make? The difference between the 3d and the 12th?

The President. Listen, if I thought that meeting on the 14th would permit him to comply fully with the United Nations resolutions, I'd be very flexible. But that's not possible.

Q. Well, what will Mr. Baker do? Is he going to negotiate? Do you want him in there early enough so that he can persuade a man who this morning said that Kuwait is part of Iraq and that is unflinching?

The President. Well, this is the problem, Ann [Ann Compton, ABC News]. I mean, he keeps making these statements that fly directly in the face of the international sanctions taken by the world, international position taken by the United Nations Security Council. So, the purpose of the talks is,

a lot of people that think they understand him don't feel that he believes we are serious. They don't feel that he thinks we will use force. Some tell me as recently as yesterday—one of the great leaders on that part of the world told me that he feels that Saddam Hussein simply does not understand the debate in this country. He thinks it means that our country is divided and that we cannot go forward to do our part in implementing the U.N. resolutions. And he's just as wrong as he can be.

So, my thought was, if a talk with 'Aziz, a talk with Baghdad would help make that clear, so much the better. That was the purpose. And if there's talks, that will be the purpose. It will not be to make concession. We've got an opportunity for a new world order, but that opportunity will be lost if an aggressor gets one single concession. It will be, and that's my view; it is the view of the coalition partners. But I still feel it is important that the man understand that we are serious about this.

Yes? Then I got to go.

Q. Mr. President, given what you just said and what Saddam said this morning once again about Province 19, may we know what you're thinking now, then, about January 15th?

The President. No. You just wait and see.

Q. At midnight January 15th? Are you more driven now to see action at that point?

The President. Well, I think at midnight, if he's not totally out of Kuwait, the U.N. sanctions must be fulfilled. So, let's see. I'm still hopeful there's a peaceful solution to this problem.

Well, thank you for your interest in labor and education. [*Laughter*] And I will now turn this—no, no more questions. No, no, no, I've been too accessible here. We're going into a Christmas mode here where I won't be doing as much of this kind of work.

Q. Sir, just something on——

Q. Just on the two nominees.

The President. No, I can't do it. I just can't do it. Can't do it.

Note: President Bush spoke at 9:30 a.m. in the Briefing Room at the White House. In his remarks, he referred to President Saddam Hussein and Foreign Minister Tariq 'Aziz of Iraq.

Remarks and a Question-and-Answer Session With Reporters Following Discussions With Allies on the Persian Gulf Crisis
December 17, 1990

The President. May I first thank the Ambassadors who are standing here at my side for being with us today. And I have a brief statement.

What you see here is living proof that the international coalition arrayed against Saddam's aggression remains deep and wide. We're talking now about some 28 countries that have committed their forces of one kind or another to this extraordinarily historic effort. Every country represented agrees that the 12 Security Council resolutions that are now on the books make clear what is required: Iraq's complete, immediate, and unconditional withdrawal from Kuwait. These same countries—and there are more than two dozen represented here today, I think maybe all 28 of us—are contributing over 200,000 individuals to the military effort against Iraq. Tens of thousands more are on their way. As has been the case from August 2d on, it is not simply the United States against Iraq; it is really Iraq against the world.

And again, none of us wants war, but none of us is prepared to accept a partial solution. It is for this reason that we all welcome Security Council Resolution 678 and its authorization that all necessary means be used after January 15th to bring about Iraq's full compliance with all that the United Nations has demanded.

Let me just add that I also used this occasion inside to brief our coalition partners on our efforts to meet directly with Iraqi officials. And thus far, Iraq's behavior underscores what I think is its lack of interest in a peaceful settlement of this crisis. For our part, we remain open to having these meetings if mutually acceptable dates can be agreed upon. And if meetings are held, I want to reiterate publicly what I said inside: namely, that what we want to do is impress upon Iraq the consequences of its aggression and the need for all Iraqi forces to leave every square inch of Kuwait. There can and will be no negotiations for concessions and no rewards for aggression.

So, thank you all very much for joining me here today. And I am glad to have had this opportunity not only to ask you to convey my respects to the leaders of state and government represented here but to tell them, please, that the United States remains steadfast and will remain steadfast in its determination to see every single United Nations resolution on this subject fulfilled without concession, without yielding 1 single inch.

Thank you all very much for coming.

Q. Mr. President, are you now open to a date beyond January 3d, sir?

The President. I've made my position very clear on that. We've given them 15 dates. He can meet on 15 minutes' notice with various people from around the world, so the matter stands right when I last talked to you about it.

Q. Mr. President, I know it's off the topic, but do you want the Education Department to rescind the——

Q. Mr. President, would you agree to the United Nations becoming involved in trying to break the impasse on the—would you agree to the United Nations getting involved, perhaps Secretary-General Perez de Cuellar?

The President. He has tried very hard, and he's working——

Q. He's already trying?

The President. Yes, he has. And he tried within the mandates of the United Nations. That is his mandate, those resolutions. And he is not about to vary from that. I talked to him about that in Paris. I think we all owe him a vote of thanks for having tried very,

very hard to convince Saddam Hussein that he ought to withdraw.

Q. I know it's off the topic, Mr. President, but would you like to see the Education Department rescind its ruling on minority scholarship?

The President. That is off the topic. I won't take the question.

Q. If Hussein does not understand, as you say—Hussein does not understand the threat against him, why are you avoiding making a specific military threat against him to make it clear that that is the choice——

The President. I just simply refer him to the United Nations Security Council resolution. And he should be interpreting that, and he ought to look at the movement of force, and he ought to draw the conclusion that he ought to get out without concession.

Q. Why shouldn't he see it as ambiguous if you won't threaten to use the military force you have arrayed?

The President. Because I'm not in a threatening mode. I don't think any of us are. We are in a determined mode, a mode that he should get out without concession. And this is the will of the world body; this is the will of the entire world, if you will, against this man. And he's got to understand it, so we're going to keep on repeating it: No concession. No negotiation for 1 inch of territory. And, Mr. Saddam Hussein, simply do what the world is calling upon you to do: Get out. We have to keep repeating it. Some people are a little slow to get the word. And we're going to just keep saying it over and over again.

Q. Well, what happens on the 15th if there have been no negotiations and if he's still there?

The President. The United Nations says use—I forget the exact wording—but whatever it takes to fulfill our resolutions.

Q. Mr. President, what do the Ambassadors in the countries who are so close to Iraq—two of them are standing right beside you, and they know a lot about that country—what do they tell you it's going to take to make him understand what you're saying?

The President. I think they are totally in accord with what I've said here. They are totally in accord with the United Nations

resolutions, and they are as determined as we are to see these United Nations resolutions fulfilled to the tee.

Q. But you have been saying this over and over and over. And it's as if he's deaf or as if he doesn't see CNN [Cable News Network]. He doesn't seem to——

The President. I agree with your assessment.

Q. But what I want to know is what do you think it will take to move it from here?

The President. I don't know. I don't know.

Q. Shooting?

The President. I would just continue down this path. I think at some point he will realize that this force, which is overwhelming, that is now being arrayed against him would be devastating; and let's hope that that brings the message home to him. That's what the United Nations stated should happen—that he ought to get out or all available means should be used. And one person cannot be rewarded for brutal aggression.

And I read this Amnesty International report—it's not released yet, it will be in a couple of days—and I hope that everybody standing out there and everybody standing here and everybody that maybe has less than the passionate interest in this satisfactory resolution to this question than I do will read that report. Because right this very minute, we're seeing a brutality in Kuwait that is unacceptable, unconscionable; and I am concerned about it. And I want to see the United Nations resolutions fulfilled right on schedule.

Q. Mr. President, how about having Baker and 'Aziz meet in a third country to break the stalemate of these talks? Is that a possibility?

The President. I hadn't thought about that; but if it would do any good, if that would help get the message to him that he has got to leave without condition, I certainly wouldn't oppose that. But what I'm not going to do is shove these meetings right up against the United Nations deadline and, thus, have the adverse effect of undermining the total fulfillment of the resolutions.

Q. The Iraqi Information Minister

seemed to suggest Saturday that if you set another date for 'Aziz to come here, that Saddam would respond with a date more acceptable to you for Baker to go to Baghdad.

The President. I think the guy's a little out of touch. We had the date set for 'Aziz. I don't know what he's talking about. I can't respond to each one of these kind of counterploys coming out of Baghdad.

Yes? This is the last one.

Q. Have the Ambassadors been able to consult with you? Did they each have a chance to speak their mind?

The President. I kind of dominated today, I'm afraid—[*laughter*]—and was a little intolerant—not of contrary opinion, because I think we're all together, but it was a time question. But let me say this: As I look around this staircase here and standing next to me at this level, I have talked to so many of their Presidents or monarchs or whatever that I feel in very close touch. And I did say that if anybody wanted to speak up in difference, why, I certainly would welcome that. But because of the time, the Ambassador from Kuwait, who also happens to be the dean of this group in terms of service,

did speak. But clearly, if somebody wants to take exception to something I've said, why, they wouldn't be alone in this country; and they'd be welcome to have their say. But I am satisfied that the coalition has never been more determined and never been firmer in what it is that we must do.

And it is so clear that—see, the optimistic side is when we prevail we have the promise of a new world order. You have a vitalized United Nations, the peacekeeping function of which, up until now, has been rather dismal, as you look over the years; and now there's a real chance. But the chance doesn't exist if we fail. So, we've got to prevail, and we will. And I think I can confidently speak for all the countries represented here. If they felt differently, I don't expect they'd be here.

Thank you all very much.

Note:President Bush spoke at 2:38 p.m. in the Rose Garden at the White House. In his remarks, he referred to President Saddam Hussein, Foreign Minister Tariq 'Aziz, and Information Minister Latif Nusayyif Jasim of Iraq; Secretary of State James A. Baker III; and Ambassador Saud Nasir Al-Sabah of Kuwait.

Message on the Observance of Christmas
December 18, 1990

At Christmas, people of every age and every walk of life celebrate with a profound sense of wonder, joy, and gratitude our Savior's birth in Bethlehem. Like the shepherds called from nearby fields and the Magi who journeyed from distant lands to welcome the Christ Child, we are drawn to this miraculous event in history.

Born in a stable and greeted by a handful of faithful and obedient men, Christ came to assume the role of a shepherd, thus fulfilling the words of the prophet Isaiah: "He shall feed His flock like a shepherd: He shall gather the lambs with His arm and carry them in His bosom."

Christ's brief time on Earth was devoted to tending the physical and spiritual needs

of His flock: healing the sick, feeding the hungry, and illuminating the path to eternal salvation. His Incarnation radically altered the course of human history by challenging men and women to live according to the will of our just and merciful Father in Heaven. Today, Christ's message of hope and redemption—first delivered on that holy night in the City of David—continues to bring peace and joy to millions of people around the world.

As we give and receive the goodwill of Christ during this holy season, let us be mindful of the true meaning of His life on earth and especially of His greatest commandment: to love God with all our heart and to love our neighbor as ourself. Events during the past year have given us a renewed sense of hope, yet in some parts of the world, peace remains an elusive blessing this Christmas. Even in some of our own cities, poverty, despair, and drug-related violence prevent families and individuals from sharing in the promise of this season. Therefore, let us strive, by following Christ's example in word and deed, to make peace on Earth a reality for all of God's children.

Barbara joins me in wishing all of our fellow Americans a Merry Christmas. May this festive and holy season be filled with the warmth of family and friends and with the deep joy of knowing God's love for mankind through the gift of His Son. God bless you.

GEORGE BUSH

The President's News Conference With Regional Reporters
December 18, 1990

The President. Let me just make a quick comment, and then I'll be glad to take some questions. But I want to just comment once again on the situation in the Gulf, because you see, ever since August 2d, the world community has been virtually united in its condemnation and its rejection of Iraqi aggression.

I've been talking about the Security Council resolutions, but the General Assembly of the United Nations, with only one vote against it—Iraq—joined in condemning what has gone on by Saddam Hussein. And I think that's a very significant point because those who were saying, "Well, it's only the Security Council," now have to recognize that what we've been saying all along is true: that it is not Saddam Hussein and the Arab world against the United States but indeed it is Saddam Hussein against the rest of the world.

And so, I mention this because we're coming down towards this U.N.-mandated deadline. I still want to see a peaceful solution to this question. You keep hearing about new initiatives—President Bendjedid of Algeria—but I gather that that has gone about as far as those initiatives that others have undertaken—Bendjedid, good credentials on all sides of this dispute, but unable to talk sense to Iraq's dictator.

So, I would just simply say that we will keep trying to find an answer. It cannot be an answer of concession. It cannot be an answer where Saddam Hussein is rewarded with one single concession, because that would fly right in the face of the rejuvenated United Nations peacekeeping effort, and it simply is unacceptable, not just to us but to the rest of our coalition partners. And you look at what the EC said yesterday—or today I guess it was—regarding the visit of Tariq 'Aziz, when they said there would be no point his coming to see them unless the visits with the United States have taken place—it shows a real solidarity because the temptation might have been the other way.

So, I think the coalition's holding. We are determined, more determined than ever. Yesterday I had a meeting with 27, I believe it was—the Ambassadors from other countries, the 28 standing together in the Gulf—represented a show of solidarity that I think was read loud and clear halfway around the world.

So, that's where we are. And there is no news to report on the proposed visit of the Secretary of State to Baghdad or, indeed, of the Foreign Minister, Tariq 'Aziz, coming here.

So, with no further ado, I'd be glad to take questions on any subjects. Let me get these first few—yes?

Persian Gulf Crisis

Q. Mr. President, are you more optimistic or less optimistic at this point about the possibilities of going to war compared to when you made the proposal to send Mr. Baker to Iraq?

The President. Well, if I had to quantify my degrees of optimism or pessimism, I'd say it's about in the same mode as when it was there. I do not believe that Tariq 'Aziz, one, has digested what he is up against in terms of this coalition force, and secondly, I think he basically is, at best, uncertain as to whether this force will be used against him. And so, what I think is essential to get to peaceful resolution is that he realizes that he simply cannot prevail. So, I guess I'm about where I was a couple of weeks ago when I made that proposal.

Q. Mr. President, I'd like to ask you a question that one of our readers of the Detroit Free Press suggested. I ask you—and it's from an 18-year-old from Birmingham, Michigan. And his question is: If the war in the Gulf escalates, how will you get the American people to support the war? And it's a common theme of our readers' questions, and it seems to ask whether you think the American public is as willing to accept war as an option as your policies seem to be?

The President. I don't want war as an option; I want peace as an option. Secondly, I think some of those questions stem from the fact that some believe this will be another Vietnam. And the agony of Vietnam is still with us. People remember a protracted war. They remember a war where individuals were asked to fight with one hand tied behind their back, in essence. This will not be, in my view, that kind of a confrontation.

And so, I think that if the United States had to do its part to implement the United Nations resolutions, I believe the country would support that. But I don't think that support would last if it were a long, drawn-out conflagration. I think support would erode, as it did in the Vietnam conquest—I mean, conflict.

But I can understand why some young kid would ask that question. I mean, they keep hearing of this prolongation and that there would be stalemate and all of this kind of thing. I don't believe that. And one of the reasons that I moved this additional force, or had it moved, was because every individual life is precious; and if there had to be some confrontation—military—I would want to be able to assure the parents and the families there is enough force there to minimize the risk to every single American kid and coalition kid—the Desert Rats,

the French Legions, and the Arabs—that we'll be fighting side by side with.

Minority Scholarships

Q. Mr. President, what prompted the administration's change of thinking—some might less kindly say flip-flop—on the question of whether financial aid can be targeted to minorities? And I have a brief follow-up, if I may.

The President. I don't think there was any flip-flop on it. There was a ruling made by a man of great integrity in the Department of Education. And when we heard about it here, I expressed a certain concern, asked that the policy be reviewed. And indeed, today the Department issued a policy statement that I think has Mr. Williams [Assistant Secretary of Education for Civil Rights], who was the promulgator of the original regulation ruling, happy. And yet it does do what I want to see, and that is to continue these minority scholarships as best we can.

I met with a group of editors earlier on today, and the question comes up, well, will there be a legal test? I'm not a lawyer, and I don't know how the courts will rule. Eventually they will rule on it. But as for now, we've worked the regulation so that we can continue to have these kinds of scholarships. I've long been committed to them; I've long been committed to affirmative action. And so, I hope the ruling, which some of it is quite technical, will accomplish that end. But I would like to think that the matter can be resolved with finality this way, but I don't think that is what we've done. I think there will probably be some court challenges to this.

You wanted a followup?

Q. Well, yes, just briefly. I think there is some question how a decision of that magnitude in the civil rights arena could have been made without the knowledge of the White House.

The President. Well, it was made without the knowledge of the White House, and I would simply refer you to Mr. Williams, who is a very able attorney over there in the Education Department. I think he explained that in his press conference.

Persian Gulf Crisis

Q. I'd like to ask you about the moral consistency of the U.S. policy on Iraq. During the 1980's, Iraq waged a war of brutal aggression against a different neighbor, Iran. It also used chemical weapons against Iranians and against its own Kurdish population. It also worked on its nuclear program. But rather than go to war against Iraq in that case, the United States took Iraq's side. In the case of the chemical weapons, the Reagan and then the Bush administrations opposed all efforts to impose sanctions in protest against the use of chemical weapons. And in the nuclear area, the United States condemned Israel for setting back Iraq's nuclear program. So, my question is: Is it hypocritical now to threaten war over conduct by the same regime when the similar conduct was condoned or even supported against different adversaries in the recent past?

The President. No, I don't think it's hypocritical whatsoever. Here you have the United Nations moving in concert. You have an unprecedented use of the peacekeeping function of the United Nations. And I was very proud that the United States was a leading component in what the Security Council did. And it is true that our administration and others previously tried to work with Iraq. But this brutal aggression—what they did here is such a clear violation of international law that the entire world was united in opposition to it. So, if there was a mistake made in trying to move them along a more civilized path by having contacts as we did, fine. But this kind of revisionistic view that that makes what's happening today wrong—I'm sorry, I don't agree with it at all. And I think we're on the right path. I think the whole world is united against this. And clearly, I'd like to have been clairvoyant so I could have seen that the man was lying when he said he wasn't going to invade Kuwait—which he did say. And he told Hosni Mubarak [President of Egypt] this, for example. But it wasn't quite that clear at the time.

Economic Stimulants

Q. Mr. President, a question of the economy. You yourself have mentioned that you would support some economic stimulants, perhaps. And I'm wondering if in the new year you're going to propose any tax cuts—capital gains, in particular—or perhaps a cut in the payroll taxes for Social Security.

The President. Well, I haven't changed my view on the fact that capital gains would be stimulative and not costly to the taxpayer. I'm hit regularly on the fact that this is a tax break for the rich. I don't believe that. But the problem you have on this is that we have under this budget agreement rigid caps, and we have to score capital gains under existing law, the way I think it's the CBO [Congressional Budget Office] or the joint committee or somebody says it has to be scored. So, we're talking about a $20 billion hit.

What I'd love to think is that we could change the way we score it to a more realistic, I would say, realistic view—the Treasury's view, for example, that shows this would lift people up, would encourage investment, and would not be a revenue loss. So, I haven't given up on my philosophical commitment to the idea that capital gains would stimulate growth. And when you have a slow or certainly a slowed-down economy, in some areas recessional, it would be good.

But we're faced with this practical problem as to what we can do not just on capital gains but on other stimulants that cost money. There is, remember, an enormous stimulant, one that I'm not very happy about; and that is about a $300 billion Federal deficit. So, I don't know where we're going to come down on our State of the Union Message, but in concept of growth and opportunity, I can guarantee you the emphasis is going to be on that. And if I can find a way to change this stultified thinking that this is deficit-creating, the capital gains cut, why, then I'd be all for that.

So, we're looking at it. I don't know where we're going to come out on it.

Q. Are you sympathetic to the idea of cutting the Social Security payroll tax at all?

The President. Well, if I can figure out a way to pay for it. One of the good things about the deficit agreement that was very controversial and for which I got a reasonable amount of criticism, I'd say, is that you have to pay for these things. And whether the same argument can be made—I haven't seen the dynamic argument made on that that I have on capital gains. So, I just don't know the answer to that one. If the offsets were there, you might. I'm a little worried—I'll be honest with you—having laid this tax question down for a while, to reopen many, many aspects of it. I've tried to draw the exception because I feel so strongly on the capital gains account.

Persian Gulf Crisis

Q. Mr. President, Saddam Hussein knows and you know that his best shot at cracking the cohesion of the coalition raid against him is to draw Israel into it, by direct attack or otherwise. General Scowcroft [Assistant to the President for National Security Affairs] indicated that there have been specific discussions with the Israelis and the coalition partners about that contingency. Can you tell us whether there's been any assurance or commitment either by the Israelis or our coalition partners that they would not crack apart if that were to happen?

The President. If——

Q. If he attacked Israel.

The President. If he attacked Israel? I'm convinced the coalition would not fall apart. I can't give you the specifics on it, but I'm absolutely convinced of it. And you can assume the way I've answered the question that we've inquired about that.

Secondly, Israel has had what I would call a low profile position in all of this, for which I salute them. It is not easy. Their security, they feel, could well be at stake from some radical act by Saddam Hussein. But I have no argument with Mr. Shamir [Prime Minister of Israel] over the way the Israelis have conducted themselves, nor do I think do the coalition partners on that particular point, regardless of what their historic relationship with Israel may have been.

Reduction of U.S. Military Forces

Q. Mr. President, as the cold war began to wind down, first in Congress and then in your own administration, there was talk of a "peace dividend." And in fact, on the very day that Saddam Hussein invaded Iraq [Kuwait], you gave a speech in which you proposed a major shift in the structure of the American military, a 25-percent drawdown over the next 5 years. With the way the force has been stretched in Operation Desert Shield, are you rethinking that? As this ends, are you going to have to take another look at whether that big a reduction in our active-duty military force is actually possible in a post-cold-war world?

The President. I believe we will be able to live with the reductions—and they were substantial—that have been worked out in the last budget agreement. And I think the fact that we have been able to move this much force this dramatically is, of its own weight, a marvelous thing. But as we restructure the defense and as defense has taken substantial hits—not, I would argue, in a peace dividend mode but more of a fiscal mode—I think I will be able to represent to the American people that we will still have this ability to rapidly deploy the best trained forces in the world.

Q. If I could follow up: If this crisis had occurred 5 years from now, when this drawdown that's been agreed on had already been largely completed, would your options have been as unlimited as they are now?

The President. Good question, and I'm not sure I can answer it. But if the question is would we have been able to deploy this much force this rapidly, I think the answer is yes. I'd want to hedge just a little bit, but I think it is yes. General Scowcroft is shaking me off a little—[*laughter*]—because we were talking about this with General Powell [Chairman of the Joint Chiefs of Staff] and Dick Cheney [Secretary of Defense]. But this is not the average disturbance, you might say, that calls for the average deployment of force. This is pushing it up to the edge of the envelope. But I think the answer is yes. I wish I could get back to you to be sure I'm not misleading you, but I felt comfortable when we had the briefing from Cheney and Powell, I think it was yesterday, on this question.

Persian Gulf Crisis

Q. Will the forces that have been taken out of Germany and deployed to the Gulf be sent back to Europe once this crisis——

The President. I'm not sure of the answer

to that question. I can't answer it. I don't know. But one thing I will say about them is: The earliest day possible, I would like to have every single American soldier out of the Gulf—for a lot of reasons. In the first place, I think the status quo ante, the return to where we were before Saddam invaded his neighbor, is unacceptable because I think you're going to see a cry for stability and order there, security and stability that cannot be met simply by return to the preinvasion borders or the status quo there. So, I think you're going to have to have some kind of peacekeeping force, and I think we're going to have to cope with the question this gentleman raised of increased nuclear capability today, beyond what it was several years ago. And so, it won't be just the way it was before.

But I would like to think it would be with some international peacekeeping force, because I think there's a problem if U.S. forces remain on the ground in the Gulf for some time. I don't feel that way about naval forces. We've been there for a long time. We will continue to stay there for a long time. We will continue to stay there, our mission being to protect freedom of passage through the Straits of Hormuz. And we have a history there of helping keep the peace and of keeping the straits open. So, I would not see any change in that force. But on whether these forces return to Germany, I think we'll have some—obviously, it might be different people, but we're going to have some big discussion over levels in post-Iraq forces in Europe. We're discussing that anyway right now.

Make it more four more—one, two, three, four. No, you regulars, no. [*Laughter*] One, two, three, four.

Q. Mr. President, are you prepared to initiate offensive action against Iraq without a declaration of war from Congress?

The President. I'm having the darnedest consultations with Congress you've ever seen. I was very pleased when the leaders at the last meeting told me that it was the best, in terms of consultations, they'd ever had. And I'll continue to do that. And I will look at—I hope I don't have to cross that bridge because I want a peaceful solution to this question. But there are so many contingencies that it's very difficult to answer that

question in one definitive way, and I'm not going to try.

Q. An article in the recent issue of Time magazine, Mr. President, says that no one in your Cabinet has a child serving in Saudi Arabia and that a disproportionate number of U.S. troops stationed on the front line hail from minorities and the working class. Is this accurate? And if it is, why does this condition exist?

The President. I don't know about the proliferation of my Cabinet and where their children are, but I don't have any service-aged kids myself. But I don't think this concept that this is a discriminatory army, or an army that is discriminating and thus sending more blacks to their fate—or minorities, Hispanics or something—is proper. I've heard it, and I reject it. And the reason I reject it is we have an all-volunteer army. We have great opportunity in this army. We have the finest kids: the best trained; the best motivated; the high achievers, not the low achievers. And so, this argument that there's some kind of racism, which I think your question implies, in this deployment—I reject it out of its—the whole cloth. It is simply not true. And if you don't believe me, believe Colin Powell. And he has pretty good credentials in this field—outstanding credentials. So, I want to gun it down just as hard as I possibly can. And I don't know about my Cabinet. I'm sorry, I can't answer that. I just don't know where their kids are.

Q. Mr. President, you've spoken of——

The President. This is an all-volunteer army; they're not draft dodging. Remember Vietnam and the allegation, which I think had a lot of truth to it. But the kid that got disproportionately there was the guy that couldn't get the exemption and came out of kind of the lower rungs of society. This is different, totally different.

And we ought to get you figures on this, because it is very, very important as to how high of quality this army is. And you'll read about one or two that say, "Well, I didn't sign up to do this; I signed up because I thought I could get a free education." He gets on the Phil Donahue show—[*laughter*]—a big hero. [*Laughter*] But that's the tiny fraction of these kids that are over there. The morale is good, and they're motivated, and they're well educated, and they're dedicated, and—if you'll excuse an old-fashioned reference—they're patriotic. And so, it isn't some cop-out armed services that they're now getting caught up in something that they were unaware of.

I'm glad we got that one because I really feel strongly on that question.

Q. You've spoken of this crisis as being not the U.S. against Iraq but, really, the world against Iraq.

The President. Yes.

Q. And I'm wondering then why the talks with Baghdad aren't being conducted by the Secretary-General of the U.N. [Javier Perez de Cuellar de la Guerra] but rather by the American Secretary of State.

The President. Good question. And the answer is the Secretary-General, as you may recall, tried; and he went to Baghdad—or I think it was in Baghdad; maybe it was in Amman. But he went there, and he went to talk within his mandate. And his mandate were the U.N. resolutions. This is before 678, or whatever the last one was. So, he has tried hard, and I salute him for that. And he would be willing—I talked to him about this in Paris—while I'm up for your question—and when we were over there for the CSCE meeting. And I asked him—he's an old friend of mine. He and I were U.N. Ambassadors at the same time. And I said, "Javier, do you think it would be worth trying this again? We're all trying for the extra step." He said, "If I felt we could make some progress within my mandate, I certainly would try again."

But it's not that people haven't tried. I just touched on it in passing about [President] Chadli Bendjedid of Algeria. You heard over and over again various people calling, as King Hussein of Jordan did, for an Arab solution. You had Tariq 'Aziz go to Moscow to talk. It isn't though people haven't tried. It is simply that as recently as today, I think it was, the last wire clip I saw, Saddam Hussein is still referring to a nation that is a member of the Arab League and a member of the United Nations as Province 19 of Kuwait [Iraq]. And therein lies the difficulty. It isn't that people haven't tried to go the extra step. But I have to give the U.N. credit for having—the

Secretary-General for really having tried on this one. And I'm sure he's quietly tried, as well as through this public mission that he undertook.

Q. What makes you think Mr. Baker will have any more luck?

The President. I'm not sure he will. I'm not sure he will. But if he can do what I referred to in the beginning, if he can convince Saddam Hussein of the truth, it will be worth the effort. Because as I've said, it's not a negotiation session, or it's certainly not a concession session. We're not going there to concede 1 single inch. Because if you do that—and you want to put it in theoretical terms—you have diminished instantly the new peacekeeping function of the United Nations, and the coalition is demoralized and falls apart. And that will not happen.

So, what he's going to do is go there and make this very clear: that there can be no concession, that the world is united, and that this force which is overwhelming is there for purpose. And I still hope that gets the message through to Saddam Hussein.

Who had the last one? Rita [Rita Beamish, Associated Press]?

Minority Scholarships

Q. Mr. President, you mentioned on the civil rights—or the minority scholarship issue the possibility of court challenges. What is your position on whether or not scholarships should be earmarked for minorities in general? And would you foresee some fine-tuning of the current new policy, which I believe now bans Federal money earmarked for minorities but not private funds?

The President. Well, as Mr. Williams pointed out, there is a legal question. My own view has been all along, in my own life and everything else, committed to this concept of minority scholarships. Clearly, it should be valid privately, and indeed, the support that we give to the historically black colleges—maybe someday will get challenged. I hope it isn't, and I hope it would sustain the challenge. Clearly, the support that we give to these institutions privately should be beyond challenge.

But I don't know the answer to your

question as to how that will work out in the courts. I don't know. We had a fascinating, almost philosophical, discussion at lunch with some of the most prominent black editors and publishers in this country, and I got into a very lively discussion on this whole question of philosophy. And what happens to some kid from one minority group if the scholarships are all allocated to one and not to another? And I don't know that answer because I'm not a lawyer.

What I do know is that I am for affirmative action and I am for trying to help the groups that have been the most disadvantaged through scholarships. And that's what I think has been resolved in the Department of Education, at least in the foreseeable future. And I hope it stands. But I don't want to mislead people in the country by suggesting that this may not receive a challenge, and then the courts are going to have to make that determination. And then, if somebody can legislatively correct it fairly, why, I'd be open for that. But I don't want to buy into a court-solution question that might happen way down the road.

But I would recommend that everybody take a look at the policy statement that just came out a little bit earlier, and I think it will define where this stands now and for how long it will continue.

Last one. Yes?

Persian Gulf Crisis

Q. Mr. President, you said the Persian Gulf will not turn into another Vietnam.

The President. Absolutely.

Q. Could you give us some projection on how long you believe the conflict would last, as far as weeks, months, years?

The President. No, you guys want to get me into talking about conflict all the time, and I understand it, and as we go down towards the 15th it will probably intensify. But I want to still talk about hoping that we can get a peaceful resolution to this question. But that means making Saddam Hussein understand what is at stake.

Secondly, I just simply cannot help you on the hypothesis. But I have looked into it enough and talked to enough of the planners and those responsible, not only in our country but leaders around the world, to be totally confident and tell the American

people we are not looking at another Vietnam. The analogy is totally different in who is supporting you, what the topography is, what the force is, what the determination of the military is—the whole array—the coalition. All of these things come together and argue very forcefully this is not another Vietnam.

And so, again, I get back to this very penetrating question by the kid that wrote you—18-year-old—because I can understand it. I can tell where a guy like that is coming from. My own kids ask that—a few grandchildren and stuff—what is this, what does it mean?

And so, it is not going to be another Vietnam. You can get all kinds of ranges in terms of how quick this guy would fold. But none that I know of are predicting anything like the long, drawn-out, bitter experience of Vietnam.

Q. Do you believe there would be far less casualties, sir, in the Persian Gulf than there were in Vietnam?

The President. Yes, but I can't document that. And they asked the question—some of you all weren't here for it, but in the press room across the street—how many? How many can you cope with? How many is enough, or how many is too much? One is too much. And so, what do you do? You plan, if you have to use force, to safeguard every single precious life. That is exactly what Colin Powell and his cohorts are doing over there, and that's what I owe the parents and the kids and the spouses. I'd particularly like to say that at this time of year, with our holidays coming up and all of that. I mean, it's a very emotional time for these families.

And I have to understand it. I've got to understand where his 18-year-old correspondent is coming from; and I've got to understand when I get these letters, mostly supportive still, but some fraught with anxiety about their own loved ones. And I can say to them, if force has to be used, we will have done everything in our power to guarantee the life of every single one of our soldiers and sailors and marines and airmen. And I will have that off my conscience. And then, clearly, it won't work out in a sanitary fashion like that; but I never would want it said that we didn't go the extra mile. So, I took some hits on moving this additional force, and that's fine. That goes with the territory. But at least I have the satisfaction in my heart of hearing from our Chairman of the Joint Chiefs and our commanding general, Norm Schwarzkopf, hey, we're doing it right. You've seen these kids out here on Thanksgiving, and we owe it to them to give them the best, give them the most to get this job done.

And the Brits are looking at it that way. I think the French are looking at it that way. The training that is going on and has gone on with some of our other coalition partners are aimed to that end, too.

Listen, thank you all for coming, and Merry Christmas to everybody.

Note: The President's 67th news conference began at 2:06 p.m. in Room 450 of the Old Executive Office Building.

Statement by Press Secretary Fitzwater on the Federal Reserve System's Reduction of the Discount Rate
December 18, 1990

We welcome the news of the lower discount rate. It should be helpful in promoting growth in the economy in the months ahead. This move appears justified by the budget agreement and the general slowdown.

Letter to Congressional Leaders on Norwegian Whaling Activities
December 18, 1990

Dear Mr. Speaker: (Dear Mr. President:)

On October 19, 1990, Secretary of Commerce Robert A. Mosbacher certified under Section 8 of the Fishermen's Protective Act of 1967, as amended (Pelly Amendment) (22 U.S.C. 1978), that Norway has conducted whaling activities that diminish the effectiveness of the International Whaling Commission (IWC) conservation program. This letter constitutes my report to the Congress pursuant to subsection (b) of the Pelly Amendment.

The certification of the Secretary of Commerce was based on the issuance by the Government of Norway of permits to its nationals, allowing the killing of North Atlantic minke whales for research purposes. At its 42nd Annual Meeting, the IWC adopted a resolution that considered that the Norwegian research program did not satisfy all criteria for research involving the take of whales. The resolution considered in particular that the research is not adequately structured so as to contribute to or mate-

rially facilitate the completion of the IWC comprehensive assessment, nor has it been established that the research addresses critically important research needs. Accordingly, the IWC invited Norway to reconsider its program. On August 10, 1990, Norway advised the IWC that it has reconsidered and has decided to proceed with its research. Research that does not meet all applicable criteria is considered inconsistent with IWC conservation policy.

Norway has made improvements in the design of its research program in each year and a reduction in the take of whales from 68 to five North Atlantic minke whales. Although the IWC is not satisfied that this program meets all applicable criteria, significant progress has been made in Norway's program and presentation. Given the progress made in the caliber of research undertaken and the efforts that have been made to improve U.S.-Norwegian scientific consultations, I am not directing that sanctions be imposed on Norwegian fish products for the whaling activities that led to certification by the Secretary of Commerce.

I am directing the Secretary of Commerce and the Secretary of State to continue consultations with Norway and our other IWC partners to ensure that the conservation program of the IWC is upheld. I hope that these actions will encourage the continued involvement of all members of the IWC in achieving the goals of this impor-

tant organization.

Sincerely,

GEORGE BUSH

Note: Identical letters were sent to Thomas S. Foley, Speaker of the House of Representatives, and Dan Quayle, President of the Senate. This letter was released by the Office of the Press Secretary on December 19.

Remarks at a White House Briefing on Drug Abuse Statistics
December 19, 1990

Thank you all very much. I am delighted to be here this morning with Lou Sullivan and John Walters to announce some very encouraging news about the state of the Nation's drug problem.

As you know, our administration remains fully committed to fighting this problem and stopping this scourge. And that was the promise I made to the American people in my Inaugural Address, and it is a promise that I intend to keep. And I continue to believe that the problem of drugs can be overcome with this clear national strategy and the hard work and combined efforts of millions of Americans. I am pleased to say that the news we have today suggests that our hard work is paying off and that our national strategy is having an effect.

In a moment, Dr. Sullivan, my Secretary at HHS, will describe for you the results of recent surveys conducted by his Department. But I wanted to emphasize how important I believe this new information is.

The national household survey and the emergency room data are the latest and most compelling evidence that drug use in America is declining significantly. And more importantly, it is declining all across the board. Overall drug use is down. Monthly cocaine use is down. Hospitals are reporting fewer drug-related emergencies. Even addictive drug use, which was once spiraling upward, has started to decline. Virtually every piece of information we have tells us that drug use trends are headed in the right direction: down. And

most importantly, we are seeing these declines among the Nation's teenagers, evidence that they are learning to say no, learning to live a life free of drugs.

All of this is wonderful and welcome news. We were confident that progress would be made, but the magnitude of the progress is impressive indeed. Nevertheless, as long as there are hospital rooms filled with drug-affected babies, neighborhoods ravaged by drug violence, or children threatened by addiction, a declaration of victory would be premature. And that is why there will be no weakening of our Federal effort to battle drugs and drug trafficking in this country. And there will be no retreat in our efforts to end the international menace of drugs.

We've come this far because of the law enforcement officials, health professionals, teachers, parents, community leaders, and individual Americans who have shown tremendous courage and determination in the face of what at one point seemed like overwhelming odds. And I'm proud to say that because of their effort, the collective effort of all, we are beating those odds. We owe all who participate a vote of gratitude; and we will continue to support them in the fight against drugs, in every neighborhood, every community, every town, every city.

I want to thank all of you very much. And I will now turn things over to Dr. Sullivan for a little more detail on this news that I think will not only be encouraging in this country but will be very well-received abroad. It'll show that we are fighting the demand side of the equation, and that will send a strong signal to our international partners.

So, Lou, thank you, sir. And, John, thank you. And now with your forbearance, I'll take off and let you elaborate on the good news. Thank you, sir. Keep up the good work.

Note: The President spoke at 10:20 a.m. in Room 450 of the Old Executive Office Building. In his remarks, he referred to John P. Walters, Acting Director of National Drug Control Policy.

Memorandum on the Certification of Countries Exporting Shrimp to the United States
December 19, 1990

Memorandum for the Secretary of State

Subject: Delegation of Authority Regarding Certification of Countries Exporting Shrimp to the United States

By virtue of the authority vested in me by the Constitution and laws of the United States of America, including section 609 of the Departments of Commerce, Justice, and State, the Judiciary, and Related Agencies Appropriations Act, 1990 (Public Law 101–162), and section 301 of title 3 of the United States Code, I hereby delegate to the Secretary of State the functions vested in me by section 609(b) of that Act. The authority delegated by this memorandum may be further redelegated within the Department of State.

The Secretary of State is authorized and directed to publish this memorandum in the *Federal Register.*

GEORGE BUSH

[Filed with the Office of the Federal Register, 11:55 a.m., January 2, 1991]

Note: This memorandum was released by the Office of the Press Secretary on December 20.

Letter to Congressional Leaders Transmitting a Report on Polar Icebreaker Requirements
December 21, 1990

Dear Mr. Chairman:

I am transmitting herewith the report on Polar Icebreaker Requirements, requested in section 23 of the Coast Guard Authorization Act of 1988 (Public Law 100–448) and in report language accompanying the 1990 Department of Defense Appropriations Act (Public Law 101–165).

This report was the result of a collaborative effort by the Departments of Transportation and Defense, the National Science Foundation, and the Office of Management and Budget.

The report concludes that the Coast Guard, which presently has two polar icebreakers, needs one additional polar icebreaker. Funds for this additional icebreaker were included in the 1990 Defense Appropriations Act.

Sincerely,

GEORGE BUSH

Note: Identical letters were sent to Ernest F. Hollings, Chairman of the Senate Committee on Commerce, Science, and Transporta-

tion, and Walter B. Jones, Chairman of the House Committee on Merchant Marine and   *Fisheries.*

Appointment of Phillip D. Brady as Assistant to the President and Staff Secretary
December 21, 1990

The President today announced his intention to appoint Phillip D. Brady as Assistant to the President and Staff Secretary, effective January 14, 1991. He would succeed James W. Cicconi.

Since 1989 Mr. Brady has served as General Counsel at the Department of Transportation. Prior to this Mr. Brady served at the White House as Deputy Assistant to the President and Director of Cabinet Affairs, 1989; Deputy Counsel to the President, 1988–1989; and Deputy Assistant to the Vice President, 1985–1988. Mr. Brady also served at the Department of Justice from 1982 to 1985. Other positions Mr. Brady has held include: Regional Director, Region IX, ACTION Agency, 1981–1982; legislative counsel for Representative Daniel E. Lungren, 1979–1981; deputy attorney general, California department of justice, 1978–1979; and an associate in the law firm of Spray, Gould and Bowers in Los Angeles, 1976–1978.

Mr. Brady graduated from the University of Notre Dame (B.A., cum laude, 1973) and Loyola University School of Law (J.D., cum laude, 1976). He was born May 20, 1951, in Pasadena, CA. Mr. Brady is married, has three children, and currently resides in Alexandria, VA.

Letter to the Speaker of the House on Modification of Provisions of the Federal Budget Agreement
December 21, 1990

Dear Mr. Speaker:

I understand that the House Democratic Caucus has approved a rule for consideration by the House that would begin to undo the recently enacted Budget Agreement.

This rule would change the new pay-as-you-go enforcement mechanism by overturning a specifically negotiated and agreed scoring provision. More important, if the proposed rule is adopted, the House of Representatives will have begun the 102nd Congress by undercutting the credibility of the entire Budget Agreement. If specifically negotiated and agreed provisions are to be undone before the ink is dry, how can we expect the Agreement to be taken seriously? Where, one might reasonably ask, is the process of erosion to stop?

Abandonment of the Agreement would undermine hard-earned confidence in the U.S. Government's improved ability to control Federal spending. To undermine such confidence in the current economic circumstances seems to me to be particularly unwise.

In order to preserve the integrity of the Budget Agreement, I urge you to prevent the adoption of any rule that would violate our Agreement. And in order to preserve confidence in that Agreement, I must advise you that I will veto any bill that contains language such as that specified in the rule approved by the Democratic Caucus.

Sincerely,

GEORGE BUSH

Note: The letter was sent to Thomas S. Foley, Speaker of the House of Representatives.

Remarks and a Question-and-Answer Session With Reporters at Camp David, Maryland, Following Discussions With Prime Minister John Major of the United Kingdom
December 22, 1990

The President. Well, let me just say that this meeting with the Prime Minister has been very fruitful, at least from the United States standpoint. As you all know, we have had a very special relationship with the United Kingdom. And I am totally convinced that not only will that relationship continue, we will work to enhance it in every way possible. And so, I feel, Mr. Prime Minister, that we've gotten off to a wonderful start, and I want to thank you for coming at this terribly busy time of year for you, just coming into office and then, of course, with the holidays just over the horizon. So, thank you for coming. And I do think it shows exactly the right sense in terms of this special relationship.

We talked about the Gulf. We talked about the changes in the Soviet Union that have dominated so much of the international news lately. We talked about the importance of resuming and successfully concluding the GATT talks. We talked about NATO and its continuing importance. And we talked about South Africa, both sides expressing encouragement on developments. So, I found common ground with Prime Minister Major on these very, very important issues.

And once again, sir, thank you for coming to Camp David in this dreary weather.

The Prime Minister. Well, Mr. President, thank you very much, indeed. If I could perhaps, firstly, express my thanks to you and Barbara for your hospitality here this weekend. It's been a remarkable occasion, a splendid opportunity to get to know one another and our thoughts and our community of interest a good deal better.

We had some splendid entertainment, if I may say so, last night from the Army chorus—an absolutely magnificent way to spend the evening. I think the only danger there is to the Anglo-American special relationship is your weather here this weekend. [*Laughter*] Other than that, it's all been absolutely splendid.

The most heartwarming part of the weekend, I think, has been the very large areas of policy where we've clearly illustrated yet again there's a very strong community of ideals as well as a community of interest. And the President has set those out. We had the opportunity of having a lengthy discussion on those: clearly, some problems to be overcome with the GATT; the Gulf self-evidently as a matter we spent some time on; and also, as the President said, the encouraging activities that are coming out of South Africa with the prospects of more to come.

So, I found it a very rewarding and worthwhile occasion, and I think it was entirely proper that one of the very first visits I was able to make as Prime Minister was here to the United States, where we've had such a long and fruitful and worthwhile relationship. And I'm grateful that it's gone so well.

The President. The Prime Minister has agreed to take a few questions, and I'll be glad to do so also.

Resignation of Soviet Foreign Minister Shevardnadze

Q. Mr. President, have you heard from President Gorbachev since the announcement?

The President. No.

Q. Mr. President, could you care to comment on the resignation of Shevardnadze and what impact you think it will have on U.S.-Soviet relationships, particularly in the Gulf?

The President. Well, again, this was a matter that Prime Minister Major and I discussed. I have no additional comment beyond what the Secretary of State said the other day and Marlin Fitzwater put out. I am convinced from what we have received so far from the Soviet Union that the policy on the Gulf will continue. I would let Prime Minister Major comment on that from their vantage point.

But we, as you know, had a very close relationship with Eduard Shevardnadze, and Jim expressed it very well—Jim Baker did. But life goes on, and we will pursue the policies in the Gulf, confident that the Soviet Union will continue on its path. And I will continue to work with this new and very encouraging bilateral relationship—work to enhance that in every way possible. So, what I'm saying is, I don't see any radical changes affecting our bilateral relationship.

And obviously, people are wondering about the concerns raised and expressed by Mr. Shevardnadze, but we will continue to deal with them in the future here as we have in the past, and hope that the changes that are taking place will be done in a very peaceful way.

Did you want to add to that?

The Prime Minister. I'll just add a word, if I may. Clearly, it's sad he's gone. He's played a remarkable part in the peacekeeping process over the past year or so. What we now need to do is to make sure that—as Mr. Gorbachev has said it will—that Soviet foreign policy continues unchanged. We'll have to wait and see how that pans out, but the early signs are encouraging. Gorbachev said that's how it would be. The Congress of Deputies voted precisely in that fashion within a matter of hours. So, we wait to see who the new Foreign Minister is.

Q. Can I ask you, both gentlemen——

Q. Mr. President, do you have any doubt, given the changes that now are occurring in the Soviet Union and the turmoil there, that if you need to make a decision to use force in the Gulf that they will be fully behind you?

The President. No, I think they—every indication we've gotten is that there will be no change in their Gulf policy.

Do you want to comment on that one?

The Prime Minister. Well, we've seen no indication of a change in the Gulf policy. There was no indication of it in the immediate comments after Mr. Shevardnadze's resignation. We hope there won't be.

Persian Gulf Crisis

Q. If I could ask you both: Saddam Hussein says he's not about to leave Kuwait. If he doesn't change his mind, is the world doomed for war?

The President. Do you want to go first?

The Prime Minister. Well, if there's going to be a conflict in Kuwait, that's really a matter for Saddam Hussein. He knows what the Security Council resolutions say. They couldn't be clearer. They've had an almost unprecedented amount of support internationally. I think one has to bear in mind what he's done is unforgivable. What he and his colleagues are doing in Kuwait at this very moment is unforgivable, as you will have seen from the Amnesty [International] report.

I hope he takes seriously the fact that the Security Council resolutions will be enforced. If he moves out, there won't be a conflict. If he doesn't, well, he knows what the consequences may be.

The President. That says it all. And that's exactly the way we feel. We are totally together on this point. And I think we're both still hoping that there will be a peaceful resolution. But I am convinced that Saddam Hussein hasn't gotten the message yet, for some odd reason, the message as to what he's up against and the message that all of us are determined to fulfill to the letter the United Nations resolutions. But let's hope he does get the message.

Q. Do you see any chance for direct talks?

Q. Mr. President, we've been getting conflicting signals this past week from General Waller [deputy commander of U.S. forces in the Persian Gulf], others in the military, in Congress, and so on as to whether the U.S. and the coalition are actually ready for war by the 15th of January. Is the U.S. ready or is the U.S. not ready?

The President. I will be discussing this matter here at Camp David on Monday, I believe it is, with Dick Cheney [Secretary of Defense] and General Powell [Chairman of the Joint Chiefs of Staff]. But put it this way: If there was some clear provocation 10 minutes from now, the allied forces are ready to respond vigorously.

Q. On a slightly different topic, there continue to be reports that American servicemen are not being allowed to wear American flag patches on their uniforms. There continues to be restrictions by the

Saudis on religious materials, entertainment. Do you go along with this position, especially during the Christmas season? And why should the Saudis be allowed to impose such narrow restrictions on those who may very likely give up their lives for mutual interests?

The President. I've discussed this with our commanding general [H. Norman Schwarzkopf], I've discussed this with the Chairman of the Joint Chiefs, and I am satisfied that our young men and women over there will be able to do what every other American family will be doing—thanking God for our many blessings at Christmas. And in terms of manifestations of their patriotism or love of country, they will be able to do what is proper.

So, I'm not worried by the sporadic reports that we get. And I think that the cultural differences are well known, but I think the Saudis and our people are working very closely to see that we are able to do what every American family does at Christmastime, and that is to worship in our own way the holidays here for other religions. And so, I've seen some reports, and then I've made inquiry, and I'm satisfied that these kids can worship their God in their own way.

Q. What about the flag patches, the American flag?

The President. I asked about that, and I forget the details of the answer, but I was satisfied that the way it was worked out is acceptable to our general officers and, thus, to the men as well.

Q. Sir, have you abandoned any hope that there will be talks before January 3d with Iraq?

The Prime Minister. Insofar as talks are concerned, there's nothing to negotiate about. Insofar as whether there's a meeting between Saddam Hussein and Secretary of State Baker is concerned, Mr. Baker's offered a whole series of dates to Saddam Hussein. He's had a wide variety to chose from; he hasn't yet chosen. But insofar as negotiations, there's nothing to negotiate about.

Q. President Bush?

The President. Exactly the same answer. We're totally together on this. We've offered up dates. We've made clear that, as

the Prime Minister has just said, that these meetings were designed to explain fully to Saddam Hussein the situation that he faces now. But we'll continue to hope that he'll be reasonable. But I see no evidence of it, if that's your question.

I see from Marlin—we're looking a little frantic, so we'll take one last one over here.

Soviet Reforms

Q. A question for both of you. Mr. Kryuchkov, the head of the KGB, has said that bloodshed may be necessary to restore order in the Soviet Union. What are your comments?

The President. What was it, again, I'm sorry?

Q. Kryuchkov, the head of the KGB, has said that bloodshed may be now necessary to restore order in the Soviet Union.

The President. Would you like to go first on that?

The Prime Minister. Well, we——

The President. This is what they call bowling us a googly. [*Laughter*]

The Prime Minister. Yes. [*Laughter*] If it's a googley, I dare say it's a curve ball for me. [*Laughter*]

Well, I think we hear a lot of comments of various sorts from the Soviet Union, some of it rather garish, of that sort. We hope very much not. What, clearly, one wants to see is the reform program continuing. It's come a long way in a short period of time, but it has a long way still to go. We hope it can travel that long road, and do so without bloodshed and peaceably.

The President. Last one. Who didn't get one?

Multilateral Trade Negotiations

Q. Have you managed to get any closer on the GATT issue at all? The trade issue?

The Prime Minister. I think there's a community of interest there. We're both aware, and so are the other community heads in the European Community, the great advantage is to get an agreement on GATT. It may not be an agreement that will have every one of us dancing in the streets on every issue. But there'll have to be a community of interest for the agreement. And I think there's a political will to make sure that it's reached.

Thank you very much.

Resignation of Soviet Foreign Minister Shevardnadze

Q. Were you surprised by Shevardnadze's resignation?

The President. Yes.

Q. Do you wish he'd stayed on board?

The President. Yes, I was surprised. And that's a matter for the internal affairs of the Soviet Union. But everybody knows of the respect we had and have for Eduard Shevardnadze. Same respect we had and have for President Gorbachev.

Q. Mr. Bush, let me ask you about Congress.

Q. Congressman Hamilton said the U.S.— he has it from U.S. officials, sir, that——

The President. This is the final—this is the last of the last. You already had one, Sandy [Sandy Gilmour, NBC News]. Go ahead. Go on, go on.

Persian Gulf Crisis

Q. I wanted to ask you about your meetings with Congress this week. What do you see the prospects that you will be seeking some sort of resolution similar to the U.N. resolution?

The President. We've had the most vigorous consultations with Congress. We will continue to have that. Congress appointed a group of 20 at the end of the last session. I

will clearly be meeting with them and soliciting their views. We're talking to all of these Members of Congress as they come back.

It's not just the President doing this— Brent Scowcroft [Assistant to the President for National Security Affairs], Jim Baker, our legislative people in the White House— and we will continue to consult in every way possible. I want Congress fully on board. I'd love to see Congress say this minute that we fully endorse the United Nations resolutions and the President should fully implement them, because I'm determined to do that and it would be very nice to send that solid signal out to Saddam Hussein. I think it would help him get the message as to what he's up against. But they've got to decide. The Congress is a separate body. They are entitled to do it any way they want. But I know the powers of the Presidency, and I've had a chance to discuss that with the key Members of Congress.

Thank you all very, very much.

The Prime Minister. Thank you.

Note: President Bush spoke at 8:20 a.m. on the helipad. In his remarks, he referred to Marlin Fitzwater, Press Secretary to the President, and President Saddam Hussein of Iraq. A tape was not available for verification of the content of these remarks.

Christmas Message to American Troops
December 24, 1990

Merry Christmas and happy holidays to you who are standing watch around the world. Never have I been prouder of our troops. Never have I been prouder to be your Commander in Chief. Because in this season of peace, it is your commitment and your courage that makes peace possible.

We think of you in the snowy fields and runways of Europe, where thanks to you millions are celebrating Christmas and Hanukkah openly for the first time in 45 years. We think of you off the coast of the Philippines and Japan and the DMZ in Korea. We

think of you in Panama, where lightning success last Christmas ended the reign of a despot and brought peace to a people. We think of you in the air, on the high seas, and at bases and Embassies around the world, who kept our country untouched and at peace throughout the long winter darkness of the cold war.

Back home, some talk of the cost of war, but it is you who understand the price of peace. Each Christmas Day, we close our eyes in prayer and think of what Harry Truman called the humble surroundings of the Nativity and how from a straw-littered stable shone a light which for nearly 20 centuries has given men strength, comfort, and peace.

It's distant in time, but close within our hearts; because on this Christmas Day, hour by hour, hand in hand, Americans will send their prayers eastward across the ocean and halfway across the world not only to the town of Bethlehem but to the sands and shores where you stand in harm's way.

We're in the Gulf because the world must not reward aggression, because our vital interests are at stake, and because of the brutality and danger of Saddam Hussein. We're there backed by 12 United Nations resolutions and the forces of 25 other countries.

Barbara and I spent Thanksgiving with our men and women over there. And when we got back, I spoke to the American people—told them of your bravery and reminded them why we're there. First, I put the immorality of the invasion of Kuwait itself. I said I was deeply concerned about what has happened and is happening there, concerned about a ruthless despot's attempt to dominate a volatile and critical region, concerned about his efforts to acquire nuclear arms, and concerned that a promising era is threatened by an international outlaw. And I told the American people something else: that we want peace, not war, and that I will do my level-best to bring you home without a single shot fired.

And let me say one other thing: The sacrifices you make will never be forgotten. America is behind you, the world is behind you, and history is behind you. When you come home—and we hope it's soon—you'll be welcomed as what you are: all-American heroes.

Today at the White House and all across America, candles burn in remembrance of you and all our troops across the country and around the world. There is no way Americans can forget the contribution you are making to world peace and to our country. Whenever we see Old Glory snapping in the breeze, we think of you. Whenever we hear the inspirational words of "The Star-Spangled Banner," we think of you. And whenever we enjoy the boundless opportunities of a free country, we think of you.

History may make men, but you are making history. I think of Lieutenant Mary Danko, the flight nurse who volunteered for Saudi Arabia. Her husband, a C–130 navigator, was already flying in support of Desert Shield. And when asked if leaving their baby with relatives was a hard thing to do, Mary said, "It's the right thing to do. We're needed." And when asked, "Now, what about the kid?" Mary explained, "We're doing it for the kid." Well, she's right. Mary's right. She knows that when peace and freedom triumph, it's not a triumph for one particular country or one particular people but a triumph for our children, a triumph for all humankind.

And so it is with the holidays, for tonight the star of Bethlehem and the candles of the menorah will cast their light in American outposts around the world with a timeless message of hope and renewal that radiates to people of all faiths. Each of you is precious. Each life is important because it touches so many other lives. And while you may be out of America's sight, rest assured no matter where you serve you will never be out of America's heart.

Merry Christmas and happy holidays to you all. God keep you and watch over you. And God bless America.

Note: This message was recorded on December 11 in Room 459 of the Old Executive Office Building. It was broadcast on the Armed Forces Radio and Television Network to American troops worldwide on Christmas Day. A tape was not available for verification of the content of these remarks.

Exchange With Reporters
December 27, 1990

The President. I really just want to wish you all a happy New Year.

Persian Gulf Crisis

Q. What about a message for Saddam Hussein, sir?

The President. No, we have no message for him.

Q. What do you mean by rabbit trails running through the snow?

The President. I mean there are a lot of false leads out there. As a matter of fact——

Q. Are you upset about the report, sir?

The President. No, but as a matter of fact, I think it would be very useful if from the President and others there were fewer comments about readiness. And I don't plan to make any comments about it at all. And I did make a comment earlier. And I feel very comfortable with the briefing I had from the Chairman of the Joint Chiefs, Colin Powell, and the Secretary of Defense. I mentioned to some earlier, I talked to General Schwarzkopf over the holidays, and there has been enough said about readiness. And I don't plan to continue to add to the debate at all. I'm very comfortable with the briefing. And the briefing I had was quite different than most of the stories I'm reading in the last day or two. So, that's what I mean about rabbit trails.

Q. Are Cheney and Powell's comments accurate? They were quoted as saying, in advising you, that U.S. troops would not be ready by——

The President. I've said all I want to say about readiness.

Soviet Union

Q. What about the Soviet Union, sir? In general terms, without divulging the confidentiality of the message, what was the word from the Ambassador today, sir?

The President. Well, if I divulge what the word was from the Ambassador, I would be breaching the confidentiality. However, there were some very friendly words of greeting from President Gorbachev. And I had a chance to ask the Ambassador to give him our best wishes for a happy New Year.

We obviously discussed some of the problems that exist there. But it was just one more in what's become a series of exchanges with the President of the Soviet Union. That's good; it's good that we keep discussing these——

Q. What's your reading on the current situation in the Soviet Union?

The President. Well, my reading is that they are having difficulties—economic difficulties, principally—difficulties in sorting out this new federation. But any time you move from a totalitarian, totally controlled state to an open state—*perestroika, glasnost*—*perestroika* in terms of reform, *glasnost* in terms of openness—you're bound to have problems. It's not just the Soviet Union; they are having problems in Eastern Europe. But the main thing is, there's a determination to keep going down this path of reform, and that's very important. But far be it from me to try to fine-tune the difficulties that they're having there.

Q. Aren't you concerned the pendulum seems to be swinging back the other way? Mr. Gorbachev wants more control. Mr. Shevardnadze was very concerned about that.

The President. Well, I think they can sort all that out.

Q. Doesn't trouble you at all, though?

Persian Gulf Crisis

Q. Why don't you straighten us out on the question of readiness and on the serious talks which Saddam said he'd like to have?

The President. Saddam keeps saying that Kuwait is Province 19 of Iraq, and that flies directly in the face of the United Nations resolutions, and I think everybody knows that. And therefore, there's no willingness to talk peace if that's the position, because there is a determination on the part of the rest of the world to see those United Nations resolutions implemented to a tee, without concession, without giving. That's not what the U.N. resolutions are about. They are very, very clear. And the United States will do its part to fulfill every single one of them.

Q. Mr. President, what message do you have to the American people regarding the January 15th—the United Nations resolution?

The President. My message to the American people, particularly at this time of year, is I hope we will have a peaceful resolution to this question. And I hope that the brutality that's going on in Kuwait this very minute, documented by that Amnesty International report, will cease. And I can guarantee to the families of those kids that are overseas that I will do absolutely everything in my power to see that their safety is maximized and that they get the full support from the American people they deserve.

Q. Has the Soviet Union reaffirmed their support for our Gulf policy, sir?

Q. Sir, you wouldn't send troops over there—commit troops over there, rather, to action unless you felt the U.S. was fully prepared and ready.

The President. Exactly, exactly.

Q. Mr. President, is it incorrect then—are the reports—in addition to being rabbit trails—are they incorrect to state that the U.S. troops will not be ready by January 15th?

The President. I read one report about what Powell and Cheney told me, and it was 180 degrees wrong. And I am not going to say any more about readiness.

Q. Which one was that? [*Laughter*]

The President. I think it was—what outfit do you work for? [*Laughter*]

Come on, I got to go.

Q. Did the Soviet Union reaffirm their support, Mr. President?

Q. You claimed Saddam——

The President. No progress. No progress on that.

Q. ——didn't seriously—that Saddam still didn't take the threat seriously.

The President. I believe that. I believe that. I think he still does not believe that we are serious and our allies are serious in fully implementing these United Nations resolutions. I read the comments he makes about war, and I find it very difficult to believe he believes them—what would happen to him. So, I don't know. But we're—I think——

Q. Well, maybe he doesn't think we're ready.

The President. I still am hopeful that he'll get the message and he'll do what he ought to do, which is get out of Kuwait by the 15th of January—totally, without condition. The world community has called on him to do that. It's enshrined now in international law as represented by the Security Council. And he tries to make it into something else.

Q. You don't believe that he can do that?

The President. Yes, I believe he can. I'm not sure I believe he will.

Q. You don't think there will be a breakthrough, diplomatically?

The President. I would hope so. I would hope so.

Q. Is there any room for compromise on the date——

The President. No compromise on anything. That's the problem. Everybody wants you to compromise. There is not going to be a compromise with this man. That would be the worst signal to send to the people around the world that are together. It wasn't just the U.N. Security Council; it was the whole General Assembly speaking up against this person.

Q. Has the U.S. promised Israel——

The President. So, the United States will do its part.

Q. Has the U.S. promised Israel that we will defend them if they are attacked?

The President. I have no comments on that.

Thank you all.

President's Schedule

Q. Will you be back between now and New Year's?

The President. I don't know. I would like to lay to rest one ugly rumor——

Q. Are you bored?

The President. ——that I'm bored to tears. [*Laughter*] I've never been happier in my life up there.

Q. So, what are you doing here?

The President. Barbara and me, we sit by the fire. We have a wonderful time. [*Laughter*] Get on the long-distance phone—dial it up.

Q. What are you doing——

Q. So, what are you doing here then?

The President. Playing wallyball.

Q. What did you get for Christmas?

The President. We have two to one—the Bush family against the marines in wallyball. There's some news, Helen [Helen Thomas, United Press International]—two victories over only one defeat.

Q. Well, listen, we should be worrying about war while you're having such a good time?

The President. That's right—I'm not. Everybody should be having a little relax here at the end between——

Q. How can they when there's a war coming?

The President. ——Christmas and the New Year. Helen, don't be so gloomy. [*Laughter*]

We'll see you. Thank you all.

Q. Will we see you——

The President. Depends if I get bored up there. [*Laughter*]

Q. ——RNC chairman?

Q. General [Brent Scowcroft, Assistant to the President for National Security Affairs], come over here. We know that you're the source of the New York Times——

The President. Get Andy out there.

Q. Who's the new RNC chairman?

The President. Scowcroft is mad at me. Scowcroft is furious at me. He was out here to see I didn't make any mistakes.

Have a good New Year.

Note: The exchange began at 1:45 p.m. on the South Lawn of the White House, prior to the President's departure for Camp David, MD. In his remarks, President Bush referred to President Saddam Hussein of Iraq; Gen. H. Norman Schwarzkopf, commander of the U.S. forces in the Persian Gulf; Aleksandr A. Bessmertnykh, Soviet Ambassador to the United States; and Eduard A. Shevardnadze, former Soviet Foreign Minister.

Presidential Determination No. 91–10—Memorandum on the Cancellation of Egyptian Military Debt
December 27, 1990

Memorandum for the Secretary of the Treasury and the Secretary of Defense

Subject: Presidential Determination on Egyptian Foreign Military Sales (FMS) Debt

Section 592(d)(1) of the Foreign Operations, Export Financing, and Related Programs Appropriations Act, 1991 (Public Law 101–513) (the "Act") authorizes me, notwithstanding any other provision of law, in the context of certain multilateral debt negotiations, to reduce to zero certain notes related to Egypt's FMS debt if other major holders of Egyptian military debt agree to equal or comparable reductions. I have concluded that such other creditors do not agree to comparable reductions in their military debt.

By virtue of the authority vested in me by section 592 of the Act, I hereby determine that it is essential to the national secu-rity interests of the United States to unilaterally cancel the requirement of Egypt to repay the United States for such Egyptian military debt; and that it is essential to the success of Desert Shield and to enhance peace and stability in the Middle East to reduce to zero the amounts described in section 592(e)(2) of the Act.

By virtue of the authority vested in me by the Constitution and laws of the United States of America, including section 592 of the Act, and section 301 of title 3 of the United States Code, I hereby delegate to the Secretary of Defense the functions under section 592(e)(2) of the Act, provided that the functions conferred by subparagraph (B) thereof shall be exercised by the Secretary of Defense in consultation with the Secretary of the Treasury.

The Secretary of the Treasury is authorized and directed to publish this determination in the *Federal Register.*

GEORGE BUSH

[*Filed with the Office of the Federal Regis-*

ter, 11:36 a.m., December 31, 1990]

Note: The memorandum was released by the Office of the Press Secretary on December 28.

Letter to Congressional Leaders on the Cancellation of Egyptian Military Debt
December 27, 1990

Dear Mr. Speaker: (Dear Mr. President:)

Pursuant to the authority vested in me by section 592(d) of the Foreign Operations, Export Financing, and Related Programs Appropriations Act, 1991 (Public Law 101–513) (the "Act"), I hereby report under paragraph (1) thereof. The basis for this report is described more fully in the attachment to this letter entitled Status of U.S. Efforts on Egyptian Debt.

I am simultaneously providing copies of a memorandum, signed by me today, in which I make certain determinations under section 592(d)(2) and 592(e)(2) of the Act. These determinations form an integral part of my report under paragraph (1) of section 592(d) of the Act. The attached Memorandum of Justification Regarding Presidential

Determinations under Section 592 sets forth more fully the basis for these determinations.

Accordingly, I have authorized the Secretary of Defense and the Secretary of the Treasury to take the appropriate steps to reduce to zero amounts owed in connection with Egypt's remaining Foreign Military Sales debt.

Sincerely,

GEORGE BUSH

Note: Identical letters were sent to Thomas S. Foley, Speaker of the House of Representatives, and Dan Quayle, President of the Senate. The letter was released by the Office of the Press Secretary on December 28.

Presidential Determination No. 91–11—Memorandum on Trade With the Soviet Union
December 29, 1990

Memorandum for the Secretary of State

Subject: Determination under Section 402(c)(2)(A) of the Trade Act of 1974, as amended—Soviet Union

Pursuant to section 402(c)(2)(A) of the Trade Act of 1974 (19 U.S.C. 2432(c)(2)(A)), as amended, (the "Act"), I determine that a waiver by Executive order of the applica-

tion of subsections (a) and (b) of section 402 of the Act with respect to the Soviet Union will substantially promote the objectives of section 402.

You are authorized and directed to publish this determination in the *Federal Register.*

[*Filed with the Office of the Federal Register, 3:30 p.m., January 14, 1991*]

Letter to Congressional Leaders on Trade With the Soviet Union
December 29, 1990

Dear Mr. Speaker: (Dear Mr. President:)

Pursuant to subsection 402(c)(2)(A) of the Trade Act of 1974 (the "Act") (19 U.S.C. 2432(c)(2)(A)), I have determined that a waiver of the application of subsections (a) and (b) of section 402 with respect to the Soviet Union will substantially promote the objectives of section 402. A copy of that determination is enclosed. I have also received assurances with respect to the emigration practices of the Soviet Union required by subsection 402(c)(2)(B) of the Act. This letter constitutes the report to the Congress required by subsection 402(c)(2).

Pursuant to subsection 402(c)(2), I shall issue an Executive order waiving the application of subsections (a) and (b) of section 402 of the Act with respect to the Soviet Union.

I note that this waiver will apply to Estonia, Latvia, and Lithuania. This in no way affects the long-standing U.S. policy of not recognizing the forcible incorporation of Estonia, Latvia, and Lithuania into the Soviet Union or our support for the right of the Baltic states to self-determination.

Sincerely,

GEORGE BUSH

Note: Identical letters were sent to Thomas S. Foley, Speaker of the House of Representatives, and Dan Quayle, President of the Senate.

Appendix A—Digest of Other White House Announcements

The following list includes the President's public schedule and other items of general interest announced by the Office of the Press Secretary and not included elsewhere in this book.

July 2

The President met with advisers at his home in Kennebunkport, ME, in preparation for the 16-nation North Atlantic Treaty Organization summit in London, United Kingdom, July 5–6, and the 7-nation economic summit in Houston, TX, July 9–11.

The President today announced his intention to appoint the following individuals to be members of the National Commission on Superconductivity:

Barbara S. Drake, of Pennsylvania. She would succeed Stephen J. Markman. Currently Mrs. Drake serves as Assistant to the Attorney General at the Department of Justice in Washington, DC.

Travis P. Dungan, of Florida. He would succeed S. Fred Singer. Currently Mr. Dungan serves as Administrator for the Research and Special Programs Administration in Washington, DC.

John K. Hulm, of Pennsylvania. He would succeed William M. Fairbank. Currently Dr. Hulm serves as chief scientist emeritus of Westinghouse Science and Technology Center in Pittsburgh, PA.

Sidney L. Jones, of Maryland. This is a new position. Currently Dr. Jones serves as Assistant Secretary of the Treasury for Economic Policy in Washington, DC.

John W. Lyons, of Maryland. He would succeed Ernest Ambler. Currently Dr. Lyons serves as Director of the National Engineering Laboratory at the National Institute of Standards and Technology in Gaithersburg, MD.

July 3

The President met with advisers at his home in Kennebunkport, ME, in preparation for the NATO summit and the Houston economic summit.

July 4

The President declared that a major disaster existed in Nebraska as a result of severe storms, tornadoes, and flooding that began June 10. He directed the Federal Emergency Management Agency to provide assistance to supplement State and local recovery efforts.

July 5

In the morning, the President arrived at Heathrow International Airport, London, for the NATO summit and went to Winfield House, home of the U.S. Ambassador, which was the President's residence during his stay in London. Later the President met with NATO Secretary General Manfred Woerner and participated in the summit's first working session at Lancaster House.

In the afternoon, the President attended a reception at Bridgewater House for NATO heads of state and Foreign Ministers and a luncheon for NATO leaders at Spencer House hosted by Prime Minister Margaret Thatcher of the United Kingdom. Following the luncheon, the President participated in a working session with NATO summit participants at Lancaster House.

In the evening, the President attended a dinner at Buckingham Palace for NATO heads of state and Foreign Ministers. At the conclusion of the dinner, the President returned to Winfield House.

The White House announced that President Bush has invited President Gnassingbé Eyadéma of Togo to make an official working visit to the United States on July 30–August 1. President Eyadéma has accepted the invitation.

The President announced that the following individuals will comprise the President's delegation to the 10th anniversary celebration of the independence of Vanuatu and the annual heads of state meeting of the South Pacific Forum, July 29–31:

Delegation Chairman:

Fred Zeder, President, Overseas Private Investment Corporation, and Martha Zeder.

Delegates:

Former Governor Hugh Gregg, of New Hampshire, and Cay Gregg.

Nancy Thawley, director of the Republican Eagles, Republican National Finance Committee.

Former State Senator William Saltonstall, of Massachusetts.

July 6

In the morning, the President had breakfast with Prime Minister Thatcher at 10 Downing Street and participated in the final working session of the NATO summit at Lancaster House.

In the evening, the President arrived at Ellington Field in Houston, TX, for the economic summit of industrialized nations and went to the Houstonian Hotel, his residence during his stay in Houston.

July 8

In the afternoon, President Bush met at the Houstonian Hotel's Manor House with President Jacques Delors of the European Community and U.S. and European Community officials.

In the evening, the President and Mrs. Bush hosted a barbecue and rodeo at the AstroArena for delegation heads and their official parties.

July 9

In the afternoon, the President went to Rice University, where he attended a reception for delegation heads at Cohen House and participated in the opening session of the economic summit at Lovett Hall.

In the evening, the President attended a working dinner for delegation heads at Bayou Bend mansion. Later, he visited a dinner for corporate sponsors of the economic summit at the Houstonian Hotel's Manor House.

July 10

The President went to Rice University, where he participated in the morning and afternoon plenary sessions of the economic summit at Herring Hall and a working luncheon at Cohen House.

In the evening, the President and Mrs. Bush hosted a reception and dinner at the Museum of Fine Arts for economic summit leaders and members of their delegations.

July 11

In the morning, the President went to Rice University for the final plenary session of the economic summit at Herring Hall.

July 12

The President met at the White House with:
—the Vice President; John H. Sununu, Chief of Staff to the President; Brent Scowcroft, Assistant to the President for National Security Affairs; and members of the CIA briefing staff;
—members of the Cabinet;
—Members of Congress;
—the Vice President, for lunch;
—John H. Sununu, Chief of Staff to the President.

The President announced that John C. McGraw, of Pennsylvania, will continue to serve as Assayer of the Mint of the United States at Philadelphia, PA. Since 1983 Mr. McGraw has served as Assayer of the United States Mint in Philadelphia.

The President announced his intention to appoint the following individuals to be members of the J. William Fulbright Foreign Scholarship Board for terms expiring September 22, 1992:

Vartan Gregorian, of Rhode Island. He would succeed Nathan Glazer. Currently Dr. Gregorian serves as president of Brown University in Providence, RI.

Margarita B. Tonkinson, of Florida. She would succeed Marvin Howard Alisky. Currently Mrs. Tonkinson serves as associate director of the office of international programs at the University of Miami in Coral Gables, FL.

The President announced his intention to appoint the following individuals to be members of the Advisory Committee on the Arts (John F. Kennedy Center for the Performing Arts). Upon appointment, they will be designated Cochairmen:

Susan Goldwater Keenan, of South Carolina. This is a new position. Currently Mrs. Keenan serves on the board of directors for Pace Industries, Inc., in Aiken, SC.

Chesley Pruet, of Arkansas. He would succeed Herb Hunter. Currently Mr. Pruet serves as president of Chesley Pruet Drilling Co. in El Dorado, AR.

The President announced his intention to appoint the following individuals to be members of the Architectural and Transportation Barriers Compliance Board for terms expiring December 3, 1992:

Porfirio C. Diaz, Jr., of California. He would succeed William J. Tangye. Currently Mr. Diaz serves as assistant director for external affairs at the department of rehabilitation in Sacramento, CA.

Scott Moore Duncan, of Texas. He would succeed Gene A. Chappie. Currently Mr. Chappie serves as a fundraiser for Duncan and Associates in Houston, TX.

Robert T. Kelly, Jr., of Florida. This is a reappointment. Currently Mr. Kelly serves as collections representative for Southern Bell in Miami, FL.

The President designated Eugene R. Sullivan to be Chief Judge of the United States Court of Military Appeals, effective October 1, 1990. He would succeed Robinson O. Everett. He was appointed to the court on May 21, 1986.

July 13

The President met at the White House with:
—the Vice President; John H. Sununu, Chief of Staff to the President; Brent Scowcroft, Assistant to the President for National Security Affairs; and members of the CIA briefing staff;
—President-elect Cesar Gaviria of Colombia;
—Secretary of State James A. Baker III;
—John H. Sununu, Chief of Staff to the President.

In the afternoon, the President went to Camp David, MD, for the weekend.

The President declared that a major disaster existed in Wisconsin as a result of severe storms, tornadoes, and floods that began June 22. He directed the Federal Emergency Management

Agency to provide assistance to supplement State and local recovery efforts.

July 15

In the afternoon, the President returned to the White House from a weekend stay at Camp David, MD.

July 16

The President met at the White House with:
—the Vice President; John H. Sununu, Chief of Staff to the President; Brent Scowcroft, Assistant to the President for National Security Affairs; and members of the CIA briefing staff;
—Secretary of Defense Richard B. Cheney;
—John H. Sununu, Chief of Staff to the President.

The White House announced that President Bush will meet with President Rodrigo Borja Cevallos of Ecuador on July 23.

The President announced his intention to appoint the following individuals to be members of the President's Foreign Intelligence Advisory Board for terms of 2 years:

Lew Allen, Jr., of California. He would succeed James Q. Wilson. Currently Dr. Allen serves as vice president of the California Institute of Technology and director of the Jet Propulsion Laboratory at the California Institute of Technology in Pasadena, CA.

John M. Deutch, of Massachusetts. He would succeed John S. Foster, Jr. Currently Dr. Deutch serves as provost and Karl Taylor Compton professor at the Massachusetts Institute of Technology in Cambridge, MA.

William G. Hyland, of New York. He would succeed Bernard A. Schriever. Currently Mr. Hyland serves as editor for the Foreign Affairs Council of Foreign Relations, Inc., in New York, NY.

Bobby Ray Inman, of Texas. He would succeed Glenn Campbell. Upon appointment he will be designated Vice Chairman. Currently Mr. Inman is self-employed as a consultant in Austin, TX.

William J. Perry, of California. He would succeed Gordon C. Luce. Currently Dr. Perry serves as chairman and chief executive officer of Technology Strategies and Alliances in Menlo Park, CA.

John G. Tower, of Texas. This is a reappointment. Upon appointment he will be designated Chairman. Currently Mr. Tower serves as a consultant in Dallas, TX.

In the evening, the President attended a baseball game between the Baltimore Orioles and the Texas Rangers at Memorial Stadium in Baltimore, MD.

July 17

The President met at the White House with:
—the Vice President; John H. Sununu, Chief of Staff to the President; Brent Scowcroft, Assistant to the President for National Security

Affairs; and members of the CIA briefing staff;
—congressional leaders;
—the Vice President, for lunch;
—members of a Japanese parliamentary delegation, to discuss Japan-U.S. relations.

The President announced that Arnold Schwarzenegger will be his representative to the opening ceremonies of the Goodwill Games on July 21 in Seattle, WA.

In the evening, the President attended the annual House Gymnasium dinner at the Cannon Office Building.

July 18

The President met at the White House with:
—the Vice President; John H. Sununu, Chief of Staff to the President; Brent Scowcroft, Assistant to the President for National Security Affairs; and members of the CIA briefing staff;
—members of the Concerned Alliance of Responsible Employers, to discuss parental leave;
—Thomas Brooks, U.S. Representative to Taiwan, and Nat Bellochi, of the American Institute of Taiwan;
—Senators Robert Dole and Arlen Specter, to discuss Middle East policy;
—directors of the Hispanic Chamber of Commerce;
—Miles S. Epling, national commander of the American Legion;
—congressional leaders, to discuss the Federal budget negotiations.

The President transmitted to the Congress the annual report of the National Corporation for Housing Partnerships and the National Housing Partnership for the fiscal year ending February 28, 1990.

The President announced his intention to appoint Dennis L. Price to be a member of the Nuclear Waste Technical Review Board for a term expiring April 19, 1994. This is a reappointment. Currently Dr. Price serves as a professor in the department of industrial engineering and operations research at Virginia Polytechnic Institute and State University in Blacksburg, VA.

July 19

The President announced his intention to appoint Gen. P.X. Kelley, USMC, Ret., to be a member of the American Battle Monuments Commission. He would succeed Andrew J. Goodpaster. Currently he serves as vice chairman of Cassidy and Associates in Washington, DC.

July 20

The President announced his intention to nominate John C. Datt to be a member of the Farm Credit Administration Board, Farm Credit Administration, for the term expiring May 21, 1996. He would succeed Marvin Duncan. Currently Mr. Datt serves as executive director of the American Farm Bureau Federation in Washington, DC.

July 21

In the afternoon, the President and Mrs. Bush traveled from Newport News, VA, to Camp David, MD, for the weekend.

July 22

The President and Mrs. Bush returned to the White House from a weekend stay at Camp David, MD.

July 23

The President met at the White House with:
—the Vice President; John H. Sununu, Chief of Staff to the President; Brent Scowcroft, Assistant to the President for National Security Affairs; and members of the CIA briefing staff;
—Secretary of the Treasury Nicholas F. Brady;
—champions from the ladies' professional golf tour;
—John H. Sununu, Chief of Staff to the President;
—Federal appeals court judge Edith Jones;
—Federal appeals court judge David H. Souter.

July 24

The President met at the White House with the Vice President; John H. Sununu, Chief of Staff to the President; Brent Scowcroft, Assistant to the President for National Security Affairs; and members of the CIA briefing staff.

The President announced that William J. Doyle III will continue to serve as Inspector General of the Railroad Retirement Board. Dr. Doyle has served as Inspector General since 1986.

July 25

The President met at the White House with:
—the Vice President; John H. Sununu, Chief of Staff to the President; Brent Scowcroft, Assistant to the President for National Security Affairs; and members of the CIA briefing staff;
—congressional leaders, to discuss Federal budget negotiations;
—congressional leaders, to discuss the defense budget.

In the morning, the President attended a fundraising reception for Representative Claudine Schneider at the Mayflower Hotel.

The President declared that a major disaster existed in north-central Vermont as a result of severe storms and flooding that began July 4. He directed the Federal Emergency Management Agency to provide assistance to supplement State and local recovery efforts.

July 26

The President met at the White House with:
—the Vice President; John H. Sununu, Chief of Staff to the President; Brent Scowcroft, Assistant to the President for National Security Affairs; and members of the CIA briefing staff;
—congressional leaders, to discuss the Federal budget negotiations;
—Jean-Pascal Delamuraz, Chief of the Department of Public Economy of Switzerland;
—the Vice President, for lunch;
—John H. Sununu, Chief of Staff to the President.

July 27

The President met at the White House with:
—the Vice President; John H. Sununu, Chief of Staff to the President; Brent Scowcroft, Assistant to the President for National Security Affairs; and members of the CIA briefing staff;
—congressional leaders, to discuss the Federal budget negotiations;
—the President's Council of Advisors on Science and Technology.

The President announced that the following individuals will comprise the U.S. delegation to the Presidential inauguration of Alberto Fujimori in Lima, Peru, July 28:

Delegation Chairman:

Lauro Cavazos, Secretary of Education, and his wife, Peggy Cavazos.

Delegates:

Chase Untermeyer, Assistant to the President and Director of Presidential Personnel.

Anthony Quainton, U.S. Ambassador to the Republic of Peru.

The White House announced that the President has decided against intervening in the possible acquisition of Semi-Gas Systems, Inc., a subsidiary of Hercules, Inc., by the Japanese corporation Nippon Sanso K.K. Semi-Gas designs, assembles, and installs gas systems to control and purify gases used in the manufacture of semiconductors.

In the afternoon, the President and Mrs. Bush traveled to their home in Kennebunkport, ME.

July 29

In the afternoon, the President returned from a weekend stay at his home in Kennebunkport, ME.

July 30

The President met at the White House with:
—the Vice President; John H. Sununu, Chief of Staff to the President; Brent Scowcroft, Assistant to the President for National Security Affairs; and members of the CIA briefing staff;
—Prime Minister Ivars Godmanis of Latvia, to discuss Latvian self-determination and economic reform;
—Pamela Barney, Department of Defense Dependents Teacher of the Year;
—Secretary of Defense Richard B. Cheney;
—John H. Sununu, Chief of Staff to the President.

In the afternoon, the President attended the National Republican Congressional Committee Spring Policy Forum luncheon at the Capital Hilton Hotel.

July 31

The President met at the White House with:
—the Vice President; John H. Sununu, Chief of Staff to the President; Brent Scowcroft, Assistant to the President for National Security Affairs; and members of the CIA briefing staff;
—congressional leaders, to discuss the Federal budget negotiations;
—John H. Sununu, Chief of Staff to the President.

In the afternoon, the President hosted a reception for the Republican Congressional Leadership Council on the State Floor.

The White House announced that the President was pleased to learn of the addition of Sybil Mobley and William Aramony to the board of directors of the Points of Light Foundation.

The President announced his intention to appoint Chandler R. Lindsley, of Texas, to be an alternate member on the part of the United States on the Roosevelt Campobello International Park Commission. She would succeed Frances Barrett Hammer. Currently Mrs. Lindsley is a ranch-owner in Era, TX.

The President announced his intention to appoint the following individuals to be members of the Advisory Committee for Trade Policy and Negotiations for terms of 2 years:

John F. Akers, of Connecticut. This is a reappointment. Currently Mr. Akers serves as chairman of the board, chief executive officer, and chairman of the corporate management board for the International Business Machines Corp. in Armonk, NY.

Robert E. Allen, of New Jersey. He would succeed Peter L. Scott. Currently Mr. Allen serves as chairman and chief executive officer of AT&T in New York, NY.

August 1

The President met at the White House with:
—the Vice President; John H. Sununu, Chief of Staff to the President; Brent Scowcroft, Assistant to the President for National Security Affairs; and members of the CIA briefing staff;
—the Vice President, for lunch;
—John H. Sununu, Chief of Staff to the President.

In the morning, the President hosted a farewell coffee in the State Dining Room for Republican Members of Congress.

The President announced his intention to appoint the following individuals to be members of the National Historical Publications and Records Commission for the terms indicated:

Charles G. Palm, of California, for the remainder of the term expiring December 26, 1991. He would succeed William A. Schambra. Currently Mr. Palm serves as associate director for library and archives at the Hoover Institution in Stanford, CA.

Frank E. Vandiver, of Texas, for a term expiring December 26, 1993. He would succeed Albert John Ossman, Jr. Currently Dr. Vandiver serves as director of the Mosher Institute for Defense Studies at Texas A&M University in College Station, TX.

The President announced his intention to appoint Samuel B. Nunez, Jr., to be a member of the Advisory Commission on Intergovernmental Relations for a term of 2 years. He would succeed John T. Bragg. Currently he serves as president pro tempore of the State senate of Louisiana.

The President announced his intention to appoint Janis Gabay, of California, to be a member of the Commission on Presidential Scholars during her tenure as National Teacher of the Year. She would succeed Mary V. Bicouvaris. Currently Ms. Gabay is a teacher at Junipero Serra High School in San Diego, CA.

The President announced his intention to appoint the following individuals to be members of the President's National Security Telecommunications Advisory Committee:

William T. Esrey, of Kansas. He would succeed Paul H. Henson. Currently Mr. Esrey serves as chairman and chief executive officer of United Telecommunications, Inc., and chairman and chief executive officer of U.S. Sprint in Kansas City, MO.

Paul G. Stern, of Maryland. He would succeed Edmund Bacon Fitzgerald. Currently Dr. Stern serves as chairman and chief executive of Northern Telecom, Ltd., in Vienna, VA.

The President announced his intention to appoint D. Warner North, of California, to be a member of the Nuclear Waste Technical Review Board for a term expiring April 19, 1994. This is a reappointment. Currently Dr. North serves as principal director and vice president of Decision Focus, Inc., in Los Altos, CA.

The President announced his intention to appoint Wales H. Madden, Jr., of Texas, to be a member of the Board for International Food and Agricultural Development for a term expiring July 28, 1993. He would succeed William E. Lavery. Upon appointment, he will be designated Chairman. Currently Mr. Madden serves as a lawyer with Madden Law Offices in Amarillo, TX.

August 2

The President met at the White House with the Vice President; John H. Sununu, Chief of Staff to the President; Brent Scowcroft, Assistant to the President for National Security Affairs; and members of the CIA briefing staff.

August 3

The President met at the White House with:
—the Vice President; John H. Sununu, Chief of Staff to the President; Brent Scowcroft, Assistant to the President for National Security Affairs; and members of the CIA briefing staff;
—national security advisers, to discuss the Iraqi invasion of Kuwait;
—John H. Sununu, Chief of Staff to the President.

The President transmitted to the Congress the annual report describing Federal actions with respect to the conservation and use of petroleum and natural gas in Federal facilities, which covered calendar year 1989, and the annual report of the National Institute of Building Sciences for 1989.

The President announced his intention to nominate the following individuals to be members of the Board for International Broadcasting for terms expiring April 28, 1991:

Cheryl Feldman Halpern, of New Jersey. She would succeed Clair W. Burgener. Currently Mrs. Halpern serves as general partner with Then as Now Limited Partnership in Livingston, NJ.

Karl C. Rove, of Texas. He would succeed Edward Noonan Ney. Currently Mr. Rove serves as president of Karl Rove and Co. in Austin, TX.

The President announced his intention to nominate the following individuals to be members of the National Commission on Libraries and Information Science for the terms indicated:

Carol K. Diprete, of Rhode Island, for the remainder of the term expiring July 19, 1991. She would succeed George H. Nash. Currently Mrs. DiPrete serves as assistant dean for academic services and library at Roger Williams College in Bristol, RI.

J. Michael Farrell, of the District of Columbia, for the remainder of the term expiring July 19, 1992. He would succeed Sally Jo Vasicko. Currently Mr. Farrell serves as a partner with the law firm of Manatt, Phelps, Rothenberg and Phillips in Washington, DC.

The President announced his intention to nominate Howard E. Simmons, of Delaware, to be a member of the National Science Board, National Science Foundation, for a term expiring May 10, 1996. He would succeed Craig C. Black. Currently Dr. Simmons serves as vice president for central research and development at E.I. Dupont de Nemours and Co. in Wilmington, DE.

The President announced his intention to nominate the following individuals to be members of the U.S. Advisory Commission on Public Diplomacy for the terms indicated:

Fitzhugh Green, of the District of Columbia, for a term expiring July 1, 1992. He would succeed Priscilla L. Buckley. Currently Mr. Green is an author and lecturer and has served as vice president and principal with the environmental consulting firm of William D. Ruckelshaus Associates.

Tom C. Korologos, of Virginia, for a term expiring July 1, 1993. This is a reappointment. Currently Mr. Korologos serves as president of Timmons and Co., Inc., in Washington, DC.

In the afternoon, the President went to Camp David, MD, for the weekend.

August 4

In the afternoon, at Camp David, MD, President Bush had telephone conversations with King Fahd bin 'Abd al-'Aziz Al Sa'ud of Saudi Arabia, President Turgut Özal of Turkey, Amir Jabir al-Ahmad al-Jabir Al Sabah of Kuwait, and Prime Minister Brian Mulroney of Canada, to discuss the Iraqi invasion and occupation of Kuwait.

August 5

In the afternoon, the President returned to the White House from a weekend stay at Camp David, MD.

In the evening, the President met with his national security advisers to discuss the Iraqi invasion and occupation of Kuwait. Following the meeting, the President received a telephone call from King Hussein of Jordan.

August 6

The President met at the White House with:
—the Vice President; John H. Sununu, Chief of Staff to the President; Brent Scowcroft, Assistant to the President for National Security Affairs; and members of the CIA briefing staff;
—Thomas S. Foley, Speaker of the House of Representatives, for a working lunch;
—John H. Sununu, Chief of Staff to the President;

—Prime Minister Brian Mulroney of Canada, to discuss the Iraqi invasion and occupation of Kuwait.

In the morning, the President visited H. Lee Atwater, chairman of the Republican National Committee, who was undergoing cancer treatment at George Washington University Hospital.

The President had telephone conversations with Secretary of Defense Richard B. Cheney, who was in Saudi Arabia, and Giulio Andreotti, Prime Minister of Italy and President of the European Community.

In the evening, the President met with his national security and economic advisers to discuss the Iraqi invasion and occupation of Kuwait.

August 7

The President met at the White House with:
—John H. Sununu, Chief of Staff to the President; Brent Scowcroft, Assistant to the President for National Security Affairs; and members of the CIA briefing staff;
—the Cabinet, to discuss the Iraqi invasion and occupation of Kuwait and Federal budget and economic matters;
—Arab-American leaders;
—John H. Sununu, Chief of Staff to the President.

In the late morning, the President traveled to the CIA Operations Center in Langley, VA, where he toured the facility, participated in briefings, and attended a working luncheon. While at the center, the President had a telephone conversation with Prime Minister Brian Mulroney of Canada to discuss the Iraqi invasion and occupation of Kuwait. In the afternoon, the President returned to the White House.

During the day, President Bush had telephone conversations with President François Mitterrand of France, President Mohammed Hosni Mubarak of Egypt, King Hassan II of Morocco, President 'Ali 'Abdallah Salih of Yemen, and Secretary of Defense Richard B. Cheney, who had met with King Fahd of Saudi Arabia and President Mubarak.

The President decided against intervening in the proposed acquisition of Norton Co. by Compagnie de Saint-Gobain, a French corporation. Norton Co. manufactures abrasive products and engineering materials, including advanced ceramics, and has engaged in extensive research and development of advanced ceramics and diamond films.

In an Oval Office ceremony, the President received diplomatic credentials from Ambassadors Tatanene Manata of Zaire, Ernesto Palazio of Nicaragua, Walid al-Moualem of Syria, James V. Hyde of Belize, Denneth Modeste of Grenada, Kazimierz Dziewanowski of Poland, and Gonzalo J. Facio of Costa Rica.

The President announced his intention to appoint the following individuals to be members of the President's Committee on Mental Retardation for terms expiring May 11, 1992:

Kenneth Lee Barun, of Illinois. He would succeed Margaret A. Depaoli. Currently Mr. Barun serves as vice president and executive director of the Ronald McDonald Children's Charities in Oak Brook, IL.

Robert E. Brown, of Ohio. He would succeed Dwight William Schuster. Currently Mr. Brown serves as director of the Ohio Department of Mental Retardation in Columbus.

Betty Barshad Osman, of New York. She would succeed Lucia L. Abell. Currently Dr. Osman serves as a psychologist for the White Plains Hospital Medical Center in White Plains, NY.

E. Duane Thompson, of Illinois. He would succeed Martin S. Appel. Currently Mr. Thompson serves as executive director of the Association for Individual Development in Aurora, IL.

The President announced his intention to appoint the following individuals to be members of the President's Commission on White House Fellowships:

Richard E. Berkowitz, of Georgia. He would succeed Thomas C. Dawson. Currently Mr. Berkowitz serves as senior vice president of Oppenheimer and Co. in Atlanta, GA.

Myron D. Emery, of California. He would succeed John Chatfield Tuck. Currently Mr. Emery serves as an attorney in the law offices of Myron D. Emery in Los Angeles, CA.

Rae Forker Evans, of the District of Columbia. She would succeed Willa Ann Johnson. Currently Mrs. Evans is the vice president of Hallmark Cards, Inc., in Washington, DC.

James L. Ferguson, of New York. He would succeed Shannon J. Wall. Mr. Ferguson has most recently served as chairman of the executive committee for the General Foods Corp., 1987–1989.

Robert H. Puckett, of Indiana. He would succeed Martha Peterson. Currently Dr. Puckett is a professor of political science at Indiana University in Terre Haute, IN.

Warren S. Rustand, of Arizona. He would succeed Irving Kristol. Currently Mr. Rustand serves as chairman of the Garrett-Sweeney Co. in Tucson, AZ.

The President announced his intention to appoint the following individuals to be U.S. Commissioners on the Pacific Salmon Commission for the terms indicated:

Joseph R. Blum, of Washington, for the remainder of the term expiring January 5, 1992. He would succeed William R. Wilkerson. Currently Mr. Blum serves as director of the Washington Department of Fisheries in Olympia.

Don W. Collinsworth, of Alaska, for a term expiring January 5, 1994. This is a reappointment. Currently Mr. Collinsworth serves as commissioner of the Alaska Department of Fish and Game in Juneau.

Guy R. McMinds, of Washington, for the remainder of the term expiring January 5, 1992. He would succeed Sherman Timothy Wapato. Currently Mr. McMinds serves as a natural resources adviser for Quinault Indian Nation in Taholah, WA.

The President announced that the following individuals will comprise the U.S. delegation to the Dominican Republic for the Presidential inauguration of Joaquin Balaguer in Santo Domingo, August 16:

Delegation Chairman:

Elizabeth Dole, Secretary of Labor.

Delegates:

Mrs. Nancy Bush Ellis, of Massachusetts.

Ricardo H. Hinojosa, U.S. District Judge for the Southern District of Texas.

Roy Pfautch, of Missouri, president of Civic Service, Inc.

Julia Rivera de Vincenty, Director of the Farmers Home Administration of Puerto Rico.

Ambassador Paul D. Taylor, U.S. Ambassador to the Dominican Republic.

The President announced his intention to appoint the following individuals:

Lois L. Evans, of New York, to be an Alternate Representative of the United States on the South Pacific Commission for a term of 2 years. She would succeed Bradford M. Freeman. Currently Mrs. Evans serves as chairman of Evans and Shea, Inc., in New York, NY.

Adm. James L. Holloway III, USN, Ret., of Maryland, to be the Representative of the United States on the South Pacific Commission for a term of 2 years. He would succeed John Henry Felix. Currently Admiral Holloway serves as president of the Naval Historical Foundation in Washington, DC.

The President announced his intention to appoint Christopher M. Weld, of Massachusetts, to be a U.S. Commissioner on the International Commission for the Conservation of Atlantic Tunas. He would succeed Michael B. Montgomery. Currently Mr. Weld serves as managing partner with Sullivan and Worcester in Boston, MA.

August 8

The President met at the White House with:
—John H. Sununu, Chief of Staff to the President; Brent Scowcroft, Assistant to the President for National Security Affairs; and members of the CIA briefing staff;
—John H. Sununu, Chief of Staff to the President;
—Federal budget advisers, to discuss the status of the budget talks and the effect of the Iraqi invasion and occupation of Kuwait on the talks.

President Bush had telephone conversations with President Zayid bin Sultan Al Nuhayyan of the United Arab Emirates, Sultan Qaboos bin Sa'id Al Said of Oman, and President Turgut Özal of Turkey, to discuss the Iraqi invasion and occupation of Kuwait.

August 9

The President met at the White House with:
—John H. Sununu, Chief of Staff to the President; Brent Scowcroft, Assistant to the President for National Security Affairs; and members of the CIA briefing staff;
—John H. Sununu, Chief of Staff to the President;
—Walter G. Hogan, Veterans of Foreign Wars commander in chief;
—Eve Launer, the Epilepsy Foundation poster child;
—Gen. Larry D. Walsh, retired Chief of Staff of the Air Force.

The President had telephone conversations with Prime Minister Margaret Thatcher of the United Kingdom and Prime Minister Robert Hawke of Australia to discuss the Iraqi invasion and occupation of Kuwait.

August 10

The President met at the White House with:
—the Vice President; John H. Sununu, Chief of Staff to the President; Brent Scowcroft, Assistant to the President for National Security Affairs; and members of the CIA briefing staff;
—the Vice President, for lunch.

In the afternoon, the President traveled to his home in Kennebunkport, ME.

August 11

In the afternoon, the President met at his home in Kennebunkport, ME, with Secretary of State James A. Baker III; John H. Sununu, Chief of Staff to the President; and Robert M. Gates, Assistant to the President and Deputy for National Security Affairs, to discuss the Persian Gulf crisis and the recent NATO Foreign Ministers meeting.

August 12

President Bush had a telephone conversation with President Hafiz al-Assad of Syria to discuss the Persian Gulf crisis.

August 13

In the morning, the President met at his home in Kennebunkport, ME, with John H. Sununu, Chief of Staff to the President; Andrew H. Card, Jr., Assistant to the President and Deputy to the Chief of Staff; and Robert M. Gates, Assistant to the President and Deputy for National Security Affairs, for his daily intelligence briefing and to discuss the Persian Gulf crisis.

Later President Bush had a telephone conversation with President Carlos Andrés Pérez of Venezuela to discuss the Persian Gulf crisis and world oil supplies.

August 14

In the afternoon, the President returned to Washington, DC, and met with advisers to discuss the Federal budget. Later he met with Foreign Minister Sabah al-Ahmad al-Jabir Al Sabah of Kuwait to discuss the Persian Gulf crisis.

The President appointed Representative Robert K. Dornan to be his personal representative at the international air show in Farnborough, England, September 2–9.

August 15

In the morning, the President met at the White House with the Committee on New Drugs for Cancer and AIDS.

In the afternoon, the President traveled to his home in Kennebunkport, ME.

August 16

President Bush telephoned President Mohammed Hosni Mubarak of Egypt to discuss President Bush's meetings with King Hussein I of Jordan and Foreign Minister Sa'ud al-Faysal Al Sa'ud of Saudi Arabia.

In the evening, the President attended a fundraising dinner in Kennebunkport, ME, for Vermont gubernatorial candidate Richard Snelling.

August 17

In the morning, the President met at his home in Kennebunkport, ME, with:
— Andrew H. Card, Jr., Assistant to the President and Deputy to the Chief of Staff, and Robert M. Gates, Assistant to the President and Deputy for National Security Affairs, for his daily intelligence briefing;
— Secretary of Health and Human Services Louis W. Sullivan; C. Boyden Gray, Counsel to the President; and Constance B. Newman, Director of the Office of Personnel Management, to discuss civil rights legislation.

August 18

In the morning, aboard the U.S. Coast Guard cutter *Monomoy* off the coast of Maine, the President met with Robert M. Gates, Assistant to the President and Deputy for National Security Affairs, and Andrew H. Card, Jr., Assistant to the President and Deputy to the Chief of Staff, for a briefing on national security issues.

Later, aboard his boat *Fidelity*, the President had a telephone conversation with Robert M. Gates, Assistant to the President and Deputy for National Security Affairs, to discuss the Iraqi statement regarding its treatment of foreign nationals.

August 19

In the afternoon, the President returned to Washington, DC, and met with national security advisers to discuss the Persian Gulf crisis.

August 20

In the morning, the President met at the White House with:
— advisers, to discuss the Federal budget negotiations;
— Deputy Secretary of Energy W. Henson Moore, to discuss the Persian Gulf crisis and U.S. energy reserves.

In the morning, the President telephoned President Turgut Özal of Turkey and Prime Minister Margaret Thatcher of the United Kingdom to discuss the Persian Gulf crisis.

The President announced his intention to appoint Robert A. Estrada, of Texas, to be a member of the Student Loan Marketing Association. He would succeed Irby Clifford Simpkins, Jr. Currently Mr. Estrada serves as chairman of the board of Estrada Securities, Inc., in Dallas, TX.

The President announced his intention to appoint the following individuals to be members of the President's Commission on White House Fellowships:

Constance Berry Newman, of Maryland. She would succeed Constance Horner. Since 1989 Ms. Newman has served as Director of the Office of Personnel Management.

Sophocles A. Hero, of Virginia. He would succeed William Milton Smith. Mr. Hero most recently served as an attorney specializing in international affairs in the Office of the General Counsel at the Department of Defense, 1959–1980.

August 21

In the morning, the President met at his home in Kennebunkport, ME, with Robert M. Gates, Assistant to the President and Deputy for National Security Affairs, and Andrew H. Card, Jr., Assistant to the President and Deputy to the Chief of Staff, for a briefing on domestic issues.

The President telephoned Brent Scowcroft, Assistant to the President for National Security Affairs, to discuss the Persian Gulf crisis and the mobilization of U.S. Reserves, and Thomas R. Pickering, U.S. Representative to the United Nations, to discuss the U.N. deliberations on the economic sanctions against Iraq.

Later in the morning, the President traveled to Woodlands Country Club in Falmouth, ME, to participate in Gov. John McKernan's 1990 Golf Classic.

In the afternoon, the President returned to Kennebunkport, ME.

August 23

In the morning, the President met at his home in Kennebunkport, ME, with Brent Scowcroft, Assistant to the President for National Security Affairs, and Andrew H. Card, Jr., Assistant to the President and Deputy to the Chief of Staff, for a briefing on domestic and national security issues.

Later in the morning, the President had telephone conversations with Chancellor Helmut Kohl of the Federal Republic of Germany and Prime Minister Robert Hawke of Australia to discuss the Persian Gulf crisis.

In the evening, the President attended a fundraising dinner in Kennebunkport, ME, for Gov. Judd Gregg of New Hampshire and congressional candidate David Emery.

August 24

The President met at his home in Kennebunkport, ME, with Secretary of the Treasury Nicholas F. Brady; Richard G. Darman, Director of the Office of Management and Budget; John H. Sununu, Chief of Staff to the President; and Andrew H. Card, Jr., Assistant to the President and Deputy to the Chief of Staff, to discuss the Federal budget negotiations.

August 25

In the morning, the President met at his home in Kennebunkport, ME, with Brent Scowcroft, Assistant to the President for National Security Affairs, for an intelligence and national security briefing.

August 28

In the afternoon, the President returned to Washington, DC, and met with Foreign Minister Yusuf bin 'Alawi bin 'Abdallah of Oman to discuss the Persian Gulf crisis.

August 29

The President met at the White House with:
—the Vice President and Brent Scowcroft, Assistant to the President for National Security Affairs, for an intelligence and national security briefing;
—advisers, to discuss the Federal budget negotiations;
—Secretary of State James A. Baker III.

The President declared that major disasters existed in New Hampshire, as a result of severe storms and flooding that began August 7, and in Illinois, as a result of tornadoes that occurred August 28. He directed the Federal Emergency Management Agency to provide assistance to supplement State and local recovery efforts.

In the afternoon, the President had a telephone conversation with Gov. Jim Thompson of Illinois, who expressed his appreciation for Federal disaster relief.

The President announced his intention to appoint the following individuals to be members of the President's Commission on the Federal Appointment Process. These are new positions:

Thomas Joseph Murrin, Deputy Secretary of Commerce. Upon appointment, he will be designated Chairman.

C. Boyden Gray, Counsel to the President of the United States.

Nancy Mohr Kennedy, Assistant Secretary of Education.

J. Michael Luttig, Acting Assistant Attorney General (Office of Legal Counsel), Department of Justice.

Constance Berry Newman, Director of the Office of Personnel Management.

Stephen D. Potts, Director of the Office of Government Ethics.

Clarence Thomas, U.S. Circuit Judge for the District of Columbia Circuit.

Charles G. (Chase) Untermeyer, Assistant to the President of the United States and Director of Presidential Personnel.

In the evening, the President hosted a dinner in the Residence for Members of Congress.

August 30

The President met at the White House with:
—Brent Scowcroft, Assistant to the President for National Security Affairs, for an intelligence and national security briefing;
—administration officials, for an energy briefing;
—national security advisers, to discuss the Persian Gulf crisis;
—Secretary of the Treasury Nicholas F. Brady and Under Secretary of the Treasury for International Affairs David Mulford.

In the afternoon, the President traveled to his home in Kennebunkport, ME.

The President announced his intention to appoint Shannon Fairbanks, of the District of Columbia, to be a member of the Board of Directors of the Federal Home Loan Mortgage Corporation for a term ending on the date of the next annual meeting of the voting common stockholders in 1991. This is a new position. Currently Mrs. Fairbanks serves as executive vice president of the American Real Estate Group in Washington, DC.

The President announced his intention to nominate Barry Zorthian, of the District of Columbia, to be a member of the Board for International Broadcasting for a term expiring May 20, 1992. He would succeed Arch Madsen. Currently Mr. Zorthian serves as a partner with the law firm of Alcalde, O'Bannon, Rousselot and Wahlquist.

August 31

In the morning, at his home in Kennebunkport, ME, President Bush had telephone conversations with King Fahd bin 'Abd al-'Aziz Al Sa'ud of Saudi Arabia, Prime Minister Margaret Thatcher of the United Kingdom, and President François Mitterrand of France to discuss the Persian Gulf crisis.

The President declared that a major disaster existed in Monroe County, WI, as a result of severe storms and flooding that occurred August 17. He directed the Federal Emergency Management Agency to provide assistance to supplement State and local recovery efforts.

The President announced his intention to appoint the following individuals to be members of the Advisory Commission on Conferences in Ocean Shipping:

Conrad H.C. Everhard, of New York. Currently Mr. Everhard serves as chairman of O.O.C.L. (U.S.A.), Inc., in New York, NY.

James J. O'Brien, of California. Currently Mr. O'Brien serves as executive director of transportation services for the Port of Oakland in California.

Paul F. Wegener, of Louisiana. Currently Mr. Wegener serves as chairman of the board of National Customs Brokers and Forwarders Association of America and as vice president of M.G. Maher and Co., Inc., in New Orleans, LA.

Roger W. Wigen, of Minnesota. Currently Mr. Wigen serves as manager of transportation policy and industry affairs for the Minnesota Mining and Manufacturing Co., Inc., in St. Paul, MN.

Raymond Paul deMember, of Virginia. Currently Mr. deMember serves as executive vice president and general counsel of the International Association of Non-Vessel-Operating Common Carriers and as an attorney in private practice in Fairfax, VA.

William P. Verdon, of the District of Columbia. Currently Mr. Verdon serves as president of United Ship Owners of America in Washington, DC.

Paul L. Crouch, of California. Currently Mr. Crouch serves as vice president of Traffic Calcot, Ltd., in Bakersfield, CA.

Samuel K. Skinner, Secretary of Transportation, will be designated Chairman. He was appointed to the Commission on October 5, 1989.

The President announced his intention to select Eugene Ronald Croisant, of Illinois, to be a member of the Board of Directors of the National Railroad Passenger Corporation for a term of 2 years. He would succeed Frank W. Jenkins. Currently Mr. Croisant serves as executive vice president for Human Resources and Administration at R.J.R. Nabisco in New York, NY.

The President announced his intention to appoint Christopher Hicks, of Maryland, to be a member of the Board for International Food and Agricultural Development for the remainder of the term expiring July 28, 1992. He would succeed Gwendolyn S. King. Currently Mr. Hicks serves as a partner with the law firm of Anderson, Hibey, Nanheim and Blair in Washington, DC.

The President announced his intention to nominate James O. Mason, of Utah, to be Representative of the United States on the Executive Board of the World Health Organization. He would succeed Frank E. Young. Currently Dr. Mason serves as Assistant Secretary for Health at the Department of Health and Human Services in Washington, DC.

The President announced his intention to appoint Robert L. Athey, of Illinois, to be Alternate Commissioner of the United States Section of the Great Lakes Fishery Commission. He would succeed Charles K. Dutcher. Currently Mr. Athey serves as vice president of Jack Nicklaus Development Corp. of Illinois in North Barrington, IL.

The President announced his intention to nominate Joan R. Challinor, of the District of Columbia, to be a member of the Board of Trustees of the James Madison Memorial Fellowship Foundation for a term of 6 years. This is a reappointment. Currently Mrs. Challinor serves as a research associate for the National Museum of American History in Washington, DC.

September 3

In the afternoon, the President and Mrs. Bush returned to Washington, DC, from their vacation in Kennebunkport, ME.

September 4

The President met at the White House with:
—the Vice President; John H. Sununu, Chief of Staff to the President; Brent Scowcroft, Assistant to the President for National Security Affairs; and members of the CIA briefing staff;
—John H. Sununu, Chief of Staff to the President;
—members of the Cabinet;
—Harold Reynolds, second baseman for the Seattle Mariners baseball team and the 195th daily Point of Light.

In the afternoon, the President participated in a swearing-in ceremony in the Oval Office for Stephen D. Potts as Director of the Office of Government Ethics.

The President announced his intention to appoint the following individuals to be members of the President's Committee on Mental Retardation for the terms indicated:

Linda Felner, of New York, for a term expiring May 11, 1992. She would succeed Alexander L. Napolitano. Currently Mrs. Felner serves as the Federal liaison for the department of intergovernmental relations in Westchester County, NY.

Thomas Gunnings, of Michigan, for a term expiring May 11, 1991. He would succeed Martin S. Ulan. Currently Dr. Gunnings serves as founder and president of the Meridian Professional Psychological Consultants, Inc., in East Lansing, MI.

J. Alfred Rider, of California, for a term expiring May 11, 1991. This is a reappointment. Currently Dr. Rider serves as an associate clinical professor for the department of internal medicine at the University of California at Davis.

The President announced his intention to appoint the following individuals to be members of the Library of Congress Trust Fund Board for the terms indicated:

Edwin L. Cox, of Texas, for the term of 5 years from March 9, 1988. He would succeed Flora Laney Thornton. Currently Mr. Cox serves as chairman of Cox Oil and Gas, Inc., in Dallas, TX.

Marguerite S. Roll, of Arizona, for the term of 5 years from March 9, 1990. She would succeed Mildred Lois Nichols Teas. Currently Mrs. Roll is a community and civic leader.

The President announced his intention to appoint Robert Boone Hawkins, Jr., of California, to be a member of the Advisory Commission on Intergovernmental Relations for a term of 2 years. This is a reappointment. Currently Dr. Hawkins serves as president of the Institute for Contemporary Studies in San Francisco, CA.

The President announced his intention to designate Richard V. Backley, of Virginia, to be Acting Chairman of the Federal Mine Safety and Health Review Commission. Mr. Backley has been a Commissioner on the Federal Mine Safety and Health Review Commission since August 31, 1978. The term of the current Chairman, Ford B. Ford, expired on August 30, 1990.

September 5

The President met at the White House with:
—the Vice President; John H. Sununu, Chief of Staff to the President; Brent Scowcroft, Assistant to the President for National Security Affairs; and members of the CIA briefing staff;
—John H. Sununu, Chief of Staff to the President;
—Members of Congress, to discuss their recent visits to the Persian Gulf region.

In the morning, the President telephoned W. Nathaniel Howell, U.S. Ambassador to Kuwait, to discuss the Persian Gulf crisis.

The President announced that Vilma Rosso Taracido, of New York, will continue to serve as Assayer of the Mint of the United States at West Point, NY.

In the evening, the President telephoned U.N. Secretary-General Javier Perez de Cuellar de la Guerra, to discuss the Secretary-General's recent diplomatic visit to the Persian Gulf region.

September 6

The President met at the White House with:
—the Vice President; John H. Sununu, Chief of Staff to the President; Brent Scowcroft, As-

sistant to the President for National Security Affairs; and members of the CIA briefing staff;
—Foreign Minister David Levi of Israel.

President Bush received telephone calls from President Turgut Özal of Turkey, Chancellor Helmut Kohl of the Federal Republic of Germany, and President François Mitterrand of France. President Bush discussed the Persian Gulf crisis and his upcoming meeting with President Mikhail Gorbachev of the Soviet Union with each foreign leader.

President Bush telephoned President Hafiz al-Assad of Syria, to discuss the Persian Gulf crisis.

The President declared that a major disaster existed in Iowa as a result of severe storms and flooding that began July 25. He directed the Federal Emergency Management Agency to provide assistance to supplement State and local recovery efforts.

The President announced his intention to nominate the following individuals to be members of the U.S. Advisory Commission on Public Diplomacy for terms expiring July 1, 1991:

William J. Hybl, of Colorado. He would succeed Richard M. Scaife. Currently Mr. Hybl serves as chairman and chief executive officer of the El Pomar Foundation in Colorado Springs, CO.

Richard B. Stone, of the District of Columbia. He would succeed E. Robert Wallach. Currently Mr. Stone serves as vice chairman, member of the board of directors, and chief executive officer of Capital Bank, N.A., in Los Angeles, CA.

The President announced his intention to nominate William H.G. Fitzgerald, of the District of Columbia, to be a member of the Board of Directors of the African Development Foundation for a term expiring February 9, 1996. He would succeed Jay Kenneth Katzen. Upon confirmation, he will be designated Vice Chairperson. Most recently, Mr. Fitzgerald served as chairman of the board of the North American Housing Corp.

September 7

The President met at the White House with:
—the Vice President; John H. Sununu, Chief of Staff to the President; Brent Scowcroft, Assistant to the President for National Security Affairs; and members of the CIA briefing staff;
—John H. Sununu, Chief of Staff to the President;
—Oskar Lafontaine, Social Democratic Party candidate for Chancellor of the Federal Republic of Germany;
—the Vice President, for lunch.

The White House announced that President Bush has invited President F.W. de Klerk of South Africa to visit Washington. President de Klerk has accepted the invitation and will meet with President Bush at the White House on September 24.

The President appointed the following individuals to be Members of the President's Committee on the Arts and the Humanities:

David B. Kennedy, of Michigan. He would succeed Stanley M. Freehling. Currently Mr. Kennedy serves as president of the Earhart Foundation in Ann Arbor, MI.

Benjamin F. Biaggini, of California. He would succeed Franklin D. Murphy. Mr. Biaggini is the former chairman of Southern Pacific Co. of San Francisco.

Richard J. Franke, of Illinois. He would succeed Charles A. Dana, Jr. Currently he serves as chairman and chief executive officer of John Nuveen and Co., Inc., in Chicago, IL.

George V. Grune, of Connecticut. He would succeed Schuyler G. Chapin. Currently Mr. Grune serves as chairman of the board and chief executive officer of the Reader's Digest Association, Inc., in Pleasantville, NY.

Donald B. Marron, of New York. He would succeed Frank Stanton. Currently Mr. Marron serves as chairman and chief executive officer of the Paine Webber Group, Inc., in New York, NY.

Konrad Henry Matthaei, of New York. He would succeed Isabel Brown Wilson. Currently Mr. Matthaei serves as director of development for the Cold Spring Harbor Laboratory in Cold Spring Harbor, NY.

Alexander K. McLanahan, of Texas. He would succeed Betsy Bloomingdale. Currently Mr. McLanahan serves as vice president of Kidder, Peabody and Co., Inc., in Houston, TX.

Raymond D. Nasher, of Texas. He would succeed Frank Sinatra. Dr. Nasher is founder and chairman of the board of the Nasher Co. in Dallas, TX.

Lynne Dominick Novack, of Oklahoma. She would succeed Karen Hansen Munro. Currently Mrs. Novack serves as an independent consultant and special project director at the International Council in Tulsa, OK.

Arthur W. Schultz, of California. This is a reappointment. Mr. Schultz is the former chairman of the board of trustees of the Art Institute of Chicago.

William E. Simon, of New Jersey. He would succeed Leonard Silverstein. Currently he serves as president of the John M. Olin Foundation and chairman of William E. Simon and Sons, Inc., in Morristown, NJ.

Jane DeGraff Sloat, of the District of Columbia. She would succeed Caroline Ahmanson.

Roger L. Stevens, of the District of Columbia. This is a reappointment. Currently Mr. Stevens is founding chairman of the John F. Kennedy Center for the Performing Arts in Washington, DC.

Oscar L. Tang, of New York. He would succeed Rawleigh Warner, Jr. Mr. Tang is cofounder, president, and chairman of the executive board of Reich and Tang, Inc., in New York, NY.

Jane Morgan Weintraub, of California. She would succeed Bill Blass.

Donald J. Hall, of Missouri. He would succeed Andrew Heiskell. Upon appointment, he will be designated chairman. Currently Mr. Hall serves as chairman of the board of Hallmark Cards, Inc., in Kansas City, MO.

Stanley S. Scott, of Louisiana. He would succeed Armand S. Deutsch. Currently Mr. Scott serves as president of Crescent Distribution Co. in Harahan, LA.

In the evening, the President and Mrs. Bush traveled to Helsinki, Finland, for President Bush's meeting with President Mikhail Gorbachev of the Soviet Union.

September 10

The President met at the White House with:
—the Vice President; John H. Sununu, Chief of Staff to the President; Brent Scowcroft, Assistant to the President for National Security Affairs; and members of the CIA briefing staff;
—Secretary of Defense Richard B. Cheney;
—John H. Sununu, Chief of Staff to the President.

The President announced his intention to appoint the following individuals to be U.S. Commissioners on the International Pacific Halibut Commission for the terms indicated:

Richard I. Eliason, of Alaska, for a term expiring December 12, 1991. This is a reappointment. Currently Senator Eliason serves as a State senator for the Alaska State Senate in Juneau, AL.

Steven Pennoyer, of Alaska, for a term expiring December 12, 1990 and also for a term expiring December 12, 1992. He would succeed Robert W. McVey. Currently Mr. Pennoyer serves as Regional Director for Alaska of the National Oceanic and Atmospheric Administration's National Marine Fisheries Service in Juneau, AK.

The President announced his intention to appoint Joan Wellhouse Stein, of Florida, to be a member of the Advisory Council on Historic Preservation for a term expiring June 10, 1994. She would succeed Robert O. Johns. Upon appointment, she will be designated vice chairman. Currently Mrs. Stein serves as chairman of the board of the Regency Group, Inc. in Jacksonville, FL.

The President transmitted to the Congress the annual report of the National Endowment for the Arts for fiscal year 1989.

September 11

The President met at the White House with:
—the Vice President; John H. Sununu, Chief of Staff to the President; Brent Scowcroft, Assistant to the President for National Security Affairs; and members of the CIA briefing staff;

—John H. Sununu, Chief of Staff to the President.

The President transmitted to the Congress the 10th annual report of the Department of Energy, which covered 1988 and 1989.

September 12

The President met at the White House with:
—the Vice President; John H. Sununu, Chief of Staff to the President; Brent Scowcroft, Assistant to the President for National Security Affairs; and members of the CIA briefing staff;
—John H. Sununu, Chief of Staff to the President;
—Judge David Souter, Supreme Court nominee;
—John H. Sununu, Chief of Staff to the President.

The President announced his intention to appoint the following individuals to be members of the President's Board of Advisors on Historically Black Colleges and Universities:

Julius W. Becton, Jr., of Texas. Currently Mr. Becton serves as president of Prairie View A&M University in Prairie View, TX.

Milton Bins, of the District of Columbia. Currently Mr. Bins serves as deputy director of the Council of Great City Schools in Washington, DC.

John Carter, of Connecticut. Currently Mr. Carter serves as president and chief executive officer of The Equitable Financial Companies in New York, NY.

James E. Cheek, of the District of Columbia. Upon appointment, he will be designated Chairman. Currently Dr. Cheek serves as president emeritus of Howard University in Washington, DC.

Edward B. Fort, of North Carolina. Currently Dr. Fort serves as chancellor of North Carolina A&T State University in Greensboro, NC.

Norman C. Francis, of Louisiana. Currently Dr. Francis serves as president of Xavier University of Louisiana in New Orleans, LA.

Edmund B. Gaither, of Massachusetts. Currently Mr. Gaither serves as director of the Museum of the National Center of Afro-American Artists in Boston, MA.

Caspa L. Harris, Jr., of Virginia. Currently Mr. Harris serves as president of the National Association of College and University Business Officers in Washington, DC.

William R. Harvey, of Virginia. Currently Dr. Harvey serves as president of Hampton University in Hampton, VA.

William E. Hogan II, of Minnesota. Currently Dr. Hogan serves as vice president of Inertial Instruments Operation for Honeywell, Inc., in Minneapolis, MN.

William P. Hytche, of Maryland. Currently Dr. Hytche serves as president of the University of Maryland Eastern Shore in Princess Anne, MD.

James A. Joseph, of Virginia. Currently Mr. Joseph serves as president and chief executive officer of the Council on Foundations in Washington, DC.

Leroy Keith, Jr., of Georgia. Currently Dr. Keith serves as president of Morehouse College in Atlanta, GA.

David Satcher, of Tennessee. Currently Dr. Satcher serves as president of Meharry Medical College in Nashville, TN.

Gloria Randle Scott, of North Carolina. Currently Dr. Scott serves as president of Bennett College in Greensboro, NC.

Carl Ware, of Georgia. Currently Mr. Ware serves as senior vice president of the Coca-Cola Co. in Atlanta, GA.

Walter Washington, of Mississippi. Currently Dr. Washington serves as president of Alcorn State University in Lorman, MS.

Carole Ann Fleming, of Texas. Upon appointment, she will be designated vice chairman. Currently Mrs. Fleming serves as an account executive for AT&T in Houston, TX. Mrs. Fleming is a member of the board of trustees of Texas Southern University.

Dorothy Irene Height, of New York. Currently Ms. Height serves as the president of the National Council of Negro Women in Washington, DC.

Ruth B. Love, of California. Currently Dr. Love serves as president of Ruth Love Enterprises in Oakland, CA.

Portia A. Scott, of Georgia. Currently Ms. Scott serves as assistant to the general manager of Atlanta Daily World in Atlanta, GA.

Arthur Edward Thomas, of Ohio. Currently Dr. Thomas serves as president of Central State University in Wilberforce, OH.

Albertine Elaine Bowie Turkson, of Texas.

Patricia Hill Williams, of New York. Currently Ms. Williams serves as assistant to the president for alumni affairs at State University of New York, College of Technology, at Farmingdale.

September 13

The President met at the White House with:
—the Vice President; John H. Sununu, Chief of Staff to the President; Brent Scowcroft, Assistant to the President for National Security Affairs; and members of the CIA briefing staff;
—John H. Sununu, Chief of Staff to the President;
—the Vice President, for lunch;
—the U.S. lacrosse team.

In the morning, the President attended a fundraising reception for U.S. senatorial candidate Patricia Saiki at the Westin Hotel.

The President announced his intention to nominate Mary Ann Mobley-Collins, of California, to be a member of the National Council on Disability for a term expiring September 17, 1991. She would succeed Joni Tada. Currently Mrs. Collins is an actress, singer, and volunteer for numerous causes in Beverly Hills, CA.

The President announced his intention to nominate Paul K. Dayton, of California, to be a member of the Marine Mammal Commission for a term expiring May 13, 1992. He would succeed

William W. Fox, Jr. Currently Dr. Dayton serves as a professor for the Scripps Institution of Oceanography at the University of California at San Diego in La Jolla, CA.

The President selected Paul Coverdell, Director of the Peace Corps, to be the Presidential representative to the International Olympic Committee meeting in Tokyo, Japan, September 16–19, to support Atlanta's bid to host the 1996 games.

The President announced his intention to nominate James R. Whelan, of Virginia, to be a member of the Board of Directors of the Inter-American Foundation for a term expiring September 20, 1994. He would succeed Harold K. Phillips. Upon confirmation, he will be designated vice chairman. Currently Mr. Whelan serves as an author and consultant in Arlington, VA.

The President transmitted to the Congress the annual report of the Tourism Policy Council, which covered fiscal year 1989.

September 14

The President met at the White House with:
—the Vice President; John H. Sununu, Chief of Staff to the President; Brent Scowcroft, Assistant to the President for National Security Affairs; and members of the CIA briefing staff;
—John H. Sununu, Chief of Staff to the President.

In the afternoon, the President went to Camp David, MD, for the weekend.

September 16

In the afternoon, the President returned to the White House from a weekend stay at Camp David, MD.

September 17

The President met at the White House with:
—the Vice President; John H. Sununu, Chief of Staff to the President; Brent Scowcroft, Assistant to the President for National Security Affairs; and members of the CIA briefing staff;
—John H. Sununu, Chief of Staff to the President;
—members of the Cabinet;
—Secretary of the Treasury Nicholas F. Brady.

In the morning, the President telephoned Linda Warsaw, the 250th daily Point of Light.

In the afternoon, in an Oval Office ceremony, the President participated in the presentation of the National Education Goals poster.

September 18

The President met at the White House with:
—the Vice President; John H. Sununu, Chief of Staff to the President; Brent Scowcroft, As-

sistant to the President for National Security Affairs; and members of the CIA briefing staff;
—John H. Sununu, Chief of Staff to the President.

In the morning, the President traveled to Denver, CO.

The President designated Jack A. Josephson, of New York, to be Chairman of the Cultural Property Advisory Committee. Mr. Josephson was appointed as a member of the Committee on June 12, 1990. Currently he serves as president of Sellers and Josephson, Inc., in Norwood, NJ.

The President designated Timothy J. McBride, of Michigan, to be a member of the Overseas Private Investment Corporation. Mr. McBride currently serves as an Assistant Secretary of Commerce for Trade Development.

September 19

In the evening, President Bush sent a personal message to President Carlos Saúl Menem of Argentina, thanking him for sending two ships to the Persian Gulf to join the international effort to enforce U.N. economic sanctions against Iraq.

September 20

The President met at the White House with:
—the Vice President; John H. Sununu, Chief of Staff to the President; Brent Scowcroft, Assistant to the President for National Security Affairs; and members of the CIA briefing staff;
—John H. Sununu, Chief of Staff to the President;
—the Vice President, for lunch.

September 21

The President met at the White House with:
—H. Lee Atwater, chairman of the Republican National Committee;
—the Vice President; John H. Sununu, Chief of Staff to the President; Brent Scowcroft, Assistant to the President for National Security Affairs; and members of the CIA briefing staff;
—John H. Sununu, Chief of Staff to the President;
—British Defense Minister Thomas King, to discuss the Persian Gulf crisis;
—congressional leaders, to discuss the Persian Gulf crisis;
—Secretary of State James A. Baker III.

The President announced his intention to nominate Katherine D. Ortega, of New Mexico, to be an Alternate Representative of the United States of America to the 45th Session of the General Assembly of the United Nations. She would succeed Barbara Franklin. Most recently, Mrs. Ortega served as Treasurer of the United States.

In the afternoon, the President and Mrs. Bush went to Camp David, MD, for the weekend.

September 23

In the afternoon, the President returned from a weekend stay at Camp David, MD.

September 24

The President met at the White House with:
—John H. Sununu, Chief of Staff to the President; Brent Scowcroft, Assistant to the President for National Security Affairs; and members of the CIA briefing staff;
—John H. Sununu, Chief of Staff to the President;
—Secretary of Defense Richard B. Cheney.

The President transmitted to the Congress the Saint Lawrence Seaway Development Corporation's annual report for 1989.

The President selected the following individuals to be delegates to the World Summit for Children at the United Nations in New York City, September 30:

James Baker, Secretary of State.

Lauro Cavazos, Secretary of Education.

Louis Sullivan, Secretary of Health and Human Services.

Antonia Novello, Surgeon General of the United States.

Clara McBride Hale. "Mother" Clara Hale founded Hale House in Harlem for infants with chemical dependence or infants infected with AIDS.

September 25

The President met at the White House with:
—John H. Sununu, Chief of Staff to the President; Brent Scowcroft, Assistant to the President for National Security Affairs; and members of the CIA briefing staff;
—John H. Sununu, Chief of Staff to the President;
—Stan Musial, former professional baseball player;
—Prime Minister Anibal Cavaco Silva of Portugal;
—members of the Boys and Girls Clubs of America;
—Robert S. Turner, commander of the American Legion.

In the evening, the President and Mrs. Bush attended the President's Club dinner at the Omni Shoreham Hotel.

September 26

The President met at the White House with:
—John H. Sununu, Chief of Staff to the President; Brent Scowcroft, Assistant to the President for National Security Affairs; and members of the CIA briefing staff;

—John H. Sununu, Chief of Staff to the President;
—the Republican congressional leadership, to discuss the Federal budget negotiations.

September 27

The President selected Secretary of Veterans Affairs Edward J. Derwinski to be his representative at the ceremonies commemorating the 30th anniversary of the independence of Cyprus, September 30–October 3.

The President announced his intention to appoint the following individuals to be members of the Board for International Food and Agricultural Development for the terms indicated:

John V. Byrne, of Oregon, for a term expiring July 28, 1993. He would succeed Jean Ruley Kearns. Currently Dr. Byrne serves as president of Oregon State University.

John A. Dibiaggio, of Michigan, for a term expiring July 28, 1993. He would succeed Hugh O. La Bounty. Currently Dr. Dibiaggio serves as president of Michigan State University in East Lansing.

Wendell G. Rayburn, of Missouri, for a term expiring July 28, 1993. This is a reappointment. Currently Mr. Rayburn serves as president of Lincoln University in Jefferson City, MO.

The President announced his intention to appoint the following individuals to be members of the President's Commission on Executive Exchange for terms of 2 years:

R. Quintus Anderson, of New York. This is a new position. Currently Mr. Anderson serves as chairman of the Aarque Companies in Jamestown, NY.

Ann Ascher, of California. She would succeed James A. Baker III. Currently Ms. Ascher serves as president of Ann Ascher, Inc., in Los Angeles, CA.

Mae Sue Talley, of Arizona. This is a new position. Most recently, Mrs. Talley served as the private sector coordinator for Latin America and the Caribbean for the Agency for International Development at the Department of State in Washington, DC.

September 28

The President met at the White House with:
—the Vice President; John H. Sununu, Chief of Staff to the President; Brent Scowcroft, Assistant to the President for National Security Affairs; and members of the CIA briefing staff;
—John H. Sununu, Chief of Staff to the President.

September 29

In the afternoon, the President and Mrs. Bush attended the National Security Council picnic at Fort McNair.

Later in the afternoon, the President and Mrs. Bush traveled to New York City. In his suite at

the Waldorf-Astoria Hotel, President Bush held bilateral meetings with:
—President Cesar Gaviria of Colombia,
—Prime Minister Salim al-Huss of Lebanon,
—President Violeta Chamorro of Nicaragua,
—Prime Minister Brian Mulroney of Canada,
—Prime Minister Tadeusz Mazowiecki of Poland, and
—Prime Minister Toshiki Kaifu of Japan.

September 30
In the afternoon, President Bush held bilateral meetings in his suite at the Waldorf-Astoria Hotel with:
—President Fernando Collor de Mello of Brazil,
—President Carlos Andrés Pérez of Venezuela,
—President Václav Havel of Czechoslovakia,
—King Baudouin I of Belgium,
—Prime Minister Felipe González Márquez of Spain,
—President Carlos Salinas de Gortari of Mexico, and
—Prime Minister Margaret Thatcher of the United Kingdom.

October 1
In the morning, President Bush held bilateral meetings in his suite at the Waldorf-Astoria Hotel with:
—President Carlos Saúl Menem of Argentina,
—President Luis Alberto Lacalle of Uruguay, and
—Secretary General Salim Salim and Chairman Yoweri Museveni of the Organization of African Unity.

Later, President Bush met at the United Nations with U.N. Secretary-General Javier Perez de Cuellar de la Guerra and U.N. General Assembly President Guido De Marco.

In the afternoon, the President had telephone conversations with Members of Congress to enlist their support for the Federal budget agreement.

President Bush held bilateral meetings in his suite at the Waldorf-Astoria Hotel with:
—Foreign Minister Eduard A. Shevardnadze of the Soviet Union,
—President Borisav Jović of Yugoslavia,
—Prime Minister Giulio Andreotti of Italy,
—President Hussain Mohammad Ershad of Bangladesh, and
—President Alfredo Cristiani Buckard of El Salvador.

October 2
The President met at the White House with:
—the Vice President; John H. Sununu, Chief of Staff to the President; Brent Scowcroft, Assistant to the President for National Security Affairs; and members of the CIA briefing staff;
—Albert J. Riccelli, Sr., president of the Sons of Italy;
—James L. Kimery, commander in chief of the Veterans of Foreign Wars;
—James W. Damon, president of the Elks;
—the Vice President, for lunch;
—John H. Sununu, Chief of Staff to the President.

Throughout the day, the President met with Members of Congress to enlist their support for the Federal budget agreement.

In an Oval Office ceremony, the President signed the United Services Organization's 50th Anniversary Commemorative Coin Act.

The President designated Norton Stevens, of New York, to be Vice Chairman of the Board of Directors of the Inter-American Foundation. Currently Mr. Stevens serves as an associate with Donaldson Enterprises in New York, NY.

In the evening, the President attended the Republican National Committee Eagles 15th anniversary fundraising dinner at the Pension Building.

October 3
The President met at the White House with:
—the Vice President; John H. Sununu, Chief of Staff to the President; Brent Scowcroft, Assistant to the President for National Security Affairs; and members of the CIA briefing staff;
—John H. Sununu, Chief of Staff to the President;
—Republican Members of Congress, to enlist their support for the Federal budget agreement;
—Peter Sampras, winner of the U.S. Open tennis tournament.

In the afternoon, the President attended a Republican fundraising luncheon at the Sheraton Carlton Hotel for Michigan congressional candidates.

Later, in an Oval Office ceremony, the President signed the 1992 Olympic Commemorative Coin Act.

The President announced his intention to appoint Michael J. Madigan, of the District of Columbia, to be a member of the District of Columbia Judicial Nomination Commission for a term of 5 years. He would succeed Carl S. Rauh. Currently Mr. Madigan serves as a partner with the law firm of Akin, Gump, Strauss, Hauer and Feld in Washington, DC.

The President announced his intention to appoint Anthony A. Lapham, of the District of Columbia, to be a member of the President's Intelligence Oversight Board. He would succeed Michael W. McConnell. Currently Mr. Lapham serves as a partner with Shea and Gardner in Washington, DC.

The President announced his intention to appoint the following individuals to be members of the Board of Trustees of the John F. Kennedy Center for the Performing Arts for terms expiring September 1, 2000:

Helen Joan Holt, of Texas. She would succeed Mrs. Theodore H. Strauss.

Marjorie S. Fisher, of Michigan. She would succeed Gerald M. Rafshoon.

Joy A. Silverman, of New York. She would succeed June Oppen Degnan.

The President announced his intention to appoint James W. Cicconi, Assistant to the President and Deputy to the Chief of Staff, to be a member of the Council of the Administrative Conference of the United States for a term of 3 years. He would succeed James H. Burnley IV.

Throughout the day, the President had telephone conversations with Republican Members of Congress to enlist their support for the Federal budget agreement.

In the evening, the President attended the National Republican Congressional Committee Leadership Council dinner at the Ritz Carlton Hotel.

October 4

The President met at the White House with:
—John H. Sununu, Chief of Staff to the President; Brent Scowcroft, Assistant to the President for National Security Affairs; and members of the CIA briefing staff;
—John H. Sununu, Chief of Staff to the President;
—Thomas S. Foley, Speaker of the House of Representatives, to discuss the Federal budget agreement;
—Republican Members of Congress, to enlist their support for the Federal budget agreement.

October 5

The President met at the White House with:
—John H. Sununu, Chief of Staff to the President; Brent Scowcroft, Assistant to the President for National Security Affairs; and members of the CIA briefing staff;
—John H. Sununu, Chief of Staff to the President;
—members of the Cabinet, to discuss the Federal budget and the closing of government operations.

In the morning, the President called African National Congress leader Nelson Mandela to discuss the recent visit of President F.W. de Klerk of South Africa.

The President announced his intention to appoint the following individuals to be members of the Competitiveness Policy Council for terms of 2 years. These are new positions:

Robert Adam Mosbacher, Secretary of Commerce.

Albert Shanker, of New York. Currently Mr. Shanker serves as president of the American Federation of Teachers in Washington, DC.

Alexander B. Trowbridge, of the District of Columbia. Currently Mr. Trowbridge serves as president of Trowbridge Partners in Washington, DC.

Throughout the day, the President spoke with congressional leaders to discuss the Federal budget.

October 6

In the evening, the President went to Camp David, MD.

October 8

In the afternoon, the President returned to the White House from Camp David, MD.

October 9

The President met at the White House with:
—the Vice President; John H. Sununu, Chief of Staff to the President; Brent Scowcroft, Assistant to the President for National Security Affairs; and members of the CIA briefing staff;
—congressional leaders, to discuss the Federal budget;
—John H. Sununu, Chief of Staff to the President.

In the morning, the President attended a fundraising breakfast for gubernatorial candidate Arliss Sturgulewski and Representative Don Young of Alaska at the Sheraton Carlton Hotel.

In the evening, the President hosted the "Art in Embassies" reception on the State Floor for supporters of the program that purchases art for display in U.S. Embassies abroad. Later, he attended the Republican Governors Association dinner at the Capital Hilton Hotel.

October 11

The President met at the White House with:
—the Vice President; John H. Sununu, Chief of Staff to the President; Brent Scowcroft, Assistant to the President for National Security Affairs; and members of the CIA briefing staff;
—John H. Sununu, Chief of Staff to the President;
—Republican congressional leaders;
—the Vice President, for lunch;
—labor leaders.

In the afternoon, the President attended a reception in the Indian Treaty Room of the Old Executive Office Building for the Texas Republican Party. He then participated in a swearing-in ceremony in the Oval Office for Wendy Gramm to continue as Chairman of the Commodity Futures Trading Commission. Later, he hosted a reception on the State Floor for Republican Members of the House of Representatives.

President Bush telephoned President François Mitterrand of France to discuss U.N. Security Council deliberations on the Persian Gulf crisis.

October 12

The President met at the White House with:
—the Vice President; John H. Sununu, Chief of Staff to the President; Brent Scowcroft, Assistant to the President for National Security Affairs; and members of the CIA briefing staff;
—John H. Sununu, Chief of Staff to the President;
—Secretary of State James A. Baker III.

The President announced his intention to nominate William W. Treat, of New Hampshire, to be a Representative of the United States of America to the 45th Session of the General Assembly of the United Nations. Currently Mr. Treat serves as chairman of Bank Meridian in Hampton, NH.

In the afternoon, the President and Mrs. Bush went to Camp David, MD, for the weekend.

October 14

In the afternoon, the President returned to the White House from a weekend stay at Camp David, MD.

October 15

The President met at the White House with:
—the Vice President; John H. Sununu, Chief of Staff to the President; Brent Scowcroft, Assistant to the President for National Security Affairs; and members of the CIA briefing staff;
—John H. Sununu, Chief of Staff to the President.

In the morning, the President traveled to Dallas, TX.

The President announced his intention to appoint John E. Reynolds III, of Connecticut, to be a member of the Advisory Council on Historic Preservation for a term expiring June 10, 1994. He would succeed Myna E. Wright. Currently Mr. Reynolds serves as a preservationist, restoration consultant, and an adaptive reuse developer in Middleton, CT.

October 16

In the afternoon, at the College of Du Page field house in Chicago, IL, the President presented the Presidential Citizen's Medal to Tony Zale, a former middleweight boxing champion, for his work with inner-city children in Chicago. He also telephoned Robert Dole, Senate minority leader, and Robert H. Michel, House Republican leader, to discuss the Federal budget.

The President announced his intention to appoint Robert Cy Laughter, of Ohio, to be a member of the American Battle Monuments Commission. He would succeed Esther Bradley. Currently Mr. Laughter serves as chairman of the board of Laughter Corp. in Dayton, OH.

October 17

The President met at the White House with:
—the Vice President; John H. Sununu, Chief of Staff to the President; Brent Scowcroft, Assistant to the President for National Security Affairs; and members of the CIA briefing staff;
—John H. Sununu, Chief of Staff to the President;
—Secretary of the Interior Manuel Lujan, Jr., chairman of the Combined Federal Campaign, to discuss the campaign;
—the Vice President, for lunch;
—Secretary of State James A. Baker III.

The President announced his intention to appoint David S. Lee, of California, to be a member of the Advisory Committee for Trade Policy and Negotiations for a term of 2 years. He would succeed James E. Burke. Currently Mr. Lee serves as president and chief executive officer of Qume Corp. in Milpitas, CA.

The President announced his intention to appoint the following individuals to be members of the Commission on Presidential Scholars:

Harry Dent, of South Carolina. He would succeed Mrs. Leslie D. Jamison. Currently Mr. Dent serves as a Christian lay minister in Columbia, SC.

Junia Doan, of Michigan. Currently Mrs. Doan serves as a partner with Doan Associates in Midland, MI.

Shirley N. Pettis-Roberson, of California. She would succeed Vivienne Raven Cooke.

Robert Melvin Worthington, of New Jersey. He would succeed Edward J. Joffe, Sr. Currently Dr. Worthington serves as an education consultant in Edgewater Park, NJ.

The President announced his intention to appoint the following individuals to be members of the U.S. Holocaust Memorial Council for the terms indicated:

Bradley A. Blakeman, of New York, for the remainder of the term expiring January 15, 1991, and for a term expiring January 15, 1996. He would succeed Marvin G. Kelfer. Currently Mr. Blakeman serves as an attorney with the law firm of Robert M. Blakeman & Associates in Valley Stream, NY.

Set Momjian, of Pennsylvania, for a term expiring January 15, 1995. He would succeed Richard Schifter. Currently Mr. Momjian serves as a marketing executive for Ford Aerospace in Arlington, VA.

October 18

The President met at the White House with:
—John H. Sununu, Chief of Staff to the President; Brent Scowcroft, Assistant to the President for National Security Affairs; and members of the CIA briefing staff;
—John H. Sununu, Chief of Staff to the President.

The President announced his intention to appoint Roger J. Whyte, of Maryland, to be a member of the National Commission for Employment Policy for a term expiring March 20, 1992. He would succeed John A. Rocco. Currently Mr. Whyte serves as a senior partner with A.T. Kearney Executive Search in Alexandria, VA.

The White House announced that the President ratified the treaty on the reunification of Germany, which was signed in Moscow on September 12.

In the evening, the President called Benjamin L. Hooks, executive director of the National Association for the Advancement of Colored People, and William T. Coleman, Jr., a representative of civil rights groups, to discuss the civil rights bill before Congress.

October 19

The President met at the White House with:
—John H. Sununu, Chief of Staff to the President; Brent Scowcroft, Assistant to the President for National Security Affairs; and members of the CIA briefing staff;
—John H. Sununu, Chief of Staff to the President;
—Yevgeniy Primakov, member of the Soviet Presidential Council, who had recently met with President Saddam Hussein of Iraq;
—Secretary of State James A. Baker III.

In the afternoon, the President met with the congressional leadership on Capitol Hill to discuss the reconciliation budget.

The White House announced that at approximately 6 p.m. the President signed the resolution providing funding for continued government operation through midnight Wednesday, October 24.

The President declared that a major disaster existed in Georgia as a result of severe storms and flooding that began October 11. He directed the Federal Emergency Management Agency to provide assistance to supplement State and local recovery efforts.

In the evening, the President and Mrs. Bush went to Camp David, MD, for the weekend.

October 21

In the afternoon, the President returned to the White House from a weekend stay at Camp David, MD.

October 22

The President met at the White House with:
—the Vice President; John H. Sununu, Chief of Staff to the President; Brent Scowcroft, Assistant to the President for National Security Affairs; and members of the CIA briefing staff;
—John H. Sununu, Chief of Staff to the President;
—Secretary of the Treasury Nicholas F. Brady.

In the afternoon, the President met in the Oval Office with American Legion representatives who were traveling to Saudi Arabia to meet with U.S. troops.

The President announced his intention to appoint Ellis D. Verink, Jr., of Florida, to be a member of the Nuclear Waste Technical Review Board for a term expiring April 19, 1994. This is a reappointment. Currently Dr. Verink serves as a consultant for the Lockheed-Georgia Co. in Gainesville, FL.

The President declared that a major disaster existed in the northern and central sections of South Carolina as a result of severe storms and flooding that occurred October 11. He directed the Federal Emergency Management Agency to provide assistance to supplement State and local recovery efforts.

October 23

In the evening, the President met at the White House with Robert Dole, Senate minority leader, and Robert H. Michel, House Republican leader, to discuss tax provisions of the deficit-reduction package.

October 24

The President met at the White House with:
—the Vice President; John H. Sununu, Chief of Staff to the President; Brent Scowcroft, Assistant to the President for National Security Affairs; and members of the CIA briefing staff;
—John H. Sununu, Chief of Staff to the President;
—members of the Cabinet;
—the Vice President, for lunch;
—Secretary of State James A. Baker III.

In an Oval Office ceremony, the President received diplomatic credentials from Ambassadors Agostino Cacciavillan of the Holy See, Candide

Pierre Ahouansou of Benin, Peter Zwack of Hungary, Sellapan Rama Nathan of Singapore, and Eduardo MacGillycuddy of Uruguay.

October 25

The President met at the White House with:
—the Vice President; John H. Sununu, Chief of Staff to the President; Brent Scowcroft, Assistant to the President for National Security Affairs; and members of the CIA briefing staff;
—Republican congressional leaders.

The President announced his intention to appoint the following individuals to be Vice Chairmen of the President's Committee on Employment of People With Disabilities:

Chad Colley, of Arkansas. He would succeed Anne H. Carlsen. Currently Mr. Colley serves as chief executive officer of the Colley Home Center, Inc., in Barling, AR.

I. King Jordan, of the District of Columbia. He would succeed Walter Y. Oi. Currently Dr. Jordan serves as the president of Gallaudet University in Washington, DC.

Lenore Miller, of New Jersey. She would succeed B. Elizabeth Tunney. Currently Mrs. Miller serves as president of Retail, Wholesale, and Department Store Unions in New York, NY.

The President announced his intention to appoint Margot E. Machol, of Illinois, to be a member of the National Commission for Employment Policy for a term expiring September 30, 1992. She would succeed Leora G. Day. Most recently Mrs. Machol served as a Commissioner of the Federal Trade Commission in Washington, DC.

The President announced his intention to appoint Clayton Yeutter, Secretary of Agriculture, to be a member of the Interagency Commission on Alternative Motor Fuels. This is a new position.

In the evening, the President traveled to Irvine, CA, where he stayed overnight.

October 26

In the afternoon, the President traveled to Honolulu, HI, for the summit meeting with representatives of 11 Pacific Island nations, October 27.

October 27

In the afternoon, the President had telephone conversations with congressional leaders to discuss passage of the budget reconciliation bill.

October 28

In the afternoon, the President traveled to San Francisco, CA, where he stayed overnight.

October 29

In the morning, the President attended a fundraising breakfast for gubernatorial candidate Pete Wilson.

October 30

The President met at the White House with:
—the Vice President; John H. Sununu, Chief of Staff to the President; Brent Scowcroft, Assistant to the President for National Security Affairs; and members of the CIA briefing staff;
—John H. Sununu, Chief of Staff to the President;
—congressional leaders, to discuss the situation in the Persian Gulf;
—national evangelical religious leaders;
—foreign policy advisers, to discuss the situation in the Persian Gulf.

October 31

The President met at the White House with:
—the Vice President; John H. Sununu, Chief of Staff to the President; Brent Scowcroft, Assistant to the President for National Security Affairs; and members of the CIA briefing staff;
—John H. Sununu, Chief of Staff to the President;
—the Vice President, for lunch;
—Secretary of State James A. Baker III.

The White House announced that the President has invited Queen Elizabeth II of the United Kingdom to make a state visit. The Queen has accepted and will meet with the President in May 1991.

November 1

The President announced that Grant C. Peterson, of Washington, will continue to serve as an Associate Director of the Federal Emergency Management Agency for State and Local Programs.

November 2

The White House announced that the President will depart November 16 for a trip that will begin in Europe and conclude November 23 in the Middle East. He will arrive in Prague, Czechoslovakia, on November 17 for meetings with President Havel and leaders of the Czech and Slovak Republics. On November 18, he will visit Germany to meet with Chancellor Kohl at the Chancellor's residence in Ludwigshafen. That afternoon he will travel to Paris for the summit meeting of the 34-nation Conference on Security and Cooperation in Europe, November 19–20. The President will then travel on to Egypt and Saudi Arabia for consultations on the situation in the Gulf with King Fahd of Saudi Arabia, President Mubarak of Egypt, and the Amir of Kuwait. He also will spend Thanksgiving Day with U.S. forces deployed in the area.

November 6

In the morning, the President attended the President's Club breakfast at the Houstonian Hotel in Houston, TX. After voting, he returned to Washington, DC.

In the afternoon, the President met at the White House with John H. Sununu, Chief of Staff to the President.

The President appointed Secretary of Veterans Affairs Edward J. Derwinski to be Chairman of the Interagency Committee for the Purchase of United States Savings Bonds for a 1-year term, effective December 1, 1990, to coordinate the 1991 governmentwide campaign. He will succeed Secretary of Housing and Urban Development Jack Kemp.

November 7

The President met at the White House with:
—the Vice President; John H. Sununu, Chief of Staff to the President; Brent Scowcroft, Assistant to the President for National Security Affairs; and members of the CIA briefing staff;
—the Vice President, for lunch;
—John H. Sununu, Chief of Staff to the President.

The President announced that Rita M. Rodriguez, of Massachusetts, will continue to serve as a member of the Board of Directors of the Export-Import Bank of the United States.

The White House announced that the President telephoned nearly 50 candidates around the country who participated in the midterm elections.

November 8

The President met at the White House with:
—the Vice President; John H. Sununu, Chief of Staff to the President; Brent Scowcroft, Assistant to the President for National Security Affairs; and members of the CIA briefing staff;
—Nancy Howe, 1990 Federal Duck Stamp Design Award winner;
—John H. Sununu, Chief of Staff to the President.

In the afternoon, the President went to Camp David, MD, for the Veterans Day weekend.

November 12

In the afternoon, the President returned to the White House from a weekend stay at Camp David, MD.

November 13

The President met at the White House with:
—John H. Sununu, Chief of Staff to the President; Brent Scowcroft, Assistant to the President for National Security Affairs; and members of the CIA briefing staff;
—John H. Sununu, Chief of Staff to the President;
—the Cabinet, to discuss the situation in the Persian Gulf, the upcoming budget process, and the legislative agenda;
—Senator Robert Dole and Representative Robert H. Michel, for lunch;
—Gabriel Aguirre, chairman of the U.S. Hispanic Chamber of Commerce.

In the afternoon, the President taped his Thanksgiving message to U.S. service personnel, which will be broadcast over the Armed Forces Radio and Television Network.

The President appointed the following individuals to be members of the President's Export Council:

Heinz C. Prechter, of Grosse Ile, MI. He would succeed Colby H. Chandler. Mr. Prechter is chairman and chief executive of ASC, Inc., in Southgate, MI. He will be designated Chairman.

Beverly F. Dolan, of Barrington, RI. He would succeed Whitney MacMillan. Mr. Dolan is chairman and chief executive officer of Textron, Inc., in Providence, RI. Mr. Dolan will be designated Vice Chairman.

Donald T. Bollinger, of Lockport, LA. He would succeed Walter F. Beran. Mr. Bollinger is chairman and chief executive officer of Bollinger Machine Shop & Shipyard, Inc., in Lockport.

Max Fisher, of Franklin, MI. He would succeed Steven A. Merksamer. Mr. Fisher is the founding chairman of the Detroit Renaissance in Detroit, MI.

Patricia S. Harrison, of Arlington, VA. She would succeed Edward A. Brennan. Mrs. Harrison is a partner in E. Bruce Harrison Co. in Washington, DC.

Robert Wood Johnson IV, of New York, NY. He would succeed Thornton A. Wilson. Mr. Johnson is chairman and chief executive officer of the Johnson Co., Inc., in New York.

Michael H. Jordan, of Dallas, TX. He would succeed Edward G. Jefferson. Mr. Jordan is chairman and chief executive officer of Pepsico Worldwide Foods, Inc., in Plano, TX.

Jonathan T. Kaji, of Gardena, CA. He would succeed John J. Murphy. Mr. Kaji is president of Kaji Associates in Gardena.

Kenneth L. Lay, of Houston, TX. He would succeed Paul Robert Locigno. Mr. Lay is chairman and chief executive officer of Enron Corp. in Houston.

John N. Palmer, of Jackson, MS. He would succeed James E. Jenkins. Mr. Palmer is chairman and chief executive officer of Mobile Telecommunications Technologies Corp. in Jackson.

Harold A. Poling, of Birmingham, MI. He would succeed Philip Caldwell. Mr. Poling is chairman and chief executive officer of Ford Motor Co. in Dearborn, MI.

Miguel R. San Juan, of Houston, TX. He would succeed Harry J. Gray. Mr. San Juan is vice president of the Greater Houston Partnership, world trade division.

William G. Spiegel, of Springfield, MO. He would succeed Van P. Smith. Mr. Spiegel is president of Spiegel Enterprises in Springfield.

Joseph Robert Wright, Jr., of New York, NY. This is a reappointment. Mr. Wright is vice chairman and director of W.R. Grace & Co. in New York.

John N. Yochelson, of Bethesda, MD. He would succeed Russell L. Hanlin. Mr. Yochelson is vice president for international business and economics at the Center for Strategic and International Studies in Washington, DC.

November 14

The President met at the White House with:

—John H. Sununu, Chief of Staff to the President; Brent Scowcroft, Assistant to the President for National Security Affairs; and members of the CIA briefing staff;

—John H. Sununu, Chief of Staff to the President;

—the congressional leadership, to discuss the situation in the Persian Gulf;

—Secretary of State James A. Baker III.

In the afternoon, the President participated in a swearing-in ceremony in the Oval Office for Roscoe B. Starek as Commissioner of the Federal Trade Commission.

The President selected David F. Girard-diCarlo, of Pennsylvania, to be a member of the Board of Directors of the National Railroad Passenger Corporation for a term of 2 years. He would succeed Samuel H. Hellenbrand. Currently Mr. Girard-diCarlo serves as a managing partner with Blank, Rome, Comisky and McCauley in Philadelphia, PA.

The President announced his intention to nominate Edward Johnson, of Michigan, to be a member of the Board of Directors of the African Development Foundation for a term expiring September 22, 1995. He would succeed William F. Pickard. Upon confirmation, he will be designated Chairperson. Currently Mr. Johnson serves as a partner with the law firm of Reynolds, Beeby and Magnuson, P.C., in Detroit, MI.

November 15

The President met at the White House with:

—the Vice President; John H. Sununu, Chief of Staff to the President; Brent Scowcroft, Assistant to the President for National Security Affairs; and members of the CIA briefing staff;

—John H. Sununu, Chief of Staff to the President.

The President selected the following individuals to represent him at the ceremonies commemorating the 20th anniversary of Oman National Day and the birthday of Sultan Qaboos, November 18–22:

Delegation Chairman:

Senator James McClure, of Idaho, and his wife, Louise McClure.

Delegates:

Robert Blake, of Lubbock, TX. Mr. Blake is a former Texas oil company executive, corporate director, and civic leader.

Richard W. Boehm, U.S. Ambassador to Oman.

Lynn M. Martin, Member of Congress from the 16th District of Illinois.

Jack Steel, of Houston, TX. Mr. Steel is a retired executive of Prudential Insurance Co. and served as special adviser to the Houston economic summit.

November 16

The President met at the White House with:

—the Vice President; John H. Sununu, Chief of Staff to the President; Brent Scowcroft, Assistant to the President for National Security Affairs; and members of the CIA briefing staff;

—John H. Sununu, Chief of Staff to the President;

—Defense Minister Lee Chong-Hu of the Republic of Korea;

—members of the American Legion.

The White House announced that the President invited George J. Mitchell, Senate majority leader; Robert Dole, Senate minority leader; Thomas S. Foley, Speaker of the House of Representatives; and Robert H. Michel, House Republican leader, to join him in celebrating the Thanksgiving holiday with U.S. troops in Saudi Arabia. The leaders have all accepted his invitation.

In the evening, the President left the White House for an 8-day trip to Czechoslovakia, Germany, France, Saudi Arabia, and Egypt.

November 19

In the morning, the President participated in the first plenary session of the Conference on Security and Cooperation in Europe (CSCE) at the Kleber Center in Paris, France. Following the session, he met with Prime Minister Ruud Lubbers of The Netherlands.

In the afternoon, the President attended a reception and luncheon with other delegation heads in the Salon des Ambassadeurs at the Palais de l'Elysée. Following the luncheon, he returned to the Kleber Center for the second plenary session of the CSCE.

The President announced his decision that the following individuals will continue to serve as members of the Commission on Presidential Scholars:

Helen Bie, of Green Bay, WI.

Robert A. Hall, Sr., of Wasilla, AK.
Evelyn W. McPhail, of Bay St. Louis, MS.

November 20

In the morning, President Bush hosted a breakfast for President Mikhail Gorbachev of the Soviet Union at the U.S. Ambassador's residence. Following breakfast, the President returned to the Kleber Center for the third plenary session of the CSCE.

In the afternoon, the President attended the fourth plenary session and final closed session of the CSCE.

The President announced his intention to appoint James C. Oberwetter, of Texas, to be a member of the International Cultural and Trade Center Commission for a term expiring August 20, 1995. He would succeed Abe Pollin. Currently Mr. Oberwetter serves as vice president of governmental and public affairs for Hunt Consolidated, Inc. (Hunt Oil Co.), in Dallas, TX.

November 21

In the morning, the President met with members of the U.S. Embassy community and returned to the Kleber Center for the CSCE signing ceremony. Following a departure ceremony at Orly Airport, he traveled to Jeddah, Saudi Arabia.

The White House announced that President Bush would meet with President Hafiz al-Assad of Syria on November 23 in Geneva, Switzerland.

In the evening, the President and Mrs. Bush arrived at King 'Abd al-'Aziz International Airport in Jeddah, Saudi Arabia, where they participated in an arrival ceremony and met informally with King Fahd bin 'Abd al-'Aziz Al Sa'ud. Later, the President attended a state dinner at the Royal Palace. Afterwards, he and King Fahd met privately and with U.S. and Saudi officials. Following the meetings, the President went to Al-Hamra Guest Palace.

November 22

In the morning, after a departure ceremony at King 'Abd al-'Aziz International Airport, the President and Mrs. Bush traveled to Dhahran, Saudi Arabia. They met informally with U.S. and Saudi officials at Dhahran International Airport and then visited U.S. troops deployed in the area.

In the evening, the President and Mrs. Bush traveled to Cairo, Egypt, and met with President Mohammed Hosni Mubarak and Mrs. Mubarak at Qubba Palace.

November 23

In the morning, the President and Mrs. Bush met at the U.S. Embassy with members of the American diplomatic community. They then participated in a formal arrival ceremony at Qubba Palace. Following the ceremony, Presidents Bush and Mubarak met privately and with U.S. and Egyptian officials.

In the afternoon, the President and Mrs. Bush attended a luncheon hosted by President and Mrs. Mubarak at Itihahdia Palace. Later, the President and Mrs. Bush traveled to Geneva, Switzerland.

In the evening, President Bush met with President Hafiz al-Assad of Syria at the Holiday Inn Crowne Plaza Hotel. Following the meeting, the President and Mrs. Bush traveled to Camp David, MD.

November 25

In the afternoon, the President and Mrs. Bush returned to the White House from a weekend stay at Camp David, MD. Later, the President had a telephone conversation with Secretary of State James A. Baker III.

November 26

In the morning, the President had breakfast at the White House with Secretary of Defense Richard B. Cheney and Gen. Colin L. Powell, Chairman of the Joint Chiefs of Staff, to discuss the President's trip to the Middle East. The President also had a telephone conversation with Secretary of State James A. Baker III.

Later in the morning, the President and Mrs. Bush traveled to Monterrey, Mexico, arriving at General Mariano Escobedo International Airport at midday. They then met President Carlos Salinas de Gortari and Mrs. Salinas in Agualeguas, where they attended the Lienzo Charro Adriana Margarita Rodeo and a Mexican folk dance presentation.

Later in the afternoon, the President and Mrs. Bush participated in a welcoming ceremony at Heroes Plaza in Monterrey. Following the ceremony, Mayor Socrates Rizzo presented President Bush with the key to the city at the Governor's Palace. The President and Mrs. Bush then went to the Holiday Inn Crowne Plaza Hotel, where they stayed overnight.

November 27

In the morning, Presidents Bush and Salinas attended a Mexican/American businessmen's breakfast in the Jalisco Room at the Holiday Inn Crowne Plaza Hotel. Following the breakfast, the two Presidents met privately and with U.S. and Mexican officials at the Museum de Nuevo León.

In the afternoon, the President and Mrs. Bush attended a dedication ceremony at the Governor's Palace for the Mexican-American Studies Program. Later, following a departure ceremony at General Mariano Escobedo International Airport, they returned to Washington, DC.

At the White House, the President called John Major, newly elected head of the Conservative

Party of England, to congratulate him on his victory.

The President declared that a major disaster existed in the State of Washington as a result of severe storms and flooding that began November 9. He directed the Federal Emergency Management Agency to provide assistance to supplement State and local recovery efforts.

November 28

The President met at the White House with:
—the Vice President; John H. Sununu, Chief of Staff to the President; Brent Scowcroft, Assistant to the President for National Security Affairs; and members of the CIA briefing staff;
—John H. Sununu, Chief of Staff to the President;
—Senator Robert Dole;
—the Vice President, for lunch;
—Secretary of State James A. Baker III, to discuss the upcoming U.N. Security Council meeting;
—Vice President Ricardo Arias Calderon of Panama.

The President declared that a major disaster existed in Palau as a result of Typhoon Mike, which struck the area November 10. He directed the Federal Emergency Management Agency to provide assistance to supplement local recovery efforts.

The President announced his intention to appoint the following individuals to be members of the President's Council on Rural America. These are new positions:

Ralph E. Bodine, of California. Upon appointment, he will be designated Chairman. Currently Mr. Bodine serves as chairman of the board of the Marlin Group in San Diego, CA.

Kay A. Orr, of Nebraska. Upon appointment, she will be designated Vice Chairman. Currently she serves as Governor of Nebraska.

Nelda L. Barton, of Kentucky. Currently Mrs. Barton serves as president and chairman of the board of Health Systems Inc. in Corbin, KY.

John E. Bourne, Jr., of South Carolina. Currently Mr. Bourne serves as mayor of North Charleston, SC.

Norman Brown, of Michigan. Currently Dr. Brown serves as president and chief programming officer of the W. K. Kellogg Foundation in Battle Creek, MI.

Hugh M. Field, of Iowa. Currently Mr. Field serves as an attorney with the law firm of Beecher, Rathest, Field, Walker and Morris in Waterloo, IA.

Ralph Hofstad, of Minnesota. Mr. Hofstad is founder of Hofstad Consultants in Edina, Minnesota, and most recently he served as president and chief executive officer of Land O'Lakes, Inc.

Charles E. Kruse, of Missouri. Currently Mr. Kruse serves as director of the Missouri Department of Agriculture in Jefferson City, MO.

Charles I. Moyer, of Kansas. Currently Mr. Moyer serves as chairman of the board and executive vice president of the First National Bank of Phillipsburg in Phillipsburg, KS.

Cathy B. Novinger, of South Carolina. Currently Mrs. Novinger serves as senior vice president of administration and government affairs for SCANA Group in Columbia, SC.

Linwood E. Palmer, Jr., of Maine. Currently Mr. Palmer serves as a lobbyist for Eaton, Peabody, Bradford and Teague in Augusta, ME.

Winthrop P. Rockefeller, of Arkansas. Currently Mr. Rockefeller serves as chairman of the board of Winrock Farms, Inc. in Little Rock, AR.

Bill Walker, of Mississippi. Currently Mr. Walker serves as president of Walker, Inc., in Jackson, MS.

The President announced his intention to nominate Edson G. Case, of Maryland, to be a member of the Defense Nuclear Facilities Safety Board for a term expiring October 18, 1995. This is a reappointment.

In the evening, the President and Mrs. Bush hosted a reception on the State Floor for newly elected Members of Congress

November 29

The President met at the White House with:
—the Vice President; John H. Sununu, Chief of Staff to the President; Brent Scowcroft, Assistant to the President for National Security Affairs; and members of the CIA briefing staff;
—Thomas S. Foley, Speaker of the House of Representatives, and Robert H. Michel, House Republican leader, for lunch;
—John H. Sununu, Chief of Staff to the President.

In the afternoon, the President participated in a swearing-in ceremony in the Oval Office for Christopher L. Koch as Chairman of the Federal Maritime Commission.

November 30

The President met at the White House with:
—the Vice President; John H. Sununu, Chief of Staff to the President; Brent Scowcroft, Assistant to the President for National Security Affairs; and members of the CIA briefing staff;
—John H. Sununu, Chief of Staff to the President;
—President John Haglelgam of Micronesia;
—Secretary of State James A. Baker III;
—Kuwaiti refugees;
—congressional leaders.

President Bush had telephone conversations with King Fahd bin 'Abd al-'Aziz Al Sa'ud of Saudi Arabia, President Mohammed Hosni Mubarak of Egypt, President Turgut Özal of Turkey, and Amir Jabir al-Ahmad al-Jabir Al Sabah of Kuwait, to discuss President Bush's remarks that morning on the Persian Gulf crisis.

The President announced his intention to appoint the following individuals to be members of the National Commission for Employment Policy for the terms indicated:

J. Fernando Niebla, of California, for a term expiring March 20, 1992. He would succeed Max Hugel. Currently Mr. Niebla serves as president and chief executive officer of INFOTEC Development, Inc., in Santa Ana, CA.

Henri S. Rauschenbach, of Massachusetts, for a term expiring February 19, 1992. He would succeed Trudy McDonald. Currently Mr. Rauschenbach serves as a Massachusetts State senator.

The White House announced that the Aggregate Report on Personnel was transmitted to Thomas S. Foley, Speaker of the House of Representatives, and Dan Quayle, President of the Senate.

In the evening, the President went to Camp David, MD, for the weekend.

December 2

In the afternoon, President Bush returned to the White House from a weekend stay at Camp David, MD. He called Chancellor Helmut Kohl of Germany to congratulate him on his party's electoral victory.

Later, the President and Mrs. Bush hosted a reception on the State Floor for musician Dizzy Gillespie, actress Katharine Hepburn, singer Risë Stevens, composer Jule Styne, and film director and writer Billy Wilder, who were the recipients of the Kennedy Center Honors for Lifetime Achievement.

In the evening, President Bush and his daughter, Dorothy LeBlond, left the White House for a 7-day trip to South America.

December 3

In the morning, President Bush arrived at Brasilia International Airport and participated in a welcoming ceremony at Planalto Palace. He and President Fernando Collor de Mello met privately and with U.S. and Brazilian officials at the palace.

In the afternoon, President Bush met with members of the American diplomatic community at the U.S. Embassy.

December 4

In the morning, President Bush participated in a departure ceremony at Brasilia International Airport before leaving for Montevideo, Uruguay.

In the afternoon, President Bush arrived at Carrasco International Airport in Montevideo, where he took part in an arrival ceremony. Afterwards, he and President Luis Alberto Lacalle met

privately and with U.S. and Uruguayan officials at the Edificio Libertad.

Later, at the Legislative Palace, President Bush participated in a welcoming ceremony, met with members of the Uruguayan Supreme Court, and received the keys to Montevideo from Mayor Tabare Vazquez and President Jorge Mazzanovich of the junta municipal. President Bush then met at the U.S. Embassy with members of the American diplomatic community.

The President announced his intention to appoint Carroll D. Besadny, secretary of the Wisconsin Department of Natural Resources, to be Commissioner of the United States Section of the Great Lakes Fishery Commission for a term expiring February 18, 1996. He would succeed James M. Ridenour.

The President announced his intention to appoint the following individuals to be members of the President's Commission on White House Fellowships:

Leslie G. Denend, of California. He would succeed Garrett D. Pagon. Currently Mr. Denend serves as executive vice president of product operations for 3COM Corp. in Santa Clara, CA.

Gail H. Klapper, of Colorado. She would succeed Donald J. Devine. Currently Mrs. Klapper serves as an attorney with the law firm of Gail H. Klapper in Denver, CO.

Elspeth Davies Rostow, of Texas. She would succeed Francis Winford Cash. Currently Mrs. Rostow serves as the Stiles professor emerita of the LBJ School of Public Affairs at the University of Texas at Austin.

Gaddi Vasquez, of California. He would succeed Sammy Lee. Currently Mr. Vasquez serves as Orange County supervisor in Santa Ana, CA.

Richard J. Leon, of the District of Columbia. He would succeed Stanley S. Scott. Currently Mr. Leon serves as a partner with the law firm of Baker and Hostetler in Washington, DC.

The President announced his intention to appoint the following individuals to be members of the Advisory Committee for Trade Policy and Negotiations for terms of 2 years:

James R. Houghton, of New York. This is a reappointment. Currently Mr. Houghton serves as chairman and chief executive officer of Corning, Inc., in Corning, NY.

Donald G. Fisher, of California. This is a reappointment. Currently Mr. Fisher serves as chairman and chief executive officer of the Gap, Inc., in San Francisco, CA.

Donald V. Fites, of Illinois. He would succeed George A. Schaefer. Currently Mr. Fites serves as chairman and chief executive officer of Caterpillar, Inc., in Peoria, IL.

Richard W. Snyder, of Texas. This is a reappointment. Mr. Snyder is founder, chairman, and chief executive officer of Snyder General Corp. in Dallas, TX.

Robert Van Dine, of California. He would succeed Harry Evans Sloan. Mr. Van Dine is founder, vice chairman, and chairman of the executive committee of St. Ives Laboratories Corp. in Rolling Hills, CA.

Rudolph A. Oswald, of Maryland. This is a reappointment. Currently Dr. Oswald serves as director of the AFL–CIO education department in Washington, DC.

The President announced his intention to appoint Dominic Man-Kit Lam, of Texas, to be a member of the President's Committee on the Arts and the Humanities. He would succeed Joan Dillon. Currently Dr. Lam serves as chairman of the board of Houston Bio-Tech, Inc., and as director of the Center for Biotechnology for Baylor College of Medicine in Woodlands, TX.

The President announced his intention to appoint Costa N. Miller, of Indiana, to be a Vice Chairman of the President's Committee on Employment of People With Disabilities. He would succeed Anne H. Carlsen. Currently Mr. Miller serves as executive director of the Indiana Association of Rehabilitation Facilities in Indianapolis, IN.

The President announced his intention to appoint the following individuals to be members of the President's Commission on Executive Exchange for terms of 2 years:

Richard G. Quick, of Pennsylvania. This is a new position. Currently Mr. Quick serves as president and chief executive officer for HVP International, Ltd., in Boalsburg, PA.

Shirley Young, of Michigan. She would succeed George P. Shultz. Currently Ms. Young serves as vice president for consumer market development for General Motors in Detroit, MI.

In the evening, President Bush traveled to Punta del Este, where he attended a dinner at the Posta del Cangrejo restaurant hosted by President and Mrs. Lacalle. Following the dinner, President Bush went to Loma Verde, where he stayed overnight.

December 5

In the morning, President Bush attended a private breakfast at the Hotel L'Auberge with President and Mrs. Lacalle before leaving for Buenos Aires, Argentina.

At midday, President Bush arrived at Aeroparque Airport in Buenos Aires, participated in a welcoming ceremony, and received the key to the city. Later, he participated in a wreath-laying ceremony at the statue of Gen. José de San Martin.

In the afternoon, at Casa Rosata, President Bush met privately with President Carlos Saúl Menem and with the international diplomatic corps. The two Presidents then participated in a working luncheon with U.S. and Argentine officials.

The President announced his intention to appoint the following individuals to be members of the President's Council on Physical Fitness and Sports:

Christine Marie Evert, of Florida. This is a new position. Ms. Evert is a retired tennis professional.

Earvin "Magic" Johnson, of California. He would succeed George W. Armstrong. Mr. Johnson is a member of the Los Angeles Lakers.

Jackie Joyner-Kersee, of California. This is a new position. Mrs. Joyner-Kersee is a professional track star.

Sammy Lee, of California. He would succeed Frederic V. Malek. Dr. Lee is a diving coach in Huntington Beach, CA.

James Lorimer, of Ohio. He would succeed Mitch Gaylord. Mr. Lorimer serves as vice president of government relations for Nationwide Insurance in Columbus, OH.

Chi Chi Rodriguez, of Florida. He would succeed Harry N. Walters. Mr. Rodriguez is a professional golfer.

The President announced his intention to nominate Eunice N. Sato, of California, to be a member of the National Advisory Council on Educational Research and Improvement for a term expiring September 30, 1991. She would succeed Noreen C. Thomas. Most recently, Mrs. Sato served as mayor of the City of Long Beach, CA.

In the evening, President Bush and President Menem attended a rodeo at the Sociedad Rural Arena.

December 6

In the morning, President Bush met at the U.S. Embassy with members of the American diplomatic community and then participated in a departure ceremony at Aeroparque Airport before leaving for Santiago, Chile.

At midday, President Bush arrived at Arturo Merino Benitez Airport in Santiago, where he took part in an arrival ceremony. Later, he and President Patricio Aylwin Azocar attended a working luncheon with U.S. and Chilean officials at President Aylwin's residence.

In the afternoon, in Valparaiso, President Bush participated in a welcoming ceremony at the Chilean Congress Building.

The White House announced that President Bush has invited Prime Minister John Major of the United Kingdom to make a visit to the United States. The Prime Minister has accepted the invitation and will meet with President Bush on December 21 and 22 at Camp David, MD.

The White House also announced that President Vytautus Landsbergis of Lithuania will meet with President Bush on December 10 in the United States.

President Bush declared that major disasters existed in Arizona, as a result of severe storms that occurred between July 8 and September 14, and in Indiana, as a result of severe storms and flooding that began November 27. He directed the Federal Emergency Management Agency to provide assistance to supplement State and local recovery efforts.

In the evening, President Bush took part in an arrival ceremony at La Moneda Palace. At the palace, he met privately with President Aylwin and with U.S. and Chilean officials.

December 7

In the morning, President Bush met at the U.S. Embassy with members of the American diplomatic community. Later, he participated in a departure ceremony at Arturo Merino Benitez Airport before leaving for Caracas, Venezuela.

In the afternoon, President Bush arrived at Simón Bolívar International Airport in Caracas where he took part in an arrival ceremony.

In the evening, President Bush and President Pérez met privately and with U.S. and Venezuelan officials at La Casona.

December 8

In the afternoon, the President met with members of the American diplomatic community at the U.S. Ambassador's residence. Following a departure ceremony at Simón Bolívar International Airport, the President returned to Washington, DC.

December 10

The President met at the White House with:
—the Vice President; John H. Sununu, Chief of Staff to the President; Brent Scowcroft, Assistant to the President for National Security Affairs; and members of the CIA briefing staff;
—newly elected officers of the Future Farmers of America;
—presidents of historically black colleges;
—Secretary of Defense Richard B. Cheney;
—John H. Sununu, Chief of Staff to the President.

In the evening, the President hosted the congressional Christmas ball on the State Floor.

December 11

The President met at the White House with:
—the Vice President; John H. Sununu, Chief of Staff to the President; Brent Scowcroft, Assistant to the President for National Security Affairs; and members of the CIA briefing staff;
—John H. Sununu, Chief of Staff to the President.

In the afternoon, the President hosted a Christmas party for White House staff on the State Floor.

The President announced his intention to nominate Robert Logan Clarke, of Texas, to be

Comptroller of the Currency, for a term of 5 years. This is a reappointment.

December 12

The President met at the White House with:
—the Vice President; John H. Sununu, Chief of Staff to the President; Brent Scowcroft, Assistant to the President for National Security Affairs; and members of the CIA briefing staff;
—John H. Sununu, Chief of Staff to the President.

The President has named the following individuals to represent him as election observers in Haiti, December 14–17:

Delegation Chairman:

William Janklow, former Governor of South Dakota and his daughter, Shonna Janklow.

Delegates:

Alvin P. Adams, Jr., United States Ambassador to Haiti.

Bernard W. Aronson, Assistant Secretary of State for Inter-American Affairs.

Walter S. Fauntroy, House of Representatives, D–DC.

Porter J. Goss, House of Representatives, R–FL.

Arturo Guzman, member of the Advisory Council of the Small Business Administration of Puerto Rico.

J. Michael Levesque, mayor, City of West Warwick, RI.

Monsignor William F. Murphy, director of the Office of Social Justice, Archdiocese of Boston.

James L. Oberstar, House of Representatives, D–MN.

Arthur E. Teele, Jr., county commissioner, Dade County, FL.

Jack Webb, senior vice president of First City Bank Corp. of TX.

The President appointed the following individuals to be Directors of the Federal Housing Finance Board. They will serve at the pleasure of the President, but no longer than the end of the next session of the Senate:

Lawrence U. Costiglio, of New York.

Daniel F. Evans, Jr., of Indiana. He will be designated chairperson.

William C. Perkins, of Wisconsin.

Marilyn R. Seymann, of Arizona.

December 13

The President met at the White House with:
—the Vice President; John H. Sununu, Chief of Staff to the President; Brent Scowcroft, Assistant to the President for National Security Affairs; and members of the CIA briefing staff;
—Jonas Savimbi, president of the National Union for the Total Independence of Angola.

In the afternoon, the President had lunch with the Vice President and Mrs. Quayle at the Vice President's residence.

In the evening, the President hosted a Christmas party for White House staff on the State Floor.

December 14

The President met at the White House with:
—the Vice President; John H. Sununu, Chief of Staff to the President; Brent Scowcroft, Assistant to the President for National Security Affairs; and members of the CIA briefing staff;
—veterans service organizations;
—Secretary of State James A. Baker III;
—the President's Council of Advisors on Science and Technology.

The President declared that a major disaster existed in the Federated States of Micronesia as a result of Typhoon Owen, which struck the area November 26–December 1. He directed the Federal Emergency Management Agency to provide assistance to supplement State and local recovery efforts.

In the afternoon, the President went to Camp David, MD, for the weekend.

December 16

In the morning, the President returned to the White House from a weekend stay at Camp David, MD.

December 17

The President met at the White House with:
—Representative Lynn Martin, nominee for Secretary of Labor;
—the Vice President; John H. Sununu, Chief of Staff to the President; Brent Scowcroft, Assistant to the President for National Security Affairs; and members of the CIA briefing staff;
—John H. Sununu, Chief of Staff to the President;
—W. Nathaniel Howell, Ambassador to Kuwait;
—the Vice President, for lunch;
—Secretary of the Treasury Nicholas F. Brady.

In the evening, the President and Mrs. Bush hosted a Christmas party on the State Floor.

December 18

The President met at the White House with:
—the Vice President; John H. Sununu, Chief of Staff to the President; Brent Scowcroft, Assistant to the President for National Security Affairs; and members of the CIA briefing staff;
—John H. Sununu, Chief of Staff to the President;
—African-American editors, for lunch;
—Ganesh Man Singh, leader of the Nepali Congress;

—William McCarthy, president of the Teamsters Union.

In the evening, the President and Mrs. Bush hosted a Christmas party on the State Floor.

December 19

The President met at the White House with:
—the Vice President; John H. Sununu, Chief of Staff to the President; Brent Scowcroft, Assistant to the President for National Security Affairs; and members of the CIA briefing staff;
—John H. Sununu, Chief of Staff to the President;
—leaders of the business community;
—Members of Congress;
—Senator Strom Thurmond of South Carolina;
—Secretary of State James A. Baker III.

In the evening, the President and Mrs. Bush hosted a Christmas party on the State Floor.

December 20

The President met at the White House with:
—the Vice President; John H. Sununu, Chief of Staff to the President; Brent Scowcroft, Assistant to the President for National Security Affairs; and members of the CIA briefing staff;
—John H. Sununu, Chief of Staff to the President;
—Secretary of State James A. Baker III and Brent Scowcroft, Assistant to the President for National Security Affairs, to discuss the resignation of Soviet Foreign Minister Eduard Shevardnadze;
—Members of Congress, to discuss the situation in the Persian Gulf;
—the Most Reverend Edmund L. Browning, presiding bishop of the Episcopal Church, to discuss the situation in the Persian Gulf.

The President announced his intention to appoint the following individuals to be members of the Commission on Presidential Scholars:

Melissa H. Chamberlain, of Missouri. She would succeed Aubyn A. Curtiss. Currently Ms. Chamberlain serves as a GOP consultant in St. Louis, MO.

Barbara Pope Dean, of South Dakota. She would succeed Brustuen H. Lien. Mrs. Dean has served as the arts development director in Rapid City, SD.

Wade Franklin III, of Ohio. He would succeed Martha C. Moore. Currently Mr. Franklin serves as director of contract compliance and affirmative action for the Columbus Public Schools in Columbus, OH.

Marge Olivia Gruenes, of Minnesota. She would succeed Virginia M. Berg. Currently Ms. Gruenes serves as principal of the Cedar Park Elementary School in Apple Valley, MN.

Jun Retsu Hatoyama, of California. He would succeed Rodney W. Wood. Currently Mr. Hatoyama serves as president of Jun R. Hatoyama and Associates, Inc., in San Francisco, CA.

Sylvia Bernstein Hermann, of Maryland. She would succeed James Andrew Dorn. Most recently, Ms. Hermann served as a member and vice chairman of the National Advisory Council on Continuing Education in Bethesda, MD.

R.L. Ireland III, of Georgia. He would succeed Anne Volz Higgins. Currently Mr. Ireland serves as a general partner for Brown Brothers Harriman and Co., in New York, NY.

Jeanne Keenan, of Washington. She would succeed Wells B. McCurdy. Currently Ms. Keenan serves as community relations director for the Washington council for economic education in Seattle, WA.

Nancy Johnson Morris, of Tennessee. She would succeed Sammie Lynn Scandlyn Puett. Most recently Ms. Morris served as a teacher at the Franklin Junior High School in Franklin, TN.

Flo Traywick, of Virginia. She would succeed Keith B. Geiger. Currently Ms. Traywick serves as a national Republican committeewoman.

Stanley Earl Wachstetter, of Mississippi. He would succeed Harold D. Weidman. Currently Pastor Wachstetter serves as pastor of the Bible Tabernacle in Clinton, MS.

Jack M. Webb, of Texas. He would succeed Joseph R. Reppert. Currently Mr. Webb serves as president of Jack Webb and Associates in Houston, TX.

The President announced his intention to appoint the following individuals to be members of National Council on Vocational Education for the terms indicated:

Bernard Baher, of Massachusetts, for a term expiring January 17, 1993. He would succeed George Johnston Ames. Upon appointment, he will be designated Chairperson. Most recently Mr. Baher served as president of the Blue Hills Foundation in Canton, MA.

Marlene Ahimaz, of Illinois, for a term expiring January 17, 1992. She would succeed Sally J. Novetzke. Currently Dr. Ahimaz serves as chief executive officer of Energy and International Development in Chicago, IL.

R. William Bramberg, Jr., of Florida, for a term expiring January 17, 1993. He would succeed William C. Hayes. Currently Mr. Bramberg serves as president of the Bramberg Management Organization in Largo, FL.

The President announced his intention to appoint Edwina P. Dalton, of Virginia, to be a member of the President's Committee on Mental Retardation for a term expiring May 11, 1993. She would succeed Howard P. Black. Currently Senator Dalton serves as a Virginia State senator.

In the evening, the President and Mrs. Bush hosted a Christmas party on the State Floor.

December 21

The President met at the White House with:
—the Vice President; John H. Sununu, Chief of Staff to the President; Brent Scowcroft, Assistant to the President for National Security Affairs; and members of the CIA briefing staff;
—John H. Sununu, Chief of Staff to the President;
—Ambassadors from member nations of the international coalition in the Persian Gulf;
—Secretary of State James A. Baker III.

In the afternoon, the President went to Camp David, MD, for the holidays.

The President announced his intention to appoint the following individuals to be members of the National Commission for Employment Policy for terms expiring September 30, 1992:

Eduardo Aguirre, Jr., of Texas. He would succeed William M. Taylor. Currently Mr. Aguirre serves as senior vice president and general manager in the international private banking division at the NCNB Texas National Bank in Houston, TX.

Lynne F. Egge, of Virginia. She would succeed Henry A. Duffy. Currently Ms. Egge serves on the Independent Union of Flight Attendants executive board as a base chairperson and as a flight attendant/purser for Pan American Airways.

The President announced his intention to appoint the following individuals to be members of the Advisory Committee for Trade Policy and Negotiations for terms of 2 years:

Roger J. Baccigaluppi, of California. This is a reappointment.

Allen E. Murray, of New York. This is a reappointment.

Jack Valenti, of the District of Columbia. He would succeed George L. Argyros. Currently Mr. Valenti serves as president and chief executive officer of the Motion Picture Association of America, Inc., in Washington, DC.

The President announced his intention to appoint the following individuals to be members of the President's Commission on Executive Exchange for terms of 2 years:

David W. Christopher, of Pennsylvania. This is a reappointment.

Wilma H. Jordan, of New York. This is a new position. Currently Ms. Jordan serves as president and chief executive officer of the Jordan Group, Inc., in New York, NY.

Lester H. Lee, of California. He would succeed George Adams Roberts. Currently Dr. Lee serves as chairman and president of Recortec, Inc., in Sunnyvale, CA.

Russell S. Reynolds, Jr., of Connecticut. This is a new position. Currently Mr. Reynolds serves as chairman of Russell Reynolds Associates, Inc., in New York, NY.

The President announced his intention to appoint the following individuals to be members of the President's Export Council:

Carol Brookins, of the District of Columbia. She would succeed J. Bonnie Newman. Currently Ms. Brookins serves as president and chief executive officer of World Perspectives, Inc., in Washington, DC.

G. *Lee Thompson,* of Connecticut. He would succeed Arthur H. Hausman. Currently Mr. Thompson serves as president and chief executive officer of the Smith Corona Corp. in New Canaan, CT.

The President announced his intention to appoint Ruth R. Miller, of Ohio, to be a member of the U.S. Holocaust Memorial Council for a term expiring January 15, 1995. She would succeed Barbaralee Diamonstein-Spielvogel. Currently Ms. Miller serves as president of the Tower City Center in Cleveland, OH.

December 22

After meeting with Prime Minister John Major of the United Kingdom, the President remained at Camp David to spend Christmas with his family.

December 24

The President declared that a major disaster existed in Guam as a result of a typhoon that occurred December 21. He directed the Federal Emergency Management Agency to provide assistance to supplement local recovery efforts.

December 26

The President met with his national security advisers to discuss the situation in the Persian Gulf.

December 27

In the morning, the President returned to the White House and met with Ambassador Aleksandr Bessmertnykh of the Soviet Union.

In the afternoon, the President went to Camp David, MD.

Appendix B—Nominations Submitted to the Senate

The following list does not include promotions of members of the Uniformed Services, nominations to the Service Academies, or nominations of Foreign Service officers.

Submitted July 10

Joseph M. McLaughlin,
of New York, to be United States Circuit Judge for the Second Circuit, vice Lawrence W. Pierce, retired.

Joe D. Whitley,
of Georgia, to be United States Attorney for the Northern District of Georgia for the term of 4 years, vice Robert L. Barr, Jr., resigned.

Anthony L. Bennett,
of Minnesota, to be United States Marshal for the District of Minnesota for the term of 4 years, vice Robert L. Pavlak, term expired.

Joyce Elaine Tucker,
of Illinois, to be a member of the Equal Employment Opportunity Commission for the remainder of the term expiring July 1, 1991, vice Clarence Thomas, resigned.

Submitted July 12

Stephen G. Milliken,
of the District of Columbia, to be an Associate Judge of the Superior Court of the District of Columbia for the term of 15 years, vice Joseph M. Hannon, deceased.

Submitted July 16

Lynn H. Duncan,
of Georgia, to be United States Marshal for the Northern District of Georgia for the term of 4 years (reappointment).

Submitted July 17

Wayne Lee Berman,
of New York, to be an Assistant Secretary of Commerce, vice D. Bruce Merrifield.

Submitted July 18

Thomas G. Nelson,
of Idaho, to be United States Circuit Judge for the Ninth Circuit, vice J. Blaine Anderson, deceased.

Submitted July 19

Steven B. Kelmar,
of Pennsylvania, to be an Assistant Secretary of Health and Human Services, vice Gerald L. Olson, resigned.

Joseph Francis Glennon,
of Florida, to be a member of the Advisory Board for Cuba Broadcasting for a term expiring October 27, 1991 (reappointment).

Kimberly A. Madigan,
of Illinois, to be a member of the National Mediation Board for the term expiring July 1, 1993, vice Walter C. Wallace, term expired.

Submitted July 23

The following-named persons to be members of the Farm Credit Administration Board, Farm Credit Administration, for the terms indicated:

For the term expiring October 13, 1994:

Billy Ross Brown, of Mississippi, vice Jim R. Billington, resigned.

For the term expiring May 21, 1996:

John C. Datt, of Virginia, vice Marvin Duncan, term expired.

Submitted July 25

David H. Souter,
of New Hampshire, to be an Associate Justice of the Supreme Court of the United States, vice William Joseph Brennan, Jr., retired.

Edward P. Brynn,
of Vermont, a career member of the Senior Foreign Service, Class of Counselor, to be Ambassador Extraordinary and Plenipotentiary of the United States of America to Burkina Faso.

Ryan Clark Crocker,
of Washington, a career member of the Senior Foreign Service, Class of Counselor, to be Ambassador Extraordinary and Plenipotentiary of the United States of America to the Republic of Lebanon.

Jerome H. Powell,
of New York, to be an Assistant Secretary of the Treasury, vice David W. Mullins, Jr., resigned.

Submitted July 31

Stephen H. Rogers,
of Virginia, a career member of the Senior Foreign Service, Class of Minister-Counselor, to be Ambassador Extraordinary and Plenipotentiary of the United States of America to the Kingdom of Swaziland.

Diane Gilbert Weinstein,
of the District of Columbia, to be a Judge of the United States Claims Court for a term of 15 years, vice Randall R. Rader, elevated.

Mary Sterling,
of Virginia, to be Inspector General, Department of Transportation, vice John W. Melchner, resigned.

Submitted August 1

Robert S. Mueller III,
of Massachusetts, to be an Assistant Attorney General, vice Edward S.G. Dennis, Jr., resigned.

Robert F. Goodwin,
of Maryland, to be a Commissioner on the part of the United States on the International Joint Commission, United States and Canada, vice Donald L. Totten, resigned.

Brig. Gen. Paul Y. Chinen, USA,
to be a member of the Mississippi River Commission.

Holland H. Coors,
of Colorado, to be a member of the Board of Trustees of the Harry S. Truman Scholarship Foundation for a term expiring December 10, 1995, vice Anita M. Miller, term expired.

The following named persons to be members of the National Science Board, National Science Foundation, for the terms indicated:

For the remainder of the term expiring May 10, 1994:

W. Glenn Campbell, of California, vice D. Allan Bromley, resigned.

For a term expiring May 10, 1996:

Perry L. Adkisson, of Texas (reappointment).
Bernard F. Burke, of Massachusetts, vice Kenneth Leon Nordtvedt, Jr., term expired.
Thomas B. Day, of California (reappointment).
James Johnson Duderstadt, of Michigan (reappointment).

Carolyn D. Leavens,
of California, to be a member of the Board of Directors of the Overseas Private Investment Corporation for a term expiring December 17, 1990, vice Allie C. Felder, Jr., term expired.

Carolyn D. Leavens,
of California, to be a member of the Board of Directors of the Overseas Private Investment Corporation for a term expiring December 17, 1993 (reappointment).

Submitted August 2

Thomas F. Kranz,
of California, to be an Associate Director of the Federal Emergency Management Agency, vice James P. McNeill, resigned.

The following named persons to be Directors of the Federal Housing Finance Board for the terms indicated:

William C. Perkins, of Wisconsin, for a term of 1 year (new position).
Marilyn R. Seymann, of Arizona, for a term of 5 years (new position).

Submitted August 3

Juliette Clagett McLennan,
of the District of Columbia, for the rank of Ambassador during her tenure of service as the U.S. Representative on the Commission on the Status of Women of the Economic and Social Council of the United Nations.

The following-named persons to be the Representative and Alternate Representatives of the United States of America to the 34th Session of the General Conference of the International Atomic Energy Agency:

Representative:

James D. Watkins, of California.

Alternate Representative:

Richard T. Kennedy, of the District of Columbia.
Michael H. Newlin, of Maryland.
Kenneth M. Carr, of California.

William B. Shubb,
of California, to be United States District Judge for the Eastern District of California, vice Raul A. Rameriz, resigned.

Gary L. Taylor,
of California, to be United States District Judge for the Central District of California, vice Ferdinand F. Fernandez, elevated.

James Ware,
of California, to be United States District Judge for the Northern District of California, vice Robert F. Peckham, retired.

Jean C. Hamilton,
of Missouri, to be United States District Judge for the Eastern District of Missouri, vice John F. Nangle, retired.

Thomas D. Rath,
of New Hampshire, to be a member of the Board of Directors of the Legal Services Corporation for a term expiring July 13, 1993, vice John N. Erlenborn, resigned.

Antonio C. Amador,
of California, to be a member of the Merit Systems Protection Board for the term of 7 years expiring March 1, 1997, vice Maria Lucia Johnson, term expired.

Richard Y. Roberts,
of Virginia, to be a member of the Securities and Exchange Commission for the term expiring June 5, 1995, vice Joseph A. Grundfest, resigned.

Paula J. Dobriansky,
of Virginia, to be an Associate Director of the U.S. Information Agency, vice Charles Edward Horner, resigned.

The following named persons to be members of the Board of Directors of the Legal Services Corporation for the terms indicated, to which positions they were appointed during the recess of the Senate from November 22, 1989, to January 23, 1990:

For a term expiring July 13, 1992:

Jo Betts Love, of Mississippi, vice Lorain Miller, term expired.
Guy Vincent Molinari, of New York, vice Claude Galbreath Swafford, term expired.
Jeanine E. Wolbeck, of Minnesota, vice Hortencia Benavidez, term expired.

For a term expiring July 13, 1993:

Howard H. Dana, Jr., of Maine, vice Thomas F. Smegal, Jr., term expired.
Luis Guinot, Jr., of Puerto Rico, vice Michael B. Wallace, term expired.
Penny L. Pullen, of Illinois, vice William Clark Durant III, term expired.
George W. Wittgraf, of Iowa, vice Paul B. Eaglin, term expired.

The following named persons to be members of the Peace Corps National Advisory Council for the terms indicated:

For the remainder of the term expiring October 6, 1990:

Meredith Morgan Dale, of the District of Columbia, vice Marc L. Holtzman.

For a term expiring October 6, 1991:

Ruth Gardner Cox, of Texas, vice Alice Roxana Thompson, term expired.
Tahlman Krumm, Jr., of Ohio, vice Colleen Toy White, term expired.

For a term expiring October 6, 1992:

Meredith Morgan Dale, of the District of Columbia (reappointment).

Submitted August 3

Arlene Render,
of Virginia, a career member of the Senior Foreign Service, Class of Counselor, to be Ambassador Extraordinary and Plenipotentiary of the United States of America to the Republic of The Gambia.

Herbert Donald Gelber,
of Florida, a career member of the Senior Foreign Service, Class of Minister-Counselor, to be Ambassador Extraordinary and Plenipotentiary of the United States of America to the Republic of Mali.

Gordon L. Streeb,
of Colorado, a career member of the Senior Foreign Service, Class of Minister-Counselor, to be Ambassador Extraordinary and Plenipotentiary of the United States of America to the Republic of Zambia.

Linton F. Brooks,
of Virginia, for the rank of Ambassador during his tenure of service as Deputy Head of Delegation to the nuclear and space talks.

David F. Levi,
of California, to be United States District Judge for the Eastern District of California, vice Edward Dean Price, retired.

Samuel B. Kent,
of Texas, to be United States District Judge for the Southern District of Texas, vice Hugh Gibson, Jr., retired.

Stephen B. Higgins,
of Missouri, to be United States Attorney for the Eastern District of Missouri for the term of 4 years, vice Thomas E. Dittmeier, term expired.

Doris Swords Poppler,
of Montana, to be United States Attorney for the District of Montana for the term of 4 years, vice Byron H. Dunbar, resigned.

Donna M. Owens,
of Ohio, to be Director of the Bureau of Justice Assistance (new position).

Scott M. Spangler,
of Arizona, to be an Assistant Administrator of the Agency for International Development, vice Charles L. Gladson, resigned.

The following named persons to be members of the Board for International Broadcasting for terms expiring April 28, 1991:

Cheryl Feldman Halpern, of New Jersey, vice Clair W. Burgener, term expired.
Karl C. Rove, of Texas, vice Edward Noonan Ney, term expired.

Gail C. McDonald,
of Oklahoma, to be a member of the Interstate Commerce Commission for a term expiring December 31, 1994, vice Paul H. Lamboley, term expired.

Charles B. DeWitt,
of the District of Columbia, to be Director of the National Institute of Justice, vice James K. Stewart, resigned.

The following named persons to be members of the National Council on the Humanities for terms expiring January 26, 1996:

Helen Gray Crawford, of Louisiana, vice Jean Vaughan Smith, term expired.
Margaret P. Duckett, of Pennsylvania, vice James V. Schall, term expired.
Henry H. Higuera, of Maryland, vice George D. Hart, term expired.
Peter Shaw, of New York, vice Charles Ray Ritcheson, term expired.

The following named persons to be members of the National Commission on Libraries and Information Science for the terms indicated:

For the remainder of the term expiring July 19, 1991:

Carol K. DiPrete, of Rhode Island, vice George H. Nash, resigned.

For the remainder of the term expiring July 19, 1992:

J. Michael Farrell, of the District of Columbia, vice Sally Jo Vasicko.

Howard E. Simmons,
of Delaware, to be a member of the National Science Board, National Science Foundation, for a term expiring May 10, 1996, vice Craig C. Black, term expired.

Andrew F. Reardon,
of Illinois, to be a member of the Railroad Retirement Board for the term of 5 years from August 29, 1988, vice John D. Crawford.

The following named persons to be members of the U.S. Advisory Commission on Public Diplomacy for the terms indicated:

For a term expiring July 1, 1992:

Fitzhugh Green, of the District of Columbia, vice Priscilla L. Buckley, term expired.

For a term expiring July 1, 1993:

Tom C. Korologos, of Virginia (reappointment).

Mary Louise Smith,
of Iowa, to be a member of the Board of Directors of the U.S. Institute of Peace for the remainder of the term expiring January 19, 1991, vice W. Bruce Weinrod, resigned.

Mary Louise Smith,
of Iowa, to be a member of the Board of Directors of the U.S. Institute of Peace for a term expiring January 19, 1995 (reappointment).

Submitted September 10

Richard A. Claytor,
of California, to be an Assistant Secretary of Energy (Defense Programs), vice Sylvester R. Foley, Jr., resigned.

Frederick Porter Hitz,
of Virginia, to be Inspector General, Central Intelligence Agency (new position).

G. Philip Hughes,
of Virginia, to be Ambassador Extraordinary and Plenipotentiary of the United States of America to Barbados, and to serve concurrently and without additional compensation as Ambassador Extraordinary and Plenipotentiary of the United States of America to the Commonwealth of Dominica, Ambassador Extraordinary and Plenipotentiary of the United States of America to Saint Lucia, and Ambassador Extraordinary and Plenipotentiary of the United States of America to Saint Vincent and the Grenadines.

George Fleming Jones,
of Texas, a career member of the Senior Foreign Service, Class of Minister-Counselor, to be Ambassador Extraordinary and Plenipotentiary of

the United States of America to the Co-operative Republic of Guyana.

William H.G. Fitzgerald,
of the District of Columbia, to be a member of the Board of Directors of the African Development Foundation for a term expiring February 9, 1996, vice Jay Kenneth Katzen, term expired.

Jeanne S. Archibald,
of Virginia, to be General Counsel for the Department of the Treasury, vice Edith E. Holiday, resigned.

James B. Loken,
of Minnesota, to be United States Circuit Judge for the Eighth Circuit, vice Gerald W. Heaney, retired.

Linda A. Akers,
of Arizona, to be United States Attorney for the District of Arizona for the term of 4 years, vice Stephen M. McNamee, resigned.

Kenneth W. Sukhia,
of Florida, to be United States Attorney for the Northern District of Florida for the term of 4 years, vice K. Michael Moore, resigned.

Todd W. Dillard,
of Maryland, to be United States Marshal for the Superior Court of the District of Columbia for the term of 4 years, vice a new position created by P.L. 100–690, dated November 18, 1988.

Craig R. Helsing,
of the District of Columbia, to be an Assistant Secretary of Commerce, vice Marc G. Stanley, resigned.

Barry Zorthian,
of the District of Columbia, to be a member of the Board for International Broadcasting for a term expiring May 20, 1992, vice Arch Madsen, term expired.

Joan R. Challinor,
of the District of Columbia, to be a member of the Board of Trustees of the James Madison Memorial Fellowship Foundation for a term of 6 years (reappointment).

James O. Mason,
of Utah, to be Representative of the United States on the Executive Board of the World Health Organization, vice Frank E. Young, resigned.

The following named persons to be members of the United States Advisory Commission on Public Diplomacy:

For terms expiring July 1, 1991:

William J. Hybl, of Colorado, vice Richard M. Scaife, term expired.
Richard B. Stone, of the District of Columbia, vice E. Robert Wallach, term expired.

Submitted September 12

Christopher L. Koch,
of Virginia, to be a Federal Maritime Commissioner for a term expiring June 30, 1995, vice James J. Carey, term expired.

The following named persons to be members of the Federal Mine Safety and Health Review Commission:

For terms of 6 years expiring August 30, 1996:

Ford Barney Ford, of Virginia. (Reappointment)
Arlene Holen, of the District of Columbia, vice James A. Lastowka, term expired.

Submitted September 13

Harmon Elwood Kirby,
of Ohio, a career member of the Senior Foreign Service, Class of Minister-Counselor, to be Ambassador Extraordinary and Plenipotentiary of the United States of America to the Republic of Togo.

Sharon Percy Rockefeller,
of West Virginia, to be a member of the Board of Directors of the Corporation for Public Broadcasting for a term expiring March 26, 1992 (reappointment).

The following named persons to be members of the National Science Board, National Science Foundation:

For terms expiring May 10, 1996:

Phillip A. Griffiths, of North Carolina, vice Annelise Graebner Anderson, term expired.
Jaime Oaxaca, of California, vice Rita R. Colwell, term expired.

William A. Geoghegan,
of Maryland, to be a member of the Advisory Board for Cuba Broadcasting for a term expiring October 27, 1992, vice Midge Decter, term expired.

The following named persons to be members of the National Council on the Humanities:

For terms expiring January 26, 1996:

Carol Iannone, of New York, vice Mary Joseph Conrad Cresimore, term expired.

Jon N. Moline, of Minnesota, vice Robert Laxalt, term expired.

William C. Andersen,
of Connecticut, to be United States Marshal for the District of Connecticut for the term of 4 years, vice P.A. Mangini, term expired.

Arthur D. Borinsky,
of New Jersey, to be United States Marshal for the District of New Jersey for the term of 4 years (reappointment).

Submitted September 17

Leonard H.O. Spearman, Sr.,
of Texas, to be Ambassador Extraordinary and Plenipotentiary of the United States of America to the Kingdom of Lesotho.

The following named persons to be Representatives and Alternate Representatives of the United States of America to the 45th Session of the General Assembly of the United Nations:

Representatives:

Thomas R. Pickering, of New Jersey.
Alexander Fletcher Watson, of Massachusetts.

Alternate Representatives:

Jonathan Moore, of Massachusetts.
Jacob Stein, of New York.
Shirin R. Tahir-Kheli, of Pennsylvania.
Milton James Wilkinson, of New Hampshire.

James R. Whelan,
of Virginia, to be a member of the Board of Directors of the Inter-American Foundation for a term expiring September 20, 1994, vice Harold K. Phillips, term expired.

John Michael Mercanti,
of Pennsylvania, to be Engraver in the Mint of the United States at Philadelphia, PA, vice Elizabeth Jones, resigned.

Paul K. Dayton,
of California, to be a member of the Marine Mammal Commission for the term expiring May 13, 1992, vice William W. Fox, Jr., resigned.

Mary Ann Mobley-Collins,
of California, to be a member of the National Council on Disability for a term expiring September 17, 1991, vice Joni Tada, term expired.

Submitted September 19

Mary Shannon Brunette,
of Virginia, to be an Assistant Secretary of Housing and Urban Development, vice Sherrie Sandy Rollins.

Submitted September 20

Branko Terzic,
of Wisconsin, to be a member of the Federal Energy Regulatory Commission for the remainder of the term expiring October 20, 1991, vice Martha O. Hesse.

Submitted September 21

John P. Leonard,
of Virginia, a career member of the Senior Foreign Service, Class of Counselor, to be Ambassador Extraordinary and Plenipotentiary of the United States of America to the Republic of Suriname.

Katherine D. Ortega,
of New Mexico, to be an Alternate Representative of the United States of America to the 45th Session of the General Assembly of the United Nations.

Oliver W. Wanger,
of California, to be United States District Judge for the Eastern District of California, vice Milton Lewis Schwartz, retired.

Roscoe Burton Starek III,
of Illinois, to be a Federal Trade Commissioner for the term of 7 years from September 26, 1990, vice Terry Calvani, term expired.

Charles L. Cragin,
of Maine, to be Chairman of the Board of Veterans' Appeals for a term of 6 years (new position— P.L. 100–687).

Submitted September 24

Robert A. Flaten,
of Minnesota, a career member of the Senior Foreign Service, Class of Minister-Counselor, to be Ambassador Extraordinary and Plenipotentiary of the United States of America to the Republic of Rwanda.

Submitted September 25

Marvin Collins,
of Texas, to be United States Attorney for the Northern District of Texas for the term of 4 years (reappointment).

Elsie V. Vartanian,
of New Hampshire, to be Director of the Women's Bureau, Department of Labor, vice Jill Houghton Emery, resigned.

Withdrawn September 25

Karen L. Gillmor,
of Ohio, to be Director of the Women's Bureau, Department of Labor, vice Jill Houghton Emery, resigned, which was sent to the Senate on March 20, 1990.

Submitted October 4

Michael Joseph Bayer,
of Ohio, to be Federal Inspector of the Alaska Natural Gas Transportation System, vice Theodore J. Garrish, resigned.

Submitted October 5

Connie Mack,
of Florida, to be a Representative of the United States of America to the 45th Session of the General Assembly of the United Nations.

Submitted October 9

Joseph R. Biden,
of Delaware, to be a Representative of the United States of America to the 45th Session of the General Assembly of the United Nations.

Walter E. Massey,
of Illinois, to be Director of the National Science Foundation for a term of 6 years, vice Erich Bloch, term expired.

Submitted October 11

Marion Clifton Blakey,
of Mississippi, to be an Assistant Secretary of Transportation, vice David Philip Prosperi, resigned.

Submitted October 12

Cecil B. Thompson,
of Virginia, to be a member of the Board of Directors of the Export-Import Bank of the United States for the remainder of the term expiring January 20, 1991, vice Simon C. Fireman, resigned.

Cecil B. Thompson,
of Virginia, to be a member of the Board of Directors of the Export-Import Bank of the United States for a term expiring January 20, 1995 (reappointment).

Submitted October 15

William W. Treat,
of New Hampshire, to be a Representative of the United States of America to the 45th Session of the General Assembly of the United Nations.

James R. McGregor,
of Pennsylvania, to be United States District Judge for the Western District of Pennsylvania, vice Gerald J. Weber, retired.

Submitted October 16

Robert William Gambino,
of Virginia, to be Director of Selective Service, vice Samuel K. Lessey, Jr., resigned.

Submitted October 17

John Leopold,
of Maryland, to be a member of the National Council on Disability for a term expiring September 17, 1991.

Dennis W. Shedd,
of South Carolina, to be United States District Judge for the District of South Carolina.

The following named persons to be members of the National Advisory Council on Educational Research and Improvement for the terms indicated:

For the remainder of the term expiring September 30, 1991:

Eugene L. Madeira, of Pennsylvania.

For a term expiring September 30, 1992:

Dale P. Gold, of Virginia.

Submitted October 18

David A. Kessler,
of New York, to be Commissioner of Food and Drugs, Department of Health and Human Services (new position—P.L. 100–607).

Submitted October 23

J. Blakeley Hall,
of Texas, to be a member of the Board of Directors of the Legal Services Corporation for a term expiring July 13, 1992, to which position he was appointed during the recess of the Senate from November 22, 1989, to January 23, 1990.

Submitted October 24

A. Pierre Guillermin,
of Virginia, to be a member of the National Advisory Council on Educational Research and Improvement for a term expiring September 30, 1993, vice Robert Lee McElrath, term expired.

Scott M. Spangler,
an Assistant Administrator of the Agency for International Development, to be a member of the Board of Directors of the African Develop-

ment Foundation for the remainder of the term expiring September 22, 1991, vice Charles L. Gladson, resigned.

George H. Oberle, Jr.,
of Oklahoma, to be a member of the National Council on Disability for a term expiring September 17, 1992 (reappointment).

William H. Kennoy,
of Kentucky, to be a member of the Board of Directors of the Tennessee Valley Authority for the term expiring May 18, 1999, vice Charles H. Dean, Jr., term expired.

Lewis W. Douglas, Jr.,
of California, to be a member of the United States Advisory Commission on Public Diplomacy for a term expiring July 1, 1993, vice Hershey Gold, term expired.

Submitted October 25

The following named persons to be members of the National Advisory Council on Educational Research and Improvement for terms expiring September 30, 1993:

Jack Raymond Reed, of Mississippi, vice Frances Mathews, term expired.

June Scobee Rodgers, of Arizona, vice Carol Pendas Whitten, term expired.

Marye Anne Fox,
of Texas, to be a member of the National Science Board, National Science Foundation, for a term expiring May 10, 1996, vice Karen J. Lindstedt-Siva, term expired.

Carl W. Vogt,
of Maryland, to be a member of the Board of Directors of the National Railroad Passenger Corporation for a term of 4 years, vice Darrell M. Trent, term expired.

Submitted October 26

John Elliott Reynolds III,
of Florida, to be a member of the Marine Mammal Commission for the term expiring May 13, 1993, vice Robert Elsner, term expired.

Submitted October 27

John A. Bushnell,
of Connecticut, a career member of the Senior Foreign Service, Class of Minister-Counselor, to be Ambassador Extraordinary and Plenipotentiary of the United States of America to the Republic of Costa Rica.

Appendix C—Checklist of White House Press Releases

The following list contains releases of the Office of the Press Secretary which are not included in this book.

Released July 3

Transcript:
Press briefing on the upcoming North Atlantic Treaty Organization summit in London, United Kingdom—by Brent Scowcroft, Assistant to the President for National Security Affairs, and John H. Sununu, Chief of Staff to the President

Released July 5

Transcript:
Interview with Brent Scowcroft, Assistant to the President for National Security Affairs, by Charles Gibson of ABC's "Good Morning America"

Released July 6

Fact sheet:
Looking ahead in conventional arms control

Fact sheet:
Multinational corps for NATO

Fact sheet:
NATO's conventional forces and strategy

Fact sheet:
NATO initiative on nuclear artillery

Fact sheet:
NATO nuclear strategy in the new age

Fact sheet:
A parliamentary body for the Conference on Security and Cooperation in Europe (CSCE): the Assembly of Europe

Fact sheet:
Reaching out to former adversaries

Fact sheet:
Strengthening the Conference on Security and Cooperation in Europe (CSCE) process

Fact sheet:
Checklist of key initiatives in the London Declaration

Transcript:
Interview with John H. Sununu, Chief of Staff to the President, by Bryant Gumbel of NBC News "Today"

Transcript:
Interview with Ambassador William H. Taft IV, U.S. Representative to the North Atlantic Treaty Organization, by Harry Smith of CBS News

Transcript:
Interview with Brent Scowcroft, Assistant to the President for National Security Affairs, by Frank Sesno of Cable News Network

Released July 8

Fact sheet:
Clean air (acid rain) bill and accord

Released July 9

Transcript:
Press briefing on the Houston economic summit—by John H. Sununu, Chief of Staff to the President

Advance text:
Remarks at the welcoming ceremony for the Houston economic summit

Transcript:
Press briefing on agricultural issues related to the economic summit—by Secretary of Agriculture Clayton K. Yeutter

Transcript:
Press briefing on trade issues related to the economic summit—by U.S. Trade Representative Carla A. Hills

Announcement:
Nomination of Stephen G. Milliken to be an Associate Judge of the Superior Court of the District of Columbia

Released July 10

Transcript:
Remarks on presentation of the economic summit political communique—by Secretary of State James A. Baker III

Press briefing on economic summit issues—by Secretary of the Treasury Nicholas F. Brady

Advance text:
Toast at the Houston economic summit dinner

Released July 11

Advance text:
Remarks at the Thank You Houston celebration in Houston, TX

Released July 12

Advance text:
Remarks to the 30th Biennial Greek Orthodox Church Clergy-Laity Congress

Released July 16

Transcript:
Press briefing on the administration's mid-session budget review—by Secretary of the Treasury Nicholas F. Brady; Richard G. Darman, Director of the Office of Management and Budget; and Michael J. Boskin, Chairman of the Council of Economic Advisers

Announcement:
Nomination of Lynn H. Duncan to be U.S. Marshal for the Northern District of Georgia

Released July 17

Announcement:
Nomination of Thomas G. Nelson to be U.S. Circuit Judge for the Ninth District

Transcript:
Press briefing on civil rights legislation—by John H. Sununu, Chief of Staff to the President, and Attorney General Dick Thornburgh

Advance text:
Remarks to the national council of La Raza

Released July 19

Advance text:
Remarks at the dedication ceremony for the Richard M. Nixon Presidential Library in Yorba Linda, CA

Announcement:
Nomination of Kimberly A. Madigan to be a member of the National Mediation Board

Announcement:
Nomination of Joseph Francis Glennon to be a member of the Advisory Board for Cuba Broadcasting

Released July 20

Advance text:
Remarks at a fundraising breakfast for senatorial candidate Allen Kolstad in Billings, MT

Advance text:
Remarks at an antidrug rally in Billings, MT

Released July 21

Advance text:
Remarks at the christening of the U.S.S. *George Washington* in Newport News, VA

Released July 23

Fact sheet:
New trade measures for Latin America and the Caribbean

Transcript:
Press briefing on President Bush's meeting with President Rodrigo Borja Cevallos of Ecuador—by Bernard W. Aronson, Assistant Secretary of State for Inter-American Affairs

Fact sheet:
Biography of David Hackett Souter

Released July 24

Advance text:
Remarks at an antidrug rally in Philadelphia, PA

Advance text:
Remarks at a Republican Party fundraising dinner in New York, NY

Released July 26

Fact sheet:
The Americans with Disabilities Act of 1990

Released July 27

Announcement:
Nomination of Diane Gilbert Weinstein to be a Judge of the U.S. Claims Court

Statement:
Possible acquisition of Semi-Gas Systems, Inc., by Nippon Sanso K.K. of Japan—by Alixe R. Glen, Deputy Press Secretary to the President

Released July 31

Announcement:
Nomination of Holland H. Coors to be a member of the Board of Trustees of the Harry S. Truman Scholarship Foundation

Announcement:
Nomination of Paul Y. Chinen to be a member of the Mississippi River Commission

Announcement:
Nomination of Carolyn D. Leavens to be a member of the Board of Directors of the Overseas Private Investment Corporation

Statement:
Appointment of Sybil C. Mobley and William Aramony to be members of the Board of Directors of the Points of Light Foundation

Press briefing on President Bush's meeting with President Gnassingbé Eyadéma of Togo—by Herman J. Cohen, Assistant Secretary of State for African Affairs

Announcement:
Nomination of five members of the National Science Board of the National Science Foundation

Announcement:
Nomination of Robert F. Goodwin to be a U.S. Commissioner on the International Joint Commission, United States and Canada

Released August 1

Announcement:
Nomination of two Directors of the Federal Housing Finance Board

Released August 2

Statement:
U.S. freeze of Iraqi and Kuwaiti assets—by Roman Popadiuk, Deputy Press Secretary to the President

Advance text:
Remarks at the Aspen Institute symposium in Aspen, CO

Released August 3

Announcement:
Nomination of James Ware to be U.S. District Court Judge for the Northern District of California

Announcement:
Nomination of William B. Shubb to be U.S. District Court Judge for the Eastern District of California

Announcement:
Nomination of three members of the Peace Corps National Advisory Council

Announcement:
Nomination of seven members of the Board of Directors of the Legal Services Corporation

Announcement:
Nomination of Juliette Clagett McLennan for the rank of Ambassador while serving as U.S. Representative on the Commission on the Status of Women of the Economic and Social Council of the United Nations

Announcement:
Nomination of Richard Y. Roberts to be a member of the Securities and Exchange Commission

Announcement:
Nomination of Thomas D. Rath to be a member of the Board of Directors of the Legal Services Corporation

Announcement:
Nomination of Antonio C. Amador to be a member of the Merit Systems Protection Board

Released August 6

Announcement:
Nomination of Stephen B. Higgins to be U.S. Attorney for the Eastern District of Missouri

Announcement:
Nomination of Doris Swords Poppler to be U.S. Attorney for the District of Montana

Announcement:
Nomination of David F. Levi to be U.S. District Judge for the Eastern District of California

Announcement:
Nomination of Linton F. Brooks for the rank of Ambassador while serving as Deputy Head of Delegation to the nuclear and space talks

Announcement:
Nomination of four members of the National Council on the Humanities

Announcement:
Nomination of Gail C. McDonald to be a member of the Interstate Commerce Commission

Announcement:
Nomination of Andrew F. Reardon to be a member of the Railroad Retirement Board

Announcement:
Nomination of Mary Louise Smith to be a member of the Board of Directors of the U.S. Institute of Peace

Released August 8

Announcement:
Nomination of Samuel B. Kent to be U.S. District Judge for the Southern District of Texas

Released August 10

Fact sheet:
Breast and Cervical Cancer Mortality Prevention Act of 1990

Released August 14

Fact sheet:
Federal budget negotiations

Released August 15

Announcement:
Nomination of Todd W. Dillard to be U.S. Marshal for the Superior Court of the District of Columbia

Advance text:
Remarks to Department of Defense employees

Released August 16

Transcript:
Remarks by King Hussein I of Jordan following discussions with the President in Kennebunkport, ME

Transcript:
Remarks by Foreign Minister Sa'ud al-Faysal Al Sa'ud of Saudi Arabia following discussions with the President in Kennebunkport, ME

Released August 20

Advance text:
Remarks at a Republican Party fundraising luncheon in North Kingstown, RI

Released August 22

Transcript:
Press briefing on the Persian Gulf crisis—by Secretary of Defense Richard B. Cheney and Gen. Colin L. Powell, Chairman of the Joint Chiefs of Staff

Released August 23

Statement:
Departure of U.S. marines from the U.S. Embassy in Kuwait—by Marlin Fitzwater, Press Secretary to the President

Released August 24

Statement:
Illness of Nancy Walker, the President's aunt—by Marlin Fitzwater, Press Secretary to the President

Released August 27

Statement:
Mechanical failure of the President's boat, *Fidelity*—by Marlin Fitzwater, Press Secretary to the President

Released September 1

Transcript:
Press briefing on the Persian Gulf crisis—by Brent Scowcroft, Assistant to the President for National Security Affairs

Released September 6

Advance text:
Remarks at a fundraising luncheon for Congressman Bill Grant in Tallahassee, FL

Announcement:
Nomination of Kenneth W. Sukhia to be U.S. Attorney for the Northern District of Florida

Announcement:
National Medal of Arts recipients

Announcement:
Nomination of James B. Loken to be U.S. Circuit Judge for the Eighth District

Announcement:
Nomination of Linda A. Akers to be U.S. Attorney for the District of Arizona

Transcript:
Press briefing on logistics for the Helsinki summit—by John Herrick, Deputy Press Secretary

Released September 11

Advance text:
Address before a joint session of the Congress on the Persian Gulf crisis and the budget deficit

Announcement:
Nomination of two members of the Federal Mine Safety and Health Review Commission

Announcement:
Nomination of Christopher L. Koch to be a Federal Maritime Commissioner

Released September 12

Transcript:
Press briefing on proposed crime legislation—by Attorney General Dick Thornburgh; Mike Moore, attorney general of Mississippi; and Richard Ieyoub, district attorney for Louisiana

Fact sheet:
Comparison of key points in the President's crime bill versus the Senate and House crime bills

Announcement:
Nomination of William A. Geoghegan to be a member of the Advisory Board for Cuba Broadcasting

Announcement:
Nomination of two members of the National Science Board

Announcement:
Nomination of two members of the National Council on the Humanities

Announcement:
Nomination of Sharon Percy Rockefeller to be a member of the Board of Directors of the Corporation for Public Broadcasting

Released September 13

Announcement:
Nomination of William C. Andersen to be U.S. Marshal for the District of Connecticut

Announcement:
Nomination of Arthur D. Borinsky to be U.S. Marshal for the District of New Jersey

Released September 17

Transcript:
Press briefing on the dismissal of Gen. Michael J. Dugan, Chief of Staff of the Air Force; the Persian Gulf crisis; and the restructuring of U.S. Armed Forces and defense spending—by Secretary of Defense Richard B. Cheney

Announcement:
Nomination of John Michael Mercanti to be Engraver at the U.S. Mint in Philadelphia, PA

Announcement:
Nomination of U.S. Representatives and Alternate Representatives to the 45th Session of the U.N. General Assembly

Released September 18

Advance text:
Remarks at a Republican Party fundraising luncheon in Denver, CO

Advance text:
Remarks at a fundraising dinner for gubernatorial candidate Pete Wilson in Los Angeles, CA

Released September 19

Announcement:
Nomination of Branko Terzic to be a member of the Federal Energy Regulatory Commission

Released September 21

Announcement:
Nomination of Oliver W. Wanger to be U.S. District Judge for the Eastern District of California

Released September 24

Fact sheet:
Executive order on educational excellence for Hispanic Americans

Transcript:
Press briefing on President Bush's meeting with President F.W. de Klerk of South Africa—by Herman J. Cohen, Assistant Secretary of State for African Affairs

Released September 25

Transcript:
Press briefing on President Bush's meeting with President Turgut Özal of Turkey—by James Dobbins, Principal Deputy Assistant Secretary of State for European and Canadian Affairs

Announcement:
Nomination of Marvin Collins to be U.S. Attorney for the Northern District of Texas

Released September 27

Advance text:
Remarks at a fundraising dinner for senatorial candidate Bill Schuette in Detroit, MI

Released September 28

Transcript:
Press briefing on the President's meeting with Amir Jabir al-Ahmad al-Jabir Al Sabah of Kuwait and the President's trip to the United Nations—by Brent Scowcroft, Assistant to the President for National Security Affairs

Released September 29

Advance text:
Remarks at the dedication ceremony for the Washington National Cathedral

Transcript:
Excerpts of Colombian President Cesar Gaviria's exchange with reporters following a meeting with President Bush in New York, NY

Transcript:
Nicaraguan President Violeta Chamorro's exchange with reporters following a meeting with President Bush in New York, NY

Transcript:
Press briefing on the President's bilateral meeting with Prime Minister Toshiki Kaifu of Japan— by Richard Solomon, Assistant Secretary of State for East Asian and Pacific Affairs

Released September 30

Advance text:
Remarks at the opening ceremony of the United Nations World Summit for Children in New York, NY

Transcript:
Press briefing on President Bush's meeting with President Carlos Salinas de Gortari of Mexico in New York, NY—by Bernard W. Aronson, Assistant Secretary of State for Inter-American Affairs

Statement:
President Bush's meetings with President Václav Havel of Czechoslovakia and King Baudouin I of Belgium in New York, NY—by Marlin Fitzwater, Press Secretary to the President

Released October 1

Transcript:
Uruguayan President Luis Alberto Lacalle's exchange with reporters following a meeting with President Bush in New York, NY

Transcript:
Press briefing on President Bush's meetings with Presidents Carlos Saúl Menem of Argentina and Luis Alberto Lacalle of Uruguay in New York, NY—by Bernard W. Aronson, Assistant Secretary of State for Inter-American Affairs

Advance text:
Address before the 45th Session of the United Nations General Assembly in New York, NY

Transcript:
Soviet Foreign Minister Eduard Shevardnadze's exchange with reporters following a meeting with the President in New York, NY

Advance text:
Remarks at the ministerial meeting in New York, NY, of the Conference on Security and Cooperation in Europe

Transcript:
Press briefing on President Bush's meeting with President Alfredo Cristiani Buckard of El Salvador in New York, NY—by Bernard W. Aronson, Assistant Secretary of State for Inter-American Affairs

Released October 4

Transcript:
Press briefing on the conventional armed forces in Europe negotiations—by Secretary of State James A. Baker III

Released October 5

Announcement:
Nomination of Connie Mack to be U.S. Representative to the 45th Session of the United Nations General Assembly

Fact sheet:
President Bush's proposed Andean Trade Preference Act of 1990

Released October 10

Advance text:
Remarks at a fundraising breakfast for Senator Jesse Helms in Raleigh, NC

Advance text:
Remarks at a rally for Gov. Bob Martinez in St. Petersburg, FL

Advance text:
Remarks at a fundraising reception for gubernatorial candidate Johnny Isakson in Atlanta, GA

Announcement:
Nomination of Senator Joseph R. Biden of Delaware to be a U.S. Representative to the 45th Session of the U.N. General Assembly

Released October 12

Announcement:
Nomination of Cecil B. Thompson to be a member of the Board of Directors of the Export-Import Bank of the United States

Released October 15

Announcement:
Nomination of James R. McGregor to be U.S. District Judge for the Western District of Pennsylvania

Released October 17

Announcement:
Nomination of Dennis W. Shedd to be U.S. District Judge for the District of South Carolina

Released October 18

Fact sheet:
U.S. assistance to Hungary

Transcript:
Press briefing on the President's meeting with Prime Minister Jozsef Antall of Hungary—by Curtis Kamman, Deputy Assistant Secretary of State for European and Canadian Affairs

Released October 19

Statement:
Resolution providing funding for continued government operation and the status of the civil rights bill—by Marlin Fitzwater, Press Secretary to the President

Released October 24

Statement:
Presidential travel plans and the Federal budget crisis—by Marlin Fitzwater, Press Secretary to the President

Released November 3

Transcript:
Press briefing on the clean air bill—by William K. Reilly, Administrator of the Environmental Protection Agency

Released November 13

Announcement:
Presentation of the National Medals of Science and Technology

Released November 14

Transcript:
Press briefing on the President's upcoming meeting with allied and Eastern-bloc leaders in Paris, France, and on the Persian Gulf crisis—by Secretary of State James A. Baker III

Released November 15

Fact sheet:
Clean Air Act amendments

Released November 16

Fact sheet:
Environmental protection, research, and education bills

Announcement:
Nomination of Wendell P. Gardner, Jr., to be an Associate Judge of the Superior Court of the District of Columbia

Released November 17

Advance text:
Remarks to the Federal Assembly in Prague, Czechoslovakia

Advance text:
Remarks in Prague, Czechoslovakia, at a ceremony commemorating the end of Communist rule

Fact sheet:
U.S. assistance to Czechoslovakia

Fact sheet:
U.S.-Czechoslovakia trade agreement

Released November 18

Advance text:
Remarks to the residents of Speyer, Germany

Transcript:
Press briefing following bilateral meeting—by Secretary of State James A. Baker III and Soviet Foreign Minister Eduard Shevardnadze

Released November 19

Transcript:
Press briefing on the conventional armed forces in Europe treaty—by Ambassador R. James Woolsey, U.S. Representative to the negotiations on conventional armed forces in Europe

Released November 21

Transcript:
Press briefing following bilateral meeting—by Secretary of State James A. Baker III and Soviet Foreign Minister Eduard Shevardnadze

Statement:
Announcement of President Bush's meeting with President Hafiz al-Assad of Syria in Geneva, Switzerland—by Marlin Fitzwater, Press Secretary to the President

Released November 22

Transcript:
Press briefing in Jeddah, Saudi Arabia, on the Persian Gulf crisis—by Secretary of State James A. Baker III

Released November 27

Transcript:
Press briefing in Monterrey, Mexico, on Mexico-U.S. meetings—by Secretary of the Treasury Nicholas F. Brady; Attorney General Dick Thornburgh; Deputy Secretary of State Lawrence S. Eagleburger; and William K. Reilly, Administrator of the Environmental Protection Agency

Advance text:
Remarks to community members in Monterrey, Mexico

Transcript:
Press briefing in Monterrey, Mexico on Mexico-U.S. trade issues—by Secretary of Commerce Robert A. Mosbacher and U.S. Trade Representative Carla Hills

Released November 28

Fact sheet:
The Cranston-Gonzalez National Affordable Housing Act

Released November 29

Fact sheet:
Immigration Act of 1990

Fact sheet:
Students Taking Action and Responsibility in Service

Released November 30

Transcript:
Press briefing on the President's trip to South America—by David C. Mulford, Under Secretary of the Treasury for International Affairs

Released December 3

Advance text:
Remarks to a joint session of the Congress in Brasilia, Brazil

Transcript:
Press briefing in Brasilia, Brazil, on the President's trip to South America—by Secretary of the Treasury Nicholas F. Brady and Deputy Secretary of State Lawrence S. Eagleburger

Released December 5

Advance text:
Remarks to a joint session of the Congress in Buenos Aires, Argentina

Advance text:
Toast at a state dinner in Buenos Aires, Argentina

Released December 6

Advance text:
Remarks to a joint session of the Congress in Valparaiso, Chile

Advance text:
Toast at a state dinner in Santiago, Chile

Released December 7

Advance text:
Remarks to the American Chamber of Commerce in Santiago, Chile

Advance text:
Toast at a state dinner in Caracas, Venezuela

Released December 8

Advance text:
Remarks to the Venezuelan-American Chamber of Commerce in Caracas, Venezuela

Released December 11

Transcript:
Press briefing on the President's meeting with Prime Minister Yitzhak Shamir of Israel—by John H. Kelly, Assistant Secretary of State for Near Eastern and South Asian Affairs

Released December 12

Fact sheet:
Export credit guarantees for the U.S.S.R.

Released December 13

Advance text:
Remarks at the presentation ceremony for the Malcolm Baldrige National Quality Awards

Fact sheet:
Volunteer liability protection initiatives

Fact sheet:
Export control measures

Fact sheet:
Enhanced proliferation control initiative

Released December 19

Fact sheet:
Norway and the Pelly amendment

Appendix D—Acts Approved by the President

Approved July 3

H.R. 1622 / Public Law 101–318
Copyright Fees and Technical Amendments Act of 1989

H.R. 3046 / Public Law 101–319
Copyright Royalty Tribunal Reform and Miscellaneous Pay Act of 1989

H.R. 3545 / Public Law 101–320
To amend the Chesapeake and Ohio Canal Development Act to make certain changes relating to the Chesapeake and Ohio Canal National Historical Park Commission

H.R. 3834 / Public Law 101–321
Selma to Montgomery National Trail Study Act of 1989

Approved July 6

H.R. 5075 / Public Law 101–322
Amtrak Reauthorization and Improvement Act of 1990

H.J. Res. 555 / Public Law 101–323
To commemorate the bicentennial of the enactment of the law which provided civil government for the territory from which the State of Tennessee was formed

S. 1999 / Public Law 101–324
To amend the Higher Education Amendments of 1986 to clarify the administrative procedures of the National Commission on Responsibilities for Financing Postsecondary Education, and for other purposes

S.J. Res. 271 / Public Law 101–325
To designate July 10, 1990 as "Wyoming Centennial Day"

S.J. Res. 315 / Public Law 101–326
For the designation of July 22, 1990, as "Rose Fitzgerald Kennedy Family Appreciation Day"

S.J. Res. 320 / Public Law 101–327
Designating July 2, 1990, as "National Literacy Day"

Approved July 8

S. 2124 / Public Law 101–328
National Space Council Authorization Act of 1990

S.J. Res. 278 / Public Law 101–329
Designating July 19, 1990, as "Flight Attendant Safety Professionals' Day"

Approved July 12

H.R. 5149 / Public Law 101–330
To amend the Child Nutrition Act of 1966 to provide that the Secretary of Agriculture may not consider, in allocating amounts to a State agency under the special supplemental food program for women, infants, and children for the fiscal year 1991, any amounts returned by such agency for reallocation during the fiscal year 1990 and to allow amounts allocated to a State for such program for the fiscal year 1991 to be expended for expenses incurred in the fiscal year 1990

Approved July 13

H.J. Res. 599 / Public Law 101–331
To designate July 1, 1990, as "National Ducks and Wetlands Day"

Approved July 16

H.R. 1028 / Public Law 101–332
Mount Rushmore Commemorative Coin Act

H.R. 4252 / Public Law 101–333
To authorize the Secretary of the Air Force to purchase certain property at Pease Air Force Base, New Hampshire

H.R. 4525 / Public Law 101–334
Ethics in Government Act Amendment of 1990

Approved July 17

H.R. 2514 / Public Law 101–335
Thrift Savings Plan Technical Amendments Act of 1990

Approved July 26

S. 933 / Public Law 101–336
Americans with Disabilities Act of 1990

Approved July 27

H.R. 2844 / Public Law 101–337
To improve the ability of the Secretary of the Interior to properly manage certain resources of the National Park System

S.J. Res. 276 / Public Law 101–338
Designating the week beginning July 22, 1990, as "Lyme Disease Awareness Week"

Approved July 31

S.J. Res. 75 / Public Law 101–339
Relating to NASA and the International Space Year

S.J. Res. 281 / Public Law 101–340
To designate September 13, 1990, as "National D.A.R.E. Day"

S.J. Res. 339 / Public Law 101–341
To designate August 1, 1990, as "Helsinki Human Rights Day"

Approved August 2

H.J. Res. 591 / Public Law 101–342
Designating the third Sunday of August of 1990 as "National Senior Citizens Day"

Approved August 3

H.J. Res. 577 / Public Law 101–343
Designating the month of November 1990 as "National American Indian Heritage Month"

Approved August 6

H.R. 2843 / Public Law 101–344
To establish the Tumacacori National Historical Park in the State of Arizona

Approved August 7

H.J. Res. 625 / Public Law 101–345
Designating August 6, 1990, as "Voting Rights Celebration Day"

Approved August 9

H.J. Res. 548 / Public Law 101–346
Designating the week of August 19 through 25, 1990, as "National Agricultural Research Week"

S.J. Res. 77 / Public Law 101–347
Recognizing the National Fallen Firefighters' Memorial at the National Fire Academy in Emmitsburg, Maryland, as the official national memorial to volunteer and career firefighters who die in the line of duty

S.J. Res. 256 / Public Law 101–348
To designate the week of October 7, 1990, through October 13, 1990, as "Mental Illness Awareness Week"

S.J. Res. 316 / Public Law 101–349
To designate the second Sunday in October of 1990 as "National Children's Day"

H.R. 5350 / Public Law 101–350
To provide for a temporary increase in the public debt limit

H.R. 5432 / Public Law 101–351
To extend the expiration date of the Defense Production Act of 1950

Approved August 10

H.R. 293 / Public Law 101–352
Fire Safe Cigarette Act of 1990

H.R. 3048 / Public Law 101–353
To designate the Agricultural Research Service, United States Department of Agriculture, animal health research building in Clay Center, Nebraska, as the "Virginia D. Smith Animal Health Research Laboratory"

H.R. 4790 / Public Law 101–354
Breast and Cervical Cancer Mortality Prevention Act of 1990

H.J. Res. 467 / Public Law 101–355
Designating September 21, 1990, as "National POW/MIA Recognition Day", and recognizing the National League of Families POW/MIA flag

S. 1046 / Public Law 101–356
Merrimack River Study Act of 1990

S. 1524 / Public Law 101–357
Pemigewasset River Study Act of 1989

S. 1543 / Public Law 101–358
To authorize the Board of Regents of Gunston Hall to establish a memorial to George Mason in the District of Columbia

S. 1875 / Public Law 101–359
To redesignate the Calamus Dam and Reservoir authorized under the Reclamation Project Authorization Act of 1972 as the Virginia Smith Dam and Calamus Lake Recreation Area

S. 2952 / Public Law 101–360
Energy Policy and Conservation Act Short-Term Extension Amendment of 1990

S.J. Res. 296 / Public Law 101–361
Designating August 7, 1990, as "National Neighborhood Crime Watch Day"

S.J. Res. 343 / Public Law 101–362
To designate August 13 through August 19, 1990, as "Home Health Aide Week"

Approved August 14

H.R. 4872 / Public Law 101–363
National Advisory Council on the Public Service Act of 1990

Approved August 15

H.R. 76 / Public Law 101–364
To amend the Wild and Scenic Rivers Act to study the eligibility of the St. Marys River in the States of Florida and Georgia for potential addition to the wild and scenic rivers system

H.R. 1159 / Public Law 101–365
Juan Bautista de Anza National Historic Trail Act

H.R. 1199 / Public Law 101–366
Department of Veterans Affairs Nurse Pay Act of 1990

H.R. 4035 / Public Law 101–367
To designate the Federal building located at 777 Sonoma Avenue in Santa Rosa, California, as the "John F. Shea Federal Building"

H.R. 4273 / Public Law 101–368
Tuberculosis Prevention Amendments of 1990

H.R. 4314 / Public Law 101–369
To implement the Inter-American Convention on International Commercial Arbitration

H.R. 5131 / Public Law 101–370
To amend the Federal Aviation Act of 1958 to extend the civil penalty assessment demonstration program, and for other purposes

H.J. Res. 515 / Public Law 101–371
Designating the week beginning September 16, 1990, as "National Give Kids a Fighting Chance Week"

H.J. Res. 554 / Public Law 101–372
Designating January 6, 1991 through January 12, 1991 as "National Law Enforcement Training Week"

H.J. Res. 627 / Public Law 101–373
Designating Labor Day weekend, September 1 through September 3, 1990, as "National Drive for Life Weekend"

S. 2461 / Public Law 101–374
Drug Abuse Treatment Waiting Period Reduction Amendments of 1990

S.J. Res. 248 / Public Law 101–375
To designate the month of September 1990 as "International Visitors' Month"

Approved August 17

H.R. 3086 / Public Law 101–376
Civil Service Due Process Amendments

H.R. 3248 / Public Law 101–377
To revise the boundary of Gettysburg National Military Park in the Commonwealth of Pennsylvania, and for other purposes

S. 666 / Public Law 101–378
To enroll twenty individuals under the Alaska Native Claims Settlement Act

Approved August 18

H.R. 498 / Public Law 101–379
Indian Law Enforcement Reform Act

H.R. 1465 / Public Law 101–380
Oil Pollution Act of 1990

S. 2240 / Public Law 101–381
Ryan White Comprehensive AIDS Resources Emergency Act of 1990

Approved August 20

H.R. 1594 / Public Law 101–382
Customs and Trade Act of 1990

Approved September 15

S. 2088 / Public Law 101–383
Energy Policy and Conservation Act Amendments of 1990

Approved September 18

S. 3033 / Public Law 101–384
To amend title 39, United States Code, to allow free mailing privileges to be extended to members of the Armed Forces while engaged in temporary military operations under arduous circumstances

Approved September 20

H.J. Res. 568 / Public Law 101–385
Designating the week beginning September 16, 1990, as "Emergency Medical Services Week"

S. 2597 / Public Law 101–386
To amend the Act of June 20, 1910, to clarify in the State of New Mexico authority to exchange lands granted by the United States in trust, and to validate prior land exchanges

S.J. Res. 285 / Public Law 101–387
To designate the period commencing September 9, 1990, and ending on September 15, 1990, as "National Historically Black Colleges Week"

S.J. Res. 289 / Public Law 101–388
To designate October 1990 as "Polish American Heritage Month"

S.J. Res. 309 / Public Law 101–389
Designating the month of October 1990 as "Crime Prevention Month"

Approved September 21

S.J. Res. 279 / Public Law 101–390
To designate the week of September 16, 1990, through September 22, 1990, as "National Rehabilitation Week"

Approved September 25

H.R. 94 / Public Law 101–391
Hotel and Motel Fire Safety Act of 1990

H.R. 7 / Public Law 101–392
Carl D. Perkins Vocational and Applied Technology Education Act Amendments of 1990

S.J. Res. 313 / Public Law 101–393
Designating October 3, 1990, as "National Teacher Appreciation Day"

S.J. Res. 331 / Public Law 101–394
To designate the week of September 23 through 29, 1990, as "Religious Freedom Week"

S.J. Res. 333 / Public Law 101–395
To designate the week of September 30, 1990, through October 6, 1990, as "National Job Skills Week"

Approved September 28

H.R. 3265 / Public Law 101–396
Federal Communications Commission Authorization Act of 1990

H.R. 1101 / Public Law 101–397
To extend the authorization of appropriations for the Water Resources Research Act of 1984 through the end of fiscal year 1994

H.R. 2174 / Public Law 101–398
Mississippi River Corridor Study Commission Act of 1989

H.R. 4501 / Public Law 101–399
To provide for the acquisition of the William Johnson House and its addition to the Natchez National Historical Park, and for other purposes

S. 963 / Public Law 101–400
Route 66 Study Act of 1990

S. 2205 / Public Law 101–401
Maine Wilderness Act of 1990

Approved October 1

H.R. 5747 / Public Law 101–402
To provide for the temporary extension of certain programs relating to housing and community development, and for other purposes

H.J. Res. 655 / Public Law 101–403
Making continuing appropriations for the fiscal year 1991, supplemental appropriations for "Operation Desert Shield" for the fiscal year 1990, and for other purposes

Approved October 2

H.R. 2761 / Public Law 101–404
United Services Organization's 50th Anniversary Commemorative Coin Act

H.R. 5755 / Public Law 101–405
To extend the temporary increase in the public debt limit

Approved October 3

H.R. 4962 / Public Law 101–406
1992 Olympic Commemorative Coin Act

Approved October 4

H.R. 5725 / Public Law 101–407
To extend the expiration date of the Defense Production Act of 1950

S. 2075 / Public Law 101–408
Indian Environmental Regulatory Enhancement Act of 1990

Approved October 5

H.R. 4773 / Public Law 101–409
White House Conference on Small Business Authorization Act

S. 535 / Public Law 101–410
Federal Civil Penalties Inflation Adjustment Act of 1990

Approved October 6

S. 3155 / Public Law 101–411
To extend the expiration date of the Defense Production Act of 1950 to October 20, 1990

Approved October 9

H.J. Res. 666 / Public Law 101–412
Making further continuing appropriations for the fiscal year 1991, and for other purposes

Approved October 11

H.J. Res. 469 / Public Law 101–413
To designate October 6, 1990, as "German-American Day"

H.J. Res. 603 / Public Law 101–414
To designate the month of October 1990 as "Country Music Month"

S.J. Res. 301 / Public Law 101–415
Designating October 1990 as "National Breast Cancer Awareness Month"

Approved October 12

H.R. 5643 / Public Law 101–416
To grant a temporary extension on the authority under which the Government may accept the voluntary services of private-sector executives; to clarify the status of Federal employees assigned to private-sector positions while participating in an executive exchange program; and for other purposes

H.J. Res. 398 / Public Law 101–417
To commemorate the centennial of the creation by Congress of Yosemite National Park

H.J. Res. 482 / Public Law 101–418
Designating March 1991 as "Irish-American Heritage Month"

S. 1738 / Public Law 101–419
To convey certain Oregon and California Railroad Grant Lands in Josephine County, Oregon, to the Rogue Community College District, and for other purposes

S. 2588 / Public Law 101–420
To amend section 5948 of title 5, United States Code, to reauthorize physicians comparability allowances

H.R. 3007 / Public Law 101–421
Drug and Alcohol Dependent Offenders Treatment Act of 1989

H.R. 3897 / Public Law 101–422
To authorize appropriations for the Administrative Conference of the United States for fiscal years 1991, 1992, 1993, and 1994, and for other purposes

S.J. Res. 57 / Public Law 101–423
To establish a national policy on permanent papers

S.J. Res. 181 / Public Law 101–424
To establish calendar year 1992 as the "Year of Clean Water"

Approved October 15

H.R. 1243 / Public Law 101–425
Department of Energy Metal Casting Competitiveness Research Act of 1990

H.R. 2372 / Public Law 101–426
Radiation Exposure Compensation Act

S. 2806 / Public Law 101–427
To redesignate The National System of Interstate and Defense Highways as The Dwight D. Eisenhower System of Interstate and Defense Highways

H.R. 5641 / Public Law 101–428
Capitol Police Retirement Act

S. 647 / Public Law 101–429
Securities Enforcement Remedies and Penny Stock Reform Act of 1990

S. 1230 / Public Law 101–430
To authorize the acquisition of additional lands for inclusion in the Knife River Indian Villages National Historic Site, and for other purposes

S. 1974 / Public Law 101–431
Television Decoder Circuitry Act of 1990

Approved October 16

H.R. 3657 / Public Law 101–432
Market Reform Act of 1990

S. 1511 / Public Law 101–433
Older Workers Benefit Protection Act

Approved October 17

H.R. 435 / Public Law 101–434
To amend the Appalachian Regional Development Act of 1965 to include Columbiana County, Ohio, as part of the Appalachian region

S. 1128 / Private Law 101–4
For the relief of Richard Saunders

S. 1229 / Private Law 101–5
For the relief of Maria Luisa Anderson

S. 1683 / Private Law 101–6
For the relief of Paula Grzyb

S. 1814 / Private Law 101–7
For the relief of Wilson Johan Sherrouse

H.R. 971 / Public Law 101–435
Telephone Operator Consumer Services Improvement Act of 1990

H.R. 2809 / Public Law 101–436
To provide for the conveyance of certain lands to the State of California, and for other purposes

Approved October 18

H.R. 1677 / Public Law 101–437
Children's Television Act of 1990

H.R. 4758 / Public Law 101–438
Rio Grande American Canal Extension Act of 1990

H.J. Res. 602 / Public Law 101–439
Designating October 1990 as "National Domestic Violence Awareness Month"

S. 247 / Public Law 101–440
State Energy Efficiency Programs Improvement Act of 1990

S. 830 / Public Law 101–441
To amend Public Law 99–647, establishing the Blackstone River Valley National Heritage Corridor Commission, to authorize the Commission to take immediate action in furtherance of its purposes and to increase the authorization of appropriations for the Commission

S. 2437 / Public Law 101–442
To authorize the acquisition of certain lands in the States of Louisiana and Mississippi for inclusion in the Vicksburg National Military Park, to improve the management of certain public lands in the State of Minnesota, and for other purposes

Approved October 19

H.R. 3468 / Public Law 101–443
Connecticut Coastal Protection Act of 1990

H.J. Res. 677 / Public Law 101–444
Making further continuing appropriations for the fiscal year 1991, and for other purposes

Approved October 22

S. 2680 / Private Law 101–8
To provide for the conveyance of lands to certain individuals in Stone County, Arkansas

H.R. 1608 / Public Law 101–445
National Nutrition Monitoring and Related Research Act of 1990

H.R. 4522 / Public Law 101–446
Firefighters' Safety Study Act

H.R. 4593 / Public Law 101–447
San Carlos Mineral Strip Act of 1990

H.R. 4985 / Public Law 101–448
To designate the Federal building located at 51 Southwest 1st Avenue in Miami, Florida, as the "Claude Pepper Federal Building"

H.R. 5070 / Public Law 101–449
To amend the John F. Kennedy Center Act to authorize appropriations for maintenance, repair, alteration and other services necessary for the John F. Kennedy Center for the Performing Arts, and for other purposes

S.J. Res. 304 / Public Law 101–450
To designate October 17, 1990, as "National Drug-Free Schools and Communities Education and Awareness Day"

S.J. Res. 317 / Public Law 101–451
To designate the week of October 14, 1990, through October 20, 1990, as "National Radon Action Week"

Approved October 24

H.R. 3787 / Public Law 101–452
Chehalis River Basin Fishery Resources Study and Restoration Act of 1990

H.R. 4279 / Public Law 101–453
Cash Management Improvement Act of 1990

S. 2017 / Public Law 101–454
Eisenhower Exchange Fellowship Act of 1990

S. 2540 / Public Law 101–455
To authorize the Board of Regents of the Smithsonian Institution to plan, design, construct, and equip space in the East Court of the National Museum of Natural History building, and for other purposes

S. 3046 / Public Law 101–456
To redesignate the Federal building located at 1 Bowling Green in New York, New York, as the "Alexander Hamilton United States Custom House"

S. 3127 / Public Law 101–457
To designate the Department of Veterans Affairs Medical Center in Albany, New York, as the "Samuel S. Stratton Department of Veterans Affairs Medical Center"

S.J. Res. 342 / Public Law 101–458
Designating October 1990 as "Ending Hunger Month"

S.J. Res. 346 / Public Law 101–459
To designate October 20 through 28, 1990, as "National Red Ribbon Week for a Drug-Free America"

S.J. Res. 349 / Public Law 101–460
Designating October 1990 as "Italian-American Heritage and Culture Month"

Approved October 25

H.J. Res. 681 / Public Law 101–461
Making further continuing appropriations for the fiscal year 1991, and for other purposes

H.R. 4757 / Public Law 101–462
To provide for the extension of certain authority for the Marshal of the Supreme Court and the Supreme Court Police

H.J. Res. 214 / Public Law 101–463
Designating the week of October 22 through October 28, 1990, as "Eating Disorders Awareness Week"

H.J. Res. 518 / Public Law 101–464
Designating October 13 through 20, 1990, as "American Textile Industry Bicentennial Week"

S.J. Res. 158 / Public Law 101–465
Designating October 21 through October 27, 1990, as "World Population Awareness Week"

H.R. 2961 / Private Law 101–9
For the relief of Sonanong Poonpipat (Latch)

Approved October 27

H.J. Res. 682 / Public Law 101–466
Waiving certain enrollment requirements with respect to any reconciliation bill, appropriation bill, or continuing resolution for the remainder of the One Hundred First Congress

Approved October 28

H.J. Res. 687 / Public Law 101–467
Making further continuing appropriations for the fiscal year 1991, and for other purposes

Approved October 30

S.J. Res. 270 / Public Law 101–468
To designate the period commencing February 17, 1991, and ending February 23, 1991, as "National Visiting Nurse Associations Week"

S.J. Res. 323 / Public Law 101–469
Designating November 11 through 17, 1990, as "Geography Awareness Week"

S.J. Res. 347 / Public Law 101–470
Designating April 7 through 13, 1991, as "National County Government Week"

S.J. Res. 351 / Public Law 101–471
To designate the month of May, 1991 as "National Trauma Awareness Month"

S.J. Res. 362 / Public Law 101–472
To designate the period commencing on November 18, 1990, and ending on November 24, 1990, as "National Adoption Week"

S.J. Res. 366 / Public Law 101–473
To designate March 30, 1991, as "National Doctors Day"

H.R. 4174 / Public Law 101–474
Administrative Office of the United States Courts Personnel Act of 1990

H.R. 5579 / Public Law 101–475
To amend section 28(w) of the Mineral Leasing Act, and for other purposes

S. 1824 / Public Law 101–476
Education of the Handicapped Act Amendments of 1990

S. 2167 / Public Law 101–477
To reauthorize the Tribally Controlled Community College Assistance Act of 1978 and the Navajo Community College Act

S. 3091 / Public Law 101–478
To amend the Act incorporating the American Legion so as to redefine eligibility for membership therein

Approved October 31

H.R. 3888 / Public Law 101–479
To allow a certain parcel of land in Rockingham County, Virginia, to be used for a child care center

H.R. 5749 / Public Law 101–480
American University Incorporation Amendments Act of 1990

H.J. Res. 519 / Public Law 101–481
Designating August 29, 1990, as "National Sarcoidosis Awareness Day"

H.J. Res. 566 / Public Law 101–482
Acknowledging the sacrifices that military families have made on behalf of the Nation and designating November 19, 1990, as "National Military Families Recognition Day"

H.J. Res. 587 / Public Law 101–483
Committing to the private sector the responsibility for support of the Civic Achievement Award Program in Honor of the Office of Speaker of the House of Representatives, and for other purposes

S. 1747 / Public Law 101–484
Ponca Restoration Act

S. 2059 / Public Law 101–485
Weir Farm National Historic Site Establishment Act of 1990

S. 2203 / Public Law 101–486
Zuni Land Conservation Act of 1990

S. 3032 / Public Law 101–487
To designate the planned Department of Veterans Affairs Medical Center in Honolulu, Hawaii, as the "Spark M. Matsunaga Department of Veterans Affairs Medical Center"

S. 3216 / Public Law 101–488
To designate the Department of Veterans Affairs Medical Center in Charleston, South Carolina, as the "Ralph H. Johnson Department of Veterans Affairs Medical Center"

S.J. Res. 293 / Public Law 101–489
To designate November 16, 1990, as "National Philanthropy Day"

S.J. Res. 307 / Public Law 101–490
Designating November 11 through November 17, 1990, as "National Women Veterans Recognition Week"

S.J. Res. 324 / Public Law 101–491
Designating June 2 through 8, 1991, as a "Week for the National Observance of the 50th Anniversary of World War II"

S.J. Res. 353 / Public Law 101–492
To designate September of 1991 as "National Rice Month"

H.R. 5209 / Public Law 101–493
Drug and Household Substance Mailing Act of 1990

H.R. 5933 / Public Law 101–494
To provide for the temporary extension of the certain laws relating to housing and community development

S. 2737 / Public Law 101–495
Korean War Veterans Memorial Thirty-Eighth Anniversary Commemorative Coin Act

S. 2753 / Public Law 101–496
Developmental Disabilities Assistance and Bill of Rights Act of 1990

S.J. Res. 388 / Public Law 101–497
Waiving certain enrollment requirements with respect to S. 2830, the Food, Agriculture, Conservation and Trade Act of 1990

Approved November 2

S. 3016 / Private Law 101–10
For the relief of Janice and Leslie Sedore and Ruth Hillman

H.R. 4111 / Public Law 101–498
Strategic and Critical Minerals Act of 1990

S. 2846 / Public Law 101–499
To authorize and direct the Secretary of the Interior to conduct a study of the feasibility of establishing a unit of the National Park System to interpret and commemorate the origins, development, and progression of jazz in the United States, and for other purposes

Approved November 3

H.R. 3386 / Public Law 101–500
Sanitary Food Transportation Act of 1990

H.R. 4151 / Public Law 101–501
Augustus F. Hawkins Human Services Reauthorization Act of 1990

H.R. 4238 / Public Law 101–502
Vaccine Immunization Amendments of 1990

H.R. 5367 / Public Law 101–503
Seneca Nation Settlement Act of 1990

H.R. 5794 / Public Law 101–504
Age Discrimination Claims Assistance Amendments of 1990

H.J. Res. 520 / Public Law 101–505
Granting the consent of Congress to amendments to the Washington Metropolitan Area Transit Regulation Compact

Approved November 5

H.R. 5268 / Public Law 101–506
Rural Development, Agriculture, and Related Agencies Appropriations Act, 1991

H.R. 5158 / Public Law 101–507
Departments of Veterans Affairs and Housing and Urban Development, and Independent Agencies Appropriations Act, 1991

H.R. 5835 / Public Law 101–508
Omnibus Budget Reconciliation Act of 1990

H.R. 5241 / Public Law 101–509
Treasury, Postal Service and General Government Appropriations Act, 1991

H.R. 4739/ Public Law 101–510
National Defense Authorization Act for Fiscal Year 1991

H.R. 5803 / Public Law 101–511
Department of Defense Appropriations Act, 1991

H.R. 5769 / Public Law 101–512
Department of the Interior and Related Agencies Appropriations Act, 1991

H.R. 5114 / Public Law 101–513
Foreign Operations, Export Financing, and Related Programs Appropriations Act, 1991

H.R. 5019 / Public Law 101–514
Energy and Water Development Appropriations Act, 1991

H.R. 5021 / Public Law 101–515
Departments of Commerce, Justice, and State, the Judiciary, and Related Agencies Appropriations Act, 1991

H.R. 5229 / Public Law 101–516
Department of Transportation and Related Agencies Appropriations Act, 1991

H.R. 5257 / Public Law 101–517
Departments of Labor, Health and Human Services, and Education, and Related Agencies Appropriations Act, 1991

H.R. 5311 / Public Law 101–518
District of Columbia Appropriations Act, 1991

H.R. 5313 / Public Law 101–519
Military Construction Appropriations Act, 1991

H.R. 5399 / Public Law 101–520
Legislative Branch Appropriations Act, 1991

H.R. 5759 / Public Law 101–521
To amend the Age Discrimination in Employment Act of 1967 to clarify the application of such Act to employee group health plans

H.R. 3840 / Public Law 101–522
To establish the Newberry National Volcanic Monument in the State of Oregon, and for other purposes

H.R. 5144 / Public Law 101–523
To provide for the study of certain historical and cultural resources located in the city of Vancouver, Washington, and for other purposes

Approved November 6

S. 3043 / Private Law 101–11
For the relief of Nebraska Aluminum Castings, Inc.

H.R. 2331 / Public Law 101–524
Deceptive Mailings Prevention Act of 1990

H.R. 5275 / Public Law 101–525
Congressional Award Amendments of 1990

H.R. 5482 / Public Law 101–526
District of Columbia Revenue Bond Act of 1990

H.R. 5702 / Public Law 101–527
Disadvantaged Minority Health Improvement Act of 1990

H.J. Res. 525 / Public Law 101–528
Designating November 18 through 24, 1990, "National Family Caregivers Week"

H.J. Res. 667 / Public Law 101–529
To designate November 16, 1990, as "National Federation of the Blind Day"

S. 1890 / Public Law 101–530
To amend title 5, United States Code, to provide relief from certain inequities remaining in the crediting of National Guard technician service in connection with civil service retirement, and for other purposes

S. 3062 / Public Law 101–531
To transfer the responsibility for operation and maintenance of Highway 82 Bridge at Greenville, Mississippi, to the States of Mississippi and Arkansas

Approved November 7

H.J. Res. 669 / Public Law 101–532
To salute and congratulate the people of Poland as they commemorate the two-hundredth anniversary of the adoption of the Polish Constitution on May 3, 1991

S. 2516 / Public Law 101–533
Foreign Direct Investment and International Financial Data Improvements Act of 1990

H.R. 3911 / Public Law 101–534
Attendant Allowance Adjustment Act

Approved November 8

H.R. 3562 / Public Law 101–535
Nutrition Labeling and Education Act of 1990

H.R. 4090 / Public Law 101–536
Pecos National Historical Park Expansion Act of 1990

H.R. 4299 / Public Law 101–537
To authorize a study of the fishery resources of the Great Lakes, and for other purposes

H.R. 5004 / Public Law 101–538
To amend the Wild and Scenic Rivers Act to designate certain segments of the Mills River in

the State of North Carolina for potential addition to the wild and scenic rivers system

H.R. 5433 / Public Law 101–539
To direct the Secretary of Agriculture to release on behalf of the United States a condition in a deed conveying certain lands to the Conservation Commission of West Virginia, and for other purposes

H.R. 5872 / Public Law 101–540
To amend title I of the Employee Retirement Income Security Act of 1974 to require qualifying employer securities to include interest in publicly traded partnerships

H.J. Res. 649 / Public Law 101–541
Approving the extension of nondiscriminatory treatment (most favored nation treatment) to the products of Czechoslovakia

S. 580 / Public Law 101–542
Student Right-To-Know and Campus Security Act

S. 1756 / Public Law 101–543
Maine Acadian Culture Preservation Act

S.J. Res. 375 / Public Law 101–544
To designate October 30, 1990, as "Refugee Day"

H.R. 3791 / Private Law 101–12
For the relief of Beulah C. Shifflett

Approved November 14

H.R. 5007 / Public Law 101–545
To designate the facility of the United States Postal Service located at 100 South John F. Kennedy Drive, Carpentersville, Illinois, as the "Robert McClory Post Office Building"

H.R. 5409 / Public Law 101–546
To designate the Post Office building at 222 West Center Street in Orem, Utah, as the "Arthur V. Watkins Post Office Building"

H.J. Res. 673 / Public Law 101–547
To designate November 2, 1990, as a national day of prayer for members of American military forces and American citizens stationed or held hostage in the Middle East, and for their families

S. 3156 / Public Law 101–548
To correct a clerical error in Public Law 101–383

Approved November 15

S. 1630 / Public Law 101–549
To amend the Clean Air Act to provide for attainment and maintenance of health protective national ambient air quality standards, and for other purposes

H.R. 1396 / Public Law 101–550
Securities Acts Amendments of 1990

H.R. 1463 / Public Law 101–551
National Capital Transportation Amendments of 1990

H.R. 2497 / Public Law 101–552
Administrative Dispute Resolution Act

H.R. 3045 / Public Law 101–553
Copyright Remedy Clarification Act

H.R. 3069 / Public Law 101–554
Displaced Homemakers Self-Sufficiency Assistance Act

H.R. 3310 / Public Law 101–555
To authorize appropriations for activities of the National Telecommunications and Information Administration for fiscal years 1990 and 1991

H.R. 4630 / Public Law 101–556
Baca Location No. 1 Land Acquisition and Study Act of 1990

H.R. 5112 / Public Law 101–557
Home Health Care and Alzheimer's Disease Amendments of 1990

H.R. 5113 / Public Law 101–558
Injury Control Act of 1990

H.R. 5419 / Public Law 101–559
To designate the Federal Building at 88 West 100 North in Provo, Utah, as the "J. Will Robinson Federal Building"

H.R. 5507 / Public Law 101–560
Regarding the Early Winters Resorts

H.R. 5667 / Public Law 101–561
To amend the Water Resources Development Act of 1974 to transfer jurisdiction of the Big South Fork National River and Recreation Area from the Secretary of the Army to the Secretary of the Interior, and for other purposes

H.R. 5708 / Public Law 101–562
To authorize acquisition of certain real property for the Library of Congress, and for other purposes

H.J. Res. 562 / Public Law 101–563
Designating October 21 through 27, 1990 as "National Humanities Week"

H.J. Res. 652 / Public Law 101–564
To designate March 25, 1991, as "National Medal of Honor Day"

H.J. Res. 657 / Public Law 101–565
Granting the consent of the Congress to amendments to the Delaware-New Jersey Compact, and for other purposes

S. 639 / Public Law 101–566
Spark M. Matsunaga Hydrogen Research, Development, and Demonstration Act of 1990

S. 1805 / Public Law 101–567
To authorize the Secretary of the Interior to reinstate oil and gas lease LA 033164

S. 3215 / Public Law 101–568
To authorize the transfer by lease of a specified naval landing ship dock to the Government of Brazil

S.J. Res. 318 / Public Law 101–569
Providing for the appointment of Ira Michael Heyman as a citizen regent of the Smithsonian Institution

S.J. Res. 369 / Public Law 101–570
Designating 1991 as the "Year of Thanksgiving for the Blessings of Liberty"

H.R. 1230 / Private Law 101–13
For the relief of Jocelyne Carayannis and Marie Carayannis

H.R. 3642 / Private Law 101–14
For the relief of Izzydor Shever

S. 620 / Private Law 101–15
For the relief of Leroy W. Shebal of North Pole, Alaska

H.R. 2419 / Public Law 101–571
To authorize the Secretary of Agriculture to exchange certain property in the Chattahoochee National Forest for the construction of facilities in the National Forest

H.R. 3656 / Public Law 101–572
Gas Related Activities Act of 1990

H.R. 4107 / Public Law 101–573
To authorize the Secretary of the Interior to permit certain uses of lands within the Colonial National Historical Park in the Commonwealth of Virginia

H.R. 4793 / Public Law 101–574
Small Business Administration Reauthorization and Amendments Act of 1990

H.R. 4808 / Public Law 101–575
Solar, Wind, Waste, and Geothermal Power Production Incentives Act of 1990

H.R. 5687 / Public Law 101–576
Chief Financial Officers Act of 1990

H.R. 5871 / Public Law 101–577
Farm Poundage Quota Revisions Act of 1990

H.R. 5796 / Public Law 101–578
To conduct certain studies in the State of New Mexico

H.J. Res. 606 / Public Law 101–579
Designating February 16, 1991, as "Lithuanian Independence Day"

S. 459 / Public Law 101–580
To amend title 35, United States Code, with respect to the use of inventions in outer space

S. 1931 / Public Law 101–581
Criminal Victims Protection Act of 1990

S. 2056 / Public Law 101–582
Year 2000 Health Objectives Planning Act

S. 2930 / Public Law 101–583
To eliminate "substantial documentary evidence" requirement for minimum wage determination for American Samoa, and for other purposes

S. 3187 / Public Law 101–584
To address immediate problems affecting environmental cleanup activities

S. 3237 / Public Law 101–585
Silver Coin Proof Sets Act

S.J. Res. 302 / Public Law 101–586
Providing for reappointment of Anne Legendre Armstrong as a citizen regent of the Smithsonian Institution

S.J. Res. 357 / Public Law 101–587
To designate October 1–31, 1991, as "Community Center Month"

Approved November 16

H.R. 3298 / Private Law 101–16
For the relief of Benjamin H. Fonorow

H.R. 29 / Public Law 101–588
Antitrust Amendments Act of 1990

H.R. 996 / Public Law 101–589
Excellence in Mathematics, Science and Engineering Education Act of 1990

H.R. 1602 / Public Law 101–590
Trauma Care Systems Planning and Development Act of 1990

H.R. 2840 / Public Law 101–591
Coastal Barrier Improvement Act of 1990

H.R. 3000 / Public Law 101–592
Fastener Quality Act

H.R. 3338 / Public Law 101–593
To direct the Secretary of the Interior to convey all interest of the United States in a fish hatchery to the State of South Carolina, and for other purposes

H.R. 3977 / Public Law 101–594
Antarctic Protection Act of 1990

H.R. 4009 / Public Law 101–595
Federal Maritime Commission Authorization Act of 1990

H.R. 4323 / Public Law 101–596
Great Lakes Critical Programs Act of 1990

H.R. 4487 / Public Law 101–597
National Health Service Corps Revitalization Amendments of 1990

H.R. 4721 / Public Law 101–598
To designate the Federal building located at 340 North Pleasant Valley Road in Winchester, Virginia, as the "J. Kenneth Robinson Postal Building"

H.R. 4888 / Public Law 101–599
To improve navigational safety and to reduce the hazards to navigation resulting from vessel collisions with pipelines in the marine environment, and for other purposes

H.R. 5140 / Public Law 101–600
School Dropout Prevention and Basic Skills Improvement Act of 1990

H.R. 5237 / Public Law 101–601
Native American Graves Protection and Repatriation Act

H.R. 5308 / Public Law 101–602
Fort Hall Indian Water Rights Act of 1990

H.R. 5497 / Public Law 101–603
To authorize the Secretary of the Interior to acquire certain lands to be added to the Fort Raleigh National Historic Site in North Carolina

H.R. 5732 / Public Law 101–604
Aviation Security Improvement Act of 1990

H.R. 5909 / Public Law 101–605
Florida Keys National Marine Sanctuary and Protection Act

S. 169 / Public Law 101–606
Global Change Research Act of 1990

S. 555 / Public Law 101–607
De Soto Expedition Trail Commission Act of 1990

S. 605 / Public Law 101–608
Consumer Product Safety Improvement Act of 1990

S. 677 / Public Law 101–609
To amend the Arctic Research and Policy Act of 1984 to improve and clarify its provisions

S. 1430 / Public Law 101–610
National and Community Service Act of 1990

S. 2287 / Public Law 101–611
National Aeronautics and Space Administration Authorization Act, Fiscal Year 1991

S. 2566 / Public Law 101–612
Smith River National Recreation Area Act

S. 2857 / Public Law 101–613
National Institutes of Health Amendments of 1990

S. 2789 / Public Law 101–614
National Earthquake Hazards Reduction Program Reauthorization Act

S. 2936 / Public Law 101–615
Hazardous Materials Transportation Uniform Safety Act of 1990

S. 2946 / Public Law 101–616
Transplant Amendments Act of 1990

S. 3069 / Public Law 101–617
Environmental Research Geographic Location Information Act

S. 3084 / Public Law 101–618
Fallon Paiute Shoshone Indian Tribes Water Rights Settlement Act of 1990

S. 3176 / Public Law 101–619
National Environmental Education Act

S.J. Res. 206 / Public Law 101–620
Calling for the United States to encourage immediate negotiations toward a new agreement among Antarctic Treaty Consultative Parties, for the full protection of Antarctica as a global ecological commons

H.R. 4559 / Public Law 101–621
Red Rock Canyon National Conservation Area Establishment Act of 1990

Approved November 21

H.R. 5264 / Public Law 101–622
To authorize modification of the boundaries of the Alaska Maritime National Wildlife Refuge

H.R. 5567 / Public Law 101–623
International Narcotics Control Act of 1990

Approved November 28

S. 2830 / Public Law 101–624
Food, Agriculture, Conservation, and Trade Act of 1990

S. 566 / Public Law 101–625
Cranston-Gonzalez National Affordable Housing Act

H.R. 987 / Public Law 101–626
Tongass Timber Reform Act

H.R. 2061 / Public Law 101–627
Fishery Conservation Amendments of 1990

H.R. 2570 / Public Law 101–628
To provide for the designation of certain public lands as wilderness in the State of Arizona

H.R. 3095 / Public Law 101–629
Safe Medical Devices Act of 1990

H.R. 3703 / Public Law 101–630
To authorize the Rumsey Indian Rancheria to convey a certain parcel of land

H.R. 4567 / Public Law 101–631
To authorize an exchange of lands in South Dakota and Colorado

H.R. 4834 / Public Law 101–632
To provide for a visitor center at Salem Maritime National Historic Site in the Commonwealth of Massachusetts

H.R. 5428 / Public Law 101–633
Illinois Wilderness Act of 1990

S. 319 / Public Law 101–634
Salt Lake City Watershed Improvement Act of 1990

S. 845 / Public Law 101–635
Food and Drug Administration Revitalization Act

S. 1859 / Public Law 101–636
To restructure repayment terms and conditions for loans made by the Secretary of the Interior to the Wolf Trap Foundation for the Performing Arts for the reconstruction of the Filene Center in Wolf Trap Farm Park in Fairfax County, Virginia, and for other purposes

S. 1893 / Public Law 101–637
Asbestos School Hazard Abatement Reauthorization Act of 1990

S. 1939 / Public Law 101–638
To extend the authorization of appropriations for the Taft Institute

S. 2628 / Public Law 101–639
Mental Health Amendments of 1990

S. 2740 / Public Law 101–640
Water Resources Development Act of 1990

S. 3012 / Public Law 101–641
Independent Safety Board Act Amendments of 1990

S.J. Res. 329 / Public Law 101–642
To designate the week of November 3, 1990, to November 10, 1990, as "National Week to Commemorate the Victims of the Famine in the Ukraine, 1932–1933", and to commemorate the Ukrainian famine of 1932–1933 and the policies of Russification to suppress Ukrainian identity

S.J. Res. 364 / Public Law 101–643
To designate the third week of February 1991 as "National Parents and Teachers Association Week"

Approved November 29

H.R. 2006 / Public Law 101–644
Indian Arts and Crafts Act of 1990

H.R. 3789 / Public Law 101–645
Stewart B. McKinney Homeless Assistance Amendments Act of 1990

H.R. 5390 / Public Law 101–646
Nonindigenous Aquatic Nuisance Prevention and Control Act of 1990

S. 3266 / Public Law 101–647
Crime Control Act of 1990

S. 303 / Public Law 101–648
Negotiated Rulemaking Act of 1990

S. 358 / Public Law 101–649
Immigration Act of 1990

Approved December 1

H.R. 5316 / Public Law 101–650
Judicial Improvements Act of 1990

Appendix E—Proclamations and Executive Orders

The texts of the proclamations and Executive orders are printed in the Federal Register (F.R.) at the citations listed below. The documents are also printed in title 3 of the Code of Federal Regulations and in the Weekly Compilation of Presidential Documents.

PROCLAMATIONS

EXECUTIVE ORDERS

Appendix F—Points of Light Recognition Program

The President named the following individuals and institutions as exemplars of his commitment to making community service central to the life and work of every American. The daily recognition program, which began on November 22, 1989, was a national tribute to voluntarism. The recipients for the period covered by this volume are listed in chronological order.

Dale Shields, of Sarasota, FL

Alpha Project, of San Diego, CA

Grand Rapids Police Department Crime Analysis Unit, of Grand Rapids, MI

Concerned Friends, Inc., of Tempe, AZ

Carol DeMayo, of Williamstown, MA

Habitat for Humanity, of Charlotte, NC

Rebecca Tinkham, of Tulsa, OK

Spartanburg County SAFE (Shelter Available for Emergencies) Homes Network, of Spartanburg, SC

Tutor Exchange, of San Jose, CA

Operation Read, of Lexington, KY

Mountaineers, Inc., of Phoenix, AZ

Harold Craig Reynolds, of Seattle, WA

Justin Lebo, of Saddle Brook, NJ

Florence Ziedman, of Buffalo Grove, IL

Lakeview Shepherd Center, of New Orleans, LA

Minerva Soerheide, of Mount Hermon, CA

Mitchell Cardell Baldwin, of Birmingham, AL

Alternatives to Domestic Violence, of Riverside, CA

Connie Harris, of Springfield, OR

Davarian Baldwin, of Beloit, WI

Gudrun "Gudy" Gaskill, of Golden, CO

Harvest House, of Lansing, MI

Ron Dickey, of El Paso, TX

David Goldstein, of Albany, NY

William and Ethel Tibbetts, of El Monte, CA

Ohioans Helping Improve Ohio (O.H.I.O.), Inc., of Cleveland, OH

Mercy Watch, of Merritt Island, FL

Orange County Rescue Mission, of Santa Ana, CA

20 Good Men, of Kansas City, KS

Berni Ehrhart, of York, PA

Project Amigos, of San Antonio, TX

Doris Wolff, of Hanover, PA

Christopher Keener, of Somers Point, NJ

Volunteers of the Huntsville Land Trust, of Huntsville, AL

Lucy Narvaiz, of Santa Fe, NM

Submarine Group 6, of the Charleston Naval Base, SC

Mountain Outreach, of Williamsburg, KY

Janet Perreira, of Bakersfield, CA

Elizabeth Carter, of East Liverpool, OH

Connecticut Hospice, Inc., of Branford, CT

Right to Read of Weld County, Inc., of Greeley, CO

John L. Oliver, of Midland, TX

Rosemont Center, of Columbus, OH

Community Service Project, of Rockland, ME

Clare Allen, of Nashville, TN

William Smith, of Donora, PA

What About Remembering Me, Inc., of Fort Worth, TX

John Booth, of Las Vegas, NV

Thora Bautz, of Scotts Valley, CA

Soaring Eagles Project, of Minneapolis, MN

Stephanie Gore, of Savannah, GA

Friends of Lubavitch of Bergen County, of Teaneck, NJ

Bridgeway, of Lakewood, CO

Castle Skip Newell III, of Laytonville, CA

Project HEAT'S ON, of Fort Wayne, IN

Bradley Free Clinic of Roanoke Valley, Inc., of Roanoke, VA

GIVE (Grandpersons Interested in Volunteering for Education), of Toledo, OH

Officer Wayne Barton, of Boca Raton, FL

Volunteers of the San Antonio Air Logistics Center—Kelly Air Force Base/Southwest Independent School District Mentoring Partnership, of San Antonio, TX

Dolores Camp, of Bismarck, ND

Larkin Street Youth Center, of San Francisco, CA

Florence Hodges, of Dothan, AL

Community Outreach Program of LeMoyne-Owen College, of Memphis, TN

Youth Alternatives, of Cheyenne, WY

Lucille Isakson, of Ogden, UT

Lorissa Dawn Keller, of Grand Rapids, MI

Linda Warsaw, of San Bernardino, CA

Special Care Parents, of Des Moines, IA

Georgia Elias, of Jacksonville, IL

Girls Incorporated, of Schenectady, NY

The Healing Place, of Eau Claire, WI

Ruby Honeycutt, of Greenville, NC

Harb-Adult, Inc., of Lancaster, PA

WRBH Radio, of New Orleans, LA

Bachman Memorial Home, of Cleveland, OH

Tripartite Tutorial and Mentoring Programs, of New London, CT

Court Designated Child Advocates, of San Jose, CA

Variety House for Children, of New York, NY

Joey LoDuca, of San Diego, CA

Mary Vandiver Moorhead, of Anderson, SC

Southern Oregon Drug Awareness, of Medford, OR

Carol McGann, of South Bend, IN

Leslie Sloan, of Springfield, IL

Samaritans on Cape Cod, Inc., of Falmouth, MA

Roxanne Black, of Atlantic City, NJ

Audine Haynes, of Greenville, MS

Student Coalition for Action in Literacy Education, of Chapel Hill, NC

Debra Walker, of Detroit, MI

Stephen Rice, of Sacramento, CA

Association for the Blind and Visually Impaired of Lehigh County, of Allentown, PA

Gerald Martin, of Bell Buckle, TN

D.C. Central Kitchen, of Washington, DC

Nations Association, Inc., of Fort Myers, FL

Tacoma Community House, of Tacoma, WA

Helping Us Grow Through Service and Smiles, of Colorado Springs, CO

Overcomers of Brevard, Inc., of Titusville, FL

Governor Mifflin Junior High School, of Shillington, PA

Adult Day Care Center, Inc., of Westerly, RI

Care and Counseling Center, of Downers Grove, IL

Caring Cuisine, of New Haven, CT

Wings of Hope, of Atlanta, GA

Katie Dykes, of Green Bay, WI

Rev. Tony McCreary, of Philadelphia, PA

Yong Kay Moua and Houa Vue Moua, of Eau Claire, WI

Barbara Frazee, of Nashville, TN

U.S.S. "Elrod," of Charleston, SC

Our House, Inc., of Little Rock, AR

Three Rivers Literacy Alliance, of Fort Wayne, IN

ITT Hartford Insurance Group, of Hartford, CT

Second Mile, of State College, PA

Bessie Spencer, of East St. Louis, IL

Seacoast Hospice Program, of Exeter, NH

Project HOPE, of Milwaukee, WI

Coach Randy Carlisle and the Kountze High School basketball team, of Kountze, TX

Ceredo-Kenova American Legion Post No. 93 and the Tolsia High School partnership, of Kenova, WV

Good Shepherd Community Center, of Vicksburg, MS

World of Work Program, of Detroit, MI

I KNOW I CAN, of Columbus, OH

Arthur Redner, of Norwalk, CT

TOP-STEP (Tutoring Others Program—Students Teaching Each Other Project), of Statesboro, GA

Thomas Sammons, of Las Vegas, NV

Chileda Institute, of La Crosse, WI

Family Outreach, of Copperas Cove, TX

Donald Edland Pringle, of Holden Beach, NC

Joseph and Penny Miller, of Spirit Lake, ID

Volunteer Action Division of the Department of Human Concerns, of Kahului, HI

Project CHARLIE, of Holland, MI

David Evans, of Cambridge, MA

Lawrence-At-Risk-Youth Mentoring Program, of Appleton, WI

Linda Smith, of Palmer, AK

Frances Peabody, of Portland, ME

Elliot Schneck, of San Francisco, CA

Joseph Agris, of Houston, TX

Kim and Wendy Roderick, of Bristol, RI

People Project, of Gillette, WY

All Saints Episcopal School, of Lubbock, TX

Marilyn Pona, of St. Louis, MO

Gloria Renda, of Steubenville, OH

Dorothy Score, of Prescott Valley, AZ

LIFE (Learning Is For Everyone), of Trenton, NJ

Mission Service Project, of Mission, TX

Ester Ryan, of Barberton, OH

Vigar Shamin, of Hillsboro, OR

C. Raymond Wilcox, of Sumter, SC

William Gulley, of Cincinnati, OH

Cities in Schools, of Charlotte, NC

Children's Home Society, of Jacksonville, FL

Step 2, of Reno, NV

Steven Workman, James Trescott, and Jim Yoak, of Parkersburg, WV

Hospice of Acadiana, of Lafayette, LA

Lafitte Garden Club, of New Orleans, LA

Pinch Hitter Project, Gate City Lodge Chapter of B'nai B'rith, of Atlanta, GA

Gennesaret Free Clinic, of Indianapolis, IN

Economic Crisis Center, of East Lansing, MI

The Eli Home, Inc., of Anaheim, CA

Deborah Stedman Arakaki, of Auburn, CA

Eleanor Hermanns, of Chula Vista, CA

Subject Index

AFL-CIO. *See* Labor & Congress of Industrial Organizations, American Federation of
AID. *See* Development Cooperation Agency, U.S. International
AIDS. *See* Health and medical care
Abortion—1049, 1052
Administration. *See other part of subject*
Administrative Conference of the U.S.—1842
Adult Day Care Center, Inc., Westerly, RI—1892
Advancement of Colored People, National Association for the—1844
Advisory committees and commissions, Federal—1281, 1589, 1829, 1830, 1835, 1836, 1839, 1843, 1854
Aeronautics and Space Administration, National—1019, 1553, 1591
Africa
 See also specific country
 Democracy and freedom—980
 Medical assistance—1324
African Americans. *See specific subject*
African Development Foundation—1836, 1847
African Unity, Organization of—1841
Agency. *See other part of subject*
Agriculture
 Administration policies—1416, 1694, 1695
 Export credit guarantees—1786, 1787
 Federal role—1696
 Grain embargoes—1724
 Grape imports—1762
 International government subsidies—962, 984, 995, 999, 1593, 1735, 1739, 1750, 1760, 1770
 President's views—1192, 1356, 1694, 1695
 Rural development—1696
 Soviet-U.S. trade agreement—1192
 Trade goals, annual report—1465
Agriculture, Department of
 Agriculture Stabilization and Conservation Service—1695
 Commodity Credit Corporation—1724, 1787
 Farmers Home Administration—1701
 Food stamp program—1695, 1696
 Forest Service—1439
 Funding—1465
 Secretary—999, 1697, 1753, 1786, 1845
Air Force, Department of the
 Chief of Staff—1241, 1263
 Former Chief of Staff—1832
 Military Airlift Command—1666
 Warren Air Force Base—1040
Air Toxics Research Center, Urban—1604
Alabama, Governor—1074, 1075
Alaska
 Maritime National Wildlife Refuge—1664
 Republican Party events—1545, 1842

Alaska Natural Gas Transportation System, Office of the Federal Inspector—1361
Algeria, President—1804, 1809
All-American Cities Awards—1102
All Saints Episcopal School, Lubbock, TX—1892
Alpha Project, San Diego, CA—1891
Alternatives to Domestic Violence, Riverside, CA—1891
Ambassador. *See specific country*
American. *See other part of subject*
American Legion—1827
Amnesty International—1382, 1413, 1802, 1821
Amtrak—1835
Andean Trade Preference Act of 1990—1362, 1363
Angola, National Union for the Total Independence of—1347, 1852
Antarctic Protection Act of 1990—1608
Appeals, U.S. Courts of
 First Circuit—1047, 1828
 Fifth Circuit—1828
Appellate Judges Conference, International—1232
Appointment Process, President's Commission on the Federal—1834
Arab Americans—1274
Arab League—1123, 1212, 1433, 1483, 1683
Architectural and Transportation Barriers Compliance Board—1826
Archives and Records Administration, National—1829
Arctic Research and Policy Act of 1984, amendments—1613
Argentina
 Economy—1735, 1752–1754, 1756, 1758
 La Nación—1731
 Nuclear weapons nonproliferation agreement—1709, 1740, 1756
 President—1709, 1735, 1748, 1752–1756, 1758, 1775, 1776, 1839, 1841, 1851
 President Bush's visit—1752, 1755, 1758, 1851
 Reforms, political and economic—1752, 1753, 1756, 1757, 1779
 Trade with U.S.—1735, 1753
 U.S. Embassy—1851
 Vice President—1755
Arizona
 Coronado National Forest—1439
 Severe storms—1851
Armed Forces, U.S.
 See also Defense and national security
 Christmas message—1818
 Europe, role. *See* Europe, U.S. military role
 Liberia deployment—1100

Name Index

Document Categories List